CONTRACT LAW

CONTRACT LAW
Cases, Materials and Commentary

SALLY WHEELER
University of Nottingham

JO SHAW
Keele University

CLARENDON PRESS · OXFORD

Oxford University Press, Walton Street, Oxford OX2 6DP

Oxford New York
Athens Auckland Bangkok Bombay
Calcutta Cape Town Dar es Salaam Delhi
Florence Hong Kong Istanbul Karachi
Kuala Lumpur Madras Madrid Melbourne
Mexico City Nairobi Paris Singapore
Taipei Tokyo Toronto
and associated companies in
Berlin Ibadan

Oxford is a trade mark of Oxford University Press

Published in the United States
by Oxford University Press Inc., New York

British Library Cataloguing in Publication Data
Data available

Library of Congress Cataloging in Publication Data
Wheeler, Sally.
Contract law: cases, materials, and commentary / Sally Wheeler, Jo Shaw.
p. cm.
Includes bibliographical references.
1. Contracts–Great Britain–Cases. 2. Contracts–Cases.
I. Shaw, Josephine. II. Title.
KD1554.41'A7W46 1994 346.41'02—dc20 [344.1062] 94–14932

ISBN 0–19–876294–1
ISBN 0–19–876295–X (pbk)

Printed in Great Britain
on acid-free paper by
Biddles Ltd, Guildford and King's Lynn

This book is dedicated to
the memory of
PATRICK WHEELER
and
WINIFRED BAXTER

Preface

This book emerged out of course materials prepared for the teaching of contract law to first-year law undergraduates at Keele University. The materials were originally conceived of as providing an alternative to the paradigm black letter approach to contract teaching which often dominates in the UK. The development of the materials was part of a general review of the core courses in the law curriculum. This review offered an opportunity to reflect upon both how best to teach students the key elements of the contractual obligation and how best to use the teaching of contract as a vehicle for broadening students' horizons about legal doctrine and legal theory generally.

Two basic approaches to teaching contract run through the selection of materials. First, we have sought to reduce to an absolute minimum the number of cases extracted and to use those which have been chosen to their full effect. Hence there are lengthy extracts from most of the chosen cases with extensive annotations, including linked extracts from secondary literature. Inevitably the selection of cases is personal, and there will be many amongst our readers who will not agree with all our choices. Some of the case extracts contain the original facts, as stated by the judges. We do not consider it appropriate for students always to use 'headnote-style' case summaries when using collections of cases. They themselves need to become accustomed to the skills of ascertaining the relevant facts. Second, we have sought to bring together contract theory and contract law. As will be apparent from Chapters 2 and 3, we have tried to take a broad and eclectic view of what is contract theory. We have generally sought not to impose our own views of the various theories but to provide a reasonably faithful representation of the increasingly rich literature. To make the theory more accessible to the first- or second-year law undergraduate, we have used a clearly recognizable and, some might say, even traditional doctrinal framework as the starting-point for theoretical discussion.

Space precluded the inclusion of chapters on a number of important aspects of contract law, including in particular illegality, restraint of trade, assignment and capacity. We hope that these omissions do not impair too greatly the usefulness of the book as a teaching text.

We have incurred many debts during the preparation of this book.

Financial support for research assistance, and towards the costs of typing and proofreading the manuscript, was made available by the Law Department of Keele University. We are particularly grateful to Tony Dugdale for his support. Members of the contract law teaching group provided helpful feedback on the teaching materials, and a number of Keele undergraduates have (largely unawares) provided useful insights on some of the materials used. We would particularly like to thank Damian Hanley, who was our research assistant during part of the summer of 1993, when the stresses and strains of moving house whilst writing a book were really beginning to take their toll. Away from Keele, colleagues in a number of law departments responded uncomplainingly to urgent requests to obtain elusive books and articles from their university libraries. Their kindness saved us from relying too much upon the vagaries of inter-library loans. We would also like to thank Messrs Steed & Steed of Sudbury for giving us early sight of the decision in *Pitt* v *PHH Asset Management*.

Our families were very supportive, and special mention should be made of Sally's sister, Zoe Collins, who looked after Leo Shaw for two weeks when his school was partially consumed by fire. Amanda Godfrey also put up with a certain amount of domestic unrest. Our final debt is to the publishers, and particularly to Richard Hart. Richard showed astonishing faith in our ability to complete this project, and we are very grateful to him for his constant encouragement from beginning to end of the production process.

None of the above are, of course, responsible for any of the failings of this book, for which we are solely and jointly responsible. The book was jointly conceived, jointly planned, and jointly written. Each chapter was drafted and redrafted with the involvement of both of us. We have endeavoured to state the law as of October 1993 when the manuscript was completed. Some later materials have been incorporated.

S.W.
J.S.

February 1994

Contents

List of Abbreviations

As far as possible we have used standard abbreviations from the *Index to Legal Periodicals*, plus the conventional abbreviations for the standard journals.

AJCL	*American Journal of Comparative Law*
Am. Soc. Rev.	*American Sociological Review*
Anglo-Am. L. Rev.	*Anglo-American Law Review*
Auckland UL Rev.	*Auckland University Law Review*
Aust. LJ	*Australian Law Journal*
BJLS	*British Journal of Law and Society*
Cal. L. Rev.	*California Law Review*
Can. Bus. LJ	*Canadian Business Law Journal*
Cardozo L. Rev.	*Cardozo Law Review*
Cin. L. Rev.	*Cincinnati Law Review*
CLJ	*Cambridge Law Journal*
CLP	*Current Legal Problems*
CML Rev.	*Common Market Law Review*
Colum. L. Rev.	*Columbia Law Review*
Conv.	*The Conveyancer*
Cornell L. Rev.	*Cornell Law Review*
Denv. LJ	*Denver Law Journal*
Duke LJ	*Duke Law Journal*
ECLJ	*European Consumer Law Journal*
Harv. L. Rev.	*Harvard Law Review*
Hastings LJ	*Hastings Law Journal*
HKLJ	*Hong Kong Law Journal*
ICLQ	*International and Comparative Law Quarterly*
Int. J. Sem. L.	*International Journal of the Semiotics of Law*
Int. J. Soc. Law	*International Journal of the Sociology of Law*
JBL	*Journal of Business Law*
JCL	*Journal of Contract Law*
JCP	*Journal of Consumer Policy*
J. Econ. Issues	*Journal of Economic Issues*
J. Inst. Th. Econ.	*Journal of Institutional and Theoretical Economics*

JL & Econ.	*Journal of Law and Economics*
JL&S	*Journal of Law and Society*
J. Leg. St.	*Journal of Legal Studies*
J. Leg. Hist.	*Journal of Legal History*
Law & Hist. Rev.	*Law and History Review*
L. & Pol. Q.	*Law and Policy Quarterly*
L&S Rev.	*Law and Society Review*
LMCLQ	*Lloyd's Maritime and Commercial Law Quarterly*
Loy. LA Int'l. & Comp. LJ	*Loyola of Los Angeles International and Comparative Law Journal*
LQR	*Law Quarterly Review*
LS	*Legal Studies*
Melb. UL Rev.	*Melbourne University Law Review*
MLR	*Modern Law Review*
NILQ	*Northern Ireland Legal Quarterly*
NLJ	*New Law Journal*
NwUL Rev.	*Northwestern University Law Review*
NYUL Rev.	*New York University Law Review*
OJLS	*Oxford Journal of Legal Studies*
Phil. & Pub. Aff.	*Philosophy and Public Affairs*
PL	*Public Law*
Pol. Q	*Political Quarterly*
Pol. Sci. Q.	*Political Science Quarterly*
S. Cal. L. Rev.	*Southern California Law Review*
Stan. L. Rev.	*Stanford Law Review*
Tenn. L. Rev.	*Tennessee Law Review*
U. Chi. L. Rev.	*University of Chicago Law Review*
U. Cin. L. Rev.	*University of Cincinnati Law Review*
U. Miss.–Kan. City L. Rev.	*University of Missouri–Kansas City Law Review*
U. Pa. L. Rev.	*University of Pennsylvania Law Review*
U. Pitt. L. Rev.	*University of Pittsburgh Law Review*
U. Toronto LJ	*University of Toronto Law Journal*
Va. L. Rev.	*Virginia Law Review*
Wis. L. Rev.	*Wisconsin Law Review*
Wm. & M. L. Rev.	*William and Mary Law Review*
Yale LJ	*Yale Law Journal*

Acknowledgements*

Grateful acknowledgement is made to all authors and publishers of extract material, and in particular to the following for permission to reprint material from the sources indicated:

The American Journal of Comparative Law: von Mehren, A., 'The Battle of the Forms: A Comparative View' (1990) 38 *AJCL*, 277.

American Sociological Review: Macaulay, S., 'Non-Contractual Relations in Business: A Preliminary Study' (1963) 28 *Am. Soc. Rev.* 56–61.

Auckland University Law Review: McClintock, R., 'Objecting in Contract' 319–20, *AULR* vol. 6 no. 3.

Blackwell Publishers: extracts from *J. Law and Society; Modern Law Review;* Pateman, *The Sexual Contact* (1988) 1–7, 55–60, *The Disorder of Women* (1988) 59–63; Twinning (ed.), *Evidence and Theory.*

Brownsword, Professor R: Adams and Brownsword, 'More in Expectation than Hope' (1991) 54 *MLR*, 'Contract Consideration and the Critical Path' (1990) 53 *MLR*, Privity and the Concept of a Network Contract' (1990) 10 *Legal Studies; Understanding Contract Law* (1987); Beyreveld and Brownsword, 'Privity, Transivity, and Rationality' (1991) 54 *MLR*; Brownsword, Howells, and Wilhelmsson (eds.), *Welfarism in Contract Law, The Philosophy of Welfarism;* 'Toward a Rational Theory of Contract' in Wilhelmsson (ed.) *Perspectives of Critical Contract Law* (1993), and 'Retrieving Reasons' (1992) 5 *JCL*.

Butterworths Australia: Brownsword, 'Retrieving Reasons' (1992) 5 *Journal of Contract Law* 83–4.

Butterworths & Co.: Adams and Brownsword, 'Privity and the Concept of a Network Contract' (1990) 10 *Legal Studies* 27–8; *All England Law Reports;* Burrows, A., *Remedies for Torts and Breach of Contract* (1987) 222; Cheshire, Fifoot and Furmston, *Law of Contract* (12th edn. 1991) 184; Collins, H., *The Law of Contract* (1st edn. pub. by Weidenfeld) 2, (2nd edn. 1993) 82–7, 289–91; Cotterrell, R., *The Sociology of Law* (2nd edn. 1992) 34, 118–19; Goodrich, *Languages of Law* (1990) 149–74; Harris, D., *Remedies in Tort Law* (1988) 115; MacDonald, E., *Exclusion Clauses: The Ambit of S.13(1) of the U.C.T. Act 1977* (1992) 13 *Legal Studies* 287, 293; Williamson, 'Contract Analysis: The Transaction Cost Approach' in Burrows and Veljanowski (ed.), *The Economic Approach to Law* (1981) 40–2, and 'Introduction' by Veljanowski, 22–5.

California Law Review, Inc: Gordley, J., 'Equality in Exchange' (1981) 69 *Cal. L. Rev.* 1588–90; Sweet, J., 'Liquidated Damages in California' (1972) 60 *Cal. L. Rev.* 86–7.

Cambridge Law Journal: Hepple, 'The Intention to Create Legal Relations' (1970) *CLJ*; Spencer, 'Signature, Consent and the Rule in L'Estrange v. Grancob' (1973) *CLJ;* Wilson, 'A Reappraisal of Quasi-Estoppel' (1965) *CLJ.*

Cambridge University Press: Barnett, R., 'Rights and Remedies in a Consent Theory of Contract' in Frey and Morris (eds.), *Liability and Responsibility* (1991) 143–5, 148–52; Reiner, R., 'Crime, Law and Deviance: The Durkheim Legacy' in S. Fenton (ed.), *Durkheim and Modern Sociology* (1984) 176–8.

Columbia Law Review: Farnsworth, 'Legal Remedies for Breach of Contract', 70 *Colum. L. Rev.* 1145 (1970); Fuller, 'Consideration and Form', 41 *Colum. L. Rev.* 799 (1941); Hale, 'Bargaining Duress and Economic Liberty', 43 *Colum. L. Rev.* 603 (1943); Kessler, 'Contracts of Adhesion – Some Thoughts About Freedom of Contract', 43 *Colum. L. Rev.* 629 (1943); Linzer, 'On the Amorality of Contract Remedies', 18 *Colum. L. Rev.* 111 (1981); Rosset, 'Partial Qualified and Equivocal Repudiation of Contract', 81 *Colum. L. Rev.*

Cornell Law Review and Fred B. Rothman & Co.: Hillman, Robert A., 'Debunking Some Myths About Unconscionability: A New Framework for U.C.C. Section 2–302', 67 *Cornell L. Rev.* 1 (1981); 'An Analysis of the Cessation of Contractual Relations', 68 *Cornell L. Rev.* 617 (1983).

Dartmouth Publishing Co. Ltd: Brownsword, Howells, and Wilhelmsson (eds.), *Welfarism in Contract Law* (1994); Wilhelmsson (ed.), *Perspectives of Critical Contract Law* (1993).

Deborah Charles Publications: Jackson, Bernard S., *Law, Fact and Narrative Coherence* (1988) (ISBN 0–951379–5) 102–6.

Earlsgate Press: Arrowsmith, S., *Civil Liability and Public Authorities* (1992) 45–52.

Foundation Press: MacNeil, I., *Contract, Exchange, Transactions and Relations* (2nd edn. 1978) 12–13.

Harper Collins (Fontana Paperbacks): Adams and Brownsword, *Understanding Contract Law* (1987) 25–6, 52–5, 109–13.

Harvard University Press: Fried, C., *Contract as Promise* (1981); Kelman, M., *A Guide to Critical Legal Studies* (1987); Unger, R., *The Critical Legal Studies Movement* (1983).

HMSO Publications and the Law Commission: 'Consultation Paper No. 121: Privity of Contract' 151–4.

Hodder & Stoughton (Edward Arnold and Co.): Kronman, a., *Max Weber* (1983) 101–2.

Illinois University Press: Hamburger, 'The Development of the Nineteenth Century Consensus Theory of Contract' (1989) 7 *L. & Hist. Rev.* 242–3; Karsten, 'The Discovery of Law by English and American Jurists' (1991) 9 *L. & Hist. Rev.* 337–9.

Journal of Consumer Policy: Wilhelmsson, T., 'Social Force Majeure' 13 *Jnl. Con. Policy* 7–12.

Journal of Law and Economics: Goldberg, V., 'Institutional Change and the Quasi-Invisible Hand' (1974) 17 *JLE* 461, 483–6.

Journal of Legal Studies: Kronman, A., 'Mistake, Disclosure, Information and the Law of Contracts' (1978) 7 *JLS* 1, 2, 5, 16, 25, 26; Posner, R., 'Gratuitous Promises in Economic and Law' (1977) 6 *JLS* 411; Posner, R. and Rosenfield, A., 'Impossibility and Related Doctrines in Contract Law: An Economic Analysis' (1977) 6 *JLS* 83, 89–111; Simpson, A. W. B., 'Quakery and Contract Law: The Case of the Carbolic Smoke Ball' (1985) 14 *JLS* 345, 376–77.

Kluwer Academic Publishers: *Critical Studies in Private Law* (1992) 72–5, 81.

Law Commission Publications: '2nd Report on Exemption Clauses' (1976) 146.

Law and Society Association: Johnston, J., 'Law, Economics and Post-Realist Explanation' (1990) *The Law and Society Review* 1245.

Little, Brown and Company: Polinsky, A., *An Introduction to Law and Economics* (2nd edn. 1987) 7.

Lloyd's of London Press: McInnis, J., 'Frustration and Force Majeure in Building Contracts' in McKendrick, E. (ed.), *Force Majeure and Frustration of Contract* (1991) 157–9.

Macmillan Ltd: Hunt, A., *The Sociological Movement in Law* (1978) 85–8.

Melbourne University Law Review: Diamond, A., 'Commerce and Contracts' (1971) *MULR*; Ham, A., 'The Rule Against Penalties in Contract: An Economic Perspective' (1990) 17 *MULR*.

J. C. B. Mohr: Goldberg, V., *Impossibility and Related Excuses* (1988) 100–1, *The Journal of Institutional and Theoretical Economics*.

New York University Law Review: Knapp, Charles L., 'Enforcing the Contract Bargain', 44 *NYUL Rev.* 637, 721–23 (1969).

Ohio State University Press: Gilmore, G., *The Death of Contract* (1974) 31–4.

Open University Press: Harden, *The Contracting State* (1992) xi–xii; Longley, *Public Law and Health Service Accountability* (1992) 42–8.

Oxford University Press: Atiyah, *Essays on Contract* (1986), *Introduction to the Law of Contract* (4th edn. 1989), *Rise and Fall of Freedom of Contract* (1979); Beatson, 'Reforming the Law of Contracts' (1992) in *Current Legal*

Problems; Collins, 'Methods and Aims of Contract Law' (1991) *OJLS*; Cumberbatch, 'In Freedoms Cause: The Contract to Negotiate' (1992) 12 *OJLS*; Dias and Markesinis, Tort Law (2nd edn. 1988); Gardner, 'Trashing with Trollope' (1992) 12 *OJLS*; Gordley, *The Philosophical Origins of Modern Contract* (1991); Harris, 'incentives to Perform Break Contracts' (1992) in *Current Legal Problems;* Hedley, 'Keeping Contract in its Place' (1985) 5 *OJLS*; Ogus, 'Remedies: English Report' in Harris and Tallon (1991); Reiter, 'The Control of Contract Power' (1981) 1 *OJLS*; Zweiget and Kotz, *Introduction to Comparative Law* (2nd edn. 1987).

Pennsylvania Law Review and Fred Rothman & Co.: Halpern, S., 'Application of the Doctrine of Commercial Impracticability' (1987) 135 *Penn, Law Rev.* 1172–3.

Pitman Publishing: Atiyah, P. S., *Sale of Goods* (8th edn. 1990) 41.

Routledge: Cornell, D., 'The Philosophy of the Limit: Systems Theory and Feminist Legal Reform' in Cornell, Rosenfeld, and Carlson (eds.) *Deconstruction and the Possibility of Justice* (1992) 73–4.

Routledge New York: Frug, *Postmodern Legal Feminism* (1992) 95–102, 116, 117.

Southern Californian Law Review: Macneil, *A Primer of Contract Planning,* 48 *S. Cal. L. Rev.* 627–704 (1975).

Sweet and Maxwell: Atiyah, 'When is an Enforceable Agreement not a Contract' (1976) 92 LQR, 175–180; Beale, 'Unfair Contracts in Britain and Europe' (1989) CLP, 205–208; Burrows, 'Contract Tort and Restitution' (1983) 99 *LQR*, 244–245; Coote, 'Exception Clauses' (1964) 137–138; Corbin, 'Contracts for the Benefit of Third Parties' (1930) *LQR*, 13–16; Duffy, 'Unfair Contract Terms and in Draft EC Directive' (1993) *Journal of Business Law*, 72–74; Flanningan, 'Privity – The End of an Era' (1987) 103 *LQR*, 567–571; Harris, Ogus, Phillips, 'Contract Remedies and the Consumer Surplus' (1979) 95 *LQR*, 583; Harrison, 'The Reform of Consideration' (1938) 54 *LQR*, 234; Jones, 'The Recovery of Benefits Gained from as Breach of Contract' (1983) 99 *LQR*, 456–457; Tabachnik, 'Anticipatory Breach of Contract' (1972) *CLP;* Treitel, 'The Law of Contract' (8th edn. 1991); Yates, 'Exclusion Clauses in Contracts' (1982) 124–5.

University of California, Hastings College of Law: Kull, A., 'Mistake, Frustration and the Windfall Principle of Contract Remedies' (1991) 43 *Hastings Law Journal* No. 1, 2; Pettit, M., 'Private Advantage and Public Power' (1987) 38 *Hastings Law Journal* No. 3, 426–28, 431.

University of Cincinnati Law Review: Jay M. Feinman, 'The Significance of Contract Theory' (1990) 58 *U. of Cin. L. Rev.* 1283.

University of Illinois Press: Hamburger, 'The Development of the Nineteenth-Century Consensus Theory of Contract', Law and History

Review (1989), 242–3; Karsten, 'The Discovery of Law of English and American Jurists in the Seventeenth, Eighteenth, and Nineteenth Centuries', in *Law and History Review* 9 (1991), 337–9.

University of Pittsburgh Law Review: Leff, A., 'Unconscionability and the Crowd – Consumers and the Common Law Tradition' (1970) 356–7.

University of Toronto Law Journal: Reiter, B., 'Courts, Consideration and Common Sense' (1977) 27 *U. Tor. L. Jnl.* 465–6; Wiegers, W., *Economic Analysis of Law and 'Private Ordering': A Feminist Critique* (1992) 190–2.

Virginia Law Review Association and Fred B. Rothman & Co.: Baird, D. and Weisburg, R., 'Rules, Standards and the Battle of the Forms' (1982) 68 *Virginia L. Rev.* .1255 and 1229; MacNeil, I., 'Efficient Breach of Contract' (1982), 68 *Virginia L. Rev.* .950–3; Schwartz, A., 'A Pre-examination of Non-substantive Unconscionability' (1977) 63 *Virginia L. Rev.* .1056–9.

Wisconsin Law Review: Gordon, 'Macauley, McNeil and the Discovery of Solidarity and Power in Contract Law' (1985) 550; Macauley, 'An Empirical View of Contract' (1985) 466–79; Mueller, 'Contract Remedies: Business Fact and Legal Fantasy' (1967) 838; Whitford, 'Structuring Consumer Protection Legislation' (1981) 1020–21, 'Ian McNeil's Contribution to Contract Scholarship' (1985) 550. Copyright 1993, by the Board of Regents of the University of Wisconsin System.

Yale Law Journal Company and Fred B. Rothman & Co. for permission to reprint from the *Yale Law Journal*: Dalton, C., An Essay in the Deconstruction of Contract Doctrine', Vol. 94, 997–1114; Fuller, L. L. and Perdue, Jr., W. R., 'The Reliance Interest in Contract Damages', Vol. 46, 52–96; Goetz,, C. J. and Scott, R. E., 'Enforcing Promises: An Examination of the Basis of Contract', Vol. 89, 1261–1322; Kronman, A., 'Contract Law and Distributive Justice', Vol. 89, 472–511, and 'Paternalism and the Law of Contract', Vol. 92, 736–98; Llewellyn, K. N., 'What Price Contract?', Vol. 40, 704–775; Schwartz, A., 'The Case for Specific Performance', Vol. 89, 271–306.

Yale University Press: MacNeil, Professor I., *The New Social Contract* (1980) 1–4, 32–5.

* Every effort was made to contact copyright holders.

Table of United Kingdom Cases

Table of Cases from Other Jurisdictions

Table of United Kingdom Legislation

Table of Legislation from Other Jurisdictions

European Community Legislation and Treaties

Table of International Instruments

PART I

Introduction

1

The System of
the Law of Obligations and
the Basis of Contract

I. WHAT IS THE LAW OF OBLIGATIONS?

The law of obligations is a body of rules 'on the protection and transfer of assets which an individual may own' (S. Hedley, 'Contract, Tort and Restitution', (1988) 8 *LS* 137 at p. 150). These assets include interests in land, other property, money, labour, the body and physical integrity, personal reputation, and human dignity. The law of obligations is a body of private law rules in that it is concerned with relations between private individuals and/or legal persons (e.g. companies), including, where appropriate, public authorities which are participating in private relationships or are operating in the market-place in the ordinary way. It is a body of law which is indispensable in a legal order based on a liberal market economy, necessary for regulating the exchange of goods and services for profit, and for determining the scope of protection which an individual may claim *vis-à-vis* the acts or omissions of others. The law of obligations works on the basis of a system of reciprocal relationships in which individuals are the subjects of duties or obligations, or the beneficiaries of rights or interests. The primary task of the law is to adjudicate upon these relationships.

II. DIVISIONS IN THE LAW OF OBLIGATIONS

The convention in English law for a century or more up to the 1970s was, as Atiyah puts it, to conceive of the law of obligations as operating within a conceptual framework in which the basic distinction has been between

P. S. Atiyah, 'Contracts, Promises and the Law of Obligations', in *Essays on Contract* (Oxford, Clarendon Press, 1986), 10

. . . obligations which are voluntarily assumed, and obligations which are imposed by law. The former constitute the law of contract, the latter fall within the purview of the law of tort. There is, in addition, that somewhat anomalous body of law which came to be known as the law of quasi-contract or, in more modern times, as the law of restitution. This body of law was accommodated within the new conceptual framework by the academic lawyers and jurists from the 1860s onwards, and, after a considerable time-lag, their ideas came to be part of the accepted orthodoxies. The law of quasi-contract, it came to be said, was part of the law of obligations which did not arise from voluntary acts of the will, but from positive rules of law. Quasi-contract thus took its place alongside tort law on one side of the great divide. Contract alone remained on the other side.

Restitution or quasi-contract has only belatedly come to achieve recognition in the English law of obligations as a separate source of obligation. Unlike contract (agreements or bargains based on promises between two or more persons, resulting in a binding commitment to bring about a particular result) or tort (unlawful wrongs causing harm), the province of restitution is not self-evident even to lawyers. It is concerned with circumstances in which the defendant is bound to restore to the plaintiff an enrichment which he has obtained unjustly, normally at the expense of the plaintiff. It has long been termed 'quasi-contract' because Blackstone, the great eighteenth-century English jurist, in his *Commentaries on the Laws of England*, rationalized the circumstances in which the defendant was bound to restore a benefit on the basis of an implied promise on the part of the defendant to pay for the benefit conferred. Since the implied promise to pay was imposed as a fiction by the court, the obligation could be classed as an involuntary one.

However, the distinction between voluntary and involuntary obligations has itself come under attack. P. Winfield (*The Province of the Law of Tort* (1931), 32) propounded the classic distinction between tort and contract as being the distinction between obligations primarily fixed by law and those primarily fixed by the parties. This has simply proved unsustainable as a description of what the courts *do*.

Dias and Markesinis explain why, in their view, the Winfield distinction alone is insufficient:

R. Dias and B.S. Markesinis, *Tort Law*, 2nd edn. (Oxford, Oxford University Press, 1989), 7–11)

This distinction may have been acceptable when contract liability was regarded as stemming from an exchange of promises only and not, as is often the case today, from the mere fact that the plaintiff has conferred a benefit on the defendant, or has incurred loss by relying on the latter's behaviour. But basing contractual obligations exclusively on the prior promises of the parties is questioned by some influential modern contract lawyers; and to the extent that this new approach is correct, it makes the division between voluntarily assumed and legally imposed obligations an 'oversimplification' of the issue. However, it is not only contract lawyers who doubt this conceptual division; tort lawyers, too, experience difficulties in dealing with certain cases of liability which are regarded as tortious, but in which the duties imposed on the defendant flow from the fact that he and the plaintiff have entered into a particular relationship. For example, the relation between an occupier of land and his lawful visitors gives rise to a duty in the former to take care. In the absence of consideration (e.g. payment of a fee), the relationship cannot be regarded as contractual. However, there is an agreement or understanding between the parties in so far as the entrant is permitted to be there, so it is impossible to say that the will of the parties is totally irrelevant to the existence of the obligation to take care. Similarly the maker of a gratuitous but careless false statement may be liable, partly because he voluntarily undertook to offer advice, and partly because the plaintiff, to his knowledge, relied on it. The reliance element here plays a crucial role, but since it can be found both in contract and tort situations it makes the dividing line between these concepts very vague. . . .

A more subtle approach to this distinction is to say that it is not the existence of the duty, but its content that is determined by the law in tort and by the parties in contract. There is a great deal of truth in this since in a contract for the sale of goods, for example, the quantity, price, and other terms will be determined in accordance with the declared or presumed intention of the parties whereas the duties in tort are fixed by law. Even this variation, however, is not wholly true, not only because the content of tort duties can be avoided or varied by means of consent, warnings, etc., but also because an increasing number of statutes require that certain obligations be implied by law in certain contracts, for example sale of goods or hire purchase. . . .

To establish a distinction between the two concepts on the basis of the difference of their avowed aims is perhaps more promising for it may help explain, though not necessarily justify, the reluctance of the common law to impose liability for omissions and to decree compensation for pure economic loss. Tort law aims at protecting life and property, whereas the law of contract is, in a sense, there to promote the further development of a person's interests. [J. A. Weir, 'Complex Liabilities' in *International Encyclopedia of Comparative Law* (Tübingen/The Hague, Mohr/Nijhoff, 1982), xi. 12, p. 5] expressed this idea: 'Contract is productive, tort law protective. In other words, tortfeasors are typically liable for making things worse, contractors for not making them better.' If this statement is taken as descriptive of a certain attitude of the English common law it is accurate. . . .

. . . Weir's formulation refers to tortfeasors being *typically* liable for making things worse and contractors *typically* liable for not making things better. We are, in other words, again talking of the traditional paradigm contract—the executory sale—where failure by the seller to deliver the goods will deprive the buyer of a gain. This approach, however, fails to pay adequate heed to the case which is both breach of contract and a tort, for example, a dentist who has extracted the wrong tooth, or a carrier who has damaged the goods being transported. Where contractual liability is imposed because of detrimental reliance by the plaintiff, he is likely to complain that he is left worse off rather than not being made richer. Can it really be said that where there is such overlap between tort and contract the solution should be governed by formal categories shaped by tradition, and that the plaintiff's rights should depend on whether his action was framed in the one branch or the other? An affirmative answer does not commend itself; and it becomes ludicrous when one remembers that until recently the choice between the contractual or tortious set of rules was determined in a manner which, though historically explicable, was little short of being capricious.

Note

It will be useful to review the final comment in this extract in the light of the decision in *Pacific Associates Inc* v. *Baxter* and the retreat from *Junior books* discussed in the next section.

The distinction between tort and contract based on the protective/ productive distinction can safely be described as the current orthodoxy in English law. This can be seen most clearly in the field of remedies, about which much more will be said in Chapters 5 and 14. The evidence put forward for the 'tort is protective' and 'contract is productive' division is that the traditional remedy for breach of contract is what is termed the expectation interest, i.e. the damages are calculated to put the plaintiff in the position he would have been in had the contract been fulfilled, whereas the traditional remedy for tort is an award of damages (called the reliance or status quo interest) calculated to protect the plaintiff by putting him back in the position he would have been in had the tort not been committed. What is happening in effect is that the consequences of the division are being fed back into the theoretical basis for the division and offered as a justification; all of this is evidence of a division, not an explanation for a division.

A. Burrows, for example, is satisfied with the current division of the law of obligations, arguing that most law falling into the boxes 'contract', 'tort', and 'restitution' can be subsumed under three cardinal principles ('Contract, Tort, and Restitution: A Satisfactory Division or Not', (1983) 99 *LQR* 217):

the fulfilment of expectations engendered by a binding promise (contract);
the compensation of wrongful harm (tort); and
the reversing of unjust enrichment (restitution).

We can add the restitutionary interest into the system of remedies described above. The fact that there exists a body of cases not falling conveniently into either the tort box or the contract box, where the judges have in fact reversed the conferring of a benefit by the plaintiff upon the defendant, or have forced the defendant to disgorge a benefit obtained at the expense of the plaintiff, has in some quarters been used as evidence of the existence of a principle of reversing unjust enrichment.

Despite its status as orthodoxy, this division has never been entirely clear-cut, for a number of reasons. In the first place, there is a substantial body of academic opinion which rejects the dominance of expectation centred remedies. Atiyah, for example, prefers a focus on the reversal of detriments suffered in reliance upon undertakings as the new paradigm of contract law. He argues that 'A more adequate and more unifying conceptual structure for the law of obligations can be built around the interrelationship between the concepts of reciprocal benefits, acts of reasonable reliance, and voluntary human conduct' ('Contracts, Promises, and the Law of Obligations', in *Essays on Contract*, rev. edn. (Oxford, Oxford University Press, 1988), 42, 43).

Other writers have made similar points about the relationship between reliance and expectations. This, for example, is the view of Reiter.

B. Reiter, 'Contracts, Torts, Relations and Reliance', in B. Reiter and J. Swan (eds.), *Studies in Contract Law* (Toronto, Butterworths, 1980), 237

If the law is to continue to support and to encourage socially desirable but complex and subtle interrelations, lawyers and judges must reject some time-honoured professed conceptions of liability in contract and tort. Instead, they must assimilate and accommodate new notions of liability growing out of relations and reliance reasonably induced. They must gradually cease to ask whether there is offer, acceptance, consideration, warranty, contract, duty, physical harm, and tort and to regard the individual answers as compelling solutions. Instead they must ask: (1) whether or not the defendant ought to be held responsible for the plaintiff's reasonable reliance or expectations based upon the defendant's words or actions; and (2) if the defendant ought to be held liable, how should the plaintiff be protected; what remedy is appropriate?

H. Collins, meanwhile, regards the key to modern contract law as lying in the working through of the complex relationship between the individual and the state, rather than solely in the bilateral relationship between the contracting parties. In *The Law of Contract*, 1st edn. (London, Weidenfeld and Nicolson, 1986, 2), for example, he argues that his work on contract law

. . . declines to classify the subject by reference to the concept of voluntary consent, promises, or the logical limits of any other system of analytical or conceptual reasoning. It endeavours to describe how the law regulates the social context of market transactions according to modern communitarian standards. In my view, our comprehension of how the law, as a system of practical reasoning regulating everyday life, effectuates its scheme of social justice is rarely served by following conceptual schemes of classification. Instead, we must examine a social context in which the practical reasoning strives toward a coherent set of solutions to problems and disputes.

Both of these views will be represented extensively in the contextual and critical discussion of the law of contract presented throughout this book.

The second reason for doubt concerning the orthodox classification is that even Burrows himself accepts that there are areas of the law which make it difficult to argue that all of the law commonly classified as falling in the contract box falls under the expectation principle, or that all the law commonly classified as falling in the tort box falls under the compensation principle. He asserts only that his cardinal principles separate most of the law falling under each head, and that consequently the present division can be regarded as satisfactory. In particular, he acknowledges that two issues conventionally studied as matters of 'contract law', namely misrepresentation (Ch. 5) and estoppel (Ch. 6), are not easily subsumed into a principle of expectation, as the law stands at present. One might add to this list also the doctrine of implied terms in contracts (Ch. 10).

III. CONTRACTUAL AND TORTIOUS RELATIONSHIPS: THE DOMINANT JUDICIAL VIEW

While it would be wrong to dismiss the two important qualifications upon the orthodox view expressed above, it is none the less true that the dominant judicial view of contractual and tortious relationships is based at present upon a strong 'boxing' of relationships according to whether they are voluntary or not. Although an expansion of tort duties was seen in a line of cases beginning with *Hedley Byrne & Co. Ltd.* v. *Heller* ([1964] AC 465), a case concerning economic loss caused by negligent advice where the adviser and the advisee were in a relationship akin to a contract, this has failed in the long term to undermine established doctrinal categories. The high point of the development of the duty of care in negligence was the case of *Junior Books Ltd.* v. *Veitchi Co. Ltd.*, which is discussed in the next section. However, the years since *Junior Books* have seen a return to orthodoxy and to clear divisions between contract and tort, with the courts in subsequent cases refusing to impose a duty of care in order to protect the plaintiff against economic loss unconnected to personal injury or physical damage except in certain narrow circumstances. These involve the making of negligent statements where the defendant has assumed a responsibility towards the plaintiff and the latter has reasonably relied upon the former's statement. In the next section, we shall use the contrasting majority and dissenting judgments in *Junior Books* and the subsequent judicial retreat from the high-water mark in *Junior Books* in order to illustrate the distinction between contractual and tortious relationships as presently conceived by the judges. In this section, we shall also use a factual situation (*Pacific Associates* v. *Baxter*) in which the inability of the plaintiffs to point to a relationship which was contractual meant that they were unable to establish any responsibility on the part of the defendant for the loss they had suffered.

Placing a particular relationship in the box marked 'contract' or the box marked 'tort' is not always what determines whether there is liability or no liability. Sometimes, tortious and contractual relationships are concurrent, although different rules apply to the two types of claim. There are different limitation periods, different rules on the remoteness of damage, and different rules on the measure of damages (Ch. 14). In particular, characterizing a relationship as tortious usually means that a plaintiff may only claim the loss which he or she has suffered in reliance upon the defendant's conduct, rather than the additional 'expectation' measure covering the extra he or she would have gained if the defendant had behaved as he had promised he would (see further Chs. 5 and 14).

Junior Books Ltd. v. *Veitchi Co. Ltd.*
[1983] 1 AC 520

The defendants were specialist floor contractors who were engaged as subcontractors to lay a floor in the plaintiffs' factory. The plaintiffs claimed that the defendants were negligent in laying the floor, which was defective as a consequence. They further contended that the defendants knew that they had relied upon the defendants' exercising skill and care as specialist contractors in selecting the materials for the floor and in its construction. The plaintiffs brought an action claiming the estimated cost of relaying the floor, and other items of consequential loss such as the cost of moving machinery and loss of profits during the period of repair. The plaintiffs chose to sue the subcontractors, because they had already settled a contractual claim against the contractors, and the terms of the compromise left the owners to bear any future costs stemming from the defective floor. This they sought to recover from the subcontractors, who were not protected by the terms of the compromise 'which barred future claims' on the part of the contractors. The House of Lords accepted by a majority of 4 to 1 that in principle the defendants owed the plaintiffs a duty of care in respect of the economic loss which they had suffered.

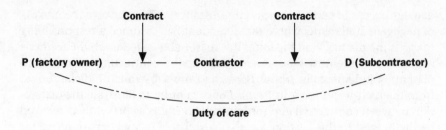

Fig. 1. The relationships in *Junior Books*

The majority of their Lordships focused on the 'proximity' of the relationship between the plaintiffs and the defendants, arguing that it was extremely close to a contractual relationship. They stressed the extent of knowledge about the plaintiffs' business which the defendants could be assumed to have. Lord Roskill even went so far as to reject any strict division between tortious and contractual relationships.

LORD FRASER . . . The proximity between the parties is extremely close, falling only just short of a direct contractual relationship. The injury to the respondents was a direct and foreseeable result of negligence by the appellants. The respondents, or their architects, nominated the appellants as specialist sub-contractors and they must therefore have relied upon their skill and knowledge. . . .

LORD KEITH OF KINKEL . . . in the present case I am of opinion that the appellants in the laying of the floor owed to the respondents a duty to take reasonable care to avoid acts or omissions which they ought to have known would be likely to cause the respondents, not only physical damage to person or property, but also pure economic loss. Economic loss would be caused to the respondents if the condition of the floor, in the course of its normal life, came to be such as to prevent the respondents from carrying out ordinary production processes on it, or, short of that, to cause the production process to be more costly than it would otherwise have been. In that situation the respondents would have been entitled to recover from the appellants expenditure incurred in relaying the floor so as to avert or mitigate their loss. . . .

. . . If the cost of maintaining the defective floor is substantially greater than it would have been in respect of a sound one, it must necessarily follow that their manufacturing operations are being carried on at a less profitable level than would otherwise have been the case, and that they are therefore suffering economic loss. That is the sort of loss which the appellants, standing in the relationship to the respondents which they did, ought reasonably to have anticipated as likely to occur if their workmanship was faulty. They must have been aware of the nature of the respondents' business, the purpose for which the floor was required, and the part it was to play in their operations. The appellants accordingly owed the respondents a duty to take reasonable care to see that their workmanship was not faulty, and are liable for the foreseeable consequences, sounding in economic loss, of their failure to do so. These consequences may properly be held to include less profitable operation due to the heavy cost of maintenance. In so far as the respondents, in order to avert or mitigate such loss, incur expenditure on relaying the floor surface, that expenditure becomes the measure of the appellants' liability. . . .

LORD ROSKILL . . . I look for the reasons why, it being conceded that the appellants owed a duty of care to others not to construct the flooring so that those others were in peril of suffering loss or damage to their persons or their property, that duty of care should not be equally owed to the respondents. The appellants, though not in direct contractual relationship with the respondents, were as nominated sub-contractors in almost as close a commercial relationship with the respondents as it is possible to envisage short of privity of contract. Why then should the appellants not be under a duty to the respondents not to expose the respondents to a possible liability to financial loss for repairing the flooring should it prove that that flooring had been negligently constructed? It is conceded that if the flooring had been so badly constructed that to avoid imminent danger the respondents had expended money upon renewing it the respondents could have recovered the cost of so doing. It seems curious that, if the appellants' work had been so bad that to avoid imminent danger expenditure had been incurred, the respondents could recover that expenditure, but that if the work was less badly done so that remedial work could be postponed they cannot do so. Yet this is seemingly the result of the appellants' contentions. . . .

. . . I think today the proper control lies not in asking whether the proper remedy should lie in contract or instead in delict or tort, not in somewhat capricious judicial determination whether a particular case falls on one side of the line or the other, not in somewhat artificial distinctions between physical and economic or financial loss when the two sometimes go together and sometimes do not—it is sometimes overlooked that virtually all damage including physical damage is in one sense financial or economic for it is compensated by an award of damages—but in the first instance in establishing the relevant principles and then in deciding whether the particular case falls within or without those principles. . . .

Turning back to the present appeal I therefore ask first whether there was the requisite degree of proximity so as to give rise to the relevant duty of care relied on by the respondents. I regard the following facts as of crucial importance in requiring an affirmative answer to that question. (1) The appellants were nominated sub-contractors. (2) The appellants were specialists in flooring. (3) The appellants knew what products were required by the respondents and their main contractors and specialised in the production of those products. (4) The appellants alone were responsible for the composition and construction of the flooring. (5) The respondents relied upon the appellants' skill and experience. (6) The appellants as nominated sub-contractors must have known that the respondents relied upon their skill and experience. (7) The relationship between the parties was as close as it could be short of actual privity of contract. (8) The appellants must be taken to have known that if they did the work negligently (as it must be assumed that they did) the resulting defects would at some time require remedying by the respondents expending money upon the remedial measures as a consequence of which the respondents would suffer financial or economic loss.

Lord Brandon's dissent provides a strong contrast in approach.

LORD BRANDON . . . The effect of accepting the respondents' contention with regard to the scope of the duty of care involved would be, in substance, to create, as between two persons who are not in any contractual relationship with each other, obligations of one of those two persons to the other which are only really appropriate as between persons who do have such a relationship between them.

In the case of a manufacturer or distributor of goods, the position would be that he warranted to the ultimate user or consumer of such goods that they were as well designed, as merchantable and as fit for their contemplated purpose as the exercise of reasonable care could make them. In the case of sub-contractors such as those concerned in the present case, the position would be that they warranted to the building owner that the flooring, when laid, would be as well designed, as free from defects of any kind and as fit for its contemplated purpose as the exercise of reasonable care could make it. In my view, the imposition of warranties of this kind on one person in favour of another, when there is no contractual relationship between them, is contrary to any sound policy requirement.

Note

In practice, it is the dissent of Lord Brandon which has endured, rather than the broad approach to the issues of principle taken by the majority. Although *Junior Books* has never been formally overruled, it has been strictly confined to its own facts by subsequent cases in the Court of Appeal and the House of Lords, where the orthodoxy has reasserted itself of confining duties of care in respect of careless *acts* (as opposed to statements) to situations involving the infliction of personal injury or physical damage to property. The 'retreat from *Junior Books*' is well documented in the tort textbooks (see e.g. *Winfield* and *Jolowicz on Tort*, 13th ed. (London, Sweet and Maxwell, 1989), 76 ff.) and can be traced through cases such as

Leigh & Sillivan Ltd. v. *Aliakmon Shipping Co. Ltd.* (*The Aliakmon*) ([1986] AC 785), *Muirhead* v. *Industrial Tank Specialities Ltd.* ([1986] QB 507), *Governors of the Peabody Donation Fund* v. *Sir Lindsay Parkinson and Co. Ltd.* ([1985] AC 210), *D. & F. Estates Ltd.* v. *Church Commissioners for England* ([1989] 1 AC 177), and *Murphy* v. *Brentwood DC* ([1991] 1 AC 398). Of greater interest to us here is the case of *Pacific Associates Inc.* v. *Baxter*, which illustrates current judicial thinking about the tort/contract boundary and about the effect of an existing contractual relationship or contractual structure upon duties of care.

Pacific Associates Inc. v. *Baxter* [1989]
2 All ER 159

The plaintiff, the 'Contractor', successfully tendered for a contract for dredging work. This contract was with the 'Employer', i.e. the person for whom he was doing the dredging work. The contract was to be supervised by the 'Engineer', i.e. a professional engineer who would, *inter alia*, ensure that the Contractor carried out the works in accordance with the contract and certify any certificates (applications) for payment that the Contractor submitted. The contract between the Contractor and the Employer provided that, in the event of a dispute between the Contractor and either the Employer or the Engineer, the dispute should be settled by an Arbitrator. This is the clause GC67 referred to in the judgments. Thus the Contractor had accepted a contract with the Employer containing terms and a particular remedial structure which did not extend to remedies against the Engineer but tied the Contractor into a contractual structure which was exhaustive of his rights. The relationship is summarized in Fig. 2.

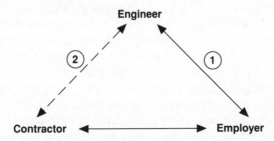

FIG 2. The relationships in *Pacific Associates Inc.* v. *Baxter*

Notes

1. Contract between Employer and Engineer under which the Employer could look to the Engineer to reimburse him for any successful claims for breach of contract against him by the contractor resulting from the Engineer's negligence.

2. No contract here, and the Court of Appeal finds that there is no assumption of responsibility by the Engineer towards the Contractor. The only action against the Engineer which the Contractor could bring must lie in tort, as there is *no* contractual relationship. The Engineer is not a party to the contract between the Employer and the Contractor.

The Contractor submitted claims to the Engineer asserting that the work was costing more than the Contractor could have envisaged at the beginning of the contract with the information then available to him. The Engineer rejected these claims. The matter was referred to the Arbitrator, who awarded the Contractor £10 million. The Contractor, on receipt of the award, agreed that it was in full and final settlement of any claims that he might have against the Employer. The Contractor then began the action against the Engineer claiming further sums (£31 million plus interest) due as a result of what he asserted to be the Engineer's failure to certify his valid claim for additional expense incurred.

All three judges in the Court of Appeal rejected the Contractor's claim on the grounds that there was no assumption of responsibility on the part of the Engineer towards the Contractor and that there was no contractual relationship between them. The Contractor had rights against the Employer under his contract with the Employer, and could not seek to establish a further relationship with the Engineer beyond his contract remedies against the Employer.

PURCHAS LJ . . . In support of his appeal counsel for the contractor submitted that on the assumptions made for the purposes of the trial of the preliminary issue the three criteria necessary to establish liability which appear from the authorities and which were marshalled in the judgment of *Bingham LJ* in *Caparo Industries plc* v. *Dickman* [1989] 1 All ER 798 were established. These were (1) foreseeability of harm, (2) proximity, (3) that as a matter of policy it is just and reasonable to impose a duty of care on the engineer in favour of the contractor. He submitted that a failure on the part of the engineer properly to discharge its duty under the contract must be taken to cause foreseeable harm to the contractor which was, under the terms of its contract with the employer dependent on the proper discharge by the engineer of his duties, inter alia, to certify the moneys due to the contractor under the contract. In addition counsel for the contractor emphasised that the employer had a right of action outside the contract and the arbitration provision in GC67 against the engineer in negligence or breach of duty . . . and that, therefore, it would not be just and reasonable if a similar right against the engineer was not enjoyed by the other party to the contract, namely the contractor. . . .

Counsel for the engineer in support of the judgment relied on the well-established proposition that there was no general liability in tort for foreseeable economic loss dissociated from physical damage. He relied on the proposition that the terms of the contract sufficiently defined the rights and liabilities arising between the engineer and the two parties to the contract; and that there was no justification for any extension of this position by superimposing a duty in tort. Furthermore, counsel relied on the disclaimer contained in cl 86 of the conditions of particular application (to which I shall refer as 'PC86') as a disclaimer on which the engineer could rely to disprove that element of acceptance of a duty of care necessary to establish liability under the principle in *Hedley Byrne*. In this case, it was submitted, the contractor's rights of protection in relation to any loss which might ensue from a failure on the part of the engineer either properly to certify or to accept a claim under GC67 were catered for under the arbitration provisions and a right of recovery against the employer under that clause. Council submitted that the remote possibility of an employer becoming bankrupt or unable to meet the liability for any damages flowing from the conduct of his agent, the engineer, was too remote a consideration to affect a general principle of whether or not liability in tort should be superimposed on the contractual position. If there was any appreciable danger of the employer failing to meet his obligations under the contract it would be open to the contractor to stipulate for a separate contractual right of action against the engineer.

On the question of reasonableness, counsel for the engineer submitted that the mere fact that the engineer accepted appointment by the employer to act under the contract was not sufficient to impose a duty in tort in favour of the contractor who had its own remedies under the contract. Furthermore, in the face of the commercial relationship and the detailed provisions of the contract, it was not just and reasonable but rather undesirable to import into a carefully structured contractual arrangement added obligations in tort. This was particularly the case where those provisions expressly provided an exclusion from liability protecting the engineer or any of its staff from liability for their acts or obligations under the contract. In support of his respondent's notice counsel submitted that in any event the engineer was entitled to immunity from suit in respect of the decision under GC67 because any miscertification at an earlier stage could then have been corrected at the GC67 stage and that in acting in pursuance of its duties under GC67 the engineer was acting in a quasi-arbitral role. . . .

. . . The engineer is a professional body and in the context of the contract assumes a responsibility towards the employer to execute its duties in a professional manner. It remains, however, to consider whether beyond this the engineer accepted a direct duty towards the contractor and whether on its part the contractor relied on the due performance of its duties under the contract by the engineer beyond giving rights to it to proceed against the employer under the contract. This question lies at the heart of this appeal and depends on whether an appropriate degree of proximity between the engineer and the contractor beyond the terms of contract is established. As I have already commented the assumption of the truth of the facts pleaded in the amended statement of claim does not determine this issue.

During the course of argument the court has been referred to a large number of authorities . . . It is clear from these authorities that there is no one touchstone with which to determine the existence or otherwise of a duty of care in any particular circumstances. Various criteria emerge which are capable of adaptation to the particular circumstances of the case under review. As a generalisation before a duty can be found to exist the circumstances in which the parties find themselves must establish a proximity of some kind that would demonstrate that the lack of care of the one will foreseeably cause pecuniary loss to the other in the context where the first has accepted responsibility for such loss, if occasioned by his negligence, and the second has in the same context relied on the exercise of due care and skill by the first so as to give rise to a direct duty to be responsible for that loss. The matter does not end there, however, because superimposed on the foregoing criteria is what has been called a policy aspect, namely that before a duty of care will be held to exist the court should find it just and reasonable to impose such a duty . . .

. . . where the parties have come together against a contractual structure which provides for compensation in the event of a failure of one of the parties involved, the court will be slow to superimpose an added duty of care beyond that which was in the contemplation of the parties at the time that they came together. I acknowledge at once the distinction, namely where obligations are founded in contract they depend on the agreement made and the objective intention demonstrated by that agreement whereas the existence of a duty in tort may not have such a definitive datum point. However, I believe that in order to determine whether a duty arises in tort it is necessary to consider the circumstances in which the parties came together in the initial stages at which time it should be considered what obligations, if any, were assumed by the one in favour of the other and what reliance was placed by the other on the first. . . .

The contractual structure against which the engineer and the contractor came into contact was substantially provided by the terms of the contract which, of course, were part of the background against which the tender was made. The contract in its general conditions contained a large number of provisions by reason of which the contractor was in a direct relationship with the engineer; examples are to be found in GC46 and GC56 and numerous other certifying conditions such as GC52, GC60 and PC60 etc. In other aspects the engineer worked solely as the agent for the employer. Instances of this were, of course, the preparation of the invitations to tender and the contract document, bills of quantities etc which accompanied it. We were told that there was no record available of any specific contract between the employer and the engineer in relation to the contract. The best information was that the engineer had for a considerable time prior to 1974 acted in relation to other contracts for the employer and that the position between them was most probably one similar to a general retainer. For the purposes of this appeal I do not think that the precise contractual arrangement between the employer and the engineer is relevant. It is sufficient to notice that there must have been some contract, expressed or implied, between the two a term of which must have been that the engineer would carry out its function with due skill and care.

It is now necessary to turn to consider some of the authorities relating to the specific position as between the contractor and the engineer. It is immediately apparent that there is no simple unqualified answer to the question 'Does the engineer owe a duty to the contractor in tort to exercise reasonable skill and care?' but that this question can only be answered in the context of the factual matrix including especially the contractual structure against which such duty is said to arise.

The central question which arises here is: against the contractual structure of the contract into which the contractor was prepared to enter with the employer, can it be said that it looked to the engineer by way of reliance for the proper execution of the latter's duties under the contract in extension of the rights which would accrue to it under the contract against the employer? In other words, although the parties were brought into close proximity in relation to the contract, was it envisaged that a failure to carry out its duties under the contract by the engineer would foreseeably cause any loss to the contractor which was not properly recoverable by it under its rights against the employer under the contract? . . .

. . . did the contractor rely on any assumption of liability in tort appearing to be accepted on the part of the engineer which would afford to it remedies beyond those which it acquired under the terms of the contract in respect of which it was to tender? One must start with the proposition that if it had required an indemnity or extra-contractual protection in respect of defaults by the engineer or insolvency on the part of the employer then it was open to the contractor to have stipulated for such protection. On the contrary, by accepting the invitation to tender on the terms disclosed in the document 'Instructions to Tenderers' and the contractual documents submitted therewith it must be taken to accept the role to be played by the engineer as defined in the contract.

The terms of the contract provided a three-stage process under which the contractor obtained payment for its work, the third stage of which (GC67) included a reference to one or more independent arbitrators who are given the power 'to open up review and revise any decision opinion direction certificate or valuation of the Engineer'. In the case of withholding by the engineer of any certificate the resort to arbitration is not postponed until after completion of the works. However in this case, as a matter of history, the claim under GC67 was not made until after the second certificate of completion. The opening words of GC67 are extremely wide: 'If any dispute or difference of any kind whatsoever shall arise between the Employer or Engineer and the Contractor . . .' No function of the engineer under or in connection with the contract was mentioned to the court during the course of argument which would escape this clause. . . .

I have come to the conclusion, for the reasons already stated, that no liability can be established in tort under which the engineer owed a direct duty to the contractor in the circumstances disclosed in this case. I emphasise, however, that in coming to this conclusion it does depend on the particular circumstances of the case not the least of which were the contractual provisions in the contract which afforded an avenue enabling the contractor to recover from the employer. I see no justification for superimposing on this contractual structure an additional liability in tort as between the engineer and the contractor. . . .

RALPH GIBSON LJ . . . The contractual duty of the engineer, owed to the employer, to act fairly and impartially is a duty in the performance of which the employer has a real interest. If the engineer should act unfairly to the detriment of the contractor claims will be made by the contractor to get the wrong decisions put right. If arbitration proceedings are necessary the employer will be exposed to the risk of costs in addition to being ordered to pay the sums which the engineer should have allowed. If the decisions and advice of the engineer, which caused the arbitration proceedings to be taken, were shown by the employer to have been made and given by the engineer in breach of the engineer's contractual duty to the employer, the employer would recover its losses from the engineer. There is, therefore, not only an interest on the part of the employer in the due performance by the engineer of the duty to act fairly and impartially but also a sanction which would operate, in addition to the engineer's sense of professional obligation, to deter the engineer from the careless making of unfair or unsustainable decisions adverse to the contractor.

IV. PROTECTING THE RESTITUTIONARY INTEREST IN THE CONTRACT

We are not concerned in this book with the whole range of restitutionary obligations. It is, however, important to see the contribution which restitutionary remedies can make in two particular sets of circumstances:

(a) two parties have embarked upon negotiations with a view to concluding a contract, performance by one has begun at the request of the other, but no formal agreement is ever reached;

(b) a contract between two parties comes to an end (e.g. it may be discharged by circumstances beyond the control of either party), and a restitutionary remedy is necessary to undo the consequences of past performance (see further Ch. 12).

The next case deals with restitutionary remedies in case (a) set out above.

British Steel Corporation v. Cleveland Bridge & Engineering Co. Ltd.
[1984] 1 All ER 504

The defendants, Cleveland Bridge and Engineering Co. (CBE), approached the plaintiffs British Steel Corporation (BSC) and asked them to manufacture certain steel fasteners and other goods. There was some discussion between the parties on the technical specifications for the goods. CBE issued a 'letter of intent'—a technical term used to describe a letter issued by one party to the other asserting their intention to enter into a contract. The defendants claimed that the contract would be on their terms and asked BSC to begin manufacture straight away. These terms were not acceptable to BSC, but they decided to object at a later date, when a formal contract offer was made. Meanwhile they began to manufacture the goods. Further discussions began over the price, specifications, delivery dates, and delivery order for the goods. Eventually, agreement was reached about the price of the goods but on little else. Several months later, when all the goods had been delivered, CBE refused to pay for them on the grounds that the goods were not delivered in accordance with the terms of the contract. BSC claimed the price of the goods or a similar sum as a *quantum meruit*, i.e. payment of a reasonable sum for the value of the benefit they had conferred on CBE. CBE counterclaimed for damages for breach of contract, arguing that some of the goods had been delivered late and others had been delivered out of the order prescribed by the contract.

Goff J's judgment makes it clear that there was nothing on the facts of the case to justify a finding of a contractual relationship between the parties. The consequence of this finding was that the claim by CBE must fail, as there was never a binding promise made by BSC on the terms of delivery. However, BSC would be entitled to a reasonable sum (*quantum meruit*) by way of a claim in restitution. If agreement had been reached, i.e. if there had been a contract between the parties extending to all terms apart from the price, then BSC would have been entitled under that contract to a reasonable sum (a *quantum meruit*) for the goods *and* CBE could have asserted their counterclaim.

GOFF J . . . two main areas of dispute developed between the parties.

First, was there any binding contract between the parties at all, under which the nodes were delivered? CBE contended that there was such a contract, which was to be found in certain documents (including a letter of intent issued by CBE dated 21 February 1979) and the conduct of BSC in proceeding with the manufacture of the nodes. BSC's primary contention was that no binding contract was ever entered into, and that they were entitled to be paid a reasonable sum for the nodes on a quantum meruit, a claim sounding not in contract but in quasi contract. The motives of the parties in putting their cases in these different ways lay primarily in the fact that, unless there was a binding contract between the parties there was no legal basis for CBE's counterclaim for damages in respect of late delivery or delivery out of sequence. So far as delivery was concerned, CBE's submission was that BSC's obligations, under the contract alleged by them to have come into existence, was to deliver the goods in the requested sequence and within a reasonable time. . . .

Now the question whether in a case such as the present any contract has come into existence must depend on a true construction of the relevant communications which have passed between the parties and the effect (if any) of their actions pursuant to those communications. There can be no hard and fast answer to the question whether a letter of intent will give rise to a binding agreement: everything must depend on the circumstances of the particular case. In most cases, where work is done pursuant to a request contained in a letter of intent, it will not matter whether a contract did or did not come into existence, because, if the party who has acted on the request is simply claiming payment, his claim will usually be based on a quantum meruit, and it will make no difference whether that claim is contractual or quasi-contractual. Of course, a quantum meruit claim . . . straddles the boundaries of what we now call contract and restitution, so the mere framing of a claim as a quantum meruit claim, or a claim for a reasonable sum, does not assist in classifying the claim as contractual or quasi contractual. But where, as here, one party is seeking to claim damages for breach of contract, the question whether any contract came into existence is of crucial importance.

As a matter of analysis the contract (if any) which may come into existence following a letter of intent may take one of two forms: either there may be an ordinary executory contract, under which each party assumes reciprocal obligations to the other; or there may be what is sometimes called an 'if' contract, ie a contract under which A requests B to carry out a certain performance and promises B that, if he does so, he will receive a certain performance in return, usually remuneration for his performance. The latter transaction is really no more than a standing offer which, if acted on before it lapses or is lawfully withdrawn, will result in a binding contract. . . .

. . . There remains the question whether, by reason of BSC carrying out work pursuant to the request contained in CBE's letter of intent, there came into existence a contract by virtue of which BSC were entitled to claim reasonable remuneration; ie whether there was an 'if' contract of the kind I have described. In the course of argument, I was attracted by this alternative (really on the basis that, not only was it analytically possible, but also that it could provide a vehicle for certain contractual obligations of BSC concerning their performance, eg implied terms as to the quality of goods supplied by them). But the more I have considered the case, the less attractive I have found this alternative. The real difficulty is to be found in the factual matrix of the transaction, and in particular the fact that the work was being done *pending* a formal sub-contract the terms of which were still in a state of negotiation. If is, of course, a notorious fact that, when a contract is made for the supply of goods on a scale and in circumstances such as the present, it will in all probability be subject to standard terms, usually the standard terms of the supplier. Such standard terms will frequently legislate, not only for the liability of the seller for defects, but also for the damages (if any) for which the seller will be liable in the event not only of defects in the goods but also of late delivery. It is commonplace that a seller of goods may exclude liability for consequential loss, and may agree liq-uidated damages for delay. In the present case, an unresolved dispute broke out between the parties on the question whether CBE's or BSC's standard terms were to apply, the former providing no limit to the seller's liability for delay and the latter excluding such liability altogether. Accordingly, when, in a case such as the present, the parties are still in a state of negotiation, it is impossible to predicate what liability (if any) will be assumed by the seller for, eg, defective goods or late delivery, if a formal contract should be entered into. In these circumstances, if the buyer asks the seller to commence work 'pend-ing' the parties entering into a formal contract, it is difficult to infer from the buyer acting on that request that he is assuming any responsibility for his per-formance, except such responsibility as will rest on him under the terms of the contract which both parties confidently anticipate they will shortly enter into. It would be an extraordinary result if, by acting on such a request in such circum-stances, the buyer were to assume an unlimited liability for his contractual per-formance, when he would never assume such liability under any contract which he entered into.

For these reasons, I reject the solution of the 'if' contract. In my judgment, the true analysis of the situation is simply this. Both parties confidently expected a formal contract to eventuate. In these circumstances, to expedite performance under that anticipated contract, one requested the other to com-mence the contract work, and the other complied with that request. If there-after, as anticipated, a contract was entered into, the work done as requested will be treated as having been performed under that contract; if, contrary to their expectation, no contract was entered into, then the performance of the work is not referable to any contract the terms of which can be ascertained, and the law simply imposes an obligation on the party who made the request to pay a reasonable sum for such work as has been done pursuant to that request, such an obligation sounding in quasi contract or, as we now say, in restitution. Consistently with that solution, the party making the request may find himself liable to pay for work which he would not have had to pay for as such if the anticipated contract had come into existence, eg preparatory work which will, if the contract is made, be allowed for in the price of the finished work.

V. THE DRAFT DIRECTIVE ON THE LIABILITY OF SUPPLIERS OF SERVICES

A different way of conceiving of the notion of responsibility or obligation is to focus on the particular person to be protected. One person who has attracted increasing protection in modern societies which are distinguished by complex supply chains of goods and high levels of technological development has been the consumer. For example, the EC Product Liability Directive adopted in 1985 has required all twelve members of the European Community to adopt legislation imposing strict liability on the manufacturer of products in respect of any defects in such products. A consumer injured by a product need only prove the existence of a defect and the causal link between the defect and the loss; manufacturers cannot escape liability by proving that they were not responsible for the defect (Consumer Protection Act 1987).

It is now proposed to extend a similar approach to the supply of services. The draft Directive extracted below would set up a reversal of the burden of proof so that persons who are injured by a service would no longer have to prove that the supplier was negligent. The reversal extends both to a person who has bought the service, and so is in a contractual relationship with the supplier, and to third parties who are injured.

Commission Proposal for a Council Directive on the liability of suppliers of services
COM(90) 482 final; **OJ 1991 C12/8**
[Recitals omitted]

Article 1

Principle

1. The supplier of a service shall be liable for damage to the health and physical integrity of persons or the physical integrity of movable or immovable property, including the persons or property which were the object of the service, caused by a fault committed by him in the performance of the service.
2. The burden of proving the absence of fault shall fall upon the supplier of the service.
3. In assessing the fault, account shall be taken of the behaviour of the supplier of the service, who, in normal and reasonably foreseeable conditions, shall ensure the safety which may reasonably be expected.
4. Whereas the mere fact that a better service existed or might have existed at the moment of performance or subsequently shall not constitute a fault.

Article 2

Definition of service

For the purpose of this Directive, 'service' means any transaction carried out on a commercial basis or by way of a public service and in an independent manner, whether or not in return for payment, which does not have as its direct and exclusive object the manufacture of movable property or the transfer of rights *in rem* or intellectual property rights.

This Directive shall not apply to public services intended to maintain public safety. It shall not apply to package travel or to waste services.

Nor shall it apply to damage covered by liability arrangements governed by international agreements ratified by the Member States or by the Community.

Article 3

Definition of supplier of services

1. The term 'supplier of services' means any natural or legal person governed by private or public law who, in the course of his professional activities or by way of a public service, provides a service referred to in Article 2.
2. Any person who provides a service by using the services of a representative or other legally independent intermediary shall continue to be deemed to be a supplier of services within the meaning of this Directive. . . .

Article 4

Definition of damage

The term 'damage' means:

(a) death or any other direct damage to the health or physical integrity of persons;
(b) any direct damage to the physical integrity of movable or immovable property, including animals, provided that this property:
    (i) is of a type normally intended for private use or consumption, and
    (ii) was intended for or used by the injured person, principally for his private use or consumption;
(c) any financial material damage resulting directly from the damage referred to at (a) and (b).

Article 5

Proof

The injured person shall be required to provide proof of the damage and the causal relationship between the performance of the service and the damage.

Article 6

Third parties and joint liability

1. The liability of the supplier of the service shall not be reduced where the damage is caused jointly by a fault on his part and by the intervention of a third party.
2. The liability of the supplier of the service may be reduced, or even waived, where the damage is caused jointly by a fault on his part and by the fault of the injured person, or a person for whom the injured person is responsible.

Article 7

Exclusion of liability

The supplier of a service may not, in relation to the injured person, limit or exclude his liability under this Directive.

. . .

Notes

1. The present status of the draft Directive is uncertain, as in its original version it encountered a good deal of criticism from professional groupings. It is already the case that the draft is limited in its application—it excludes from its ambit liability for pure economic loss, thus excluding most of the 'clean hands' professions such as lawyers and accountants. Since the publication of the draft, doctors and the construction industry, led by architects, have argued vigorously, and probably successfully, for their services to be dealt with in separate sectoral directives. Publication of the revised drafts is still awaited.

2. As Article 1(3) points out, the standard of the supply of services is set by 'reasonable expectations'. It is worth considering whether these 'expectations' are the same for persons who have contracted to receive services, who may have particular expectations because, for example, they have paid for a high-cost, high-quality service, for third parties who are coincidentally injured by a defective service (e.g. a pedestrian injured by a car which has been defectively repaired). The justification for protecting the third party in this case is that, as a consumer, he has come within the sphere of risk created by the service.

3. See further on recent important contract law developments affecting consumers: G. Howells, 'Contract Law: The Challenge for the Critical Consumer Lawyer', in T. Wilhelmsson (ed.), *Perspectives of Critical Contract Law* (Aldershot, Dartmouth, 1993), 327.

VI. THE ESSENCE OF AGREEMENT

We have located contract within the law of obligations by focusing on its nature as a voluntary agreement. In the final section of this introductory chapter, we aim to provide the student with the basic tools of analysis with which to understand the notion of an agreement and the closely related idea of the 'promise'.

J. Rinkes and G. Samuel, *Contractual and Non-Contractual Obligations in English Law* (Nijmegen, Ars Aequi Libri, 1992), 103–5

English judges and academics state from time to time that the English law of contract is about enforceable agreements and it has to be said at once that there is a certain truth in this view. Thus most English commercial contract documents superficially look little different from the commercial agreements to be found anywhere in Europe, and even the legislator in the United Kingdom occasionally uses the language of agreement. Yet a strict legal analysis of English contract law will reveal, as we have already indicated, that it is not the notion of *convention* but the notion of *pollicitatio* or *promissum* that forms the focal point of liability; the English contractor is liable in damages at common law for breach of promise rather than non-performance of an agreement.

In fact a close look at the nineteenth century cases reveals that the English law of contract was, in its formative days at least, founded on two ideas. First there was a general principle that 'if a man has made a deliberate statement, and another has acted upon it, he cannot be at liberty to deny the truth of the statement'. Secondly, there was the principle that any contractual promise was *prima facie* actionable even if it lacked an object and a cause in the French law sense of these terms. Accordingly if a person was contractually to promise that it shall rain the next day he would be liable not only on the basis that he ought not to be allowed to go back on his word but also on the basis that he has assumed a risk and must bear the consequences. These two ideas give rise to a law of contract in England which is really very much more objective in its foundation than the French model which is founded on the subjective notion of consent. . . .

. . . The standard definition of an English contract remains 'a promise or set of promises which the law will enforce'.

Note

The point Rinkes and Samuel are making here is that the particular focus of English law of contract on promise is a product of history, not a moral choice (although see the work of Charles Fried where a contrary position is taken, below Ch. 2). One of the questions which we shall be addressing in

Chapter 2 concerns the types of factors which have influenced that histori-cal evolution, including philosophical, economic, political, and social developments.

The practical implications of these insights are worked through neatly in the following extract from Adams and Brownsword. This extract is based on the fairy-tale of Jack and the Beanstalk. In the story, Jack takes his poverty-ridden family's last cow to market. On the way there he exchanges it for some beans which are described as magic, much to his mother's annoyance. He plants the magic beans and a huge beanstalk grows from them. Jack climbs the beanstalk and after several trials and tribulations (their exact nature depends on the version of the story) the magic beans do indeed become a passport to riches for Jack and his family.

J. Adams and R. Brownsword, *Understanding Contract Law* (London, Fontana, 1987), 25–6

Consider, the following three categories of promise:

(i) A strictly unilateral (gratuitous) promise, e.g. Jack (of 'Jack and the Beanstalk') promises to give away his mother's last cow to the butcher whom he meets on the way to the market, Jack (contrary to the story) ask-ing for nothing in return for the cow.

(ii) A promise-in-return-for-an-act, e.g. Jack (again contrary to the story) promises to give the butcher the cow if the butcher can grow a beanstalk, climb up it, kill the giant who lives in the land at the top of the beanstalk, and return safely with the giant's riches.

(iii) A promise-in-return-for-a-promise, e.g. Jack (this time more or less as in the story) promises to give the butcher the cow if the butcher promises to give him some magic beans in return.

Promise (i) *requires* no reciprocal act (as in (ii)). Nor does it *require* any recip-rocal promise of performance by the promisee (as in (iii)). It could be straight-forwardly unconditional, as in our example, or it could be conditional, but not in a way that makes a return demand on the promisee (e.g. where Jack promises to give the cow to the butcher if it rains the following day). What really matters about promise (i) is not so much whether it is unconditional or conditional, but that it requires no return act or promise of performance from the promisee. Promises (ii) and (iii), by contrast, are 'reciprocal-conditional' precisely because they do stipulate some return act or promise of performance.

Next, we can distinguish between the following three senses of agreement:

(i) Agreement-as-acceptance, meaning a promisee's willingness to stand in the position of promisee with respect to a particular promise (e.g. the butcher indicates that he agreed to accept Jack's gratuitous promise to give him his brown cow—maybe the butcher would not have so accepted a gratuitous promise to give him a white elephant).

(ii) Agreement-as-bargain-form, meaning a form of reciprocal arrangement (e.g. Jack proposes to give his cow to the butcher in return for some reciprocal act or promise of performance).

(iii) Agreement-as-commitment, meaning a promisee's indication of his commitment to an agreement-as-bargain-form, where the promisor has stipulated the making of a reciprocal promise.

To what extent can these three senses of agreement be found where we are dealing with each of the three categories of promise previously identified?

First, if Jack gratuitously promises to give away his cow to the butcher, the butcher can either accept or not accept. Assuming that the butcher accepts Jack's gift, there is agreement-as-acceptance. However, there can never be agreement in either of the other two senses, for both these senses presuppose a return condition for the promisee, and this is missing in the gratuitous promise. Next, if Jack promises to give the butcher his cow only if the butcher grows a beanstalk, climbs up it, kills the giant who lives in the land at the top of the beanstalk and returns safely with the giant's riches, then Jack's proposal is an agreement-as-bargain-form, and this stands irrespective of whether the butcher accepts Jack's challenge. If the butcher accepts the challenge, then there is also agreement-as-acceptance. What there cannot be, however, is agreement-as-commitment, since this presupposes a promise-in-return-for-a-promise. Finally, if Jack promises to give his cow to the butcher if the butcher promises to give Jack some magic beans, then, regardless of whether the butcher so promises, Jack's proposal constitutes an agreement-as-bargain-form. Assuming that the butcher makes the return promise, there is also agreement-as-acceptance and agreement-as-commitment. The promise-in-return-for-a-promise alone has the potential to yield agreement in all three senses.

These abstract distinctions are reflected in the doctrinal watershed between enforceable and unenforceable promises. English law . . . exhibits a tension between the policy: (a) to enforce only promises which form part of an agreed exchange; (b) to enforce promises which induce reliance and change of position; and (c) to enforce a restricted number of gift and other gratuitous promises.

Note

The policy choices raised by Adams and Brownsword in their final paragraph are examined further in Chapter 6, when we consider in detail the doctrine of consideration.

Tweddle v. *Atkinson* provides a useful introduction to some of these ideas.

Tweddle v. *Atkinson* (1861)
1 B. & S. 393

William Guy and John Tweddle contracted with each other to confer a benefit (a sum of money) upon Tweddle's son, William, on the occasion of the younger Tweddle's marriage to Guy's daughter. Tweddle senior paid his son the promised money but Guy did not. The amount was still outstanding at Guy's death and Tweddle junior sued his estate for the amount.

WIGHTMAN J Some of the old decisions appear to support the proposition that a stranger to the consideration of a contract may maintain an action upon it, if he stands in such a near relationship to the party from whom the consideration proceeds, that he may be considered a party to the consideration. . . . But there is no modern case in which the proposition has been supported. On the contrary, it is now established that no stranger to the consideration can take advantage of a contract, although made for his benefit.

CROMPTON J . . . The modern cases have, in effect, overruled the old decisions; they shew that the consideration must move from the party entitled to sue upon the contract. It would be a monstrous proposition to say that a person was a party to the contract for the purpose of suing upon it for his own advantage, and not a party to it for the purpose of being sued.

Note

Two doctrines are illustrated here. First is the concept of consideration, seen here as the idea that the putative promisee (Tweddle junior) has to provide something in return for the promise. It is clear that he has not (the marriage is not sufficient). An alternative way of determining enforceability is to view Tweddle junior as a stranger to the contract between the two fathers. The (contractual) doctrine under which the contract is viewed as a closed obligation which does not confer rights or enforceable benefits on third parties is termed privity of contract (Ch. 7). On either test, the contract cannot be enforced by Tweddle junior.

Questions

1. Why did the House of Lords retreat from *Junior Books*?

2. What solution does restitution provide to the problems which arise when parties fail to reach a final agreement but one party, at least, begins performing what he thinks are his obligations?

3. The draft Directive on the liability of suppliers of services does not distinguish between damage occurring in the context of a contractual relationship between plaintiff and defendant and damage where there is no contract between the two parties. What consequences would this have

in the context of the current structure of the law of obligations in England?

4. Can we explain the result in *Tweddle* v. *Atkinson* using the approach to agreements and promises elaborated by Adams and Brownsword using the 'Jack and the Beanstalk' scenario?

2

Contract Theory

I. INTRODUCTION: LEGAL THEORY AND CONTRACT

The general objective of the next two chapters is to offer the reader a map of contract theory which will act as a guide and a source of reference points throughout the subsequent chapters dealing with the substance of the law of contract. We would not want to suggest that there is a linear progression of themes flowing through the different sections of this chapter, or a hierarchy of ideas. On the contrary, it will soon be apparent that the theories represented here and throughout the book operate at a diversity of levels; and consequently, although links can and should be drawn between the different sections, it would be wrong to view the theories as falling into a particular fixed framework of relationships. To this end, we begin with an extract which celebrates the complex phenomenon of law as a discipline, and identifies one possible rough typology of theoretical work which emphasizes the point that our working conception of contract theory is intended to be inclusive rather than exclusive in nature.

W. Twining, 'Evidence and Legal Theory', in W. Twining (ed.), _Legal Theory and Common Law_ (Oxford, Blackwell, 1986), 62–5

One's view of the nature and role of legal theory depends upon one's view of the discipline of law. In this context general definitions are not very helpful. Just as law as a social institution shades off and overlaps with other social phenomena in extraordinarily complex ways, so law as a subject cannot and should not have rigid boundaries that segregate it from other disciplines. For certain purposes, in some contexts, lines have to be drawn; but as often as not precise definitions and sharp boundaries do more harm than good. In relation to other disciplines, the study of law is a complex, varied and amorphous part of a general intellectual enterprise, the direct end of which is the advancement of knowledge and understanding. As a practical matter there has to be a rough division of intellectual labour; there need to be specialized institutions, and individual specialists. But when these artificial boundaries become institutionalized or rigidified, the theorist has a much more important role to play in subverting divisions and building intellectual bridges than in settling lines of demarcation.

Academic law can also be seen as the intellectual and scholarly branch of law-related activities in the real world—whether it is related to the concerns of professional lawyers or of other specialized participants in legal and law-related social processes; or to the unspecialized and enormously diverse concerns of non-specialists who become involved in such processes. Here again specialization has its uses: one does not expect, for example, many judges or solicitors or policemen or plaintiffs to be academic experts in jurisprudence or indeed in most fields of law. But one function of legal theorizing is to break down institutional barriers, habits of action, or ways of thought that divide off the academic from the applied, theory from practice, the law in books from the law in action.

Law is a fascinating, complex, important and pervasive phenomenon in society. Professional legal practice is a quite varied and influential form of specialized activity which is by no means coextensive with the law in action. The discipline of law is also wide-ranging, varied, amorphous and important. It is potentially enormously interesting, even if in practice it is sometimes made unforgivably boring.

If one looks at law as a discipline in these terms, it is hardly surprising that its relationship both with other disciplines and with the world of affairs is perennially problematic. Such problems are close to the core of the concerns of many legal theorists—whether they proceed by agonized introspection, over-confident assertion (usually reading one part as the whole), eye-catching polemics, grand theorizing or patient reflection about quite small questions. The primary task of the jurist is to study the assumptions underlying legal discourse; many of those assumptions lie at key points of contact between the world of learning and the worlds of practical affairs. . . .

. . . One way of looking at legal theorizing is as an activity directed to a variety of tasks all of which are directly concerned with understanding. These tasks occur at various levels and require different kinds of knowledge, skills and aptitudes. They can be characterized in various ways and the list could be quite long. For present purposes . . . a brief restatement of the tasks might go as follows:

(1) Intellectual history, that is the systematic study and criticism of the heritage of legal thought and critical study of the work of individual thinkers.
(2) High Theory, that is to say the exploration of fundamental general questions related to the subject-matter of law as a discipline, such as questions about the nature and functions of law, the relations between law and justice, or the epistemological foundations of different kinds of legal discourse. This is the particular sphere of legal philosophy.
(3) Middle-order theorizing, prescriptive as well as descriptive; in particular:
    (a) the development of general hypotheses about legal or law-related phenomena capable of being tested by empirical methods; and
    (b) the development of prescriptive working theories for various kind of participants in legal processes, such as prescriptive theories of legisla-

tion, adjudication and legal reasoning.

(4) The conduit function, that is to say the systematic exploration at a general level of the relationship between law and at least the more general aspects of all other disciplines relevant to law. This is approximately equivalent to Julius Stone's view of jurisprudence as 'the lawyer's extraversion'.

(5) The integrative or synthesizing function, that is to say, the task of exploring and articulating frames of reference which provide a *coherent* basis for law as a discipline, for legal discourse generally and for particular parts of it.

The list is incomplete and there are many overlaps. But this formulation helps to bring out a number of points that are worth stressing in the present context.

First, legal theory in this broad sense encompasses a great diversity of questions. These questions arise from quite different concerns at different levels in varied contexts; appropriate responses to such questions are correspondingly diverse. Confusion of levels and conflation of questions foster the kind of artificial polemics to which jurisprudence is particularly prone. This way of mapping legal theory is, I think, more helpful and far less misleading than classifications in terms of 'schools' and 'isms' and 'ists'.

Secondly, this kind of map is a safeguard against the error of treating one part as if it were the whole. The most common version of this error today is the tendency to treat legal philosophy as coextensive with legal theory. It is unduly narrow, and impoverishes the discipline of law, to equate jurisprudence with legal philosophy or to treat philosophical questions as being the only, or the primary, worthwhile concern of every serious jurist. Questions which one kind of philosopher or another would treat as philosophical questions occupy a special place in legal theorizing. These are questions about the most general and, in a loose sense, the most fundamental assumptions of legal discourse. Such questions stand at the centre of legal theory; they also represent a critical point where boundaries between disciplines break down. For questions about justice or the nature of law or rights or reasonings, for example, are shared by philosophers, political theorists, social scientists and jurists on an almost equal footing. However, there are many general questions about law which also deserve to be treated as theoretical questions, but which are not peculiarly or exclusively philosophical. Prescriptive working theories for participants (e.g. a theory of appellate advocacy or judging); middle-order theories about legal phenomena (for example, a cross-cultural theory of litigation or dispute settlement) or a theoretical framework for a particular field of law or an area of legal discourse (such as a theory of contract or of criminal law) are examples of theorizing and theories which belong to jurisprudence, but fall outside, or at least go beyond legal philosophy—though they all, of course, have philosophical dimensions.

This view is not anti-philosophical. But it does strongly suggest that overconcentration on legal philosophy—on the more abstract problems of legal theory—may lead to the neglect of some other functions of legal theorizing, such as the construction and criticism of middle-order theories, of working theories for participants, and the devising of mapping theories, that is coherent frames of reference for law-as-discipline and for particular sectors thereof.

Notes

1. Twining's essay is part of his contribution to two important debates within legal education—namely the distinction between legal philosophy and the broader enterprise of legal theory (which Twining, but not all writers, treats as synonymous with 'jurisprudence') and the place of legal theory once defined within the legal curriculum.

2. Twining and MacCormick, another important writer in this field, argue for the continuing importance of separate 'theory courses' in legal education, so long as they do not become too highly abstracted from the practical concerns reflected in individual subject-based courses such as the law of contract. In their view, the 'pervasive approach' does not allow the five functions of legal theory earlier identified by Twining to be achieved as economically or as efficiently as the approach which uses a special course.

D. N. MacCormick and W. Twining, 'Theory in the Law Curriculum', in W. Twining (ed.), *Legal Theory and Common Law* **(Oxford, Blackwell, 1986), 248–9**

It is difficult to see how intellectual history or central questions of legal philosophy can be dealt with systematically or in depth other than by direct study. Certain kinds of middle-order theorizing can no doubt be accommodated in other course; for example, it may be possible to accommodate theories of adjudication or legislation, or even some aspects of the sociology of the legal profession, within courses on legal institutions or legal process or legal method. But, insofar as such courses deal adequately with those topics they become in effect 'theory courses'. Furthermore, it is not easy to get to grips with, for example, Ronald Dworkin's theory of adjudication or the nature of legal reasoning if one is divorced from the context of broader theoretical debates. Similarly, while a broad approach to family law or criminal law or constitutional law inevitably involves drawing on material from other disciplines, a more systematic exploration of the relationships between law and these other disciplines requires attention to be focused directly on such relationships at a higher level of generality than would be appropriate for most standard law courses. Most important of all is the integrative function. One role of 'theory' within a course on contract or torts or constitutional law is to provide a coherent view of the subject as a whole. But it is difficult to see how a coherent view of law as a whole or, more mundanely, of all the subjects studied by an individual student within his or her degree course can be achieved other than by direct study. Whatever other educational objectives are served by separate theory courses, perhaps their most important function is to provide an opportunity to students to stand back from the detailed study of particular topics and to look at their subject as a whole at a higher level of generality and from a variety of perspectives. Such a course, whatever it is called, which draws on and feeds into all other courses in the curriculum and thereby helps to provide the basis for an integrated educational experience, is performing one of the main jobs of jurisprudence.

3. A. Hunt, in contrast, argues that there should ideally be no need for a theory course as a 'compartmentalized ingredient' within the curriculum. However, he accepts that

since the ramifications of espousing the central role of theory constitute an attack on the prevailing naive empiricism which dominates legal education, it may, in the short term at least, be necessary to design and teach 'theory' courses as core elements within the curriculum. ('Jurisprudence, Philosophy and Legal Education: Against Foundationalism', (1986) 6 *LS* 292 at 301).

Whatever the merits of separate courses, none of the writers quoted here would deny the importance of ensuring that theory is present in courses such as the law of contract. One very strong reason is that the pervasive approach makes it impossible for theoretical perspectives to be marginalized in respect of the legal education of any law student, whatever the core content of her law degree and whatever the options she chooses, and this is a view which we firmly support.

4. The Twining typology of legal theory is valuable in so far as it portrays the system of ideas which underlie the discipline of law as a multi-dimensional structure. One point which he does not make explicitly, but which is implicit in point (4), is that legal theory cannot be understood in isolation from the theories of other disciplines. For example, the substance of contract law cannot be understood at any level of abstraction above the purely descriptive without reference to social, economic, and political theories which have sought to explain the nature and role of 'contract', understood as more than simply a legal phenomenon.

A few caveats should be entered about the sections which follow. First, it will be immediately apparent that relatively little of the work used relates directly to the English law of contract. On the contrary, it is generally North American legal thought which dominates in this sphere, with a few notable exceptions such as the work of Patrick Atiyah. However, the insights of the work used are in general terms broadly applicable, in particular to English law, which shares a common law heritage with the United States. Second, the classifications used and the order of the sections are to some extent arbitrary. Other classifications could have been used with equal validity, and there are always some writers and some theories which are difficult to classify. We have tried to counteract the dangers of rigid compartmental-ization and of intellectual isolationism by cross-referencing between sec-tions, and between this chapter and the rest of the book. Finally, there is no such thing as 'pure description' of a theory. Inevitably, some theoretical work is represented via our interpretations and those of other writers who came later. This is especially true of those theorists whose work does not offer easily digestible and succinct statements of their key ideas!

II. CONTRACT AND SOCIO-ECONOMIC STRUCTURE

A. Introduction

The questions 'Why are there contracts?' and 'What is the nature of con-tract?' have long preoccupied those who have studied social behaviour. Many writers have pointed to a close connection between the incidence of contractual exchanges and the changing socio-economic structure of soci-ety. For example, a number of nineteenth-century writers, including Weber, Durkheim, Maine, and Marx, associated the 'growing importance of con-tracts as a source of legal rights with the expansion of the market as a form of economic organisation' (A. Kronman, *Max Weber* (London, Edward Arnold, 1983), 96). This in turn points to a link between contract and the ideology of individualism which underpins the constitution of the 'free market', a point illustrated by Cotterrell with a number of pertinent examples.

R. Cotterrell, *The Sociology of Law*, 2nd edn. (London, Butterworths, 1992), 118–19

'Our [English] law,' wrote the comparative lawyer H. C. Gutteridge, 'has not hesitated to place the seal of its approval upon a theory of the extent of individ-ual rights which can only be described as the consecration of the spirit of unre-stricted egoism' (Gutteridge 1933: 22). It is the *individualism* of Western law and society which has appeared as its hallmark. . . .

The idea is expressed in the jurist Sir Henry Maine's celebrated late nineteenth-century thesis that the history of progressive societies had hitherto been one of movement from social relations based on status to relations of contract (Maine 1861); in the German sociologist Ferdinand Tönnies' concep-tion of modern societies as based on impersonal, instrumental, limited and temporary social relations of *Gesellschaft* (association) rather than on the inti-mate, universalistic, and permanent ones of *Gemeinschaft* (community) (Tönnies 1957); . . . Ehrlich writes, 'the ideal of justice of individualism is the individual and his property, the individual who has an untrammeled power of disposition over his property, who recognizes no superior but the state, and is not bound by anything but the contracts he has entered into' (1936: 235).

Note

The classic works referred to by Cotterrell are: H. Gutteridge, 'Abuse of Rights', (1933) 5 *CLJ* 22; H. Maine, *Ancient Law* (London, Dent, 1861); F. Tönnies, *Community and Society*, trans. Loomis (East Lansing, Mich. Michigan State University Press, 1957); E. Ehrlich, *Fundamental Principles of the Sociology of Law*, trans. Moll (New York, Arno Press, 1975 edn.).

Casting the net wider, Cohen examines critically the 'economic argument for contractualism', in which individualism forms one strand running through the justifications commonly advanced.

M. Cohen, 'The Basis of Contract', (1933) 44 *Harv. L. Rev.* 553 at 562–4

. . . a régime in which contracts are freely made and generally enforced gives greater scope to individual initiative and thus promotes the greatest wealth of a nation. Three arguments have been used in defense of this view.

The first was based on the eighteenth century optimism that assumed, on religious and metaphysical grounds, a preestablished harmony between man's selfish pursuit of gain and the common good.

> Thus God and Nature planned the general frame
> And bade self love and social be the same

But this was soon seen to be contrary to fact when factory and mine owners began to exploit men, women, and children in a way that a nation like Great Britain could not tolerate. Factory legislation thus followed as a refutation of the optimistic dogma.

The second argument, the psychologic one of Bentham, rested on the assumption that as happiness consists in a maximum of pleasure, and that as each man knows best what will please him most, a contract in which two parties freely express what they prefer is the best way of achieving the greatest good of the greatest number. This argument blandly ignores the fact that though men may be legally free to make whatever contract they please, they are not actually or economically free. The mere fact of litigation, of appeal to the courts for enforcement, proves that the parties did not achieve real agreement or that their compact has not been found to serve the interest of one of the parties. Men in fact do not always know what will turn out to their advantage, and some of them have a talent for exploiting the ignorance or the dire need of their neighbors to make the latter agree to almost anything.

The psychologic argument has therefore been succeeded by the biologic doctrine of natural selection and the survival of the fittest. The old Providence

bership in such a group as a given family is based upon natural relationship, which is socially and economically regarded as a special and intrinsic quality and is attributed to him by the law independently of his own acts of consociation. . . .

. . . The present-day significance of contract is primarily the result of the high degree to which our economic system is market-oriented and of the role played by money. The increased importance of the private law contract in general is thus the legal reflex of the market orientation of our society. But contracts propagated by the market society are completely different from those contracts which in the spheres of public and family law once played a greater role than they do today. In accordance with this fundamental transformation of the general character of the voluntary agreement we shall call the more primitive type 'status contract' and that which is peculiar to the exchange or market economy 'purposive contract' (*Zweck-Kontrakt*).

The distinction is based on the fact that all those primitive contracts by which political or other personal associations, permanent or temporary, or family relations are created involve a change in what may be called the total legal situation (the universal position) and the social status of the persons involved. To have this effect these contracts were originally either straightforward magical acts or at least acts having a magical significance. For a long time their symbolism retained traces of that character, and the majority of these contracts are 'fraternization contracts.' By means of such a contract a person was to become somebody's child, father, wife, brother, master, slave, kin, comrade-in-arms, protector, client, follower, vassal, subject, friend, or, quite generally, comrade (*Genosse*). To 'fraternize' with another person did not, however, mean that a certain performance of the contract, contributing to the attainment of some specific object, was reciprocally guaranteed or expected. Nor did it mean merely that the making of a promise to another would, as we might put it, have ushered in a new orientation in the relationship between the parties. The contract rather meant that the person would 'become' something different in quality (or status) from the quality he possessed before. For unless a person voluntarily assumed that new quality, his future conduct in his new role could hardly be believed to be possible at all. Each party must thus make a new 'soul' enter his body. At a rather late stage the symbolism required the mixing and imbibing of blood or spittle or the creation of a new soul by some animistic process or by some other magical rite. . . .

. . . The agreements of fraternization as well as other forms of status contract were oriented toward the total social status of the individual and his integration into an association comprehending his total personality. This form of contract with its all-inclusive rights and duties and the special attitudinal qualities based thereon thus appears in contrast to the money contract, which, as a specific, quantitatively delimited, qualityless, abstract, and usually economically conditioned agreement, represents the archetype of the purposive contract. As a non-ethical purposive contract the money contract was the appropriate means for the elimination of the magical and sacramental elements from legal transactions and for the secularization of the law.

Note

Kronman explicates the status/purposive distinction in the following terms:

A. Kronman, *Max Weber* (London, Edward Arnold, 1983), 101–2

Weber draws three related distinctions between status and purposive contracts. First, a status contract effects a total change in the personalities of the individuals involved, an 'all-inclusive' change in the 'universal position' of the parties, as a result of which each acquires a new soul and becomes another person. By contrast, a purposive contract merely establishes 'a new orientation' in the parties' relationship; it does not involve a change in their 'total legal situation'. Unlike status contracts, which have as their object the creation of an 'all-inclusive fraternal relationship', purposive contracts are 'delimited' in the sense that they 'neither [affect] the status of the parties nor [give] rise to new qualities of comradeship but [aim] solely . . . at some specific (especially economic) performance or result.'

Second, status contracts are contracts of fraternization: they seek to establish a relationship of brotherhood or comradeship between the individuals involved. As the term fraternization implies, relationships of this sort are quasi-familial; they are patterned after and take as their model some natural relationship existing between the members of a household. Status contracts may therefore be said to have their foundation in the household community. A purposive contract, on the other hand, does not require the establishment of a fraternal bond between the parties (who are, and remain, strangers). 'In sharp contrast to all other groups which always presuppose some measure of personal fraternization or even blood kinship, the market is fundamentally alien to any type of fraternal relationship.' Thus, 'where the market is allowed to follow its own autonomous tendencies', individuals engaged in market relationships 'do not look toward the persons of each other but only toward the commodity; there are no obligations of brotherliness or reverence, and none of those spontaneous human relations that are sustained by personal unions. They all would just obstruct the free development of the bare market relationship, and its specific interests serve, in their turn, to weaken the sentiments on which these obstructions rest.' The 'bare' or 'abstract' market-oriented exchange contract is not modelled, even fictively, on the blood relationships that exist between members of a household community; it thus stands in the sharpest possible contrast to all status contracts whose fundamental aim is to establish a real or imaginary bond of the latter sort.

Third, it is characteristic of status contracts that they are effected by magical or supernatural means. According to Weber, 'one whose thinking is embedded in magic cannot imagine any other than a magical guaranty for the parties to conform, in their total behaviour, to the intention of the "fraternization" they contracted.' Even after primitive animistic conceptions have died away, it is still thought necessary 'to place each party [to a status contract] under the dominion of a supernatural power, which power constitutes not only their collective protection but also jointly and severally threatens them in case of anti-fraternal conduct.' This explains why the oath, 'which originally appears as a person's conditional self-surrender to evil magical forces [and] subsequently assumes the character of a conditional self-curse, calling for the divine wrath to strike . . . remains even in later times one of the most universal forms of all fraternization pacts.' By contrast, the market-oriented money contract—the 'archetype' of all purposive contracts—has been an important factor in the *elimination* of 'magical and sacramental elements' from the law. Unlike status contracts, which 'were originally either straightforward magical acts or at least acts having a magical significance', purposive contracts are self-consciously anti-magical and wherever they have gained recognition have tended to accelerate the disenchantment of the legal order.

Notes

1. Marriage provides perhaps the archetypal example of the status contract, and, as R. Cotterrell notes, 'the law of marriage appears to be a latecomer to "contractualisation" among areas of Western legal doctrine' (*The Sociology of Law*, 2nd edn. (London, Butterworths, 1992), 122). As we shall see, in particular in Chapter 4, Section I, much of what occurs within the family (in the private sphere) has historically been seen as outside the scope of formal 'public' law, perhaps ironically so, since marriage is above all a *public* commitment.

2. One feature of Weber's analysis is the rigid line he draws between status and purposive contracts. To that extent, purposive contracts can be seen as closely linked to the modern paradigm of the bargain-based exchange—a paradigm which was visible in *Tweddle* v. *Atkinson* ((1861) 1 B. & S.393) in Chapter 1. Weber's analysis rigidly divides the co-operative and competitive sides of human social activity—a division which enjoys continuing currency in legal thinking but one which has been challenged by, for example, the work of the French sociologist Émile Durkheim which we shall examine below, and those modern writers whose work has been influenced by Durkheim's insights about co-operation and mutuality in contract.

3. The status/contract debate has been a continuing one. It has been widely argued that, under the advanced welfare state, the position of the

individual once again becomes defined according to status (e.g. single parent, disabled person). On the other hand, in recent years there has been revival of 'contractarian' arguments within welfare politics, which might suggest that the tide has changed (see J. Wiseman, 'The Welfare State: A Public Choice Perspective', in T. Wilson and D. Wilson (eds.), *The State and Social Welfare* (London, Longman, 1991), 55). Similarly, in the law of contract, the role of status in determining the legal position of the parties has been advocated (see R. Childres and S. Spitz, 'Status in the Law of Contract', (1972) 47 *NYU L. Rev.* 1).

Weber goes on to discuss certain limitations upon freedom of contract, which he places in two categories. First are restrictions upon an individual's freedom to bind herself. A person may not sell herself into slavery; there are also restrictions upon sexual freedom and freedom of testation, all areas where the degree of freedom of contract has tended to decline. Second, Weber discusses in detail the relationship between freedom and coercion.

Weber, *Economy and Society,* 729–31

The development of legally regulated relationships toward contractual association and of the law itself toward freedom of contract, especially toward a system of free disposition within stipulated forms of transaction, is usually regarded as signifying a decrease of constraint and an increase of individual freedom. It is clear from what we have been saying, in how relative a sense this opinion is formally correct. The possibility of entering with others into contractual relations the content of which is entirely determined by individual agreement, and likewise the possibility of making use in accordance with one's desires of an increasingly large number of type forms rendered available by the law for purposes of consociation in the widest sense of the word, has been immensely extended in modern law, at least in the spheres of exchange of goods and of personal work and services. However, the extent to which this trend has brought about an actual increase of the individual's freedom to shape the conditions of his own life or the extent to which, on the contrary, life has become more stereotyped in spite, or, perhaps, just because of this trend, cannot be determined simply by studying the development of formal legal institutions. The great variety of permitted contractual schemata and the formal empowerment to set the content of contracts in accordance with one's desires and independently of all official form patterns, in and of itself by no means makes sure that these formal possibilities will in fact be available to all and everyone. Such availability is prevented above all by the differences in the distribution of property as guaranteed by law. The formal right of a worker to enter into any contract whatsoever with any employer whatsoever does not in practice represent for the employment seeker even the slightest freedom in the determination of his own conditions of work, and it does not guarantee him any influence on this process. It rather means, at least primarily, that the more powerful party in the market, i.e., normally the employer, has the possibility to set the terms, to offer the job "take it or leave it," and, given the normally more pressing economic need of the worker, to impose his terms upon him. The result of contractual freedom, then, is in the first place the opening of the opportunity to use, by the clever utilization of property ownership in the market, these resources without legal restraints as a means for the achievement of power over others. The parties interested in power in the market thus are also interested in such a legal order. Their interest is served particularly by the establishment of "legal empowerment rules." This type of rules does no more than create the framework for valid agreements which, under conditions of formal freedom, are officially available to all. Actually, however, they are accessible only to the owners of property and thus in effect support their very autonomy and power positions. . . .

. . . The increasing significance of freedom of contract and, particularly, of enabling laws which leave everything to "free" agreement, implies a relative reduction of that kind of coercion which results from the threat of mandatory and prohibitory norms. Formally it represents, of course, a decrease of coercion. But it is also obvious how advantageous this state of affairs is to those who are economically in the position to make use of the empowerments. The exact extent to which the total amount of "freedom" within a given legal community is actually increased depends entirely upon the concrete economic order and especially upon the property distribution. In no case can it be simply deduced from the content of the law. . . .

. . . Formally, the market community does not recognize direct coercion on the basis of personal authority. It produces in its stead a special kind of coercive situation which, as a general principle, applies without any discrimination to workers, enterprisers, producers and consumers, viz., in the impersonal form of the inevitability of adaptation to the purely economic "laws" of the market. The sanctions consist in the loss or decrease of economic power and, under certain conditions, in the very loss of one's economic existence. The private enterprise system transforms into objects of "labor market transactions" even those personal and authoritarian-hierarchical relations which actually exist in the capitalistic enterprise. While the authoritarian relationships are thus drained of all normal sentimental content, authoritarian constraint not only continues but, at least under certain circumstances, even increases. The more comprehensive the realm of structures whose existence depends in a specific way on "discipline": that of capitalist commercial establishments, the more relentlessly can authoritarian constraint be exercised within them, and the smaller will be the circle of those in whose hands the power to use this type of constraint is concentrated and who also hold the power to have such authority guaranteed to them by the legal order. A legal order which contains ever so few mandatory and prohibitory norms and ever so many "freedoms" and "empowerments" can nonetheless in its practical effects facilitate a quantitative and qualitative increase not only of coercion in general but quite specifically of authoritarian coercion.

Notes

1. Weber cuts through the purely formal analysis of law, and draws attention instead to power relations within society (see A. Hunt, *The Sociological Movement in Law* (London, Macmillan, 1978) 129). Coercion continues, and indeed grows, despite the presence of enabling legal norms. A similar insight was developed later by American Legal Realists, such as Hale, who argued that property and contract together inevitably operate in a 'coercive' fashion, although not one which necessarily justifies the intervention of the court to protect the weaker party in a bargaining process (see R. Hale, 'Coercion and Distribution in a Supposedly Non-Coercive State', (1923) 38 *Pol. Sci. Q.* 470 and 'Bargaining, Duress and Economic Liberty', (1943) 43 *Colum. L. Rev.* 603). Hale's work is discussed in Chapter 8. The problem of power introduced by Weber is one of the general themes of Part III of this book.

2. As a sociologist of law, Weber has been immensely influential, not only through his specific writings on contract, but even more so through his articulation of forms of authority in law, his work on legal classification, and his explanation of rationality in law. In so far as his historical analyses of social change have offered a functional method which can be used to pursue radical objectives, he has, along with Marx, been a major influence upon the school of critical legal studies which has offered some of the most far-reaching critiques of contract doctrine developed in recent years (see Section VII).

C. Émile Durkheim and Solidarity in Contract

Durkheim's work on contract forms one part of a larger project in which the 'analysis of legal doctrine provides a route towards an understanding of social cohesion' (Cotterrell, *The Sociology of Law*, 76). What distinguishes Durkheim from Weber is not only his view of contract as an essentially social instrument but also his view of society as a moral phenomenon, and his position on the role of law as an integrative mechanism. It is therefore important to situate Durkheim's work on contract within his general sociology of law. Reiner summarizes Durkheim's position in the following terms:

**R. Reiner, 'Crime, Law and Deviance: The Durkheim Legacy', in
S. Fenton, *Durkheim and Modern Sociology* (Cambridge, Cambridge
University Press, 1984), 176–8**

Law was a fundamental concept in the thesis developed in Durkheim's first book, *The Division of Labour in Society*, Durkheim's main concern here, as elsewhere in his work, was with understanding the problems and preconditions of social solidarity in complex, differentiated, industrial societies. Central to his account was the distinction he developed between two contrasting forms of solidarity—'mechanical' and 'organic'. 'Mechanical' solidarity is said to be characteristic of simple societies with only a rudimentary division of labour. The individual members of society are uniformly enveloped within a common 'conscience collective', sharing the same values, beliefs and roles. Notions of individual difference, rights and responsibilities are only weakly developed, if at all. Solidarity of such societies is mechanical in that it arises from the similarity of the different atoms constituting the whole.

'Organic' solidarity, by contrast, is that which develops on the basis of an advanced and complex division of labour. Such societies are characterized by the interdependence of units differentiated by economic and social function. Although organically solidary societies do not have a pervasive collective conscience like that associated with mechanical solidarity, the practical interdependence arising out of the division of labour, if combined with an appropriate social ethic recognizing and based upon respect for the individual differences produced by specialized functions, could bind such societies into tightly knit, albeit differentiated, social organisms.

Durkheim . . . brings law explicitly and centrally into his discussion of solidarity for methodological reasons. He observes that 'social solidarity is a completely moral phenomenon which, taken by itself, does not lend itself to exact observation nor indeed to measurement'. Empirical research requires an externally observable and measurable indicator of solidarity, which cannot be directly apprehended in itself. 'We must substitute for this internal fact which escapes us an external index which symbolises it and study the former in the light of the latter. This visible symbol is law.'

This usage of law as the index of social solidarity is based upon a highly tendentious conception of the law–society relation, which Durkheim explicitly elaborates and defends.

Social life, especially where it exists durably, tends inevitably to assume a definite form and to organise itself, and law is nothing else than this very organisation in so far as it has greater stability and precision. The general life of society cannot extend its sway without juridical life extending its sway at the same time and in direct relation. We can thus be certain of finding reflected in law all the essential varieties of social solidarity.

Durkheim recognizes that there may be rules and relations in society which 'fix themselves without assuming a juridical form' and are based on custom.

But he sees these as 'assuredly secondary: law produces those which are essential and they are the only ones we need to know'. . . .

Law itself is not explicitly defined by Durkheim. But the implication is that law is the set of rules which are more or less formally promulgated and enforced in a society. It is a kind of legal positivism in that rules need not have any particular substantive content nor any specific formal character to count as law. What is tendentious is the direct linking of law to the moral consensus of a society. This rules out by definitional fiat the exploration of such issues as the conflicting social interests which law might serve, or an adequate account of the process of legislation which may reflect struggles between competing interests and conceptions of morality. The methodological strategy of assuming law to be an index of solidarity seems to presuppose a consensus view of law, even though later in the same book, when discussing the forced division of labour, Durkheim acknowledges that legal rules may reflect and even exacerbate class conflict.

The importance of Dukheim's detailed work on contract, which is dispersed across two of his major books, is drawn out by Hunt.

A. Hunt, *The Sociological Movement in Law* (London, Macmillan, 1978), 85–8

Durkheim returns on a number of occasions to the discussion of the nature and function of contract. In both *The Division of Labour* and in *Rules* his treatment is essentially polemical. His treatment is characteristically Durkheimian; he takes a phenomenon which as conventionally viewed seems to imply a fairly obvious and direct explanation, but he promptly seeks to demonstrate that a true understanding of the phenomenon is to be found in some diametrically opposed analysis. Contract bears all the characteristics of the pre-eminently individualist act as the expression of individual free will. But he is insistent that contracts are inherently social rather than individual in character.

In *Division of Labour* great importance is attached to contract because of the central role that it has played in the individualist, and particularly utilitarian, social theory. Indeed it is necessary to recognise the major role that the concept 'contract' played in nineteenth century thought, in economics, philosophy, sociology and in jurisprudence. His attacks are in particular directed against Spencer and, by implication, Maine.

For Durkheim contract is essentially social.

A contract is not sufficient unto itself, but is possible only thanks to the regulation of the contract which is originally social.

Instead of the conventional two-party analysis he insists on a three-party model with the third party, namely society, laying down in advance the permitted framework of contractual activity. His insistence is upon the social institu-

tion of contract, what he describes as 'the non-contractual elements of contract'.

If the contract has power to bind, it is society which gives this power to it. . . . Moreover
it lends this obligatory force only to contracts which have in themselves a social value.

So far his treatment of contract has not gone beyond his characteristic assertion of the social character of the institution. He draws support for this view
from the extent to which the social character of contract is winning wider
recognition both in legal practice and in juristic thought in particular through
the growth of such concepts as duress and undue influence and, of particular
importance, the rapid advance of the doctrine of 'public policy'.

His next step is also fairly unexceptional; he relates contract to the advance
of the division of labour.

Contractual relations necessarily develop with the division of labour, since the latter is
not possible without interchange and the contract is the juridical form of exchange.

The more contentious aspect of his elaboration is to be found in *Professional
Ethics*. Here he is at his most challenging, if not necessarily at his most convincing. He draws together apparently disparate elements of social reality and
spans the epochs of social evolution in order to produce a very distinctive
account of the historical evolution of contract. So crucial a role has contract
played in social thought that it appears today to exist as a 'natural institution', a
permanent and inevitable component of human society. But he is anxious to
show that it is a relatively recent innovation. If its primary social function is as a
means of acquisition of property, he argues that the earliest form of such acquisition was through inheritance. This he sees as giving way before the advance
of contract. He is particularly vehement against the institution of inheritance.
His attack upon it was his only enduring link with the socialists; its abolition he
demanded as a pre-condition of the realisation of a meritocratic society.

He posits the evolution of contract as passing through two distinct stages.
Using terminology very similar to that used by Maine he labels this transition as
the change from 'status-contract' to 'will-contract'.

On the one hand we have relations in due form according to law, having as their origin
the status of persons or of things, or of the modifications so far latent in this status; on
the other, relations according to law having as their origin wills that are in agreement to
modify their status.

The earlier form of contract, based on status, is religious in origin, the parties
or the subject matter being endowed with a sacred character. It is this sacred-
ness which provides the basis of the obligatory nature of the undertaking. His
central concern is to explain how the transition to 'will contract' takes place.
The essence of the problem is to determine what it is that makes agreement
between two wills binding. The crucial role is played by ritual. Ritual may surround the parties to the contract, for example the sharing of a meal, shaking
hands or drinking from the same cup, or it may surround the subject matter, for

example the ritualistic character of transfer of realty in many societies. Such ritual gives a sacred character to the act of exchange. The decisive step is to endow the undertaking *itself* with a sacred and hence binding character. Thereby the declaration of will is given an exteriority; a ritual form of promise emerges, for example the universal appearance of the oath and other magico-sacred formulas. The undertaking is thus marked by 'sacred formalism'; the next step is for 'juridical formalism' to replace sacred formalism. Here the symbolic act becomes the substitute for the actual transference of property.

The symbolism represents only a decadence that comes when the primary meaning of the custom is lost. Customs begin by being active causes, and not symbols, of social relations.

The truly consensual contract arises only when the ritual and symbolic element declines in importance and finally disappears. He recognises that factors such as the quantitative increase in the number of transactions plays some part in his process, but it is significant that he explicitly resists a 'determinist' position.

The mere fact that an institution is required does not mean it will appear at a given moment out of the void. There must be something to make it of, that is, current ideas must allow it to come about and existing institutions must not oppose it but, rather, supply the material needed to shape it. So it is not enough for the consensual contract to be demanded by the advance of economic life: the public mind, too, had to be ready to conceive it as possible.

In order to assess his thesis it is necessary to recognise that the analysis fits fairly consistently with, for example, the historical development of contract in English law. However his overzealous efforts to avoid 'determinism' tends to leave the theory somewhat nebulous. A crucial feature for a consistent sociological theory of contract must start from the study of the type of exchange relations which have in fact manifested themselves as a consequence of the development of economic activity. An understanding of the economic form and content is a necessary pre-condition for an explanation of the role of ritual and formalism in evolution of contract. Durkheim tends simply to presume that exchange is a natural and invariant consequence of the division of labour. Whereas in reality the transition from simple barter to developed capitalistic exchange spans major changes which necessarily had some impact upon the legal expression of these transactions.

The consensual contract, which Durkheim sees as reflecting a growing secularisation of society, rests no longer on the words used; the obligation becomes based on the intentions of the parties. The words as such are not formally binding; they are evidence of intention.

The consensual contract amounts to a revolutionary innovation in the law.

So crucial a role has it played that a wide range of social relations have been subsumed under a contractual form. Of particular importance is the employer-employee relationship; to view such a relationship in purely contractual terms has major ideological implications and Durkheim stresses the unfree basis upon which this exercise of 'free will' is based.

The consensual contract did not mark the end of the evolution of contract; Durkheim posits a new stage, that of a 'contract of equity' which reflects an increasing awareness of social interest in not only the nature but the consequences of contractual activity. This process is reflected in the extension of the factors vitiating contracts, the emergence of the doctrine of public policy and the general movement towards increasing social intervention addressed towards the objective of 'just contracts'. Such a thesis has close resemblance to Pound's insistence upon the emergence of a new stage of the 'socialisation of law'.

Durkheim's model of the ideal society is of a system of socially just contracts as opposed to freewill contracts. This development he sees impeded by the pernicious institution of inheritance. This he sees as the cause although it is more correct to argue that it is a reflection of social inequality. Thus while rejecting the social doctrine of individualist utilitarianism his projected society rests firmly upon contractual foundations, but with the proviso that such contracts must first pass the test of being socially just.

Notes

1. Durkheim's analysis of modern contractual relations shares certain common features with that of Weber. For example, they are united in identifying the secularization of society and of contract as marking a distinctive stage of development. In contract, Durkheim offers an idealistic picture of the role of law in social relations, insisting that obligatory force should only be lent to what he terms 'contracts of equity'. Weber, on the other hand, while identifying a state of strong solidarity within a group such as a family, sees contract between strangers dealing at arm's length as unrestricted by ethical concerns.

2. S. Lindenberg and H. de Vos ('The Limits of Solidarity: Relational Contracting in Perspective and Some Criticism of Traditional Sociology', (1985) 141 *J. Inst. Th. Econ.* 558) have argued that a split has arisen in social science between economics—focused on an analysis of exchange relations—and sociology—aimed at the identification of systems of solidarity. This duality has rarely been broken down by those whose focus is on contract. An example of a scholar who has sought to do this is Ian Macneil, whose work on relational contracting will be examined in more detail in Section IV below and in subsequent chapters. Here we extract the opening paragraphs of his book *The New Social Contract* in order to give a flavour of the framework within which he is functioning.

I. Macneil, *The New Social Contract* (New Haven, Conn., Yale University Press, 1980), 1–4

Primal Roots of Contract

SOCIETY. We shall start at the beginning. In the beginning was society. And ever since has been society. This surely must be the most forgotten fact in the modern study of contracts, whether in law or in economics. . . . For nowhere in human history or prehistory has there been only Adam or even Adam and Eve, but always there has been human society.

If we wish to understand contract, we must return from our self-imposed intellectual isolation and absorb some basic truths. Contract without the common needs and tastes created only by society is inconceivable; contract between totally isolated, utility-maximizing individuals is not contract, but war; contract without language is impossible; and contract without social structure and stability is—quite literally—rationally unthinkable, just as man outside society is rationally unthinkable. The fundamental root, the base, of contract is society. Never has contract occurred without society; never will it occur without society; and never can its functioning be understood isolated from its *particular* society.

Specialization of labor and exchange. The second primal root of contract is specialization of labor and exchange. . . . specialization of labor is something we seem unable to overlook in our daily lives. We cannot so much as tell a story about a cab driver, or say that we are studying to be lawyers, or discuss farm subsidies, or complain about the reluctance of auto manufacturers to install anti-pollution devices, without constantly calling specialization to our attention. And yet we can and do overlook it; even when we see it we are blissfully able to ignore it. Until the women's movement, or even since, how many people consciously recognized the housewife as a highly specialized laborer within the family unit? . . .

One form of exchange, the measured reciprocal exchange—in which we engage every time we go to the supermarket—is clearly an exchange under anyone's definition. But discrete exchange is *not* the primal root of contract. While it has far deeper historical and prehistorical antecedents than is sometimes recognized, discrete exchange is but one of the subspecies forming the exchange part of this second primal root. The broad generic concept of exchange traceable far back into history and prehistory simply recognizes that specialization requires some process of reciprocal distribution of product for the specialization to be worthwhile. Indeed, in extensive specialization where individuals do not produce for themselves everything needed to continue living and producing, each *must* receive the product of others to continue specializing. *How* such exchange occurs is irrelevant to this foundation notion of the concept and to understanding it as a basic root of contract. Exchange can happen in countless ways other than measured reciprocal exchange, ways such as following custom, the Pharaoh's feeding of the pyramid-building slaves, a socialist centralized rationing system, or the intricacies of complex employment relations. But whatever the particular technique of exchange, without it the system of specialization will come to a grinding halt. Everyone will then become unspecialized subsistence farmers, or, more likely, small group hunters and gatherers. . . .

CHOICE. The third primal root of contract is a sense of choice, the concept of some freedom to elect among a range of behaviors. In its absence, speaking of even rudimentary contract is futile despite the existence of specialization of labor and exchange. The social insects, particularly ants, rather than humans, clearly are the world's leading contractors if choice is omitted from the concept of contract. Without freedom of will—real, imagined, or postulated—contract becomes conceptually indistinguishable from their genetically programmed specialization of labor and exchange of product. Note, however, that a concept of contract does not require that choice be real, only that we act as if it is.

AWARENESS OF FUTURE. The rudiments of contract exist in a society with specialization and exchange, coupled with a sense of choice. But it is not until addition of the fourth root, conscious awareness of a future, that contract can come into full bloom. Once mankind has this awareness, and with it an increasing sense of himself as a choosing creature, the potentiality for a full development of contract comes into being. Now, specialization of labor and exchange, a sense of choice, and a consciousness of the future, all completely embedded and intertwined in a society, make contract possible.

Using this analysis as a base, Macneil argues for a conception of contracts principally as 'relations' within which the primary goal is co-operation rather than the pursuit of pure self-interest by the parties, who are seen in this model as interdependent rather than wholly autonomous beings. This is in comparison to what is often termed the 'neo-classical' paradigm of contract as the 'spot' or 'discrete' exchange epitomized by the sale of a newspaper in a shop. Macneil's argument is that relations underpin all exchanges, although he has been criticized by writers such as D. Campbell ('The Society Theory of Relational Contract: Macneil as the Modern Proudhon', (1990) 18 *Int. J. Soc. L.* 75) for failing to explain in sufficient detail exactly how he blends together two such apparently contradictory terms as 'relation' and 'exchange', i.e. how he rationalizes the two streams of human nature epitomized by these terms: co-operation and conflict. However, the passage quoted here from *The New Social Contract* clearly owes much to the insights of Durkheim's sociology.

3. Identifying the essence of social order is, of course, a perennial difficulty for social theorists: how, for example, to reconcile two conflicting views of social order—the pursuit of self-interest, instrumentalism, and free choice, which underlies the classical political economy perception of society, and

the doctrines of legitimacy and consensus, which postulate models of society as essentially cohesive. A difficulty arises also for lawyers, since it raises the question of the function of legal rules: are they instruments to facilitate merely the pursuit of private interest, or do they serve some broader public interest concerned with the development and maintenance of solidarity? Achieving a synthesis between these two conceptions has long troubled legal theorists (see R. Unger, *Law in Modern Society* (New York, Free Press, 1976), esp. 23–7, 262–5).

4. Durkheim's continuing influence on contracts scholarship can also be seen in the empirical work of Stewart Macaulay (see Section V below).

5. Other perspectives on the roots of contract will be examined in Chapter 3, where the focus will be on the different aspects of the relationship between the contractual phenomenon and the state. In particular, we shall discuss the work of so-called 'contractarians' who have used contract to describe the basis of government in democracies (the 'social contract').

III. THE HISTORICAL ACCOUNT OF THE EVOLUTION OF CONTRACT LAW AND THE EMERGENCE OF THE MODERN PARADIGM OF CONTRACT

A. The Modern Paradigm and Neo-classical Contract

The modern paradigm of contract is centred around, but not wholly dominated by, the concept of 'bargain'. M. Eisenberg describes the bargain in the following terms ('The Bargain Principle and its Limits', (1982) 95 *Harv. L. Rev.* 741 at 742): 'By bargain, I mean an exchange in which each party views the performance that he undertakes as the price of the performance undertaken by the other.' As we shall see, many substantive doctrines of the law of contract are heavily influenced by the concept of bargain, including in particular the doctrine of consideration (see *Tweddle* v. *Atkinson* in Chs. 1 and 6). Equally, there are many occasions on which the bargain paradigm, while still formally recognized, is in practice set aside by the courts, because the circumstances demand that other principles, such as the protection of the consumer, take precedence.

It is certainly true that the modern paradigm of contract owes much to what is often termed the 'classical law of contract', a body of rules principally formulated in the nineteenth century, in the search to set out a coherent and consistent operating framework for the exercise of private autonomy through agreement. On the other hand, the modern law of contract is frequently described in literature from the United States as the 'neo-classical law of contract', suggesting, as Feinman puts it, a 'partial accommodation' with the classical law, which he describes in the following terms:

J. Feinman, 'The Significance of Contract Theory', (1990) 58 *U. Cin. L. Rev* 1283 at 1286–8

Classical law in general was structured by a series of dichotomies which defined the relationships among legal actors. For example, the federal government and state governments had separate spheres of authority, as did legislatures and courts. The most fundamental dichotomy was between the individual and the community. Therefore, relations among individuals were governed by private law, which was distinct from public law, which regulated relations between individuals and the state. Within private law, contract law embodied the dichotomy between individual and community by imagining a realm of private agreement in which individual freedom was protected from state coercion. The image that motivated this realm was the isolated bargain between independent, self-interested individuals. Steely-eyed bargainers carefully calculated their interests in a particular exchange, gave a promise or performance only in return for something else, and embodied their transaction in an agreement that carefully defined the terms of performance and therefore could provide the basis for a determinate remedy in case of breach.

Accordingly, as conceived by classical contract law, liability was always voluntarily assumed by the individual through his making of a promise or an agreement, unlike in tort law, in which liability was imposed by the legal system without regard for the individual's consent. Contract doctrines such as narrow formation rules and bargain consideration followed logically from these principles and assured that the individual actually had consented to a bargained-for exchange. When courts mechanically applied these abstract, formal doctrines, they protected the individual's right to assume contractual obligation or to avoid it at the same time as they provided a predictable basis for commercial transactions.

The problems of classical contract law quickly became apparent to judicial and scholarly commentators. Contractual liability, like all other legal liability, did not arise solely from the individual's choice but came from the court's imposition of legal obligation as a matter of public policy; a contract was binding because the court determined that imposing liability served social interest, not because the individual had voluntarily assumed liability through his manifestation of assent. Nor could the parties' words in creating the contract exclusively define the scope of liability; courts had to interpret, fill gaps, and even impose pre-contractual and quasi-contractual liability, either to make the parties' contract meaningful in its commercial context or to serve social interests other than individual choice, such as fairness. Because of the inherent limits of language and the infinite variability of facts, courts could not state doctrinal rules in such a way that they could be mechanically applied to all fact situations that might arise; moreover, the changing needs of commerce made it undesirable to attempt to do so. . . .

As with classical law, neoclassical law can be evoked by presenting the image of its prototypical case as well as by describing its substance, method, and social role. The prototype of neoclassical contract posits parties in an economic relationship that is neither entirely isolated nor wholly encompassing. The parties seek individual advantage through the transaction, but their individual advantage is tied to the success of their mutual venture. The relationship arises through voluntary bargaining which defines the basic terms of the agreement, but the terms can only be understood by examining the context within which the agreement is reached, so that context sometimes supplies interpretations and additional terms.

Proceeding from this image, as a matter of substantive principle neoclassical contract law attempts to balance the individualist ideals of classical contract with communal standards of responsibility to others. The core remains the principle of freedom of contract, distinguishing contract from tort and other areas, but this principle is "tempered both within and without [contract's] formal structure by principles, such as reliance and unjust enrichment, that focus on fairness and the interdependence of parties rather than on parties' actual agreements." In deciding the scope of contractual liability, courts weigh the classical values of liberty, privacy, and efficiency against the values of trust, fairness, and cooperation, which have been identified as important by post-classical scholars.

Neoclassical contract accommodates these conflicting values through a method that is flexible and pragmatic. Logic and analytic rigor remain important in contract law because they are a source of legal authority and an important element of professional culture. In contrast to classical law, though, neoclassical law tempers rigid logic by the use of policy analysis, empirical inquiry, and practical reason. Contract doctrine, more often formulated as general standards rather than mechanical rules, guides judges, sometimes quite strongly, but it allows them enough discretion in hard cases to reach just, socially desirable results.

Through this flexible body of principles and methods for their application, neoclassical contract serves the important social goal of supporting and regulating economic transactions. It does this in two general ways. First, it provides a framework for parties who engage in business planning. The framework helps them to create legal relations, to determine their content, to avoid them altogether, and to sort out difficulties when planning goes awry. Second, it provides a background set of norms for fair market relations. Even without the direct threat of enforcement, these norms are used by business people to set standards and limits for their conduct.

Notes

1. Feinman writes in relation to the law of contract in the United States. There is no single 'American' law of contract, since this area of private law

falls within the competence of the States rather than the federal government. Two centralizing tendencies can, however, be discerned which make it possible to generalize at least in part about the law in the United States. There is, first, the Restatement of Contracts, a privately organized 'codification' of underlying principles and, second, the Uniform Commercial Code (UCC), adopted in almost all the states to regulate sales transactions in a common fashion, in the interests of facilitating cross-US trade (see on these the more detailed comments in Ch. 4, where parts of the Restatement and the UCC are extracted). In so far as it is possible to generalize about US law, it should be noted, by way of a word of warning, that the English law of contract retains a stronger thread of the classical law and firmer commitment to the principles of party autonomy, particularly in commercial transactions.

2. The picture painted of the modern law is of a body of rules which, while eminently reasonable and generally flexible in operation, rather lacks a theoretical substructure which would explain in a coherent way the interactions between the competing individual and societal interests identified by Feinman. To put it another way, the modern law can be depicted as an atheoretical attempt to incorporate the insights of thinking like that of Durkheim into the law, without, however, altering the basic paradigm. Feinman takes this accusation further later in his article.

Feinman, 'The Significance of Contract Theory', 1295

Neoclassical contract can be described as anti-theoretical and multi-dimensional. The two attributes go together. Neoclassical law is a part of everyday legal discourse, a mode of discourse that is relatively unsystematic and not rigidly controlled by disciplinary structures. Theory much more abstract than modest generalizations about black-letter law simply does not fit within such a mode of discourse. Typically, the mainstream of contract law and scholarship celebrates rather than condemns the lack of systematic theory; the mainstream counter-attack against the new contract theories reflects that attitude. The aversion to systematic theory makes neoclassical law multi-dimensional. The lack of a strict disciplinary framework means that, in contract law discourse, anything goes; arguments of great variety about authority, rights, utility, policy, and fairness are common. Of course, it is an exaggeration to say that anything goes. Some arguments and types of arguments are excluded by convention, and different arguments have different persuasive value. However, the conventions are loosely defined, and they are not determined by a rigorous theoretical framework.

Notes

1. It is arguable that Feinman's criticism is too harsh. Using the typology of legal theory offered by Twining, even 'modest generalizations about black letter law' can be classed as theory, albeit at a low level. Moreover, some writers have sought to elaborate a firmer theoretical grounding for the modern law and to offer some sort of consistent rationalization of why the courts sometimes do and sometimes do not interfere in the bargain agreed between the parties. For example, Eisenberg argues that there are limits to the bargain principle, and that these can be discerned using a form of market analysis. He summarizes his conclusions thus:

M. Eisenberg, 'The Bargain Principle and its Limits', (1982) 95 *Harv. L. Rev.* 741 at 799

[The bargain] principle, which in the typical case is supported by considerations of both fairness and efficiency, finds its fullest justification in the exemplary case of a half-completed bargain made in a perfectly competitive market. Bargains made in other kinds of markets are not intrinsically suspect. Nevertheless, that a market is less than perfectly competitive does set the stage for transactions in which the bargain principle loses much or all of its force, because it is supported by neither fairness nor efficiency. For example, a market that involves a monopoly sets the stage for the exploitation of distress; a market in which transactions are complex and differentiated rather than simple and homogeneous sets the stage for the exploitation of transactional incapacity; a market in which actors do not simply take a price established by a general market and are susceptible to transient economic irrationality sets the stage for unfair persuasion; a market that involves imperfect price-information sets the stage for the exploitation of price-ignorance.

Eisenberg's argument is that beyond the limits of the bargain principle a new paradigm has emerged in US law, namely the principle of unconscionability. This provides not only a *post hoc* rationalization of existing legal doctrines which give the courts licence to intervene in the bargaining process (see e.g. the doctrines of mistake and misrepresentation examined in Ch. 5 and the doctrines of duress and undue influence examined in Ch. 9) but also a blueprint for future development. This principle cannot be applied to English law as it stands, but in Chapter 8 and following, we attempt to provide some theoretical insights into the state of 'contractual justice' as presently understood and applied by the courts.

2. The paradigm described in this section, while dominant in judicial thinking and amongst many commentators, including, in particular, those responsible for most of the major textbooks, is not wholly uncontested.

Much of the rest of this chapter is concerned with the presentation of alternative models of contract, of alternative methods of analysis which differ from black-letter case and statute analysis, and of a range of goals for contract law which go beyond the provision of a framework for planned and adversarial exchanges. We begin the process of widening the focus beyond the dominant paradigm by assessing a number of histories of contract law which have offered differing explanations of the evolution of the modern law. A particular emphasis has been placed on understanding what happened in the nineteenth century to the law of contract.

3. For further reflection on the modern paradigm and the classic works of exposition within the law of contract see D. Campbell, 'The Undeath of Contract: A Study in the Degeneration of a Research Programme', (1992) 22 *HKLJ* 20; J. Adams and R. Brownsword, *Understanding Contract Law* (London, Fontana, 1987), 15–20. An interesting general work on the expository tradition is D. Sugarman, 'Legal Theory, the Common Law Mind and the Making of the Textbook Tradition', in W. Twining (ed.), *Legal Theory and Common Law* (Oxford, Blackwell, 1986), 26.

B. Historical Perspectives: General Comments

As A. W. B. Simpson puts it ('Contract: The Twitching Corpse', (1981) 1 *OJLS* 265 at 273): 'all those who have written on nineteenth century contract law . . . are agreed that something very significant did happen in the nineteenth century; they have tried to say what is was, and explain the process.' The difficulty is that they have not always been in agreement on how and when the classical law evolved, on the earlier legal background against which it evolved, on the extent to which it ever provided a coherent explanation of the nature of the contractual obligation and on the extent to which nineteenth-century developments have produced a satisfactory conceptual structure for the modern law. What all such writers have shared, however, has been a common belief that there can be no understanding of the present without a full understanding of the past.

Hamburger identifies two distinct and different perspectives on doctrinal change which emerge through the scholarship on the history of contract law:

P. Hamburger, 'The Development of the Nineteenth Century Consensus Theory of Contract', (1989) 7 *Law & Hist. Rev.* 241 at 242–3

By far the more influential point of view asserts that legal doctrine is the product of social and economic forces, including intellectual trends that reflect those forces. In past centuries, this perception has been explored by historians as different as Robert Brady and A. V. Dicey, and by political economists as diverse as Adam Smith and Karl Marx. In this century, the approach has become more sharply focused in the works of such historians as P. S. Atiyah, L. Friedman, M J. Horwitz, and W. Hurst. These exponents of what can be a called a societal approach are noteworthy for their emphasis on the economic and related intellectual influences upon law.

Although the various proponents of the societal theory take very different views of it, its principal advocates appear to share a belief that the law directly and promptly reflected societal forces. For example, Horwitz argues that the bench and bar in nineteenth-century America united to promote commercial interests and were able to alter doctrine for this purpose because they had an "instrumental" understanding of law. Atiyah explains changes in nineteenth-century English contract doctrine as a reflection of liberal economic thought and ideology. For these historians, law was a product of societal forces, hardly ever an impediment.

A rather different approach is apparent in the work of other historians, of whom A. W. B. Simpson can be taken as an example. Simpson has carefully examined contract doctrine and how it has changed. His general approach is not necessarily inconsistent with the societal perspective, but it suggests at the very least that an accurate explanation of law's relationship to society requires a firm grasp of how legal doctrine changes. In connection with contract, Simpson is explicit about the need to understand the nature of doctrinal change.

Underlying Simpson's concern about doctrine and its capacity for change is an important assumption or observation about the nature of judge-made doctrine: it is somewhat conservative. That judges cannot innovate—that they find the law rather than make it—is one of the profound half-truths of the common law. To state the proposition more accurately, discontinuities in doctrine can only occur if they are imperceptible or are sufficiently well disguised that they can be plausibly denied. Unlike legislative alterations, undisguised changes in judge-made doctrine or common law have not typically been accommodated by the Anglo-American legal system—particularly when such changes were perceived to be inconsistent with prior doctrine.

Here we shall take the work of Patrick Atiyah as illustrative of the first school of thought, and the work of James Gordley as illustrative of the second.

C. Patrick Atiyah

Patrick Atiyah's major work of legal history, *The Rise and Fall of Freedom of Contract* (Oxford, Oxford University Press, 1979), attempts to offer an account of the key interactions between legal doctrine and socio-economic forces in the period 1770–1970. The basic thesis of the book emerges already in its title. Against a background of political, economic, and intellectual history, Atiyah charts the emergence of a distinctive concept of freedom of contract, the period of its dominance within the doctrinal structure of the law between 1770 and 1870, and its subsequent decline.

In his textbook on contract, Atiyah summarizes the ruling concept of freedom of contract as understood in the core period of 1770–1870 when, he argues, it held sway in English contract law.

P. S. Atiyah, *An Introduction to the Law of Contract*, 4th edn. (Oxford, Clarendon Press, 1989), 9–10

. . . the law of contract was designed to provide for the enforcement of the private arrangements which the contracting parties had agreed upon. In general the law was not concerned either with the fairness or justice of the outcome, nor with the possibility that the contract might not be in the public interest. The function of contract law was merely to assist one of the contracting parties when the other broke the rules of the game and defaulted in the performance of his contractual obligations. In other words the judge was just a sort of umpire whose job it was to respond to the appeal 'How's that?' when something went wrong. As applied to the law of contract these ideas meant encouraging almost unlimited freedom of contracting, and thus the shibboleths 'freedom of contract' and 'sanctity of contract' became the foundations on which the whole law of contract was built. It would, however, be wrong to conclude that the judges of this period were uninterested in justice: they thought that it *was* just to enforce contractual duties strictly according to the letter. It would be equally mistaken to think that the judges were indifferent to the public interest. They simply thought that, in nearly all cases, it *was* in the public interest to enforce private contracts. Indeed, it was widely thought that this was proved by fundamental economic principles. As late as 1875 one of the greatest judges of the nineteenth century, Sir George Jessel, declared that, 'if there is one thing more than another which public policy requires, it is that men of full age and competent understanding shall have the utmost liberty of contracting and that their contracts, when entered into freely and voluntarily, shall be held sacred and shall be enforced by Courts of Justice'. . . .

Like most shibboleths, that of 'freedom of contract' rarely, if ever, received the close examination which its importance deserved, and even today it is by no means easy to say what exactly the nineteenth-century judges meant when they used this phrase. At least it may be said that the idea of freedom of contract embraced two closely connected, but none the less distinct, concepts. In the first place, it emphasized that contracts were based on mutual agreement, while in the second place, it stressed that the creation of a contract was the result of a free choice unhampered by external control such as government or legislative interference.

It is implicit in the idea of the 'rise' of freedom of contract that things were not always thus. In *Rise and Fall*, Atiyah argues that in eighteenth-century England a number of rival theories of promissory obligation were struggling for supremacy.

Atiyah, *The Rise and Fall of Freedom of Contract*, 141–2

On the one hand, there were the newer notions about the inherently binding nature of promises, but at the same time there were still the traditional ideas in which promises were neither necessary nor sufficient conditions for the creation of obligations. In this older scheme, duties arose out of relationships or transactions; even where the relationship or transaction was itself a consensual one, such as a simple sale, the obligations that arose out of the transaction were, in a sense, the consequence of the law, not simply of the parties' intentions. A sale, for example, created a debt, but although it was the act of the parties which created the sale, it was the law which created the debt. . . .

A second respect in which eighteenth-century contract theory differed fundamentally from that which grew up later, was in its treatment of the part executed contract, rather than the wholly executory contract, as its paradigm case. Ever since the nineteenth century the law has adopted the wholly executory contract as its typical case; contracts are assumed to be arrangements which are made for future performance. The separation of the making of the contract—the creation of the legal tie, or obligation—from the performance of the contract is an absolutely central feature of modern contract theory. It was barely present in eighteenth-century theory.

The third respect in which the eighteenth-century model of contract differed from that of the present day concerned the nature of the remedy which a plaintiff was given for a breach of contract. In modern English contract law a plaintiff is assumed to have—as a matter of course—a claim for damages for his 'loss' as a result of a breach of contract. This 'loss' is, in principle, defined by the *expectations* which the plaintiff was entitled to have as a result of the making of the contract. The fact that the plaintiff has or has not acted to his prejudice in reliance on the defendant is generally regarded as immaterial, except to the purely arithmetical calculations; the fact that the defendant has or has not received a benefit as a result of some act of performance by the plaintiff, is also treated as, in principle, immaterial in modern English law. . . . But my concern at present is not with modern theory but with that of the eighteenth century; and my suggestion is that at that time there was a much closer relationship between the nature of the liability sought to be imposed on a defendant, and the ground of the plaintiff's claim. In particular, if liability was sought to be imposed—as could quite typically be imposed in any contractual action today—for breach of a wholly executory and unrelied-upon promise, the reaction of the courts was still fundamentally hostile. The notion that a promisee was entitled to have his *expectations* protected, purely and simply as such, as a result of a promise and nothing else, was not generally accepted in eighteenth-century law.

Notes

1. A 'wholly executory contract' is one formed on the basis of mutual promises of future performance. It is a key concept in the doctrine of consideration, in so far as it defines the scope of the enforceability of promises (see Ch. 6).

2. The central part of Atiyah's thesis here is where he explicitly ties together 'free market' and 'free contract'. He links the emergence of an abstract body of general contract law, applicable, at least in principle, to all contracts and enunciated in a set of propositions set down in authoritative textbooks, to the rise of the free-market economy and the demands which this places on the law.

Atiyah, *The Rise and Fall of Freedom of Contract*, 400–2

There seems no doubt that all this generality, this attempt to state the law in terms of abstract principle, fitted well with the new political economy. It was a law suited to the free market, in which the subject matter of the contract was immaterial. During the course of this century, that is between 1770 and 1870, this general law of contract did very largely create a body of rules applicable to all contracts alike. . . .

This emphasis on contract law as the law of the market was, in England at least, well established by 1870, although in America it may have been a later development. One of its principal characteristics was its abstractness, its lack of particularity, its attempt to treat all contracts as being of the same general character. 'This abstraction', it has been said by an American scholar of the parallel development in the United States,

is not what people think of when they criticise the law as being too abstract, implying that the law is hypertechnical or unrealistic (though often it is). The abstraction of classical contract law is not unrealistic; it is a deliberate renunciation of the particular, a deliberate relinquishment of the temptation to restrict untrammeled individual autonomy or the completely free market in the name of social policy. [L. Friedman, *Contract Law in America* (Madison, Wis., University of Wisconsin Press, 1965), 20–1]

Some have, indeed, seen a positive virtue, a sign of judicial impartiality, in this abstract application of the law of the market place. The emphasis on the fixed rules of contract law, the emphasis on the abstract nature of these rules and their applicability to all people and all subject-matter alike, has been treated as part of the very nature of certain and predictable rules as opposed to more flexible, but more unpredictable discretionary justice. The rule of the market place is thus equated with the Rule of Law itself. Whatever may be thought of the value-judgments implicit in such an equation in the modern world, there seems little doubt that historically the equation is correct. . . .

In general terms, this equation of general principles of contract law with the free market economy led to an emphasis on the framework within which individuals bargained with each other, and a retreat from interest in substantive justice or fairness. The model of contract theory which implicitly underlay the classical law of contract—for such we may now call it—was thus the model of the market.

Note

These historical assertions have been criticized. For example, for Ian Macneil ('Relational Contract: What We Do and Do Not Know', [1985] *Wis. L. Rev.* 483 at 511–12), these are 'essentially unproved and questionable hypotheses which are nevertheless regularly cited as if they were established fact'. On the other hand, Atiyah warns the reader in his preface that, as someone qualified only in law, he does not necessarily possess all the tools of analysis necessary to evaluate the interdisciplinary material he has drawn upon. Moreover, it has been commented that Atiyah's thesis works better as a history of ideology rather than as an attempt to match the histories of legal doctrine and capitalist economic development (see e.g. B. Mensch, 'Freedom of Contract as Ideology', (1981) 33 *Stan. L. Rev.* 733).

The final part of Atiyah's thesis concerns the decline of freedom of contract since 1870, according to Simpson,

a period during which, it is argued, the importance attached to the enforcement of freely negotiated contracts was progressively reduced, leaving us today with a fossilized body of contractual doctrine which is no longer in tune with contemporaneously held values' ('Contract: The Twitching Corpse', 275).

Interestingly, in the most recent edition of his textbook *An Introduction to the Law of Contract* (4th edn., 1989), Atiyah observes that there has been, since 1980, in effect a 're-rise' of freedom of contract, in particular in legislative policy, where many privatization and deregulation measures have aimed to leave economic actors free to make their own agreements (pp. 30–9) (see further Ch. 3).

The aim of Atiyah's work has been not only to provide a historical reconstruction of the evolution of modern contract doctrine, and of the influences upon it, but also to provide a distinctive theory of contractual obligation which in turn learns from the lessons of history. In the introduction to *Rise and Fall*, Atiyah acknowledges that his historical work has made it necessary to re-examine the basis of promissory liability and to reconsider the current framework of the law of obligations—a point we touched upon in Chapter 1. It is the touchstone of Atiyah's work that the law of obligations should be organized around three general principles: protection of reasonable reliance, restoration of benefits conferred, and the voluntary creation and extinction of liabilities. To this end, Atiyah's work has revealed an important parallelism between the protection of reliance under pre-nineteenth-century contract law and the resurgence of reliance-based liabilities in the twentieth century, such as liability for negligent misrepresentations (see Ch. 5) and the enforcement of promises relied upon by the promisee (see Ch. 6). These ideas are explored further by Atiyah in 'Contracts, Promises and the Law of Obligations', (1978) 94 *LQR* 193, where he offers a set of answers to the question why promises should be enforced which is distinctively different to those offered by the modern bargain-based paradigm.

Work similar to that of Atiyah, but with a broader substantive focus, has been undertaken in the United States by Morton Horwitz (see *The Transformation of American Law, 1780–1860* (Cambridge, Mass., Harvard University Press, 1977); *The Transformation of American Law, 1870–1960* (New York, Oxford University Press, 1992), esp. ch. 2). See also L. Friedman, *Contract Law in America* (Madison, Wis., University of Wisconsin Press, 1965).

D. James Gordley

The work of James Gordley offers a contrast to that of Atiyah. In *The Philosophical Origins of Modern Contract Doctrine*, Gordley advances a thesis about the evolution of the present doctrinal structures of contract law in both *civil law* and *common law* countries. At the outset, the question Gordley asks himself is as much an issue of comparison as of history: what is it that explains the common doctrinal structures of contract shared by civil law and common law systems alike?

J. Gordley, *The Philosophical Origins of Modern Contract Doctrine* (Oxford, Clarendon Press, 1991), 3–9

This study will provide an answer, although not one that fits easily with many popular notions about legal history. In the sixteenth and early seventeenth centuries, a fairly small group of theologians and jurists centred in Spain self-consciously attempted to synthesize the Roman legal texts with the moral theology of Thomas Aquinas. The fundamental concepts and doctrines of private law with which we are familiar are a simplification of the synthesis they achieved. This book will show that this is the origin of present-day contract doctrine, and I believe a similar story can be told of the emergence of the modern law of property and tort.

Thomas Aquinas was a thirteenth-century Dominican friar. Shortly before his birth, Aristotle's works on metaphysics, physics, politics, and ethics first became available in the West. They touched off the sort of storm we associate with the work of Newton or Darwin. Thomas, it is commonly said, baptized Aristotle. He achieved a synthesis between the Greek philosophical tradition that Aristotle represented and the religious tradition of Christianity.

The *Corpus iuris civilis* of Justinian had been rediscovered and had become the object of academic study about two hundred years before Thomas was born. This revival of Roman law affected almost every aspect of medieval religious and political life. Intellectually, it contributed to a preoccupation with law that is apparent in the work of Thomas. Nevertheless, no genuine synthesis between Roman law and Thomistic or Aristotelian philosophy took place until the end of the Middle Ages.

In the sixteenth and early seventeenth centuries, a synthesis finally was achieved by a group of theologians and jurists known to historians as the 'late scholastics' or the 'Spanish natural law school'. The greatest representatives of this school were Francesco de Vitoria, Diego de Covarruvias, Domingo de Soto, Luis de Molina, and Leonard Lessius. They built a system of doctrines Thomistic and Artistotelian in ground plan and Roman in much of its detail. They thus gave Roman law a systematic doctrinal organization which it had previously lacked. . . .

In the seventeenth and eighteenth centuries, the doctrines of the late scholastics were taken over and popularized by members of the northern natural law school such as Hugo Grotius, Samuel Pufendorf, and Jean Barbeyrac. From the works of these authors, or of those they influenced such as Jean Domat and Robert Pothier, these doctrines made their way into the modern common and civil law. In the nineteenth century, for the first time, common lawyers wanted a doctrinal system. They created one by borrowing extensively from Grotius, Pufendorf, Barbeyrac, Domat, and Pothier. They then cited English cases to illustrate the doctrines they had borrowed—doctrines which the courts surely did not have in mind when these cases were decided. The drafters of the French Civil Code borrowed almost two-thirds of that document and nearly all the provisions on contracts from Pothier and Domat. These provisions were then declared to be 'the will of the legislator', and almost all the efforts of nineteenth-century French jurists were devoted to interpreting them. Nineteenth-century German jurists devoted their energy to building as perfect a doctrinal system as they could. They did so by refashioning the doctrinal system they had inherited from the previous century. The doctrines of the nineteenth-century common and civil lawyers, with various modifications, endured into the twentieth century and have now been disseminated throughout the world.

This account of the origins of modern legal doctrine will seem odd to those who are used to economic explanations of legal change. None of the changes we shall consider had much economic significance. What did change was the way contract law was understood. . . .

It is . . . a surprising story. Its most surprising feature is that doctrines which, in modified form, now govern most of the world were founded on philosophical ideas that fell from favour centuries ago. Indeed, in their original form these doctrines depended directly on Aristotelian and Thomistic moral conceptions about virtue and metaphysical conceptions about the nature or essence of things. Making a contract, for example, was an exercise of the virtue of liberality by which one enriched another, or of the virtue of commutative justice by which one exchanged things of equal value. Each type of contract had a certain 'nature' or 'essence' from which certain obligations followed. In the seventeenth century, even as these doctrines were being disseminated in northern Europe, the moral and metaphysical ideas on which they were based were called into question by Descartes, Hobbes, Locke, and others. This attack ultimately broke the authority of Aristotle. In the mid-seventeenth century, Hobbes complained that 'the Philosophy-schooles, through all the Universities of Christendome', followed Aristotle. Pufendorf complained that most educated people regarded Aristotelian philosophy as a summit beyond which the human mind could scarcely advance. By the mid-eighteenth century that philosophy had lost its hold on the schools and on educated people alike. By the nineteenth century it was all but unintelligible.

One would have expected the legal doctrines founded on this philosophy to fall along with it or else to be reformulated under the influence of more modern philosophical ideas. But that is not what happened. As we will see, throughout the seventeenth and eighteenth centuries the doctrines remained much as the late scholastics had left them. Jurists such as Pufendorf and Barbeyrac jettisoned Aristotle's metaphysics and moral philosophy, adopted various principles from the philosophies of their own day, but made only minor changes in the doctrines themselves. The doctrines drifted, cut off from their old philosophical moorings and left without any real tie to the professed philosophical beliefs of the jurists who were now disseminating them.

These doctrines were finally reformulated in the nineteenth century, but with little relation to the philosophy of Bentham, Kant, or any other thinker then popular. English, American, French, and German jurists eliminated concepts that had meaning in the context of Thomistic and Aristotelian philosophy but, in the nineteenth century, seemed wrong or unintelligible. They then bent and stretched the concepts they retained to make them do the work of those they had rejected.

In the field of contract law, with which we shall be concerned, the result was what have been called 'will theories' of contract. The will of the parties became, in Simpson's words, a sort of *Grundnorm* from which as many rules of contract law as possible were to be inferred. The late scholastics and the natural lawyers had recognized as fundamental the principle that contracts are entered into by the will or consent of the parties. They had formulated general doctrines of mistake, fraud, and duress by considering how these influences affect the will.

The nineteenth-century innovation was not to pay attention to the will but to reject other concepts of Aristotelian origin that had previously figured in contract doctrine. Making a contract was regarded simply as an act of will, not as the exercise of a moral virtue. The parties were bound simply to what they willed, not to obligations that followed from the essence or nature of their contract. . . .

In the twentieth century, a doctrinal crisis began that is still with us. Even as Western law spread throughout the world, Western legal scholars wondered if it was possible to have coherent legal doctrine. In the field of contract law, as we shall see, the problem was that the nineteenth-century jurists had borrowed part of the earlier doctrinal system and had not managed to make that part work by itself. They claimed to be interpreting positive law. But the positive law did not simply enforce whatever the parties willed and only what they willed—nor could it. The positive law distinguished gift from exchange and one type of exchange from another. It held the parties to obligations that depended on the type of contract they had made even if they had not willed these obligations expressly. It sometimes released the victims of unequal bargains from obligations they had willed expressly. Twentieth-century critics pointed out that the will theories could not explain these aspects of contract law. In fact, they were the very aspects that the late scholastics had explained with the Aristotelian notions of essence and virtue that the nineteenth-century jurists had discarded.

The crisis has continued because the critics found themselves unable to rebuild the edifice they had razed. Grant Gilmore summed up the current state of contract law by saying: 'The systems have come unstuck and we see, presently, no way of glueing them back together again.' Yet the nineteenth-century doctrines drift on, riddled with twentieth-century qualifications and exceptions.

It is indeed surprising that our modern legal doctrines were founded originally on philosophical ideas discarded long ago. It is also surprising that in all these years no adequate substitute for these ideas has been found. Nevertheless, we can understand the history of Western legal doctrine only when we recognize that this is so.

Notes

1. Gordley gives a very different explanation for the development of the so-called 'will theories' of contract, which underlay the classical law, from that proposed by Atiyah. The latter sees will theory—or the 'tendency to attribute all the consequences of a contract to the will of those who made it' (*Rise and Fall*, 405)—as simply one of the principal characteristics of the classical contract theory which arose as much in response to the ideological demands of the market as in response to an intellectual history,

although he does make reference to the Natural Law School of thinkers. Gordley sees modern contract doctrine as taking its present form in civil law and common law countries despite rather than because of the developments in the nineteenth century, and it is a central plank of his thesis that this has contributed to the absence of a coherent theory of contract today.

2. Although Gordley claims that his work is principally diagnostic and historical, in the final chapter of his book he takes the argument two steps further. First, he dismisses new versions of the will theories in the guise of Fried's theory of 'contract as promise' (see Section VI) and the law-and-economics scholarship of Posner and others (see Section V) as failing to provide an intellectually coherent system. Like the original will theories, they fallaciously attempt to build contract around a single organizing principle of choice or commitment, a task which is simply impossible, according to Gordley. Second, he suggests that his insights can lead to the building of a new theoretical edifice—one can envisage, perhaps, a theory which uses the concepts of Aristotelian justice in order to incorporate ideas of a just price and of distributive justice. In other words, it would be a theory under which promises would be enforced only if they satisfied some form of substantive fairness criterion.

3. The work of Brian Simpson also broadly falls within the same strand of thinking as Gordley's, in his focus on the importance of doctrine. See his 'Innovation in Nineteenth Century Contract Law', (1975) 91 *LQR* 247 and 'The Horwitz Thesis and the History of Contracts', (1979) 46 *U. Chi. L. Rev.* 533.

IV. THE THEORY OF RELATIONAL CONTRACT AND THE ROLE OF EMPIRICAL METHODOLOGIES

A. Introduction

In this section we examine two closely related topics: the first is a way of conceiving of contractual relations and the second a method of studying them. Relational contract theory offers a challenge to the modern paradigm, but operates at a rather different level from the critique of bargain presented by, for example, reliance theories. It is concerned, not with identifying the type of interest protected by the enforcement of promissory obligations, but with offering a different model for understanding the process and practice of contracting. Relational contract theory argues that modern contractual relations are typically characterized by ongoing long-term relationships in which co-operation between the parties is a stronger factor than conflict and self-interest. The modern law tends, in contrast, to continue to be organized, with few exceptions, around a paradigm of the 'discrete transaction', the type of contractual arrangement described by Macneil as 'sharp in by clear agreement; sharp out by clear performance' ('The Many Futures of Contracts', (1974) 47 *S. Cal. L. Rev.* 691 at 738). In other words, the modern law is singularly ill-equipped to deal with the reality of modern contractual relations, as it is premissed on a model of the adversarial, arm's-length bargain between strangers in which the rights and duties of the parties are eternally fixed at the point of formation. This is a feature of the law which Macneil describes as 'presentiation' (e.g. Macneil, 'Restatement (Second) of Contracts and Presentiation', (1974) 60 *Va. L. Rev.* 589). The arguments of relational-contract scholars, led by Macneil, have sought not only to draw attention to this lack of it between reality and legal framework but also to show the extent to which the practices of relationalism now underlie most exchanges. Here their work intersects with empirical studies, largely pio-neered by Stewart Macaulay, whose work examines, at a micro level, the role of contract in particular business relationships. This idea is sometime called the 'living law', to use a term coined by Ehrlich, in contradistinction to the law in the courts, the traditional focus of 'black-letter' contract scholars. The central insight of empirical scholars is that the role of con-tract law cannot be taken for granted in exchange relationships, and that businessmen are frequently indifferent to the question of whether or not they are operating within the bounds of legal enforceability.

B. Macneil and Relational Contract Theory

Ian Macneil has elaborated a theory of relational contract in an extensive body of books and articles (see D. Campbell, 'The Social Theory of Relational Contract: Macneil as the Modern Proudhon', (1990) 18 *Int. J. Soc. Law* 75 for a lengthy bibliography of Macneil's publications) of which the key works are probably the following: 'The Many Futures of Contracts', (1974) 47 *S. Cal. L. Rev.* 691; 'A Primer of Contract Planning', (1975) 48 *S. Cal. L. Rev.* 627; *The New Social Contract* (New Haven, Conn., Yale University Press, 1980); 'Economic Analysis of Contractual Relations: Its Shortfalls and the Need for a "Rich Classificatory Apparatus"', (1981) 75 *NwUL Rev.* 1018. Macneil's theory has developed over the years, and his style of presentation is somewhat opaque and elusive. Here we present a simple description by Macneil of the characteristics of discrete transactions and relational contracts, an application and amplification of these ideas by Brown in the context of labour relations, and a summary by Feinman of the theory behind relational contract. A review of the impact and implications of Macneil's work follows the section on empirical methodologies.

I. Macneil, *Contract: Exchange Transactions and Relations,* 2nd edn. (Mineola, NY, Foundation Press, 1978),12–13

Contractual ordering of economic activity takes place along a spectrum of transactional and relational behavior. At one end are discrete transactions. Discrete transactions are contracts of short duration, involving limited personal interactions, and with precise party measurements of easily measured objects of exchange, for example, money and grain. They require a minimum of future cooperative behavior between the parties and no sharing of benefits or burdens. They bind the two parties tightly and precisely. The parties view such transactions as deals free of entangling strings, and they certainly expect no altruism. The parties see virtually everything connected with such transactions as clearly defined and presentiated. If trouble is anticipated at all, it is anticipated only if someone or something turns out unexpectedly badly. The epitome of discrete contract transactions: at noon two strangers come into town from opposite directions, one walking and one riding a horse. The walker offers to buy the horse, and after brief dickering a deal is struck in which delivery of the horse is to be made at sundown upon the handing over of $10. The two strangers expect to have nothing to do with each other between now and sundown; they expect never to see each other thereafter; and each has as much feeling for the other as has a Viking trading with a Saxon. A modern example with many of these characteristics is a purchase of nonbrand name gasoline in a strange town one does not expect to see again.

At the other end of the contract spectrum are ongoing relations. Being more diverse than well-honed discrete transactions, they are more difficult to describe concisely, but the following are typical characteristics. The relations are of significant duration (for example, franchising). Close whole person relations form an integral part of the relation (employment). The object of exchange typically includes both easily measured quantities (wages) and quantities not easily measured (the projection of personality by an airline stewardess). Many individuals with individual and collective poles of interest are involved in the relation (industrial relations). Future cooperative behavior is anticipated (the players and management of the New York Yankees). The benefits and burdens of the relation are to be shared rather than entirely divided and allocated (a law partnership). The entangling strings of friendship, reputation, interdependence, morality, and altruistic desires are integral parts of the relation (a theatrical agent and his clients, a corporate management team). Trouble is expected as a matter of course (a collective bargaining agreement). Finally, the participants never intend or expect to see the whole future of the relation as presentiated at any single time, but view the relation as an ongoing integration of behavior to grow and vary with events in a largely unforeseeable future (a marriage; a family business). . . .

D. Brown, 'Contract Remedies in a Planned Economy: Labour Arbitration Leads the Way', in B. Reiter and J. Swan (eds.), *Studies in Contract Law* (Toronto, Butterworths, 1980), 96–9

A typical "transaction" is the exchange of a particular good or service for a fixed sum of money. The exchange is simple, and it is possible in advance of the exchange to define fully the performance which each party must undertake. The price, quantity of goods, and time for delivery are likely to be described quite completely. However, the limits of language often render planning incomplete in minor ways. In addition, the effect that changes in surrounding circumstances will have upon contractual obligations is not usually considered, nor are the risks of non-performance addressed frequently.

Advance planning of the substance of the exchange is the essence of a transaction but several other characteristics are important. The exchange is carefully measured. The price of the goods will be stated in dollars or cents per unit. This measured reciprocity is the parties' sole purpose as there are no other rights or obligations arising out of the arrangement. Each participant may hope to engage the other in future dealings, but even this interest will be of little importance in a competitive market. There is little need for further cooperation after the bargain is struck because delivery and payment are all that remain to be done. The major benefit derived from the bargain is financial gain and the parties' attachment to one another is primarily economic. Most transactions involve only two participants. . . .

Relational arrangements frequently survive for long periods and they may be continually renegotiated. The performance called for by the contract is seldom fully planned at the outset. The manner in which collective agreements regulate employment is illustrative. These agreements do not arrange for any particular employee to work for a defined period. Employees may quit and management retains the power to terminate and to hire workers subject to the rules of the contract. Management decisions that impinge upon employment are controlled in two ways. One category of rules concerns the volume of work performed by persons protected by the agreement. The "recognition clause" defines the tasks which must be done by persons within the bargaining unit when the work is performed under the employer's direction. These jobs may not be carried out by supervisory personnel or by other employees who are not members of the unit. . . .

The second category of rules which govern employment decisions by management provides guidelines for the identification of the individuals to whom work is to be assigned. . . .

A collective agreement does not arrange an exact exchange in the same way as a simple sales contract defines a bargain. The function of a collective agreement is quite different. It lays down mutually acceptable rules to guide the employment relationship but these rules do not require the engagement of particular workers. Employees may quit and management retains considerable discretion to adjust the number of jobs in response to market and technological forces and to select or discharge workers. The agreement does structure the outcome by permitting or prohibiting certain kinds of management action and by establishing procedural safeguards.

This approach is typical of relational arrangements. The substance of the exchange is seldom mapped out in detail at the outset, largely because the relation is too broad in scope and duration to be fully anticipated. This does not mean that the relation is unplanned. Rather, advance planning lays down the framework within which the relation will take shape and guides future performance by allocating discretionary powers, not by precisely describing what is to be done. Constitutional and procedural matters replace substantive concerns. Most of the substance of the exchange will be determined later as it is carried out, although some aspects of the performance to be rendered may be determined from the start. Only general standards are set down to regulate employment under a collective agreement but remuneration is stated in dollars and cents. Similarly, a franchise agreement may exactly define the hours and location of the franchisee's operation, but it is not likely to fix the quantity of goods to be supplied by the franchisor. . . .

How are the full contours of contractual performance mapped out? Some matters may be reserved for unilateral decision. A buyer may determine the quantity to be delivered under a requirements contract just as an employer may decide the volume of employment. Mutual planning will also continue throughout the life of the contract. On occasion the contract may be renegotiated. More important, consultation will be required to fill gaps in the original agreement. The application of contractual language to diverse circumstances will constantly throw up questions for resolution. The parties will often disagree as to the facts or the correct interpretation of their agreement. Consider a shopping centre lease which defines exclusive merchandising jurisdictions for each tenant. The right to sell furniture kits might be claimed by both the hardware merchant and the furniture retailer. The agreement will probably offer no easy answer as to whose claim should prevail because it will not precisely define the meaning of "furniture" and of "hardware". The retailers must attempt to reach a mutually acceptable solution if confrontation is to be avoided.

The agreement will sometimes provide expressly for consultation. This requirement may be a condition precedent to the exercise of a unilateral power. The obligation of an employer to consult the union before subcontracting work frequently does not prohibit management action if an accommodative solution is not reached.

J. Feinman, 'The Significance of Contract Theory', (1990) 58 *U. Cin. L. Rev.* at 1299–1302

Relational contract theory, largely developed by Ian Macneil, is widely mis-understood and, as misunderstood, is usually shrugged off by mainstream scholars. Part of the misunderstanding may arise from Macneil's style of pre-sentation, which usually does not observe the style of traditional legal scholar-ship; the greater share of the misunderstanding is due to the fundamental opposition between the goals and methods of relational contract theory and those of neoclassical scholarship.

In the mainstream view, the core assertions of relational contract theory are that the dominant form of contract, relational contract, "occurs over time through continuous interactions between parties," so that "one must investigate the social conditions that form the foundation of parties' bargains in order to comprehend the relational norms and hence to understand contract." Classical contract, with its focus on a distinct moment of contract formation, could not accommodate these concerns. However, mainstream scholars assert that, con-trary to the opinion of relational extremists, modern contract law recognizes the existence of relational contracts, though not their dominance, and is well equipped to investigate the social contexts of such agreements to determine their legal effect. For example, where an actress in a TV series suddenly becomes very popular, whether her employer is required to renegotiate her contract depends on the parties' intentions, which can be determined accu-rately through neoclassical methods and doctrines by examining course of dealing, usage of trade, and the meaning of good faith in the context. Thus neo-classical contract already embodies the important parts of relational contract; the rest consists of unnecessary flights of theoretical fancy.

If this view of relational contract was correct, one wonders how Macneil could have acquired a reputation as one of our finest scholars. After all, Karl Llewellyn wrote about the importance of relations and contexts at about the time Macneil was born. However, the mainstream view of relational contract is simplistic and partial.

Relational contract theory begins with some very basic observations and insights about people's interaction in organized society. Any society in which specialization of labor exists will include exchange, and exchange always occurs in a relational context. In any society, even the most capitalistic, individ-ualistic one, the production and distribution of goods and services is carried on through a variety of exchange mechanisms, of which discrete, self-maximizing exchange on a market (the paradigm of neoclassical contract) will be a very small part. More commonly, exchange occurs within relations that involve more elements and are of longer duration than does an isolated, discrete exchange. Moreover, even the most discrete contract is an event that is always situated within a framework of non-discrete relations which must be examined to understand the discrete contract. Accordingly, as an initial empirical and conceptual matter, thinking about contract ought to begin with relational exchange, not discrete contract. Recognizing, as neoclassical contract does, that some contracts are more extensive than discrete bargains is not enough; relational contract theory stresses that all contracts are relational to some extent, and truly relational contracts predominate.

The second step in relational contract theory is to examine in more detail the behavior exhibited by parties along the spectrum of discrete and relational exchange. All exchanges require certain kinds of behavior, such as a common means of communication between the parties, a minimum amount of solidarity, and some reciprocity. Some exchanges are relatively discrete, involving short duration, limited party interactions, and precise measurement of the value of the objects exchanged. Other exchanges are more relational, involving significant duration, many facets of the parties' lives, and the exchange of values that cannot easily be quantified. The distinction between discrete and relational exchanges is perhaps the most important way of categorizing exchanges.

The different types of exchange behavior observed give rise to norms, "a case of an 'is' creating an 'ought.'" The norms parallel the categories of behavior that have been conceptualized; some norms are common to all exchanges, while others are associated more strongly with discrete and relational exchanges, respectively. Solidarity and reciprocity, for example, are norms that are common to all contracts. In discrete contracts the norms of implementation of planning and effectuation of consent are intensified by the distinctive elements of discrete exchanges. On the other hand, in relational contracts other common contract norms, such as maintaining the integrity of one's role within the relation and harmonizing the relation with the surrounding social matrix, are more important because of the more extensive characteristics of relational exchanges.

In Macneil's view, these immanent norms can be developed and applied to constitute "more precise, intellectually coherent principles which are nevertheless sufficiently open-textured for effective use in the law of modern contractual relations." When used to analyze a particular situation, this conceptual framework certainly emphasizes different elements than does neoclassical law, and arguably provides a richer analysis. In addition, the framework brings to light certain features of many exchanges that neoclassical law undervalues or ignores because of its emphasis on relatively discrete, value-maximizing agreements. Values other than wealth maximization figure importantly in exchanges, even discrete contracts and market exchanges because the non-economic, non-market aspects of relations pervade market transactions. Sometimes relations are not mutually favorable to all parties because they arise out of social situations of inequality, so the values may include elements of coercion and dependence, contrary to the neoclassical assumption of rough equality. In other situations, values such as trust, cooperation, reciprocity, and role integrity are essential to the relationship.

Notes

1. Campbell and Harris introduce a note of caution into the assessment of Macneil's work, suggesting that his view of co-operation is perhaps slightly idealistic.

D. Campbell and D. Harris, 'Flexibility in Long-Term Contractual Relationships: The Role of Co-operation', (1993) 20 *JL&S* 166 at 182

There are certain elements in Macneil's work which, in our opinion, rather undercut the power of this notion of contracts as 'instruments for social co-operation'. These turn on a failure to appreciate the limits to the co-operation which can be brought about by contracts properly understood as the legal expression of *capitalist* exchange. The nature of the co-operation arrived at through capitalist competition is, of course, overlaid by many themes of conflict. However, in terms of showing that co-operation is an essential and irreducible element of *efficient* long-term contracting behaviour, we regard Macneil's work as a foremost contribution to the social theory of the modern economy. It requires, however, empirical examination and possible factual corroboration of its co-operative hypothesis if its status is to be accepted.

2. Macneil's work is closely associated with a strand of work in the field of economics termed 'transaction cost' or 'neo-institutional' economics. In Section V we shall review this work, which, in the contracts field, is principally associated with Oliver Williamson and Victor Goldberg.

3. In this book we shall make reference to relational contract analysis in order to broaden and deepen the understanding of substantive doctrines of the law of contract. A particularly good example is offered by the adjustment of long-term contractual relationships, as this demonstrates the size of the gap between neo-classical accommodation of the relational elements of contract and 'true' relational analysis. The former sees the contract as something which is essentially fixed in form and content, although changeable if the parties agree. With each change to the contract, it is anew 'presentiated'. Under relational contract, the substance is never finally fixed, but always open and mutable (see further Ch. 6). There is no single great 'meeting of minds' (see W. Whitford, 'Ian Macneil's Contribution to Contracts Scholarship', [1985] *Wis. L. Rev.* 545 at 546).

4. After years of relative neglect, there is now a small but growing body of literature applying Macneil's analysis to specific types of contracts. See e.g. Campbell and Harris, 'Flexibility in Long-Term Contractual Relationships'.

Macneil also appears frequently in the bibliographies to the individual contributions in T. Wilhelmsson (ed.), *Perspectives of Critical Contract Law* (Aldershot, Dartmouth, 1993), which emphasizes the point which Macneil himself makes that all critical studies work is invariably relational, since it is written from a standpoint of 'holistic, historical social analysis' ('Relational Contract: What We Do and Do Not Know', [1985] *Wis. L. Rev.* 483 at 513–14). On critical legal studies in contract, see further Section VII.

5. An interesting example, which could be termed 'relational contract in action' is offered by so-called social work contracts which can be used to structure the relationships between social workers and their clients with a view to ensuring that social work interventions are more purposeful and based on stronger lines of communication between the parties. Social work contracts are not legally binding and differ in many formal and substantive respects from legally enforceable contracts, but they provide an example of how an agreement can give a structure to an attempt at cooperation which evolves over time. See generally on this J. Corden and R. Preston-Shoot, *Contracts in Social Work* (Aldershot, Gower, 1987).

C. Stewart Macaulay and Empirical Studies

In 1984 the Wisconsin Law School held a symposium to mark the 21st anniversary of the publication of one of the most celebrated and most cited works of contracts scholarship—Stewart Macaulay's 'Non-contractual Relations in Business', (1963) 28 *Am. Soc. Rev.* 55. The papers given at the symposium were subsequently published, prefaced by a review by Macaulay himself, in which he reflects upon his earlier article and upon the effects of the passage of time upon what he said then. It is perhaps ironic that a paper which is acclaimed as a work of contracts scholarship should have been published in a sociology journal and should have as its central tenet the project of identifying the extent to which contractual relations are relevant in business practice—a question to which Macaulay was obliged to give the answer: 'not very'. Details of what Macaulay called his tentative findings about the contractual or non-contractual relationships of a sample of manufacturing companies, mainly based in Wisconsin, USA, are included in Chapters 10 and 14. The data was gathered on the basis of interviews with managers and lawyers within the companies in question, and Macaulay acknowledges from the beginning the somewhat provisional nature of the methodology. Notwithstanding this, Macaulay's work has been enormously influential, both in opening up new ways of 'knowing' about contract and in offering an empirical dimension to the relational contract theory of Macneil. The work of the two scholars is commonly now discussed in tandem (see the extract from Gordon below). Examples of empirical analysis of contract in the UK context include H. Beale and A. M.

Dugdale, 'Contracts between Businessmen: Planning and the Use of Contractual Remedies', (1975) 2 *BJLS* 45, and T. Daintith, 'The Design and Performance of Long Term Contracts', in Daintith and G. Teubner (eds.), *Contract and Organisation* (Berlin, De Gruyter, 1986), 164.

S. Macaulay, 'An Empirical View of Contract', [1985] *Wis. L. Rev.* 465 at 466–72, 475, 477–9

The 1963 article challenges a model of contract law's functions, explicit or implicit in the work of contracts scholars and social theorists. This model makes contract law far more central than its actual role in society. One version of the model suggests that in a state of nature we are all selfish. Law supports needed interdependence by coercing us to honor obligations to others. The historical story is that we begin with trading within real communities. Capitalism breaks this up, and we become alienated strangers. Then the legal system supplies a kind of synthetic community based on rights and duties enforced by courts. A variant of the story is that market capitalism changes all personal relations into autonomous market trades—capitalism replaces a spirit of interdependence by "what's in it for me?" Contract law supplies the needed glue to hold individualists to their bargains.

More particularly, writers assume a number of things about the institution of contract. First, there is careful planning of relationships in light of legal requirements and the possibilities of nonperformance. We must spell out everything because parties will perform only to the letter of a contract, if they go that far. Second, contract law is a body of clear rules so that it can facilitate planning. It provides formal channels so that we know the right way to proceed to produce desired legal consequences. Finally, contract litigation is a primary means of deterring breach and directly and indirectly resolving disputes. Without contract law and the state's monopoly of the legitimate use of force, performance of contracts would be highly uncertain.

However, all of these assumptions about history and about human relationships are just wrong or so greatly overstated as to be seriously misleading. Contract planning and contract law, at best, stand at the margin of important long-term continuing business relations. Business people often do not plan, exhibit great care in drafting contracts, pay much attention to those that lawyers carefully draft, or honor a legal approach to business relationships. There are business cultures defining the risks assumed in bargains, and what should be done when things go wrong. People perform disadvantageous contracts today because often this gains credit that they can draw on in the future. People often renegotiate deals that have turned out badly for one or both sides. They recognize a range of excuses much broader than those accepted in most legal systems.

There are relatively few contracts cases litigated, and those that are have special characteristics. Few of those cases litigated produce anything like adequate compensation for the injuries caused. Frequently, limitations on liability in written contracts block remedies based on the reasonable expectations of the party who did not draft the instrument. At best, formal legal procedures usually are but a step in a larger process of negotiation. Filing a complaint and pre-trial procedure can be tactics in settlement bargaining; appeals often prompt reversals and remands, leaving the parties to settle or face continuing what seems to be an endless process. When final judgments are won, often they cannot be executed because of insolvency.

How do we explain this gap between the academic model and an empirical description of the system of contract law in action? Academic writers often make individualistic assumptions. Their theories rest on words of discrete transactions where people respond to calculations of short-term advantage. However, people engaged in business often find that they do not need contract planning and contract law because of relational sanctions. There are effective private governments and social fields, affected but seldom controlled by the formal legal system. Even discrete transactions take place within a setting of continuing relationships and interdependence. The value of these relationships means that all involved must work to satisfy each other. Potential disputes are suppressed, ignored, or compromised in the service of keeping the relationship alive.

While we often read that increasing bureaucratic organization has made the world impersonal, this is not always the case. Social fields cutting across formal lines exist within bureaucracies, creating rich sanction systems. Individuals occupying formal roles ignore organizational boundaries as they seek to overcome formal rationality to achieve goals, gain rewards, and avoid sanctions. Social networks serve as communications systems. People gossip, and this creates reputational sanctions.

Power, exploitation and dependence also are significant. Continuing relationships are not necessarily nice. The value of arrangements locks some people into dependent positions. They can only take orders. The actual lines of a bureaucratic structure may be much more extensive than formal ones. Seemingly independent actors may have little real freedom and discretion in light of the costs of offending dominant parties. Once they face sunk costs and comfortable patterns, the possibility of command rather than negotiation increases. In some situations parties may see relational sanctions as inadequate in view of the risks involved. However, instead of contract law, they usually turn to other techniques to provide security, ranging from collateral to vertical integration. . . .

American contract remedies are limited and reflect a fear of awarding too much. Our courts rarely order specific performance of contracts. One must prove one's damages with reasonable certainty, and in most states the injured party cannot recover the lost anticipated profits of "a new business." . . .

Limiting remedies can benefit a weaker party, making breach of contract less burdensome. However, often it benefits stronger parties. They have less need for legal remedies to achieve their ends because they have other-than-legal leverage. Limited remedies allow stronger parties to walk away from burdensome obligations at low or no cost. Courts frequently find that a stronger [party] has breached a contract, but so limit the remedy awarded the weaker that the victory is hollow.

Even when contract law might offer a remedy, the legal system in operation promotes giving up or settling rather than adjudicating to vindicate rights. One must pay for one's own lawyer, and one must win enough to offset all the costs of the endeavor. Thus, using the legal process always is a gamble. Furthermore, crafty lawyers use delay and procedural technicality for advantage. Galanter has discussed what he calls "megalaw." Those who can afford to play invest in the skills of large law firms. They play the litigation game by expanding procedural complexity to draw out the process. Others who cannot afford to invest as much must drop out. This kind of power is not distributed equally. In another famous article, Galanter tells us "why the 'haves' come out ahead." The "haves" are repeat players who can spread the costs of litigation over many similar transactions. They can afford to play for rules and treat disputes as test cases which may help them in the future. They can run up the costs of a particular case in order to reinforce their reputation as difficult defendants to sue. . . .

III. In 1984, what should be added to this picture?

The original article does not rest on naive functionalist assumptions of harmony. Nevertheless, today I would stress that relational sanctions do not always produce cooperation or happy situations. Trust can be misplaced. There are always failures to perform and mistakes. Usually, business people take an insurance approach. They write off these incidents as long as there are not too many or one of them does not involve too much money. Business scandals always have been with us, and they prompt attempts to use care and countermeasures. By and large, the contracting system works well enough. However, even large famous business corporations can suffer major losses as the result of incomplete planning and trusting the wrong people.

When long-term continuing relationships do collapse, those disadvantaged often turn to contract law and legal action. We have seen litigation prompted by major shocks to the world economic system. OPEC and the energy crises of the 1970s provoked many cases where contracts had rested on relational sanctions and assumptions about the costs of energy. Relational considerations gave way to the large amounts of money that businesses would have lost had they performed their commitments. Westinghouse, for example, promised electric utilities buying its nuclear reactors that it would guarantee the price of fuel. A world cartel sent the price soaring far beyond the price Westinghouse had guaranteed. Westinghouse found a plausible excuse in the Uniform Commercial Code and announced that it would not perform. After elaborate rituals before the courts, the cases were settled. Westinghouse injured its reputation, but the alternative might have been the destruction of a major multinational corporation. Contract doctrine played a part in the resolution of this dispute, but it would be hard to call it the principal actor. . . .

While our court reports have registered a great deal of contracts litigation in recent years, all of these attempts to use contract law have revealed that the second part of my 1963 critique still has force. The legal system in operation simply fails to vindicate rights or offer much to those who seek redress from the courts. Often it offers only symbolic victories, probably producing great frustration. For example, . . . we have enacted statutes granting rights to dealers who hold franchises to sell automobiles, gasoline, and the like. Members of the trade associations that worked to pass this legislation saw enactment as a great victory. Yet again and again the courts have read these statutes narrowly so that franchisors escape real harm. The statutes may have had indirect impact. Franchisors may have modified the behaviour of their agents to avoid atrocity cases that might prompt courts to interpret the new rights broadly, but this is only supposition. . . .

IV. What difference does all this make and to whom?

What should we make of this gap between the academic model of contract law and the system as it works? At minimum, we need a complex model of contract law in operation if we wish to be descriptively accurate. Contract law operates at the margins of major systems of private government through institutionalized social structures and less formal social fields. We must establish rather than assume the actual influence of this doctrine. Contract law as discussed by scholars frequently is but a rhetorical ploy in a much larger struggle. Lawyers may use its vocabulary in the process of dealing with a dispute. Often, however, the real issue between the parties is transformed to fit a law school model far removed from the transaction. As such, classic doctrine may affect negotiations, but not in the way assumed by most scholars. Perhaps lawyers skilled in playing the contract game do better for their clients, but defenders of orthodoxy must prove this. Perhaps bargaining in the shadow of the law implements those values explicit or implicit in contract doctrine to some degree. This cannot be assumed but must be established by investigation.

The contract process in action seldom is a neutral application of abstract rationality. The party with the best argument as judged by a contracts professor will not necessarily win the case. An opponent with a plausible argument, little need to settle, and resources to play the lawyering game is unlikely to bow to arguments favored by law professors at elite schools. Indeed, all an attorney may need are arguments that seem more or less plausible to judges and other lawyers. Even those disliked by scholars such as "unilateral contract" and "the meeting of the minds" often will do in the actual dispute resolution process.

We cannot be sure what functions orthodox contract doctrine serves. However, what we know so far suggests that contract doctrine incorporates major conflicting strands of political philosophy. It does not stand apart from the cross currents of political debate over time. At a particular time, one conception is emphasized. Later, as time change, another view takes its turn.

At the most basic level, contract law promises to remedy breaches of contract and provide security of expectations. It does this only indirectly and imperfectly. It helps reassure us about the stability of an ever changing and frightening world. It deters breach by those unaware that counterrules neatly match most contract rules or that most contract rules are qualitative and open-ended. Much of law operates under the Wizard of Oz principle of jurisprudence—you will recall that the Great Oz was a magnificent and wonderful wizard until Dorothy's dog knocked over the screen so all could see that the Wizard was a charlatan.

Nonetheless, contract law curbs power to some degree. Those who can command may not want to appear arbitrary and all powerful. It is good public relations to channel their actions into the forms of contract to gain the symbolism of bargain and free choice. Even this modest effort offers a degree of leverage for limiting the exercise of power. Scholarly notions of free contract are a frail defense against those with power seeking to achieve illegitimate ends. Nonetheless, there are few other defenses short of revolution.

Perhaps classic contracts scholarship can safely ignore the way the contract system works. This scholarship may be irrelevant to most of practice, and so it does not matter how articles are written. However, this scholarship has influence in some instances, and this leaves us with a puzzle. In the face of many studies challenging its descriptive accuracy, many scholars and theorists continue to paint a simple instrumental picture. What purposes are being served by all this traditional scholarly effort? Perhaps it is a form of denial. The formal contract system claims to be neutral and autonomous and to rest on simple rationality. A descriptively accurate model of the process challenges these assumptions. We must remember that long-term continuing relations are not always nice situations for those short of power. Instead of free individuals making informed choices, many are dependent and must choose between unpleasant options. Courts seldom come close to putting aggrieved parties in the position they would have been had the contract been performed. Cases are often won by lawyer ploys and the strategic and tactical advantages flowing from greater wealth. Instead of vindicating rights, our legal system offers deals. As a result, often one party feels cheated while the other thinks he got away with something.

At least in the United States, we want to believe that a lawyer, armed only with reason, can champion the weak and overcome the powerful. This myth drew many of us to law school, and it is hard to give up. A descriptive model reduces many lawyers to little more than captive intellectuals serving those who control significant resources in society. In short, classical contracts scholarship allows us to maintain a comforting image of what it is that typical lawyers do. A system of individual rights prompts higher thought. Descriptive accuracy requires us to confront the dark side of the society and its legal system.

Notes

1. The Westinghouse litigation reappears in Chapter 12, in the discussion of 'excuse doctrines', where it is discussed by Campbell and Harris in their article on long-term contracting referred to above. It is given as an example of how unhelpful law can be in the resolution of disputes under long-term contracts.

2. Macaulay can speak authoritatively about what he calls the 'dark side' of the legal system because he can lay claim to 'descriptive accuracy' when he paints his rather gloomy picture of contract in action. It should not be taken for granted that empirical studies, although generally welcomed by contract scholars, have received universal acclaim, even from those concerned with maintaining a socio-economic perspective on the legal system.

R. Cotterrell, *The Sociology of Law*, 2nd edn. (London, Butterworths, 1992), 34

How useful is the concept of 'living law' itself as a guide for research? It seems to invite inquiries of seemingly boundless scope. In fact it becomes useful only if thought of as the *alter ego* of lawyers' law; the 'real-life' parallel to the rules written in the law books (cf. Gurvitch 1947: 121). It follows that living law—if it is not to be equated with the whole range of studies in descriptive sociology—can be studied only in relation to the categories established in lawyers' law. It is a concept devised solely for polemical purposes, by a lawyer concerned to organise the data of social life in a way that would directly challenge lawyers' conceptions and categories. Paradoxically, to achieve this the data had to be organised in terms of those conceptions and categories.

The essence of Cotterrell's criticism is that studies such as Macaulay's do not in fact take the understanding of legal concepts and legal frameworks any further forward, since the work is trapped by the very 'lawyer's law' categories which it seeks to expose as absurd or meaningless. In other words, while at one level Macaulay may describe, he does not theorize any more purposefully than the black-letter lawyers whose work he quite explicitly criticizes for its irrelevance and for its pernicious influence. Whether or not this criticism is valid depends perhaps rather on the nature of the claims for its findings that any particular empirical study makes, and on what was taken in the first instance as the field of enquiry. Arguably, Macaulay's work does not fall foul of Cotterrell's criticisms, as his claims for his work do not lead him beyond speculation as to what *are* in fact the functions of contract doctrine, given that it is demonstrably irrelevant to much business practice.

3. The strong message emerging from Macaulay's review of his own work is that he is no longer as sanguine about the *reality* of trust and co-operation as defining elements of non-contractual relations in the fields he has studied. On the other hand, Macaulay's original findings are supported also by Macneil's work on relational contract. The balancing act between wealth maximization and human sociality is well summed up by Whitford's review of what he calls one of the 'great messages' of Macneil's work.

W. Whitford, 'Ian Macneil's Contribution to Contracts Scholarship', [1985] *Wis. L. Rev.* 545 at 550

That message, which has had a lesser impact in the world of contracts scholarship, is that parties in relational contracts frequently temper wealth maximization goals with other objectives.

Consider, for example, Macneil's recurrent assertion that parties to relational contracts desire to preserve their relationship. Preservation of the relationship can be a means to wealth maximization. As parties establish regular ways of conducting their business, and as they commit what the economists call idiosyncratic investments to the relationship, the transaction costs of finding a substitute for an existing relationship can become great. A manufacturer with a regular supplier will have worked out many understandings over the years that make particular exchanges more efficient. Rarely will a switch to a new supplier not involve extra costs as similar understandings are developed anew. Hence, making extensive efforts to preserve relationships, the behavior pattern that Macneil observes, is frequently the course indicated by wealth maximization goals.

Yet wealth maximization concerns are not the only reason parties desire to preserve relations. Humans are social animals and their identities (that is, self-concepts relating to their character and place in society) are partly constituted by their relationships. Not all relationships are enjoyable, and at times the parties will prefer separation to a continued relationship. But if the relationship is an important one, termination will inevitably entail a partial change in identity. Perhaps franchise termination provides the best example. For the franchisee, termination often means the end of a career, and therefore is an event often carrying emotional costs well beyond the wealth costs of establishing a new career.

D. Relationalism and Empiricism in Perspective

Gordon reviews the work of Macneil and Macaulay in tandem, drawing together their insights to provide a powerful critique of classical and neo-classical contract law.

R. Gordon, 'Macaulay, Macneil, and the Discovery of Solidarity and Power in Contract Law', [1985] *Wis. L. Rev.* 565 at 569–74

Organic Solidarity. . . . What Macneil and Macaulay brought to surface aware-ness was that the images of classical contract law described at best a small and residual body of contract dealings: "discrete transactions" (in Macneil's phrase) between strangers. The common type of commercial exchange was among participants in continuing relations, members of interactive communities whose projects themselves, as well as expectations about how they will be carried out, are partially created by the community. In classical contract, individuals have no obligations to each other save those created by the coercive rules of the state or their own promises: if contract law outcomes are therefore to be ratio-nalized on the preferred grounds of consent rather than those of public policy, the outcomes must appear to flow from the parties' promises, from their ex ante allocations of performance obligations and risks, or at least from a plausi-ble implication (or transaction-cost-saving legal approximation) of such promises. In the "relational" view of Macaulay and Macneil, parties treat their contracts more like marriages than like one-night stands. Obligations grow out of the commitment that they have made to one another, and the conventions that the trading community establishes for such commitments; they are not frozen at the initial moment of commitment, but change as circumstances change; the object of contracting is not primarily to allocate risks, but to signify a commitment to cooperate. In bad times parties are expected to lend one another mutual support, rather than standing on their rights; each will treat the other's insistence on literal performance as willful obstructionism; if unexpected contingencies occur resulting in severe losses, the parties are to search for equitable ways of dividing the losses; and the sanction for egregiously bad behaviour, is always, of course, refusal to deal again.

The work of Macaulay and Macneil thus picks up a recurrent if usually muted contrapuntal theme in liberal social science: that certain kinds of cul-tural-social understandings and institutions, to maintain them, have been important conditions of the successful operation of capitalist economies. To put it another way, expectations of mutual advantage (narrowly conceived), reinforced only by coercive state enforcement of property-and-contract rights, fashion insufficiently durable bonds to induce cooperative social action on any large scale. Something else must be at work to create the foundations of mutual trust and solidarity upon which economic planning depends. Macneil's work in particular is close to Durkheim's in its emphasis upon the norms of solidarity and reciprocity, "organic solidarity," that can emerge from continuing relations. . . .

Domination. . . .In the messy and open-ended world of continuing contract relations, where the contours of obligation are constantly shifting, the effects of power imbalances are not limited to the concessions that parties can extort in the original bargain. Such imbalances tend to generate hierarchies that can gradually extend to govern every aspect of the relation in performance. This is the potential dark side of continuing contract relations, as organic solidarity is the bright side: what starts out as a mere inequity in market power can be deepened into persistent domination on one side and dependence on the other. This is not slavery, since the parties are legally free to exit; but the whole perspective of relational contract suggests that sunk costs can matter tremendously, that the trauma of abandoning a relationship around which a company has structured all its operations, hiring, investment, and planning decisions, can keep it tied into a dependence that its members experience as all the more corrupting because it is in some sense voluntary.

Modern contracts scholars tend to see such relations of domination as aberrational situations, which, for good or evil (depending on whether one is liberally or conservatively inclined) contract law has evolved various curative doctrines to police. In other words, there is not that much of a problem, and contract law can take care of what problem there is. Macaulay and Macneil . . . follow the lead of the more unsparingly cold-eyed Realists such as Hale, Kessler, and Dawson, who find coercion and domination to be pervasive in market relations. Their reactions to this knowledge differ somewhat. Macaulay's reaction (which I feel more confident that I can describe than I do Macneil's) is to assimilate continuing contract relations to a general conception of political struggle. In Macaulay's view, contract parties—such as the automobile manufacturers and their suppliers or dealers, or the oil companies and gas-station franchisees—appear both as social groups locked into relations of hierarchy and as political interest-groups trying strategically to manipulate outside institutions (including courts) to improve their basic bargaining positions. On the whole, Macaulay is a depressed liberal; he wishes that the weaker parties to these relationships could transform them into more egalitarian ones, but is very pessimistic about their ability to do so, because he believes that most of the institutional structures through which the struggle is carried on tend to work to the advantage of wealth and power.

Discontinuity and Marginality of "Contract Law". All their other challenges to standard contracts work might have been forgiveable, if Macneil and Macaulay had not implacably insisted upon demonstrating, over and over again, the relative insignificance for contracts-in-action of the traditional materials of legal scholarship, the decisions of common law contracts courts. This demonstration has two aspects:

(a) The marginality of state-enforced norms and sanctions in the governance of contract relations. This was of course the theme of Macaulay's famous 1963 article which described businessmen who did not rely on legal norms to define or sanctions to enforce their relations because they had their own, more effective, norms and sanctions. Macneil's approach has been somewhat different. It has been to contrast the detailed normative premises in traditional contract law with those emerging from relational contracting, and show that despite limited concessions to relationalism, modern contract law remains wedded to unrealistic models of the discrete transaction. Both men picture contract law and its enforcement as a world removed from, and only indirectly related to, the normal expectations of contracting parties. . . . Macaulay in particular pictures the occasional resort by private parties to formal legal sanctions as mostly opportunistic and tactical: by going to law, the parties are not appealing to shared values embodied in legal rules, or seeking moral vindication of their position or a just settlement of their disputes; they are usually engaged in maneuvers to improve their bargaining positions. The "law", to such parties, its norms, rules, procedures, costs, etc., appears in a completely alienated form as a set of games, strategies and hurdles. From this point of view, the only thing that matters about a legal form is whether it can help give one leverage or slow the other side down. Parties with a lot of resources, for example, do not mind general equitable standards even if the substance of such standards cuts against them because they cannot practically be enforced without a lot of expensive evidence. . . . Macaulay's businessmen may be seen as inhabiting overlapping and to some extent mutually contradicting moral universes of contracting rules, one of which (their private order) supplies the norms that they actually internalize, the other (the legal order) furnishing an arsenal of strategic weapons in case the relation breaks down. His work reveals, then, a radical discontinuity between official ways of thinking about law, as a repository of values and sanctions controlling social behavior, and the expectations of the inhabitants of the "semi-autonomous social fields" (in Sally Moore's phrase) that the law is supposed to affect. Even more interesting and disturbing, it reveals that quite often the professionals of the legal system themselves adopt the outsiders' rather than the official view: Macaulay shows lawyers, and even sometimes judges, accepting the chilling and amoral vision of the law as nothing but a storehouse of bargaining chips.

(b) The marginality of the common law of contract within the body of state-enforced norms and sanctions. Macneil and Macaulay go well beyond the familiar point that general contract law has fallen from its nineteenth century primacy in the governance of private ordering to the relatively trivial status of a body of law employed to fill in the interstices left by the big new systems of specialized legislative and administrative regulation. Macneil points out that from the relational perspective, any body of law that helps to structure contracting behavior ought to be considered as part of contract law: this would include corporation law and labor law for example. Macaulay's view of contract relations as periodic political conflict, sees common law contract courts as simply one among the many institutional battlegrounds on which the parties carry on their struggle. The perspectives of both men suggest that even those who think legal scholarship should be confined to the study of state-enforced norms, are not looking at enough of the contract law that matters if they stick to the common law (and UCC) alone. . . .

With their discovery of relational contract-in-action, Macneil and Macaulay imported a new element into contracts discourse, the element of society, which cannot be accounted for entirely as the product of individual or constitutional-democratic-state choices, but which exists in some respects prior to such choices, and which helps to condition both what is chosen and the structures within which choices are played out. To express this in another way, their work shows how economic purposes and actions are deeply embedded in social fields, in densely woven webs of local customs, conventional morals, bonds of loyalty and entrenched power hierarchies. Of course, nobody could claim that Macneil and Macaulay discovered contracting societies. Mainstream contract law, especially in its post-Realist forms, repeatedly recognizes the existence of social background conditions to contracting. For example, consider the "course of dealing, course of performance, and usage of trade" or the "commercial reasonableness" that may be consulted as supplementary guides to contractual intent, or the sometimes pervasive inequalities between parties in information, bargaining skill, or market alternatives that make up what the courts like to call "unequal bargaining power." But in mainstream contract law, such conditions only occupy the background; they are what will govern the transaction only until the parties or the state choose otherwise; they are canvases which individual intent or state policy may paint over at discretion. Macneil's and Macaulay's accomplishment has been to bring contracting societies into the foreground, and by so doing to show that you cannot even begin to understand contractual expectations without understanding the social conditions of their generation, change, and termination. Moreover, they demonstrate that such conditions are not supplementary, but primary, sources of contracting norms and sanctions. Finally, not only are those social conditions not readily trumped by the state-enforced norms and sanctions of contract law, but they are often simply not affected by contract law at all.

Notes

1. Points of linkage to other sections of this chapter should be noted: these include in particular the association between the work of Macneil and that

of Durkheim on the issue of solidarity and the role of society in contractual relations, and the analysis of relations of power and domination put forward most strongly by Macaulay, which links relational work to that of the Legal Realists and to the more recent Critical Legal Scholars.

2. The issue of 'marginality' is picked up again at a number of points in the book, but in particular in Chapter 14, where we discuss the importance of 'non-legal' sanctions for breach of contract.

V. THE ECONOMIC ANALYSIS OF CONTRACTUAL RELATIONS

A. Introduction

Economic analysis of contract is more than simply placing contract in its economic context. That has been done by many of the scholars whose work has been extracted so far in this chapter. The point was perhaps made most pithily by the American legal theorist Roscoe Pound when he said that 'wealth, in a commercial age, is made up largely of promises' (*An Introduction to Legal Philosophy* (New Haven, Conn., Yale University Press, 1922), 236). Moreover, lawyers have for some time been aware of the importance of economics as a discipline for law. Lon Fuller is famous for saying that 'law is the only human study having no distinctive end of its own. Where its ends can be regarded as grounded in reason . . . they must be derived not from law itself but from ethics, sociology and economics' (*The Anatomy of Law* (New York, Praeger, 1968), 4).

The study of law by economists and the application of economists' tools of analysis to law by economic-minded lawyers has come to offer one of the most important strands of thinking about contract in recent years. It offers a vast and complex literature which often seems impenetrable but which none the less exercises a degree of influence on some of the leading courts in the common law jurisdictions. This is particularly so in the United States, where key law-and-economics scholars such as Richard Posner, Robert Bork, and Frank Easterbrook have themselves become judges.

The objectives of this review of law-and-economics literature are threefold: first, to identify the type of assumption and general framework of analysis shared by economists of all persuasions; second, to demonstrate the utility of economic analysis in contract law, in so far as it asks questions which differ from those typically asked by lawyers and consequently, in the answers it gives, offers an additional layer of analysis which can be useful in the formulation and evaluation of legal policy. Finally, we shall seek to identify some of the main streams of work *within* the broad field of economic analysis.

B. The Purposes of Economic Analysis

If economics can be defined as 'the science which studies human behaviour as a relationship between ends and scarce means which have alternative users' (L. Robbins, quoted by C. Veljanovski in *The New Law-and-Economics* (Oxford, Centre for Socio-Legal Studies/SSRC, 1982), 18), then economic analysis of law must involve the study of the interaction between legal rules and institutions and the behaviour of rational economic actors, which individuals are assumed by economists to be.

Most economic analysis of law is organized around the 'efficiency principle' which, in the abstract, 'simply means achieving ends in the best possible way' (Veljanovski, *The New Law-and-Economics*, 37). Although economists recognize a variety of different types of efficiency, the key to the concept is its link with the maximization principle. Polinsky defines what he describes as a 'popular' and 'intuitive' concept of efficiency, which he used as the basis for his introductory analysis of law-and-economics, and contrasts it to the concept of 'equity'.

A. Polinsky, *An Introduction to Law and Economics*, 2nd edn. (Boston, Little, Brown, 1989), 7

. . . the term *efficiency* [refers] to the relationship between the aggregate benefits of a situation and the aggregate costs of the situation; the term *equity* [refers] to the distribution of income among individuals. In other words, efficiency corresponds to "the size of the pie," while equity has to do with how it is sliced. Economists traditionally concentrate on how to maximize the size of the pie, leaving to others—such as legislators—the decision how to divide it. The attractiveness of efficiency as a goal is that, under some circumstances, everyone can be made better off if society is organized in an efficient manner.

As Feinman puts it:

J. Feinman, 'The Significance of Contract Theory', (1990) 58 *U. Cin. L. Rev.* 1283 at 1296

Economic analysis of law begins with the hypothesis that people seek to maximize their welfare. It is implicit in this hypothesis that people respond to incentives, altering their behavior to increase their welfare. When people are allowed to shape their behavior to maximize their welfare, especially through voluntary exchanges with others, resources gravitate to their most valuable uses, increasing what is known as allocative efficiency. Allocative efficiency provides the economic criterion for evaluating legal doctrines and decisions.

Although the concept of allocative efficiency is commonly associated with what is termed 'normative economics', in fact the economic analysis of law can have a number of different objectives.

J. Coleman, 'Efficiency, Auction and Exchange', in *Markets, Morals and the Law* (Cambridge, Cambridge University Press, 1988), 67–8

Three distinct but related activities fall within the domain of law-and-economics: Two of these are conceptual in nature; one is normative. Analytic law-and-economics may be either descriptive or positive. Descriptive law-and-economics is concerned with the principle of economic efficiency as an explanatory tool by which existing legal rules and decisions may be rationalized or comprehended. Richard Posner's "Theory of Negligence" is characteristic of this approach. In his essay, Posner attempts to show that a large number of negligence cases were decided along lines of economic efficiency. His view is not that judges articulated and invariably applied an economic standard of adjudication. Instead, he claims that these cases may be rationalized or reconstructed in light of an economic theory of adjudication.

Positive law-and-economics is concerned less with the actual explanatory power of economic efficiency than it is with the capacity of market models to provide a conceptual apparatus within which traditional legal problems may be conceived. Typical is Isaac Ehrlich's work on crime. Ehrlich presents the interplay between the criminal, viewed as engaged in an economic activity—namely, committing crimes—and the criminal law and the rules and strategies governing its enforcement as the medium through which consumers—namely, possible victims of crime—express their decisions about how much crime they are willing to accept at various prevention prices.

Normative law-and-economics is the home of reformers. Existing legal rules are evaluated and new ones fashioned in terms of their economic efficiency. Guido Calabresi's *The Costs of Accidents* is an exemplary text in normative law-and-economics. It sets out and evaluates various systems of accident law according to the capacity of each to minimize the sum of the costs of accidents and the costs of avoiding them.

Notes

1. Normative economics is sometimes also called welfare economics, and it looks at social policy choices on the basis of a postulate of rationality. It is when economists or lawyers using economic analysis slip from the 'is' to the 'ought' that they encounter the harshest criticism, mainly on the grounds that their model of human behaviour admits of only a limited range of human responses to the problem of choice. For example, to argue that the common law *ought* to be efficient may be to overstate the role of economic analysis, for it claims that efficiency alone can provide an

adequate moral basis for a system of rules which lays claim to the enforcement power of the state to maintain its force.

2. Equally, there are some difficulties with descriptive economic analysis as, unlike positive economics, which is basically a means for ensuring that economics offers accurate predictions, and which therefore need not be built on accurate or realistic assumptions, descriptive economics is dangerously misleading if the assumptions on which it is built are not satisfactory. According to Veljanovski:

C. Veljanovski, *The New Law-and-Economics*, (Oxford, Centre for Socio-Legal Studies/SSRC, 1982), 26

A major problem with the predictive approach is that it lacks descriptive content, and hence as a conceptual system to analyze *specific* laws it has severe limitations. 'Viewed as a language,' says Friedman (1953, p. 26). '[positive economic] theory has no substantive content. It is a set of tautologies. Its function is to serve as a filing system for organizing empirical material and facilitating our understanding of it; and the criteria by which it is judged are those appropriate to a filing system.'

It is therefore clear that the descriptive use of economics must be judged by a different criterion for two reasons. First, since its purpose is to *describe* the existing system of law, rather than to predict the impact of changes in the law, the assumptions upon which the theory is built must be descriptively accurate, and these assumptions need to be subject to empirical verification. Thus the statement that 'common law is efficient', is a hypothesis that can be tested by showing that its benefits exceed its costs. In practice, however, the descriptive analyses have tended instead to adopt assumptions concerning the efficiency of the market which are not empirically verified propositions at all. They have, in other words, retained the descriptive unrealism of assumptions which characterizes predictive economics. Second, descriptive economic theories of law have not been subject to the type of rigorous empirical testing which is deemed appropriate to predictive economics, and there are serious doubts as to whether the descriptive theories are even potentially refutable in this way. The difficulty of testing the theories strengthens the need for descriptive accuracy, otherwise neither assumptions nor conclusions will be subject to verification.

Note

This is a criticism which has been made of Richard Posner's descriptive work, which rationalizes the body of the common law as efficient, but only, it is argued, by dint of positing an unrealistic picture of what that common law is, ironing out the contradictions and discontinuities (see e.g. Mary Joe Frug's criticisms of Posner's 'impossibility analysis' in Ch. 12).

C. The Economist and the Contract

While caution in the application of the methodology of economics may always be warranted, there can be no doubt that the economist's general perspective on the phenomenon of the contract and on the economic activity of exchange will always offer valuable food for thought to the lawyer.

C. Veljanovski and D. Harris, 'The Use of Economics to Elucidate Legal Concepts: The Law of Contract', in T. Daintith and G. Teubner (eds.), *Contract and Organisation* (Berlin, De Gruyter, 1986), 109–18

Contract Law Viewed as a Framework for the Making of Voluntary Transactions

The economist offers explanations for the overall purpose of the law of contract. He says that parties enter into legally binding contracts because they expect to obtain a benefit from doing so. The law makes promises in contracts legally binding because that enables parties to improve their "welfare": the ability to make binding promises decreases future uncertainty and generates beneficial reliance on each other's promise. Formal rules of law are needed to facilitate the making and enforcement of promises, because the parties cannot themselves make arrangements which adequately guard against the risk of a promise being broken.

By the use of an ideal "model" of contract, the economist can also explain the need for external pressure (for example, courts) to enforce contractual promises. In the hypothetical, ideal world in which each party was fully informed about all the circumstances and could accurately predict the future, and the costs of negotiating were negligible, the parties would draw up a "complete contingent contract", that is, one which exhaustively specified all the parties' rights and obligations in every possible situation, and which provided a set of procedures and penalties to deal with every conceivable aspect of non-performance. . . . In practice, such a contract would be very costly (in both time and expense) to draw up and to enforce; and even if the parties had made such an "ideal" contract, they could still encounter two principal difficulties in the course of performance of the contract—verification of the relevant facts, and enforcement of the promise against an unwilling party. First, the contract may contain a clause purporting to deal with a particular contingency but one party may dispute that the facts specified in the clause have occurred. If this dispute cannot be settled by agreement, some third-party resolution (by a judge or arbitrator) will be needed to decide it. Secondly, many contracts are not self-enforcing, in the sense that each party could "enforce" the other's promise without assistance from third parties. Most contracts require some third-party mechanism (such as courts) to be organised by society in order either to induce the party contemplating a breach to perform his promise or else to force him to pay the penalties for breach agreed in the contract. Frequently, market or other forces, such as fear of the loss of business reputation, will be sufficient to induce performance of contracts . . . but in some cases of breach of promise an external enforcement mechanism would be needed even with the ideal, model contract. Accordingly, the law of contract provides a framework within which voluntary arrangements agreed between the parties can, if the parties so wish, be turned into binding arrangements subject to external or third-party enforcement. The law thus facilitates the making of arrangements which the parties could not achieve on their own, without the assistance of the law.

Minimisation of Transaction Costs

In the context of contract, "transaction costs" is a term used by economists to cover the time, effort, trouble, and other costs incurred by the parties in negotiating agreement upon the terms of their contract, or in negotiating the settlement of, or litigating the adjudication of, a contractual dispute. The economist assumes that rational men will strive to avoid or minimise transaction costs. . . .

Although the economist may, for some purposes, use the idea of a complete contingent contract . . . he accepts that in practice most contracts are incomplete, in that they fail to provide expressly for many contingencies which even a layman could anticipate. A simple reason for this is that it would be too costly for the parties to negotiate agreement on a comprehensive set of precisely-defined obligations for many situations when they know that most of these situations would never occur; another reason is that it would often be beyond the capacity of the parties to anticipate the less likely contingencies. Usually the parties specify only the main aspects of their relationship and leave unspecified many less important aspects. By doing this, they tacitly agree that, if in the course of performance a secondary aspect does become important and they cannot then agree on how to deal with it, they will rely on the law to resolve the problem. From this point of view, a vital function of the law of contract is to provide a set of standard clauses or rules to cover the contingencies for which the parties have not made precise arrangements in their contract. The legal rules are a ready-made or standardised set of clauses which the parties can use if they do not want a completely "tailor-made" or "custom-built" contract. Use of the standard clauses saves the parties much time in negotiating contracts, thus minimising transaction costs. If a dispute about the contract later arises between the parties, their attempts to negotiate a private settlement of the dispute out of court will also be explained by their self-interested desire to minimise transaction costs.

The Cost of Information

The economist also views the institution of contract and the provisions of contract law as encouraging the production of the optimal amount of information.

There is a general tendency among lawyers and legislators to assume that information is costless, but economists understand that it is very costly to acquire information (new facts) and to minimise mistakes. Contract law can be seen as part of the incentive system designed to encourage people to acquire and produce new information about market opportunities and mutually beneficial exchanges. . . . The cost of supplying correct information and the corresponding costs of relying on incorrect information underlie the legal rules on representations made by one party to induce the other to enter the contract, and the rules on the effect of mistakes (where one or both parties have entered the contract on the assumption of incorrect facts). It has been argued that the legal rules should be designed to impose liability on the party best able to avoid such mistakes in future, viz. the party who can more cheaply gather or produce the relevant information (Kronman [see Ch. 5]).

Bargaining around the Law

Another insight to be gained from the economist is that laws which regulate specific terms of a contract may be circumvented by adjustment in other terms by the parties. If a term is regulated by the law, the beneficial effects of the regulation may be offset by adjustments in other terms so that the net improvement in the welfare of the favoured party will be less than initially anticipated by the legislator, and may even be negligible. . . . For instance, legislation designed to protect consumers may prohibit special clauses which exclude the normal legal liability of the other party, or, on the other hand, may require the other party to undertake a liability which he would not voluntarily undertake (e.g. legislation requiring manufacturers to provide guarantees with the products they sell); but consumers may not benefit much since the price may be adjusted to offset the increased costs which these legal requirements impose on the other party. In general, there will be a tendency for the parties to bargain around a legal requirement when it does not encourage value-maximizing (i.e. efficient) contracts; in other words, the party bearing the higher costs will have an incentive to shift them on to the other party. Thus it is not possible to assume (as most lawyers tend to) that, because a law is designed to favour one party, its ultimate impact will also be beneficial to that party.

Perhaps the best documented example of a law designed to favour one group which rebounded to their disadvantage is rent control. The belief underlying rent control legislation appeared to be that controlling the price of a commodity will not lead to adjustments in the behaviour of the supplier. But economics informs us that controlling the price of a commodity such as rented accommodation, so that the real rate of return to investment in it falls, will merely encourage landlords to seek other ways of increasing the income from their properties. They will try, for example, to demand key or deposit money, or will require the tenant to pay for repairs and other expenses. If these clauses are also controlled, landlords will either withdraw their properties from the rented accommodation market or allow the quality of their properties to fall by not maintaining them. The result of this type of legal intervention is that tenants as a group are harmed by shortages in rented accommodation or by the poor quality of the accommodation which is available.

Contract Law Viewed as a System of Incentives

Another way in which economists can teach lawyers to view the law of contract is as a system of incentives and disincentives to influence decisions whether or not to make, and whether or not to perform contractual promises. The law is seen as an important influence on the behaviour of the parties, particularly in the decisions which they take in the course of the contractual period: the legal rules will affect their choices between the different course of action open to them. Although the law-maker may not have thought of the influence which the rules of contract law might have on the behaviour of citizens, once those rules exist and are known to the parties, they will function as incentives to behave in certain ways and *not* to behave in other ways. (It is easy to think of the penalties of the criminal law as a system of incentives *not* to commit crimes. The economist considers that all civil law can function in a similar way—to the extent that citizens know the legal rules, that knowledge will influence how they decide to act.)

The sorts of questions which this approach poses for the contract lawyer are: Do the rules on breach of contract and on the remedies for breach provide sufficient incentives to promisors who may be deciding whether or not to perform their promises? Here, the promisor's anticipation of what the legal consequences of breach might be, and of the cost to him of those consequences, may be the crucial factor in influencing his decision one way or the other. . . . Once this approach is followed further questions arise. In which types of situation do we wish to have a legal remedy which compels the promisor actually to perform his promise according to its terms (in England law, the remedies of specific performance . . . and injunction)? In which types of situation is it sufficient for the disappointed promisee to be confined to money compensation for the net loss which he has suffered as a result of the breach (after taking account of his ability to obtain substitute performance from a third party—the doctrine of mitigation which has a ready application in the market situation)? If there is no available market (e.g. because the contractual performance was designed for the unique requirements of the promisee, as in the building of a house to specified plans on a specific site), in which circumstances should the legal remedy give the disappointed promisee the full cost of his getting substitute performance from a third party who contracts to complete the work (e.g. building the house) which the contract-breaker undertook but failed to complete?

The Concept of Risk-taking

Often, of course, contractual promises cannot be fulfilled despite the best efforts of the promisor, and in this situation the concept of the law as an incentive system will obviously not apply. But another economic concept is available to the lawyer to clarify his thinking about involuntary breach of contract—the concept of risk-taking. Much of the future we face is uncertain, but one way of partially reducing that uncertainty is to obtain binding promises from other people that they will perform (or refrain from performing) certain acts in the future. A contract is often a reciprocal allocation of specified risk and an efficient system of contract law should facilitate risk-sharing by upholding the allocation of risks made by the contract. . . . This approach justifies the result that, even where the failure to perform was an event beyond the control of the party in breach, the loss should nevertheless be imposed on him (Posner and Rosenfield [see Ch. 12]). It must be assumed that in the usual case, where both parties are risk-averse, they will have allocated the risk of an anticipated loss caused by nonperformance to the party better able to bear it or to insure against it, who will typically be the party making the promise. The only exception to this approach would be where the event preventing performance was an unusual one, beyond the scope of the normal risks contemplated by the parties, in which case the doctrine of frustration will operate under English law to terminate further performance of the contract (thus making the parties share the risk). . . .

The Use of Contract Law in Negotiating out-of-Court Settlements

Most of the writers who apply economic perspectives to the law of contract have implicitly assumed that a breach of contract immediately and automatically brings a legal sanction into operation. But lawyers know that, although there are many occasions in which disputes arise between parties to contracts, there are relatively few occasions when these disputes are settled in the formal setting of the courtroom, by judges applying the rules of the law of contract. The vast majority of contractual disputes are settled by direct negotiations between the parties (with or without the assistance of lawyers), in which compromises are reached in the light of all the factors which the parties consider relevant, especially any desire on their part to maintain an existing relationship between them; they are not limited to the "legal" considerations which the judge may properly take into account when reaching a judgment. The contract-breaker knows that the procedure for taking the claim to a full hearing in court involves cost and delay, which he can exploit to his own advantage in the negotiations. If the claimant is under financial pressure, he will obviously be more willing to accept the immediate payment of a lower sum, than to face continuing pressure and uncertainty in the hope that a court will award a greater sum (often an unknown amount) at some unknown time in the future. Fear of the expense of pursuing or defending a claim may obviously induce a compromise. Again, people differ greatly in their psychological make-up, and in their ability to face uncertainty (which economists call their attitudes towards risks). The emotional strain of a dispute, or the fear of being involved in a public court hearing, may also exert some pressure on one or both parties to settle. Thus, the parties' imperfect appreciation of what the formal law of contract would say about their problem is usually only one of many relevant factors, and its force is often outweighed by other factors. The formal legal rules, and the anticipated costs of litigation if the dispute were taken to court, provide only the background to the parties' negotiations: the law merely casts a distant shadow on their negotiating positions.

It will be argued by some that the possibility of a judicial resolution of the dispute offers adequate protection to a party who feels that the pressure of these extra-legal factors is unfair to him. Empirical studies, however, show that the fear of delay, expense and uncertainty in using the courts frequently out-weighs the apparent advantage that the eventual judgment should, in theory, ignore all extra-legal considerations. A party must make a crude cost-benefit analysis of the pros and cons of an early compromise of his dispute, and it is not surprising that the other advantages of a compromise usually outweigh the disadvantage that the impact of extra-legal factors cannot be avoided. One consequence is that, even where lawyers are involved in negotiating the settlement, the legal rules are often applied by them without any precision, because if other factors are likely to prevail, it is a waste of time and expense to investigate the precise legal position.

The economist explains this situation by saying that the disputing parties realise that extra-legal methods of resolving contractual disputes are usually much cheaper, and that rational individuals will always choose the cheapest method of dealing with a dispute (minimising transaction costs. The relevant question is then whether each mode of dispute resolution (renegotiation, arbitration, settlement or compromise, litigation, etc.) is designed so that it imposes the minimum necessary costs on each party and does not distort the incentives to perform. It would clearly not make economic sense either to settle all contractual disputes out-of-court, or to refer all to adjudication. In theory, there will be an 'optimal' level of litigation which reflects the social costs and benefits of using the courts compared with using other settlement processes. An appreciation of this situation should lead contract lawyers to the conclusion that legal rules on remedies for breach of contract should be designed to take into account the fact that in the vast majority of cases the rules will be used to guide out-of-court settlements and to induce compromises. This means that the law-maker (whether judge or legislator) should consider the effect of any proposed rule on the relative negotiating strength of the parties, and, in particular, how the rule will affect the distribution of the "bargaining chips" or advantages between the parties. In particular, he should aim primarily at the potential use of the rules in a two-party, "direct negotiations" situation, rather than at their use by an impartial, third party arbitrator or judge.

The law-maker, at least in England, has assumed that the rules of contract law will be applied in an independent way, and that the impartiality of the judge will prevent any apparent inequality between the parties in court; it is assumed that the ideal of equality before the law will be achieved by the judge ignoring the relative wealth of the parties, their business or financial strength, their reputations, political support, or other extra-legal circumstances. The independence of the judiciary is avowedly designed to neutralise the inequalities of the parties' negotiating strength in the market-place outside the court. But if contract law is used in out-of-court negotiations much more frequently than in court, the law-maker should realise that the assumption of impartial, third-party application of the rules will seldom apply; and that his rules will usually be applied in a "dirty" world where extra-legal factors may predominate. Relative bargaining strength is the crucial factor here, and, if there is an inequality, there is no third party to protect the weaker party.

We can illustrate the problem by reference to some English rules on contract law. In the last fifty years, there has been a tendency for new rules of law to give discretion to the judge, by enabling him to decide what is "fair" or "just" or "reasonable". These rules may work well in disputes which are resolved by judgment in court. But when they are used in out-of-court negotiations between the parties, they obviously create uncertainty in predicting how a judge would decide. In these negotiations this uncertainty gives an advantage to the contract-breaker (the defendant to the claim). Because there is no assurance that the judge would award any particular sum of money as compensation for breach, the defendant can usually persuade the claimant to accept a much lower sum than he claims as representing his loss. The uncertainty is very likely to lead to a "discount" or reduction in the agreed compensation. Unfortunately there will be other discounts in addition, because there will usually be other uncertainties facing the claimant—uncertainty about the facts, if there is a dispute over the evidence; uncertainty about the length of the delay before the dispute could be settled by a judge; and uncertainty about the legal costs of going to court. The contract-breaker can use each uncertainty and the delay involved in litigation to extract from the other party a settlement for a sum which is substantially less than the courts would award. Rules which may work well when applied by an impartial third-party, may confer unfair advantages on one or other party in the context of direct, two-party negotiations.

Notes

1. These observations show very clearly how, even at a very pragmatic level, the approach of the economist can enrich the lawyer's understanding of the legal rules governing contracts and the legal institutions for the enforcement of contracts. In this book we shall use examples of economic

analysis very much in such a spirit of pragmatic enquiry—hence the cross-references to Chapter 5 (Kronman on the disclosure of information) and Chapter 12 (Posner and Rosenfield on the economics of 'impossibility'). Links can also be made to the analysis of protective rules which restrict the parties' freedom of contract to bargain out beneficial rules (see the analysis of implied terms in Ch. 10 and of exclusion clauses in Ch. 11). Equally, economic analysis can be combined powerfully with empirical studies to enhance our understanding of why parties often opt for extra-legal sanctions rather than use the mechanisms of the court system (Ch. 14). Finally, some of Veljanovski and Harris's closing comments on the effects of open-textured standards of reasonableness and fairness upon parties' calculations of behaviour offer another strand of reflection to the analysis of mechanisms of control of powerful or abusive behaviour in the contractual context (Chs. 8 and 9) and of the control of exclusion clauses (Ch. 11).

2. At one level, it is perhaps a little misleading for Veljanovski and Harris to posit the mysterious and apparently monolithic figure of 'the economist'. For, like any discipline, economics does not offer a single methodology or a single perspective, but encompasses a plethora of different ideas and approaches. Within the body of work often called the 'new law-and-economics', which has grown up since the 1960s, the dominant strand of economics has been 'neo-classical' economics which, in the field of contract, has emerged as a form of work often described as 'bargain-based' or 'market economics'. On the other hand, there also exists a contrasting approach—'neo-institutionalist' or 'transaction cost' economics—which, while sharing many of the assumptions of neo-classical economics, such as the centrality of the wealth-maximization principle, the goal of efficiency, and the key framework of market analysis, none the less takes a sufficiently different perspective on these assumptions to lead to contrasting conclusions about the law of contract.

D. Market-Based and Transaction Cost Analysis of Contract Law

The distinction between market-based and transaction cost analyses of contract law is explained by Williamson, one of the foremost proponents of the latter.

O. Williamson, 'Contract Analysis: The Transaction Cost Approach', in P. Burrows and C. Veljanovski (eds.), *The Economic Approach to Law* (London, Butterworths, 1981), 39 at 40–2

The market-based approach

The paradigm transaction for the market-based approach is the discrete transaction. Anthony Kronman and Richard Posner . . . offer two examples, one very simple, the other more complex. The simple illustration has *A* buying a newspaper from news-vendor *B*. The more complex illustration involves *B* contracting to build a house for *A*. Whereas the first involves coincident exchange of money for goods of known quality, the second does not and requires more self-conscious attention to the structure of the exchange.

According to Posner, the law of contracts helps to facilitate exchanges of the latter kind in three respects. First, it imposes costs on those who would attempt to exploit such agreements, e.g., by accepting payment and refusing to deliver. Secondly, it reduces 'the complexity and hence cost of transactions by supplying a set of normal terms that, in the absence of the law of contracts, the parties would have to negotiate expressly'. . . . Thirdly, it furnishes 'prospective contracting parties with information concerning the many contingencies that may defeat an exchange, and hence . . . [assists] them in planning their exchange sensibly. The parties, through their lawyers, are guided around the pitfalls in the process of exchange revealed by the opinions in decided contract cases'. . . . ,

Very simple transactions excepted, this market-based view of contracting suggests that commercial transactions are greatly dependent on and governed by legal forms and rules. The transactions cost approach sketched below relaxes this dependency and addresses itself to a wider set of transactions and governance structures than are captured by the discrete contracting approach.

The transaction cost approach

As Kenneth Arrow . . . puts it, transaction costs are the 'costs of running the economic system'. Such costs 'impede and in particular cases completely block the formation of markets'. Nonmarket or market-assisted forms of organization arise on this account. Attention is thus focused less on technology than on the comparative costs of planning, adapting and monitoring task completion under alternative forms of contracting.

A wider conception of economic organization is contemplated by the transaction cost approach. Although market exchange remains important, it is only one of several governance structures. The importance of legal rules, moreover, varies with the nature of the transaction. This broader conception of contract owes its origins to a larger view of economics associated with the names of John R. Commons . . . , Ronald Coase . . . , and Friedrich Hayek . . . . Lawyers such as Karl Llewellyn . . . , Lon Fuller . . . , Stewart Macaulay . . . and Ian Macneil . . . have independently recognized the need to expand contract law beyond its technical features in order to include a more general concern with the contractual purposes to be served.

Commons took the position that the transaction rather than the commodity was the basic unit of analysis. Although conflicting interests among parties to a transaction were assumed to be natural, they were not taken as fixed. On the contrary, the object was to devise institutions that served to harmonize interests or at least to achieve order where otherwise there would be conflict. Legal institutions served these purposes, but so did other organizing structures.

Specifically, as Coase recognized, the business firm is an alternative to markets as a means for organizing transactions. The decision whether to organize transactions within a firm rather than across a market interface depends on the transaction costs that attend each. Coase also recognized that adapting transactions efficiently to changing circumstances easily gives rise to strain if the parties are autonomous and each appropriates a separate profit stream.

The importance of change and of the need to adapt effectively to uncertainty were even more prominently featured in Hayek's treatments of the economic problem. Rather than concentrate on equilibrium, Hayek emphasized disequilibrium and the need to understand the adaptation processes that were set in motion by disturbances. Comprehensive planning efforts were held to be ill-advised because human agents had limited capacities and, similarly, because specialized (idiosyncratic) knowledge of events and circumstances was in the possession of individuals and could not be costlessly disclosed to, much less apprehended by, central planners. These reasons, together with the 'marvel' of the price system—whereby changing economic opportunities are accurately signalled by relative prices—formed the basis for Hayek's preference for a market-based economy.

My transaction cost approach follows Commons by making the transaction the basic unit of analysis. Also, like Commons, I am interested in the design of institutions, legal and otherwise, that serve to promote the renewal or continuity of exchange relations. I follow Coase by regarding the firm as an important alternative to the market for governing economic activity, and I share Hayek's views on the limits of human agents and on the importance of organizing transactions in such a way as to realize more assuredly the productive values embedded in idiosyncratic human and physical assets. To be sure, legal rules and market processes remain important under this extended view of contract, but informal procedures and nonmarket organization also perform important governance functions. Moreover, and crucially to the exercise, *governance structures are matched with transactional attributes in a discriminating way* under the transaction cost approach to contracting set out here.

Not only does the transaction cost approach make allowance for a broader set of governance structures but it also makes allowance for a more diverse set of transactions than is admitted under the market-based model of contracting favored by Posner, which emphasizes relatively discrete trades between A and B. Both the attributes of human agents and of the trading environment come under scrutiny when this larger viewpoint is adopted. Given that contracts are negotiated and executed under conditions of uncertainty, the object is to assign governance structures to transactions so as to promote effective adaptation to changing circumstances without incurring unneeded costs.

Notes

1. Burrows and Veljanovski offer further elucidation of the market/trans-action cost distinction.

P. Burrows and C. Veljanovski, 'Introduction: The Economic Approach to Law', in Burrows and Veljanovski (eds.), *The Economic Approach to Law* **(London, Butterworths, 1981), 1 at 22–5**

The neo-institutional [or 'transaction-cost'] approach embodies the following characteristics. First, it is taxonomical. It lists a set of economically relevant categories that are useful for examining the law. It thus remedies one of the failings of neo-classical market approaches, that of being over-general and incapable of dealing convincingly with specific legal phenomena. As Markovits . . . notes: '[A]t least in part, the failings of conventional economics reflect a simplistic vocabulary that fails to distinguish a large number of phenomena that need to be analysed separately'. And hence we see a new vocabulary being developed, particularly by Williamson, for this purpose. Secondly, and related to this, the approach is more microanalytical. It focuses on the details of the environment in which transactions take place, and it suggests an empirical approach that requires the collection of more detailed data on individual trans-actions rather than data on quantitative aggregates. It is able, for example, to integrate and use constructively the sociological evidence on how businessmen contract and use contract law originally provided by Macaulay. . . . Thus, while the market approach focuses on impersonal, aggregative forces, the neo-institutional approach focuses on individual or small number transactions where personality, relations and power are important. Thirdly, in terms of methodology it comes closer to qualitative biology than to the physical sci-ences that have greatly influenced neoclassical economics. It is therefore process-orientated, dynamic, tends to be evolutionary, and seeks to identify the principal factors that have been responsible for institutional development. Stated somewhat differently it rejects (market) equilibrium analysis and instead places emphasis on the adaption to disequilibrium, hypothesizing that 'ineffi-ciency' gives rise to adaptive efforts to minimize costs. Lastly, it investigates specifically legal/institutional phenomena, and uses these to develop concep-tual categories rather than evidence to verify an efficiency-type hypothesis.

The differences between market and neo-institutional approaches are best illustrated by their respective treatment of contractual relations. The evolving economics of contractual relations recognizes that it is the inherently temporal character of contract that gives rise to the need for contract law. In situations where the exchange of obligations and performance is not simultaneous, and extends over periods of varying duration, there is a need for some enforcement mechanism. The temporal element of these contracts, and the fact that many contracts are formed with less than complete information and much uncertainty, gives rise to the possibility that one party may breach the contract even when it is inefficient to do so. In the neoclassical framework the allocative goal of contract law is to promote the efficient allocation of resources. Thus contract law is seen as having a set of efficiency-related purposes. . . . The economic function of contract law is also to reduce transaction costs and uncertainty by supplying a set of standard (implied) terms, thereby avoiding the costs of explicit negotiation and alerting the parties to potential difficulties that will assist them in contract planning. Finally, contract law provides a framework for the regulation of abuses in the contracting process such as fraud, misrepresentation and duress, that impede or are poorly controlled by market forces.

Although this market-based approach has provided a number of excellent analyses of contract law, it does not come to grips with many issues relevant to a large subset of contractual activity. While the market-based approach recognizes that it is the temporal element that necessitates contract law, it is nonetheless based on a timeless model of contract and treats the sale of goods contract as the paradigm case. The neo-institutional approach emphasizes time, uncertainty and the frictions associated with sale of goods contracts, which it regards as a special and not particularly interesting case, and non-market (or relational) contracts. The transactions costs of writing and executing contracts are interpreted as emanating from two related sources: uncertainty and bounded rationality on the one hand, and lack of competitive pressures (small number of contractors) on the other. The combination of these factors give rise to 'opportunism', which is 'effort(s) to realise individual gains through lack of candour or honesty in transactions' (Williamson, Wachter and Harris) . . . and to the need for 'governance structures' (law, arbitration, the market) that will discourage parties from being opportunistic. The emphasis of this approach is not on a utility maximizing contract where the 'law' fills in terms that the parties would have agreed to had they addressed the problem at the contract formation stage, but on adjustment processes that will preserve continuing contractual relations in the face of opportunism and deal with cases where contracts are incompletely specified.

The neo-institutional approach, it will be recalled, stems partially from the same basis as the market-based analysis and it therefore should not be surprising if it is vulnerable to some of the same criticisms. It also attempts to 'explain' everything in terms of 'efficiency'. However, the concept of efficiency used is quite different—it is not that of replicating ideal market results, but *procedural* efficiency in adjusting to an uncertain and changing environment. The approach is in fact less committed to the market than it would appear, and often provides persuasive economic reasons why activities should be sheltered from market forces. . . . Unlike the market-based approach it does not assert that the law or institutions are efficient, but usually only attempts to identify the efficiency attributes of various institutional arrangements, and to hypothesize that there is a tendency for institutions to evolve to exploit opportunities for improving the efficiency with which market and non-market goals are pursued.

Notes

1. The authors themselves define 'bounded rationality' as the 'cognitive limits of individuals to deal comprehensively with the complex decisions they are required to make' (ibid., n. 56, p. 28).

2. The key works of Posner and Kronman where the market-based approach to the economic analysis of contract is to be found are: R. Posner, *The Economic Analysis of Law*, 3rd edn. (Boston, Little, Brown, 1986) and A. Kronman and R. Posner, *The Economics of Contract Law* (Boston, Little, Brown, 1979). See also A. Polinsky, *An Introduction to Law and Economics*, 2nd edn. (Boston, Little, Brown, 1989) and S. Lowry, 'Bargain and Contract Theory in Law and Economics', (1976) 10. *J. Econ. Issues* 1. Examples of this type of work can be found in Chapters 5 (Kronman), 6 (Posner), 10 (Trebilcock and Kronman), 11 (Schwartz), and 14 (efficient breach theory).

3. Transaction cost economics is closely associated with the work on the relational paradigm of contract pioneered by Macneil (see Section IV above), although Macneil's work differs from that of the economists not only in the weight which he places on the relational element of contract but also in 'his depiction of the phenomena he describes as relations not as obstructive costs but as facilitative structures' (D. Campbell, 'The Social Theory of Relational Contract: Macneil as the Modern Proudhon', (1990) 18 *Int. J. Soc. Law* 75 at 78). What distinguishes Macneil from writers such as Williamson or Goldberg (see Chs. 10 and 12) or Goetz and Scott (see Ch. 6), who have pursued similar relationally based approaches, is his emphasis on the *social* features of relational contract. In other words, his starting-point differs from that of the economists.

4. For a statement of Goldberg's position, see V. Goldberg, 'Toward an Expanded Theory of Contract', (1976) 10. *J. Econ. Issues* 45.

5. Examples of relational analysis can be found in Chapter 10, where the problem of incomplete contracts lends itself particularly clearly to this type of approach.

6. Mention should be made also of an emerging third stream of law-and-economics analysis, which to an extent gives the lie to the constant objection that this type of scholarship is irrevocably wedded to the market economy in its purest form, and that in reality it presents a conservative ideology which eschews questions of distributive justice and social responsibility. A more interdisciplinary strand of economic analysis is beginning to develop in which writers have used the insights of social psychology (see

Farber on exclusion clauses in Ch. 11) or of game theory to enrich the economic critique. Johnston explains briefly how the latter has grown out of transaction cost economics.

J. Johnston, 'Law, Economics, and Post-Realist Explanation', (1990) 24 *L. & S. Rev.* 1217 at 1245

. . . in viewing law as an environmental variable which affects private ordering, transaction cost economics has made clear the potential enormous relevance of game theory to the law. Game theory is concerned with strategic interaction between rational actors, in a world where what is best for me to do depends not only on what you do but what we each believe about what the other will do. Many situations with this general strategic structure can also not be fully described without specifying the relevant legal environment: not only in antitrust, where the desirability of cartel and collusive behavior obviously depends in large part on the law's attitude toward such behavior, but also in the law of contracts and cooperative ventures such as corporations, partnerships, and marriages, where negotiations at all stages are importantly influenced by what agreements the law will enforce and how it enforces them. Game theory is relevant not only to situations involving cooperation, but also conflict, as is indicated by its increasing application to analyze rational behavior by litigants.

E. Economic Analysis and Its Sceptics

Economic analysis of law does not lack critics, including some who reject the entire project and others who acknowledge the valuable insights which economics can offer but counsel caution in the application of those insights for policy purposes. Trenchant criticism of the world view of law-and-economics, in particular as personified by Posner, comes from the critical legal studies writer Kelman.

M. Kelman, *A Guide to Critical Legal Studies* (Cambridge, Mass., Harvard University Press, 1987), 118–20

As social theory, Law and Economics starts with the supposition that values and desires are the arbitrary assertion of individuals. . . . Though wealth maximization is the preferred collective goal for the legal economists, it is preferred not because it is a morally right end but because, as a factual matter, following a collective wealth-maximizing strategy ought to rebound to each person's whimsically selfish benefit in the rather short run.

Legal economics claims further that one can construct a state that is consistent with the premise that values are arbitrary yet does not suffer from what Unger calls the problem of "order". . . . First, rules are established without regard to morality: end states either are the product of actual negotiation or are established in accord with hypothetical negotiations. Similarly, people's initial lots are altered, in this social theory, only when there is actual consent (explicit contract), implied consent, or hypothetical consent, at least at some level of generality. Thus, victorious plaintiffs in tort suits are deemed to consent to compensated losses (that is, compensation is supposed to be set at a level that would have induced prior consent to injury had bargaining been plausible). . . . Thus, the smoothly functioning system permits no harm, allows no room for worry that the selfish will "grab" benefits.

The sense of contradiction that dominates CLS writing is utterly absent in legal economic literature. At the technical level of the choice of *form* of legal pronouncement, the rules-standards "dilemma" is reduced to an argument over the relative costs of substantively misgoverned conduct and administratively costly case-by-case fact-finding. At the philosophical level, the conflict between individualism and altruism simply disappears, because the very notion of altruism is unfathomable. It is simply reduced to (even perhaps defined as) an individual's arbitrary taste to incorporate the interests of others in making his own selfish calculations, and like other tastes it is neither to be condemned nor encouraged. To the extent that (apparent) altruism is ever to be applauded, it is simply in situations in which one party (for example a helpless child) is transactionally disabled from negotiating with others to purchase help; thus, a parent's emotional concern for a child is needed solely because we cannot readily substitute enforceable contracts in which a child agrees to trade some of the future wages she will earn if cared for in exchange for better care in early life. Finally, as I have indicated, the fear of disorder or excessive individualism simply disappears: proper background rules can restrain harm, ensure that everyone's interests are properly accounted for in the incentive structures each of us faces.

Wiegers adds a further layer of criticism, attacking neo-classical economics in particular from a feminist perspective.

W. Wiegers, 'Economic Analysis of Law and "Private Ordering": A Feminist Critique', (1992) 42 *U. Toronto LJ* 170 at 170, 190–2

'Economic man,' like the 'reasonable man' in law, has been the subject of feminist critique. As constructed in neoclassical economic thought, he is an individual who knows what will maximize his utility or satisfaction in life and who is motivated to seek it. His preferences are stable but always constrained in that the satisfaction of some wants must come at the expense or sacrifice of others. In theory, he is neither naturally superior nor inferior to other 'economic men,' though his preferences are entitled to be weighed in the market only so far as they are backed by willingness to pay. His world-view is dominated by market exchanges and trade-offs.

Neoclassical economics offers a vision of 'human' behaviour that many women have felt excluded by and from. While recognizing that 'economic man' is an abstraction, the classical model of competitive individualism that emerged in the nineteenth century clearly failed to describe or reflect the reality of women. Historically, women have been assumed and expected to be all that 'economic man' is not—emotional, vulnerable, passive, empathic, caring, and nurturant. The central ideas in neoclassical economic theory were formulated by men and were intended to explain behaviour in traditional markets that have always been male-dominated. Until the mid-nineteenth century or later, married women were legally subordinate to their husbands, denied the right to hold property or to enter into or sue upon contracts in their own right, as well as denied the right to engage in trades and occupations. Although women have always been involved in labour markets, the family home is still socially regarded as our primary sphere of responsibility. . . .

The 'real story' of gender relations—of women's subordination to men—has often been described in terms of an exchange. Through marriage, women have exchanged sexual access to their bodies, their reproductive capacity, household services, and often their wage labour for physical and economic security from men. Viewing marriage as a 'bargain,' however, tends falsely to imply that women got what they 'bargained for' rather than what they were forced to live with. The 'guarantee of lifelong security' for married women has often meant a subsistence income or less and also physical violence if not death. The concept of 'bargain' also implies that women were 'free' and equal parties to such arrangements. But if many, if not most, women have married for economic security rather than for love, they have done so because they have had few alternative means of support. Moreover, women have not been equal participants in fashioning or determining the limited set of life options and alternatives available to them.

Historically, women's response to male dominance in Western societies has included active resistance, submission, and collaboration. If consent is defined only in terms of rational, deliberate choice, women could be said to have largely 'consented' to their subordinate social roles. Whether these choices were voluntary or free, however, depends upon the conditions under which choice was exercised. The consent, submission, or accommodation by women to a system of male dominance has been secured through a number of means including physical force, socialization, a lack of education and economic alternatives, and economic incentives, as well as through the stigma and physical danger facing non-conforming women. . . .

Market methodology will likewise tend to obscure the extent to which women's choices reflect a 'structured inequality of life conditions.' Thus, Richard Posner's description of the traditional sexual division of labour as a voluntary and efficient exchange ignores entrenched barriers to the equal participation of women in the workplace, such as unequal pay, sex discrimination, and a sex-segregated labour market, as well as the refusal of men and male-dominated institutions to accommodate, support, and perform child care.

Posner's analysis not only obscures the extent to which choice is structured by such factors, but simultaneously validates and reinforces market outcomes by presenting them as consensual or as the result of 'free' choice. In his analysis, choice plays a legitimizing role in rendering market outcomes fair, acceptable, or deserved.

Note

In Chapter 3, we shall see that Carole Pateman likewise addresses the supposedly consensual relationship underlying women's subordination. However, she approaches the contradiction of consent and coercion from a different perspective, looking at the 'sexual contract' as throwing into relief the 'social contract', said by some political theorists to provide the basis of social and political order. Further feminist critiques of contract law appear in Chapter 4 (Dalton on cohabitation contracts; see also Section VII) and Chapters 11 and 12 (Frug on exclusion clauses and impossibility doctrine).

Other writers who have offered a wide-ranging ideological critique of the disciplines of law-and-economics include E. Baker, 'The Ideology of Economic Analysis of Law', (1975) 5 *Phil. & Pub. Aff.* 3, and B. White, 'Economics and Law: Two Cultures in Tension', (1986) 54 *Tenn. L. Rev.* 161. Measured criticism of economic analysis also comes from A. Leff, 'Economic Analysis of Law: Some Realism about Nominalism', (1974) 60 *Va. L. Rev.* 451, and J. Johnston, 'Law, Economics and Post-Realist Explanation'.

VI. PROMISE-CENTRED THEORIES OF CONTRACTUAL OBLIGATION

A. Introduction

Earlier in this chapter, we noted the evolution of the will theory of contractual obligation to explain why promises should be enforceable. Contracts were constituted by a 'meeting of minds'. Depending upon one's view of the history of legal doctrine, we can take will theory to be an ideological phenomenon which arose under certain economic conditions (cf. Atiyah) or a complex and somewhat confused response to the abstraction of contract doctrine in the age of the philosophy of the individual. One reason for the failure of the will theory adequately to explain the basis of contract lay in its inability to reconcile the subjective idea of the mind or of the will with the practical need of the law to point to objective and observable phenomena such as speech acts and actions. This point will be pursued further in Chapter 5, when we look at the so-called 'objective test of agreement'. A species of 'will theory' has seen a recent renaissance in the form of the work of Charles Fried, in *Contract as Promise*, and Randy Barnett, who has elaborated a 'consent theory' of contract.

B. Contract as Promise

The thesis of Fried's *Contract as Promise* is that promises are enforceable because of the moral worth of promising, not because other people have relied upon them, or because they form part of a 'bargain'.

C. Fried, *Contract as Promise* (Cambridge, Mass., Harvard University Press, 1981), 14–17

The Moral Obligation of Promise

Once I have invoked the institution of promising, why exactly is it wrong for me then to break my promise?

My argument so far does not answer that question. The institution of promising is a way for me to bind myself to another so that the other may expect a future performance, and binding myself in this way is something that I may want to be able to do. But this by itself does not show that I am morally obligated to perform my promise at a later time if to do so proves inconvenient or costly. That there should be a system of currency also increases my options and is useful to me, but this does not show why I should not use counterfeit money if I can get away with it. In just the same way the usefulness of promising in general does not show why I should not take advantage of it in a particular case and yet fail to keep my promise. That the convention would cease to function in the long run, would cease to provide benefits if everyone felt free to violate it, is hardly an answer to the question of why I should keep a particular promise on a particular occasion.

David Lewis has shown that a convention that it would be in each person's interest to observe if everyone else observed it will be established and maintained without any special mechanisms of commitment or enforcement. Starting with simple conventions (for example that if a telephone conversation is disconnected, the person who initiated the call is the one who calls back) Lewis extends his argument to the case of language. Now promising is different, since (unlike language, where it is overwhelmingly in the interest of all that everyone comply with linguistic conventions, even when language is used to deceive) it will often be in the interest of the promisor *not* to conform to the convention when it comes time to render his performance. Therefore individual self-interest is not enough to sustain the convention, and some additional ground is needed to keep it from unraveling. There are two principal candidates: external sanctions and moral obligation. . . .

Considerations of self-interest cannot supply the moral basis of my obligation to keep a promise. By an analogous argument neither can considerations of utility. For however sincerely and impartially I may apply the utilitarian injunction to consider at each step how I might increase the sum of happiness or utility in the world, it will allow me to break my promise whenever the balance of advantage (including, of course, my own advantage) tips in that direction. The possible damage to the institution of promising is only one factor in the calculation. Other factors are the alternative good I might do by breaking my promise, whether and by how many people the breach might be discovered, what the actual effect on confidence of such a breach would be. There is no a priori reason for believing that an individual's calculations will come out in favor of keeping the promise always, sometimes, or most of the time. . . .

The obligation to keep a promise is grounded not in arguments of utility but in respect for individual autonomy and in trust. Autonomy and trust are grounds for the institution of promising as well, but the argument for *individual* obligation is not the same. Individual obligation is only a step away, but that step must be taken. An individual is morally bound to keep his promises because he has intentionally invoked a convention whose function it is to give grounds—moral grounds—for another to expect the promised performance. To renege is to abuse a confidence he was free to invite or not, and which he intentionally did invite. To abuse that confidence now is like (but only *like*) lying: the abuse of a shared social institution that is intended to invoke the bonds of trust. A liar and a promise-breaker each *use* another person. In both speech and promising there is an invitation to the other to trust, to make himself vulnerable; the liar and the promise-breaker then abuse that trust. The obligation to keep a promise is thus similar to but more constraining than the obligation to tell the truth. To avoid lying you need only believe in the truth of what you say when you say it, but a promise binds into the future, well past the moment when the promise is made. There will, of course, be great social utility to a general regime of trust and confidence in promises and truthfulness. But this just shows that a regime of mutual respect allows men and women to accomplish what in a jungle of unrestrained self-interest could not be accomplished. If this advantage is to be firmly established, there must exist a ground for mutual confidence deeper than and independent of the social utility it permits.

The utilitarian counting the advantages affirms the general importance of enforcing *contracts*. The moralist of duty, however, sees *promising* as a device that free, moral individuals have fashioned on the premise of mutual trust, and which gathers its moral force from that premise. The moralist of duty thus posits a general obligation to keep promises, of which the obligation of contract will be only a special case—that special case in which certain promises have attained legal as well as moral force. But since a contract is first of all a promise, the contract must be kept because a promise must be kept.

To summarize: There exists a convention that defines the practice of promising and its entailments. This convention provides a way that a person may create expectations in others. By virtue of the basic Kantian principles of trust and respect, it is wrong to invoke that convention in order to make a promise, and then to break it.

Notes

1. Other writers have appraised the significance of promises *in* contracts (e.g. P. S. Atiyah, *Promises, Morals and Law* (Oxford, Clarendon Press, 1981); J. Raz, 'Promises in Morality and Law', (1982), 95 *Harv. L. Rev.* 916); only Fried has articulated a comprehensive theory *equating* contract and promise.

2. Following from Fried's basic thesis of promising, he asserts general support for the autonomy of the parties to shape their own contracts: 'Since the terms of obligation are freely invented and imposed by the parties on themselves, they may mould them as they wish' (p. 132). Moreover, his argument also leads him to draw a sharp distinction between contractual and tortious obligation. *Contract as Promise* speaks sharply against the thesis that contract has no proper autonomous sphere of concern. On the other hand, Fried does not purport to argue that the whole of the law, *as it stands*, is logically consistent with a promise principle. He finds gaps in the law, which he argues are irrational. For example, he argues against the doctrine of consideration, as the criterion by which the enforceability of promises is judged, as unnecessary if the moral obligation of promise as such is accepted (see Ch. 6).

3. Fried's position on promising has been criticized as 'a form of moral paternalism', since it alleges 'that the advantages of a society in which promises are kept outweigh the proper concern for liberty' (see H. Collins, 'Contract and Legal Theory', in W. Twining (ed.), *Legal Theory and Common Law* (Oxford, Blackwell, 1986), 144). In other words, without an assumption about the desirability of such a society, what Collins calls 'choice theories' (i.e. those based principally on the personal responsibility of the parties to the obligation) 'cannot reconcile the basic liberal precept that private autonomy should be respected as far as possible with the practice of legally enforcing all promising' (ibid. 143).

4. For further criticism of Fried see J. Gordley, *The Philosophical Origins of Modern Contract Doctrine* (Oxford, Clarendon Press, 1991), 237–8.

C. Consent Theory

Randy Barnett has proposed a 'consent theory' of contract which is closely related to that of Fried in that it too identifies a (different) moral component of contractual obligation, in this instance 'consent'. In the following passage, Barnett explains how consent theory differs from will theory.

R. Barnett, 'Rights and Remedies in a Consent Theory of Contract', in R. Frey and C. Morris (eds.), *Liability and Responsibility* **(Cambridge, Cambridge University Press, 1991), 135 at 143–5**

At first blush, a consent theory of contract may appear to some to be a version of a "will theory." A will theory bases contractual obligation on the fact that an obligation was freely assumed. Understanding the fundamental differences between the two approaches, therefore, will assist an appreciation of the comparative virtues of the consent theory. A theory that bases contractual obligation on the existence of a "will to be bound" is hard-pressed to justify contractual obligation in the absence of an actual exercise of the will. It is difficult to see how a theory that bases the enforceability of commitments on their willful quality can justify enforcing objectively manifested agreements when one of the parties did not subjectively intend to be bound. Yet the enforcement of such agreements is, and has always been, widely accepted. In contrast to a will theory, a consent theory's recognition of the dependence of contractual obligation on a rights analysis is able to account for the normal relationship between objective and subjective considerations in contract law.

The concept of rights or entitlements is a social one whose principal function is to specify boundaries within which individuals may operate freely to pursue their respective individual ends and thereby provide the basis for cooperative interpersonal activity. The boundaries of individual discretion that are defined by a system of clear entitlements serve to allocate decision-making authority among individuals. Vital information is thereby conveyed to all those who might wish to avoid disputes and respect the rights of others, provided they know what those rights are. Potential conflicts between persons who might otherwise vie for control of a given resource are thus avoided. Therefore, to fulfill its social function, entitlements theory demands that the boundaries of protected domains be ascertainable, not only by judges who must resolve disputes that have arisen, but, perhaps more importantly, by the affected persons themselves before any dispute occurs.

In contract law this informational or "boundary-defining" requirement means that an assent to alienate rights must be *manifested* in some manner by one party to the other to serve as a criterion of enforcement. Without a manifestation of assent that is accessible to all affected parties, the aspect of a system of entitlements that governs transfers of rights will fail to achieve its main function. At the time of the transaction, it will have failed to identify clearly and communicate to both parties (and to third parties) the rightful boundaries that must be respected. Without such communication, parties to a transaction (and third parties) cannot accurately ascertain what constitutes rightful conduct and what constitutes a commitment on which they can rely. Disputes that might otherwise have been avoided will occur, and the attendant uncertainties of the transfer process will discourage reliance.

Although requiring the consent of the rights-holder as a condition of a valid transfer of rights is absolutely vital . . . , whether one has consented to a transfer or rights under such a regime, however, generally depends not on one's subjective opinion about the meaning of one's freely chosen words or conduct, but on the ordinary meaning that is attached to them. If the word "yes" ordinarily means *yes*, then a subjective and unrevealed belief that "yes" means *no* is generally immaterial to a regime of entitlements allocation. Only a general reliance on objectively ascertainable assertive conduct will enable a system of entitlements to perform its allotted boundary-defining function.

Given that the function of a rights theory is to facilitate human action and interaction in a social context by defining the boundaries of permitted actions and resolve competing claims, a coherent rights theory should allocate rights largely on the basis of factors that minimize the likelihood of generating conflicting claims. In this regard, objectively manifested conduct, which usually reflects subjective intent, provides a sounder basis for contractual obligation than do subjectively held intentions. Evidence of subjective intent that is extrinsic to the transaction and was unavailable to the other party is relevant, if at all, only insofar as it helps a court to ascertain the objective meaning of certain terms. . . .

The consent that is required is a *manifestation of an intention to alienate rights.* In a system of entitlements where consent to transfer rights is what justifies the legal enforcement of agreements, any such manifestation implies that one intends to be legally bound to adhere to one's commitment. Therefore, the phrase "a manifestation of an intention to be legally bound" neatly captures what a court should seek to find before holding that an enforceable transfer of alienable rights has been effected.

Notes

1. Consent theory does not see contract as an isolated obligation, but as part of a broader system of legal entitlements, where the boundaries of individual entitlements (e.g. to property) are set by a moral criterion of consent, defined as an external manifestation of assent. Barnett argues that this accounts for the objective theory of agreement (see Ch. 5), and his thesis also leads him to accept a wider range of social acts (e.g. including reliance) as constituting the basis for enforcing promises than does, for example, Fried (see Ch. 6).

2. See further on Barnett's theory 'A Consent Theory of Contract', (1986) 86 *Colum. L. Rev.* 269.

VII. CRITICAL LEGAL STUDIES AND CONTRACT THEORY

A. Introduction

The term 'critical legal studies' is generally used to denote a diverse body of scholarship which is centred around all or some of the following precepts about law. Law is not a neutral tool of social ordering, but has an ideological power which reinforces a dominant hierarchy of values and interests within society (e.g. based on class, race and gender). However, the critical perspective on contract is not simply a claim to reveal the intimacy of the association between the modern capitalist economy, exchanges between individuals, and the legal institution of contract. Nor is it simply an argument for a socially and procedurally just contract law (see Ch. 8). Critical perspectives on contract also challenge the very notion of *a* theory of contract, in the sense of proclaiming the 'death of Grand Theory' in which all internal inconsistencies and contradictions within contract as a legal doctrine and social phenomenon are conveniently ironed out. According to T. Wilhelmsson ('Questions for a Critical Contract Law—and a Contradictory Answer', in Wilhelmsson (ed.), *Perspectives of Critical Contract Law* (Aldershot, Dartmouth, 1993), 13–14), what he calls 'alternative dogmatics' 'emphasises and cherishes the internal contradictions of law as one of the main sources for developing new ideas'. In other words, the idea of a critical theory is not simply to substitute new ideas for old (reliance for bargain, substantive justice for procedural justice, etc.) but to recognize the strictly limited nature of the new models themselves. Critical contract scholars are united more closely in their rejection of the adequacy of the classical or neo-classical models of contract than they are either in the nature of their attempts to offer an alternative explanatory framework or in the assumptions which they bring to the task of building theory. One key uniting factor is that they would acknowledge the centrality of those assumptions in shaping the law, and would not adhere to what they would argue is a spurious claim that the law can be some sort of value-free instrument for enforcing order within society.

B. Dichotomies within Contract Law

One insight shared by a number of critical authors is that much of the modern law of contract is made of dichotomies or, as Roberto Unger (*The Critical Legal Studies Movement* (Cambridge, Mass., Harvard University Press, 1986) puts it, principles and counterprinciples. For every principle that supposedly governs the basis of contract (e.g. freedom of contract), there exists another counterprinciple which at the very least circumscribes the application of the principle (e.g. the concept of community) (see the discussion of Unger in Ch. 4). On the other hand, as Wilhelmsson points out, if these counterprinciples or 'modern tendencies' are viewed, not as exceptions but as themselves the starting-point for contractual obligation, the basis exists for a new model centred around concepts of social co-operation.

T. Wilhelmsson, 'Questions for a Critical Contract Law—and a Contradictory Answer', in Wilhelmsson (ed.), *Perspectives of Critical Contract Law* (Aldershot, Dartmouth, 1993), at 38–41

[An] analysis of the anomalies within the traditional models . . . [reveals] that each of the central features of the models encounter an opposite tendency within existing contract law. There are at least the following tensions between traditional contract law and modern tendencies:

Traditional contract law	Modern tendencies
Content-neutrality	Content-orientation
Static approach	Dynamic approach
Antagonism	Cooperation
Atomism	Collectivism
Abstract approach	Person-oriented approach

Each of these supplements can give rise to new contract models, when elevated from the position as an exception to a starting point of contractual reasoning. Depending on which aspect of the new thinking one emphasizes, one can reach different types of models, ranging from content-oriented models of just social practice, and doctrines of social-typical conduct to models emphasizing cooperation and collectivism. The different models are not necessarily different only as to emphasis. It is quite possible to construct models which retain the traditional approach as a main rule on some point and are anti-traditionalist on some other point. Various combinations are possible.

In order to test the idea of creating a new all-embracing contract model, it is tempting to confront the traditional paradigm with a construction that emphasizes all the new elements of the dichotomies mentioned above. . . . Many other versions could be structured, depending on the weight one attaches to the various supplements.

The building of a new model, which would mainly rest on the opposite elements, could choose to put the thought of contract as cooperation in a central position, for example with regard to the changed realities of contract practice and in conformity with views expressed in modern contract doctrine. The concept of cooperation is here used of course in the same broad sense as above, not only focusing on continuing cooperation in long-term contracts but also on demands for loyality and disclosure in momentary relationships. . . .

The dynamic approach of modern contract law would thereby underline the flexible character of the cooperation, leaving room for changes when the circumstances change. As an anti-traditional cooperation model would be person-oriented, changes in the social and economic needs of the parties should also be taken into account. The collectivist approach again would emphasize the relation of the cooperation to the social and legal networks to which the parties are attached, as well as to other contracting of the parties. Summarizing these points, one could speak about a cooperation within and with regard to its dynamic context.

In an anti-traditionalist cooperation model, the legal analysis would focus on the content of the cooperation. This element is obviously not connected by logical necessity with a model of contract as cooperation as such. However, it is not easy to judge . . . cooperation only on the basis of content-neutral criteria. The thought of contract as a flexible and changing form of cooperation therefore as such tends to favour a content-oriented approach to the problem of the binding force of contracts. In addition, one may claim that "real" and need-oriented cooperation is not compatible with the domination of one party over the other. A content-oriented approach is needed to eliminate or diminish the possibilities of such domination.

As the anti-traditionalist model is not atomistic, the cooperation cannot be judged only on the basis of its successfulness in relation to the needs and desires of the parties. A collectivist—or perhaps rather: anti-atomistic or societal—approach easily implies the thought of contract as a tool of rational distribution of goods, services and capital on the market. Such a societal approach would also as such explain the shift from content-neutrality to at least some form of content-orientation of contract law. . . .

Summarized in a short formulation, an anti-traditionalist model could therefore picture contract as a form of flexible and changing cooperation between and with regard to different actors on the market, enforced as a tool of rational distribution in the society.

Notes

1. Wilhelmsson might appear at first sight to defy his own injunction against Grand Theory-building. On the other hand, as he points out later in his paper, his model does not necessarily serve only progressive ends oriented towards the left of the political spectrum. The most extreme example he gives is that of 'person orientation', where the contents of contracts and the criteria for enforceability can be made to depend upon the personal characteristics of the parties, thus allowing the protection of weak and

vulnerable parties. Person orientation can also be used, he observes, for fascist purposes, noting the example of Nazi Germany where Jews were deprived of their status as full persons under the civil law (p. 46). Consequently, it is easy to see the objection of the liberal to a project such as Wilhelmsson's: expressly imparting a value content to legal rules in this way removes the bulwark function of the rule of law, as law becomes simply a pawn in a political game, susceptible to swings in accordance only with the whims of the politically dominant hierarchy.

2. There are clear links between critical contract theory and the paradigm of relational contract pioneered by Macneil and empirically investigated by Macaulay and others. Macneil himself describes critical work on contract law as adopting a relational perspective, and indeed in a sense the work of Wilhelmsson (e.g. on social *force majeure*—see Ch. 12) takes Macneil's work on contract as an evolving and flexible relation to its logical conclusion, in which parties may be released from their obligations if excessive hardship would accrue to them if they were not.

3. The relationship between classical contract law and what can be termed the 'critical' project in contract is further explored by Collins (see Ch. 8).

C. Dalton and Deconstruction

Another example of 'critical' work on contract is Clare Dalton's 'An Essay of Deconstruction of Contract Doctrine', which focuses its particular explanatory force on the operation of certain dichotomies in contract law: public/private, objective/subjective, form/substance. These dualities, she argues, lie behind the inconsistencies and indeterminacies of contract doctrine. These points can be briefly illustrated in relation to the first duality: public/private.

C. Dalton, 'An Essay in the Deconstruction of Contract Doctrine', (1985) 94 *Yale L. J.* 997 at 1010–11

The opposing ideas of public and private have traditionally dominated discourse about contract doctrine. The underlying notion has been that to the extent contract doctrine is "private" or controlled by the parties, it guarantees individual autonomy or freedom; to the extent it is "public," or controlled by the state, it infringes individual autonomy.

Since at least the mid-nineteenth century, the discourse of contract doctrine has tried to portray contract as essentially private and free. At all times, nonetheless, traditional doctrine has uneasily recognized a public aspect of contract, viewing certain state interests as legitimate limitations on individual freedom. But this public aspect has traditionally been assigned a strictly supplemental role; indeed, a major concern of contract doctrine has been to suppress "publicness" by a series of doctrinal moves.

The public aspect of contract doctrine is suppressed differently in each area of that doctrine, and in each historical period. The method of suppression is generally either an artificial *conflation* of public and private, in which the public is represented as private, or an artificial *separation* of public from private, which distracts attention from the public element of the protected "private" arena by focusing attention on the demarcated (and limited) "public" arena.

Dalton expands upon the techniques of *separation* and *conflation* in relation to the doctrines of duress and unconscionablility, supposedly part of contract law, in order to express a *public* interest in maintaining restraints upon the legitimate exploitation of *private* power through free contract. She explains the point thus:

Dalton, 'An Essay in the Deconstruction of Contract Doctrine', 1011

The separation of duress and unconscionability from the main body of contract doctrine diverts attention from the fact that the entire doctrine of consideration reflects societal attitudes about which bargains are worthy of enforcement. But even as the technique of separation marks out duress and unconscionability as public exceptions to private contract doctrine, within duress and unconscionability doctrine public and private are conflated—the public grounds for disapproving bargains recast as evidence that there is no private bargain to be enforced. In this arena, the techniques of separation and conflation serve to camouflage critical issues of power—the power of the state to police private agreements, and the power of one private party over another.

Dalton deconstructs the dualities of contract law with a clear vision in mind—to demonstrate that contract law is about power and knowledge. She concludes:

Dalton, 'An Essay in the Deconstruction of Contract Doctrine', 1113

My story reveals the world of contract doctrine to be one in which a comparatively few mediating devices are constantly deployed to displace and defer the otherwise inevitable revelation that public cannot be separated from private, or form from substance, or objective manifestation from subjective intent. The pain of that revelation, and its value, lies in its message that we can neither know nor control the boundary between self and other.

Note

Put thus, contract—as a basic expression of human sociality—can be seen as a symbol of human weakness. Contract doctrine, according to Dalton, mystifies the key epistemological problems which 'concretely hamper our ability to live with another in society'. However, Dalton's is an exercise in deconstruction: she does not offer any mechanism by which a better, more social world can be built, but simply a means of identifying the particular ways whereby human freedom and self-determination are currently restricted.

Questions

1. Using the typology developed by Twining to highlight the different tasks of legal theory, assign the readings in this chapter to one or more of his categories. NB: you may find it useful to return to this typology as you work through this book.

2. If you found that you needed to assign a reading to more than one category, or if you experienced difficulty in deciding which category or categories applied to a particular reading, consider why this happened.

3. To what extent do the various approaches to the notion of the contract developed by writers such as Durkheim and Weber contribute to modern approaches to the law of contract?

4. How does Gordley's approach to using historical material differ from that of writers such as Atiyah?

5. What are the chief features of relational contracts and what distinguishes them from discrete transactions? You may find it easiest to approach this question using practical examples of contracts with which you are familiar (sales, tenancies, hiring arrangements, etc.).

6. The work of Stewart Macaulay attracts the label 'empirical'. Why is it given this label, and why is the label not attached to much of the other work discussed in this chapter? What is the value of this type of scholarship for contract law?

7. Do promise-centred theories of contractual obligation have more in common with the bargain-based paradigm or the reliance-based alternative?

8. Feminist and critical legal scholars (amongst others) have argued against economic analyses of contract law on the grounds that they offer too narrow a picture of human nature. Do you agree with these criticisms?

3

Contract and State

I. INTRODUCTION

In this chapter we examine some of the interactions between contract and the state. These operate at a number of different levels from the merely functional—organs of the state can and do make contracts governed, at least in English law, for a large part by the *general* law of contact (Section III)—to the realms of political philosophy and the notion of the 'social contract' (Section II). None of this is new, and it does not in itself justify a separate chapter on 'contract and state'. As the extracts from Atiyah in Section II show, 'social contractarianism' can be linked to the general rise of contract as a mechanism of social ordering the eighteenth century, if the theory of political and economic change propounded by Atiyah is followed (cf. Ch. 2 and the extracts from Gordley). What is more novel, however, is the increasing use of 'contract' by government both as a way of stimulating market activity (e.g. within the national health service) and as a surrogate for certain aspects of citizenship, as a means of structuring the entitlements and expectations of individuals in relation to public services. These issues will be addressed in Section IV.

II. SOCIAL CONTRACTARIANISM

A. The Idea of the Social Contract

In the *Concise Encyclopedia of Western Philosophy and Philosophers*, 2nd edn., (ed. J. Urmson and J. Rée (London, Unwin Hyman, 1989), 198), social contract theories are defined as those which 'attempt to explain the duty of obedience to the laws and civil authority by reference to a contract or compact or promise to obey made for the sake of the benefits gained from the civil society thereby instituted'. The idea of structuring social order around a contract has existed since Plato, but it was the philosophers of the English Reformation (e.g. Hobbes and Locke) and of the Enlightenment (e.g. Rousseau) who developed the distinctive modern versions of the

theory, although these versions do differ on key questions such as the identity of the parties to the contract (the people contracting amongst themselves or the people contracting with the sovereign), the nature of the
consent given by the parties (implicit or explicit), and the core terms of the
contract.

Atiyah argues that there are links between the rise of social contract
theory and the emergence of a more distinctive and dominant conception
of contract based on consent and will in the eighteenth century.

P. S. Atiyah, *The Rise and Fall of Freedom of Contract* (Oxford, Oxford University Press, 1979), 36–41

In the eighteenth century the notion of contract, and the role of contract in
society, were a great deal broader than they are today. Men thought their
relationships with each other, and their relationship with the State, to be of a
similar character. And over and above that, there is a sense in which they
perceived the role of choice or consent in the one relationship to be the
precondition for the proper role of choice or consent in the other. They *chose* to
create a society in which free choice was one of their principal goals; they
voluntarily created a society in which the voluntary creation of relationships
would be permitted and respected; they *freely* instituted a society for the protection of their property in order that they could be free to acquire, exploit, or
dispose of property to their best advantage. . . .

There have always been two separate relationships which have, at various
times, been treated under the general head of the Social Contract. On the one
hand there is the relationship, in any political society, between the governors
and the governed, and on the other hand there is the relationship between the
people themselves. Some theorists held that the relationship between the
people was contractual; that political society was—or was to be treated as if—
it had been instituted by an agreement by which the people abandoned their
'natural' freedoms and constituted themselves into one body politic. Everybody
submitted himself to this new constitutional and legal order, thereby gaining
the right to the due protection of its laws. Other theorists fastened on the relationship between sovereigns and subjects. Nobody, of course, had any doubt
that a subject owed obligations to his sovereign, but there was a great deal
more difficulty over the question of reciprocal obligations. Did a sovereign owe
'duties' to his people? And if so, who was to be the judge of the due performance of those duties, and how were they to be enforced? . . .

 . . . what was new in contractual theory was not the idea of a relationship
involving mutual rights and duties, but the idea that the relationship was created by, and depended on, the free choice of the individuals involved in it. The
waning of the medieval Aristotelian concept of man as an essentially political
and social being, necessarily involved (without his choosing) in a network of

communal and social relationships, inevitably brought with it a need to explain how societies existed at all. As Tawney put it:

The difference between the England of Shakespeare, still visited by the ghosts of the Middle Ages, and the England which emerged in 1700 from the fierce polemics of the last two generations, was a difference of social and political theory even more than of constitutional and political arrangements. Not only the facts, but the minds which appraised them, were profoundly modified . . . The natural consequence of the abdication of authorities which had stood, however imperfectly, for a common purpose in social organization, was the gradual disappearance from social thought of the idea of purpose itself. Its place in the eighteenth century was taken by the idea of mechanism. The conception of men as united to each other, and of all mankind as united to God, by mutual obligations, arising from their relation to a common end, ceased to be impressed upon men's minds.

In short, the new man of the eighteenth century, who was the true descendant of post-Reformation man, was an individualist; and one of the essential differences between the social and political theory of the pre- and post-Reformation eras concerned the way in which individuals make up a community. It was only through the free choice of these free individuals that societies and political communities existed at all.

A similar argument is elaborated by Pateman who links social contract theory not only to economic and social developments, but also the concept of promise. She develops her argument specifically in the context of John Locke's social contract theory, contained in his *Two Treatises of Government*, first published in 1689.

C. Pateman, 'Justifying Political Obligation', in *The Disorder of Women* (Cambridge, Polity, 1989), 59–63

Political theories in which consent and the associated idea of the social contract were central and fundamental became prominent, as everyone knows, in the seventeenth and eighteenth centuries. Nor is this surprising. Political ideas and concepts, notwithstanding the way in which they are treated by so many political theorists, do not exist in a separate, timeless world of their own, but help to constitute specific forms of social life. Social contract and consent theories were formulated at a time of great socio-economic development and change, at a time when the capitalist market economy and the liberal constitutional state were beginning to emerge. As part of these developments, individuals and their relationships began to be seen in a new and revolutionary way. The contract theorists began their arguments from the premise that individuals are 'born free and equal' or are 'naturally' free and equal to each other. Such a conception was in complete contrast to the long-prevailing view that people were born in a God-created and 'natural' hierarchy of inequality and subordination. Within this traditional perspective, although disputes could frequently arise about the scope of specific rulers' right of command, there was scarcely room for general doubts about political obedience; rulers and political obedience were part of God's way with the world. But once the idea gained currency that individuals were born free and equal or were 'naturally' so (and how were they freely to enter contracts and make equal exchanges in the market, and pursue their interests as they saw fit, if they were not?) then a very large question was also raised about political authority and political obedience. . . .

Making promises is one of the most basic ways in which free and equal individuals can freely create their own social relationships. As part of their social and moral education, individuals learn how to take part in the social practice of promising and so develop as persons with certain kinds of capacities. These capacities include the ability to engage in the rational and reasoned deliberation required to decide whether, on this occasion, a promise ought to be made, and also the ability to look back and critically evaluate their own actions and relationships; sometimes a promise may justifiably be broken or altered or revised in some way. Now, if political obligation is like, or is a form of, promising there is an important question to be asked; namely, how can citizens assume their political, like their other, obligations for themselves; what form of political system would make this possible? In short, it must be asked what is the political counterpart of the social practice of promising. . . .

The hypothesis of the contract is a way of showing how 'in the beginning' free and equal individuals can rationally agree to live under political authority. However, the *liberal* social contract has two stages and the significance of each stage is very different. It is the first part of the contract story that shows how the 'dispersed' individuals form a new political community. This part of the social contract establishes an obligation between, and places authority in the hands of, the members of the community themselves. Thus the first stage of the contract, taken by itself, is related to the question about the comparison with promising. Locke treats the first part of the contract as necessary (a political community must be created) but as an unimportant preliminary. It is the second stage of the contract that is fundamental to liberal theory The second stage embodies the assumption that it is necessary for the members of the new community to alienate their right to exercise political authority to a few representatives. The free agreement of the contract thus becomes an agreement that a few representatives shall decide upon the content of individuals' political obligation. Self-assumed obligation becomes an obligation to let others decide upon one's political obligation. The comparison with promising now begins to appear misplaced and, furthermore, political obligation is now owed to the state and its representatives, not by citizens to each other.

Locke could not complete his theory with the idea of the social contract. He had to meet the patriarchalists' objection that an agreement of the fathers could not bind sons, not if the latter were truly born free and equal. Locke had, therefore, to introduce the notion of consent into his theory. The sons had, in their turn, voluntarily to consent or agree to the political arrangements made by their fathers. Locke had to answer the same problems as contemporary theorists: given a legitimate political system, how can individuals be said to consent to it? From what aspect of their actions can their political obligation be inferred?

In his discussion of consent, Locke remarks that no one doubts that express consent gives rise to political obligation and makes an individual the subject of government. The difficulty about consent arises 'where he has made no Expressions of it at all.' Locke solves this problem by his famous claim that the tacit consent of the members of the community can be inferred from their peaceful everyday interactions under the protection of government.

Notes

1. Locke's approach to the social contract conceives of the relationship between rules and subjects as one of trust. The notion of trust defines the limits of legitimate governmental activity and defines the obligations of those who govern. Resistance to tyrannical government is therefore justified, and in this respect Locke is to be distinguished from Thomas Hobbes, whose major work on social contract, *Leviathan*, was first published in 1651. Hobbes argued that once the people, in a state of nature, have constituted themselves into a political association, a community, they then invest all power and authority in a sovereign (whom he called Leviathan), who is not subject to any limits. The absolute authority of the sovereign was for Hobbes the ideal alternative to the fear of death that haunts men in a state of nature. Indeed, Hobbes is perhaps most famous for warning that he life of man could be 'solitary, poor, nasty, brutish, and short'. A third strand of social contract theory should also be mentioned, and that is the work of Jean-Jacques Rousseau, the French idealist thinker. In his *Du contrat social*, first published in 1762, Rousseau argued that government is only legitimate if sovereignty remains with the people. This required the people to give express consent to be governed.

2. Our interest in social-contract theory does not so much concern an understanding of theories of political obligation but rather arises out of the continuing relevance of contractarianism for the modern concept of contract. Four aspects stand out. First, social-contract theory as conceived by Hobbes, in particular, is above all a theory of individualism. Individuals are conceived of as 'naturally' antagonistic, and consequently in need of a civilizing influence such as contract to exit from a savage state of nature. The individualism of social-contract theory continues to find an echo in the dominance of individualism in neo-classical contract doctrine today.

Second, consent theories of political obligation have recently been revived, in particular by John Rawls's *Theory of Justice* (Cambridge, Mass.,

Harvard University Press, 1971). The link to modern contract doctrine arises because Rawls bases his assessment of individual entitlements on a consideration of what individuals *would* agree to if they reverted to an 'original position' (Rawls's words). He explicitly links the contractarian idea with the promise of equal protection and fairness for all individuals, since he argues that the principles which we would be led by our self-interest to choose as the terms of a contractarian framework for society would, in an ideally fair situation, themselves be fair. The importance of Rawls's argument in the contract context is the link it makes between wider political and philosophical notions of justice and the more limited conception of contractual justice which we consider in more detail in Chapter 8.

Third, a metaphorical link can be drawn between contracts as an exercise in communication and social contract theory. In Chapter 4 we discuss work by Peter Goodrich which uses the 'postal rule' governing the communication of acceptances by letter as a metaphor for the role of language in social order.

The fourth aspect of social contract theory which we shall consider here concerns the questions which it begs: 'contract between whom and about whom?' and 'whose consent is needed and given?' These questions have been analysed from a feminist perspective by Pateman, whose argument we shall now examine.

3.   For a much more detailed account of social-contract theory, see N. Lessnoff, *Social Contract* (Basingstoke, Macmillan, 1986).

B. Social Contract Theory and its Critics

Social contract theory has not been without its critics. For example, David Hume argued that the idea of a social contract is simply unrealistic. He also challenged the use of theory to justify the legitimacy of states, even granted that they were originally founded upon a contract. Locke used a concept of consent, including tacit consent, to deal with this problem, but Hume sought to demonstrate that the assumption that states which begin in a legitimate way remain legitimate so long as they continue in the same way, regardless of the consent of individual citizens, is just that—an assumption (*Of the Original Contract,* first published in 1748).

Pateman's challenge to standard social-contract theory begins with the revelation of the so-called 'sexual contract', the hidden half of the social contract.

C. Pateman, 'Contracting In', in *The Sexual Contract* (Cambridge, Polity Press, 1988), 1–7

The original contract is a sexual-social pact, but the story of the sexual contract has been repressed. Standard accounts of social contract theory do not discuss the whole story and contemporary contract theorists give no indication that half the agreement is missing. The story of the sexual contract is also about the genesis of political right, and explains why exercise of the right is legitimate—but this story is about political right as *patriarchal right* or sex-right, the power that men exercise over women. The missing half of the story tells how a specifically modern form of patriarchy is established. The new civil society created through the original contract is a patriarchal social order.

Social contract theory is conventionally presented as a story about freedom. One interpretation of the original contract is that the inhabitants of the state of nature exchange the insecurities of natural freedom for equal, civil freedom which is protected by the state. In civil society freedom is universal; all adults enjoy the same civil standing and can exercise their freedom by, as it were, replicating the original contract when, for example, they enter into the employment contract or the marriage contract. Another interpretation, which takes into account conjectural histories of the state of nature in the classic texts, is that freedom is won by sons who cast off their natural subjection to their fathers and replace paternal rule by civil government. Political right as paternal right is inconsistent with modern civil society. In this version of the story, civil society is created through the original contract after paternal rule—or patriarchy—is overthrown. The new civil order, therefore, appears to be anti-patriarchal or post-patriarchal. Civil society is created through contract so that contract and patriarchy appear to be irrevocably opposed.

These familiar readings of the classic stories fail to mention that a good deal more than freedom is at stake. Men's domination over women, and the right of men to enjoy equal sexual access to women, is at issue in the making of the original pact. The social contract is a story of freedom; the sexual contract is a story of subjection. The original contract constitutes both freedom and domination. Men's freedom and women's subjection are created through the original contract—and the character of civil freedom cannot be understood without the missing half of the story that reveals how men's patriarchal right over women is established through contract. Civil freedom is not universal. Civil freedom is a masculine attribute and depends upon patriarchal right. The sons overturn paternal rule not merely to gain their liberty but to secure women for themselves. Their success in this endeavour is chronicled in the story of the sexual contract. The original pact is a sexual as well as a social contract: it is sexual in the sense of patriarchal—that is, the contract establishes men's political right over women—and also sexual in the sense of establishing orderly access by men to women's bodies. The original contract creates what I shall call, following Adrienne Rich, 'the law of male sex-right'. Contract is far from being opposed to patriarchy; contract is the means through which modern patriarchy is constituted.

One reason why political theorists so rarely notice that half the story of the original contract is missing, or that civil society is patriarchal, is that 'patriarchy' is usually interpreted patriarchally as paternal rule (the literal meaning of the term). So, for example, in the standard reading of the theoretical battle in the seventeenth century between the patriarchalists and social contract theorists, patriarchy is assumed to refer only to paternal right. Sir Robert Filmer claimed that political power was paternal power and that the procreative power of the father was the origin of political right. Locke and his fellow contract theorists insisted that paternal and political power were not the same and that contact was the genesis of political right. The contract theorists were victorious on this point; the standard interpretation is on firm ground—as far as it goes. Once, more, a crucial portion of the story is missing. The true origin of political right is overlooked in this interpretation; no stories are told about its genesis. . . . Political right originates in sex-right or conjugal right. Paternal right is only one, and not the original, dimension of patriarchal power. A man's power as a father comes after he has exercised the patriarchal right of a man (a husband) over a woman (wife). The contract theorists had no wish to challenge the original patriarchal right in their onslaught on paternal right. Instead, they incorporated conjugal right into their theories and, in so doing, transformed the law of male sex-right into its modern contractual form. Patriarchy ceased to be paternal long ago. Modern civil society is not structured by kinship and the power of fathers; in the modern world, women are subordinated to men *as men*, or to men as a fraternity. The original contract takes place after the political defeat of the father and creates modern *fraternal patriarchy*.

Another reason for the omission of the story of the sexual contract is that conventional approaches to the classic texts, whether those of mainstream political theorists or their socialist critics, give a misleading picture of a distinctive feature of the civil society created through the original pact. Patriarchal civil society is divided into two spheres, but attention is directed to one sphere only. The story of the social contract is treated as an account of the creation of the public sphere of civil freedom. The other, private, sphere is not seen as politically relevant. Marriage and the marriage contract are, therefore, also deemed politically irrelevant. To ignore the marriage contract is to ignore half the original contract. In the classic texts . . . the sexual contract is displaced onto the marriage contract. The displacement creates a difficulty in retrieving and recounting the lost story. All too easily, the impression can be given that the sexual contract and the social contract are two separate, albeit related, contracts, and that the sexual contract concerns the private sphere. Patriarchy then appears to have no relevance to the public world. On the contrary, patriarchal right extends throughout civil society. The employment contract and (what I shall call) the prostitution contract, both of which are entered into in the public, capitalist market, uphold men's right as firmly as the marriage contract. The two spheres of civil society are at once separate and inseparable. The public realm cannot be fully understood in the absence of the private sphere, and, similarly, the meaning of the original contract is misinterpreted without both, mutually dependent, halves of the story. Civil freedom depends on patriarchal right. . . .

Some knowledge of the story of the sexual contract helps explain why singular problems arise about contracts to which women are a party. The problems are never mentioned in most discussions of the classic texts or by contemporary contract theorists. Feminists have been pointing out the peculiarities of the marriage contract for at least a century and a half, but to no avail. The standard commentaries on the classic stories of the original contract do not usually mention that women are *excluded* from the original pact. Men make the original contract. The device of the state of nature is used to explain why, given the characteristics of the inhabitants of the natural condition, entry into the original contract is a rational act. The crucial point that is omitted is that the inhabitants are sexually differentiated and, for all the classic writers (except Hobbes), a difference in rationality follows from natural sexual difference. Commentaries on the texts gloss over the fact that the classic theorists construct a patriarchal account of masculinity and femininity, of what it is to be men and women. Only masculine beings are endowed with the attributes and capacities necessary to enter into contracts, the most important of which is ownership of property in the person; only men, that is to say, are 'individuals'.

In the natural condition 'all men are born free' and are equal to each other; they are 'individuals'. This presupposition of contract doctrine generates a profound problem: how in such a condition can the government of one man by another ever be legitimate; how can political right exist? Only one answer is possible without denying the initial assumption of freedom and equality. The relationship must arise through agreement and . . . contract is seen as the paradigm of free agreement. But women are not born free; women have no natural freedom. The classic pictures of the state of nature also contain an order of subjection—between men and women. . . . Sexual difference is political difference; sexual difference is the difference between freedom and subjection. Women are not party to the original contract through which men transform their natural freedom into the security of civil freedom. Women are the subject of the contract. The (sexual) contract is the vehicle through which men transform their natural right over women into the security of civil patriarchal right. . . .

Surprisingly little attention has been given to the connection between the original contract—which is generally agreed to be a political fiction—and actual contracts. The social contract, so the story goes, creates a society in which individuals can make contracts secure in the knowledge that their actions are regulated by civil law and that, if necessary, the state will enforce their agreements. Actual contracts thus appear to exemplify the freedom that individuals exercise when they make the original pact. According to contemporary contract theorists, social conditions are such that it is always reasonable for individuals to exercise their freedom and enter into the marriage contract or employment contract or even, according to some classic and contemporary writers, a (civil) slave contract. Another way of reading the story . . . is that the social contract enables individuals voluntarily to subject themselves to the state and civil law; freedom becomes obedience and, in exchange, protection is provided. On this reading, the actual contracts of everyday life also mirror the original contract, but now they involve an exchange of obedience for protection; they create what I shall call *civil mastery* and *civil subordination*.

Since women were excluded from the original contract, but rather were the subjects of at least one portion of that contract—the hidden portion—Pateman argues that it is not surprising that women's status as parties to actual contract is somewhat ambiguous. Cornell explains Pateman's argument thus:

D. Cornell, 'The Philosophy of the Limit: Systems Theory and Feminist Legal Reform', in D. Cornell, M. Rosenfeld, and D. Carlson (eds.), *Deconstruction and the Possibility of Justice* (New York, Routledge, 1992), 73–4

Carole Pateman . . . has argued that the so-called social contract, which has continued to serve as a useful fiction in liberal jurisprudence, is itself yet another patriarchal construct. . . . for Pateman the very basis of social order is an implicit *sexual contract* that gives men access to women. Once this sexual contract is noted, it is then possible to give a different meaning to the public/private distinction as it has been traditionally developed in social contract theory. For Pateman, access to women including violent access to women, is rendered beyond the scope of the terms of the male social pact. Contract only regulates relations between men, not between men and women. Implicit in this idea of the contract is that what men do with women is considered "private" and, thus, not to be regulated by the state. After all, what rational man would even hypothetically agree to have his "affairs" with women regulated? Women, by definition, cannot be equal to men under this arrangement. They can never be subjects of the social contract; they can only be subjected to it. Thus, Pateman argues that gender consolidation influences our conceptualization of civil society. The political significance of Pateman's analysis is that we cannot hope to change our social order if we do not take sexual difference into account. As Pateman explains, "To argue that patriarchy is best confronted by endeavouring to render sexual difference politically irrelevant is to accept the view that the civil (public) realm and the 'individual' are uncontaminated by patriarchal subordination." Obviously, the actual law of most

Western democracies has changed, allowing women to enter into contracts in their own name. Pateman, however, is suggesting that this change alone does not alter the patriarchal "foundation" of the myths which justify civil society. If Pateman's analysis is correct, it is not surprising that Mary Joe Frug could so graphically show the masculine bias that continues to underpin much of our current doctrine in contract law.

Note

Frug's feminist analysis of contract doctrine appears in *Postmodern Legal Feminism* (New York, Routledge, 1992) and is extracted in Chapters 11 and 12.

Pateman herself neatly summarizes the ambiguity of women's position in relation to contract.

C. Pateman, 'Contract, the Individual and Slavery', in *The Sexual Contract* (Cambridge, Polity Press, 1988), 60

Women are property, but also persons; women are held both to possess and to lack the capacities required for contract—and contract demands that their womanhood be both denied and affirmed.

The argument is also developed by Pateman into a deeper challenge to contract as the 'paradigm of free agreement'. The problem stems, she argues, from the treatment of individuals who are separate and isolated as the base unit of society. This leads her to question the conventional understanding of exchange itself.

Pateman 'Contract, the Individual and Slavery', 955–9

The first question that must be asked is why contract is seen as the paradigm of free agreement. The answer can best be ascertained by starting with the 'individual' as found in Hobbes' theory and in contemporary contractarianism, who is seen as naturally complete in himself. That is to say, the boundaries that separate one individual from another are so tightly drawn that an individual is pictured as existing without any relationships with others. The individual's capacities and attributes owe nothing to any other individual or to any social relationship; they are his alone. The contractarian individual necessarily is the proprietor of his person and his attributes, or, in C. B. Macpherson's famous description, he is a possessive individual. The individual owns his body and his capacities as pieces of property, just as he owns material property. According to this view, each individual can and must see the world and other individuals only from the perspective of his subjective assessment of how best to protect his property, or, as it is often put, from the perspective of his self-interest. . . .

The individual's task is thus to ensure that his property right is not infringed. Individual self-protection is the problem that has to be solved in the state of nature—and the solution is contract. More precisely, since the problem has to be solved for every individual, it is the problem of social order . . . , and the solution is the original contract. But why *contract*?

If the individual owns his capacities, he stands in the same external relation to this intimate property as to any other. To become the owner of the property in his person, the individual must create a relation between himself and his property, he must take possession of himself and put his will into his person and capacities to make them 'his'. Similarly, if the individual has no natural relation with any other, then all relationships must be conventional, the creation of individuals themselves; individuals must will their social relationships into existence. They do this if, and only if, they can protect their property by creating a relationship. A necessary condition of such protection is that each individual recognize the others as property owners like himself. Without this recognition others will appear to the individual as mere (potential) property, not owners of property, and so equality disappears. Mutual recognition by property owners is achieved through contract: 'contract presupposes that the parties entering it recognize each other as persons and property owners' [Hegel] . . .

If property is to be protected, one individual can have access to the property of another only with the latter's agreement. An individual will allow the use of his property by another, or rent it out or sell it, only if his protection is not infringed, if it is to his advantage. If this is the case for two individuals they will make a contract with each other. Both parties to the contract enter on the same basis, as property owners who have the common purpose, or common will, to use each other's property to mutual advantage.

Individuals recognize each other as property owners by making mutual use of, or *exchanging*, their property. Exchange is at the heart of contract; as Hobbes states, 'all contract is mutual translation, or change of right.' Each individual gains through the exchange—neither would alienate his property unless that were the case—so the exchange is therefore equal. Socialist critics of the employment contract and feminist critics of the marriage contract have attacked the claim that, if two individuals make a contract, the fact that the contract has been made is sufficient to show that the exchange must be equal. The critics point out that, if one party is in an inferior position (the worker or the woman), then he or she has no choice but to agree to disadvantageous terms offered by the superior party. However, socialist and feminist criticism of the inequality of the participants in the employment and marriage contracts takes for granted the character of the exchange itself. What does the 'exchange' in the contracts in which I am interested consist in? What exactly is exchanged?

In principle, the exchange could take a variety of forms and any kind of property could be exchanged, but the contracts that have a prominent place in classic social contract theory are not only about material goods, but property in the peculiar sense of property in the person, and they involve an exchange of obedience for protection. This exchange does not immediately have much connection with the pictures conjured up in stories of the state of nature, in which two individuals bargain over property in the woods and, for example, one exchanges some of the nuts he has gathered for part of a rabbit killed by the other. Talk of 'exchange' can be misleading in the context of property in the person. Contract theory is primarily about a way of creating social relationships constituted by subordination, not about exchange. To be sure, exchange is involved, but again, what is at issue is 'exchange'—or more accurately, two exchanges—in a special sense.

First, there is the exchange constitutive of contract and a social relationship. Unless certain signs of the commitment of the will are seen as property, this exchange does not involve property. Rather, the contract is concluded and the relationship is brought into being through the exchange of words, that is, through the performance of a speech act (or the exchange of other signs, such as signatures). Once the words are said, the contract is sealed and individuals stand to each other in a new relationship. Thus, in the social contract, natural male individuals transform themselves into civil individuals (citizens); in the employment contract, men turn themselves into employer and worker; and, in the marriage contract, women become wives and men become husbands by virtue of saying 'I do'. . . . The second 'exchange' could not be more different from the first. The new relationship is structured through time by a permanent exchange between the two parties, the exchange of obedience for protection. . . . The peculiarity of this exchange is that one party to the contract, who provides protection, has the right to determine how the other party will act to fulfill their side of the exchange. . . . , as an . . . illustration of this point, consider the employment contract.

I noted earlier that the contractarian conception of social life implies that there is contract 'all the way down'; social life is nothing more than contracts between individuals. Economic life should thus be structured accordingly. The fact that contractarians treat the employment contract as the exemplary contract suggests that economic institutions provide an example of their ideal. But in a capitalist firm, as Coase's neo-classical analysis makes clear, if a workman moves from one department to another, this is not because he has freely bargained with the employer and made a new contract; he moves 'because he is ordered to do so'. A firm is not, as it were, a contractarian society in miniature, constituted through a continual series of discrete contracts; as Coase writes, 'for this series of contracts is substituted one.' The employer contracts only once with each worker. In the employment contract, the worker 'for a certain remuneration (which may be fixed or fluctuating) agrees to obey the direction of an entrepreneur *within certain limits*. The essence of the contract is that it should only state the limits to the powers of the entrepreneur'. Coase notes that if there were no limits the contract would be a contract of voluntary slavery. Coase also emphasizes that, the longer the period for which the employer contracts to use the services of the worker, the more desirable it is that the contract should not be specific about what the employer can command the worker to do; it is the employer's prerogative to direct the worker in his work, and, for Coase, this is the essence of the employment contract. Contract creates a relation of subordination.

Notes

1. Pateman's analysis of employment and marriage as relationships is strongly reminiscent of Weber's concept of 'status contracts' discussed in Chapter 2. The difference is that Pateman's critique of individualism, developed through a feminist analysis of the 'original contract', leads her to conclude that the permanent exchange necessarily creates a relationship of subordination, not of equality. In that sense, Pateman adds to Weber's social analysis.

2. The message of Pateman's work is of the important connection between the relationships which constitute the basis of social order and political legitimacy (the idea that we consent to be governed) and the contractual relationships which structure so much of everyday life. One cannot be understood in isolation from the other. In other words, state and market are irrevocably intertwined, a point developed at length by Hugh Collins in *The Law of Contract*, 2nd edn. (London, Butterworths, 1986).

3. A further important strand of Pateman's work concerns the role of consent, both in theories of political obligation and in the realities of women's lives (e.g. consent and rape). See further 'Women and Consent', in *The Disorder of Women* (Cambridge, Polity Press, 1989), 71ff. These ideas are also explored by Wiegers, 'Economic Analysis of Law and "Private Ordering": A Feminist Critique', (1992) 43 *U. Toronto LJ* 170, extracted in Chapter 2.

III. GOVERNMENT AND CONTRACT

The state/contract relationship operates not only at the ideological level but also on a much more mundane plane. The state makes use of the mechanism of contract in order to participate within the market order. Arrowsmith offers a review of government use of contracts in the United Kingdom.

S. Arrowsmith, *Civil Liability and Public Authorities* (Winteringham, Earlsgate Press, 1992), 45–9

The government today makes considerable use of contract in carrying out its policies and activities. First, contract is used in many situations in which it is also used in the private sphere. Thus the government employs many servants to carry out its business, and the relationship between the government and these individuals is often contractual, though there are also important cases where it may not be . . . . Public bodies also make contracts to obtain goods and services from outside suppliers—office equipment, weapons for the army, and advertising and construction services are just a few examples of the huge range of products and services normally obtained from independent contractors. These contracts, called contracts of procurement, are of enormous economic significance: in 1984 the central government market was estimated to be worth close to £15000 million (Turpin, *Government Procurement and Contracts* (1989) at p.x). They have become more important in recent years at both central and local level, as there has been increased emphasis on "contracting out" as the best method of obtaining value for money, both at central level (see Turpin at pp. 206–207 and 257) and at local government level, where obligations to contract out many functions have been imposed by legislation . . . . Obviously the scope of modern government's activity makes its contractual activities as employer and as purchaser of considerable importance, both to the large number of individuals engaged by the government, or who seek government business or employment, and to the public generally, who pay for these contracts and stand to benefit from their performance.

Most contracts of employment and procurement are freely negotiated in that, first, there is no legal requirement to deal with the government at all, and, second, terms are set by negotiation, although, of course, the government, like some powerful private persons, may often have considerable bargaining power in practice. Thus, the terms of employment contracts, for example, are often determined through collective bargaining . . . . Procurement contracts are generally made on standard forms drawn up by the government after consultation with suppliers' representatives, and the price and some other terms determined by competitive procedures or negotiation with individual suppliers . . . . It has often been pointed out that, for the central government, at least, there is no need to use the market or even the contractual method to obtain the services of employees and independent contractors, since it has legislative powers at its disposal. Contract is chosen, however, as a device which generally enables government needs to be met, whilst also providing a useful framework to ensure that those dealing with the government receive fair treatment. The only case where the government's legislative powers are regularly invoked in peacetime to obtain its needs is in relation to the acquisition of land; clearly this is necessary because of the relatively unique nature of land, which means that needs cannot be adequately met through the market. Legislative powers are, of course, invoked in war time, providing both for military conscription and an adequate supply of other goods and services from the private sector (as to the latter see the former Ministry of Supply Act 1939 s. 7(3)). . . . there is also some legislative direction on how the terms of certain types of contracts are to be determined.

As well as purchasing, the government frequently makes contracts to sell or supply goods or services. For example, contract governs its relationship with its tenants, whether of council houses or business premises. There is also often a contract between the government and the user of a public service—for example, of public recreation facilities. Public utilities such as gas, water or electricity, whether in public hands, or in private hands as at present, have since the nineteenth century generally been subject to statutory obligations to supply their products to certain persons, with the terms of supply often regulated . . . . However, the courts have tended, in these cases, to say that the supply relationship is not a contractual one . . . .

A rather different use of contract in the public sphere is as a method for regulating behaviour, a use which has attracted attention for the important constitutional issues which it raises . . . . The traditional method of regulation is by direct legislative prescription backed by legislative sanctions: for example, a fine, imprisonment or loss of benefits such as a right to trade. The government may also, however, use its contractual powers to control behaviour in various ways. We may distinguish between contracts of which the main object is regulation of subject behaviour, and the use of contract bargaining power to regulate matters which are not connected with the main object of the contract.

Illustrations of the first category are licensing agreements which create a contractual relationship between the government and a trader, in which rules for the protection of the public are laid out in the licence as contractual conditions. In such cases legal sanctions for enforcement derive from the legal force of the contract. An example is the case of contracts awarded to companies wishing to operate on the independent television network. . . . Local authorities have also used the method of the contractual licence to regulate the conduct of market traders, with sanctions for non-compliance being, for example, the termination or suspension of the licence under the terms of the contract. . . .

The government also uses its contract power to further policies which have nothing to do with the main object of the contract in question. An illustration is the use the government has made of its enormous influence as a purchaser of goods and services from the private sector to induce compliance with government policy . . . . Perhaps the most famous example was the government's use of procurement power between 1975 and 1979 in relation to its anti-inflation policy—firms paying wages regarded as excessive were refused government business . . . . Compliance with government policies may be enforced not only by refusing contract awards but also by imposing conditions in contracts which are awarded. For example, compliance with existing statutory obligations to refrain from racial discrimination has been made a term of many government contracts . . . . Procurement power is used also to achieve "secondary" policies in ways which are not aimed at changing individual behaviour—so that they cannot really be classified as "regulatory"—but which forward some secondary policy simply by their implementation. For example, awards have in the past been made to domestic suppliers to maintain a domestic capability, or to prison or sheltered workshops to maintain the viability of these institutions . . . .

The importance of procurement as an instrument for achieving secondary policies has declined recently as the United Kingdom government has increasingly chosen to emphasise value for money as the main objective of procurement. In addition some (though not all) secondary policies are now precluded by European Community law . . . and, in international law, by the General Agreement on Trade and Tariffs. Domestic legislation, as well as common law developments, have also placed restrictions on local government's powers to take account of non-commercial considerations . . . .

Finally, it may be observed that "contractual type" arrangements have been used increasingly in recent years in the UK to regulate and formalise the relationship between certain government agencies, notably in relation to the "next steps" programme. In some of these cases the contractual analogy has an important symbolic function as an expression of the formality of the relationship and of the independence of the entities concerned. . . . these relationships do not, however, give rise to private law contractual relationships . . .

Notes

1. Some 'public services' are provided on the basis of contract, such as those provided by British Telecom. However, even after privatization, there is nothing in legislation such as the Water Act 1989 or the Gas Act 1986 to suggest that the *ordinary consumer* is supplied with these commodities by the utilities on the basis of a contract.

2. Arrowsmith describes in more detail the 'next steps' programme.

Arrowsmith, *Civil Liability and Public Authorities*, 52

The aim of this programme is to separate the policy making functions of central government from the function of implementing, or administering, decided policies, its objective being to increase efficiency in management: it is expected that the separation will produce better monitoring and accountability in relation to the management function, will raise the status of civil service managers and will give managers greater autonomy in their sphere of expertise. To this end in the last three years a number of separate agencies have been set up within government departments, each headed by a Chief Executive, to be responsible for the administration of policies set at the political level. The most famous example is the Benefits Agency, set up from 1991 to administer benefits which come under the auspices of the Department of Social Security. The relationship between the minister and agency is governed by a "framework document", similar to a contract: the contractual analogy is seen as a suitable basis for the governance of the relationship. However, it seems clear that there is no private law contractual relationship between a Minister and the "next step" agencies, since these agencies have no legal identity which is separate from that of the Minister. As indicated earlier, the framework document serves primarily as a symbol of the intended formality of the relationship and of the perceived independence of the parties to it; their position is intended as far as possible to be analogous to that of parties to a private law commercial contract, even though there do not exist parallel methods of legal enforcement.

Note

See further D. Goldsworthy, *Setting Up Next Steps* (London, HMSO, 1991).

3. The role of the 'contractual type' arrangements which are not enforceable in regulating behaviour and in particular in building a market framework into bureaucratic agencies will be assessed in more detail in the final section of this chapter, which examines certain recent ideological uses of the 'contract' figure.

The typical government contract is a long-term relationship, such as a procurement contract, under which quantities of goods are obtained from suppliers as and when needed. This situation resembles that of Macaulay's business contractors, and many of the same principles of co-operative action apply. According to C. Turpin (*Government Procurement and Contracts*, 2nd edn. (Harlow, Longman, 1989), 70–1: 'The aims and principles of government procurement require a middle way between a detached, impersonal conduct of business and an almost symbiotic relationship.' Relational contract values must therefore operate within such a context, although informed by the special nature of the relationship between a public body and a private individual.

As is well known, the years since the election of Margaret Thatcher's first government in 1979 have seen a radical programme of privatization of public services and public utilities. This means that government may now be procuring more public services on the basis of contract, out of the private sector. One of the most controversial recent examples of this is the introduction of private prisons, run on the basis of an Agreement between the Home Office and security firms such as Group 4. Such an arrangement means that a public function, undertaken for the protection of the public on the basis of the hierarchical structures of public sector management, is now run on the basis of a contract between government and a private-sector firm. Public attention was attracted to the nature of these arrangements by the report of the Chief Inspector of Prisons, Judge Stephen Tumim, on The Wolds Remand Prison, published in August 1993. Judge Tumim criticized certain 'weaknesses' in the Agreement (*Wolds Remand Prison*, Report by HM Chief Inspector of Prisons (London, Home Office, 1993), 1) which resulted in the remand prisoners at the Wolds leading rather purposeless lives. He also expressed surprise that after thirteen months of operation the details of the Agreement remained unclear, for example, as to who was responsible for the cost of vandal damage. The absence of a system of financial control also made it impossible to assess whether the privately managed prison was offering value for money, which has, of course, been the central, publicly expressed objective of the Conservative Government's privatization programme (see para. 7.06 of the Report).

Two interesting points emerge from this. First, issues of public policy, such as the proper treatment of remand prisoners and consequently the underlying purpose of imprisonment on remand, are expressed in the language of contract rather than the language of public policy. Second, it would appear that the evidence of incompleteness and uncertainty identified in relation to business contracts by Macaulay, Beale, and Dugdale is not unique to the private sector, but appears to be tolerated by the contracting parties in relationships within the public sector.

IV. CONTRACT, CITIZENSHIP, AND THE CONSTITUTION

A. NHS Contracts

In *The Contracting State*, Ian Harden gives a detailed analysis of the recent increase in the use of contractual frameworks for the delivery of public services by government, including the creation of the National Health Service internal market, the use of compulsory competitive tendering by local authorities, and the next steps programme. He argues that the use of contract in the public services domain has two distinct facets.

I. Harden, *The Contracting State* (Buckingham, Open University Press, 1992), pp. xi–xii

One is the pursuit of specific political objectives. In relation to these, the language of contract has a largely ideological significance. 'Contract' connotes individual rights and freedom of choice. It is also essential to the functioning of the market system. Hence it is associated with consumer sovereignty over decisions about what shall be produced and with efficiency in the process of supply. These are things that are of fundamental importance in terms of constitutional values. However, 'contract' does not refer to a clear legal framework which can be applied directly, or by analogy, so as to realize them in the context of public services.

In contrast, the other aspect of the contractual approach is a genuine potential for promoting constitutional values through an institutional separation of functions. Specifically, responsibility for deciding what services there shall be is distinguished from responsibility for delivering the services. This separation of the roles of 'purchaser' and 'provider' offers the opportunity not only to pursue economy, efficiency and effectiveness, but also to enhance both individual rights and the accountability of government for policy decisions. However, the contractual approach cannot bring about these results by itself. It can do so only as part of a broader legal and constitutional framework for public services which, at present, does not exist. The ambiguity of the book's title reflects the danger that results. Without an appropriate framework, the contractual approach may lead to a contraction of public services, or to a loss of their 'public' aspect.

It is the first rather than the second of these two facets which has so far been more highly developed. The creation of an internal market within the NHS is a good example. The role of contract under the NHS reforms is explained by Longley.

D. Longley, *Public Law and Health Service Accountability* (Buckingham, Open University Press, 1992), 42–3

In an effort to induce greater efficiency in the use of resources, the main focus of the reforms has been the creation of a 'provider or internal market'. The pivot of the new organization is the imposed use of contract as the vehicle which underpins the implementation of policy and provision of health services from April 1991. The contract mechanism is seen as having two main advantages. It separates the role and the responsibilities of purchasers of health care from that of providers. Just as importantly, by formally setting out criteria and targets for delivery, it is seen to provide a means of focusing both purchaser and provider attention on the quality of health care and supplying a catalyst for improvement.

There are significant differences between the private law contract which is the subject of this book and many of the contracts which are concluded within the framework of the NHS internal market. The most distinctive contractual mechanism is the 'NHS contract', governed by s. 4 of the National Health Service and Community Care Act 1990, the main legislative plank of the Conservative Government's NHS reforms. NHS contracts are concluded between District Health Authorities, now responsible for 'purchasing' the health-care services which are required by those living in the area and fund-holding General Practitioners on the one hand, and health service bodies outside the health authorities management structure—NHS Trusts—on the other hand. As Hughes comments, these are 'contracts' which differ from the classical private law model in many respects: the introduction of NHS contracts is not the product of market forces, but of legislative innovation. They were not a response to the pressures of the market, but an artificial construct designed to simulate market conditions (D. Hughes, 'The Reorganisation of the National Health Service: The Rhetoric and Reality of the Internal Market', (1991) 54 *MLR* 88 at 90). Moreover, normal contractual enforcement mechanisms do not apply in the case of NHS contracts, for these are expressly stated by the legislation not to give rise to any contractual duties or liabilities at law.

Longley, *Public Law and Health Service Accountability*, 46–8

Such contracts are ultimately to be enforced not through the courts, but through arbitration powers exercised by the Secretary of State or a person appointed by him. . . .

Guidance from the NHS management executive on resolving disputes states that all NHS contracts should be constructed so as to minimize the risk of dispute, but should include clauses for agreed arbitration if either party believes a contract has been broken. The parties to the contract should specify the arbitrator, who will usually be the Regional General Manager, but there appears to be no obstacle to the parties agreeing to private arbitration. They may also agree the terms on which arbitration may take place, including 'pendulum' arbitration where the arbitrator can only accept one or other of the parties' position in full. This has the effect of forcing any compromises to be made before arguments are put to the arbitrator. Arbitration clauses do not, however, alter the right of either party to use the formal dispute resolution procedure where informal procedures have failed.

Unusually, arbitration powers extend to pre-contractual negotiation if either party believes the other is making use of an unfair advantage. Where disputes arise over the terms of proposed contracts there is no agreed arbitration system. In that case, to obtain an impartial view of the proposed terms both parties are expected to seek the assistance of their Regional General Manager as conciliator. Once contract negotiations have begun neither party can withdraw without the permission of the other or the Secretary of State. This procedure is radically different from any in private law where regulation of this stage of contracting is unknown . . . . The executive sees these arrangements, supported by a shared objective of securing effective health services as reducing the need for use of the formal dispute resolution process.

Where there is no apparent alternative to involving the formal procedure disputes will be referred to the Secretary of State. Cases where the Secretary of

State decides to appoint an adjudicator to resolve a dispute are governed by The National Health Service Contracts (Dispute Resolution) Regulations (1991 SI 1991/725). The adjudicator may adopt a written procedure and may consult anyone whom he considers will assist him. The principles of natural justice are observed in the procedures. Each party is entitled to make representations, to see and comment on those made by the other party and to make observations on the results of any consultation. The adjudicator's decision has to be written and must be accompanied by reasons. Any determination of the Secretary of State, who has the power to vary the terms of the contract or to bring it to an end, is final and binding, although the above dispute-resolution powers are judicially reviewable. . . .

. . . there is a discretion not to delegate formal disputes to an adjudicator in which case the Regulations do not apply. Support is lent to this view by the fact that the Secretary of State is potentially an interested party rather than an independent arbiter in disputes because of his constitutional position in relation to health service authorities . . . .

The effect of the above powers is that the actual degree of contractual freedom of purchasers and providers is ultimately determined centrally by executive decision, not by the market. The true nature of the contract mechanism in the health service therefore is not an undertaking of any commercial risk but merely another strategem for administrative planning. It is important that this is recognized because without the elements of risk and liability normally associated with contracting and competition, the growth between purchasers and providers of informal and therefore unaccountable 'orderings' to protect their mutual interest is likely to be sustained.

Notes

1. See further on the use of contract in the regulatory context, M. Freedland, 'Government by Contract and Public Law', [1994] *PL* 86; N. Lewis, 'The Citizen's Charter and Next Steps: A New Way of Governing', (1993) 64 *Pol. Q* 361; N. Lewis, 'Reviewing Change in Government: New Public Management and Next Steps' [1994] *PL* 105.
2. For a further discussion of anti-competitive collusion in the context of the NHS internal market, see F. Miller, 'Competition Law and Anti-Competitive Professional Behaviour Affecting Health Care', (1992) 55 *MLR* 453.

Hughes suggests ('The Reorganisation of the National Health Service', 90) that this type of *sui generis* mechanism, where the 'contract' is something more than just a symbol or a metaphor, but less than a fully binding and enforceable exchange of promises as per the classic private law model, may well set a trend for the introduction of market conditions within areas of 'public provision not amenable to privatisation' (cf. the discussion of the Wolds Prison Report in Section III above).

On the other hand, Harden's conclusion is that the use of contracts to regulate the provision of public services is some way from achieving the new constitutional settlement which he is looking for.

Harden, *The Contracting State*, 77–8

The mechanism of contract can itself play a valuable role, within a broader legal and constitutional framework. Both accountability and individual rights can be promoted by an organizational separation of decisions as to what services there should be from the delivery of those services, and by these responsibilities being negotiated in a binding agreement between the organizations concerned.

Harden proposes the creation of a new generally applicable 'public law contract' which could provide the basis for the organizational independence and accountability which should, he argues, be the real objective in public service provision.

Harden, *The Contracting State*, 75

Such a public law contract, with its own principles governing formation, pricing and dispute-resolution, is appropriate to a particular kind of independence for public sector organizations. That is one in which express secondary contractual provisions are dependent for their interpretation and application on shared values and purposes that go beyond those of—even long-term—commercial self-interest.

Yet again the analysis carries us back to the principles of relational contracting, and the values identified by Macneil (see Ch. 2). Perhaps, therefore, what is needed is not an artificial split between public and private law but a law of contract which is sensitive to context and to the specific and distinctive characteristics of different types of relationship. From that perspective, contract may have much more to offer public law than if a one-dimensional concept of individual autonomy and exchange is used.

B. Contract and Citizenship

There is evidence that the contractual metaphor is being carried some way beyond the simulation of market conditions within bureaucracies such as the NHS and the BBC (which has generated its own internal market without need for legislative intervention, in the form of 'Producer Choice'). The evidence can be drawn from the so-called Citizen's Charter, 'a programme of legislative and administrative reform directed towards ensuring quality in the services delivered to the public by central government, local authorities, the NHS and the public utilities' (A. Barron and C. Scott, 'The Citizen's

Charter Programme', (1992) 55 *MLR* 526). Barron and Scott describe the programme, set out in a July 1991 White Paper (Cm. 1599), as a 'blending of New Right concerns with restricting the power of bureaucracy and extending individual choice, with more widespread concerns to make government bureaucracies more responsive to the needs of users' (ibid.). A key to understanding the rhetoric and meaning of the Citizen's Charter is to uncover the conception of citizenship implicit in the programme, a conception which Barron and Scott argue is closely related to contract, and derived from a core concern with individual liberty to be found in the work of F. A. Hayek (see *The Road to Serfdom*, first published in 1944).

A. Barron and C. Scott, 'The Citizen's Charter Programme', (1992) 55 *MLR* 526 at 543–5

. . . the New Right's panacea for the perceived inefficiency and ineffectiveness of the public sector has been to implement measures designed to introduce market rationality into processes of public decision making. So far as service provision is concerned, these measures have been justified on the basis that they are calculated to improve the quality of the service received by the user. The White Paper adopts this line, emphasising the benefits of marketisation for the user as the reason for, rather than merely a possible outcome of, public sector reform. But this, we would argue, involves a series of discursive manoeuvres, the implications of which for the theory and practice of citizenship in the UK are more far-reaching than might appear at first sight. Firstly, the White Paper achieves a subtle redefinition of the user as a consumer: the recipient of services, the provision of which has hitherto been justified by a conception of citizenship as entitlement based on need, is reconceived as a paying customer, who as such is entitled to expect the level of quality which would be guaranteed were the provider constrained by the pressure of competition in the marketplace. The second, and more interesting, rhetorical move is that which resurrects the category of the citizen in order then to graft it onto the identity of this consumer, who as such is not the bearer of needs, but an economic actor. What this suggests, in turn, is that the consumer's legitimate expectation of quality in the context of contracts for services may in fact be akin to a constitutional *right* where those services are provided by public sector agencies. The ideological cement which constitutes the link between citizen and consumer is the ideal of freedom and, ultimately, it is in respect of the association of markets with freedom that the concept of citizenship has mutated into a useful technique for the legitimation of the government's strategy with regard to public services.

The insistence upon the right to liberty as the fundamental right of the citizen, coupled with the claim that liberty is best secured through participation in the process of exchange, suggests that the insulation of markets from 'coercive' state intervention is itself an aspect of, rather than a retreat from, the ideal of citizenship. It carries with it, further, a coherent justification for the provision of those services which remain in public hands: their *raison d'être* is to satisfy the wants/preferences of the citizen *as if* the latter were a consumer in the market-place, and in this way to discharge a *contractual* obligation to the citizen. The relationship between state and citizen is implicitly conceptualised in the Citizen's Charter programme in terms of a contractual nexus; services are pro-vided by the state as a *quid pro quo* for the taxes paid by the citizen, and this of course permits a further link to be forged between the tax yield and the level of provision. Indeed, contract provides the model for a whole series of relation-ships structuring the provision of public services which hitherto have been understood in bureaucratic or organisation terms: those between state and (public or private sector) provider, provider and employee, and provider and user. In each case, the device of the contract is intended both to enable the expression of consumer choices and to discipline the provider: it is a means of imposing obligations as well as a recognition of rights. . . .

. . . it is chiefly through an appeal to the capacity of the service provider/user 'contract' to empower users and thus enhance citizenship that the programme is explained and justified. The implications of this argument merit further clarifi-cation. Firstly, the service contract individualises the right to be served, and to object when the standard of service is unsatisfactory: the collective protest is displaced by the individual complaint. On one level, this ignores the structural imbalance of power that may exist between provider and user, the effects of which can only effectively be dealt with, it would seem, through the interven-tion of regulatory authorities. But more fundamentally, its effect is to detach the ideal of citizenship from active participation by the citizen within the institu-tions of the state, as well as from membership of a political community, where the latter signifies a political entity unified by reference to a finite set of common purposes and shared needs. For the Right, community, if it means anything at all, means a conglomeration of equally autonomous and rational agents, each pursuing her/his own ends within a common framework of rules designed to preserve the market order. . . . The function of politics is to facilitate participation in this—private—realm, and in that way to make citizenship meaningful. The right to participate in political life is merely an instrument for the achievement of that end.

Finally, to emphasise the satisfaction of consumer preferences as the primary objective of public service provision seems implicitly to deny that the moral basis of such provision, or citizenship itself, could be entitlement based on need: it therefore suggests that the meeting of needs may no longer be regarded as essential to the ideal of citizenship. The argument against a needs-based conception of welfare is primarily driven by antipathy to the professional determination of need within bureaucratic structures. . . . If persons are regarded as having 'needs' rather than 'wants,' then they must be assumed to be characterised by dependence rather than autonomy. Yet, for the Hayekian liberal, the equality of persons consists precisely in the capacity of each person for autonomous action: the capacity to choose implies, firstly, that a need can only be a preference in disguise (ie, that which is needed is in fact the object of a choice); and secondly, that the subject is prior to the objects of its choices. Indeed, the achievement of contemporary New Right thinking has been to reinterpret the identity of the citizen in terms of the capacity to own and exchange property, and to reduce the rights of the citizen to one: the right to buy.

In a sense we have come full circle, from the original contract from which political legitimacy is derived to a contract which structures the entitlements of citizens. The use of contract as a surrogate for managerial techniques and for conceptions of citizenship demonstrates the enduring appeal of this doctrinal figure, and represents an appropriate point at which we can leave the introductory framework of the first three chapters and embark upon the substantive discussion which will occupy the remainder of this book.

Questions

1. What additional dimension does the work of Pateman add to traditional social contract analysis?
2. How, if at all, has the role of contract changed in the public domain?

PART II

The Creation of Contracts

4

The Formatio

long insisted o
enforceability
Anson—see
from the d
v. Carbo
the do
imp
juri

I. INTRODUC

We shall begin this chapter, which examines the various
formation of contracts, by looking at the so-called threshold req
for enforceability, termed intention to create legal relations. Second,
take a brief glance at the nature of the pre-contractual relationship, highlighting a possible contradiction between doctrine and practice. Finally,
we cover the conventional ground of formation of contracts, using cases
and extracts to illustrate some of the ways in which judges determine
whether or not a contract exists.

II. INTENTION TO CREATE LEGAL RELATIONS

Conventional contract doctrine states that it is a condition of the enforceability of an agreement that the parties should have intended to create
legal relations. Intention will be presumed in the context of agreements
made in a commercial context, unless clear words are used to rebut that
presumption and to carry an agreement outside the reach of legal enforceability. In the case of agreements made in a social or domestic context, it
will normally be presumed that there is no intention to create legal relations, although in practice the courts have generally proved willing to
enforce agreements which have already been executed (or performed) and
where one party has undertaken a serious act of detrimental reliance (e.g. a
widowed parent sells his or her home with a view to buying a joint home
with a child, but the arrangement breaks down).

A. Intimate and Domestic Relationships and the Law

The *locus classicus* of the judicial doctrine of intention to create legal relations is *Balfour* v. *Balfour*. It is this case which contains the clearest assertion of the requirement of an intention to create legal relations as a test of
the enforceability of an agreement. However, certain academic writers had

the requirement of intention as a basic criterion of (e.g. nineteenth-century writers such as Leake, Pollock, and S. Hedley, (1985) 5 *OJLS* 391 at 403ff), and there is evidence istinction drawn between 'mere puffs' and 'promises' in *Carlill ic Smoke Ball Co.* (Section II (B) below) of judicial recognition of ctrine. It is accepted that intention to create legal relations was an rt from the civil law systems of continental Europe, whose eminent sts exercised a considerable influence upon those responsible for the ormulation in the nineteenth century of a body of general principles of the law of contract (see the extract from Gordley in Ch. 2). The view is also well supported that the common law has no need of the concept of intention, since the application of the bargain principle through the doctrine of consideration gives courts all the tools they need in order to sort out the enforceable from the unenforceable promises. While convincing in themselves, these arguments do not explain why in practice the doctrine of intention to create legal relations was given a judicial boost in *Balfour* v. *Balfour* and why it is now regarded as an immovable aspect of modern doctrine.

Balfour v. *Balfour* [1919]
2 *KB* 571

On her doctor's advice, Mrs Balfour chose to remain in England when her husband returned to Ceylon after a period of leave from his post as a civil engineer. The parties agreed on this arrangement amicably (it was not a separation) and Mr Balfour agreed to pay his wife £30 per month while he worked abroad. Some time later the husband proposed a permanent separation. After obtaining a divorce, and an order for alimony, Mrs Balfour sued her husband upon the terms of the agreement made before he returned to Ceylon. After succeeding at first instance, on the grounds that her consent to the arrangement constituted good consideration for the promise of the husband, her claim was rejected on appeal.

WARRINGTON L J . . . we have to say whether there is a legal contract between the parties, in other words, whether what took place between them was in the domain of a contract or whether it was merely a domestic arrangement such as may be made every day between a husband and wife who are living together in friendly intercourse. It may be, and I do not for a moment say that it is not, possible for such a contract as is alleged in the present case to be made between husband and wife. The question is whether such a contract was made. . . . All I can say is that there is no such contract here. These two people never intended to make a bargain which could be enforced in law. The husband expressed his intention to make this payment, and he promised to make it, and was bound in honour to continue it so long as he was in a position to do so.

The wife on the other hand, so far as I can see, made no bargain at all. That is in my opinion sufficient to dispose of the case. . . .

DUKE LJ . . . it is impossible to disregard in this case what was the basis of the whole communications between the parties under which the alleged contract is said to have been formed. The basis of their communications was their relationship of husband and wife, a relationship which creates certain obligations, but not that which is here put in suit. There was a discussion between the parties while they were absent from one another, whether they should agree upon a separation. In the Court below the plaintiff conceded that down to the time of her suing in the Divorce Division there was no separation, and that the period of absence was a period of absence as between husband and wife living in amity. An agreement for separation when it is established does involve mutual considerations. . . .

. . . in this case there was no separation agreement at all. The parties were husband and wife, and subject to all the conditions, in point of law, involved in that relationship. It is impossible to say that where the relationship of husband and wife exists, and promises are exchanged, they must be deemed to be promises of a contractual nature. In order to establish a contract there ought to be something more than mere mutual promises having regard to the domestic relations of the parties. It is required that the obligations arising out of that relationship shall be displaced before either of the parties can found a contract upon such promises . . . .

. . . The proposition that the mutual promises made in the ordinary domestic relationship of husband and wife of necessity give cause for action on a contract seems to me to go to the very root of the relationship, and to be a possible fruitful source of dissension and quarrelling. I cannot see that any benefit would result from it to either of the parties, but on the other hand it would lead to unlimited litigation in a relationship which should be obviously as far as possible protected from possibilities of that kind. I think, therefore, that in point of principle there is no foundation for the claim which is made here, and I am satisfied that there was no consideration moving from the wife to the husband or promise by the husband to the wife which was sufficient to sustain this action founded on contract. I think, therefore, that the appeal must be allowed. . . .

ATKIN L J . . . it is necessary to remember that there are agreements between parties which do not result in contracts within the meaning of that term in our law. The ordinary example is where two parties agree to take a walk together, or where there is an offer and an acceptance of hospitality. Nobody would suggest in ordinary circumstances that those agreements result in what we know as a contract, and one of the most usual forms of agreement which does not constitute a contract appears to me to be the arrangements which are made between husband and wife. It is quite common, and it is the natural and inevitable result of the relationship of husband and wife, that the two spouses should make arrangements between themselves—agreements such as are in dispute in this action—agreements for allowances, by which the husband agrees that he will pay to his wife a certain sum of money, per week, or per month, or per year, to cover either her own expenses or the necessary expenses of the household and of the children of the marriage, and in which the wife promises either expressly or impliedly to apply the allowance for the purpose for which it is given. To my mind those agreements, or many of them, do not result in contracts at all. . . . they are not contracts because the parties did not intend that they should be attended by legal consequences. To my mind it would be of the worst possible example to hold that agreements such as this resulted in legal obligations which could be enforced in the Courts. It would mean this, that when the husband makes his wife a promise to give her an allowance of 30s. or 2l. a week, whatever he can afford to give her, for the maintenance of the household and children, and she promises so to apply it, not only could she sue him for his failure in any week to supply the allowance, but he could sue her for non-performance of the obligation, express or implied, which she had undertaken upon her part. All I can say is that the small Courts of this country would have to be multiplied one hundredfold if these arrangements were held to result in legal obligations. They are not sued upon, not because the parties are reluctant to enforce their legal rights when the agreement is broken, but because the parties, in the inception of the arrangement, never intended that they should be sued upon. Agreements such as these are outside the realm of contracts altogether. The common law does not regulate the form of agreements between spouses. Their promises are not sealed with seals and sealing wax. The consideration that really obtains for them is that natural love and affection which counts for so little in these cold Courts. The terms may be repudiated, varied or renewed as performance proceeds or as disagreements develop, and the principles of the common law as to exoneration and discharge and accord and satisfaction are such as find no place in the domestic code.

Notes

1. The judgments are couched in terms of what the parties 'intended' when they made their agreement. In fact, this notion of intention is no more than the presumption of the judges about what they consider, with the benefit of hindsight, that the parties must have had in contemplation when embarking upon the arrangement. In practice it is an utterly unreal question, since in all probability the parties did not consider the question at the time of the inception of the agreement and, moreover, the answer to this question does not necessarily provide a convincing justification for giving or denying a legal remedy once the agreement has been put into operation.

Consequently, in a situation where two family members have entered into property arrangements involving one party relinquishing his or her own home in order to move in with the other family member in return for a share in the latter's home, the courts have been inclined to protect such a serious act of (potentially detrimental) reliance. In doctrinal terms, the court will find in such a case that the presumption that agreements between family members are not intended to create legal relations has been rebutted (see e.g. *Parker* v. *Clark* [1960] 1 All ER 93).

2. Not all acts of reliance will be protected, however. In *Jones* v. *Padvatton* ([1969] 2 All ER 616) a woman agreed to give up her well-paid job and home in the USA at her mother's request to move to the UK to study for the Bar. In return, her mother agreed to pay her fees and maintenance, and later to place a house she owned in London at her disposal. After repeated failed attempts by the daughter to pass the Bar exams, the mother sued for possession of the house. An order was granted, the majority of the Court of Appeal holding that there was no binding contract to allow the daughter to occupy the property, since this was a family arrangement which was not susceptible to legal enforcement. Furthermore the agreement was too vague to be enforceable. The daughter's reaction to the commencement of the action for possession by her mother was to refuse to allow her entrance to the property and to state in evidence before the trial judge that 'a normal mother does not sue her daughter in court'. Yet from the facts Fenton Atkinson LJ felt able to infer that the daughter 'never for a moment contemplated the possibility of the mother or herself going to court to enforce legal obligations and that she felt it quite intolerable that a purely family arrangement should become the subject of proceedings in a court of law'. The result of the case was that the daughter's alleged contractual right took second place to the mother's property right.

3. A case such as *Jones* v. *Padvatton* could not have been dismissed on the grounds that the daughter gave no consideration. The act of relinquishing a home and job falls well within the recognized scope of consideration in English law. Even in *Balfour* v. *Balfour* itself, Atkin LJ and Duke LJ did seem prepared to accept the finding of Sargant J at first instance that the wife had given consideration by consenting to the arrangement, although it is difficult to see what she had promised or what she had lost, or what the husband had gained by the arrangements. Understandably, *Balfour* v. *Balfour* itself has been criticized on the basis that the doctrine of intention is an unnecessary supplement to the dominant paradigm of bargain, under which the notion of consideration makes it possible to distinguish between enforceable and unenforceable promises (see R. Unger, 'Intent to Create Legal Relations, Mutuality and Consideration', (1956) 19 *MLR* 96, and B. Hepple, 'Intention to Create Legal Relations', [1970] *CLJ* 122). A bargain-based approach can also provide a solution to *Jones* v. *Padvatton*; this was

the approach taken by Salmon LJ, who held the agreement prima facie enforceable but implied a term allowing it to lapse after a reasonable time, during which the daughter could be expected to complete her studies. In this case he defined a reasonable time as five years, and as five years had elapsed, Salmon LJ was able to reach the same conclusion on the facts as Fenton Atkinson and Danckwerts LJJ.

While it is easy to criticize the criterion of intention to create legal relations as a misfit in the common law of contract, more useful is an attempt to identify what might be the policy arguments which lie behind its invocation. A good starting-point is the colourful language of Atkin LJ in *Balfour* v. *Balfour* itself, and Atiyah's comment that in cases such as that one the result depends 'not so much on the lack of intention to create legal relations, as on the court's view that it would be unseemly and distressing to allow husbands and wives, while still living together, to use the court as an arbiter for their matrimonial differences' (P. S. Atiyah, *An Introduction to the Law of Contract*, 4th edn. (Oxford, Clarendon Press, 1989), 165).

  Hedley sees intention to create legal relations as the tool which the courts have used to control the use of contract in the context of social and domestic arrangements where remedies had previously been the province of equity alone.

S. Hedley, 'Keeping Contract in its Place: *Balfour* v. *Balfour* and the Enforceability of Informal Agreements', (1985) 5 *OJLS* 391 at 403

The judges wanted contract let into domestic contexts, but only on their terms; and they found the perfect device for achieving this in the solution Atkin LJ had adopted, of postulating a doctrine of 'intent to create legal relations'. If liability were thought appropriate on certain facts, it could plausibly be made out as 'intended'; if not, it would be easy to deny the existence of the requisite intention. I am not saying that the judges consciously thought along these lines, though some of them may well have done. But this was the effect. The 'legal relations' doctrine gave the judges *carte blanche* to impose or refuse contractual liability in unfamiliar contexts. . . .

Clare Dalton has offered a sustained critique of the lack of coherence in the 'intention' argument in the context of US cases on 'cohabitation contracts'. In the next extract, a cohabitation contract is defined broadly as a more or less detailed oral or written arrangement between two cohabiting parties about the basis on which they are to cohabit, including, in some cases, provision for the disposal of joint property and dissolution of the arrangement. A cohabitation contract in this form may be either a supplement to or an alternative to marriage.

C. Dalton, 'An Essay in the Deconstruction of Contract Doctrine', (1985) 94 *Yale LJ* 997 at 1098–1100

One possible explanation for this presumption against finding contracts is that it accords with the parties' intentions. It can be argued that cohabitants generally neither want their agreements to have legal consequences, nor desire to be obligated to one another when they have stopped cohabitating. It can further be presented as a matter of fact that their services are freely given and taken within the context of an intimate relationship. . . .

This intention-based explanation, however, coexists . . . with two other, more overtly public, explanations that rest on diametrically opposed public policies. The first suggests that the arena of intimate relationships is too private for court intervention through contract enforcement to be appropriate. In *Hewitt* [*Hewitt* v. *Hewitt* 77 Ill. 2d 49 (1979)], for example, the Illinois Supreme Court suggests that "the situation alleged here was not the kind of arm's length bargain envisioned by traditional contract principles, but an intimate arrangement of a fundamentally different kind."

While it has some intuitive appeal, the argument that intimate relationships are too private for court enforcement is at odds with the more general argument that all contractual relationships are private and that contract enforcement merely facilitates the private relationships described by contract. To overcome this apparent inconsistency, we must imagine a scale of privateness on which business arrangements, while mostly private, are still not as private as intimate arrangements. But then the rescue attempt runs headlong into the other prevailing policy argument, which separates out intimate arrangements because of their peculiarly public and regulated status. Under this view, it is the business relationship that by and large remains more quintessentially private.

According to this second argument, the area of non-marital agreements is too public for judicial intervention. The legislature is the appropriate body to regulate such arrangements; courts may not help create private alternatives to the public scheme. In *Hewitt*, the supreme court directly follows its appeal to the intimate nature of the relationship with an acknowledgement of the regulated, and hence public, character of marriage-like relations. With respect to intimate relations conceived as public, the judiciary can then present itself as either passive or active. The argument for passivity is that judges should "stay out" of an arena already covered by public law. The argument for activity is that judges should reinforce public policy by deterring the formation of deviant relationships, either because they fall outside the legislative schemes organizing familial entitlement and property distribution, or because they offend public morality.

Neither the private nor the public arguments for the absence of contract in this setting are conclusive. Both private and public counterarguments are readily available. If the absence of contract is presented as flowing from party intention, competing interpretations of intention can be used to argue the presence of contract. If, within a more public framework, the court categorizes the concerns implicated by the relationship as private, then an argument can be made that within the boundaries expressly established by legislation, the parties should be free to vary the terms of their relationship without interference by the state. If the focus is the place of cohabitation agreements within the publicly-regulated sphere of intimate relationships, then an argument can be made that certain kinds of enforcement in fact extend and implement public policy rather than derogate from it.

Notes

1. It is clear from the brief quotation from the Illinois Supreme Court in the case of *Hewitt* that the intermingling of contractual and domestic relationships has provoked similar reactions amongst US judges to those displayed in *Balfour* v. *Balfour* in England. While Dalton deconstructs the doctrinal approach on 'intention', finding it entirely indeterminate, she also exposes the policy choices as contradictory in so far as they are based on a dichotomy between the public and the private spheres. It is difficult to say that intimate relations are too private to be regulated by contract, since the classic justification for contract law is that it provides a mechanism for facilitating private ordering *par excellence*. On the other hand, if intimate relationships are a matter of public concern, which they clearly are in so far as the institution of marriage has evolved to give a publicly regulated form to such relationships, it is possible that they are too 'public' to be regulated by a judicially imposed contract even if it expresses the will of the parties.

2. Dalton's arguments on doctrine and policy demonstrate that there is a need for sustained debate about the reach of the law of contract. It should not be taken for granted that contract is either a 'natural' or an 'unnatural' method of regulating any human relationship, be it 'domestic' or 'economic' in nature. Fictions of 'intention' should not be a substitute for serious policy choices. Feminist commentators, in particular, have addressed this issue at both the general and the specific level. Pateman, for example as we saw in Chapter 2, not only criticizes contractarian thought as being fundamentally male-oriented, but also rejects contractarian solutions as not providing a route to sexual equality for women. A more focused debate has concerned the desirability of legally enforceable cohabitation contracts, and whether, if used as an alternative or supplement to marriage, they can provide a means for men and women to move towards more egalitarian interpersonal relationships which are not irrevocably tainted by endemic and structural sexual inequalities affecting men and women in general. Much of this debate has centred on the inevitability of the market as the forum within which contractual exchange, and the consequential

'marketization' of family life that occurs if contractual relations are used to structure intimate relationships.

These discussions have carried the protagonists in the debate a long way from spurious concepts of individual intention, which in contrast seem a crude and narrow measure of the appropriate reach of the law. On cohabitation contracts, see E. Kingdom, 'Cohabitation Contracts and Equality' (1990) 18 *Int. J. Soc. Law* 287; F. Olsen, 'The Family and the Market: a Study of Ideology and Legal Reform', (1983) 96 *Harv. L. Rev.* 1497; L. Weitzman, *The Marriage Contract: Spouses, Lovers and the Law* (London, Collier, 1981).

B. Intention and Policy

Outside the realm of domestic arrangements, arguments based on intention have had limited appeal to the judges. In *Ford Motor Co. Ltd.* v. *Amalgamated Union of Engineering and Foundry Workers* ([1969] 1 WLR 339; [1969] 2 All ER 481), Geoffrey Lane J used a blend of arguments based on the intentions of the parties and broader considerations of policy in order to conclude that a collective agreement between a large industrial company and various trade unions representing the employees of the company concerning many aspects of their employment was not enforceable.

GEOFFREY LANE J If one applies the subjective test and asks what the intentions of the various parties were, the answer is that, so far as they had any express intentions, they were certainly not to make the agreement enforceable at law. If one applies an objective test and asks what intention must be imputed from all the circumstances of the case, the answer is the same. The fact that the agreements prima facie deal with commercial relationships is outweighed by the other considerations, by the wording of the agreements, by the nature of the agreements, and by the climate of opinion voiced and evidenced by the extra-judicial authorities. Agreements such as these, composed largely of optimistic aspirations, presenting grave practical problems of enforcement and reached against a background of opinion adverse to enforceability, are, in my judgment, not contracts in the legal sense and are not enforceable at law. Without clear and express provisions making them amenable to legal action, they remain in the realm of undertakings binding in honour.

Notes

1. Hepple notes:

It would be open to the House of Lords in an appropriate case to review the cases since *Balfour* v. *Balfour* and to reject or modify the requirement of additional proof of an intention to create legal relations. A possible obstacle, however, is that the device of constructive "intention" is superficially attractive because it enables the courts to cloak policy decisions in the mantle of private contractual autonomy. (Hepple, 'Intention to Create Legal Relations', [1970] *CLJ* 122 at 134)

2. The particular policy problem raised by collective agreements is now resolved by statute (Trade Unions and Labour Relations (Consolidation) Act 1992, s. 179) which provides that collective agreements will be conclusively presumed not to be enforceable unless they are in writing and contain an express provision stating the intention of the parties that the agreement should be a legally enforceable contract.

3. It is none the less instructive to review the approach of Geoffrey Lane J, for prior to his judgment it had not been commonly thought that the parties to a commercial agreement needed to evince a positive intention to be bound by their promises before entering the realm of contract law. The empirical evidence reviewed in Chapter 2 demonstrates, of course, that parties to commercial relationships are frequently exceedingly ambivalent about the precise nature of their relationships, but only because certain other features of those relationships and certain other values are of greater day-to-day interest. It seems odd that Geoffrey Lane J needs to take the general climate of opinion which is hostile to enforceability by the parties as evidence of some form of 'objective intention', instead of seizing on what has always been the largely uncontested public policy that the unenforceability of collective agreements goes to the very heart of the tradition of British industrial relations as the true basis for his decision.

C. Commercial Agreements

It can be clearly demonstrated that the use of intention to create legal relations in domestic and social contracts as a criterion of enforceability represents a thinly disguised and largely unnecessary smokescreen for policy choices about the correct scope of the law and legal sanctions. In *Ford*, the decision of the judge to regard intention as a necessary positive element of every contract likewise led to a strange diversion from the ordinary meaning of 'intention'. In commercial agreements proper, the role of intention as a criterion of enforceability has an even more limited role, as the Court of Appeal pointed out in *Kleinwort Benson*.

Kleinwort Benson Ltd. v. *Malaysia Mining Corp. Bhd*
[1988] 1 All ER 714 (QBD); [1989] 1 All ER 785

The defendants ('MMC') decided to set up a subsidiary company ('Metals Ltd.') to trade in tin on the London Metal Exchange. In order to finance this subsidiary company, the defendants sought from the plaintiff bank a loan of £5 million to supplement the existing capital of the subsidiary of £1.5 million. The loan was subsequently increased to £10 million. Before making the first loan, the plaintiffs asked the defendants for a guarantee of their subsidiary's indebtedness to them. Their commission charge for the loan was then 0.375% per annum. After negotiations, the defendants refused to give a guarantee to the plaintiffs but suggested instead a 'comfort letter'. This was supplied by the plaintiffs with some amendments from the defendants. The plaintiffs increased their commission charge to 0.5% per annum. There were three relevant paragraphs in the letter:

[1] We hereby confirm that we know and approve of these facilities and are aware of the fact that they have been granted to Metals Ltd. because we control directly or indirectly Metals Ltd.

[2] We confirm that we will not reduce our current financial interest in Metals Ltd. until the [loans] have been repaid or until you have confirmed that you are prepared to continue the facilities with new shareholders.

[3] It is our policy to ensure that the business of Metals Ltd. is at all times in a position to meet its liabilities to you under the above arrangement.

When the tin market collapsed in 1985 the plaintiffs were owed the whole amount by Metals Ltd. They sought to recover this amount from the defendants under the comfort letters, which they maintained had legal force. The defendants denied this. The judgment at first instance was delivered by Hirst J ([1988] 1 All ER 714).

Hirst J The main question which I have to decide is whether, as KB contend, and MMC deny, the crucial paragraph [3] was contractual in status; if it is, the subsidiary question arises as to its proper construction. . . .

The general principle is clearly and concisely defined in *Chitty on Contracts* (25th edn, 1983) para 123 under the heading 'Contractual Intention' as follows:

'An agreement, even though it is supported by consideration, is not binding as a contract if it was made without any intention of creating legal relations. Of course, in the case of ordinary commercial transactions it is not normally necessary to prove that the parties in fact intended to create legal relations. The onus of proving that there was no such intention "is on the party who asserts that no legal effect is intended, and the onus is a heavy one". Where such evidence is adduced, the courts normally apply an objective test: for example, where the sale of a house is not "subject to contract", either party is likely to be bound even though he subjectively believed that he would not be bound until the usual exchange of contracts had taken place. The courts also attach weight to the importance of the agreement to the parties, and to the fact that one of them has acted in reliance on it.'

The quotation in the third sentence of this paragraph is derived from the decision of Megaw J in the case of *Edwards v. Skyways Ltd* [1964] 1 All ER 494 at 500. . . .

. . . [The plaintiffs] submitted, far from there being any pointers against an intention to create contractual relations, all the circumstances pointed to the contrary. In particular: (a) the language was formal and appropriate to legal obligations; (b) the letters of comfort were matters of importance to KB, and something on which they plainly relied in granting the facilities, in the instance for up to £5m, and subsequently up to no less than £10m, to a company with a fully paid up capital of only £1.5m. It was also treated by MMC as important and as of significance, as shown by the board's resolution; (c) the extra ⅛% commission reflected the contrast between a contractual term, giving rise in case of breach to no more than a claim in damages, and a full-blooded guarantee, which gave rise to a monetary claim which was much more easily quantifiable and enforceable; (d) if it was intended not to be legally binding, MMC could and should have said so, in which case KB could have considered their position. . . .

The main gravamen of [counsel for the defendants'] argument was that he was able to satisfy the burden of establishing non-contractual status for the crucial paragraph on three main grounds. (i) The court started with an equal and opposite presumption that, where (as he submitted was the case here) ambiguous words had to be construed, they must be construed contra proferentem, and here, he submitted, KB were the proponents. (ii) As a matter of construction the contrast between the opening words of para (1), 'we hereby confirm . . .', and particularly those of the admittedly contractual para (2) ('we confirm that we will not . . .') showed clearly that the weaker phraseology in para (3) beginning 'it is our policy to ensure . . .' was intended to be non-contractual. (iii) The surrounding circumstances, and in particular the common appreciation by both sides that MMC were not prepared either to accept joint and several liability or to enter into a guarantee, strongly supported displacement of the presumption. . . .

As to the language used, he submitted that the wording of para (3) was not the language of contract, in stark contrast to para (2), which bore all the hallmarks of contract with its express confirmation at the outset. If the former were intended to be contractual, he asked, why depart from the language of the latter? The real reason was that KB knew perfectly well that MMC would not agree to the equivalent of a guarantee. . . .

(ii) The wording of the crucial paragraph is unequivocal and categorical. Far from being expressed other than in the language of contract, as counsel for the defendants submitted, I think that the phraseology is fully apt to express a legal obligation. I see no magic in the opening words 'we confirm that we will not . . .' in para (2), or their omission from para (3): put another way, I do not think that any greater strength would have been added to para (3) if it had begun 'We confirm that it is our policy . . .' Thus I reject counsel's argument based on comparison of the various paragraphs, and consider the wording of the crucial paragraph completely apt to constitute a contractual undertaking. . . .

. . . The suggestion that, in effect, commercial 'amour propre' might have ruled out MMC being willing to enter into a contractually binding obligation under the crucial paragraph is severely undermined by the admitted fact that they did so in the preceding one; and, while it might be some solace to KB (if they were forced to accept a term binding only in honour) that it would be embarrassing for MMC to renege in normal circumstances, a legally binding obligation would obviously exert greater force. . . .

On the other side, a number of considerations to my mind strongly reinforce the presumption, namely: (a) KB clearly acted in reliance, inter alia, on this paragraph in agreeing to advance first £5m and then £10m; (b) it was of paramount importance to KB that MMC should ensure that Metals were at all times in a position to meet their liabilities under the facility arrangements. Leaving aside any question of catastrophe, commodity markets like tin are of their very nature speculative and volatile, and prone to yield sharp and substantial losses as well as profits. The original facility was over thrice Metals' paid up capital, and the extended facility almost seven fold, and was provided, without security, entirely for the purpose of furnishing working capital for such operations in the tin market. It is thus hard to imagine anything of greater commercial importance than a contractually binding ability to have recourse to the holding company should the subsidiary default; (c) it was also treated as a matter of importance by MMC, as is shown by their formal board resolution. . . .

For the above reasons, I have come to the conclusion, and I hold, that the crucial paragraph on its proper construction, in its context, did have contractual status.

As to its interpretation, that seems to me to be crystal clear without embellishment. It is an undertaking that, now and at all times in future, so long as Metals are under any liability to KB under the facility arrangements, it is and will be MMC's policy to ensure that Metals is in a position to meet those liabilities. . . .

When the blow fell at the end of 1985, and Metals were unable to meet their obligations, MMC made it abundantly plain that it was no longer their policy so to ensure. This was a clear breach of contract, for which the plaintiffs are entitled to recover damages.

Notes

1. Hirst J appears to approach the case by asking two questions: first, whether the parties had intended to create legal relations and second, what was the effect of what they had agreed in paragraph 3? He decides that in a business relationship such as this the presumption of an intention to create legal relations had to be rebutted by the defendants rather than proved by the plaintiffs. In his view, the defendants failed successfully to rebut the presumption. Having decided that paragraph 3 of the comfort letter has

contractual force, he goes on to conclude that the effect of the paragraph has made the defendants liable to the plaintiffs.

2. The extract below is from the decision of the Court of Appeal ([1989]] 1 All ER 785) and demonstrates a very different approach.

RALPH GIBSON LJ For my part, I am persuaded that the main criticisms of the judgment of Hirst J advanced by counsel for the defendants are well founded and I would, for the reasons which follow, allow this appeal. In my judgment the defendants made a statement as to what their policy was, and did not in para 3 of the comfort letter expressly promise that such policy would be continued in future. It is impossible to make up for the lack of express promise by implying such a promise, and indeed, no such implied promise was pleaded. My conclusion rests on what, in my judgment, is the proper effect and meaning which, on the evidence, is to be given to para 3 of the comfort letters. . . .

Counsel for the plaintiffs before Hirst J had placed strong reliance on *Edwards v Skyways Ltd* and his submission was recorded by Hirst J as follows: '. . . there was a heavy onus on [the defendants] to prove that there was no intention to create contractual relations.'

In my judgment counsel for the defendants is right in his submission that the presumption described in *Edwards v Skyways Ltd* had no application to the issues in this case once the plea of a separate agreement or understanding to the effect that the comfort letters should have no legal effect had disappeared from the case for want of evidence to support it. The introduction of that plea into the case appears to have served only to distract attention from what, if I am right, are the clear merits of the defendants' case as to the meaning and effect of para 3 of the comfort letters.

To explain why, in my view, the presumption applied by Hirst J had no application to this case it is necessary to examine in some detail the issues in *Edwards v Skyways Ltd*. In that case Skyways Ltd, the defendants, found it necessary to declare redundant some 15% of the pilots in their employ. The secretary of Skyways Ltd, at a meeting with representatives of the airline pilots union, agreed that—

'Pilots declared redundant and leaving the company would be given an ex gratia payment equivalent to the company's contribution to the Pension Fund [and, in addition] . . . a refund of their own contributions to the fund.'

(See [1964] 1 All ER 494 at 497.) Edwards, in reliance on that agreement, left the company and claimed payment under it. The company purported to rescind its decision to make the ex gratia payment on the ground that it had obligations to creditors and the promised ex gratia payments were not enforceable in law. The company admitted that a promise had been made to make the payments and that the promise was supported by consideration, but contended (in reliance on *Rose & Frank Co v J R Crompton & Bros Ltd* [1923] 2 KB 261 at

288) that the promise or agreement had no legal effect because there was no intention to enter into legal relations in respect of the promised payment. It was argued that the mere use of the phrase 'ex gratia', as part of the promise to pay, showed that the parties contemplated that the promise when accepted would have no binding force in law and, further, that there was background knowledge, concerned with the tax consequences of legally enforceable promises to pay, and present to the minds of the representatives of the parties, which gave unambiguous significance to the word 'ex gratia' as excluding legal relationships. Megaw J rejected these arguments on the facts and on his construction of the meaning in the context of the words 'ex gratia'. The company thus failed to show that what was otherwise admittedly a promise, supported by consideration, was to be denied legal effect because of the common intention of the parties that it should not have such effect and, accordingly, the company failed to displace the presumption. Megaw J was not dealing with the sort of question which is raised in this case, namely whether, given that the comfort letter was intended to express the legal relationship between the parties, the language of para 3 does or does not contain a contractual promise. . . .

The concept of a comfort letter was, as counsel for the defendants acknowledged, not shown to have acquired any particular meaning at the time of the negotiations in this case with reference to the limits of any legal liability to be assumed under its terms by a parent company. A letter, which the parties might have referred to at some stage as a letter of comfort, might, after negotiation, have emerged containing in para 3 in express terms the words used by Hirst J to state the meaning which he gave to para 3. The court would not, merely because the parties had referred to the document as a comfort letter, refuse to give effect to the meaning of the words used. But in this case it is clear, in my judgment, that the concept of a comfort letter, to which the parties had resort when the defendants refused to assume joint and several liability or to give a guarantee, was known by both sides at least to extend to or to include a document under which the defendants would give comfort to the plaintiffs by assuming, not a legal liability to ensure repayment of the liabilities of its subsidiary, but a moral responsibility only. Thus, when the defendants by Mr John Green in June 1984 told the plaintiffs that Mr Green would recommend that credit lines for Metals be covered by a letter of comfort rather than by guarantee, the response of Mr Irwin, before any draft or a comfort letter had been prepared, was '. . . that a letter of comfort would not be a problem, but that [he] would probably have to charge a higher rate'. The comfort letter was drafted in terms which in para 3 do not express any contractual promise and which are consistent with being no more than a representation of fact. If they are treated as no more than a representation of fact, they are in that meaning consistent with the comfort letter containing no more than the assumption of moral responsibility by the defendants in respect of the debts of Metals. There is nothing in the evidence to show that, as a matter of commercial probability or common sense, the parties must have intended para 3 to be a contractual promise, which is not expressly stated, rather than a mere representation of fact which is so stated.

Next, the first draft of the comfort letter was produced by the plaintiffs. Paragraph 1 contained confirmation that the defendants knew of and approved of the granting of the facilities in question by the plaintiffs to Metals, and para 2 contained the express confirmation that the defendants would not reduce their current financial interest in Metals until (in effect) facilities had been paid or the plaintiffs consented. Both are relevant to the present and future moral responsibility of the defendants. If the words of para 3 are to be treated as intended to express a contractual promise by the defendants as to their future policy, which Hirst J held the words to contain, then the recitation of the plaintiffs' approval and the promise not to reduce their current financial interest in Metals, would be of no significance. If the defendants have promised that at all times in the future it will be the defendants' policy to ensure that Metals is in a position to meet its liabilities to the plaintiffs under the facility, it would not matter whether they had approved or disapproved, or whether they had disposed of their shares in Metals. Contracts may, of course, contain statements or promises which are caused to be of no separate commercial importance by the width of a later promise in the same document. Where, however, the court is examining a statement which is by its express words no more than a representation of fact, in order to consider whether it is shown to have been intended to be of the nature of a contractual promise or warranty, it seems to me to be a fact suggesting at least the absence of such intention if, as in this case, to read the statement as a contractual promise is to reduce to no significance two paragraphs included in the plaintiffs' draft, both of which have significance if the statement is read as a representation of fact only.

That point can be made more plainly thus: if para 3 in its original or in its final form was intended to contain a binding legal promise by the defendants to ensure the ability of Metals to pay the sums due under the facility, there was no apparent need or purpose for the plaintiffs, as bankers, to waste ink on paras 1 and 2. . . .

. . . The evidence showing the context in which the comfort letters were produced, as set out in the judgment of Hirst J, was evidence of the factual background known to the parties at or before the date of the contract and of the 'genesis' and 'aim' of the transaction . . ., in short the provision of a comfort letter by the defendants, as the parent company of Metals to which the plaintiffs were intending to provide finance, in circumstances in which the defendants had refused to assume legal liability for the repayment of money lent to Metals by the plaintiffs, whether in the form of joint and several liability or of a guarantee. Those facts are not available to show merely that the defendants did not themselves subjectively intend to assume legal liability and that, therefore, the words eventually included in the comfort letter provided by the defendants should be construed so as to exclude such liability. . . .

With that evidence before the court I find it impossible to hold that the words in para 3 were intended to have any effect between the parties other than in accordance with the express words used. For this purpose it seems to me that the onus of demonstrating that the affirmation appears on evidence to have been intended as a contractual promise must lie on the party asserting that it does, but I do not rest my conclusion on failure by the plaintiffs to discharge any onus. I think it is clear that the words of para 3 cannot be regarded as intended to contain a contractual promise as to the future policy of the defendants. If para 3 had been drafted by the plaintiffs and submitted in the form in which Hirst J formulated its meaning, namely as—

'an undertaking that, now and at all times in future, so long as Metals are under any liability to [the plaintiffs] under the facility arrangements, it is and will be [the defendants'] policy to ensure that Metals is in a position to meet those liabilities',

it must have appeared to both parties, in the context proved in evidence, as a radically different term from that which was in fact submitted and accepted. Such an undertaking does not fit, as a matter of commercial probability, with the factual background. I do not suggest that people only act in accordance with apparent commercial probability; the plaintiffs might have submitted such an undertaking which, in the light of the prior refusal to give a guarantee, was likely to be rejected and the defendants, contrary to what seemed likely, might have accepted it, but the plaintiffs in fact submitted the words we see in para 3. The plain meaning of those words, without the addition contained in Hirst J's formulation of its meaning, does fit the factual background. Most importantly, that factual background explains, notwithstanding the commercial importance to the plaintiffs of security against failure by Metals to pay and the plaintiffs' reliance on the comfort letter, why the plaintiffs drafted and agreed to proceed on a comfort letter which, on its plain meaning, provided to the plaintiffs no legally enforceable security for the repayment of the liabilities of Metals. I therefore find it impossible to hold that by the words of para 3 the parties must be held to have intended that the plaintiffs be given that security. . . .

If my view of this case is correct, the plaintiffs have suffered grave financial loss as a result of the collapse of the tin market and the following decision by the defendant company not to honour a moral responsibility which it assumed in order to gain for its subsidiary the finance necessary for the trading operations which the defendants wished that subsidiary to pursue. The defendants have demonstrated, in my judgment, that they made no relevant contractual promise to the plaintiffs which could support the judgment in favour of the plaintiffs. The consequences of the decision of the defendants to repudiate their moral responsibility are not matters for this court.

I would allow this appeal.

Notes

1. Discussions of the case both at first instance and in the Court of Appeal include A. Tettenborn, 'Commercial Certainty: A Step in the Right Direction', [1988] *CLJ* 346; B. Davenport, 'A Very Comfortable Comfort Letter', [1988] *LMCLQ* 290; A. Ayres and A. Moore, '"Small Comfort" Letters: Kleinwort Benson'", [1989] *LMCLQ* 182; and I. Brown, 'The Letter of Comfort: Placebo or Promise?', [1990] *JBL* 281.

2. For the Court of Appeal, intention to create legal relations is not an issue. The judgment of Ralph Gibson LJ concentrates on the meaning of paragraph 3 of the comfort letter in order to ascertain whether the defendants have made a *promise* of a contractual nature or simply a statement about their current policy towards their subsidiary company. In other words, a claim that the statement was not intended to have a contractual effect (if such had been its meaning as construed by the courts) was not even considered by the Court of Appeal. There was no evidence that the parties to the arrangements did not intend them to fall within the scope of adjudication of a court. The Court of Appeal declined to follow the approach of Hirst J which seemed to build on the misguided approach of Geoffrey Lane J in *Ford* in so far as it takes intention to create legal relations as a necessary positive element of contractual formation, albeit one presumed to be present in the commercial sphere. The judgment of Ralph Gibson LJ shows much in common with the approach of critics of the intention doctrine, who point to the notion of bargain as the key to the seriousness of promises.

3. There does remain a limited category of cases in which arrangements are intentionally carried outside the law's reach by very clear words used by the parties: *Rose and Frank Company Ltd.* v. *J. R. Crompton & Bros. Ltd.* ([1923] 2 KB 261 (CA); [1925] AC 445 (HL)) is perhaps the best-known example. The case involved a sole agency agreement between the parties which was expressed not to be subject to the jurisdiction of the courts and to be binding in honour only. The Court of Appeal and the House of Lords agreed that there was no binding agency contract, although in order to protect the parties in respect of their past dealings the House of Lords held that individual orders for goods made by the plaintiff and accepted by the defendants constituted legally binding contracts such that the defendants were bound to deliver the goods as ordered.

4. In the light of *Kleinwort Benson*, it would perhaps be better to regard such cases not as cases of a rebutted presumption of a fictitious intention to create legal relations in commercial agreements but as cases where an apparent bargain is carried outside the law's reach by the clear intentions of the parties. The extent to which the parties should be permitted to do

this could then be judged in the light of the principles of autonomy, equality of bargaining power (was exemption from the courts actually imposed by one party?), and the protection of detrimental reliance in the case of an executed agreement.

5. The view of letters of comfort as not constituting contractual promises put forward by the Court of Appeal in *Kleinwort Benson* is by no means incontrovertible. In the factually similar case of *Banque Brussels Lambert SA* v. *Australian National Industries Ltd.* ((1989) 21 NSWLR 502), the Commercial Division of the New South Wales Supreme Court reached the opposite conclusion on the effect of a letter of comfort. The court concluded that it was wholly wrong to subject such letters to minute textual analysis, as this ignored their status as commercial documents which are little different from letters of guarantee. It is for accounting reasons that such letters are not termed guarantees.

6. Further details on the tests used for distinguishing between contractual promises and other statements are given in Chapter 10.

D. Conclusion and Reflection

It must be concluded, therefore, that the role of the subjective intentions of the parties in determining the scope of the legal enforceability of agreements is exceedingly limited. In the social and domestic context, the 'apparent intentions' of the parties are no more than a smokescreen for policy choices about the relationship between law and the private, domestic sphere, which seem based on unsophisticated assumptions about what is 'natural' in that context. Collective agreements provide an anomalous category of complex multi-party arrangements which fit uneasily into a bargain scenario and which are now regulated by statute. Commercial agreements offer the only true example of party intention having an impact on enforceability. Even a bargain in the common law sense may not be enforceable if the parties have deliberately carried it outside the reach of the law, rejecting the 'natural' sanctions for the enforcement of bargains, those of the law.

Roberto Unger (see Ch. 2) seeks to explain the law of contract as a system of principles and counterprinciples. He has applied this conceptual structure to the rules on intention to create legal relations in the following terms.

R. Unger, *The Critical Legal Studies Movement* (Cambridge, Mass., Harvard University Press, 1983), 61–4

The first principle is that of the freedom to enter or to refuse to enter into contracts. More specifically, it is the faculty of choosing your contract partners. It might be called, for short, the freedom to contract. . . .

Other areas of law and doctrine, however, do circumscribe the principle of freedom to contract on behalf of an entirely different idea. They embody a counterprinciple: that the freedom to choose the contract partner will not be allowed to work in ways that subvert the communal aspects of social life. . . .

The most instructive application of the counterprinciple lies . . . in . . . the rules of contract law that discourage contract in noncommercial settings. These rules express a reluctance to allow contract law to intrude at all upon the world of family and friendship, lest by doing so it destroy their peculiar communal quality. Let us approach the issue indirectly, through the norms that govern the interpretation of the intent to contract. These norms elucidate more clearly than any others the boundaries of the principle of freedom to contract and the vision of human coexistence within and outside commerce that these boundaries imply.

The general first-level rule in contemporary Anglo-American contract law is that a declaration of intent to be legally bound may be unnecessary, although a declaration of intent not to be held at law may be effective. Those who devote themselves to self-interest in the harsh business world are presumed to want all the help they can get to avoid being done in by their contract partners. A second-level rule guides and qualifies the interpretation of the first-level one. Whenever possible a court construes intention in a manner that protects justified reliance and reads the parties out of a situation in which they stand at each other's mercy. Thus, if the bargain is one for separate deliveries over a long period and one party has seriously relied upon continued supply, the court may be expected to lean over backward to interpret the exclusion of liability as narrowly as possible. A third-level rule limits the scope of both the first-level and second-level ones. As a qualification to the latter, it affirms that the impulse to interpret intent so as to avoid delivering one party into another's hands will be suppressed in noncommercial contexts. As a limitation upon the former, it reverses in family life or friendship the presumption of intent to be legally bound; an explicit assertion of intent will be required. "Social arrangements," it is said, either are rarely intended to have legal consequence or ought not to have such consequences. Intent should be construed accordingly. In one sense this third-level criterion is prior to the other two, for it determines the scope of their application. Its apparent justification lies in the attempt to defend private community against the disruptive intervention of the law and of the regime of rigidly defined rights and duties that the law would bring in its wake. Just why private community needs this defense is something that we can explain only after making explicit the vision that underlies the interplay between the principle of freedom to contract and its counterprinciple. . . .

The relation of principle and counterprinciple in contract law can be interpreted as an expression of two different views of how people can and should interact in the areas of social life touched by contract law: one crude and easy to criticize, the other more subtle and justifiable. The crude view is the one displayed most clearly by the rules that try to keep contract out of the realm of "social arrangements." It contrasts an ideal of private community, meant to be realized chiefly in the life of family and friendship, to the ideal of contractual freedom, addressed to the world of self-interested commerce. The social realm is pictured as rich in precisely the attributes that are thought to be almost wholly absent from the economic sphere. The communal forms in which it abounds, islands of reciprocal loyalty and support, neither need much law nor are capable of tolerating it. For law in this conception is the regime of rigidly defined rights that demarcate areas for discretionary action.

The idea that there is a field of experience outside the serious world of work, in which communal relations flourish, can be made to justify the devolution of practical life to the harshest self-interest. The premises to this devolution recall the contrast between Venice and Belmont in *The Merchant of Venice*. In Venice people make contracts; in Belmont they exchange wedding rings. In Venice they are held together by combinations of interest, in Belmont by mutual affection. The wealth and power of Venice depend upon the willingness of its courts to hold men to their contracts. The charm of Belmont is to provide its inhabitants with a community in which contracts remain for the most part superfluous. Venice is tolerable because its citizens can flee occasionally to Belmont and appeal from Venetian justice to Belmontine mercy. But the very existence of Belmont presupposes the prosperity of Venice, from which the denizens of Belmont gain their livelihood. This is the form of life classical contract theory claims to describe and seeks to define—an existence separated into a sphere of trade supervised by the state and an area of private family and friendship largely thought not wholly beyond the reach of contract. Each half of this life both denies the other and depends upon it. Each is at once the other's partner and its enemy.

The large imaginative background to this contrast is a vision of social life that distinguishes more or less sharply among separate models of human connection. These models are meant to be realized in separate areas of social life: democracy for the state and citizenship, private community for family and friendship, and an amalgam of contract and impersonal technical hierarchy for the everyday world of work and exchange. The most remarkable feature of this vision is its exclusion of the more morally ambitious models of human connection from the prosaic activities and institutions that absorb most people most of the time. These models are democracy and private community. Their moral ambition consists in their promise of a partial reconciliation between the competing claims of self-assertion and attachment to other people—a reconciliation, in fact, between two competing sides of the experience of self-assertion itself. According to the logic of the vision, any attempt to extend these ideals beyond their proper realm of application into everyday life will meet with disaster. Not only will the extension fail, but the practical and psychological conditions that enable the higher ideals to flourish on their own ground may also be destroyed in the course of the attempt.

Note

Understood as an expression of a counterprinciple operating as a fetter upon the principle of freedom to contract or not to contract, the doctrine of intention to create legal relations can be theorized either as a relatively crude measure of the reach of the law or as a more sophisticated measure of the key values underlying the social activity of contract ('the everyday world of work and exchange'). Drawing a line between the public and private spheres leads, on Unger's analysis, to a relative impoverishment of the world of contract and exchange on a moral plane, because it results in the exclusion from that world of the more sophisticated means of reconciling the competitive and co-operative sides of human nature which have developed in the worlds of the family and the community.

III. GOOD FAITH AND THE BARGAINING PROCESS

The next section considers whether legal status can or should be ascribed to the negotiations between parties prior to their reaching what is formally recognized by the law as an enforceable agreement. In the event of an enforceable agreement being concluded by the parties, prior negotiations may become the subject of dispute in areas such as misrepresentation and mistake and, as such, are considered in later chapters. Here we are concerned with the situation where, despite perhaps extended negotiations, the parties do not reach agreement sufficient to constitute a contract. Of particular concern is the status of 'agreements to agree' or 'contracts to bargain' where the parties purport to bind themselves to reach an agreement. This was the situation in *Walford* v. *Miles*.

Walford v. *Miles*
[1992] 1 All ER 453

The case concerned the proposed sale by the respondents, Mr and Mrs Miles, of their company PNM, which carried on a photographic processing business at its premises in London. Mr Miles became ill and consequently decided to sell the business and its premises in 1985. He entered negotiations with P and K, the company's auditors, with a view to their purchasing the company but this proved fruitless. In 1986 the business was again offered for sale and P and K made an offer of £1.9 million. The appellants, Mr Walford and his brother, heard of the proposed sale and were anxious to purchase the business as they considered it a bargain. Mr and Mrs Miles, for their part, were prepared to warrant that the cash resources in the company's bank account on completion would be £1 million, and that in the first year of trading after completion the company's profits would be £300,000. Mr Miles was to continue working in the business for twelve months after completion, as the appellants knew nothing about the photographic processing business. The purchase price was agreed as £2 million. Mr Miles agreed that, if the appellants could provide a comfort letter from their bank to the effect that they would be able to purchase the business for £2 million, then he and Mrs Miles would not negotiate with anybody else or consider any alternative offers. The text of this agreement was incorporated into paragraph 5 in the appellants' statement of claim. The comfort letter was provided. However, five days later the appellants were told by Mr Miles that he was not proceeding with the sale but was selling to somebody else. The business was sold for £2 million to P and K.

The appellants brought an action for breach of contract. They contended that the contract was constituted by Mr Miles's 'promise not to negotiate with or consider offers from third parties in exchange for a comfort letter from their bank.

Lord Ackner

The pleaded case

The appellants relied upon an oral agreement, collateral to the negotiations which were proceeding to purchase the company and the land it occupied 'subject to contract'. The consideration for this oral agreement was twofold: firstly, the appellants agreeing to continue the negotiations and not to withdraw and, secondly, their providing the comfort letter from their bankers in the terms requested. . . .

As thus pleaded, the agreement purported to be what is known as a 'lock-out' agreement, providing the appellants with an exclusive opportunity to try and come to terms with the respondents, but without expressly providing any duration for such an opportunity. . . .

For reasons which will become apparent hereafter it was decided to amend [paragraph 5 of the statement of claim] by the following addition:

'It was a term of the said collateral agreement necessarily to be implied to give business efficacy thereto that, so long as they continued to desire to sell the said property and shares, the [first respondent] on behalf of himself and the [second respondent] would continue to negotiate in good faith with the [appellants].'

Thus the statement of claim alleged that, not only were the respondents 'locked out' for some unspecified time from dealing with any third party, but were 'locked in' to dealing with the appellants, also for an unspecified period. . . .

The validity of the agreement alleged in para 5 of the statement of claim as amended

The justification for the implied term in para 5 of the amended statement of claim was that, in order to give the collateral agreement 'business efficacy', Mr Miles was obliged to 'continue to negotiate in good faith'. It was submitted to the Court of Appeal and initially to your Lordships that this collateral agreement could not be made to work, unless there was a positive duty imposed upon Mr Miles to negotiate. It was of course conceded that the agreement made no specific provision for the period it was to last. It was however contended, albeit not pleaded, that the obligation to negotiate would endure for a reasonable time, and that such time was the time which was reasonably necessary to reach a binding agreement. . . .

Apart from the absence of any term as to the duration of the collateral agreement, it contained no provision for the respondents to determine the negotiations, albeit that such a provision was essential. It was contended by Mr Naughton [Counsel for the Walfords] that a term was to be implied giving the respondents a right to determine the negotiations, but only if they had 'a proper reason'. However, in order to determine whether a given reason was a proper one, he accepted that the test was not an objective one: would a hypothetical reasonable person consider the reason a reasonable one? The test was a subjective one: did the respondents honestly believe in the reason which they gave for the termination of the negotiations? Thus they could be quite irrational, so long as they behaved honestly. . . .

. . . Although the cases in the United States did not speak with one voice your Lordships' attention was drawn to the decision of the United States Court of Appeals, Third Circuit in *Channel Home Centers Division of Grace Retail Corp v Grossman* (1986) 795 F 2d 291 as being 'the clearest example' of the American cases in the appellants' favour. That case raised the issue whether an agreement to negotiate in good faith, if supported by consideration, is an enforceable contract. I do not find the decision of any assistance. While accepting that an agreement to agree is not an enforceable contract, the United States Court of Appeals appears to have proceeded on the basis that an agreement to negotiate in good faith is synonymous with an agreement to use best endeavours and, as the latter is enforceable, so is the former. This appears to me, with respect, to be an unsustainable proposition. The reason why an agreement to negotiate, like an agreement to agree, is unenforceable is simply because it lacks the necessary certainty. The same does not apply to an agreement to use best endeavours. This uncertainty is demonstrated in the instant case by the provision which it is said has to be implied in the agreement for the determination of the negotiations. How can a court be expected to decide whether *subjectively*, a proper reason existed for the termination of negotiations? The answer suggested depends upon whether the negotiations have been determined in good faith! However, the concept of a duty to carry on negotiations in good faith is inherently repugnant to the adversarial position of the parties when involved in negotiations.

Each party to the negotiations is entitled to pursue his (or her) own interest, so long as he avoids making misrepresentations. To advance that interest he must be entitled, if he thinks it appropriate, to threaten to withdraw from further negotiation or to withdraw in fact in the hope that the opposite party may seek to reopen the negotiations by offering him improved terms. Mr Naughton, of course, accepts that the agreement upon which he relies does not contain a duty to complete the negotiations. But that still leaves the vital question: how is a vendor ever to know that he is entitled to withdraw from further negotiations? How is the court to police such an 'agreement'? A duty to negotiate in good faith is as unworkable in practice as it is inherently inconsistent with the position of a negotiating party. It is here that the uncertainty lies. In my judgment, while negotiations are in existence either party is entitled to withdraw from these negotiations, at any time and for any reason. There can be thus no obligation to continue to negotiate until there is a 'proper reason' to withdraw. Accordingly, a bare agreement to negotiate has no legal content. . . .

. . . I believe it is helpful to make these observations about a so-called 'lock-out' agreement. There is clearly no reason in English contract law why A, for good consideration, should not achieve an enforceable agreement whereby B agrees for a specified period of time not to negotiate with anyone except A in relation to the sale of his property. There are often good commercial reasons why A should desire to obtain such an agreement from B. B's property which A contemplates purchasing may be such as to require the expenditure of not inconsiderable time and money before A is in a position to assess what he is prepared to offer for its purchase or whether he wishes to make any offer at all. A may well consider that he is not prepared to run the risk of expending such time and money unless there is a worthwhile prospect, should he desire to make an offer to purchase, of B, not only then still owning the property, but of being prepared to consider his offer. A may wish to guard against the risk that, while he is investigating the wisdom of offering to buy B's property, B may have already disposed of it or, alternatively, may be so advanced in negotiations with a third party as to be unwilling or for all practical purposes unable to negotiate with A. But I stress that this is a negative agreement—B, by agreeing not to negotiate for this fixed period with a third party, locks himself out of such negotiations. He has in no legal sense locked himself *into* negotiations with A. What A has achieved is an exclusive opportunity, for a fixed period, to try and come to terms with B, an opportunity for which he has, unless he makes his agreement under seal, to give good considerations. I therefore cannot accept Mr Naughton's proposition, which was the essential reason for his amending para 5 of the statement of claim by the addition of the implied term, that without a positive obligation on B to negotiate with A the lock-out agreement would be futile.

Notes

1. Lord Ackner expressly rejects the idea that to use 'best endeavours' and

to negotiate 'in good faith' amount to the same thing. In what way they are different is not made clear. For the House of Lords, a primary objection to 'agreements to agree' is that they are too uncertain. How, their Lordships ask themselves, can a court be expected to decide whether, subjectively, a proper reason existed for the termination of negotiations? That the answer lies in whether the negotiations have been terminated in good faith is rejected as being outside the 'adversarial position' of parties in negotiation. The difference that 'best endeavours' would make to the 'adversarial position' of the parties is not articulated.

2. To consider parties negotiating a contract to be in an adversarial position is to take a very one-dimensional view of how contracts are concluded. The parties here were not embarking upon a wholly discrete exchange. The proposed sale had certain relational characteristics in that Mr Miles was to continue working in the business for twelve months for the appellants and had warranted how much profit the business would make. It is unlikely that a working relationship would be reached in these circumstances by arm's length 'hard bargaining'. As Cumberbatch points out,

J. Cumberbatch, 'In Freedom's Cause: The Contract to Negotiate', (1992) 12 *OJLS* 586 at 588

[T]he adversarial position of negotiating parties would seem, with respect, to have been overstated. While it must be conceded that each party seeks to obtain the best deal for himself, this is not usually effected through actively ensuring the worst possible deal for the other party, and, further, it would be the exceptional context in which a party who was 'bound' himself to negotiation, commonly understood to involve proposal, consideration and counterproposal, could be said to be performing his contractual obligation by, as Lord Ackner suggests, refusing to negotiate. There would seem, therefore, to be much to counter their Lordships' view that the agreement to negotiate is too uncertain as a matter of principle and, it might be argued, the decision was probably based on latent considerations of policy.

A relational agreement as in *Walford* v. *Miles* involves continued co-operation between the parties (see the extracts from Macneil and Macaulay in Ch. 2 and more generally I. Macneil, 'A Primer of Contract Planning', (1975) 48 *S. Cal. L. Rev.* 627).

3. A more relevant point may be that Mrs Miles explained the conduct of herself and her husband towards the appellants in terms of wishing to abandon the proposed relational exchange with them in favour of a discrete exchange with the eventual purchasers. Perhaps it was in the minds of their Lordships that to hold the respondents to the proposed relational

exchange on the grounds that the agreement to agree was enforceable would be to impinge on their freedom to contract. This point is neatly expressed by Cumberbatch.

Cumberbatch, 'In Freedom's Cause: The Contract to Negotiate', 589

It may be tentatively suggested in light of the assertions that 'each party . . . is entitled to pursue his . . . own interest' and that 'there can be no obligation to continue to negotiate until there is a proper reason to withdraw', that the relevant aspect of public policy is the freedom of the individual (and other entities) to contract or not to contract with whoever he wants, whenever he wants and on the terms he wants. At first blush, it might seem odious, and a flagrant infringement of this freedom, to force one party to negotiate with another. However, once it is accepted that the source of such an obligation is the serious promise of that same party, freely given, in a commercial context and for good consideration, much of the objection is removed. It would be vain to argue that a party should not be allowed to restrict this freedom, as Parliament and the courts have done, as social relationships have become increasingly more sophisticated.

4. On the question of uncertainty and the role of the courts in determining whether one party has a proper reason to withdraw from 'the agreement to agree', some useful observations are offered by Knapp, writing in the context of US law, on how these difficulties could be overcome.

C. Knapp, 'Enforcing the Contract to Bargain', (1969) 44 *NYU L. Rev.* 673 at 721–3. Reproduced with kind permission of the New York University Law Review

Good Faith Bargaining

What sort of conduct will be regarded as "bad faith" in the context of a contract to bargain? . . . Withdrawal merely because a better offer has been received from a third party . . .seems the most obvious case of bad faith. Somewhat less obvious, but an example of bad faith nevertheless, would be a withdrawal, . . . for no reason other than a change of heart. On the other hand, withdrawal after substantial negotiations have failed to produce agreement on the reserved terms . . . should not be regarded as bad faith, and should produce no liability on the part of the withdrawing party.

Consideration of the "good faith" standard for performance of the contract to bargain suggests two related objections which may be raised to judicial recognition of such contracts. The device may be used to penalize a party merely for "insufficient bargaining." There is, of course, some danger that a party's withdrawal from a contemplated transaction after what he regards as a complete breakdown of negotiations might later be viewed as a failure to bargain long enough, or "reasonably" enough, thus constituting a breach of contract. Plaintiff, however, bears the burden of proof both as to the existence of a contract and as to its breach. In the absence of any additional factors to indicate bad faith (such as acceptance of a better offer from a third party), a court might well find that plaintiff had failed to demonstrate defendant's lack of good faith.

This leads to the second objection that whenever an extraneous factor, such as a better offer from a third party, makes withdrawal from the contract materially advantageous to one party, that party runs the risk of being held liable even if he withdraws from the transaction only after extensive bargaining has failed to produce a complete agreement. Two factors, however, seem to minimize the likelihood of such occurrences. One is the possibility of creating a record of bargaining sufficient to demonstrate that agreement clearly could have been reached had the plaintiff really desired it; second, even those courts willing to recognize the contract to bargain will do so with extreme caution, and only where the justice of plaintiff's claim is virtually beyond question. These two factors suggest that a contract to bargain is likely to be enforced only where there has been either a unilateral withdrawal from negotiations or at least an insistence on terms so clearly unreasonable that they could not have been advanced with any expectation of acceptance, coupled with some demonstrable advantage to be gained by defendant in avoiding the contemplated transaction.

5. Lord Ackner in his judgment discusses lock-out agreements, which he defines as A agreeing with B, for good consideration, that B should not negotiate with anyone except A for a fixed period of time. He indicates that this sort of arrangement is enforceable in English law. He describes it as a lock-out agreement because he sees B as locked out of negotiating with third parties *but* not as locked into negotiating with A. Presumably he feels that the inclusion of a fixed time period will overcome the problems of when either party can withdraw from the negotiations, which so troubled him in *Walford* v. *Miles*. For Lord Ackner, the significance of B being locked-out rather than locked-in could be that he does not see B as being forced to agree with A; it is up to A to convince B to contract with him, and B does not have to do so if he does not so wish. This would answer the point raised by Cumberbatch about the breakdown of contract. However, the social matrix of negotiations is such that they are not one-sided. Whether we describe B as locked-out from negotiations with third parties or locked into negotiations with A, surely the practical effect is the same; A and B are negotiating with each other, to the exclusion of others, to conclude an agreement with contractual force.

If we construct a lock-out agreement on the facts of *Walford* v. *Miles*, we find Mr Miles locked-out from negotiations with anyone other than the appellants for a fixed period. At the end of the period Mr Miles withdraws and contracts with a third party. The appellants may have an enforceable agreement according to Lord Ackner, but how can they enforce it unless the court is prepared to imply a good faith requirement into the negotiations? Without this, Mr Miles could have refused to answer any correspondence or return phone calls from the appellants without incurring any sanctions, provided that he did not communicate with third parties until the period had elapsed. To say that enforceability rests on Mr Miles not talking to anyone else rather than on whether or not he talks to the appellants would seem to reduce a 'lock-out' agreement to a meaningless agreement.

See further on these problems I. Brown, 'The Contract to Negotiate: A Thing Writ in Water?', [1992] *JBL* 353; R. Buckley, 'Walford v Miles: False Certainty About Uncertainty—An Australian Perspective', (1993) 6 *JCL* 58; and P. Neill, 'A Key to Lock-Out Agreements?', (1992) 108 *LQR* 405.

6. The reasoning on lock-out agreements in *Walford* v. *Miles* was applied by the Court of Appeal in *Pitt* v. *PHH Asset Management* [1993] 4 All ER 961. The lock-out agreement in this case concerned a prospective house purchaser who wished to prevent the vendor from negotiating with a third party for a fixed period of two weeks. The agreement was broken by the vendor within the two-week period, when a sale to a third party was agreed. The Court of Appeal in this case expressed very strongly their desire to protect the plaintiff from the avaricious nature of the defendant, but protection was only possible on the basis of breach of the agreement within the time period; if the period expired without resolution of the sale, the vendor would have become free to sell to a third party.

7. The appellants were seeking to claim £3 million as damages for breach of contract. This was their expectation loss. The purchase price of the business was £2 million and the appellants felt that it was worth £3 million. They were asking to be put in the position they would have been in had the contract been performed "– if, in other words," they had been able to purchase an asset for £2 million which they felt was in fact worth £3 million. In fact, the House of Lords was not required to consider the issue of quantum, as this was left to be determined had the issue of liability been decided in their favour. We can then only speculate on whether the decision would have been any different if the appellants had been able to show detrimental reliance on the 'agreement to agree', perhaps in the form of foregoing other opportunities or entering into other contracts (e.g. recruiting skilled staff). The position of the appellants was that what they lost by the respondents' actions was the chance to snap up what they considered to be a real bargain in the commercial sense. The key question is whether the law should protect this kind of speculation.

Consider the facts and outcome of the following case in comparison to the result in *Walford* v. *Miles*.

Blackpool and Fylde Aero Club Ltd. v. *Blackpool BC*
[1990] 3 All ER 25

Blackpool Borough Council owned and managed Blackpool Airport. As a revenue-raising exercise, the Council was in the habit of granting a concession (a right to use) to an air operator to operate pleasure flights from the airport. Blackpool and Fylde Aero Club had been granted the concession on the three previous occasions it had been awarded by the Council. Its present concession was about to expire, and the Council prepared an invitation to tender. This was sent to seven parties connected in some way with the airport. The arrangements for replying to the tender invitation were that the tender had to be placed in the envelope provided by the Council and delivered to them by 12 noon on Thursday 17 March 1983. The tender invitation made it clear that no tenders received after this time would be considered. The Aero Club prepared its tender and duly delivered it.

The Council staff did not open the box containing the delivered tenders on 17 March. They did so on 18 March and, on finding the tender from the Aero Club, they marked it late. It was not considered, and the tender was awarded to a third party. After some discussion between the Council and the Aero Club, the Council's mistake was discovered and the Council proposed to go through the tendering exercise again. The third party to whom the concession had been awarded threatened to sue the Council for breach of contract on the grounds that its tender had been accepted and so a contract had been made. The Aero Club then began an action for breach of contract against the Council, on the basis that the Council had warranted that all tenders in the prescribed form and in by the due date would be considered. The Court of Appeal rejected the Council's appeal against a finding of liability in favour of the Aero Club.

BINGHAM LJ A tendering procedure of this kind is, in many respects, heavily weighted in favour of the invitor. He can invite tenders from as many or as few parties as he chooses. He need not tell any of them who else, or how many others, he has invited. The invitee may often, although not here, be put to considerable labour and expense in preparing a tender, ordinarily without recompense if he is unsuccessful. The invitation to tender may itself, in a complex case, although again not here, involve time and expense to prepare, but the invitor does not commit himself to proceed with the project, whatever it is; he need not accept the highest tender; he need not accept any tender; he need not give reasons to justify his acceptance or rejection of any tender received. The risk to which the tenderer is exposed does not end with the risk that his tender may not be the highest (or, as the case may be, lowest). But whereas here, tenders are solicited from selected parties all of them known to the invitor, and where a local authority's invitation prescribes a clear, orderly and familiar procedure (draft contract conditions available for inspection and plainly not open to negotiation, a prescribed common form of tender, the supply of envelopes designed to preserve the absolute anonymity of tenderers and clearly to identify the tender in question and an absolute deadline) the invitee is in my judgment protected at least to this extent: if he submits a conforming tender before the deadline he is entitled, not as a matter of mere expectation but of contractual right, to be sure that his tender will after the deadline be opened and considered in conjunction with all other conforming tenders or at least that his tender will be considered if others are. Had the club, before tendering, inquired of the council whether it could rely on any timely and conforming tender being considered along with others, I feel quite sure that the answer would have been 'of course'. The law would, I think, be defective if it did not give effect to that.

It is of course true that the invitation to tender does not explicitly state that the council will consider timely and conforming tenders. That is why one is concerned with implication. But the council does not either say that it does not bind itself to do so, and in the context a reasonable invitee would understand the invitation to be saying, quite clearly, that if he submitted a timely and conforming tender it would be considered, at least if any other such tender were considered.

Notes

1. The remedy claimed by the appellants in *Walford* v. *Miles* was their expectation loss of £3 million. In other words, they were asking the court to put them in the position they would have been in had they been able to purchase the business. They had offered £2 million to the respondents but believed that the business was worth £3 million. In the *Blackpool Airport* case it is not clear what remedy the plaintiffs were seeking. The question of damages was deferred at first instance and not discussed in the Court of Appeal. There would appear to be four alternatives that the plaintiffs could have pursued:

(i) The rerun of the tendering exercise, which may then have left the Council open to an action for breach of contract from the previously successful third party. This type of recovery can be termed either reliance-based, as it is by J. Adams and R. Brownsword ('More in Expectation than Hope: The Blackpool Airport Case', (1991) 54 *MLR* 281), or indeed expectation-based, as it would have had the effect of putting the Aero Club in the position it would have been in had the contract been performed, in that the Club would have had a chance of winning the concession.

(ii) A similar approach is to award the Club the money equivalent of a rerun of the tendering exercise. This could be calculated as the loss of profit (taken from the profit figures obtained on the previous awards of the concession to the Club) less a discount for the possibility that it would not have secured the contract for the concession.

(iii) The loss of profit on the concession contract. This is obviously the most favourable remedy for the Aero Club, but it is difficult to argue that this should be the measure of damages, since the contract which the Court of Appeal did in fact imply was a contract between the Aero Club and Blackpool BC that the Club's tender would be considered if presented in the correct form. The effect of awarding loss of profit on the concession contract would be to award expectation loss on a contract which is wholly fictional.

(iv) The cost of preparing the tender. This is the least favourable remedy for the Aero Club, and reflects the recovery of purely reliance loss.

IV. OFFER AND ACCEPTANCE

We now turn to look at the legal mechanisms involved in creating a contract. The extract from Lewis below gives an overview of what is required: an offer and an acceptance of that offer form an agreement which is recognized as a legally binding contract.

R. Lewis, 'Contracts Between Businessmen: Reform of the Law of Firm Offers and an Empirical Study of Tendering Practices in the Building Industry', (1982) 12 *JLS* 153 at 156

Offer and Acceptance

The classical concepts of offer and acceptance derive from a few cases decided in the late eighteenth and early nineteenth centuries. Traditionally, they have been one of the first subjects studied by a law student in the initiation into the mysteries of contract. The rites of the subject begin with an investigation of the formation of contract and this involves study of "the phenomena of agreement" which deals with the nature of the communications between the parties. These general rules "wear the rich deep polish of a thousand classrooms". They demand that in order for any contract to be formed, one party must make an offer which is mirrored in an acceptance given in return by the other. The general impression is one of free bargaining, an unregulated market with each side able to make overtures to the other about any matter whatsoever; counter offers destroy earlier offers until negotiations either break down or arrive at that consensus necessary to achieve the label of contract and the protection of court enforceability.

Until an unequivocal acceptance is made, the offeror is free to do as he pleases so that he can vary the terms of the offer or even revoke it if he wishes. According to classical ideas of freedom of contract, an offer is by its nature revocable until it is accepted so that an offeror is not to be kept to his promise if he has indicated in good time that he will not be bound by it. This means that before an offer is relied upon, an acceptance should be sent so as to close tightly the jaws of the contract and secure any expectations to which the offer may give rise.

Contract law has developed rules on what constitutes an offer; it would seem that an offer has to be a statement, (written or oral) or some other form of definite indication that a person is prepared to be legally bound without further negotiation. This offer has to be certain and firm enough to be capable of acceptance. For example, if Sally offers to sell her house to Jo and Jo accepts, then, to be an offer capable of acceptance, Sally's offer must contain at least the price.

In order that those involved in negotiating contracts do not find themselves bound at an unexpectedly early stage, contract law does not regard all statements or conduct expressing a willingness to be bound as offers. Preliminary negotiations between parties are said to amount to invitations to treat. The distinction between an invitation to treat and an offer is central to contract law, and was an issue in *Gibson* v. *Manchester City Council.*

A. Locating Offer and Acceptance

Gibson v. *Manchester City Council*
[1979] 1 All ER 972

In 1970 the defendant Council began a policy of selling council houses to tenants; Mr Gibson entered into negotiations with the Council to purchase the house he was renting by applying on a printed form supplied by the Council for details of the price of the house and mortgage terms available from the Council. Before negotiations for the sale of Mr Gibson's house were complete, political control of the Council switched to the Labour Party, which reversed the policy of council house sales. Details of the correspondence between the parties, on the basis of which Mr Gibson claimed that he had a contract with the Council, are given in Lord Diplock's judgment. The plaintiff brought an action for specific performance of this contract. He succeeded at first instance and in the Court of Appeal ([1978] 2 All ER 583), where Lord Denning MR made a number of unorthodox comments about the formation of contracts (see the judgment of Lord Edmund-Davies below). The defendants appealed to the House of Lords.

LORD DIPLOCK The only question in the appeal is of a kind with which the courts are very familiar. It is whether in the correspondence between the parties there can be found a legally enforceable contract for the sale by the Manchester Corporation to Mr Gibson of the dwelling-house of which he was the occupying tenant at the relevant time in 1971. That question is one that, in my view, can be answered by applying to the particular documents relied on by

Mr Gibson as constituting the contract, well settled, indeed elementary, principles of English law. This being so, it is not the sort of case in which leave would have been likely to be granted to appeal to your Lordships' House, but for the fact that it is a test case. The two documents principally relied on by Mr Gibson were in standard forms used by the council in dealing with applications from tenants of council houses to purchase the freehold of their homes under a scheme that had been adopted by the council during a period when it was under Conservative Party control. Political control passed to the Labour Party as a result of the local government elections held in May 1971. The scheme was then abandoned. It was decided that no more council houses should be sold to any tenant with whom a legally binding contract of sale had not already been concluded. At the date of this decision there were a considerable number of tenants, running into hundreds, whose applications to purchase the houses which they occupied had reached substantially the same stage as that of Mr Gibson. The two documents in the same standard form as those on which he principally relies had passed between each one of them and the council. So their rights too are likely to depend on the result of this appeal. . . .

. . . The particulars of claim alleged an offer in writing by the council to sell the freehold interest in the house to Mr Gibson at a price of £2,180 and an acceptance in writing of that offer by Mr Gibson. The judge . . . followed the conventional approach to the question that fell to be decided. He looked to see whether there was an offer of sale and an acceptance. He held that, on their true construction, the documents relied on as such in the particulars of claim did amount to an offer and an acceptance respectively and so constituted a legally enforceable contract. He ordered specific performance of an open contract for the sale to Mr Gibson of the freehold interest in the house at the price of £2,180.

The council's appeal against this judgment was dismissed by a majority of the Court of Appeal (Lord Denning MR and Ormrod LJ); Geoffrey Lane LJ dissented. Lord Denning MR rejected what I have described as the conventional approach of looking to see whether on the true construction of the documents relied on there can be discerned an offer and acceptance. One ought, he said, to 'look at the correspondence as a whole and at the conduct of the parties and see therefrom whether the parties have come to an agreement on everything that was material'. . . .

Ormrod LJ, who agreed with Lord Denning MR, adopted a similar approach but he did also deal briefly with the construction of the document relied on by Mr Gibson as an unconditional offer of sale by the council. On this he came to the same conclusion as the county court judge.

Geoffrey Lane LJ in a dissenting judgment, which for my part I find convincing, adopted the conventional approach. He found that on the true construction of the documents relied on as constituting the contract, there never was an offer by the council acceptance of which by Mr Gibson was capable in law of constituting a legally enforceable contract. It was but a step in the negotiations for a contract which, owing to the change in the political complexion of the council, never reached fruition.

My Lords, there may be certain types of contract, though I think they are exceptional, which do not fit easily into the normal analysis of a contract as being constituted by offer and acceptance; but a contract alleged to have been made by an exchange of correspondence between the parties in which the successive communications other than the first are in reply to one another is not one of these. I can see no reason in the instant case for departing from the conventional approach of looking at the handful of documents relied on as constituting the contract sued on and seeing whether on their true construction there is to be found in them a contractual offer by the council to sell the house to Mr Gibson and an acceptance of that offer by Mr Gibson. I venture to think that it was by departing from this conventional approach that the majority of the Court of Appeal was led into error.

The genesis of the relevant negotiations in the instant case is a form filled in by Mr Gibson on 28th November 1970 enquiring what would be the price of buying his council house at 174 Charlestown Road, Blackley, and expressing his interest in obtaining a mortgage from the council. The form was a detachable part of a brochure which had been circulated by the council to tenants who had previously expressed an interest in buying their houses. It contained details of a new scheme for selling council houses that had been recently adopted by the council. The scheme provided for a sale at market value less a discount dependent on the length of time the purchaser had been a council tenant. This, in the case of Mr Gibson, would have amounted to 20%. The scheme also provided for the provision by the council of advances on mortgage which might amount to as much as the whole of the purchase price.

As a result of that enquiry Mr Gibson's house was inspected by the council's valuer and on 10th February 1971 the letter which is relied on by Mr Gibson as the offer by the Council to sell the house to him was sent from the city treasurer's department. It was in the following terms:

'Dear Sir,

'Purchase of Council House
'*Your Reference Number 82463 03*

'I refer to your request for details of the cost of buying your Council house. *The Corporation may be prepared to sell the house to you at the purchase price of £2,725 less 20% = £2,180 (freehold).*

'Maximum mortgage the Corporation may grant:

	£2,177 repayable over 20 years.
'Annual fire insurance premium:	£2.45
'Monthly Repayment charge calculated by:—	
(i) flat rate repayment method:	£19.02

'If you wish to pay off some of the purchase price at the start and therefore require a mortgage for less than the amount quoted above, the monthly instalment will change; in these circumstances, I will supply new figures on request. The above repayment figures apply so long as the interest rate charged on home loans is 8½%. The interest rate will be subject to variation by the Corporation after giving not less than three months' written notice, and if it changes, there will be an adjustment to the monthly instalment payable. This letter should not be regarded as firm offer of a mortgage.

'If you would like to make formal application to buy your Council house, please complete the enclosed application form and return it to me as soon as possible.

'Yours faithfully,
'(Sgd) H. R. Page
'City Treasurer

'Mr. Robert Gibson.'

My Lords, the words I have italicised seem to me, as they seemed to Geoffrey Lane LJ, to make it quite impossible to construe this letter as a contractual offer capable of being converted into a legally enforceable open contract for the sale of land by Mr Gibson's written acceptance of it. The words 'may be prepared to sell' are fatal to this; so is the invitation, not, be it noted, to accept the offer, but 'to make formal application to buy' on the enclosed application form. It is, to quote Geoffrey Lane LJ, a letter setting out the financial terms on which it may be the council would be prepared to consider a sale and purchase in due course.

Both Ormrod LJ and the county court judge, in reaching the conclusion that this letter was a firm offer to sell the freehold interest in the house for £2,180, attached importance to the fact that the second paragraph, dealing with the financial details of the mortgage of which Mr Gibson had asked for particulars, stated expressly, 'This letter should not be regarded as a firm offer of a mortgage'. The necessary implication from this, it is suggested, is that the first paragraph of the letter *is* to be regarded as a firm offer to sell despite the fact that this is plainly inconsistent with the express language of that paragraph. My Lords, with great respect, this surely must be fallacious. If the final sentence had been omitted the wording of the second paragraph, unlike that of the first, with its use of the indicative mood in such expressions as 'the interest rate *will* change', might have been understood by council tenants to whom it was addressed as indicating a firm offer of a mortgage of the amount and on the terms for repayment stated if the council were prepared to sell the house at the stated price. But, whether or not this be the explanation of the presence of the last sentence in the second paragraph, it cannot possibly affect the plain meaning of the words used in the first paragraph.

Mr Gibson did fill in the application form enclosed with this letter. It was in three sections: section A headed 'Application to buy a council house', section B 'Application for a loan to buy a council house', and section C 'Certificate to be completed by all applicants'. He left blank the space for the purchase price in section A and sent the form to the council on 5th March 1971 with a covering letter in which he requested the council either to undertake at their own expense to carry out repairs to the tarmac path forming part of the premises or to make a deduction from the purchase price to cover the cost of repairs. The letter also intimated that Mr Gibson would like to make a down payment of £500 towards the purchase price instead of borrowing the whole amount on mortgage. In reply to the request made in this letter the council, by letter of 12th March 1971, said that the condition of the property had been taken into consideration in fixing the purchase price and that repairs to the tarmac by the council could not be authorised at this stage. This letter was acknowledged by Mr Gibson by his letter to the council of 18th March 1971 in which he asked the council to 'carry on with the purchase as per my application already in your possession'.

My Lords the application form and letter of 18th March 1971 were relied on by Mr Gibson as an unconditional acceptance of the council's offer to sell the house; but this cannot be so unless there was a contractual offer by the council available for acceptance, and, for the reason already given I am of opinion that there was none. It is unnecessary to consider whether the application form and Mr Gibson's letters of 5th and 18th March 1971 are capable of amounting to a contractual offer by him to purchase the freehold interest in the house at a price of £2,180 on the terms of an open contract, for there is no suggestion that, even if it were, it was ever accepted by the council. Nor would it ever have been even if there had been no change in the political control of the council, as the policy of the council before the change required the incorporation in all agreements for sale of council houses to tenants of the conditions referred by Lord Denning MR in his judgment and other conditions inconsistent with an open contract. . . .

LORD EDMUND-DAVIES My Lords, it was on the basis of the foregoing documents and correspondence that Mr Gibson instituted proceedings in the county court in September 1974 for specific performance of what he, in effect, submitted was an open contract whereby the council had agreed to sell to him the freehold of his dwelling for £2,180. It was pleaded that the council had so offered by their letter of 10th February 1971 and the accompanying application form, the acceptance (as I understand) being conveyed by Mr Gibson's completing and returning that form and later 'unconditionally accepted the said offer by letter to the defendants dated 18th March 1971'. Reliance was also sought to be laid on an internal memorandum passing between two of the council's departments which was said to constitute an admission by the council that they had (presumably by *that* date) sold the freehold to Mr Gibson. It is convenient to mention also at this stage that both in the county court and in the Court of Appeal the plaintiff relied further on the fact that during 1971 the town clerk, in the course of a letter he sent a city councillor who had espoused Mr Gibson's case, had written regarding the treasurer's letter of 10th February 1971:

'*Mr. Gibson accepted this offer,* but before the papers could be passed to me for preparation of the formal contract the local elections intervened. Since then no more contracts
have been prepared, pending a formal decision being taken by the present Council
regarding the policy to be adopted in relation to the sale of Council houses . . .'

It is, however, right to observe that, later in his same letter, the town clerk
wrote of the unwisdom of Mr Gibson's having carried out certain alterations
'before there was a binding contract in existence', although these words may,
or may not, have been intended to refer to the absence of any 'formal contract',
a fact to which the writer also adverted.

The pleaded defence was simple: the council had made no offer; alternatively, if they had, Mr Gibson had not accepted it; the internal memorandum
constituted no admission . . . There was at best no more than an invitation by
the council to tenants to apply to be allowed to purchase freeholds . . . . even
had there been an offer, I hold that counsel for the council was right in submitting that there followed no acceptance, but nothing more than an application to
buy at an unstated price, coupled with an application for a loan.

The offer and acceptance approach obviously presenting certain difficulties,
the majority held in the Court of Appeal that it was not the only one,—

Lord Denning MR said that in such cases—

'You should look at the correspondence as a whole and at the conduct of the parties
and see therefrom whether the parties have come to an agreement on everything that
was material. If by their correspondence and their conduct you can see an agreement
on all material terms, which was intended thenceforward to be binding, then there is a
binding contract in law even though all the formalities have not been gone through. For
that proposition I would refer to *Brogden* v *Metropolitan Railway Co* [(1877) 2 App. Cas.
666]'.

On that alternative basis, Lord Denning MR concluded that the parties had in
truth contractually bound themselves. His first ground for so concluding was
the nature of the correspondence between the parties, and I have already indicated why, for my part, I hold that of itself this disclosed the making of no contract. His second ground was that, in the belief that a contract to sell would
emerge, Mr Gibson did much work in repairing and improving his house and
premises. But no evidence was called as to when such work had been done,
and it appears from the correspondence that, although as far back as June
1970 Mr Gibson had enquired whether he might proceed to improve the property, '. . . to the mutual benefit of the City and myself until such time as my case
comes up for consideration', the council's reply in the following October gave
no encouragement to the tenant to execute any improvements, and concluded,
'If at any time you decide to withdraw your application I should be obliged if
you would let me know'. It is therefore impossible to conclude that improvements were executed on the basis that the council had already committed
themselves to sell. Nor, with respect to Lord Denning MR, can it be material
that, entirely unknown to Mr Gibson, the council at one stage took 174

Charlestown Road off the list of houses being maintained by them and put it on the list of 'pending sales', for that action had been taken in February 1971 in relation to all cases where the direct works department had been notified that sales were 'proceeding'. And it has to be observed that this alteration in the list was effected a month earlier than the time when, according to Mr Gibson's pleaded case, he accepted the council's 'offer' to sell. And, finally, the town clerk's letter to the city councillor already referred to cannot in my judgment have relevance to the matter of consensus ad idem. I have already sought to show that, read as a whole, its wording is equivocal; and, even were it clear, the proper question is not whether the town clerk considered that a contract had been concluded but whether this was so in fact and in law.

Notes

1. The difference between the reasoning of the Court of Appeal and the House of Lords centres upon what each feels is sufficient for a contract to be said to exist. The factual situation was that the parties were already in a relational nexus with each other (i.e. as landlord and tenant) and were negotiating towards a contract. In this instance, the majority of the Court of Appeal appeared prepared to say that there is no need for one component in the transaction to be specifically identifiable as an 'offer' and another as an 'acceptance'. Rather, the transaction can be assessed as a whole. The House of Lords adopts a more traditional approach and rejects the 'whole transaction analysis'.

2. If the whole transaction approach is rejected, it then becomes crucial to identify which event in any scenario amounts to an offer. Above, we defined an offer as an expression of intent which, if accepted, will bind the offeror without further negotiation; as such it must be firm and certain. It is clear, however, from some cases that simply identifying an event with these characteristics is not sufficient. We need to look further and examine the consequences of labelling a particular event an offer. This is best illustrated by a group of cases involving shop sales.

3. *Pharmaceutical Society of Great Britain* v. *Boots Cash Chemists (Southern) Ltd.* ([1953] 1 QB 401) concerned sales of drugs in a self-service pharmacy. The customer selected the goods she wished to buy and took them to the cash desk, where the cashier added up the price and took the customer's money. Some of the goods on sale were required by statute to be sold under the supervision of a pharmacist. There was a pharmacist present at the cash desk who supervised transactions concerning such goods. The question for the court to determine was when the contract was made; it was argued that if the display of goods constituted an offer and the selection of them by the customer an acceptance, then a contract was

made at that point and the pharmacist had no jurisdiction at the cash desk to prevent the sale of particular goods to unsuitable customers.

A display of goods in a shop looks as though it fulfils all the criteria we have identified for an offer. However, the consequences of labelling it as such were, according to Somervell LJ, that

once an article has been placed in the receptacle [i.e. shopping basket or trolley], the customer himself is bound and would have no right, without paying for the first article, to substitute an article which he saw later of a similar kind and which he perhaps preferred. ([1953] 1 QB 401 at 406)

Other objections that have been put forward are that a shop is a place where bartering over the price might take place, and that a shopkeeper would be obliged by construing the display as an offer to sell more goods than he has if he receives more acceptances. Atiyah points out (*An Introduction to the Law of Contract*, 65) that none of these reasons is really sufficient, but rather the approach of the Court is an *ex post facto* justification for a policy choice. In the event, the Court of Appeal decided that the display was only an invitation to treat, and that the offer was made by the customer in taking the goods to the cash desk and accepted there by the cashier.

It can therefore be seen that, according to the definition of an 'offer' provided by the cases, the offer could have occurred when the goods were displayed, when they were selected by the customer, or when they were taken to the cash desk by the customer. Acceptance could take place when the cashier processed the transaction or when the customer paid the price asked for. The Court of Appeal shifted the label 'offer' to a point in the scenario other than the one which at first sight seemed most obvious, and that enabled the court to reach a particular result which it presumably considered to be preferable in the circumstances. This type of reasoning is defined by Atiyah as conceptual.

P. S. Atiyah, *An Introduction to the Law of Contract*, 4th edn. (Oxford, Clarendon Press, 1989), 64–5

Put very briefly, conceptual reasoning usually takes the form of reasoning *forwards* from legal concepts to the solution of particular dispute. For instance, if a plaintiff claims that the defendant has broken a contract and the defendant denies that there was any contract, the court may approach the case by asking whether the defendant's words or conduct amount to an offer or an acceptance. If this question is answered in the negative, the court then *deduces* that no contract was made.

But this is not the only way in which such questions can be approached; for an alternative—and less conceptual—method of approach is to reason *back-*

wards. For instance, if the court thinks that the plaintiff ought to have a legal remedy against the defendant for what happened, the court may reason thus: if the plaintiff is to be given a legal remedy, we must hold that there was a contract; but in order to hold that there was a contract we must first hold that the defendant's conduct amounted to an offer (or an acceptance). *Therefore* we hold that the defendant's conduct did amount to an offer (or an acceptance).

In practice, courts in this country have traditionally adopted the first approach in preference to the second, but there is no doubt that this has some disadvantages. It tends to lend an air of inevitability to the decisions of the courts which is most misleading. The decision only appears to be inevitable because most of the real issues are not discussed at all; though they may weigh with the courts in arriving at their decisions, their reasoning is not openly and consciously displayed. Instead, a number of other reasons which may be more or less convincing are offered for the decision. . . .

Thus in strict logic the way in which a fact or a particular piece of conduct should be conceptualized by having a legal label attached to it, should depend on the result which it is desired to achieve. But it must be recognized that lawyers and courts often reason in a way which suggests that they do not accept the strictly logical position. They frequently attach the label first, and give every appearance of thinking that the selection of the correct label is something which must be done without reference to the result.

Notes

1. A different way of explaining how and why judges reach their decisions and why there are differences in the ways in which they reason their decisions is offered by Adams and Brownsword:

J. Adams and R. Brownsword, 'More in Expectation than Hope: The Blackpool Airport Case', (1991) 54 *MLR* 281 at 285–6

Contractual Ideologies

. . . we have argued that an understanding of contract involves an appreciation of various competing ideologies. This claim has two dimensions: first, that contractual doctrines presuppose certain ideological positions (in particular, 'market-individualism' and 'consumer-welfarism'); and, second, that where judges are required to settle issues of contract law, they operate within a field of ideological tensions comprising 'formalism,' 'market-individualist realism' and 'consumer-welfarist realism.' . . .

. . . The distinction between formalism and realism is irrelevant for the purposes of analysing the ideological underpinnings of contractual doctrine. . . . Quite simply, formalism and realism represent two kinds of *judicial approach* to cases; they are not ideological categories into which legal doctrines can be organised. As categories of judicial approach, however, we regard formalism and realism as the starting point for understanding adjudication; and, in this sense, we regard them as infinitely more important than market-individualism or consumer-welfarism. Let us explain why this is so.

. . .we distinguished between a formalist and a realist approach in terms of 'following the rule-book' (formalism) as against 'result-orientation' (realism). We can put this rather more precisely. The fundamental question for any judge, in any kind of case, is whether fidelity to the formal doctrines, rules, principles and the like (the 'law' as legal positivists would have it) is to be treated as an over-riding value for decision-makers. In other words the question is whether the formal materials are to be applied even though, as the judge believes, such an application violates some background value (utility, justice, convenience or whatever). Where judges treat fidelity to the formal materials as an overriding value, they follow a formalist approach; where judges do not accord fidelity to these materials such an overriding value, they follow a realist approach. This distinction, it must be emphasised, is fundamental in that it is applicable irre-spective of the substantive area of law concerned (ie, contract or otherwise). In other words, at this level, *general judicial ideologies* are involved. Within the two basic approaches, further discriminations can be drawn. The formalist approach can be sub-divided into 'textual-formalist' (where the language of statutes and precedents is strictly observed) and 'purposive-formalist' (where the language of the materials is treated simply as evidence of the underlying purpose, intent or principles of the law). The realist approach can also be sub-divided, into 'weak realist' (where fidelity to the formal materials is accorded some, but not overriding value) and 'strong realist' (where fidelity to the formal materials is accorded no value whatsoever). Accordingly, in any case, in any area of law, we can classify general judicial approaches in terms of textual-formalism, purposive-formalism, weak realism and strong real-ism. . . .

. . . we need to say that, in conjunction with the general judicial ideologies, *particular ideologies* operate within the various fields of law. These particular ideologies are especially important for the purposes of interpreting realist approaches, because they give direction to realist decision-making. However, such particular ideologies are specific to each area of substantive law. In other words, unlike the general ideologies which are applicable across the whole range of law, the particular ideologies have only a local relevance. Accordingly, whilst market-individualism and consumer-welfarism seem to us to be ideolo-gies with particular significance in relation to contractual disputes, they have no relevance in deciding, say, criminal law disputes (where such ideologies as crime control and due process would be appropriate). Our ideological frame-work, therefore, has a general part (the formalist–realist axis) which must be supplemented from one substantive area of law to another by the appropriate particular ideologies.

2. The reasoning of the House of Lords in *Gibson* can be described as formalist.

3. Adams and Brownsword expand their definition of realist reasoning to incorporate two general ideologies which they believe decisions made on the basis of realist reasoning might exhibit.

J. Adams and R. Brownsword, *Understanding Contract Law* (London, Fontana, 1987), 52–3, 54–5

If we focus on the realist approach . . . it will be appreciated that we could conceive, in principle, of any number of criteria to serve as the measure of fitness of particular results. In our contention, however, two realist philosophies dominate contractual thinking in practice. These are what we shall term 'market-individualism' and 'consumer-welfarism'.

Market-individualism has two limbs, a market philosophy and an individualistic philosophy. The market philosophy sees the function of the law of contract as the facilitation of competitive exchange. This demands clear contractual ground rules, transactional security, and the accommodation of commercial practice. The individualistic side of market-individualism enshrines the landmark principles of 'freedom of contract' and 'sanctity of contract', the essential thrust of which is to give the parties the maximum licence in setting their own terms, and to hold parties to their freely made bargains. One particularly important entailment of market-individualism is that judges should offer no succour to parties who are simply trying to escape from a bad bargain, for the sum total of freely negotiated bargains is the good of society as a whole in that it results in an economically efficient use of resources.

The tenets of consumer-welfarism cannot be stated so crisply. In the most abstract terms, consumer-welfarism stands for reasonableness and fairness in contracting. More concretely, this is reflected in a policy of consumer-protection and a pot-pourri of specific principles. For example, consumer-welfarism holds that contracting parties should not mislead one another, that they should act in good faith, that a stronger party should to exploit the weakness of another's bargaining position, that no party should profit from his own wrong or be unjustly enriched, that remedies should be proportionate to the breach, that contracting parties who are at fault should not be able to dodge their responsibilities, and so on. Crucially, consumer-welfarism subscribes to the paternalist principle that contractors who enter into bad bargains may be relieved from their obligations where justice so requires. To this extent, and at the price of some over-simplification, consumer-welfarism may be said to treat justice as more important than freedom (and *vice versa* for market-individualism). . . .

Our two ideal-typical judicial approaches (formalism and realism) can be combined with our two contractual philosophies (market-individualism and consumer-welfarism) to yield the following interpretive framework of judicial ideology:

	Formalism	*Realism*
Market-Individualism	Rule-book approach (rules in rule-book reflecting market-individualism)	Result-orientated approach (guided by market-individualism
Consumer-Welfarism	Rule-book approach (rules in rule-book reflecting consumer-welfarism)	Result-orientated approach (guided by consumer-welfarism)

The recent Court of Appeal decision in *G. Percy Trentham Ltd.* v. *Archital Luxfer Ltd.* ([1993] 1 Lloyd's LR 25) offers further food for thought on judicial reasoning styles in relation to questions of offer and acceptance, and gives a hint that the approach of the Court of Appeal in *Gibson* may be about to undergo a renaissance.

The *Trentham* case involved an alleged subcontract between the plaintiffs, who were main contractors engaged in designing and building some industrial units, and the defendants, who were manufacturers, supplies, and installers of aluminium windows and doors. The parties agreed that the window works allegedly contracted for had been carried out by the defendants and paid for by the plaintiffs. However, when the plaintiffs claimed damages for breach of contract, arguing that there were defects in the window works, the defendants denied liability on the grounds that there had never existed a binding subcontract between the parties for any of the phases of the work actually carried out. On a preliminary issue of liability, the Court of Appeal unanimously reached the conclusion that there had been a contract in respect of all the different phases of the work. The sole judgment was delivered by Steyn LJ who, while not dismissing the possibility of an 'offer and acceptance' approach such as was undertaken by the first instance judge, stressed instead the importance of this being an executed commercial transaction, where the actual performance rendered was, in his view, only explicable in terms of an established and binding agreement. The inference is that in his mind the centrality of this factor as pointing towards the existence of a binding contract overrode any niceties involved in the 'offer and acceptance' approach. Certain general points which Steyn LJ made about issues of contract formation under English law are extracted here.

It seems to me that four matters are of importance. The first is the fact that English law generally adopts an objective theory of contract formation. That means that in practice our law generally ignores the subjective expectations and the unexpressed mental reservations of the parties. Instead the governing criterion is the reasonable expectations of honest men. And in the present case that means that the yardstick is the reasonable expectations of sensible businessmen. Secondly, it is true that the coincidence of offer and acceptance will in the vast majority of cases represent the mechanism of contract formation. It is so in the case of a contract alleged to have been made by an exchange of correspondence. But [it] is not necessarily so in the case of a contract alleged to have come into existence during and as a result of performance. See *Brogden* v. *Metropolitan Railway* . . . *Gibson* v. *Manchester City Council* . . . . The third matter is the impact of the fact that the transaction is executed rather than executory. It is a consideration of the first importance on a number of levels. . . .The fact that the transaction was performed on both sides will often make it unrealistic to argue that there was no intention to enter into legal relations. It will often make it difficult to submit that the contract is void for vagueness or uncertainty. Specifically, the fact that the transaction is executed makes it easier to imply a term resolving any uncertainty, or, alternatively, it may make it possible to treat a matter not finalised in negotiations as inessential. In this case fully executed transactions are under consideration. Clearly, similar considerations may sometimes be relevant in partly executed transactions. Fourthly, if a contract only comes into existence during and as a result of performance of the transaction it will frequently be possible to hold that the contract impliedly and retrospectively covers pre-contractual performance.

Notes

1. The objective theory of contract is dealt with in detail in Chapter 5; here it suffices to highlight the weight which Steyn LJ places upon an objectified 'business approach' to issues of contract formation. The existence of a contract is for him almost a 'common-sense' matter in the type of subcontracting situation at issue in *Trentham*, a point which he reinforces by reference to the role of intention to create legal relations. Yet it is precisely such arguments about the so-called 'intentions' of commercial contractors which are refuted by empirical research such as that undertaken by Macaulay and by Beale and Dugdale, who argue that businessmen are frequently either indifferent to the existence of legal sanctions or sometimes even positively hostile to the imposition of a legal structure.

2. It is significant that Steyn LJ sees some evidence of a looser approach to contract formation in certain contexts. In this respect he stresses the importance of contract performance, suggesting thereby the argument that the legitimate expectations of the parties can only be protected by a *contractual* remedy, as opposed to one based on restitution or tort. This, of course, was certainly not the approach taken in the *British Steel* case ([1984] 1 All ER 504 discussed in Ch. 1), which was not cited in *Trentham*. The point here is that an undertaking to provide works of a certain

standard and without defects cannot be made good through a restitution-ary remedy as easily as an assumed undertaking to pay for goods supplied, which can simply be converted into a restitutionary obligation to restore the reasonable value of the goods. Damages based on contract are the only clear answer to the plaintiff's difficulties.

The stress placed upon the executed nature of the transaction provides a clear example of backwards reasoning. In other words, issues of contract formation are not being interpreted and applied by the judge in such a way as to deny a remedy to a clearly deserving plaintiff who probably has no other effective remedy under the law of obligations.

B. Styles of Judicial Reasoning and Unilateral Contracts

While the next case is commonly taken to be a leading case on offer and acceptance in the context of unilateral, it can, as we shall see, equally well be analysed in terms of the different styles of judicial reasoning which are adopted by the members of the Court of Appeal.

A preliminary note on unilateral contracts. The unilateral contract, or 'if contract' as it is sometimes called, is a two-sided arrangement, but only a one-sided obligation. It is a promise (e.g. to pay money) in return for a stip-ulated act. The most commonly used example is that of the reward offered to anyone who finds and returns a lost pet. The *Blackpool Airport* case con-tains an example of an attempt to 'imply' a unilateral contract along the lines of 'If you tender to provide pleasure flights before the closing date, complying with the condition quoted by the Council, we promise to con-sider your tender along with all the others'. *Carlill* v. *Carbolic Smoke Ball Co.* concerns an analogous situation, except that here it was an express promise which was at issue.

Carlill v. *Carbolic Smoke Ball Co.*
[1891–4] All ER Rep. 127

The defendants, who produced a medical preparation called the Carbolic Smoke Ball which was intended to protect the user against influenza, pub-lished an advertisement in a newspaper in which they stated they would pay £100 to anyone who caught 'flu after using the Ball in a specified man-ner for a specified period. They also stated that they had deposited £1,000 with a bank, as a sign of their good faith. Having seen the advertisement, the plaintiff bought one of the balls, used it as required by the instructions for two weeks, but contracted 'flu. She brought an action to recover the £100 offered by the defendant.

LINDLEY LJ—This is an appeal by the defendants against a decision of Hawkins, J., rendering them liable to pay the plaintiff £100 under the circumstances to which I will allude presently. The defendants are interested in selling as largely as possible an article they call the "Carbolic smoke ball." What that is I do not know. But they have great faith in it as an effectual preventive against influenza and colds, or any diseases caused by taking cold, and as also useful in a great variety of other complaints. They are so confident in the merits of this thing that they say in one leaflet that the carbolic smoke ball never fails to cure all the diseases therein mentioned when used strictly according to these directions. Like other tradespeople they want to induce the public to have sufficient confidence in their preparation to buy it largely. That being the position they put this advertisement into various newspapers. . . . The appeal has been argued with great ingenuity by the defendants' counsel, and his contentions are reduced in substance to this—that, put it as you will, this is not a binding promise. . . .

. . . Read this how you will, and twist it about as you will, here is a distinct promise, expressed in language which is perfectly unmistakeable, that £100 reward will be paid by the Carbolic Smoke Ball Co. to any person who contracts influenza after having used the ball three times daily, and so on. One must look a little further and see if this is intended to be a promise at all; whether it is a mere puff—a sort of thing which means nothing. Is that the meaning of it? My answer to that question is "No," and I base my answer upon this passage: "£1,000 is deposited with the Alliance Bank, Regent Street, showing our sincerity in the matter." What is that money deposited for? What is that passage put in for, except to negative the suggestion that this is a mere puff, and means nothing at all? The deposit is called in aid by the advertisers as proof of their sincerity in the matter. What do they mean? It is to show their intention to pay the £100 in the events which they have specified. I do not know who drew the advertisement, but he has distinctly in words expressed that promise. It is as plain as words can make it.

Then it is said that it is a promise that is not binding. In the first place it is said that it is not made with anybody in particular. The offer is to anybody who performs the conditions named in the advertisement. Anybody who does perform the conditions accepts the offer. I take it that if you look at this advertisement in point of law, it is an offer to pay £100 to anybody who will perform these conditions, and the performance of these conditions is the acceptance of the offer. That rests upon a string of authorities, the earliest of which is that celebrated advertisement case of *Williams* v. *Carwardine* [(1833) 4 B. & Ad. 621], which has been followed by a good many other cases concerning advertisements of rewards. But then it is said: "Supposing that the performance of the conditions is an acceptance of the offer, that acceptance ought to be notified." Unquestionably as a general proposition when an offer is made, you must have it not only accepted, but the acceptance notified. But is that so in cases of this kind? I apprehend that this is rather an exception to the rule, or, if not an exception, it is open to the observation that the notification of the acceptance need not precede the performance. This offer is a continuing offer. It was never revoked, and if notice of acceptance is required (which I doubt very much, for I rather think the true view is that which is as expressed and explained by Lord Blackburn in *Brogden* v. *Metropolitan Rail. Co.*), the person who makes the offer receives the notice of acceptance contemporaneously with his notice of the performance of the conditions. Anyhow, if notice is wanted, he gets it before his offer is revoked, which is all you want in principle. But I doubt very much whether the true view is not, in a case of this kind, that the person who makes the offer shows by his language and from the nature of the transaction that he does not expect and does not require notice of the acceptance apart from notice of the performance.

We have, therefore, all the elements which are necessary to form a binding contract enforceable in point of law subject to two observations on vagueness and consideration. . . .

It appears to me, therefore, that these defendants must perform their promise, and if they have been so unguarded and so unwary as to expose themselves to a great many actions, so much the worse for them. For once in a way the advertiser has reckoned too much on the gullibility of the public. It appears to me that it would be very little short of a scandal if we said that no action would lie on such a promise as this, acted upon as it has been. The appeal must be dismissed with costs.

Bowen, LJ—The first observation that arises is that the document is not a contract at all. It is an offer made to the public. The terms of the offer, counsel says, are too vague to be treated as a definite offer, the acceptance of which would constitute a binding contract. He relies on his construction of the document, in accordance with which he says there is no limit of time fixed for catching influenza, and that it cannot seriously be meant to promise to pay money to a person who catches influenza at any time after the inhaling of the smoke ball. He says also that, if you look at this document you will find great vagueness in the limitation of the persons with whom the contract was intended to be made—that it does not follow that they do not include persons who may have used the smoke ball before the advertisement was issued, and that at all events, it is a contract with the world in general. He further says, that it is an unreasonable thing to suppose it to be a contract, because nobody in their senses would contract themselves out of the opportunity of checking the experiment which was going to be made at their own expense, and there is no such provision here made for the checking. He says that all that shows that this is rather in the nature of a puff or a proclamation than a promise or an offer intended to mature into a contract when accepted.

Counsel says that the terms are incapable of being consolidated into a contract. But he seems to think that the strength of the position he desires to adopt is rather that the vagueness of the document shows that no contract at all was intended. It seems to me that in order to arrive at this contract we must read it in its plain meaning as the public would understand it. It was intended to be issued to the public and to be read by the public. How would an ordinary person reading this document construe it upon the points which the defendant's counsel has brought to our attention? It was intended unquestionably to have some effect, and I think the effect which it was intended to have was that by means of the use of the carbolic smoke ball the sale of the carbolic smoke ball should be increased. It was designed to make people buy the ball. But it was also designed to make them use it, because the suggestions and allegations which it contains are directed immediately to the use of the smoke ball as distinct from the purchase of it. It did not follow that the smoke ball was to be purchased from the defendants directly or even from agents of theirs directly. The intention was that the circulation of the smoke ball should be promoted and that the usage of it should be increased.

The advertisement begins by saying that a reward will be paid by the Carbolic Smoke Ball Co. to any person who contracts influenza, and the defendants say that "contracts" there does not apply only to persons who contract influenza after the publication of the advertisement, but that it might include persons who had contracted influenza before. I cannot so read it. It is written in colloquial and popular language. I think that the expression is equivalent to this, that £100 will be paid to any person who shall contract influenza after having used the carbolic smoke ball three times daily for two weeks. It seems to me that that would be the way in which the public would read it. A plain person who read this advertisement would read it in this plain way, that if anybody after the advertisement was published used three times daily for two weeks the carbolic smoke ball and then caught cold he would be entitled to the reward. . . .

Was the £100 reward intended to be paid? It not only says the reward will be paid, but it says: "We have lodged £1,000 to meet it." Therefore, it cannot be said that it was intended to be a mere puff. I think it was intended to be understood by the public as an offer which was to be acted upon, but counsel for the defendants says that there was no check on the persons who might claim to have used the ball and become entitled to the reward, and that it would be an insensate thing to promise £100 to a person who used the smoke ball unless you could check his using it. The answer to that seems to me to be that, if a person chooses to make these extravagant promises, he probably does so because it pays him to make them, and if he has made them the extravagance of the promises is no reason in law why he should not be bound by them.

It is said it is made to all the world, i.e., to anybody. It is not a contract made with all the world. There is the fallacy of that argument. It is an offer made to all the world, and why should not an offer be made to all the world which is to ripen into a contract with anybody who comes forward and performs the conditions? It is an offer to become liable to anyone, who before it is retracted performs the conditions. Although the offer is made to all the world the contract is made with that limited portion of the public who come forward and perform the conditions on the faith of the advertisement. This case is not like those cases in which you offer to negotiate, or you issue an advertisement that you have got a stock of books to sell or houses to let, in which case there is no offer to be bound by any contract. Such advertisements are offers to negotiate, offers to receive offers, offers "to chaffer," as a learned judge in one of the cases has said: per Willes, J, in *Spencer* v. *Harding* [(1870) LR 5 CP 561]. If this is an offer to be bound on a condition, then there is a contract the moment the acceptor fulfils the condition. That seems to me to be sense, and it is also the ground on which all these advertisement cases have been decided during the century. It cannot be put better than in Willes J's judgment in *Spencer* v. *Harding*, where he says (L.R. 5 C.P. at p. 563):

"There never was any doubt that the advertisement amounted to a promise to pay the money to the person who first gave information. The difficulty suggested was that it was a contract with all the world. But that, of course, was soon overruled. It was an offer to become liable to any person who, before the offer should be retracted, should be the person to fulfil the contract of which the advertisement was an offer or tender. That is not the sort of difficulty which presents itself here. If the circular had gone on 'and we undertake to sell to the highest bidder,' the reward cases would have applied, and there would have been a good contract in respect of the persons."

As soon as the highest bidder presents himself—says Willes, J, in effect—the person who was to hold the vinculum juris on the other side of the contract was ascertained, and it became settled.

Then it was said that there was no notification of the acceptance of the offer. One cannot doubt that as an ordinary rule of law an acceptance of an offer made ought to be notified to the person who makes the offer, in order that the two minds may come together. Unless you do that, the two minds may be apart, and there is not that consensus which is necessary according to the English law to constitute a contract. But the mode of notifying acceptance is for the benefit of the person who makes the offer as well as for the opposite party, and so the person who makes the offer may dispense with notice to himself if he thinks it desirable to do so. I suppose there can be no doubt that where a person in an offer made by him to another person expressly or impliedly intimates that a particular mode of acceptance is sufficient to make the bargain binding, it is only necessary for the person to whom the offer is made to follow the indicated method of acceptance. And if the person making the offer expressly or impliedly intimates in his offer that it will be sufficient to act on the proposal without communicating acceptance of it to himself, and the offer is one which in its character dispenses with notification of the acceptance, then according to the intimation of the very person proposing the contract, performance of the condition is a sufficient acceptance without notification.

That seems to me to be the principle which lies at the bottom of the acceptance cases, of which an instance is the well-known judgment of Mellish LJ, in *Harris* v. *Nickerson* [(1873) LR 8 QB 286] and Lord Blackburn's opinion in the House of Lords in *Brogden* v. *Metropolitan Rail. Co.* It seems to me that that is exactly the line which he takes.

If that is the law, how are you to find out whether the person who makes the offer does intimate that notification of acceptance will not be necessary in order to constitute a binding bargain? In many cases you look to the offer itself. In many cases you extract the answer from the character of the business which is being done. And in the advertisement cases it seems to me to follow as an inference to be drawn from the transaction itself that a person is not to notify his acceptance of the offer before he performs the conditions, but that, if he performs the conditions at once, notification is dispensed with. It seems to me, also, that no other view could be taken from the point of view of common sense. If I advertise to the world that my dog is lost and that anybody who brings him to a particular place will be paid some money, are all the police or other persons whose business is to find lost dogs to be expected to sit down and write me a note saying that they have accepted my proposal? Of course they look for the dog, and as soon as they find the dog, they have performed the condition. The very essence of the transaction is that the dog should be found. It is not necessary under such circumstances, it seems to me, that in order to make the contract binding, there should be any notification of acceptance. It follows from the nature of the thing that the performance of the condition is sufficient acceptance without the notification of it. A person who makes an offer in an advertisement of that kind makes an offer which must be read by the light of that common sense reflection. In his offer he impliedly indicates that he does not require notification of the acceptance of the offer.

Notes

1. Two issues of principle are dealt with in the extracts from the judgments, namely (1) whether there was a 'promise' to pay £100 if the user of the ball contracted 'flu, and (2) whether such a promise, if there was one, had 'ripened' into a binding contract between Mrs Carlill and the Smoke Ball company. The first issue is one of 'intention'; according to Simpson:

A. W. B. Simpson, 'Quackery and Contract Law: The Case of the Carbolic Smoke Ball', (1985) 14 *J. Leg. St.* 345 at 376–7

. . . [U]ntil Mrs. Carlill brought her action there was no case which had clearly recognized the requirement of an intention to create legal relations; her case did. It was indeed explicitly argued in this trial by Asquith [Counsel] that "the advertisement was a mere representation of what the advertisers intended to do in a certain event. The defendants did not by issuing it mean to impose upon themselves any obligations enforceable by law." In all probability he took the idea from one of the text writers. This argument was firmly rejected by the trial judge, who relied in particular on the fact that the advertisement had stated that £1,000 had been deposited in the Alliance Bank "showing our sincerity in the matter." This, he argued, "could only have been inserted with the object of leading those who read it to believe that the defendants were serious in their proposal." In the Court of Appeal the same view was taken. . . .

The fact that the judges found it necessary to make this point entailed their acceptance of the idea that without an intention to create legal relations there could be no actionable contract. In fact in the argument before the Court of Appeal little was made of the point. . . . But Lindley's opinion was so framed as to enable the case to be used as an authority for the view that . . . [the] doctrine [of intention to create legal relations] was part of English law.

2. The 'ripening' of the promise into a binding contract required the judges to engage in extensive attempts to fit together the conventional rules of offer and acceptance and the somewhat anomalous category of unilateral contracts in order to find some form of 'agreement' which never in truth existed, at least in the conventional sense of the word. Simpson explains the difficulties raised for conventional contract doctrine, and identifies the process whereby *Carlill* has attained the status of *locus classicus* of the formation of unilateral contracts. Significantly, he attributes the success of the judges in satisfying themselves that there was an agreement and that there was no unacceptable departure from classical principles not to the compelling force of their logic, but to their conviction, amply demonstrated in the judgments and related documentation, that the defendants were not 'gentlemen' and did not deserve to win. One point of particular note showed by Simpson is that *Carlill* is not a conventional 'reward' case. However, it is interesting to note that this word is used in the headnote of the Law Report.

Simpson, 'Quackery and Contract Law: The Case of the Carbolic Smoke Ball', 78

[M]ost contracts that concern the courts involve two-sided agreements, two-sided in the sense that the parties enter into reciprocal obligations to each other. A typical example is a sale of goods, where the seller has to deliver the goods and the buyer to pay for them. The doctrines of nineteenth-century contract law were adapted to such bilateral contracts, but the law also somewhat uneasily recognized that there could be contracts in which only one party was ever under any obligation to the other. The standard example was a published promise to pay a reward for information on the recovery of lost property: £10 to anyone who finds and returns my dog. In such a case obviously nobody is obligated to search for the dog, but if they do so successfully, they are entitled to the reward. Such contracts seem odd in another way; there is a promise, but no agreement, for the parties never even meet until the reward is claimed. Promises of rewards, made to the world at large, will not involve an indefinite number of claims—there is only one reward offered—and the courts will uphold the claimant's right to the reward although he has never communicated any acceptance of the promise. Classified as "unilateral" contracts, such arrangements presented special problems of analysis to contract theorists, whose standard doctrines had not been evolved to fit them. Thus it was by 1892 orthodox to say that all contracts were formed by the exchange of an offer and an acceptance, but it was by no means easy to see how this could be true of unilateral contracts, where there was, to the eyes of common sense, no acceptance needed.

The analytical problems arose in a particularly acute form in the smoke ball case. Thus it seemed very peculiar to say there had been any sort of agreement between Mrs. Carlill and the company, which did not even know of her existence until January 20, when her husband wrote to them to complain. There were indeed earlier cases permitting the recovery of advertised rewards; the leading case here was *Williams v. Carwardine*, where a reward of £20 had been promised by handbill for information leading to the conviction of the murderer of Walter Carwardine, and Williams, who gave such information, successfully sued to recover the reward. But this was long before the more modern doctrines had become so firmly embodied in legal thinking, and in any event the case was quite distinguishable. It concerned a reward, whereas Mrs. Carlill was seeking compensation. There could be at most only a few claimants for this, but there is no limit on the number of those who may catch influenza. Furthermore, the Carbolic Smoke Ball Company had had no chance to check the validity of claims, of which there could be an indefinite number; much was made of this point in the argument. But the judges were not impressed with these difficulties, and their attitude was no doubt influenced by the view that the defendants were rogues. They fit their decision into the structure of the law by boldly declaring that the performance of the conditions was the acceptance, thus fictitiously extending the concept of acceptance to cover the facts. And, since 1893, law students have been introduced to the mysteries of the unilateral contract through the vehicle of *Carlill v. Carbolic Smoke Ball Co.* and taught to repeat, as a sort of magical incantation of contract law, that in the case of unilateral contracts performance of the act specified in the offer constitutes acceptance, and need not be communicated to the offeror.

3. One particular 'offer and acceptance' problem which the judges encountered in *Carlill* was the problem of notification of acceptance. It is intriguing that they were content to use the very different factual circumstances of *Brogden* v. *Metropolitan Railway* to assist them in resolving the

issue. It was essential to the factual novelty of *Carlill* that, aside from the 'impersonal' act of purchasing the ball, there was no contact between the parties until Mr Carlill wrote to complain to the company about the misfortune which had befallen his wife. The parties in *Brogden* were in a long-standing commercial relationship under which Brogden had supplied coal to the Company. The Company's agent sent Brogden a draft agreement of the supply of 250 tonnes of coal per week from 1 January 1872 at 20*s*. per tonne, with an option for the Company to purchase up to 350 tonnes. Brogden filled in some blanks on the form, wrote 'approved' on the draft, and returned it to the Company, whose manager filed it in his desk. The Company then commenced ordering coal from January 1872, but when delays in deliveries arose Brogden refused to supply any further coal.

The Company brought an action for breach of contract and the key question of law became whether or not the Company had accepted the offer made by the defendants. As Lindley LJ states the proposition in *Carlill*, the conclusion that there was a contract was dependent upon the principle that there may be circumstances in which an offeror waives the right to be expressly notified of acceptance, but indicates that actual performance will be sufficient. There is some doubt regarding the extension of a rule of convenience in business affairs, which recognized the reality of the continuing relationship between the coal-supplier and the railway company, to cover a situation such as this; however, the effect of the extension is that the judges can now happily state as a 'proposition of law' that in unilateral contracts the contract can be said to come into existence when the offeree performs the stipulated act without the offeror knowing of this fact. The point can even be extended a stage further to allow courts to conclude that, once performance has begun, the offer must be kept open to allow the offeree to complete performance (*Errington* v. *Errington* [1952] 1 All ER 149).

4. The judgments of the Court of Appeal deal also with two additional elements which are essential to the creation of an enforceable contract, namely certainty and consideration. It was argued that there could be no binding contract, as it was not clear at what point the 'protection' offered by the ball was supposed to cease so that the user could no longer claim if he or she contracted 'flu. Bowen LJ inclined to the view that the protection would cease when the user ceased using the ball; Lindley LJ added to this period a reasonable time for the infection to germinate. A. L. Smith LJ declined to express a view since, in any case, Mrs Carlill had been using the ball when she caught 'flu. The final point of discussion concerned the issue whether she had done anything 'in return for' the promise. The Court concluded that using the ball constituted sufficient consideration for the promise to pay £100 (see further Ch. 6).

C. The Battle of the Forms

We began our discussion of offer and acceptance with an extract from Lewis. One of the points that Lewis makes in his overview of contract formation is that 'in order for a contract to be formed one party must make an offer which is mirrored in an acceptance given in return by the other.' What is meant here is that an offeree cannot pick and choose which parts of an offer he accepts; acceptance must be for the whole contents of the offer, or it will amount not to an acceptance but to a counter-offer which can then be accepted or rejected by the original offeror. The significance of this rule is illustrated in the facts and judgment in the following case.

Butler Machine Tool Co. Ltd. v. *Ex-Cell-O Corporation (England) Ltd.* [1979] 1 All ER 965

This case concerned the attempted imposition of a price variation clause by the sellers of a machine. The key question was whether the sellers had made the contract on their terms of sale or not. The detailed facts are stated in the judgment of Lord Denning MR, who begins by summarizing the decision of the first instance judge.

LORD DENNING MR. . . . The judge held that the price variation clause in the sellers' form continued through the whole dealing and so the sellers were entitled to rely on it. . . . The judge said that the sellers did all that was necessary and reasonable to bring the price variation clause to the notice of the buyers. He thought that the buyers would not 'browse over the conditions' of the sellers, and then, by printed words in their (the buyers') document, trap the sellers into a fixed price contract.

I am afraid that I cannot agree with the suggestion that the buyers 'trapped' the sellers in any way. . . . The case was decided on the documents alone. I propose therefore to go through them.

On 23rd May 1969 the sellers offered to deliver one 'Butler' double column plano-miller for the total price of £75,535, 'DELIVERY: 10 months (Subject to confirmation at time of ordering) Other terms and conditions are on the reverse of this quotation'. On the back there were 16 conditions in small print starting with this general condition:

'All orders are accepted only upon and subject to the terms set out in our quotation and the following conditions. These terms and conditions shall prevail over any terms and conditions in the Buyer's order.'

Clause 3 was the price variation clause. It said:

'. . . Prices are based on present day costs of manufacture and design and having regard to the delivery quoted and uncertainty as to the cost of labour, materials etc. during the period of manufacture, we regret that we have no alternative but to make it a condition of acceptance of order that goods will be charged at prices ruling upon date of delivery.'

The buyers, Ex-Cell-O, replied on 27th May 1969 giving an order in these words: 'Please supply on terms and conditions as below and overleaf.' Below there was a list of the goods ordered, but there were differences from the quotation of the sellers in these respects: (i) there was an additional item for the cost of installation, £3,100; (ii) there was a different delivery date: instead of 10 months, it was 10 to 11 months. Overleaf there were different terms as to the cost of carriage, in that it was to be paid to the delivery address of the buyers; whereas the sellers' terms were ex warehouse. There were different terms as to the right to cancel for late delivery. The buyers in their conditions reserved the right to cancel if delivery was not made by the agreed date, whereas the sellers in their conditions said that cancellation of order due to late delivery would not be accepted.

On the foot of the buyers' order there was a tear-off slip:

'ACKNOWLEDGEMENT: Please sign and return to Ex-CELL-O CORP. (England) LTD. We accept your order on the Terms and Conditions stated thereon—and undertake to deliver by . . . Date . . . Signed . . .'

In that slip the delivery date and signature were left blank ready to be filled in by the sellers.

On 5th June 1969 the sellers wrote this letter to the buyers:

'We have pleasure in acknowledging receipt of your official order dated 27th May covering the supply of one 'Butler' Double Column Plano-Miller . . . This is being entered in accordance with our revised quotation of 23rd May for delivery in 10/11 months, ie March/April, 1970. We return herewith, duly completed, your acknowledgement of order form.'

The enclosed the acknowledgment form duly filled in with the delivery date, March/April 1970, and signed by the Butler Machine Tool Co Ltd.

No doubt a contract was then concluded. But on what terms? The sellers rely on their general conditions and on their last letter which said 'in accordance with our revised quotation of 23rd May' (which had on the back the price variation clause). The buyers rely on the acknowledgment signed by the sellers which accepted the buyers' order 'on the terms and conditions stated thereon' (which did not include a price variation clause).

If those documents are analysed in our traditional method, the result would seem to me to be this: the quotation of 23rd May 1969 was an offer by the sellers to the buyers containing the terms and conditions on the back. The order of 27th May 1969 purported to be an acceptance of that offer in that it was for the same machine at the same price, but it contained such additions as to cost of installation, date of delivery and so forth, that it was in law a rejection of the offer and constituted a counter-offer. That is clear from *Hyde v Wrench*. . . . The letter of the sellers of 5th June 1969 was an acceptance of that counter-offer, as is shown by the acknowledgment which the sellers signed and returned to the buyers. The reference to the quotation of 23rd May 1969 referred only to the price and identity of the machine.

. . . The important thing is that the sellers did not keep the contractual date of delivery which was March/April 1970. The machine was ready about September 1970 but by that time the buyers' production schedule had to be rearranged as they could not accept delivery until November 1970. Meanwhile the sellers had invoked the price increase clause. They sought to charge the buyers an increase due to the rise in costs between 27th May 1969 (when the order was given) and 1st April 1970 (when the machine ought to have been delivered). It came to £2,892. The buyers rejected the claim. The judge held that the sellers were entitled to the sum of £2,892 under the price variation clause. He did not apply the traditional method of analysis by way of offer and counter-offer. He said that in the quotation of 23d May 1969 'one finds the price variation clause appearing under a most emphatic heading stating that it is a term or condition that is to prevail'. So he held that it did prevail.

I have much sympathy with the judge's approach to this case. In many of these cases our traditional analysis of offer, counter-offer, rejection, acceptance and so forth is out-of-date. . . .The better way is to look at all the documents passing between the parties and glean from them, or from the conduct of the parties, whether they have reached agreement on all material points, even though there may be differences between the forms and conditions printed on the back of them. As Lord Cairns LC said in *Brogden v Metropolitan Railway Co*:

. . . 'there may be a *consensus* between the parties far short of a complete mode of expressing it, and that *consensus* may be discovered from letters or from other documents of an imperfect and incomplete description.'

Applying this guide, it will be found that in most cases when there is a 'battle of forms' there is a contract as soon as the last of the forms is sent and received without objection being taken to it. . . . The difficulty is to decide which form, or which part of which form, is a term or condition of the contract. In some cases the battle is won by the man who fires the last shot. He is the man who put forward the latest term and conditions: and, if they are not objected to by the other party, he may be taken to have agreed to them. . . . That may however go too far. In some cases, however, the battle is won by the man who gets the blow in first. If he offers to sell at a named price on the terms and conditions stated on the back and the buyer orders the goods purporting to accept the offer on an order form with his own different terms and conditions on the back, then, if the difference is so material that it would affect the price, the buyer ought not to be allowed to take advantage of the difference unless he draws it specifically to the attention of the seller. There are yet other cases where the battle depends on the shots fired on both sides. There is a concluded contract but the forms vary. The terms and conditions of both parties are to be construed together. If they can be reconciled so as to give a harmonious result, all well and good. If differences are irreconcilable, so that they are mutually contradictory, then the conflicting terms may have to be scrapped and replaced by a reasonable implication.

In the present case the judge thought that the sellers in their original quotation got their blow in first; especially by the provision that 'These terms and conditions shall prevail over any terms and conditions in the Buyer's order'. It was so emphatic that the price variation clause continued though all the subsequent dealings and that the buyer must be taken to have agreed to it. I can understand that point of view. But I think that the documents have to be considered as a whole. And, as a matter of construction, I think the acknowledgment of 5th June 1969 is the decisive document. It makes it clear that the contract was on the buyers' terms and not on the sellers' terms: and the buyers' terms did not include a price variation clause.

I would therefore allow the appeal and enter judgment for the buyers.

LAWTON LJ. The modern commercial practice of making quotations and placing orders with conditions attached, usually in small print, is indeed likely, as in this case, to produce a battle of forms. The problem is how should that battle be conducted? The view taken by the judge was that the battle should extend over a wide area and the court should do its best to look into the minds of the parties and make certain assumptions. In my judgment, the battle has to be conducted in accordance with set rules. . . .

. . . By letter dated 5th June 1969 the sales office manager at the sellers' Halifax factory completed that tear-off slip and sent it back to the buyers.

. . . the return of [the] printed [tear-off] slip was accompanied by a letter which had this sentence in it: 'This is being entered in accordance with our revised quotation of 23rd May for delivery in 10/11 months.' I agree with Lord Denning MR that, in a business sense, that refers to the quotation as to the price and the identity of the machine, and it does not bring into the contract the small print conditions on the back of the quotation. Those small print conditions had disappeared from the story. That was when the contract was made. At that date it was a fixed price contract without a price escalation clause.

As I pointed out in the course of argument to counsel for the sellers, if the letter of 5th June which accompanied the form acknowledging the terms which the buyers had specified had amounted to a counter-offer, then in my judgment the parties never were ad idem. It cannot be said that the buyers accepted the counter-offer by reason of the fact that ultimately they took physical delivery of the machine. By the time they took physical delivery of the machine, they had made it clear by correspondence that they were not accepting that there was any price escalation clause in any contract which they had made with the plaintiffs.

I agree with Lord Denning MR that this appeal should be allowed.

BRIDGE LJ. . . . this is a case which on its facts is plainly governed by what I may call the classical doctrine that a counter-offer amounts to a rejection of an offer and puts an end to the effect of the offer.

The first offer between the parties here was the sellers' quotation dated 23rd May 1969. The conditions of sale in the small print on the back of that document, as well as embodying the price variation clause, to which reference has been made in the judgments already delivered, embodied a number of other important conditions. There was a condition providing that order should in no circumstances be cancelled without the written consent of the sellers and should only be cancelled on terms which indemnified the sellers against loss. There was a condition that the sellers should not be liable for any loss or damage from delay however caused. There was a condition purporting to limit the sellers' liability for damage due to defective workmanship or materials in the goods sold. And there was a condition providing that the buyers should be responsible for the cost of delivery.

When one turns from that document to the buyers' order of 27th May 1969, it is perfectly clear not only that that order was a counter-offer but that it did not purport in any way to be an acceptance of the terms of the sellers' offer dated 23rd May. In addition, when one compares the terms and conditions of the buyers' offer, it is clear that they are in fact contrary in a number of vitally important respects to the conditions of sale in the sellers' offer. Amongst the buyers' proposed conditions are conditions that the price of the goods shall include the cost of delivery to the buyers' premises, that the buyers shall be entitled to cancel for any delay in delivery, and a condition giving the buyers a right to reject if on inspection the goods are found to be faulty in any respect.

The position then was, when the sellers received the buyers' offer of 27th May, that that was an offer open to them to accept or reject. They replied in two letters dated 4th and 5th June respectively. The letter of 4th June was an informal acknowledgment of the order, and the letter of 5th June enclosed the formal acknowledgment, as Lord Denning MR and Lawton LJ have said, embodied in the printed tear-off slip taken from the order itself and including the perfectly clear and unambiguous sentence: 'We accept your order on the Terms and Conditions stated thereon.' On the face of it, at that moment of time, there was a complete contract in existence, and the parties were ad idem as to the terms of the contract embodied in the buyers' order.

Counsel for the sellers has struggled manfully to say that the contract concluded on those terms and conditions was in some way overruled or varied by the references in the two letters dated 4th and 5th June to the quotation of 23rd May 1969. The first refers to the machinery being as quoted on 23rd May. The second letter says that the order has been entered in accordance with the quotation of 23rd May. I agree with Lord Denning MR and Lawton LJ that that language has no other effect than to identify the machinery and to refer to the prices quoted on 23rd May. But on any view, at its highest, the language is equivocal and wholly ineffective to override the plain and unequivocal terms of the printed acknowledgment of order which was enclosed with the letter of 5th June. Even if that were not so and if counsel for the sellers could show that the sellers' acknowledgment of the order was itself a further counter-offer, I suspect that he would be in considerable difficulties in showing that any later circumstance amounted to an acceptance of that counter-offer in the terms of the original quotation of 23rd May by the buyers. But I do not consider that question further because I am content to rest on my view that there is nothing in the letter of 5th June which overrides the plain effect of the acceptance of the order on the terms and conditions stated thereon.

I too would allow the appeal and enter judgment for the buyers.

Notes

1. The Court of Appeal described the buyers' order as a counter-offer which destroyed the sellers' original offer made in their quotation. The mirror image rule in contract is that a contract can only be formed if the acceptance corresponds to the offer. In addition to this rule, an acceptance which does not correspond to the terms of the offer destroys the original offer, and the offeree cannot purport to accept it at a later date. An acceptance which does not correspond to the offer may also be considered a counter-offer, i.e. an offer in its own right (see *Hyde* v. *Wrench* (1840) 3 Beav. 334). However, a request by an offeree for further information from an offeror will not amount to a rejection of the offer or a counter-offer, and so does not preclude subsequent acceptance of the offer (see *Stevenson, Jacques & Co.* v. *MacLean* (1880) 5 QBD 346). The dividing line between what constitutes a request for further information and what gives rise to a counter-offer is not a particularly clear one. For example, a request about methods of payment is more likely than not to be regarded as a request for further information, whereas a question about price is more likely to be regarded as a counter-offer. Clearly it is crucial to the question on whose terms the contract is made to determine what constitutes a counter-offer.

2. Bridge LJ and Lawton CJ deal with this case by applying the traditional (or perhaps formalist) approach of looking for a stage in the transaction which can bear the label 'offer' and another stage which can bear the label 'acceptance'. Clearly, the result would have been different if they had been minded to place the label 'offer' on the sellers' letter accompanying the order acknowledgement, or if they had been prepared to give effect to the sellers' attempt to entrench their terms in their quotation. Their strict application of the mirror-image approach led them to decide, however, that the order placed on the buyers' terms destroyed the sellers' offer in the quotation entirely, including the entrenchment terms. The criticism of this approach is that it encourages businessmen to carry on sending their terms and conditions to each other in an effort to impose their terms on the contract. This view presupposes a particular role for contract law in the behaviour of business parties which you may like to compare with the work of Stewart Macaulay extracted in Chapter 2. See further on this R. Rawlings, 'The Battle of Forms' ((1979) 42 *MLR* 715).

3. Lord Denning MR presents his approach as an alternative to the traditional one, and one could describe it as realist. He feels that it is necessary to look at the transaction as a whole. The approach he applies to the facts of this case does not admit, unlike the trial judge Thesiger J, the validity of the sellers' attempt to entrench their terms. In this respect, he retains the traditional approach to the mirror-image rule and counter-offers. The weakness of Lord Denning's approach is evident from the number of alternative results he feels may occur. It offers little more than the approach of the majority. Businessmen, if we believe that contract law influences their behaviour, will, under Lord Denning's approach, still be seeking to ensure that their standard terms prevail over those of their trading partner.

4. Lawton LJ makes the point in his judgment that if the return of the order acknowledgement and the accompanying letter by the sellers to the buyers was a counter-offer, then the parties could never be said to be '*ad idem*'. That is, there was no meeting of their minds sufficient to constitute acceptance and consequently there could not be any contract between the parties. The consequences of this proposition are not discussed by the Court of Appeal, but they have been discussed extensively in the secondary literature. Atiyah (*An Introduction to the Law of Contract*, 74–5) makes the point that the Court of Appeal did not correctly construe the sellers' accompanying letter, which he feels was intended by them to reimpose their terms; consequently, in his view, the only conclusion that a court which forced itself to reason in terms of offer and acceptance could have come to was that there was no contract between the parties. He condemns this view as absurd. However, as Chapter 6 will show in more detail, Atiyah's view of the reach of contractual obligations is rather more expansive than some of the more traditional theorists. The more traditional view on the point is expressed by W. Howarth ('Contract, Reliance and Business Transactions', [1981] *JBL* 122 at 126–7), who makes the point that the production of a machine should not make any difference to the court in deciding whether or not there was a contract between the parties; when assessing the formation issue, contract theory draws no distinction between executory and executed subject matter.

5. If the Court of Appeal had held that there was no contract in the case, then the parties would have been thrown back on seeking a *quantum meruit* remedy in restitution (see the extracts from *British Steel Corporation* v. *Cleveland Bridge Engineering & Co. Ltd.* [1984] 1 All ER 504, in Ch. 1). E. McKendrick ('The Battle of the Forms and the Law of Restitution', (1988) 8 *OJLS* 197 at 208) provides an informative and interesting discussion of the complexities of answering a *Butler*-type contract problem, with solutions drawn from the field of restitution.

6. Attempts have been made to clarify or to improve upon the traditional approach to battle of the forms based on the literal matching of the offer and acceptance. This approach is not confined to English law but is shared, for example, by French law, under which a purported acceptance containing different or additional terms which are essential to the contract is treated as a counter-offer. Examples of attempted clarifications include Article 19 of the UN Convention on Contracts for the International Sale of Goods, which is in force in over twenty countries.

(1)　A reply to an offer which purports to be an　acceptance　but contains additions, limitations or other modifications is a rejection of the offer and constitutes a counter-offer.

(2)　However, a reply to an offer which purports to be an acceptance but contains additional or different terms which do not materially alter the terms of the offer constitutes an acceptance, unless the offeror, without undue delay, objects orally to the discrepancy or dispatches a notice to that effect. If he does not so object, the terms of the contract are the terms of the offer with the modifications contained in the acceptance.

(3)　Additional or different terms relating, among other things, to the price, payment, quality and quantity of the goods, place and time of delivery, extent of one party's　liability to the other or the settlement of disputes are considered to alter the terms of the offer materially.

Broadly, this provision adopts the traditional approach and sets out in detail the types of additional or different terms which materially alter the terms of the offer. A less directive approach is found in §2-207 of the US Uniform Commercial Code, which contains a set of common provisions governing many commercial transactions which have been promulgated as law by almost all the States.

(1)　A definite and seasonable expression of acceptance or a written confirmation which is sent within a reasonable time operates as an acceptance even though it states terms additional to or different from those offered or agreed upon, unless acceptance is expressly made conditional on assent to the additional or different terms.

(2)　The additional terms are to be construed as proposals for addition to the contract. Between merchants such terms become part of the contract unless:
(a)　the offer expressly limits acceptance to the terms of the offer;
(b)　they materially alter it; or
(c)　notification of objection to them has already been given or is given within a reasonable time after notice of them is received.

(3)　Conduct by both parties which recognizes the existence of a contract is sufficient to establish a contract for sale although the writings of the parties do not otherwise establish a contract. In such case the terms of the particular contract consist of those term on which the writings of the parties agree, together with any supplementary terms incorporated under any other provisions of this Act.

Note

The rationale for the UCC was to provide a single legal framework throughout the US for commercial transactions. The philosophy of its original drafters, one of whom was Karl Llewellyn, was to provide for flexibility within a common framework. The objective is to allow commercial practices to evolve within the law, with the courts moving in to readjust the interpretation of the UCC over the decades. Nevertheless, the extent to which §2-207 contains an innovatory approach to the battle of the forms has been the subject of exclusive debate. Von Mehren, for example, sees §2-207 as innovatory, describing the approach in broad terms in the following propositions:

A. von Mehren, 'The "Battle of the Forms": A Comparative View', (1990) 38 *AJCL* 265 at 277

(1) a contract can arise between the parties if they have indicated their intention to contract even though they knew, or should have known, that their positions differed with respect to certain terms and these differences are material; (2) where a contract is formed despite an unresolved disagreement, neither party's expression prevails at least to the extent that divergent terms are contained in the other party's expressions; (3) in these cases, the issues of formation and content are separated and the court must complete the contract drawing upon such sources as suppletive rules of law, usage, and the court's conception of what is fair and just.

The key to the operation of §2-207 has lain in the willingness of courts to find 'expressions of acceptance' under §2-207(1), and to impose strict requirements on parties who wish to signal their reluctance to contract on the offeror's terms. Otherwise the contract will treat 'the deal as on' but, crucially, will not necessarily treat the contract as formed on the basis of either party's terms exclusively. The 'deal is on' philosophy, which focuses on an underlying willingness to contract, can be coupled with an innovative approach under which the court has recourse to 'background law' to complete the contract:

Von Mehren, 'The "Battle of the Forms": A Comparative View', 296

So far as the judicial effort involved in supplying terms is concerned, battles-of-the-forms cases typically should be no more—and are often less—

burdensome than ordinary incomplete or indefinite contract cases. The court needs only to define the area of party disagreement and then draw on background law. The parties have reached agreement on many essential elements of their transaction—price, quantity, duration, and the like; the terms that remain open because the parties' forms are not in agreement are usually susceptible of being established by reference to objective standards such as trade practices and suppletive rules of law. The approach to the "battle of the forms" that has emerged under UCC §2-207 and in German law thus ordinarily does not entail the undue administrative burdens that enforcing contracts which are incomplete or unclear with respect to such issues as price, quantity, and duration can impose upon the judicial system.

Notes

There are three difficulties with this approach:

1. Von Mehren makes an assumption about the elements which the parties will have agreed upon, including, in particular, price. Yet the archetypal battle of the forms problem is one of disagreement on price (see *Butler*), and since it seems that von Mehren does not envisage the court supplying the price from 'background law', it is difficult to see how this approach carried us any further forward than the traditional mirror-image approach.

2. As Baird and Weisberg point out in their criticism of §2-207, the approach supported by von Mehren may encourage 'sloppiness' on the part of contracting parties when dealing with each other's terms, and discourages the parties from seeking their own resolution in advance of differences in expectations, rather than relying upon an *ex post facto* resolution by the court.

D. Baird and R. Weisberg, 'Rules, Standards and the Battle of the Forms: A Reassessment of §2-207', (1982) 68 *Va. L. Rev.* 1217 at 1255

Thus, under any legal provision, including the mirror-image rule, market forces reduce a merchant's ability to use wholly biased, preprinted forms. Indeed, the mirror-image rule, compared to other possible approaches, takes maximum advantage of these market forces. It makes printed forms matter more by encouraging or even forcing parties receiving documents to read them more carefully. The rule thereby encourages parties sending documents to make them attractive to their intended recipients.

3. The interpretation and application of §2-207 may be decisively shaped by whether its provisions are understood as containing 'rules' or 'standards'. Baird and Weisberg explain the difference between rules and standards in the following terms:

Baird and Weisberg, 'Rules, Standards and the Battle of the Forms: A Reassessment of §2-207', 1227-9

A. *The Choice Between Formal Rules and Open Standards*

The evolution from the common-law rules of offer and acceptance to 2-207 marks a major shift from formal rules to relatively unconstraining legal standards. Therefore, we begin with a brief review of how "rules" and "standards" governing private transactions differ in both principle and practice.

In establishing and applying criteria for resolving contract disputes, legislatures and courts generally try to encourage people to engage in mutually beneficial transactions. This truism simply states an end and leaves lawmakers with the difficult choice of means. On the one hand, people may feel most encouraged to transact when they have seen the judiciary carry out their wishes and intentions in particular cases. Courts and legislatures that take this view would create very general criteria that leave judges broad power to examine the circumstances of particular cases—to see whether the parties indeed struck a bargain and to identify the terms on which the parties' minds met. On the other hand, attempting to recognize the bargain-in-fact in every case might breed uncertainty about the likely outcome of contract cases and thus discourage people from entering into transactions. Lawmakers therefore might prefer to create formal rules of contract formation, and the courts might enforce these rules rigidly.

The tension between these two approaches to contract law is, of course, a tension in all jurisprudence. . . .

Dean Murray has been perhaps the most ardent proponent of the view that Article 2 generally favors the "standards" approach. The Code, he stresses, eschews formal rules that focus on the precise language of the parties' documents. Instead, it invites and requires courts to look to all available evidence of the parties' intent, including their course of dealing with the customs of their trade, to uncover the essential bargain-in-fact:

The *true* bargain in fact must be laid bare because only it is deserving of the legally recognized status of a "contract" between the parties—only the bargain-in-fact should be made operative by the courts.

The true agreement, in this view, is a living organism subject to growth through modifications of the parties' expression and conduct. The formal writings are but one stage in the life of the agreement and offer only a partial description of it:

All of these . . . manifestations of the underlying philosophy of Article 2 (and attendant sections of Article 1) manifest the same goal: a more precise and fair identification of the actual or presumed intent of the parties.

. . . Any other goal is hostile to the nature of intention, bargain and assent. The only other possible route to fairness is the government administered contract which not only strips the "agreement" of individual freedom of choice but may well prove to be unworkable and, therefore, ultimately unfair. [J. Murray, 'Another Word about Incipient Unconscionability', (1978) 39 *U. Pitt. L. Rev.* 597 at 648]

Another way of understanding the distinction is to see rules as containing 'closed' conditions for the application of a particular legal consequence, whereas a standard is 'open-textured', allowing the applier to exercise an element of discretion. English courts have encountered similar difficulties in settling on an appropriate judicial approach to the provisions of the Unfair Contract Terms Act 1977, in particular the so-called 'reasonableness' test. This point is considered in Chapter 11.

D. Communication of Acceptance

In *Carlill* v. *Carbolic Smoke Ball Co.*, the discussion of unilateral contracts revealed that one of the difficulties with concluding that there was a contract between Mrs Carlill and the Company was that it was not known to the Company until after the event that Mrs Carlill was using the Ball in accordance with the prescribed instructions. Mrs Carlill had not *communicated* to the Company her intention to take up their offer. For classical contract lawyers, the special difficulties posed by unilateral contracts require an exception to be made to the general rule that acceptance must be communicated to be effective, and that acceptance takes effect when and where it is communicated to the offeror, regardless of whether the parties are dealing face-to-face or at a distance. The next case applies these principles in the light of modern methods of communication.

Brinkibon Ltd. v. *Stahag Stahl und Stahlwarenhandelgesellschaft GmbH* [1982] 1 All ER 293

The appellant buyers wished to purchase from the respondent sellers a quantity of steel bars. The sellers were an Austrian company. The sellers sent the buyers a telex with their terms of sale. The buyers telexed their acceptance. The contract was not performed and the buyers decided to bring an action for breach of contract. To commence an action, the buyers had to serve a writ on the sellers. They applied to the English court for leave (i.e. permission) to do this outside the jurisdiction. At first instance, the buyers were given leave, but this was reversed by the Court of Appeal on the ground that the contract was made outside the jurisdiction—in other words, in Austria. The buyers appealed to the House of Lords.

LORD WILBERFORCE . . . In the present case it seems that if there was a contract (a question which can only be decided at the trial), it was preceded by and possibly formed by a number of telephone conversations and telexes between London and Vienna, and there are a number of possible combinations on which reliance can be placed. At this stage we must take the alternatives which provide reasonable evidence of a contract in order to see if the test is satisfied. There are two. (i) A telex dated 3 May 1979 from the sellers in Vienna, said to amount to a counter-offer, followed by a telex from the buyers in London to the sellers in Vienna dated 4 May 1979, said to amount to an acceptance. (ii) The above telex dated 3 May 1979 from the sellers followed by action, by way of opening a letter of credit, said to have amounted to an acceptance by conduct.

The first of these alternatives neatly raises the question whether an acceptance by telex sent from London but received in Vienna causes a contract to be made in London or in Vienna. If the acceptance has been sent by post, or by telegram, then, on existing authorities, it would have been complete when put into the hands of the Post Office, in London. If on the other hand it had been telephoned, it would have been complete when heard by the offeror, in Vienna. So in which category is a telex communication to be placed? Existing authority of the Court of Appeal decides in favour of the latter category, ie a telex is to be assimilated to other methods of instantaneous communication: see *Entores Ltd v Miles Far East Corp* [1955] 2 QB 327. The buyers ask that this case, which has stood for 30 years, should now be reviewed.

Now such review as is necessary must be made against the background of the law as to the making of contracts. The general rule, it is hardly necessary to state, is that a contract is formed *when* acceptance of an offer is communicated by the offeree to the offeror. And if it is necessary to determine *where* a contract is formed (as to which I have already commented) it appears logical that this should be at the place where acceptance is communicated to the offeror. In the common case of contracts, whether oral or in writing inter praesentes, there is no difficulty; and again logic demands that even where there is not mutual presence at the same place and at the same time, if communication is instantaneous, for example by telephone or audio communication, the same result should follow.

Then there is the case (very common) of communication at a distance, to meet which the so-called 'postal rule' has developed. I need not trace its history: it has firmly been in the law at least since *Adams v Lindsell* (1818) 1 B & Ald 681. The rationale for it, if left somewhat obscure by Lord Ellenborough CJ, has since been well explained. Mellish LJ in *Harris's Case* (1872) LR 7 Ch App 587 at 594 ascribed it to the extraordinary and mischievous consequences which would follow if it were held that an offer might be revoked at any time until the letter accepting it had been actually received: and its foundation in convenience was restated by Thesiger LJ in *Household Fire and Carriage Accident Insurance Co Ltd v Grant* (1879) 4 Ex D 216 at 223. In these cases too it seems logical to say that the place, as well as the time, of acceptance should be *where* (as *when*) the acceptance is put into the charge of the post office.

In this situation, with a general rule covering instantaneous communication inter praesentes, or at a distance, with an exception applying to non-instanta-neous communication at a distance, how should communications by telex be categorised? In *Entores Ltd v Miles Far East Corp* the Court of Appeal classified them with instantaneous communications. Their ruling, which has passed into the textbooks, . . . appears not to have caused either adverse comment, or any difficulty to businessmen. I would accept it as a general rule. Where the condi-tion of simultaneity is met, and where it appears to be within the mutual inten-tion of the parties that contractual exchanges should take place in this way, I think it a sound rule, but not necessarily a universal rule.

Since 1955 the use of telex communication has been greatly expanded, and there are many variants on it. The senders and recipients may not be the prin-cipals to the contemplated contract. They may be servants or agents with lim-ited authority. The message may not reach, or be intended to reach, the designated recipient immediately: messages may be sent out of office hours, or at night, with the intention, or on the assumption, that they will be read at a later time. There may be some error or default at the recipient's end which pre-vents receipt at the time contemplated and believed in by the sender. The mes-sage may have been sent and/or received through machines operated by third persons. And many other variations may occur. No universal rule can cover all such cases; they must be resolved by reference to the intentions of the parties, by sound business practice and in some cases by a judgment where the risks should lie . . . .

The present case is, as *Entores Ltd v Miles Far East Corp* itself, the simple case of instantaneous communication between principals, and, in accordance with the general rule, involves that the contract (if any) was made when and where the acceptance was received. This was on 3 May 1979 in Vienna. . . .

LORD FRASER . . . The question is whether acceptance by telex falls within the general rule that it requires to be notified to the offeror in order to be binding, or within the exception of the postal rule whereby it becomes binding when (and where) it is handed over to the Post Office. The posting rule is based on considerations of practical convenience, arising from the delay that is inevitable in delivering a letter. But it has been extended to apply to telegrams sent through the Post Office, and in strict logic there is much to be said for applying it also to telex messages sent by one business firm directly to another. There is very little, if any, difference in the mechanics of transmission between a private telex from one business office to another and a telegram sent through the Post Office, especially one sent from one large city to another. Even the element of delay will not be greatly different in the typical case where the oper-ator of the recipient's telex is a clerk with no authority to conclude contracts, who has to hand it to his principal. In such a case a telex message is not in fact received instantaneously by the responsible principal. I assume that the present case is a case of that sort.

Nevertheless I have reached the opinion that, on balance, an acceptance sent by telex directly from the acceptor's office to the offeror's office should be treated as if it were an instantaneous communication between principals, like a telephone conversation. One reason is that the decision to that effect in *Entores Ltd v Miles Far East Corp* seems to have worked without leading to serious difficulty or complaint from the business community. Secondly, once the message has been received on the offeror's telex machine, it is not unreasonable to treat it as delivered to the principal offeror, because it is his responsibility to arrange for prompt handling of messages within his own office. Thirdly, a party (the acceptor) who tries to send a message by telex can generally tell if his message has not been received in the other party's (the offeror's) machine, whereas the offeror, of course, will not know if an unsuccessful attempt has been made to send an acceptance to him. It is therefore convenient that the acceptor, being in the better position, should have the responsibility of ensuring that his message is received. For these reasons I think it is right that in the ordinary simple case, such as I take this to be, the general rule and not the postal rule should apply. But I agree with both my noble and learned friends that the general rule will not cover all the many variations that may occur with telex messages. . . .

LORD BRANDON Counsel invited your Lordships to hold that the *Entores Ltd* case was wrongly decided and should therefore be overruled. In this connection he said that it was well-established law that when acceptance of an offer was notified to an offeror by post or telegram the concluding of the contract took place when and where the letter of acceptance was posted or the telegram of acceptance was dispatched. He then argued that the same rule should apply to cases where the acceptance of an offer was communicated by telex, with the consequence that the contract so made should be regarded as having been made at the place from which the telex was sent and not the place where it was received.

My Lords, I am not persuaded that the *Entores Ltd* case was wrongly decided and should therefore be overruled. On the contrary, I think that it was rightly decided and should be approved. The general principle of law applicable to the formation of a contract by offer and acceptance is that the acceptance of the offer by the offeree must be notified to the offeror before a contract can be regarded as concluded . . . . The cases on acceptance by letter and telegram constitute an exception to the general principle of the law of contract stated above. The reason for the exception is commercial expediency . . . . That reason of commercial expediency applies to cases where there is bound to be a substantial interval between the time when the acceptance is sent and the time when it is received. In such cases the exception to the general rule is more convenient, and makes on the whole for greater fairness, than the general rule itself would do. In my opinion, however, that reason of commercial expediency does not have any application when the means of communication employed between the offeror and the offeree is instantaneous in nature, as is the case when either the telephone or telex is used. In such cases the general principle relating to the formation of contracts remains applicable, with the result that the contract is made where and when the telex of acceptance is received by the offeror.

It follows from what I have said that, in my opinion, counsel for the buyers' contention that the present case falls within para (f) of Ord 11, r 1(1) of the Rules of the Supreme Court on service fails and must be rejected.

Notes

1. The decision in *Brinkibon* is notable among recent contract cases for the more or less uniformly 'classical' or 'formalist' reasoning of the judgments. It has been described by J. Wightman ('Does Acceptance Matter?' in J. Adams (ed.), *Essays for Clive Schmitthoff* (Abingdon, Professional Books, 1983), 145) as 'one of the dwindling number of recent cases which are fit, on account of their uninhibited general application, to find their way into the books on the general principles of contract'. The judgment of Lord Wilberforce in particular is reasoned in terms of a basic rule (the requirement that acceptance be communicated), an exception to the rule (the 'postal rule'), and a return to the general rule justified in the interests of commercial expediency for instantaneous forms of communication, although with further exceptions to the general rule envisaged, to cover the problems of defective equipment or inadequate supervision of telex (or fax) machines. These are necessary in order to encompass within the classical structure of the law a new form of communication.

2. *Brinkibon* raises greater difficulties when the question discussed by the House of Lords is seen in its proper context. Wightman, for example, challenges (at p. 147) whether it is appropriate to use a rule of contract law on acceptance to solve what is essentially a policy question. The policy question is whether this is one of the restricted category of cross-jurisdictional cases where it is appropriate to allow service of a writ outside the jurisdiction. The difficulty with a contract-based approach is that it does not easily permit a court to have regard to the well-established policy factors which would normally influence that type of decision. These include whether a foreign court has jurisdiction, where the witnesses and evidence are most easily accessible, and whether proceedings have already begun in a different court, as well as the concern that the service of writs should not be seen to interfere unduly in the sovereignty of other nations. In other words, it is not clear why a rule of contract law should be used to determine an issue which has nothing to do with contract, namely the issue of jurisdiction.

3. As the judgments of Lords Wilberforce and Fraser indicate, it is scarcely likely to be the general rule that telex acceptances are complete on com-

munication which proves to be of particular significance in the future, but more probably the exceptions to that general rule generated to cover the problems of defective equipment or lack of supervision. However, in the tradition of the common law, no 'universal rule' or exhaustive list of exceptions is enunciated by the House of Lords. While their Lordships were prepared to use contract analysis to solve a jurisdictional problem, thereby confirming a new chapter in the contract notebook opened by *Entores* in 1955, their judgments do not greatly enhance legal certainty, since they provide no clear guidelines on what are undoubtedly the real practical problems of modern forms of instantaneous communication.

4. The traditional justifications for the postal rule are centred around theories of agency and risk. For a detailed examination of these justifications see D. Evans, 'The Anglo-American Mailing Rule: Some Problems of Offer and Acceptance in Contracts by Correspondence', (1966) 15 *ICLQ* 553.

5. A more cynical approach is to say that the postal rule is simply an arbitrary rule created to solve a practical problem (see G. Treitel, *Law of Contract*, 8th edn. (London, Sweet and Maxwell, 1991), 24; Atiyah, *An Introduction to the Law of Contract*, 77), namely that one party must bear the risk of the letter being lost in the post. By the same token, French and German law, which do not have a postal rule but which apply the communication rule unconditionally, could be seen as having made the alternative choice of burdening the offeree rather than the offeror. The practical significance of the rule has been diminished by decisions such as that in *Holwell Securities Ltd.* v. *Hughes* ([1974] 1 WLR 155). Here the Court of Appeal was asked to consider the status of the postal rule in relation to an option clause which was described as exercisable 'by notice in writing to' the offeror. It decided that the postal rule was excluded by the words used, which were intended to mean that notice had actually to be received by the offeror to be effective. It appears that the postal rule can be 'contracted out of' by the offeror's use of appropriate words, or through the offeror simply decreeing the form which communication of acceptance must take or decreeing that acceptance must actually be received.

6. A further alternative rationale for the postal rule and the subsequent developments in the rules on communication of acceptance is put forward by Gardner, who bases his argument on the history of the post as a means of communication.

S. Gardner, 'Trashing with Trollope: A Deconstruction of the Postal Rules', (1992) 12 *OJLS* 170 at 178–93

1840 was the year in which the uniform penny post was introduced, and the circumstances surrounding this event may have much significance for appreciating the decisions of that decade.

The uniform penny post had been proposed in 1837, in a pamphlet entitled *Post Office Reform: Its Importance and Practicability*, published by Rowland Hill. The idea was that there should be a uniform rate of letter postage of 1d across the whole country. Hill's argument was taken up by Robert Wallace MP, who since 1833 had himself been crusading for the reform of the national's postal arrangements. . . .

It is important to understand that the introduction of the penny post was not a random event. It was—and was contemporarily regarded and supported as—an element in the general programme of liberal reform of the age. Robert Wallace was the new MP for Greenock, a town newly enfranchised under the Reform Act, and Wallace was a free-trader, concerned for the economic development of his constituency. Given its remote location, he felt, an efficient system of postage was essential to providing its traders with what is nowadays called 'a level playing-field'; or perhaps, more positively, to their being able to contribute fully to the prosperity of the nation. Hill too was a liberal, though more of the ideological kind: his designs for the postal service seem to have sprung from his concern for the education and general civilization of the people; he regarded the post as a means of disseminating knowledge, and free trade principles as a means of improving its effectiveness. And it was the huge public support for Hill's scheme, especially from amongst the then Whig government's liberal supporters, which in 1838–9 persuaded the government—somewhat against, as we have seen, the Select Committee's advice—that it should be enacted.

This popular support for Hill's scheme may be an important part of the explanation for the rule which the courts were to adopt by their decisions in the 1840s. The general perception seems to have been that the scheme provided something of a panacea, by which the postal service would become in every way thoroughly wonderful. . . . it is quite clear that very substantial improvements in postal efficiency were indeed occurring at this time, partly from the recommendations of the 1835 Commission, but above all from the fact that from 1830 the mail began to be carried on the new railways, which by 1846 had entirely superseded the slower and less reliable coach system on routes to and from London.

The contemporary perception may have played a substantial part in the decisions in which the courts established the acceptance rule in the 1840s. In these terms, the basis of the rule might have been not a preference for posting over delivery as the dispositive act. It might have been an idea that delivery was self-evidently important, but that in the newly prevailing conditions posting and delivery were little different: that once posted, a letter was as good as delivered. But there is a certain weakness about this. Despite the great improvements in efficiency to which reference has been made, equating posting with delivery on purely empirical grounds would have been a little foolish: indeed, the reason why these cases came to court at all was because the equation had failed.

However, some of Hill's other innovations added a further dimension to this constructive identification of posting with delivery. One was a dramatic shift towards prepayment of postage. In March 1839, only 14 per cent of letters sent by the London General Post were prepaid, leaving 86 per cent for which payment had to be collected from the addressee. By February 1840 these figures had been precisely reversed. Prepayment was endorsed by none other than Queen Victoria herself, abandoning the privilege of free use of the mail. A year later still, the unpaid element had fallen further to 8 per cent. A second was the further facilitation of prepayment by the introduction in 1840 of the self-adhesive postage stamp: another measure which entranced the public. Of the February 1841 prepaid total of 92 per cent, 45 per cent comprised letters for which the payment was by this means. A third important innovation was the cutting of letter-boxes in front doors of houses, so that letters no longer needed to be handed to their addressee; this too captured the public imagination.

Taken together, these measures may have great significance. Until 1840, the delivery of a letter typically required that the addressee should manually receive it and pay for it. This was not, of course, a significant practical hurdle, but it sat in symbolic contrast with the new position, whereby the sender had only to affix his stamp and post the letter, and it would go through to its destination *without further subvention from outside the system*. So these three innovations of 1840 may be seen as predicating a radically new perception of the nature of the post: the notional equation of the posting of a letter with its delivery. They may thus have been a very powerful influence towards the courts affirming the acceptance rule in the way that they did in that decade. (The empirical efficiency of the system still matters to some extent, in that the argument would not work unless the system was perceived as at least adequately efficient; but we have seen that in the 1840s this was the case.) . . .

Later decisions, have generally drifted away from the equation of posting with delivery. In terms of the present thesis, that would be very understandable. The further one gets from the 1840 reforms, and in particular the more one has access to instantaneous modes of communication such as became available in 1878–80, the less natural one would find that equation. The development of additional new modes of remote communication has further discredited the old equation of posting with delivery, and it is noticeable that cases dealing with these new technologies increasingly marginalize the postal acceptance rule. The decisions on telex communications, for example, explicitly treat the rule for postal acceptance as artificial, and an exception.

The only surprise may be that [the] newer decisions [*Entores, Brinkibon*] have any time for the postal acceptance rule at all. After all, our contemporary culture, justly or not, tends to emphasize the possibility that a letter will be lost or delayed in the post, the very reverse of the old equation. But of course, the rule remains the law until the decisions establishing it are overruled, and since it seems to present no real practical difficulty they are unlikely to be. . . .

So explained, the postal acceptance rule may be regarded as something of a museum piece. It is worth noticing, however, that there is a chance of history repeating itself. One of the newest forms of telecommunication, the fax, seems greatly to have captured the public's imagination. It seems to be perceived as rather wonderful. There may be a general feeling that the act of sending off a fax and receiving from the machine the message 'transmission OK' is in effect conclusive that the message has got through to the addressee. All this would be quite analogous to the picture presented here of the origin of the rules about letters in the Victorians' perception of their reformed postal service. It would not be surprising, therefore, if fax communications were treated along the lines of the postal acceptance rule. This is not, however, an argument that they should be. Even were it right for the law to be shaped by popular perceptions in this way, some degree of realism about fax technology would be called for: and it is clear enough that the message 'transmission OK' (or the opposite) does not always amount to the truth. In fact, it would be preferable for the rule to be settled by reference to considerations about business convenience and the allocation of risks. From this point of view, there seems much to be said for a rule on the same lines as that adopted for telexes. In principle this requires delivery rather than mere transmission, though there are two qualifications based on business practicality. When the message is sent during times when the addressee's machine can be expected to have been watched, the message need only be shown to have reached the machine, rather than to have come to the addressee's own eyes; and when the sender believes the message to have arrived ('transmission OK') but it has not, and the addressee unreasonably fails to alert the sender, the message is treated as having been delivered.

The next extract discusses the postal rule in a very different way. Whereas Gardner seeks to explain the social phenomenon of the postal rule in its specific historical context, Goodrich uses it in a metaphorical sense to achieve a much broader end. He seeks to explain the journey from the contractarian tradition (see the discussion of contractarianism in Ch. 3) to the construction of legal contract doctrine. The journey takes Goodrich through an examination of Rousseau's *Essay on the Origin of Languages* (the Essay referred to in the text) to show that formal contract law, as evidence by the postal rule, reflects the passing of tradition from the law of God, in the form of a convenant, to the law of commerce, in the form of a written contract or exchange between two parties. Goodrich's analysis is a historical linguistic one; his starting-point is Rousseau's starting-point, that speech is the 'first' institution which underlies society (the 'social contract'). From there, Rousseau explains the development of law through speech and ultimately writing. This development gives us a contract tradition, in which we are steeped, where

linguistic, social and legal traditions 'fix in advance' standard meanings and proper references to words and texts and pass them down. We are both the recipients and custodians of the lawful knowledge of tradition, faithful to its system of commerce and communication. Our own contracts perform the repetitive permanence of institutional language and bind us to the law. (C. Douzinas and R. Warrington, 'Posting the Law: Social Contracts and the Postal Rule's Grammatology', (1991) *Int. J. Sem. L.* IV/11, 115 at 118).

P. Goodrich, *Languages of Law: From Logics of Memory to Nomadic Masks* (London, Weidenfeld and Nicolson, 1990), 149–74

An early nineteenth-century common law doctrinal development . . . held that an epistolary acceptance of a contractual offer becomes binding once placed in the course of the post. . . . The postal rule, a product of the classical law of contract, paradoxically reminds us that the system of circulation of messages, the means of communication or objectified text, is often of greater significance than its apparent subjective content. When it is a question of contract and so of law, the postal rule may serve to indicate that the letter, the contractual act, may have an existence independent both of its sender and of its destination.

The paradoxical character of the postal rule is emblematic of a more general series of questions that need to be raised as part of a postmodern account of contract and of the contractarian tradition. Even at the height of the ascendancy of *laissez-faire* economics and of its corresponding doctrine of freedom of contract, the postal rule uneasily testifies to the intrinsically social character of the contract. It is a relationship made by reference to and via the avenue of the law. It is a communication that passes from one subject to the other via the objectification—the textual relay—of the post and of all the qualifications and supplements that are the inevitable consequences of a centrally organised system of social communication. It entails thereby a series of epistolary and more broadly linguistic questions that are the essential subject matter of any critical history of the contractarian tradition and its concept of law. . . .

Our concern with the postal rule is with a metaphor for the institutional character of contract, within which institution it is frequently impossible rigorously to distinguish legal contract from social contract. They are both legal forms of association, of *societas*, and both equally imply participation in a tradition, within a system of communication or, better, of transmission governed by law. . . . we may simply note that postal communication entailed—by virtue of statutory and case law provisions—that each word used was fixed in advance, that it belonged to a standard or recognised form, that it referred to its proper, legally designated referent.

The institutional implications of the post do not stop with the objectified form or language of the writ or letter. To use the post is in the first instance to enter into a specific, centrally regulated jurisdiction, a specific domain of discourse subject to rules of both lexical and semantic scope requiring, at the minimum, a specific textual form and more normally a legally prescribed and recognised content as well. Post or *postea* also, of course, means after or afterwards. A second aspect to our invocation of postal communication concerns the temporal charter whereby our communication comes, in a dual sense, afterward. . . . In social terms, speech is also already a part of tradition, a participant in a conventionally regulated network. As regards tradition and its transmission, we are involved in the receipt and sending on of received forms; we are both recipients and custodians of the lawful knowledge of tradition and of its representation, its language. The letter of *signum* becomes a token of participation in a juridically defined sociality. It betokens at the very least that we come after and are faithful to—are users of—the postal network, or more generally of the tradition, of the system of commerce and communications. . . .

To recapitulate, the form of tradition and the form of our participation in it are both linguistic and symbolic. They are governed by certain rules of reference but also by a theory of origin and image that is concerned as much with temporality, with a charter designating lineage or lineal relations between before and after, as with reference. In a purely descriptive sense we may chart the contract in terms of its progression from theocratic pact or covenant of biblical derivation requiring obedience to an unwritten law (nature), to the more positive and legalistic contract or social treaty establishing political sovereignty and a coincidental power of secular nomination. The desire to elicit and question the more fundamental forms of the social contract, to enquire as to the linguistic contract or the veridical language that underpins juridical rule, leads us from the post to the letter: that is to say, from the institution to the word, from the network to its elements of conduction. . . .

. . . By fixing meaning in advance, by deciding the forms of interpretation before reading the material text of tradition, we are asked by the contract to keep faith with a temporal charter—a particular sense of time as deferral of death—and to belong to a specific track, a stretch of text or territory, a space or expanse of land, a region or nation, that will serve as the sign of our identity and as the mark of that through which 'we' will live on. . . .

In the material terms . . . the contract as mark, note or grapheme has a dual significance. On one hand, the instrument is a physical object, a symbol in the sense of a sign or token that circulates within the institution and according to an economy of writing or politics of scriptural accumulation and exchange. In crude material terms, the contract is produced by and is by and large accessible to the legal profession alone; it belongs to a specific textual community and its institutional significance should be traced in terms of that community. On the other hand, the contract is an epistle or note and as such is an act of communication; it is not simply a form but also a content. As regards the content of contract, the relevant grammatological themes concern writing and repetition, reference and faith; in short, the question of linguistic content concerns the rhetorical and more broadly semantic conditions under which a particular writing system becomes monumental and its texts become party to a tradition, thereby escaping history to join the repetitive permanence of institutional language. . . .

The first order of justification of the contract is linguistic. The contract acts as simple writing, as a mark or note that is capable of representing and preserving the ephemeral phonic substance of speech. In this view, speech is prior to script and is the substance of the contractual mark which notes and remembers the anterior event. Such is the fable (*histoire*) presented in Rousseau's theory of the origin of language, a work which states at its very beginning that 'speech, being the first social institution, owes its form to natural causes alone'. The invocation of nature as the source of speech immediately establishes the elements of a hierarchy of oppositions which moves in Rousseau's text from the natural to the artificial, from passion to reason (law) and from rhetoric to writing. . . .

. . . Following certain other readings of Rousseau, we have elaborated the thesis that the theory of the origins of language places a linguistic contract at the basis of the occidental juridico-political tradition. Language is the first contract of sociality, the original bond or institution, and it lies therefore at the basis of tradition as its hidden source. The implications of the relationship of language to law, of speech to norm and of text to institution can be analysed initially in terms of the governing relation of rhetoric to writing specified in the closing chapters of the *Essay*. . . .

In positive terms, the simulation of a point of origin, the postulation of a contract as the source of tradition, suggests a move from the rule of God to the rule of law, from covenant to contract. The shift is one of laicisation rather than of secularisation, a change of terminology rather than of function: law as the direct expression of God's will, as concession or donation, is replaced by an apparently positive notion, that of reference to a contract, an agreement, a mutual bond upon the strength of which a new series of institutional guarantees—of points of transmission—can replace an antique Christian order with the rational universalities of law. It is the people, by means of the general will, that now guarantee sovereignty, order and law. It is the people, in the split form of the contract, that now send and receive the message of law: the contract establishes the two parties to an exchange and then indicates the bond or tie that binds them together in the form of obligation. . . .

The issue of postmodernity can itself be formulated as that of systematically raising the question of how we have been contracted, which is to say how we have been made to speak and upon what terms we participate in the institutional text. We will end by reviewing in general terms the principal tenets of the contract as writing, always noting that here the contract has further connotations as something put out. To put out a contract is to send a missive, to advertise an intention and equally to threaten with death, to put out a contract on someone meaning prospectively to sign his death warrant and by extension to symbolise his end. The crucial relations are here temporal and spatial. The contract endeavours to govern the future and as writing it seeks to communicate beyond the lifetime of its author: the legislator 'should found his judgment not upon what he sees, but upon what he foresees, nor should he stop so much at the actual state of the population but rather at that which it ought naturally to attain'. To write is to preserve, to delay, to create a monument to posterity whereby the simulated figure of the father can continue to lay down the law on no stronger ground than that of tradition: that is the role (*officium*) of paternity, that is why the contract must be obeyed. . . .

. . . The contract, in establishing the genre of law, acts as an antidote to other discourses. The written law comes to represent the idea or ideal whereby original and image, real and imagined, inside and outside, conscious and unconscious, society and nature, take their places within the tradition. We receive the tradition 'in the normal course of the post'. The contract, as was observed at the outset, is binding once posted . . . . When literature plays the law we are entitled to expand the invocation of the postal rule determining the formation—the communication—of a contract. The emblem of the postmodern contract would be that of the undelivered letter, of the letter that does not arrive . . .

E. Unilateral Contracts and the Tendering Process

The final case in this chapter brings together some of the observations which have been made so far on the nature and role of offer and acceptance analysis, both in the formation of contracts and in the regulation and structuring of different types of exchange transactions.

Harvela Investments Ltd. v. *Royal Trust Co. of Canada Ltd.*
[1986] AC 207; [1985] 2 All ER 966

The plaintiff and the second defendant (Sir Leonard Outerbridge) were rival offerors for a parcel of shares held by the first defendants, the vendors, who invited both parties to submit by sealed offer or confidential telex a 'single offer' for the whole parcel by a stipulated date. The vendors stated in the invitation to bid that 'we bind ourselves to accept [the highest] offer' received by them which complied with the terms of the invitation. Harvela tendered a bid of C$2,175,000. The second defendant tendered a bid of C$2,100,000 or 'C$101,000 in excess of any other offer . . . expressed as a fixed monetary amount, whichever is the higher'. The vendors accepted the second defendant's bid, as being a bid of C$2,276,000, and entered into a contract with him for the sale of the shares. Harvela commenced proceedings against the vendors and Sir Leonard, arguing that the latter's bid was invalid, and claiming a declaration that there was a binding contract between them and the vendors for the sale of the shares for the sum of C$2,175,000 and for specific performance of that contract.

LORD TEMPLEMAN Where a vendor undertakes to sell to the highest bidder, the vendor may conduct the sale by auction or by fixed bidding. In an auction sale each bidder may adjust his bid by reference to rival bids. In an auction sale the purchaser pays more than any other bidder is prepared to pay to secure the property. The purchaser does not necessarily pay as much as the purchaser was prepared to pay to secure the property. In an auction a purchaser who is prepared to pay $2.5m. to secure a property will be able to purchase for $2.2m. if no other bidder is prepared to offer as much as $2.2m.

In a fixed bidding sale, a bidder may not adjust his bid. Each bidder specifies a fixed amount which he hopes will be sufficient, but not more than sufficient, to exceed any other bid. The purchaser in a fixed bidding sale does not necessarily pay as much as the purchaser was prepared to pay to secure the property. But any bidder who specifies less than his best price knowingly takes a risk of being outbid. In a fixed bidding sale a purchaser who is prepared to pay $2.5m. to secure the property may be able to purchase for $2.2m. if the purchaser offers $2.2m. and no other bidder offers as much as $2.2m. But if a bidder prepared to pay $2.5m. only offers $2.2m. he will run the risk of losing the property and will be mortified to lose the property if another bidder offers $2.3m. Where there are two bidders with ample resources, each determined to secure the property and to prevent the other bidder from acquiring the property, the stronger will prevail in the fixed bidding sale and may pay more than in an auction which is decided not by the strength of the stronger but by the weakness of the weaker of the two bidders. On the other hand, an open auction provides the stimulus of perceived bidding and compels each bidder, except the purchaser, to bid up to his maximum.

Thus auction sales and fixed bidding sales are liable to affect vendors and purchasers in different ways and to produce different results. The first question raised by this appeal, therefore, is whether Harvela and Sir Leonard were invited to participate in a fixed bidding sale, which only invited fixed bids, or were invited to participate in an auction sale, which enabled the bid of each bidder to be adjusted by reference to the other bid. A vendor chooses between a fixed bidding sale and an auction sale. A bidder can only choose to participate in the sale or to abstain from the sale. The ascertainment of the choice of the vendors in the present case between a fixed bidding sale and an auction sale by means of referential bids depends on the presumed intention of the vendors. That presumed intention must be deduced from the terms of the invitation read as a whole. The invitation contains three provisions which are only consistent with the presumed intention to create a fixed bidding sale and which are inconsistent with any presumed intention to create an auction sale by means of referential bids.

By the first significant provision, the vendors undertook to accept the highest offer; this shows that the vendors were anxious to ensure that a sale should result from the invitation. By the second provision, the vendors extended the same invitation to Harvela and Sir Leonard; this shows that the vendors were desirous that each of them, Harvela and Sir Leonard, and nobody else would be given an equal opportunity to purchase the shares. By the third provision, the vendors insisted that offers must be confidential and must remain confidential until the time specified by the vendors for the submission of offers had elapsed; this shows that the vendors were desirous of provoking from Sir Leonard an offer of the best price he was prepared to pay in ignorance of the bid made by Harvela and equally provoking from Harvela the best price they were prepared to pay in ignorance of the bid made by Sir Leonard.

A fixed bidding sale met all the requirements of the vendors deducible from the terms of the invitation. A fixed bidding sale was bound to result in a sale of shares save in the unlikely event of both Harvela and Sir Leonard failing to respond to the invitation. A fixed bidding sale gave an equal opportunity to Harvela and Sir Leonard to acquire the shares. A fixed bidding sale provoked the best price, or at any rate something approximate to the best price, which the purchaser was prepared to pay to secure the shares and to ensure that the rival bidder did not acquire the shares. On the other hand, if the invitation is construed so as to create an auction sale by means of referential bids, the requirements of the vendors deducible from the terms of the invitation could not be met.

First, if referential bids were permissible, there was a danger, far from negligible, that the sale might be abortive and the shares remain unsold. The shares would only be sold if at least one bidder submitted a fixed bid and the other bidder based his referential offer on that fixed bid. In the events which happened, Harvela put forward a fixed bid of $2,175,000 and Sir Leonard made a referential bid of $101,000 more than Harvela's fixed bid, thus enabling Sir Leonard's referential bid to be quantified at $2,276,000. But if Sir Leonard's referential bid had not been expressed to be based on Harvela's fixed bid, or if Harvela had not made a fixed bid but only a referential bid, then Sir Leonard's bid could not have been quantified. Similarly, if Harvela had made a referential bid not expressed to be tied to Sir Leonard's fixed bid, or if Sir Leonard had not made a fixed bid but only a referential bid, then Harvela's bid could not have been quantified. The sale would have been abortive although both bidders were anxious to purchase and submitted offers.

Secondly, if referential bids were permissible, there was also a possibility, which in fact occurred, that one bidder would never have an opportunity to buy. In the present case Harvela, by putting forward a fixed bid, could never succeed in buying the shares although the invitation had been extended to them. Harvela's only part in the sale was unwittingly to determine the price at which Sir Leonard was entitled and bound to purchase the shares. Harvela could not win and Sir Leonard could not lose. There was nothing in the invitation to warn Harvela that they must submit a referential bid if they wished to make sure of being able to compete with Sir Leonard. There was nothing in the invitation which indicated to Sir Leonard that he was entitled to submit a referential bid. But no one has argued that the invitation did not invite fixed bids; indeed, Sir Leonard submitted a fixed bid, albeit as an unsuccessful alternative to his referential bid. . . .

. . . The task of the court is to construe the invitation and to ascertain whether the provisions of the invitation, read as whole, create a fixed bidding sale or an auction sale. I am content to reach a conclusion which reeks of simplicity, which does not require a draftsman to indulge in prohibitions, but which obliges a vendor to specify and control any form of auction which he seeks to combine with confidential bidding. The invitation required Sir Leonard to name his price and required Harvela to name their price and bound the vendors to accept the higher price. The invitation was not difficult to understand and the result was bound to be certain and to accord with the presumed intentions of the vendors discernible from the express provisions of the invitation. Harvela named the price of $2,175,000; Sir Leonard failed to name any price except $2,100,000 which was less than the price named by Harvela. The vendors were bound to accept Harvela's offer. . . .

Lord Diplock The construction questions turns upon the wording of the telex of 15 September 1981 referred to by Lord Templeman as "the invitation" and addressed to both Harvela and Sir Leonard. It was not a mere invitation to negotiate for the sale of the shares in Harvey & Co. Ltd. of which the vendors were the registered owners in the capacity of trustees. Its legal nature was that of a unilateral or "if" contract, or rather of two unilateral contracts in identical terms to one of which the vendors and Harvela were the parties as promisor and promisee respectively, while to the other the vendors were promisor and Sir Leonard was promisee. Such unilateral contracts were made at the time when the invitation was received by the promisee to whom it was addressed by the vendors; under neither of them did the promisee, Harvela and Sir Leonard respectively, assume any legal obligation to anyone to do or refrain from doing anything.

The vendors, on the other hand, did assume a legal obligation to the promisee under each contract. That obligation was conditional upon the happening, after the unilateral contract had been made, or an event which was specified in the invitation; the obligation was to enter into a synallagmatic [or bilateral] contract to sell the shares to the promisee, the terms of such synallagmatic contract being also set out in the invitation. The event upon the happening of which the vendor's objection to sell the shares to the promisee arose was the doing by the promisee of an act which was of such a nature that it might be done by either promisee or neither promisee but could not be done by both. The vendors thus did not by entering into the two unilateral contracts run any risk of assuming legal obligations to enter into conflicting synallagmatic contracts to sell the shares to each promisee.

The two unilateral contracts were of short duration; for the condition subsequent to which each was subject was the receipt by the vendors' solicitors on or before 3 p.m. on the following day, 16 September 1981, of a sealed tender or confidential telex containing an offer by the promisee to buy the shares for a single sum of money in Canadian dollars. If such an offer was received from each of the promisees under their respective contracts, the obligation of the promisor, the vendors, was to sell the shares to the promisee whose offer was the higher; and any obligation which the promisor had assumed to the promisee under the other unilateral contract came to an end, because the event the happening of which was the condition subsequent to which the vendors' obligation to sell the shares to that promisee was subject had not happened before the unilateral contract with that promisee expired.

Since the invitation in addition to containing the terms of the unilateral contract also embodied the terms of the synallagmatic contract into which the vendors undertook to enter upon the happening of the specified event, the consequence of the happening of that event would be to convert the invitation into a synallagmatic contract between the vendors and whichever promisee had offered, by sealed tender or confidential telex, the higher sum. . . .

The answer to the construction question itself, however, appears to me to present no difficulties in so far as it leads to the conclusion that the condition subsequent to which the vendors' obligations under the unilateral contracts were subject was incapable of being fulfilled by either promisee except by a self-contained offer of a purchase price for the shares expressed as a fixed sum of money which did not necessitate, for its quantification, reference to offers made by any other bidders. . . .

The invitation invited each promisee to whom it was addressed to specify by a fixed hour on the following day the price at which he was willing to accept the promisor's offer to sell the shares upon the terms set out in the invitation. Such price was to be specified, not by an offer of which the other promisee could obtain knowledge, but by sealed tender or confidential telex the contents of which the promisor undertook should not be disclosed to the other promisee until it was too late for him to make a timeous offer.

The whole business purpose of unilateral contracts inviting two or more promisees to submit sealed tenders of a purchase price for property which are not to be disclosed to any competing promisee and imposing on the promisor a legal obligation to transfer the property to the promisee whose tender specifies the highest price is that each promisee should make up his mind as to the maximum sum which he estimates the property is worth to him, not a sum of money the amount of which cannot be determined except by reference to amounts specified in sealed tenders received from other promisees of which, under the terms of the unilateral contract, he is to be denied all knowledge before the time for making his own tender has expired. That business purpose would be defeated by a tender which took the form of an offer to purchase the property not for a specified fixed sum of money but for a sum greater by some specified amount than the fixed sum specified in the sealed tender lodged by some other promisee by the terms of a unilateral contract in identical terms. What other sensible reason could there be for making it a term of each unilateral contract that the promisee should be kept in ignorance of the amounts offered by any other promisees?

Notes

1. Lord Diplock describes his judgment as being 'in the nature of footnotes . . . designed to indicate the way in which . . . the solutions . . . reached by this House are compatible with current juristic analyses of contractual obligations as they have developed in the course of the last twenty five years'. To this end, his analysis is focused upon showing how a fixed bidding sale can be explained in terms of offer and acceptance analysis. In principle, an invitation to receive tenders is an invitation to treat. In the eyes of Lord Diplock, the only way in which the first defendants can be found to accept the highest single offer is because they have contracted to do so; otherwise the doctrine of the free revocability of offers (*Dickinson* v. *Dodds* (1876) 2 Ch. D. 463) would allow the first defendants to withdraw any offer to sell to the highest bidder. To reach this conclusion he must therefore use the artificially contrived concept of an implied unilateral or 'if' contract between the parties. The use of the unilateral contract in this context shows how this legal device, which was in its infancy at the time of *Carlill* v. *Carbolic Smoke Ball Co.*, can also be used in the type of tendering situation to create the desired patterns of legal obligations.

2. In contract, the approach of Lord Templeman is much more straightforward. He uses a policy-based argument (backwards reasoning?) which examines the differences between fixed bidding sales and auctions in order to justify his conclusion about the legal nature of the first defendants' confidential telex, and the advisability and effectiveness of the referential bid made by Sir Leonard Outerbridge. He focuses in particular on the consequences which might follow in these circumstances from allowing the referential bid to form the basis of the contract of sale, rather than attempting a strict doctrinal analysis of why the first defendants could not accept the referential bid as the basis of what to them in the circumstances appeared to be the most advantageous contract of sale. It is worthwhile recalling that in a case where the result appeared obvious to a unanimous House of Lords, the Court of Appeal unanimously reached the opposite conclusion on the admissibility of the referential bid. In the House of Lords, Counsel for the plaintiffs suggested that the Court of Appeal had misunderstood the nature of sealed competitive bidding and wrongly assumed that it was a rare occurrence ([1986] 1 AC 207 at 211). This perhaps suggests that, despite the

intellectual gymnastics undertaken by Lord Diplock to satisfy the conceptual demands of offer and acceptance, the real basis for the decision was in
fact commercial convenience and the demands of business practice.

3. 'Tendering' is a term which is used to describe a variety of different
types of commercial arrangements, under which contractors negotiate to
get the best price for goods and/or services which they wish to buy or sell.
The *Blackpool Airport* case, where the structure of the tender invitation
was held to generate a duty to consider all validly submitted tenders, is
another example of this common business practice. A rather different, and
more factually complex system of tendering arises where the tenders are
made by subcontractors ('subs') in order to form part of a bid made by a
main contractor ('generals') to secure a project (e.g. to build a hospital or a
power station). The 'offer and acceptance' issue which arises in this context concerns whether or not the tendering subcontractors are bound by
the price and terms which they quoted originally, in particular if they have
expressed this quotation as a 'firm offer' by which they intend to be bound.

Legal analysis, of course, suggests that an offer alone is insufficient and
that it can be withdrawn provided withdrawal is communicated (*Byrne* v.
Leon Van Tienhoven (1880) 5 CPD 344). Conversely, the main contractor
will not want to commit himself to buying the goods or services offered by
the subcontractor, at least until he has secured the main contract for the
project. The alternatives are buying (for money) an option in order to
ensure that the price quoted and used in order to calculate the price duly
quoted for the main contract will be the final price. However, this is expensive and cumbersome, particularly where subcontractors and contractors
are making large numbers of unsuccessful tenders for projects.

Consequently, the Law Commission has considered whether a 'firm
offer' should be regarded as binding on the offeror and has recommended
the introduction of the concept of the 'firm offer' in relation to offers made
for interests in land in the course of business (Law Commission Working Paper on Firm Offers No. 60, 1975). However, empirical evidence
gathered by Lewis has shown that the difficulties experienced at the level
of legal doctrine are by no means considered significant in business
practice.

R. Lewis, 'Contracts Between Businessmen: Reform of the Law of Firm Offers and an Empirical Study of Tendering Practices in the Building Industry', (1982) 12 *JL&S* 153 at 160–9

A detailed questionnaire was sent to 20 generals (9 of whom replied) and 20
subs (11 of whom replied) all from the Cardiff area. The sample, although relatively small, comprised a significant percentage of local firms which for various
reasons were likely to have experience of subcontract problems. . . .

Withdrawal by a sub and the action a general may take

How common is the problem of withdrawal by the sub after the general has used his bid? Most of the generals noted that at some time they had encountered the problem, and one small firm even remarked that withdrawal "is the great difficulty with sub-contracting today". The others, however, doubted whether the problem was very common, one of them commenting "we have never (in 30 years) known a sub-contractor withdrawing his bid before an award" [of the main contract to the general. This does not exclude withdrawal after the award.]

There are certain precautions that could be taken by generals in advance of submitting their own bids to ensure that a sub's bid is reliable. Firstly a general could create an option contract and threaten the use of legal sanction in order to bind the sub to his bid. This would necessitate the general obtaining the sub's agreement that in exchange for a nominal fee the sub's bid would be kept firm for a set period. In the survey this had been considered only by one general, being the exceptional firm which had stated that it had found withdrawal of bids a common practice. Even this small firm had only considered and not actually attempted to use option contracts. Its failure to do so may be related to the inconvenience of building into the tendering system an option procedure, especially when bids are received late. But the difficulties of employing such a technique are not insuperable, especially with regard to those subs from whom it is usual to expect tenders. The reason for the failure of generals to establish a legal sanction to prevent withdrawal of a bid before acceptance must lie elsewhere.

A second method of protection for the general is for him to demand from the sub a sum of money as a guarantee of "bid bond". In large international contracts it is common to find a requirement that the tenderer should submit together with his bid a deposit of around one per cent of the contract sum. "The purpose inherent in this machinery is the protection of the employer against default by the contractor, whom it would be difficult to sue owing to his being outside the jurisdiction of the employer's country. The 'bid bond' is forfeit if, upon being offered a contract on the basis of his tender, the tenderer refuses to enter upon the contract." However the survey revealed that such precautions were not adopted by generals for those domestic contracts with subs which form the basis of the present investigation.

Although withdrawal was uncommon, what would be the attitude of a general towards a sub who did try to revoke his bid? Five of the nine generals believe that before the award of the main contract the sub was free to do as he liked; after all, within certain limits the general was also free to change his bid at this time. However, after the award six generals considered that a sub should be bound to his bid, and only three felt he was free to withdraw. A similar majority of subs agreed that they felt bound to their bid. Eight of the eleven said that after the award they were committed to performing the work at the price quoted. However, their commitment was not influenced by the legal position: they would keep to their bid either because they felt morally bound not to revoke, or because they feared loss of their business reputation. Only two subs considered themselves legally bound to perform, although one of these had gone so far as to ensure that liability would not arise by stating that his bid was only an estimate and did not form a legally binding undertaking to keep his price firm.

What action would a general take against a sub who withdrew his bid? . . . no general mentioned threat of legal action, but nearly all considered that if they had a continuing relationship with a sub they could bring pressure to bear. Persuasion "might well pay dividends if he is already doing work for you or hopes to in the future." If the sub could not be persuaded to change his mind "we would have serious reservations about inviting him to tender for future work," or ultimately, "we would strike him off our list". Other action "would depend a lot upon the size of job, size of subcontractor relative to the size of job, and the difference between the price of the lowest sub's tender and the next lowest. If the financial implications were not much relatively, we would accept the second lowest tender. If they were serious we would approach the clients' Quantity Surveyors and try to reach an agreement with them on a revised tender".

The survey so far suggests that withdrawal of offers in the building contract context is not a widespread problem and that generals can exercise their own informal control over it in any case. However, this is by no means the whole picture. . . .

The use made by generals of the bidding procedure

Withdrawal of a bid by a sub reveals only one side of the problem for the general similarly may be guilty of what some consider unethical or improper practice which in turn can injure the sub. . . . The general can take advantage of the open nature of the tendering procedure and the fact that a contract with a sub is not formed until some time after the award of the main contract. As a result of this delay in the formation of contract the general has the opportunity after receiving a bid to disclose it to other subs and thus put pressure upon them to undercut the price quoted ("bid shopping"). Alternatively the initiative may be taken by the other subs themselves in inquiring of the general as to the lowest bid submitted. If the general provides the information he may be encouraging the subs to make a lower offer ("bid peddling"). Both practices reveal that a general in fact may not rely upon employing the sub whose bid he has used in computing his tender, and it is then more difficult for him to claim that in justice the sub should be bound to his bid whilst he remains free to do as he pleases. To what extent does the general fail to use the sub on whose bid he has relied or to what extent does he try to change that bid? Several questions in the survey were aimed at investigating this aspect of the problem.

After receiving a sub's tender all the generals agreed that sometimes the lack of detail in the bid led to further negotiations taking place and these could continue even after the general had been awarded the main contract. . . . Six of the nine generals admitted that occasionally they had been involved in further negotiations about the price and that this happened both before and after they had been awarded the main contract. This may simply reflect that there were indeed matters which had been left vague in the subs' original bids, but it could also indicate that generals were shopping around for a lower price. The subs confirmed that such shopping was taking place, one of them stating that "[i]t is almost common practice for a large number of general contractors to request further negotiations regarding the price prior to their placing an order. They are usually trying to obtain a reduction."

Further evidence of the generals not always relying upon subs' bids came from their admission that even after using a bid they were quite willing to switch subs if necessary. . . . For their part the subs recognised the generals' legal entitlement to switch subcontractors but they were almost unanimous in expressing disapproval of generals who did so after informing other subs of the state of the bidding market and thus encouraging price cutting. . . . Three of the generals admitted to giving information but all qualified their statements: one said he would let his usual subs know "if he received a bid from an unknown sub", another said he would give details only if asked by other subs, and a third remarked that "without giving details of prices we will give an indication of competitiveness". Other generals strongly opposed bid shopping and denied that they were involved in it: one said "if subs became aware of a firm doing this, it would not take long before they would refuse to tender," another noted it was "company policy" not to release details of bids and a third commented that he "was a great believer in getting the quality of work you pay for". Others expressed similar fears of a price cutting war by subs leading to poorer quality in their workmanship and the general eventually suffering. . . .

Very little action is taken by subs to minimise the risk of what they see as misuse of their bids. They are not in a position to do anything because they usually do not know to what use their bids have been put. However, one sub said that he would confer with other specialist subs in a serious case and several noted that they no longer tendered to certain contractors who had acquired a bad reputation. Bid shopping provides a good reason for the sub sending in his bid as late as possible so that the general has less time to encourage other bids. One sub specifically noted that the only preventative action he had been able to take was by "getting the tender in on time and not before". . . .

Summary

In a private construction contract withdrawal of a firm bid by a sub . . . cannot occur where there is direct nomination of a sub, nor where a sub's bid is not stated to be firm as in a third of the cases in the survey. Even where there are firm bids generals do not necessarily rely upon the figures supplied by the lowest tendering sub when computing their own bid. Instead of being troubled by an enforced change of sub resulting from withdrawal, generals are as likely to initiate such a change themselves by encouraging undercutting of original tenders.

The infrequency of the problem of withdrawal undoubtedly influences attitudes towards the introduction of legal sanctions to control it. But it may also be that the informal control methods that already exist make formal legal regulation unnecessary. At least it is important to observe that the potential which exists for making use of the legal system has not been exploited. Generals have either not devised standard tender forms or allow subs to ignore them. They do not use option contracts or bid bonds and they do not close a deal as soon as possible so as to create a contract and threaten legal sanction to prevent withdrawal. Resort to a court to determine rights and liabilities was not mentioned as a possible remedy. Instead the sanctions discussed were informal: renegotiation and applying economic pressure; arbitration by a third party such as a quantity surveyor or architect; and, as an ultimate deterrent, the severing of trade relations between the respective firms. The same pattern emerged with regard to the subs' attitudes to generals "misusing" the bidding procedure, although the subs were generally thought to be in a weaker economic position. The final question in the survey was biased in favour of relying upon formal remedies based upon legal rights and it carried with it a balance and appearance of justice which might be thought superficially to appeal to the contractors surveyed. Despite this its legal solution [was] rejected either as impractical, easily avoided and difficult to enforce, or as unfair and too inflexible in not making allowance for the several excuses which contractors recognised as good reasons for non-performance. The informal remedies which already existed, whether cost cutting by subs or the use of economic "muscle" by generals, emerged as more important methods of regulating the commercial relationship.

Note

One of the difficulties with applying offer and acceptance analysis to the tendering situation, or with making certain firm offers binding in law, is that it certainly appears to offer a greater degree of security to the general contractor without taking into account the broader context of the negotiations which might have taken place prior to the closing of a deal. Thus it deals with the possibility of abuse by one side of the tendering process without addressing the equally serious possibility of abuse by the other side. It illustrates the danger of piecemeal legal intervention into business practices which may have grown up in the shadow of the law, where the parties have shown no particular inclination to use existing legal sanctions.

F. Conclusions

The cases and extracts in this section seek to expose different methods of judicial reasoning which manifest themselves in the positioning of the labels 'offer' and 'acceptance'. These are not watertight categories but simply observable phenomena which particular judges feel, for the reasons they give, are able adequately to bear the burden of being described as 'offers' and 'acceptances' (*Gibson*; *Butler*). Other judges may interpret the same observable phenomena in quite a different way by, for example, labelling a particular statement as an invitation to treat as opposed to an offer. It could be said that the explanation for such differences of approach can be found in the degree to which certain judges are willing to depart from a classical view of the contract founded upon a perfect consensus *ad idem* between the parties. For example, it is difficult to subsume the doctrinal figure of the unilateral contract within the matrix of offer and acceptance without in many cases effectively 'inventing' a moment of agreement (*Carlill*). On the other hand, the unilateral contract has proved a useful device for the formalist judge determined to adhere to the principle of the free revocability of offers, and the preservation of maximum freedom to negotiate for the parties (*Harvela*).

Equally, an explanation for many of the cases may lie in the fact that very often they are not 'true' contract cases. They are cases where the device of offer and acceptance analysis is being used as a smokescreen for policy decisions such as the desirability of self-service pharmacies (*Boots*), the degree to which the political ideology of one local council should bind its successors (*Gibson*), or the desirability of allowing service outside the jurisdiction (*Brinkibon*). Consequently, differing judicial ideologies may be as decisive for the conclusions reached in particular cases (cf. Adams and Brownsword) as are differing methods of reasoning.

Questions

1. What conception of 'agreement' dominates the rules on the formation of contracts, and do these rules offer the judges a workable framework within which to determine whether or not a contract has been concluded between two parties?

2. Would you say that the absence of a duty to bargain in good faith has influenced the approaches of the judges in any of the cases extracted in Section III? If so, how, and if not, why not?

3. What do the empirical observations made by Lewis, as well as by Macaulay and others (Ch. 2) about contract in the commercial context tell us about the effectiveness and appropriateness of the legal rules on formation?

4. Using the various economic theories presented in Chapter 2, consider how economists would view the different judicial approaches to contract formation.

5. Can you identify any common strands of thinking in the extracts from Dalton, Unger, and Goodrich in this chapter? Are there useful comparisons to be made between their approaches to contract formation and the more general theory of Pateman discussed in Chapter 3?

5

Formation Problems

I. INTRODUCTION

In this chapter we look at the type of events which may enable one party to a contract to assert that there is in fact no contract or to escape from a contract, either because there was no agreement between the parties or because the agreement was induced by a misrepresentation made by one party to the other. The substantive areas of contract law under discussion are what is variously called 'agreement', 'formation', or 'communication' mistake and misrepresentation.

A first task is to delimit the scope of mistake doctrine as considered in this chapter. It has become accepted practice to separate out three areas of 'mistake' in contract. Difficulties, however, frequently arise because a common terminology is not used by either the writers or the courts. In the first situation (called unilateral mistake by Cheshire, Fifoot, and Furmston's *Law of Contract*, 12th edn. (London, Butterworths, 1991)) one party is mistaken and the other party knows of the mistake. Any exchange which takes place on this basis could be described as 'involuntary' (R. Cooter and T. Ulen, *Law and Economics*, (Glenview, Ill., Scott, Foresman, 1988), 257). In the second situation, the parties are at cross-purposes with each other and there is no 'consensus *ad idem*' or 'meeting of minds' which can be identified as forming the subject of the contract. The third situation is rather different; here the parties have made the *same* mistake. We can say that they have reached an agreement, but the question then becomes whether the mistake is so important that the contract should be set aside. In that case, the issue of policy is to determine which party should take the risk of a contingency for which the parties had failed to plan when they concluded their contract. We deal with this latter type of mistake, generally termed 'common mistake', in Chapter 12.

It will be clear from the readings and discussion which follow that, although we can identify three types of mistake, it is not always clear in the cases and, indeed, in some of the secondary literature which type of mistake is being referred to. Not all contract writers separate out the strands of mistake in the way we have described. They may, for example, seek to offer a clarification based on operative/non-operative mistake or mistake nullifying consent and mistake negating consent (see G. Treitel, *The Law of Contract*, 8th edn. (London, Sweet and Maxwell, 1991), 249 ff.) or distinguish principally between mistake in law and mistake in equity (see Anson's *Law of Contract*, 26th edn. (Oxford, Oxford University Press, 1984), ch. 8).

The approach adopted in this chapter links formation mistake formally to the issue of offer and acceptance and the concept of agreement. A contract entered into under a formation mistake is 'void *ab initio*', that is, it is treated as if it had never come into being.

Misrepresentation is a closely related legal doctrine; one party alleges that his consent was induced by the misrepresentation of the other and was therefore imperfect. Such a contract can in principle be brought to an end (rescinded) by the party whose consent was induced. In certain circumstances damages are available for loss caused by the misrepresentation. The readings illustrate that there are close factual relationships between the circumstances in which mistakes and misrepresentation can be pleaded, and indeed they may frequently be pleaded as alternatives, where, for example, the mistake is *actively* induced by the other party. Equally, there may be a fine distinction between a (mis)representation and a promise: that is, a statement by one party which is incorporated into the contract and becomes the basis for a breach of contract. In practice, mistake is rarely pleaded nowadays, and it succeeds even more rarely, because the doctrine is narrowly circumscribed in English law.

The case law on mistake is factually and legally intricate. Given how rarely mistake succeeds in practice, it might be questioned by the student why this area should be subjected to close analysis at all. There does, however, remain a convincing justification for studying mistake, and that is the insight which it provides into the construction and operation of what is termed the 'objective theory of contract'. Mistake, perhaps more than any other issue in contract, raises questions of evidentiary inference; simply because the facts would suggest the existence of a mistake by one party known to the other does not mean that this can be proved. This is because the classical law of contract has regard to manifestations of intent, not to the pure subjective will of the parties.

In the following extract, Dalton examines problems which are inherent in the practice of 'communication' and its interpretation by the courts, and then moves into a discussion of the dominant doctrine of objectivity in the Anglo-American common law.

II. THE OBJECTIVE THEORY OF CONTRACT

C. Dalton, 'An Essay in the Deconstruction of Contract Doctrine', (1985) 94 *Yale LJ* 997 at 1039–44

To the extent judges attempt to describe communication in doctrinal terms, they are forced into accounts that tend to distort what we imagine the actual process of communication between the contracting parties to have been. To the extent the doctrinal model leaves judges without guidance, they are left ascribing meaning according to unarticulated criteria. Both these problems emphasize the gap between the contract as the parties may have understood it and the contract as ultimately described by the court.

At the root of these difficulties lies the problem of knowledge—the gulf between self and other, subject and object. Translated into doctrinal discourse, this becomes the distinction between subjectivity, substance, and intent on one hand, and objectivity, form, and manifestation on the other. Our legal culture appreciates the difference between what someone subjectively intends, and the form in which he makes that intention available to others (the objective representation of his thought or wish). That we concede the possibility of "misunderstanding" demonstrates our awareness of this dichotomy and our recognition that the signs can be read to manifest something other than the "actual" or "real" intent of their author. Appreciating the difference, our legal culture has explicitly opted to favor objective over subjective, form over substance, and manifestation over intent . . . . Yet the suppressed subjective constantly erupts to threaten the priority accorded the objective, is subdued, and erupts again. . . .

Doctrinal obsession with the competing claims of objective and subjective, manifestation and intent, dates perhaps from the time at which a "will theory" of contract, initially conceived as emphasizing the subjective "meeting of the minds," was "objectivized" by the likes of Holmes and Williston. In this second incarnation, while the subjective intentions of the parties were still felt to provide the legitimating basis of contractual obligation, the measure of intention became overwhelmingly objective. . . .

The *Second Restatement* provides an up-to-the-minute account of how [the tension between subjectivity and objectivity] is managed today. We see that objectivity is still accorded an initial priority. Take, for example, the *Restatement*'s formulation of "promise" as "a manifestation of intention to act or refrain from acting in a specified way, so made as to justify a promisee in understanding that a commitment has been made."[1] Here the *Second Restatement* directs us to focus, not on all intentions, but only on manifested ones. The commentary elaborates on the significance of this distinction: "The

---

[1] RESTATEMENT (SECOND), *supra* note 6, § 2(1).

phrase 'manifestation of intention' adopts an external or objective standard for interpreting conduct; it means the external expression of intention as distinguished from undisclosed intention."[1] At first glance, this constrained notion of intent seems pragmatic. To base contract interpretation on undisclosed intention is surely to invite chaos, perjury, a whole catalog of evils. At a more theoretical level, we might also imagine a concern with undisclosed intention to be senseless. At some point the undisclosed must be disclosed or we can have no concrete knowledge of it. Intent, in this view, is wholly dependent on manifestation—the only questions left are: What count as manifestations? To whom must they be made? In what form? At what time?

But even while objectivity retains its priority, subjectivity is accorded a vital and subversive supplementary role. According to the *Restatement* scheme, recognizing a manifestation requires a knowledge of intent. The *Restatement* demands that we categorize manifestations: Only manifestations of *intent* qualify as promises,[2] only manifestations *of assent* qualify as assent.[3] Doctrinally we cannot, it turns out, sort or interpret manifestations without reference to an intent we have already acknowledged to be beyond our grasp save through the graspable reality of manifestations that we cannot comprehend without recourse to an unknowable intent . . . and so on. . . .

Intention Ousted: The Objective Theory of Contract

A standard history of contract doctrine represents that, from the sixteenth to the early nineteenth century, contract formation depended upon a subjective "meeting of the minds." Despite the accordance of this subjective theory with the nineteenth-century "will theory" of contract, by the middle of the nineteenth century "the tide had turned in favor of an objective theory of contract." To see the sequence as one in which objectivism replaced subjectivism is to discount the crucial, although supplementary, role that subjective will as a *source* of obligation continued to play. But the story accurately portrays the increased insistence on objectivity as an interpretive standard.

Holmes' article, *The Theory of Legal Interpretation*, illustrates the fundamental challenge of objectivism to the subjective theory it came to overshadow.[4] According to Holmes, the "intent" of the parties was never the issue in any case of contract interpretation. To determine the meaning of a word used in a contractual situation, Holmes believed the first step should be to consider its meaning in the context of surrounding words. But this was an exercise in applying the "general usages of speech", and did not reflect any concern with the "idiosyncrasies of the writer."[5] Admitting evidence of circumstances, and reading a contractual document in light of them, was also not about divining the

---

[1] *Id.* § 2(1) comment b.   [2] *Id.* § 2(1).   [3] *Id.* § 18.
[4] Holmes, The Theory of Legal Interpretation, 12 *Harv. L. Rev.* 417 (1899).
[5] *Id.* at 417.

intent of the parties. We were to ask instead, Holmes suggested, what the words used by the speaker would mean "in the mouth of a normal speaker of English, using them in the circumstances in which they were used."[1] In the case where the speaker uses a proper name that could refer to more than one person or thing (because there are, for example, two Blackacres or ships Peerless), Holmes saw the inquiry into circumstance revealing which of two different *words* the speaker used, rather than revealing the speaker's intention.

Mainstream twentieth-century thinkers came to accept the most extreme manifestations of the Holmesian doctrine. "It is even conceivable," Williston observes, "that a contract may be formed which is in accordance with the intention of neither party."[2] Learned Hand puts it more vividly when he suggests:

A contract is an obligation attached by the mere force of law to certain acts of the parties, usually words, which ordinarily accompany and represent a known intent. If, however, it were proved by twenty bishops that either party, when he used the words, intended something else than the usual meaning which the law imposes upon them, he would still be held [to the usual meaning] . . .[3]

This analysis forces us to ask what justifies the departure from intent. The central argument advanced is that replacing the unknowable and possibly idiosyncratic intentions of the contracting party with "that stubborn anti-subjectivist, the 'reasonable man,'"[4] is an advance. It seems insufficient to suggest that this substitution merely satisfies an aesthetic impulse. At one level the substitution can be seen as a shift to a "responsibility" model: You are responsible for what you would appear to the reasonable man to be saying, rather than for what you actually meant to say. In this sense the standard seems tortious rather than contractual, even as "reliance" strikes us as a tortious notion. But at another level it can be reconciled with intention and the contractual model. If the reasonable man is a businessman assessing the words and conduct of businessmen, then in most instances appearance and reality will converge. Alternatively, if the ranking of manifestations is seen as a tool available to businessmen in their contract planning, they will be sure to shape in the proper legal form the deal they intended to make.

It seems fair to say that the credibility of these arguments depends on two things: First, on the extent to which we can believe in the "reasonable man," as represented by his interpreters, the jurors and trial judges. As Frank puts it:

[W]e must recognize, unless we wish to fool ourselves, that although one area of subjectivity has been conquered, another remains unsubdued. . . . We ask judges or juries to

---

[1] *Id.* at 417–18.   [2] 1 S. Williston, *Law of Contracts* § 95 (3d ed. 1957).
[3] *Hotchkiss* v. *National City Bank*, 200 F. 287, 293 (S.D.N.Y. 1911), *aff'd*, 201 F. 664 (2d Cir. 1912), *aff'd*, 231 U.S. 50 (1913).
[4] *Ricketts* v. *Pennsylvania* R.R., 153 F. 2d 757, 761 (2d Cir. 1946) (Frank, J., concurring).

discover that "objective viewpoint"—through their own subjective processes. Being but human, their beliefs cannot be objectified, in the sense of being standardized.[1]

Second, the credibility of these arguments depends on our valuing objectivity and stability (to the extent we think the rule does or can promote them) more than we value the effort at divining "real" intention, in situations where the intention appears from the evidence to have been understood by both parties, but is different from the intention objectively constructed.

Notes

1. In the United States, most of the central areas of private law fall within the competence of the various States, rather than under federal law. Where, as with contract, for example, the several laws of the States are, with a few exceptions, built directly on the foundation of the English common law, there has remained powerful unifying influence. The so-called 'Restatements' also form an important element in the sense of there being some sort of 'common' American law.

K. Zweigert and H. Kötz, *An Introduction to Comparative Law*, 2nd edn. (Oxford, Oxford University Press, 1987), ii. 259–60

Another indication of the unitary basis of American private law, despite all the local variants, is the success with which it has for some time been being compiled in the so-called 'Restatements'. Since the increasing flood of precedents was making the law cumbrous and unmanageable it seemed sensible to record it in a clearly ordered and systematically constructed 'Restatement'; this task was entrusted to the 'American Law Institute', founded in 1923 by the American Bar Association in conjunction with judges and law teachers. The following procedure was adopted. A leading scholar is selected a 'Reporter' for each legal topic; his task is to absorb all the existing case-law, to extract general rules, and, in association with a group of advisers including experienced lawyers, judges, and professors, to formulate a text which needs the endorsement of certain committees of the American Law Institute before it is published as a 'Restatement'. The task of the reporter is to lay down the law in its *present positive form* and not to improve or modernize it. Nevertheless in cases where the rules of the various states are inconsistent they may choose the solution which seems to them to be the more progressive, even if it obtains only in a minority of states. By this means Restatements have been produced for all important areas of American private law except family law and the law of succession—for example, the general law of contract, tort, trusts, conflicts of law—and many of them have already appeared in a second edition.

---

[1] *Zell v. American Seating Co.*, 138 F.2d 641, 647 (2d Cir. 1943), *rev'd*, 322 U.S. 709 (1944) (*per curiam*).

Restatements are rather like the Civil Law codes in their systematic structure of abstractly formulated rules, and in many cases the Continental jurist can use them as a means of easy access to the rules of American private law in the first instance. Warning should be given, however, not to use them too uncritically, for the only way to be sure whether a particular rule is in force in a particular state is by consulting the judicial decisions of that state. If the problem in question has not yet been decided or clearly decided in that state, an American judge will often have recourse to the Restatement, but will normally accord it only fractionally more weight than he would to a leading textbook, and that, in a Common Law country, is not very much.

2. Dalton talks of a 'standard history of contract doctrine' which sees the formation of contract shifting from a subjective meeting of minds, via the will theory, to an objective theory of contract. These intellectual developments have been decisive in shaping both the role of the courts in construing the agreements reached between contracting parties and the evolution of doctrines such as mistake, which focus on the consent of the parties and which therefore require a standard against which that consent is to be tested.

However, it is a matter of considerable controversy amongst legal historians precisely when the shifts between the various theories occurred, at least within the case law and the literature, and what exactly were the external influences upon the common law which provoked or underlay the changes. It seems most likely that the shifts which produced the present governing perception of the basis of contract were a combination of socio-economic factors including the rise of *laissez-faire* capitalism in the nineteenth century, the dominance of liberal political philosophy, and the spread of ideas emanating from the Roman law-dominated civil-law legal systems on the continent of Europe (see generally P. Hamburger, 'The Development of the Nineteenth Century Consensus Theory of Contract', (1989) 7 *L. & Hist. Rev.* 241, and the literature discussed therein, especially Atiyah, *The Rise and Fall of Freedom of Contract*, rev. edn. (Oxford, Oxford University Press, 1985); M. Horwitz, *The Transformation of the American Law 1780–1860* (Cambridge, Mass., Harvard University Press, 1977); A. W. B. Simpson, 'Innovation in Nineteenth Century Contract Law', (1975) 91 *LQR* 247; see also discussion of Gordley in Chapter 2 for a rather different perspective).

3. Classical English contract doctrine would not subscribe to the position of extreme objectivity put forward by Justice Learned Hand. For this comment suggests that the use of an objective standard which examines the external and manifested conduct or statements of the parties to discover their meaning implies a complete abandonment of the commitment to the importance of the subjective intentions of the parties as the original basis

for agreement. It treats what should normally be regarded as an evidentiary convenience as a substantive standard of the 'truth' of a contract.

It is possible to find in the case law support for three different approaches to objectivity: promisor objectivity; promisee objectivity; and detached or fly-on-the wall objectivity. These positions are summarized in the next extract.

R. McClintock, 'Objectivity in Contract', (1988–91) 6 *Auckland UL Rev.* 317 at 319–20

Promisor Objectivity

A simple formulation of the theory of promisor objectivity is that the promise, representation or expression of agreement is to be viewed from the position of the maker thereof. An element of objectivity is added by requiring that the promisor's interpretation reasonably held is considered, not her actual interpretation. Wherever adopted, however, the position is further mitigated by requiring regard to the promisee's reception of the promise. Otherwise the test is excessively weighted in favour of the promisor. A typical formulation is given by the American Restatement of Contracts:

Where there is no integration [formal agreement], words or other manifestations of intention forming an agreement . . . are given the meaning which the party making the manifestations should reasonably expect that the other party would give to them [para. 227]

Framed in this way the theory stops short of completely objectifying the view of the promisor. The interpretation need only be within the range of reasonable interpretations. The theory could be objectified further by substituting the reasonable person for the promisor.

Promisee Objectivity

Here the viewpoint of the promisee or representee is taken. A degree of objectivity is imported by requiring that the view taken be reasonable. But again objectivity could be hardened by requiring that the reasonable person take the place of the promisee. The classical view is expressed by Spencer [1973] *CLJ* 104 at 106:

Words are to be interpreted as they were reasonably understood by the *man to whom they were spoken.*

As under promisor objectivity, if the requirement of objectivity is simply to provide reasonable bounds then the actual understanding or agreement of the party remains important.

In contrast, Pollock, for example, suggests a more fully objective position:

We must look to the state of things as known to and affecting the parties at the time of the promise, including their information and competence with regard to the matter in hand, and then see what expectation the promisor's words, as uttered in that state of things, would have created in the mind of a reasonable man in the promisee's place and with the same means of judgment. The reasonable expectation thus determined gives us the legal effect of the promise.

On this formulation the place for the actual intentions and understandings of the parties is extremely limited. First, the data from which the viewpoint is to be constructed is taken from that available to both parties. Second, the reasonable person is fixed with this information and placed in the shoes of the promisee.

Detached Objectivity

Only under this theory is a completely objective approach taken. Here the viewpoint is that of a third party: the judge or the reasonable person. Within the English jurisdiction, this position has been associated with Lord Denning. The locus classicus is *Solle v Butcher* ([1950] 1 KB 671 at 691):

once a contract has been made, that is to say, once the parties, whatever their inmost states of mind, have to all outward appearances agreed with sufficient certainty in the same terms on the same subject-matter, then the contract is good.

This has been termed the "fly on the wall" theory. No place is given for the intentions and understandings of the parties themselves in the construction of the promise or agreement between them.

III. THE OBJECTIVE THEORY AND MISTAKE AS TO TERMS

The next case (*Smith* v. *Hughes*) offers some support for forms of objectivity based on the perceptions of both the promisor and the promisee as being determinative of the content of an 'agreement'. It therefore opens the possibility for one party to claim that his consent is vitiated by a mistake. Moreover, because the perceptions are 'objectivized', it is the understanding of the reasonable person in the position of the promisor or the promisee, whose hypothetical beliefs are decisive. It is also possible to derive some support from the judgments for exceptions to the standards of promisor or promisee objectivity—whichever is chosen—in circumstances where one party has induced the other party into making the mistake, or where one party unfairly takes advantage of the other party's mistake. These points will be explored in more detail in the notes following *Smith* v. *Hughes*, but it should be noted that these exceptions have led Adams and Brownsword to characterize the approach of the English courts in *some* cases as one of 'modified subjectivism', an approach which rests on 'inter-subjective understanding and thereby militates against one party exploiting another's known misunderstanding' (*Understanding Contract Law* (London, Fontana, 1987), 62). This should not be confused with detached objectivity, which does not receive any consistent doctrinal support (see the debates of *Howarth* and *Vorster*).

Smith v. *Hughes* is an important and useful case for a number of reasons. First, it consists of three lengthy judgments in which the judges take slightly contrasting approaches. Second, while the case itself is illustrative of quite a narrow point of construction concerning the nature of a sale by sample, the judgments range over a number of issues concerned with the test of agreement, and situated themselves firmly within the philosophical and intellectual traditions of the time. Hannen J, for example, cites the political philosopher Daley. There is also reference to Roman law doctrines by leading counsel for the plaintiff which obviously influence the judges. Finally, *Smith* v. *Hughes* offers a constellation of facts which are dogged by the additional ambiguities generated by jury trial. In principle, the appeal by the plaintiff sought to challenge the judge's direction to the jury; yet, in their judgments, the members of the Court of Appeal seem to concentrate rather on second-guessing the factual assessment made by the jury. The reason for this may be that, although the jury was given two specific directions by the judge, depending upon what they concluded were the words used and the beliefs held by the parties, they were not asked to make separate findings of fact, i.e. to reveal the basis upon which they eventually found for the defendant.

Smith v. *Hughes*
(1871) LR 6 QB 597

The plaintiff was a farmer and the defendant was an owner and trainer of race-horses. The plaintiff approached the defendant with a view to selling him oats. He showed him a sample and the defendant, having looked at the sample, bought his entire stock. The defendant then discovered that the oats were new oats, and refused to accept them on the grounds that he had wanted old oats. The farmer sued for the price. There was conflicting evidence as to whether the word 'old' had been used. The plaintiff asserted that he talked in terms of oats only, and that he did not know that race-horse trainers had little use for new oats. The defendant's manager asserted that the plaintiff had used the word 'old' when describing the oats. The price of the oats was high for new oats, but there was evidence that oats were very scarce at the time. The judge directed the jury that they had to decide whether either party had used the word 'old'. If their view was that the word had been used, then they had to find for the defendant. If they thought that the word had not been used, then they had to decide whether the plaintiff believed the defendant to believe or to be under the impression that he was contracting for the purchase of old oats. If this was the case, then they had to find for the defendant. If they found neither of these scenarios to apply, then they had to find for the plaintiff.

The jury found for the defendant.

CockBURN, CJ It is to be regretted that the jury were not required to give specific answers to the questions so left to them. For, it is quite possible that their verdict may have been given for the defendant on the first ground; in which case there could, I think, be no doubt as to the propriety of the judge's direction; whereas now, as it is possible that the verdict of the jury—or at all events of some of them—may have proceeded on the second ground, we are called upon to consider and decide whether the ruling of the learned judge with reference to the second question was right.

For this purpose we must assume that nothing was said on the subject of the defendant's manager desiring to buy *old* oats, nor of the oats having been said to be old; while, on the other hand, we must assume that the defendant's manager believed the oats to be old oats, and that the plaintiff was conscious of the existence of such belief, but did nothing, directly or indirectly, to bring it about, simply offering his oats and exhibiting his sample, remaining perfectly passive as to what was passing in the mind of the other party. The question is whether, under such circumstances, the passive acquiescence of the seller in the self-deception of the buyer will entitle the latter to avoid the contract. I am of opinion that it will not.

The oats offered to the defendant's manager were a specific parcel, of which the sample submitted to him formed a part. He kept the sample for twenty-four hours, and had, therefore, full opportunity of inspecting it and forming his judgment upon it. Acting on his own judgment, he wrote to the plaintiff, offering him a price. Having this opportunity of inspecting and judging of the sample, he is practically in the same position as if he had inspected the oats in bulk. It cannot be said that, if he had gone and personally inspected the oats in bulk, and then, believing—but without anything being said or done by the seller to bring about such a belief—that the oats were old, had offered a price for them, he would have been justified in repudiating the contract, because the seller, from the known habits of the buyer, or other circumstances, had reason to infer that the buyer was ascribing to the oats a quality they did not possess, and did not undeceive him.

I take the true rule to be, that where a specific article is offered for sale, without express warranty, or without circumstances from which the law will imply a warranty—as where, for instance, an article is ordered for a specific purpose—and the buyer has full opportunity of inspecting and forming his own judgment, if he chooses to act on his own judgment, the rule caveat emptor applies. If he gets the article he contracted to buy, and that article corresponds with what it was sold as, he gets all he is entitled to, and is bound by the contract. Here the defendant agreed to buy a specific parcel of oats. The oats were what they were sold as, namely, good oats according to the sample. The buyer persuaded himself they were old oats, when they were not so; but the seller neither said nor did anything to contribute to his deception. He has himself to blame. The question is not what a man of scrupulous morality or nice honour would do under such circumstances. . . .

. . . If, indeed, the buyer, instead of acting on his own opinion, had asked the question whether the oats were old or new, or had said anything which intimated his understanding that the seller was selling the oats as old oats, the case would have been wholly different; or even if he had said anything which shewed that he was not acting on his own inspection and judgment, but assumed as the foundation of the contract that the oats were old, the silence of the seller, as a means of misleading him, might have amounted to a fraudulent concealment, such as would have entitled the buyer to avoid the contract. Here, however, nothing of the sort occurs. The buyer in no way refers to the seller, but acts entirely on his own judgment. . . .

It only remains to deal with an argument which was pressed upon us, that the defendant in the present case intended to buy old oats, and the plaintiff to sell new, so the two minds were not ad idem; and that consequently there was no contract. This argument proceeds on the fallacy of confounding what was merely a motive operating on the buyer to induce him to buy with one of the essential conditions of the contract. Both parties were agreed as to the sale and purchase of this particular parcel of oats. The defendant believed the oats to be old, and was thus induced to agree to buy them, but he omitted to make their age a condition of the contract. All that can be said is, that the two minds were not ad idem as to the age of the oats; they certainly were ad idem as to the sale and purchase of them. Suppose a person to buy a horse without a warranty, believing him to be sound, and the horse turns out unsound, could it be contended that it would be open to him to say that, as he had intended to buy a sound horse, and the seller to sell an unsound one, the contract was void, because the seller must have known from the price the buyer was willing to give, or from his general habits as a buyer of horses, that he thought the horse was sound? The cases are exactly parallel.

The result is that, in my opinion, the learned judge of the county court was wrong in leaving the second question to the jury, and that, consequently, the case must go down to a new trial.

BLACKBURN J In this case I agree that on the sale of a specific article, unless there be a warranty making it part of the bargain that it possesses some particular quality, the purchaser must take the article he has bought though it does not possess that quality. And I agree that even if the vendor was aware that the purchaser thought that the article possessed that quality, and would not have entered into the contract unless he had so thought, still the purchaser is bound, unless the vendor was guilty of some fraud or deceit upon him, and that a mere abstinence from disabusing the purchaser of that impression is not fraud or deceit; for, whatever may be the case in a court of morals, there is no legal obligation on the vendor to inform the purchaser that he is under a mistake, not induced by the act of the vendor. And I also agree that where a specific lot of goods are sold by a sample, which the purchaser inspects instead of the bulk; the law is exactly the same, if the sample truly represents the bulk, though, as it is more probable that the purchaser in such a case would ask for some further warranty, slighter evidence would suffice to prove that, in fact, it was intended there should be such a warranty. On this part of the case I have nothing to add to what the Lord Chief Justice has stated.

But I have more difficulty about the second point raised in the case. I apprehend that if one of the parties intends to make a contract on one set of terms, and the other intends to make a contract on another set of terms, or, as it is sometimes expressed, if the parties are not ad idem, there is no contract, unless the circumstances are such as to preclude one of the parties from denying that he has agreed to the terms of the other. . . . If, whatever a man's real intention may be, he so conducts himself that a reasonable man would believe that he was assenting to the terms proposed by the other party, and that other party upon that belief enters into the contract with him, the man thus conducting himself would be equally bound as if he had intended to agree to the other party's terms.

The jury were directed that, if they believed the word "old" was used, they should find for the defendant—and this was right; for if that was the case, it is obvious that neither did the defendant intend to enter into a contract on the plaintiff's terms, that is, to buy this parcel of oats without any stipulation as to their quality; nor could the plaintiff have been led to believe he was intending to do so.

But the second direction raises the difficulty. I think that, if from that direction the jury would understand that they were first to consider whether they were satisfied that the defendant intended to buy this parcel of oats on the terms that it was part of his contract with the plaintiff that they were old oats, so as to have the warranty of the plaintiff to that effect, they were properly told that, if that was so, the defendant could not be bound to a contract without any such warranty unless the plaintiff was misled. But I doubt whether the direction would bring to the minds of the jury the distinction between agreeing to take the oats under the belief that they were old, and agreeing to take the oats under the belief that the plaintiff contracted that they were old.

The difference is the same as that between buying a horse believed to be sound, and buying one believed to be warranted sound . . . . I agree, therefore, in the result that there should be a new trial.

HANNEN, J. . . . It is essential to the creation of a contract that both parties should agree to the same thing in the same sense. Thus, if two persons enter into an apparent contract concerning a particular person or ship, and it turns out that each of them, misled by a similarity of name, had a different person or ship in his mind, no contract would exist between them . . . .

But one of the parties to an apparent contract may, by his own fault, be precluded from setting up that he had entered into it in a different sense to that in which it was understood by the other party. Thus in the case of a sale by sample where the vendor, by mistake, exhibited a wrong sample, it was held that the contract was not avoided by this error of the vendor . . . .

But if in the last-mentioned case the purchaser, in the course of the negotiations preliminary to the contract, had discovered that the vendor was under a misapprehension as to the sample he was offering, the vendor would have been entitled to shew that he had not intended to enter into the contract by which the purchaser sought to bind him. The rule of law applicable to such a case is a corollary from the rule of morality which Mr. Pollock cited from Paley, that a promise is to be performed "in that sense in which the promiser apprehended at the time the promisee received it," and may be thus expressed: "The promiser is not bound to fulfil a promise in a sense in which the promisee knew at the time the promiser did not intend it." And in considering the question, in what sense a promisee is entitled to enforce a promise, it matters not in what way the knowledge of the meaning in which the promiser made it is brought to the mind of the promisee, whether by express words, or by conduct, or previous dealings, or other circumstances. If by any means he knows that there was no real agreement between him and the promiser, he is not entitled to insist that the promise shall be fulfilled in a sense to which the mind of the promiser did not assent.

If, therefore, in the present case, the plaintiff knew that the defendant, in dealing with him for oats, did so on the assumption that the plaintiff was contracting to sell him old oats, he was aware that the defendant apprehended the contract in a different sense to that in which he meant it, and he is thereby deprived of the right to insist that the defendant should be bound by that which was only the apparent, and not the real bargain. . . .

. . . It may be assumed that the defendant believed the oats were old, and it may be suspected that the plaintiff thought he so believed, but the only evidence from which it can be inferred that the plaintiff believed that the defendant thought that the plaintiff was making it a term of the contract that the oats were old is that the defendant was a trainer, and that trainers, as a rule, use old oats; and that the price given was high for new oats, and more than a prudent man would have given.

Having regard to the admitted fact that the defendant bought the oats after two days' detention of the sample, I think that the evidence was not sufficient to justify the jury in answering the question put to them in the defendant's favour, if they rightly understood it; and I therefore think there should be a new trial.

Notes

1. On one level, *Smith* v. *Hughes* is a case about the duties of the seller and the expectations of the buyer in the context of sale by sample. The case was

decided on the basis that the buyer had bought the oats in reliance upon his inspection of the sample. While there may have been some sparse evidence that the seller knew that the buyer wanted old oats, in the absence of a specific finding of fact by the jury to the effect that the word 'old' had been used, there was no reason to depart from the assumption that the buyer's reliance was upon his inspection and not upon the seller and from the normal rule of *caveat emptor* (let the buyer beware). Sale by sample is now dealt with by section 15 of the Sale of Goods Act 1979, which provides:

(2) In the case of a contract for sale by sample there is an implied condition—
    (a) that the bulk will correspond with the sample in quality; . . .
    (b) that the buyer will have a reasonable opportunity of comparing the bulk with the sample.

Cockburn CJ's judgment in particular indicates that these conditions would be complied with on the facts.

2. The short extract from Atiyah which follows explains the only grounds on which the buyer may seek to escape the obligation to pay for the thing for which he had apparently contracted.

P. S. Atiyah, *Sale of Goods*, 8th edn. (London, Pitman, 1990), 41

In ordering a new trial on the ground of misdirection, the court drew a distinction between these two possibilities:

(a) If the defendant mistakenly thought that the goods were old then, in the absence of warranty by the plaintiff, the defendant would be bound by the contract even though the plaintiff was aware of the mistake.

(b) On the other hand, if the defendant mistakenly thought that the plaintiff was offering to sell him the oats *as old oats*, and the plaintiff was aware of the mistake, then the defendant would not be liable for refusing to accept the oats.

The most, however, which the judges are prepared to assume on the part of the defendant buyer in *Smith* v. *Hughes*, on the facts as they appeared, was that he may have made a mistake about the quality of the oats and, indeed, that the seller *may* have been aware of that mistake. However, he was not mistaken about the *terms* upon which the seller was offering the goods. This reveals two key aspects of what is generally known as the doctrine of unilateral mistake:

That the mistake must be as to the *terms* on which the other party intends to contract; and
that the other party must 'know' of the mistake.

Spencer indicates the linkage between agreement and mistake as to the question of determining the terms of a contract.

**J. Spencer, 'Signature, Consent and the Rule in *L'Estrange* v. *Graucob*',
[1973] *CLJ* 104 at 105**

[*Smith* v. *Hughes*] . . . usually features in books in the chapter headed "mistake"
rather than in the one headed "agreement." However, when the common law
deals with the sort of mistake where P thought the terms of the contract to be
ABC and D thought them to be XYZ . . . it solves the problem by asking which
set of terms (if any) are those to which, as a matter of law, the parties agreed. In
other words, mistake is often no more than the other side of agreement. So
Smith v. *Hughes* is an authority quite as relevant to agreement as it is to mistake.

The key to *Smith* v. *Hughes* is that the court concluded that, on the facts,
the quality of the oats was merely collateral to the sale by sample.

3. The judges in *Smith* v. *Hughes* appear to take slightly different views
about how the promises of the parties are to be understood. Compare in
particular the views of Blackburn J and Hannen J. Blackburn J focuses on
the apprehensions of a reasonable man about the conduct of the party
(promisee objectivity), while Hannen J's approach is less clear but appears
to provide some support for a more subjective approach. He draws a distinction, for example, between the 'apparent' and the 'real' bargain. In
consequence of these differences of view, the same two judges seemed to
have different perceptions of the duties of the seller and what is meant by
an awareness of the other party's mistake. Discussion of these points is
largely hypothetical in *Smith* v. *Hughes*, but other cases seem to bear out
the view, probably most closely supported by Blackburn J's approach, that
either the mistake must be 'induced' or it must be one which in all the circumstances (e.g. the trade background) the other party could not be
allowed to take advantage of.

Cases which are sometimes cited as authority for the proposition that
'snapping up' a bargain based on a known mistake as to terms by the other
party is not permitted can be explained on other grounds. For example, in
Hartog v. *Colin and Shields* ([1939] 3 All ER 566), the seller of hare-skins
made a mistake when he offered them at a 'price per pound', rather than a
'price per piece', as was the trade custom. The effect of this mistake was
that the skins were offered for sale at about one-third of their market price.
It was held that the buyers could not enforce a contract on the terms of
'price per pound' because they should have realized that a mistake had
been made. The prior negotiations between the parties and the general
trade background led Singleton J to refuse to draw a distinction between
the plaintiff's constructive (i.e. assumed) knowledge and his actual knowledge. It might be helpful also in understanding this case to note that the
principle of *caveat emptor* would not apply to the buyer snapping up a
good bargain at the expense of the seller.

A case which is taken to illustrate the reverse point (i.e. whether a seller can take advantage of a buyer's mistake) is *Scriven* v. *Hindley* ([1913] 3 KB 564). Here the buyer bid at an auction for a commodity he believed to be hemp, which was in fact tow. The price offered was well above the market price for tow, and the jury found as a fact that the auctioneer believed that the buyer had made a mistake, but only a mistake as to the value the buyer put upon the commodity as tow. The buyer refused to accept the tow and refused to pay for it. The seller brought an action for the price but failed. In addition, to the knowledge of the auctioneers, it was significant that the court found that the form of the sale catalogue and the method of exhibiting the lots contributed to the mistake (more than one third party who attended the auction gave evidence to this effect).

4. In *Smith* v. *Hughes*, Cockburn CJ deals with the argument that, because the plaintiffs were intending to sell new oats, and the defendants to buy old oats, there was no consensus *ad idem* and consequently no contract. This illustrates a factual situation which rarely arises in practice, namely where the statements of the parties are so incontrovertibly at cross-purposes that no 'agreement' can be derived from them, even based on the reasonable expectation of each party, when they receive the statements of the other. Since there was an undoubted agreement between the parties in *Smith* v. *Hughes* as to the sale of a particular parcel of oats, it was clearly never likely that what would now be described as a claim of 'mutual mistake' would succeed. Mutual mistake only arises if there is a complete breakdown of the objective test of agreement, which arises very rarely. *Scriven* v. *Hindley* is treated by some writers as a case of the cross-purposes doctrine (an offer to sell tow and an offer to buy hemp), but both perspectives on the facts (i.e. complete confusion or a known mistake) lead to the conclusion that the buyer can avoid the imposition of a contract to buy tow. More illumination of the problems of distinguishing the two doctrines and of determining whether there was any form of agreement between the parties might have come from an attempt by the buyers to enforce a contract for the sale of hemp at the price they offered to buy at.

Little additional edification can be gleaned from a study of *Raffles* v. *Wichelhaus* (1864) 2 H. & C. 906, the classic case of the two ships named *Peerless* referred to in Dalton (above). In this case, the buyers and sellers made what was in effect a primitive futures contract about cotton due to arrive from India 'ex *Peerless*'.

Difficulties arose because there were two ships *Peerless* plying the cotton trade between Liverpool and India, although the sellers only had a consignment of cotton on the second one, which arrived in December 1867. The buyers claimed that they had meant the first ship, which had arrived in October of that year, and refused to accept and pay for a consignment from the second ship. It is perhaps a little odd that they had not attempted to enforce a delivery from the first ship when none arrived but, as Simpson ('Contracts for Cotton to Arrive: the Case of the Two Ships *Peerless*', (1989) 11 *Cardozo L. Rev.* 287) has shown, this may well have been because the market for cotton at that time was extremely volatile, and by the time the cotton arrived at Liverpool the buyers might well have been looking for any excuse to escape from what had turned out to be a bad bargain. They may have been extremely relieved when they were not asked to take cotton from the first ship. The buyers successfully resisted the demand that they take cotton from the second ship, although the basis of the decision is not clear, since there is no proper judgment in this respect, merely a recitation of counsels' arguments with some interpretations by the judges and a brief statement of the decision itself.

Simpson's detailed historical researches on the cotton trade and the shipping trade stand in sharp contrast to the treatment which *Raffles* v. *Wichelhaus* has conventionally received in the textbooks, where it has acquired the status of the classic case of mutual mistake—statements by the parties from which an unambiguous agreement cannot be derived, even if the statements are looked at objectively from the perspective of each party. Simpson's research has now demonstrated that the case should be looked at in its context, and the following are among the most important findings of general and specific historical context which he has discovered:

It was not unusual for there to be two or more ships with the same name, and the conventional method of distinguishing between them was to put the captain's name afterwards: hence we have *Peerless* (Major) (arrived in October) and *Peerless* (Flavin) (arrived in December).

Consequently, the facts of the case should not be thought of as entirely out of the ordinary. In the primitive cotton futures market, with an extremely volatile price, it was of the first importance to buyers to know which ship they had ordered cotton from. The vague designation used—'to arrive'—was simply a product of the absence of technology making it possible to predict when a ship might arrive. Hence those who criticize *Raffles* v. *Wichelhaus* for being excessively subjective, pointing out that in fact there was only one consignment of cotton available for the sellers, and that objectively the buyer could get what he wanted from the second ship, underestimate the importance of this factor.

As the cotton trader, Raffles the seller had certain informational advantages over the buyers, as he would have known earlier than they that there were to be two ships sailing from India with cotton. It may be that this fact influenced the court when it refused to enforce a contract for cotton from the second ship.

Raffles v. *Wichelhaus* remains an enigmatic case. Simpson has not succeeded, for example, in clarifying one key point—namely when the contract was made—which would have revealed much additional information about the assumptions of the parties. However, now that we know more, it is perhaps best to treat *Raffles* as a transaction specific judgment which is not in itself, in the common law tradition, capable of being made into an abstract authority for any wider point of mutual mistake.

5. The following observations by Willett provide an analysis of *Smith* v. *Hughes*-type situations within the framework of judicial behaviour put forward by Adams and Brownsword (see Ch. 4).

C. Willett, 'Uninduced Misapprehensions in Contract Law', (1992) 5 *JCL* 157 at 161–2

The interpretive scheme for contract law provided by Adams and Brownsword provides an illuminating means of understanding the dilemma faced by the courts in this type of situation. They talk of 'consumer welfarism' and 'market individualism' as being influential and usually conflicting philosophies in adjudication of contract law disputes. Of course, there need not be an all-pervading conflict between them. For instance all things being equal (that is, assuming no inequality of bargaining power between the parties, which a consumer welfarist might wish to be taken into account) the normal objective rule as expressed in *Smith v Hughes* appears to satisfy both camps. The market individualist is happy because the transaction is secure; competitive exchange has been fostered and the sphere of influence of two free economic beings has been maximised. Equally the consumer welfarist (unless of a very extreme kind) is unlikely to feel any strong paternalistic urges towards a party who is perfectly capable of looking after himself, but has made a mistake, through no fault of the other party.

The conflict arises in such 'frontier' type situations as . . . *Hartog v Colin and Shields*. The market individualist wants such agreements to stand in the pursuit of the very interest mentioned above. The consumer welfarist, on the other hand will wish to set the agreement aside on the grounds that there has been an abuse of an informational advantage.

IV. MISTAKES OF IDENTITY

A rather different problem occurs when the source of the mistake made by a seller is the identity or characteristics of the other party to the exchange (the buyer) rather than the subject-matter of the contract, where this mistake has occurred because of the actions of the buyer in engendering the mistake in the seller. The usual scenario compounds this mistake by the original buyer then contracting with a third party to sell the subject-matter of the contract. The original buyer then disappears, leaving the third party and the original seller to dispute ownership of the subject-matter of the contract.

This problem manifests itself in the line of cases known as the 'identity' cases. The original seller's argument is one based in conversion: the buyer did not acquire good title from him, as the contract was 'void *ab initio*' owing to ineffective consent based on a mistake as to the identity of characteristics of the buyer. Therefore the third party could not acquire good title from the rogue buyer. In these situations the court has to make a choice between the original seller and the third party.

Citibank NA v. Brown Shipley & Co. Ltd.
[1991] 2 All ER 690

WALLER J. . . . there is in issue which of the innocent parties should bear the loss from a fraud.

The facts are broadly as follows. Certain fraudsters, probably the same fraudsters, managed to induce Citibank NA on three occasions (only two of which are relevant) and then Midland Bank plc to issue banker's drafts in favour of Brown Shipley & Co Ltd.

Brown Shipley made some checks on each occasion with the issuing banks, the extent of which, and result of which, are in issue. Brown Shipley then collected payment, and paid out very substantial sums in cash to the fraudsters.

Citibank and Midland seek to recover from Brown Shipley the value of the drafts as damages in conversion. Put simply, Citibank and Midland say that title in the drafts was never transmitted to Brown Shipley, and that therefore the act of presenting them for payment was a conversion, and the correct measure of damage is the face value of the drafts.

Brown Shipley's answer is that title did pass . . . .

The issues are as follows. (1) Did the title of the drafts at all times remain in Citibank or Midland Bank? . . .

THE FACTS

Citibank acted as bankers for Economou Co Ltd and for Neptune Maritime of Monrovia (Neptune), for whom Economou Co Ltd acted as agents. Neptune apparently had two accounts with Citibank, number 400432 and number 980242. By letter dated 25 March 1980 the mandate on behalf of Neptune in respect of these accounts specified four Swiss gentlemen as signatories. By letter dated 31 August 1982 Neptune authorised Citibank to transfer funds between accounts on the 'telephonic instructions from a person identifying himself as G Economou or A Economou, R Radin, L Ryall . . . All instructions given to you . . . will be confirmed in writing by authorised signatories.'

There was it appears a widening of the mandate by a course of conduct, under which by similar telephonic instructions, payments could be made from the said accounts in relation to running expenses of any of Neptune's ships identified by name at the time of the giving of the instructions to known large commercial entities such as Shell, British Petroleum and Mitsubishi.

There are examples in the papers of such instructions being confirmed in writing, all of which are on Neptune headed paper, and bear the signatures of two of the Swiss gentlemen, as one would expect as a result of the mandate.

It is also of relevance that Economou Co Ltd had an account or accounts at Citibank, and that the authorised signatories of that or those accounts were George Economou, Angelo Economou, Miss Ann Lynch, Richard Radin and E Firman. Citibank had examples of those signatures on the relevant signature card.

The first transaction

In mid-December 1986 Mr Trigg of Brown Shipley received a number of telephone calls from an individual who gave his name as 'Economou', about the possibility of Brown Shipley supplying about £150,000 worth of dollars. Mr Trigg consulted Mr Glitz, the chief cashier of Brown Shipley, and the so-called Mr Economou was informed that either a sterling draft, a banker's payment or a dollar draft drawn on the London dollar clearing system would be needed. These conversations culminated in a conversation on 23 December 1986 at 10.13 am.

Following that conversation it would appear that someone, whom Mr Burge of Citibank believed to be Mr George Economou, telephoned Mr Burge of Citibank. The caller asked Mr Burge to prepare a banker's draft in favour of Brown Shipley for the sum of $US225,000. Mr Burge was convinced and still remains convinced that he was talking to Mr George Economou. No evidence was given as to what Mr Burge was told that the draft was needed for. In accordance with the instructions received, Mr Burge prepared a draft, numbered 117538153 in favour of Brown Shipley, drawn on Citibank (New York State) NA for $US225,000.

On the morning of 23 December 1986 Mr Burge was asked to go downstairs to meet a messenger from Economou Co Ltd and he did so. The person he met there was he thought a messenger from that company, and he handed the draft to him and in return received a letter on Economou & Co headed paper dated 22 December 1986. That letter purported to confirm the telephone instructions, but that letter was different from any other confirmation letter previously received. It was on Economou paper. It was signed by four people, purporting to be signatories for Economou Co Ltd, three of whose signatures bore a close resemblance to those of G Economou, A Economou and R Radin examples of whose signatures Citibank had. The fourth signature purported to be that of D A Lloyd, who was not an authorised signatory so far as Citibank was concerned, either of Neptune or of Economou Co Ltd. The letter was addressed to Mr Burridge crossed out with 'Burge' put in its place. It referred to an inward transfer of funds expected to come not later than 30 December

1986. It was thus (a) patently not in accordance with any mandate from Neptune, (b) contained a signature which was not in accordance with any mandate even from Economou Co Ltd and (c) contained signatures of persons authorised to sign on behalf of Economou Co Ltd which no one within Citibank actually checked against signatures that they had. . . .

[Someone whose identity was never discovered telephoned Mr Burge and Brown Shipley and arranged for the dollar draft to be replaced with a sterling one.]

In the result the same messenger returned to Citibank with the dollar draft, saw Mr Burge, who in the meanwhile had prepared a sterling draft. That sterling draft for £154,532 was drawn on Citibank's Strand branch and was exchanged by Mr Burge for the dollar draft. The messenger then went to Brown Shipley, where he handed over the sterling draft to Mr Trigg and left it with him saying he would return in the morning to collect the cash (as Mr Trigg had previously arranged with the caller purporting to be Mr Economou).

Mr Trigg took the draft to Mr Glitz, who in accordance with his normal practice rang up Citibank and asked for the department responsible for the issue of drafts. He spoke to a female, who was clearly Angela Byrne, whose name he wrote on the back of the draft. He told Miss Byrne that Brown Shipley were holding a draft. He gave purely the name of the payee and the date and refused to give more information as he wanted Citibank to supply all the details in order that Brown Shipley could satisfy itself that the draft was in order. She [gave] . . . Mr Glitz the number and the amount of the draft, which tallied with the draft that Mr Glitz held. She was then asked by Mr Glitz (according to him) to confirm that the draft had been issued in the ordinary course of business, and she responded with a Yes. . . .

In the result Brown Shipley sent a messenger round on 23 December 1986 to Citibank, with the draft, and received a banker's payment dated 24 December 1986 drawn on Citibank's Old Jewry branch. Brown Shipley was thus able to obtain funds through their own clearing bank, National Westminster Bank plc, on 24 December 1986. On 24 December 1986, in the morning, at 9.30, the same man calling himself Economou rang Mr Trigg at Brown Shipley . . . . He was told that he would get the cash as soon as possible and definitely by 10.30 am.

The cash was handed over by Mr Trigg in an envelope to the messenger, a Mr Castle, who in return for that envelope, signed a copy of the contract with Brown Shipley.

The second transaction

That a second transaction was in contemplation was referred to in the caller's conversation with Mr Trigg at 9.30 on 24 December 1986 in relation to the first transaction. That caller suggested that he needed further cash, which would not be available from Citibank until Wednesday, 31 December 1986, whereas he needed it on Monday, 29 December 1986. Mr Trigg advised him to obtain a dollar draft on the London dollar clearing system, pointing out that there must have been an exchange loss on the first transaction. . . .

[A dollar draft was obtained but, owing to a discrepancy in the figures on the draft and the amount requested, it was exchanged for a sterling draft.]

. . . the sterling draft was delivered to Brown Shipley . . . . it was . . . seen by Mr Trigg . . . on Monday, 29 December 1986.

The confirmation letter received by Mr Burge was this time in manuscript. It was again on Economou headed paper. It did not purport to bear signatures of any of the Swiss gentlemen. It purported to be signed by G Economou, A Economou and D A Lloyd.

Again it was (1) patently not in compliance with any mandate from Neptune, (2) it contained a signature which was not relevant to Economou or Neptune and (3) it contained signatures which Citibank did not trouble to check against the genuine signatures that they held.

In the event on Monday, 29 December 1986, following Mr Trigg taking the sterling draft to Mr Glitz, Mr Glitz had a further conversation with someone at Citibank about that sterling draft. . . . His evidence was that on 24 December 1986, when the second transaction was first mentioned to him, he was 'slightly uneasy, simply because of the large amounts involved'. . . . [He] took the view that since Citibank had confirmed that the first transaction was satisfactory and payment had been made there was no basis for Brown Shipley to press the matter further with Citibank.

It would also seem that the transaction was unusual enough for Mr Trigg to mention it to the senior treasury manager at Brown Shipley, Mr Ralph Rosen. They spoke to Brown Shipley's director of treasury, Mr Jean-Louis Luyks, who evidently had said that if Brown Shipley were in possession of cleared funds then Brown Shipley could proceed with the transactions in question.

The fact is that these were somewhat unusual transactions for Brown Shipley, in that, whoever Brown Shipley were dealing with, they were not customers, they were what is called a casual and the figures supplied by them of transactions of an equivalent size of supplying notes to casuals shows these transactions to be out of the norm. Brown Shipley, what is more, had done nothing themselves to identify the persons or companies with whom they were dealing. But the terms of the conversations between Mr Trigg and whomever he was talking to so far as recordings remain show the matter being treated as one of routine so far as Brown Shipley were concerned.

In any event Mr Glitz carried out his normal practice. In accordance with that practice, he again telephoned Citibank. . . . The normal practice involved getting . . . details of the draft . . . . Having received the details he also asked whether the drafts were issued by Citibank in the ordinary course of business, and received an unequivocal assurance in that regard.

Again I see no reason not to accept Mr Glitz's evidence. From that evidence it is clear that he did not say that he or Brown Shipley had any uneasy feeling at any stage, and nor did he give the details of the transaction known only to Brown Shipley, ie that the customer was a casual and notes were being handed out in return for the draft. It is clear that overall he was convinced that all was well, and what convinced him was what had in fact happened on the first transaction, ie in short, the issue of the dollar draft by Citibank, exchange for a sterling draft by Citibank, confirmation by Citibank that all was well and a meeting of the payment to Brown Shipley and then a similar pattern on the second transaction. . . .

The third transaction

I will not deal in any detail with the third transaction, because it was ineffective from the fraudster's point of view. . . .

The Midland transaction

Eight months later, the fraudsters (and on the balance of probabilities I find they were the same fraudsters) struck again.

This transaction commenced with a telephone call to a Mr Hart of Brown Shipley on 5 August 1987. The speaker purported to be a Mr Watton speaking on behalf of the Willmott Group wanting to buy £236,000 of Deutschmarks in bank notes. This was in fact the first transaction of this size between Brown Shipley and a non-customer since the previous fraud. But it is not a transaction which caused any surprise at Brown Shipley, as can be seen from the terms of the conversation held at 15.53 on 5 August with Mr Hart. Furthermore, the terms of the next conversation again with Mr Hart, but this time with a person purporting to be a Mr John Bayliss, secretary and director of Willmott, show the matter to be one of routine so far as Brown Shipley were concerned. That conversation took place at 16.15 on the same day. In that conversation arrangements were made between Mr Hart and the caller for a banker's draft to be delivered to Brown Shipley the next day, in return for which Brown Shipley would sell the Deutschmarks as previously arranged with Mr Watton.

That same evening a person describing himself as Peter Willmott rang Mr Cooper of Midland Bank at Hitchin. . . . So far as Midland were concerned, a company, John Willmott Administration Ltd of Hitchin Road, Shefford, Bedfordshire, were customers, and the name of that company was changed to Willmott Dixon Administration Ltd from 1 May 1987. The authorised signatories of the company, to which I shall refer as 'Administration' do not include Peter Willmott or John Bayliss.

Peter Willmott was a signatory on a joint account at the same branch of Midland with other individuals according to a mandate dated 9 September 1986, and John Bayliss appears to have had a personal account at the same branch.

It would appear there were substantial funds in Administration's account on or about 5–6 August 1986.

The conversation which Mr Cooper had with the person calling himself Peter Willmott related to methods of transferring money. On the next day, 6 August, between 9.00 and 9.30 am, the same person rang and asked Mr Cooper to arrange for a banker's draft for £236,000 to be issued and made payable to Brown Shipley. The draft was to be collected by the Willmott messenger. Mr Cooper asked for a letter of confirmation and the caller said that the letter would be signed by himself and John Bayliss. . . . Mr Cooper then authorised a Miss Owen to issue a banker's draft, but stated that only telephonic instructions had as yet been received, and it was important that Midland received proper written authorisation. Midland's standing instructions would seem to have required Midland to have telephoned the customer back on a number known only to Midland. . . . it is clear that Mr Cooper did not make any such telephone call.

A messenger . . . came to the Midland branch and was handed by Miss Howkins the draft in return for a letter of confirmation. This letter of confirmation bears signatures purporting to be those of Peter Willmott and John Bayliss, which Miss Howkins says she recognised as they had often signed for Willmott before.

This letter of confirmation was headed John Willmott Holdings Ltd, 34 Upper Brook Street, London W1Y 1EE. It instructed Midland to debit 'our Wilmot Dixon Holdings Ltd account'; it will be noted that there is a single 'l' in Wilmot, and on the letter Holdings is struck out in manuscript, and 'Admin' inserted, and this was apparently done by Midland. Neither John Bayliss nor Peter Willmott were authorised signatories for the Administration account. The signatures on the confirmation letters were passable forgeries of John Bayliss and Peter Willmott, but no one at Midland checked either the terms of Midland's authority or whether the signatures were the actual signatures of those individuals.

Again, as with Citibank, there was so far as Midland was concerned a total non-compliance with their mandate. . . .

[Someone purporting to be John Bayliss took the draft to Brown Shipley. Glitz sought assurances from the Midland Bank about the number of the draft and its amount. He maintained that they were forthcoming with this information and about the fact that the draft was issued in the ordinary course of business.]

THE LAW

The question of title

The cornerstone of Mr Jonathan Hirst QC's submissions [for the issuing banks] on this aspect is *Cundy v Lindsay* (1878) 3 App Cas 459. He submits that if

Brown Shipley were to obtain title to the banker's drafts, they can only do so through the fraudsters. He submits that the fraudsters had no title because on the principle of *Cundy v Lindsay* there was no contract between them and Citibank, or them and Midland, under which even a voidable title was transmitted.

Apart from authority which I must refer to in a moment and which Mr Hirst suggested supported his approach, it seemed to me that there were fallacies in Mr Hirst's approach.

First the *Cundy v Lindsay* principle only reaches the result of no title at least in a bilateral contract situation where the findings of fact are (i) A thinks he has agreed with C because he believes B with whom he is negotiating, is C; (ii) B is aware that A did not intend to make any agreement with him; and (iii) A has established that the identity of C was a matter of crucial importance.

Where A issues a document promising to pay B under which he fully intends to promise to pay B, and which is only to take effect on its delivery to B, but which he gives to C thinking he is D, and which he expects (as happens) will be delivered to B, the question arises as to which contract it is alleged the *Cundy v Lindsay* principle should render void. The 'title' of B does not seem to me to be derived through C or D at all. C or D would seem to me to be little more than a conduit pipe carrying what at that stage is an inchoate instrument; the instrument only becomes a valid instrument on delivery to B (see s 21(1) of the Bills of Exchange Act 1882). Delivery to be effective must be made either by or under the authority of party drawing (see s 21(2)), but a valid and unconditional delivery is presumed until the contrary is proved (s 21(3)). It would seem to me that only if it could be established that delivery was without authority would there be no quite separate contract on which B could rely as against A. That contract, ie the one between A and B, may be voidable, but once B has had the instrument delivered to him with the authority of A, it seems to me that a contract comes into existence between A and B (as A intended) under which, as between those two, B has a good title. So far as authority is concerned, it will usually be very difficult for A to establish that it was of crucial importance to him who actually physically transported the draft to B. In this case, for example, delivery might have been done by post; it might have been done by one or other of the banks' messengers; it might have been done by some other messenger. It so happened that in this case that it was done by someone thought to be the customer or his messenger, but that was not of crucial importance. That being so, the authority, as it seems to me, albeit induced by fraud, would not be void; the authority would be actual, even if voidable.

I must turn now to the authorities to see what effect they have on the thoughts expressed above.

(1) I have been referred to the cases relating to mistake in the *Cundy v Lindsay* sense, eg *Lake v Simmons* [1927] AC 487, *Phillips v Brooks Ltd* [1919] 2 KB 243, *Ingram v Little* [1960] 3 All ER 332 and *Lewis v Averay* [1972] 1 QB 198.

I do not think at the end of the day the last three cases assist very much, save to emphasise (1) that each case rests on its own facts, (2) that in the bilateral contract context for no title to pass it must be established that there is no contract under which such a title can pass and (3) the no contract situation, as opposed to a voidable contract, only arises if it is fundamental to the contract that one party to the contract should be who he says that he is. That is easier to establish where contracts are made entirely by documents and is less easy to establish in an inter praesentes position. . . .

Returning now to the facts of the instant case, it seems to me that the key lies in whether there was any authority to deliver the banker's drafts to Brown Shipley. The presumption is in favour of there being authority. The *Cundy v Lindsay* principle could be applied so as to negative that authority (as per *Lake v Simmonds*), but only if the precise identity of the bailee and possibly also the identity of the person to whom the banker's draft was to be delivered were mistaken *and* proved to be of fundamental importance. Neither Midland nor Citibank were under any mistake or misapprehension as to whom the draft was to be delivered. Furthermore, the bailee who physically carried the draft was a messenger whose precise identity was unimportant. Even if it could be suggested that it is going too far to say his precise identity was unimportant, it seems to me that neither Citibank nor Midland have established to the degree required that it was fundamental to them that the bailee was a particular person about whom they were mistaken, as opposed to a person whose attributes did not include authority from their customer as they believed. Once there was authority, title to the banker's drafts was, as I see it, transmitted directly from Citibank or Midland to Brown Shipley, on the drafts becoming valid instruments as a result of delivery through whomever the messenger was.

My conclusion on the first question accordingly is that Brown Shipley did not convert the drafts by presenting them for payment.

[In the second part of the judgment Waller J deals with an alternative submission by Brown Shipley that might have protected them against an action for conversion even if he had found that title did not pass. In the light of the first part of the judgment these comments are *obiter* but provide a useful insight into the evaluation of commercial risk made by Waller J.

Brown Shipley claimed that the issuing banks had made representations to them regarding the propriety of the transactions that they were entitled to rely upon. The issuing banks countered this by saying that Brown Shipley lost their entitlement to rely upon the representations because they had disclosed insufficient information about the transactions and had they done so, the issuing banks would not have made the representations. Waller J went on:]

Citibank: first transaction

The following are the facts which it is alleged Brown Shipley should have revealed. First, the fact that Brown Shipley were dealing with a casual, ie a non-customer, whom they had not met; second, that Brown Shipley were exchanging for the drafts a very large sum in cash; and third, that Brown Shipley had made no inquiries whatever as to the bona fides of the persons with whom they were dealing.

My view is that, as between banks, Citibank must have appreciated that they were being rung up in order to get a confirmation that the drafts were (a) not forgeries and (b) issued in the ordinary course of business, so that Brown Shipley could rely on them as cash. I do not feel that it would have struck any reasonable banker in Brown Shipley's position, or for that matter in Citibank's position, that there should have been revealed, as between the banks, details of a transaction which Brown Shipley were about to do with a customer of Citibank. The whole purpose of ringing was to put Citibank on notice that Brown Shipley wanted comfort, and, it seems to me, that if Citibank wished before confirming to have details of the transaction, then it should have asked for them. The facts were not *so* unusual as to give rise to any suspicion of fraud which would of course have put a totally different complexion on Brown Shipley's duty.

Citibank: second transaction

This transaction does give rise to slightly different considerations because of the admission by Mr Glitz that at some stage he did have a 'slightly uneasy' feeling. . . . In other words, from Mr Glitz's viewpoint, Citibank had two occasions on which to examine the transaction. Furthermore, from Mr Glitz's viewpoint, Citibank had done precisely the same in the previous transaction and thus must have been aware of all the facts of which Mr Glitz was aware in relation to the size of the transaction, save the fact that possibly Brown Shipley were going to pay cash against the draft. Thus before Mr Glitz telephoned Citibank in accordance with his normal practice in relation to the second transaction, his feeling of unease had been considerably relieved by what Citibank have already done. His practice involved seeking details of the draft thus confirming it was not a forgery, and then asking whether the draft was issued in the normal course of business. If anyone within Citibank had done the least check in relation to that question, they would have discovered the answer, ie that these drafts had been issued patently outside their mandate.

Once again it seems to me that it would not be reasonable to expect Brown Shipley to disclose details of the transaction, or to disclose some rather nebulous feeling of unease, which to some extent had already been assuaged. Brown Shipley were known in the market to be bankers who dealt in notes, and

Brown Shipley gave every opportunity by asking two questions for Citibank to carry out the checks that were necessary.

Thus in relation to the second transaction, I would also have held that Brown Shipley should not be precluded from relying on the representation received by virtue of any non-disclosure. . . . Mr Glitz gave full opportunity to the employees of Midland to check the matter out, and any reasonable check at that time would in fact have disclosed that the draft had been issued patently outside Midland's mandate.

In the event, it seems to me that Brown Shipley should not be disentitled from relying on the representation that they received from Midland at this time.

Conclusion

In the circumstances, the actions of Citibank and Midland fail.

Notes

1. Waller J refers to *Cundy* v. *Lindsay* in his judgment and decides that it is not applicable to the facts of Citibank. The facts of *Cundy* v. *Lindsay* were that

B. Jackson, *Law, Fact and Narrative Coherence* (Liverpool, Deborah Charles, 1988), 102

a rogue called Blenkarn, representing himself to be 'Blenkiron & Co.' (the latter being an existing and reputable local firm), wrote a letter to the plaintiff, ordering goods. On receiving them, Blenkarn resold them to the defendant, who bought them in good faith. On discovery of the facts, the plaintiffs sued the defendants for recovery of the goods. The appeal courts held that the plaintiff had intended to contract only with Blenkiron & Co., and not with whoever traded at the address to which the goods were to be sent. Therefore, the contract was void (ab initio), and the plaintiff was able to recover the goods from the innocent third party purchaser.

There are clear similarities between *Cundy* v. *Lindsay* and *Citibank* in contradistinction to the other identity mistake cases. In both cases there was arms-length dealing, and yet the result is different. This difference in result can be seen in the unilateral mistake cases where there are face-to-face dealings. For example, in *Phillips* v. *Brookes*, *Lake* v. *Simmonds* and *Lewis* v. *Averay* the court found for the third party who acquired the goods and in *Ingram* v. *Little* the court found for the original seller. Clearly the key to these decisions cannot be found in a crude distinction between arms-length dealing and face-to-face dealing. Nor does it lie in attempts to draw a distinction between identity and attributes. As Lord Denning MR points out in *Lewis* v. *Averay* this is an unhelpful distinction; identity is merely a collection of attributes. In practice, those few cases where an identity mistake has been held to make the contract void are cases where the court has construed the identity of the other contracting party as crucial to the party who made the mistake. This emerges from a comparison of *Cundy* v. *Lindsay* and *King's Northern Metal Co. Ltd.* v. *Edridge, Merrett & Co. Ltd.*, (1897) 14 TLR 98. In *Cundy* it was the deliberate linkage to a known reputable firm which induced the mistaken consent of Cundy. In *King's Norton* a rogue sought to work a similar fraud by posing as the representative of a non-existent firm (Hallam & Co.) which had previously done business as Hallam & Co., and had duly paid for goods on invoice. He had simply induced the belief that Hallam & Co. was reputable, and not created a confusion as to identity.

A more helpful way of rationalizing the cases can be found by applying the statements of Waller J in *Citibank* and Pearce LJ in *Ingram* v. *Little* that each case is to be decided on its facts. By looking at the cases in this way, we can decide which of the two parties (the original seller or the third party) is best able to guard against the risk of dealing with a fraudster. In assessing this risk, the crucial issues are the access to and use of information. For example in *Cundy* v. *Lindsay* the original sellers followed their (and presumably many other manufacturers') standard practice of supplying goods with an invoice and expecting payment to follow. There was no reason for them to make any extra checks, as they were encouraged to believe by the fraudster that the person they were dealing with was a well-known, reputable merchant who would pay in the ordinary course of business. If this merchant did not settle his bills in this way, then he would not have the reputation he did. In *Citibank*, however, the issuing banks had mechanisms (such as signatures, etc.) to protect themselves from exactly the kind of fraud that occurred, and yet declined to use them.

Waller J points out at the end of his judgment that Brown Shipley were entitled to assume that Citibank had used the information available to them but not to Brown Shipley in order to exclude the possibility of fraud. It is, of course, true that the situation in *Citibank* is unusual in the sense that the defrauded parties were in contact with each other. Hence the receiving bank was able to inquire directly about the issuing bank's information. The type of information that Citibank had available to them and the type of checks they could be expected to make were, as Waller J indicates, part of specialized banking practice. In *Phillips* v. *Brookes* the original seller, a jeweller, was not able to assert, like the sellers in *Cundy* v. *Lindsay*, that he was following standard business practice when he allowed the rogue to take the jewellery away; he had no reason to assume that Sir George Bullough was any more honest than anybody else who walked into the shop.

2. Are there any context-specific factors which help us to understand the different results reached by the Court of Appeal in the seemingly factually

similar cases of *Ingram* v. *Little* and *Lewis* v. *Averay*, involving sales of motor cars between private individuals? In both cases the sellers are taken in by the conduct of seemingly reputable buyers who persuaded them to part with the car without waiting for payment to be assured. In both cases the asset in question is relatively important financially to the person who is selling it. In both cases the checks made by the sellers were futile in the sense that they would never have revealed the ability to pay of the people the fraudsters claimed to be.

However the crucial difference between the cases lies in the attitudes the court expected a seller in the private market to take. It is expected that a man of 25 will realize that there are rogues about and take precautions accordingly—hence the result in *Lewis* v. *Averay*. In *Ingram* v. *Little*, it is not obligatory for the old lady sellers to show healthy scepticism and a knowledge of the potential hazards of dealing in the second-hand car market.

In the following extract Jackson assumes that the Court of Appeal had found a distinction such as the one identified above between the position of the sellers in *Lewis* v. *Averay* and *Ingram* v. *Little*, and seeks to identify how the court signals through the use of language in the judgments the existence of that distinction.

Jackson, *Law, Fact and Narrative Coherence*, 102–6

. . . consider the decision-making in the case of *Ingram* v. *Little*. Here, the sellers were defrauded into parting with their car by a rogue who presented himself in person, claiming to be P. G. M. Hutchinson of a certain address. The sellers had not heard of P. G. M. Hutchinson, but took the trouble of verifying from the telephone directory that there was a P. G. M. Hutchinson at the address the rogue had given, before accepting the rogue's cheque. When the cheque turned out to be worthless, they sought recovery of the car from the innocent third party to whom the rogue had, in the meantime, resold it. Here, the court held that the contract was void, and not merely voidable, so that the sellers were able to recover the car. . . .

. . . In *Phillips* v. *Brooks Ltd.*, the seller seeking to recover his goods was a shopkeeper, while in *Ingram* v. *Little* the sellers were private individuals (two sisters) disposing of their secondhand car. In terms of comparison with narrative frameworks, the judges have at least two alternatives. On the one hand, there is the narrative of the shopkeeper—here, almost by definition, a retailer of fairly valuable commodities (such as the jeweller in *Phillips* v. *Brooks Ltd.*) not the corner sweetshop—who, in the course of business, is bound on occasion to part with goods in return for worthless cheques, and on the other hand the story of the 'innocent' (in both sense) private seller, defrauded by an (habitual) rogue.

What influenced the choice between these two stock narratives, in terms of comparison with the 'facts' of *Ingram* v. *Little*? The comparison is informed not only by neutral perceptions of degree of similarity, but by the force or pertinence (or 'relevance') of these particular narrative traits which distinguish the two schemes. And this relevance is a function of an *evaluation* of the situation. . . . narratives come laden with tacit social evaluations. In [the case of] the shopkeeper defrauded by a dud cheque, though our sympathies may be with him, we do not sympathise with him as fulfilling the role of an innocent victim in the same way that we do when regarding the narrative of the private individual who has been defrauded by the same means. The representation of the plaintiffs as "two sisters" (impliedly of the elderly maiden variety) evokes further sympathy, and reinforces our evaluation that they are victims who ought to be assisted (even as against an innocent third party purchaser).

. . . In *Lewis* v. *Averay*, the rogue posed as Richard Greene, a well-known film actor (who played Robin Hood in the television series of that name—information provided by Lord Denning). As proof of identity he produced an admission pass to a leading British film studio, Pinewood, bearing the name 'Richard A. Green', a photograph (of the rogue) and an official stamp. The plaintiff then handed over the car and its log-book in exchange for a (stolen) cheque signed R. A. Green. By the time the fraud came to light, the car had been resold to an innocent purchaser, from whom the plaintiff then sought to recover it. The Court of Appeal . . . chose . . . to follow *Phillips* v. *Brooks Ltd.* and disapprove *Ingram* v. *Little*: the contract was merely voidable, had not been avoided in time, and therefore the innocent third party purchaser was protected against the claims of the original owner.

At the level of legal doctrine, the result is confusing, unless one simply takes a predictive view based upon the weight of authority *after Lewis* v. *Averay*, and concludes that in practice *Ingram* v. *Little* is unlikely to be followed in future cases: doctrinally, it is not distinguishable from the other cases, but must be treated simply as an anomaly. If, however, we look at these cases against typical narratives with their accompanying social evaluations, the results of the decision-making may not appear quite so strange. Even the different results in *Ingram* v. *Little* and *Lewis* v. *Averay* become intelligible. Although in both, the plaintiff was a private individual, not a retailer, in the one case we sympathise with the victim of the fraud (the two sisters in *Ingram* v. *Little*) while in the other we are amused: the plaintiff here appears more as a stupid dupe than as a victim. How many people would believe a stranger when he turned up out of the blue and told them he was a famous actor? If he was so famous, the plaintiff should not have been fooled; he should not have accepted the evidence of the admission pass; and he should have realised that the name on the cheque presented to him was spelled differently from that of the real Richard Greene.

This is reinforced by Lord Denning's narrative constructions of the parties in this case: the plaintiff was "a young man who is a postgraduate student of

chemistry", while the defendant was also young: "at the time under
a music student in London at the Royal College of Music." In ten
the two "innocent" parties competing not to carry the loss, there wa
to choose. But added point is given to the underlying narrative pat
fact that the duped plaintiff was a person of some intelligence (if it i
ble so to construct postgraduate students of chemistry). Hence, when it comes
to comparison of the litigants, the plaintiff's youth is suppressed: "Now Mr
Lewis, the original owner of the car, sues young Mr. Averay."

The overall impression given by the narratives in *Ingram* v. *Little* and *Lewis* v.
Averay is therefore different: the two sisters may have been defrauded, but Lewis
was actually *fooled*. That being so, the contest between plaintiff and defendant is
no longer one between two equally innocent parties: it is between a fool and an
innocent, and the fool is at least partly the victim of his own stupidity. The culpability of the plaintiff here may not amount to that required by the law to
deprive him of a remedy: i.e. that the true situation would have been *obvious* to a
reasonable person. Nevertheless, decision-making reflects the social evaluation
of the case, which is typified by laughter rather than sympathy.

3. It may be asked why the plaintiffs in *Citibank,* or indeed in the other
mistaken identity cases, did not seek to follow the factually more obvious
route of arguing that the contract had been rescinded because it was
entered into as a result of a fraudulent misrepresentation by the rogues.
Why did the plaintiffs choose to argue the much narrower doctrine of mistake? The reason for this lies in the difference between a void and a voidable contract. If the process of formation of a contract is undermined by
the operation of a mistake, whether unilateral or mutual, it is treated as if it
had never existed. Consequently, title to the goods defrauded cannot pass
to the rogue, and from there to the innocent third party. However, if the
formation of a contract is vitiated by the operation of a misrepresentation,
it is merely voidable. That is, it is presumed effective until rescinded by the
seller, and so long as the contract has not been rescinded, the rogue buyer
has title to the goods which he can in turn pass to the innocent third party.
The latter is then immune to an action in conversion, since he is truly now
the owner of the goods. Collins summarizes the context in which mistake
remains a useful doctrine in the following terms:

H. Collins, 'Methods and Aims of Comparative Contract Law', (1991) 11 *OJLS* 396 at 400

. . . the mistake cases are those where the mistake is an unusual one because
it has not been induced by the other contracting party by words or conduct
constituting representations for the law of misrepresentation or promises for
the law of warranties. In other words, mistake is only pleaded in order to avoid
the limitations of the law of misrepresentation and warranties. Often the

mistake cases are those where misrepresentation affords an inadequate remedy to the plaintiff because it merely renders the contract voidable, not void, and in a dispute over title to property, the plaintiff seeks the advantage of securing title to goods by persuading the court to declare the contract void.

Rescission is a self-help remedy, in that the victim of a misrepresentation is entitled to tell the other party that he is treating the contract as at an end. There are some difficulties with this in cases of fraud where the rogue has disappeared: the seller cannot communicate with him, and he has no idea, usually, what has become of the good until it reappears in the hands of an innocent third party. In the case of car purchase fraud, it was held by the Court of Appeal in *Car and Universal Finance Co. Ltd.* v. *Caldwell* ([1965] 1 QB 525) that immediately informing the police and the Automobile Association, which keeps a register of stolen cars, that a car has been stolen through a cheque fraud will be sufficient to rescind a contract for misrepresentation, thus preventing a *later* purchaser without notice of the fraud from acquiring good title. According to Davies LJ it is implicit in the transaction between the rogue and the seller that the latter is entitled to rescind by the best means possible, if the goods and the rogue have disappeared (at p. 558). However, this construction is entirely fictitious, since rescission cannot in any real sense have been said to be *communicated* to the purchaser. He has no actual notice of the fact that the car is stolen, since by definition he is claiming good faith. The most that can be said is that the purchaser on the second hand car market has some sort of duty to check that his or her proposed purchase is not in any of the available registers of stolen cars. This construction may be reasonable in the context of stolen cars, but should it operate in the context of other goods in which there is not such a lively second hand market in stolen goods (e.g. household goods such as fridges, cookers, and washing machines)?

V. THE ROLE OF MISREPRESENTATION IN THE LAW OF OBLIGATIONS

In Chapter 1 we explained that contract had to be seen in the matrix of the law of obligations. We posited there and in the following chapter the idea that contract was influenced heavily by Victorian values of *laissez-faire* and reflects a bargain-based approach to liability. Tort, on the other hand, reflects a reliance-based approach. The doctrinal approach to misrepresentation illustrates very well the interplay between tort and contract in terms of creating liability for misrepresentation. The cases and readings in this section were chosen to highlight the importance of remedies, and the effect of the different remedial structures offered by different doctrinal categories of liability upon the construction of arguments within cases.

This brief extract from Atiyah places the evolution of misrepresentation in its historical context.

P. S. Atiyah, 'The Resurgence of Reliance-Based Liabilities', *The Rise and Fall of Freedom of Contract*, rev. edn. (Oxford, Oxford University Press, 1985), 771–3

In the shadow of nineteenth century individualism, lawyers still pay lip service (and sometimes more) to the fundamental belief that a man should rely on himself, and not on others. But in practice, in actual decisions, and in actual legislation, it is evident that this individualism no longer represents the values underlying the law. . . .

One of the first areas of the law to show signs of retreat from the high water mark of Victorian individualism was the law of misrepresentation. In the last few decades of the nineteenth century, this was a much litigated area of the law, perhaps partly because of the need to reconcile the hitherto differing approaches of common law and Equity; but partly also . . . because values were changing. The older notion that a man could say what he liked to a prospective contracting party, so long only as he refrained from positively dishonest assertions of fact, seems to have come up against a new morality in the late nineteenth century. The Courts began to insist on the duty of a party not to mislead the other party by extravagant or unjustified assertions, and they also seem to have been influenced by a desire to impose some form of control on the new types of advertisement now appearing in the mass press. There was, of course, a clash between these two moralities. The older one was still very much alive, especially among common lawyers; it led . . . to the decision in *Derry* v. *Peek* in 1889 . . . . the newer ideas were . . . very influential from the 1870s onwards, and, indeed, in their determination to stamp out the laxer business morality which gave wide latitude to misrepresentation, the Courts decided some cases in a way which even today, may seem to go too far. *Redgrave* v. *Hurd*, for example, is still regarded as a leading case on the law of misrepresentation, standing for the proposition that a man cannot escape the consequences of a misrepresentation merely because the representee could have discovered the truth by reasonable care. But the actual decision was a very strong one, for the plaintiff had bought the defendant's house and his practice as a solicitor, in reliance on some casual assertions about the value of the practice, without any examination of the books. Even today that would seem such a remarkable want of due precaution on the part of the buyer that the actual decision may well be of dubious validity.

Perhaps because of the clash of these two moralities, the law of misrepresentation unfortunately became bogged down in a mass of technicalities. Judges, and textbook writers, drew distinctions between 'statements of fact' and

ents of 'mere opinion' which were difficult to apply, and anyhow did not ately reflect the essential point that justifiable reliance depended on a much wider set of factors. Similarly, the distinctions drawn between warranties and mere representations became almost impossible of application as the Courts insisted that all depended on the 'intention of the parties'. . . . By the 1960s the law of misrepresentation had become so unsatisfactory that an attempt was made at reform by the Misrepresentation Act, 1967. Although this Act may prove a workable instrument, in that it largely gives the Court the freedom, or discretion, to treat misrepresentations as a ground for rescission, or for damages, as it sees fit, the Act has unfortunately not simplified the conceptual apparatus of the law. The distinction between misrepresentation and warranty survives, and so too does the distinction between statements of opinion and statement of fact. What has gone wrong here is the failure of lawyers to appreciate the nature of the issues raised by misrepresentation cases. Instead of asking whether, having regard to the various circumstances, the representee was justified in placing any reliance on the other party, or whether he should have rested on his own judgment (or purchased expert advice in the market) they have continued to pursue the highly technical and abstract distinctions of older cases.

Atiyah refers to the 'highly technical and abstract distinctions of older cases'. The rise of misrepresentation as a head of liability from Victorian *laissez-faire* values has been a difficult one. The boundary between tortious and contractual liability has proved problematic, and at times the inadequate remedial structure has led plaintiffs to try to argue their way out of misrepresentation and into some other category of liability, for example, breach of contract. To understand misrepresentation and its doctrinal significance fully, it is necessary to look closely at its evolution.

VI. THE DOCTRINAL MECHANISMS OF MISREPRESENTATION

It is necessary to decide what type of statements may give rise to liability on behalf of the representor. A distinction we need to draw is between so-called 'mere puffs' which are considered to be statements of no legal effect and promissory representations. A mere puff can be defined colloquially as a 'salesman's hype', for example, 'it's glorious to be in this house in summertime' or 'Smart Wash washing powder washes whitest of all'.

We can take as our definition of misrepresentation a false statement of fact made by a person in the content of pre-contractual negotiations which induces the other party to enter into a contract. It is necessary to know whether a statement is a misrepresentation or a term of the contract.

A. Burrows, 'Contract, Tort and Restitution: A Satisfactory Division or Not?', (1983) 99 *LQR* 217 at 244–5

Misrepresentations

An immediate question that has rarely been adequately examined, is how does the law distinguish a promise, which is at the roof of breach of contract and promissory estoppel, from a representation, which is at the root of the torts of deceit and negligent misrepresentation, and of the Misrepresentation Act 1967. Clearly there is the vital *similarity* that both promises and representations concern statements or actions which may engender expectations in others. But the crucial distinction is that a promise is a statement or action by which the speaker or actor appears to accept an obligation to do or not to do something; a representation, on the other hand, is a statement or action asserting the truth of particular facts.

Clearly not every statement or action regarding the future conduct of the speaker or actor is a promise. Promises differ not only from representations, but also from mere statements (or actions) of intention, because they involve the apparent acceptance of an obligation to do what one has said (or acted as if) one is going to do; that is, promises involve the apparent acceptance that one should not change one's mind regarding some future conduct, whereas mere statements (or actions) of intention do not involve this apparent acceptance of an obligation.

The emphasis, in our definition of a promise, on the *appearance* of accepting an obligation to do or not to do something, reflects the legal position that it is the objective intention and not the subjective intention that always holds sway. In most situations, the objective and subjective intention coincide, but even where the "promisor" can show that despite appearances he has not in fact accepted an obligation to do or not to do something, it is still the appearance that counts. And once one recognises the objectivity of the test, then one must also recognise that the decision, as to whether a promise has been made or not, rests to some extent on the value judgments of the courts. In deciding whether a reasonable bystander would think that by his words and action, the speaker or actor was accepting an obligation to do or not to do something, the courts must use their own understanding of people's behaviour and hence their own understanding of the attitudes of the times.

Note

See further on the nature of terms Chapter 10.

We need to know which category a statement falls into, as the remedial structure for each is different.

In the past, remedies for misrepresentation were substantially weaker than they are now—for example, a representee who could not show that there had been fraud in the conduct of the representor would find that there was no remedy of damages available to him in misrepresentation. It was necessary to argue a breach of contract to obtain damages. The representee's position was enhanced by the fact that once breach of a contract term is established it is often not necessary to establish any fault or negligence on the part of the representor.

For example, car dealers who stated that the car they sold was fitted with a replacement engine and gearbox with a relatively low mileage were held to have contractually promised the truth of the statement (*Dick Bentley Productions Ltd* v. *Harold Smith (Motors) Ltd.* [1965] 2 All ER 65). An alternative mechanism which was employed by the courts to reach the same result was the collateral contract or warranty device (hence Atiyah's reference in the above extract to the distinction between warranties and representations); the statement was construed not as a term of the main contract but as one forming the subject-matter of a separate ancillary contract. Damages awarded in this context were, of course, founded in contract, and so were based on the expectation measure. The decision below on negligent misrepresentation explains in greater detail that there is now a damages remedy for some types of non-fraudulent misrepresentation. The damages awarded will be assessed on a tortious basis—the reliance loss. The need to argue that a representation is a breach of contract (evidentially more difficult to prove than arguing misrepresentation) will now only arise in very limited contexts—see the notes following *Royscot* v. *Rogerson* ([1991] 3 All ER 294) for some examples.

Once we have distinguished between a term of the contract and a representation, the doctrinal boundaries of actionable *mis*representation are relatively simple if technical in detail. Atiyah in the extract above criticizes these boundaries as difficult to apply, which is true in some respects. However, in the main, Atiyah's criticism stems from the fact that he would prefer to see the boundaries of misrepresentation drawn not by technical rules but by an overarching principle of reliance—that liability would be imposed whenever reliance by the representee would be reasonable. In fact, the application of the boundary rules does in some instances reflect the reliance principle. The first requirement is an unambiguous statement of fact, not of intention or opinion. A statement in this sense can be constituted by conduct, such as the deliberate concealment of visible defects in a house. Normally, non-disclosure or silence does not amount to a misrepresentation.

However, failing to disclose a material change in circumstances which changes the basis of a representation previously made can amount to an actionable misrepresentation. In *Esso Petroleum Co. Ltd.* v. *Mardon* ([1976] QB 801) Esso failed to correct a throughput estimate when they became aware that the garage they were building would not have direct vehicular access from the main road.

The line between statements of fact and opinion can also be fine, and the court may be influenced by the fact that the representor making what he now alleges to be a statement of opinion had what J. Adams and R. Brownsword call 'informational advantages' over the representee (*Understanding Contract Law* (London, Fontana, 1987), 136). *Esso Petroleum* v. *Mardon* also illustrates this point. Clearly, an oil company is in a much better position to use its experience as a landlord of petrol stations to estimate the annual throughput of a new petrol station than a new tenant.

One factor which has conventionally influenced the evolution of misrepresentation doctrine has been the principle of *caveat emptor*, which would tend to place the burden upon a buyer to check the condition of the item to be purchased and, arguably, the correctness of any statements made by the seller. This underlies the non-disclosure principle discussed above. It also influences the requirement that the misrepresentation must induce the contract, and that the reliance upon the misrepresentation must normally be reasonable. That must be balanced against the principle of encouraging fair play in negotiations. Atiyah tells us (above) that there is no duty on the representative to check the statements made. Although Atiyah doubts the present-day validity of the authority traditionally used for this proposition (*Redgrave* v. *Hurd* (1881) 20 Ch.D. 1), there is no indication that it would not be followed.

A. Rescission

The conventional contractual remedy potentially available for all types of misrepresentation, regardless of whether fraud can be shown or not, is rescission, i.e. the right to set aside the contract which results in the restoration of the parties to the contract to their pre-contractual positions. This can only happen if the subject-matter of the contract still exists. If it does not, then a return to pre-contract positions is impossible. Rescission is a drastic remedy in the sense that it undoes the entire contract, but it is also inadequate in that it does not permit the recovery of consequential loss. The availability of rescission as a remedy is affected by events which follow the misrepresentation in question. Rescission will be unavailable in the following circumstances:

(a) A lapse of time before the plaintiff sought recovery. What constitutes a lapse of time sufficient to bar rescission depends on what is reasonable on the facts of the case. In cases of fraud, however, lapse of time is not considered to be a bar on rescission.
(b) Previous affirmation of the contract by the plaintiff. The representor is

entitled to know his position, and consequently it is considered unfair for the plaintiff later to go back on his decision to carry on with the contract.

(c) Third-party rights. For example, if the subject-matter of the contract has already been sold to someone else, rescission is unavailable. This was explained in the previous section on mistake.

B. Types of Misrepresentation

It is common to distinguish between types of misrepresentation according to the state of mind of the representor. The categories conventionally used are fraudulent, negligent, and innocent. Each category has its own system of remedies.

Fraud. In the words of Lord Herschell in *Derry* v. *Peek* ((1889) 14 App. Cas. 337 at 374), 'fraud is proved when it is shown that a false representation has been made (1) knowingly, or (2) without belief in its truth or (3) recklessly, careless whether it be true or false'. Liability under this head gives rise to a right to damages for the tort of deceit. Damages will be assessed on the tortious measure. The common-law remedy of rescission is also available.

Negligent Misrepresentation. Prior to 1964 there was no such category and consequently no remedy. A plaintiff had a choice between fraud as set out above and, if that could not be proved, innocent misrepresentation, for which there was not and still is not a remedy in damages, but only a right to rescind.

In 1964 the House of Lords decided *Hedley Byrne & Co. Ltd.* v. *Heller and Partners Ltd.* [1964] AC 465). Here the plaintiffs were advertising agents who relied (to their eventual detriment) on statements made by the defendants, who were the bankers of one of the plaintiffs' clients, about the financial situation of these clients. The defendants made the statement negligently. The plaintiffs dealt with the bank's clients as a result of the representations and lost money. The defendants were protected from liability by an effective disclaimer. The House of Lords decided that what was needed to create liability was a voluntary assumption of responsibility by the defendants towards the plaintiff which resulted in reliance by the plaintiffs on the defendants' statements. If the reliance was reasonable, the court may decide that a special relationship exists between the parties giving rise to a duty of care. This type of action has been labelled the tort of negligent misstatement. In 1976 in *Esso* v. *Mardon* the Court of Appeal accepted the application of the *Hedley Byrne* doctrine to pre-contractual misrepresentations which induced the representee to enter into a contract. The effect of the development of negligent misstatement in this way was to give a remedy in tort damages, in addition to the common law remedy of rescission, to the plaintiff who could demonstrate the criteria for the existence of a special relationship and breach of the duty arising out of that relationship by the defendant.

These developments, however, were largely neutralized by the advent of the Misrepresentation Act 1967. The Act, through section 2(1), gives a remedy of damages for negligent misrepresentation. The text of section 2(1) is set out in the extract from the judgements in *Royscot* v. *Rogerson* below. The notes following the judgment extracts explain how the award of damages will be assessed. Here it is sufficient to say that they will be awarded by means of the tort reliance measure. The crucial difference between an action under *Hedley Byrne* principles for negligent misstatement and an action for negligent misrepresentation under the Misrepresentation Act 1967 is that section 2(1) of the Misrepresentation Act 1967 reverses the burden of proof; far from asking a plaintiff to prove the existence of a special relationship, it places the burden of proof on the defendant by imposing liability unless the defendant can show that his belief in the truth of the statement was reasonable. According to the Court of Appeal in *Howard Marine* v. *Ogden* ((1978) QB 574), the defendant must show objectively reasonable grounds for believing that the representation was true. The plaintiff is left with proving that he is within the other doctrinal boundaries drawn around misrepresentation. The common law remedy of rescission is also available.

These factors, together with an enhanced position on remoteness of damage explained in the notes following *Royscot* v. *Rogerson*, means that a *Hedley Byrne*-type action is not attractive to plaintiffs. The only circumstances in which it would be preferable to use such an action is where no contract results from the parties' dealings or there is a three-party situation, where the party making the statement in question is not a party to the eventual contract. In these cases the Misrepresentation Act 1967 does not apply.

Innocent Misrepresentation. There is no right to damages in respect of wholly innocent misrepresentations where the defendant is able to establish that he had reasonable grounds to believe in the truth of his statement. The only remedy is rescission at common law. It is possible that this may be supplemented by the award of an 'indemnity', that is, a sum of money intended to cover expenditure which the representee necessarily incurred as a result of entering into the contract induced by the representor (e.g. ground rent on a property may be covered by an indemnity but not the cost of making good a defect in a property which had been the subject of a misrepresentation).

Misrepresentation Act 1967, section 2(2)

Where a person has entered into a contract after a misrepresentation has been made to him otherwise than fraudulently, and he would be entitled, by reason of the misrepresentation, to rescind the contract, then, if it is claimed, in any proceedings arising out of the contract, that the contract ought to be or has been rescinded, the court or arbitrator may declare the contract subsisting and award damages in lieu of rescission, if of the opinion that it would be equitable to do so having regard to the nature of the misrepresentation and the loss that would be caused by it if the contract were upheld as well as to the loss that rescission would cause to the other party.

This section deals with the draconian nature of the rescission remedy by giving the court a discretion in the context of negligent and innocent misrepresentation to declare the contract subsisting and to award damages instead of rescission. It will be most appropriate for the court to do this where the plaintiff has overvalued the subject-matter of the contract as a result of the misrepresentation, but can adequately be compensated by damages without the need to return both parties to their starting-block positions.

The only situation in which a plaintiff may prefer rescission to an award of damages is where restitution is more valuable than compensation. Consider the situation where a plaintiff has parted with an asset at what he now knows to be an undervalue, and that asset is one which will increase in value, e.g. an antique table. As the discretion is the court's, we do not know how relevant the plaintiff's views on the desirability of rescission will be.

There is no question of a plaintiff who recovers damages under sections 2(1) and 2(2) recovering more than a plaintiff who obtains an award of damages under section 2(1) and rescission. Section 2(3) deals with this problem by instructing the court that an award of damages under 2(2) has to be taken into account when calculating an award under 2(1).

There is some ambiguity in the wording of section 2(2) as to exactly when the court's discretion will operate but the better view is probably that damages can only be awarded under section 2(2) where rescission is actually possible. If rescission is barred for one of the reasons given above, then 'damages in lieu of rescission' cannot be awarded, since there is no rescission for which damages are substituted.

The measure of damages under section 2(2) is as yet unclear. The choice would appear to be between tort damages or a restitutionary measure with no allowance for consequences. The more popular view is that the damages awarded will be tort damages—see J. Cartwright, 'Damages for Misrepresentation', [1987] *Conv.* 423. See also Fig. 3.

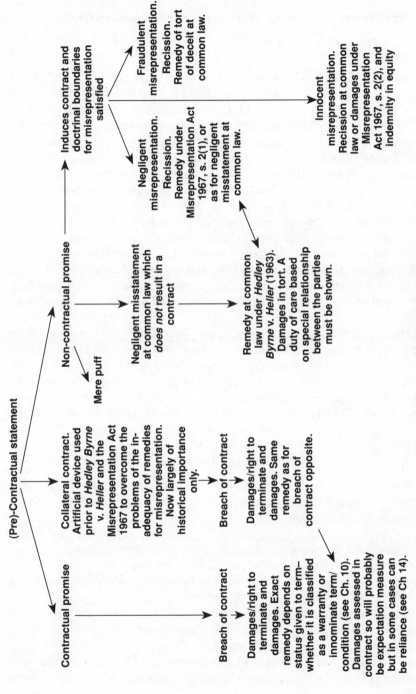

Fig. 3. Contours of liability for statements

C. The Measure of Damages for Negligent Misrepresentation

Royscot Trust Ltd. v. *Rogerson*
[1991] 3 All ER 294

The first defendant agreed to buy a second-hand car from the second defendant, a car dealer. The first defendant wished to purchase the car on hire purchase terms. The plaintiff finance company required all would be purchasers to pay 20 per cent of the car's price as a deposit. The dealer represented to the plaintiff finance company that the car cost £8,000, and that the first defendant had paid £1,600 by way of deposit leaving a balance of £6,400. In fact the purchase price of the car was £7,600 and the defendant paid £1,200 as a deposit, leaving a balance of £6,400. The dealer represented the figures in the way he did so as to create the impression that the requirement of the 20 per cent deposit had been fulfilled.

In reliance on the misrepresentation, which all parties accepted was not made fraudulently, the plaintiffs entered into a hire-purchase agreement with the first defendant and paid the second defendant £6,400. The first defendant sold the car in breach of the agreement and twelve months later defaulted on the agreement. The plaintiffs issued proceedings against both defendants.

The first defendant's liability was calculated simply as the value of the agreement minus the instalments that had been paid. The position of the second defendant was more complicated. The second defendant's position was that the plaintiffs had suffered no loss in its dealings with them; the plaintiffs had paid over £6,400 and recovered back title to a car worth at least £6,400. The plaintiffs' view was the dealer should reimburse them the difference between what they had paid to him (£6,400) and what the first defendant has repaid (£2,774.76), i.e. £3,625.24.

The Court of Appeal applied the plaintiffs' view of the damages question.

BALCOMBE LJ The finance company's cause of action against the dealer is based on s 2(1) of the Misrepresentation Act 1967. This subsection reads (so far as relevant) as follows:

'Where a person has entered into a contract after a misrepresentation has been made to him by another party thereto and as a result thereof he had suffered loss, then, if the person making the misrepresentation would be liable to damages in respect thereof had the misrepresentation been made fraudulently, that person shall be so liable notwithstanding that the misrepresentation was not made fraudulently . . .'

. . . there was some doubt whether the measure of damages for an innocent misrepresentation giving rise to a cause of action under the 1967 Act was the tortious measure, so as to put the representee in the position in which he would have been if he had never entered into the contract, or the contractual measure, so as to put the representee in the position in which he would have been if the misrepresentation had been true, and thus in some cases give rise to a claim for damages for loss of bargain. . . . there is now a number of decisions which make it clear that the tortious measure of damages is the true one. Most of these decisions are at first instance and will be found in *Chitty on Contract* (26th edn, 1989) para 439, note 63 and in *McGregor on Damages* (15th edn, 1988) para 1745. One at least, *Chesneau v Interhome Ltd* (1983) 134 NLJ 341 is a decision of this court. The claim was one under s 2(1) of the 1967 Act and the appeal concerned the assessment of damages. In the course of his judgment Eveleigh LJ said ([1983] CA Transcript 238):

'. . . [damages] should be assessed in a case like the present one on the same principles as damages are assessed in tort. The subsection itself says: ". . . if the person making the misrepresentation would be liable to damages in respect thereof had the misrepresentation been made fraudulently, that person shall be so liable . . ." By "so liable" I take it to mean liable as he would be if the misrepresentation had been made fraudulently.'

In view of the wording of the subsection it is difficult to see how the measure of damages under it could be other than the tortious measure and, despite the initial aberrations referred to above, that is now generally accepted. Indeed counsel before us did not seek to argue the contrary.

The first main issue before us was: accepting that the tortious measure is the right measure, is it the measure where the tort is that of fraudulent misrepresentation, or is it the measure where the tort is negligence at common law? The difference is that in cases of fraud a plaintiff is entitled to any loss which flowed from the defendant's fraud, even if the loss could not have been foreseen: see *Doyle v Olby (Ironmongers) Ltd* [1969] 2 All ER 119, [1969] 2 QB 158. In my judgment the wording of the subsection is clear: the person making the innocent misrepresentation shall be 'so liable', ie liable to damages as if the representation had been made fraudulently. . . . This is also the effect of the judgment of Eveleigh LJ in *Chesneau v Interhome Ltd* [1983] CA Transcript 238 already cited: 'By "so liable" I take it to mean liable as he would be if the misrepresentation had been made fraudulently.'

This was also the original view of the academic writers. In Atiyah and Treitel 'Misrepresentation Act 1967' (1967) 30 MLR 369 at 373–374 it says:

'The measure of damages in the statutory action will apparently be that in an action of deceit . . . But more probably the damages recoverable in the new action are the same as those recoverable in an action of deceit . . .'

Professor Treitel has since changed his view. In *Law of Contract* (7th edn, 1987) p 278 he says:

'Where the action is brought under section 2(1) of the Misrepresentation Act, one possible view is that the deceit rule will be applied by virtue of the fiction of fraud. But the preferable view is that the severity of the deceit rule can only be justified in cases of actual fraud and that remoteness under section 2(1) should depend, as in actions based on negligence, on the test of foreseeability.'

The only authority cited in support of the 'preferable' view is *Shepheard v Broome* [1904] AC 342, a case under s 38 of the Companies Act 1867, which provided that in certain circumstances a company director, although not in fact fraudulent, should be 'deemed to be fraudulent'. As Lord Lindley said ([1904] AC 342 at 346): '. . . To be compelled by Act of Parliament to treat an honest man as if he were fraudulent is at all times painful', but he went on to say: 'but the repugnance which is naturally felt against being compelled to do so will not justify your Lordships in refusing to hold the appellant responsible for acts for which an Act of Parliament clearly declares he is to be held liable . . .' The House of Lords so held.

It seems to me that that case, far from supporting Professor Treitel's view, is authority for the proposition that we must follow the literal wording of s 2(1), even though that has the effect of treating, so far as the measure of damages is concerned, an innocent person as if he were fraudulent. *Chitty on Contracts* (26th edn, 1989) para 439 says:

'. . . it is doubtful whether the rule that the plaintiff may recover even unforeseeable losses suffered as the result of fraud would be applied; it is an exceptional rule which is probably justified only in cases of actual fraud.'

No authority is cited in support of that proposition save a reference to the passage in Professor Treitel's book cited above.

Professor Furmston in *Cheshire Fifoot and Furmston's Law of Contract* (11th edn, 1986) p 286 says:

'It has been suggested [and the reference is to the passage in Atiyah and Treitel's article cited above] that damages under section 2(1) should be calculated on the same principles as govern the tort of deceit. This suggestion is based on a theory that section 2(1) is based on a "fiction of fraud". We have already suggested that this theory is misconceived. On the other hand the action created by section 2(1) does look much more like an action in tort than one in contract and it is suggested that the rules for negligence are the natural ones to apply.'

The suggestion that the 'fiction of fraud' theory is misconceived occurs in a passage which includes the following (p 271):

'Though it would be quixotic to defend the drafting of the section, it is suggested that there is no such "fiction of fraud" since the section does not say that a negligent misrepresentor shall be treated for all purposes as if he were fraudulent. No doubt the wording seeks to incorporate by reference some of the rules relating to fraud but, for instance, nothing in the wording of the subsection requires the measure of damages for deceit to be applied to the statutory action.'

With all respect to the various learned authors whose works I have cited above, it seems to me that to suggest that a different measure of damage applies to an action for innocent misrepresentation under the section than that which applies to an action for fraudulent misrepresentation (deceit) at common law is to ignore the plain words of the subsection and is inconsistent with the cases to which I have referred. In my judgment, therefore, the finance company is entitled to recover from the dealer all the losses which it suffered as a result of its entering into the agreements with the dealer and the customer, even if those losses were unforeseeable, provided that they were not otherwise too remote . . . .

Accordingly, I would dismiss the dealer's appeal. I would allow the finance company's cross-appeal, set aside the judgment of 22 February 1990 and direct that in its place judgment be entered for the finance company against the dealer in the sum of £3,625.24 together with interest. The finance company accepts that it will have to give credit for any sums that it may receive from its judgment against the customer.

Notes

1. Balcombe LJ in his judgment makes the point that it is accepted by both parties that the misrepresentation was not made fraudulently. He then refers to the misrepresentation as 'an innocent misrepresentation'. By 'innocent misrepresentation' he means a statement which is not made fraudulently in the common-law sense. As has been explained earlier, prior to the decision in *Hedley Byrne* v. *Heller* misrepresentations were categorized either as fraudulent or innocent. Balcombe LJ's use of the description 'innocent' has its origins here. There is no doubt that he treats, if not describes, the misrepresentation as a negligent one: this is clear from his use of the Misrepresentation Act 1967, section 2(1) to supply the remedy. Ralph Gibson LJ, whose judgment is not extracted, described the misrepresentation as negligent.

2. Balcombe LJ indicates that it is the tortious measure of damages that will be awarded in a successful action under the Misrepresentation Act 1967, section 2(1). He describes the plaintiff as being returned to the position he would have been in had the *contract* never been made. On the facts of *Royscot* v. *Rogerson* it can safely be assumed that had the plaintiffs known the truth they would never have entered into a contractual relationship with the first and second defendants in this form, if at all. However misrepresentation under the Misrepresentation Act 1967, section 2(1) is in effect a statutory tort, and what the plaintiff is being compensated for is the misrepresentation and the effect that has on the bargain that he eventually made. There will be many situations where the plaintiff will be in the position of asserting that the misrepresentation made a difference to the value he put on the subject-matter of the contract, rather than claiming that he would not have entered the contract at all, or entered it only on very different terms, had he known the truth. Imagine the situation of a house-purchaser who is informed that the property she is looking at was recently rewired. She buys the house for this and other reasons. She discovers that the house had not been rewired. A successful action under the

Misrepresentation Act 1967, section 2(1) would compensate her for the difference in value between what she paid for a house with new electrical wiring and what the house is worth *without* the new wiring. This example provides a case where the court may choose to exercise its discretion under section 2(2) and award damages in lieu of rescission, as from the nature of the misrepresentation it would seem draconian to allow rescission of the contract for the sale of the house when the effect of the misrepresentation can be remedied.

The equation of the misrepresentation and ending the contract for the purposes of damages works on the facts of *Royscot* v. *Rogerson*, but there will be many cases where it does not. Balcombe LJ's formulation can be dismissed as a slip of the tongue resulting from the facts of *Royscot* v. *Rogerson*.

3. The designation of the measure of damages as tortious gives the plaintiff his reliance loss and not his loss of bargain. For example, consider a plaintiff who buys a picture for £85 on the grounds that there is a label attached to it describing it as having been exhibited as a Constable. He thinks that he has made a very good bargain. However, he later discovers that the painting is not by Constable. The tortious measure of damages would give the plaintiff the difference between the £85 he paid for the painting and what it is worth now, which is unlikely to be less than £85. Consequently, he will recover very little. The contract measure of damages, however, would place the plaintiff in the position he expected to be in as a result of the contract. This would give him the difference in value between the worth of the painting as an original and the £85 he paid for it.

4. The difference between tort and contract damages outlined above creates the impression that those who have made a good bargain will be better off trying to argue that the misrepresentation became a term of the contract so that they may recover damages for breach of contract. This may in some circumstances be true, but it is worth considering the effect of Balcombe LJ's formulation of remoteness of damage under the Misrepresentation Act 1967, section 2(1).

Remoteness of damage means the extent of the consequences of a particular act that can be recovered as damages. The test for remoteness of damage for fraudulent misrepresentation has always been that any loss flowing directly from the misrepresentation can be recovered whether foreseeable or not; a requirement of foreseeability was considered inappropriate in relation to an intentional tort (see *Doyle* v. *Olby (Ironmongers) Ltd* [1969] 2 All ER 119). The test of remoteness under the negligent misstatement tort created by the decision in *Hedley Byrne* v. *Heller* (above) was the negligence test of reasonable foresight; that is, only foreseeable damage following from the statement could be recovered. Balcombe LJ held that the much wider test of all loss flowing directly from the misrepresentation was the appropriate test for negligent misrepresentation under section 2(1) of the Misrepresentation Act 1967. This, together with the reversal of the burden of proof, considerably enhances the attraction of pleading negligent misrepresentation under section 2(1).

The formulation of remoteness adopted by Balcombe LJ also compresses the role of fraudulent misrepresentation. Successful actions for fraudulent misrepresentation and misrepresentation under section 2(1) of the Act will now both result in damages assessed under the tortious measure, with the test of remoteness of damage encompassing all the loss flowing directly from the misrepresentation. An action under section 2(1) has the added benefit to the plaintiff of a reversal of the burden of proof.

By adopting the same remoteness rule for both fraudulent and negligent misrepresentation, Balcombe LJ has signalled that no distinction should be drawn between the culpability of the representor who is negligent, reckless, or dishonest. This leaves us with very much a consumer welfarist perspective on liability for misrepresentation. In other words, what is important is the loss to the representee and compensation for that loss, not the culpability of the representor. The application, through the fiction of fraud construction, of the fraud rules on remoteness results in the harshest possible result for representors. While we can point to the compensatory aims of tort law, it is difficult to justify Balcombe LJ's position on the liability of the negligent misrepresentor; tort law has traditionally distinguished between the fraudulent/intentional tortfeasor and the negligent tortfeasor by restricting the liability of the negligent tortfeasor for consequential loss.

5. In deciding what the remoteness of damage rule was for negligent misrepresentation, Balcombe LJ had to construe the meaning of section 2(1)—the so-called 'fiction of fraud'. In doing so he adopted a literal approach to the statute: he examined the words of the section to see if, in his view, there were any words which indicated that negligent misrepresentation was to be construed any differently from fraudulent misrepresentation. He concluded that there were not. It is interesting that he eschews a more purposive approach to statutory interpretation, although he refers to academic writers who have taken such an approach. In not taking a purposive approach he avoids a consideration of the intentions of Parliament and related policy issues, such as whether Parliament intended the statute to have a purely compensatory function and whether it intended to place fraudulent and negligent representors and victims of fraudulent and negligent representations in very similar positions. (See Fig. 4 and Table 1.)

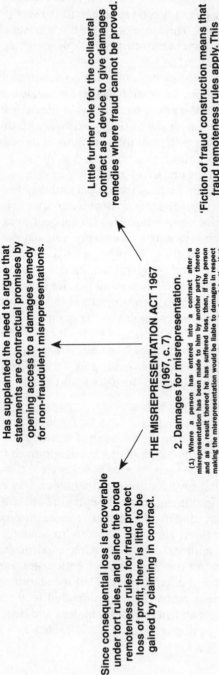

Has supplanted the need to argue that statements are contractual promises by opening access to a damages remedy for non-fraudulent misrepresentations.

Little further role for the collateral contract as a device to give damages remedies where fraud cannot be proved.

'Fiction of fraud' construction means that fraud remoteness rules apply. This undermines the need to use *fraud*, as s. 2(1) gives an equally good remedy.

THE MISREPRESENTATION ACT 1967
(1967, c. 7)

2. Damages for misrepresentation.

(1) Where a person has entered into a contract after a misrepresentation has been made to him by another party thereto and as a result thereof he has suffered loss, then, if the person making the misrepresentation would be liable to damages in respect thereof had the misrepresentation been made fraudulently, that person shall be so liable notwithstanding that the misrepresentation was not made fraudulently, unless he proves that he had reasonable ground to believe and did believe up to the time the contract was made that the facts represented were true.

Since consequential loss is recoverable under tort rules, and since the broad remoteness rules for fraud protect loss of profit, there is little to be gained by claiming in contract.

Burden of proof makes s. 2(1) more attractive than fraud where the burden falls on the plaintiff. Fraud is hard to prove.

Scope for application of the common-law principles of *Hedley Byrne* v. *Heller* much reduced by the rules on remoteness of damage and burden of proof. The only role is where there is no contract concluded, or where a contract is concluded but the misrepresentation was made by a third party

Fig. 4. Section 2(1) of the Misrepresentation Act 1967

Table 1. *Summary of liability for statements and conduct amounting to representations*

Type of statement	Burden of proof		Type of damages available	Basis of damages liability	Type of remoteness	Rescission/termination available	Bars to rescission
Mere puff			Not actionable				
Contractual promise	Promisee must show that statement was a term and that it was breached.	May not have to prove fault.	Contract damages: usually the expectation, but sometimes reliance (see Ch. 14)	Common law	Contract (see Ch. 14)	Termination if the statement is a condition or an 'innominate term' and the breach is sufficiently serious (see Ch. 10)	n.a.
Collateral contract or warranty	Promisee		As above	Common law	Contract (see Ch. 14)		n.a.
Representation *not* resulting in a contract	Representee must prove duty of care based on a special relationship and breach		Tortious damages: the reliance measure	Common law (*Hedley Byrne v. Heller*)	Foreseeability	No	n.a.
Fraudulent misrepresentation	Representee, using the test in *Derry v. Peak*		Tortious damages: the reliance measure	Common law	Direct consequences	Yes, at common law. Indemnity available.	(1) Affirmation (2) Third-party rights (3) Restitution impossible
Negligent misrepresentation	*Representor* under s.2(1) has to show objectively reasonable belief in the truth of the statement (*Howard Marine v. Ogdens*)		Tortious damages: the reliance measure	S. 2(1) of the Misrepresentation Act 1967	Direct consequences	Yes, but it may be bought off under s. 2(2). What is not clear is whether s. 2(2) confers any rights where there are bars to rescission and so rescission is not available as a remedy. Indemnity available	(1) Affirmation (2) Lapse of time (3) Third-party rights (4) Restitution impossible
Innocent misrepresentation	Representee		Undecided, but probably tortious damages under s. 2(2). The alternative is a restitutionary measure with no allowance for consequences	No *right* to damages. S. 2(2) may result in the court allowing the buy-off of rescission with damages. But this is not the same as a right to damages.	Not decided		Rescission may be replaced at discretion of court by an award of damages under s. 2(2).

Exercise

This section concludes with an exercise which brings together many of the ideas in this chapter. It uses the facts of a case decided at first instance by Waller J, but not the judgments. Read the exercise, and answer the questions set out at the end. You will want to consult the answers at the end of the chapter; you may then compare your answers and our answers with the approach taken by Waller J. You may well reach a different conclusion from the judge, or the same conclusion by different means. This does not matter; issues such as quantum of damages are highly contestable. We have chosen to use a real case rather than a hypothetical situation, and to use the full judgment facts rather than a headnote summary, because this demonstrates the factual evaluation which the judge must undertake.

Naughton v. *O'Callaghan*
[1990] 3 All ER 191

WALLER J. In September 1981 the first plaintiff (Mr Naughton) and the second plaintiff (Mr Kilkenny) were intent on buying a yearling at the September sales at Newmarket. Their intention was to put such yearling in training in Ireland with Mr Adrian Maxwell with whom they had had previous horses in training, and it was Mr Maxwell who was to bid and advise on the purchase of the horse. No one remembers precise details of the way the purchase came about, but in conformity with normal practice it would seem that the catalogue would arrive with Mr Maxwell and he would consider in relation to various clients, including the plaintiffs, what horses might be suitable for his various clients to be purchased at the sale. He would mark in the catalogue those horses which he would be prepared to advise the plaintiffs to buy.

In the catalogue, lot 200 to be sold on Wednesday evening, 30 September 1981, was a chestnut colt named Fondu. A full description of the colt and its pedigree is set out in the agreed documents, but in particular the description was of a colt whose sire was Nonalco and whose dam was Habanna whose sire in turn was Habitat.

Habanna, as the description in the catalogue confirms, was itself a good class racehorse having won two races including a listed race and having been placed second in a group 2 race. As the evidence before me showed, for the purposes of a description in the catalogue, races have been categoried in order of merit, Group 1, Group 2, Group 3 and listed races. The indication 'LR' or 'GRI' or 'GRII' or 'GRIII' appears in black type, and it is common ground that the black type is of significance to anyone reading the catalogue and selecting a horse for which to bid at auction.

Mr Maxwell picked out Fondu in the catalogue as suitable for the plaintiffs because of the Habitat line in the pedigree. He may well have discussed the matter with the first plaintiff who was also attracted by the Habitat line. There is no question, and it is common ground, that the Habitat line was an attractive one in 1981, both because of Habanna's own record and because Habitat was itself building up an increasing reputation as a sire of winners or class horses. Furthermore, Habitat was beginning, but only beginning, to build up a reputation as a sire of brood mares, that is to say a sire of mares themselves producing foals that turned out to be successful racehorses.

As I have said, Mr Maxwell was acting for various clients at the September sales, and he went over early in order to confirm what recommendation to give to his clients. He went and inspected Fondu and confirmed that it was the horse for his particular clients, the plaintiffs, but there is no doubt that he relied particularly on the pedigree as described in the catalogue.

In the event, the first plaintiff and Mr Maxwell attended this sale at Newmarket and Mr Maxwell bid for Fondu. . . . Fondu was purchased for the sum of 26,000 guineas.

. . . Fondu was taken to Ireland and put into training with Mr Maxwell. The first race for which Fondu was entered was in September 1982 in Ireland, and it raced three times that year, all in Ireland. Fondu was not a success on the racecourse during that season, it being placed seventh in its first race, twelfth in its second race and fourth in its third race.

At the end of 1982 Mr Maxwell left Ireland to go and train in the United States . . . . A decision was taken to put Fondu in training in England at Upper Lambourne near Newbury in Berkshire with Mr Charles Nelson. In 1983 Fondu was entered for three races in England, but fared no better than it had done in Ireland. It was placed eleventh in its first race at Bath, seventeenth in its second race at Bath, and in its third race in May 1983 it was placed eighteenth. . . .

Discovery of Fondu's true pedigree

In about June or July 1983 the plaintiffs discovered that they had not bought a colt as described in the catalogue at all. It appears that at the stud where Fondu was produced as a foal, being the stud of the third parties in this action, some error had been made. Fondu was not the son of Habanna at all. The fact was that Fondu's dam was Moon Min (USA) whose sire was First Landing whose dam was Capelet . . . .

Having discovered this error, one might have thought that there would have been an immediate reaction from the plaintiffs, either themselves or from advisers on their behalf. But the sequence of events thereafter is that Fondu was kept in training with Mr Nelson until October 1983, and the second plaintiff then kept Fondu at home from 1 November 1983 to 4 April 1984. Thereafter Fondu was placed by the first plaintiff (as he explained in the hope that it would be a point-to-point horse for his son) with Rodney Simpson's racing stables from about 5 April 1984. The first plaintiff received invoices for training fees and keep right through 1984 from Rodney Simpson, up until 31 July 1984. Thereafter he received a further invoice for Fondu's keep from Jane

Webber of Great Shefford near Newbury in August 1984. It also appears from documents in the bundle relating to charges made to the first plaintiff by Weatherbys that Fondu actually continued to be entered for races during 1984, the last race being on 30 June 1984, but Fondu never in fact raced during 1984. These entries, it was suggested, must have been due to some overzealousness on the part of an employee of Mr Simpson.

Only on 7 June 1984 did solicitors on behalf of the plaintiffs write to the defendant, the seller of Fondu at the Newmarket sales. In that letter the solicitors, having referred to the purchase by their client of Fondu, stated that their clients had discovered midway through the 1983 season that the dam line was not as shown in the catalogue. The letter then suggested that the horse was taken out of training and that it had been of no use or interest to the plaintiffs since. It further stated that they would not have bid for Fondu if they had known the true breeding, since they were impressed by what the catalogue showed. They set out the loss suffered by their clients at £31,500, that being the purchase price plus VAT, and the training fees and expenses of £14,734. That figure appears to be the fees and expenses charged by Mr Maxwell in 1981 and the charge by Mr Nelson from November 1982 to October 1983, plus the cost of keeping Fondu at home for a period from 1 November 1983. The letter invited the defendant to take the horse back and settle with the plaintiffs by paying the purchase price plus the training fees. In default the letter suggested that the plaintiffs would sell the horse at public auction and look to the defendant for the difference between the net sale proceeds and the aforesaid figures. The horse was not taken back by the defendant and nor has it in fact been sold at public auction. It remained after 1984 with the second plaintiff, where it still is. . . .

. . . It is common ground that by May/June 1983, when the true pedigree was discovered, Fondu by virtue of its record on the track was worth about £1,500. . . . In my judgment, if the true pedigree had become known before Fondu was raced, there is no question that the plaintiffs would have sought to reject Fondu or otherwise dispose of the colt. I say that because albeit Moon Min had a good pedigree, so far as Mr Maxwell was concerned that related in the main to horses which had been successful on the dirt tracks in America, rather than on the turf in Europe. It equally follows that I am quite clear that if Fondu had been described in the catalogue as out of Moon Min, there is no question of Mr Maxwell having advised the plaintiffs to bid for the horse and no question thus of this horse having been purchased with its true description in the catalogue.

It is also right to say however, and it is this that makes for the difficult point of law, that if Fondu had been correctly described in the catalogue as out of Moon Min, it would have had a substantial value to persons other than the plaintiffs. On the defendant's side, Major Philipson gave evidence that the value of Fondu correctly described would, in his opinion, have been at least the price paid for Fondu incorrectly described in September 1981. On the plaintiffs' side, Mr

Anderson confirmed that if he had been advising a buyer who wanted to buy Fondu as correctly described out of Moon Min, he would have advised them to go to something in the region of £5,000 less than the price that he would advise a buyer to go in relation to Fondu as incorrectly described.

The problem is thus a neat one. (1) The price paid for Fondu as it was described was 26,000 guineas, and no one suggested that that was other than a reasonable price. (2) The price that might have been obtained for Fondu as it ought to have been described was about the same or, as I find, slightly less than the 26,000 guineas, say 23,500 guineas. (3) The price of Fondu when it was discovered that it had been incorrectly described in June/July 1983 and after it had proved a failure on the racecourse was (as agreed) £1,500.

The plaintiffs thus claim (a) the difference between 26,000 guineas and £1,500 and (b) the cost of training and keeping Fondu up until discovery of the true pedigree and some reasonable period thereafter. . . .

It is perhaps also helpful to mention at this stage . . ., *Johnson v Agnew* [1980] AC 367 esp. at 400–401, where Lord Wilberforce said:

'The general principle for the assessment of damages is compensatory, ie that the innocent party is to be placed, so far as money can do so, in the same position as if the contract had been performed. Where the contract is one of sale, this principle normally leads to assessment of damages as at the date of the breach, a principle recognised and embodied in s 51 of the Sale of Goods Act 1893. But this is not an absolute rule; if to follow it would give rise to injustice, the court has power to fix such other date as may be appropriate in the circumstances. In cases where a breach of a contract for sale has occurred, and the innocent party reasonably continues to try to have the contract completed, it would to me appear more logical and just rather than tie him to the date of the original breach, to assess damages as at the date when (otherwise than by his default) the contract is lost. . . '

. . . Section 53 of the Sale of Goods Act 1979 seems to me to be the appropriate section and not s 51 as contended for by the plaintiffs. Section 53 provides:

'. . . (2) The measure of damages for breach of warranty is the estimated loss directly and naturally resulting, in the ordinary course of events, from the breach of warranty.

(3) In the case of breach of warranty of quality such loss is prima facie the difference between the value of the goods at the time of delivery to the buyer and the value they would have had if they had fulfilled the warranty . . .'

Subsection 3 is only a prima facie rule and in accordance with Lord Wilberforce's speech in *Johnson* v *Agnew* . . . . which I have already quoted above, if it is unjust to apply that rule it will not be applied.

Questions

1. What have Fondu's owners lost?
   In assessing what they have lost, bear in mind the following points:

(a) The different values which could be attached to Fondu:

26,000 guineas (the amount the plaintiffs paid) (purchase price):
23,000 guineas (the amount at which the judge notionally values a horse of Fondu's actual pedigree if it had been sold by auction at the same time) (bloodstock price);
£1,500 (the agreed value of Fondu when the mistake about her breeding was discovered) (end price);

(b) any difference in assessment of loss which occurred before or after the mistake was discovered;

(c) the inherent risk that any thoroughbred racehorse might not win races;

(d) the swiftly depreciating nature of the value of an unsuccessful racehorse.

2. How should Fondu's owners have framed their action to get the best possible result?

3. Is it possible for the owners to return the horse to the sellers and to reclaim the price? Would this be a desirable course of action?

VII. INFORMATION AND THE LAW OF CONTRACT

This section draws together the strands of the previous sections on defects in formation by highlighting the central problem of information—and in particular its retention and disclosure. With the possible exception of *Raffles* v. *Wichelhaus*, all the cases extracted or discussed in this chapter share a common feature: one party knows something that the other does not. In legal terms, the question is to determine the extent to which the knowing party may take advantage of the informational imbalance, and whether he or she can be forced to disclose the information by the giving of remedies to the other party in the event of non-disclosure.

Kronman provides some useful introductory thoughts on the role of information in contracts.

A. Kronman, 'Mistake, Disclosure, Information, and the Law of Contracts', (1978) 7 *J. Leg. St.* 1 at 2–5

Mistake and the Allocation of Risk

Every contractual agreement is predicated upon a number of factual assumptions about the world. Some of these assumptions are shared by the parties to the contract and some are not. It is always possible that a particular factual assumption is mistaken. From an economic point of view, the risk of such a mistake (whether it be the mistake of only one party or both) represents a cost. It is a cost to the contracting parties themselves and to society as a whole since the actual occurrence of a mistake always (potentially) increases the resources which must be devoted to the process of allocating goods to their highest-valuing users. . . .

Information is the antidote to mistake. Although information is costly to produce, one individual may be able to obtain relevant information more cheaply than another. If the parties to a contract are acting rationally, they will minimize the joint costs of a potential mistake by assigning the risk of its occurrence to the party who is the better (cheaper) information-gatherer. Where the parties have actually assigned the risk—whether explicitly, or implicitly through their adherence to trade custom and past patterns of dealing—their own allocation must be respected. Where they have not—and there is a resulting gap in the contract—a court concerned with economic efficiency should impose the risk on the better information-gatherer. This is so for familiar reasons: by allocating the risk in this way, an efficiency-minded court reduces the transaction costs of the contracting process itself.

It will be apparent from the discussion throughout this chapter that two parties in contractual negotiations are normally entitled to keep to themselves information which motivates them to conclude a contract. That is clearly not an absolute principle, because there is a narrow category of unilateral mistake by the offeree as to the terms of an offer where the offeror is aware of the mistake, which renders a contract void *ab initio* (see notes to *Smith* v. *Hughes* above). There is also one major exception to the nondisclosure rule, namely so-called contracts *uberrimae fidei* (contracts of utmost good faith). The best example is the contract of insurance, where the insured and insurer are under a mutual duty to disclose material facts. A breach of the duty gives the 'deceived' party the right to rescind the contract, even if the non-disclosure occurred entirely innocently. The next case is concerned with a failed attempt to extrapolate from the duty of disclosure in an insurance contract something more—namely a right to damages to compensate the 'deceived' party for loss which he or she alleges flowed from the failure to disclosure.

Banque Financière de la Cité SA v. *Westgate Insurance Co. Ltd.*
[1989] 2 All ER 952 (CA)

B. controlled four companies. Over a period of two years he obtained loans for his companies totalling 80 million Swiss francs from a number of bank syndicates. As protection against B's failure to repay the loans, the banks took gemstones and credit insurance policies as security (see Fig. 5).

The litigation in this case concerned the insurance policies. In some of the policies the Bank was actually the insured, i.e. it was insuring the risk

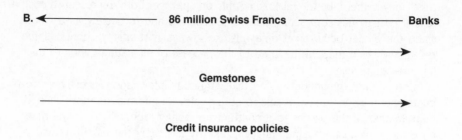

Fig. 5. The facts of *Banque Financière*

that B would not be able to pay. In the other policies B was technically the insured but the bank was assigned the policy. This made no material difference, as in all cases the insurers knew that the banks were, if not technically the insured, the interested party under the policies. The polices were arranged by L (Mr Lee the broker) who acted on behalf of the insured to find an insurer. L was able to arrange insurance cover for only part of the loan. Unless he could obtain full cover, the whole deal would fall apart and his employers (Notcutts) would lose their commission. The cover that could be arranged was provided by D (Dungate, the underwriter) through his employers. D agreed to provide insurance cover for the outstanding loans for fourteen days only. This enabled the loan transactions to be completed. After the expiry of the fourteen days there was no insurance cover for part of the loans, but L represented to the banks that they were fully covered and issued false cover notes to this effect.

By chance D found out about L's dishonest behaviour and forced him to destroy the false cover notes. The effect of this was to return his employer's exposure on the loan to its previous agreed level and to leave the banks exposed. D, however, did not know that the banks were exposed by lack of insurance cover, as he believed that L had at that point obtained full cover. Nevertheless, L's issue of false cover notes was never properly explained by him and D did not tell anyone else of this. He continued to do business with L.

The banks continued to lend money to B. By the end of 1981 it was clear that B had perpetrated a massive fraud and neither he nor the money could be found. The banks tried to reclaim their money under the insurance policies, but all the policies contained clauses which rendered them inoperable in the event of fraud (in this case B's is the relevant fraud). This led to the banks abandoning their claims under the policies. They settled actions against L's employers (the brokers). However, they began actions against the insurers under several heads (set out below), all founded on D's non-disclosure of his dealings with L and the false cover notes.

To make the facts more complicated, D changed employers during his dealings with L—he worked first for 'Hodge' then 'Skandice'. The banks (with one exception) were represented by the same counsel, and are referred to in the judgment as the 'banks' or 'Keysers'. Slade LJ gives judgment on behalf of the Court of Appeal. He divides his judgment into eleven issues. For our purposes it is necessary to look only at issues 4–8. To clarify the judgment, we have added a number of subheadings.

[SLADE LJ]
[The obligation to disclose and the remedy of rescission]

Issue (4)

We begin with a statement of basic principle of the English law of contract:

'Ordinarily the failure to disclose a material fact which might influence the mind of a prudent contractor does not give the right to avoid the contract. The principle of caveat emptor applies outside contracts of sale. There are certain contracts expressed by the law to be contracts of the utmost good faith, where material facts must be disclosed; if not, the contract is voidable. Apart from special fiduciary relationships, contracts for partnership and contracts of insurance are the leading instances. In such cases the duty does not arise out of contract; the duty of a person proposing an insurance arises before a contract is made, so of an intending partner.'

(See *Bell v Lever Bros Ltd* [1932] AC 161 at 227 per Lord Atkin.)

The common features of contracts which are classified by the law as contracts uberrimae fidei is that by their very nature one party is likely to have the command of means of knowledge not available to the other. In the leading case of *Carter v Boehm* (1766) 3 Burr 1905 at 1909 Lord Mansfield CJ described the rationale behind the duty of disclosure falling on the insured in the case of contracts of insurance as follows:

'Insurance is a contract upon speculation. The special facts, upon which the contingent chance is to be computed, lie most commonly in the knowledge of the *insured* only: the under-writer trusts to his representation, and proceeds upon confidence that he does not keep back any circumstance in his knowledge, to mislead the under-writer into a belief that the circumstance does not exist, and to induce him to estimate the risque, as if it did not exist. The keeping back such circumstance is a *fraud*, and therefore the policy is *void*. Although the suppression should happen through *mistake*, without any fraudulent intention; yet still the under-writer is *deceived*, and the policy is *void*; because the risque run is really different from the risque understood and intended to be run, at the time of the agreement.' (Lord Mansfield CJ's emphasis.) . . .

In our judgment, there is no doubt that the obligation to disclose material facts is a mutual one imposing reciprocal duties on insurer and insured. . . .

It is no less clear that where there is obligation to disclose material facts it is an absolute one which is not negatived by the absence of fraud or negligence. The law requires a party to an insurance contract to state not only all those material circumstances within his knowledge which he believes to be material, but those which are in fact so: . . . . Thus, the [merely] accidental failure to disclose facts, if material facts, will involve a breach of duty.

The authorities show that, in relation to the duty of disclosure falling on the insured, every fact is material which would influence the judgment of a prudent insurer (not the particular insurer. . . . in deciding whether to accept the particular risk for the particular insured and, if so, at what premium. . . . in the case of commercial contracts, broad concepts of honesty and fair dealing, however laudable, are a somewhat uncertain guide when determining the existence or otherwise of an obligation which may arise even in the absence of any dishonest or unfair intent . . . . More importantly, in our judgment, it would be too broad a proposition to state that any fact is material if it is 'calculated to influence the decision of the insured to conclude the contract of insurance'. To give one example, it might well be that in a particular case proposed insurers would be aware of another reputable underwriter who would be prepared to underwrite the same risk at a substantially lower premium. In our judgment the mere existence of the relationship of insurers and insured would not place on them the duty to inform the insured of this fact.

In adapting the well-established principles relating to the duty of disclosure falling on the insured to the obverse case of the insurer himself, due account must be taken of the rather different reasons for which the insured and the insurer require the protection of full disclosure. In our judgment, the duty falling on the insurer must at least extend to disclosing all facts known to him which are material either to the nature of the risk sought to be covered or the recoverability of a claim under the policy which a prudent insured would take into account in deciding whether or not to place the risk for which he seeks cover with that insurer. . . .

The facts known by Mr Dungate demonstrating the dishonesty of the broker through whom the banks were negotiating with him were thus material facts which it was his duty to disclose to them before they concluded the contractual arrangements with the insurers which were concluded on 24 June 1980.

It follows that in our judgment (a) Hodge, through Mr Dungate, was in breach of this duty of disclosure owed to the banks in June 1980, (b) in the absence of supervening events depriving them of this right, the banks, on discovering the non-disclosure, would have had the right to rescind the further contract of insurance concluded on 24 June 1980 and to demand the return of the further premium paid by them in September 1980.

However, this is not the relief arising out of the non-disclosure which Keysers seek. A claim for the return of the premium raised in its respondent's notice has not been pursued in this court. Instead, Keysers seek damages for breach of the obligation of disclosure. To this claim we now turn.

[Non-disclosure as a breach of contract: a remedy in damages?]

Issue 5

If the failure of Mr Dungate in June 1980 and afterwards to disclose to the banks the information possessed by him as to Mr Lee's dishonest past conduct had itself constituted the tort of deceit, the banks would have had a claim for damages against Mr Dungate's employers in the ordinary way. However, the general rule is that, subject to certain exceptions, mere passive non-disclosure of the truth, however deceptive, does not amount to deceit in law: see *Salmond and Heuston on the Law of Torts* (19th edn, 1987) pp 435–436. None of the exceptions apply in the present case. Keysers have not advanced any claim in deceit and they have no statutory right to disclosure. They have therefore been obliged to seek other routes by which to pursue their claims to monetary compensation.

The first of these routes rests on the submission that the breach of a party to a contract uberrimae fidei of his obligation of disclosure is itself capable of giving rise to an action for damages in an appropriate case. This is a novel claim as yet entirely unsupported by any decision of the courts of this country beyond the judgment of the judge. And indeed we have been told that after research no authority of any common law court has been discovered which supports it. . . .

Keysers' claim under the present head may thus perhaps at first sight appear a bold one. Nevertheless, as was submitted on behalf of the banks, the entire absence of any authority directly supporting (or indeed rejecting) a claim of this nature is not perhaps entirely surprising. By the very nature of insurance cases allegations of non-disclosure of material facts are more likely to be made by the insurers than by the insured; in the ordinary course insurers will know of no material facts of which the insured himself is ignorant. And in the ordinary course the right to avoid the policy will be an adequate remedy for the aggrieved insurer.

In the rare case where there has been non-disclosure of a material fact *by* the insurer the position may be rather different. Avoidance of the policy and the return of the premium may well constitute entirely sufficient relief for the insured if he becomes aware of the non-disclosure before the occurrence of the contingency against which he has intended to insure. If, however, he becomes aware of it only after the occurrence of the contingency, relief of this nature may be quite inadequate. . . .

It was further argued on behalf of the banks that, unless the bilateral duty of disclosure gives rise to a remedy in damages, the contract is 'unbalanced', since rescission of the policy, while an adequate remedy for the insurer, is no adequate remedy for the insured. We are not convinced that rescission of the policy is necessarily an adequate remedy even for the insurer if, for example, the non-disclosure has led him to accept a risk at a far lower premium that he would otherwise have charged. In any event, in our judgment, the so-called lack of balance of the contract throws no further light on the legal origin of the right of either party to demand full disclosure. . . .

If, however, this obligation does not arise under contract or statute and no fiduciary relationship between the parties is asserted, a breach of the obligation must, in our judgment, itself constitute *a tort* if it is such as to give rise to a claim for damages.

There is no authority whatever to support the existence of such a tort and, quite apart from such lack of authority, there are in our judgment . . . reasons why this court should not by its present decision create a novel tort of this nature. First, we have already concluded that the powers of the court to grant relief where there has been non-disclosure of material facts in the case of a contract uberrimae fidei stems from the jurisdiction originally exercised by the courts of equity to prevent imposition. The powers of the court to grant relief by way of rescission of a contract where there has been undue influence or duress stem from the same jurisdiction. Since duress and undue influence as such give rise to no claim for damages, we see no reason in principle why non-disclosure as such should do so.

Fourth, as we have already stated, in the case of a contract uberrimae fidei, the obligation to disclose a known material fact is an absolute one. It attaches with equal force whether the failure is attributable to 'fraud, carelessness, inadvertence, indifference, mistake, error of judgment, or even to [the] failure to appreciate its materiality': see Ivamy *General Principles of Insurance Law* (5th edn, 1986) p 156 and the cases there cited. A decision that the breach of such an obligation in every case and by itself constituted a tort if it caused damage could give rise to great potential hardship to insurers and even more, perhaps, to insured persons. An insured who had in complete innocence failed to disclose a material fact when making an insurance proposal might find himself subsequently faced with a claim by the insurer for a substantially increased premium by way of damages before any event had occurred which gave rise to a claim. In many cases warranties given by the insured in the proposal form as to the truth of the statements made by him might afford the insurers the same remedy, but by no means in all cases. In our judgment it would not be right for this court by way of judicial legislation to create a new tort, effectively of absolute liability, which could expose either party to an insurance contract to a claim for substantial damages in the absence of any blameworthy conduct.

No relevant breach of contract has been established and fraud is not alleged against Mr Dungate or Hodge. We accordingly hold that, if the breach by Hodge, through Mr Dungate, of its duty of full disclosure is to give rise to a claim for damages at the suit of Keysers, this claim must be based on (innocent) misrepresentation or the tort of negligence. . . .

[Is there conduct amounting to a misrepresentation?]

Issue (6)

Mr Dungate, it was said, . . . made an implied representation to [the banks] that Mr Lee was, so far as he (Mr Dungate) knew, a suitable and trustworthy broker. This representation, it was claimed, fell to be treated as a misrepresentation from 2 June 1980 onwards, when Mr Dungate learnt of its untruth but nevertheless failed to inform the banks of its untruth. . . .

[Slade LJ concluded that the only misrepresentation was one of silence.]

If a person is to [bring] a claim for misrepresentation said to have been made by conduct, he must, in our judgment, at very least show that he relied on the representation in question. In the present case Keysers have not shown either (a) that they were led by Mr Dungate to believe that he was making any representation as to Mr Lee's honesty or (b) that they relied on any such representation. So far as we are aware, no evidence was called on behalf of any of the banks suggesting that Mr Dungate in any way led them to understand that he was vouching for Mr Lee's honesty. This, in our judgment, is the short answer to the claim based on this first head of alleged misrepresentation. . . .

[Do contracts of insurance contain implied representations that full disclosure has been made?]

The second head pursued by Keysers in this court . . . is of a different character. The submission, as developed in argument, is that in the case of any contract of insurance there is deemed to be an implied representation by each party that he has made full disclosure of all material facts. The representation is said to arise *by operation of law* in every such case. As counsel for Chemical Bank pithily put the point in argument. 'Where there is a duty to disclose silence in law constitutes a misrepresentation.' Accordingly it is submitted, Hodge must be treated as having induced the banks to enter the new insurance arrangements of June 1980 by the untrue representation that it had made disclosure of this nature.

A number of textbook writers, having stated that silence or non-disclosure on its own does not constitute misrepresentation, go on to state as a matter of general principle that it will constitute a misrepresentation in a case where the contract requires the utmost good faith: see eg *Cheshire Fifoot and Furmston's Law of Contract* (11th edn, 1986) pp 260–262 and *Chitty on Contracts* (25th edn, 1983) paras 399, 460.

Counsel who presented the main argument for the banks of misrepresentation, submitted that this statement of general principle derives support from judicial dicta in insurance cases. . . .

In our judgment [the cases] lend no support whatever to the proposition that a breach of the duty of disclosure in the case of contracts uberrimae fidei always as a mater of law falls to be treated as constituting a misrepresentation.

The proposition, if correct, could have far-reaching consequences. The supposed misrepresentation might presumably fall to be treated as made not only to the parties to a written contract but to other persons who would in the future be relying on its terms as recorded in the contract. The proposition, however, is in our judgment untenable. It derives no support from authority. . . . Most of the reasons which we have stated for rejecting the proposition that the failure to disclose a material fact constitutes a breach of an implied term of a contract uberrimae fidei support, mutatis mutandis, the rejection of the proposition that such failure constitutes a misrepresentation deemed to arise by operation of law.

We reject this proposition and answer issue (6) in the negative.

[Non-disclosure and the Misrepresentation Act 1967]

Issue (7)

Section 2(1) of the Misrepresentation Act 1967, which is the subsection relied on by Keysers, provides:

'Where a person has entered into a contract after a misrepresentation has been made to him by another party thereto and as a result thereof he has suffered loss, then, if the person making the misrepresentation would be liable to damages in respect thereof had the misrepresentation been made fraudulently, that person shall be so liable notwithstanding that the misrepresentation was not made fraudulently, unless he proves that he had reasonable ground to believe and did believe up to the time the contract was made that the facts represented were true.'

Under issue (6) we have referred to the two heads of alleged misrepresentation still pursued by Keysers and have concluded that neither head has been established as a matter of fact or law. If these conclusions be correct, Keysers' claims for damages based on the 1967 Act must necessarily fail for that reason, if no other, and issue (7) does not arise.

There are, however, at least two further reasons why these heads of claim could, in our judgment, give rise to no claim for damages under the 1967 Act, even if the misrepresentation alleged had been proved.

First, as the wording of s 2(1) shows, one of the conditions which has to be satisfied if a remedy under that subsection is to be available is that 'the person making the misrepresentation would be liable to damages in respect thereof had the misrepresentation been made fraudulently'. Thus, in the words of counsel for Hodge, the ingredients of a fraudulent misrepresentation have to be present save for the ingredient of dishonesty. However, one of the essential ingredients of a misrepresentation if it is to give rise to a cause of action for deceit is that it should be made with the intention that it should be acted on by the other party (see *Clerk and Lindsell on Torts* (15th edn, 1982) para 17–32). It was never alleged against Mr Dungate, let alone proved, that he made any misrepresentation to the banks with the intention that they should act on it. This, in our judgment, would be an answer to both heads of claim based on the 1967 Act.

As regards the second head of claim, we think there would be a further answer. If s 2(1) is to apply at all, a misrepresentation has to have been 'made' to the complainant by the other party. The expression 'misrepresentation . . .

made' (which is repeated in several later sections of the 1967 Act) would, in our judgment, on the ordinary meaning of words be inapt to refer to a misrepresentation which had not been made in fact but was (at most) merely deemed by the common law to have been made. If it had been the intention of the legislature that a mere failure to discharge the duty of disclosure in the case of a contract uberrimae fidei would fall to be treated as the 'making' of a representation within the meaning of the 1967 Act, we are of the opinion that the legislature would have said so.

We accordingly answer issue (7) in the negative.

[Has there been a negligent misstatement within the boundaries set by *Hedley Byrne* v. *Heller*?]

Issue (8)

We now come to what counsel for Skandia called the heart of the case. Did Hodge owe the banks a common law duty of care in negligence? The judge has held that they did. . . .

The decision of the House of Lords in *Hedley Byrne & Co Ltd v Heller & Partners Ltd* and subsequent decisions founded on its principles establish that, where in the particular circumstances of a case one party is shown to have assumed a voluntary responsibility to another, the court may hold that a special relationship exists between them giving rise to a duty of care, the breach of which is capable of giving rise to a claim for damages for purely economic loss.

The facts of the *Hedley Byrne* case, which arose out of a negligent misrepresentation, are too well known to require repetition. While that case established that economic loss resulting from a negligent misrepresentation may be recovered in tort, there are two conditions for recoverability. The first is that the defendant should have assumed a voluntary responsibility towards the plaintiff in making the statement or representation. The second is that the plaintiff should have relied on it. . . .

Now if the facts of the present case had been that Mr Dungate had carelessly misrepresented to the banks that Mr Lee was an honest man, the *Hedley Byrne* principles would, in our judgment, plainly have applied, subject to the conditions we have mentioned, even though the misrepresentation was made in a pre-contractual setting.

On the facts of many cases, the conclusion of a contract will preclude the parties from relying on the law of tort to provide them with any greater protection than that which the contract itself has expressly or impliedly conferred on them. . . . However, the decision of this court in *Esso Petroleum Co Ltd v Mardon* establishes that in appropriate circumstances liability in tort may be imposed on one contracting party to another for misrepresentations made before the signing of a written contract. As Shaw LJ succinctly put it ([1976] QB 801 at 832–833):

'It is difficult to see why, in principle, a right to claim damages for negligent misrepresentation which has arisen in favour of a party to a negotiation should not survive the event of the making of a contract as the outcome of that negotiation. It may, of course, be that the contract ultimately made either expressly or by implication shows that, once it has been entered into, the rights and liabilities of the parties are to be those and only those which have their origin in the contract itself. In any other case there is no valid argument apart from legal technicality for the proposition that a subsequent contract vitiates a cause of action in negligence which had previously arisen in the course of negotiation.'

It would have been possible for the parties in the *Esso Petroleum* case to make express provision as to the effect of the pre-contractual representations in their contract. Indeed such provision is not uncommon in commercial contracts. But that possibility was held not to exclude liability in tort. By the same token, in the present case it would have been possible, though highly unlikely, for the parties in concluding the contract of 24 June 1980 to have included an express warranty by Hodge as to the honesty of the broker's employee. Like the judge, we would not regard that possibility as sufficient in itself to exclude a duty of care in tort, if we were otherwise minded to find such a duty.

Accordingly, if Mr Dungate had carelessly misrepresented to the banks that Mr Lee was an honest man, the *Hedley Byrne* principles would, in our judgment, have enabled Keysers to succeed in their claim in negligence if, though only if, they could have proved a voluntary assumption of responsibility in respect of such representation by Mr Dungate coupled with reliance by the banks. It is to be observed that in the *Esso Petroleum* case Lord Denning MR and Ormrod LJ specifically referred to an assumption of responsibility by the defendant. In many cases where a misrepresentation has been made to another person, particularly by a professional man acting in the course of his profession, the assumption of responsibility may be readily inferred.

But on the view of the facts taken by the judge and by this court there has been no misrepresentation in the present case. The essence of the banks' case is that they are seeking to recover damages for economic loss which they say they suffered as the result of Mr Dungate's *failure* to inform them of Mr Lee's dishonesty.

Can a mere failure to speak ever give rise to liability in negligence under *Hedley Byrne* principles? In our view it can, but subject to the all-important proviso that there has been on the facts a voluntary assumption of responsibility in the relevant sense and reliance on that assumption. These features may be much more difficult to infer in a case of mere silence than in a case of misrepresentation. . . .

We can see no sufficient reason on principle or authority why a failure to speak should not be capable of giving rise to liability in negligence under *Hedley Byrne* principles, provided that the two essential conditions are satisfied.

A hypothetical example may illustrate the point. Suppose that a father employs an estate agent for a fee to advise his son on the proposed purchase of a house and the estate agent negligently fails to inform the son that a motorway is shortly to be constructed within a few hundred yards of the property.

We would not doubt that in such a case the son, knowing of the estate agent's duty and relying on it, could have a claim in negligence under *Hedley Byrne* principles. To draw a distinction on those particular facts between misinformation and a failure to inform would be to perpetuate the sort of nonsense in the law which Lord Devlin condemned in the *Hedley Byrne* case.

So in so far as Keysers' case is based on *Hedley Byrne* principles, the question comes to this. Did Mr Dungate in fact assume responsibility towards the banks? If so, did the banks rely on that assumption of responsibility? The answer to each part of the question must surely be No.

We can see no justification for holding that Mr Dungate, who made no representation, assumed any responsibility at all in relation to Mr Lee's honesty or dishonesty. Counsel for the banks other than Chemical Bank argued that a voluntary assumption of responsibility is to be found in Mr Dungate's voluntary conduct in continuing to deal with Mr Lee. We do not agree. The phrase 'voluntary assumption of responsibility' in this context means what it says: conduct by the party signifying that he assumes responsibility for taking due care in respect of the statement or action. No doubt, in deciding whether there has been such an assumption of responsibility the conduct of the party may be objectively construed. To deal in the ordinary way with an agent without any relevant communication to his principal cannot, we think, be held to be an assumption of responsibility because the party has done nothing which signifies assumption of responsibility in the relevant sense.

Nor is there any evidence that the banks relied on any assumption of responsibility by the insurers in respect of Mr Lee's honesty. We need not repeat what we have already said in that connection under issue (6). It must follow that, in the absence of any voluntary assumption of responsibility and reliance by the banks, no duty of care on the part of the insurers can be established under *Hedley Byrne* principles. . . .

[General observations on non-disclosure]

The general principle that there is no obligation to speak within the context of negotiations for an ordinary commercial contract (though qualified by the well-known special principles relating to contracts uberrimae fidei, fraud, undue influence, fiduciary duty etc) is one of the foundations of our law of contract, and must have been the basis of many decisions over the years. There are countless cases in which one party to a contract has in the course of negotiations failed to disclose a fact known to him which the other party would have regarded as highly material, if it had been revealed. However, ordinarily in the absence of misrepresentation, our law leaves that other party entirely without remedy. Lord Atkin gave some striking examples in *Bell v Lever Bros Ltd* [1932] AC 161 at 224 (we have added the numbering to his examples):

'[1] A. buys B.'s horse; he thinks the horse is sound and he pays the price of a sound horse; he would certainly not have bought the horse if he had known as the fact is that the horse is unsound. If B. has made no representation as to soundness and has not contracted that the horse is sound, A. is bound and cannot recover back the price. [2] A. buys a picture from B.; both A. and B. believe it to be the work of an old master, and a high price is paid. It turns out to be a modern copy. A. has no remedy in the absence of representation or warranty. [3] A. agrees to take on lease or to buy from B. an unfurnished dwelling-house. The house is in fact uninhabitable. A. would never have entered into the bargain if he had known the fact. A. has no remedy, and the position is the same whether B. knew the facts or not, so long as he made no representation or gave no warranty. [4] A. buys a roadside garage business from B. abutting on a public thoroughfare: unknown to A., but known to B., it has already been decided to construct a byepass road which will divert substantially the whole of the traffic from passing A.'s garage. Again A. has no remedy.'

Example 2 is common mistake. In examples 1, 3 and 4, B, if he had directed his mind to the matter, either might well have realised that A was proceeding under a misapprehension or knew that that was so, and that this misapprehension was likely to cause a loss. Nevertheless, in our judgment, it would be wholly contrary to principle to suggest, at least in the case of an ordinary contract made between persons in an ordinary relationship, that B, having undertaken no relevant contractual obligation to A, should be treated as having assumed a responsibility which could give rise to a liability to A in tort. To reach such a decision as to the effect of a non-disclosure in the course of contractual negotiations would run counter to the general principle of caveat emptor on which our law of contract is founded. As Blackburn J said in *Smith v Hughes* (1871) LR 6 QB 597 at 607:

'. . . even if the vendor was aware that the purchaser thought that the article possessed [some particular] quality, and would not have entered into the contract unless he had so thought, still the purchaser is bound, unless the vendor was guilty of some fraud or deceit upon him, and . . . a mere abstinence of disabusing the purchaser of that impression is not fraud or deceit; for, whatever may be the case in a court of morals, there is no legal obligation on the vendor to inform the purchaser that he is under a mistake, not induced by the act of the vendor.'

By the same token we would hold that no legal obligation on the part of Mr Dungate to inform the banks of Mr Lee's dishonesty arose, either in contract or in tort, merely because there was an 'established business relationship' between the parties, and because the insurers continued to transact further business with the banks. That factor does not turn a pure omission into a misrepresentation, in tort any more than in contract. It would not justify the court treating Mr Dungate as having assumed a duty or responsibility to speak, in tort, which was not imposed on him by the law of contract. . . .

[The inadequacy of the contract remedy and the unavailability of a tortious remedy]

This brings us to what was, in our view, the most forceful submission made on behalf of the banks . . . . The very nature of the contract which was being negotiated, it is said, gives rise to a special relationship between the negotiating parties which justifies the imposition of a duty of care. . . . We do not think that the nature of the contract as one of the utmost good faith can be used as a platform to establish a common law duty of care. Parliament has provided that in the case of marine insurance the consequence of a failure to disclose a material fact, and by inference the *only* consequence, is that the contract may be avoided. It is not suggested that the consequences in non-marine insurance should be different. In those circumstances it is not, we think, open to the court to assist the banks by providing a supplementary remedy in tort. No doubt, on the very unusual facts of the present case, the statutory remedy of rescission seems inadequate. This is unfortunate for the banks. But the banks' misfortune is of the same kind as the misfortune suffered by the injured party in the various instances given by Lord Atkin in *Bell v Lever Bros Ltd*, where the law affords no remedy at all. What the banks cannot do in our judgment is to invoke the nature of the contract as one of good faith, with its limited contractual remedy, to bridge the gap so as to give them a cause of action in tort. The error in the submission made for the banks is that it ignores the nature of the special obligation imposed in contracts of utmost good faith. The obligation does not, if we are right, create a duty to speak for breach of which the law attaches the consequences which flow from an ordinary breach of duty, whether statutory or otherwise. It is a rule of law which provides, and provides only, that certain stated consequences (namely the insured party's right to avoid the contract) will follow if utmost good faith be not observed.

Furthermore, despite the eloquent submissions of counsel for the banks . . . in this context, we are not satisfied that justice and reasonableness imperatively require the finding of a duty of care owed by Hodge to Keysers. This is not a case in which the denial to the banks of a cause of action in negligence will mean that the banks are left without any remedy at all. For Notcutts, the firm of brokers by whom Mr Lee was employed, and on whom the banks placed reliance for the honesty of Mr Lee, were vicariously liable for the actions of Mr Lee; and Mr Ballestero and his fraudulent associates were also liable for the loss which they directly caused to the banks. It is true that Mr Ballestero and his associates have either disappeared or are not worth suing. But Notcutts were well worth suing and were sued, although in the event the banks chose to settle their claims against them on the terms which we have already mentioned. This, therefore, is far from being a case where the invocation of the law of tort against the banks was the only way by which the courts could have afforded them a remedy. It is possible to exaggerate the hardship which Keysers will suffer if this court declines to give them a remedy against Hodge.

This having been said, we can well understand the banks' desire to demonstrate that, by failing to take any action with reference to Mr Lee's known dishonesty, the insurers failed to prevent the wrongs subsequently inflicted on the banks by Mr Ballestero. Counsel made much of the fact that what we are concerned with here was dishonesty on the part of Mr Lee, and dishonesty which was proven, not merely suspected. It was said that it ought to be the policy of the law to promote honesty and probity in business dealings, particularly in the insurance market. We accept that Mr Dungate's failure to inform the banks of Mr Lee's dishonesty was morally reprehensible. By any decent standards of commercial morality the disclosure should have been made. His view of contemporary morality was supported by the expert witnesses who said that it was part of Mr Dungate's professional duty to inform the banks.

But this, to our minds, is one of those many cases where the legal obligation falls short of the moral imperatives. No doubt liability for negligence is based 'upon a general public sentiment of moral wrongdoing for which the offender must pay' (see *Donoghue v Stevenson* [1932] AC 562 at 580). But it must be remembered that Lord Atkin went on to say, in the very next sentence, that—

'acts or omissions which any moral code would censure cannot in a practical world be treated so as to give a right to every person injured by them to demand relief.'

The law cannot police the fairness of every commercial contract by reference to moral principles. It frequently appears with hindsight, as in this case, that one contracting party had knowledge of facts which, if communicated to the other party, would have protected him from loss. However, subject to well-recognised exceptions, the law does not and should not undertake the reopening of commercial transactions in order to adjust such losses.

Notes

1. The banks' appeal to the House of Lords was unsuccessful. In much briefer judgments ([1990] 2 All ER 947) the House of Lords concluded that there was indeed no *Hedley Byrne*-type duty owed by the insurers to the banks; their Lordships also indicated that much of the earlier discussion of Steyn J and the Court of Appeal was misconceived, since they refused to accept that it was L's fraud which caused the loss to the banks. The speeches proceed on the basis that the only relevant cause of the loss was B's fraud. For comments on *Banque Financière* see D. Allen, 'Non-Disclosure: Hairshirt or Halo?', (1992) 55 MLR 96; F. Trindade, 'Commercial Morality and the Tort of Negligence', (1989) 105 LQR 191; Trindade, 'The Skandia Case in the House of Lords', (1991) 107 LQR 24.

2. In the context of the insurance contract, it is typically to be expected that the duty of disclosure operates to protect the insurer against a deficit of information in the calculation of the risk. For the insurer, the ability to treat the insurance contract as at an end and to refuse to cover the risk is a good enough remedy. Moreover, it is the insured person who will normally have access to information which is material to the calculability of the risk. Construing the duty of disclosure as a mutual duty may seem a fair-minded and logical way to proceed, but in practice it alone will avail the

insured little if, as is clear from *Banque Financière*, there is almost no chance that a right to damages in contract or tort to cover consequential loss flowing from the failure will arise from breach of that duty. In that sense it is a meaningless duty.

3. The way in which the judges in the Court of Appeal reach their conclusions displays strong characteristics of formalist reasoning. The type of policy factors which they (and the House of Lords subsequently) cite to support their conclusions show the law of contract principally as a neutral facilitative framework for commercial transactions: turning the duty of disclosure into a positive contractual duty takes it too far, and may upset the established contractual balance; misrepresentations under the Misrepresentation Act 1967 follow the common law and do not include omissions; and the duty of care under *Hedley Byrne* v. *Heller* only applies where there is a voluntary assumption of responsibility and reliance by the other party. No matter that turning round the duty of disclosure reveals that the remedy, namely rescission, cannot effectively be turned round. It is no part of the law of tort to remedy gaps in the framework of contractual remedies.

Commercial morality is seen as largely irrelevant and, if relevant, one-dimensional. Encouraging the banks to be more careful in their lending habits by denying them a remedy against the insurers may be productive of greater efficiency. But does telling the insurers that their duty of disclosure is virtually meaningless make for high standards of commercial morality, since it encourages underwriters such as Dungate to keep dangerous pieces of information about the conduct of the insurance market to themselves and not to share it with the consumers so that they can decide how and whether to conclude transactions on that market? Perhaps the most convincing answer to this point focuses on the assessment of risk made by the underwriters. They had *refused* a risk beyond SF 10 million. Imposing a duty of care would in fact have carried their liability well beyond the risk which they had deemed to be the limit of their potential responsibility. It is perhaps interesting to note, however, that in reaching the opposite conclusion on the duty of care point, Steyn J at first instance ([1987] 2 ALL ER 923 at 944) asked whether good faith and fair dealing required disclosure of the information by Dungate. Those terms are textually identical to those employed in §161 of the US Restatement (Second) of Contracts, which imposes a limited duty in respect of non-disclosures, in the same terms as if they were misrepresentations, if non-disclosure would offend against the principle of fair dealing and good faith. There is no space for such open-textured standards in the formalist approaches of the Court of Appeal and the House of Lords.

Dungate came by the information about L. apparently by chance. Kronman offers us a framework of analysis to assess the disclosure of information which focuses on the manner by which that information was 'discovered'.

A. Kronman, 'Mistake, Disclosure, Information, and the Law of Contracts', (1978) 7 *J. Leg. St.* 1 at 13–18, 22, 25–6

Allocative efficiency is promoted by getting information of changed circumstances to the market as quickly as possible. Of course, the information doesn't just "get" there. Like everything else, it is supplied by individuals (either directly, by being publicized, or indirectly, when it is signalled by an individual's market behavior).

In some cases, the individuals who supply information have obtained it by a deliberate search; in other cases their information has been acquired casually. A securities analyst, for example, acquires information about a particular corporation in a deliberate fashion—by carefully studying evidence of its economic performance. By contrast, a businessman who acquires a valuable piece of information when he accidentally overhears a conversation in a bus acquires the information casually.

As it is used here, the term "deliberately acquired information" means information whose acquisition entails costs which would not have been incurred but for the likelihood, however great, that the information in question would actually be produced. These costs may include, of course, not only direct search costs (the cost of examining the corporation's annual statement) but the costs of developing an initial expertise as well (for example, the cost of attending business school). If the costs incurred in acquiring the information (the cost of the bus ticket in the second example) would have been incurred in any case—that is, whether or not the information was forthcoming—the information may be said to have been casually acquired. The distinction between deliberately and casually acquired information is a shorthand way of expressing this economic difference. Although in reality it may be difficult to determine whether any particular item of information has been acquired in one way or the other, the distinction between these two types of information has—as I hope to show—considerable analytical usefulness.

If information has been deliberately acquired (in the sense defined above), and its possessor is denied the benefits of having and using it, he will have an incentive to reduce (or curtail entirely) his production of such information in the future. . . .

It might be claimed that whenever the benefits of possessing any kind of information are either increased or decreased, one would expect to find *some* overall adjustment in the level of investment in the production of such information. If he is not permitted to benefit from the information he acquires, even the bus rider will in the future pay less attention to the conversations going on around him (although it would certainly be strange if he stopped riding buses altogether). But while it is true that in reality every adjustment (upwards or downwards) in the benefits of possessing a particular kind of information will have an incentive effect of some sort, the effect may vary in magnitude—it may be greater or lesser. Strictly speaking, casually acquired information (as I have used the term up to this point) represents the ideal limit of a continuum—the case in which the change in magnitude that results from eliminating one of the benefits of possessing certain information is zero. In any real case there will be incentive effects which fall somewhere along the continuum. However, where the decline in the production of a certain kind of information which is caused by denying its possessor the right to appropriate the information for his own benefit is small, it is likely to be more than offset by the corresponding social gain that results from the avoidance of mistakes. In the argument that follows, I shall use the term "casually acquired information" in a somewhat looser sense than I have used it so far to refer to information of this sort.

One effective way of insuring that an individual will benefit from the possession of information (or anything else for that matter) is to assign him a property right in the information itself—a right or entitlement to involve the coercive machinery of the state in order to exclude others from its use and enjoyment. The benefits of possession become secure only when the state transforms the possessor of information into an owner by investing him with a legally enforceable property right of some sort of other. . . .

One (seldom noticed) way in which the legal system can establish property rights in information is by permitting an informed party to enter—and enforce—contracts which his information suggests are profitable, without disclosing the information to the other party. Imposing a duty to disclose upon the knowledgeable party deprives him of a private advantage which the information would otherwise afford. A duty to disclose is tantamount to a requirement that the benefit of the information be publicly shared and is thus antithetical to the notion of a property right which—whatever else it may entail—always requires the legal protection of private appropriation. . . .

In addition, since it would enable the seller to appropriate the buyer's information without cost and would eliminate the danger of his being lured unwittingly into a losing contract by one possessing superior knowledge, a disclosure requirement will also reduce the seller's incentive to search. Denying the buyer a property right in deliberately acquired information will therefore discourage both buyers and sellers from investing in the development of expertise and in the actual search for information. The assignment of such a right will not only protect the investment of the party possessing the special knowledge, it will also impose an opportunity cost on the other party and thus give him an incentive to undertake a (cost-justified) search of his own.

If we assume that courts can easily discriminate between those who have acquired information casually and those who have acquired it deliberately, plausible economic considerations might well justify imposing a duty to disclose on a case-by-case basis (imposing it where the information has been casually acquired, refusing to impose it where the information is the fruit of a deliberate search). A party who has casually acquired information is, at the time of the transaction, likely to be a better (cheaper) mistake-preventer than the mistaken party with whom he deals—regardless of the fact that both parties initially had equal access to the information in question. One who has deliberately acquired information is also in a position to prevent the other party's error. But in determining the cost to the knowledgeable party of preventing the mistake (by disclosure), we must include whatever investment he has made in acquiring the information in the first place. This investment will represent a loss to him if the other party can avoid the contract on the grounds that the party with the information owes him a duty of disclosure.

If we take this cost into account, it is no longer clear that the party with knowledge is the cheaper mistake-preventer when his knowledge has been deliberately acquired. Indeed, the opposite conclusion seems more plausible. In this case, therefore, a rule permitting nondisclosure (which has the effect of imposing the risk of a mistake on the mistaken party) corresponds to the arrangement the parties themselves would have been likely to adopt if they had negotiated an explicit allocation of the risk at the time they entered the contract. The parties to a contract are always free to allocate this particular risk by including an appropriate disclaimer in the terms of their agreement. Where they have failed to do so, however, the object of the law of contracts should be (as it is elsewhere) to reduce transaction costs by providing a legal rule which approximates the arrangement the parties would have chosen for themselves if they had deliberately addressed the problem. This consideration, coupled with the reduction in the production of socially useful information which is likely to follow from subjecting him to a disclosure requirement, suggests that allocative efficiency is best served by permitting one who possesses deliberately acquired information to enter and enforce favorable bargains without disclosing what he knows.

A rule which calls for case-by-case application of a disclosure requirement is likely, however, to involve factual issues that will be difficult (and expensive) to resolve. . . . The cost of administering a disclosure requirement on a case-by-case basis is likely to be substantial.

[Kronman then develops his argument through specific examples based on US law:

(1) The purchase of land by a purchaser who knows that the land is more valuable than the seller thinks it is.
(2) Sale of land by a seller who knows of latent defects in the property.
(3) Transactions completed where one party has information about market conditions that the other does not possess.]

Courts frequently have stated that in the absence of a confidential or fiduciary relation between buyer and seller, "a purchaser [of real estate], though having superior judgment of values, does not commit fraud merely by purchasing without disclosing his knowledge of value." A rule of this sort makes economic sense where the buyer's judgment is based upon his prediction of the likelihood of various future uses to which the property might be put. Although a buyer's "knowledge of value" is not always based upon deliberately acquired information, the number of entrepreneurs involved in professional real estate speculation makes it plausible to assume that such knowledge is often (if not typically) acquired in a deliberate manner. (Real estate speculators, by matching buyers and sellers, facilitate the movement of real property to its most efficient use. The information on which their predictions of future use are based should therefore be regarded as a social asset.) . . .

Where the seller actually knows of the defect, and the buyer does not, the seller is clearly the party best able to avoid the buyer's mistake at least cost— unless the seller has made a deliberate investment in acquiring his knowledge which he would not have made had he known he would be required to disclose to purchasers of the property any defects he discovered. A seller, of course, may make a substantial investment in acquiring information concerning a particular defect: for example, he may hire exterminators to check his property for termites. But even so, it is unlikely that his principal aim in acquiring such information is to obtain an advantage over potential purchasers. Typically, homeowners conduct investigations of this sort in order to protect their own investments. In most cases, a homeowner will have an adequate incentive to check for termites even if the law requires him to disclose what he discovers; furthermore, many termite infestations are discovered by simply living in the house—something the owner will do in any event. A disclosure requirement is unlikely to have a substantial effect on the level of investment by homeowners in the detection of termites: the point is not that information regarding termites is costless (it isn't), but that a disclosure requirement would not be likely to reduce the production of such information. . . .

A seller of goods might argue that a rule requiring him to disclose latent defects will discourage him from developing (socially useful) expertise regarding the qualities or attributes of the goods he is selling: if he cannot enjoy its fruits by selling without disclosure, what incentive will he have to acquire such expertise in the first place? This argument is rather unconvincing. A seller benefits in many different ways from his knowledge of the various attributes which his goods possess. For example, expertise of this sort enables him to be more efficient in purchasing materials, and reduces the likelihood that he will fail to identify any special advantage his goods enjoy (and therefore undersell them). Because the benefits which he derives from such knowledge are many and varied, it is unlikely that a duty to disclose latent defects will by itself seriously impair a seller's incentive to invest in acquiring knowledge regarding the attributes of what he sells.

By contrast, the usefulness of market information (as distinct from information regarding the attributes of goods held for sale) is substantially reduced by imposing a duty to disclose on its possessor. It is doubtful whether the benefits of market information which are not eliminated by a disclosure requirement are sufficient by themselves to justify a deliberate investment in its production. Consequently, even if we regard these two kinds of information—market information and product information—as equally useful from a social point of view, a legal rule requiring disclosure is likely to have a different impact upon the production of each. It follows from what I have just said that a rule permitting nondisclosure of market information is sensible whether the party possessing the information is a buyer or a seller. . . . Although economic considerations would appear to support similar treatment for buyers and sellers possessing market information, these same considerations may justify different treatment where product information is involved. It should be clear, from what I have already said, that there is no inconsistency in requiring sellers to disclose latent defects, while not requiring buyers to disclose latent advantages.

Note

Kronman justifies his theory by reference to a discussion of US cases on unilateral mistake and non-disclosure, concluding that many of the so-called unilateral mistake cases, where one party can rescind because of a mistake of which the other party is aware, involve information which has become available by chance. It should be noted that some of the US cases on unilateral mistake are perhaps more generous to the mistaken party than are their English equivalents.

One criticism of Kronman is that he only endeavours in his article to apply his theory to relatively simple two-party cases involving buyers or sellers with informational advantages over their respective partners. Yet in reality even the case of the seller who fails to reveal a latent defect becomes more complicated, in view of the fact that buyers commonly employ (or those from whom they borrow money employ on their behalf) persons whose primary role is to ensure that the buyer makes a good bargain (i.e. the surveyor). The question arises, therefore, whether Kronman's theory can be adapted to three or multi-party situations.

Equally, applying Kronman's theory to *Banque Financière* reveals another respect in which it could be said to be working at one level only. Kronman himself distinguishes elsewhere in his article between non-disclosure as a ground for avoiding a contract and non-disclosure as the basis of a remedy for consequential loss, essential if, as here, rescinding the contract provides a patently inadequate remedy. Dungate's information is acquired casually. According to Kronman, this should give 'the party without the information the right to rescind', as indeed the Court of Appeal clearly believes that it does (the House of Lords, incidentally, is not quite so sure). But this leaves open the question of whether a distinction between casually or deliberately acquired information provides any useful clues as to whether a further remedy of damages should be available.

Answers to Exercise

1(*a*). At first sight the most obvious statement of the owners' loss in respect of the value of the horse is the difference between 26,000 guineas (£27,300) (plus VAT) and £1,500 = £25,800. Yet this simplicity deceives, since at the time of the purchase, correctly described, Fondu would probably have fetched around 23,500 guineas (£24,675) (plus VAT). The reason for the excessively low price of £1,500 after two seasons' racing was that Fondu had proved herself singularly inept at racing, and therefore had depreciated dramatically in price.

1(*b*). The cost of keeping Fondu in training is clearly a quantifiable loss. Care should be taken on two counts in assessing whether it is recoverable: first, there would seem to be no reason for the owners to claim racehorse training fees (as opposed to a bare amount for upkeep) as they have discovered the default which makes Fondu unsuitable for racing on grass tracks; second, they would almost certainly have bought a racehorse at the sales, even if not Fondu if she had been correctly described. Can the training fees which they have incurred anyway really be described as a loss?

1(*c*). More speculative is the loss they suffered in the form of disappointment that Fondu proved unsuccessful as a racehorse. But is this an inherent risk of horse-racing, given that any racehorse, even with very good breeding, can be unsuccessful?

1(*d*). It is also not easy to point to any certain loss of prize money resulting from a correctly described horse winning races. This is probably too speculative an expectation to be recoverable.

1(*e*). Likewise, the owners' loss of the chance that by winning races Fondu might have increased her value as a future brood mare must be discounted as too speculative.

It therefore seems likely that the only legally recoverable loss would be (*a*) and (*b*), and that (*c*)–(*e*) would be excluded by the rules of damages which we shall examine in Chapter 14. Consequently we shall restrict our focus to heads (*a*) and (*b*).

2. Damages could be available for either (*a*) breach of contract or (*b*) misrepresentation, either (i) fraudulent misrepresentation, (ii) negligent misrepresentation, or (iii) innocent misrepresentation, if section 2(2) of the Misrepresentation Act 1967 is applied. Consult Figs. 3 and 5.

2(*a*). *Breach of contract.* It could clearly be a term of the contract that Fondu corresponds to the description in the catalogue. Breach of such a term arises strictly without proof of fault. While damages for breach of contract are prima facie assessed on the basis of the expectation loss, and this clearly includes the loss in value, an additional complexity results from the possible application of section 53 of the

Sale of Goods Act 1979, which limits the damages, in this case drastically. However, the application of this section by the court is only discretionary. It should be noted that if the larger measure of loss of value is given, Fondu's owners would in effect be protected against the risk that any racehorse might prove unsuccessful and therefore depreciate in value. While heads (*c*)–(*e*) above are in the nature of expectation loss, they are, we noted, rather speculative in nature. Looked at contractually, it might also be hard to include the training fees as consequential loss, since such fees would have been incurred anyway.

2(*b*). *Misrepresentation*. Under the general heading of misrepresentation, it would appear that the statement in the catalogue is an actionable misrepresentation in the sense of being a statement of fact which induces the contract. It remains to consider what type of misrepresentation is at issue.

   (i) *Fraudulent misrepresentation*. It is hard to imagine that fraudulent behaviour would be a plausible explanation for what happened. Correctly described, Fondu was still a valuable horse and could have been sold. This is therefore discounted on a basis of claim.

   (ii) *Negligent misrepresentation*. More likely is the possibility of negligence on the part of the sellers, and indeed claiming under section 2(1) of the Misrepresentation Act 1967 has the distinct advantage over fraudulent misrepresentation of the reversal of the burden of proof and does not have more disadvantageous recovery rules. In relation to the loss of value, the task is to put the plaintiffs back in the position they would have been in if the tort had not been committed. This seems a clearer argument than under contract for allowing the larger measure of loss of value because section 53 of the Sale of Goods Act 1979 does not apply. Fraud remoteness rules apply, but even so it is difficult to conceive of recovery under the direct-consequences test of consequential loss beyond the training fees.

   (iii) *Innocent misrepresentation*. The availability of damages under the discretion of the court probably depends on rescission being available in principle. As the next section shows, this is doubtful. This would have applied if the sellers had been able to prove they were not negligent.

3. Returning the horse several years later in return for the purchase price is a desirable way of avoiding arguments about what is the 'real' loss in value. However, two difficulties arise. First, it is not clear that the buyers have any grounds for now undoing the contract. Second, there may be no grounds for recovering consequential loss.

3(*a*). *Rescission for misrepresentation.* While prima facie possible, it may well be that rescission is barred by either lapse of time (the period of time between the misrepresentation being made and the discovery of the defect) or affirmation (the choice of the buyer not to sue immediately upon discovery of the defect but to wait and see whether Fondu would make a point-to-point horse). Only the latter applies to fraudulent misrepresentation. The right to rescind for misrepresentation would not preclude a separate recovery of damages, although these would be discounted to prevent double recovery if rescission had taken place.

3(*b*). Is there a case for arguing mistake? Unilateral mistake is excluded, because the sellers do not know that the buyers are making a mistake. There is no mutual mistake, since objectively both parties are dealing with Fondu as described in the catalogue (we have discounted fraud, so at the most the sellers honourably but negligently believe in the description). There remains the possibility of claiming common mistake (dealt with in detail in Ch. 12). Both parties make the same mistake about a contingency (i.e. the possibility of misdescription) for which they have not planned. The problem is that there is probably only a mistake of quality, which does not suffice for mistake to be operative at common law, even though relief might be given in equity. In any case, there is little advantage to the buyer, since there is no basis for a claim of consequential loss once the contract is set aside.

Questions

1. What are the advantages and disadvantages of the adoption of an objective theory of contract formation in legal doctrine? Can an approach based on objectivity provide a complete and coherent account of formation mistake doctrine?

2. Look back through the cases which you have already studied in this book. Can you find any examples of narrative constructions of the type discussed by Jackson? If so, how, if at all, does his approach assist you in reaching a better understanding of these cases?

3. Do you agree with Balcombe LJ's decision in *Royscott Trust* v. *Rogerson* not to take a purposive approach to the interpretation of the Misrepresentation Act 1967? Would it have produced a more balanced decision if the court had refused to adopt the 'fiction of fraud' in the context of the remoteness rules?

4. Would an analysis of insurance contracts which started from the proposition that they were relational contracts lead to different conclusions

on the legal evaluation of the management of information to those adopted in *Banque Financière*? In what ways do insurance contracts differ from the paradigm of relational contract as elaborated by writers such as Macneil?

5. To what category of 'law-and-economics' scholarship would you assign Kronman's analysis of information? To what extent to you think it is vulnerable to the types of criticisms of law-and-economics scholarship outlined in Chapter 2?

6

Consideration and the Enforceability of Promises

I. INTRODUCTION

Our examination of *Tweddle* v. *Atkinson* ((1861) 1 B. 7 S. 393) in Chapter 1 indicated that not all promises are considered as binding by the law. Contract law requires that a promise should fulfil several formal criteria before it becomes binding. One of these criteria is examined in this chapter: consideration. The extract from Fuller below casts some light on the need for formal requirements as a threshold to enforceability.

A definition of consideration is provided by Lord Dunedin (himself quoting from Pollock, *Principles of Contract Law*, 13th edn., 133) in *Dunlop* v. *Selfridge* ([1915] AC 847 at 855): 'An act or forbearance of one party, or the promise thereof, is the price for which the promise of the other is bought, and the promise thus given for value is enforceable.' This enshrines the bargain principle of contract, a view propounded by some academics, such as C. J. Hamson, 'The Reform of Consideration' ((1938) 54 *LQR* 233).

Of all the enforceability criteria, consideration is the one which has given rise to most academic debate and discussion. The extracts in Sections II and III below indicate that not all contract scholars see consideration as inexorably linked to the bargain principle: Fried, for example, continues to argue—following on from the position extracted in Chapter 2—that promise is the basis of contract, and not bargain. He rejects bargain because he finds that it contains inherent contradictions centred on exchange and freedom of contract; for him, liability exists for the simple reason that the promisor has accepted that it does.

A quite different position is taken by Atiyah, who is of the view that foreseeable reliance on a promise is good consideration regardless of whether this reliance was requested by the promisor. The point being made here is one which has wider implications for contract law as a whole. The basis of the difference expressed is in the reason for enforcing promises: Atiyah sees the reason for enforcing promises as reliance on the promise and consequently the remedy for breach of promise as reliance damages—the position the plaintiff would have been in had the contract never been made; in contrast, Treitel sees the reason for enforcing promises as the expectation of the promisee and consequently the remedy for breach of the promise as expectation damages—the position the plaintiff would have been in had the contract been performed. This links the concept of consideration back to the key distinctions within the law of obligations discussed in Chapter 1. Much more is said about this in Chapter 14 on remedies; but it is important at this point to be aware of the expectation/reliance debate and its consequences.

The cases and secondary literature extracted below illustrate that, in addition to the continuing theoretical controversy as to the very nature of consideration, the debate in practice now centres on two main areas: the interplay between consideration and promissory estoppel and the definition of benefit over and above that already contractually promised.

A. Sufficiency and Adequacy

A range of legal principles surrounding consideration has been formulated over the last three centuries. The quotation from *Dunlop* v. *Selfridge* above refers to the 'forbearance on one party'; in some textbooks the definition of consideration is formulated as benefit and detriment—one party gives up something which is received as a benefit by the other party. Traditionally, the value which the promisee places upon the benefit is immaterial. The benefit has to be one which is within the legal definition of benefit; so, for example, 'natural affection' (see *White* v. *Bluett* (1853) 23 LJ Ex. 36) is not sufficient consideration. Contract law looks for sufficiency of consideration but not adequacy. Sufficiency of consideration requires the consideration to have some economic value, but the refusal to examine adequacy leaves the parties free to decide the precise nature of the consideration. Contract law looks for a bargain to be made but is uninterested by questions of the merits of the bargain (see *Chappell and Co. Ltd.* v. *Nestlé Co. Ltd.* [1960] AC 87).

B. Past Consideration

The terms 'executory' and 'executed' are important in relation to consideration. Executed consideration is the name given to the performance of the promise (including forbearance). An executory contract or consideration is an exchange of promises where performance has not yet occurred. In this situation, both parties to the contract can be viewed as promisor and promisee. Past consideration has to be distinguished from both of these situations. This is consideration given for a promise already made or performed, and it is not regarded as sufficient consideration (see *Roscorla* v. *Thomas* (1842) 3 QB 234).

C. Duty Situations

The case law can be grouped into three: (*a*) a promise to perform a duty imposed by law; (*b*) a promise to perform a duty already contractually owed; and (*c*) a promise to a third party to perform a duty already contractually owed.

In situation (*a*) it seems that, for reasons of public policy, a promise to perform a duty already imposed by law cannot be good consideration (see *Collins* v. *Godefroy* (1831) 1 B. & Ad. 950). In situation (*b*) the position is more complicated. The *locus classicus* position has always been that of *Stilk* v. *Myrick* ((1809) 2 Camp. 317, 6 Esp. 129), a case which, as leading textbooks point out, is capable of two interpretations, depending upon which report is used.

The Espinasse Report would appear to cast *Stilk* as a policy decision based on fears about the use of duress to obtain benefits over and above those already contractually promised. The Campbell report is much wider in its ambit, giving the reason for the decision as one of a failure to provide extra consideration over and above that already contractually promised. This is the approach that English law has favoured, and Gilmore (*The Death of Contract* (Columbus, Oh., Ohio State University Press, 1974), 22–8) provides a view on how the 'decision in *Stilk*' developed into the 'rule in *Stilk*'.

The fate of the Espinasse Report is rather ironic, as *Stilk* now has to be read in the light of *Williams* v. *Roffey Bros. & Nicholls (Contractors) Ltd.* ([1990] 1 All ER 512), extracted below in Section III, which would appear to suggest that an important question for the court in deciding whether something extra is being provided over and above that already contractually promised is whether or not there has been duress (see generally Ch. 9 and in particular the extracts from *Atlas Express* v. *Kafco* [1989] 1 All ER 641).

The adoption of Campbell's version of *Stilk* is consistent with the refusal of contract law to accept part payment of a debt as discharge of the whole amount due. The rule in *Pinnel's Case* ((1602) 5 Co. Rep. 117a) is that any discharge is not binding, as the debtor has not given consideration of the promise; consideration can be provided by paying the lesser amount earlier, by an altered mode of payment, or by providing something additional.

In situation (*c*) the rule appears to be that performance of an existing duty contractually owed to a third party is good consideration (see *Scotson* v. *Pegg* (1861) 6 H. & N. 295). It is hard to see any underlying policy reasons for the distinction between this situation and situation (*b*).

II. THEORIES OF CONSIDERATION

Perhaps more than any other doctrine of the law of contract, consideration operates as the litmus test of the position of any given commentator on the nature of the contractual obligation. Consequently, the extracts that follow build upon the introduction to the ideas of contractual obligation and the theories of contract presented in Chapters 1 and 2. The three dominant theories of 'bargain', 'reliance', and 'will/promise' are represented, as is an attempt to go beyond the traditional established theories by Barnett ('Rights and Remedies in a Consent Theory of Contract', in R. Frey and C. Morris (ed.), *Liability and Responsibility: Essays in Law and Morals* (Cambridge, Cambridge University Press, 1991). As we have commented in earlier chapters, it is not possible to draw strict lines to divide up contract theorists, and consequently it is important to remember that there are diverse opinions within broad strands of theory, and theorists whose work straddles the conventional boundaries.

A. Bargain Theories

C. J. Hamson, 'The Reform of Consideration', (1938) 54 *LQR* 233 at 234

What is today the significance of consideration in the law of simple contract? So far from being an additional and unnecessary mystery, an accidental tom-tit in an otherwise rational theory of contract, consideration in its essential nature is an aspect of the fundamental notion of bargain, other aspects of which, no less but no more important, are offer and acceptance. Consideration, offer and acceptance are an indivisible trinity, facets of one identical notion which is that of bargain. Indeed, consideration may conveniently be explained as merely the acceptance viewed from the offeror's side. Acceptance is defined to be the doing of that act (which may be the giving of a promise or the rendering of a performance) which is *requested* by the offeror in exchange for his promise; it is the *response* to the offer. An act done at the request of the offeror in response to his promise is consideration; and consideration in its essence is nothing else but response to such a request. To a gratuitous promise the common law notion of offer and acceptance does not apply. We can no doubt separate offer, acceptance and consideration for our convenience in treating of them: but they are logical and interdependent entities abstracted from the one entire reality which is bargain. We can no more abolish one without destroying the others than we can think of a circle without a circumference.

Notes

1. Hamson's view is illustrative of a bargain-based theory of consideration, evidenced by the paid-for promise. On that basis, it is relatively straightfor-

ward in principle to apply the doctrine of consideration in order to distinguish bargains from non-bargains (i.e. gratuitous promises). This is perhaps the orthodox view of consideration, at least in so far as it is propounded (often implicitly rather than explicitly) by the courts. It is closely linked to the protection of the expectation interest as the paradigm remedy for breach of contract. Like the other theories of consideration, of course, bargain theory is self-generating in its assertions, in the sense that it depends for the logic of its argument upon an assertion of the essence of contractual obligation, without necessarily stating why contractual obligation should arise in that form and only in that form.

2. Perhaps the most straightforward explanation is the following: contract law is intended to protect people's expectations, and expectations are engendered in the ordinary course of events by bargains. This is a view closely associated with the classical law of contract, linked to 'its ideology of autonomous agents striking their bargains in the market place', symbolizing the 'positive aspirations of liberal society itself' (R. Brownsword, 'Liberalism and the Law of Contract', *Archiv für Rechts- und Sozialphilosophie*, Beiheft 36 (1990), 86 at 86) with its emphasis upon the free choice of individuals. This view is represented in English law by commentators such as J. C. Smith, who calls consideration 'the price tag on the promise' (*The Law of Contract* (London, Sweet and Maxwell, 1993, 2nd edn.), 67 ff.). It is, however, above all in the USA that bargain theory has received close attention in what has been described as a 'rich normative literature emphasising the social utility of bargains' (C. Goetz and R. Scott, 'Enforcing Promises: An Examination of the Basis of Contract', (1980) 89 *Yale LJ* 1261 at 1282; see also E. Patterson, 'An Apology for Consideration', (1958) 58 *Colum. L. Rev.* 929). Bargain-based theory seeks to draw a distinction between onerous and non-onerous or donative transactions (e.g. gifts) which it dubs 'economically sterile' in that 'they do not serve, at least directly, to produce wealth' (A. von Mehren, 'A General View of Contract', *International Encyclopedia of Comparative Law* (Tübingen/The Hague, Mohr/Nijhoff, 1982), vol. vii, ch. 1, p. 22). Of course, as we shall see later, not all economists would agree that donative or gratuitous promises should not be enforceable simply because they are not bargains in the conventional sense (see Posner, below).

B. Reliance Theories

P. S. Atiyah, 'Contracts, Promises and the Law of Obligations', (1978) 94 *LQR* 193 at 201–3

Let me turn now to a more challenging question. To what extent is it true to say that contractual liabilities arise from agreement or promises or depend on the voluntary assumption of obligation? I want to begin by suggesting that the power of the classical model here derives largely from its stress on the executory contract. If two parties do exchange promises to carry out some performance at a future date, and if, immediately on the exchange of promises, a binding legal obligation comes at once into existence, then it seems inexorably to follow that the obligation is created by the agreement, by the intention of the parties. If they have done nothing to implement the agreement, if no actions have followed the exchange of promises, then manifestly the legal obligation cannot arise from anything except the exchange of promises. Thus far the classical model appears to be impregnable. But closer examination suggests that the area of impregnability is really rather small.

The first point to note is that wholly executory contracts are rarer, more ephemeral in practice, and somewhat less binding than the classical model of Contract would suggest. In the classical model as I have suggested, the executory transaction lies at the very heart of Contract. It is precisely because the classical model largely defines Contract in terms of executory transactions that it necessarily locates the source of contractual liability in what the parties intend rather than in what they do. But large numbers of contracts are regularly made in which the making and the performance, or at least part performance, are simultaneous or practically simultaneous events. Consider such simple transactions as the boarding of a bus, or a purchase of goods in a supermarket, or a loan of money. Is it really sensible to characterise these transactions as agreements or exchanges of promises? Is it meaningful or useful to claim that a person who boards a bus is promising to pay his fare? If so, would it not be just as meaningful to say that when he descends from the bus and crosses the road he promises to cross with all due care for the safety of other road users? I do not, of course, deny that all these transactions involve some element of voluntary conduct. People do not generally board buses, buy goods in a supermarket, or borrow money in their sleep. But they involve much else besides voluntary conduct. They usually involve the rendering of some benefit, or actions of detrimental reliance, or both. A person who is carried by a bus from point A to point B after voluntarily boarding the bus can normally be presumed to have derived some benefit from the arrangements. Does his liability to pay his fare have nothing to do with this element of benefit? A person who borrows money and actually receives the loan is, according to the classical model of Contract, liable to repay the money merely because he promised to repay it. The fact that he received the money appears to be largely irrelevant. It is not, indeed, wholly irrelevant in law, because of the doctrine of consideration, but in the classical model it is the intention or agreement or promise which is the source of the liability and not the consideration. The consideration is either a historical anachronism, a meaningless technicality, or if it has any rational function at all today, it is merely to provide evidence of the seriousness of a promise. Thus a person who borrows £100 is liable to repay it *because* he has promised; the actual receipt of the money is merely evidence of the seriousness of the promise. . . .

Consider next the possibility of detrimental reliance by the promise. Is it not manifest that a person who has actually worsened his position by reliance on a promise has a more powerful case for redress than one who has not acted in reliance on the promise at all? A person who has not relied on a promise (nor paid for it) may suffer a disappointment of his expectations, but he does not actually suffer a pecuniary loss. The disappointment of an expectation may of course be treated as a species of loss by definition, as indeed, the law generally does treat it, if the expectation derives from Contract. But no definitional jugglery can actually equate the position of the party who suffers a diminution of his assets in reliance on a promise, and a person who suffers no such diminution.

Notes

1. The concept of reliance has a long history in the law of contract. It can be dated back to the ancient common law action of assumpsit. Until the late eighteenth century courts espoused an 'equivalence approach' to value in contracts, enforcing only those which were substantively fair and protecting the reliance of the promisee. We do not know the exact process whereby consideration assumed its present doctrinal form, but we do know that a gap in the law emerged which left unprotected the unrequested reliance of the promisee upon a promise. Part of the key to the emergence of the executory contract as the paradigm form of contract can be found in the economic and social forces of the period. This assists us in setting Atiyah's work in its historical context.

2. In Chapter 2 we examined the 'classical' conception of contract best expressed by the work of Adam Smith and others who promoted the idea of a liberal, *laissez-faire* economic ideology supported by minimum state intervention in the realm of exchange but with strong support for the enforceability of bargains and for the protection of the buyer's expectation interest. Adam Smith's treatise *The Wealth of Nations* was published in 1776, during a period of rapid industrial expansion and consequent social change. As well as by those we now class as economists, the values of an individualistic model of contract were also assumed by utilitarians, such as Jeremy Bentham, who, if they addressed concepts such as contract at all, justified the classic model in terms of principles of utility. The central tenets of this classical model were a presumption that contract was the predominant form of relationship, that the parties to a contract enjoyed equality of bargaining power, and that agreement was based on free choice. These ideas lie behind both bargain theory and will theory.

As we indicated in Chapter 2 it was this model that Durkheim attacked by refuting a concept of contract that gave effect to an individualist, self-interested position rather than one which reflected social solidarity. To follow Durkheim requires recognition of inequality of bargaining power and regulation of the same. As a complete contrast, we saw that Weber's reaction to the classical model was to condemn it as too simplistic; it offered a model of society where expansion of markets was fed by freedom of contract. For Weber, freedom of contract could not occur without rules on property distribution and the use of those resources.

Atiyah (*The Rise and Fall of Freedom of Contract*, rev. edn. (Oxford, Oxford University Press, 1985), 4, 404 f.) uses the classical model of contract to illustrate the ascendency of expectation-based recovery and as evidence of the lack of development of reliance-based recovery. Atiyah argues that reliance loss, unless expressly bargained for, had no place in the dominant market-place culture of the day, and could not be recovered unless sought as the subject of an action in tort or restitution. He sees this period, which he identifies as 1770–1870, as the zenith of expectation-based liability in contract.

After 1870, Atiyah sees an upsurge in the recognition of reliance-based liability and recovery. As evidence of this he cites (*Rise and Fall*, 771 f., cited in Ch. 5 above) the development of reliance-based liabilities such as the Misrepresentation Act 1967 and the tort of negligent misstatement (e.g. *Esso Petroleum Ltd.* v. *Mardon* [1976] 2 All ER 5); these are used by Atiyah to illustrate the emergence of a model of contract based on recognition of unequal bargaining power, and the relational rather than the discrete nature of many contractual relationships. Perhaps most important for Atiyah is the establishment of actions founded on estoppel evidenced by reliance. The development of this action and its links with the traditional consideration model are examined in Sections IV and V. Other developments in contract law relied upon by Atiyah as evidencing the importance today of the reliance model are statutory interventions such as the Trade Descriptions Act 1968 and presumably also the Supply of Goods and Services Act 1982, although this is not expressly mentioned, all of which point away from the principle of 'buyer beware'. He also includes common law doctrines such as the imposition of liability for breach of implied terms.

Central to the idea of the growth of a model of contract based on reliance is the idea that contract is coming closer to the other two heads of civil obligation, tort and restitution, with all three now based on ideas of reliance and the reasonableness of that reliance—a theme we introduced in Chapter 1. Similar views on the subsuming of contract into the other reliance-based doctrines are expressed by writers such as Grant Gilmore (*The Death of Contract*, 90) and B. Reiter ('Contracts, Torts, Relations and Reliance', in Reiter and J. Swan (eds.), *Studies in Contract Law* (Toronto,

Butterworths, 1980)), who point to the decline of the true voluntary obligation in contract and the tendency within tort to focus on voluntary relationships (e.g. the 'special' relationship in the tort of negligent misstatement) in the duty context.

3. As we have seen, the problem with this view is that in recent years the courts have begun to swing back against this drawing together of obligations to recognize once more the unique nature of the voluntary obligation in contract. Often termed as the retreat from *Junior Books* v. *Veitchi* ([1983] 1 AC 520), this can be seen in cases such as *Pacific Associates Inc.* v. *Baxter* ([1989] 2 All ER 159) discussed in Chapter 1. In this case and a number of others the court asserted the primacy of the contractual obligation, and rejected the option of imposing a duty of care in tort where there is an underlying contractual structure.

C. Will Theories

In common with reliance theory, the will theory of contract sees little, if any, role for the doctrine of consideration. Fried, for example, considers whether consideration offers a rational alternative to his theory of promissory liability and concludes that it does not. It should be noted that will theorists are closely related to the bargain school, in the sense that both see contract law as upholding the expectations of the promisee, and both would endorse expectation damages as the primary remedy for breach of contract (see L. Fuller and W. Perdue, 'The Reliance Interest in Contract Damages', (1936) 46 *Yale LJ* 52). Recovery of expectation loss encourages exchange at the highest price. However, there is a distinction to be drawn between the two schools: where they differ is in their starting-point. For the will theorists, the reason for enforcing promises is internal, namely the promise itself. For the bargain theorists, the reason is external, namely the decision to enforce any bargains as binding contracts. The will theorists depend upon a moral principle of social ordering (people ought to keep their promises); the bargain theorists depend upon an economic principle of social ordering (paid-for promises constitute the core of the market order).

C. Fried, *Contract as Promise* (Cambridge, Mass., Harvard University Press, 1981), 29, 35–8

It is the doctrine of consideration that leads some to see contract as distinct from promise; it is consideration that leads people to say that promise may be all well and good as a ground of moral obligation, but the law is concerned with different and more serious business. What is this more serious business? One intuitive idea is that exchanges are enforced because one who welches on an exchange is a kind of cheat or thief: He has obtained a benefit and now refuses to pay for it. . . . this intuitive sense does not fit the facts—at least in the many cases of executory contracts where the "cheat" has not yet received anything in exchange for his promise except the "victim's" own promise. Where you have given in exchange for my promise nothing more than your own return promise, it is a bootstrap argument to reason that you must be allowed to recover because I by my breach appropriate to myself a value without rendering the agreed-upon exchange. The only value I have received or you given is just your promise, and so I benefit at your expense only on the premise that your promise is enforceable. But that premise is inadmissible in an argument designed to show that promises are enforceable only so far as necessary to prevent one party from deriving a one-sided benefit. This is not to say that exchanges of promises are not truly exchanges, only that the prevention of unjust enrichment cannot be the basis for enforcing such promissory exchanges. An analogous argument obtains to block the suggestion that the doctrine of consideration shows that the law of contracts is concerned not to enforce promises but to compensate harm suffered through reliance.

Exactly what kind of challenge does the doctrine of consideration pose to my thesis of contract as promise? If consideration implies a basis other than promise for contractual obligation, what exactly is that basis? To answer these questions and thus take the measure of the challenge, we must examine the present doctrine in some detail. The doctrine comprises two propositions: (A) The consideration that in law promotes a mere promise into a contractual obligation is something, or the promise of something, given in exchange for the promise. (B) The law is not at all interested in the adequacy of the consideration. The goodness of the exchange is for the parties alone to judge—the law is concerned only that there *be* an exchange. Thus the classic conception seeks to affirm both exchange and freedom of contract. . . .

I conclude that the standard doctrine of consideration . . . does not pose a challenge to my conception of contract law as rooted in promise, for the simple reason that that doctrine is too internally inconsistent to offer an alternative at all. The matrix of the inconsistency is just the conjunction of propositions A and B. Proposition B affirms the liberal principle that the free arrangements of rational persons should be respected. Proposition A, by limiting the class of arrangements to bargains, holds that individual self-determination is not a sufficient ground of legal obligation, and so implies that collective policies may after all override individual judgments, frustrating the projects of promisees after the fact and the potential projects of promisors. Proposition A is put forward as if it were neutral after all, leaving the parties their "freedom of contract." But there is a sense in which any promisor gets something for his promise, if only the satisfaction of being able to realize his purpose through the promise. Freedom of contract *is* freedom of promise, and, as my illustrations show, the intrusions of the standard doctrines of consideration can impose substantial if random restrictions on perfectly rational projects. . . .

. . . why is my enforceable promise to sell my brother-in-law my automobile less sterile than my promise to give it to my nephew? The law recognizes the *completed* transaction (after I actually hand over or sign over the automobile), presumably in recognition of my right to do with my property as I choose. In a sense the completed transaction in both cases is quite fertile enough: It is an expression of my will, it increases my satisfaction in some broad sense, and it does so by increasing the satisfaction of my nephew or brother-in-law. Both actual transfers are useful just in the sense that any freely chosen, significant act of mine is useful to me, and therefore is of net utility to society until it harms someone else. Allowing people to *make* gifts (let us assume freely, deliberately, reasonably) serves social utility by serving individual liberty. Given the preceding chapter's analysis of promise, there simply are no grounds for not extending that conclusion to *promises* to make gifts. I make a gift because it pleases me to do so. I promise to make a gift because I cannot or will not make a present transfer, but still wish to give you a (morally and legally) secure expectation.

I conclude that the life of contract is indeed promise, but this conclusion is not exactly a statement of positive law. There are too many gaps in the common law enforcement of promises to permit so bold a statement. My conclusion is rather that the doctrine of consideration offers no coherent alternative basis for the force of contracts, while still treating promise as necessary to it. Along the way to this conclusion I have made or implied a number of qualifications to my thesis. The promise must be freely made and not unfair. . . . It must also have been made rationally, deliberately. The promisor must have been serious enough that subsequent legal enforcement was an aspect of what he should have contemplated at the time he promised.

Notes

1. Fried accepts that his theory is not an explanation of the law as it presently stands, either in the USA or in England. However, his work finds support in proposals which have been made to abolish the doctrine of consideration and to replace it solely by a test of contractual intention or of formality (see Lord Wright, 'Ought the Doctrine of Consideration to be Abolished from the Common Law?', (1936) 49 *Harv L. Rev.* 1225; Sixth Interim Report (Statute of Frauds and the Doctrine of Consideration) of the Law Revision Committee, Cmd. 5449 (1937)). We dealt with the difficulties of applying a test of intention in Chapter 4, and the close relationship between consideration and formalities is addressed by Fuller and by Barnett below.

2. Fried himself does not propose unlimited enforcement of promises (see the last paragraph of the extract). He excludes so-called 'social promises'—the invitation to dinner, etc.—and bases his conclusion on a test of

'serious' intention. As with any test of this nature, serious evidentiary problems would arise in practice.

3. Closely related to Fried in his emphasis on the role of the will of the promisor is Posner, whose economic analysis of gratuitous promises is used here to illustrate his general position on the field of contract law occupied by the doctrine of consideration.

R. Posner, 'Gratuitous Promises in Economics and Law', (1977) 6 *J. Leg. St.* 411 at 411–12, 414–15

The Economics of "Gratuitous" Promises

Why would "economic man" ever make a promise without receiving in exchange something of value from the promisee, whether it be money, a promise of future performance beneficial to the promisor, or something else of value to him? It is tempting to answer this question simply by invoking "interdependent utilities." Since people may indeed derive utility or welfare from increases in the utility or welfare of family members, or for that matter of strangers, interdependence may explain why (some) gifts or transfers are made. But it cannot explain why a *promise* to make a transfer in the future is made. Promises, as distinct from transfers, seem related to situations of bilateral performance, of exchange. A promises B $25,000 in exchange for B's building a house for A. B will not build without a promise of payment in advance; A will not pay in advance without B's promise to build. But if A wanted merely to transfer $25,000 to B (his favorite charity), why would he *promise* B to make the transfer in the future? Why not wait until he is ready to make the transfer and just do it? The purpose of a promise seems to be to induce performance of some sort by the promisee; if reciprocal performance is not desired, there seems no reason to make a promise.

The approach taken here is that a gratuitous promise, to the extent it actually commits the promisor to the promised course of action (an essential qualification), creates utility for the promisor over and above the utility to him of the promised performance. At one level this proposition is a tautology: a promise would not be made unless it conferred utility on the promisor. The interesting question is how it does so. I shall argue that it does so by increasing the present value of an uncertain future stream of transfer payments.

To illustrate, suppose A promises to give $1000 a year for the next 20 years to the B symphony orchestra. The value of the gift to B is the discounted present value of $1000 to be paid yearly over a 20-year period in the future. Among the factors that will be used by B in discounting these expected future receipts to present value is the likelihood that at some time during the 20-year period A will discontinue the annual payments. Depending on B's estimation of A's fickleness, income prospects, etc., the present value of the gift of $1000 a year may be quite small; it may not be much more than $1000. But suppose the gift is actually worth more to B because A is certain to continue the payments throughout the entire period, though this fact is not known to B. If A can make a binding promise to continue the payments in accordance with his intention, B will revalue the gift at its true present worth. The size of the gift (in present-value terms) will be increased at no cost to A. Here is a clear case where the enforcement of a gratuitous promise would increase net social welfare. . . .

Optimal Rules for Enforcing "Gratuitous" Promises

The analysis in Part I may seem to imply that *all* promises, whether compensated or "gratuitous," should be enforced; or at least that enforceability should not depend on whether the promise is one or the other. The second implication has, as we shall see, appeal; but the first is questionable because it ignores the costs to the legal system of enforcing promises. The design of optimal rules of substantive law must always take into account the costs of enforcement. Promises should not be enforced where the enforcement cost—to the extent not borne by the promisor—exceeds the gain from enforcement. The qualification is, of course, essential: if the promisor bore the full costs of enforcement, it would be a matter of indifference to society whether he chose to make enforceable a promise that seemed to confer on him but trivial utility relative to enforcement costs. But it is in fact unlikely—quite apart from the public subsidy of the court system—that such a promisor would bear those costs fully: if he reneged on his promise, and the promisee brought suit against him, the promisor would not be required to defray the promisee's costs of suit. Another category of enforcement costs that are not fully internalized consists of the costs of legal error. Here the focus is not on the promisor but on the mistaken or dishonest "promisee" who imposes on his "promisor" the costs of defending a groundless suit, at the same time incurring litigation costs of his own which have no social value either.

The question whether it is economical for society to recognize a promise as legally enforceable thus requires a comparison of the utility of the promise to the promisor with the social cost of enforcing the promise. The utility of a "gratuitous" promise (a term I shall continue to use for the sake of convenience) would seem to depend primarily on (1) the size of the promised transfer and (2) the optimal length of the period for completing the transfer (the longer the period, the greater will be the loss of utility from having to substitute an immediate transfer if the promise is not enforceable). The social costs of enforcing the promise depend first of all on the administrative costs of enforcement. These in turn are a function in part of the size of the promised transfer, for expenditures on litigation are an investment in its outcome and therefore tend to be larger, the greater the stakes in the litigation. The social costs of enforcement also depend on the likelihood of an error—*e.g.*, of finding a promise where none in fact was made.

The criteria developed above should probably be applied to *categories* of promises, rather than to individual promises on a case-by-case basis. Great (and costly!) uncertainty would be created if a gratuitous promisor, in order to know whether his promise was enforceable, would have to predict how a court would apply the criteria directly to the circumstances in which the promise was made.

Note

Posner's analysis represents an assessment of cost v. benefit which compares the social utility generated by the autonomous exercise of will with the costs of enforcement. In J. Gordley's words, 'any disposition of property should be deemed valuable simply because the owner has chosen it, whether he chooses to use the property himself, to give it away, or to destroy it' (*The Philosophical Origins of Modern Contract Doctrine* (Oxford, Clarendon Press, 1991), 238).

D. Consent Theory

In the next extract, Barnett provides an alternative paradigm—'consent'—which, he argues, overcomes the weakness of the other theories. Like the will theorists, Barnett begins with the intention of the promisor to be bound to a transfer of rights based on contract, but distances himself from their arguments by pointing out the difficulties of reconciling will theory with the judicial practice of recognizing objectively manifested agreements which conflict with the subjective intentions of the parties (see the Objective Theory of Contract, discussed in Ch. 5). Under consent theory, the parties are bound by *manifested* intent.

Barnett, 'Rights and Remedies in a Consent Theory of Contract', in R. Frey and C. Morris (eds.), *Liability and Responsibility: Essays in Law and Morals* (Cambridge, Cambridge University Press, 1991), 135 at 148–52

In a consent theory . . . proof of consent to transfer alienable rights is legally sufficient to establish the existence of a contractual obligation. Consent is prima facie binding both because of its usual connection with subjective assent (which protects the autonomy of the promisor) and because people usually have access only to the manifested intentions of others (which protects the reliance of the promisee and others as well as the security of transactions). There are two ways to manifest one's intention to be legally bound. The first is to deliberately "channel" one's behavior through the use of a legal formality in such a way as to convey explicitly a certain meaning—that of having an intention to be legally bound—to another. This is the formal means of consenting. The second and, perhaps, more common method is by indirectly or implicitly conveying this meaning by other types of behavior. This is the informal means of consenting.

Formal consent.

For a considerable part of the history of the common law, the principal way of creating what we now think of as a contractual obligation was to cast one's agreement in the form of a sealed writing. The emergence of assumpsit as the principal action of contractual enforcement required the development of a doctrinal limitation on the enforcement of commitments—that is, the doctrine of consideration. This development eventually resulted in the ascendancy of the bargain theory of consideration, which had the unintended consequence of creating doctrinal problems for the enforcement of formal commitments where there was no bargained-for consideration. Notwithstanding their ancient history, formal commitments, such as those under seal, came to be thought of as "exceptions" to the "normal" requirement of consideration. Expressions such as "a seal imports consideration" or is "a substitute for consideration" became commonplace. In a climate of opinion dominated by notions of "bargained-for consideration" and "induced reliance," when there is no bargain and no demonstrable reliance to support enforcement, formal promises have had an uncertain place in the law of contract.

A consent theory of contract, however, provides the missing theoretical foundation of formal contracts and explains their proper place in a well-crafted law of contract. The voluntary use of a recognized formality by a promisor manifests to a promisee an intention to be legally bound in the most unambiguous manner possible. . . .

The same holds true for nominal consideration and for false recitals of consideration. A consent theory acknowledges that, if properly evidenced, the exchange of one dollar or a false recital by the parties that consideration exists may fulfill the channeling function of formalities, whether or not any bargained-for consideration for the commitment in fact exists. If it is widely known that the written phrase "in return for good and valuable consideration" means that one intends to make a legally binding commitment, then these words will fulfill a channeling function as well as, and perhaps better than, a seal or other formality. . . .

Informal consent.

. . . The enforcement of informal commitments where evidence of legally binding intentions is more obscure, however, has plagued contract law for centuries. . . .

Bargaining as evidence of consent.

Within a consent theory, the fact that a person has received something of value in return for a promise may indeed indicate that this promise was an expression of intention to transfer rights. Moreover, in some circumstances where gratuitous transfers are unusual, the receipt of a benefit in return for a promise should serve as objective notice to the promisor that the promise has been interpreted by the other party to be legally binding.

Although the existence of a bargain or other motivation for a transaction may be good evidence of the sort of agreement that has been made, in a consent theory the absence of consideration does not preclude the application of legal sanctions if other indicia of consent are present. So if it can be proved, for example, that a party voluntarily consented to be legally bound to keep an offer to transfer rights open, to release a debt, to modify an obligation, or to pay for past favors, the lack of bargained-for consideration will not bar enforcement of these kinds of commitments in a consent theory. . . .

Reliance as evidence of consent.

A consent theory also identifies those circumstances where the presence of reliance provides an adequate substitute for the traditional requirement of consideration. . . . Expenditures made by a promisee in reliance on the words and conduct of the promisor may prove as much about the nature of this transaction as the existence of consideration, especially where the reliance is or should be known to the promisor.

E. Consideration and Formalities

Some of the issues concerning the relationship between consideration and formalities are discussed in more detail by Fuller.

L. Fuller, 'Consideration and Form', (1941) 41 *Colum. L. Rev.* 799 at 799–806

That consideration may have both a "formal" and a "substantive" aspect is apparent when we reflect on the reasons which have been advanced why promises without consideration are not enforced. It has been said that consideration is "for the sake of evidence" and is intended to remove the hazards of mistaken or perjured testimony which would attend the enforcement of promises for which nothing is given in exchange. Again, it is said that enforcement is denied gratuitous promises because such promises are often made impulsively and without proper deliberation. In both these cases the objection relates, not to the content and effect of the promise, but to the manner in which it is made. Objections of this sort, which touch the form rather than the content of the agreement, will be removed if the making of the promise is attended by some formality or ceremony, as by being under seal. On the other hand, it has been said that the enforcement of gratuitous promises is not an object of sufficient importance to our social and economic order to justify the expenditure of the time and energy necessary to accomplish it. Here the objection is one of "substance" since it touches the significance of the promise made and not merely the circumstances surrounding the making of it. . . .

The Functions Performed by Legal Formalities

The Evidentiary Function.—The most obvious function of a legal formality is, to use Austin's words, that of providing "evidence of the existence and purport of the contract, in case of controversy." The need for evidentiary security may be satisfied in a variety of ways: by requiring a writing, or attestation, or the certification of a notary. . . .

The Cautionary Function.—A formality may also perform a cautionary or deterrent function by acting as a check against inconsiderate action. The seal in its original form fulfilled this purpose remarkably well. The affixing and impressing of a wax wafer—symbol in the popular mind of legalism and weightiness—was an excellent device for inducing the circumspective frame of mind appropriate in one pledging his future. To a less extent any requirement of a writing, of course, serves the same purpose, as do requirements of attestation, notarization, etc.

The Channeling Function.—Though most discussions of the purposes served by formalities go no further than the analysis just presented, this analysis stops short of recognizing one of the most important functions of form. That a legal formality may perform a function not yet described can be shown by the seal. The seal not only insures a satisfactory memorial of the promise and induces deliberation in the making of it. It serves also to mark or signalize the enforceable promise; it furnishes a simple and external test of enforceability. . . .

Interrelations of the Three Functions. . . . it is obvious that there is an intimate connection between [the three functions of legal form]. Generally speaking, whatever tends to accomplish one of these purposes will also tend to accomplish the other two. He who is compelled to do something which will furnish a satisfactory memorial of his intention will be induced to deliberate. Conversely, devices which induce deliberation will usually have an evidentiary value. Devices which insure evidence or prevent inconsiderateness will normally advance the desideratum of channeling, in two different ways. In the first place, he who is compelled to formulate his intention carefully will tend to fit it into legal and business categories. In this way the party is induced to canalize his own intention. In the second place, wherever the requirement of a formality is backed by the sanction of the invalidity of the informal transaction (and this is the means by which requirements of form are normally made effective), a degree of channeling results automatically. Whatever may be its legislative motive, the formality in such a case tends to effect a categorization of transactions into legal and non-legal. . . .

When are Formalities Needed? The Effect of an Informal Satisfaction of the Desiderata Underlying the Use of Formalities . . . In what situations does good legislative policy demand the use of a legal formality? One part of the answer to the question is clear at the outset. Forms must be reserved for relatively important transactions. We must preserve a proportion between means and end; it will scarcely do to require a sealed and witnessed document for the effective sale of a loaf of bread.

But assuming that the transaction in question is of sufficient importance to support the use of a form if a form is needed, how is the existence of this need to be determined? A general answer would run somewhat as follows: *The need for investing a particular transaction with some legal formality will depend upon the extent to which the guaranties that the formality would afford are rendered superfluous by forces native to the situation out of which the transaction arises*—including in these "forces" the habits and conceptions of the transacting parties.

Whether there is any need, for example, to set up a formality designed to induce deliberation will depend upon the degree to which the factual situation, innocent of any legal remolding, tends to bring about the desired circumspective frame of mind. An example from the law of gifts will make this point clear. To accomplish an effective gift of a chattel without resort to the use of documents, delivery of the chattel is ordinarily required and mere donative words are ineffective. It is thought, among other things, that mere words do not sufficiently impress on the donor the significance and seriousness of his act. . . .

So far as the channeling function of a formality is concerned it has no place where men's activities are already divided into definite, clear-cut business categories. Where life has already organized itself effectively, there is no need for the law to intervene. It is for this reason that important transactions on the stock and produce markets can safely be carried on in the most "informal" manner. At the other extreme we may cite the negotiations between a house-to-house book salesman and the housewife. Here the situation may be such that the housewife is not certain whether she is being presented with a set of books as a gift, whether she is being asked to trade her letter of recommendation for the books, whether the books are being offered to her on approval, or whether—what is, alas, the fact—a simple sale of the books is being proposed. The ambiguity of the situation is, of course, carefully cultivated and exploited by the canvasser. Some "channeling" here would be highly desirable, though whether a legal form is the most practicable means of bringing it about is, of course, another question.

Notes

1. For a review of alternatives to consideration, see E. Patterson, 'An Apology for Consideration', (1958) 58 *Colum. L. Rev.* 929 at 956.

2. As regards other ways of fulfilling the channelling function of form, see now the development of a distinctive 'consumer law'. In the context of consumer protection, informality is less willingly tolerated, and legislative

regulation has taken a number of interesting forms other than the restrictions on 'house-to-house' sales hinted at in Fuller's final paragraph.

For example, statute has created the category of 'cancellable agreements': these are certain credit and hire agreements which, during a statutorily prescribed 'cooling-off period' can be terminated unilaterally by the debtor or hirer by giving notice to the other party (ss 67 f. of the Consumer Credit Act 1974). A cancellable agreement is one made off trade premises (typically in the home of the debtor/hirer), following antecedent oral negotiations involving representations made by the creditor or his agent to the debtor or a relative.

The effect of statute intervening in this manner is to police not the bargain itself but the context in which it is formed. The limits of consumer protection are policing the formation of the bargain, not regulating the price paid for the bargain. For further techniques of consumer protection, see further Part III especially Ch. 11.

III. FINDING CONSIDERATION

A. Introduction

In the previous section, we have seen how the concept of consideration interacts with core theoretical debates within the law of contract. For the law student, in contrast, the study of consideration is less the analysis of theoretical debate and more the elaborate game of doctrinal hide-and-seek entitled 'finding consideration'. This section begins with extracts by Atiyah and Treitel, from their respective textbooks, which shed light upon the role of the court in the search for consideration. It should be noted that, for Atiyah, in this doctrinal rather than theoretical contract, consideration is simply a reason for enforcing promises (see 'Consideration: A Restatement', in *Essays on Contract* (Oxford, Oxford University Press, 1986), 241). This is a position he broadly shares with a number of US theorists (see A. Corbin, 'Does a Pre-existing Duty Defeat Consideration?', (1917–18) 27 *Yale LJ* 362). In the extract, however, he acknowledges the continued vitality, if inconsistency, of the juristic concept of consideration, and the fact that the student must take as an act of faith the differences in treatment accorded by courts to gratuitous or quasi-gratuitous promises. Treitel offers the notion of 'invented' consideration to fulfil much the same role, and although this notion has encountered criticism from Atiyah himself (see *Essays*, 181–3), both writers point to the difficulties faced by students in trying to reconcile cases such as *Shadwell* v. *Shadwell* ((1860) 9 CBNS 159) and *Offord* v. *Davies* ((1862) 12 CBNS 748).

These extracts are followed by a brief review by Karl Llewellyn of what he calls the 'troublesome classes' of case, where the concept of consideration presents difficulties to the courts. Although Llewellyn's analysis was addressed to the state of US law in the 1930s, it still largely holds true for English law in the 1990s.

P. S. Atiyah, *An Introduction of the Law of Contract,* 4th edn. (Oxford, Clarendon Press, 1989), 134–7

In 1839 it was held that the surrender of a document which turned out to be legally invalid and of no inherent value was good consideration for a promise to pay £9,600. If the defendant chose to promise this enormous sum for a valueless piece of paper that (according to the court) was his business. In 1908 it was held that a newspaper which published readers' queries together with their own replies derived sufficient benefit to support an implied promise to take reasonable care in their reply. In a more recent case chocolate manufacturers offered a gramophone record to anyone who sent in some 50 odd pence and three chocolate wrappers; it was held that the wrappers (though worthless and thrown away on receipt) involved some benefit to the manufacturers and were part of the consideration. So it seems that anything should be a good consideration if it is judged so by the promisor who wants it.

But this leads to a contradiction or inconsistency in the law. Obviously, in one sense, any person who makes a promise does so, if he is a rational being, because he thinks that making the promise will be preferable to not making it, or (as an economist might say) because making the promise makes him better off. Even a gratuitous promise is made for some *reason* which seems a good enough reason to the promisor. But if *any* reason for making a promise were recognized as a good consideration on these grounds, this would be tantamount to abolition of the entire doctrine. And, indeed, there are some modern theorists, who, in their renewed faith in classical principles, wish to go this far, and insist that the present law is fundamentally inconsistent. But the law itself continues to recognize that the doctrine of consideration exists, so this will not do. The mere fact that the promisor thought it worth his while, thought it desirable, to make a promise, is not enough to show that it is given for good consideration. It must be shown that a consideration has some real 'value'. . . .

[After an analysis of a number of inconsistent cases on 'economic value' such as *White* v. *Bluett* ((1853) 23 LJ Ex. 36) and *Ward* v. *Byham* ([1956] 1 WLR 496), Atiyah concludes that]

[I]t does not seem possible to insist that consideration must always be of economic value, or is it possible to say that anything of economic value can be a good consideration. And it is very doubtful if any other general rule can be found which can reconcile the apparent inconsistencies in the law. It must simply be recognized that certain gratuitous promises (such as promises to charities, or promises to make gifts to members of the promisor's family) are likely to be treated as without consideration (at any rate unless they are relied upon to the detriment of the promisee), while other promises of little or no economic value may be treated as valid because the promisor is deemed to be capable of deciding for himself what something is worth. So, too, there are a number of technical rules concerning the sufficiency of consideration in special circumstances, which will be considered below, which preclude any easy attempt at reconciliation with some universal rule as to the value of consideration.

G. Treitel, *The Law of Contract*, 8th ed. (London, Sweet and Maxwell, 1991), 67

Invented consideration

Normally, a party enters into a contract with a view to obtaining the consideration provided by the other: for example, the buyer wants the goods and the seller the price. In the United States it has been said that this is essential, and that "Nothing is consideration that is not regarded as such by both parties."[1] But English courts do not insist on this requirement and often regard an act or forbearance as the consideration for a promise even though it may not have been the object of the promisor to secure it. They may also regard the possibility of some prejudice to the promisee as a detriment without regard to the question whether it has in fact been suffered. These practices may be called "inventing consideration," and the temptation to adopt one or the other of them is particularly strong when the act or forbearance which was actually bargained for cannot be regarded as consideration for some reason which is thought to be technical and without merit. In such cases the practice of inventing consideration may help to make the operation of the doctrine of consideration more acceptable; but the practice may also be criticised[2] on the ground that it gives the courts a wide discretion to hold promises binding (or not) as they please. Thus the argument that the promisee *might* have suffered prejudice by acting in reliance on a promise is in some cases made a basis of decision,[3]

---

[1] *Philpot* v. *Gruninger*, 14 Wall, 570, 577 (1872); Restatement, *Contracts* § 75(1); Restatement *Contracts 2d* § 71(1) and (2); Williston, *Contracts* (rev. ed.), Vol. 1, at p. 320; Corbin, *Contracts*, § 172, is more sceptical. The Restatement, *Contracts* 2d § 72 also supports the converse proposition, *viz.* that anything is consideration if it is bargained for, even if there is no element of benefit or detriment; but this is subject to important exceptions, especially where what is bargained for is the performance of an existing duty or the settlement of an invalid claim: §§ 73, 74. . . .

[2] Holmes, *The Common Law*, p. 292. In the United States there is less need to invent consideration because of the existence of a broad doctrine of promissory estoppel: see Restatement, *Contracts*, and *Contracts 2d*, § 90.

[3] *Shadwell* v. *Shadwell* (1860) 9 C.B. (n.s.) 159, 174: the consideration was said by Erle C.J. to consist of the possibility that the promisor "*may* have made a most material change in his position . . ."

while in others precisely the same argument is rejected.[1] The courts have not been very consistent in the exercise of this discretion and its existence is a source of considerable uncertainty in this branch of the law.

Note

See further on the Atiyah/Treitel debate: Atiyah, *Consideration in Contracts: A Fundamental Restatement* (Canberra, Australian University Press, 1971); Treitel, 'Consideration: A Critical Analysis of Professor Atiyah's Fundamental Restatement', (1976) *50 Aust. LJ* 439; Atiyah, 'Consideration: A Restatement', in *Essays on Contract* (Oxford, Clarendon Press, 1986).

K. Llewellyn, 'What Price Contract? An Essay in Perspective', (1931) 40 *Yale LJ* 704 at 742

Four troublesome classes of cases remain. There are business promises such as "firm offers," understood to be good for a fixed time, but revoked before. They are frequent; they are and should be relied on. As to them our consideration doctrine is badly out of joint. Closely related in orthodox doctrine, less so in practice, is the second class: promises which call for acceptance by extended action (such as laying twenty miles of track), revoked while the work is in process. A third and hugely important class is that of either additional or modifying business promises made after an original deal has been agreed upon. Law and logic go astray whenever such dealings are regarded as truly comparable to new agreements. They are not. No business man regards them so. They are going-transaction adjustments, as different from agreement-formation as are corporate organization and corporate management; and the line of legal dealing with them which runs over waiver and estoppel is based on sound intuition. The fourth main trouble-making class has only a doctrinal connection with business; it lies chiefly in the field of family affairs; it includes the promise made and relied on, but which did not bargain for reliance, and in the case of promises to provide it laps over into the third party beneficiary problem. As to all of these classes but the first, a distinct but very uneven tendency is observable in the courts to strain by one dodge or another toward enforcement. That tendency is healthy. It may be expected to increase. It has already had some effects on orthodox doctrine, and may be expected to have more.

Notes

1. For an analysis of firm offers, see Chapter 4, Section IV, E. Unilateral contracts are also touched upon in that chapter, although the difficulties

---

[1] In *Offord* v. *Davies* (1862) 12 C.B. (n.s.) 748: the argument of counsel (at p. 750) that "the plaintiff *might* have altered his position in consequence of the guarantee" was rejected. Erle C.J. being again a member of the court.

which they raise for the doctrine of consideration are not considered there. Family arrangements likewise appear in Chapter 4, Section II. The doctrines of promissory and proprietary estoppel, dealt with in Sections IV and V, are also relevant in this context.

2. To the extent that applying the doctrine of consideration to the modifications of contractual relationships produces results which are unpredictable and contrary to business practice, it is dysfunctional and, arguably, should be abandoned. For a Canadian perspective on the same problem, see B. Reiter, 'Courts, Consideration and Common Sense' ((1977) 27 *U Toronto LJ* 439). The remainder of this section is devoted to a detailed case-study of the process of finding consideration in the context of the modification of pre-existing contractual relationships where one party is merely reaffirming his or her willingness to perform while seeking improved performance from the other side. The shift from *Stilk* v. *Myrick* to *Williams* v. *Roffey* (below) demonstrates that the process of 'finding' consideration cannot operate in isolation from other factors such as the nature of the relationship being varied, and the evolution of other contractual doctrines such as duress.

Stilk v. Myrick
(1809) 2 Camp. 317 (see also 6 Esp. 129; 170 Eng. Rep. 1168).

This was an action for seaman's wages, on a voyage from London to the Baltic and back.

By the ship's articles, executed before the commencement of the voyage, the plaintiff was to be paid at the rate of £5 a month; and the principal question in the cause was, whether he was entitled to a higher rate of wages?—In the course of the voyage two of the seamen deserted; and the captain having in vain attempted to supply their places at Cronstadt, there entered into an agreement with the rest of the crew, that they should have the wages of the two who had deserted equally divided among them, if he could not procure two other hands at Gottenburgh. This was found impossible; and the ship was worked back to London by the plaintiff and eight more of the original crew, with whom the agreement had been made at Cronstadt.

Garrow for the defendant insisted, that this agreement was contrary to public policy, and utterly void. In West India voyages, crews are often thinned greatly by death and desertion; and if a promise of advanced wages were valid, exorbitant claims would be set up on all such occasions. This ground was strongly taken by Lord Kenyon in *Harris* v. *Watson*, Peak. Cas. 72, where that learned Judge held, that no action would lie at the suit of a sailor on a promise of a captain to pay him extra wages, in consideration of his doing more than the ordinary share of duty in navigating the ship; and his Lordship said, that if such a promise could be enforced, sailors would in many cases suffer a ship to sink unless the captain would accede to any extravagant demand they might think proper to make. . . .

LORD ELLENBOROUGH.—I think *Harris* v. *Watson* was rightly decided; but I doubt whether the ground of pubic policy, upon which Lord Kenyon is stated to have proceeded, be the true principle on which the decision is to be supported. Here, I say, the agreement is void for want of consideration. There was no consideration for the ulterior pay promised to the mariners who remained with the ship. Before they sailed from London they had undertaken to do all that they could under all the emergencies of the voyage. They had sold all their services till the voyage should be completed. If they had been at liberty to quit the vessel at Cronstadt, the case would have been quite different; or if the captain had capriciously discharged the two men who were wanting, the others might not have been compellable to take the whole duty upon themselves, and their agreeing to do so might have been a sufficient consideration for the promise of an advance of wages. But the desertion of a part of the crew is to be considered an emergency of the voyage as much as their death; and those who remain are bound by the terms of their original contract to exert themselves to the utmost to bring the ship in safety to her destined port. Therefore, without looking to the policy of this agreement, I think it is void for want of consideration, and that the plaintiff can only recover at the rate of £5 a month.

Note

For an interesting view of the construction of the 'rule in *Stilk* v. *Myrick*, see G. Gilmore, *The Death of Contract*, 22–8.

Williams v. *Roffey Bros. & Nicholls (Contractors) Ltd.*
[1990] 1 All ER 512

The defendants were a large firm of building contractors who had entered into a contract to refurbish a block of flats. They subcontracted the carpentry work to the plaintiff for £20,000. The plaintiff soon found himself in difficulties: partly because of pricing the work too low in the first place and partly because of poor supervision of his work-force, the plaintiff had received some 80 per cent of the subcontract price but had completed only 20 per cent of the work. The defendants were aware of both of the plaintiff's problems, and were anxious for him to finish. In the event that he defaulted on the contract or was late in completing the work, the defendants would become liable to the flats' owner on a liquidated damages clause. The defendants offered the plaintiff a bonus of some £10,000, a proportion of which was payable on the completion of each flat. The plaintiff completed eight of the remaining flats but did not receive all the bonus that had been promised. The plaintiff stopped work and sued for the out-

standing bonus. The defendants relied upon the plaintiff's existing contractual obligation as a defence to non-payment of the bonus. The Court of
Appeal found in the plaintiff's favour.

GLIDEWELL LJ It is common ground that by the end of March 1986 the plaintiff
was in financial difficulty. The judge found that there were two reasons for this,
namely: (i) that the agreed price of £20,000 was too low to enable the plaintiff to
operate satisfactorily and at a profit. Mr Cottrell, a surveyor employed by the
defendants, said in evidence that a reasonable price for the works would have
been £23,783; (ii) that the plaintiff failed to supervise his workmen adequately. . . .

*Was there consideration for the defendant's promise made on 9 April 1986 to pay an
additional price at the rate of £575 per completed flat?*

The judge made the following findings of fact which are relevant on this
issue. (i) The sub-contract price agreed was too low to enable the plaintiff to
operate satisfactorily and at a profit. Mr Cottrell, the defendants' surveyor,
agreed that this was so. (ii) Mr Roffey, the managing director of the defendants,
was persuaded by Mr Cottrell that the defendants should pay a bonus to the
plaintiff. The figure agreed at the meeting on 9 April 1986 was £10,300.

The judge quoted and accepted the evidence of Mr Cottrell to the effect that
a main contractor who agrees too low a price with a sub-contractor is acting
contrary to his own interests. He will never get the job finished without paying
more money.

The judge therefore concluded:

'In my view where the original sub-contract price is too low, and the parties subsequently agree that the additional moneys shall be paid to the sub-contractor, this agreement is in the interests of both parties. This is what happened in the present case, and in
my opinion the agreement of 9 April 1986 does not fail for lack of consideration.'

Counsel for the defendants relies on the principle of law which, traditionally,
is based on the decision in *Stilk* v *Myrick*. . . .

In *North Ocean Shipping Co Ltd v Hyundai Construction Co Ltd, The Atlantic
Baron* [1979] QB 705 Mocatta J regarded the general principle of the decision
in *Stilk* v *Myrick* as still being good law. He referred to two earlier decisions of
this court, dealing with wholly different subjects, in which Denning LJ sought to
escape from the confines of the rule, but was not accompanied in this attempt
by the other members of the court.

In *Ward* v *Byham* [1956] 1 WLR 496 the plaintiff and the defendant lived
together unmarried for five years, during which time the plaintiff bore their
child. After the parties ended their relationship, the defendant promised to pay
the plaintiff £1 per week to maintain the child, provided that she was well
looked after and happy. The defendant paid this sum for some months, but
ceased to pay when the plaintiff married another man. On her suing for the

amount due at £1 per week, he pleaded that there was no consideration for his agreement to pay for the plaintiff to maintain her child, since she was obliged by law to do so . . . . The county court judge upheld the plaintiff mother's claim, and this court dismissed the defendant's appeal.

Denning LJ said ([1956] 1 WLR 496 at 498):

'I approach the case, therefore, on the footing that, in looking after the child, the mother is only doing what she is legally bound to do. Even so, I think that there was sufficient consideration to support the promise. I have always thought that a promise to perform an existing duty, or the performance of it, should be regarded as good consideration, because it is a benefit to the person to whom it is given. Take this very case. It is as much a benefit for the father to have the child looked after by the mother as by a neighbour. If he gets the benefit for which he stipulated, he ought to honour his promise, and he ought not to avoid it by saying that the mother was herself under a duty to maintain the child. I regard the father's promise in this case as what is sometimes called a unilateral contract, a promise in return for an act, a promise by the father to pay £1 a week in return for the mother's looking after the child. Once the mother embarked on the task of looking after the child, there was a binding contract. So long as she looked after the child, she would be entitled to £1 a week.'

However, Morris LJ put it rather differently. He said ([1956] 1 WLR 496 at 498–499):

'Counsel for the father submits that there was a duty on the mother to support the child, that no affiliation proceedings were in prospect or were contemplated, and that the effect of the arrangement that followed the letter was that the father was merely agreeing to pay a bounty to the mother. It seems to me that the terms of the letter negative those submissions, for the father says: "providing you can prove that [the child] will be well looked after and happy and also that she is allowed to decide for herself whether or not she wishes to come and live with you." The father goes on to say that the child is then well and happy and looking much stronger than ever before. "If you decide what to do let me know as soon as possible". It seems to me, therefore, that the father was saying, in effect: Irrespective of what may be the strict legal position, what I am asking is that you shall prove that the child will be well looked after and happy, and also that you must agree that the child is to be allowed to decide for herself whether or not she wishes to come and live with you. If those conditions were fulfilled the father was agreeable to pay. On those terms, which in fact became operative, the father agreed to pay £1 a week. In my judgment, there was ample consideration there to be found for his promise, which I think was binding.'

Parker LJ agreed. As I read the judgment of Morris LJ, he and Parker LJ held that, though in maintaining the child the plaintiff was doing no more than she was obliged to do by law, nevertheless her promise that the child would be well looked after and happy was a practical benefit to the father, which amounted to consideration for his promise.

[The second case discussed is *Williams* v. *Williams* [1957] 1 WLR 148.]

There is, however, another legal concept of relatively recent development which is relevant, namely that of economic duress. Clearly, if a sub-contractor has agreed to undertake work at a fixed price, and before he has completed the work declines to continue with it unless the contractor agrees to pay an increased price, the sub-contractor may be held guilty of securing the contractor's promise by taking unfair advantage of the difficulties he will cause if he does not complete the work. In such a case an agreement to pay an increased price may well be voidable because it was entered into under duress. Thus this concept may provide another answer in law to the question of policy which has troubled the courts since before *Stilk v Myrick* and no doubt led at the date of that decision to a rigid adherence to the doctrine of consideration.

This possible application of the concept of economic duress was referred to by Lord Scarman, delivering the judgment of the Judicial Committee of the Privy Council in *Pao On v Lau Yiu* ([1980] AC 614 at 632). He said:

'Their Lordships do not doubt that a promise to perform, or the performance of, a pre-existing contractual obligation to a third party can be valid consideration. In *New Zealand Shipping Co Ltd v A M Satterthwaite & Co Ltd* [1975] AC 154 at 168 the rule and the reason for the rule were stated as follows: "An agreement to do an act which the promisor is under an existing obligation to a third party to do, may quite well amount to valid consideration: . . . the promisee obtains the benefit of a direct obligation . . . This proposition is illustrated and supported by *Scotson v Pegg* which their Lordships consider to be good law." Unless, therefore, the guarantee was void as having been made for an illegal consideration or voidable on the ground of economic duress, the extrinsic evidence establishes that it was supported by valid consideration. Counsel for the defendants submits that the consideration is illegal as being against public policy. He submits that to secure a party's promise by a threat of repudiation of a pre-existing contractual obligation owed to another can be, and in the circumstances of this case was, an abuse of a dominant bargaining position and so contrary to public policy . . . This submission found favour with the majority in the Court of Appeal. Their Lordships, however, consider it misconceived.'

Lord Scarman then referred to *Stilk v Myrick* and its predecessor *Harris v Watson* (1791) Peake 102 and to *Williams v Williams* ([1957] 1 All ER 305), before turning to the development of this branch of the law in the United States of America. He then said) [1980] AC 614 at 634–635):

'Their Lordships' knowledge of this developing branch of American law is necessarily limited. In their judgment it would be carrying audacity to the point of foolhardiness for them to attempt to extract from the American case law a principle to provide an answer to the question now under consideration. That question, their Lordships repeat, is whether, in a case where duress is not established, public policy may nevertheless invalidate the consideration if there has been a threat to repudiate a pre-existing contractual obligation or an unfair use of a dominating bargaining position. Their Lordships' conclusion is that where businessmen are negotiating at arm's length it is unnecessary for the achievement of justice, and unhelpful in the development of the law, to invoke such a rule of public policy. It would also create unacceptable anomaly. It is unnecessary because justice requires that men, who have negotiated at arm's length, be held to their bargains unless it can be shown that their consent was vitiated by fraud, mistake or duress. If a promise is induced by coercion of a man's will, the doctrine of duress suffices to do justice. The party coerced, if he chooses and acts in time, can avoid the contract. If there is no coercion, there can be no reason for avoiding the contract where there is shown to be a real consideration which is otherwise legal. . . .

It is true that *Pao On v Lau Yiu* is a case of a tripartite relationship, ie a promise by A to perform a pre-existing contractual obligation owed to B, in return for a promise of payment by C. But Lord Scarman's words seem to me to be of general application, equally applicable to a promise made by one of the original two parties to a contract.

Accordingly, following the view of the majority in *Ward v Byham* and of the whole court in *Williams v Williams* and that of the Privy Council in *Pao On v Lau Yiu* the present state of the law on this subject can be expressed in the following proposition: (i) if A has entered into a contract with B to do work for, or to supply goods or services to, B in return for payment by B and (ii) at some stage before A has completely performed his obligations under the contract B has reason to doubt whether A will, or will be able to, complete his side of the bargain and (iii) B thereupon promises A an additional payment in return for A's promise to perform his contractual obligations on time and (iv) as a result of giving his promise B obtains in practice a benefit, or obviates a disbenefit, and (v) B's promise is not given as a result of economic duress or fraud on the part of A, then (vi) the benefit to B is capable of being consideration for B's promise, so that the promise will be legally binding.

As I have said, counsel for the defendants accepts that in the present case by promising to pay the extra £10,300 the defendants secured benefits. There is no finding, and no suggestion, that in this case the promise was given as a result of fraud or duress.

If it be objected that the propositions above contravene the principle in *Stilk v Myrick*, I answer that in my view they do not: they refine and limit the application of that principle, but they leave the principle unscathed, eg where B secures no benefit by his promise. It is not in my view surprising that a principle enunciated in relation to the rigours of seafaring life during the Napoleonic wars should be subjected during the succeeding 180 years to a process of refinement and limitation in its application in the present day.

It is therefore my opinion that on his findings of fact in the present case, the judge was entitled to hold, as he did, that the defendants' promise to pay the extra £10,300 was supported by valuable considerable, and thus constituted an enforceable agreement. . . .

RUSSELL LJ Can the defendants now escape liability on the ground that the plaintiff undertook to do no more than he had originally contracted to do although, quite clearly, the defendants, on 9 April 1986, were prepared to make the payment and only declined to do so at a later stage? It would certainly be unconscionable if this were to be their legal entitlement. . . .

. . . While consideration remains a fundamental requirement before a contract not under seal can be enforced, the policy of the law in its search to do justice between the parties has developed considerably since the early nineteenth century when *Stilk v Myrick* was decided by Lord Ellenborough CJ. In the late twentieth century I do not believe that the rigid approach to the concept of consideration to be found in *Stilk v Myrick* is either necessary or desirable. Consideration there must still be but in my judgment the courts nowadays should be more ready to find its existence so as to reflect the intention of the parties to the contract where the bargaining powers are not unequal and where the finding of consideration reflects the true intention of the parties. . . .

For my part I wish to make it plain that I do not base my judgment on any reservation as to the correctness of the law long ago enunciated in *Stilk v Myrick.* A gratuitous promise, pure and simple, remains unenforceable unless given under seal. But where, as in this case, a party undertakes to make a payment because by so doing it will gain an advantage arising out of the continuing relationship with the promisee the new bargain will not fail for want of consideration. . . .

PURCHAS LJ In my judgment, the rule in *Stilk v Myrick* remains valid as a matter of principle, namely that a contract not under seal must be supported by consideration. Thus, where the agreement on which reliance is placed provides that an extra payment is to be made for work to be done by the payee which he is already obliged to perform, then unless some other consideration is detected to support the agreement to pay the extra sum that agreement will not be enforceable. *Harris v Watson* and *Stilk v Myrick* involved circumstances of a very special nature, namely the extraordinary conditions existing at the turn of the eighteenth century under which seamen had to serve their contracts of employment on the high seas. There were strong public policy grounds at that time to protect the master and owners of a ship from being held to ransom by disaffected crews. Thus, the decision that the promise to pay extra wages even in the circumstances established in those cases was not supported by consideration is readily understandable. Of course, conditions today on the high seas have changed dramatically and it is at least questionable, counsel for the plaintiff submitted, whether these cases might not well have been decided differently if they were tried today. The modern cases tend to depend more on the defence of duress in a commercial context rather than lack of consideration for the second agreement. In the present case, the question of duress does not arise. The initiative in coming to the agreement of 9 April came from Mr Cottrell and not from the plaintiff. It would not, therefore, lie in the defendants' mouth to assert a defence of duress. Nevertheless, the court is more ready in the presence of this defence being available in the commercial context to look for mutual advantages which would amount to sufficient consideration to support the second agreement under which the extra money is paid. . . . I consider that the modern approach to the question of consideration would be that where there were benefits derived by each party to a contract of variation even though one party did not suffer a detriment this would not be fatal to the establishing of sufficient consideration to support the agreement. If both parties benefit from an agreement it is not necessary that each also suffers a detriment. In my judgment, on the facts as found by the judge, he was entitled to reach the conclusion that consideration existed and in those circumstances I would not disturb that finding. . . .

Notes

1. Note that one of the crucial steps away from the hard 'no consideration' rule in *Stilk* v. *Myrick*, towards an acceptance of commercial arrangements as bargains supported by consideration unless there is evidence of economic duress, was made by the Privy Council in *Pao On* v. *Lau Yiu Long*.

Pao On owned shares in Shing On, a private limited company, which had as its major asset a building under construction. Lau Yiu Long was the major shareholder in Fu Chip, a public limited company, which wished to acquire the building by buying shares in Shing On. An arrangement was made between Fu Chip and Pao On, whereby Fu Chip would buy shares in Shing On and Pao On would buy shares in Fu Chip. It was a condition of the agreement that Pao On must retain the shares for one year. There was, however, a danger that the value of these shares might drop, and therefore a second agreement was reached between Pao On and Lau Yiu Long whereby the latter would buy back the shares at a guaranteed price. This was not necessarily a good bargain for Pao On, for if the value of the shares rose they would be unable to realize a profit. They were only protected against a loss. Consequently, they refused to complete the first agreement until the second agreement was cancelled and replaced with an indemnity agreement which would protect Pao On against loss, but would allow them to make a profit if the value rose by selling on the market rather than to Lau Yiu Long. Lau Yiu Long agreed to this change because they feared delays and a consequent loss of confidence in Fu Chip. Later the value of the shares fell, and so Pao On tried to make use of the indemnity. Lau Yiu Long resisted, claiming that Pao On had given nothing in return for the indemnity, but had simply agreed to complete an agreement which they were contractually bound to complete with Fu Chip. Pao On brought an action to enforce the agreement.

Such a tripartite relationship fell within the established principles governing the enforceability of promises made in return for promises to perform a contractual duty *to a third party*. Consequently, the Privy Council was able to find good consideration. It also refused to invoke a principle of public policy—the same principle, it was argued by the defendant in *Pao On*, as lay at the heart of *Stilk* v. *Myrick*, at least as it emerges from the

Espinasse Report—in order to negative an otherwise valid assertion of consideration given that there was no proven economic duress. This development was carried through to one of its logical conclusions (i.e. the quasi-abandonment of the rule in *Stilk* v. *Myrick*) in *Williams* v. *Roffey*.

For further reflections on *Pao On* and an earlier case of duress by threatened breach of contract, (*North Ocean Shipping Co. Ltd.* v. *Hyundai (The Atlantic Baron)*) see Coote, 'Duress by Threatened Breach of Contract', [1980] *CLJ* 40.

2. It is interesting to consider why it is that both Glidewell LJ and Russell LJ can conclude that matters have changed sufficiently since *Stilk* v. *Myrick* to warrant a departure from or qualification of the strict rule elaborated on the basis of the Campbell Report that the performance of or promise to perform an existing duty owed to the promisor is not good consideration for a promise. What changes have triggered the shift from a focus on legal benefit to the factual benefit derived by the promisor? The technical answer is, of course, the articulation of a wider conception of duress which extends to the use of economic power, and in particular the threat of breach of contract. The effectiveness of economic duress in this context is, however, merely an assertion on the part of the judiciary, and it is an assertion which has not in any way been empirically tested. Arguably, the most that can be said about the judgments in *Williams* v. *Roffey* is that they represent a shift from formalist to realist reasoning, within the framework of contractual analysis advanced by Adams and Brownsword (see Ch. 4). The difficulty with the shift is that it leads the judges to make bold but unsupported statements of policy.

3. *Williams* v. *Roffey* is occasioning a revival of the academic debate regarding the desirability of abolishing the doctrine of consideration, with the proposal coming from R. Halson ('Sailors, Sub-Contractors and Consideration', (1990) 106 *LQR* 183) that it should logically be replaced by the notion of economic duress. Such calls are tempered by A. Phang ('Consideration at the Crossroads', (1991) 107 *LQR* 21, building on an earlier article 'Whither Economic Duress? Reflections on Two Recent Cases', (1990) 53 *MLR* 107), who argues that it is unhelpful to consider simply 'substituting one vague doctrine for another'. Although Phang asserts that 'the doctrine of economic duress does, as compared with that of consideration, appear more consonant with present-day commercial needs', before it can realistically be adopted as a comprehensive test of contractual enforceability, it requires further concretization by the courts. There will be further detailed discussion of duress in Chapter 9.

4. A useful perspective on judicial unwillingness (in Canada as well as England) to shift the form of debate from consideration to duress is provided by Reiter.

B. Reiter, 'Courts, Consideration and Common Sense', (1977) 27 *U. Toronto LJ* 439 at 465–6

It may be suggested that the pre-existing duty rule is justified by its functioning to insulate courts from the need to make the difficult and unpleasant decisions of fact or law required by the more sophisticated 'pressure doctrines.' Since 'gratuitous' modification promises present strong possibilities of having been procured improperly, a strict rule requiring refusal of enforcement generally renders unnecessary inquiry into the circumstances of any individual case: 'because of the likelihood that the promise was obtained by an express or implied threat to withhold performance of a legal duty, the promise does not have the presumptive social utility normally found in a bargain' [Restatement (Second) of Contracts].

This suggestion [cannot] be supported . . . . First, the basic assumption that a businessman will insist upon the strict fulfilment of his legal rights however dramatically circumstances have changed for the other party and that only pressure will force him to yield to suggestions that he ought to help absorb unforeseen and onerous changes suffered by his obligee, reflects an unrealistic and unduly pernicious view of modern business ethics. Second, the general assumption of pressure as the producer of modifications fails to distinguish between the quite different circumstances in which such adjustments are made. While vigilance may be appropriate where no more appears than that a price is raised, even suspicion of pressure may be unjustifiable where the circumstances alone and without further evidence of good faith suggest legitimate motivations for the concession. Where future dealing is important a buyer might well accede to a supplier's request for more, fearing that the supplier might fail otherwise or esteeming valuable future good will more highly than modest present inconvenience. Where a price increase is being passed on industry-wide, there may be little incentive to insist upon delivery at original prices. Many modification cases provide the promisee with no greater leverage than he would have had if there had been no prior on-going relation: the 'real opportunity for overreaching' requires virtually irreversible reliance on the pre-existing duty, present in only a small handful of the many situations in which modification promises are made. Third, if investigation reveals that no unfair pressure was applied, the modifying promise has that same social importance and decisive claim to enforcement as has any other commercial bargain: it ought to go unenforced only for compelling reasons.

The function of the law is seriously misapprehended when it is felt that the convenience of the judges is a sufficient reason to force businessmen to accomplish permissible and desired ends only in legally appointed ways. The convenience of the judges is selectively served by a rule banning enforcement to save decision on duress.

The next case, *Foakes* v. *Beer*, is not concerned with the modification of long-term contractual relationships, but with the variation of a debt. However, the commentary from Adams and Brownsword which follows it indicates the potentially radical impact of *Williams* v. *Roffey* outside its narrow factual scenario.

Foakes v. *Beer*
(1884) 9 App. Cas. 605

The respondent was awarded judgment for a debt of £1090 19*s*. against the appellant. Some fifteen months later, the two parties entered into an agreement whereby the appellant paid £500 at once and undertook to pay £300 per year in two instalments until the debt was satisfied, and the respondent undertook not to take proceedings to recover the debt. The appellant paid the full debt, but the respondent claimed interest.

EARL OF SELBORNE L.C. . . . . [T]he agreement of the judgment creditor . . . is that she "will not take any proceedings whatever on the judgment," if a certain condition is fulfilled. What is that condition? Payment of the sum of £150 in every half year, "until the whole of the said sum of £2090 19*s*." (the aggregate amount of the principal debt and costs, for which judgment had been entered) "shall have been fully paid and satisfied." A particular "sum" is here mentioned, which does not include the interest then due, or future interest. Whatever was meant to be payable at all, under this agreement, was clearly to be payable by half-yearly instalments of £150 each; any other construction must necessarily make the conditional promise nugatory. But to say that the half-yearly payments were to continue till the whole sum of £2090 19*s*., "and interest thereon," should have been fully paid and satisfied, would be to introduce very important words into the agreement, which are not there, and of which I cannot say that they are necessarily implied. Although, therefore, I may (as indeed I do) very much doubt whether the effect of the agreement, as a conditional waiver of the interest to which she was by law entitled under the judgment, was really present to the mind of the judgment creditor, still I cannot deny that it might have that effect, if capable of being legally enforced.

But the question remains, whether the agreement is capable of being legally enforced. Not being under seal, it cannot be legally enforced against the respondent, unless she received consideration for it from the appellant, or unless, though without consideration, it operates by way of accord and satisfaction, so as to extinguish the claim for interest. What is the consideration? On the face of the agreement none is expressed, except a present payment of £500, on account and in part of the larger debt then due and payable by law under the judgment. The appellant did not contract to pay the future instalments of £150 each, at the times therein mentioned; much less did he give any new security, in the shape of negotiable paper, or in any other form. The promise de futuro was only that of the respondent, that if the half-yearly payments of £150 each were regularly paid, she would "take no proceedings whatever on the judgment." No doubt if the appellant had been under no antecedent obligation to pay the whole debt, his fulfilment of the condition might have imported some consideration on his part for that promise. But he was under that antecedent obligation; and payment at those deferred dates, by the forbearance and indulgence of the creditor, of the residue of the principal debt and costs, could not (in my opinion) be a consideration for the relinquishment of interest and discharge of the judgment, unless the payment of the £500, at the time of signing the agreement, was such a consideration. As to accord and satisfaction, in point of fact there could be no complete satisfaction, so long as any future instalment remained payable; and I do not see how any mere payments on account could operate in law as a satisfaction ad interim, conditionally upon other payments being afterwards duly made, unless there was a consideration sufficient to support the agreement while still unexecuted. Nor was anything, in fact, done by the respondent in this case, on the receipt of the last payment, which could be tantamount to an acquittance, if the agreement did not previously bind her.

The question, therefore, is nakedly raised by this appeal, whether your Lordships are now prepared, not only to overrule, as contrary to law, the doctrine stated by Sir Edward Coke to have been laid down by all the judges of the Common Pleas in *Pinnel's Case* in 1602, and repeated in his note to Littleton, sect. 344, but to treat a prospective agreement, not under seal, for satisfaction of a debt, by a series of payments on account to a total amount less than the whole debt, as binding in law, provided those payments are regularly made; the case not being one of a composition with a common debtor, agreed to, inter se, by several creditors. . . . The doctrine itself, as laid down by Sir Edward Coke, may have been criticised, as questionable in principle, by some persons whose opinions are entitled to respect, but it has never been judicially overruled; on the contrary I think it has always, since the sixteenth century, been accepted as law. If so, I cannot think that your Lordships would do right, if you were now to reverse, as erroneous, a judgment of the Court of Appeal, proceeding upon a doctrine which has been accepted as part of the law of England for 280 years.

The doctrine, as stated in *Pinnel's Case*, is "that payment of a lesser sum on the day" (it would of course be the same after the day), "in satisfaction of a greater, cannot be any satisfaction for the whole, because it appears to the Judges, that by no possibility a lesser sum can be a satisfaction to the plaintiff for a greater sum." . . .

. . . If the question be (as, in the actual state of the law, I think it is), whether consideration is, or is not, given in a case of this kind, by the debtor who pays down part of the debt presently due from him, for a promise by the creditor to relinquish, after certain further payments on account, the residue of the debt, I cannot say that I think consideration is given, in the sense in which I have always understood that word as used in our law. It might be (and indeed I think it would be) an improvement in our law, if a release or acquittance of the whole debt, on payment of any sum which the creditor might be content to receive by way of accord and satisfaction (though less than the whole), were held to be, generally, binding, though not under seal; nor should I be unwilling to see equal force given to a prospective agreement, like the present, in writing though not under seal; but I think it impossible, without refinements which practically alter the sense of the word, to treat such a release or acquittance as supported by any new consideration proceeding from the debtor. . . . What is called "any benefit, or even any legal possibility of benefit," in Mr. Smith's notes to *Cumber* v. *Wane*, is not (as I conceive) that sort of benefit which a creditor may derive from getting payment of part of the money due to him from a debtor who might otherwise keep him at arm's length, or possibly become insolvent, but is some independent benefit, actual or contingent, of a kind which might in law be a good and valuable consideration for any other sort of agreement not under seal.

My conclusion is, that the order appealed from should be affirmed, and the appeal dismissed, with costs, and I so move your Lordships. . . .

LORD BLACKBURN . . . where a matter paid and accepted in satisfaction of a debt certain might by any possibility be more beneficial to the creditor than his debt, the Court will not inquire into the adequacy of the consideration. If the creditor, without any fraud, accepted it in satisfaction when it was not a sufficient satisfaction it was his own fault. And that payment before the day might be more beneficial, and consequently that the plea was in substance good, and this must have been decided in the case.

There is a second point stated to have been resolved [in *Pinnel's Case*], viz.: "That payment of a lesser sum on the day cannot be any satisfaction of the whole, because it appears to the judges that by no possibility a lesser sum can be a satisfaction to the plaintiff for a greater sum." This was certainly not necessary for the decision of the case; but though the resolution of the Court of Common Pleas was only a dictum, it seems to me clear that Lord Coke deliberately adopted the dictum, and the great weight of his authority makes it necessary to be cautious before saying that what he deliberately adopted as law was a mistake . . . .

. . . But as this has very seldom, if at all, been the ground of the decision even in a Court of the first instance, and certainly never been the ground of a decision in the Court of Exchequer Chamber, still less in this House, I did think it open in your Lordships' House to reconsider this question. And, notwithstanding the very high authority of Lord Coke, I think it is not the fact that to accept prompt payment of a part only of a liquidated demand, can never be more beneficial than to insist on payment of the whole. And if it be not the fact, it cannot be apparent to the judges. . . .

What principally weighs with me in thinking that Lord Coke made a mistake of fact is my conviction that all men of business, whether merchants or tradesmen, do every day recognise and act on the ground that prompt payment of a part of their demand may be more beneficial to them than it would be to insist on their rights and enforce payment of the whole. Even where the debtor is perfectly solvent, and sure to pay at last, this often is so. Where the credit of the debtor is doubtful it must be more so. I had persuaded myself that there was no such long-continued action on this dictum as to render it improper in this House to reconsider the question. I had written my reasons for so thinking; But as they were not satisfactory to the other noble and learned Lords who heard the case, I do not now repeat them nor persist in them.

I assent to the judgment proposed, though it is not that which I had originally thought proper.

Notes

1. Adams and Brownsword, in their case note on *Williams* v. *Roffey* reflect upon the implications of the decision for venerable rules of the common law such as the rule on the part payment of debts in *Pinnel's Case* and the doctrine of frustration (see Ch. 12), as well as for newly emerging doctrinal frameworks such as economic duress. Their comments locating *Williams* v. *Roffey* within a changing conception of consideration find an interesting reference in the dissenting comments of Lord Blackburn in *Foakes* v. *Beer*, making a point about business practice which is echoed by Wilson below.

J. Adams and R. Brownsword, 'Contract, Consideration and the critical Path', (1990) 53 *MLR* 536 at 540–2

Consider Glidewell LJ's six propositions, but with the factual situation turned on its head:

(i) if A has entered into a contract with B to do work for, or to supply goods or services to, B in return for payment by B, and

(ii) at some stage before B has completely performed his obligations under the contract, A has reason to doubt whether B will, or will be able to, complete his side of the bargain (ie whether B will be able to pay); and

(iii) A thereupon promises B that, in return for B's promise to pay such a sum, he will accept a lesser payment from B; and

(iv) as a result of giving his promise, A obtains in practice a benefit, or obviates a disbenefit; and

(v) A's promise is not given as the result of economic duress or fraud on the part of B; then

(vi) the benefit to A is capable of being consideration for A's promise, so that the promise will be legally binding.

It is submitted that the logic of *Williams* v *Roffey* is that, in a case which instantiates these elements, the court must hold the creditor (A) to his word. If this is correct, landmark decisions such as *Pinnel's* case and *Foakes* v *Beer* will have to be reconsidered. After all, the parallel is obvious: whether you are dealing with a stricken creditor or a stricken debtor, in certain circumstances, the economic imperatives may dictate that financial adjustments should be made (the doctrine of consideration notwithstanding). It is arguable, of course, that, in such a situation free of duress or fraud, the doctrine of equitable estoppel may be utilised to protect the debtor. Indeed, in *Williams* v *Roffey*, Russell LJ indicated that he would have welcomed the development of just such a line of argument. However, this omission may have been a blessing in disguise, for it resulted in the court squarely facing up to the doctrine of consideration and its place in the commercial world.

This leaves a number of unresolved cases, especially past consideration and the promise of a gift. Although the court in *Williams* v *Roffey* advocates a more flexible approach towards the requirement of consideration, it is emphasised that a gratuitous promise, pure and simple, remains unenforceable. Quite probably, past consideration and the promise of a gift are seen as falling into this category. For, whilst the detriment requirement has been abandoned, the likelihood is that, at least in the short term, some kind of 'objective' benefit requirement will be deployed to hold the line. In other words, it will not be enough for the promisee to argue that the (gratuitous) promisor derived some kind of subjective, intangible, benefit from his promise.

. . . *Williams* v *Roffey* represents an important staging post in the transformation of our conception of consideration. Judicial rhetoric still clings to the remnants of an exchange model, of benefit being derived in return for the promise. However, the driving force behind the recent decisions on the existing duty question quite clearly has been a mixture of considerations of fairness and commercial utility (aided by the developing doctrine of economic duress). In *Williams* v *Roffey*, the court appreciated both that the defendants' promise was commercially necessary and that it would be unconscionable for them to go back on their word. Moreover, not only did the court appreciate these matters, it was prepared to act on them.

The implications of the court's robust approach, however, extend beyond the doctrine of consideration. For instance, it may become necessary to review the application of the frustration principle, which, in its modern manifestation, firmly sets its face against assisting a contractor to re-negotiate an underpriced contract, despite the underpricing arising through circumstances beyond the control of the parties. Yet, in *Williams* v *Roffey*, the court bends over backwards to indemnify a contractor against the effects of underpricing in circumstances where the underpricing is entirely within his control. The most immediate question, though, concerns the doctrine of economic duress. The point is that relaxation of the consideration requirement (as betokened by *Williams* v *Roffey*) entails that economic duress becomes the primary regulative principle in relation to price re-negotiation. This raises large questions; but a brief comment must suffice.

As Andrew Phang has recently observed . . . the burgeoning case-law dealing with economic duress has failed to put the doctrine on a clear footing. There are two leading issues. First, what are the necessary and sufficient conditions for the principle to apply? And, second, do these criteria (whatever they are) apply universally to all contractual situations? In response to the first question, the relevant conditions appear to revolve around three elements: the conduct of the party applying the pressure; the conduct, position and response of the party to whom the pressure is applied; and the balance of the resulting agreement. Such is the formal structure of this question, but the substantive jurisprudence will take some time to take shape. The second question is no less difficult. Should the doctrine of economic duress be applied uniformly to all transactions, so that no discrimination is made between agreements and re-negotiated agreements, between commercial and consumer agreements, and so on? In the face of such uncertainties, it is tempting to think that we might, perhaps, be better off with the old law. After all, contractors at least knew where they stood. Such a view, however, would be a mistake. The old law bought calculability only at the price of ignoring commercial reality. In this sense, *Williams* v *Roffey*, in conjunction with the doctrine of economic duress, represents both an opportunity and a challenge. For, by weakening the consideration requirement, *Williams* v *Roffey* presents the opportunity for reasonable re-negotiations to be enforced, while the doctrine of economic duress challenges us to determine which re-negotiations we judge to be unreasonable.

For further contrasts between the approach taken in *Williams* v. *Roffey* to the risk of underpricing and the treatment of external contingencies which render performance more onerous under the doctrine of frustration, see R. Halson, 'Sailors, Sub-contractors and Consideration', (1990) 106 *LQR* 183.

2. It is worth considering whether it would be correct to suggest that the policy of the law is to encourage the party whose performance turns out to be underpriced (whether or not through some fault of his own) to persuade the other party (provided only that no unfair pressure is used) to agree to a renegotiation, rather than to seek to treat the contract as at an end and face a possible action for wrongful repudiation.

3. Whether this analysis should be extended to the debt scenario of *Foakes* v. *Beer*, as argued by Adams and Brownsword, requires further consideration. As we shall see, promissory estoppel is already in use in situations akin to that posed by Adams and Brownsword as suitable for the transposition of the *Williams* v. *Roffey* approach. The doctrine enables the adjustment of price, but subject to a restriction prohibiting unconscionable conduct (see *D. & C. Builders* v. *Rees* [1966] 2 QB 617). Brady ('Performance of Pre-existing Contractual Duty as Consideration', (1975) 52 *Denv. LJ* 433 at 438) has in fact sought to distinguish the *Foakes* v. *Beer* scenario from the other 'existing legal obligation' cases, arguing that the rule in *Pinnel's*

Case is a rule of the law of debt not the law of contract. If this point is accepted, then the policy arguments behind the proposal by Adams and Brownsword lose their force, since debt is a very different type of fixed legal obligation from the types of relational contract which have typically been varied using the promissory estoppel doctrine.

4. It is clear that in cases such as *Stilk* v. *Myrick* and *Williams* v. *Roffey*, what the courts are struggling with is the articulation of some concept capable of regulating the adjustment of longer-term contracts such as the contract of employment and the contract for work and materials, i.e. contracts which typify the relational side of contracting (see Ch. 2). The event in respect of which the adjustment is desired is what economists term the 'regret contingency', i.e. the possibility that one party may regret the bargain and wish to negotiate a better price. It is also implicit in the cases which are litigated that adjustment has not been planned or envisaged at the outset. The contract rule-book does provide a mechanism for co-operative adjustment; but in the absence of performance or a right to terminate, it takes a further contract to vary or discharge an earlier contract. Consequently, consideration, as an indispensable element of contract formation must be present not only at the inception but also during the currency of a relational contract if there is a variation of price, performance, or other obligation. It is precisely the tendency of courts to treat as equal the inception and variation of an agreement which was criticized by Reiter throughout the essay extracted above.

From this perspective, it may well be that economic duress (or indeed promissory estoppel—the alternative canvassed by Russell LJ in *Williams* v. *Roffey* but not discussed in the parts of the decision extracted in this chapter—a specifically relational concept which attaches to a pre-existing legal relationship) is a mechanism better able to police the continuing health of a bargain than a concept such as consideration, which is more oriented towards classical discrete transaction (*the* prima facie *unadjustable* price for a promise). However, it is Ian Macneil's argument that, wherever a system of relational contract law requires the boundaries of the neoclassical law to be overstepped,

somewhere along the line of increasing duration and complexity, trying to force changes into a pattern of original consent becomes both too difficult and too unrewarding to justify the effort, and the contractual relation escapes the bounds of the neoclassical system. That system is replaced by very different adjustment processes of an on-going administrative kind . . . ('Contracts: Adjustment of Long Term Economic Relations under Classical, Neoclassical and Relational Contract Law', (1978) 72 *NwUL Rev.* 854 at 901)

The general thrust of the relational contracts scholarship on the adjustment of long-term contracts is that courts should enforce adjustments such as to protect the parties' expectations and enforce commitments (see R. Hillman, 'Court Adjustment of Long-Term Contracts: An Analysis under Modern Contract Law', [1987] *Duke LJ* 1).

5. The analysis of Goetz and Scott in the concluding extract in this section would seem to indicate that it would be unfortunate (from the perspective of the maximization of efficient promising) if English law were solely to go down the road of balancing the existence of consideration against economic duress, rather than exploring the wider avenues of promissory liability pursued by US law.

Goetz and Scott postulate the goal of contract law as achieving efficiency in interactions between promisor and promisee, by reducing the transaction costs of both. They use the example of consideration and the modification of existing contractual terms to illustrate their optimal enforcement model. Their analysis, which is merely descriptive in character and does not posit an alternative model, explains current patterns of promissory liability and the interaction of consideration and promissory estoppel (albeit in the US setting, but with general implications for all common-law jurisdictions). They expressly eschew setting a limit upon the enforceability of promises. The difficulty with promissory estoppel, as we shall see, is that it is not a reciprocal relationship, and consequently there is no incentive for the parties to accommodate the contingencies and costs which arise in the course of their relationship. As Vincent-Jones indicates (Section VI), this matter falls to the court for *ex post facto* determination.

C. Goetz and R. Scott, 'Enforcing Promises: An Examination of the Basis of Contract', (1980) 89 *Yale LJ* 1261 at 1292–4, 1300–1

[B]argaining tends to produce the optimal amount of promissory reliance even when the legal rule deviates from the optimal reliance principle. By modifying contractual terms, the parties can vary the standard liability rule in order to maximize net reliance benefits.

What effects can be predicted from full enforcement of reciprocal bargain promises? . . . [A]pplication of sanctions for breach imposes the risk of the regret contingency on the promisor. As the promisor's potential liability is increased, he is encouraged to take precautionary action to minimize the expected liability, by conditioning promises more carefully in negotiations. The promisee, in turn, may bargain for a less restricted promise by paying explicitly for the additional reassurance provided by a compensation award.

Alternatively, a rule denying enforcement of a bargained-for promise reduces precautionary costs incurred by promisors seeking to minimize the risks of regret, because it shifts that risk to the promisee. The promisee may adapt to this increased uncertainty by discounting the price he is willing to pay for the promise. If the promise is actually worth more than the promisee estimates, the promisor will incur costs up to the expected value of the promise in order to assure the promisee of the true worth of the promise. These additional reassurance costs induced by the promisee's adaptive behavior could include the voluntary assumption of legal liability through collateral guarantees or performance bonds.

Thus, because bargainers will attempt to allocate the risk of regret optimally themselves, the effects of enforcement rules depend on the transaction costs of risk allocation. Evaluation of these costs requires an analysis of how bargainers adapt to the risks of regret contingencies. If in certain transactions precautionary efforts by promisors would be more expensive than reassurance, nonenforcement enables the parties to shift the risk of regret more cheaply. Alternatively, when reassurance is more costly, fully enforcing promises induces cheaper precautionary conduct. . . .

The design of the Bargain Paradigm

. . . Not all promises made in a bargaining context are presumptively enforceable. Indeed, the reciprocal bargain or consideration model is considerably more limited than the larger exchange context that it occupies. For example, . . . promises to discharge contractual obligations are traditionally unenforceable even though they are made in the context of a bargain. . . .

Dissatisfaction with the mechanical rules of the common law has induced courts and commentators to offer more flexible alternatives. For example, detrimental reliance has been urged as a basis for imposing discretionary liability for broken promises made in a bargaining context. The current liability design of the consideration model appears to rest on crucial assumptions about bargainers' risk preferences and relative abilities to minimize risk. The indeterminacy of these empirical assumptions may explain the rigidity of the common law pattern. Liability based on future actions such as those in reliance increases bargaining uncertainty, the cost of which reduces the social value of the exchange. Whenever the outcome of private bargaining is unpredictable, liability rules that clearly specify the consequences of alternative actions will minimize uncertainty. By sharply distinguishing fully enforceable bargains from unenforceable promises, the formal rules of consideration permit bargainers to choose the outcome that minimizes expected bargaining costs.

The preceding analysis explains only the basic design of the consideration model. It does not help identify where to draw the line between enforcement and nonenforcement. At common law the category of enforceable bargained-for promises was rigidly narrow. . . .

[H]owever, . . . the recent expansion of promissory liability is consistent with the judgment that, for certain types of bargain promises, a large core of liability can be defined without causing a significant increase in enforcement costs.

IV. CONSIDERATION AND ESTOPPEL DOCTRINES

A. Promissory Estoppel

Whatever view of consideration is held by those who support the 'reliance school' of thought, the orthodox position is that it encapsulates the idea of bargain: a promise which has not been paid for cannot be enforced. As we saw, this orthodox view gives rise to a gap in the law—i.e. that the doctrine of consideration is unable to offer protection to the promisee who has relied on a promise but not offered consideration in the bargain sense. Where the parties are in a legal relationship with each other and one party has indicated that he will not enforce his strict legal position, the other party, if he relies upon that promise, can prevent the promisor returning to his strict legal position. This is the doctrine of promissory estoppel. The outline above is misleading in its simplicity—there is considerable divergent opinion about how the affected party has to rely upon the promise (whether detrimentally or not) and whether the promisor is kept out of his strict legal rights permanently or temporarily. These issues are examined more fully in the notes following the two cases in this section. The central feature of promissory estoppel is that it can be used to enforce a promise not to stand on strict legal rights, but only as a defence by the promisee against an attempted return by the promisor to his strict legal rights. This is in contrast to an action by the promisee on the promise. It is essential for traditional contract law to draw this distinction—otherwise a promisee who has paid for his promise and one who has merely relied upon a promise would find themselves in the same position.

Alan (W. J.) & Co. Ltd. v. *El Nasr Export and Import Co.*
[1972] 2 All ER 127

The sellers contracted to sell two shipments of coffee, one in September/October and one in October/November. The contract stated that payment would be by way of an irrevocable letter of credit in Kenyan shillings. However, the credit was opened in pounds sterling, which then enjoyed parity with the Kenyan currency. The first shipment was made and payment claimed by the sellers. The second shipment was made, and the sellers prepared an invoice in pounds sterling. This invoice was presented to the bank, but in the mean time sterling had been devalued. The sellers received payment from the bank in pounds sterling, a payment which, because of the devaluation, was less than the sale price in Kenyan shillings. The sellers claimed the difference between the payment they had originally received for the second shipment in pounds sterling and the original contract price in Kenyan shillings.

LORD DENNING MR. . . . [I]n many cases—and our present case is one—the letter of credit does not conform. Then negotiations may take place as a result of which the letter of credit is modified so as to be satisfactory to the seller. Alternatively, the seller may be content to accept the letter of credit as satisfactory, as it is, without modification. Once this happens, then the letter of credit is to be regarded as if it were a conforming letter of credit. It will rank accordingly as conditional payment.

There are two cases on this subject. One is *Panoutsos v Raymond Hadley Corpn of New York*, but the facts are only to be found fully set out in Commercial Cases. The other is *Enrico Furst & Co v W E Fischer Ltd*. In each of those cases the letter of credit did not conform to the contract of sale. In each case the non-conformity was in that it was not a confirmed credit. But the sellers took no objection to the letter of credit on that score. On the contrary, they asked for the letter of credit to be extended; and it was extended. In each case the sellers sought afterwards to cancel the contract on the ground that the letter of credit was not in conformity with the contract. In each case the court held that they could not do so.

What is the true basis of those decisions? Is it a variation of the original contract or a waiver of the strict rights thereunder or a promissory estoppel precluding the seller from insisting on his strict rights or what else? In *Enrico Furst* Diplock J said it was a 'classic case of waiver'. I agree with him. It is an instance of the general principle which was first enunciated by Lord Cairns LC in *Hughes v Metropolitan Railway Co* ((1877) 2 App. Cas. 439), and rescued from oblivion by *Central London Property Trust Ltd v High Trees House Ltd* ([1947] KB 130). The principle is much wider than waiver itself; but waiver is a good instance of its application. The principle of waiver is simply this: if one party, by his conduct, leads another to believe that the strict rights arising under the contract will not be insisted on, intending that the other should act on that belief, and he does act on it, then the first party will not afterwards be allowed to insist on the strict legal rights when it would be inequitable for him to do so . . . . There may be no consideration moving from him who benefits by the waiver. There may be no detriment to him by acting on it. There may be nothing in writing. Nevertheless, the one who waives his strict rights cannot afterwards insist on them. His strict rights are at any rate suspended so long as the waiver lasts. He may on occasion be able to revert to his strict legal rights for the future by giving reasonable noting in that behalf, or otherwise making it plain by his conduct that he will thereafter insist on them: see *Tool Metal Manufacturing Co Ltd v Tungsten Electric Co Ltd* ([1955] 2 All ER 657). But there are cases where no withdrawal is possible. It may be too late to withdraw; or it cannot be done without injustice to the other party. In that event he is bound by his waiver. He will not be allowed to revert to his strict legal rights. He can only enforce them subject to the waiver he has made.

Instances of these principles are ready to hand in contracts for the sale of goods. A seller may, by his conduct, lead the buyer to believe that he is not insisting on the stipulated time for exercising an option . . . . A buyer may, by requesting delivery, lead the seller to believe that he is not insisting on the contractual time for delivery . . . . A seller may, by his conduct, lead the buyer to believe that he will not insist on a confirmed letter of credit . . . but will accept an unconfirmed one instead . . . . A seller may accept a less sum for his goods than the contracted price, thus inducing him to believe that he will not enforce payment of the balance: see *Central London Property Trust Ltd v High Trees House Ltd* and *D & C Builders Ltd v Rees*. In none of these cases does the party who acts on the belief suffer any detriment. It is not a detriment, but a benefit to him, to have an extension of time or to pay less, or as the case may be. Nevertheless, he has conducted his affairs on the basis that he has that benefit and it would not be equitable now to deprive him of it.

The judge rejected this doctrine because, he said, 'there is no evidence of the [buyers] having acted to their detriment'. I know that it has been suggested in some quarters that there must be detriment. But I can find no support for it in the authorities cited by the judge. The nearest approach to it is the statement of Viscount Simonds in the *Tool Metal* case that the other must have been led 'to alter his position', which was adopted by Lord Hodson in *Emmanuel Ayodeji Ajayi v R T Briscoe (Nigeria) Ltd* [[1964] 1 WLR 1326]. But that only means that he must have been led to act differently from what he otherwise would have done. And, if you study the cases in which the doctrine has been applied, you will see that all that is required is that the one should have '*acted* on the belief induced by the other party'. That is how Lord Cohen put it in the *Tool Metal* case, and is how I would put it myself. . . .

Conclusion

Applying the principle here, it seems to me that the sellers, by their conduct, waived the right to have payment by means of a letter of credit in Kenyan currency and accepted instead a letter of credit in sterling. It was, when given, conditional payment; with the result that, on being duly honoured (as it was) the payment was no longer conditional. It became absolute, and dated back to the time when the letter of credit was given and acted on. The sellers have, therefore, received payment of the price and cannot recover more. . . .

MEGAN LJ The offer made by the confirming bank . . . did not comply, in several respects, with what the sellers were entitled to require. However, the only non-conforming aspect of the offer which I regard as relevant for the purposes of this appeal is the term of the offer in respect of currency. That, in my view, is not only relevant, it is vital. The confirming bank's offer, made to the sellers with the knowledge of, and on the instructions of, the buyers, was an offer which involved sterling, not merely as the currency of payment, but as the currency of account, in respect of that transaction. The sellers accepted the conforming bank's offer, including its terms as to currency, by submitting invoices and drafts with the form and contents which I have already described.

As I see it, the necessary consequence of that offer and acceptance of a sterling credit is that the original term of the contract of sale as to the money of account was varied from Kenyan currency to sterling. The payment, and the sole payment, stipulated by the contract of sale was by the letter of credit. The buyers, through the confirming bank, had opened a letter of credit which did not conform, because it provided sterling as the money of account. The sellers accepted that offer by making use of the credit to receive payment for a part of the contractual goods. By that acceptance, as the sellers must be deemed to have known, not only did the confirming bank become irrevocably bound by the terms of the offer (and by no other terms), but so also did the buyers become bound. Not only did they incur legal obligations as a result of the sellers' acceptance—for example, an obligation to indemnify the bank—but also the buyers could not thereafter have turned round and said to the sellers (for example, if Kenyan currency had been devalued against sterling) that the bank would thereafter pay less for the contractual goods than the promised sterling payment of £262 per ton. If the buyers could not revert unilaterally to the original currency of account, once they had offered a variation which had been accepted by conduct, neither could the sellers so revert. The contract had been varied in that respect.

The sellers, however, contend that they were, indeed, entitled to make use of the non-confirming letter of credit offered to them, without impairing their rights for the future under the original terms of the contract, if and when they chose to revert. They seek to rely on the analogy of a sale of goods contract where the goods are deliverable by instalments, and one instalment falls short of the prescribed quality. The buyer is not obliged, even if in law he could do so, to treat the contract as repudiated. He is not, it is said, even obliged to complain. But he is in no way precluded from insisting that for future instalments of the goods the seller shall conform with the precise terms of the contract as to quality. That is not, in my opinion, a true analogy. The relevant transaction here is not one of instalments. It is a once-for-all transaction. It is the establishment of a credit which is to cover the whole of the payment for the whole of the contract. Once it has been accepted by the sellers, the bank is committed, and is committed in accordance with its accepted terms, and no other terms. Once the credit is established and accepted it is unalterable, except with the consent of all the parties concerned, all of whose legal rights and liabilities have necessarily been affected by the establishment of the credit. Hence the sellers cannot escape from the consequences of the acceptance of the offered credit by any argument that their apparent acceptance involved merely a temporary acquiescence which they could revoke or abandon at will, or on giving notice. It was an acceptance which, once made, related to the totality of the letter of credit transaction; and the letter of credit transaction was, by the contract of sale, the one and only contractual provision for payment. When the letter of credit was accepted as a transaction in sterling as the currency of account, the price under the sale contract could not remain as Kenyan currency.

For the buyers it was submitted further that, if there were not here a variation of the contract, there was at least a waiver, which the sellers could not, or did not properly revoke. I do not propose to go into that submission at any length. On analysis, it covers much the same field as the question of variation. In my view, if there were no variation, the buyers would still be entitled to succeed on the ground of waiver. The relevant principle is, in my opinion, that which was stated by Lord Cairns LC in *Hughes v Metropolitan Railway Co.* The acceptance by the sellers of the sterling credit was, as I have said, a once-for-all acceptance. It was not a concession for a specified period of time or one which the sellers could operate as long as they chose and thereafter unilaterally abrogate; any more than the buyers would have been entitled to alter the terms of the credit or to have demanded a refund from the sellers if, after this credit had been partly used, the relative values of the currencies had changed in the opposite way. . . .

On the simple form of contractual provision for payment in this sale contract with which we are concerned, the sellers, in my view, have no right of requiring payment (I am not, of course, speaking of damages for breach) otherwise than in accordance with, and by means of, a confirmed irrevocable letter of credit: so long, at any rate, as no default is made by the bank in its performance of the letter of credit obligations. There are cases in which a contract on its true construction imposes on the buyer a potential liability to make payment direct to the seller in certain circumstances, outside or in addition to payment by the bank under a duly established letter of credit. An example is to be found in the facts of *Urquhart Lindsay & Co Ltd v Eastern Bank Ltd.* But there is no scope for such an implication in the present contract of sale. Here the contractual obligation is 'payment by confirmed, irrevocable letter of credit . . .' If such a credit is duly established, and if payment is duly made in accordance with its terms, I see no scope for any liability on the part of the buyers to make, or on the part of the sellers to require, any other or additional payment. Here the credit was, it is true, not duly established. But the non-compliance of the credit with the contract of sale was, in my opinion, unquestionably waived, and irrevocably waived, by the sellers. On the facts of this case, then the credit which was established has to be treated as a conforming credit. On the terms of this contract of sale, there remains no obligation on the buyers to make any payment to the sellers, because they have discharged the whole of their contractual obligation as to payment when a conforming credit has been established and payment has actually been made under that credit, in accordance with its terms, to the full extent that the sellers have properly sought to draw on it. It follows that, even if there were no variation or relevant waiver in respect of the terms of the contract of sale, I should hold that the sellers' claim fails on that quite separate and independent ground. . . .

STEPHENSON LJ Where, as here, the letter of credit by which the buyers' liability to pay was to be discharged did not conform to the contract, it only became binding on the sellers if they accepted or agreed to it. That they could do unequivocally and in full satisfaction of the buyers' liability or pro tanto and in part satisfaction if it did not conform in respect of the price including (as here) the currency of account. Alternatively, they could reject the letter of credit or insist on its amendment to conform with the sale contract. But if the sellers wanted to accept the letter of credit and payment under it without prejudice to their right to the full price (in the currency of account) from the buyers, they must say so and not allow buyers and sub-buyers, issuing and confirming banks to act on it. Otherwise they must be taken to have accepted the letter of credit and its terms of payment in pounds sterling as the currency of account as well as the currency of payment, and to have accepted them beyond the possibility of unilateral revocation. . . .

By not objecting to the non-conforming letter of credit, by obtaining payment on it in sterling from the bank and by extending it the sellers clearly accepted and agreed to it and were treated as having done so not only by the bank but by the buyers, who may be presumed (although there was no evidence about it) to have paid charges and incurred liabilities such as a liability to indemnify the bank. The sellers never indicated any reservations about the change from Kenya shillings to pounds sterling or asked for any adjustment, probably for the simple reason that they considered sterling as good as Kenya shillings if not better. When after devaluation of sterling they invoiced the balance of the goods against part payment of the balance of the price and claimed the difference created by devaluation from the buyers, they were attempting to assert a liability which, whether by variation or waiver, they had allowed the buyers to alter. . . . I would leave open the question whether the action of the other party induced by the party who 'waives' his contractual rights can be any alteration of his position, as Lord Denning MR has said, or must, as the judge thought, be an alteration to his detriment, or for the worse, in some sense. In this case the buyers did, I think, contrary to the judge's view, act to their detriment on the sellers' waiver, if that is what it was, and the contract was varied for good consideration, which may be another way of saying the same thing; so that I need not, and do not, express a concluded opinion on that controversial question.

Notes

1. The same result is reached by all three Court of Appeal judges—that the sellers cannot revert to the originally intended contract currency of Kenyan shillings—but by markedly different routes. Megaw and Stephenson LJJ

take a conventional approach based on contract doctrine. The letter of credit is offered by the buyers to the sellers, and once they have accepted this arrangement in pounds sterling and used it, the sellers are then contractually bound to accept payment in pounds sterling. In other words, the parties agreed to a modification of the original arrangements. If the change in exchange rates had made it advantageous to the sellers to receive pounds sterling and disadvantageous to the buyers to pay in that form, the sellers could have sued the buyers to enforce their position, as the arrangement was contractual and so the promise could be sued on. In contrast, Lord Denning MR sees the case as involving promissory estoppel: the sellers by accepting pounds sterling waived their rights to recover to their original position and were estopped from claiming payment in Kenyan shillings.

In reaching these conclusions, the judges interpreted the facts slightly differently. For Megaw and Stephenson LJJ the transaction was driven by the buyers' conduct in offering to the sellers this method of payment. For Lord Denning the initiative lay with the sellers who accepted payment in this form.

2. Lord Denning makes reference in his judgment to the effect of the sellers' conduct-whether it should be suspensory or permanent. If promises not to rely on strict legal rights have permanent effect, then there is an obvious conflict with *Foakes* v. *Beer* which suggests that, in the absence of consideration to support a promise not to rely on strict legal rights, a reversion to the strict legal position is always possible. In a broader sense, it is important to know within the matrix of relational contract whether a waiver of rights destroys the original position permanently in favour of the new (see I. Macneil, 'Contracts', (1978) 72 *NwUL Rev.* 854 at 874).

Within the promissory estoppel cases themselves, there is support for the view that the effect should be merely suspensory (see *Tool Metal Manufacturing Co. Ltd.* v. *Tungsten Electric Co. Ltd.* and *Ajayi* v. *R. T. Briscoe (Nigeria) Ltd.*), with the promisor being able to return to his original position on giving reasonable notice. Confusion arises as a result of dicta of Denning J in *Central London Property Trust Ltd.* v. *High Trees House Ltd.*, which suggest that the effect of the promise is to extinguish the original rights.

What Lord Denning appears to be telling us here is that there is no clear answer and we have to look at the context of the particular agreement; there can only be a reversion to strict legal rights if it would not be inequitable to do so in the context of the promise. In *High Trees House* the promise by the landlords was to waive their rights to the full rent during the war years; this was clearly a situation which could not change, and it was inequitable for the landlord later to go back on the promise. The same may not be the case if the promise is made because of circumstances which may change. For example, Jo promises not to enforce payment of a debt in full against Sally because she has been made redundant; when Sally obtains employment again, Jo may revert to her original position because the circumstances which gave rise to the promise no longer exist. In most cases it would appear that the context of the promise not to rely will allow a return to original rights on the giving of reasonable notice following a change in circumstances. This is consistent with a doctrine founded in equity.

3. An undecided question in relation to promissory estoppel is whether mere reliance by the promisee on the promise by the promisor not to enforce strict legal rights is sufficient for the estoppel to be operative, or whether that reliance has to be detrimental in some way to the promisee. It is hard to see how the buyers relied to their detriment in *Alan* v. *El Nasr*; if anything, they gained from the waiver by the sellers of their strict legal rights. Indeed, Lord Denning seems to indicate that mere reliance is good enough to estop the promisor. An approach more consistent with the nature of an equitable doctrine is offered by Goff J in *The Post Chaser* ([1982] 1 All ER 19). This moves the focus from the nature of reliance by the promisee onto the nature of the present relation between them by suggesting the requirement of 'inequity'; the promisor cannot return to his original position if to do so would be inequitable to the promisee. The difference between 'inequity' and 'detriment' is that for there to be 'inequity' it would probably be sufficient to show that the promisee had embarked upon a course of action which he would not otherwise have undertaken. If this is the preferred approach, then the conduct of the buyers in reliance on the promise of the sellers in *Alan* v. *El Nasr* would appear to stand right at the outer edge of the doctrine of promissory estoppel.

4. In the United States, §90 of the Restatement (Second) of Contracts reads as follows:

Promise Reasonably Inducing Action or Forbearance
(1) A promise which the promisor should reasonably expect to induce action or forbearance on the part of the promisee or a third person and which does induce such action or forbearance is binding if injustice can be avoided only by enforcement of the promise. The remedy granted for breach may be limited as justice requires.
(2) A charitable subscription or a marriage settlement is binding under subsection (1) without proof that the promise induced action or forbearance.

Thus the promisee is specifically protected, in circumstances where he has relied upon the promise and that reliance is reasonable, since enforcement of the promise is allowed if injustice cannot be avoided. For the reliance school of thought, both such specific legislative protection as is offered in the USA or the judicial protection provided in English law are unnecessary, as reliance should be thought of as good consideration. However, on the view put forward in the Restatement, the distinction between promises supported by consideration being enforceable in a positive sense and promises supported by reliance providing only a defence is containable.

5. As the previous section explained, *Williams* v. *Roffey* has seen the Court of Appeal give a considerably wider definition to consideration. This will inevitably lessen the role of promissory estoppel. The range of cases in which the promisee will not be able to show consideration will be fewer. It is worth noting that if in *Williams* v. *Roffey* the subcontractor had not been able to show that he had given good consideration, he would have had no way of enforcing the main contractor's promise to pay a bonus, as that would have involved using promissory estoppel to found a cause of action. This is not permitted (see *Combe* v. *Combe* [1951] 2 KB 215). Conversely, it could be said that what *Williams* v. *Roffey* shows is that in most commercial contexts, if the court is prepared to apply a broad test of factual benefit, there may be little, if any, scope for arguments based on promissory estoppel. As the next two sections show, on the other hand, estoppel may have a brighter future either in the proprietary context or where it is applied in combination with notions of unconscionability.

B. Proprietary Estoppel

Proprietary estoppel is another equitable doctrine which has been used by the courts to deal with promises made in relation to property rights. The threshold criteria necessary to create a situation in which proprietary estoppel can operate are rather different from promissory estoppel. First, the two doctrines apply, as their names suggest, to two different types of promise: in promissory estoppel, the estoppel arises out of an existing legal relationship between the parties and the promise by one of them not to rely on their strict legal rights; in proprietary estoppel, the estoppel can *only* arise in the context of promises *or conduct* relating to land or other property. Second, the party raising proprietary estoppel must have acted in the mistaken belief that he had or would obtain an interest in property belonging to the other party. Third, the party raising proprietary estoppel must have altered his position to his detriment by either expending money or otherwise incurring a detriment in support of his mistaken belief, e.g. fencing or clearing a piece of land he believed to be his or divesting himself of his only access to water in the belief that he had a right to water from his neighbour's land. Fourth, the party against whom proprietary estoppel is raised must have either actively encouraged the mistaken party in his erroneous belief or have stood by passively while he acted to his detriment.

The final and most important difference is that proprietary estoppel can be used to found a cause of action and is in this respect the complete opposite of promissory estoppel. In *Crabb* v. *Arun DC*, proprietary estoppel is used by the plaintiff to obtain a right of access that the defendants had led him to believe they had already granted.

Crabb v. *Arun DC*
[1975] 3 All ER 865

The plaintiff owned a piece of land. The adjacent piece of land was owned by the defendant council. Both pieces of land had originally been in the same ownership but had been sold separately to the plaintiff and the defendants. The defendants built a road running between the two plots of land. The plaintiff was granted a right of way over the road and access at point A. The plaintiff decided to divide his land into two. He needed a second access point to the defendants' road. He discussed the matter with the defendants at a meeting in July 1967, and was given to understand that he would be granted access at point B. No formal agreement was entered into. The defendants built a new road and fenced it off, leaving a gap in the fence for the plaintiff's access. The plaintiff, believing that he had a right of access at point B, sold the portion of his land served by access at point A and did not reserve for himself any right of access. He then became totally dependant on access point B. The defendants fenced off access point B and refused to reopen it or to grant the plaintiff any access right except on payment of money. The plaintiff commenced proceedings against the defendants for an injunction restraining refusal of the right of access.

The Court of Appeal decided in favour of the plaintiff and, in view of the lapse of time between the plaintiff losing access at point B and the court hearing as well as the conduct of the defendants in withdrawing access and failing to reach an agreement with the plaintiff, granted the plaintiff a right of access at point B.

LORD DENNING MR Summing up the evidence, as accepted by the judge, the result of the meeting on July 22, 1967, was that there was an agreement in principle that the plaintiff should have an additional access at point B to the land, because it was envisaged that he would sell his two acres of land in two portions: the front portion with access at point A to the new road, and the back portion with access at point B to the new road. But the judge found there was no definite assurance to that effect, and, even if there had been, it would not have been binding in the absence of either writing or consideration. . . .

. . . The defendants made no formal grant to the plaintiff of any access at point B or any easement over the new road. But, nevertheless, the parties acted in the belief that he had or would be granted such a right. During the winter of 1967 the defendants erected a fence along the line of the agreed boundary, but they left gaps at point A with access to the front portion of the plaintiff's land at point B with access to the back portion. These two gaps were used by lorries which went in and out at points A and B as if they were exits and entrances. . . .

On February 6, 1968, there was an important development. The defendants gave orders for gates to be constructed at points A and B, and they were in fact constructed. . . . The gateposts were set firmly in concrete at points A and B, and were clearly intended to be permanent.

Some months later, in the autumn of 1968, the plaintiff agreed to sell the front portion of his land to a purchaser and assigned to the purchaser the right of access at point A. But, here is the important matter. In the conveyance of the front portion of October 4, 1968, the plaintiff did not reserve any right for himself (as the owner of the back portion) to go over the front portion so as to get out at point A. The plaintiff thought that he already had a right of access at point B (where gates had already been erected) and so he did not need to reserve any right to get to point A . . . .

But then, in January 1969, there was a new development. The plaintiff put a padlock on the inside of the gate at point B. The defendants were incensed by this. But they did not say a word to the plaintiff. They went on to his land. They took down the gates at point B. They pulled them out of the concrete. They took them away and filled the gap with extra posts and a close-boarded fence to match the existing fence. In short, they shut up the access at point B. . . .

In June 1971 the plaintiff brought this action claiming a right of access at point B and a right of way along the estate road. He had no such right by any deed or conveyance or written agreement. So, in strict law, on the conveyance, the defendants were entitled to their land, subject only to an easement at point A, but none at point B. To overcome this strict law, the plaintiff claimed a right of access at B on the ground of equitable estoppel, promissory or proprietary. . . .

When Mr. Millett, for the plaintiff, said that he put his case on an estoppel, it shook me a little: because it is commonly supposed that estoppel is not itself a cause of action. But that is because there are estoppels and estoppels. Some do give rise to a cause of action. Some do not. In the species of estoppel called proprietary estoppel, it does give rise to a cause of action. . . .

The basis of this proprietary estoppel—as indeed of promissory estoppel—is the interposition of equity. Equity comes in, true to form, to mitigate the rigours of strict law. . . . it will prevent a person from insisting on his strict legal rights—whether arising under a contract, or on his title deeds, or by statute—when it would be inequitable for him to do so having regard to the dealings which have taken place between the parties.

What then are the dealings which will preclude him from insisting on his strict legal rights? If he makes a binding contract that he will not insist on the strict legal position, a court of equity will hold him to his contract. Short of a binding contract, if he makes a promise that he will not insist upon his strict legal rights—then, even though that promise may be unenforceable in point of law for want of consideration or want of writing—then, if he makes the promise knowing or intending that the other will act upon it, and he does act upon it, then again a court of equity will not allow him to go back on that promise: . . . . Short of an actual promise, if he, by his words or conduct, so behaves as to lead another to believe that he will not insist on his strict legal rights—knowing or intending that the other will act on that belief—and he does so act, that again will raise an equity in favour of the other; and it is for a court of equity to say in what way the equity may be satisfied. The cases show that this equity does not depend on agreement but on words or conduct. . . .

The question then is: were the circumstances here such as to raise an equity in favour of the plaintiff? True the defendants on the deeds had the title to their land, free of any access at point B. But they led the plaintiff to believe that he had or would be granted a right of access at point B. At the meeting of July 26, 1967, Mr. Alford and the plaintiff told the defendants' representative that the plaintiff intended to split the two acres into two portions and wanted to have an access at point B for the back portion; and the defendants' representative agreed that he should have this access. I do not think the defendants can avoid responsibility by saying that their representative had no authority to agree this. They entrusted him with the task of setting out the line of the fence and the gates, and they must be answerable for his conduct in the course of it . . . .

The judge found that there was "no definite assurance" by the defendants' representative, and "no firm commitment," but only an "agreement in princi-ple," meaning I suppose that, as Mr. Alford said, there were "some further processes" to be gone through before it would become binding. But if there were any such processes in the mind of the parties, the subsequent conduct of the defendants was such as to dispense with them. The defendants actually put up the gates at point B at considerable expense. That certainly led the plaintiff to believe that they agreed that he should have the right of access through point B without more ado. . . .

In the circumstances it seems to me inequitable that the council should insist on their strict title as they did; and to take the high-handed action of pulling down the gates without a word of warning: and to demand of the plaintiff £3,000 as the price for the easement. If he had moved at once for an injunction in aid of his equity—to prevent them removing the gates—I think he should have been granted it. But he did not do so. He tried to negotiate terms, but these failing, the action has come for trial. And we have the question: in what way now should the equity be satisfied?

Here equity is displayed at its most flexible, see *Snell's Principles of Equity*, 27th ed. (1973), p. 568, and the illustrations there given. If the matter had been finally settled in 1967, I should have thought that, although nothing was said at the meeting in July 1967, nevertheless it would be quite reasonable for the defendants to ask the plaintiff to pay something for the access at point B, perhaps—and I am guessing—some hundreds of pounds. But, as Mr. Millett pointed out in the course of the argument, because of the defendants' conduct, the back land has been landlocked. It has been sterile and rendered useless for five or six years: and the plaintiff has been unable to deal with it during that time. This loss to him can be taken into account. And at the present time, it seems to me that, in order to satisfy the equity, the plaintiff should have the right of access at point B without paying anything for it.

I would, therefore, hold that the plaintiff, as the owner of the back portion, has a right of access at point B . . . without paying compensation. I would allow the appeal and declare that he has an easement, accordingly.

SCARMAN LJ . . . If the plaintiff has any right, it is an equity arising out of the conduct and relationship of the parties. In such a case I think it is now well settled law that the court, having analysed and assessed the conduct and relationship of the parties, has to answer three questions. First, is there an equity established? Secondly, what is the extent of the equity, if one is established? And, thirdly, what is the relief appropriate to satisfy the equity? . . . In pursuit of that inquiry I do not find helpful the distinction between promissory and proprietary estoppel. This distinction may indeed be valuable to those who have to teach or expound the law; but I do not think that, in solving the particular problem raised by a particular case, putting the law into categories is of the slightest assistance . . .

I come now to consider the first of the three questions which I think in a case such as this the court have to consider. What is needed to establish an equity? . . . [He quotes dicta from] Lord Kingsdown [in *Ramsden* v. *Dyson* (1866)], L.R. 1 HL 129, 170:

"The rule of law applicable to the case appears to me to be this: If a man, under a verbal agreement with a landlord for a certain interest in land, or, what amounts to the same thing, *under an expectation, created or encouraged by the landlord*,"—my italics—"that he shall have a certain interest, takes possession of such land, with the consent of the landlord, and upon the faith of such promise or expectation, with the knowledge of the landlord, and without objection by him, lays out money upon the land, a court of equity will compel the landlord to give effect to such promise or expectation."

That statement of the law is put into the language of landlord and tenant because it was a landlord and tenant situation with which Lord Kingsdown was concerned; but it has been accepted as of general application. While *Ramsden* v. *Dyson* may properly be considered as the modern starting-point of the law of equitable estoppel, it was analysed and spelt out in a judgment of Fry J. in 1880 in *Willmott* v. *Barber* (1880) 15 Ch. D. 96 . . . Mr. Lightman for the defendants sought to make a submission in reliance upon the judgment. Fry J. said, at pp. 105–106:

"It has been said that the acquiescence which will deprive a man of his legal rights must amount to fraud, and in my view that is an abbreviated statement of a very true proposition. A man is not to be deprived of his legal rights unless he has acted in such a way as would make it fraudulent for him to set up those rights. What, then are the elements or requisites necessary to constitute fraud of that description? In the first place the plaintiff must have made a mistake as to his legal rights. Secondly, the plaintiff must have expended some money or must have done some act (not necessarily upon the defendant's land) on the faith of his mistaken belief. Thirdly, the defendant, the possessor of the legal right, must know of the existence of his own right which is inconsistent with the right claimed by the plaintiff. If he does not know of it he is in the same position as the plaintiff, and the doctrine of acquiescence is founded upon conduct with a knowledge of your legal rights. Fourthly, the defendant, the possessor of the legal right, must know of the plaintiff's mistaken belief of his rights. If he does not, there is nothing which calls upon him to assert this own rights. Lastly,"—if I may digress, this is the important element as far as this appeal is concerned—"the defendant, the possessor of the legal right, might have encouraged the plaintiff in his expenditure of money or in the other acts which he has done, either directly or by abstaining from asserting his legal right."

. . . . "Fraud" was a word often in the mouths of those robust judges who adorned the bench in the 19th century. It is less often in the mouths of the more wary judicial spirits today who sit upon the bench. But it is clear that whether one uses the word "fraud" or not, the plaintiff has to establish as a fact that the defendant, by setting up his right, is taking advantage of him in a way which is unconscionable, inequitable or unjust. . . .

The court therefore cannot find an equity established unless it is prepared to go as far as to say that it would be unconscionable and unjust to allow the defendants to set up their undoubted rights against the claim being made by the plaintiff. In order to reach a conclusion upon that matter the court does have to consider the history of the negotiations under the five headings to which Fry J. referred. I need not at this stage weary anyone with an elaborate statement of the facts. I have no doubt upon the facts of this case that the first four elements referred to by Fry J. exist. The question before the judge and now in this court is whether the fifth element is present: have the defendants, as possessor of the legal right, encouraged the plaintiff in the expenditure of money or in the other acts which he has done, either directly or by abstaining from asserting their legal rights? The first matter to be considered is the meeting on site of July 26, 1967. . . .

. . . Clearly the plaintiff and Mr. Alford [the plaintiff's architect] came away from that meeting in the confident expectation that a right would in due course be accorded to the plaintiff. Mr. Alford did foresee "further processes." Of course, there would be further processes. The nature of the legal right to be granted had to be determined. It might be given by way of licence. It might be granted by way of easement. Conditions might be imposed. Payment of a sum of money might be required. But those two men, the plaintiff and his architect, came away from the meeting in the confident expectation that such a right would be granted upon reasonable conditions. . . . The confident expectation with which the plaintiff and Mr. Alford left the meeting in July remained remarkably undisturbed by the meeting of January 1968. Indeed it was reinforced because there on the ground, plain for all to see, was a fence with gaps which accorded exactly with the agreement in principle reached in the previous July. Ten days later the defendants ordered gates, and by March the gates were installed. I ask myself: as at March 1968 had these defendants encouraged the plaintiff to think that he had or was going to be given a right? To use the language of Fry J., had they done it directly or had they done it by abstaining from asserting a legal right? Their encouragement of the belief in the mind of the plaintiff and Mr. Alford was both direct and indirect. It was direct because of what they had done on the ground. It was indirect because ever since the July meeting they had abstained from giving the plaintiff or his architect any indication that they were standing on their rights, or had it in mind to go back, as, of course, they were entitled at that stage to go back, upon the agreement in principle reached at that meeting. . . . In September 1968, without telling the defendants or giving them any notice, so far as I am aware, the plaintiff entered into a contract to sell the northern piece of land without reservation over that land of any right of way. This was the act which was detrimental to the interests of the plaintiff. He did it in the belief that he had or could enforce a right of way and access at point B in the southern land.

. . . Does the fact that the defendants had no notice of the sale of the northern land before it was completed destroy the equity? Mr. Lightman will concede, as I understand this part of his argument, no more than this: that the plaintiff might have been able to establish an equity if he had referred to the defendants before binding himself to the purchaser of the northern land: for that would have given the defendants an opportunity of disabusing the mind of the plaintiff before he acted to his detriment. The point is worthy of careful consideration. I reject it because, in my judgment, in this sort of proceedings, the court must be careful to avoid generalisation. I can conceive of cases in which it would be absolutely appropriate for a defendant to say: "But you should not have acted to your detriment until you had had a word with me and I could have put you right." But there are cases in which it is far too late for a defendant to get himself out of his pickle by putting upon the plaintiff that sort of duty; and this, in my judgment, is one of those cases. If immediately following the July meeting the clerk to the defendant authority had written saying: "I have had a report of the meeting with the assistant engineer and I must inform you that whether or not there is to be an easement or a licence is a matter which can only be decided by the council," the plaintiff would not now establish his equity: in selling the northern land without reservation of a right of way, he would have acted at his own risk. But one has to look at the whole conduct of the parties and the developing relationship between them. By September 1968, 13½ months after the initial meeting, the plaintiff must really and reasonably have been attaching importance to the abstention of the defendants from declaring to him in correspondence, or by telephone to his agent, their true position, namely, that there would be no acceptance in principle of a right until the matter had been considered by the authority itself. By that time there had been, as well, the laying out of the fence and the installing of the gates. It is for those reasons—the passage of time, the abstention and the gates—that I think the defendants cannot rely upon the fact that the plaintiff acted, without referring to the defendants, on his intention—an intention of which they had had notice ever since their agent was informed of it at the meeting in July 1967. I think therefore an equity is established.

I turn now to the other two questions—the extent of the equity and the relief needed to satisfy it. There being no grant, no enforceable contract, no licence, I would analyse the minimum equity to do justice to the plaintiff as a right either to an easement or to a licence upon terms to be agreed. I do not think it is necessary to go further than that. Of course, going that far would support the equitable remedy of injunction which is sought in this action. If there is no agreement as to terms, if agreement fails to be obtained, the court can, in my judgment, and must, determine in these proceedings upon what terms the plaintiff should be put to enable him to have the benefit of the equitable right which he is held to have. . . .

In the present case the court does have to consider what is necessary now in order to satisfy the plaintiff's equity. Had matters taken a different turn, I would without hesitation have said that the plaintiff should be put upon terms to be agreed if possible with the defendants, and, if not agreed, settled by the court. But, as already mentioned by Lord Denning MR and Lawton LJ, there has been a history of delay, and indeed high-handedness, which it is impossible to disregard. In January 1969 the defendants, for reasons which no doubt they thought good at the time, without consulting the plaintiff, locked up his land. They removed not only the padlocks which he had put on the gates at point B, but the gates themselves. In their place they put a fence—rendering access impossible save by breaking down the fence. I am not disposed to consider whether or not the defendants are to be blamed in moral terms for what they did. I just do not know. But the effect of their action has been to sterilise the plaintiff's land; and for the reasons which I have endeavoured to give, such action was an infringement of an equitable right possessed by the plaintiff. It has involved him in loss, which has not been measured; but, since it amounted to sterilisation of an industrial estate for a very considerable period of time, it must surpass any sort of sum of money which the plaintiff ought reasonably, before it was done, to have paid the defendants in order to obtain an enforceable legal right. I think therefore that nothing should now be paid by the plaintiff and that he should receive at the hands of the court the belated protection of the equity that he has established. Reasonable terms, other than money payment, should be agreed; or, if not agreed, determined by the court.

For those reasons I also would allow the appeal.

Notes

1. The remedy awarded to the plaintiff was the grant of a right of access at point B. At first sight it seems that the remedies afforded in proprietary estoppel are more flexible than under contract. An example of a seemingly very generous remedy is *Pascoe* v. *Turner* ([1979] 1 WLR 431). The defendant in that case had received a promise from the plaintiff that the house which she had shared with him and its contents were hers when he ceased to live there. In reliance on this promise, the defendant spent around £230 on decorating the house. The plaintiff later sued for possession of the house and the defendant raised proprietary estoppel as a defence and by way of counter-claim. The Court of Appeal upheld this claim and ordered the house to be conveyed to the defendant. Clearly, there were other remedies that the Court of Appeal could have ordered which might perhaps have better reflected the amount of the defendant's modest expenditure, such as a life interest in the house. Perhaps the key to the award of a remedy of this type can be seen from the final paragraph of Scarman LJ's judgment in *Crabb* v. *Arun DC*. The Court of Appeal in that case may have felt that the grant of a right of access was the only way in which the plaintiff's equity could be satisfied.

The remedy that is usually awarded in contract is expectation damages, or, if an award in these terms is insufficient to compensate the injured party, specific performance or an injunction (see generally Ch. 14), thereby also protecting the expectation interests of the plaintiff. In proprietary estoppel the remedy appears to be whatever is necessary to put the plaintiff in the position he thought he was in. The plaintiff in *Crabb* v. *Arun DC* thought at the outset that he would have to pay the defendant Council a sum of money for access at point B. What persuaded the court that the plaintiff should not have to negotiate and pay an appropriate sum was the conduct of the defendants and the amount of time during which the plaintiff's industrial estate had been landlocked. In other words, without this additional feature an order to reach agreement on terms would have been sufficient. The idea of fashioning a remedy to put the injured party in the position he thought he was in would appear to have the same effect as the remedies available in contract.

2. The two extracts which follow are taken from case notes written on *Crabb* v. *Arun DC*. One of the commentators, Millett QC (as he then was), was leading counsel for the plaintiff before the Court of Appeal. The extracts demonstrate the divergent views of the reliance school (Atiyah) and the exchange or bargain school (Millett). Millett indicates that he is not averse to viewing the traditional boundaries of consideration as too narrow; however, he is clearly not prepared to go as far into the reliance camp as Atiyah and he does see a 'separate language' for estoppel and considera-

tion. Thus we can assume that he subscribes to the view that consideration must involve something more than mere reliance.

P. S. Atiyah, ' "When Is an Enforceable Agreement Not a Contract?" Answer: When It Is an Equity', (1976) 92 *LQR* 174, 175–80

[In *Crabb* v. *Arun*] Lord Denning suggest that the plaintiff was led to believe that a right of way would be granted, and both he and Scarman L.J. quoted the words of Lord Kingsdown in *Ramsden* v. *Dyson* at p. 170 to the effect that there was a verbal agreement, or "what amounts to the same thing," an "expectation created or encouraged" by the defendants. . . .

With this finding of fact, it might have been thought that the plaintiff could have had a simple contract remedy. . . . What, one may ask, has gone wrong with the law of contract, that a claim based on an agreement could not be enforced as a contract? There are probably three reasons why the plaintiff chose to argue estoppel rather than contract. First, it may have been thought that a claim based on contract would have required proof of a more positive promise or undertaking by the defendants, rather than the vague creation of an expectation. Secondly, there may have been doubts about the doctrine of consideration. [Third reason omitted.]

Yet it is difficult to understand why . . . these . . . difficulties need have proved insurmountable in a claim overtly based on contract any more than in a claim based on estoppel. Let me take them in turn. The first difficulty is surely non-existent. It has been standard contractual doctrine for at least a hundred years that the intention of a party is to be deduced from the way he has conducted himself, and from what he has said. If a party leads another to suppose that he has granted an undertaking or made a promise, it is immaterial that he did not, in his own mind, intend to commit himself. There is nothing peculiarly equitable about this doctrine. Indeed, the paradoxical truth is that it is the doctrine of estoppel which has dragged its feet on this point, and not the common law rules of contract. . . .

Most probably, however, the plaintiff's advisers were more concerned about the difficulty of establishing consideration if they openly sued on a contract. But this too does not seem an insurmountable difficulty. For one thing, the plaintiff could have argued that the agreement was based on a price to be fixed, and was thus a perfectly good bilateral contract. . . .

[I]s there any reason why the plaintiff should not have been able to set up his action in reliance on the undertaking or agreement, as a valid consideration? The standard doctrine is clear enough: consideration does not have to be a benefit to the promisor, it is enough that there is a detriment to the promisee. Here, plainly, there was a detriment, *viz.* the action of the plaintiff in selling the northern portion of his land without reserving a right of way. Why would that action in reliance not have been a sufficient detriment to constitute a consideration? The only possible answer must be: because the plaintiff's sale of the land was not requested or specified as the consideration required by the defendants. Although the defendants knew that the plaintiff was contemplating the sale of part of his land the actual sale was made without the defendants' knowledge, or request. . . .

It seems clear . . . that the problem of what is, in any given case, a sufficient action in reliance to justify holding a party bound by an undertaking or promise or expectation he has created, cannot be magically wafted away by calling the case estoppel instead of contract.

P. Millett, '*Crabb* v. *Arun* DC: A Riposte', (1976) 92 *LQR* 342 at 342–5

The plaintiff's claim as originally pleaded did in fact rest on simple contract. It ran into immediate difficulties. When the defence was served, it denied the existence of any enforceable contract on at least four separate grounds, each of which appeared to be unassailable. These were: (i) that there was in fact no agreement; (ii) that if there was an agreement it was unsupported by consideration; [grounds 3 and 4 were respectively a technical requirement under the Law of Property Act 1925 and an argument based on agency; neither is relevant for our purposes].

Faced with this defence, the plaintiff changed his ground. By his reply, he alleged an estoppel; and at the opening of the case at first instance his counsel expressly disclaimed any reliance upon the existence of a contract. . . .

The grounds for the concession may now be considered in turn.

(i) *Lack of any agreement.* . . . A contract must bind *both* parties, not one only; and the defendant council could not, by voluntary acts on its part not requested by the plaintiff, impose contractual obligations upon him. Nor could it be relied upon as constituting an "offer" by conduct, capable of "acceptance" by the plaintiff. It was not so intended by the defendant council nor so understood by the plaintiff, and was not "accepted" by any conduct on his part. But it could be relied upon as confirming the reasonable expectation in the plaintiff's mind that his request for a new access point would be granted. That expectation having been thus created, once the plaintiff, in reliance thereon, had irreversibly prejudiced his position in a manner which was reasonably to be foreseen, it was clearly inequitable to allow the expectation to be defeated. But this is the language of estoppel, not of contract.

(ii) *Lack of consideration.* The plaintiff might have been willing to pay a reasonable sum for the access he desired, if it had been asked for, but it was not; and he certainly never expressly or by implication agreed to do so. The discussion at the initial meeting never reached this stage. Professor Atiyah suggests that the plaintiff's conduct in disposing of the portion of his land, which deprived the remaining portion of all access, could be regarded as constituting sufficient consideration for the grant of the new access which he has sought.

This is not the place to consider whether the traditional definition of consideration may not be too narrow; but Professor Atiyah's suggestion appears to
deprive it of all sensible meaning. The plaintiff's disposal of his own land, and
the terms of disposal, were matters of complete indifference to the defendant
council. The disposal was not sought by, or even known to, the council. More
to the point, it formed no part of the arrangements for the provision of the new
access, and was in no sense a *quid pro quo*. The plaintiff disposed of his land
without reserving a right of way, not because he understood that this was part
of any arrangement he had entered into with the council, but because he had
been encouraged to believe that he already had, or would shortly be granted, a
new access to his remaining land. Again, this is the language of estoppel, not of
contract.

3. In *Crabb* v. *Arun DC* there is no pre-existing legal relationship between
the litigating parties and, as mentioned in the introduction to proprietary
estoppel, it is a feature of the doctrine that this is *not* a condition of its
operation. We also saw in our discussion of promissory estoppel that the
exact nature of the reliance necessary to support the doctrine—i.e. whether
it must be detrimental or not—is not conclusively settled. It appears that in
proprietary estoppel the reliance must be detrimental and must arise out
of the words or the conduct of the other party which foster the expectation
in the mistaken party that he owns either the land or an interest in the
land. It is important to note that, while promissory estoppel is concerned
with issues that arise in the context of pre-existing relationships, proprietary estoppel focuses solely on the expectation of the promisee and *how*
that expectation arose. To this end, a failure by the other party to correct
the promisee's mistaken assumption can be sufficient for rights under proprietary estoppel to arise.

4. In the extracts from *Crabb*, Scarman LJ made the observation that he
did not find the drawing of distinctions between different types of estoppel
helpful. One interpretation of that dictum is to say that he is of the view
that these two doctrines are so similar that they could be combined.
Another is that he is saying nothing so bold, and is referring instead to the
common base of the two doctrines, namely that in both effect is given to
promises where there has been reliance and where it would be unconscionable to allow the promisor to rely upon his strict legal rights. The latter view is the preferable one. The two doctrines have developed on
distinct lines in English law, and apply to different situations and different
types of promise. If Scarman LJ had been advocating the merging of the
two doctrines, it is likely that he would have used considerably more
expansive language to justify his position.

The most fundamental difference between the two doctrines is that
while promissory estoppel is defensive in nature, rights under proprietary

estoppel can be used to found a cause of action. There are several reasons for this difference. The first is that to allow promissory estoppel to found a cause of action would be to recognize that reliance was in effect good consideration—usually for the variation of an existing contract. This lies behind the argument of the reliance school that there is no need for a doctrine such as promissory estoppel. The second reason is that proprietary estoppel is concerned not only with the promise made and the fact of the promisee's reliance but also with the conduct of the other party in either acquiescing or encouraging the promisee in his mistaken belief. Thirdly, there is the possibility of unjust enrichment in proprietary estoppel; it is possible that the promisee acting under his mistaken belief will have improved the other party's land or expended money on it. This is less likely to occur in promissory estoppel.

The Australian case which follows—*Waltons Stores (Interstate) Ltd.* v. *Maher*—takes the common base of the doctrines in equity to its extreme, and appears to allow recovery in a factual situation which matches neither proprietary estoppel nor promissory estoppel as conventionally understood in England.

5. For further discussion of proprietary estoppel see P. S. Atiyah, 'Consideration and Estoppel: The Thawing of the Ice', (1975) 38 *MLR* 65; J. Dewar, 'Licences and Land Law: An Alternative View', (1986) 49 *MLR* 471; I. Duncanson, 'Equity and Obligations', (1976) 39 *MLR* 268; S. Moriarty, 'Licences and Land Law: Legal Principles and Public Policies', (1984) 100 *LQR* 376; M. Thompson, 'From Representation to Expectation: Estoppel as a Cause of Action', [1983] *CLJ* 257; and A. Teh, 'Promissory Estoppel as a Sword', (1984) 13 *Anglo-Am. L. Rev.* 47.

C. A New Approach to Estoppel?

Waltons Stores (Interstate) Ltd. v. *Maher*
(1988) 62 ALJR 110

The respondents were the owners of commercial property. They negotiated with the appellants to demolish the latters' current commercial premises and construct new ones which the appellants would lease. The respondents' solicitors supplied the appellants' solicitors with the relevant documentation 'by way of exchange'. They heard nothing from the appellants and proceeded to perform their part of the agreement, viz. the demolition of the old premises and the construction of new ones. During the construction of the new premises the appellants informed the respondents that they did not wish to go ahead with the lease arrangement. The respondents began an action for a declaration that there was a valid and enforceable agreement for the lease. They sought specific performance but were

awarded damages in lieu by the first instance judge, Kearney J, who held
that the appellants were estopped from denying that a concluded contract
by way of exchange existed. The appellants appealed to the New South
Wales Court of Appeal, where their appeal was dismissed, and thence to
the High Court of Australia. The following extracts are taken from the judgments of the members of the High Court who dismissed the appeal.

MASON CJ and WILSON J The estoppel set up by the respondents and found
by the primary judge was a common law estoppel in the form of a representation by the appellant constituted by its silence in circumstances where it should
have spoken. . . .

If there is any basis at all for holding that common law estoppel arises where
there is a mistaken assumption as to future events, that basis must lie in reversing *Jorden v Money* (1854) 5 HLC 185 and in accepting the powerful dissent of
Lord St Leonards in that case. The repeated acceptance of *Jorden v Money*
over the years by courts of the highest authority makes this a formidable exercise. We put it to one side as the respondents did not present any argument to
us along these lines.

This brings us to the doctrine of promissory estoppel on which the respondents relied in this Court to sustain the judgment in their favour. Promissory
estoppel certainly extends to representations (or promises) as to future conduct
. . . . So far the doctrine has been mainly confined to precluding departure from
a representation by a person in a pre-existing contractual relationship that he
will not enforce his contractual rights, whether they be pre-existing or rights to
be acquired as a result of the representation: *Ajayi v Briscoe* . . . . But Denning J
in *Central London Property Trust Ltd v High Trees House Ltd*, treated it as a wide-
ranging doctrine operating outside the pre-existing contractual relationship . . . .
In principle there is certainly no reason why the doctrine should not apply so as
to preclude departure by a person from a representation that he will not
enforce a non-contractual right . . .

There has been for many years a reluctance to allow promissory estoppel to
become the vehicle for the positive enforcement of a representation by a party
that he would do something in the future. Promissory estoppel, it has been said,
is a defensive equity (*Hughes v Metropolitan Railway Co* (1877) 2 App Cas 439 at
448; *Combe v Combe* [1951] 2 KB 215 at 219–220) and the traditional notion has
been that estoppel could only be relied upon defensively as a shield and not as
a sword . . . . But this does not mean that a plaintiff cannot rely on an estoppel.
Even according to traditional orthodoxy, a plaintiff may rely on an estoppel if
he has an independent cause of action, where in the words of Denning LJ in
Combe v Combe, the estoppel "may be part of a cause of action, but not a cause
of action in itself".

But the respondents ask us to drive promissory estoppel one step further by
enforcing directly in the absence of a pre-existing relationship of any kind a

non-contractual promise on which the representee has relied to his detriment. For the purposes of discussion, we shall assume that there was such a promise in the present case. The principal objection to the enforcement of such a promise is that it would outflank the principles of the law of contract . . . Denning LJ in *Combe v Combe*, after noting that "The doctrine of consideration is too firmly fixed to be overthrown by a side-wind", said (at 220) that such a promise could only be enforced if it was supported by sufficient consideration. . . .

There is force in these objections and it may not be a sufficient answer to repeat the words of Lord Denning MR in *Crabb v Arun District Council* [1976] Ch 179 at 187, "Equity comes in, true to form, to mitigate the rigours of strict law". True it is that in the orthodox case of promissory estoppel, where the promisor promises that he will not exercise or enforce an existing right, the elements of reliance and detriment attract equitable intervention on the basis that it is unconscionable for the promisor to depart from his promise, if to do so will result in detriment to the promisee. . . .

The point is that, generally speaking, a plaintiff cannot enforce a voluntary promise because the promisee may reasonably be expected to appreciate that, to render it binding, it must form part of a binding contract.

Crabb was an instance of promissory estoppel. It lends assistance to the view that promissory estoppel may in some circumstances extend to the enforcement of a right not previously in existence where the defendant has encouraged in the plaintiff the belief that it will be granted and has acquiesced in action taken by the plaintiff in that belief. . . . As Oliver J pointed out in *Taylors Fashions Ltd v Liverpool Victoria Trustees Co Ltd* [1982] QB 133 at 153, the Court of Appeal treated promissory estoppel and proprietary estoppel or estoppel by acquiescence as mere facets of the same general principle. . . . In *Taylors Fashions* Oliver J also remarked (at 153) that what gave rise to the need for the court to intervene was the defendants' unconscionable attempt to go back on the assumptions which were the foundation of their dealings. Indeed, Scarman LJ in *Crabb* saw the question in terms of whether an equity had arisen from the conduct and relationship of the parties (at 193–194), concluding that the court should determine what was "the minimum equity to do justice to the plaintiff" (at 198). . . .

The decision in *Crabb* is consistent with the principle of proprietary estoppel applied in *Ramsden v Dyson* . . . And it should be noted that in *Crabb*, as in *Ramsden v Dyson*, although equity acted by way of recognising a proprietary interest in the plaintiff, that proprietary interest came into existence as the only appropriate means by which the defendants could be effectively estopped from exercising their existing legal rights.

One may therefore discern in the cases a common thread which links them together, namely, the principle that equity will come to the relief of a plaintiff who has acted to his detriment on the basis of a basic assumption in relation to which the other party to the transaction had "played such a part in the adoption of the assumption that it would be unfair or unjust if he were left free to ignore it" . . . Equity comes to the relief of such a plaintiff on the footing that it would be unconscionable conduct on the part of the other party to ignore the assumption. . . .

The foregoing review of the doctrine of promissory estoppel indicates that the doctrine extends to the enforcement of voluntary promises on the footing that a departure from the basic assumptions underlying the transaction between the parties must be unconscionable. As failure to fulfil a promise does not of itself amount to unconscionable conduct, mere reliance on an executory promise to do something, resulting in the promisee changing his position or suffering detriment, does not bring promissory estoppel into play. Something more would be required. *Humphrey's Estate* [[1987] AC 114] suggests that this may be found, if at all, in the creation or encouragement by the party estopped in the other party of an assumption that a contract will come into existence or a promise will be performed and that the other party relied on that assumption to his detriment to the knowledge of the first party. *Humphrey's Estate* referred in terms to an assumption that the plaintiff would not exercise an existing legal right or liberty, the right or liberty to withdraw from the negotiations, but as a matter of substance such an assumption is indistinguishable from an assumption that a binding contract would eventuate. On the other hand the United States experience, distilled in the *Restatement* (2d §90), suggests that the principle is to be expressed in terms of a reasonable expectation on the part of the promisor that his promise will induce action or forbearance by the promisee, the promise inducing such action or forbearance in circumstances where injustice arising from unconscionable conduct can only be avoided by holding the promisor to his promise. . . .

. . . the crucial question remains: was the appellant entitled to stand by in silence when it must have known that the respondents were proceeding on the assumption that they had an agreement and that completion of the exchange was a formality? The mere exercise of its legal right not to exchange contracts could not be said to amount to unconscionable conduct on the part of the appellant. But there were two other factors present in the situation which require to be taken into consideration. The first was the element of urgency that pervaded the negotiation of the terms of the proposed lease . . . The respondents' solicitor had said to the appellant's solicitor on 7 November that it would be impossible for Maher to complete the building within the agreed time unless the agreement were concluded "within the next day or two". The outstanding details were agreed within a day or two thereafter, and the work of preparing the site commenced almost immediately.

The second factor of importance is that the respondents executed the counterpart deed and it was forwarded to the appellant's solicitor on 11 November. The assumption on which the respondents acted thereafter was that completion of the necessary exchange was a formality. The next their solicitor heard from the appellant was a letter from its solicitors dated 19 January, informing him that the appellant did not intend to proceed with the matter. It had known, at least since 10 December, that costly work was proceeding on the site.

It seems to us, in the light of these considerations, that the appellant was under an obligation to communicate with the respondents within a reasonable time after receiving the executed counterpart deed and certainly when it learnt on 10 December that demolition was proceeding. It had to choose whether to complete the contract or to warn the respondents that it had not yet decided upon the course it would take . . . . It was unconscionable for it, knowing that the respondents were exposing themselves to detriment by acting on the basis of a false assumption, to adopt a course of inaction which encouraged them in the course they had adopted. To express the point in the language of promissory estoppel the appellant is estopped in all the circumstances from retreating from its implied promise to complete the contract.

BRENNAN J . . . an equitable estoppel is a source of legal obligation. It is not enforceable against the party estopped because a cause of action or ground of defence would arise on an assumed state of affairs; it is the source of a legal obligation arising on an actual state of affairs. An equitable estoppel is binding in conscience on the party estopped, and it is to be satisfied by that party doing or abstaining from doing something in order to prevent detriment to the party raising the estoppel which that party would otherwise suffer by having acted or abstained from acting in reliance on the assumption or expectation which he has been induced to adopt. Perhaps equitable estoppel is more accurately described as an equity created by estoppel. . . .

. . . Mr Maher expected that Waltons would execute and deliver the original deed of Agreement for Lease and would thereby make a binding contract. Mr Maher either assumed that a contract had been made or expected that, the matter having passed beyond the stage of negotiations, Waltons would execute and deliver the original deed and was not free at that stage to withdraw. Kearney J found that the Mahers "believed that they had an agreement" because they had assumed "that the exchange would be duly completed". In reliance on that assumption or expectation Mr Maher proceeded to clear the site and build the store. Waltons discovered that Mr Maher was performing the work required under the proposed contract, and it must have known that Mr Maher would not have commenced that work if he had not assumed that a contract had been made or expected that Waltons was bound to enter into a contract. Waltons intended that he should act on that assumption or expectation by continuing to build the store in order that Waltons should enjoy the option of completing the exchange and proceeding to take the lease if it should appear expedient to do so. It was not disputed in this Court that the Mahers would suffer detriment if Mr Maher's expectation were to go unfulfilled.

Is this sufficient to create an equity in the Mahers . . . [?]

The element which both attracts the jurisdiction of a court of equity and shapes the remedy to be given in unconscionable conduct on the part of the person bound by the equity, and the remedy required to satisfy an equity varies according to the circumstances of the case . . . . However, in moulding its decree, the court, as a court of conscience, goes no further than is necessary to prevent unconscionable conduct. What, then, is unconscionable conduct? An exhaustive definition is both impossible and unnecessary, but the minimum elements required to give rise to an equitable estoppel should be stated.

Some indication of what constitutes unconscionable conduct can be gleaned from the instances in which an equity created by estoppel has been held to arise. If cases of equitable estoppel are in truth but particular instances of the operation of the general principles of equity, there is little purpose in dividing those cases into the categories of promissory and proprietary estoppel which are not necessarily exhaustive of the cases in which equity will intervene. Like Scarman LJ in *Crabb v Arun District Council*, I do not find it generally helpful to divide into classes the cases in which an equity created by estoppel has been held to exist. However, the familiar categories serve to identify the characteristics of the circumstances which have been held to give rise to an equity in the party raising the estoppel. In cases of promissory estoppel, the equity binds the holder of a legal right who induces another to expect that that right will not be exercised against him . . . In cases of proprietary estoppel, the equity binds the owner of property who induces another to expect that an interest in the property will be conferred on him . . . .

In all cases where an equity created by estoppel is raised, the party raising the equity has acted or abstained from acting on an assumption or expectation as to the legal relationship between himself and the party who induced him to adopt the assumption or expectation. The assumption or expectation does not relate to mere facts, whether existing or future. (An assumption as to a legal relationship may be an assumption that there is no legal relationship, as in the cases where A builds on B's land assuming it to be his own.) Though the party raising the estoppel may be under no mistake as to the facts, he assumes that a particular legal relationship exists or expects that a particular legal relationship will exist between himself and the party who induced the assumption or expectation. The assumption or expectation may involve an error of law. Thus a promissory or a proprietary estoppel may arise when a party, not mistaking any facts, erroneously attributes a binding legal effect to a promise made without consideration. But, if the party raising the estoppel is induced by the other party's promise to adopt an assumption or expectation, the promise must be intended by the promisor and understood by the promisee to affect their legal relations. . . .

. . . it is important to observe that the doctrine has no application to an assumption or expectation induced by a promise which is not intended by the promisor and understood by the promisee to affect their legal relations . . . .

Parties who are negotiating a contract may proceed in the expectation that the terms will be agreed and a contract made but, so long as both parties recognise that either party is at liberty to withdraw from the negotiations at any time before the contract is made, it cannot be unconscionable for one party to do so. Of course, the freedom to withdraw may be fettered or extinguished by agreement but, in the absence of agreement, either party ordinarily retains his freedom to withdraw. It is only if a party induces the other party to believe that he, the former party, is already bound and his freedom to withdraw has gone that it could be unconscionable for him subsequently to assert that he is legally free to withdraw. . . .

The unconscionable conduct which it is the object of equity to prevent is the failure of a party, who has induced the adoption of the assumption or expectation and who knew or intended that it would be relied on, to fulfil the assumption or expectation or otherwise to avoid the detriment which that failure would occasion. The object of the equity is not to compel the party bound to fulfil the assumption or expectation: it is to avoid the detriment which, if the assumption or expectation goes unfulfilled, will be suffered by the party who has been induced to act or to abstain from acting thereon.

If this object is kept steadily in mind, the concern that a general application of the principle of equitable estoppel would make non-contractual promises enforceable as contractual promises can be allayed. A non-contractual promise can give rise to an equitable estoppel only when the promisor induces the promisee to assume or expect that the promise is intended to affect their legal relations and he knows or intends that the promisee will act or abstain from acting in reliance on the promise, and when the promisee does so act or abstain from acting and the promisee would suffer detriment by his action or inaction if the promisor were not to fulfil the promise. When these elements are present, equitable estoppel almost wears the appearance of contract, for the action or inaction of the promisee looks like consideration for the promise on which, as the promisor knew or intended, the promisee would act or abstain from acting. . . .

But there are differences between a contract and an equity created by estoppel. A contractual obligation is created by the agreement of the parties; an equity created by estoppel may be imposed irrespective of any agreement by the party bound. A contractual obligation must be supported by consideration; an equity created by estoppel need not be supported by what is, strictly speaking, consideration. The measure of a contractual obligation depends on the terms of the contract and the circumstances to which it applies; the measure of an equity created by estoppel varies according to what is necessary to prevent detriment resulting from unconscionable conduct.

In *Combe v Combe* Denning LJ limited the application of promissory estoppel, as he expounded the doctrine, to ensure that it did not displace the doctrine of consideration. His Lordship's solution of the problem was to hold that the promise should not itself be a cause of action, but merely the foundation of a defensive equity. He said (at 220):

"Seeing that the principle never stands alone as giving a cause of action in itself, it can never do away with the necessity of consideration when that is an essential part of the cause of action. The doctrine of consideration is too firmly fixed to be overthrown by a side-wind."

The remedy offered by promissory estoppel has been limited to preventing the enforcement of existing legal rights. In *Crabb v Arun District Council* Lord Denning MR said, at 188, that if a person

"by his word or conduct, so behaves as to lead another to believe that he will not insist on his strict legal rights—knowing or intending that the other will act on that belief— and he does so act, that again will raise an equity in favour of the other; and it is for a court of equity to say in what way the equity may be satisfied".

If the object of the principle were to make a promise binding in equity, the need to preserve the doctrine of consideration would require a limitation to be placed on the remedy. But there is a logical difficulty in limiting the principle so that it applies only to promises to suspend or extinguish existing rights. If a promise by A not to enforce an existing right against B is to confer an equitable right on B to compel fulfilment of the promise, why should B be denied the same protection in similar circumstances if the promise is intended to create in B a new legal right against A? There is no logical distinction to be drawn between a change in legal relationships effected by a promise which extinguishes a right and a change in legal relationships effected by a promise which creates one. Why should an equity of the kind to which *Combe v Combe* refers be regarded as a shield but not a sword? The want of logic in the limitation on the remedy is well exposed in Mr David Jackson's essay "Estoppel as Sword" in (1965) 81 *Law Quarterly Review* 84, 223 at 241–243.

Moreover, unless the cases of proprietary estoppel are attributed to a different equity from that which explains the cases of promissory estoppel, the enforcement of promises to create new proprietary rights cannot be reconciled with a limitation on the enforcement of other promises. If it be unconscionable for an owner of property in certain circumstances to fail to fulfil a non-contractual promise that he will convey an interest in the property to another, is there any reason in principle why it is not unconscionable in similar circumstances for a person to fail to fulfil a non-contractual promise that he will confer a non-proprietary legal right on another? It does not accord with principle to hold that equity, in seeking to avoid detriment occasioned by unconscionable conduct, can give relief in some cases but not in others. . . .

. . . the better solution of the problem is reached by identifying the unconscionable conduct which gives rise to the equity as the leaving of another to suffer detriment occasioned by the conduct of the party against whom the equity is raised. Then the object of the principle can be seen to be the avoidance of that detriment and the satisfaction of the equity calls for the enforcement of a promise only as a means of avoiding the detriment and only to the extent necessary to achieve that object. So regarded, equitable estoppel does not elevate non-contractual promises to the level of contractual promises and the doctrine of consideration is not blow away by a side-wind. Equitable estoppel complements the tortious remedies of damages for negligent mis-statement or fraud and enhances the remedies available to a party who acts or abstains from acting in reliance on what another induces him to believe. . . .

In my opinion, to establish an equitable estoppel, it is necessary for a plaintiff to prove that (1) the plaintiff assumed or expected that a particular legal relationship exists between the plaintiff and the defendant or that particular legal relationship will exist between them and, in the latter case, that the defendant is not free to withdraw from the expected legal relationship; (2) the defendant has induced the plaintiff to adopt that assumption or expectation; (3) the plaintiff acts or abstains from acting in reliance on the assumption or expectation; (4) the defendant knew or intended him to do so; (5) the plaintiff's action or inaction will occasion detriment if the assumption or expectation is not fulfilled; and (6) the defendant has failed to act to avoid that detriment whether by fulfilling the assumption or expectation or otherwise. For the purposes of the second element, a defendant who has not actively induced the plaintiff to adopt an assumption or expectation will nevertheless be held to have done so if the assumption or expectation can be fulfilled only by a transfer of the defendant's property, a diminution of his rights or an increase in his obligations and he, knowing that the plaintiff's reliance on the assumption or expectation may cause detriment to the plaintiff if it is not fulfilled, fails to deny to the plaintiff the correctness of the assumption or expectation on which the plaintiff is conducting his affairs. . . .

GAUDRON J . . . the assumption that contracts would be exchanged is also an assumption as to future rights. An assumption as to a future right may provide the basis for the operation of an equitable estoppel. . . .

Whether an assumption as to a future contractual right will found an equitable estoppel may depend on whether proprietary estoppel and promissory estoppel are discrete categories of equitable estoppel based on definitional differences as to the circumstances in which they operate or are merely illustrative of different assumptions as to rights (for example, an assumption as to a right possessed or to be possessed as distinct from an assumption as to the manner in which a right possessed or to be possessed by another will be exercised) and the different ways in which adherence to those different assumptions will be compelled. In *Crabb*, Scarman LJ appears to have favoured the latter view saying (at 192–193):

"If the plaintiff has any right, it is an equity arising out of the conduct and relationship of the parties. In such a case I think it is now well settled law that the court, having analysed and assessed the conduct and relationship of the parties, has to answer three questions. First, is there an equity established? Secondly, what is the extent of the equity, if one is established? And, thirdly, what is the relief appropriate to satisfy the equity?"

There is, I think, much to be said for the view expressed by Scarman LJ . . . .

Accordingly, I am of the view that because of the appellant's imprudence in failing to inform the respondents that exchange might not occur, the respondents adopted and acted upon the assumption that exchange had taken place, and it would be unjust or unfair to allow departure from that assumption. The appellant is estopped from asserting any matter contrary to that assumption.

By reason that the appellant is estopped from denying that exchange had taken place, the rights and liabilities of the parties are to be determined on the basis that it had in fact taken place.

Notes

1. The four judges whose judgments are extracted above decide the case on the basis of 'general estoppel' (our words). The fifth judge (Deane J)—whose judgment is not extracted—reached the same result as the other four judges, but by means of a different route the content of which does not really concern us. However, he expressed sentiments similar to those of the other four concerning the desirability of a general doctrine of estoppel rather than one divided into different heads with different operational criteria.

2. Gaudron J, in common with Mason CJ, Wilson and Brennan JJ, decides that the appellants were estopped by virtue of the operation of promissory estoppel from denying that there was a lease agreement. There is a slight difference in their interpretations of the facts. According to Mason CJ and Wilson and Brennan JJ, estoppel arose primarily from the fact of receipt of the documents by the appellants and their subsequent failure to inform the respondents that exchange had not taken place and of their change of plan. According to Gaudron J, this alone would not be sufficient to estop the appellants. Grounds for estoppel only arise, in Gaudron J's view, when it comes to the appellants' attention that demolition work was being carried out by the respondents; the appellants should have been aware that the respondent had a reasonable expectation that exchange would take place and were under a duty to inform them that they, the respondents, had changed their minds.

3. One of the problems faced by the High Court in *Waltons Stores* is that the factual situation confronting the judges fitted a conventional application neither of promissory estoppel nor of proprietary estoppel. There was no pre-existing legal relationship between the parties nor a promise by the appellants to waive strict legal rights, both considered necessary for

promissory estoppel to operate. There was also no mistaken belief by the respondents as to an interest in land which is considered necessary for proprietary estoppel. Instead, the two doctrines are pushed together to form a general estoppel doctrine which seems to turn on unconscionability. There is no detailed discussion on how the doctrinal differences between proprietary and promissory estoppel, or, indeed, the reasons for these differences, are to be overcome. There would to be appear no reason for the description by Mason and Wilson of *Crabb* v. *Arun DC* as a promissory estoppel case. On conventional criteria, it is a proprietary estoppel case, but it avails the creation of their general doctrine more arbitrarily to reclassify this case in this way. The most succinct statement of this general doctrine is to be found in Brennan J.'s six-point guide to 'equitable estoppel'.

4. The problems of allowing promises based on reliance to be actionable under the heading of estoppel have already been examined. An interesting point concerning this arises in Brennan J's judgment. He observes that the argument that consideration is undermined by allowing promises founded on reliance to become a cause of action through estoppel, is answered by looking at the basis of the court's intervention in the case of estoppel. According to Brennan J, intervention occurs not because of any right derived from the promise that the promisee may possess but on the grounds of the unconscionable conduct of the promisor. This is certainly a novel approach; it seems to create an additional form of obligation over and above the three related civil obligations we identified in Chapter 1. A criticism is that it appears to create the result of allowing promises based on reliance and promises based on consideration to confer the same advantages on the promisee, so leaving us with no distinction between the paid-for promise and the relied-upon promise. Brennan J appears to attempt to head off this criticism by presenting the remedy that will be obtained in an action based on the unconscionable conduct of the promisor as one which will enforce the promise only to the extent that detriment to the promisee is avoided. It must follow from this that, if reliance is not detrimental, then the promise cannot found a course of action. For further discussion of the evolution of unconscionability into a basis of liability, see M. Eisenberg, 'The Bargain Principle and its Limits', (1982) 95 *Harv. L. Rev.* 741.

The difficulty with this type of remedy is identifying the circumstances in which the remedy to alleviate the promisee's detriment will not be simply the enforcement of the promise or the award of the expectation interest. In *Waltons Stores* we know that the respondents obtained an award of damages in lieu of specific performance with quantum to be assessed by the Master, and a declaration that there was in existence a valid agreement for a lease. This was not a case where the promisor was unjustly enriched because of the reliance of the promisee, or where the change of position enjoyed by the promisee was irretrievable. The respondents had expended money to improve their own land by constructing new commercial premises which they would be able to let out in the future at a rent reflecting their improvements. A remedy which would distinguish between promises supported by reliance and promises supported by consideration would be an award of damages calculated to compensate the plaintiffs for any loss of rent and the opportunity to rent, but not one which put them in the same financial position as if the lease had been entered into. The conduct of the appellants induced the respondents to think for a period of months that they had leased their property to the appellants—there was no evidence given that the property could not be re-marketed and leased to new tenants. Relief from unconscionable conduct on the part of the appellants would support a remedy in these terms but not a more extensive one. Equitable doctrines traditionally afford flexible remedies.

5. It if appears that there is a partial contradiction between, on the one hand, the 'contract-related' remedy awarded to the plaintiffs and, on the other hand, the attempt to found the liability on a general principle of protection against unconscionable conduct which is closer to tort than to contract, then this perhaps stems from the fact that the parties were in an incipient contractual relationship. It is surely this that explains why a form of promissory liability is fed into the principle of unconscionability to produce at least the perception that the plaintiff was deprived of an expectation. If we take a narrow view of *Waltons Stores* as a case about unconscionability in equity, the case may yet leave the established doctrinal categories of promissory liability as recognized in English law largely untouched.

V. CONSIDERATION, ESTOPPEL, AND THE CONTRACT RULE-BOOK

One of the central difficulties with contracts scholarship in the consideration field is the prevalence of assertions unsupported by empirical evidence about the significance of the established doctrinal categories. The extract from Goetz and Scott in Section III demonstrated the role of economic analysis in providing a model for the contract rule-book based on allocative efficiency, but in their work Goetz and Scott specifically disavow any intention to define what should be the limits of enforceability. The theoretical contributions considered in Section II, while highlighting the centrality of the basis of enforceability within theories of contractual obligation, likewise shed little light on the evolution of the contract rule-book in the context of consideration and promissory estoppel, and on the empirical or other consequences of that rule-book. This section contains four short extracts which provide contrasting perspectives, exemplifying the process of norm construction in the consideration context, and the commercial and distributional consequences of the interaction of promissory estoppel and consideration and of the outer limits of promissory obligation. These extracts should help the reader to understand some of the reasons why consideration and promissory estoppel have consistently remained topics of doctrinal and theoretical debate, and why so many of those questions remain unresolved.

Gilmore illustrates the process of constructing a rule—that in *Foakes* v. *Beer*—which limits the ability of creditor and debtor to reach an accommodation of their respective interests within the framework of a legal obligation. Wilson explains the position of this same rule in the context of commercial contracting by asserting that it is simply one which businessmen do not litigate upon because they regard themselves as bound within the context of such accommodations. Epstein's approach is to refute the relevance of the promise v. reliance conflict at the heart of consideration by asserting, once more without evidence, that the distributional consequences of that division are minimal. Finally, Vincent-Jones, who uses empirical evidence collected by others to support his argument, concludes likewise that the central difference between consideration (promise) and promissory estoppel (reliance) lies not in the differing role of law as an external guarantee of sanctions in each case but rather in the extent to which the different types of relation will permit and encourage advance planning, instead of being subject simply to adjudication after the event by a court.

G. Gilmore, *The Death of Contract* (Columbus, Oh., Ohio State University Press, 1974), 31–4. © Ohio State University Press, 1974.

On its facts, *Foakes v. Beer* . . . was, to say the least, ambiguous. It was by no means clear that Mrs. Beer, the judgment creditor, had ever promised to release Dr. Foakes, her debtor, from paying interest, provided that he paid the principal amount of the debt in installments over several years (as in fact he did). There are suggestions in the case that if Mrs. Beer on receipt of the last installment had given Dr. Foakes an "acquittance"—that is, an acknowledgment of payment in full—that would have been binding on her. However, what came to be the most celebrated passage in the *Foakes v. Beer* opinions was Lord Blackburn's resurrection of a dictum attributed to Lord Coke in *Pinnel's Case* (1602):

And it was resolved by the whole Court, that payment of a lesser sum on the day in satisfaction of a greater, cannot be any satisfaction for the whole, because it appears to the Judges that by no possibility, a lesser sum can be a satisfaction to the plaintiff for a greater sum: but the gift of a horse, hawk, or robe, &c, in satisfaction is good.

He was persuaded, Blackburn wrote in effect, that the decision he and his colleagues were about to give was wrong but, of course, if Lord Coke had said in 1602 that a part could never be satisfaction for the whole, why that was the end of the matter. Giving effect to the dictum in *Pinnel's Case* meant disregarding what Coke had said in a later case as well as a good many other holdings scattered over the ensuing two and a half centuries—but, what must be, must be.

The House of Lords, evidently, had its doubts. The theorists had none, and *Foakes v. Beer*—or, rather the rule in *Foakes v. Beer*—was promptly installed as one of the brightest jewels in the crown of the common law. We may, as always, pursue the rule to its ultimate abstraction in Williston:

Since a debtor incurs no legal detriment by paying part or all of what he owes, and a creditor obtains no legal benefit in receiving it, such a payment if made at the place where the debt is due in the medium of payment which was due, and at or after maturity of the debt, is not valid consideration for any promise. The question most commonly arises when a debtor pays part of a liquidated debt in return for the creditor's agreement that the debt shall be fully satisfied. Such an agreement on the part of the creditor needs for its support other consideration besides the mere part payment.

The rule, Williston noted, "has not infrequently been criticized by courts and law writers; and in a few jurisdictions . . . has been changed by decision or statute." He concluded on a note of somewhat muted triumph:

But the rule of the common law has at least the merit of consistency with the general rule of consideration governing the formation and discharge of contracts.

Apparently the best that could be said for the rule is that it had "at least" the merit of being logically consistent with other rules.

J. Wilson, 'A Reappraisal of Quasi-Estoppel', [1965] *CLJ* 98, 112–14

[T]here is a clear distinction between a pure donation and a commercially recognised gratuitous promise, which is widely regarded as part of normal business practice. Reductions in rent, waiver of time stipulations and other modifications of existing contractual obligations in favour of a debtor because of financial or other difficulties are everyday occurrences in the business world and their enforcement would accord with normal commercial morality. Yet it is claimed that none of them is binding in law unless it is put under seal or some artificial consideration is imported, *e.g.*, by reducing the length of a lease by one day. But the use of a seal is not practical in modern business, while the parties may not be aware of the opportunities provided by a manipulation of the consideration concept.

The result is that where two businessmen have reached a firm agreement gratuitously to modify a contract in favour of one of them with the intention that such an agreement should be binding and that the party relieved should conduct his affairs in the future on that basis, there is no provision in the doctrine of consideration to bar the creditor at a later date from enforcing his strict rights under the original contract. In these circumstances the honest merchant will tend to regard himself as bound by his word, while litigation will generally be confined to the unscrupulous. The position is reminiscent of that under the Statute of Frauds before the abolition of the writing requirement in contracts of sale by the Law Reform (Enforcement of Contracts) Act, 1954. It is not difficult to find the reason why there are so few commercial cases reported in the law reports after *Foakes* v. *Beer* in which an agreement of this type is involved, or why the Commercial Court Users' Conference reported in 1961 that business-men preferred arbitration to the uncertainties involved in a court action. Moreover, the few cases which have arisen support the thesis that the busi-nessman considers himself bound by such a promise. . . . In the remaining com-mercial cases reported, the court either found that no definite promise of the type alleged had been made, or that the agreed period for remission had ended—thus providing the reason why the actions had been brought. The reluctance of businessmen to repudiate a promise of this type has had the unfortunate result that no attempt has yet been made to challenge the effec-tiveness of such a definite promise in the courts. Consequently all reference to the equitable relief available in such circumstances is necessarily confined to *obiter dicta*.

It is submitted that, against the background of commercial practice, it is unrealistic . . . to contend . . . that the "promise had no legal effect, and if the debtor was rash enough to act as though it had, he must bear the result of his folly." It is undesirable that the law on this subject should be out of touch with commercial practice since the whole purpose of the law of contract is to give effect to the reasonable expectations of the contracting parties—provided that they do not conflict with basic considerations of public policy. No principle of public policy is involved here, and consequently effect should be given to the intention of the contracting parties wherever possible. This result has been achieved by the courts, to a large extent, by skilful manipulation of the consid-eration doctrine (*e.g.*, to enforce compositions between creditors).

R. Epstein, 'The Social Consequences of Common Law Rules', (1982) 95 *Harv. L. Rev.* 1717 at 1744–8

Much of the internal logic of contract law is devoted to defining appropriate spheres for the operation of strict consideration doctrine and promise-based reliance. . . . Consideration is a narrow, cautious doctrine reflecting the legal system's determination to define and control a class of enforceable agree-ments. It has . . . been ranked with offer and acceptance as part of the "indivisi-ble trinity" of doctrines that organize contract law. Promissory estoppel, on the other hand, is characterized by its advocates as a welcome, if belated, recogni-tion and mitigation of the undue harshness and uncompromising technicality that consideration imposes on the common law.

There are . . . two threshold questions relevant to an assessment of claims that a given rule is economically efficient or that it benefits a dominant social class. First, what proportion of transactions are treated differently by the two principles? Second, what potential does the choice of rules have to enhance overall output or to redistribute wealth? It is not my purpose to take sides in this perennial debate, but to counsel that the stakes involved in the choice of rules are so small that it is pointless to convert the doctrinal dispute into an essay on distributional or allocative programs.

Whether or not the doctrine of promissory estoppel is accepted, the requirement of consideration will be satisfied as a matter of course in nearly every contractual transaction. Consideration is built into the definition of most standard contracts. A sale is defined, for example, as a transfer of ownership of goods in exchange for a money consideration—the price. Contracts for hire, for barter, for employment, for a loan with interest, for insurance, or for partnership necessarily import consideration. Indeed, human self-interest is so persistent that most promises falling outside these well established categories will also be supported by consideration; true gifts are not often made outside family or charitable settings. The doctrine of promissory estoppel, therefore, is relegated to influencing marginal family arrangements—in which the law of wills and its demands for formality exert a heavy influence—and some fringe commercial transactions. Without the corrective of promissory estoppel in these borderline cases, the insistence upon consideration might introduce a jarring element into contractual relations, and the variance between legal doctrine and commercial practice might set traps for the unwary. Even here, however, promissory estoppel may be less significant than social pressures in influencing commercial behavior. How often, for instance, would a bank try to collect a forgiven interest payment, stating as its sole reason the want of consideration?

The consideration debate is also of little consequence from the perspective of wealth redistribution and allocative efficiency. This point is amply demonstrated by the potential for evasion. Suppose, for the moment, that the rules of contract formation are of vital social concern. What is the real bite of a consideration requirement? In most cases, a simple insertion of nominal consideration, or an elementary restructuring of contractual terms, allows the parties to escape whatever restrictions the law may impose. . . . Consideration has, for just this reason, been viewed as a matter less of judicial regulation than of "form," like the requirement of a writing or seal. It therefore follows that parties involved in any important, recurrent contractual arrangement will practice the standard evasions as a matter of course, at a minuscule cost per transaction.

One must thus conclude that the two rules of contract formation differ chiefly in matters of style and nuance. These contrasts are hardly sufficient to achieve substantial social or economic impact. In the commercial context, the rules' effect on efficiency is apt to be dwarfed by a host of other institutional characteristics, such as the degree of cohesion, custom, and trust between persons and within industries. The English have maintained a thriving commercial system for many years without fully endorsing the doctrine of promissory estoppel . . . . Nor does the articulation of principles for marginal cases yield distributional consequences; most commercial transactions and nearly all family transactions are between parties of the same class. However one tries to spin a story about the larger social consequences of this persistent doctrinal tension, it will remain a story, and no more.

P. Vincent-Jones, 'Contract and Business Transactions: A Socio-legal Analysis', (1989) 16 *JL&S* 166 177–8

Theory is lagging behind practice in two senses. First, as has been amply demonstrated in the empirical studies, businesses do not generally engage in formal planning in the manner suggested by the classical model, and even if they do, they tend (in the unlikely event of dispute) not to resort to contractual remedies. Such remedies will not be available, even if desired, if there is no contract between the parties—which will be exactly the case where the parties have not planned their relationship 'contractually', and may also be the case where they have so planned but there is some defect in the contractual bond. Again, with regard to adjustment of exchange relationships, the empirical studies showed little evidence of businesses regarding the obligations of the other party as 'promises' to which they should be bound, either legally or morally.

Secondly, developments both within contract and in other areas of law 'indicate a decline in the central role of the executory contract'. The basis of liability is now increasingly not so much the frustration of an expectation, deriving from the other party's breach of promise, as the fact of conferment of a benefit on that party (as in quasi-contract, restitution), or action in reasonable detrimental reliance on something said or done by that party (as in misrepresentation, promissory and proprietary estoppel). Liability need not depend, therefore, on 'contractual' planning, but may be incurred at an earlier stage in the transaction process, irrespective of whether an 'agreement' is eventually reached.

The relevance of this analysis for the foregoing discussion lies in the suggestion that Macaulay's model of 'contractual' relations appears to be based, at least to some extent, on classical contract theory, raising the possibility that 'legal relations' were not detected precisely because business relations are *not* predominantly legal in the sense of the contractual model, although they *may* be legal in some other sense. What is being suggested is that private law rights and obligations do not have to be planned in advance of a particular transaction, but arise from the *de facto* behaviour of the parties. Therefore, even the most apparently 'non-legal' business relationship may, by the very fact of its existence, be guaranteed by (potential) resort to law, whatever the parties may or may not have 'agreed' beforehand. Reliance-based liability is as much a form of 'external guarantee' as contractual liability. A 'legal proposition' still determines that a certain factual situation may have certain legal consequences, and enables the individual to engage in purpose-rational calculations accordingly. The difference appears to lie in the fact that the individual does not determine the exact nature of legal consequences *a priori*, since these may only be decided *ex post facto* at a later stage by the court in the event of dispute.

Notes

Using an empirical survey of contracting practice in a variety of US companies conducted in 1988, R. Weintraub ('A Survey of Contract Practice and Policy', [1992] *Wis. L. Rev.* 1) concludes that many of the current operating rules of contract should be reformed to be made more functional in the light of the needs of business. In particular, the bargain model of consideration should be rejected in favour of an approach which sees consideration as encapsulating a requirement that there should be a compelling social need before any agreement will be enforced.

VI. CONSIDERATION, CONTRACTS, AND PUBLIC POLICY

In large part, everything so far in this chapter—whether case extracts or commentaries—has accepted as given the basic exchange model of contract, although modified to a greater or lesser extent by the reliance principle. Only the relational contract scholarship referred to seriously challenges this paradigm. The two extracts in this final section pose a countervision of the contractual relation which rejects the market paradigm (Unger), and critiques the policies operating within the consideration context which determine the proper scope of personal autonomy in relation to the role of the state (Collins).

Seen from these perspectives, choices about which rules are best are at root political choices, and the answers will therefore depend upon the political position taken by the individual protagonist in the contract debate. Determining the limit of the enforceability of personal commitments and relations of interdependence becomes in that analysis a determination of community goals and a definition of what is the 'community' (compare with this the commentary by Unger on the doctrine of intention to create legal relations in Ch. 4). Is the 'community' for example, simply a market order, or is it possible to shape the rules of contract law around a countervision such as that proposed by Unger? In both extracts, the role of the state in relation to private ordering through contracts is explicitly recognized, and the state is seen as a significant actor (through its legal processes, for example). Yet in classical contracts scholarship, the state is

largely ignored. For Collins, in contrast, the context of contracting is decisively shaped by the extent to which the state intervenes to limit the freedom of the individual to escape unwanted liability, and for Unger the
proper scope of promissory liability should be understood within the constraints of the principle and counterprinciple discussed in Chapter 2—the
principle of freedom to contract and the counterprinciple that the exercise
of this freedom should not subvert the communal aspects of social life
('the first counterprinciple' referred to in the extract).

R. Unger, *The Critical Legal Studies Movement* (Cambridge, Mass., Harvard University Press, 1983), 80–2

. . . The dominant approach to contract problems assumes that obligations
have two main sources: the unilateral imposition of a duty by the state (as in
many forms of tort liability) and the articulated agreement in full conformity to
the established procedures for contracting. Contract theory treats any additional source, including relations of interdependence, as either an uncertain
penumbra of the articulated agreement or an equitable qualification to the
basic principles of the law. The theory of rights that fits this view of the sources
of obligation is one that sees an entitlement as designing a zone of discretionary action whose limits are set at the moment of the initial definition of the
entitlement. The boundary lines may be subject to dispute in a given context of
actual or threatened exercise of the right, but not to major extension or retrac-
ing. A concern with the effects of the exercise upon another party would turn
concrete relations of interdependence into sources of obligations that could
complete or even supersede bargained terms.

The countervision depends upon very different premises. It implies that
obligations do arise primarily from relationships of mutual dependence that
have been only incompletely shaped by government-imposed duties or explicit
and perfected bargains. The situations in which either of these shaping factors
operates alone to generate obligations are, on this alternative view, merely the
extremes of a spectrum. Toward the center of this spectrum, deliberate agreement and state-made or state-recognized duties become less important, though
they never disappear entirely. The closer a situation is to the center, the more
clearly do rights acquire a two-staged definition: the initial, tentative definition
of any entitlement must now be completed. Here the boundaries are drawn
and redrawn in context according to judgments of both the expectations generated by interdependence and the impact that a particular exercise of a right
might have upon other parties to the relation or upon the relation itself.

Within this view of the sources of obligation and the nature of rights the
countervision of contract has a secure place. . . . It incorporates the analysis of
explicit statements or promises into a more comprehensive framework that
also takes into account the merit and measure of the promisee's reliance and

the moral quality of the promisor's claim to discharge. This framework develops the first counterprinciple and relates it to the principle of freedom to contract in ways that emphasize the intersection of contract and community.

H. Collins, *The Law of Contract*, 2nd edn. (London, Butterworths, 1993), 82–7

Rationale of Reliance Model

At first sight the co-existence of two general tests of enforceability within the same legal system suggests a degree of confusion, or even contradiction. But do these two models in fact represent different values guiding the law, or merely a different emphasis among the same values according to the relevant fact situation? The answer to this question depends upon the rationale of the reliance model as a test of enforceability. . . .

Can a teleological explanation of tests of enforceability shed any light on the rationale for the reliance model? Is it possible, for example, to fit this model into the framework of state support for value-enhancing transactions? This argument appears plausible if we regard the reliance model as providing legal security for transactions and economic associations which elude the category of simple exchange. Many of the cases which employ the reliance model fit the pattern of grappling with complex economic associations between numerous parties which cannot be distilled into a series of discrete exchange transactions.

This standard feature of the cases stands out in a common instance of the application of the reliance model in America in disputes between building contractors illustrated by *Drennan* v. *Star Paving Co.* [51 Cal 2d 409 (1958)] A general contractor, in preparing a tender for building work, solicited bids from specialist sub-contractors for portions of the work. The general contractor then computed all the costs of the work and submitted a bid for the whole job, which was accepted. One of the sub-contractors had made a mistake in the quotation for his specialized work and refused to carry it out. It was clear that the general contractor had not formally accepted the sub-contractor's bid, so the doctrine of consideration had not been satisfied, but all the parties were aware that the general contractor would rely upon the quotation in putting forward his tender. The California Supreme Court held that, despite the absence of reciprocal promises, the sub-contractor's bid was binding, because it was reasonably foreseeable that it would be relied upon by the general contractor and had in fact been relied upon. These practices of the construction industry involve complex arrangements between numerous independent contractors, and, for this system of production to work effectively, sometimes parties must be protected in their reliance upon others at a point earlier than the establishment of formal exchange relations. To obtain the general efficiency advantages of a competitive tendering system for construction work, the general contractors must be able to rely upon the accuracy of bids by sub-contractors. To this extent, the reliance model may display a response to concerns for economic efficiency and value-enhancing market transactions.

The difficulty with this interpretation lies in the problem of accounting for its application in cases where the facts reveal no more than a donative promise followed by reasonable detrimental reliance. In cases such as *Pascoe* v. *Turner*, for instance, the enforcement of the promise to convey the house looks like a sterile transaction, not deserving of support as a value-enhancing exchange. We noted above, however, that not all donative promises are sterile, for it is possible that the recipient of the intended gift will value the property more highly than the donor. This opens up the possibility that the presence of unrequested detrimental reliance reveals that in fact the donee values the property more highly than the promisor. On this view, the fact that the deserted mistress in *Pascoe* v. *Turner* made improvements to the house evidences the greater value which she placed upon the property. But even supposing that detrimental reliance does evidence the donee's greater valuation of the property, the argument must overcome the problem that the absence of detrimental reliance does not prove the contrary point that the donee places no greater value on the property. The presence or absence of detrimental reliance appears an inept test of the relative utilities of the property between the parties.

The final rationale for tests of enforceability, the libertarian strand, which emphasises the choice of the parties, runs against the grain of the reliance model. The source of the problem in cases like *Crabb* v. *Arun District Council* and *Waltons Stores (Interstate) Ltd* v. *Maher* lies precisely in the desire of one party to avoid legal relations, but who nevertheless encourages detrimental reliance. It is to prevent a strict insistence upon rights and freedom from unwanted legal obligations that the reliance model has been developed.

But this failure of the libertarian rationale can provide an insight into the forces shaping the reliance model. The decisive rejection of the libertarian stance suggests that the reliance model represents a weakening of the law's concern to protect individuals from unwanted contractual obligations. Instead of envisioning society as a collection of antagonistic individuals trading exclusively in the light of self-interest, the modern law recognizes the need to protect individuals who co-operate in relations of economic interdependence and trust. The role of the law is not simply to facilitate exchanges, but to regulate relations of economic dependence and to prevent abuses of trust. Inevitably, this more communitarian vision leads to a reduction in the scope of individual liberty, in the sense of freedom from unwanted obligations, by clouding the hard lines drawn by the classical law between binding exchange relations and uninhibited freedom of action.

Even so, respect for individual liberty still pervades the legal reasoning which fashions the reliance model. Not every case of economic interdependence engenders duties to encourage concern for the interests of others. The reliance model confines the state's power to impose legal obligations to cases where one person through words or conduct has deliberately encouraged the detrimental reliance by another. The dimension of unconscionability which emphasizes a requirement of bad faith also serves to limit this restriction upon autonomy.

This discussion of the rationale of the reliance model suggest that its justification lies primarily in a new interpretation of the values which shaped the exchange model in the doctrine of consideration. Here again the harm to the promisee in the form of detrimental reliance comprises a vital element in the justification for the imposition of a legal obligation. But the libertarian limitation upon the types of harm which may justify a legal obligation has been expanded from those which have been requested to encompass those which have been foreseen and encouraged. The advent of the reliance model thus symbolizes a decline in the importance attached to the freedom of individuals from unwanted contractual obligations. The hesitation which surrounds this weakening of the libertarian strand in the law accounts for the courts' unwillingness to provide redress unless they also perceive conduct amounting to bad faith and regard the result as producing injustice in the form of irretrievable harm.

Questions

1. Is it necessary for the law of contract to have a concept of consideration? Structure your answer on the basis of the various theories of consideration which you have studied.

2. What other legal mechanisms could fulfil Fuller's criteria for the formal enforceability of contracts?

3. What, if any, changes to the classical model of consideration can be deduced from *Williams* v. *Roffey*? Was it significant that *Williams* v. *Roffey* involved a commercial transaction, envisaging an extended relation between the parties? What, if any, impact might *Williams* v. *Roffey* have upon *Foakes* v. *Beer*?

4. Identify the features in the judgments of the High Court of Australia in *Waltons Stores* which make it unlikely that this type of decision would be handed down by the House of Lords at the present time. You may wish to review your answer to this question after completing work on Chapters 8 and 9.

5. In what respects do the approaches to consideration and promissory estoppel taken by Epstein and Vincent-Jones differ from those of the theorists whose positions on bargain and reliance were outlined at the beginning of the chapter?

6. Linking the discussions by Unger and Collins to the outline of critical legal studies work on contract given in Chapter 2, identify what you think are the principal features of the 'critical legal' approach to the enforceability of promises.

7

Privity of Contract

I. INTRODUCTION

In the chapter on consideration, we identified the mechanisms used by the courts to distinguish between binding and non-binding promises. That chapter illustrated the first of the two propositions which can be derived from *Tweddle* v. *Atkinson* ((1861) 1 B. & S. 393) (see Ch. 1), namely that the son-in-law had not bought his father-in-law's promise. The second proposition is that the son-in-law was unable to enforce the promise because he was a stranger to the contract between the two fathers. This is the doctrine of privity of contract which prevents a person from enforcing a benefit due to him under a contract to which he is not a party. It also prevents a non-party from relying upon the protective provisions of a contract to which he is not privy, such as defences and limitation or exclusion clauses, in order to resist an action brought in tort or for breach of another contract. This latter aspect will be explored in Section III.

The doctrine of privity is closely related to, but conceptually distinct from, consideration, as the first extract from Beatson (below) shows. It is one thing to address the question of what types of promise are unenforceable and quite another to determine who may enforce them. Convention has it that *Tweddle* v. *Atkinson* is the primary historical source of the doctrine in English common law, although some would doubt the extent to which it truly addresses the privity issue (see the extract from Flannigan, below). It is certainly treated as such by the courts today, and Karsten provides some insights as to how and why the evolution of the English common law should have followed this course.

P. Karsten, 'The Discovery by Law by English and American Jurists in the Seventeenth, Eighteenth, and Nineteenth Centuries: Third-Party Beneficiary Contracts as a Test Case', (1991), 9 *Law & Hist. Rev.* 327 at 337–9

Tweddle v. *Atkinson* (1861) is viewed as the leading case in England. It is an excellent example of the "doctrinal" mind at work, the approach that increasingly characterized the English cases. Two fathers orally agreed to provide gifts of 100 and 200 pounds respectively to the son of one and the daughter of the other on the eve of their marriage. After the marriage they reduced this agreement to writing, giving the young couple a right to sue for the monies if either party to the covenant failed to pay. One did, and the husband sued. The law courts had become increasingly unwilling to allow creditor-beneficiaries from whom no consideration had moved to sue; in *Tweddle*, for the first time, an English court turned away a donee-beneficiary on those same grounds, decisively overruling *Dutton v. Poole* [(1678) 2 Lev. 210; 83 ER 523]. Crompton J, observed that "the modern and well-established doctrine of the action of assumpsit" did not permit a stranger to the consideration to sue. He offered a solidly doctrinal explanation for the change:

At the time when the cases which have been cited were decided the action of assumpsit was treated as an action of trespass upon the case, and therefore in the nature of a tort; and the law was not settled, as it now is, that natural love and affection is not a sufficient consideration for a promise upon which an action may be maintained; nor was it settled that the promisee cannot bring an action unless the consideration moved from him. The modern cases have, in effect, overruled the old decisions; they shew that the consideration must move from the party entitled to sue upon the contract. It would be a monstrous proposition to say that a person was a party to the contract for the purposes of suing upon it for his own advantage, and not a party to it for the purpose of being sued. . . . by reason of the principles which now govern the action of assumpsit, the present action is not maintainable. [(1861) 1 B. & S. 396 at 398]

Crawford Hening maintained that the English jurists of the fifteenth and sixteenth centuries had allowed third-party beneficiaries to sue in account because "the judicial instinct recognized" that such persons "ought to recover"; but if such behavior characterized English jurists in the era of the Tudors, the same certainly could not be said of their Victorian descendants. English jurists almost never offered dicta concerning the economic or social appropriateness of their decisions, whether it be for or against the third-party beneficiary plaintiff. What they did offer was considerable attention to precedent, logic, and "the principles" of contract. As such, they constitute examples of the power of "taught legal tradition."

There is a revealing exception to the statement that English jurists addressing third-party beneficiary suits almost never offered dicta regarding the economic implications of their decisions, an exception that may underscore my point about the decidedly doctrinal nature of their thought. *Hybart v. Parker* (1858) involved a suit by a third-part beneficiary, a cost-book mining company's purser, who sought to compel a shareholder to honor a contract with the corporation. Despite the observation of the purser's counsel that "this is a question of vital importance to cost-book mining companies," William J, turned the suit away because of the purser's lack of privity. He allowed that "it may be . . . that the law operates hardly in the case of these companies," but "if it be a hardship, the remedy must be sought at the hands of the legislature" [[*Hybart* v. *Parker*

(1858) 4 CB 209 at 214]. Parliament made new law; not Common Pleas. Jurists merely interpreted the received legal doctrines; they did not "make" them, even when cost-book mining companies might benefit from such a making.

But it is not surprising that nineteenth-century English jurists behaved doctrinally; few have argued that Jeremy Bentham's utilitarian critique of the procedure-bound common law had a truly significant impact on England's judicial community (excepting someone like Lord Denning). And English jurists showed little inclination to respond to the arguments of American legal realists regarding "instrumentalism" or "law making." In fact, when Arthur Corbin ['Contracts for the Benefit of Third Persons', (1930) 46 *LQR* 13] attempted to convince English jurists to abandon the rule in *Tweddle* and to turn away from the fictions that the contract had made the defendant either an "agent" or a "trustee" of the third-party beneficiary, it was reported by English legal specialists that, although Corbin "had a powerful influence on our legal development," that influence was precisely contrary to what he had hoped. In the words of L. C. B. Gower, professor of law at the London School of Economics, "Alas, once Professor Corbin drew [English jurists'] attention to what they were doing, they hastily recoiled, and since his article appeared there has been a recession rather than a further advance" [Gower, Review of *Corbin on Contract*, (1952) 61 *Yale LJ* 1103].

Note

Karsten's discussion of the approach of the judges in *Tweddle* argues that they took what we could define as a 'formalist' (see Ch. 4) approach to legal reasoning, demonstrating the power of 'taught legal tradition' (i.e. the 'contract rule-book'). He contrasts this approach with the 'instrumentalist' approach, which is similar to the approach which Adams and Brownsword define as 'realist'.

Privity can be a harsh doctrine in that, applied strictly and without exceptions, it can deny a third party the right to enforce a benefit under a contract even if the parties can conclusively be proved to have intended to confer such a benefit, and even if the third party has relied upon the expectation of the benefit to his detriment. The conventional doctrinal arguments in favour of privity of contract are summarized in the following extract from Treitel.

G. Treitel, *The Law of Contract*, 8th edn. (London, Sweet and Maxwell, 1991), 527–8

Reasons for the Doctrine

There are two aspects of the doctrine of privity: no one except a party to a contract can acquire rights under it; and no one except a party can be

subjected to liabilities under it. The reason for the second aspect of the doctrine is obvious: a person should not, as a general rule, have contractual obligations imposed on him without his consent. The first aspect of the doctrine is
less easy to explain. One possible reason for it is that a contract is a personal
affair, affecting only the parties to it; but this is rather a restatement of the doctrine than a reason for its existence. Another possible reason is that it would be
unjust to allow a person to sue on a contract on which he could not be sued;
but the law enforces unilateral contracts, to which the same argument applies.
A third possible reason is that, if third parties could enforce contracts made for
their benefit, the rights of contracting parties to rescind or vary such contracts
would be unduly hampered: this reasoning has certainly been influential in
limiting the development of one of the exceptions to the doctrine. Yet a fourth
possible reason is that the third party is often a mere donee. A system of
law which does not give a gratuitous promisee a right to enforce the promise is
not likely to give this right to a gratuitous beneficiary who is not even a
promisee.

Note

Treitel offers reasons for the doctrine of privity which are exclusively linked
to the nature of the contractual obligation. In his final point he highlights
the alleged link to consideration, a point taken up in the next extract from
Beatson. By way of contrast, Atiyah suggests that there were good economic reasons for the development of the privity doctrine at a time of
increasing complexity in commercial relationships. The appearance of
middlemen in all types of commercial situations served to separate the
parties at either end of the transaction, and it was generally accepted that
no privity existed between them. Economically, this may have served a
useful purpose in that it encouraged the development of a market-based
concept of enterprise liability (Atiyah, *The Rise and Fall of Freedom of
Contract* (Oxford, Oxford University Press, 1979), 85). It may, for example,
have encouraged each economic operator to drive 'a hard bargain' with the
person with whom he contracted; but, more regrettably, privity also
enables the supplier of a consumer good or service to hide behind one or
more middlemen (in contract law, at least) from the ultimate consumer.
The difficulties which this generates are discussed in more detail in the
final section of the chapter.

With such a contested doctrine, it is not surprising to find many arguments
ranged against its continued application. These are summarized by
Beatson.

J. Beatson, 'Reforming the Law of Contracts for the Benefit of Third Parties: A Second Bite at the Cherry', [1992] *CLP* 1 at 4–5

There are three main arguments of principle. First and foremost, the present law defeats the intentions of parties to a contract who wish to benefit a third party; when both parties have agreed to benefit a third party, allowing the third party an enforceable claim gives effect to their intention and promotes the idea of agreement as a source of obligation. In *Dunlop* v. *Selfridge* [[1915] AC 847 at 855], the case in which the House of Lords restated the third party rule, Lord Dunedin said that the rule made 'it possible for a person to snap his fingers at a bargain deliberately made, a bargain not in itself unfair, and which the person seeking to enforce it has a legitimate interest to enforce'. When combined with the rule that the contracting party can generally only recover damages for his own loss, the third party rule can produce the unacceptable result that in a contract for the benefit of a third party the only person who has suffered loss is unable to sue whereas the person able to sue has suffered no loss and so cannot recover substantial damages. In the absence of any alternative remedy, such as specific performance, there is, in such cases, no legal sanction for non-performance or defective performance by the promisor and it is hard to regard the agreement as a fully enforceable contract.

Secondly, the denial of third party rights is linked to an imperial all-embracing doctrine of consideration which erroneously allowed two separate issues of principle to be conflated. It was argued (and this was possible on the cases) that the third party rule and consideration are inextricably bound together and that only a person who has provided consideration can enforce a contract. However, as the Law Revision Committee recognized, the issue of which promises create a legally enforceable contract is distinct from the issue of who may enforce a contract. The former is the province of the doctrine of consideration; the latter of the doctrine of privity. The identification of this difference between the two doctrines is part of the process of ceasing to regard consideration as the Swiss army knife of the law, performing many functions in an ingenious but imperfect way. . . . But although the issue of third party rights emerged as a separate issue in the nineteenth century, and the balance of authority does not regard it as part and parcel of the doctrine of consideration, the historical link with consideration led to what can only be regarded as an unfortunate error of principle; the refusal to give effect to the clear intentions of the parties.

Thirdly, the denial of third party rights does not recognize that third parties will organize their affairs on the faith of the contract; that is, they will rely on the contract. Thus, for instance, where liability insurance is taken out by a main contractor for the benefit of all involved in a project, it is likely that subcontractors will decide not to take out their own insurance.

Note

As Beatson comments, there have been those who have argued that privity and consideration are simply different facets of the same rule. Now that privity is generally recognized as a separate requirement, it is possible to focus more precisely on the arguments in favour of its abolition. Isolating the doctrine of privity as a separate concept is a prerequisite to identifying the circumstances in which to allow third parties to enforce certain contractual promises; it is not an attack upon the essence of the contractual obligation. To put it another way, it becomes possible to argue for limited legislative or judicial abolition of the doctrine without destroying the conventional view of contract as bargain. Whether such arguments are either successful or convincing is a point to be pursued in the next section.

II. THE *TRIDENT* CASE

The main body of this chapter is shaped around a decision of the High Court of Australia (the highest Australian court) in which the judges adopted sharply contrasting attitudes to privity of contract (*Trident General Insurance Co. Ltd.* v. *McNiece Bros. Proprietary Ltd.* Prior to this case, the position in Australia could be regarded as materially identical to the position under the English common law. Consequently, this decision can in some senses be analysed as if it were a decision of the House of Lords in which some judges opted for the 'conservative' position of adhering strictly to privity of contract, while others chose the 'radical' approach of substantially weakening privity of contract.

What is particularly intriguing about studying this case is that *Trident* is not an English case, and indeed it is highly unlikely at the present time that the House of Lords would go down the same route as the Australian High Court, even though a number of judges have expressed dissatisfaction with the strict workings of the privity doctrine. Their Lordships have opted instead to wait upon the actions of Parliament, calling on a number of occasions for legislative action. While there are already in place quite a number of specific legislative exceptions to privity which allow third parties to sue on the benefit of, for example, motor vehicle insurance policies (Road Traffic Act 1988, s. 148(7)), general legislative action has not been forthcoming, although it was recommended in 1937 by the Law Revision Committee and in 1991 by the Law Commission. *Trident* illustrates the continuing possibilities of judicial intervention under the common law to achieve a similar effect, as well as providing a full survey of the doctrine itself, its scope, nature, and effects. It also provides the possibility of linking together judicial attitudes to privity and general judicial conceptions of the nature of contract.

Trident General Insurance Co. Ltd. v. *McNiece Bros. Proprietary Ltd.* (1988) 165 CLR 107

In 1977 Blue Circle took out an insurance policy with Trident. The policy was stated to provide insurance cover for Blue Circle and all of its subsidiary companies, contractors and subcontractors in the carrying out of specified construction contracts. In 1979 a worker, H, was injured while working on one of the designated sites. H was under the direction of a McNiece Bros. employee but was not himself employed by them. H brought an action against McNiece and recovered A$541,768.16, less the state benefits he had already received. McNiece sought to recover an indemnity from Trident for the amount they had paid H Trident denied liability and thus action was begun.

The first instance court decided that McNiece was in a contractual relationship with Trident, and that McNiece was therefore entitled to an indemnity from Trident. Trident appealed to the New South Wales Court of Appeal which held (McHugh JA giving the principal judgment) that there was no contractual relationship between McNiece and Trident but that nevertheless McNiece could recover. The Court of Appeal reached this conclusion on the grounds that privity of contract did not apply in situations where commercial convenience and practice dictated that it should not. According to the court, this was one of those situations.

Trident appealed to the High Court of Australia. The seven judge court dismissed Trident's appeal by a majority, and held that Trident was liable to indemnify McNiece.

A Summary of the Judgments

Mason CJ and Wilson J: this is a joint judgment in which they decide that the privity of contract rules do not apply. Look carefully at whether they intend this as a general proposition or as one confined to the facts of the case.

Brennan J (dissenting): he decides that the privity rule is firmly entrenched and that the only exceptions are well-documented applications of other doctrines such as trust and agency. He allows Trident's appeal on the grounds that the facts do not come within the exceptions, that no great hardship will be caused, and that reform is the role of the legislature not of the judiciary.

Deane J: he deals with the privity issue by examining an argument which McNiece had attempted to argue in the Court of Appeal but had been refused leave to do so, namely that a trust of the insurance policy existed and that Trident was the trustee and McNiece the beneficiary. Deane J feels that this argument may have succeeded, and that further evidence needs to be adduced before the case can finally be disposed of. He does not accept the arguments on privity of Mason CJ and Wilson J or Toohey J.

Dawson J (dissenting): this judge also delivers a dissenting judgment on broadly similar grounds as Brennan J, and his judgment is omitted here.

Toohey J: this is a fierce attack on the credibility of the privity doctrine in general terms. However, read the last paragraph of the judgment, where Toohey J appears in the end to confine himself to the facts of the case.

Gaudron J: she looks at the facts of the case from the viewpoint of restitution; Trident will be unjustly enriched if they do not indemnify McNiece.

This is the order in which the judgments are delivered and are published, but not the order in which we consider them here. We start with Brennan J as an expression of the traditional view. We then move through the judgments in an order which we feel takes us on a journey from tradition to novelty. What we are trying to show by using the judgments in this way is the paths of judicial reasoning that are open to judges when confronted with a conceptual structure like that of the privity doctrine.

BRENNAN J (dissenting) . . . The declaration by the Court of Appeal that policies of liability insurance are a common law exception to the doctrine of privity of contract and that the exception has existed for some time may come as a surprise to those who have seen no reference to such an exception in the books. . . .

If policies of liability insurance are to be recognized as an exception to the doctrine, what are the features which might make them so? Excluding the principles of agency, trust and estoppel from consideration, what makes a "non-party assured" who has furnished no consideration for a policy of loss insurance different from any other third party mentioned in a contract between promisor and promisee as a party who is to have the benefit of a promise? The difference suggested by McHugh JA [in the NSW Court of Appeal] was that commercial necessity, practice and widespread use, strengthened by analogy with modern statutes, established policies of loss insurance as exceptions to the doctrine of privity of contract. The fact that policies of loss insurance are frequently expressed to cover losses sustained by persons who are not parties to the contract and the fact that insurers ordinarily honour those contracts do not establish the kind of commercial practice that evokes the creation of a new principle of the common law. It may be that, where the voluntary acceptance of liability by an insurer does not account for the commercial practice and use of which his Honour spoke, those factors are to be accounted for by operation of the law of agency, trusts and estoppel. His Honour's proposition that it is commercially necessary to admit an exception to the doctrine of privity would be more supportable if it were found that those principles when applied in conjunction with the doctrine leave the law powerless to prevent or remedy injustice. But it was impossible to demonstrate such a defect in this case where agency was negatived on the facts and no occasion arose to consider the application of the principles of trust and estoppel.

Nor is the argument for a judicially created exception advanced by considering modern statutory provisions. As Dawson J [at first instance] points out, s. 48 of the *Insurance Contracts Act 1984 (Cth)* weakens rather than strengthens the proposition that a common law exception exists. That section creates in a person who is not a party to a contract of general insurance a statutory right to recover the amount of his loss directly from the insurer if he was specified or referred to in the contract as a person to whom the insurance cover was provided. But the Parliament did not make that provision retrospective, and it cannot be inferred that the Parliament contemplated that cases arising before the Act came into force (this case being one of them) would be governed by provisions of the common law identical with those in the Act. . . .

Privity is a doctrine which is both settled and fundamental, though it was not settled in England until the nineteenth century. . . . In 1861, *Tweddle* v. *Atkinson* was decided. The law was then settled that "no stranger to the consideration can take advantage of a contract, although made for his benefit" per Wightman J. . . . The rule was affirmed by the House of Lords in *Dunlop Pneumatic Tyre Co. Ltd.* v. *Selfridge & Co. Ltd.* Viscount Haldane LC said [[1915] AC 847 at 853]:

"My Lords, in the law of England certain principles are fundamental. One is that only a person who is a party to a contract can sue on it. Our law knows nothing of a jus quaesitum tertio arising by way of contract. Such a right may be conferred by way of property, as, e.g., under a trust, but it cannot be conferred on a stranger to a contract as a right to enforce the contract in personam. A second principle is that if a person with whom a contract not under seal has been made is to be able to enforce it consideration must have been given by him to the promisor or to some other person at the promisor's request. These two principles are not recognized in the same fashion by the jurisprudence of certain Continental countries or of Scotland, but here they are well established. A third proposition is that a principal not named in the contract may sue upon it if the promisee really contracted as his agent. But again, in order to entitle him so to sue, he must have given consideration either personally or through the promisee, acting as his agent in giving it." . . .

The doctrine of privity has been treated as settled not only by the House of Lords: *Beswick* v. *Beswick* [[1968] AC 58] but also by the Supreme Court of Canada: *Greenwood Shopping Plaza Ltd.* v. *Beattie* [(1980) 111 DLR (3rd ed) 257] and by this Court. In *Wilson* v. *Darling Island Stevedoring & Lighterage Co. Ltd.* [(1956) 95 CLR 43 at 80] Kitto J spoke of "the elementary general rule that the only persons entitled to the benefits or bound by the obligations of a contract are the parties to it": . . . The doctrine of privity has long been settled and it was settled as a doctrine of general application. . . .

In this case, unless the Court determines that the doctrine of privity be reopened and a new doctrine substituted, the appeal must be allowed. The Court of Appeal ought to have allowed the appeal to it. However, the doctrine of privity was directly challenged, at least to the extent of allowing an exception in he case of liability insurance where the third party is named in the policy. In my view, for reasons which will appear, to admit such an exception involves the overthrow of the doctrine. The true question for decision is, therefore, whether this Court should now decide to overrule the settled and fundamental doctrine of privity.

It is submitted that the doctrine of privity sometimes produces unjust results and that this Court should re-examine it in the light of the criticisms the doctrine has attracted. . . .

To admit a third party's right to sue into the common law, it would be necessary to postulate a new source of legal rights and obligations arising independently of contract and equity and to create a new set of rules prescribing the availability of the rights and the limits of the obligations to which the third party promise gives rise. And if such a new source of legal rights were postulated, our laws with respect to agency, trusts, estoppel and damages which have been constructed around the doctrine of privity of contract would have to be reworked. . . .

The subsidiary rules which the courts have developed to solve the problems raised by a third party promise are sometimes described as exceptions to the doctrine of privity, but (as Lord Reid suggested) the apparent exceptions are in truth applications of other legal principles to the contractual relationship of promisor and promisee. . . . Neither the principles of trust nor the principles of agency are exceptions to the doctrine of privity. In their application to a third party promise, those principles proceed on the footing that the legal contractual right is vested solely in the promisee. There is no true exception to the doctrine of privity. If an exception were now introduced and a jus quaesitum tertio were recognized in respect of some contracts, the exception would raise at least as many problems as it might solve. The field of jus quaesitum tertio may look greener, but the brambles are no fewer. . . .

When a third party promise is in a contract to which the third party is not a party, the promise can be enforced only by an action brought by the promisee or to which the promisee is a party. The legal cause of action against the promisor is vested solely in the promisee. Double recovery is impossible. Where the promisor has promised to pay money to or otherwise to confer a benefit on the third party directly, the promisee may compel him specifically to perform his promise, for damages would be an imperfect remedy for the promisee: *Beswick* v. *Beswick*. The availability of specific performance goes a long way towards shutting out injustice. Where damages are the appropriate remedy for breach of a promise to pay money to the promisee for the benefit of a third party, the promisee may recover the whole of the amount promised where the promisee is a trustee for the third party: *Beswick* v. *Beswick* or an agent who is authorised by the contract to sue on behalf of the principal: *Woodar Ltd.* v. *Wimpey Ltd.* [[1980] 1 WLR 277]. These may not be the only cases in which a promisee may recover the full amount promised. It is still an open question whether a promisee who is neither a trustee for nor an agent of a third party can recover in some circumstances more than nominal damages if the promisor's breach of a promise which is intended to confer a benefit on a third party causes the promisee no personal loss: *Woodar Ltd.* v. *Wimpey Ltd.* The speech of Lord Diplock in *The Albazero* [[1977] AC 774], raises the question whether a promisee may recover in full what was lost by a third party provided the promisee is accountable to the third party for what he recovers. It is not appropriate in this case to decide the limits of the promisee's remedies. It is sufficient to note that the possibility of injustice which might be thought to flow from the effect of the doctrine of privity on the promisee's remedies depends on the rules relating to the measure of damages. . . . A development of the rules relating to damages rather than the acceptance of a third party's right to sue offers the prospect of an orderly development of the law if such a development be needed to avoid injustice.

If a third party were to complain of injustice on the ground that he has no right to cause the promisee to enforce a policy of loss insurance, the supposed injustice must arise because there is no relevant relationship between the third party and the promisee. Such a case can arise only if the third party is one (a) for whom the promisee is not an agent, fiduciary or trustee, (b) who has no relevant contractual relationship with the promisee, and (c) who has not been induced to assume or expect that the policy covers the risk of loss by the third party by any representation made by the promisor or the promisee in circumstances which would entitle the third party to claim the benefit of the policy by estoppel: see *Waltons Stores (Interstate) Ltd.* v. *Maher* [(1988) 164 CLR 387].

Notes

1. Brennan J refers to s. 48 of the Insurance Contracts Act 1986, an Australian Federal Statute. As he explains, this section deals with the situation which arose in *Trident* by giving the injured party a right to recover directly from the insurance company if he or she was not a party to the insurance contract, provided that the injured person was referred to in the contract as a person to whom the insurance cover was provided. The Insurance Contracts Act came into force prospectively and did not cover the *Trident* case. Brennan J takes the fact that the Act had prospective force only to mean that the legislature intended the common law rules to be applied strictly to events outside the scope of the Act. Exactly the opposite view of the effect of the prospective nature of the legislation is taken by

Mason CJ and Wilson J in their judgment. Their view is that, just because there has been legislation to deal with the situation, this is not a reason to apply strict ('unjust' in their words) common law rules to situations which the Act does not cover.

2. Brennan J highlights the use of other doctrines as a way of overcoming the strictures of the privity doctrine. These require some further explanation.

Agency. The idea behind agency is that one party—the principal—(P) can appoint an agent (A) to conclude a contract on his behalf with a third party (T). A cannot sue or be sued on the completed contract but P can. The contract in effect is between P and T. Courts have, from time to time, avoided the effect of the privity doctrine by 'imputing' an agency relationship between P and A, thus bringing P into a contractual relationship with T, while at first sight he might have been thought to be a stranger to the relationship between A and T. For further details, see Cheshire, Fifoot, and Furmston's *Law of Contract*, 12th edn. (London, Butterworths, 1991), ch. 15.

Trust. This is an equitable concept creating an obligation on the part of one party to hold property for another. If A and B contract with each other to confer a benefit on C, and A then does not confer the benefit, there is a breach of contract. The right to sue on the contract is B's right. However, if we use the concept of a trust then we say that B holds the right to sue on C's behalf. This would allow C to sue on the contract and recover the benefit that should have been conferred under the contract. The judgment of Deane J is couched in terms of trust, and this concept will be looked at in more detail in a note to that judgment.

Specific Performance. This is an equitable remedy for breach of contract and is thus discretionary. The defaulting party can be compelled by the court to perform his promise, including conferring a benefit on a third party. It is considered in more detail in the chapter on remedies; here, it is sufficient to note that it is only available in relation to certain types of promise and thus has limited usefulness as a means of surmounting the difficulties created by the privity doctrine. It is also of little assistance when the contract has been performed but only defectively. The most obvious difficulty with specific performance as a remedy is that it is only available where damages are insufficient as a remedy. As the promisee is suing to recover for *his loss* in the benefit not being conferred, not the third party's loss, nominal damages are likely to be considered an adequate remedy, thus excluding the possibility of specific performance.

Brennan J refers to 'specific performance [as going] a long way towards shutting out injustice', and cites *Beswick* v. *Beswick* as authority for this. In *Beswick* v. *Beswick* the plaintiff sued in two capacities, as administratrix of the estate of the deceased Mr Beswick (B in our example above), and in her personal capacity (C in our example above). She recovered in her capacity as administratrix, the House of Lords holding that the privity doctrine prevented her from recovering in her personal capacity. Whether damages were inadequate or not is a moot point; as administratrix she had suffered no loss and so damages should have been nominal. However, another way of looking at the facts is to say that in her personal capacity she was entitled to a weekly sum for the rest of her life and as this could not be calculated into a lump sum, damages were an inadequate remedy. The House of Lords took the latter view and ordered specific performance.

Specific performance has not been extensively used as a remedy to the problems of privity. A major reason why this is so may be that there is no way of compelling B in our example to sue and request a specific performance remedy on behalf of C. The facts of *Beswick* v. *Beswick*, where both parties are in reality the same person, are unlikely to come about very often. In the light of this fact, it is hard to justify the role that Brennan J attributes to specific performance.

Estoppel. Brennan J appears to be referring to estoppel not as a general principle of reliance but as a specific instance of representation. His argument is that at some point a representation is made to the third party, for example, that he is covered by an insurance policy and that there is no need to obtain further insurance cover. The difficulty with using estoppel to overcome privity is that, as we saw in the last chapter, it is not clear whether estoppel can be used to found a cause of action. In order to rely on estoppel, a plaintiff has to make out a case similar to negligent misstatement.

3. Brennan J wishes to see a development of the law on damages to overcome any injustices caused by the privity doctrine. He does not indicate what form the development might take. It is hard to see how this equates with the very traditional views expressed in his judgment. He appears to be saying that a plaintiff who does not come within the categories outlined in the last paragraph of his extracted judgment has no 'relevant relationship' and yet at the same time to be arguing that damages can be developed to get around the problem caused by privity. It would seem that a development of damages as a remedy could only take the form of allowing B to recover for C's loss, and such a development in fact completely abrogates the privity doctrine. We move now to Deane J's judgment.

DEANE J At the time of the establishment of this Court, the common law of England and of this country was long settled in its insistence upon the principle of privity of contract, that is to say, the general rule that only the parties to a contract are bound by, and entitled to enforce, its terms. Thus, in the first edition of *Principles of the English Law of Contract* published in 1879, Sir William Anson commenced a sometime tentative identification of the limits of contractual obligation (Pt III, Ch. I, p. 195) with the unequivocal statement that we "may safely lay down the general rule that a person, who is not a party to a contract, cannot be included in the rights and liabilities which the contract creates so as to enable him to sue or be sued upon it"; see, to the same effect, Pollock, *Principles of Contract at Law and Equity*, 1st ed. (1876), pp. 167, 190–191. "This", Professor Anson went on to say, "is not only established by decided cases, but seems to flow from the very conception which we form of contract". In subsequent editions of the work published before his death in 1914, Professor Anson consistently stressed that "the general rule" of privity constitutes "an integral part of our conception of contract".

In the course of the present century, the "decided cases" have served only to reinforce the principle of privity of contract as a fundamental rule of the common law. Those subsequent cases include decisions of the House of Lords, of the Privy Council and of this Court. In the House of Lords and Privy Council, the principle has been described as "fundamental", "elementary", "established", "as well established as any in our law" and "firmly built into the structure of English law" see *Dunlop Pneumatic Tyre Co. Ltd.* v. *Selfridge & Co. Ltd.*; *Vandepitte* v. *Preferred Accident Insurance Corporation of New York* [[1933] AC 70]; *Midland Silicones Ltd.* v. *Scruttons Ltd.* [[1962] AC 446]. In this Court, the requirement of privity as a general rule has never been doubted. . . .

Circumstances can undoubtedly arise in which accepted processes of legal reasoning require a court, usually a final appellate court, to reverse the development of the law by disowning established principle. However, where the established principle is as entrenched, by authority and in legal conception, as is the principle of privity, such a reversal can only be justified by precisely defined and compelling reasons advanced as part of a plainly identified process of legal reasoning. No such reasons are available to justify a wholesale abrogation of the general common law rule of privity of contract. . . .

If, within the confines of the law of contract, a third party who would be benefited by the performance of a contractual promise is left without redress, other principles of law operate (unhindered by the rule of privity) upon or within the context of contractual rights and obligations to avoid injustice in particular categories of case. . . . It is, however, unnecessary in the present case to embark upon a detailed examination of questions of estoppel by conduct or to seek to identify what, if any, circumstances could found an action in unjust enrichment by the third party against an insurer who has refused to honour the indemnity which he has been paid to provide. The reason why that is so is that it has not been suggested in the present case that Trident is estopped by its conduct from relying upon the rule of privity to deny liability to McNiece or that the circumstances are such as might arguably give rise to a right of action (in McNiece) founded on unjust enrichment. Nor has any reliance been placed, either in the judgments in the Court of Appeal or in argument in this Court, upon the doctrine of estoppel by conduct or (except to the extent that they are reflected in the law of trusts) upon principles of unjust enrichment. If there be a doctrinal basis for the recognition by the Court of Appeal of a right of action in the third party assured to enforce the insurer's promise of indemnity in the present case, it must be found, either directly or by way of analogy, in the law of trusts. . . . Indeed, the "reluctance" of courts to find a trust in such cases seems often to have been caused by a misunderstanding of the nature of equity's requirement of an intention to create an express trust, or put differently, by a failure to appreciate the innate flexibility of the law of trusts . . . .

A trust can attach to the benefit of the whole contract or of the whole or part of some particular contractual obligation. In the case of a policy of liability insurance under which the insurer agrees to indemnify both a party to the contract and others, there is no reason in principle or in common sense why the party to the contract should not hold the benefit of the insurer's promise to indemnify him on his own behalf and the benefit of the promise to indemnify others respectively upon trust for those others. Where the benefit of a contractual promise is held by the promisee as trustee for another, an action for enforcement of the promise or damages for its breach can be brought by the trustee. In such an action, the trustee can recover, on behalf of the beneficiary, the damages sustained by the beneficiary by reason of breach. If the trustee of the promise declines to institute such proceedings, the beneficiary can bring proceedings against the promisor in his own name, joining the trustee as defendant. . . .

The question whether a particular contract itself creates a trust of the benefit of one or more of the promises which it contains is primarily a question of the construction of the terms of the contract. Those terms must, however, be construed in context and a trust of a contractual promise will obviously be more readily discerned in the terms of some classes of contracts than it will in others. It is difficult to envisage a class of contract in which the creation of such a trust would be more readily discernible than the type of contract which is involved in the present case, namely, a policy of liability insurance indemnifying both a party to the contract and others who are designated either by specific identification or by their membership of an identified group. In the case of such a policy, the terms of the contract itself will, in the context of the nature of insurance, ordinarily manifest an intention to the effect that each non-party assured is to be fully entitled to the benefit of the promisor's promise to indemnify him, that is to say, that the promisee should hold the chose in action constituted by the right to enforce that promise upon trust for the relevant non-party assured: . . . The intention so manifested will commonly be a joint intention of promisor and promisee. . . .

The relevant terms of the policy of insurance in the present case are set out or summarized in the judgment of McHugh JA in the Court of Appeal and in the joint judgment of Mason CJ and Wilson J in this court. It is unnecessary that I repeat them. It suffices to say that, in the context of the nature of liability insurance, those contractual terms manifest an unmistakable intention that each assured should be entitled to the benefit of the insurer's promise to indemnify it against the specified loss and should be itself entitled to insist upon enforcement of that promise. That intention is properly to be construed in legal terms as an intention that the chose in action constituted by the benefit of Trident's promise to indemnify each contractor and sub-contractor on the identified sites in respect of specified loss should be held by the promisee ("Blue Circle") upon trust for the relevant contractor or sub-contractor. Prima facie, the contract operated to give effect to that intention which it manifested. That being so, the prima facie effect of the policy itself in the events which occurred (i.e. McNiece becoming a designated contractor or sub-contractor) was to create a trust for McNiece of the benefit of Trident's promise to indemnify it against relevant loss. . . .

. . . My refusal to take the final steps of recognizing, in a case such as the present and in the absence of some applicable statutory provision, a direct right of action in the third party against the insurer to enforce the contract is not based on an insistence upon matters of form or procedure. It flows from an inability to see such a direct right of action in contract otherwise than as inconsistent with the established legal position. For present purposes, a refusal to take that final step is significant in at least two distinct ways. First, the defeasibilty and extent of the third party assured's rights under a trust of the insurer's promise are as defined by the law of trusts and not as laid down by some new judicial prescription. Secondly, the existence of an intention to create such a trust (manifested by a contract, not directly binding between the parties to it on the one hand and a third party on the other) could be negatived or modified by other circumstances. That being so, it would be unfair to hold in the present case that McNiece was entitled to succeed in an action against Trident on the basis of a trust without extending to Trident any opportunity at all of establishing the existence of further circumstances which could negative or modify the creation or effect of any such trust.

Nor, in my view, does there exist any acceptable justification for the alteration of that established legal position by the creation, by judicial decision as distinct from legislative reform, of a direct right of action in a third party assured under a policy of liability insurance to enforce a contract to which he is not a party. As has been seen, it has long been the settled law of this country that it is of the very nature of a contract that it does not, of itself, confer any direct right of enforcement upon a person who is not a party to it. In the light of the provisions of s. 48 of the *Insurance Contracts Act 1984 (Cth)*, the only real point to be served by the judicial creation of such a direct right of enforcement would seem to be its retrospective application to any hard cases that might have arisen before the commencement of that Act. Even that doubtful point is, however, of doubly doubtful validity since it is far from apparent that there are, in fact, any such outstanding cases in which an insurer, who has invoked absence of privity to decline indemnity to a third party assured, is beyond the reach of doctrines of trust and estoppel or the principles of unjust enrichment. . . . [I]t is necessary to decide what are the appropriate orders which should be made for the disposal of the appeal in view of my conclusion that the policy itself prima facie created a trust in McNiece's favour of the benefit of Trident's promise to indemnify it. . . . The appropriate course is to give McNiece leave to join Blue Circle as a respondent to the proceedings in this Court and to stand the matter over to allow McNiece to file a notice of contention alleging the existence of a trust and to allow Trident, if it can, to place before this Court material showing that it has an arguable case, based on further evidence, that there are circumstances which have the effect of precluding or modifying the trust which the policy of insurance would otherwise have sufficed to create. If, as would seem likely, . . . Trident is unable to place such material before the Court, the appropriate order would then be for the appeal to be dismissed.

Notes

1. From Deane J's reference to Anson at the beginning of his judgment, we can see that he, like Brennan J, is taking a traditional view of contract as a bargain, enforceable only by parties who have exchanged promises or who have bought the promise of the other.

2. As Deane J points out, the subject of a trust can be a promise—in the instance he describes, a contractual promise. The recipient of the promise (B) then becomes trustee for the person on whom the benefit is to be conferred (the beneficiary) (C). In the event of the benefit not being conferred, B can sue the promisor (A) to recover the C's loss. The problem that was alluded to in relation to specific performance—that B may not wish to sue and cannot be forced to do so—does not arise as C can sue A as beneficiary, joining the trustee/promisee to the action.

A difficulty with supplementing the contract relationship which A and B thought they had entered into with one of trust is that it may confer rights on the beneficiary of the promise which A and B never intended to confer. For example, A and B may agree that they for some reason no longer intend to be bound by the contract. If the relationship they thought they had entered into (the contract) is construed as creating also a trust, then they cannot simply end their relationship without exposing themselves to the risk of action by C.

3. This type of problem has led the House of Lords to indicate on several occasions that the imposition of the fiction of a trust is inappropriate. It has restricted the use of the trust concept by requiring the party alleging that there is a trust to show an intention to create a trust. If the requisite degree of intention can be shown, there would also be sufficient intention to create a contract directly between A and C.

In 1930 Arthur Corbin, one of the foremost proponents of the recognition of contracts for the benefit of third parties in the United States, argued that, while lip-service was paid to the privity rule in the English cases, in practice the courts would always evade the rule if the interests of justice in a particular case demanded it. In the following extract, Corbin's general credo concerning the development of the common law is followed by his view of the use of the trust device and his proposal that this fiction be abandoned.

A. Corbin, 'Contracts for the benefit of Third Persons', (1930) 46 *LQR* 12 at 13–16, 45

. . . The living law consists of the great stream of decision and application. In so far as there is uniformity in decision and application, there is 'law.' Jurists observe varying degrees of such uniformity and attempt to state the rules thereof in words, very frequently assuming or asserting an absolute and unchanging character for the rule which they believe themselves to have discovered and expressed. Other jurists accept these stated rules as absolute and unchanging, and attempt with some success to keep the flowing stream within the banks represented by the stated rules. But we must also realize that the stream determines its own banks; the rules are merely a statement of the uniformity of the stream, and they are continually undermined and re-established elsewhere as the tide of decisions ebbs and flows with the needs, feelings, and desires of mankind. . . .

. . . The American Law Institute has made it safe to say in the United States that two parties can by contract confer an enforceable right upon a third. Can it not be made safe in England also? Have not the English Courts in fact recognized and enforced such rights? This can be determined only by a review of decisions, searching them out with respect to what they have done, and not merely with respect to what they may have said. The Chancery and the Exchequer, as well as the King's Bench and Common Bench, must be considered, and also the work of the Supreme Court and the House of Lords since the Judicature Act. It will appear at once that the decisions at common law, using that term to exclude equity, were variable and inconsistent. *Tweddle* v. *Atkinson* was decided with such positive severity that it still controls the stated generalizations of the leading law writers. But . . .the Court of Chancery found a way to do something for the third party; and the common law Courts followed in some degree Chancery's lead. . . .

If . . . it can be shown that the beneficiary of a contract has any remedy under existing law for the enforcement of a promise made for his benefit, he has a legal right. If a Court will give judgment that money promised by a party to the contract shall be paid to the beneficiary, he has a legal right. And if the only operative facts leading to this judicial action are the making of a promise by the defendant for a consideration given by the promisee, the beneficiary's

legal right is as clearly one created by the contract as is the right of the immediate promisee himself. . . . The definition and classification of such fundamental terms as right and duty depend upon results reached, and not upon
formalities of the procedure used in reaching them. And, finally, nothing to the
contrary is to be found in the fact that in order to reach the result and award
the money to the beneficiary, the Court may think it necessary to call the
promisee a 'trustee' for the third party's benefit. If this appellation is a mere
device for reaching the result that the promisor shall pay the money to the beneficiary, and if the operative facts consist wholly of a promise by the defendant
for a consideration given by the promisee, it is merely a verbal or procedural
complication . . . .

It may well be that the expansion of the trust concept . . . is an instance of
the growth of law by fiction. It has often been by fiction that old rules have
been avoided, discredited, and finally broken down. No one familiar with the
history of debt and assumpsit can doubt the growth of law through the giving of
new meanings to old terms or can doubt the beneficence of the process. The
result is the same whether reached by fiction or not. It is merely a question as
to when independent judicial minds will openly recognize the fact that fiction
has been employed, that a change has been worked in the law by its use, and
that the time has come to state the result in terms that will no longer mislead
able judges and mystify the lawyers who must advise their clients and predict
judicial action.

Note

The fate of Corbin's proposals has already been alluded to in the extract by
Karsten (above). It was in the decision in *Vandepitte* v. *Preferred Accident
Insurance Corporation of New York* that the Privy Council is credited with
refuting Corbin's challenge to doctrinal orthodoxy, and since then the trust
doctrine has rarely been used by the English courts for the reasons given in
the notes above. Further details on the bifurcation of the English and
American common laws of contract in the matter of the recognition of contracts for the benefit of third parties by the US courts and in the US
Restatement of Contract are given in the notes to Toohey J's judgment
below. We now extract the joint judgment of Mason CJ and Wilson J.

MASON CJ and WILSON J . . . Trident's case in this Court is that the rules that
only a party to a contract can sue on it and that consideration must move from
the promisee are fundamental principles of the common law of contract. These
principles evolved in the course of the nineteenth century in the development
in England of the law of contract and they have been consistently applied, not
only in England but also in Australia, to contracts for the benefit of third parties,
including insurance contracts. The argument is that the principles are so well

accepted and so embedded in our law of contract that they should not be over-
turned by judicial decision, even if their application to contracts for the benefit
of third parties is not altogether satisfactory, a matter which Trident by no
means concedes. According to Trident, the recognition in appropriate circumstances by the courts of the trust of a contractual promise provides an adequate mechanism for protecting the rights of the third party under a third party
contract. The concept of the trust of a contractual promise, it is said, overcomes any serious problem which might otherwise arise if the common law
principles alone were to govern third party contracts.

Although the principle that only a party to a contract can sue on it is
described as fundamental, the early common law permitted third parties to
enforce contracts made for their benefit: With reference to the common law
before 1861, Windever J. observed in *Coulls* v. *Bagot's Executor & Trustee Co.
Ltd.* [(1967) 119 CLR 460 at 498]

"The law was not in fact 'settled' either way during the two hundred years before 1861.
But it was, on the whole, moving towards the doctrine that was to be then and thereafter taken as settled."

The received doctrine is that *Tweddle* v. *Atkinson* decided that a third party
cannot sue on a contract for his benefit . . ..

These "fundamental" traditional rules, where they survive, have been under
siege throughout the common law world. In the United Kingdom the Law
Revision Committee, which included many distinguished lawyers under the
chairmanship of Lord Wright, recommended the abolition of the consideration
rule and the privity rule in its Sixth Interim Report. . . . The Committee stated
that the English common law (an expression which, in the context of the
Report in 1937, may be taken to include the Australian common law) was
alone among modern systems of law in its insistence on the privity rule and
observed that the United States had taken steps to mitigate the rigour of the
rule. Even in England, the Committee noted, Parliament had found it necessary
to create legislative exceptions: par. 41. The Committee went on to make the
point that the trust concept as applied to the promise for the benefit of the third
party had not proved to be a satisfactory solution because there was uncertainty surrounding the approach of the courts to the recognition of a trust: par.
44. Another criticism of the trust concept was that, once created, the trust was
not revocable by the promisor or the promisee: par. 47. A third comment was
that insistence on the privity rule casts doubts on the enforceability of bankers'
commercial credits by sellers of goods as against the banker setting up the
credit: par. 45. The final point made by the Committee was that the position of
the third party is more analogous to that of an assignee of a contractual right
than to that of a cestui que trust: para. 46.

The Committee recommended that the statutory recognition of third party
rights should be carefully limited. The proposed limitations were: (1) no third

party right should be acquired unless given by the *express* terms of the contract; (2) the promisor should be able to raise against the third party any defence available against the promisee; and (3) the right of the promisor and of the promisee to cancel the contract at any time should be preserved unless the third party has received notice of the agreement and has adopted it. It might be noted that this regime is much like that which has developed in the United States. There, the problems arising from the traditional rules have been avoided by not requiring that consideration move from the promisee to the promisor . . . . As it stands now in most American states, third parties can sue directly upon contracts made for their benefit by others: see generally *Restatement* (2d), *Contracts* (1979), Ch. 14.

Despite the criticisms and the proposals for reform, the traditional rules survive in the United Kingdom: see, e.g., *Midland Silicones Ltd.* v. *Scruttons Ltd.*; *Beswick* v. *Beswick*; *Woodar Investment Ltd.* v. *Wimpey Ltd.* Legislative procrastination prompted Lord Reid in 1968 to suggest that, if there were to be a further long delay, then the House of Lords might be compelled to deal with the question: *Beswick.* Similarly, Lord Scarman, supported by Lord Keith of Kinkel, expressed the view in 1980 that the House of Lords might "reconsider *Tweddle* v. *Atkinson* and the other cases which stand guard over this unjust rule": *Woodar.* In *Swain* v. *Law Society* [[1983] 1 AC 598 at 611], Lord Diplock described the doctrine of privity as "an anachronistic shortcoming that has for many years been regarded as a reproach to English private law". . . .

In Western Australia dissatisfaction with those rules has resulted in the enactment of s. 11 of the *Property Law Act 1969 (W.A.)*, which confers in certain circumstances a right on a third party to sue on a contract for his benefit. In 1973 the Queensland Law Reform Commission recommended that the law be amended so as to allow that a contract conferring a benefit on a third party should be enforceable by him in his own name: see Report No. 16, cl. 55 of the draft bill and the commentary on that provision. The recommendation was adopted and is expressed in s. 55 of the *Property Law Act 1974 (Q.).* And in New Zealand the *Contracts (Privity) Act 1982 (N.Z.),* like the Queensland Act, allows the third party to enforce a contract made for his benefit by imposing an obligation on the promisor in favour of the third party where the parties intend that the third party should be able to enforce the provision for his benefit. . . .

There is much substance in the criticisms directed at the traditional common law rules as questions debated in the cases reveal. First, there is the vexed question whether the promisee can recover substantial damages for breach by the promisor of his promise to confer a benefit on the third party. The orthodox view is that ordinarily the promisee is entitled to nominal damages only because non-performance by the promisor, though resulting in a loss of the third party benefit, causes no damage to the promisee. . . .

Next, there is the question whether the contract to confer a benefit on the third party is capable of specific performance . . . As Lord Upjohn noted in

Beswick, "Equity will grant specific performance when damages are inadequate to meet the *justice* of the case" (our emphasis) . . . . There is no reason to doubt that the courts will grant specific performance of a contract of indemnity or insurance, even if it involves payment of a lump sum, at least where the payment is to be made to a third party, damages being an inadequate remedy. But, even if we assume the availability of specific performance at the suit of the promisee in a wide variety of situations, there are nonetheless situations . . . where specific performance is not a suitable remedy and damages are inadequate. In these situations the incapacity of the third party to sue means that the law gives less protection to the promisee and the third party than the promisor. . . .

Then there is there trust of the contractual promise on which the appellant places particular reliance as a palliative of the difficulties generated by the common law principles. . . . [C]ritics of the common law rules have pointed to the uncertainty surrounding the circumstances in which the courts will recognize a trust in contracts for the benefit of third parties as a reason for rejecting the trust concept as a sufficient answer to the difficulties caused by those rules. . . .

This apparent uncertainty should be resolved by stating that the courts will recognize the existence of a trust when it appears from the language of the parties, construed in its context, including the matrix of circumstances, that the parties so intended. . . .

In order to justify the privity and consideration rules in the face of these problems, three practical policy considerations are sometimes invoked. First, they preclude the risk of double recovery from the promisor by the third party as well as the promisee. If the third party is permitted to sue the risk of double recovery arises from the possibility that the one party make seek specific performance after another has recovered damages. The risk is insignificant; joinder of all parties in the first action will make the resulting decision binding on all.

The second point is that the privity requirement imposes an effective barrier to liability on the part of a contracting party to a vast range of potential plaintiffs . . . .

The third matter is more important. The recognition of an unqualified entitlement in a third party to sue on the contract would severely circumscribe the freedom of action of the parties, particularly the promisee. He may rescind or modify the contract with the assent of the promisor, arrive at a compromise or assign his contractual rights. He may even modify the contract so that he diverts to himself the benefit initially intended for the third party. . . .

Should it be a sufficient foundation for the existence of a third party entitlement to use on the contract that there is a contractual intention to benefit a third party? Or, should an intention that the third party should be able to sue on the contract be required? Under s. 48 of the *Insurance Contracts Act 1984 (Cth)* and in the United States an intention to benefit a third party alone is necessary and that seems to be the position in Western Australia. But in Queensland (*Property Law Act 1974*, ss. 55(1), 55(6)(c)(ii)) and in New Zealand (*Contracts (Privity) Act 1982*, ss. 4, 8) an intention that the third party should be able to sue is required. This requirement again seems to have its origin in the recommendations of the English Law Revision Committee. As the contracting parties are unlikely to turn their attention to the enforcement by the third party, the ascertainment of this intention may well be fraught with similar problems to those that have surrounded the trust concept.

The variety of these responses to the problems arising from contracts to benefit a third party indicate the range of the policy choices to be made and that there is room for debate about them. A simple departure from the traditional rules would lead to third party enforceability of such a contract, subject to the preservation of a contracting party's right to rescind or vary, in the absence of reliance by the third party to his detriment, and to the availability in an action by the third party of defences against a contracting party. The adoption of this course would represent less of a departure from the traditional exposition of the law than other legislative choices which have been made. Moreover, as we have seen, the traditional rules, which were adopted here as a consequence of their development in the United Kingdom, have been the subject of much criticism and of legislative erosion in the field of insurance contracts. Regardless of the layers of sediment which may have accumulated, we consider that it is the responsibility of this Court to reconsider in appropriate cases common law rules which operate unsatisfactorily and unjustly. The fact that there have been recent legislative developments in the relevant field is not a reason for continuing to insist on the application of an unjust rule as it stood before its alteration by the *Insurance Contracts Act 1984 (Cth)*.

In the ultimate analysis the limited question we have to decide is whether the old rules apply to a policy of insurance. The injustice which would flow from such a result arises not only from its failure to give effect to the expressed intention of the person who takes out the insurance but also from the common intention of the parties and the circumstance that others, aware of the existence of the policy, will order their affairs accordingly. We doubt that the doctrine of estoppel provides an adequate protection of the legitimate expectations of such persons and, even if it does, the rights of persons under a policy of insurance should not be made to depend on the vagaries of such an intricate doctrine. In the nature of things the likelihood of some degree of reliance on the part of the third party in the case of a benefit to be provided for him under an insurance policy is so tangible that the common law rule should be shaped with that likelihood in mind.

This argument has even greater force when it is applied to an insurance against liabilities which is expressed to cover the insured and its sub-contractors. It stands to reason that many sub-contractors will assume that such an insurance is an effective indemnity in their favour and that they will refrain from making their own arrangements for insurance on that footing. That, it seems, is what happened in the present case. But why should the respondent's rights depend entirely on its ability to make out a case of estoppel?

In the circumstances, notwithstanding the caution with which the Court ordinarily will review earlier authorities and the operation of long-established principle, we conclude that the principled development of the law requires that it be recognized that McNiece was entitled to succeed in the action.

For the foregoing reasons, we would dismiss the appeal.

Notes

1. In their relaxation of the strict doctrine of privity, Mason CJ and Wilson J make reference to and summarize the unimplemented 1937 proposals of the Law Revision Committee in the United Kingdom, amongst other attacks upon the doctrine. In the 1990s the doctrine came under renewed scrutiny from law reformers in the United Kingdom, and the Law Commission issued a Consultation Paper (Law. Com. No. 121) in November 1991 which contains provisional recommendations for reform. The Law Commission Paper is discussed in detail by Beatson (himself a Law Commissioner) in 'Contracts for the Benefit of Third Parties' ([1992] *CLP* 1) from which we have taken a number of extracts. Given the earlier work of the Law Revision Committee, the initial question arises: 'why not implement the Committee's original proposals?'

J. Beatson, 'Contracts for the Benefit of Third Parties', [1992] *CLP* 1 at 22

There are several good reasons for a fresh look at the topic. As we have seen, there has been much doctrinal development albeit within the framework of the third party rule. In any event, the Law Revision Committee's report has not escaped criticism. It has been said to be too narrow in its requirement that the benefit be conferred on the third party by the 'express terms' of the contract. Secondly, although the promiser was to be allowed any defence against the third party which he would have had against the promisee, there is no requirement that the promisee be joined as a party to the action.

Thirdly, the Committee's proposal that the contract could be revoked or varied by the parties before 'adoption' by the third party has been said to be too narrow since, in some circumstances, it is arguable that the parties should not be able to cancel. The concept of 'adoption' has also been said to lack precision. The experience of several Commonwealth jurisdictions which have legislatively abolished the rule provides useful and more up to date guidance.

Some examples of the experience of other Commonwealth countries in the privity field are described by Mason CJ and Wilson J in their judgment, and these are referred to also throughout the Law Commission Consultation

Paper. Some of the approaches taken by other jurisdictions were rejected, such as the introduction of legislation which simply provides that privity should not be a bar to a third party's action (the solution adopted at common law by the majority of the judges in *Trident*, and the general approach taken in the USA) in favour of a more detailed legislative scheme.

The main features of the scheme proposed by the Law Commission, which is so far provisional in nature, are the following:

Beatson, 'Contracts for the Benefit of Third Parties', 3–4

The Commission's provisional view is that a third party should be able to sue if that is what the contractors intended and that legislation should make provision for the rights of contracting parties to modify or terminate the contract, promisors' defences, and the types of remedy available to third parties. The alternative possibilities, the relative merits of the different approaches, and the provisional recommendations are set out in Part V of the Consultation Paper. The main features of the scheme are:

1. The test of enforceable benefit should be a double intention test; that the parties intend (*a*) that the third party should receive the benefit of the proposed performance and (*b*) to create a legal obligation enforceable by the third party.
2. The rights created against a contracting party should include the following rights: to receive the promised performance where appropriate, to pursue any remedies for delayed or defective performance, and to rely on any provisions of the contract restricting or excluding the third party's liability as if the third party were a party to the contract.
3. The rights created should be governed by the contract. They should accordingly be valid only to the extent that it is valid and be subject to any defences, set-offs, and counter-claims which would have been available to the promisor. Although the parties should not be able to impose duties on a third party, they may impose conditions upon the enjoyment of any benefit by him.
4. The rights may be created in a third party even though he is not in existence or ascertained at the time the contract is made.
5. The legislation should make it clear whether, and if so, when the contracting parties may vary or cancel the contract. No view is expressed as to whether irrevocability should depend on acceptance, adoption, or material reliance by the third party.
6. Existing legislative exceptions to the third party rule should be preserved.

The third party's claim is viewed as a contractual claim, governed by the provisions of the contract, including any relevant defences. The key to enforcing a benefit lies in the intentions of the contracting parties, not, for example, in the reliance on the part of the third party or in the creation of a reasonable expectation of a benefit on the part of the third party by the contracting parties. The so-called double or dual intention test must be satisfied. To that extent, the Law Commission's proposals are located within a traditional framework of contract based on the will of the parties. They do not offer support for the reliance theories discussed below. For further comment on the proposals see A. Tettenborn, 'Privity of Contract: The Law Commission's Proposals' ([1992] *LMCLQ* 182).

2. Towards the end of their judgment, Mason CJ and Wilson J refer to the reliance approach in the context of insurance policies. In their view, where the likelihood of reliance 'is so tangible', the common law rules should be shaped with reliance in contemplation. The approach of Mason CJ and Wilson J can therefore be contrasted with that of Brennan J and Deane J who take a traditional view of the scope of contract liability. Mason CJ and Wilson J seem to be close to using reliance as a general theory of contractual obligation, that is, to finding that contracts can be enforced by those who have relied upon promises as well as by those who have paid for contractual promises. In the previous chapter we were looking at situations where a party had received a promise and relied upon it but not actually paid for it. In situations where privity of contract creates a problem the position is rather different, as the third party has relied upon a promise made to the promisee. However, for a true reliance theorist the trigger for liability is not the receipt of a promise but reliance. It should make no difference that the promise relied upon was received by someone else. Under such a theory, there is simply no scope for a privity doctrine. The question of whether the promisor needs to know of that reliance, or can be deemed to know, depends on how we redraw the boundaries of contractual liability once the privity rule has been abandoned. We look at this issue in more detail in the notes following Toohey J's judgment and in Section III.

3. The case that Mason CJ and Wilson J are adopting a reliance-based approach to contract should not be overstated. They refer to the intention test as the criterion of an enforceable benefit. They also refer to the 'limited question we have to decide' and to the impact of the Insurance Contracts Act 1984, which gives their judgment a more cautious flavour. Toohey J's judgment provides a strong contrast

TOOHEY J [T]his Court is concerned with the application of the doctrine of privity of contract only in relation to a public liability indemnity policy. It is not called upon to deal with the doctrine in all its aspects. Still, it would be unreal to think that a decision upholding the Court of Appeal would not have implications for privity of contract in other situations. And the disposition of this appeal inevitably takes the Court into areas that lie outside the field of insurance.

The proposition that ". . . only a person who is a party to a contract can sue on it" (Viscount Haldane L.C. in *Dunlop Pneumatic Tyre Co. Ltd. v. Selfridge & Co. Ltd.*) has been the subject of much criticism by judges, academics and law reform agencies. Its origin is of doubtful legitimacy, as Professor Flannigan has demonstrated in "Privity—The End of an Era (Error)", (1987) 103 *Law Quarterly Review*, 564. The law, although still fluid by the middle of the nineteenth century, is generally taken to have been settled by *Tweddle v. Atkinson* in favour of the view that at common law a third party cannot sue on a contract made for his benefit. Nevertheless doubts surround the true ratio of this case. It may be that it was decided on the basis that the plaintiff was a stranger to the consideration rather than on the ground that he was not a party to the agreement . . . or, as the defendant argued in *Tweddle*, on both grounds. The reports of the case do not provide a conclusive answer. . . . [T]he issue which lies at the heart of this appeal as I see it, is whether the principled development of the common law supports the conclusion of the Court of Appeal that "this Court should now declare that at common law a non-party assured is, and has been for some time at common law, able to sue on a written policy of liability insurance": McHugh JA, with whom Hope and Priestley JJA agreed.

Even when courts have expressed their impatience with the limitations imposed by privity of contract, they have applied the doctrine. At the same time they have not withheld approval from developments in the law that have by-passed privity of contract, so that, for instance, a promisee might be regarded as holding his right under a contract on trust for a third person to whom a benefit had been promised and might be required to exercise that right at the instance of the third person. . . . But, in the present case, no trust was pleaded and the Court of Appeal refused to allow an amendment to the statement of claim to raise such an issue. The decision of the Court of Appeal did not involve sidestepping privity of contract; rather it rejected the notion in its application to contracts of insurance.

In my view, the proposition enunciated by the Court of Appeal that for some time at common law a non-party assured has been able to sue on a written policy of liability insurance is not supported by authority. . . .

To hold, as in the present case, that a person not a party to a contract of insurance may sue on that contract represents a change in the common law and that must be acknowledged. Against the background of the decisions of this Court . . . it is not, I think, a change to be made by an intermediate court of appeal. The change is not disguised by pointing to the various ways in which third parties have been permitted to sue, whether by way of trust, agency or the like. . . .

In a quite different context, that of hearsay evidence, Lord Reid said in *Myers v. Director of Public Prosecutions* [[1965] AC 1001 at 1021]

"The common law must be developed to meet changing economic conditions and habits of thought, and I would not be deterred by expressions of opinion in this House in old cases. But there are limits to what we can or should do. If we are to extend the law it must be by the development and application of fundamental principles. We cannot introduce arbitrary conditions or limitations: that must be left to legislation. And if we do in effect change the law, we ought in my opinion only to do that in cases where our decision will produce some finality or certainty. . ... The most powerful argument of those who support the strict doctrine of precedent is that if it is relaxed judges will be tempted to encroach on the proper field of the legislature, and this case to my mind offers a strong temptation to do that which ought to be resisted."

Can it be said that, in the present case, to uphold the Court of Appeal is to encroach on what is the proper field of the legislature, given the very strong preponderance of authority against the enforcement of a contract by a person who is not a party thereto? . . .

I do not accept that a non-party assured is, as the common law presently stands, able to sue. But equally I accept that the law which precludes him from doing so is based on shaky foundations and, in its widest form, lacks support both in logic or in jurisprudence. My concern is whether the law is so well entrenched that nothing short of legislative interference can fairly budge it.

My conclusion is that the law is not so well entrenched as to be incapable of change. Lord Reid commented in *Tomlinson (A) (Hauliers) Ltd. v. Hepburn* [[1966] AC 451 at 470]

"No doubt the principle preventing jus quaesitum tertio has been firmly established for at least half a century. But it does not appear to me to be a primeval or necessary principle of the law of England."

It is true that his Lordship added: "We must uphold it until it is altered." But I do not understand Lord Reid to be excluding the possibility of alteration judicially as well as legislatively . . . .

At common law apparent exceptions have been recognized in the fields of agency, assignment of choses in action, carriage of goods, commercial letters of credit, covenants concerning land, claims in tort and proprietary or possessory rights . . . .

The Supreme Judicial Court of Massachusetts, in *Choate, Hall and Stewart v. S.C.A. Services Inc.* [(1979) 392 NE (2d) 1045], took the step which had been taken more than a hundred years earlier by the New York Court of Appeals in *Lawrence v. Fox* [(1859) 20 NY 268] of permitting a plaintiff to sue on a contract to which he was not a party. In the Massachusetts case Kaplan J referred to the various exceptions to privity of contract that had grown up, some of which he described as "rationalization[s] after the event" and continued [at p. 1051]

"The rather confusing patchwork should be supplanted by the general rule now prevalent, [a reference to the rule prevailing in other State jurisdictions allowing third party enforcement] which avoids circuity of action and is calculated to accord with the probable intentions of the contracting parties and to respond to the reasonable reliance of the third party creditor."

. . . [W]hen a rule of the common law harks back no further than the middle of the last century, when it has been the subject of constant criticism and when, in its widest form, it lacks a sound foundation in jurisprudence and logic and further, when that rule has been so affected by exceptions or qualifications, I see nothing inimical to principled development in this Court now declaring the law to be otherwise in the circumstances of the present case . . . .

. . . The appellant entered into a contractual obligation with Blue Circle Southern Cement Ltd. and it did so with the intention that the benefit of that obligation should extend to those involved with Blue Circle as contractors and sub-contractors on the work sites in question. That is borne out by the terms of the policy. The respondent was sufficiently identified as one of those involved. The policy was intended by both the appellant and Blue Circle to be a basis of insurance in respect of the work being carried out on the sites and Blue Circle and its contractors and sub-contractors could be expected to arrange their business in that light.

Certainly a court must look long and hard at the implications of declaring the law to be otherwise than hitherto accepted. In particular the court must consider the impact of any change on existing rights and obligations. But in the present case, to allow the respondent to sue the appellant is to give effect to the presumed intention of the appellant at the time it issued the insurance policy. . . .

The proposition which I consider this Court should now indorse may be formulated along these lines. When an insurer issues a liability insurance policy, identifying the assured in terms that evidence an intention on the part of both insurer and assured that the policy will indemnify as well those with whom the assured contracts for the purpose of the venture covered by the policy, and it is reasonable to expect that such a contractor may order its affairs by reference to the existence of the policy, the contractor may sue the insurer on the policy, notwithstanding that consideration may not have moved from the contractor to the insurer and notwithstanding that the contractor is not a party to the contract between the insurer and assured.

No doubt, a decision upholding the Court of Appeal will itself give rise to a number of questions. Are there other situations in which a third party may sue on a contract when consideration has not moved from the third party to the promisor? What defences are available to the promisor in such cases? These are questions which do not now require an answer. Other situations must await another day; the terms on which special leave to appeal was granted preclude a decision in wider terms than have been expressed in these reasons. The defences available to an insurer against whom action may lie at the suit of a third party do not have to be explored for none was advanced on behalf of the appellant before this Court.

The appeal should be dismissed.

Notes

1. Toohey J considers that privity of contract *does not* have a history which renders it unimpeachable. This is a much stronger attack on the doctrine

than that mounted by Mason CJ and Wilson J. He refers to the fact that in legal terms the doctrine is not of great antiquity, as it is only since 1861 and the decision in *Tweddle* v. *Atkinson* that commentators have referred to a 'rule' of privity. Yet even now, it is not entirely clear on what basis *Tweddle* v. *Atkinson* was decided. For example, we referred in the introduction to the chapter to the debate about whether *Tweddle* is simply authority for the proposition that consideration must flow from the promisee or whether it in fact creates a privity of contract rule in addition. We set out the case for two separate rules, in an extract from Beatson. A rather different historical view of how the two rules were linked together is provided by Flannigan.

R. Flannigan, 'Privity: The End of an Era (Error)', (1987) 103 *LQR* 564 at 567–71

This brings us to *Twedle* v. *Atkinson*. It is this 1861 case that has been taken to be the one which finally ended the uncertainty and confirmed that a third party cannot sue on a contract between two others even though it was made for the benefit of the third party. . . .

The Entrenchment of the Doctrine of Privity

. . . contrary to popular legal opinion, *Twedle* v. *Atkinson* really does not stand as an authority for an independent privity doctrine. The case was one decided exclusively on the absence of consideration moving from the third party. . . . But let us look to the judgments and consider just how the matter of the third party beneficiary was dealt with.

It is apparent that the court in *Twedle* v. *Atkinson* was not in possession of all the relevant authorities. Wightman J had this to say:

"Some of the old decisions appear to support the proposition that a stranger to the consideration of a contract may maintain an action upon it, if he stands in such a near relationship to the party from whom the consideration proceeds, that he may be considered a party to the consideration. The strongest of those cases is that cited in *Bourne* v. *Mason* (1 Ventr. 6), in which it was held that the daughter of a physician might maintain assumpsit upon a promise to her father to give her a sum of money if he performed a certain cure. But there is no modern case in which the proposition has been supported. On the contrary, it is now established that no stranger to the consideration can take advantage of a contract, although made for his benefit."

The fact is that, apart from *Dutton* v. *Poole*, the old decisions were *not* qualified on the "near relationship" basis . Moreover, . . . the proposition that a third party could enforce a contract *had* been supported in modern cases.

[For example, Flannigan cites *Marchington* v. *Vernon*, (1797) Bos & P. 101 and a footnote to the judgment in *Piggott* v. *Thompson* (1802) 3 Bos. & P. 147.]

Lastly, prior to this decision, it had hardly been satisfactorily established that "no stranger to the consideration can take advantage of a contract, although made for his benefit." . . . Nothing about the general right of a third party to take action is decided here. The lack of a general right, premised on a lack of consideration, is simply assumed.

Crompton J does purport to give one reason for debarring the third party. According to him, it would be a "monstrous proposition to say that a person was a party to the contract for the purpose of suing on it for his own advantage, and not a party to it for the purpose of being sued." . . . There is a promise made *to* benefit the third party; but there is no promise of performance made *by* the third party which could be enforced against him or her. The original parties were obviously aware of this at the time they contracted. Is the original promisor somehow prejudiced by being compelled to perform? Most decidedly not. The promisor got what he bargained for from the promisee or, if not, he is entitled to get it in an action against the promisee. Then consider the alternative. Is it not markedly more "monstrous" that, having received performance, the promisor could ignore his or her own promise?

If we look at Justice Blackburn's judgment it is made patently clear that, in fact, the court wasn't even being asked to choose between generally allowing or disallowing third party actions. Apparently on the authority of *Price* v. *Easton*, counsel for the third party had conceded the general rule and sought only to argue a *Dutton* v. *Poole* "near-relationship" exception:

"Mr. Mellish admits that in general no action can be maintained upon a promise, unless the consideration moves from the party to whom it is made. But he says that there is an exception; namely, that when the consideration moves from a father, and the contract is for the benefit of the son, the natural love and affection between the father and son gives the son the right to sue as if the consideration had proceeded from himself. And *Dutton and Wife* v. *Poole* was cited for this."

It seems entirely unsatisfactory that the general third party right of action should be lost on an unnecessary concession. Yet this is what happened if *Twedle* v. *Atkinson* is the decisive case. The result of the concession, of course, was to allow the court to forgo any penetrating analysis of the issue.

Twedle v. *Atkinson* was subsequently treated as having decided that a third party had no right of action. As we have seen, it was actually an assumption by the court rather than decision. Nevertheless, the court's assumption is based on a supposed need for consideration. There was no talk of an independent "privity" rule here.

Historical arguments notwithstanding, judges none the less experience difficulties in 'budging' (to use the terminology of Toohey J) the privity rule, even if they dislike its effects. The question arises whether *Trident*, and the judgment of Toohey J in particular, give the green light to a new direction not just in the Australian but also in the English common law.

2. In the United States, privity of contract enjoys a much more precarious existence than in other common law jurisdictions, although the attacks upon its general application have come from the courts, taking their cue from the 1855 decision of the New York Court of Appeals in *Lawrence* v. *Fox*, rather than from the legislature. Even so, it took 100 years for the courts of all the state jurisdictions to recognize the concept of the contract for the benefit of third parties, although by 1932 the concept had been enshrined in the First Restatement of Contracts, and was significantly expanded in the Second Restatement published in 1981. The Law Commission examined the developments in the United States, before deciding not to follow that approach on the grounds that it was productive of uncertainty, concluding that, after so many years and many hundreds of cases, significant issues still remain undecided. We extract here the Commission's summary of the US position, and of the major unresolved issues.

Law Commission, Consultation Paper No. 121, *Privity of Contract*, 1991, 151–4

15. Since the decision of the New York Court of Appeals in *Lawrence* v. *Fox*, it has become generally accepted that a third party is able to enforce a contractual obligation made for his benefit. However, the problem of defining what is meant by a third party beneficiary has never adequately been solved. Section 133 of the first Restatement of Contracts published in 1932 distinguished donee beneficiaries, creditor beneficiaries, and incidental beneficiaries: only donee and creditor beneficiaries could enforce contracts made for their benefit. A person was a "donee beneficiary" if the purpose of the promisee was to make a gift to him, or to confer upon him a right not due from the promisee. A person was a "creditor beneficiary" if performance of the promise would satisfy an actual or asserted duty of the promisee to him. A person was an incidental beneficiary if the benefits to him were merely incidental to the performance of the promise.

16. It became apparent that a number of third party beneficiaries did not fall within the "donee" and "creditor" categories, such that some courts simply disregarded the categorisation approach and allowed beneficiaries to recover who were neither creditors nor donees. The inflexibility of the categorisation approach led to changes in the second Restatement of Contracts published in 1981, under which intended beneficiaries, who can enforce contracts, are contrasted with incidental beneficiaries, who cannot. Section 302 of the Restatement (Second) provides:

"(1) Unless otherwise agreed between promisor and promisee, a beneficiary of a promise is an intended beneficiary if recognition of a right to performance in the beneficiary is appropriate to effectuate the intention of the parties and either,

(a) the performance of the promise will satisfy an obligation of the promisee to pay money to the beneficiary; or

(b) the circumstances indicate that the promisee intends to give the beneficiary the benefit of the promised performance.

(2) An incidental beneficiary is a beneficiary who is not an intended beneficiary."

17. However, the Restatement (Second) fails properly to explain the distinction between intended and incidental beneficiaries, given that "the parties, or more simply the promisee, may intend a third party to receive a benefit but not intend that party to have standing to enforce that promise." The "intent to benefit" test has, in practice, failed to achieve consistent results . . . .

18. Other difficult questions under the Restatement (Second) include the following. Should reference be made to the contract alone, or to all the prevailing circumstances when determining whether the appropriate intention exists? The case law is divided on this point, although the better view would appear to favour the latter option. Another issue is that of whose intent is required. Section 302(1) refers to the intentions of the parties, although section 302(1) (b) refers to the promisee's intention. Different jurisdictions apply different tests: one requires proof only of the promisee's intention; another focuses upon the intent of both parties; a third requires additionally that the promisor have reason to know of the promisee's intent to benefit a third party.

19. On the question whether the contracting parties may vary or revoke their promise, section 311 of the Restatement (Second) provides that the contracting parties may create rights that cannot be modified, but that otherwise they are free to modify unless the beneficiary "materially changes his position in justifiable reliance on the promise or brings suit on it or manifests assent to it at the request of the promisor or promisee".

3. The judgment of Toohey J provides further evidence of the attitudes of the judges to privity, like consideration, being led by their conceptions of the basis of contractual liability. There are a number of indications in his judgment that Toohey J shares the views of Mason CJ and Wilson J on the role of reliance. See e.g. his citation of the judgment of the Supreme Judicial Court of Massachusetts in *Choate, Hall and Stewart* v. *S.C.A. Services Inc.*, which refers to the protection of the reasonable reliance of the third party. Like Mason CJ and Wilson J, Toohey J also seems to revert in his conclusion to a narrow response to the questions raised before the High Court, namely the applicability of privity in the context of liability insurance arrangements. The final paragraph of his judgment does, however, allude to the wider issues which he has raised. Abandoning the

privity rule leaves open two principal questions—determining the range of potential beneficiaries who may enforce the contract and identifying the conditions under which the claim may be brought. As we have seen, the Law Commission has proposed a double intention test to limit the range of beneficiaries, and has proposed that the claim be subject to the terms of the contract. Collins identifies a rather different mechanism for limiting the range of beneficiaries—one which tends to draw together the claim of the third party beneficiary on the contract and a claim in tort.

H. Collins, *The Law of Contract*, 2nd edn. (London, Butterworths, 1993), 289–91

A much more substantial objection to an abolition of the rule that third parties cannot sue upon a contract points out that the numbers of third parties interested in suing may be considerable and engender unexpectedly enormous liabilities. . . .

The American case, *Martinez* v. *Socoma Companies, Inc,* [II Cal 3d 394, 521 P 2d 841 (1974)] illustrates this problem well. Under the Economic Opportunity Act of 1964 (as amended) the United States Congress designated certain neighbourhoods which had large concentrations of low income persons and unemployment as Special Impact Areas and made federal funds available for government contracts with local private industry. The defendants entered into such a contract with the government and undertook to train and employ a specified number of local residents. The plaintiffs were members of the class intended to benefit from legislative aid who alleged that the company had failed to comply with its contractual obligation to hire and train the required number of local residents. The plaintiffs claimed a right to sue the company as intended beneficiaries under the contract. The California Supreme Court denied their claim on the ground that from the terms of the contract it did not appear that the government intended to make a gift to the plaintiffs or to confer on them a legal right against the defendants. The plaintiffs were simply incidental beneficiaries of the contract, and the company's responsibility did not extend so far. It is evident that the court feared to extend rights to such a wide class of beneficiaries, that is, all the poor and unemployed persons in the Special Impact Area, and that this fear provided the reason for preserving a modified privity rule. . . .

The law of tort encounters the same problem of limiting the range of liability. When a lawyer negligently drafts a will which is invalid as a result, thereby depriving the intended beneficiaries of their expected inheritance, the beneficiaries can win compensatory damages against the lawyer if they satisfy the test that the lawyer owed the beneficiaries a duty of care. . . . a Californian court in *Lucas* v. *Hamm* [56 Cal 2d 583 (1961)] also permitted the disappointed beneficiaries under an invalid will to sue as third party beneficiaries of the contract between the testator and the lawyer on the ground that they were intended to benefit from the contract to draft a will. This decision reveals that, once the courts permit third party beneficiaries to sue upon a contract, the problem of limiting the range of liability is similar in contract and tort. The question then presses upon us whether it makes sense to use the same test for determining the range of liability, namely the test of reasonable foreseeability . . . .

The most significant justification for the doctrine of privity thus boils down to the simple point that the law of contract must draw a line at some point to set limits to the range of liability to third parties. English law established the line firmly at the point where a person was a party to the agreement.

Note

Martinez v. *Socoma Companies Inc.* involves an application of the Restatement (First) of Contracts discussed in the Law Commission extract above.

Trident involved a relatively straightforward matrix of contractual arrangements and a definable range of beneficiaries. It must have been possible for the insurance company to define the outer limits of its potential liability and to calculate the insurance premiums accordingly. *Martinez*, on the other hand, raises the difficulties which arise where there is an indeterminate category of beneficiaries. Collins suggests a test of reasonable foreseeability in such circumstances, drawing together liability in tort and contract. One difficulty, however, with treating the claim of the third party as if it were a tort claim is that the claim, although arising out of the contractual promise, could not be governed by it, and so the defences and exclusions contained in the contract would not be applicable. This may be unfair on the promisor and force him to accept a greater risk than he originally contracted to take.

In the final section of this chapter we shall address the problems and possibilities of relaxing privity in more complex contractual matrices, where all three parties are linked by one or more contracts, but where there is no contract between the alleged third-party beneficiary and the promisor.

The final judgment extracted, that of Gaudron J, takes a rather different approach to privity problems.

GAUDRON J In my view a promisor who has accepted an agreed consideration for a promise to benefit a third party comes under an obligation to the third party to fulfil that promise and the third party acquires a right to bring an action to secure the benefit of that promise. The right of the third party is not a right to sue on the contract: rather, it is a right independent of, but ordinarily corresponding in content and duration with, the obligation owed under the contract by the promisor to the promisee.

The doctrine of privity of contract and the related requirement that consideration should be provided by the person seeking to enforce a contractual obligation do not deny the binding nature of a contractual promise the performance of which will benefit a third party. Breach of the contractual obligation may sound in damages at the suit of the promisee. However, it is not clear on existing authority whether the promisee is restricted to recovering damages for his loss only or whether damages can also be recovered by the promisee for the third party's loss: *Coulls v. Bagot's Executor & Trustee Co. Ltd.*; ... *Beswick v. Beswick.* ... If damages are an inadequate remedy, the promisee may obtain a decree of specific performance of the contract: *Coulls; Beswick.* ... The third party, however, cannot institute an action for breach of contract or for specific performance unless he can bring himself within one of the recognized exceptions to or qualifications of the rules. Commonly the position of the third party is expressed in terms of inability to sue on the contract . . . .

The source of the obligation to perform a contractual promise is the contract itself, but there is no reason in logic or in law why the existence of a contract should preclude the existence of another obligation ordinarily corresponding in content and duration with the contractual obligation, but having its source in law rather than in the contract. . . .

Where the consideration is wholly executed in favour of a promisor under a contract made for the benefit of a third party a rule that the third party may not bring action to secure the benefit of the contract permits of the possibility that the promisor may be unjustly enriched to the extent that the promise is not fulfilled. . . .

In my view it should now be recognized that a promisor who has accepted agreed consideration for a promise to benefit a third party is unjustly enriched at the expense of the third party to the extent that the promise is unfulfilled and the non-fulfilment does not attract proportional legal consequences. Although exceptions to and qualifications of the rules of privity and consideration and the doctrines of trust and estoppel operate in certain circumstances to preclude any unjust enrichment, the exceptions, qualifications and doctrines should not be seen as reasons to impede the development of legal principle which will obviate all possibility of unjust enrichment. Rather, their existence should be seen as demonstrating the necessity for the recognition of such an obligation.

The possibility of unjust enrichment is obviated by recognition that a promisor who has accepted agreed consideration for a promise to benefit a third party owes an obligation to the third party to fulfil that promise and that the third party has a corresponding right to bring action to secure the benefit of the promise. . . .

To recognize an obligation on the part of a promisor who has accepted agreed consideration for a promise to benefit a third party, is not to abrogate the doctrine of privity of contract. It is merely to confine it to the only area in which it can properly operate, viz. the area of rights and obligations having their source in contract. The matter can be put another way. A right to enforce an obligation imposed by law by reason of the acceptance of agreed consideration for a promise to benefit a third party is no more a right to sue on the contract than an action to recover a debt on an executed consideration is an action upon a contract. . . .

On the basis that the appellant received the agreed consideration specified in the policy of insurance—a matter that has not been disputed—it came under an obligation to the respondent to fulfil its promise to indemnify it as provided in the policy. The respondent is entitled to maintain an action to enforce that obligation. Accordingly the appeal should be dismissed.

Notes

1. The basis of Gaudron J's judgment in McNiece's favour is very different from that of the other judges. She decides the case by using the principles of restitution. Privity of contract does not cause a problem because the type of claim she is advocating does not arise from the contract. It is an entirely separate claim, which the third party can bring on the grounds that Trident have agreed with Blue Circle and accepted consideration to the effect that they will benefit certain third parties, i.e. McNiece and other contractors. If Trident then do not confer that benefit, according to Gaudron J, they will have been unjustly enriched at the expense of the third party, McNiece. Gaudron J sees restitution as a doctrine to be used to supplement privity in the same way as the trust and agency mechanisms examined earlier in the chapter. Consequently, where restitution cannot be used, privity of contract still defines the limits of recovery.

2. This approach appears to solve the privity of contract problems very neatly. However, it has attracted considerable criticism on the grounds that it extends the concept of 'unjust enrichment at the expense of the plaintiff' beyond its accepted limit without any supporting authority, and that in any event it provides a solution to the privity problem only in limited circumstances. See K. Soh, 'Privity of Contract and Restitution', (1989) 105 *LQR* 4. However, for support for the approach of Gaudron J., see Collins, *The Law of Contract*, 2nd edn., 300.

3. One of the difficulties for Australian lawyers is that *Trident* has left the law in a state of considerable uncertainty. Six of the judges appear to split 3–3 on the issue of whether the privity of contract doctrine should be relaxed within the context of insurance contracts, and Gaudron J's judgment is difficult to classify. For the moment, the *Trident* case is no more than persuasive authority which can be cited before the English courts, but it does seem unlikely that the judges would be persuaded to shift from their pattern of adherence to traditional doctrines by what is, in sum, an equivocal decision of the High Court of Australia. It does, however, provide us with an interesting insight into the types of judicial approach that can be taken to this issue.

III. EXPANDING THE CONTRACTUAL MATRIX

In *Trident*, McNiece Bros. sought to take advantage of the substance of a contract between Trident and Blue Circle, by claiming the benefit of the insurance policy from Trident. As far as the *insurance arrangements* were concerned there was no contractual link between McNiece and Blue Circle. This is what Beyleveld and Brownsword call a 'single-contract setting', where A, *a gratuitous third party beneficiary*, seeks to enforce a contract between B and C (D. Beyleveld and R. Brownsword, 'Privity, Transitivity and Rationality', (1991) 54 *MLR* 48 at 69) (the text uses their letters). *Tweddle* v. *Atkinson* is similar. However, problems with privity of contract, and consequently privity-avoiding devices, arise also in 'multi-contract settings', where 'A, *who is in contract with B*, seeks to enforce a contract between B and C'. In such circumstances, it is more difficult to dismiss the claims of A as an undeserving third party who has not paid for the promise (he may well have paid indirectly), or as a complete stranger to the relationship between B and C. In Chapter 1, in *Junior Books* v. *Veitchi* ([1983] 1 AC 520) and *Pacific Associates* v. *Baxter* ([1989] 2 All ER 504), we saw two contrasting approaches to the situation of A through the medium of tort. The dominant judicial view in England now is to deny a tortious remedy; thus, for example, a building owner who has a contract with a main building contractor, and who suffers pure economic loss as a consequence of the negligence of a subcontractor with whom he has no contract, will not be able to sue the subcontractor for damages in tort, but must sue down the contractual chain via the main contractor. Privity of contract prevents an action by the owner on the contract between the main building contractor and the subcontractor.

However, the privity principle can also work harshly against the subcontractor. Suppose the subcontractor causes damage to the building owner's property, then under the ordinary principles of tort he will be liable, since he will owe a duty of care in negligence to the building owner in respect of damage to his property, as opposed to pure economic loss (*Donoghue* v. *Stevenson* [1932] AC 562). In that case, he would also be precluded by privity of contract from relying upon any clause in the contract between the owner and the main contractor under which the risk of damage to the owner's property was allocated to the owner rather than to the contractor. Put in the terms used above, C (the defendant subcontractor) may not rely on defences contained in contracts to which A (the plaintiff building owner) is party, including the contract with B, with whom C is also in contract. It was a similar type of contractual chain which was at issue in *The Eurymedon*, and in that case the House of Lords, by a bare majority, stretched the boundaries of the notion of implied contract in order to protect the defendants.

New Zealand Shipping Co. Ltd. v. *A. M. Satterthwaite & Co. Ltd.* (*The Eurymedon*)
[1975] AC 154 (Privy Council on appeal from the New Zealand Court of Appeal)

LORD WILBERFORCE (majority judgment) The facts of this case are not in dispute. An expensive drilling machine was received on board the ship *Eurymedon* at Liverpool for transhipment to Wellington pursuant to the terms of a bill of lading no. 1262 dated June 5, 1964. The shipper as the maker of the drill, Ajax Machine Tool Co. Ltd. ("the consignor"). The bill of lading was issued by agents for the Federal Steam Navigation Co. Ltd. ("the carrier"). The consignee was A. M. Satterthwaite & Co. Ltd. of Christchurch, New Zealand ("the consignee"). For several years before 1964 the New Zealand Shipping Co. Ltd. ("the stevedore") had carried out all stevedoring work in Wellington in respect of the ships owned by the carrier, which was a wholly owned subsidiary of the stevedore. In addition to this stevedoring work the stevedore generally acted as agent for the carrier in New Zealand; and in such capacity as general agent (not in the course of their stevedoring functions) the stevedore received the bill of lading at Wellington July 31, 1964. Clause 1 of the bill of lading, on the construction of which this case turns, was in the same terms as bills of lading usually issued by the stevedore and its associated companies in respect of ordinary cargo carried by their ships from the United Kingdom to New Zealand. The consignee became the holder of the bill of lading and owner of the drill prior to August 14, 1964. On that date the drill was damaged as a result of the stevedore's negligence during unloading.

At the foot of the first page of the bill of lading the following words were printed in small capitals:

"In accepting this bill of lading the shipper, consignee and the owners of the goods, and the holders of this bill of lading agree to be bound by all of its conditions, exceptions and provisions whether written, printed or stamped on the front or back hereof."

On the back of the bill of lading a number of clauses were printed in small type. It is only necessary to set out the following. The first and third paragraph of clause 1 provided:

"This bill of lading shall have effect (*a*) subject to the provisions of any legislation giving effect to the International Convention for the unification of certain rules relating to bills of lading dated Brussels, August 25, 1924, or to similar effect which is compulsorily applicable to the contract of carriage evidenced hereby and (*b*) where no such legislation is applicable as if the Carriage of Goods by Sea Act 1924, of Great Britain and the rules scheduled thereto applied hereto and were incorporated herein. Nothing herein contained shall be deemed to be a surrender by the carrier of any of his rights or immunities or an increase of any of his responsibilities or liabilities under the provisions of the said legislation or Act and rules (as the case may be) and the said provisions shall not (unless and to the extent that they are by law compulsorily applicable) apply to that portion of the contract evidenced by this bill of lading which relates to forwarding under clause 4 hereof. If anything herein contained be inconsistent with or repugnant to the said provisions, it shall to the extent of such inconsistency or repugnance and no further be null and void. . . .

"It is hereby expressly agreed that no servant or agent of the carrier (including every independent contractor from time to time employed by the carrier) shall in any circumstances whatsoever be under any liability whatsoever to the shipper, consignee or owner of the goods or to any holder of this bill of lading for any loss or damage or delay of whatsoever kind arising or resulting directly or indirectly from any act neglect or default on his part while acting in the course of or in connection with his employment and, without prejudice to the generality of the foregoing provisions in this clause, every exemption, limitation, condition and liberty herein contained and every right, exemption from liability, defence and immunity of whatsoever nature applicable to the carrier or to which the carrier is entitled hereunder shall also be available and shall extend to protect every such servant or agent of the carrier acting as aforesaid and for the purpose of all the foregoing provisions of this clause the carrier is or shall be deemed to be acting as agent or trustee on behalf of and for the benefit of all persons who are or might be his servants or agents from time to time (including independent contractors as aforesaid) and all such persons shall to this extent be or be deemed to be parties to the contract in or evidenced by this bill of lading."

Clause 11 provided:

"The carrier will not be accountable for goods of any description beyond £100 in respect of any one package or unit unless the value thereof shall have been stated in writing both on the broker's order which must be obtained before shipment and on the shipping note presented on shipment and extra freight agreed upon and paid and bills of lading signed with a declaration of the nature and value of the goods appearing thereon. When the value is declared and extra freight agreed as aforesaid the carrier's liability shall not exceed such value or pro rata on that basis in the event of partial loss or damage."

No declaration as to the nature and value of the goods having appeared in the bill of lading, and no extra freight having been agreed upon or paid, it was acknowledged by the consignee that the liability of the carrier was accordingly limited to £100 by the application of clause 11 of the bill of lading. Moreover, the incorporation in the bill of lading of the rules scheduled to the Carriage of Goods by Sea Act 1924 meant that the carrier and the ship were discharged from all liability in respect of damage to the drill unless suit was brought against them, within one year after delivery. No action was commenced until April 1967, when the consignee sued the stevedore in negligence, claiming £880 the cost of repairing the damaged drill.

The question in the appeal is whether the stevedore can take the benefit of the time limitation provision. The starting point, in discussion of this question, is provided by the House of Lords decision in *Midland Silicones Ltd.* v. *Scruttons Ltd.* There is no need to question or even to qualify that case in so far as it affirms the general proposition that a contract between two parties cannot be sued on by a third person even though the contract is expressed to be for his benefit. . . .

Clause 1 of the bill of lading, whatever the defects in its drafting, is clear in its relevant terms. The carrier, on his own account, stipulates for certain exemptions and immunities: among these is that conferred by article III, rule 6, of the Hague Rules which discharges the carrier from all liability for loss or damage unless suit is brought within one year after delivery. In addition to these stipulations on his own account, the carrier as agent for, inter alios, independent contractors stipulates for the same exemptions. . . .

If the choice, and the antithesis, is between a gratuitous promise, and a promise for consideration, as it must be in the absence of a tertium quid, there can be little doubt which, in commercial reality, this is. The whole contract is of a commercial character, involving service on one side, rate of payment on the other, and qualifying stipulations as to both. The relations of all parties to each other are commercial relations entered into for business reasons of ultimate profit. To describe one set of promises, in this context, as gratuitous, or nudum pactum, seems paradoxical and is prima facie implausible. . . .

In their Lordships' opinion the present contract presents much less difficulty than many . . . It is one of carriage from Liverpool to Wellington. The carrier assumes an obligation to transport the goods and to discharge at the port of arrival. The goods are to be carried and discharged, so the transaction is inherently contractual. It is contemplated that a part of this contract, viz. discharge, may be performed by independent contractors—viz. the appellant. By clause 1 of the bill of lading the shipper agrees to exempt from liability the carrier, his servants and independent contractors in respect of the performance of this contract of carriage. Thus, if the carriage, including the discharge, is wholly carried out by the carrier, he is exempt. If part is carried out by him, and part by his servants, he and they are exempt. If part is carried out by him and part by an independent contractor, he and the independent contractor are exempt. The exemption is designed to cover the whole carriage from loading to discharge, by whomsoever it is performed: the performance attracts the exemption or immunity in favour of whoever the performer turns out to be. There is possibly more than one way of analysing this business transaction into the necessary components; that which their Lordships would accept is to say that the bill of lading brought into existence a bargain initially unilateral but capable of becoming mutual, between the shipper and the appellant, made through the carrier as agent. This became a full contract when the appellant performed services by discharging the goods. The performance of these services for the benefit of the shipper was the consideration for the agreement by the shipper that the appellant should have the benefit of the exemptions and limitations contained in the bill of lading. . . . whether one describes the shipper's promise to exempt as an offer to be accepted by performance or as a promise in exchange for an act seems in the present context to be a matter of semantics. . . .

3. The appellant submitted, in the alternative, an argument that, quite apart from contract, exemptions from, or limitation of, liability in tort may be

conferred by mere consent on the part of the party who may be injured. As their Lordships consider that the appellant ought to succeed in contract, they prefer to express no opinion upon this argument: to evaluate it requires elaborate discussion. . . .

VICCOUNT DILHORNE [dissenting] In the course of its discharge from the ship at Wellington, the drilling machine was damaged by the negligence of the appellant, the stevedore, and the question for determination in this appeal is whether the appellant is exempted from liability for its negligence by the terms of the bill of lading. That depends on the construction to be placed on and the effect of clause 1 of the conditions printed on the back of the bill of lading . . . .

The clause does not in my opinion either expressly or impliedly contain an offer by the shipper to the carrier to enter into an agreement whereby if the appellant performed services in relation to the goods the shipper would give it the benefit of every exemption from and limitation of liability contained in the bill of lading. I see no difficulty in expressing such an offer in clear and unequivocal language, and if the clause contained such an offer, I would have been in favour of allowing the appeal.

What the clause records is not an offer but an agreement, and one agreement only, made between the shipper and the carrier acting in a dual capacity, on its own behalf and on behalf of all persons who were or might be its servants or employed by it as independent contractors, and an agreement to which all such persons are or are to be deemed to be parties.

I agree with Turner P. in thinking that the terms of clause 1 cannot be read as constituting such an offer. If the terms of the expressed agreement fail to constitute a legally binding contract between the shipper and the appellant, to read them as merely constituting an offer by the shipper capable of acceptance by conduct by the appellant is to rewrite the clause. . . .

The appellant's second contention recognises that at the time of the issue of the bill of lading there was no legally binding contract between the consignor and the appellant. It was not suggested that the agreement set out in clause 1 was not a legally binding contract between the consignor and the carrier and so this contention involves reading the one agreement, to which the consignor on the one hand and the carrier and whomsoever it chose to employ are or are to be deemed to be parties, as a valid contract between the consignor and the carrier and at the same time as a bargain not amounting to a valid contract between the consignor and all those who were at the time employed or who might be employed by the carrier. I do not know of any precedent for construing one agreement in writing in these two different ways.

What was the alleged bargain? If I understood the argument correctly, it was that the consignor would exempt any person employed by the carrier in the carriage and discharge of the drill from all liability if that person performed any services in relation to the carriage and discharge of the drill. The contention was that if such services were performed, that constituted acceptance of the consignor's offer to exempt and consideration for it; and so by performance the bargain was converted into a full contract.

I admire the ingenuity of the argument. It attempts to overcome the difficulty that clause 1 is expressed to contain an agreement and not an offer and it attempts to overcome the lack of consideration on which in my opinion the appellant's first contention founders; but I do not myself see any material difference between A offering B money if B does work for A and a bargain between A and B that A will pay B money if B does work for A. In each case A is making an offer which B can accept by doing the work.

In my view one really cannot read the agreement set out in clause 1 as stating any such bargain. . . .

Clause 1 of the bill of lading in this case, construed strictly, cannot be read in my opinion as the appellant desires. Anxiety to save negligent people from the consequences of their negligence does not lead me to give an unnatural and artificial meaning to the clause and a meaning which the words it contains do not bear. . . .

Notes

1. In order to 'construct' a contractual relationship between the stevedores (C) and the consignee (A), Lord Wilberforce, on behalf of the majority, was forced to stretch the conventional concepts of offer and acceptance, as well as to 'find' consideration for the consignee's promise. In contrast, Viscount Dilhorne and Lord Simon (dissenting) refused to contemplate such artificialities. There is an alternative to such a cosmetic privity-avoided device, proposed by Beyleveld and Brownsword, and that is to treat the relationship between the C and A as itself contractual, because they are linked indirectly by contracts via the carriers (B). This flows, in their view, from treating the relationships as 'transitive' ((1991) 54 *MLR* 48 at 50–1). This implies inferring from the two existing contractual relationships, A–B and B–C, the same type of relationship linking A and C, where there are sufficiently strong reasons for doing so. This approach involves an avowed relaxation of privity through the inference of a contractual relationship; however, the relaxation is two-sided in that not only is A permitted to sue C in contract, but C is able to set up as a defence any of the provisions contained in the contracts, A–B and B–C.

Beyleveld and Brownsword use the facts of *Junior Books* (see Ch. 1) in order to illustrate their points. They point to the sets of circumstances in which treating the relationship as transitive is justified, calling these the 'breakdown principle' and the 'subsumption principle'. They are principally concerned to question whether, on their analysis, A (the building owner) would have a claim in contract against the subcontractor (C), (their question G1) and whether, if so, C can rely upon exonerating terms in the head contract (A–B), or in the subcontract (B–C), (their questions G2 and G3).

D. Beyleveld and R. Brownsword, 'Privity, Transitivity and Rationality', (1991) 54 *MLR* 48 at 64–70

The breakdown principle is easily explained and, in effect, it involves an immanent critique of the reasoning which has underpinned the retrenchment from *Junior Books*. In a number of the cases where A has been refused a tortious remedy against C, the point has been taken that A has an alternative means of recovering his losses, particularly by suing back down the chain of contracts. In other words, A should pursue his remedy by suing B in contract, leaving B to sue C in contract. Thus, in *Simaan General Contracting Co.* v. *Pilkington Glass Ltd (No. 2)* [[1988] 1 All ER 791], where the relevant contractual chain comprised a building owner, Sheikh Al-Oteiba, (A), a main contractor, Simaan, (B), a subcontractor, Feal, (C), and a manufacturer of glass units to be incorporated in the building, Pilkington, (D), Bingham LJ said:

I do not think it just and reasonable to impose on Pilkington a duty of care towards Simaan of the scope contended for [ie to account directly to Simaan for their purely economic loss] . . . Just as equity remedied the inadequacies of the common law, so has the law of torts filled gaps left by other causes of action where the interests of justice so required. I see no such gaps here because there is no reason why claims beginning with the sheikh should not be pursued down the contractual chain . . . ending up with a contractual claim against Pilkington. That is the usual procedure. It must be what the parties contemplated when they made their contracts. I see no reason for departing from it.

Hence, Simaan, having a contractual avenue of recourse against Feal, were not to be permitted to use the tortious route directly against Pilkington.

It will be appreciated, however, that the basis of the thinking in *Simaan* was not that the plaintiffs should have no remedy. Far from it, the thinking was that the plaintiffs should have a remedy and that this was better delivered by the ordinary contractual route rather than by the *Junior Books* tortious route. But, what if, for some reason, the ordinary contractual route were blocked? For example, what if the subcontractor in *Simaan* were insolvent, or protected by exemption clauses? Or what if the action in contract were time-barred, or if, as in *Junior Books*, there were a settlement which precluded any further contractual claim? In such circumstances, the implication of *Simaan* is not that the tortious route should necessarily be opened up but that it should be made available to the plaintiff if, all things considered, this were required 'in the interests of justice.' . . . the point to be extracted from *Simaan* is its implicit recognition of the principle that, in a *Junior Books* situation, the plaintiffs should have a remedy, ordinarily sounding in contract (down the chain of contracts) but, in some exceptional circumstances, sounding directly in tort.

We can reformulate this as our breakdown principle as follows: in a *Junior Books* situation, in response to question G1, A should have a direct remedy against C in circumstances where A's ordinary avenue of contractual recourse against B is barred. . . .

. . . it may be objected that such a direct remedy would be manifestly incompatible with the interests of justice. . . .

[This] objection picks up Lord Brandon's point in *Junior Books*, where . . . his Lordship argued that a direct remedy for A against C would be unfair if A were to be able, thereby, to outflank exemption clauses in the chain of contracts. This is a point well-taken. Accordingly, as we intimated in our earlier discussion of this point, a corollary of giving question G1 an affirmative answer is that we must give affirmative answers, too, to questions G2 and G3. In other words, where the breakdown principle comes into play we must treat the contractual relationships as transitive, thus allowing C to rely on any of the contractual exempting provisions in order to answer A's claim. Hence, the privity rules are not relaxed in a one-sided fashion and the opportunity to address the demands of the interests of justice is fully preserved. . . .

There is a second reason for thinking that A should have a direct remedy against C, our so-called 'subsumption' principle. To introduce this principle, we can return to one of the cornerstones of Lord Roskill's speech in *Junior Books*, the idea that there was a special relationship between the respondent clients and the appellant subcontractors. The appellants in *Junior Books*, as his Lordship remarked,

though not in direct contractual relationship with the respondents, were as nominated sub-contractors in almost as close a commercial relationship with the respondents as it is possible to envisage short of privity of contract . . .

The situation in *Junior Books* involves a special relationship between the parties (A and C), because the *contracts* to which they are parties are specially related. The subcontract is already, so to speak, contained within, or subsumed under, the main contract. Moreover, the subsumption of the subcontract in relation to the main contract can be viewed both functionally and causally. Functionally, the subcontract draws its purpose from the main contract, in the sense that the main contract sets out the client's needs and the subcontract is dedicated to securing the performance of some of these needs. Causally, the very existence of the subcontract depends upon the main contract; the latter is the raison d'être of the former. In short, the main contract and the subcontract are, so to speak, organically related. . . .

Now, it cannot be said that, in the course of the retrenchment from *Junior Books*, the Courts have failed to attend to the question of contractual structure. On the contrary, one of the leading themes in the recent case-law is the emphasis on the significance of the particular contractual structure. Where a chain of contracts has formed the background to A's direct negligence claim against C, the Courts have treated the contractual structure as militating against A's claim. In our contention, this misreads the significance of the structural consideration. Where the contracts are organically related, the significance of the contractual structure is not to put distance between A and C, but to involve C in the main contract enterprise. Instead of conceiving of the contractual structure thus '(A–B) and (B–C),' we should think of it as '(A–(B–C)–B)'; in other words, we should regard C's subcontract performance as a component of the main contract performance. Viewed in this way, the logic of the contractual structure can only be that C has been co-opted into the work and that A should have a direct remedy against C.

Although the subsumption principle joins with the breakdown principle in supporting a direct remedy for A against C, it should be noted that the principles are not co-extensive. In one sense, the breakdown principle is broader than the subsumption principle, for it can apply wherever there is a chain of contracts, even though the contracts are not organically related. For example, suppose that A buys defective goods from B, the goods having been manufactured and sold to B by C. These contracts are not organically related. Nevertheless, the breakdown principle argues that, where A's claim against B is barred, then A should be entitled to recover his financial loss by direct action against C. In another sense, however, the breakdown principle is narrower than the subsumption principle. Whereas, under the former principle, A has no direct action against C unless his action against B is blocked, under the latter principle, A has a direct action against C simply in virtue of the logic of the contractual structure. In other words, under the subsumption principle, A has a direct recourse against C irrespective of whether the ordinary contractual channel of recovery (against B) is blocked. . . .

In multi-contract contexts, our proposal would involve a substantial re-writing of the law. Because many commercial transactions (eg, in the field of construction and carriage) are implemented through a cluster of main contracts, subcontracts, sub-subcontracts, and the like, many such clusters would fall within the scope of the subsumption principle. In this light, one of the modern mainstays of the privity doctrine, the line taken by the majority of their Lordships in *Scruttons*, would have to be revised. . . . The implications of the breakdown principle would be no less important. Quite apart from facilitating direct claims in commercial contractual settings (ie, in those settings where the subsumption principle did not apply), it would open the way for consumers to bring direct claims for purely economic loss against others than the immediate suppliers of defective goods and services. Of course, suing back down the chain of contracts would remain the standard avenue of recourse, but where this avenue failed (in circumstances where, other things being equal, it would have been available to the consumer) the breakdown principle would bring a back-up remedy into play. Although this would be something of an innovation in the Common Law, it would not be altogether out of step with either the everyday practice of pursuing claims directly against the manufacturers of defective goods, or with a number of statutory interventions aimed at giving consumer purchasers effective remedies.

This approach is equally applicable to *The Eurymedon*. The relationship between the stevedores and the consignees would be treated as contractual under the subsumption principle, which subsumes the stevedoring arrangement under the bill of lading. However, using the allocation of risk agreed between the parties in the bill of lading and accepted by the consignees when they accepted the bill of lading, the consignees will be denied a remedy. This reverses the effect of the privity doctrine in these circumstances, which is to treat the ordering mechanisms contained in contracts as strictly bilateral and private, by restricting them to the parties to the contract alone.

2. A similarly functional approach to the problem of restrictions based on privity in multi-contract situations is taken by Adams and Brownsword, who propose treating linked contracts as 'networks'. Networks are composed of 'a cluster of contracts set up to serve a principal organising purpose' ('Privity of Contract: That Pestilential Nuisance', (1993) 56 *MLR* 722 at 727).

J. Adams and R. Brownsword, 'Privity and the Concept of a Network Contract', (1990) 10 *LS* 12 at 27–8

1. A network contract is a contract forming part of a set of contracts.
2. The set of contracts has the following characteristics:
    (i) there is a principal contract (or, there are a number of principal contracts) within the set giving the set an overall objective;
    (ii) other contracts (secondary and tertiary contracts, and so on) are entered into, an object of each of which is—directly or indirectly—to further the attainment of this overall objective; and,
    (iii) the network of contractors expands until a sufficiency of contractors are obligated, whether to the parties to the principal contract or to other contractors within the set, to attain the overall objective.

Building contracts and carriage contracts are paradigms of network contracts, as are many credit and commercial financing arrangements. In each of these cases, it is possible to discern a common underlying purpose so that we can say that the set of contracts as a whole comprises a single network.

In common with the transitivity proposal, this approach has the advantage of bringing about a two-sided relaxation of the privity doctrine, protecting C against excessive liability by allowing him to rely upon any of the provisions of the contracts within the network which allocate the risk of loss elsewhere. However, unlike transitivity, which is *inferred* from the facts, Adams and Brownsword have proposed that networks should only arise where they are specifically or implicitly designated by the parties. This constitutes a comprehensive reply to the criticism that by relaxing the privity requirements the courts would be interfering with the contract price, or with 'transactional justice', as Adams and Brownsword put it. For, in fact, the court would be giving effect to an agreed allocation of risks, by granting not only a claim to the plaintiff but also the protection of exemption clauses to the defendant. In that way, the courts would be reaching a solution which was both fair and commercially sensible. (See further Adams and Brownsword, 'Privity of Contract', at 722).

3. Collins suggests a further privity-avoiding device which recognizes the economic reality of the relations between the parties. He points out how different the approach taken to *The Eurymedon* could have been if the judges had taken notice of the fact that the carriers were a wholly owned subsidiary of the stevedores.

H. Collins, 'Ascription of Legal Responsibility to Groups in Complex Patterns of Economic Integration', (1990) 53 *MLR* 731 at 734–6, 744

The recurrent problem has been that formal separations of legal personality, usually in the legal form of discrete companies, place narrow limits on the scope of legal responsibility when viewed in the economic context of close integration of production. The courts have been striving to overcome these artificial barriers by imposing liabilities in ways which make sense in the context of economic integration, despite being prohibited from so doing by the ordinary principles of legal responsibility. . . .

. . . The doctrine of privity of contract normally precludes the contract from vesting rights in third parties. But where one party to the contract and the third party are in reality both members of a complex economic organisation, the case for discovering routes which circumvent privity in order to give the notional third party rights appears particularly pressing. For example, one reason that the subtle combination of agency and collateral contract proved successful in *New Zealand Shipping Co. Ltd.* v *Satterthwaite & Co. Ltd. (The Eurymedon)* may have been due to the fact that the carrier, a party to the main contract and at the same time the purported agent for a collateral contract, was the wholly owned subsidiary of the stevedores, the third party to the main contract and alleged principals to the collateral contract. Of course, if the Privy Council had been prepared to recognise that the carrier and the stevedore in reality comprised two members of a multinational group of companies which could be conceived as a single legal entity for the purposes of establishing contractual responsibility, then the problems presented by the doctrine of privity would not have arisen at all. . . .

. . . Because owners of capital enjoy an unrestricted freedom to determine the shape and size of legal personalities which bear the burden of legal responsibility, they can exercise their freedom to avoid obligations or restrict another's rights by adopting patterns of vertical disintegration for productive activities. In the absence of statutory intervention, the common law permits this evasion of legal responsibility, for it does not usually penetrate the formal separation of legal identities.

Note

The problem of corporate group structure and of whether groups should be regarded as one economic unit or as composed of distinct legal entities is one which, as Collins points out in the remainder of his article, has troubled company lawyers for a considerable time (see e.g. A. Berle, 'The Theory of Enterprise Entity', (1947) 47 *Colum. L. Rev.* 343). Case law development has followed the formalist route of viewing corporate group members as distinct legal entities (see e.g. *Bank of Tokyo Ltd.* v. *Karoon*, [1987] AC 45). Statutory intervention has been piecemeal. One example is s. 253(2) of the Companies Act 1985, which deals with corporate group accounts. If the conditions of s. 253(2) are not met, the members of a corporate group have to present accounts as a group and not as individual legal entities. Under s. 253 it is not sufficient simply for one company to have an interest in another. The operation of the section depends on the existence of actual control or dominant control exercised by one company over another. It is important to note that companies within a group may make their own management decisions, and may in fact carry on business in a very different area from that of their parent company. To hold that in these circumstances a parent company should be liable for its subsidiary would be as unfair as asserting that there was never any responsibility.

4. In its proposals, the Law Commission has taken an intention-based approach to the problem of privity and defences which is similar to its approach to the third-party beneficiary restriction. In para. 5.17 of the Consultation Paper, the right to reply, for example, on an exemption clause in a bill of lading which would be treated analogously to a benefit conferred on a third party (the stevedore) and thus subject to an intention test. Thus C will be able to benefit from defences found in a contract between A and B in an action brought by A against C, if it was the intention of the parties that C should benefit from the defence.

Questions

1. How would *Trident* and *The Eurymedon* be decided under English law if the Law Commission's proposals were adopted as they stand?

The Creation of Contracts

2. What is it that leads certain common law judges to say that there is a rule of privity of contract which cannot be 'budged'? Is it related to a conception of the judicial role in the law-making process or to the nature of the contractual obligation?

PART III

Contract, Power, and Justice

8

Contractual Justice

I. INTRODUCTION

In the first two parts of this book, one of the key underlying themes has been the nature of the agreements which the law of contract will enforce. Although its position has not gone unchallenged in the modern law, the central paradigm of the bargain has, to a large extent, shaped the rules on formation of contracts and on the enforceability of promises. However, as we have seen, concepts such as reliance have increasingly undermined the classical law, and indeed reliance can lay claim to be a competing paradigm of formation and enforceability.

Similar tensions and themes can be seen as we transfer our attention to the contents of the contract, the obligations of and risks incumbent upon the parties, and then, in Part IV, to issues of performance, termination, and breach, with associated remedies. Here again, bargain has been the underlying paradigm of the classical law; but other models have achieved some level of recognition in the law, acknowledging or demanding a much greater level of intervention on the part of the state in the shaping of the contractual relations between individuals (see below Collins on the extent of the 'transformation' of contract law). M. Eisenberg ('The Bargain Principle and its Limits', (1982) 95 *Harv. L. Rev.* 741) goes so far as to assert that 'unconscionability' now represents an alternative paradigm to bargain, allowing us to explain why and how courts should intervene in certain types of transaction, either because they were not freely made or because they result in an unacceptably unfair outcome for one of the contracting parties. Eisenberg's arguments in relation to US law have been echoed by writers on English law, and some have argued that a more comprehensive doctrine of inequality of bargaining power could be elaborated to fulfil a similar controlling function.

The theme of this chapter is to consider to what extent there is a notion of contractual justice which assists us in determining whether it is right to enforce a contract simply because it encapsulates a bargain (or a promise relied upon), in the conventional sense. We introduce some of the basic concepts of contractual justice, such as the distinction between substantive and procedural justice and the relationship between bargain and coercion, and offer an outline of some of the different positions commonly taken in relation to the thorny problems of deciding 'which contracts?' and 'whose justice?' are to be enforced. Views which could be described as libertarian, liberal, and critical/radical are described here; at this stage we have left them largely uncommented upon, offering them as points of reference which will stimulate reflection in the context of the substantive chapters which follow. We begin with von Mehren, who offers what could be described as an orthodox liberal position on the role and effect of justice in the realm of contract.

II. CONTRACTUAL JUSTICE: BASIC CONCEPTS

A. von Mehren, 'Contractual Justice', in 'A General View of Contract',
International Encyclopedia of Comparative Law **(Tübingen/The Hague, Mohr/Nijhoff, 1982), vol. vii, ch. 1, pp. 64–7**

Definition. In various ways and to varying degrees, all legal orders that accept the institution of contract are concerned with contractual justice. This justice is not, it should be noted, a synonym for social and economic justice. The existing distribution of wealth and power in a society may be perceived as unjust. Such injustice is basically neither enhanced, nor diminished, by transactions that satisfy the criteria of contractual justice. Requirements of contractual justice serve to preserve, rather than change, the economic and social *status quo*; views of social and economic justice raise, on the other hand, the issue whether the *status quo* should be changed.

What then is meant when a given transaction is said to violate the canons of contractual justice? When is autonomous ordering—for which contract provides the mechanism—just?

The justice of autonomous ordering of production and distribution decisions can be considered from two perspectives—one procedural, the other substantive. Contract, regardless whether the ordering in question is one- or two-sided, implies autonomous ordering. The ordering should, therefore, be done by parties who act with a degree of awareness, independence, and responsibility. Where these qualities are not present in requisite measure, the requirements of procedural justice immanent in the concept of contract are not met.

When onerous transactions are in question, an exchange standard of justice is also inherent in the concept of contract. Onerous transactions are designed to permit a party to change the form of his wealth without, at least in the subjective evaluation of that party, reducing its total value. A contract is not, therefore, just unless each party receives, in terms of his own evaluation, a value at least equivalent to the value he gives up.

These two types of contractual justice—procedural and exchange—need not overlap. A contract can satisfy procedural standards and be unjust as an exchange; conversely, a just exchange can result from an unjust contracting process.

Procedural contractual justice. . . . the very concept of contract as autonomous ordering implies a concern for the process out of which contracts arise. A concern for procedural justice derives as well from various of the explanations advanced for the enforceability of contracts. For example, where contract is grounded on the individual's choice . . . transactions in which a party's will is unduly influenced or his choice is based on a mistake are plainly open to question. Similarly, if contract is explained from social and economic perspectives, the institution's justification requires that the contractual process be procedurally just. The use of contract to enlist individual initiative and elicit and discipline the myriad of discrete decisions required to allocate and distribute resources . . . becomes problematical if the contracting process is procedurally unfair. Accordingly, demonstration of the transaction's substantive justice cannot redeem a contract that does not satisfy the applicable standards of procedural justice. In many contexts, on the other hand, if the requirements of procedural justice are met, there is at least a strong presumption that the transaction is substantively just . . .

Thinking about the problem of procedural contractual justice has traditionally proceeded in terms of situations involving two-sided ordering. Jurists have given great attention to determining and defining what procedural justice requires in such cases. . . . It suffices to observe here that, although there are areas of controversy, certain procedural standards are, in principle, well recognized. For example, in particular situations, a transaction is unenforceable because of defects—*e.g.* fraud, duress, or mistake—in the contracting process. In addition, certain categories of persons—*e.g.* minors—are accorded special protection in their exercises of private autonomy, so that contracts they conclude may be wholly or partially unenforceable (*ibidem*). Finally, the proposition has been advanced that significant "inequality of bargaining power," in and of itself, constitutes a basis for setting contracts aside.

More recently, special protection has been accorded to parties to contracts where "aggressive" negotiating techniques—*e.g.* door-to-door canvassing—are used. Such techniques typically exploit, for one party's advantage, widely prevailing traits: a reluctance to say "no", and a tendency to undertake commitments without full reflection where psychological pressure inheres in the situation. Accordingly, there is a need to ensure that the party towards whom the aggressive technique was directed has fully considered his decision. The cautionary purpose is typically served by allowing the purchaser to cancel within a limited period (*e.g.* a week) from the time the contract was concluded. In other contexts, the cautionary function is served by requiring the use of formalities designed to induce reflection.

The standards of procedural justice developed for two-sided contractual ordering are applied . . . with varying degrees of adjustment, to one-sided ordering (standard form contracts). . . . Thus, a party who accepts a standard form contract may be bound by general conditions to which his attention was not specifically directed if the conditions in question had been brought, in an appropriate fashion, to the attention of the general public. . . .

The general economic and social assumptions accepted by societies that prefer the principle of private autonomy generally support the proposition that value for the purpose of applying the equivalence principle is properly measured in terms of the evaluations made by the immediate parties to the transaction. In economic theory, assuming that the requirements of procedural justice are met, each party will, by his own lights, be better off when the transaction takes place on terms to which both parties have agreed.

It does not follow, however, that liberal economic theory necessarily precludes recourse to standards of value that take into account evaluations other than those of the immediate parties to the transaction when an issue of substantive contractual justice has arisen. Indeed, there may be

"a general decline in the belief that individuals know their own interests best, and . . . an increased awareness of a great range of factors which diminish the significance to be attached to an apparently free choice or to consent. Choices may be made or consent given without adequate reflection or appreciation of the consequences; or in pursuit of merely transitory desires; or in various predicaments when the judgment is likely to be clouded; or under inner psychological compulsion or under pressure by others of a kind too subtle to be susceptible of proof in a law court. . . ."[1]

In part because social and economic life has become increasingly complex and interrelated, the "idea of a free and self-responsible individual, . . ., can not be accepted unconditionally for us today, for the task of holding one's own as a person, of understanding the consequences of one's actions, and of being responsible for them has become much more difficult."[2]

Accordingly, even though a transaction satisfies the equivalence principle in that each party has, in his view, received at least the equivalent of what he has given up, the legal order could, in theory, be concerned that certain parties, individually or as a class, are such poor traders that the other party to the transaction will almost always obtain the best terms possible within the range of terms upon which the contract could be concluded. No general economic principle has been developed that requires a particular distribution of these possible gains between the traders in question; the more skilled or more fortunate bargainer keeps the gains that he obtains from the trade when he gives less than he would be willing to pay in order to obtain the return performance. But it does not follow from the lack of an economic theory respecting the "correct" distribution of gains from trade that contract law, in dealing with the problem of substantive justice, must take the same view. . . .

[1] *Hart,* Law, Liberty and Morality (London 1963).
[2] *Raiser,* Vertragsfreiheit heute: JZ 1958, 1–8, 3.

When does procedural justice warrant the substantive justice of a contract?—If the requirements of procedural justice are met, the equivalence principle is necessarily satisfied in onerous transactions where the performances either have market values or the legal order is prepared to accept the parties' evaluations as the standard against which substantive justice is to be measured. There are obvious advantages in not reviewing transactions in terms of substantive justice but rather seeing in a satisfaction of requirements of procedural justice a warrant that the equivalence principle is satisfied. From a social and economic perspective, the institution of contract is a more easily administered, a less complex, and a more complete method of achieving autonomous ordering if the parties, rather than courts or other agents of society, determine what is contractually just. The very premise of the will theory precludes consideration of the issue of substantive justice where the party's will was exercised in circumstances satisfying the requirements of procedural justice; a free and enlightened exercise of the will justifies the enforceability of the resulting transaction.

Accordingly, on both practical and theoretical grounds it is understandable why, during the nineteenth century, contract law concerned itself very little, if at all, with the substantive—as distinct from procedural—justice of individual transactions. General conditions and standard forms—which pose most sharply the problem of substantive justice . . . were far less usual than they later became. The liberal concept of society and of the state, then so widely held, gave citizens full freedom to pursue their interests; the state was not to interfere. Its function was to protect order and to ensure security in transactions.

"To neutrality as to the content of the contract was thus added the firm (*entschiedene*) protection of what was agreed upon in the contractual forum. Both were to find their limits only where the contract violated a statutory prohibition or infringed good morals." [Raiser]

Although not all doubts were stilled, the comfortable proposition that a transaction's substantive justice is guaranteed if the contract results from a procedurally fair process of contracting dominated the law of contract for decades. In the twentieth century, however, a major exception is being carved out for one-sided—in particular, standardized—contracts. Two considerations explain this development. In the first place, the requirements of procedural justice applicable to one-sided ordering do not furnish the same warrant as in cases of two-sided ordering that the evaluations made by each party will be carefully considered and, hence, reliable. The psychological and sociological situation of the party who accepts without bargaining the terms of a contract is typically such that he considers less carefully and fully than he would in a two-sided transaction the value to him of the performance in question. In addition, certain requirements of procedural justice may be less strict where ordering is not two- but one-sided. In particular, in view of the functions served by standardized transactions in contemporary economic life . . . and the lack of importance, so far as negotiating is concerned, of actual knowledge of particular terms to many parties to such transactions, the law may not require that these terms be communicated to a party if appropriate steps have been taken to bring the terms to the attention of the general public. It follows that satisfaction of the requirements of procedural justice applicable to one-sided ordering does not establish that the quality of both parties' evaluation is such that they can be relied upon to establish the substantive justice of the transaction.

The question whether gains from trade . . . are equitably distributed between the parties is also particularly troubling in one-sided transactions. In two-sided transactions, presumably the bargaining process normally prevents one party monopolizing these gains for his benefit. On the other hand, in one-sided transactions, the party setting the terms may well obtain all these gains. Accordingly, there is a stronger argument for the legal order intervening, in the name of substantive justice, to ensure their "fair" allocation.

An additional reason why a legal order may be prepared to consider the substantive justice of standardized contracts is that groups or classes of transactions rather than highly individualized contracts are in question. Accordingly, a decision can resolve the issue of substantive justice for the group or class in question. The task facing the legal order is thus more manageable than the general review of all contracts in terms of substantive justice.

Notes

1. The type of analytical approach taken by von Mehren makes it possible to link the issue of justice back to the underlying theme of contractual obligation, which dominated Parts I and II above. In particular, von Mehren notes the relationship between the will theory of contract and the willingness of courts to control the process whereby contracts have been made. Some of the devices have already been considered (e.g. misrepresentation) and others are considered in this part (e.g. duress).

2. In general, von Mehren makes a case for less intervention in the context of 'two-sided contractual ordering', where the idea of contract is encapsulated in the negotiated and bargained-for exchange. He acknowledges that the idea of bargain operates only uneasily in the context of 'one-sided contractual ordering' or standard-form contracts. These are considered in greater detail in Chapter 10.

3. Atiyah makes some further comments upon the link between substantive and procedural justice.

P. S. Atiyah, *Essays on Contract* (Oxford, Oxford University Press, 1988), 334–5.

. . . ideas of procedural and substantive fairness feed upon each other. Imagine a society in which fraud is regarded as a permissible bargaining procedure and negotiating parties are simply expected to be more careful of trusting anything the other party says. Perhaps this leads to inefficiency since both parties have to devote more resources to ascertaining the facts from more trustworthy sources. Still, it is an imaginable state of affairs; as I recollect my schoolboy days, the market in comics and marbles was conducted somewhat along these lines. Naturally, if skill in lying and dissembling is an accepted attribute of the bargaining procedure, the outcome of bargains will be different. But it will not only be different in fact, it will probably seem acceptably different. It is unlikely that such a bargaining procedure would be found acceptable except in a society which had some admiration for the plausible rogue, the skill of the lying cheat. What is a fair outcome may thus depend on our views about fair procedures.

The process also works in the reverse direction. Suppose a contract in which the outcome favours one party vastly more than the other; our natural reaction today is to believe that something must have gone wrong with the bargaining process. How could a rational person have entered into this contract if he had known what he was about, had not been subject to undue pressures, or the like? We may be so sceptical that such a contract could have been the result of the ordinary and proper bargaining processes that we examine the case with a strong, almost conclusive presumption that a sufficiently unfair contract must have been the result of improper procedures. This is partly, but only partly, because there is a reasonable presumption of fact that a very unfair or imbalanced contract was the result of some procedural improprieties; but it is also partly due to a normative idea. We want people to behave like reasonable people; our laws and institutions are based on the assumption that man is a rational being—and a rational being with particular characteristics. One of these characteristics is that a person is presumed not to want or intend to give away his property without some good reason. When the most plausible explanation of a contract is that one of the parties must have behaved in an irrational manner, something clearly has gone wrong and there is a lack of fit between what ought to have happened and what has happened. So in this way also there are serious problems about drawing a sharp line between procedural and substantive fairness or procedural and substantive unconscionability.

Another major group of concepts of contractual justice is discussed by Hale in the next extract. These are the ideas of power, bargain, and freedom in a market order. Hale begins by illuminating the bargain process as a dynamic interaction between the owners of property and money for mutual advantage, albeit an interaction to which they are in some way 'coercively' committed by the market order. In sections of the article which are not extracted in this book, Hale goes on to demonstrate that the close relationship between coercion and bargain helps us to understand the operation of the concept of duress as a vitiating factor in the formation of contracts, showing how difficult it is to characterize any participation in the market order as either totally free or totally forced. We shall return to these issues in Chapter 9.

R. Hale, 'Bargaining, Duress and Economic Liberty', (1943) 43 *Colum. L. Rev.* 603 at 603–6, 626–8

That men may live, they must either be in a position each to produce the material necessities of life for his own use, or there must be some adequate incentive for production of the goods and services which people other than the producers may enjoy, and some means by which individual consumers can acquire some portion of them. In thinly settled lands it may be possible for each family to produce most of the things needed to satisfy its own wants. The law has only to recognize each family's property right in its farm and its products, and protect that property from interference. But in a land as thickly settled as ours, such individualistic methods of providing for wants would be wholly inadequate. We have to resort to the more efficient process of machine production, with its widespread division of labor. Almost every article or service that is produced is the fruit of the combined efforts of countless people, each working on a fractional part of the product. But the product is consumed only in small part, if at all, by its producers. Other people consume it, and the producers of this product consume the products of other people's labor. Goods are turned out collectively and consumed individually. Individuals could conceivably be conscripted to contribute their respective efforts to the collective process of production, and the products could be rationed out to each for his individual consumption. These are not the methods of our free economy. We rely instead, for the most part, on bargaining.

There are few, if any, who own enough of the collective output of goods ready for consumption to satisfy their needs for more than a brief period in the future. Some persons own more than enough of certain types of goods, but they must perforce acquire the use of other types as well. The owner of a shoe factory is in no danger of going ill-shod—he may wear his own shoes. But he cannot live on shoes alone. Like everyone else, he must *buy* food or starve. Even the producer and owner of food must as a rule buy other forms of food than those in which he has specialized. Any person, in order to live, must induce some of the owners of things which he needs, to permit him to use them. The owner has no legal obligation to grant the permission. But if offered enough money he will probably do so; for he, too, must obtain the permission of other owners to make use of *their* goods, and for this purpose he too needs money—more than he has at the outset. He needs it more than he needs his surplus of shoes. Indeed he values his right of ownership in the shoes solely for the power it gives him to obtain money with which to buy other things which he does not yet own.

The owner of the shoes or the food or any other product can insist on other people keeping their hands off his products. Should he so insist, the government will back him up with force. The owner of the money can likewise insist on other people keeping their hands off his money, and the government will likewise back *him* up with force. By *threatening* to maintain the legal barrier against the use of his shoes, their owner may be able to obtain a certain amount of money as the price of not carrying out his threat. And by threatening to maintain the legal barrier against the use of his money, the purchaser may be able to obtain a certain amount of shoes as the price of not withholding the money. A bargain is finally struck, each party consenting to its terms in order to avert the consequences with which the other threatens him. . . .

How, then, does any purchaser obtain the money that will enable him to consume? We have already seen that the owner of products obtains it, by selling his products to buyers. But how did he come to be the owner of the products? The answer which first suggests itself is that he produced them. To the extent that this is true, it indicates that he made his contribution to the productive process, not by first making a bargain with consumers, but because he anticipated that his efforts would put him in a favorable position to make future bargains. But the answer is not wholly true. The owner did not produce the shoes by his own efforts alone. Other people have taken part in the production too—not only his employees, but those who have advanced the necessary capital, or taken any part in the production of the raw materials and fuel which he uses, or in transporting them to his factory.

Yet of all these innumerable producers of the shoes, only the owner of the factory acquires title to them. The others have all, at one time or another, waived their claims to any share in the ownership of the shoes. They have done so in a series of bargaining transactions, in which they received money, or promises to pay money. Through this series of bargains, the owner of the plant has acquired the full right of ownership in the shoes. This right enables him, if he is successful, to obtain from his customers more than enough to repay all the outlays he has made to the other participants—enough more to compensate him for his risk and labor in organizing and managing the plant, and perhaps even more than this.

As a result of these innumerable bargains, the owner and the other participants in the production obtain their respective money incomes, and these money incomes determine the share that each may obtain of the total goods and services turned out by the collective efforts of all the other members of society. And it is as a result of these bargains, or in anticipation of them, that each participant in these collective productive efforts makes his contribution. We rely on the bargaining process to serve the conflicting interests of individuals in securing a share of the collective output of society, and also to serve their common interest in the creation of that collective output.

Though these bargains lead to vast differences in the economic positions of different persons, whether as producers or as consumers, these differences have all resulted from transactions into which each has entered without any explicit requirement of law that he do so. But while there is no explicit legal requirement that one enter into any particular transaction, one's freedom to decline to do so is nevertheless circumscribed. One chooses to enter into any given transaction in order to avoid the threat of something worse—threats which impinge with unequal weight on different members of society. The fact that he exercised a choice does not indicate lack of compulsion. Even a slave makes a choice. The compulsion which drives him to work operates through his own will power. He makes the "voluntary" muscular movements which the work calls for, in order to escape some threat; and though he exercises will power and makes a choice, still, since he is making it under threat, his servitude is called "involuntary." And one who obeys some compulsory requirement of the law in order to avoid a penalty is likewise making a choice. If he has the physical power to disobey, his obedience is not a matter of physical necessity, but of choice. Yet no one would deny that the requirement of the law is a compulsory one. It restricts his liberty to act out of conformity to it.

Government has power to compel one to choose obedience, since it can threaten disobedience with death, imprisonment, or seizure of property. Private individuals are not permitted to make such threats to other individuals, save in exceptional circumstances such as self-defense. But there are other threats which may lawfully be made to induce a party to enter into a transaction. In the complex bargains made in the course of production, some parties who deal with the manufacturer surrender a portion of their property, others their liberty not to work for him, in order to avert his threat to withhold his money, while he, in turn, surrenders some part of the money he now owns, or some part of his right to keep from them money he may obtain in the future, to avert their threats of withholding from him their raw materials or their labor. And he may have surrendered property in the past, and the freedom to abstain from labor, in order to attain his position as owner of the plant and its products, and so to obtain the money with which to avert the threats of owners of the things he wishes to consume, to withhold those things from him. In consenting to enter into any bargain, each party yields to the threats of the other. In the absence of corrective legislation, each party, in order to induce the other to enter into a transaction, may generally threaten to exercise any of his legal rights and privileges, no matter how disadvantageous that exercise may be to the other party....

As a result of governmental and private coercion under what is mistakenly called *laissez faire*, the economic liberty of some is curtailed to the advantage of others, while the economic liberty of all is curtailed to some degree. Absolute freedom in economic matters is of course out of the question. The most we can attain is a relative degree of freedom, with the restrictions on each person's liberty as tolerable as we can make them. It would be impossible for everyone to have unrestricted freedom to make use of any material goods of which there are not enough to go round. If some exercised a freedom to take all the goods they desired, the freedom of others to consume those goods would be gone. There can be no freedom to consume what does not exist, or what other consumers have already appropriated. To protect a consumer's liberty from annihilation at the hands of other consumers, the law curtails it in a more methodical and less drastic way, by forbidding the use of goods without the consent of the owner. In practice this means that the liberty to consume is conditioned on the payment of the market price. When, as in time of war, a price high enough to keep the demand down to the amount is deemed to place too great a limitation on the freedom of the less well-to-do consumer, the price is kept down by law. We then add a supplementary restriction on the freedom to consume, in order to protect it from being destroyed by the activities of hoarders. Freedom to consume is then conditioned, not only on the possession of money, but also on the possession of rationing coupons.

Liberty to consume would be restricted far more drastically than it is were there no restrictions on that other aspect of economic liberty, freedom to abstain from producing. We do not have slave labor, but there are nevertheless compulsions which force people to work. These compulsions affect different people in varying degree, and are usually far more tolerable than slavery, or than the famine which would doubtless ensue were there no compulsions to work at all. In our industrial society, an employee works in order to make a bargain with his employer and thus obtain the money with which to free himself from some of the restrictions which other people's property rights place on his freedom to consume. He induces the employer to pay him his wage by *threatening* not to work for him, and then not carrying out his threat. Not carrying it out involves temporary surrender of his liberty to be idle. He *must* surrender that liberty, under penalty of not having freedom to consume more than his present means would enable him to. . . .

The employer's power to induce people to work for him depends largely on the fact that the law previously restricts the liberty of these people to consume, while he has the power, through the payment of wages, to release them to some extent from these restrictions. He has little power over those whose freedom to consume is relatively unrestricted, because they have large independent means, or who can secure freedom to consume from other employers, because of their ability to render services of a sort that is scarce and in great demand. Those who own enough property have sufficient liberty to consume, without yielding any of their liberty to be idle. Their property rights enable them to exert pressure of great effectiveness to induce people to enter into bargains to pay them money. The law endows them with the power to call on the governmental authorities to keep others from using what they own. For merely not exercising this power, they can obtain large money rewards, by leasing or selling it to someone who will utilize it. These rewards may in many instances amount only to postponed payments for services which the owners have rendered in the past in the process of production, but frequently they greatly exceed any such amount. In fact the owner may have rendered no services whatever himself, but may have acquired his property by government grant or by virtue of the fact that the law assigns property rights to those named in the will of the previous owner, or, if he makes no will, according to the intestacy laws. Bargaining power would be different were it not that the law endows some with rights that are more advantageous than those with which it endows others.

It is with these unequal rights that men bargain and exert pressure on one another. These rights give birth to the unequal fruits of bargaining. There may be sound reasons of economic policy to justify all the economic inequalities that flow from unequal rights. If so, these reasons must be more specific than a broad policy of private property and freedom of contract. With different rules as to the assignment of property rights, particularly by way of inheritance or government grant, we could have just as strict a protection of each person's property rights, and just as little governmental interference with freedom of contract, but a very different pattern of economic relationships. Moreover, by judicious legal limitation on the bargaining power of the economically and legally stronger, it is conceivable that the economically weak would acquire greater freedom of contract than they now have—freedom to resist more effectively the bargaining power of the strong, and to obtain better terms.

Notes

1. Hale offers a more macro perspective upon systems of contractual justice than von Mehren, by highlighting how all of us are tied into a system of bargaining by the market order and how the bargaining process can be characterized as a system of interrelated threats and consents. His explanation of the coercive power of the market shows why courts will always find it extremely difficult to police exchange transactions by reference to nebulous concepts such as fairness and inequality of bargaining (see further on this Section V below), and he throws down a challenge to government to consider how it should protect the weak and the vulnerable by ensuring that they have greater 'real' freedom when it comes to bargaining.

2. Hale identifies the key interaction in the market order as being the relationship between production and property. It is this interaction, of course, which engenders what is popularly known today as 'wealth creation'. It

could be commented, with the benefit of hindsight fifty years later, that Hale's work ignores the equally crucial relationship between production and the environment, a relationship which cannot be described by reference to models of contract and bargain, but only as a relation of exploitation.

3. For further details on Hale's work, until recently little known in the UK, see N. Duxbury, 'Robert Hale and the Economy of Legal Force', (1990) 53 *MLR* 421.

4. Hale's view of power in the contractual context as being not simply linear, but as being composed of complex networks and webs, is echoed by Foucault's abstract frame of analysis for power.

M. Foucault, 'Two Lectures', in Foucault, *Power/Knowledge*, ed. Gordon, (Brighton, Harvester, 1980), 98

Power must be analysed as something which circulates, or rather as something which only functions in the form of a chain. It is never localised here or there, never in anybody's hands, never appropriated as a commodity or piece of wealth. Power is employed and exercised through a net-like organisation. And not only do individuals circulate between its threads; they are always in the position of simultaneously undergoing and exercising this power. They are not only its inert or consenting target; they are always also the elements of its articulation. In other words, individuals are the vehicles of power, not its points of application.

In the next extract, Macneil takes Foucault's analysis further by examining how power operates within different models of contractual relationships. He contrasts the discrete transaction—the paradigm of classical contract law—and 'modern contractual relations', discussed elsewhere in this book as 'relational contract'.

I. Macneil, *The New Social Contract: An Inquiry into Modern Contractual Relations*, (New Haven, Conn., Yale University Press, 1980), 32–5

By power I mean the ability to impose one's will on others irrespective of or by manipulating their wishes. . . .

Specialization and the exchange necessary to make it viable inevitably create dependence, each specialist depending upon other kinds of specialists for essential goods and services. To the extent that specialists exercise significant control over their products they acquire power to prevent those dependent on them from taking the product at will. Consider, for example, truck drivers and trucking companies. The drivers own their own time, and the companies own capital. Property and personal rights inhibit seizure of either of these assets by the other group, thereby conferring on both drivers and companies power over each other. An opportunity is provided, however, for exercising power beyond simply the negative power of preventing seizure. Each can exercise power by insisting upon particular terms of exchange, the drivers demanding, for example, $25 an hour, the companies demanding an hour's work for $10. When they finally agree on $15 an hour, while each is doing something that on balance it wants to do, the power created by dependence has nevertheless caused it to reach a result worse than it preferred. The exchange resulted from a vectoring of both willingness and unwillingness producing an affirmative balance in favor of willingness.

It should be obvious that, other things being equal, the terms of the exchange will depend upon relative balances of dependence. If, for example, the companies are unorganized and the drivers form a united front, the latter are, for practical purposes, relatively independent, and the power of the companies is relatively modest, although not nonexistent or even insignificant. Indeed, although it is fashionable in some circles to speak, for example, of the powerlessness of consumers or of unorganized workers, they are always far from powerless, far from total unilateral dependence. They are only relatively less powerful, because they are relatively more dependent.

The exchange we have been discussing is a bilateral exercise of power. It does not, therefore, ordinarily create a hierarchy or command position, by which I mean power exercisable unilaterally. For either drivers or companies to exercise their power *so as to gain thereby* they must convince the other of the desirability of permitting the exercise. Nevertheless, contracts also create unilateral power. Indeed, that is true even of the discrete transaction whenever exchange is projected into the future, in other words, whenever there is anything at all to the exchange besides the present bilateral transfer of goods. And, of course, there always is—for example, in a supermarket sale if the steak is tainted or the money paid is counterfeit we soon see some future aspects to what looked like a simple present exchange. Suppose the meat *is* bad, and the customer is made seriously ill; the customer now has the power, by threat or actual use of legal process, to command the supermarket to pay damages, whether it desires to do so or not.

Thus, even in a discrete transaction, unilateral power exists between the time when promises are made and when they are kept. This is a commonplace to lawyers, but one often subtly evaded in economic models. During the period of unperformed promises whoever is owed performance is indeed in a position of command and the relation can thus be one of hierarchy. Indeed it will be whenever only one party remains obligated, or whenever one party desires not to proceed while the other party wants performance. Whether the command is a potent one or a weak one will depend upon the sanctions available.

What differentiates bilateral exercise of power in contractual relations from that of the discrete transaction is its dynamic quality. The relative balance of dependence in the discrete transaction is a static phenomenon; it is a given.

But the balance of dependence in relations is in significant measure a product of the relations themselves. For example, a young welder about to go to work for an industrial plant has, as a result of numerous existing factors, a certain balance of interdependence with prospective employer, and the terms of employment acceptable to both sides will reflect that relatively static situation. But twenty years later countless changes in the employment relation itself will have created a totally different picture of interdependence. Aging, for example, may have made the welder far more dependent on the employer than he was at the start. But the change need not be only in such a direction; unionization may, for example, have made the employer far more dependent on the employee, since dealing with him involves dealing with the whole labor force.

The foregoing phenomenon is by no means limited to circumstances which we may be prone to consider as relatively unbalanced. It is also so common in the industrial and financial world among relative equals that Wachter and Williamson have coined a new phrase to describe it: obligational market contracting. A neat term that; it captures nicely the vectoring of willingness and unwillingness mentioned earlier, as well as the dynamic dependence of ongoing relations, together with a hint of the command and hierarchy also so very common in contractual relations.

This discussion of power may be summarized as follows in terms of the axes between discrete transactions and modern relational contract. In the discrete transaction bilateral power is exercised initially at the time the deal is made, the exercise being affected by whatever the power status quo is then. Between then and complete performance one or both parties may have unilateral power. Thus while power may be assumed away in theoretical models of the discrete transaction, in fact it is always present and important.

In contractual relations similar bilateral and unilateral power is also regularly present, but the status quo is dynamic, and power relations are always in a state of flux. Given also the presence of continuing command and hierarchical structures, coupled with ongoing conditions of dependence, power becomes a far more complex phenomenon internally. Power of this kind is a dominant feature of modern contractual relations.

Note

Macneil's analysis demonstrates that power is often not a static phenomenon in the contractual context. Power depends upon the evolution of the contractual relationship, and vice versa. The fact that two people are linked by a contract of employment means that their mutual rights and obligations will develop in ways in which those of two people who are strangers and dealing at arm's length would not. The practical as well as legal interdependence of employer and employee influence the degree to which each has power over the other, and this power will change over time in response to external events such as economic growth, changes in market conditions, and unemployment, as well as internal factors such as an increase in the level of skill offered by the employee. Consequently, it is impossible to build a snapshot picture of bargaining power in a relational contract—a moving picture is a better analogy. This analysis, too, recalls the 'web framework' articulated by Foucault.

III. MODELS OF CONTRACT

Von Mehren enters a plea that the law of contract is easier to administer (and to understand?) in so far as it principally respects the autonomy of the parties to order their lives privately, without interference from the state. Atiyah, as we have seen, links the rise of 'freedom of contract' as a doctrinal model for the law with a particular stream of *laissez-faire* economic ideology. Kronman describes an alternative perspective, that of the libertarian, who justifies his private arrangements by reference to a standard of almost absolute personal autonomy.

A. Kronman, 'Contract Law and Distributive Justice', (1980) 89 *Yale LJ* 472 at 475–6

The libertarian theory of contract law is premised upon the belief that individuals have a moral right to make whatever voluntary agreements they wish for the exchange of their own property, so long as the rights of third parties are not violated as a result. For a libertarian, there are only two grounds on which an agreement to exchange property may be impeached: first, that it infringes the rights of someone not a party to the agreement itself, and second, that one of the individuals agreeing to the exchange was coerced into doing so, and thus did not give his agreement voluntarily. Imagine a judge charged with responsibility for enforcing contracts between the members of a particular community. So long as the judge acts in a way consistent with libertarian principles, he need ask himself only two questions whenever a contract dispute arises: Did the party now said to be in breach voluntarily agree to do what the other party wants him to do? Will performance of the agreement violate the rights of third parties? If the answers are "yes" and "no," respectively, the contract must be enforced, regardless of its consequences for the welfare of the individuals involved. If the judge refuses to enforce a particular contract merely because it has certain distributional consequences, or if he adopts a general rule invalidating an entire class of contracts for similar reasons, his actions are indefensible on libertarian grounds. Taking distributional effects into account in this way is inconsistent with the libertarian conception of individual freedom and violates the basic entitlement on which that conception rests.

Unger expands upon the voluntarist vision by incorporating it into the market structure of economic exchange.

R. Unger, *The Critical Legal Studies Movement* (Cambridge, Mass., Harvard University Press, 1983), 67–8

A regime of contract is just another legal name for a market. It ceases to exist when inequalities of power and knowledge accumulate to the point of turning contractual relations into the outward form of a power order. The ability of the contracting parties to bargain on their own initiative and for their own account must be real. On the other hand, a commitment to cancel out every inequality of power or knowledge as soon as it arose would also undermine a contract system. Real markets are never just machines for instantaneous transactions among economic agents equally knowledgeable and equally able to await the next offer or to withdraw from current courses of dealing. Continued success in market transactions shows partly in the buildup of advantages of power or knowledge that enable their beneficiaries to do that much better in the next round of transactions. If everyone were quickly restored to a situation of equality within the market order, the method responsible for this restoration would be the true system of resource allocation. Such a method would empty market transactions of much of their apparent significance.

At first these two boundaries—allowing the inequalities to accumulate unrestrictedly and correcting them as soon as they emerge—may seem to leave so large an intermediate space of solution that they hardly constrain the organization of a contract regime. There are any number of points within them at which the compromise between correction and allowance might be struck. The decision to draw the line at one place rather than another cannot itself be deduced from the abstract idea of a market. But when the analysis of this tension combines with the thesis that the market lacks any inherent institutional structure, the joint result begins to look far more consequential. The distance between the boundaries does not remain constant as the institutional character of the market changes. Some market regimes, taken in their actual political and social settings, may regularly generate or incorporate so much inequality that the minimum of correction needed to prevent them from degenerating into power orders amounts to more than the maximum correction compatible with the autonomy of decentralized market decisions. . . . The real solution is then to change the institutional character of the market. In the absence of such a revision, attempts must be made to find moderating solutions, either by singling out the most serious problems for special treatment (such as labor law) or by preferring vague slogans (such as good faith, unconscionability) that can be used to support limited, ad hoc corrective interventions. Both of these responses have the capacity to limit the subversive impact of correction upon the central though shrinking and porous body of contract law.

Note

Unger's approach to the role of contract law within the market is based on his system of principles and counterprinciples (see Chs. 2, 4, and 6 above). Control of the market operates through the interaction of the second pair of principles/counterprinciples, namely the freedom of the parties to choose their own terms for their contracts (the freedom principle) and the refusal of the law to enforce unfair bargains (the fairness principle). Since contract and market are irrevocably linked, the possibilities of addressing power relations in contract law are limited by the extent to which the market system itself is capable of institutional reform. Unger subsequently goes on to give some examples of the application of the counterprinciple of fairness which, in his words, 'serve as surrogates for institutional reconstruction' (of the market). These include the doctrine of economic duress, considered in Chapter 9. Wilhelmsson likewise makes out a strong case for an interventionist role for the law.

T. Wilhelmsson, *Critical Studies in Private Law* (Dordrecht, Kluwer, 1992), 12–15, 72–5

A common criticism of the general principles and concepts of private law is that they are insensitive to the concrete needs that the legal system ought to fulfil. . . . Private law is criticised on good grounds for its excessively high level of abstraction. The abstract concepts used in private law hamper discussion of the actual parties' economic and social needs and the importance of these for the legal decisions. It can also be maintained that the use of more general concepts of law increases the relative autonomy of the legal system in relation to society. One goal of an emancipatory dogmatics of private law, attempting to bring juridical discourse closer to societal (to give the substantive elements greater weight in relation to the formal elements of the legal system), should therefore be to create *new* concepts of law and new arguments which break through the abstract façade of private-law principles. It is not enough merely to use the accepted concepts in a new way.

The high abstraction level of private law is maintained by, among other things, the *concepts of juridical roles* . . . . One speaks of seller A and buyer B, creditor C and debtor D, owner E and non-owner F, and so on, without regard to who in the actual case is hidden behind these concepts; thus in a traditional analysis of private law we less frequently run across Professor of Law A, docker B, the big industrial company C, Fatty D, small-town resident E, etc. The criticism just mentioned of the general principles of private law obviously focuses on precisely the way the parties have been described within the system of private law. This becomes an important point of attack for a legal dogmatics that is attempting to enhance the potential of private law to deploy substantive arguments in connection with the circumstances of the actual parties. The objective is to lessen "the gap between legal subjectivity . . . and life-factual subjectivity". . . .

Towards a "social private law"

The creation of a new systematics for private law posits a choice of objectives that in the final instance is political moral. . . . The goal is to work towards a private law in which the ideology of the *"welfare state"* is taken at its word; the production of *certain elements* of a *social private law.*

Much used in the literature of private law, this term "social private law" generally expresses mainly the materialization of private law in the form of norms for protecting the weaker party in a legal relationship. The goals of the welfare state are perceived as appearing in private law through precisely this principle of protection. . . . however, such regulations of contract law, in which the principle of protection appears, can only partly be viewed as realizing this social idea: redistributive welfare goals are not realized through such rules. The question is, however, how far such goals, typical for social security law, could be promoted directly *within the framework* of private law and contract law. How far can one speak of *social private law in this sense* (or perhaps even further on of "private social law")? Or, to use a more pretentious formulation: how far can the *autonomy* of traditional contract law be replaced with the *solidarity* of social law when creating general principles of contract law?

In more concrete terms the issue is here formulated as follows: *to what extent can and should a party's economic and social position be taken account of as a legal fact in contract law?* Can norms of contract law be developed which strengthen the position of economically and socially weak social groups or—using a different formulation—which (to some extent) fulfil the economic and social needs of such groups? The key concept is thus *need-orientation* . . . .

Need-orientation and person-related norms

Need-orientation is a diffuse concept. The goal of taking account of concrete and real needs of the members of society can in practice support a number of different strategies. These may conflict with each other but may also very well be imagined as being complementary.

The needs in question may be entirely general in a society or may exist at least in the great majority of its physical persons. Such needs are non-person-related. In argumentation based on non-person-related needs one refers, for example, to different kinds of physical and mental needs of "people in general", to consumers' "normal requirements" etc. As the development of contract law in the welfare state—including the latest good example: consumer law—indicates, such satisfying of normal requirements by legal means is an important and indispensable element of the private law of a welfare state. The principle of protection of the weaker party in contract law is perhaps the fore-most expression of just this aspect of welfare-state contract law . . . .

However, this non-person-related aspect of the contract law of the welfare state, important though it may be, is not the concern of the present work. The focus here is on that aspect of welfare-state thinking that has not hitherto been permitted to penetrate private law, viz. the concern with *person-related* needs. . . . By need-orientation is here meant the attaching of legal relevance to a party's actual needs arising from his poverty, low income, illness, unemploy-ment etc. The question is whether such specific concrete and actual needs, of self-evident relevance in social security law, can be taken into account in con-tract law also.

Here some further justification for the above delimitation of the term need-orientation in this work should be given:

Private law has traditionally managed to preserve an appearance of consisting of a relatively "unpolitical" collection of norms. To this end it has used its abstract way of describing the persons to whom the norms are to be applied. The abstract personal concepts of "contracting party", "seller" and "buyer", "creditor" and "debtor" and so on determine the structure of private law . . . . General needs, which are not person-related, can often be made objects of law without giving up the use of such abstract person concepts. A more radical break with the traditional conceptual structure cannot occur until relevance is also attached to person-related needs. If one wishes to investigate the *limits of a need-oriented pri-vate law*, it is thus precisely person-related needs that should be the object of attention. In this way the outermost limits of the applicability of welfare-state ideology in private law can also be explored. . . . an alternative legal dogmatics should direct its attention precisely to the limits of what is legally possible . . . .

In modern critical literature on contract law one often meets in the descrip-tion of the contract law of the welfare state expressions such as "solidarity", "altruism", "community", "a fair distribution of wealth", etc. These concepts, too, are vague and may be interpreted in many ways. It is obvious, however, that one of their aspects comprises observance of the concrete, person-related needs of individual parties. The type example of an altruistic or solidarity-based action is the giving of a benefit to a person not because he has earned it but merely because it can contribute to meeting his needs. "Community", too, is characterized by action that takes account of participants' personal needs.

In contract law one party's gain is always the other's loss. It can therefore be said that a need-oriented contract law in the meaning intended here expresses a kind of "Robin Hood morality": taking from the rich and giving to the poor. This endeavour has an old tradition in Western societies as a popularly cher-ished alternative-moral attitude. An alternative legal dogmatics with this per-spective could function as a weapon of a modern *Robin Hood, J.*

A law of contract that stresses the parties' economic position, etc., could conceivably be criticised for *extreme individualism*, for breaking society down into private individuals with specific characteristics. At first sight this may appear to be so, but the point is that conceptual change need not stop at the individual-centred concepts. From these, it is a short step to concepts at collective level that describe, for example, social classes. One can say that a breaking-down of the prevailing abstract conceptual structure in private law, using person-related concepts, is a condition for the development of relevant new collective concepts.

Notes

1. Wilhelmsson identifies two steps which contract law may take if it moves away from the abstract model. It can take into account general classes of persons—e.g. consumers, tenants, and 'weaker parties' (a well-recognized concept in the Nordic tradition from which Wilhelmsson himself comes). Much 'liberal' thinking on contract incorporates such a perspective (see H. Collins, 'Contract and Legal Theory', in W. Twining (ed.), *Legal Theory and Common Law* (Oxford, Blackwell, 1986), 144 ff.) in so far as it views the values of liberalism—autonomy, choice, and self-determination—as relative and limited by the principle that the exercise of free choice should not harm the interests of others. As Collins states, this leads inevitably to a discussion of distributive justice, i.e. to a debate as to which interests and whose interests should be protected. At that point, the façade of neutrality for contract law posited by the libertarians breaks down completely. Contract ceases simply to be a 'private' matter concerned with relations between individuals, and becomes a matter of public concern, namely the distribution of public goods and resources, a point made strongly by Clare Dalton ('An Essay in the Deconstruction of Contract Doctrine', (1985) 94 *Yale LJ* 997) (see Ch. 2).

Wilhelmsson's second step is to focus on the individual characteristics of the contracting parties so as to develop person-based, need-oriented general principles. We shall return to a specific application of this principle when we discuss the concept of social *force majeure* in Chapter 12. The idea lying behind this concept is to allow persons to escape transactions (e.g. onerous consumer debts) if they are prevented from fulfilling their obligations by some unfortunate change in their circumstances such as illness or unemployment.

2. Justice of this latter nature is not a new idea in contract law. Gordley's historical research has identified the nature and influence of the Aristotelian concepts of commutative and distributive justice.

J. Gordley, 'Equality in Exchange', (1981) 69 *Cal. L. Rev.* 1587 at 1588–90

Pre-nineteenth-century jurists and philosophers developed the doctrine of equality in exchange by drawing upon two different authorities. One was a theory of exchange proposed by Aristotle in his *Nichomachean Ethics*, the other was a Roman text in the *Corpus iuris civilis* of Justinian, which provided a legal remedy for those who sold land at less than half its just price. . . .

Distributive justice, according to Aristotle, "is manifested in distributions of honor or money or other things that fall to be divided among those who have a share in the constitution." Commutative justice "plays a rectifying part in transactions between man and man." Distributive justice follows a geometrical proportion. Each citizen receives a share of whatever there is to be divided. It is the mathematics of dividing a pie. Aristotle noted that there is no one correct principle for determining the share each person should receive. Rather, a particular society will adopt a principle consistent with its political regime. Democracies favor the principle that each citizen should receive an equal share. Aristocracies tend to divide goods according to "excellence." Even an illegitimate regime will have a characteristic principle. In an oligarchy, which Aristotle regarded as the corruption of an aristocracy, goods are divided according to the principle that "them that has, gets": the mere possession of wealth and power is recognized as a claim to receive them.

Commutative justice, in contrast, follows an arithmetic proportion. It is concerned not with sharing resources, but with preserving each citizen's share. Therefore, the party who has lost resources to another has a claim for the amount necessary to restore his original position. It is the mathematics of addition and subtraction, of balancing accounts.

To paraphrase Aristotle only slightly, commutative justice operates on the principle that no one should gain by another's loss. This principle later made its way into Roman law in a famous passage of the *Corpus iuris*: "By nature it is equitable that no one should be made richer by another's loss or injury." The text eventually played a major role in developing the modern law of unjust enrichment.

3. For a proper understanding of the role of rules of contract law which attempt to intervene directly in the relationship between the parties, it is essential to appreciate that the shift from Step 1 to Step 2 in Wilhelmsson's analysis entails an entirely different conception of contract. The liberal precept of avoiding harm to others can still make use of a tradition which perceives contract as a competitive opportunity (see Brownsword, 'The Philosophy of Welfarism and Its Emergence in the Modern English Law of Contract', on which this discussion draws heavily). Interventions are consequently restricted to those which 'perfect' the competitive opportunity, by ensuring that no one who goes into the marketplace to undertake a contractual exchange does so lacking the essential prerequisites of contractual capacity to the extent that he or she will be unable to participate even on a presumptively equal basis in economic exchange. This is the 'basic entry requirement', but it is supplemented by 'first aid for casualties', described by Brownsword in the following terms:

R. Brownsword, 'The Philosophy of Welfarism and Its Emergence in the Modern English Law of Contract', in R. Brownsword, Howells, and T. Wilhelmsson (eds.), *Welfarism in Contract Law* **(Aldershot, Dartmouth, 1994), 21 at 34**

The law of contract should seek to protect those who are not properly (i.e., minimally) prepared for the contract competition (e.g. minors) or who are otherwise vulnerable (e.g. those who are subject to undue influence—such persons being incapable of exercising free, self-interested, contractual choices); secondly, it should protect those who are situated below the Plimsoll line (e.g. the poor, and the ignorant); thirdly, it should prohibit contractual outcomes which threaten to push contractors below the line (e.g. exclusions of liability for negligently inflicted personal injury, penalty clauses etc.); fourthly, it should adopt excusing conditions (such as the Scandinavian doctrine of social force majeure) which are sensitive to economic hardship; and, finally, it should imply into contracts such terms as are necessary to secure minimum conditions for the party at risk.

This model could be said to come close to that represented by the modern English law of contract which will be described in the following chapters. It is certainly the philosophy which underlies the Unfair Contract Terms Act 1977, the central plank of legislative intervention in the field of contractual justice (see in particular Ch. 11). In contrast to the above, Step 2 in Wilhelmsson's analysis leaves the realm of contract as an intrinsically competitive relationship, and sees it instead as a paradigmatically co-operative exercise in which each contracting party is equally interested in the outcome for the other party as in his or her own benefit from the exchange. On this analysis, if contract is an instrument of 'social solidarity' (Brownsword), then the outcome can be judged as akin to the 'contracts of equity' sought by Durkheim, in the work extracted in Chapter 2.

IV. THE TRANSFORMATION OF THE LAW OF CONTRACT

Here we extract a summary from Collins which helps us to understand the extent to which the nature of contract law has been transformed by the type of developments charted in this section of the book. To put this extract in context, it will assist the reader to know that Collins is discussing what precisely constitutes the 'critical' programme in contract law, i.e. a programme which challenges the centrality of contract as a 'natural' form of human interaction and rejects the mask of legitimacy in respect of underlying social inequalities which the law of contract lends to competitive exchanges (see further Ch. 2). Collins's discussion calls for critical scholars to be clearer in their identification of the types of value which should be enshrined in a critical contract law, in order in particular to distinguish their work from that of economists whose theory of contract law is based on a model of market and market failure. It is hoped that, after reading the subsequent chapters, you will be better equipped to decide whether it is the transformation thesis or the conservative re-interpretation based on economic analysis which most strongly influences the current state of English law in this field.

H. Collins, 'Ascription of Responsibility for Contractual Obligations', in T. Wilhelmsson (ed.), *Perspectives of Critical Contract Law* (Aldershot, Dartmouth, 1993), 293–6

One theme of this critical programme has been to ask whether new values now infuse the law of contract. This investigation suggests that the traditional law of contract was based upon ideals such as freedom of contract, or more generally on the justice of market exchange relationships, which were associated in their development during the nineteenth century with a belief in the laissez-faire principles of political economy and a libertarian attachment to freedom of the individual. The critical theory of contract law then suggests that the basic values of the law of contract have been transformed as society itself has progressively abandoned its commitment to laissez-faire economics and rugged individualism. The law of contract, which comprises the principles governing the constitution and regulation of markets, should betray signs of this transformation in its rejection of the ideals of freedom of contract in all its ramifications. The underlying transformation should be discernible in the basic values embraced by the law, and perhaps also in the form of law itself . . . .

The initial plausibility of this transformation thesis stems from wider political developments. As liberal societies introduced the tax and benefit structures of the Welfare State, it seems likely that other aspects of the law including the law of contract were modified to bring them into line with the new scheme of values. The transformation thesis can then be expounded by examining legal doctrines which appear to qualify or replace a straightforward attachment to the nineteenth century adherence to the idea of freedom of contract. At this point, however, the critical programme encounters two predictable difficulties.

In the first place, exponents of the transformation thesis cannot agree on the content and weight of the new values which are said to infuse the law. One interpretation might claim that the principal change which has arisen is that the law has embraced a notion of substantive fairness or equivalence in exchange for the sake of distributive justice, and has developed corresponding techniques by which to invalidate unfair contracts . . . . Another interpretation might suggest that the law has dropped the idea of an unsituated person, which was the key assumption of the libertarian framework, and replaced it with a recognition that persons enter contracts with the abilities and disadvantages of their class or group, such as consumers, employees, and tenants. The result is that a differentiated law of contract emerges, with the universalistic principles of nineteenth century doctrine superseded by particularistic principles tied to particular social categories. Yet a third interpretation of the transformation might seize upon the claim that the key alteration of legal doctrine has been with regard to the time frame of the legal analysis of contractual relations . . . . Instead of contracts being regarded as instantaneous transactions, they are treated as social and economic relations which develop gradually and persist long after any formal actions under the contract have been performed. This development signifies a deeper respect on the part of legal doctrine to the diffuse bonds of social solidarity.

It should not be supposed that these rival interpretations are necessarily incompatible. The truth may lie in some combination of these and other interpretations. But the critical programme should be aware of the tensions between these different perspectives. Consider, for example, the possible interpretations of the development of regulations designed to prohibit or control exclusion clauses in contracts which are offered by the three versions of the transformation thesis described above. On the first view, the control of exclusion clauses represents an attempt to redistribute wealth, here located in liability for the risk of loss, away from those who enjoy the resources to impose standard form contracts on others, as part of a scheme of just loss distribution. The second interpretation insists rather that the legal controls seek to protect certain disadvantaged groups, particularly consumers, from their own folly in making disadvantageous contracts. The third interpretation views the control of exclusion clauses as a measure designed to ensure that contracting parties take account of each other's interests. These rival interpretations of the legal control of exemption clauses suggest different outcomes for particular cases. For example, where the exclusion clause is contained in a commercial contract between rich corporations, only the third interpretation is likely to support control over exclusion clauses and to regard this as central to the law's purposes.

I conclude from this discussion that the critical programme needs to become much clearer about the nature and content of the new values which are said to inform the modern law of contract. . . .

But it has to be said, and this is the second difficulty which immediately confronts the transformation thesis, that more conservative interpretations of the law have not lain impoverished and moribund in the meantime. On the contrary, as well as the blunt denials that anything has changed in the values underlying the law of contract at all, the conservative interpretation has embraced the new faith of economic analysis of law. Whilst acknowledging that some changes have taken place in the law of contract at the margins, this conservative interpretation insists that these changes represent an even deeper commitment to the nineteenth century scheme of values. The new legal regulations are conceived as responses to market failure. They are designed to rectify instances of breakdowns in the competitive market.

Within this framework of economic analysis, measures such as the control of exclusion clauses become reanalysed as attempts to restore the competitiveness and efficiency of markets. It is observed, for instance, that ordinary consumers often lack the requisite skills to understand and compare the possible contracts on offer by different manufacturers and retailers. There is a danger in these circumstances, in the absence of competition between sellers with respect to the terms of their standard form contracts, that they will be tempted to cut costs covertly by drastically restricting their obligations under contracts by means of sweeping exclusion clauses . . . . To avoid this market failure, and therefore to restore a competitive market, the law may respond in two ways . . . . Either the law may compel sellers to highlight and explain the content of such clauses, so that consumers may make an informed choice between competing terms; or, alternatively, the law may invalidate some or all of these clauses, which will then force sellers to compete in areas which consumers understand better, such as the price of goods and services.

I have little doubt that it would be possible to explain most modern developments in the law of contract by reference to this idea of market failure. Given that the market is riddled with instances of non-competitive behaviour, there must always be some instance of informational asymmetry or bargaining handicap which might justify legal intervention. This analysis of the values of modern contract law therefore presents a substantial challenge to the critical programme. It can explain and justify all kinds of regulation of contracts within a basic commitment to the traditional values associated with freedom of contract. The only real problem for this market failure analysis is knowing how to justify some limits to legal regulation, for if the slightest hint of non-competitive behaviour might justify legal regulation, then there would be little space left for freedom of contract. Where the limits of legal regulation should be set seems to rest on a political judgment, which balances the respect for freedom of contract and the need to preserve incentives for capital investment against the degree of risk and the deleterious consequences (judged by reference to efficiency) of market failure.

V. ADJUDICATING CONTRACTUAL JUSTICE

In the classical paradigm of the law of contract, justice is to be done on an individual basis, taking into account the circumstances of that particular transaction alone and having an impact upon the subsequent validity and enforceability of that transaction alone. It is also assumed that the need for adjudication will arise because one individual chooses to litigate in response to an occurrence of loss attributable to a breach of the contract. Of course, it is normally open to parties to a contract to agree that a dispute will be resolved by arbitration or some other form of alternative dispute resolution; legislatures also sometimes open up new avenues of complaint for consumers, for example, complaints to administrative authorities such as the Swedish Consumer Ombudsman. However, the normal forum for resolving disputes concerning contractual justice remains the court, and it is to the role of the judge in controlling contract power that we turn to in this final section. We begin with a comment by Leff on the futility of individualized consumer litigation as a mechanism for altering the terms on which goods are offered for sale or for improving and enforcing guarantees of the quality of such goods.

A. Leff, 'Unconscionability and the Crowd: Consumers and the Common Law Tradition', (1970) 31 *U. Pitt. L. Rev.* 349 at 356–7

The problem is . . . with the common-law tradition itself when sought to be used to regulate the quality of transactions of a case-by-case basis, each one of which is economically trivial (so that you need free legal help for the consumer, and the seller can almost always avoid nasty precedent by an early surrender or settlement), and each one of which depends upon several doses of "the total context of the fact situation" and "copious examination of the manifestations of the parties and the surrounding circumstances followed by a balancing effort." It is as if there were some breakdown in the competitive structure which permitted, even fostered, the production of shoddy goods—not dangerous, just crummy—and one sought to have an impact upon that disutility by encouraging individual suits by individual buyers for individual product insufficiences on (often) very individual factual patterns. One cannot think of a more expensive and frustrating course than to seek to regulate goods or "contract" quality through repeated lawsuits against inventive "wrongdoers." Wouldn't it be easier and far more effective, *if* one finds these . . . clauses . . . offensive in consumer transactions, just to face one's conclusion and regulate them out of existence, in a manner no lawyer could conscientiously avoid? Wouldn't it be better, finally, to face the political problems and pass a statute that deals with cross-collateral clauses, negotiable-note and waiver-of defense financing, abusive collection devices, a wide panoply of quasi-crooked marketing devices, and so on, and maybe even gross overpricing (on analogy to the civil-law *laesio enormis* progeny) and tuck in, along with private causes of action for the victims, an administrative enforcement arm to police these repetitive nasty practices (and perhaps get compensation for the whole class of bilked consumers theretofore identifiably bilked)? Isn't there some economy of scale in that approach? Remember, the idea is to change as many nasty forms and practices

as possible, not merely to add to the glorious common law tradition of eventually coping. Wouldn't more be changed by explicit positive law, administratively interpreted and enforced, than by the feed-back from easily
distinguishable, easily stallable, exceedingly expensive *cases*?

Note

We leave Leff on a question. Answers will be easier to formulate when you
have studied the materials in the next three chapters and assessed some of
the different devices both in terms of varied forms of judicial control and
the alternative regulatory mechanisms considered briefly in Chapter 11.
Leff himself concludes that 'case-by-case sniping, while unlikely to do
much good, is equally unlikely to do any harm'. Reiter, who is sceptical
about the broader impact of the judicial control of contract power, is none
the less more positive about the need to theorize the judicial role.

B. Reiter, 'The Control of Contract Power', (1981) 1 *OJLS* 347 at 363–7

. . . if the judicial control of contract power is unlikely to be effective in respect
of widespread or repeated problems, why should we bother to attempt to construct a full and proper theory of this phenomenon? This question can be
addressed only through consideration of the appropriate role of judicial control.
It is important to appreciate from the outset that in many fields nominally dele-
gated to private autonomy, the market and other related pressures operate to
produce socially acceptable levels of performance. While contracts as written
may well seem to be quite harsh, few businesses could survive if the harsh
terms reflected the level of performance that the term-imposer anticipated
delivering, (or more importantly, the level of performance actually achieved).
While these pressures may not change the written terms of contracts, they
serve to establish customary levels of performance that are acceptable in the
vast majority of cases. As well, the effects of the developments at the macro
level . . . must be appreciated: in most fields subject to recurring difficulties, legislation and administrative regulation assure that despite the failure of economic and related pressures to produce acceptable levels of performance,
unfairness does not result.

    The problem areas that remain are interstitial and marginal. They are areas
where economic and social pressures do not operate adequately and where
legislative activity has either not yet occurred, or is impractical. More
specifically, they involve markets with substantial information inefficiencies;
markets populated by fly-by-night operators unaffected by market pressures;
markets in transition; and markets where the individuals likely to be harmed are
too diffuse or too inarticulate to be able to secure legislated solutions. They
tend to involve individuals too weak to compete effectively and those who
would prey upon them in the market; or individuals taken by surprise by

deficient performance in the context of a market where information is under-produced or is likely to be processed in an inadequate fashion. The social and economic characteristics of our society, allowing opportunities for innovation and necessarily involving information inefficiencies, entail that some individuals will suffer from socially unacceptable contracting behaviour. I submit that it is for these individuals that a theory of judicially created and elaborated control of contract power is relevant.

But a further objection is raised against the courts' playing even such a limited, interstitial role. It is argued that even if all of the above be admitted, it would be unwise to trust the matter to courts. It is suggested that courts have no interest in tackling the different issues that must be involved and that lacking the appropriate resources, they will undoubtedly err as they go about the task, an essentially political one.

I, on the other hand, see no alternative but to leave such issues to courts. First, the courts are the only 'front line' redress mechanism in our society. If it is accepted that it would be unwise to legislate about every aspect of society, or (at a more practical level) that the limits to human foresight and time mean that some aspects of social life meriting legislative regulation must escape it, cases must occur in which 'everyone' believes an individual to have been treated unfairly in the course of primary social activity. Assume that the courts refuse to act to assist such a person. Even if the legislature acts to 'change the law' once the problem area has been revealed through the law suit, its legislation is unlikely to be retroactive, and the 'new law' will therefore not assist the justly aggrieved individual who called the matter to legislative attention in the first place. . . .

The argument that the control of contract power must be left to the legislature neglects the important fact that our legal institutions are not fungible: each institution is specialized. Courts are uniquely skilled at dealing with the particular, generalizing from analogy: it is not appropriate to waste our biggest institutional gun on the sorts of problems that come up in unconscionability cases.

A further objection to leaving the matter to the legislature derives from the very inadequate state of our understanding of modern political society. We have only a very limited knowledge of what demands are likely to be met with legislative responses. For instance, the question of how the consumer interest can be expected to fare in the legislative process is most vexed. It is cavalier and irresponsible to assume that the victims of unconscionability will receive the same sort of treatment within the framework of two such different institutions as courts and legislatures. . . .

Nor do I accept the argument that it is impossible to elaborate useful criteria for the proper exercise of judicial control over contract power. This argument claims first, that the courts have provided few useful criteria despite many years of attempting to control contract power (if what I have said above is correct); second, that the courts have produced many wrong decisions, and third, that ultimately the matter involves picking winners and losers, a political, rather than a judicial task.

The view that the courts have provided no useful criteria is true only in its own terms and to a very limited extent. While the courts have had to cope with a legal theory denying them the right to control contract power, they have obviously been unable to express openly the criteria they have been employing, and the due discussion and development of criteria have been retarded accordingly. 'Covert tools are never reliable tools'.

Yet in my view, particularly in consumer cases, the courts have generally reached very desirable results through the manipulation of the legal techniques that they have had available. These cases provide the rough contours of a doctrine of limits to contract power that are reasonably apparent though not enunciated clearly in the judgments. I accept that the courts have achieved a number of unsatisfactory results in commercial cases (though the number of such unsatisfactory decisions has often been exaggerated). This should be expected: while judges may be able to appreciate the expectations of consumers by virtue of judges' being individuals living their own daily lives, they are less sensitive to what fairness might involve in a commercial context. Lacking evidence that could help them decide whether or not contract power has been abused in a particular case, the courts have occasionally jumped to conclusions. There is a chicken-and-the-egg problem here. The courts require counsel to lead evidence to explain commercial background and practice if they are to perform effectively in commercial cases. But it is only when the courts declare openly that they propose to exercise the jurisdiction I would give them that counsel will understand that such evidence is relevant. It is in aid of the breaking of this circle that I support explicit judicial or legislative development of a theory of limits to contract power. But even so, I would expect that the notion of control should have far less play in commercial cases than it has in consumer and family contract cases. The market does tend to be an efficient place in commercial matters, where the information needed to make important decisions is available (or is available to those willing to pay for it) and where alternatives can generally be found by those not wishing to yield to pressures they regard as extravagant. In short, I suggest that the open recognition of a judicial role can serve to improve the development of criteria and to prevent the recurrence of the few unwise decisions that have been rendered in their absence.

Notes

1. Reiter makes a strongly stated plea for a judicial role in the control of contract power. You will be able to judge for yourselves at the end of this part of the book whether his assertions concerning current judicial activity are correct. His thesis is essentially that current practice will reach maturity and

offer an effective and consistent form of recourse if judges are able to act overtly in order to fetter abuses of market power. We suggest you reread his broad-brush comments about the contrasting levels of success in consumer and commercial cases when you have studied the cases on the 'reasonable-ness' test applied under the Unfair Contract Terms Act 1977 in Chapter 11.

2. Reiter considers courts to be in the 'front line' as a mechanism for redress. That is not a popular perception of the role of the courts in the UK. It is worth bearing in mind that Reiter's cultural background is North American. There may not be the same approach by consumers to court involvement in Canada as there is in the UK, but see the empirical findings of Iain Ramsey, 'Small Claims Courts in Canada: A Socio-Legal Approach', in C. Whelan (ed.), *Small Claims Courts: A Comparative Study* (Oxford, Oxford University Press, 1990), which would appear to offer a different pic-ture. We have, when reading this extract, to bear in mind the role and work of consumer agencies (see the study by R. Cranston, *Regulating Business* (London, Macmillan, 1979). These questions may fall outside the scope of Reiter's enquiry into the judicial role, but none the less they are issues which impinge upon the viability of his argument.

3. If Reiter is correct about the role of the judge, then it appears to be confined to a restricted range of areas where market failure occurs. But in practice, legislation frequently leaves a wide margin of discretion to the judiciary, which they must again exercise subject to the caveats of the futil-ity of individual cases highlighted by Leff. One point which Reiter does not address is access to justice: he may well have correctly identified the most vulnerable group who are indeed dependent upon the courts as the 'front line' of justice within society. Yet they are also the group most frequently failed by the system and its institutional constraints, in particular the costs of going to law. These caveats notwithstanding, some avenues of redress which are opened up by strategic litigation—or at least the threat of litiga-tion—are explored by Whitford.

W. Whitford, 'Structuring Consumer Protection Legislation to Maximise Effectiveness', [1981] *Wis. L. Rev.* 1018 at 1020–1

It is a fair conclusion that vague, admonitory legislation usually has little impact on the general character of merchant-consumer transactions. Certainly that would be an appropriate conclusion respecting the unconscionability provi-sion. It is possible to argue, of course, that almost anything is unconscionable. But it has proven very difficult to obtain a judicial precedent about the meaning of unconscionability that has a substantial impact on a large number of transac-tions. This is partly because the unconsionability section, in its only really clear message, provides that a court must consider all the surrounding circumstances before deciding whether a contract provision or practice is unconscionable. As a result it is nearly always possible to distinguish any precedent on the ground that some circumstance or another is different. Furthermore, in litigation to establish a principle of potential general application in unconscionability cases, a merchant stands to be affected in many transactions, while a consumer litigant will be benefited in only one or a few. Merchants can generally justify greater expenditures on the litigation than the consumers, therefore, which probably causes decisions to be more favorable to merchant interests than they would be if each side invested equally in the litigation. For the same reason a merchant can more easily justify the expense of circumventing any undesirable precedent that is established by attempting to distinguish it in future cases.

Though vague, standardless legislation is not likely to have significant effect on the great mass of transactions, it can have a conclusive, yet often unrecognized, effect on the outcome of particular litigation. Because there is always some argument that a transaction is unconscionable, it is virtually always possible for a plaintiff to impose some risk of losing a lawsuit on a defendant by raising an issue of unconscionability. More important, since nearly everything is relevant to a determination of unconscionability, interjecting the issue into a lawsuit may make available an opportunity for extensive discovery, with all the expense that can impose on the defendant. A consumer plaintiff, however, usually must make a considerable investment in legal resources to seek extensive discovery. As a consequence, this litigational ploy tends not to be used, except where legal resources are inexpensive or costless to the plaintiff, such as when the consumer is entitled to legal aid of some type. Moreover, jurisdictions vary in the availability of extensive discovery in small actions; others have restricted discovery in unconscionability actions where the consumer is unable, prediscovery, to make a prima facie showing of unconscionability. Where the discovery ploy is available and used, a common outcome is a settlement in which the merchant agrees to satisfy all or most of the particular consumer's claim, but in a way that does not establish a precedent for other claims, and the consumer withdraws all discovery requests.

In sum, vague admonitory legislation is probably mostly symbolic in its effects, having little impact on the general situation of consumers. It can provide a useful tool for obtaining a favorable litigation result by a consumer with access to low cost legal services. Ironically, the more vague the legislation the more useful it may be in this respect, since increasing vagueness may increase the kinds of information reachable on discovery. There are already many vague principles available to consumer litigants, however, so that any additional legislation of this type may not have even the limited marginal impact of enhancing the individual consumer's litigation position.

Notes

1. The notion of 'unconscionability' is a multi-textured standard against which the fairness of bargains can be judged. Its importance in English law

is much more restricted than in US law, where it has a key role as the basis against which judges test the validity of all manner of onerous contractual terms including exclusion clauses (see Chs. 9 and 11). The unconscionability provision to which Whitford refers is §2-301 of the US Uniform Commercial Code, discussed in Chapter 9.

2. Whitford's comments are, of course, addressed to the situation in the USA, where rules on discovery of evidence differ from the UK. However, the general strategic gains to be made in *individual* cases will be similar in any system where courts are asked to apply a broad discretionary standard, and the threat of litigation may provoke a settlement where the possibility of an unfavourable decision might be very undesirable from the perspective of the supplier.

Questions

1. What are the key ways in which the approaches of von Mehren and Hale to issues of contractual justice differ? Would you agree with the comment that they provide complementary perspectives upon the problem of power in contractual relations?

2. Does the interventionist critique put forward by Wilhelmsson and others offer a sustained and convincing argument for the widespread application of a substantive concept of contractual justice?

3. What structural problems exist within many legal systems which make it difficult in practice to apply a standard of contractual justice?

9

Duress and Unconscionability

I. INTRODUCTION

At the level of doctrine, this chapter is principally concerned with two rather narrowly circumscribed doctrines of contract law, which enable courts to exercise some direct control over fairness in contracts. These are duress—in particular economic duress—and undue influence. Duress is a common law doctrine which formally operates as a vitiating factor in relation to the contract: the presence of duress attacks the very existence of the contract, casting doubt upon the nature of the consent of the party upon whom the duress has operated. In that respect, therefore, duress should be seen as closely linked to the other formation defects discussed in Chapter 5. Undue influence operates in equity to protect the position of certain categories of persons deemed to be especially vulnerable to the adverse influence of the party with whom they are contracting, or a third party. It can sometimes be termed unconscionability, but this latter term is perhaps better reserved to describe a more generalized doctrine of contractual fairness operating under §2-203 of the US Uniform Commercial Code which allows courts a broad discretion to control 'unconscionable' contracts. This doctrine will be discussed in Section IV.

While at first sight the type of doctrines which operate in English law would seem principally if not solely concerned with issues of procedural rather than substantive unfairness, we shall see in our discussion of the cases how difficult it is, in reality, for judges rigidly to separate issues of fairness in the bargaining process and the 'fair' or 'unfair' content of the bargain which results from that process.

Beyond the level of English and American doctrine, this chapter is concerned with many of the conceptual questions introduced in the previous chapter. It is in particular concerned with the problem of power.

C. Dalton, 'An Essay in the Deconstruction of Contract Doctrine', (1985) 94 *Yale LJ* 997 at 1024–7

The story of the doctrines of duress and unconscionability reveals efforts over time to create a private domain in which individuals can reach binding agreements and courts can enforce them, despite the difficulties presented by the problem of power. In the context of duress and unconscionability, doctrine wrestles with the power of contracting parties over one another, and the power of the state over both.

The doctrines of duress and unconscionability are self-consciously "public" insofar as they are designed to police the limits of "fair" bargain. They legitimate the exercise of state power to prevent one contracting party from exercising an illegitimate power over the other. Thus, the private deal of the parties—or what appears to be the private deal of the parties—may be overridden in the name of a norm that, under appropriate circumstances, trumps the otherwise prevalent norm of non-intervention.

In a discourse so protective of its private or non-interventionist status, this is a dangerous move that raises a number of interesting questions: Why should contract have to harbor such a public aspect? When is intervention justified? How has this public aspect of contract been reconciled over time with the rest of "private" contract doctrine? What does this particular story reveal about the body of doctrine to which it bears such a dangerously supplemental relationship? . . .

The "why" question has both a private and a public answer. The private answer is that since privacy in contract is conceived of as a guarantor of freedom, contracts entered into under coercion are not deserving of that privacy—indeed, under those circumstances, state intrusion becomes the guarantor of freedom. The public answer is that we have some values that occasionally trump our desire for a system of contract in which each party bears full responsibility for protecting his own interests. We conceive some limit to self-interest, some requirement that under certain circumstances contracting parties should look out for one another, and we are prepared to use the power of the state to enforce that obligation.

The "when" question reveals the extent of the problem of power. Three different approaches to the question are embedded in contract doctrine as it has evolved since the nineteenth century. One approach is to focus on the disfavored party, and ask whether that party's assent to the transaction was genuine. Another approach is to focus on the behavior of the favored party, and to rule that some kinds of behavior between contracting parties are unacceptable. A third approach is to look at the terms of the transaction itself, and to determine that some deals are just too lopsided to be enforceable.

The first approach—determining whether the disfavored party genuinely assented—is rendered unworkable by the problem of knowledge. We cannot directly know or ascertain the subjective intent of the disfavored party. Our inquiry therefore becomes indirect—we turn to objective evidence of the party's subjective intent. But in our search for objective evidence we find ourselves abandoning our initial focus, and focusing instead, as the second and third approaches suggest, on the other party's behavior and the terms of the resulting deal. Could anyone resist the pressure exerted by *that* threat, *those* circumstances? Would anyone have voluntarily agreed to *that* deal?

The second and third approaches each embody an assumption that we can distinguish the acceptable from the unacceptable; the attempt to make this distinction throws us directly into the problem of power. We live with two convictions—that we should take care of ourselves and that we should take care of others—and we lack any conceptual or instrumental scheme sufficiently persuasive in its neutrality or its appeal to consensual values to regulate when one impulse should predominate. How, then, should we determine that some self-interested behavior is beyond the pale, but some other is not? How should we determine that some transactions are acceptable in their terms but others are not?

These questions go to the heart of the problem of power—the power of the state to control private arrangements and to evaluate private power relations. Doctrine attempts to deny that these questions can be answered only by recourse to non-neutral and non-consensual choices. Since doctrine's devices for denial suppress the public aspect of duress and unconscionability, they also serve to reconcile those doctrines with the otherwise private face of contract.

One device, at once evasive and reconciliatory, conflates public and private by shifting attention from the behavior of the favored party or the terms of the transaction back to the subjective assent of the disfavored party—a seemingly private inquiry. The refuge provided by this technique is scarcely adequate, of course, for reasons just explored: Because any search for subjective intent encounters the problem of knowledge, doctrine cannot remain lodged in the subjective, but must venture out again into the territory of the objective, where the problem of power remains.

Alternatively, another favored device is to present duress and unconscionability as doctrines policing process, not substance. This technique of separation admits public involvement, but reassures that the public decisions are being made in neutral and consensual territory—the territory of bargaining process. To the extent that this illusion can be maintained, the dangerous questions of substance are left in the private sphere. The problem is that found in any shift from substance to form: We are incapable of identifying form, let alone distinguishing the proper from the defective form, without recourse to the very substance we were hoping to escape.

An important illustration of this latter technique is the translation of bad behavior into a procedural concern. Sometimes privacy is presented as inhering above all in the power of private individuals to set the substantive terms of their exchanges. Accordingly, to protect privacy, courts must scrupulously avoid evaluating those terms. A focus on bad behavior, presented as a policing of bargaining *process*, thereby becomes a less problematic intrusion than a focus on the substance of the resulting exchange. The substantive nature of judging behavior is thus disguised, or the norms of conduct presented as more neutral and/or consensual than any norm of exchange.

A final device is to acknowledge the difficulties and dangers of public duress and unconscionability doctrine, but to reassure by limitation: These doctrines are to be applied only in the extreme case; they stand in glaring contrast to the rest of (private) contract doctrine. Actually, this inquiry ultimately reveals how all of contract doctrine is as "public" as these supposedly exceptional cases. Or, it would be equally true to say, duress and unconscionability turn out to be just as private as the rest of contract doctrine—which is not nearly as private as traditional theory would have it.

Note

Dalton introduces the public/private dimension of the power debate. That is, when is it right that the state should intervene—through the courts and through legislation—to restrict the power of private individuals freely to make contracts on terms chosen by themselves, where that power is acknowledged to be unevenly distributed? Dalton stresses that contract law has attached its flag to a ship of objectivity—a state of presumed, as opposed to real, knowledge about the intentions and motives of the parties (cf. Ch. 5). She suggests that classical contract law would wish to circumscribe the impact of doctrines such as economic duress and unconscionability (in the US sense) by highlighting how they deviate from traditional non-interventionist standards. In fact, as our discussions of the origins of consideration in Chapter 6 and the extract from Gordley in Chapter 8 illustrate, it is by no means so exceptional, in a historical context, for courts to police the underlying fairness of contracts. There is a historical precedent from eighteenth-century England, when courts of equity readily relieved parties from harsh and unconscionable bargains without reference to the question whether they had freely given their consent (see further J. Gordley, *The Philosophical Origins of Modern Contract Doctrine* (Oxford, Oxford University Press, 1991), 146 ff.).

II. DURESS

The modern law of duress has been marked by a gradual broadening of the common law doctrine to encompass not just threats to property and persons but also threats to the economic interests of the victim, such as a threat not to perform a contract unless it is renegotiated on terms more favourable to the party threatening breach.

Atlas Express Ltd. v. *Kafco (Importers and Distributors) Ltd.*
[1989] 1 All ER 641

TUCKER J By their statement of claim the plaintiffs, Atlas Express Ltd, claim against the defendants, Kafco (Importers and Distributors) Ltd, £17,031.83 plus interest, as outstanding payments due to them under a number of invoices submitted to the defendants. It is admitted that some of this has since been paid, and the sum now claimed is £10,970.37.

The plaintiffs are well-known carriers of goods by road in the United Kingdom. They offer a parcels delivery service. The defendant company . . . imports basketware from abroad and supplies it to retailers in the United Kingdom.

On 24 June 1986 the plaintiffs entered into a general trading agreement with the defendants whereby the plaintiffs agreed to deliver cartons of the defendants' basketware at a rate per carton depending on the number of cartons in the load. By October 1986 the defendants had entered into an agreement to supply their basketware to Woolworth shops in the United Kingdom. The defendants wished the plaintiffs to make the deliveries for them, and the plaintiffs agreed to do so. The terms of this agreement were contained in a trading agreement signed by Mr Armiger on the defendants' behalf on 20 October 1986. The rate agreed was expressed as being £1.10 per carton. There was a minimum charge of £7.50 per consignment but this referred to the delivery to each branch. The agreement was silent as to the size of the cartons or as to the number of cartons necessary to constitute a load. The rate was expressed to be effective from 10 October 1986 to a review on 31 May 1987. The case proceeded on the basis that this was a concluded agreement. . . .

The rate agreement was that orally agreed between Mr Armiger and Mr Hope, the manager of the plaintiffs' depot in Wellingborough. They met at the defendants' warehouse at Tinker's Drove, Wisbech, on 10 October 1986. Mr Hope had gone there to see a sample of the goods his company were being asked to deliver. He was shown a range of cartons of the sort the defendants used. He cannot say what size the largest carton was which he then saw, because he did not take any measurements. The trailers which the plaintiffs used were 40 feet long. Mr Hope says he calculated the rate per carton on the basis that the plaintiffs would be transporting a minimum of 400 cartons, and possibly as many as 600, on each trailer, thus producing a minimum return of £440 per load. In order to achieve this quantity per load, it would be necessary that no carton should exceed a measurement of 2ft 6in in any dimension. Mr Hope said that to the best of his memory, he and Mr Armiger discussed the basis on which the rate was calculated, though later he agreed that he was not sure they had had a conversation about a load of 400. Mr Armiger was firmer in his evidence. He said that the sizes of the cartons were never discussed and nothing was said about the number of cartons which would be carried, and that he could not have agreed a figure of 400 because he never knew what revenue the plaintiffs expected, and he did not know how many cartons could be loaded onto a trailer.

I prefer Mr Armiger's evidence on this point. I think his recollection of the conversation is clearer than Mr Hope's, and I believe him. . . .

In any event, the plaintiffs' counsel said that he did not rely on any knowledge by Mr Armiger of the basis on which the calculation was made. This was not part of his pleaded case, and he did not submit that this was a term of the contract between the parties, or that it was a representation made by or on behalf of the defendants.

Much more important is the question of the sample or mix of cartons which Mr Hope saw at the defendants' warehouse at Tinker's Drove, Wisbech. . . . I find that Mr Hope saw a fair and representative mix of the kind of cartons which his company was being asked to deliver, and that he was given every opportunity of inspecting what was there, so as to enable him to calculate the rate to be quoted. It may be that Mr Hope mistakenly believed that he could load more cartons on to a trailer than was physically possible but, in fixing the rate of £1.10 per carton, he was not in any way misled by the defendants and he should not have been deceived by the sample and mix of cartons which he saw.

In pursuance of the written agreement, the plaintiffs proceeded to make the first delivery. When Mr Hope saw the load from the defendants, he said he was surprised to see how large the cartons were and how many large cartons were included in the load. He said they were far larger than the parties had contemplated, and because of this there were fewer of them, only 200 instead of the 400 he had anticipated. He said he had no prior knowledge that cartons of that size would be included. I find that he is wrong about this. I accept Mr Armiger's evidence that the load was representative of the type of cartons which Mr Hope had seen at the warehouse, and that the cartons were no larger than those inspected by him.

However, Mr Hope was convinced that it would not be financially viable to carry such a load at the rate agreed. He contacted Mr Armiger about it, in an attempt to renegotiate the rate. I find that the two of them met to discuss it, and that Mr Hope made it plain to Mr Armiger that the plaintiffs would not carry any more goods under the Woolworth agreement unless the defendants agreed to pay at least a minimum rate of £440 per trailer load. I find that if the defendants had refused, the plaintiffs would not have made any further deliveries. However, I find that no agreement to renegotiate the terms of the contract was reached at this stage.

The defendants were a small company and their three directors were personally committed to its success. They had secured a large order from Woolworth and had obtained a large quantity of goods in order to fulfil it. It was essential to the defendants' success and to their commercial survival that they should be in a position to make deliveries. I find that this was obvious to

Mr Hope, and was known by him. It was now early November, a time of year when demands on road hauliers and deliveries are heaviest.

It would have been difficult, if not impossible, for the defendants to find alternative carriers in time to meet their delivery dates. . . .

[On] 18 November, one of the plaintiffs' drivers arrived at the defendants' premises with an empty trailer. He brought with him a document entitled 'Amended/Transferred Account Details'. Mr Hope had written in the new rates, which now specified a minimum charge of £400 per trailer. Mr Armiger did not want to agree to this, and he had not done so at the meeting. He queried it with the driver, who said that he had instructions that if the defendants did not sign the agreement he was to take the trailer away unloaded. Mr Armiger had done his best at the meeting to persuade Mr Hope to reduce his demands, but the only concession he had achieved was that the minimum charge would not apply to deliveries within the five counties nearest to the plaintiffs' depot at Wellingborough. Mr Armiger tried to contact Mr Hope on 18 November, but he was unable to do so. Mr Hope was unavailable. I infer that this was deliberate. It prevented the defendants from protesting to him. In these circumstances, Mr Armiger justifiably felt himself to be in a situation of 'take it or leave it'. He could not afford to lose the plaintiffs' services, with all the consequences that would ensue, so he signed the agreement. Before doing so, he wrote in the concession which he had obtained.

I find that when Mr Armiger signed that agreement he did so unwillingly and under compulsion. He believed on reasonable grounds that it would be very difficult, if not impossible, to negotiate with another contractor. He did not regard the fact that he had signed the new agreement as binding the defendants to its terms. He had no bargaining power. He did not regard it as a genuine armslength renegotiation in which he had a free and equal say and, in my judgment, that view was fully justified.

. . . he felt that he was 'over a barrel'. . . . I accept the evidence of the Woolworth manager, Mr Graham, that if the defendants had told them they could not supply the goods Woolworth would have sued them for loss of profit and would have ceased trading with them. I find that this was well known to the defendants' directors.

After Mr Armiger signed the agreement, the plaintiffs' driver agreed to load a delivery. Thereafter the plaintiffs carried the defendants' goods and delivered them to Woolworth until 29 December 1986. The plaintiffs knew that the defendants would not be paid by Woolworth until deliveries were completed, and the plaintiffs agreed that they would not expect payment from the defendants until the defendants had been paid by Woolworth. Mr Hope recognised that this would not be before 30 January 1987.

On 2 February 1987 the defendants sent to the plaintiffs a cheque for £10,000, expressed as being a payment on account. I do not regard that as an acceptance of the new terms. The defendants made their position quite clear through their solicitors, who wrote to the plaintiffs on 2 March 1987, saying that the revised contract was signed under duress. This was three months before the plaintiffs commenced proceedings.

The issue which I have to determine is whether the defendants are bound by the agreement signed on their behalf on 18 November 1986. The defendants contend that they are not bound, for two reasons: first, because the agreement was signed under duress; second, because there was no consideration for it.

The first question raises an interesting point of law, i.e. whether economic duress is a concept known to English law.

Economic duress must be distinguished from commercial pressure, which on any view is not sufficient to vitiate consent. The borderline between the two may in some cases be indistinct. But the authors of *Chitty on Contracts* (25th edn, 1983) and of *Goff and Jones on the Law of Restitution* (3rd edn, 1986) appear to recognise that in appropriate cases economic duress may afford a defence, and in my judgment it does. It is clear to me that in a number of English cases judges have acknowledged the existence of this concept.

Thus, in *D & C Builders Ltd* v. *Rees* [1966] 2 QB 617 at 625 Lord Denning MR said: 'No person can insist on a settlement procured by intimidation.' And in ◦*Occidental Worldwide Investment Corp* v. *Skibs A/S Avanti, The Siboen and the Sibotre* [1976] 1 Lloyd's Rep 293 at 336 Kerr J appeared to accept that economic duress could operate in appropriate circumstances. A similar conclusion was reached by Mocatta J in *North Ocean Shipping Co Ltd* v. *Hyundai Construction Co Ltd, The Atlantic Baron* [1979] QB 705 at 719.

In particular, there are passages in the judgment of Lord Scarman in *Pao On* v. *Lau Yiu* [1980] AC 614 at 635–636, which clearly indicate recognition of the concept, where Lord Scarman said:

'Duress, whatever form it takes, is a coercion of the will so as to vitiate consent. Their Lordships agree with the observation of Kerr J in *The Siboen and The Sibotre* that in a contractual situation commercial pressure is not enough. There must be present some factor "which could in law be regarded as a coercion of his will so as to vitiate his consent". . . . In determining whether there was a coercion of will such that there was no true consent, it is material to enquire whether the person alleged to have been coerced did or did not protest; whether, at the time he was allegedly coerced into making the contract, he did or did not have an alternative course open to him such as an adequate legal remedy; whether he was independently advised; and whether after entering the contract he took steps to avoid it. All these matters are . . . relevant in determining whether he acted voluntarily or not. In the present case there is unanimity amongst the judges below that there was no coercion of Lau's will. In the Court of Appeal the trial judge's finding (already quoted) that Lau considered the matter thoroughly, chose to avoid litigation, and formed the opinion that the risk in giving the guarantee was more apparent than real was upheld. In short, there was commercial pressure, but no coercion. . . . It is, therefore, unnecessary for the Board to embark on an enquiry into the question whether English law recognises a category of duress known as "economic duress". But, since the question has been fully argued in this appeal, their Lordships will indicate very briefly the view which they have formed. At common law money paid under economic compulsion could be recovered in an action for money had and received. The compulsion had to be such that the party was deprived of "his freedom of exercising his will". It is doubtful, however, whether at common law any duress other than duress to the person sufficed to render a contract voidable; see Blackstone's Commentaries (12th edn, 1793) vol 1, pp 130–131 and *Skeate* v. *Beale* (1841) 11 Ad & El 983. American law (Williston on Contracts (3rd edn, 1970) ch 47) now recognises that a contract may be avoided on the ground of economic duress. The commercial pressure alleged to constitute such duress must, however, be such that the victim must have entered the contract against his will, must have had no alternative course open to him, and must have been confronted with coercive acts by the party exerting the pressure: see Williston on Contracts ch 47, s 1603. American judges pay great attention to such evidential matters as the effectiveness of the alternative remedy available, the fact or absence of protest, the availability of independent advice, the benefit received, and the speed with which the victim has sought to avoid the contract. Recently two English judges have recognised that commercial pressure may constitute duress the presence of which can render a contract voidable [Lord Scarman then referred to the judgments of Kerr and Mocatta JJ to which I have referred and continued:] Both stressed that the pressure must be such that the victim's consent to the contract was not a voluntary act on his part. In their Lordship's view, there is nothing contrary to principle in recognising economic duress as a factor which may render a contract voidable, provided always that the basis of such recognition is that it must amount to a coercion of will, which vitiates consent. It must be shown that the payment made or the contract entered into was not a voluntary act.' . . .

Reverting to the case before me, I find that the defendants' apparent consent to the agreement was induced by pressure which was illegitimate and I find that it was not approbated. In my judgment that pressure can properly be described as economic duress, which is a concept recognised by English law, and which in the circumstances of the present case vitiates the defendants' apparent consent to the agreement.

In any event, I find that there was no consideration for the new agreement. The plaintiffs were already obliged to deliver the defendants' goods at the rates agreed under the terms of the original agreement. There was no consideration for the increased minimum charge of £440 per trailer.

Notes

1. It seems from Tucker J's judgment above that two elements have to be considered when duress is raised as a defence to breach of contract. First, the pressure has to be assessed to see whether it amounts to coercion of the will, and second, the pressure has to satisfy the criterion of being 'illegitimate'. In both these cases, the courts have to undertake a difficult balancing act to determine the dividing line between legitimate commercial pressure and illegitimate duress.

More assistance on the requirements for illegitimacy is provided by Lord

Scarman in *Universe Tankships Inc. of Monrovia* v. *International Transport Workers Federation (The Universe Sentinel)* [1983] 1 AC 366 at 400–1.

It is, I think, already established law that economic pressure can in law amount to duress; and that duress, if proved, not only renders voidable a transaction into which a person has entered under its compulsion but is actionable as a tort, if it causes damage or loss: *Barton* v. *Armstrong* and *Pao On* v. *Lau Yiu Long*. The authorities upon which these two cases were based reveal two elements in the wrong of duress: (1) pressure amounting to compulsion of the will of the victim; and (2) the illegitimacy of the pressure exerted. There must be pressure, the practical effect of which is compulsion or the absence of choice. Compulsion is variously described in the authorities as coercion or the vitiation of consent. The classic case of duress is, however, not the lack of will to submit but the victim's intentional submission arising from the realisation that there is no other practical choice open to him. This is the thread of principle which links the early law of duress (threat to life or limb) with later developments when the law came also to recognise as duress first the threat to property and now the threat to a man's business or trade. . . .

The real issue . . . is, therefore, as to the second element in the wrong duress: was the pressure applied . . . in the circumstances of [the] case one which the law recognises as legitimate? For, as Lord Wilberforce and Lord Simon of Glaisdale said in *Barton* v. *Armstrong* [1976] A.C. 104, 121D: "the pressure must be one of a kind which the law does not regard as legitimate."

. . . in life, including the life of commerce and finance, many acts are done "under pressure, sometimes overwhelming pressure": but they are not necessarily done under duress. That depends on whether the circumstances are such that the law regards the pressure as legitimate.

In determining what is legitimate two matters may have to be considered. The first is as to the nature of the pressure. In many cases this will be decisive, though not in every case. And so the second question may have to be considered, namely, the nature of the demand which the pressure is applied to support.

The origin of the doctrine of duress in threats to life or limb, or to property, suggests strongly that the law regards the threat of unlawful action as illegitimate, whatever the demand. Duress can, of course, exist even if the threat is one of lawful action: whether it does so depends upon the nature of the demand. Blackmail is often a demand supported by a threat to do what is lawful, e.g. to report criminal conduct to the police. In many cases, therefore, "What [one] has to justify is not the threat, but the demand . . .": see *per* Lord Atkin in *Thorne* v. *Motor Trade Association* [1937] A.C. 797, 806.

From this we can see that it is not necessary for the pressure applied to be unlawful to amount to duress. There is no perfect match between what constitutes in tort an illegal commercial activity which amounts to an 'economic tort' such as conspiracy and what in contract constitutes duress. The linking of the two elements of coercion and illegitimacy will result in the courts having to embark upon a lengthy, case-specific enumeration of the facts to see, for example, exactly what choices the aggrieved party had and what information was known by the alleged aggressor.

2. It is still not entirely clear from the authorities that English law has totally left behind the traditional approach to duress based on coercion of the will and vitiation of consent. The case against this approach is well summarized by Halson.

R. Halson, 'Opportunism, Economic Duress and Contractual Modifications', (1991) 107 *LQR* 649 at 664–7

The most popular test used by English courts to determine whether an agreement is compelled or not relies on the absence of consent by the "victim." His will is said to be coerced in a way which vitiates his consent. In *Pao On* v. *Lau Liu Long* Lord Scarman, delivering the opinion of the Board, agreed that economic duress rendered a contract voidable provided that the duress amounted to a coercion of the will which vitiated consent. The same test has been used in a number of decisions at first instance and in the Court of Appeal. It was at one time popular in the United States and it seems that the influence of the test persists. This is surprising in view of the judicial statement of Holmes J. exposing the speciousness of its reasoning. For the consent obtained by a threat is in every meaningful sense a real consent. All that has happened is that a party has been faced with a choice between two evils, submission to a demand or the threatened consequences of resistance. It is true that it is a choice which the law deprecates. However, that should not lead courts to the conclusion that the consent was unreal. Indeed, there is a sense in which one can say that the more extreme the threatened wrong and the concomitant desire of the victim to avoid it, the more "real" the consent obtained. Therefore the consent obtained as the result of a threat is a more sincere, more genuine consent than is generally manifested by so-called voluntary agreements.

In view of the wealth of academic opinion against the vitiation of consent test and the judicial statements of Holmes J., it is perhaps surprising to see the test adopted by the English courts so readily and uncritically. It is even more surprising when the analysis of consent in a criminal case, *D.P.P. for Northern Ireland* v. *Lynch* [1975] AC 653 is considered. The House of Lords in that case had rejected the idea that duress in some way overbears the individual's will to deprive him of the ability to give a genuine consent. . . .

The case against the vitiation of consent test is, I submit, overwhelming. If taken literally it is illogical and meaningless. It has been suggested that the test was never intended to be applied literally, but was just legal shorthand for the judicial finding that a party has been subjected to an improper motive for his action. Indeed there is some evidence to support this view. Lord Scarman in *The Universal Sentinel* notes that

"The classic case of duress is however not the lack of will to submit but the victim's intentional submission arising from the fact that there is no other practical choice open to him."

From this statement it would appear that Lord Scarman was aware of the fallacy . . . others have exposed; but at other points in the same judgment he speaks of "pressure amounting to compulsion of the will of the victim." . . .

The evidence that the vitiation of consent formula was never intended to be applied mechanistically is at best equivocal. Even if it were unequivocal it would be open to all the criticisms that can be levelled at rules which do not directly address the "policy" issues behind them; the law squanders the opportunity to expand and develop doctrines in a coherent way; it fails to generate debate; the predictive value of the law to counsel and contracting parties is lessened; finally there is the danger that a subsequent court may try to apply the rule mechanistically, in ignorance of the policy factors to which previous judges have adverted.

3. The effect of a successful plea of duress is to render the contract voidable. As Chapter 5 showed when we examined the doctrine of mistake, the distinction between void and voidable contracts is a crucial one. If the application of a doctrine renders a contract voidable, then the right of the innocent party to treat the contract as at an end is restricted by factors such as lapse of time and third-party rights. For example, if Jo induces Sally to sell her widgets at a very reduced price by threatening not to buy any from her without a price reduction, and Jo then sells them to a third party who buys them in good faith, then, although the contract is voidable at the instance of Sally if Jo's pressure amounted to economic duress, the widgets themselves will not be recoverable from the third party (see Cartwright, *Unequal Bargaining* (Oxford, Oxford University Press, 1991), 168–9). Other limitations on the rescission of a voidable contract are affirmation by the innocent party (expressly or impliedly consenting to the continued existence of the contract) and the impossibility of restoring the parties to their original positions because of a change in the nature of the subject-matter of the contract.

In other words, duress operates as a vitiating factor in relation to contracts in the same way as misrepresentation or fraud. Consequently, in so far as a remedy of damages is required in respect of conduct amounting to duress—a particularly crucial issue if rescission is barred—it must be sought in the realm of tort, in particular the economic torts such as conspiracy, intimidation, and other deliberate interferences in the economic interests of the victim which have been held to be actionable.

4. In a throwaway comment at the end of his judgment, Tucker J notes that 'in any event, I find that there was no consideration for the new agreement'. This comment indicates that in English law, as presently constituted, there exist two separate doctrinal devices for testing the enforceability of attempted modifications of existing contracts—consideration and economic duress. This parallelism emerged in Chapter 6 in relation to the examination of *Williams* v. *Roffey*, where the Court of Appeal was happy to apply a relaxed test of *de facto* benefit to the requirement of consideration, in the absence of the inference of duress. *Atlas Express* lies, in the view of Tucker J, on the other side of the boundary between enforceability and unenforceability on both counts.

This raises a number of points. For example, it is necessary to ascertain whether there are two separate spheres of application for the two doctrines or whether in fact the two doctrines, which appear very different in form, are in fact to be applied concurrently. The earlier analysis of *Williams* v. *Roffey* would appear to indicate that the courts still see consideration as providing a separate test of enforceability which is more than merely technical, and which allows the court to determine the range of 'genuine' modifications based on an analysis of real benefit.

Of course, it is easier to apply a clear 'rule' of nominal or indeed 'real benefit' consideration to assess the enforceability of bargains than it is for a court to try to apply open-ended standards which require them to express a position on the underlying justice of a contract. Nominally, the doctrine of economic duress is concerned solely with process, and with the nature of the threat which results in the conclusion of a contract. In the contractual modification scenario, however, Tucker J in *Atlas Express* seemed to drift inexorably towards an assessment of substance by looking at the nature of the bargain. He lays great stress on the efficiency of the pricing exercise carried out by the plaintiffs' employee; that he had not measured the cartons, that he had perhaps underestimated how many cartons could be loaded onto a trailer, etc. The inference is that the plaintiffs made a bad bargain due to their own carelessness and then tried to improve their position by pressurizing the defendants.

The analysis by Tucker J was, however, an unsophisticated one, raising the question of whether economic duress is in truth a more finely tuned doctrine for controlling the fairness of modern commercial contracting—a suggestion made by A. Phang ('Whither Economic Duress?', (1990) 53 *MLR* 115). At present, what is required in terms of judicial analysis is some indication of how the two doctrines can be meshed together, since the difficulty with the analyses of the two closely related cases of *Williams* v. *Roffey* and *Atlas Express* is that, in applying the two different doctrines, each court offered no more than a cursory reference to the other doctrine.

5. The facts of *Atlas Express* can be fitted into what Trebilcock describes as a 'situational monopoly'.

M. Trebilcock, 'An Economic Approach to Unconscionability', in B. Reiter and J. Swan (eds.), *Studies in Contract Law* (Toronto, Butterworths, 1980), 392–6

Structurally Impaired Markets

What is contemplated here is the case of a market which is so structurally impaired as to preclude the behaviour of one or other of the parties to a contract being effectively disciplined in his behaviour towards the other party by market (competitive) forces. . . . there is the case of what might be called situational (or "spot") monopolies where special circumstances have arisen giving one contracting party abnormal market power with respect to the other, albeit perhaps not in relation to other parties in the same market. . . .

(i) Situational Monopolies
This class of case is approximately coterminous with those circumstances often considered as falling under the doctrine of duress . . . .

In a recent English decision, *Occidental World-Wide Investment Corp.* v. *Skibs A/S Avanti* ([1976] 1 Lloyds LR 293), the court held that the doctrine of duress was not confined to duress to the person and duress of goods but could comprehend other forms of compulsion. However, "the court must in every case at least be satisfied that the consent of the other party was overborne by compulsion so as to deprive him of any *animus contrahendi*." . . .

As the scope of the doctrine of duress has moved from the narrow case of physical threats to less clearly specified cases of "economic duress," it has become more important to define precisely what it is that will constitute unacceptable forms of coercion. The failure to articulate the essence of the concept of duress in meaningful economic terms has led courts to rely on a variety of dubiously useful criteria. For example, in the *Occidental* case, the emphasis on whether the coercion had vitiated the consent of the party pleading duress seems unhelpful. In any operational sense, clearly consent has been forthcoming to the transaction. Indeed, even in the physical threat cases, the consent of the party threatened is entirely real. To attach significance to the absence of a protest by a party to an allegedly coerced agreement, as was also suggested in *Occidental*, again seems of doubtful soundness if it was clear that a protest would be futile. Yet again, to talk of these transactions as "one-sided" is also unhelpful, because even in the extreme example of a contract induced by physical threat, there are substantial mutual advantages to the transaction. Finally, to attach redemptive significance to the presence of independent advice in a situation where it is acknowledged that the presence of independent advice does "nothing to expand the choices open" to the party alleging duress seems again mistaken.

It is submitted that the relevant test in all of the so-called duress cases is whether the conduct of the party against whom the doctrine is pleaded was such as to remove from, or to take advantage of the absence of, effective access by the other party to a workably competitive range of alternative choices. For example, in the salvage cases, what may be objectionable about the terms exacted by a tug owner from the owner or captain of a sinking ship is that the latter faces no realistic alternative suppliers of the demanded service. Similarly, in cases where one contracting party threatens to suspend performance unless the other party agrees to a variation in the contract. Here, again, the latter may face a form of situational monopoly if the nature of the contract and the stage of performance is such that he cannot readily obtain an alternative supplier to complete the contract, (and is unlikely to obtain full compensation through a damages award. . . .

The extension of the doctrine of duress to any form of monopolistic threat would seem a promising and defensible line of development for the doctrine to take. Beyond rationalizing all the various classes of cases hitherto subsumed under the doctrine of duress, a doctrine so functionally defined has the advantage of posing a relatively realistic inquiry for the courts to embark upon. In cases of situational monopolies, the circumstances directly surrounding the particular transaction between the two parties in question will generally yield reliable inferences as to the extent of the monopoly power possessed by one in relation to the other. . . .

First, despite the monopoly that exists in these cases some of these transactions may be value maximizing; what has happened is that the monopolist has taken all or almost all the consumer surplus in rents (*e.g.*, in the salvage cases). Thus, these transactions may not be so much allocatively inefficient as distributively "unfair." What makes them distributively unfair cannot avoid a value judgment, although economic analysis might suggest some caution in intervention where excessive profits merely signal a transition to a new equilibrium or where excessively blunt intervention may eliminate incentives to supply the product or service in question. Second, in a number of the standard duress cases, the circumstances are more accurately characterized, economically, not as simple monopolies but as bilateral monopolies. For example, even in the salvage cases, depending on the circumstances, it may be the case that both the owners of the tug and the vessel in distress each possess abnormal market power in relation to the other. That is to say, the tug owner may be the only supplier of salvage services readily accessible to the distressed vessel, but in turn, the distressed vessel may be the only readily available demander of the tug's services.

What is not clear from the facts of *Atlas Express* is whether or not the plaintiffs knew that there was no alternative for the defendants. We are told that it would be difficult for the defendants to find another carrier, but we do not know whether they tried to find one or, had they been able to find one, the price at which the transportation would have been available. The analysis offered in the case does not enable us to answer the question of whether the £440 demanded by the plaintiffs was in fact a fair market price for the service provided. However, Tucker J finds that the plaintiffs knew of the importance of the defendants' contractual arrangements to supply their goods to a large chain store. It may be that he decided to focus not on the allocation of resources and value-maximizing behaviour but on the distributional consequences of the plaintiffs' behaviour. As Trebilcock points out, this involves a value judgment, and it is this which led Tucker J to find in favour of the defendants.

6. We could speculate whether the plaintiffs could have avoided the enforcement of the original unfavourable contract by raising the claim of 'snapping-up' analogous to the argument of the seller in *Hartog* v. *Colin and Shields* ([1939] 3 All ER 566), who escaped from a contract made when he mistakenly offered to sell hareskins at a price well below the normal market price (see Ch. 5). To succeed in such a claim, the plaintiffs would have had to admit that their calculation was flawed but that this mistake was known to the defendants. If this claim were successful, it would be apparent that there would be nothing untoward in the plaintiffs seeking to revert to the normal market price, since the original contract would be void *ab initio* for mistake and therefore unenforceable. On this analysis, Atlas Express would simply be seeking to charge what other carriers would have charged, and the defendants would be precluded from taking advantage of their known mistake by enforcing the original contract. Knowledge on the part of the defendants could be proved if there were evidence that Kafco had obtained a number of quotations for the work, and that Atlas's quotation was significantly and inexplicably out of line with quotations from their competitors. An analysis of this nature, which focuses on opportunistic behaviour at the outset by Kafco, lends a slightly different tenor to the assessment of Atlas's later attempt to revert to a normal market price (on the assumption that this was what Atlas Express later tried to charge).

7. In Chapter 8, we reviewed Unger's analysis of modern contract law in the guise of a corrective mechanism balancing between freedom of contract and contractual fairness. He has applied his approach to the law of duress.

R. Unger, *The Critical Legal Studies Movement* (Cambridge, Mass., Harvard University Press, 1983), 69–71

The counterprinciple of fairness reappears in the rules and doctrines that police the bargaining process itself. An agreement will be enforced only if it results from an indispensable minimum of free and considered decision by all parties concerned. The obvious attraction of this tactic is that it seems to dispense with the need to second-guess the equivalence of the performances. It therefore minimizes the market-subverting effects of interventionist correction. Besides, it merely extends into contract law the same quest for neutral process that characterizes the traditional liberal case for established institutions and the ruling methods of liberal political philosophy. Here as elsewhere this search runs into trouble. The heart of the trouble lies in what must be done to reconcile the idealized bargaining picture with the existing institutional forms of the market economy. The attempted reconciliation ends up requiring—however sporadically and indirectly—the very policing of contract terms that the emphasis on bargaining procedures is meant to avoid. No branch of contract law presents these themes more clearly than the law of duress.

The modern Anglo-American doctrine of duress tends to cross each of the three frontiers that surround its traditional territory. It has developed on the border between aberrational and structural inequality—the case of the drowning man and the case of the poor one—in a way that casts doubt upon the very distinction between the two. It has shown a greater willingness to impose a standard of good faith upon the exercise of formal rights. It has demonstrated a more or less explicit concern with the rough equivalence of the performances, though it often treats the gross failure of equivalence as a mere trigger for stricter scrutiny of the bargaining process.

The most characteristic result of this multiple expansion has been the doctrine of economic duress with its key concept of equal bargaining power. According to this doctrine, a contract may be voidable for economic duress whenever a significant inequality of bargaining power exists between the parties. Gross inequalities of bargaining power, however, are all too common in the current forms of market economy, a fact shown not only by the dealings between individual consumers and large corporate enterprises, but also by the huge disparities of scale and market influence among enterprises themselves. Thus, the doctrine of economic duress must serve as a roving commission to correct the most egregious and overt forms of an omnipresent type of disparity. But the unproven assumption of the doctrine is that the amount of corrective intervention needed to keep a contractual regime from becoming a power order will not be so great that it destroys the vitality of decentralized decision making through contract. If this assumption proved false, no compromise between correction and abstention could achieve its intended effect. The only solution would be the one that every such compromise is meant to avoid: the remaking of the institutional arrangements that define the market economy. The doctrinal manifestation of this problem is the vagueness of the concept of economic duress. The cost of preventing the revised duress doctrine from running wild and from correcting almost everything is to draw unstable, unjustified, and unjustifiable lines between the contracts that are voidable and those that are not. In the event, the law draws these lines by a strategy of studied indefinition, though it might just as well have done so—as it so often does elsewhere—through precise but makeshift distinctions.

Note

The superficial attraction of policing the bargaining process is that difficult judgments about the equivalence of what is exchanged by the two parties are thereby avoided. In practice, the doctrine of duress drifts into the substantive realm where it exhibits the potential to curb all instances of misuses of power. In reality, however, the courts tread a fine line between preventing unfairness and encouraging exchange. Consequently, the reality of duress doctrine is a compromise based on indeterminate distinctions between what is allowed and what is not. These are the type of distinctions displayed in the contrast between *Atlas Express* and *Williams* v. *Roffey*. When we examine the law of undue influence in the next section, we shall also see another good example of a corrective mechanism, this time restricted not through vague and indeterminate definitions but through 'precise but makeshift distinctions' (Unger) within a highly rule-bound structure.

III. UNDUE INFLUENCE

A. Introduction

The doctrine of undue influence developed, like many of the equitable doctrines of the law of contract, as a counterweight to a strict common law doctrine. In this case it was the doctrine of duress, which originally recognized only physical threats as grounds for avoiding a contract. The sphere of application of 'actual undue influence', under which the party seeking to avoid a contract must prove the exercise of some form of illegitimate pressure resulting in a transaction from which he now wishes to escape, covers much the same ground as the developing doctrine of economic duress. More difficult is defining the sphere of 'presumed undue influence', in which the dominated party is able to point to a relationship between herself and the dominator where it is more likely than in, for example, an arm's-length commercial relationship that the dominator might derive a particular advantage by placing pressure on the other party. This is the type of relationship where one party displays a particular vulnerability or where the other party has a particular responsibility (e.g. parent/child, solicitor/client, doctor/patient). The law has recently been clarified by the House of Lords to demonstrate that presumed undue influence can also arise in the context of relationships which one party can prove to have involved a tendency towards domination (e.g. relationships between spouses or cohabitees, whether heterosexual or gay). In both of these cases, it is not necessary for the victim to prove that undue influence actually occurred. The operation of this presumption is an important exception to the normal requirement that it is for the party seeking to escape from the contract to prove why it should not be enforced.

The first case in this section concerns an attempt by the House of Lords in 1986 to place the law of undue influence on a firmer doctrinal footing. The approach taken in *National Westminster Bank plc* v. *Morgan* was to resist some attempts by lower courts to develop a more generous approach to victims of alleged pressure who found themselves in relationships which could broadly be described as based on confidence or trust, such as banker and client. As we shall see later in the section, the case, while still good law, may require reconsideration in the light of the revised approach to undue influence taken by the House of Lords in *Barclays Bank plc* v. *O'Brien* ([1993] 4 All ER 417) and *CIBC Mortgages plc* v. *Pitt* ([1993] 4 All ER 433).

B. *Morgan* and Subsequent Developments

National Westminster Bank plc v. *Morgan*
[1985] 1 All ER 821

Mr Morgan was a self-employed businessman of mixed fortunes. He held both his business and private bank accounts with the National Westminster Bank (the 'bank'). It appeared to him that his business fortunes were improving, but unfortunately the Abbey National Building Society, which had a mortgage over his home, was beginning proceedings for possession of the house due to non-payment of the mortgage. Mr Morgan and his wife, who jointly owned the home, were very concerned not to lose it, and thus approached the bank for help. The bank was prepared to help by paying off the mortgage to the building society, and taking as security for themselves an unlimited charge over the property. By the time these arrangements were in place, the building society had obtained a possession order.

Mr Barrow, the manager of the relevant branch of the bank, visited Mrs Morgan at her home to obtain her signature on the charge. Mrs Morgan made it clear to Mr Barrow that she had little confidence in her husband's business abilities and did not want the legal charge to secure any business liabilities. She was assured, erroneously, by Mr Barrow that the charge would cover only the money advanced by the bank on their home. Mrs Morgan did not obtain legal advice about the nature of the charge before she signed it.

Mr and Mrs Morgan fell into arrears with their repayments and the bank obtained an order for possession of the house. Mr Morgan then died, and at the time of his death there was no business indebtedness outstanding.

Mrs Morgan appealed, successfully, to the Court of Appeal against the possession order, claiming that she was persuaded to execute the charge because of undue influence on the part of the bank. The bank appealed to the House of Lords.

LORD SCARMAN . . . The bank appeals with the leave of the House. Two issues are said to arise: the first, the substantive issue, is whether the wife has established a case of undue influence; the second, said to be procedural, is whether, if she has, she ought properly to be granted equitable relief, and the nature of any such relief. The two issues are, in truth, no more than different aspects of one fundamental question: has the wife established a case for equitable relief? For there is no longer any suggestion that she has a remedy at law. Unless the transaction can be set aside on the ground of undue influence, it is unimpeachable. . . .

The trial judge set the scene for the critical interview by these findings of fact: husband and wife were looking for a rescue operation by the bank to save the home for themselves and their children; they were seeking from the bank only a breathing space of some five weeks; and the wife knew that there was no other way of saving the house.

Mr Barrow's visit to the house lasted 15 to 20 minutes. His conversation with the wife lasted only five minutes. The wife's concern was lest the document which she was being asked to sign might enable the husband to borrow from the bank for business purposes. She wanted the charge confined to paying off the Abbey National and to the provision of bridging finance for about five weeks. She told Mr Barrow that she had no confidence in her husband's business ability and did not want the mortgage to cover his business liabilities. Mr Barrow advised her that the cover was so limited. She expressed her gratitude to the bank for saving their home. The judge found that the bank was not seeking any advantage other than to provide on normal commercial terms but at extremely short notice the bridging finance necessary to secure their home. He rejected the suggestion that the wife had any misgivings on the basis that she would prefer the house to be sold. He accepted that it was never the intention of Mr Barrow that the charge should be used to secure any other liability of the husband.

The atmosphere in the home during Mr Barrow's visit was plainly tense. The husband was in and out of the room, 'hovering around'. The wife made it clear to Mr Barrow that she did not want him there. Mr Barrow did manage to discuss the more delicate matters when he was out of the room.

Such was the interview [ie the interview in which she signed the charge] in which it is said that Mr Barrow crossed the line which divides a normal business relationship from one of undue influence. I am bound to say that the facts appear to me to be a far cry from a relationship of undue influence or from a transaction in which an unfair advantage was obtained by one party over the other. The trial judge clearly so thought, for he stated his reasons for rejecting the wife's case with admirable brevity. He made abundantly clear his view that the relationship between Mr Barrow and the wife never went beyond that of a banker and customer, that the wife had made up her own mind that she was ready to give the charge, and that the one piece of advice (as to the legal effect of the charge) which Mr Barrow did give, though erroneous as to the terms of the charge, correctly represented his intention and that of the bank. The judge dealt with three points. First, he ruled on the submission by the bank that the transaction of loan secured on the property was not one of manifest disadvantage to the wife since it provided what to her was desperately important, namely the rescue of the house from the Abbey National. He was pressed, of course, with the contrast between the unlimited terms of the legal charge and the assurance (to which at all times the bank adhered) by Mr Barrow that the charge was limited to paying off the Abbey National and the bridging finance. He considered the balance to be between the 'enormous' advantage of preserving the home from the Abbey National and the 'essentially theoretical' disadvantage of the terms of the written charge, and accepted the submission that the transaction was not manifestly disadvantageous to the wife.

Second, he rejected the submission made on behalf of the wife that Mr Barrow put pressure on her. In his view the pressure on her was the knowledge that Abbey National were on the point of obtaining possession with a view to the sale of her home. It was, however, suggested that Mr Barrow had made a mistake in the advice which he gave her as to the nature of the charge. Mr Barrow's mistake was not as to the bank's intentions but as to the wording of the charge. He accurately stated the bank's intention and events have proved him right. I would add in passing that no case of misrepresentation by Mr Barrow was sought to be developed at the trial and the case of negligence is not pursued.

The judge recognised that Mr Barrow did not advise her to take legal advice; but he held that the circumstances did not call for any such advice and that she was not harried into signing. She was signing to save her house and to obtain short-term bridging finance. 'The decision,' the judge said, 'was her own.'

Third, he rejected the submission that there was a confidential relationship between the wife and the bank such as to give rise to a presumption of undue influence. Had the relationship been such as to give rise to the presumption, he would have held, as counsel for the bank conceded, that no evidence had been called to rebut it. He concluded that the wife had failed to make out her case of undue influence.

The Court of Appeal disagreed. The two Lords Justices who constituted the court (Dunn and Slade LJJ). . . . put an interpretation of the facts very different from that of the judge; they also differed from him on the law.

As to the facts, I am far from being persuaded that the trial judge fell into error when he concluded that the relationship between the bank and the wife never went beyond the normal business relationship of banker and customer.

Both Dunn and Slade LJJ saw the relationship between the bank and the wife as one of confidence in which she was relying on the bank manager's advice. Each recognised the personal honesty, integrity, and good faith of Mr Barrow. Each took the view that the confidentiality of the relationship was such as to impose on him a 'fiduciary duty of care'. It was his duty, in their view, to ensure that the wife had the opportunity to make an independent and informed decision; but he failed to give her any such opportunity. They, therefore, concluded that it was a case for the presumption of undue influence.

My Lords, I believe that Dunn and Slade LJJ were led into a misinterpretation of the facts by their use, as is all too frequent in this branch of the law, of words and phrases such as 'confidence', 'confidentiality', 'fiduciary duty'. There are plenty of confidential relationships which do not give rise to the presumption of undue influence (a notable example is that of husband and wife: see *Bank of Montreal* v. *Stuart* [1911] AC 120); and there are plenty of non-confidential relationships in which one person relies on the advice of another, e.g. many contracts for the sale of goods. Nor am I persuaded that the charge, limited as it was by Mr Barrow's declaration to desiring the loan to pay off the Abbey National debt and interest during the bridging period, was disadvantageous to the wife. It meant for her the rescue of her home on the terms sought by her: a short-term loan at a commercial rate of interest. The Court of Appeal has not, therefore, persuaded me that the judge's understanding of the facts was incorrect.

But, further, the view of the law expressed by the Court of Appeal was, as I shall endeavour to show, mistaken. Dunn LJ, while accepting that in all the reported cases to which the court was referred the transactions were disadvantageous to the person influenced, took the view that in cases where public policy requires the court to apply the presumption of undue influence there is no need to prove a disadvantageous transaction (see [1983] 3 All ER 85 at 90). Slade LJ also clearly held that it was not necessary to prove a disadvantageous transaction where the relationship of influence was proved to exist. Basing himself on the judgment of Cotton LJ in *Allcard* v *Skinner* (1887) 36 Ch D 145 at 171 he said ([1983] 3 All ER 85 at 92):

'Where a transaction has been entered into between two parties who stand in the relevant relationship to one another, it is still possible that the relationship and influence arising therefrom has been abused, even though the transaction is, on the face of it, one which, in commercial terms, provides reasonably equal benefits for both parties.'

I can find no support for this view of the law other than the passage in Cotton LJ's judgment in *Allcard* v. *Skinner* to which Slade LJ referred. The passage is as follows:

'The question is—Does the case fall within the principles laid down by the decisions of the Court of Chancery in setting aside voluntary gifts executed by parties who at the time were under such influence as, in the opinion of the Court, enabled the donor afterwards to set the gift aside? These decisions may be divided into two classes—First, where the Court has been satisfied that the gift was the result of influence expressly used by the donee for the purpose; second, where the relations between the donor and donee have at or shortly before the execution of the gift been such as to raise a presumption that the donee had influence over the donor. In such a case the Court sets aside the voluntary gift, unless it is proved that in fact the gift was the spontaneous act of the donor acting under circumstances which enabled him to exercise an independent will and which justifies the Court in holding that the gift was the result of a free exercise of the donor's will. The first class of cases may be considered as depending on the principle that no one shall be allowed to retain any benefit arising from his own fraud or wrongful act. In the second class of cases the Court interferes, not on the ground that any wrongful act has in fact been committed by the donee, but on the ground of public policy, and to prevent the relations which existed between the parties and the influence arising therefrom being abused.'

The transactions in question in *Allcard* v. *Skinner* were gifts; it is not to be supposed that Cotton LJ was excluding the applicability of his observations to other transactions in which disadvantage or sacrifice is accepted by the party influence. It is significant for the proper understanding of his judgment that gifts are transactions in which the donor by parting with his property accepts a disadvantage or a sacrifice, and that in *Allcard* v. *Skinner* the donor parted with almost all her property. I do not, therefore, understand Cotton LJ, when he accepted that Miss Allcard's case fell into the class where undue influence was to be presumed, to have treated as irrelevant the fact that her transaction was manifestly disadvantageous to her merely because he was concerned in the passage quoted to stress the importance of the relationship. If, however, as Slade LJ clearly thought, Cotton LJ in the last sentence quoted should be understood as laying down that the transaction need not be one of disadvantage and that the presumption of undue influence can arise in respect of a transaction which provides 'reasonably equal benefits for both parties', I have with great respect to say that in my opinion Cotton LJ would have erred in law; principle and authority are against any such proposition. . . .

. . . Whatever the legal character of the transaction, the authorities show that it must constitute a disadvantage sufficiently serious to require evidence to rebut the presumption that in the circumstances of the relationship between the parties it was procured by the exercise of undue influence. In my judgment, therefore, the Court of Appeal erred in law in holding that the presumption of undue influence can arise from the evidence of the relationship of the parties without also evidence that the transaction itself was wrongful in that it constituted an advantage taken of the person subjected to the influence which, failing proof to the contrary, was explicable only on the basis that undue influence had been exercised to procure it.

The principle justifying the court in setting aside a transaction for undue influence can now be seen to have been established by Lindley LJ in *Allcard* v. *Skinner*. It is not a vague 'public policy' but specifically the victimisation of one party by the other. It was stated by Lindley LJ in a famous passage (36 Ch D 145 at 182–183):

'The principle must be examined. What then is the principle? It is that it is right and expedient to save persons from the consequences of their own folly? or is it that it is right and expedient to save them from being victimised by other people? In my opinion the doctrine of undue influence is founded on the second of these two principles. Courts of Equity have never set aside gifts on the ground of the folly, imprudence, or want of foresight on the part of donors. The Courts have always repudiated any such jurisdiction. *Huguenin* v *Baseley* ((1807) 14 Ves 273) is itself a clear authority to this effect. It would obviously be to encourage folly, recklessness, extravagance and vice if persons could get back property which they foolishly made away with, whether by giving it to charitable institutions or by bestowing it on less worthy objects. On the other hand, to protect people from being forced, tricked or misled in any way by others into parting with their property is one of the most legitimate objects of all laws; and the equitable doctrine of undue influence has grown out of and been developed by the necessity of grappling with insidious forms of spiritual tyranny and with the infinite varieties of fraud.'

When Lindley LJ came to state the circumstances which give rise to the presumption, he put it thus (36 Ch D 145 at 183):

'As no Court has ever attempted to define fraud so no Court has ever attempted to define undue influence, which includes one of its many varieties. The undue influence which Courts of equity endeavour to defeat is the undue influence of one person over another; not the influence of enthusiasm on the enthusiast who is carried away by it, unless indeed such enthusiasm is itself the result of external undue influence . . . .

The wrongfulness of the transaction must, therefore, be shown: it must be one in which an unfair advantage has been taken of another. The doctrine is not limited to transactions of gift. A commercial relationship can become a relationship in which one party assumes a role of dominating influence over the other. . . . Similarly, a relationship of banker and customer may become one in which the banker acquires a dominating influence. If he does and a manifestly disadvantageous transaction is proved, there would then be room for the court to presume that it resulted from the exercise of undue influence.

This brings me to *Lloyds Bank Ltd* v. *Bundy* [1975] QB 326. It was, as one would expect, conceded by counsel for the wife that the relationship between banker and customer is not one which ordinarily gives rise to a presumption of undue influence; and that in the ordinary course of banking business a banker can explain the nature of the proposed transaction without laying himself open to a charge of undue influence. This proposition has never been in doubt, though some, it would appear, have thought that the Court of Appeal held otherwise in *Lloyds Bank Ltd* v. *Bundy*. If any such view has gained currency, let it be destroyed now once and for all time. . . . The question which the House does have to answer is: did the court in *Lloyds Bank Ltd* v. *Bundy* accurately state the law?

Lord Denning MR believed that the doctrine of undue influence could be subsumed under a general principle that English courts will grant relief where there has been 'inequality of bargaining power'. He deliberately avoided reference to the will of one party being dominated or overcome by another. The majority of the court did not follow him; they based their decision on the orthodox view of the doctrine as expounded in *Allcard* v. *Skinner*. This opinion of Lord Denning MR, therefore, was not the ground of the court's decision, which has to be found in the view of the majority, for whom Sir Eric Sachs delivered the leading judgment.

Nor has counsel for the wife sought to rely on Lord Denning MR's general principle; and, in my view, he was right not to do so. The doctrine of undue influence has been sufficiently developed not to need the support of a principle which by its formulation in the language of the law of contract is not appropriate to cover transactions of gift where there is no bargain. The fact of an unequal bargain will, of course, be a relevant feature in some cases of undue influence. But it can never become an appropriate basis of principle of an equitable doctrine which is concerned with transactions 'not to be reasonably accounted for on the ground of friendship, relationship, charity, or other ordinary motives on which ordinary men act . . .' (see *Allcard* v. *Skinner* 36 Ch D 145 at 185 Lindley LJ). And even in the field of contract I question whether there is any need in the modern law to erect a general principle of relief against inequality of bargaining power. Parliament has undertaken the task (and it is essentially a legislative task) of enacting such restrictions on freedom of contract as are in its judgment necessary to relieve against the mischief: for example, the hire-purchase and consumer protection legislation, of which the Supply of Goods (Implied Terms) Act 1973, the Consumer Credit Act 1974, the Consumer Safety Act 1978, the Supply of Goods and Services Act 1982 and the Insurance Companies Act 1982 are examples. I doubt whether the courts should assume the burden of formulating further restrictions.

I turn, therefore, to consider the ratio decidendi of Sir Eric Sachs's judgment.

In so far as Sir Eric appears to have accepted the 'public policy' principle formulated by Cotton LJ in *Allcard* v. *Skinner*, I think for the reasons which I have already developed that he fell into error if he is to be understood as also saying that it matters not whether the transaction itself was wrongful . . . . But in the last paragraph of his judgment where Sir Eric turned to consider the nature of the relationship necessary to give rise to the presumption of undue influence in the context of a banking transaction, he got it absolutely right. He said [1975] QB 326 at 347):

'There remains to mention that counsel for the bank, whilst conceding that the relevant special relationship could arise as between banker and customer, urged in somewhat doom-laden terms that a decision taken against the bank on the facts of this particular case would seriously affect banking practice. With all respect to that submission, it seems necessary to point out that nothing in this judgment affects the duties of a bank in the normal case where it obtains a guarantee, and in accordance with standard practice explains to the person about to sign its legal effect and the sums involved. When, however, a bank, as in the present case, goes further and advises on more general matters germane to the wisdom of the transaction, that indicate that it may—not necessarily must—be crossing the line into the area of confidentiality so that the court may then have to examine all the facts including, of course, the history leading up to the transaction, to ascertain whether or not that line has, as here, been crossed. It would indeed be rather odd if a bank which vis-à-vis a customer attained a special relationship in some ways akin to that of a "man of affairs"—something which can be a matter of pride and enhance its local reputation—should not, where a conflict of interest has arisen as between itself and the person advised be under the resulting duty now under discussion. Once, as was inevitably conceded, it is possible for a bank to be under that duty, it is, as in the present case, simply a question for "meticulous examination" of the particular facts to see whether that duty has arisen. On the special facts here it did arise and it has been broken.'

This is good sense and good law . . . . the relationships which may develop a dominating influence of one over another are infinitely various. There is no substitute in this branch of the law for a 'meticulous examination of the facts'.

A meticulous examination of the facts of the present case reveals that Mr Barrow never 'crossed the line'. Nor was the transaction unfair to the wife. The bank was, therefore, under no duty to ensure that she had independent advice. It was an ordinary banking transaction whereby the wife sought to save her home; and she obtained an honest and truthful explanation of the bank's intention which, notwithstanding the terms of the mortgage deed which in the circumstances the trial judge was right to dismiss as 'essentially theoretical', was correct; for no one has suggested that Mr Barrow or the bank sought to make the wife liable, or to make her home the security, for any debt of her husband other than the loan and interest necessary to save the house from being taken away from them in discharge of their indebtedness to the building society.

For these reasons, I would allow the appeal. In doing so, I would wish to give a warning. There is no precisely defined law setting limits to the equitable jurisdiction of a court to relieve against undue influence. This is the world of doctrine, not of neat and tidy rules. The courts of equity have developed a body of learning enabling relief to be granted where the law has to treat the transaction as unimpeachable unless it can be held to have been procured by undue influence. It is the unimpeachability at law of a disadvantageous transaction which is the starting point from which the court advances to consider whether the transaction is the product merely of one's own folly or of the undue influence exercised by another. A court in the exercise of this equitable jurisdiction is a court of conscience. Definition is a poor instrument when used to determine whether a transaction is or is not unconscionable: this is a question which depends on the particular facts of the case.

Notes

1. The general approach of Lord Scarman's judgment could be described as formalist and rules-based. He denies a role for public policy in the interpretation and application of undue influence doctrines and provides no special treatment for married women or cohabitees. The tenor of the judgment is strongly against the use of 'inequality of bargaining power' as a general principle to guide the application of the vitiating factors such as duress and undue influence. The continuing influence of such a principle will be taken up again in the subsequent discussion of *Barclays Bank plc* v. *O'Brien* and in the discussion of the broader principle of unconscionability in Section IV.

2. Unfortunately, the approach taken by Lord Scarman did not fully clarify the scope of undue influence. In particular, while stressing the importance of the distinction between actual and presumed undue influence, the case does not explain exactly the contours of application of either these concepts or that of 'manifest disadvantage', such that since *Morgan* there has been considerable confusion about the scope of the law. It has been this which has led more recently to further House of Lords intervention in the form of *Barclays Bank* v. *O'Brien* and *CIBC Mortgages* v. *Pitt*. In the following notes we attempt to clarify the scope of *Morgan* and to identify what the position now is.

3. Lord Scarman's approval of the dictum of Cotton LJ in *Allcard* v. *Skinner* confirms that the analysis of undue influence is based on the distinction between actual and presumed undue influence, regardless of whether the transaction under scrutiny is a gift or a contract. One of the difficulties presented by *Morgan* is that Lord Scarman does not make it entirely clear whether the undue influence allegedly practised upon Mrs Morgan by the bank manager would have fallen into the 'actual' or the 'presumed' category. What is clear is that the banker/customer relationship is not one that normally falls into the presumed category; the old equity cases which determine the scope of this category conventionally treated this relationship as one of debtor/creditor. Lord Scarman's comments at the end of his judgment about Mr Barrow not 'crossing the line' appear to indicate that, had the bank manager conducted himself such as to generate a more 'confidential relationship' between himself and Mrs Morgan, the relationship could have been one benefiting from the presumption of undue influence. This, according to Lord Scarman, is the correct explanation for the decision of the Court of Appeal in *Lloyds Bank* v. *Bundy*, where the border into the 'special relationship' had been crossed because the father who gave the bank a guarantee in respect of his son's business debts, and used his home as security, placed himself, on the facts, entirely in the hands of the bank manager. This explanation of *Morgan* is clearly support-

able in the light of the subsequent subdivision of the category of presumed undue influence, confirmed by the House of Lords in *Barclays Bank* v. *O'Brien* ([1993] 4 All ER 417 at 423), into what are termed 'Class 2A' and 'Class 2B' instances of presumed undue influence. It will be apparent from the next extract that the allocation of relationships between spouses and cohabitees to Class 2B occurs in the context of a relatively sympathetic policy environment favouring wives who are put under pressure by husbands to allow charges over jointly owned matrimonial homes to cover the husband's business debts or to act as sureties for such debts, a factual situation which has arisen in a number of the recent cases, including *O'Brien* itself.

We quote here from Lord Browne-Wilkinson's consideration of these important social factors, and his use of policy considerations to shape the law of undue influence in a decisive way.

Barclays Bank plc v. *O'Brien*
[1993] 4 All ER 417 at 422–4

LORD BROWNE-WILKINSON

Policy considerations

The large number of cases of this type coming before the courts in recent years reflects the rapid changes in social attitudes and the distribution of wealth which have recently occurred. Wealth is now more widely spread. Moreover a high proportion of privately owned wealth is invested in the matrimonial home. Because of the recognition by society of the equality of the sexes, the majority of matrimonial homes are now in the joint names of both spouses. Therefore in order to raise finance for the business enterprises of one or other of the spouses, the jointly owned home has become a main source of security. The provision of such security requires the consent of both spouses.

In parallel with these financial developments, society's recognition of the equality of the sexes has led to a rejection of the concept that the wife is subservient to the husband in the management of the family's finances. A number of the authorities reflect an unwillingness in the court to perpetuate law based on this outmoded concept. Yet, as Scott LJ in the Court of Appeal rightly points out, although the concept of the ignorant wife leaving all financial decisions to the husband is outmoded, the practice does not yet coincide with the ideal (see [1992] 4 All ER 983 at 1008). In a substantial proportion of marriages it is still the husband who has the business experience and the wife is willing to follow his advice without bringing a truly independent mind and will to bear on financial decisions. The number of recent cases in this field shows that in practice many wives are still subjected to, and yield to, undue influence by their husbands. Such wives can reasonably look to the law for some protection when their husbands have abused the trust and confidence reposed in them.

On the other hand, it is important to keep a sense of balance in approaching these cases. It is easy to allow sympathy for the wife who is threatened with the loss of her home at the suit of a rich bank to obscure an important public interest, viz the need to ensure that the wealth currently tied up in the matrimonial home does not become economically sterile. If the rights secured to wives by the law renders vulnerable loans granted on the security of matrimonial homes, institutions will be unwilling to accept such security, thereby reducing the flow of loan capital to business enterprises. It is therefore essential that a law designed to protect the vulnerable does not render the matrimonial home unacceptable as security to financial institutions.

With these policy considerations in mind I turn to consider the existing state of the law. . . .

Undue influence

A person who has been induced to enter into a transaction by the undue influence of another (the wrongdoer) is entitled to set that transaction aside as against the wrongdoer. Such undue influence is either actual or presumed. In *Bank of Credit and Commerce International SA* v *Aboody* (1988) [1992] 4 All ER 955 at 964, . . . the Court of Appeal helpfully adopted the following classification.

Class 1: actual undue influence. In these cases it is necessary for the claimant to prove affirmatively that the wrongdoer exerted undue influence on the complainant to enter into the particular transaction which is impugned.

Class 2: presumed undue influence. In these cases the complainant only has to show, in the first instance, that there was a relationship of trust and confidence between the complainant and the wrongdoer of such a nature that it is fair to presume that the wrongdoer abused that relationship in procuring the complainant to enter into the impugned transaction. In class 2 cases therefore there is no need to produce evidence that actual undue influence was exerted in relation to the particular transaction impugned: once a confidential relationship has been proved, the burden then shifts to the wrongdoer to prove that the complainant entered into the impugned transaction freely, for example by showing that the complainant had independent advice. Such a confidential relationship can be established in two ways, viz:

Class 2A. Certain relationships (for example solicitor and client, medical advisor and patient) as a matter of law raise the presumption that undue influence has been exercised.

Class 2B. Even if there is no relationship falling within class 2A, if the complainant proves the de facto existence of a relationship under which the complainant generally reposed trust and confidence in the wrongdoer, the existence of such relationship raises the presumption of undue influence. In a class 2B case therefore, in the absence of evidence disproving undue influence, the complainant will succeed in setting aside the impugned transaction merely by proof that the complainant reposed trust and confidence in the wrongdoer without having to prove that the wrongdoer exerted actual undue influence or otherwise abused such trust and confidence in relation to the particular transaction impugned.

As to dispositions by a wife in favour of her husband, the law for long remained in an unsettled state. In the nineteenth century some judges took the view that the relationship was such that it fell into class 2A, i.e. as a matter of law undue influence by the husband over the wife was presumed. It was not until the decisions in *Howes* v. *Bishop* [1909] 2 KB 390 and *Bank of Montreal* v. *Stuart* [1911] AC 120 that it was finally determined that the relationship of husband and wife did not as a matter of law raise a presumption of undue influence within class 2A. . . .

An invalidating tendency?

Although there is no class 2A presumption of undue influence as between husband and wife, it should be emphasised that in any particular case a wife may well be able to demonstrate that de facto she did leave decisions on financial affairs to her husband thereby bringing herself within class 2B, i.e. that the relationship between husband and wife in the particular case was such that the wife reposed confidence and trust in her husband in relation to their financial affairs and therefore undue influence is to be presumed. Thus, in those cases which still occur where the wife relies in all financial matters on her husband and simply does what he suggests, a presumption of undue influence within class 2B can be established solely from the proof of such trust and confidence without proof of actual undue influence.

In the appeal in *CIBC Mortgages plc* v. *Pitt* [1993] 4 All ER 433 Mr Price QC for the wife argued that in the case of transactions between husband and wife there was an 'invalidating tendency', i.e. although there was no class 2A presumption of undue influence, the courts were more ready to find that a husband had exercised undue influence over his wife than in other cases. Scott LJ in the present case also referred to the law treating married women 'more tenderly' than others. This approach is based on dicta in early authorities. In *Grigby* v *Cox* (1750) 1 Ves Sen 517, 27 ER 1178 Lord Hardwicke LC, whilst rejecting any presumption of undue influence, said that a court of equity 'will have more jealousy' over dispositions by a wife to a husband. In *Yerkey* v *Jones* (1939) 63 CLR 649 at 675 Dixon J refers to this 'invalidating tendency'. He also refers (at 677) to the court recognising 'the opportunities which a wife's confidence in her husband gives him of unfairly or improperly procuring her to become surety'.

In my judgment this special tenderness of treatment afforded to wives by the courts is properly attributable to two factors. First, many cases may well fall into the class 2B category of undue influence because the wife demonstrates that she placed trust and confidence in her husband in relation to her financial affairs and therefore raises a presumption of undue influence. Second, the sexual and emotional ties between the parties provide a ready weapon for undue influence: a wife's true wishes can easily be overborne because of her fear of destroying or damaging the wider relationship between her and her husband if she opposes his wishes.

For myself, I accept that the risk of undue influence affecting a voluntary disposition by a wife in favour of a husband is greater than in the ordinary run of cases where no sexual or emotional ties affect the free exercise of the individual's will.

Applying this terminology, Mrs Morgan would have been closer to successfully establishing the presumption of undue influence if she had been able to prove a Class 2B relationship between her and the bank manager, on the facts. Another example of Class 2B undue influence, approved by the House of Lords in *O'Brien*, is *Avon Finance Co. Ltd.* v. *Bridger* ([1985] 2 All ER 281), where a son had procured the signature of his elderly parents on a document which pledged their retirement home as security for a loan to himself. It was out of this loan that he contributed to the purchase price of the house. He told the parents that the papers related to their own mortgage on the property and not to the loan which he had taken out, which was not supposed to be secured on the house. The transaction was set aside for undue influence since it was not possible for the son to rebut the presumption, given that the parents had not received independent legal advice.

4. Lord Browne-Wilkinson's approach is couched in terms of close emotional and sexual relationships. Tiplady's analysis of the presumption in the next extract is posed in wider terms, and explicitly includes commercial and professional relationships. It is certainly arguable that Lord Scarman's approach was quite unsympathetic to the claims of Mrs Morgan, for where a bank manager comes to a customer's house with the express purpose of procuring her signature on a document and assures her confidently of certain aspects of the transaction, there is a strong case for treating such a relationship as generating an enhanced right to protection for the party alleging that undue influence was exercised. Tiplady explains why this might be so.

D. Tiplady, 'The Limits of Undue Influence'
(1985) 48 *MLR* 579 at 580–1

The constant feature of those relationships which attract the doctrine of undue influence is that, no matter how divergent the facts, in each, one party is given to believe that he can rely upon another for disinterested advice and guidance, and that, ultimately, the position, well-being and welfare of the party under this belief will be placed foremost. It is a relationship in which the dominant party can be expected to display altruism, a relationship of "candour and protection"; of "care and providence." Typically, therefore, although the relevant nexus may often be professional, it will transcend the merely commercial. A commercial relationship can, however, pass into this higher plane, either in general, or at specific points. This will happen if it is established that one party has not been asked merely for advice or guidance, but has in effect agreed to step over to the other's side, to see things from his point of view, and, in short, decide the crucial matter for him. One would not however, normally expect a business-man to assume this degree of reliance.

Since the House of Lords decision in *O'Brien*, the onus now falls on the bank in such situations to ensure that the wife is advised to take independent legal advice on the implications of the charge she is being asked to sign.

5. Mrs Morgan's most serious difficulty was that she was unable to demonstrate that the transaction was 'manifestly disadvantageous' or 'unfair' to her. This, according to Lord Scarman, is a threshold require-ment, without which the presumption of undue influence cannot arise. The requirement of manifest disadvantage was taken one step further by the Court of Appeal in *Bank of Credit and Commerce International* v. *Aboody* ([1992] 4 All ER 955), which held that it was also a necessary ele-ment of a successful plea of *actual undue influence.* This part of *Aboody* has now been overruled by the House of Lords in *CIBC Mortgages* v. *Pitt*, on the grounds that undue influence is a species of fraud. According to Lord Browne-Wilkinson ([1993] 4 All ER 433 at 439):

Like any other victim of fraud, a person who has been induced by actual undue influence to carry out a transaction which he did not freely and knowingly enter into is entitled to have that transaction set aside as of right . . . A man guilty of fraud is no more entitled to argue that the transaction was beneficial to the per-son defrauded than is a man who has procured a transaction by misrepresenta-tion. The effect of the wrongdoer's conduct is to prevent the wronged party from bringing a free will and properly informed mind to bear on the proposed transaction which accordingly must be set aside in equity as a matter of justice.

This approach accords with that suggested by Cartwright (*Inequality of Bargaining Power* (Oxford, Clarendon Press, 1991), 177), who pointed out that in the context of the other vitiating factors such as duress, fraud, and misrepresentation all that need be proved are the basic elements of the claim and a causal link between the threat, the lies, or the misinformation and the conclusion of the contract.

6. Certain aspects of Lord Browne-Wilkinson's judgment in *Pitt* invite fur-ther attacks upon the 'manifest disadvantage' criterion in presumed undue influence, as he suggests that 'the exact limits of the decision in *Morgan*

may have to be considered in the future' ([1993] 4 All ER 433 at 439). There are a number of reasons why the manifest disadvantage criterion may be abandoned, either because it is illogical, unworkable, or unfair.

7. First and foremost, it is illogical to apply the criterion to one type of undue influence and not to both. Since the presumption of undue influence is simply a shifting of the burden of proof which relieves the victim of the burden of proving any form of victimization, it is not clear why a criterion relating to the nature of the transaction rather than the relationship between the parties should apply in one case and not the other. If it is dismissed as alien to the concept of fraud in the context of actual undue influence, then it must be equally out of place in the context presumed undue influence (i.e. presumed fraud). In practice, the law at present may allow recovery more readily by a plaintiff who can prove actual undue influence than by one who would normally benefit from the presumption except that she must demonstrate that she has been manifestly disadvantaged. This must surely not be the intention of those who acknowledge an invalidating tendency in favour of plaintiffs such as the wife who is about to lose her home because of her husband's business failures.

8. Second, it is possible to prove extreme uncertainty in relation to the actual operation of the manifest disadvantage criterion. It might seem relatively unproblematic for Lord Scarman to conclude that Mrs Morgan had not been disadvantaged, as she had saved her house from the Abbey National in 1978 and was not encumbered with additional business debts when the possession proceedings were taken by the bank. However, looking at the different bases for determining the point in time at which manifest disadvantage is to be ascertained reveals its indeterminacy as a criterion of recovery. Three possible bases can be identified:

(i) Was the transaction one which, when it was entered into, appeared in all the circumstances to be disadvantageous? In Mrs Morgan's case this was clearly not so, since the transaction was one which secured her home—the consequence she desperately wished to achieve. The fact that it could have resulted in her being encumbered with other debts is more difficult. It is likely that, had the nature of the transaction been explained to her and had she consequently insisted that she and her husband look elsewhere for financing, she would have discovered that every sensible lending institution would have required an unlimited charge, given Mr Morgan's borrowing record and given that his only means of support and of repaying the loan was through self-employment for which he required overdraft facilities. Consequently, even though Mrs Morgan potentially faced the encumbrance of business debts, it is not absolutely clear whether, looked at from this perspective, it would have been manifestly to her disadvantage.

(ii) Looked at from the perspective of the worst-case scenario shortly after the transaction was entered into, was the possibility that business debts might in future be secured on the house manifestly disadvantageous to Mrs Morgan? This perspective would permit the court to assess whether Mrs Morgan could have escaped from the transaction had she discovered, before any business debts were run up, exactly what the nature of the charge was. However, given what was said above about the advantages which Mrs Morgan did derive and her chances of obtaining finance elsewhere on better terms for herself, it seems that even from this perspective manifest disadvantage is not clear.

(iii) The third approach is to look at the transaction with the benefit of hindsight. Assessed at the time when the claim of undue influence was raised, had the transaction proved to be manifestly disadvantageous? The answer in Mrs Morgan's case was, of course, 'no', but the answer might have been different if business debts had accumulated. Again, what was said above about the balance of advantage and disadvantage in the transaction does not necessarily indicate that she would have satisfied the requirements laid down by the House of Lords even if she had been saddled with her husband's business debts.

The normal practice of the courts is to assess the terms of a contract at the time when it is made (see Ch. 11 and the discussion of the Unfair Contract Terms Act 1977). The tradition of classical contract law of presentiation (see Ch. 2) excludes the subsequent actual or potential effects of a term or of a contract as a whole from consideration, creating the fiction that the contract as it was concluded between the parties was a perfect rendering of their intentions for ever more. Yet the difficulty with approach (i) is that it does appear less generous to the victim of presumed undue influence than to the victims of other defects in the formation process.

A rather more generous assessment of manifest disadvantage is made by the Court of Appeal in *Cheese* v. *Thomas* ([1994] 1 All ER 35). The plaintiff had purchased a house with his great-nephew, the defendant. The plaintiff had put his total accrued capital of some £43,000 into the house and his nephew had taken out a mortgage for £40,000. This arrangement enabled the plaintiff to move back to Hayes, where he wished to live but could not afford to do so. He got exactly what he expected from the transaction at the time it was made, which was a house to live in, in an area he wished to live in. However, the Court of Appeal later held the transaction to be one of manifest disadvantage for the plaintiff on three grounds; first, the plaintiff had parted with all his capital; second, if the plaintiff wanted to live elsewhere he could not compel the defendant to repay his capital or sell the house, as it was in the defendant's name; and third, the plaintiff would be in difficulty if the defendant did not keep up the mortgage payments. Yet if the time for the assessment of manifest disadvantage is in fact as described in points (i) or (ii) above, it is hard to see how the plaintiff here was in a worse position than Mrs Morgan. For a further discussion of remedies for undue influence, see note 3 to *Barclays Bank* v. *O'Brien* below.

9. One aspect of the law on which *Morgan* offers little clarification is what is *undue* influence. However, Lord Scarman does indicate that the basis of the doctrine is not 'vague public policy' but 'actual victimization' of one party by the other. More guidance is offered on the meaning of undue influence by the Court of Appeal in *Barclays Bank* v. *O'Brien*. In the case of presumed undue influence, it is for the alleged dominator to prove that there as no victimization and, as Tiplady comments ('The Limits of Undue Influence', 581): 'the presumption that a dominant party used his influence improperly will often be decisive, since the typical undue influence case is one in which that dominance is of so subtle and insidious a kind that it is impossible to prove it was not in fact at work.

It is perhaps useful to recapitulate the principles of undue influence in terms of a flow-chart (Fig. 6) and to conclude the discussion of *Morgan* with some comments upon the detailed schema.

The schema in Fig. 6 confirms that English law approaches the problems of victimization in the context of the bargaining process by using a rule-based framework. Setting these hurdles which the claimant must surmount not only is relatively ungenerous to the victim but also emphasizes that English law does not use a generalized standard of unfairness or unconscionability which the judges could apply at their discretion in the light of the circumstances of each particular case. This is the approach taken in the United States under §2–203 of the Uniform Commercial Code, which will be discussed in Section IV. This applies *in addition* to the conventional common law and equitable remedies also recognized in English law. The argument against such an approach is always that it offers flexibility only at the expense of certainty; however, it is arguable that not only is the framework outlined above sufficiently complex but it is also still sufficiently unclear, notwithstanding the recent House of Lords case law, for a charge of uncertainty to be sustainable.

C. Undue Influence and Third Parties

The type of factual situation which arose in *Morgan*, where the alleged wrongdoer was the bank's employee, is relatively rare. The general run of cases are those in which it is the husband who exercises the influence, but the key legal question is whether or not the bank which has taken the charge can enforce it *vis-à-vis* the wife who alleges undue influence. The situation is not entirely unlike those discussed in cases such as *Lewis* v.

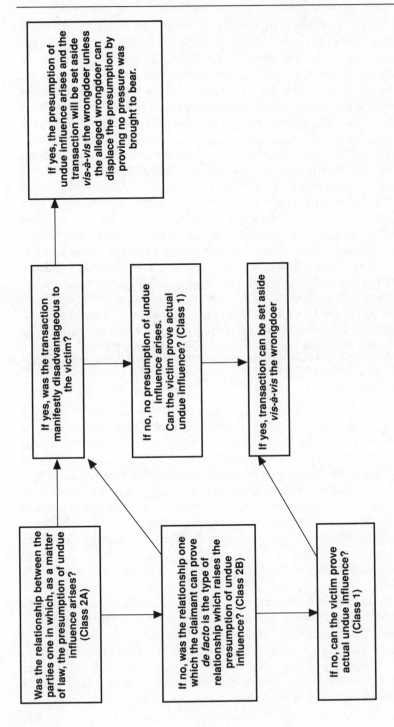

Fig. 6   Undue Influence

Averay ([1971] 3 All ER 907; see Ch. 5) where the court must choose between an innocent party who has been defrauded out of his goods and an innocent party who has bought the stolen goods. The court resolves the choice by determining whether or not the contract between the innocent seller and the rogue is void for mistake or voidable for misrepresentation, thus allowing the rogue, in the latter situation, to pass good, albeit voidable, title to the third party. Here the key question is whether the bank is affected in some way by wrongdoing of the husband; this is the situation which arose in *Barclays Bank* v. *O'Brien*, albeit that the alleged wrongdoing in that case involved a misrepresentation, not undue influence. In fact the same principles apply, and the House of Lords made it clear in their resolution of the case that the policy context was the same—namely one of sympathetic treatment of the wife in the face of the bureaucratic organization of the bank. The Court of Appeal and the House of Lords reached the same result in *O'Brien* and also shared a similar policy approach to the question of the protection of married women, although Lord Browne-Wilkinson explicitly extended his approach to cover *all* cohabitees. The principal difference between the two decisions lies in the technical approach to the legal position of the bank. Here we extract *in extenso* the Court of Appeal judgment, for it contains an interesting discussion of the position of women under the law, a point taken up in the notes which follow.

Barclays Bank plc v. *O'Brien*
[1992] 4 All ER 983

SCOTT LJ . . . This appeal . . . raises yet again a problem that has been before the Court of Appeal on a number of occasions over the past ten years or so. The problem arises where a debtor is required by a creditor to provide security for his indebtedness; the debtor and creditor agree that the security will be provided by some third party; the relationship between the debtor and the third party, typically husband and wife, makes it likely that the third party's assistance will be forthcoming; the debtor procures the third party's consent by some material misrepresentation or by exerting undue pressure or influence of some kind; the third party signs the necessary security documents without any independent advice and without any explanation from the creditor of the true effect of the documents; the third party subsequently, as a defence to the creditor's attempt to enforce the security documents, contends that he or she was induced to sign by the debtor's material misrepresentation, or did not properly understand the import of the documents, or that his or her consent was not a true consent having regard to influence or pressure exerted by the debtor. The question for the courts in these cases is whether the third party can escape from the effect of the documents that he or she has signed. In most cases the relationship between debtor and third party is that of husband and wife. In some, however, it is that of adult child and elderly parent. In none of the cases has the relationship between the debtor and the third party been such that, in law, undue influence is to be presumed until rebutted.

Some of the cases to which I have referred suggest that the answer to the problem depends on whether or not the debtor can be regarded as having been appointed by the creditor to act as agent of the creditor in procuring the consent of the third party to the proposed security transaction.

This approach has, to my mind, lent an air of unreality to some of the arguments addressed to the court. In a typical case in which a husband, seeking a bank advance for his business purposes, is told by his bank manager that security in the form of a charge over the jointly owned matrimonial home must be provided, it would astonish both the husband and the bank manager to be told that the husband had been appointed by the bank as its agent to obtain the wife's consent to the proposed charge. It may be that a court of equity will regard the bank as affected by equities arising out of the manner in which the husband persuades his wife to agree to the proposed transaction. And it may be that the extent to which the bank has left it to the husband to procure the wife's consent and to explain the transaction to her will be a critical feature of the case. But to describe the issue as one which depends on whether or not the bank must be taken to have appointed the husband as its agent to deal with the wife and to procure her consent serves, in my opinion, to mask the basis upon which in certain cases creditors have failed to enforce their security against the third parties and upon which in other cases they have succeeded.

I think it convenient in this judgment first to set out the salient facts of the case, as found by the judge, and then to consider the authorities from which must be extracted the principles of law and equity to be applied to the facts.

The facts

Mr and Mrs O'Brien were married in 1963. For the past 16 years or so their matrimonial home has been 151 Farnham Lane, Slough. They had purchased the property in December 1974 in their joint names with the aid of a building society mortgage. By 1987 the amount outstanding on the building society mortgage was £25,000 or thereabouts.

Mr O'Brien is a chartered accountant who, in 1987, was in practice as a sole practitioner. He had also an interest in a company, Heathrow Fabrications Ltd, and was the company's auditor. He was not a director. He was, however, negotiating with the other shareholders to take an increased stake in the company. . . .

The company had agreed an overdraft facility with the bank that by December 1986 had been raised to £40,000. The company frequently exceeded its agreed overdraft limit and, in December 1986, the debt balance on its account stood at about £57,000. . . .

In April 1987 discussions took place between Mr Tucker and Mr O'Brien in which Mr O'Brien was endeavouring to obtain an increase in the overdraft facilities available to the company. Mr Tucker [manager of the bank] agreed to allow an overdraft facility of £60,000 for one month. His note of 2 April 1987 records:

'I have agreed to mark an overdraft facility of £60,000 for one month, as O'Brien is presently in the course of remortgaging his house to raise the £60,000. If there is any problem with this (wife may be the problem) his son has already raised £40,000 which if necessary will be in substitution of the £60,000.'

This note shows that Mr O'Brien was offering the house as security but that the bank was aware that Mrs O'Brien might not agree to the proposal.

The agreed £60,000 overdraft was utilised by the company but the additional security was not forthcoming. . . .

In this state of affairs an important meeting took place between Mr Tucker and Mr O'Brien on 22 June 1987. Mr O'Brien wanted an increased overdraft facility for the company. Mr Tucker wanted additional security. It was eventually agreed that the company would be allowed an overdraft facility of £135,000, reducing to £120,000 after three weeks. As security it was agreed that Mr O'Brien would guarantee the payment by the company of its indebtedness and that his liability under the guarantee would be secured by a second charge over the house, which was believed to have an equity of about £100,000. . . .

Mr Tucker gave instructions for the necessary security documents to be prepared. These included a guarantee to be signed by Mr O'Brien and a legal charge of the house to be signed by both Mr and Mrs O'Brien. When the documents were ready, Mr Tucker sent them to the Burnham branch (Burnham was a sub-branch of Slough) to await signature by Mr and Mrs O'Brien. Together with the documents he sent an important memorandum to the Burnham sub-branch. The memorandum said:

're: Mr and Mrs N E O'Brien 2nd Charge
    151 Farnham Lane, Slough, Berkshire
Our above named customers will be calling at your sub branch Burnham on Wednesday 1st July 1987 to sign the enclosed documentation. We would be obliged if you could witness our customers' signatures where appropriate and ensure that they are fully aware of the documentation signed. The second charge over the property is to be held in support of Mr O'Brien's balance of account guarantee liability to Heathrow Fabrications Limited who bank with us. The company is currently afforded an overdraft facility of £107,000, and we are in the process of agreeing to increase this facility in the near future to £135,000. Thus our customers should be advised of the current level of facilities granted and that soon the maximum facilities to be granted to the company will be £135,000 and we will be looking to the guarantee for this sum which in turn is supported by the charge over the above property. Please ensure that our customers are fully aware of the nature of the documentation

to be signed and advise that if they are in any doubt they should contact their solicitors before signing.

Enclosed are the following forms which should be completed as follows:—

Original

To be signed by Mr O'Brien and witnessed by yourselves, Mr & Mrs O'Brien to acknowledge receipt of copies at foot of page.

with side letter on reverse

Side letter to be signed to ensure that there is no doubt that charge is to be in support of the guarantee liability. Mr & Mrs O'Brien to sign at foot and across join at top.

copies

Copy guarantees for customers' records.' . . .

Mr O'Brien brought his wife to the sub-branch. The documents, already signed by Mr O'Brien, were produced by the same clerk. . . . The clerk failed to follow Mr Tucker's instructions. Mrs O'Brien signed the legal charge and the side-letter. The clerk witnessed her signature. No explanation of the documents or of their effect was given to Mrs O'Brien. She did not read the documents before signing.

The guarantee signed by Mr O'Brien was a guarantee, unlimited in amount, of the liabilities of the company to the bank. The legal charge, signed by both Mr and Mrs O'Brien, contained a charge of 151 Farnham Lane to secure the payment of any liabilities of Mr O'Brien to the bank. The guarantee and the legal charge were dated 3 July 1987. The side letter, also signed by both Mr and Mrs O'Brien, was not dated and reads as follows:

'We hereby agree acknowledge and confirm as follows:—(1) That we have each received from you a copy of the Guarantee dated 3rd July 1987 (a copy of which is attached hereto) under which Nicholas Edward O'Brien guarantees the payment and discharge of all monies and liabilities now or hereafter due owing or incurred by Heathrow Fabrications Limited to you. (2) That the liability of the said Nicholas Edward O'Brien to you pursuant to the said Guarantee is and will be secured by the Legal Charge dated 3rd July 1987 over the property described above made between (1) Nicholas Edward O'Brien (2) Nicholas Edward O'Brien and Bridget Mary O'Brien and (3) Barclays Bank PLC. (3) That you recommended that we should obtain independent legal advice before signing this letter.

Yours faithfully . . .'

A copy of the guarantee was not given to either Mr O'Brien or Mrs O'Brien. No one recommended to Mrs O'Brien that she should obtain legal advice. She did not read the side letter before signing it. She did, of course, have an opportunity of doing so. The judge found that—

'no steps were taken [by the clerk] to ensure that either of the defendants was aware of the nature or effect of the documents they were signing, and no suggestion was made to them that independent legal advice ought to be sought.'

On the strength of these security documents the bank allowed the company's overdraft, which was standing at about £107,000 when the documents were signed, to increase to £135,000. But the company's indebtedness continued to grow and soon exceeded the £135,000 figure. By October 1987 the indebtedness was over £154,000 and in November formal demand was served on Mr O'Brien calling for payment pursuant to the guarantee. . . .

Mr Tucker did not . . . . himself deal with Mrs O'Brien. She was not a customer of Barclays Bank. Her knowledge of the proposed legal charge, the reasons for it and the desirability of her signing it came exclusively from her husband. It is important, however, to notice that Mrs O'Brien does not fit the now rather outmoded pattern of the down-trodden, uneducated wife, subservient to her husband and his wishes and unable to understand financial matters or to take practical business-like decisions. Mrs O'Brien had, in her youth, passed GCE and secretarial examinations. She had worked as a secretary before, at the age of 19 years, marrying Mr O'Brien. In 1987 she was in her early 40s. Between 1980 and 1981 she had worked in Dunstable as an office manager. For some years Mr O'Brien worked in Saudi Arabia and, in his absence, Mrs O'Brien had to manage the household finances. On the evidence before the learned judge, Mrs O'Brien cannot in my opinion, be described as a lady in a particularly vulnerable position vis-à-vis her husband.

The circumstances in which Mrs O'Brien was persuaded by her husband to sign the legal charge are set out in some detail in the learned judge's judgment. Mrs O'Brien made, broadly, two complaints. First, she contended that her husband put her under undue pressure to sign and that she finally succumbed to the pressure. Second, she contended that her husband misrepresented to her the effect of the legal charge. She knew she was signing a mortgage of the matrimonial home but she believed, from what Mr O'Brien had told her, that the security was limited to £60,000 and would last only three weeks. . . .

[Scott LJ rejects at the beginning of his judgment any idea that the bank could have appointed Mr O'Brien its agent. Consequently there is no need for him to discuss the issue of Mr O'Brien's misrepresentation, as it did not bind the bank. He concentrated instead on a line of cases to show that equity is more generous to wives who guarantee their husband's debts than to others.]

The equitable principle applied in *Turnbull & Co* v. *Duva* [[1902] AC 429] and *Chaplin & Co Ltd* v. *Brammall* [[1908] 1 KB 233] seems to be that if a wife signs a security document at her debtor husband's request the creditor will be unable to enforce the security unless either the debtor or the creditor has taken positive steps to try and ensure that the wife understands the import of the security documents or unless she has obtained independent advice. The two cases contrast oddly with *Bainbrigge* v. *Brown* [(1881) 18 Ch. D. 188], where no such requirement was imposed on the father's mortgagees and, since there was no undue influence or misrepresentation by the debtor, cannot, in my opinion, be explained by treating the debtor as the creditor's agent. . . .

There is, to my mind, no doubt at all but that the *Turnbull* v. *Duval* line of cases demonstrate a treatment of wives who have given security to support their husband's debts more tender than that which would have been applied to other third party sureties. Under the general law a surety is expected to satisfy himself or herself of the extent of the risk proposed to be undertaken. Contracts of suretyship are not uberrimae fidei. Misrepresentation or undue influence for which the debtor is responsible will not, unless the creditor had knowledge of what had happened, or unless the creditor was, via agency or some like route, a party to what had happened, prejudice the enforceability by the creditor of the security given by the surety. . . . But this was not the approach where security had been given by wives in support of their husbands. In neither *Turnbull & Co* v. *Duval* nor *Chaplin & Co Ltd* v. *Brammall* was there misrepresentation or undue influence. But in each case the wife lacked a full understanding of the security transaction into which she had entered and had had no independent advice. The reason in both cases why the security given was unenforceable was that (a) the security was given by the wife of the debtor, (b) the creditor knew of the relationship, (c) the creditor had done nothing to ensure that the wife understood the transaction, (d) the wife did not properly understand the transaction and (e) she had had no independent advice. In those circumstances, equity did not permit the security to be enforced against the wife. . . .

In *Yerkey* v *Jones* (1939) 63 CLR 649 Dixon J expressed the opinion, supported by a carefully researched argument, that the tenderness to wives exhibited by the cases was attributable to two factors. First, although the Married Women's Property Acts had given wives power to dispose of their separate property, nonetheless the courts viewed with suspicion gratuitous transactions by wives for the benefit of their husbands. Dixon J observed (at 674):

'It seems that the assimilation of dispositions by a wife in favour of her husband to transactions between strangers was not so complete. It was not supposed that they dealt at arm's length.'

He then cited the passage from *Story's Equity Jurisprudence* and made the comment to which I have already referred. Secondly, there is the principle, espoused by Romilly MR in *Hoghton* v. *Hoghton* (1852) 15 Beav 278 at 298–299 that 'where one person obtains, by voluntary donation, a large pecuniary benefit from another, the person taking the benefit is bound to show that the donor knew and understood what he was doing' (see per Dixon J (at 679)). This wide principle was, as Dixon J shows, not accepted as sound law but nonetheless 'contributed to the . . . view that unless it appears that the wife clearly understood the effect of an instrument conferring a voluntary benefit on her husband it may be invalidated' (at 680). . . .

In *Kingsnorth Trust Ltd* v. *Bell* [1986] 1 All ER 423 a husband and wife agreed to charge their jointly owned matrimonial home to secure an advance made to the husband for the purposes of his business. The responsibility of procuring the execution of the charge by the wife was left to the husband. He misrepresented to her the purpose of the advance. She received no independent advice. The Court of Appeal held that in those circumstances the security could not be enforced against the wife. The leading judgment was given by Dillon LJ, who described as 'clear law' the proposition that—

'if a creditor, or potential creditor, of a husband desires to obtain, by way of security for the husband's indebtedness, a guarantee from his wife or a charge on property of his wife, and if the creditor entrusts to the husband himself the task of obtaining the execution of the relevant document by the wife, then the creditor can be in no better position than the husband himself, and the creditor cannot enforce the guarantee or the security against the wife if it is established that the execution of the document by the wife was procured by undue influence by the husband and the wife had no independent advice.'

(See [1986] 1 All ER 423 at 427.)

This statement of law is, I observe, entirely consistent with the approach suggested by Dixon J in *Yerkey* v. *Jones*. It is also to be observed that the proposition as stated by Dillon LJ would not be applicable in the law of suretyship generally and is an implicit recognition of the special protection given by equity to married women who provide security in support of their husbands' debts. . . . [After discussing a number of recent cases on undue influence, including *Bank of Baroda* v. *Shah* ([1988] 3 All ER 24) and *Bank of Credit and Commerce International SA* v. *Aboody* ([1992] 4 All ER 955), Scott LJ went on:]

These authorities seem to me to leave the developing law, if not at the crossroads, at least at the junction of two diverging roads. One road would treat the special protection previously provided by equity for married women who provide security for their husbands' debts as now of only historical interest. . . . Third party security taken by creditors would be impeachable on account of misrepresentation or undue influence by the debtor only if the creditor had knowledge of the relevant facts or if the debtor had been acting as the agent of the creditor. A true agency would be necessary, not a spurious finding of agency in order to enable apparent justice to be done in hard cases. The creditor would not be concerned with the question whether or not the surety had an adequate understanding of the transaction. The surety would have to look after himself or herself, as most sureties have always had to do. The foundations of this road would have been laid by . . . . *Bank of Baroda* v. *Shah* and *Bank of Credit and Commerce International SA* v. *Aboody*.

Travellers along the other road would recognise that, for the historical reasons identified by Dixon J in *Yerkey* v. *Jones,* equity has in the past treated married women differently and more tenderly than other third parties who provide security for the debts of others. They would notice that *Avon Finance Co Ltd* v. *Bridger* had added to the protected class a case in which vulnerable elderly parents had agreed to provide security for the debts of their adult son. And they would, I think, conclude that, if a protected class is to continue to be recognised, the class ought, logically, to include all cases in which the relationship between the surety and the debtor is one in which influence by the debtor over the surety and reliance by the surety on the debtor are natural and probable features of the relationship. In cases falling within this protected class, security given by the surety would, in certain circumstances, be unenforceable notwithstanding that the creditor might have had no knowledge of and not have been responsible for the vitiating feature of the transaction. *Turnbull & Co* v. *Duval, Chaplin & Co Ltd* v. *Brammall, Avon Finance Co Ltd* v. *Bridger, Kingsnorth Trust Ltd* v. *Bell* . . . all, in my opinion, provide support for this road.

In cases falling within this protected class, equity would hold the security given by the surety to be unenforceable by the creditor if: (i) the relationship between the debtor and the surety and the consequent likelihood of influence and reliance was known to the creditor; and (ii) the surety's consent to the transaction was procured by undue influence or material misrepresentation on the part of the debtor or the surety lacked an adequate understanding of the nature and effect of the transaction; and (iii) the creditor, whether by leaving it to the debtor to deal with the surety or otherwise, had failed to take reasonable steps to try and ensure that the surety entered into the transaction with an adequate understanding of the nature and effect of the transaction and that the surety's consent to the transaction was a true and informed one.

These requirements emerge, in my opinion, from the authorities to which I have referred.

The choice between the two roads cannot, in my opinion, be made simply by reference to binding authority. Binding authority can be found to justify either. The choice should, I think, be a matter of policy. Ought the law to treat married women who provide security for their husband's debts, and others in an analogous position, as requiring special protection? The position of married women today, both generally and vis-à-vis their husbands, is very different from what it was when the equitable principles underlying [the cases] were being formulated. It is arguable that married women no longer need the protection afforded to them by cases like these. Many women, it is true, do not. But the tendency in households for business decisions to be left to the husband and for the wife, whether or not she is a joint owner of the matrimonial home and whether or not she has a separate job, to have the main domestic responsibilities still persists. And, in the culturally and ethnically mixed community in which we live, the degree of emancipation of women is uneven.

The likelihood of influence by a husband over his wife and of reliance by a wife on her husband to make the business decisions for the family was the justification in the first place for the tenderness of equity towards married women who gave their property as security for their husband's debts. In my opinion, that justification is still present. I, for my part, would take the second of the two roads. . . . None of the modern cases has . . . explicitly stated that married women who provide security for their husband's debts are in no different position from other sureties. . . .

Each case within the protected class must, in the end, depend on its own facts. But I would regard a clear written recommendation to the surety to take independent advice before signing the security document as advisable in most cases. I would regard it as inadvisable for the security document to be sent to the surety for signature unless accompanied by a recommendation to that effect. I would regard it as particularly inappropriate for the creditor simply to entrust the security document to the debtor with a view to the debtor obtaining the surety's signature. If the surety is invited to sign the security document in the creditor's offices, the creditor should, before the document is signed, explain its nature and effect to the surety. The background to all of this is knowledge on the part of the creditor that security is being taken from the surety for the benefit of the debtor and that the surety is a person who is likely to be influenced by and to have some degree of reliance on the debtor. In these circumstances the creditor should be seeking to ensure that unfair advantage is not taken of the surety. If, however, a creditor has taken reasonable steps, such as advising the surety to take independent advice, or, if the surety declines to do so, offering a fair explanation of the security document before the surety signs it, I can see no reason why equity should intervene.

It goes without saying that, if the debtor has employed undue influence or misrepresentation in order to persuade the surety to enter into the transaction and the creditor has knowledge that this has happened, the security will be unenforceable. It will be unenforceable also if the facts justify a finding that the debtor has been appointed the creditor's agent. The debtor's misfeasance will then the be the creditor's misfeasance. But this, I think, will, in the class of case I am considering, be very rare. Banks, building societies and finance houses do not appoint their debtors as their agents for the purpose of procuring additional security. They may, and often do, inform their debtors that loan facilities will be available if certain security can be provided. They may, and often do, leave it to the debtors to see if they can procure the additional security. But, in my opinion, that is no basis for an inference of agency. . . .

There is one final comment I would make. In a case of the class I have been considering, the creditor will often, I think, find itself in a position of having to explain the security transaction to the proposed surety if an unimpeachable security is to be obtained. The creditor should not, in my opinion, be taken in so doing to have assumed a duty of care. If the surety is a customer or if the creditor assumes the role of adviser, it may be that the creditor will be found to have owned a contractual or tortious duty of care to the surety. . . . But, if there is no more than that the creditor, in an attempt to satisfy itself that the surety properly understands the proposed transaction and that the transaction will not subsequently be impeachable, offers an explanation of the transaction and of the security document, I do not think that the creditor should be taken to have assumed a tortious duty of care. If the explanation was inadequate, the security might not be enforceable but it would not follow that liability in damages would attach. . . .

The present case

I now apply to the present case the principles that I have spent overlong in trying to identify.

The learned judge declined to find that Mr O'Brien had been appointed as agent of the bank. I agree. No doubt the bank left it to Mr O'Brien to procure his wife to agree to enter into the security transaction. But I, like the judge, decline to regard that as justifying an inference that Mr O'Brien was appointed the bank's agent. . . .

As the judge found, Mr O'Brien misrepresented to his wife the effect of the charge. He told her that it was limited to secure £60,000 and would be released in a short time. Neither was true. But he did not, in my judgment, do these things, all done to procure his wife to agree to sign, as the bank's agent. As to the causation point, the judge found that Mr O'Brien's misrepresentation was 'material'. That can only mean that he found it, on the balance of probabilities, to have had a causative effect. I do not think his remarks later in his judgment detract from this finding.

The judge did not find that undue influence had been established. His main point, applying *National Westminster Bank plc* v. *Morgan* [1985] 1 All ER 821, [1985] AC 686, was that the transaction was not manifestly to Mrs O'Brien's disadvantage. This may be so. But for my part I would reject the undue influence case on the ground that the influence brought to bear by Mr O'Brien was not, in the context of a normal husband and wife relationship and bearing in mind Mrs O'Brien's character and capabilities, sufficiently undue. Mr O'Brien was, Mrs O'Brien said, extremely insistent that she should sign. He made an emotional scene on the day she signed and told her that, if she did not sign, the company would be bankrupt and her son John would lose his home. These were heavy family pressures but not particularly unusual nor sufficient, in my opinion, to overset and bear down the will of Mrs O'Brien. She signed because she was persuaded that it was the right thing to do, not because her husband's pressure deprived her consent of reality.

In any event, the bank had no knowledge of the circumstances that, in the event, persuaded Mrs O'Brien to sign. Even if the pressure had constituted undue influence, it would not, in my judgment, have affected the bank.

If the first of the two roads had been the right one to take, that would be an end of the matter. The appeal would be dismissed. But that is not, in my judgment, the end of the matter. The bank knew, of course, that Mrs O'Brien was Mr O'Brien's wife. She was being asked to provide security for the debts of the company in order, as the bank knew, to advance her husband's business inter-ests. The bank knew that Mr O'Brien was likely to have some influence on her and that she was likely to place some reliance on him and his business judg-ment. In the event, due to Mr O'Brien's misrepresentation, Mrs O'Brien did not have an adequate understanding of the effect of the charge. She thought it was limited to securing £60,000 and would only continue in force for a few weeks. In these circumstances it is necessary to ask whether the bank took reasonable steps to try and ensure that she had an adequate comprehension of the effect of the charge. The answer to this question must, in my opinion, be that the bank did not. If the instructions given by Mr Tucker to the Burnham sub-branch had been carried out, my answer would have been otherwise. The side-letter advised her to take independent advice. But the clerk did not do anything to see that she read the letter and she did not read it. No explanation of the effect of the charge or of the sum intended to be thereby secured was offered to her. She was not invited to read the charge. The pages of the charge were folded back leaving open the page on which she was to sign. Not only did she not read the charge but the folding back of the pages would have tended to dis-courage her from doing so. The bank knew, through the clerk, that she signed the charge without reading it.

Although it was not what Mr Tucker had intended, the bank did, in the event, leave it entirely to Mr O'Brien to explain the transaction to his wife and to pro-cure her consent to it. In the event she misunderstood the effect of the transac-tion. Her misunderstanding derived from her husband's misrepresentation. He was not the bank's agent. But the equitable principles established by the author-ities require, in my judgment, the creditors who take from married women security for their husband's debts take reasonable steps to see that they under-stand the transactions they are entering into. This the bank failed to do. . . .

In view of Mrs O'Brien's misunderstanding of the transaction the transaction was not, in my judgment, enforceable against her, save to the extent of £60,000. Events which took place in the course of the proceedings below resulted in the bank recovering, on account of its charge, £60,000. As against Mrs O'Brien, therefore, the security must be treated as satisfied.

I would allow this appeal.

Notes

1. In the House of Lords Lord Browne-Wilkinson, while rejecting the appeal by the plaintiffs, nevertheless disapproved of what he called Scott LJ's 'special equity' route to giving relief to the wife. He argued that the bank had constructive notice of the husband's misrepresentation of the legal effect of the charge, and fell under a specific obligation to protect the interests of the wife by advising her to take independent legal advice. Lord Browne-Wilkinson concludes his judgment with a summary of his

findings—one must assume, for the assistance of County Court judges who will frequently be asked to apply this reasoning to cases before them.

Barclays Bank plc v. *O'Brien*
[1993] 4 All ER 417 at 428–32

LORD BROWNE-WILKINSON

Conclusions

(a) Wives

My starting point is to clarify the basis of the law. Should wives (and perhaps others) be accorded special rights in relation to surety transactions by the recognition of a special equity applicable only to such persons engaged in such transactions? Or should they enjoy only the same protection as they would enjoy in relation to their other dealings? In my judgment, the special equity theory should be rejected. First, I can find no basis in principle for affording special protection to a limited class in relation to one type of transaction only. Second, to require the creditor to prove knowledge and understanding by the wife in all cases is to reintroduce by the back door a presumption of undue influence of class 2A (which has been decisively rejected). Third, although Scott LJ found that there were two lines of cases one of which supported the special equity theory, on analysis although many decisions are not inconsistent with that theory the only two cases which support it are *Yerkey* v. *Jones* and the decision of the Court of Appeal in the present case. Finally, it is not necessary to have recourse to a special equity theory for the proper protection of the legitimate interests of wives as I will seek to show.

In my judgment, if the doctrine of notice is properly applied, there is no need for the introduction of a special equity in these types of cases. A wife who has been induced to stand as a surety for her husband's debts by his undue influence, misrepresentation or some other legal wrong has an equity as against him to set aside that transaction. Under the ordinary principles of equity, her right to set aside that transaction will be enforceable against third parties (e.g. against a creditor) if either the husband was acting as the third party's agent or the third party had actual or constructive notice of the facts giving rise to her equity. Although there may be cases where, without artificiality, it can properly be held that the husband was acting as the agent of the creditor in procuring the wife to stand as surety, such cases will be of very rare occurrence. The key to the problem is to identify the circumstances in which the creditor will be taken to have had notice of the wife's equity to set aside the transaction.

The doctrine of notice lies at the heart of equity. Given that there are two innocent parties, each enjoying rights, the earlier right prevails against the later right if the acquirer of the later right knows of the earlier right (actual notice) or would have discovered it had he taken proper steps (constructive notice). In particular, if the party asserting that he takes free of the earlier rights of another knows of certain facts which put him on inquiry as to the possible existence of the rights of that other and he fails to make such inquiry or take such other steps as are reasonable to verify whether such earlier right does or does not exist, he will have constructive notice of the earlier right and take subject to it. Therefore where a wife has agreed to stand surety for her husband's debts as a result of undue influence or misrepresentation, the creditor will take subject to the wife's equity to set aside the transaction if the circumstances are such as to put the creditor on inquiry as to the circumstances in which she agreed to stand surety.

It is at this stage that, in my view, the 'invalidating tendency' or the law's 'tender treatment' of married women, becomes relevant. As I have said above in dealing with undue influence, this tenderness of the law towards married women is due to the fact that, even today, many wives repose confidence and trust in their husbands in relation to their financial affairs. This tenderness of the law is reflected by the fact that voluntary dispositions by the wife in favour of her husband are more likely to be set aside than other dispositions by her: a wife is more likely to establish presumed undue influence of class 2B by her husband than by others because, in practice, many wives do repose in their husbands trust and confidence in relation to their financial affairs. Moreover the informality of business dealings between spouses raises a substantial risk that the husband has not accurately stated to the wife the nature of the liability she is undertaking, i.e. he has misrepresented the position, albeit negligently.

Therefore, in my judgment a creditor is put on inquiry when a wife offers to stand surety for her husband's debts by the combination of two factors: (a) the transaction is on its face not to the financial advantage of the wife; and (b) there is a substantial risk in transactions of that kind that, in procuring the wife to act as surety, the husband has committed a legal or equitable wrong that entitles the wife to set aside the transaction.

It follows that, unless the creditor who is put on inquiry takes reasonable steps to satisfy himself that the wife's agreement to stand surety has been properly obtained, the creditor will have constructive notice of the wife's rights.

What, then are the reasonable steps which the creditor should take to ensure that it does not have constructive notice of the wife's rights, if any? Normally the reasonable steps necessary to avoid being fixed with constructive notice consist of making inquiry of the person who may have the earlier right (i.e. the wife) to see if whether such right is asserted. It is plainly impossible to require of banks and other financial institutions that they should inquire of one spouse whether he or she has been unduly influenced or misled by the other. But in my judgment the creditor, in order to avoid being fixed with constructive notice, can reasonably be expected to take steps to bring home to the wife the risk she is running by standing as surety and to advise her to take independent advice.

As to past transactions, it will depend on the facts of each case whether the steps taken by the creditor satisfy this test. However for the future in my judgment a creditor will have satisfied these requirements if it insists that the wife attend a private meeting (in the absence of the husband) with a representative of the creditor at which she is told of the extent of her liability as surety, warned of the risk she is running and urged to take independent legal advice. If these steps are taken in my judgment the creditor will have taken such reasonable steps as are necessary to preclude a subsequent claim that it had constructive notice of the wife's rights. I should make it clear that I have been considering the ordinary case where the creditor knows only that the wife is to stand surety for her husband's debts. I would not exclude exceptional cases where a creditor has knowledge of further facts which render the presence of undue influence not only possible but probable. In such cases, the creditor to be safe will have to insist that the wife is separately advised. . . .

If the law is established as I have suggested, it will hold the balance fairly between on the one hand the vulnerability of the wife who relies implicitly on her husband and, on the other hand, the practical problems of financial institutions asked to accept a secured or unsecured surety obligation from the wife for her husband's debts. In the context of suretyship, the wife will not have any right to disown her obligations just because subsequently she proves that she did not fully understand the transaction: she will, as in all other areas of her affairs, be bound by her obligations unless her husband has, by misrepresentation, undue influence or other wrong, committed an actionable wrong against her. In the normal case, a financial institution will be able to lend with confidence in reliance on the wife's surety obligation provided that it warns her (in the absence of the husband) of the amount of her potential liability and of the risk of standing surety and advises her to take independent advice.

Mr Jarvis QC for the bank urged that this is to impose too heavy a burden on financial institutions. I am not impressed by this submission. The report by Professor Jack's Review Committee on *Banking Services: Law and Practice* (1989), (Cmnd 622) recommended that prospective guarantors should be adequately warned of the legal effects and possible consequences of their guarantee and of the importance of receiving independent advice. Pursuant to this recommendation, the Code of Banking Practice (adopted by banks and building societies in March 1992) provides in para 12.1 as follows:

'Banks and building societies will advise private individuals proposing to give them a guarantee or other security for another person's liabilities that: (i) by giving the guarantee or third party security he or she might become liable instead of or as well as that other person; (ii) he or she should seek independent legal advice before entering into the guarantee or third party security. Guarantees and other third party security forms will contain a clear and prominent notice to the above effect.'

Thus good banking practice (which applies to all guarantees, not only those given by a wife) largely accords with what I consider the law should require when a wife is offered as surety. The only further substantial step required by law beyond that good practice is that the position should be explained by the bank to the wife in a personal interview. I regard this as being essential because a number of the decided cases show that written warnings are often not read and are sometimes intercepted by the husband. It does not seem to me that the requirement of a personal interview imposes such an additional administrative burden as to render the bank's position unworkable.

(b) Other persons

I have hitherto dealt only with the position where a wife stands surety for her husband's debts. But in my judgment the same principles are applicable to all other cases where there is an emotional relationship between cohabitees. The 'tenderness' shown by the law to married women is not based on the marriage ceremony but reflects the underlying risk of one cohabitee exploiting the emotional involvement and trust of the other. Now that unmarried cohabitation, whether heterosexual or homosexual, is widespread in our society, the law should recognise this. Legal wives are not the only group which are now exposed to the emotional pressure of cohabitation. Therefore if, but only if, the creditor is aware that the surety is cohabiting with the principal debtor, in my judgment the same principles should apply to them as apply to husband and wife.

In addition to the cases of cohabitees, the decision of the Court of the Court of Appeal in *Avon Finance Co Ltd* v. *Bridger* shows (rightly in my view) that other relationships can give rise to a similar result. . . .

Summary

I can therefore summarise my views as follows. Where one cohabitee has entered into an obligation to stand as surety for the debts of the other cohabitee and the creditor is aware that they are cohabitees: (1) the surety obligation will be valid and enforceable by the creditor unless the suretyship was procured by the undue influence, misrepresentation or other legal wrong of the principal debtor; (2) if there has been undue influence, misrepresentation or other legal wrong by the principal debtor, unless the creditor has taken reasonable steps to satisfy himself that the surety entered into the obligation freely and in knowledge of the true facts, the creditor will be unable to enforce the surety obligation because he will be fixed with constructive notice of the surety's right to set aside the transaction; (3) unless there are special exceptional circumstances, a creditor will have taken such reasonable steps to avoid being fixed with constructive notice if the creditor warns the surety (at a meeting not attended by the principal debtor) of the amount of her potential liability and of the risks involved and advises the surety to take independent legal advice.

I should make it clear that in referring to the husband's debts I include the debts of a company in which the husband (but not the wife) has a direct financial interest.

The failure of the bank to follow its own procedures on advising spouses, which are those of good banking practice, was decisive in persuading Lord Browne-Wilkinson to find in favour of Mrs O'Brien. By way of contrast to *O'Brien*, Mrs Pitt in the linked case of *CIBC Mortgages* v. *Pitt* was able to prove actual undue influence by her husband but could not show that the bank had any notice of the impropriety. The key distinction between the cases is factual: in *Pitt* the transaction related to a mortgage of the matrimonial home, to raise money for Mr Pitt to play the stock market, which he managed successfully until the 1987 market crash. As far as the bank was concerned, the transaction was a simple mortgage to raise money, for what reason they knew not, with the proceeds taking the form of a cheque made payable to both husband and wife. The bank had no notice of the pressure brought to bear by Mr Pitt upon Mrs Pitt.

2. The basis of the House of Lords decision in *O'Brien* is rather clearer than the somewhat vague equitable jurisdiction to which Scott LJ resorted in order to find in favour of Mrs O'Brien. This is a jurisdiction which seeks to protect the interests of married women (and analogously vulnerable categories of persons) in situations such as these. It requires financial institutions to ensure that those against whose property they take a legal charge as security against a third party's debts receive independent legal advice or are otherwise apprised of the nature and effect of the documents they have signed, thereby shielding women in Mrs O'Brien's situation not only from incidences of *actual undue* influence but also from *any* form of influence exercised by their husbands. However, the existence of an equitable jurisdiction in the form in which it was exercised by the first instance judge and by the Court of Appeal is by no means self-evident, and a stricter approach was followed by a differently constituted Court of Appeal in the similar case of *Barclays Bank plc* v. *Khaira* ([1993] 1 Fam. 343), where a defence raised by a wife faced by circumstances akin to those of Mrs O'Brien, based on an alleged duty on the part of the bank to explain the transaction was essentially treated as unarguable. Consequently, it is unsurprising that the House of Lords returned to more orthodox legal principles.

3. Mrs O'Brien is given relief against the bank in terms that the bank is unable to rely on the full scope of the charge. The part of the arrangement that Mrs O'Brien was unaware of is severed from the rest of the charge and set aside. The rest of the charge had already been satisfied prior to the hearing. This looks very much like the remedy of rescission on terms which we shall encounter once more in Chapter 12 on risk in relation to common mistake in equity.

This type of approach would not have assisted Mrs Morgan had the

House of Lords decided to award her a remedy. The portion of the charge in that case which allowed Mr Morgan to borrow further monies for his business secured on the family home—the effect which Mrs Morgan did not want—did not account for any of the money that Mrs Morgan currently owed the bank; there was no outstanding business borrowing. To set aside the bank's charge in full in these circumstances would be to give Mrs Morgan the windfall of owning her home unencumbered. It may be that the question of what remedy was appropriate influenced the court in deciding that the transaction with the bank did not manifestly disadvantage Mrs Morgan. Would it be, then, that had Mrs Morgan raised the defence of undue influence during the lifetime of her husband, when there had been business borrowing, the court might then have been prepared to set aside that part of the transaction, if the prerequisites for the defence were present?

In *Cheese* v. *Thomas* the Vice-Chancellor emphasized that the setting aside of transactions on the ground of undue influence involved a restitutionary remedy (see further Chs. 1 and 14) and not compensatory damages. In his view, this enabled the court to achieve a practically just outcome while still having in sight the aim of restoring each party to its original position. In *Cheese* v. *Thomas*, restoring the parties to their original position would have meant returning to the plaintiff his capital stake of £43,000; the difficulty with this was that the house had lost one-third of its purchase value. If the plaintiff received his full £43,000 the defendant would bear all the consequences of the loss in value. The Court of Appeal ordered the parties to participate in the sale proceeds of the house in accordance with their shares of 43 : 40, and this had the effect of splitting the loss in value of the property between them. The Court seems to set some store by the conduct of the defendant: he is described as an 'innocent fiduciary', and it is made clear that the trial judge found that no impropriety on the defendant's behalf had occurred. This may well have persuaded the Court to split the loss on the property between the two parties. If the remedy was one of damages, then presumably the conduct of the defendant would have been immaterial beside the plaintiff's loss.

4. Unlike some judges, Scott LJ is quite explicit about the policy reasons which he sees as underlying his adjudication of the respective rights and interests of Mrs O'Brien and the bank. His is the archetypal consumer-welfarist judgment based on his assessment of the particular needs of a vulnerable group. Of course, the very essence of the equitable jurisdiction of undue influence is paternalist, in so far as it concentrates on restricting the exercise of power in the context of unequal relationships. Cretney, for one, was not convinced by Scott LJ's analysis of gender relations in the modern (partnership) marriage as the basis for his conclusions on the operation of the equitable jurisdiction.

S. Cretney, 'The Little Woman and the Big Bad Bank' (1992) 108 *LQR* 534 at 536–8

It is respectfully suggested that the extension of the pre-First World War case law which clearly did give special protection to married women (see, *e.g. Turnbull* v. *Duval* . . . .; *Chaplin & Co. Ltd.* v. *Brammall* . . . .) to others who are "vulnerable" reveals the underlying weaknesses of the Court of Appeal's decision. To make protection depend exclusively on the status of marriage would today be open to two rather different objections. First, such a solution would do nothing to protect the growing numbers who prefer to enjoy a domestic relationship outside marriage. Secondly, it would ignore the changing nature of domestic relationships: the parties to a marriage can now fairly be said to start and continue on a footing of social, domestic and economic equality (*per* Rougier J., *R.* v. *J—(Rape: Marital Exemption)* [1991] 1 All E.R. 759 at p. 760). So the Court of Appeal accepted that the class to be protected has to be extended to include other cases in which influence by one over another and reliance by the one on the other are "natural and probable features of the relationship." But if the test is to be whether the relationship is *in fact* one in which the circumstances are such as to suggest dependency coupled with mutual trust and confidence (see the illuminating judgment of Morritt J. in *Simpson and others* v. *Simpson and another* [1992] 1 F.L.R. 601) why should it be assumed that married women are necessarily vulnerable? Why not leave the matter to be decided on the facts of the particular case? The effect of the Court of Appeal's decision will be to give unnecessary and unwarranted protection to married women such as Mrs. O'Brien (said by Scott L.J. not to be a lady who was in a particularly vulnerable position *vis-à-vis* her husband).

. . . A rule which will require banks to treat married women, regardless of the particular facts, in a manner appropriate to children not yet emancipated from their father's control (see *Bainbrigge* v. *Browne* (1881) 18 Ch. D. 188, 196 *per* Fry J.) seems totally inappropriate at this stage in the evolution of family structures.

Why should Scott LJ and Cretney reach such divergent conclusions about the role of the law in protecting married women, notwithstanding that they share a common assessment of Mrs O'Brien's character and her own standing as a woman? Under the approach taken by Scott LJ, Mrs O'Brien is protected simply because she is a wife, although she herself is a capable and independent woman. She receives the protection due to all married women because Scott LJ perceives the inequality of women as a continuing reality in the 'culturally and ethnically mixed community' which is the United Kingdom today. Cretney, in contrast, starts with a legal rather than a factual model—the model of equal partnership in marriage which is used as the modern paradigm. This is a model which he projects onto the law of undue influence, and from which he can construct the proposition that married women should not receive special protection, because it perpetuates unacceptable and outmoded stereotypes.

This contrast in approach closely mirrors one of the perennial debates within feminist approaches to law: should men and women be treated the same because they are equal in the eyes of the law? Or should the differences between the sexes, including not only biological differences but also differences in socio-economic standing stemming from the historical oppression of women, justify different treatment extending, where appropriate, to special rights for women, such as protection against pregnancy discrimination in employment or positive measures to promote women's employment? It is the difficulty of subsuming Mrs O'Brien's own individual standing as an emancipated woman into a collective system of protective rights which troubles Scott LJ, and to achieve his objective he is forced to have recourse to a body of law which embodies paternalism and the disenfranchisement of women rather than the reversal of historic disadvantage, which is his objective. Consequently, aping the nineteenth-century judges, he talks of law's tenderness towards married women, telling the story of Mrs O'Brien so as to evoke sympathy for women generally in her position, embroidering this by generating anger about the way that banks manage situations such as these and against husbands who recklessly endanger the family home. We can learn much about how Scott LJ reconciles the individual/collective conflict by dismissing the (individual) plea of undue influence and finding a broader equity protecting the (collective) situation of married women from the way he relates the narrative. We reach the conclusion that Mrs O'Brien was in an impossible dilemma but that it was not *fair* that she had to resolve that dilemma without information, information denied her by the all-powerful bank. This approach echoes that of Lord Denning in the case of *Lewis* v. *Averay* discussed in Chapter 5.

The difficulty with the manner in which Scott LJ chooses to correct the perceived unfairness of Mrs O'Brien's situation is that, having recognized the separation of the wife from the husband, including the possibility of a conflict of interests between them, Scott LJ then delivers the wife up into the tutelage of the state, a situation of paternalist protection which many women simply find insulting and unacceptable. The difficulties experienced by Scott LJ and Cretney exemplify the problems identified by Pateman in Chapter 3: it is not an easy task to subsume into a neo-classical contract law framework a group of individuals—women—who were excluded from the original conception of the contract. This point is taken up also by Frug in Chapters 11 (exclusion clauses) and 12 (impossibility doctrine).

5. Another way of looking at the policy-based analysis of Scott LJ is to see it as resurrecting in another form the spirit of Lord Denning's inequality of bargaining power approach in *Lloyds Bank* v. *Bundy*, which the House of Lords must have regarded as effectively destroyed after *Morgan*. Indeed, in

neither *O'Brien* nor *Pitt* was that case discussed by the House of Lords. Yet even though in those cases their Lordships chose to follow a more restricted route to the same result, it seems unlikely that the perennial conflict between broad-based standards and rule-based frameworks exemplified by the conflict in approach between *Morgan* and *Bundy* will now disappear for ever. There is an unresolved tension between applying rules based on closed categories of beneficiaries satisfying static tests of entitlement and open-textured standards benefiting an evolving class of beneficiaries defined according to policy criteria. This debate has been alluded to before in the context of the US approach to the battle of the forms, in comparison with that taken in English law (see Ch. 4). The US approach to the types of conduct regulated in English law by the doctrine of undue influence is likewise greatly influenced by a standards approach. It is to the general principle of unconscionability applicable under the Uniform Commercial Code that we now turn in the final section of this chapter, in order to offer a contrast to the largely rule-bound framework of English law.

IV. UNCONSCIONABILITY

As a legal term, unconscionability does have some restricted meaning and usage in English law, as there is an ancient equitable jurisdiction to set aside certain unconscionable bargains where one party is in a position to exploit a weakness of the other. Poor and ignorant persons and expectant heirs have benefited from this protection, but one of the few modern examples of relief being given is *Cressell* v. *Potter* ([1978] 1 WLR 255), where a wife who had left her husband and conveyed her half-share in the matrimonial home to him, in return for being released from liability under the mortgage, later successfully claimed a half-share when her husband sold the property. Megarry J classed her as the modern equivalent to a 'poor and ignorant person' who had been taken advantage of by her husband.

In the United States, unconscionability has developed along rather different and much broader lines into a general principle which many would argue allows the courts to set aside any contract where, in the view of the court, its continued performance would be unfair or inequitable to one party. The most important unconscionability provision is contained in §2-302 of the Uniform Commercial Code. This applies to all sales transactions covered by the Code and will be examined below. Other provisions of note include §1–203, which states that 'every contract or duty . . . imposes an obligation of good faith in its performance or enforcement'. Individual State legislatures have put more flesh on the bones of unconscionability by defining in greater detail the types of transaction or trading practice which are unfair and therefore unlawful.

§2–302 UCC provides:

(1) If the court as a matter of law finds the contract or any clause of the contract to have been unconscionable at the time it was made the court may refuse to enforce the contract, or it may enforce the remainder of the contract without the unconscionable clause, or it may so limit the application of any unconscionable clause as to avoid any unconscionable result.

(2) When it is claimed or appears to the court that the contract or any clause thereof may be unconscionable the parties shall be afforded a reasonable opportunity to present evidence as to its commercial setting, purpose and effect to aid the court in making the determination.

G. McLaughlin, 'Unconscionability and Impracticability: Reflections on Two U.C.C. Indeterminacy Principles', (1992) 14 *Loy. LA Int'l. & Comp. LJ* 439 at 440–4.

. . . section 2-302(1) demonstrates that unconsionability must exist at the time the contract for sale is made, not at some later time. Consequently, if a contract for sale is found to be fair and balanced at the time the contract is entered into, it will not be considered unconscionable, even if at the time of performance the contract is found to be unfair and unbalanced. . . .

. . . section 2-302(2) requires that a court allow the parties to present evidence regarding the commercial setting, purpose, and effect of a contract in order to aid the court in determining whether unconscionability exists. This commercial evidence can give needed context to business practices that might otherwise appear harsh. For example, a price term in a contract for sale may appear excessive when viewed in isolation. A seller of goods, however, may be able to show that unusually high manufacturing or production costs justified the high price term in the sale contract.

Finally, section 2-302 gives a court a wide range of remedial options once it finds unconscionability. The court "may refuse to enforce the contract, or it may enforce the remainder of the contract without the unconscionable clause, or it may so limit the application of any unconscionable clause as to avoid any unconscionable result." Courts that have construed this language have ruled that the section does not permit an award of money damages upon a finding of unconscionability. . . .

By now, however, one thing should be obvious. While section 2-302 reveals much about the clothing of unconscionability, it reveals little about the nature of the doctrine beneath that clothing. Section 2-302 does not contain a definition, or even a standard, to determine whether the terms of a contract are in fact unconscionable. In the Official Comments to section 2-302, the drafters did provide some guidance as to the nature of unconscionability, but even here the guidance is less than optimal. For example, Official Comment 1 states that the principle underlying unconscionability is "the prevention of oppression and unfair surprise and not of disturbance of allocation of risks because of superior bargaining power." At another place in Official Comment 1, the drafters describe the "basic test" of unconscionability as whether the clauses are "so one-sided" as to be unconscionable. . . . None of these explications, however, is particularly helpful in predicting the outcome of cases in which parties seek to be excused on the ground of unconscionability.

Explaining the standard of conduct required by §2-302, the Supreme Court of New Jersey in *Kugler* v. *Romain* commented:

The standard of conduct contemplated by the unconscionability clause is good faith, honesty in fact and observance of fair dealing. The need for application of the standard is most acute when the professional seller is seeking the trade of those most subject to exploitation: the uneducated, the inexperienced and people on low incomes. (279 A. 2d 640 at 652 (1970))

Consequently, US courts at various times have used the unconscionability clause not only in the 'pressure' situations covered by duress and undue influence in English law but also to invalidate exclusion clauses, to set aside transactions on grounds of price, and to condemn instalment sales containing terms which allowed the retailer to repossess all the goods sold to the consumer if the latter defaulted on any element of the repayments.

McLaughlin goes on to describe the basic two-pronged analytical framework which academic commentators have developed to provide a scheme for understanding the scope of application of unconscionability. This is the distinction between procedural and substantive unconscionability, developed principally by Leff on the basis of an early analysis of the unconscionability doctrine as applied up to that point and subsequently applied by many courts to structure their analysis (see A. Leff, 'Unconscionability and the Code: The Emperor's New Clause', ((1967) 117 *U. Pa. L. Rev.* 485). McLaughlin explains and critiques this distinction.

McLaughlin, 'Unconscionability and Impracticability: Reflections on Two U.C.C. Indeterminacy Principles', 444–6

The First Prong: Procedural Unconscionability

The first prong of unconscionability analysis, referred to as "procedural unconscionability," deals with what Leff calls "bargaining naughtiness." To determine whether procedural unconscionability exists, a court should consider various factors, including (1) the age, literacy, and business sophistication of the party claiming unconscionability (usually the buyer); (2) the bargaining tactics of the other party to the contract (usually the seller); and (3) the commercial setting of the sales contract, particularly whether the buyer could have obtained the goods from an alternative source. Textual support for "procedural unconscionability" can be found in the Official Comment's phrase "unfair surprise." If age or literacy precludes a buyer from giving meaningful assent to the terms of a sale contract, then it is fair to conclude that the buyer will be unfairly surprised by the terms of that contract. Similarly, if a seller's boilerplate language is so deceptive or convoluted that it prevents a buyer from meaningfully assenting to the terms of the contract, then again it is fair to conclude that the buyer will be unfairly surprised.

The Second Prong: Substantive Unconscionability

The second prong of unconscionability analysis identified by Leff is "substantive unconscionability." Substantive unconscionability examines the nature of the terms that result from the bargaining process. Textual support for this second component is rooted in the words "oppression" and "one-sided" found in Official Comment 1 to U.C.C. section 2-302. Most courts find excessively high prices and unfair remedy terms, including broad disclaimer of warranty provisions, substantively unconscionable because they are harsh and oppressive to buyers.

The Indeterminate Nature of the Two-Pronged Analysis

It is important to remember that this two-pronged analytical framework for unconscionability is just that—an analytical framework. It does not, and indeed cannot, substitute for a definition of unconscionability. In fact, the two prongs—procedural unconscionability and substantive unconscionability—are themselves indeterminate. For example, the existing case law on procedural unconscionability has not catalogued the factors that must be considered before a court will find "bargaining naughtiness." Even when relevant factors are listed, the case law does not indicate what weight should be afforded to each of these factors. Further, given that no precise definition of procedural unconscionability exists, courts are basically free to pick and choose among a range of factors in order to achieve a fair result.

The same can be said of substantive unconscionability. The Official Comment of U.C.C. section 2-302 states that the principle of unconscionability is "one of the prevention of oppression . . . not of disturbance of allocation of risks because of superior bargaining power." Obviously, superior bargaining power can produce a one-sided allocation of risks. The Official Comment, however, fails to provide courts with a bright-line distinction between oppressive, and therefore unconscionable, contractual terms, and burdensome, but still acceptable, contractual terms resulting from superior bargaining power. Therefore, courts again have great freedom to determine when contractual terms are not only burdensome but oppressive, and thus substantively unconscionable.

The indeterminacy that exists when procedural and substantive unconscionability are considered separately also exists when they are considered in combination. Most courts and scholarly commentators are of the view that before there can be a finding of section 2-302 unconscionability, both procedural and substantive unconscionability must be present. Others, however, believe that section 2-302 unconscionability can be found when substantive unconscionability alone is present.

Note

McLaughlin's analysis indicates that Leff's framework has not really answered any of the key questions about how a court should apply such an open standard; it is a useful basis for identifying the different types of advantage within the contractual process which might justify excusing one party from performance. In that sense, it is a similar distinction to that drawn between substantive and procedural fairness or justice, but just as we noted that these concepts cannot easily be separated, so courts and scholars generally acknowledge that elements of both forms of unconscionability are what justify judicial intervention—an objectively bad or unbalanced bargain, unfair because it was obtained in circumstances where one party took advantage of the other. Some have argued that unconscionability should only 'allow the courts to police the process whereby private arrangements are formed' and should not allow them 'to act as roving commissions to set aside those agreements whose substantive terms they find objectionable' (see R. Epstein, 'Unconscionability: A Critical Reappraisal', (1975) 18 *JL & Econ.* 293 at 294–5).

So far there has been little evidence from the US experience to suggest why the unconscionability approach would provide a better system for dealing with the types of problem in policing the contract and the bargaining process encountered throughout this part of the book. Further criticism comes from Hillman, who identifies the difficulties caused when courts prefer to use the unconscionability doctrine instead of the existing common law vitiating factors such as fraud and duress.

R. Hillman, 'Debunking some Myths about Unconscionability: A New Framework for U.C.C. Section 2–302', (1982) 67 *Cornell. L. Rev.* 1 at 16–19. © Copyright 1982, Cornell University.

The unconscionability provision of section 2–302 was a victory for the proponents of broad legislative drafting over those who counselled the need for specificity in commercial law. A principal argument made in favor of unconscionability is that it enables courts to decide cases directly on fairness grounds without resorting to manipulation of existing legal rules. Manipulation should be avoided, the argument goes, because it renders a rule more ambiguous and therefore less helpful in cases where traditional application of the rule is appropriate. Moreover, direct invocation of a fairness standard establishes minimum levels of commercial decency and discourages the use of offensive clauses or contracts.

Obviously, manipulation of doctrine should be avoided. The manipulation vice, however, has been overemphasized in arguments in support of the present unconscionability approach. Manipulation occurs when the focus of the court's concern is the fairness of the terms of the agreement and not the bargaining process. When the bargaining process *is* the primary problem in the case—and it is the primary concern in many unconscionability cases— common law doctrines are available to deal with the problem without manipulation.

Technically, courts often manipulate the facts of a case to fit a particular doctrine rather than manipulate the doctrine itself. For example, courts have found general disclaimers of liability ambiguous, and have thereby permitted injured parties to cover for the other contracting parties' negligence despite the disclaimers. Other courts have held that limitations of liability on the back of claim checks for deposited property are unenforceable on the theory that the offerees never assented to such terms. If, in fact, the disclaimer of liability was plainly worded, or if a reasonable person would have been alerted to the limitation on the back of the claim check—and if the court's actual aim is to avoid enforcement of the disclaimer or limitation—the court's decision will create confusion among contracting parties in the future as to whether their clearly drafted agreements will be enforced. Nevertheless, if the facts of the case do support the findings, there is no manipulation and the doctrine should be applied. In fact, virtually all of the cases involving bargaining ills can be resolved without manipulation by applying common law doctrines.

In some cases, the broadening of a common law doctrine may not represent manipulation in the pejorative sense. Instead, the court's decision may simply illustrate the normal common law growth process under which rules are adapted to fit new factual situations. The proper test for determining whether a rule is manipulated or properly employed is whether its application furthers the goals of the particular area of the law and contributes to the clarity of that law. This point is particularly relevant to a second argument made by supporters of the present approach to section 2-302. Unconscionability is needed, they argue, because traditional contract doctrines inevitably must be manipulated to deal with changing developments in the modern commercial world of standardized contracts of adhesion. This argument ignores, however, the proper role of the common law in adapting to change. For example, one of the principal problems that emanates from the world of mass-produced contracts is the need for disclosure. As previously demonstrated, the problem of disclosure can be addressed adequately through the development—not the manipulation—of existing common law doctrines.

The point here is not that unconscionability is superfluous, but that its usage should reflect the underlying purposes of the doctrine. Manipulation of facts or doctrine to reach just results based on a hidden motive of the court—the nullification of unfair contract terms—should be avoided. If manipulation is the evil to which the doctrine of unconscionability is directed, employment of common law doctrines should not be criticized when the facts support their application without manipulation. Employment of common law doctrines is, in fact, beneficial, because it contributes to the certainty of the unconscionability inquiry.

Notes

1. Hillman alludes in this extract to a number of different control devices for unconscionable behaviour. We have discussed information problems in Chapter 5 (mistake and misrepresentation), have looked at duress and undue influence in this chapter, and shall examine the incorporation and interpretation of different types of contract term in more detail in Chapters 10 and 11. English law shares in broad outline the doctrines applicable in US law which Hillman uses here as illustrations, and thus it is not difficult to see how the argument raised by Hillman would apply in English law were a general unconscionability clause to be introduced by Parliament.

2. Using Hillman, it can be concluded that an unconscionability clause can be useful in order to prevent a particular type of mischief. However, unconscionability should not be stretched beyond its underlying purpose. We conclude this section with an extract from Leff which seeks to identify the specific domain of unconscionability, explaining why the doctrine has caused difficulties for academic commentators and courts alike.

A. Leff, 'Thomist Unconscionability', (1979) 4 *Can. Bus. LJ* 424 at 424–8

It seems to me that the real question underlying and masked by "the unconscionability problem" is this: ought one be allowed by the law to reap material gain from some advantage for which one is not responsible, that is, which one did not, commendably *or* evilly, cause? To put it another way, should a person be allowed to arrogate to himself the fruits of being just smarter, or just stronger, or just luckier than the someone else with whom he is doing a deal?

Notice, this is a question about unachieved advantages. About those that are the product of the possessor's efforts, there is some cultural unanimity. It is, for example, widely accepted that a person is entitled to be paid for work, and to be paid more for superior work. If a person makes a better product, or distributes it more conveniently, so that people want it more and want more of it, it is generally conceded that if he takes advantage of his advantage he is entitled to do so, even if he makes an above-normal profit, even, indeed, if he grows stinking rich. And, this includes the "work" of acquiring superior information—about products, production, or markets. . . .

Similarly, it is pretty well accepted that a man cannot be allowed to take advantage of achieved advantages which were achieved through force or fraud. If a man has better information than the other party to a deal because he lied to that other, or if he finds himself with a strong market position because he forcibly bars the other party from getting to his competitors, then "we" disapprove—strongly enough to render deals made under those conditions void, voidable, or unenforceable. The law will deny to defrauder and the thug his above-normal profit; in the more pallid language of the law, common law fraud and knife-at-the-throat duress are valid defences to actions upon a contract.

Nor indeed, when it comes to "achieved" commercial advantages, has our law gotten stuck at these crude species of lying and forcing. The law, developing through centuries, has given pejorative juridical significance to modes of "achievement" beyond pure intentional and knowing lies and business propositions in the form "buy my widgets or I'll cut your throat". One can in fact display quite a large number of contract defences so that things would look (in descending order of clear moral naughtiness) something like this:

Comparative Defects in Complainant's Information	*Comparative Defects in Complainant's Freedom*
Common Law Fraud	Common Law Duress
Intentional Misrepresentation	Duress by Imprisonment
Negligent Misrepresentation	Duress of Goods
Innocent Misrepresentation	Conspiratorial Monopoly
Duty to Volunteer	Inequality of Bargaining
Material Information	Power . . .

. . . look at the last term in each column. The "fraud" line first. If there were indeed a general duty to volunteer to the other party in a deal *all* relevant information that you have and he does not, then there could be no pay-off for investment in superior information—or training or skill. *A fortiori* there could be no profit from mere accidental information advantages, or lucky guesses, or a better natural business head.

And what if one took seriously the last entry in the "duress" line, and actually made "inequality of bargaining power" a contract defence? If withholding information were in general a defence, that would remove from capitalist profit any return to search and training. But if inequality of bargaining power were taken seriously, then no one could be allowed to profit from any market deformation, any momentary declination of any market from textbook perfection, even if it were the product of forces over which neither party had any control. When demand outran supply for a time, one could not increase one's prices so as to take advantage of the temporary misfit of desire and satisfaction. But that is one of the most common states of any reasonably competitive market, and one not ordinarily caused by any anticompetitive conspiracy at all.

One can see how dramatic an effect actual widespread application of these last items on each chart would have by asking for a moment how one would *know* if a party had failed to disclose material information, or was profiting from an inequality of bargaining power. Simple: any differentiation of the price from that normally charged would conclusively prove either superior information or superior power; if both parties had equal knowledge and equal freedom there would be only one price, the normal market price. So (if the last lines were taken seriously) any deal at any higher price would be unenforceable under the law.

Moreover, it is by now pretty well understood that every term in a contract is part of the price, in the sense that every term is part of the total deal, and thus every changed term will have to be reflected some place in the total exchange ratio. Hence, every abnormal contract *is* a contract at a non-normal price, and it would be, under the above reasoning, legally unenforceable.

What follows is this: both a general duty to volunteer all information material to a transaction, and a general concept of inequality of bargaining power are, in fact, not the culminations of the fraud and force lines of contract defences at all. They belong, instead, to the grand old third line of historic contract-control legal devices, the line in the middle so to speak, the line of illegality (and its little brother "against public policy"). It is here that we find those defences that have nothing really to do with information or freedom defects, that have nothing to do with trying to create efficient markets, that operate instead without proof of any fraud-like or force-like activities. It is here that today we find usury, but usury is just the last pale left-over emanation from that great monument of medieval commercial law, the fair price doctrine.

And that is where we find unconscionability, or rather, that is what unconscionability means: a bad deal not brought about by any determinable bad conduct (the finding of which would render the use of unconscionability superfluous), but rather bad only because of its intrinsic badness: its out of the ordinary "price". It is what one uses when one wants to say "you cannot take advantage of any advantage you have, no matter how, or how innocently, your advantage was brought about".

That then, I think, is why the unconscionability doctrine continues to fascinate and torment us. It is not an extension of market-perfecting, capitalism facilitating law, but its covert enemy. The other contract defences—fraud and all the little "fraudlets", duress and all the lesser pressures—are market-process oriented; in the economist's terms, they look to *efficiency of allocation*. But the "middle line"—usury, fair price and, yes, unconscionability—is result oriented; in economic terms, it looks toward *fairness of distribution*. Our problem is that we want *simultaneously* to produce and protect market efficiency *and* to achieve non-exploitative market results. But (given individual differences among people, and innocently achieved superior information, market power, and pure luck) *we cannot have both at the same time*.

In effect, we want to have the world so arranged that everyone will be motivated to get as good a deal for himself as possible by being as informed and efficient as he can be, but that no one will have to get a bad deal in the process. But the payoff for the former necessitates, indeed entails, the latter. Hence doing both is not a technical problem—how do you define unconscionability, how do you specify unfairness in a short statute—but a cultural one: we cannot have perfect freedom and perfect fairness at once. What we have, instead, is "unconscionability", a legal device that allows us, inconsistently and with only symbolic impact, an occasional evasive bow in the direction of our incoherent hearts' desires.

Note

Leff concludes that unconscionability is a form of public policy intrusion into free contract, explicable on the basis neither of abuse of information nor of abuse of power. As such, it is inimical to the system of free enterprise which underlies the US (and English) law of contract, and therefore its application by the courts will perpetually be a source of difficulty and dissatisfaction.

Questions

1. Which, if any, of the doctrines discussed in this chapter do you see as offering a convincing method for distinguishing between the legitimate and illegitimate use of bargaining power?

2. The types of relationship in which the doctrine of undue influence typically operates to provide protection are ongoing and largely co-operative rather than adversarial in nature. Does this help to explain the difficulties experienced by the English courts in seeking to establish a tight framework of rules for the operation of this doctrine?

3. Do you agree with Leff's criticisms of the indeterminate and flawed nature of the unconscionability doctrine? Do they help to illuminate some of the problems encountered in the English law of duress and undue influence?

10

The Terms of the Contract

I. INTRODUCTION

In this chapter, two distinctive approaches to the issues raised by the contents of the contract—the terms—are developed. We deal, principally through an analysis of illustrative cases—with the main doctrinal difficulties, including certainty of terms, the determination of the precise contents of the contract, implied and express terms, and the relative importance of terms. Second, using contextual and theoretical materials, we offer an outline introduction to some aspects of contract planning and the use of contract in different contexts to structure exchanges. To this end, we focus on standard-form contracts (sometimes called contracts of adhesion), on the responses of relational contract theory to the problems of incomplete contracts, and on the empirical investigation of the nature of business contracting.

II. CERTAINTY OF TERMS

Certainty of terms is a doctrinal notion closely related to the basic prerequisites of contract formation (see e.g. the discussion of *Walford* v. *Miles* in Ch. 4). No statement or promise can form part of a contract unless it is sufficiently clear and unambiguous for its meaning to be capable of determination.

Scammell v. *Ouston*
[1941] 1 All ER 14

The respondents approached the appellants with a view to purchasing a van from them. Part of the purchase price was to be offset by a van offered in part exchange. After some discussion of the price and the allowance for the old van, the respondents submitted a formal offer. The appellants accepted this, indicating that the outstanding purchase price would be paid over two years on hire-purchase terms. The details of the hire-purchase terms were never discussed or finalized. The respondents claimed delivery of the new van and the appellants raised in their defence the issue that there never was a contract between them, the hire-purchase term being too vague to bear any specific meaning.

VISCOUNT MAUGHAM It is a regrettable fact that there are few, if any, topics on which there seems to be a greater difference of judicial opinion than those which relate to the question whether, as the result of informal letters or like documents, a binding contract has been arrived at. Many well-known instances are to be found in the books, the latest being that of *Hillas & Co., Ltd.* v. *Arcos, Ltd.* [(1932) 147 LT 503]. The reason for these different conclusions is that laymen unassisted by persons with a legal training are not always accustomed to use words or phrases with a precise or definite meaning. In order to constitute a valid contract, the parties must so express themselves that their meaning can be determined with a reasonable degree of certainty. It is plain that, unless this can be done, it would be impossible to hold that the contracting parties had the same intention. In other words, the *consensus ad idem* would be a matter of mere conjecture. This general rule, however, applies somewhat differently in different cases. In commercial documents connected with dealings in a trade with which the parties are perfectly familiar, the court is very willing, if satisfied that the parties thought that they made a binding contract, to imply terms, and, in particular, terms as to the method of carrying out the contract, which it would be impossible to supply in other kinds of contract.

My Lords, it is beyond dispute that, if an alleged contract is partly verbal and partly in writing, it is necessary to take the whole of the negotiations into consideration for the purpose of seeing whether the parties are truly agreed on all material points, for, if they are not, there is no binding contract. Nor is it right to construe a letter or other document forming a part of the negotiations in such a case without regard to the verbal statements which also form a part of them. To construe the language of such a letter, so to speak, *in vacuo* might easily result in giving to the words, as used by the writer, a meaning which, in the circumstances of the case, he did not intend the words to bear, or one which the recipient of the letter did not attribute to them. Accordingly, the words in the letter, "This order is given on the understanding that the balance of purchase price can be had on hire-purchase terms over a period of 2 years," must be read together with the parole evidence of J. G. Ouston in order to give those words their true meaning. . . .

We come . . . to the question as to the effect of the so-called purchase being on "hire-purchase terms," and here we are confronted with a strange and confusing circumstance. The term "hire-purchase" for a good many years past has been understood to mean a contract of hire by the owner of a chattel conferring on the hirer an option to purchase on the performance of certain conditions . . . . There is in these contracts—and this is, from a business standpoint, a most important matter—no agreement to buy within the Factors Act, 1889, or the Sale of Goods Act, 1893. . . . It is inaccurate and misleading to add to an order for goods, as if given by a purchaser, a clause that hire-purchase terms are to apply, without something to explain the apparent contradiction. Moreover, a hire-purchase agreement may assume many forms, and some of the variations in those forms are of the most important character—*e.g.*, those which relate to termination of the agreement, warranty of fitness, duties as to repair, interest, and so forth.

Bearing these facts in mind, what do the words "hire-purchase terms" mean in the present case? They may indicate that the hire-purchase agreement was to be granted by the appellants, or, on the other hand, by some finance company acting in collaboration with the appellants. They may contemplate that the appellants were to receive by instalments a sum of £168 spread over a period of 2 years upon delivering the new van and receiving the old car, or, on the other hand, that the appellants were to receive from a third party a lump sum of £168, and that the third party, presumably a finance company, was to receive from the respondents a larger sum than £168, to include interest and profit spread over a period of 2 years. Moreover, nothing is said (except as to the 2-years' period) as to the terms of the hire-purchase agreement—for instance, as to the interest payable, and as to the rights of the letter, whoever he may be, in the event of default by the respondents in payment of the instalments at the due dates. As regards the last matters, there was no evidence to suggest that there are any well-known "usual terms" in such a contract, and I think that it is common knowledge that in fact many letters, though by no means all of them, insist on terms which the legislature regards as so unfair and unconscionable that it was recently found necessary to deal with the matter in the Hire-Purchase Act, 1938. These, my Lords, are very serious difficulties, and, when we find, as we do, in this curious case, that the trial judge and the three Lords Justices, and even the two counsel who addressed your Lordships for the respondents, were unable to agree upon the true construction of the alleged agreement, it seems to me that it is impossible to conclude that a binding agreement has been established by the respondents. . . . The appeal must, I think, succeed, and the action for damages must be dismissed, with costs here and below. . . .

LORD WRIGHT There are, in my opinion, two grounds on which the court ought to hold that there never was a contract. The first is that the language used was so obscure and so incapable of any definite or precise meaning that the court is unable to attribute to the parties any particular contractual intention. The object of the court is to do justice between the parties, and the court will do its best, if satisfied that there was an ascertainable and determinate intention to contract, to give effect to that intention, looking at substance, and not mere form. It will not be deterred by mere difficulties of interpretation. Difficulty is not synonymous with ambiguity, so long as any definite meaning can be extracted. The test of intention, however, is to be found in the words used. If these words, considered however broadly and technically, and with due regard to all the just implications, fail to evince any definite meaning on which the court can safely act, the court has no choice but to say that there is no contract. Such a position is not often found, but I think that it is found in this case. My reason for so thinking is not only based on the actual vagueness and unintelligibility of the words used, but is confirmed by the startling diversity of explanations, tendered by those who think there was a bargain, of what the bargain was. I do not think it would be right to hold the appellants to any particular version. It was all left too vague. There are many cases in the books of what are called illusory contracts—that is, where the parties may have thought they were making a contract, but failed to arrive at a definite bargain. It is a necessary requirement than an agreement, in order to be binding, must be sufficiently definite to enable the court to give it a practical meaning. Its terms must be so definite, or capable of being made definite without further agreement of the parties, that the promises and performances to be rendered by each party are reasonably certain. In my opinion, that requirement was not satisfied in this case.

However, I think that the other reason, which is that the parties never in intention, nor even in appearance, reached an agreement, is a still sounder reason against enforcing the claim. In truth, in my opinion, their agreement was inchoate, and never got beyond negotiations. They did, indeed, accept the position that there should be some form of hire-purchase agreement, but they never went on to complete their agreement by settling between them what the terms of the hire-purchase agreement were to be. The furthest point they reached was an understanding or agreement to agree upon hire-purchase terms. However, as Lord Dunedin said in *May & Butcher, Ltd.* v. *R* ([1934] 2 KB 103 (reported in a note to *Foley* v. *Classique Coaches, Ltd.* ([1934] 2 KB 1) at p. 21:

To be a good contract there must be a concluded bargain, and a concluded contract is one which settles everything that is necessary to be settled and leaves nothing to be settled by agreement between the parties. Of course it may leave something which still has to be determined, but then that determination must be a determination which does not depend upon the agreement between the parties.

. . . It was not even clear who were to be parties to the hire-purchase agreement, or what their respective roles were to be. The respondents, it is clear, were necessary parties. The appellants also were necessary parties, because it was their chattel which was being dealt with. The finance company was also a necessary party. However, there were at least two possible ways of carrying out the deal. The hire-purchase agreement might be in such terms that the appellants were the letters and the respondents the hirers, and the purchase price was to be discharged by periodic instalments in the form of negotiable instruments, payable to the appellants to discount the bills with the finance company, who, on the security of the bills drawn by the respondents and indorsed by the appellants, would pay the appellants the purchase price at once, keeping as their eventual profit the extra amount which was added to the price for interest and bank charges. Such an arrangement must obviously involve the making of a special tripartite agreement. Another possible method would be for the appellants to agree with the respondents to sell the van to the finance company on the stipulation that the latter should agree to let the van to the respondents under a hire-purchase agreement. Clearly in that case also a special tripartite agreement would be necessary. There was perhaps a third possible mode under which the appellants sold the van for cash (at least as regards the balance, for the transaction was, in part, barter) to the respondents, who, having become purchasers, then transferred the van to the finance company on a hire-purchase agreement in consideration of the company advancing the price. Even in such a case, the appellants would, I think, in practice be a necessary party, because the finance company would require the undertaking of the appellants to transfer the van direct to them and the respondents' concurrence in that undertaking. Otherwise, the finance company would be paying cash without at once obtaining their security in the form of the van. Thus a tripartite agreement would be necessary. However, I need not consider that case, because it was clearly not contemplated by the parties. The correspondence shows that the terms of the hire-purchase agreement were to be matters of joint concern to the three parties who were to agree upon them. What is clear is that, while a hire-purchase agreement was being demanded, its exact form and its exact terms were left for future agreements. . . .

. . . For instance, if it were stipulated that there should be "a usual" hire-purchase agreement, the court might be able, if supplied with appropriate evidence, to define what are the terms of such an agreement. However, there was nothing of the sort in this case, and I reserve my opinion on any such hypothetical case. I think this appeal should be allowed.

Notes

1. A major reason for denying that the agreement reached between the parties was sufficiently certain to amount to a binding contract was the bewildering variety of explanations given to their Lordships about what it was supposed to mean. For the Court of Appeal, this was not an insuperable obstacle. According to McKinnon LJ:

It is quite true that the form of the agreement might have been in one or other of two or three forms. The essential stipulation implied was that it should be in a reasonable form. Either one of two variant forms, if in a reasonable form, would have sufficed for satisfaction of the defendants' [the sellers] obligation. ([1940] 1 All ER 59 at 66)

The Court of Appeal concurred with Tucker J at first instance in concluding that there was a complete and enforceable agreement.

Such a conflict of judicial evaluation of a factual situation provides a good example of the contrast between realist and formalist reasoning as identified by Adams and Brownsword (see Ch. 4).

2. Perhaps the explanation for the conflict lies at least in part in the nature of the transaction. Elsewhere in his judgment, Lord Wright comments that MacKinnon LJ in the Court of Appeal cites *Hillas & Co. Ltd.* v. *Arcos Ltd.* in support of his conclusion. The crucial difference between that case and *Scammell* v. *Ouston* is that there the court was able to identify a contract for the supply of Russian timber for 1931 on the basis of the parties' continuing business relationship, including in particular an executed contract for the supply of Russian timber for 1930 and a rather vaguely worded option clause in that contract. With the help of expert evidence, the Court 'joined the dots' in order to put together a completed contract, by interpreting the key phrase 'fair specification over the season'. In *Scammell* v. *Ouston*, the court was constructing the contract from almost nothing and not giving effect to what was intended to be an ongoing relationship.

III. CONTRACTUAL INTENTION

Evans (Portsmouth) Ltd. v. *Andrea Merzario Ltd.*
[1976] 2 All ER 930

The plaintiffs were importers of machinery from Italy. They had, since 1959, had a contractual relationship with the defendants to arrange transportation of the machinery from Italy to Portsmouth. The machinery was carried by sea for the final part of its journey. During the sea voyage, prior to 1967, the machines were carried in crates below deck as the plaintiffs were worried that on-deck travel would cause the machines to rust. In 1967, the defendants proposed to the plaintiffs that further sea travel should be in containers rather than crates. The defendants orally assured the plaintiffs that the containers would be shipped below deck.

The plaintiffs changed to container transport. A container was shipped on deck due to an oversight by the defendants. An unexpected wave caused the container to fall from the deck and it sank to the sea bed. The machinery was irretrievably lost. The plaintiffs alleged that the oral assurance about below-deck shipment was a term of the contract and claimed damages. The defendants claimed that the oral assurance did not enjoy the status of a contractual term and that, even if it was construed in this way, the defendants' liability was limited and possibly excluded by the contents of the printed terms in the contract of carriage between the two parties.

LORD DENNING MR [A]fter [the] containers fell off the deck into the water, the English importers, through their insurers, claimed damages against the forwarding agents. In reply the forwarding agent said there was no contractual promise that the goods would be carried under deck. Alternatively, if there was, they relied on the printed terms and conditions. The judge held there was no contractual promise that these containers should be carried under deck. He thought that, in order to be binding, the initial conversation ought to be contemporaneous, and that here it was too remote in point of time from the actual transport; furthermore that, viewed objectively, it should not be considered binding. The judge quoted largely from the well-known case of *Heilbut, Symons & Co* v. *Buckleton* ([1913] AC 30) in which it was held that a person is not liable in damages for an innocent misrepresentation; and that the courts should be slow to hold that there was a collateral contract. I must say that much of what was said in that case is entirely out of date. We now have the Misrepresentation Act 1967 under which damages can be obtained for innocent misrepresentation of fact. This Act does not apply here because we are concerned with an assurance as to the future. But even in respect of promises as to the future, we have a different approach nowadays to collateral contracts. When a person gives a promise, or an assurance to another, intending that he should act on it by entering into a contract, and he does act on it by entering into the contract, we hold that it is binding: see *Dick Bentley Productions Ltd* v. *Harold Smith (Motors) Ltd* ([1965] 2 All ER 65). That case was concerned with a representation of fact, but it applies also to promises as to the future. Following this approach, it seems to me plain that Mr Spano gave an oral promise or assurance that the goods in this new container traffic would be carried under deck. He made the promise in order to induce Mr Leonard to agree to the goods being carried in containers. On the faith of it, Mr Leonard accepted the quotations and gave orders for transport. In those circumstances the promise was binding. There was a breach of that promise and the forwarding agents are liable—unless they can rely on the printed conditions. . . . The cases are numerous in which oral promises have been held binding in spite of written exempting conditions . . . The most recent is *Mendelssohn* v. *Normand Ltd* [1969] 2 All ER 1215 at 1218, where I said: 'The printed condition is rejected because it is repugnant to the express oral promise or representation.' During the argument Roskill LJ put the case of the Hague Rules. If a carrier made a promise that goods would be shipped under deck and, contrary to that promise, they were carried on deck and there was a loss, the carrier could not rely on the limitation clause. Following these authorities, it seems to me that the forwarding agents cannot rely on the condition. There was a plain breach of the oral promise by the forwarding agents. I would allow the appeal.

Roskill LJ [Here] one is not concerned with a contract in writing (with respect, I cannot accept counsel for the defendants' argument that there was here a contract in writing) but with a contract which, as I think, was partly oral, partly in writing and partly by conduct. In such a case the court does not require to have recourse to lawyers' devices such as collateral oral warranty in order to seek to adduce evidence which would not otherwise be admissible. The court is entitled to look at and should look at all the evidence from start to finish in order to see what the bargain was that was struck between the parties. That is what we have done in this case. . . . When one does that, one finds first, as I have already mentioned, that these parties had been doing business in transporting goods from Milan to England for some time before; secondly, that transportation of goods from Milan to England was always done on trailers which were always under deck; thirdly, that the defendants wanted a change in the practice—they wanted containers used instead of trailers; fourthly, that the plaintiffs were only willing to agree to that change if they were promised by the defendant that those containers would be shipped under deck, and would not have agreed to the change but for that promise. The defendants gave such a promise which to my mind against this background plainly amounted to an enforceable contractual promise. In those circumstances it seems to me that the contract was this: 'If we continue to give you our business, you will ensure that those goods in containers are shipped under deck'; and the defendants agreed that this would be so. Thus there was a breach of that contract by the defendants when this container was shipped on deck; and it seems to me to be plain that the damage which the plaintiffs suffered resulted from that breach. That being the position, I think that counsel for the defendants' first argument fails.

I will deal very briefly with the second point, with which Lord Denning MR has already dealt fully. It is suggested that even so these exemption clauses apply. . . . I think that is an impossible argument. . . . the defendants' promise that the container would be shipped on deck would be wholly illusory. . . . It is a question of construction. Interpreting the contract as I find it to have been, I feel driven to the conclusion that none of these exemption clauses can be applied, because one has to treat the promise that no container would be shipped on deck as overriding any question of exempting condition. Otherwise, as I have already said, the promise would be illusory. . . .

GEOFFREY LANE LJ. I agree, for the reasons already expressed, that the effect of the conversation between Mr Spano of the defendants and Mr Leonard for the plaintiffs in the autumn of 1967 was to produce a binding obligation on the defendants to ensure that the plaintiffs' machinery in containers would be carried under deck between Rotterdam and Tilbury. This was not a collateral contract in the sense of an oral agreement varying the terms of a written contract. It was a new express term which was to be included thereafter in the contracts between the plaintiffs and the defendants for the carriage of machinery from Italy. Given that premise, the question which remains is whether the defendants' printed trading conditions affect that new express term in favour of the defendants. It seems to me that no great matter of principle is involved. There is no dispute that the terms of the printed contract had by the time of this particular incident, by the course of dealings, become a part of each individual contract between the plaintiffs and the defendants insofar as they were apposite. There is equally no doubt that if they are to be applied to this new express term and applied literally, they would render that term valueless to the plaintiffs. . . . The two are logically inconsistent with each other. The express new term must be taken to override the printed condition. Clauses 11 and 12 would have the effect of restricting the defendants' liability for a breach of this term to the circumstances in which such breach was due to their wilful default or wilful negligence. Whatever that may mean, the chances of the plaintiffs ever being compensated for breach of the term would be remote in the extreme. Taking the facts of the present case, for example, the undoubted breach of the term when this container was shipped on deck and therefore fell overboard was due to the defendants failing to ensure that their sister company in Rotterdam had insisted on under deck stowage. It was careless, it was inefficient, but that would not have been enough to allow the plaintiffs to succeed if conditions 11 and 12 are to be applied. It seems to me that whether the test is an objective or a subjective one, whether one takes the view of the officious invisible bystander, or the view of Mr Spano or the view of Mr Leonard himself as to the effect of the meeting in autumn 1967, the answer would be the same. The effect of their agreement was to remove from the new term the restrictions or exemptions contained in those trading conditions. Any other conclusion would be to destroy the business efficacy of the new agreement from the day it started. . . .

For these reasons I agree that this appeal succeeds.

Notes

1. Lord Denning MR decided that the oral assurance given to the plaintiffs formed a separate collateral contract, while the other two judges avoided the collateral contract device and held that the assurance was an express term of the main contract. Collateral contracts have been used in the past as a way of overcoming the problems caused by the limited remedies for misrepresentation. Because of the operation of the parole evidence rule, under which this type of oral evidence contradicting the terms of a written contract should have been excluded, the courts previously have not been so generous as the majority here in admitting terms created in this way into the main contract, and hence the need arose to place them outside in a separate contract. However, as the judgments of Roskill and Geoffrey Lane LJJ show, this is no longer considered a problem, with a more relaxed approach being taken to the strict requirements of evidence. In any case, the remedy is the same whichever approach is taken; breach of a term in the main contract and breach of a collateral contract will attract an award of damages assessed on the contractual expectation basis.

2. Had the Court of Appeal held that the oral assurance did not have contractual force, then the plaintiffs would have been thrown back on the remedies for misrepresentation. Lord Denning indicated that they would not have been able to found an action for misrepresentation, and the other two judges are silent on this point. It is worth remembering that the plaintiffs were not arguing the case in misrepresentation and that, if they had been doing so, they might have presented their evidence rather differently.

3. According to Roskill and Geoffrey Lane LJJ, the contract between the parties is partly oral, partly written, and partly based on conduct; the test they seem to be applying to construct the contents of the contract appears to be that of the officious bystander: what would a person looking at the dealings between the parties assert was part of the contract? Geoffrey Lane LJ goes as far as to say that on *any* test the oral assurance would have become part of the contract. As far as the dividing line between what will be considered a term and what will remain a so-called 'mere representation' without contractual effect is concerned, the Court of Appeal does not appear to offer a definitive test. The traditional approach is that of intention: did the parties intend a particular statement to be part of the contract (*Heilbut, Symons & Co.* v. *Buckleton*)? However, since in practice it is difficult to ascertain the intentions of two parties whose interests may be in conflict, in the light of the dominant objective theory of agreement, particular types of factor are given weight in the assessment of what constitute the terms of a contract. These include time—when was the representation made and when was the contract concluded?—the relative importance of the term for the two parties, the type of contract at issue, and the special knowledge and bargaining power of the two parties. In this case, using these factors, it could be said that the oral assurance was very important to the plaintiffs. It was also held to override the printed terms in the contract and the fact that the representation was made in the context of an ongoing contractual relationship must have been a significant factor in this context. It could not, therefore, be seen as a matter unrelated to the conclusion of the contract.

4. The refusal by the Court of Appeal to allow the defendants to stand on the printed terms of the contract and to deny liability shows us that a contract can in reality be found in a fluid relationship between parties. It may not be possible in many relational commercial situations to produce a single document, or, indeed, set of documents, and then to assert that these exclusively fix the contents of the contractual relationship. One way in which the classical law of contract has recognized this point is in its acceptance that a term may be incorporated into the contract by a consistent course of dealings (see Geoffrey Lane LJ's judgment).

IV. INCORPORATION OF TERMS

If terms have not been specifically negotiated and agreed between the parties, but rather form part of a body of terms proffered by one party for acceptance by the other, the question arises as to what the party proffering the terms must do to ensure that they are effectively incorporated into the contract.

Interfoto Picture Library Ltd. v. *Stiletto Visual Programmes Ltd.*
[1988] 1 All ER 348

The defendants were an advertising agency. They required photographs of the 1950s for a client presentation. To obtain suitable pictures, they telephoned the plaintiffs, who ran a library of photographic transparencies and with whom they had not previously dealt. The plaintiffs delivered to them on the same day 47 transparencies, together with a delivery note setting out their terms and conditions. The conditions stated, *inter alia*, that the transparencies were only on loan for 14 days, and that after that time there would be a charge of £5 plus VAT per day per transparency for their retention. The defendants did not use any of the transparencies but did not return them to the plaintiffs until 19 days after the return date. The plaintiffs submitted an invoice for £3,783.50 for the overdue period. The defendants refused to pay and the plaintiffs brought an action for the amount of the invoice. The Court of Appeal found for the defendants.

DILLON LJ The plaintiffs' claim is based on conditions printed on their delivery note. . . .

It is addressed to Mr Beeching of the defendants at the defendants' address and in the body of it the 47 transparencies are listed by number. In the top right-hand corner the date of dispatch is given as 5 March 1984 and the date for return is clearly specified as 19 March. Across the bottom, under the heading 'Conditions' fairly prominently printed in capitals, there are set out nine conditions, printed in four columns. Of these the important one is no 2 in the first column, which reads as follows:

'All transparencies must be returned to us within 14 days from the date of posting/ delivery/collection. A holding fee of £5.00 plus VAT per day will be charged for each transparency which is retained by you longer than the said period of 14 days save where a copyright licence is granted or we agree a longer period in writing with you.'

Condition 8 provides:

'When sent by post/delivered/collected the above conditions are understood to have been accepted unless the package is returned to us immediately by registered mail or by hand containing all the transparencies whole and undefaced and these conditions shall apply to all transparencies submitted to you whether or not you have completed a request form.' . . .

The sum of £3,783.50 is calculated by the plaintiffs in strict accordance with condition 2 as the fee for the retention of 47 transparencies from 19 March to 2 April 1984. It is of course important to the plaintiffs to get their transparencies back reasonably quickly, if they are not wanted, since if a transparency is out with one customer it cannot be offered to another customer, should occasion arise. It has to be said, however, that the holding fee charged by the plaintiffs by condition 2 is extremely high, and in my view exorbitant. The judge held that on a quantum meruit a reasonable charge would have been £3.50 per transparency per week, and not £5 per day, and he had evidence before him of the terms charged by some ten other photographic libraries, most of which charged less than £3.50 per week and only one of which charged more (£4 per transparency per week) . . . .

The primary point taken in the court below was that condition 2 was not part of the contract between the parties because the delivery note was never supplied to the defendants at all. That the judge rejected on the facts; he found that the delivery note was supplied in the same Jiffy bag with the transparencies, and that finding is not challenged in this court. He made no finding however that Mr Beeching or any other representative of the defendants read condition 2 or any of the other printed conditions, and it is overwhelmingly probable that they did not.

. . . The contract came into existence when the plaintiffs sent the transparencies to the defendants and the defendants, after opening the bag, accepted them by Mr Beeching's phone call to the plaintiffs at 3.10 on 5 March. The question is whether condition 2 was a term of that contract.

There was never any oral discussion of terms between the parties before the contract was made. In particular there was no discussion whatever of terms in the original telephone conversation when Mr Beeching made his preliminary inquiry. The question is therefore whether condition 2 was sufficiently brought to the defendants' attention to make it a term of the contract which was only concluded after the defendants had received, and must have known that they had received the transparencies *and* the delivery note.

This sort of question was posed, in relation to printed conditions, in the ticket cases, such *Parker* v. *South Eastern Rly Co* (1877) 2 CPD 416 in the last century. At that stage the printed conditions were looked at as a whole and the question considered by the courts was whether the printed conditions as a whole had been sufficiently drawn to a customer's attention to make the whole set of conditions part of the contract; if so the customer was bound by the printed conditions even though he never read them.

More recently the question has been discussed whether it is enough to look at a set of printed conditions as a whole. When for instance one condition in a set is particularly onerous does something special need to be done to draw customers' attention to that particular condition? In an obiter dictum in *J Spurling Ltd* v. *Bradshaw* [1956] 2 All ER 121 at 125 Denning LJ stated:

'Some clauses which I have seen would need to be printed in red ink on the face of the document with a red hand pointing to it before the notice could be held to be sufficient.'

Then in *Thornton* v. *Shoe Lane Parking Ltd* [1971] 2 QB 163 both Lord Denning MR and Megaw LJ held as one of their grounds of decision, as I read their judgments, that where a condition is particularly onerous or unusual the party seeking to enforce it must show that that condition, or an unusual condition of that particular nature, was fairly brought to the notice of the other party. . . . Megaw LJ deals with the point where he says ([1971] 2 QB 163 at 172–173):

'. . . at least where the particular condition relied on involves a sort of restriction that is not shown to be usual in that class of contract, a defendant must show that his intention to attach an unusual condition *of that particular nature* was fairly brought to the notice of the other party. How much is required as being, in the words of Mellish LJ [in *Parker* v. *South Eastern Rly Co* (1877) 2 CPD 416 at 424], "reasonably sufficient to give the plaintiff notice of the condition", depends on the nature of the restrictive condition. In the present case what has to be sought in answer to the third question is whether the defendant company did what was reasonable fairly to bring to the notice of the plaintiff, at or before the time when the contract was made, the existence of this particular condition. This condition is that part of the clause—a few words embedded in a lengthy clause— which Lord Denning MR has read, by which, in the midst of provisions as to damage to property, the defendants sought to exempt themselves from liability for any personal injury suffered by the customer while he was on their premises. Be it noted that such a condition is one which involves the abrogation of the right given to a person such as the plaintiff by statute, the Occupiers' Liability Act 1957. True, it is open under that Act for the occupier of property by a contractual term to exclude that liability. In my view, however, before it can be said that a condition of that sort, restrictive of statutory rights, has been fairly brought to the notice of a party to a contract there must be some clear indication which would lead an ordinary sensible person to realise, at or before the time of making the contract, that a term of that sort, relating to personal injury, was sought to be included. I certainly would not accept that the position has been reached today in which it is to be assumed as a matter of general knowledge, custom, practice, or whatever is the phrase that is chosen to describe it, that when one is invited to go on the property of another for such purposes as garaging a car, a contractual term is normally included that if one suffers any injury on those premises as a result of negligence on the part of the occupiers of the premises they shall not be liable.' (My emphasis.)

Counsel for the plaintiffs submits that *Thornton* v. *Shoe Lane Parking Ltd* was a case of an exemption clause and that what their Lordships said must be read as limited to exemption clauses and in particular exemption clauses which would deprive the party on whom they are imposed of statutory rights. But what their Lordships said was said by way of interpretation and application of the general statement of the law by Mellish LJ in *Parker* v. *South Eastern Rly Co* and the logic of it is applicable to any particularly onerous clause in a printed set of conditions of the one contracting party which would not be generally known to the other party.

Condition 2 of these plaintiffs' conditions is in my judgment a very onerous clause. The defendants could not conceivably have known, if their attention was not drawn to the clause, that the plaintiffs were proposing to charge a 'holding fee' for the retention of the transparencies at such a very high and exorbitant rate.

At the time of the ticket cases in the last century it was notorious that people hardly ever troubled to read printed conditions on a ticket or delivery note or similar document. That remains the case now. In the intervening years the printed conditions have tended to become more and more complicated and more and more one-sided in favour of the party who is imposing them, but the other parties, if they notice that there are printed conditions at all, generally still tend to assume that such conditions are only concerned with ancillary matters of form and are not of importance. In the ticket cases the courts held that the common law required that reasonable steps be taken to draw the other parties' attention to the printed conditions or they would not be part of the contract. It is in my judgment a logical development of the common law into modern conditions that it should be held, as it was in *Thornton* v. *Shoe Lane Parking Ltd*, that, if one condition in a set of printed conditions is particularly onerous or unusual, the party seeking to enforce it must show that that particular condition was fairly brought to the attention of the other party.

In the present case, nothing whatever was done by the plaintiffs to draw the defendants' attention particularly to condition 2; it was merely one of four columns' width of conditions printed across the foot of the delivery note. Consequently condition 2 never, in my judgment, became part of the contract between the parties.

I would therefore allow this appeal and reduce the amount of the judgment which the judge awarded against the defendants to the amount which he would have awarded on a quantum meruit on his alternative findings, i.e. the reasonable charge of £3.50 per transparency per week for the retention of the transparencies beyond a reasonable period, which he fixed at 14 days from the date of their receipt by the defendants.

BINGHAM LJ In many civil law systems, and perhaps in most legal systems outside the common law world, the law of obligations recognises and enforces an overriding principle that in making and carrying out contracts parties should act in good faith. This does not simply mean that they should not deceive each other, a principle which any legal system must recognise; its effect is perhaps most aptly conveyed by such metaphorical colloquialisms as 'playing fair', 'coming clean' or 'putting one's cards face upwards on the table'. It is in essence a principle of fair and open dealing. In such a forum it might, I think, be held on the facts of this case that the plaintiffs were under a duty in all fairness to draw the defendants' attention specifically to the high price payable if the transparencies were not returned in time and, when the 14 days had expired, to point out to the defendants the high cost of continued failure to return them.

English law has, characteristically, committed itself to no such overriding principle but has developed piecemeal solutions in response to demonstrated problems of unfairness. Many examples could be given. Thus equity has intervened to strike down unconscionable bargains. Parliament has stepped in to regulate the imposition of exemption clauses and the form of certain hire-purchase agreements. The common law also has made its contribution, by holding that certain classes of contract require the damage but are in truth a disguised penalty for breach, and in many other ways. The well-known cases on sufficiency of notice are in my view properly to be read in this context. At one level they are concerned with a question of pure contractual analysis, whether one party has done enough to give the other notice of the incorporation of a term in the contract. At another level they are concerned with a somewhat different question, whether it would in all the circumstances be fair (or reasonable) to hold a party bound by any conditions or by a particular condition of an unusual and stringent nature.

[Bingham LJ went on to examine *Parker* v. *South Eastern Rly Co.*, concluding that the judgments appear 'to base the law very firmly on consideration of what is fair in all the circumstances'.]

McCutcheon v. *David MacBrayne Ltd* [1964] 1 All ER 430 is a case out of the common run because the document containing the contractual exemption was neither issued nor signed. The interest of the case for present purposes lies in two passages in the speeches of Lord Reid and Lord Pearce. Lord Reid said ([1964] 1 All ER 430 at 432:

'If it could be said that when making the contract Mr McSporran knew that the respondents always required a risk note to be signed and knew that the purser was simply forgetting to put it before him for signature, then it might be said that neither he nor his principal could take advantage of the error of the other party of which he was aware. But counsel frankly admitted that he could not put his case as high as that.'

Lord Pearce expressed a similar opinion ([1964] 1 All ER 430 at 440):

'This is not a case where there was any bad faith on the part of the appellant or his agent. Had the appellant's agent snatched at an offer that he knew was not intended, or deliberately taken advantage of the respondents' omission to proffer their usual printed form for his signature, the situation would be different and other considerations would apply.'

Here again, as it seems to me, one finds reference to a concept of fair dealing that has very little to do with a conventional analysis of offer and acceptance. . . .

The tendency of the English authorities has, I think, been to look at the nature of the transaction in question and the character of the parties to it; to consider what notice the party alleged to be bound was given of the particular condition said to bind him; and to resolve whether in all the circumstances it is fair to hold him bound by the condition in question. This may yield a result not very different from the civil law principle of good faith, at any rate so far as the formation of the contract is concerned.

Turning to the present case. . . . Once the Jiffy bag was opened and the transparencies taken out with the delivery note, it is in my judgment an inescapable inference that the defendants would have recognised the delivery note as a document of a kind likely to contain contractual terms and would have seen that there were conditions printed in small but visible lettering on the face of the document. To the extent that the conditions so displayed were common form or usual terms regularly encountered in this business, I do not think the defendants could successfully contend that they were not incorporated into the contract.

The crucial question in the case is whether the plaintiffs can be said fairly and reasonably to have brought condition 2 to the notice of the defendants. . . . In my opinion the plaintiffs did not do so. They delivered 47 transparencies, which was a number the defendants had not specifically asked for. Condition 2 contained a daily rate per transparency after the initial period of 14 days many times greater than was usual or (so far as the evidence shows) heard of. For these 47 transparencies there was to be a charge for each day of delay of £235 plus value added tax. The result would be that a venial period of delay, as here, would lead to an inordinate liability. The defendants are not to be relieved of that liability because they did not read the condition, although doubtless they did not; but in my judgment they are to be relieved because the plaintiffs did not do what was necessary to draw this unreasonable and extortionate clause fairly to their attention. I would accordingly allow the defendants' appeal and substitute for the judge's award the sum which he assessed on the alternative basis of quantum meruit.

Notes

1. The defendants succeeded on the ground that the term was considered so unusual and onerous by the Court of Appeal that the plaintiffs had not done sufficient to bring it to their attention and consequently it was not effectively incorporated into the contract between them. On one level, as Bingham LJ points out, incorporation is simply a matter of contractual analysis—i.e. looking at offer and acceptance. Prior to the passing of the Unfair Contract Terms Act 1977, it was the most obvious way to strike down an exclusion clause simply to argue that it had never become part of the contract. Of course, this approach can still be used but, as Chapter 11 will show, the consequences of not being able to strike an exclusion clause down on the basis of non-incorporation are not so serious for a plaintiff as before. The issue remains important, however, for so-called onerous terms.

Before we reach the discussion of whether there is sufficient notice of the term in question, there are two threshold hurdles to be overcome. The first is that the clause in question has to be contained in a document which was intended to have contractual force. Whether this is the case or not is a question of fact. The court's adjudication will take into account issues such as current commercial or consumer practice (see *Chappleton* v. *Barry UDC* [1940] 1 KB 532). The defendants in *Interfoto* did not dispute that the delivery note with the transparencies had contractual force. The second hurdle is that the notice of the term must be given at the time the contract is made and not imposed at a later point after offer and acceptance have coincided. This is the position for all terms, not just onerous terms (*Olley* v. *Marlborough Court Ltd.* [1949] 1 KB 532); terms can only be added to the contract after formation if they are implied by the court (see Section VI).

Two other methods of incorporation should be mentioned. The first is signature; a person is bound by a document which he or she has signed, provided that the signature is not induced by fraud or misrepresentation (*L'Estrange* v. *Graucob Ltd.*, [1934] 2 KB 394). The second is incorporation through a course of dealing. *McCutcheon* v. *David MacBrayne Ltd.*, referred to by Bingham LJ, is an example of this. What exactly is required to constitute a course of dealing has never been made entirely clear by the courts, but the House of Lords in *McCutcheon* indicated that it must be a consistent course of dealing to the extent that a combination of oral and written transactions will not be considered enough. On this point, see further E. MacDonald, 'Incorporation of Contract Terms by a Consistent Course of Dealing', (1988) 8 *LS* 48; and 'The Duty to Give Notice of Unusual Contract Terms', [1988] *JBL* 375.

2. The defendants in *Interfoto* do not appear on the facts we are given in the report to have been deceived, coerced, or unduly influenced in any way by the plaintiffs. Protection for them can only be advocated on the basis of Bingham LJ's point about fair dealing or 'good faith'. On this footing we have then to focus on the clause in question rather than on any actual conduct of the plaintiffs. The clause is criticized by the Court of Appeal and classified as onerous on the grounds that the late-return charge is significantly higher than that applied by other agencies. It is difficult to know whether to commend the Court of Appeal for taking into account some evidence about the market place or to chastise the judges for the incompleteness of their analysis. Other points which the Court of Appeal could have looked at were the following:

The scarcity of the transparencies;
the fact that the defendants had never dealt with this agency before (did they do so on this occasion because only this agency could supply them?);
whether the transparencies in question were irreplaceable, and if so

whether this explained the charge as high enough to encourage borrowers to return them;

whether these particular transparencies were in great demand, sufficient to explain the high charge;

whether this lending agency had a reputation to maintain as providing a high-speed service. This would not have been possible if transparencies were regularly not returned on time. In those circumstances a high late-return charge might be permissible as a way of guaranteeing the service.

3. Bingham LJ refers to the implicit and 'piecemeal' recognition of the good faith principle. We have already encountered an instance where good faith is *not* recognised in English law, and that is in the formation of contracts (see *Walford* v. *Miles* [1992] 1 All ER 453, discussed in Chapter 4). We shall return to the question of the importation of good faith as a principle from the civil law systems in the discussion of the EC Directive on unfair terms in consumer contracts in the final section of Chapter 11.

4. The cases referred to in the judgment concerned mainly exclusion clauses purporting to exclude liability for personal injury or substantial property damage. It is perhaps to be expected that the courts have been quite eager to offer protection in these circumstances to parties who are unlikely to understand the contract conditions which they are given, or who do not expect to find a clause of such a serious nature amongst the conditions. *Interfoto*, on its facts, would seem a little different. It may well be that, had the defendants read the conditions, they would have returned the transparencies immediately on the grounds that the borrowing terms were unacceptable. On the other hand, they were in the position of having an onerous term imposed upon them, not one which excluded liability for personal injury. Finally, the defendants were not consumers as such; they were another company acting in the course of their business. To that extent, they were not deserving of special protection.

V. A COMMENTARY ON STANDARD FORM CONTRACTS

1. The parties in *Interfoto* traded on the plaintiff's standard terms and conditions. A contract formed in this way is often referred to as a contract of adhesion. The extract from Rakoff below sets out the typical characteristics of a contract of adhesion. Much of the debate about contracts of adhesion assumes that they are not contracts made in inter-business transactions or, if they are, that one party is more experienced or has greater bargaining power than the other. We do not know whether this was the case in *Interfoto*. We saw in Chapter 4 that exchanges between firms of standard-form contract documents could result in the so-called battle of the forms. We have to balance this against the empirical findings of S. Macaulay, in 'Non-

Contractual Relations in Business: A Preliminary Study', ((1963) 28 *Am. Soc. Rev.* 55) which were that businessmen frequently did not read the contents of standard form contracts. This appears to have been the case in *Interfoto*.

T. Rakoff, 'Contracts of Adhesion: An Essay in Reconstruction', (1983) 96 *Harv. L. Rev.* 1173 at 1176–7.

The term "contract of adhesion" has acquired many significations and therefore needs definition. One of the factors that intuitively lie at the core of the concept is the use of standard form documents. But that element is certainly not sufficient; two parties could employ standard forms as the basis for a negotiating session, and no one would be concerned. Another of the central factors is the presentation of demands on a take-it-or-leave-it basis. That too, considered alone, is not enough; sellers quote prices on a nonnegotiable basis in many quite unobjectionable contexts. It is the combination of the two elements that characterizes the problem. More precisely spelled out, the following seven characteristics define a model "contract of adhesion":

(1) The document whose legal validity is at issue is a printed form that contains many terms and clearly purports to be a contract.

(2) The form has been drafted by, or on behalf of, one party to the transaction.

(3) The drafting party participates in numerous transactions of the type represented by the form and enters into these transactions as a matter of routine.

(4) The form is presented to the adhering party with the representation that, except perhaps for a few identified items (such as the price term), the drafting party will enter into the transaction only on the terms contained in the document. This representation may be explicit or may be implicit in the situation, but it is understood by the adherent.

(5) After the parties have dickered over whatever terms are open to bargaining, the document is signed by the adherent.

(6) The adhering party enters into few transactions of the type represented by the form—few, at least, in comparison with the drafting party.

(7) The principal obligation of the adhering party in the transaction considered as a whole is the payment of money.

2. The following two extracts can be taken to illustrate the tensions between the freedom of contract paradigm and the situation of exploitation assumed by some to be created by standard-form contracts. The position expounded is that, whatever the benefits that society as a whole can derive from the use of standard form contracts, they are evidence of stronger, if not monopoly, market power, and in that sense the weaker party cannot be said to have voluntarily entered into the contractual relationship. Other exponents of this view are O. Kahn-Freud (Introduction to K. Renner, *The Institutions of Private Law and their Social Functions* (London, Routledge and Kegan Paul, 1949) and von Mehren (see Ch. 8).

F. Kessler, 'Contracts of Adhesion: Some Thoughts about Freedom of Contract', (1943) 43 *Colum. L. Rev.* 629

The development of large scale enterprise with its mass production and mass distribution made a new type of contract inevitable—the standardized mass contract. A standardized contract, once its contents have been formulated by a business firm, is used in every bargain dealing with the same product or service. The individuality of the parties which so frequently gave color to the old type contract has disappeared. The stereotyped contract of today reflects the impersonality of the market. It has reached its greatest perfection in the different types of contracts used on the various exchanges. Once the usefulness of these contracts was discovered and perfected in the transportation, insurance, and banking business, their use spread into all other fields of large scale enterprise, into international as well as national trade, and into labor relations. It is to be noted that uniformity of terms of contracts typically recurring in a business enterprise is an important factor in the exact calculation of risks. Risks which are difficult to calculate can be excluded altogether. . . .

In so far as the reduction of costs of production and distribution thus achieved is reflected in reduced prices, society as a whole ultimately benefits from the use of standard contracts. And there can be no doubt that this has been the case to a considerable extent. The use of standard contracts has, however, another aspect which has become increasingly important. Standard contracts are typically used by enterprises with strong bargaining power. The weaker party, in need of the goods or services, is frequently not in a position to shop around for better terms, either because the author of the standard contract has a monopoly (natural or artificial) or because all competitors use the same clauses. His contractual intention is but a subjection more or less voluntary to terms dictated by the stronger party, terms whose consequences are often understood only in a vague way, if at all. Thus, standardized contracts are frequently contracts of adhesion; they are *à prendre ou à laisser*. Not infrequently the weaker party to a prospective contract even agrees in advance not to retract his offer while the offeree reserves for himself the power to accept or refuse; or he submits to terms or change of terms which will be communicated to him later. To be sure, the latter type of clauses regularly provide for a power to disaffirm, but as a practical matter they are acquiesced in frequently, thus becoming part of the "living law". Lastly, standardized contracts have also been used to control and regulate the distribution of goods from producer all the way down to the ultimate consumer. They have become one of the many devices to build up and strengthen industrial empires.

Trebilcock provides us with a synopsis of Lord Diplock's judgment in *Schroeder Publicity Co. Ltd.* v. *Macaulay* ([1974] 1 WLR 1308), which is the classic judicial exposition of the exploitation thesis.

M. Trebilcock, 'An Economic Approach to Unconscionability', in B. Reiter and J. Swan (eds.), *Studies in Contract Law* **(Toronto, Butterworths, 1980, 397–8**

The judgment of Lord Diplock [in *Schroeder* v. *Macaulay]* is particularly instructive in its treatment of the alleged abuses of market power flowing from the use of standard form contracts. His Lordship said that standard forms of contract are of two kinds. The first, of early origin, are widely used in commercial transactions, are the result of extensive prior negotiations by the parties, and are adopted because "they facilitate the conduct of trade." Examples cited were bills of lading, charter parties, insurance policies, and contracts of sale in the commodity markets. Here, his Lordship said, there is a strong presumption that the terms of these contracts are fair and reasonable because they are used by parties "whose bargaining power is fairly matched."

As to the second class of standard form contracts (essentially consumer-type transactions) such a presumption was said not to apply. These were said to be of comparatively modern origin and are *"the result of the concentration of particular kinds of business in relatively few hands."* Said to exemplify this category were the ticket cases. The identifying characteristics of contracts falling into this category were described as follows:

"The terms of this kind of standard form contract have not been the subject of negotiation between the parties to it, or approved by an organization representing the interests of the weaker party. They have been dictated by that party whose bargaining power, *either exercised alone or in conjunction with others providing similar goods and services,* enables him to say: 'If you want these goods or services at all, these are the only terms on which they are obtainable. Take it or leave it.' To be in a position to adopt this attitude toward a party desirous of entering into a contract to obtain goods or services provides a classic instance of superior bargaining power."

His Lordship went on to point out that the fact that the defendants' bargaining power vis-à-vis the plaintiff was strong enough to enable them to adopt this take-it-or-leave-it attitude raised no presumption that they had used it to drive an unconscionable bargain but that special vigilance on the part of the court was called for to see that they had not. The fact that in the result the court struck down the contract means, of course, that in the court's view the defendants' superior bargaining power had in fact been abused in the terms it had exacted from the plaintiff.

A complete contrast to this judicial approach is offered by Goldberg.

V. Goldberg, 'Institutional Change and the Quasi-Invisible Hand', (1974) 17 *JL & Econ.* **461 at 483–4**

If people voluntarily enter into contracts it is because it is in their best interest to do so. If the terms of one producer are unsatisfactory, the customer will shop around for others; if information on contract terms were costlessly available (and could be analyzed costlessly) he would continue shopping until he received precisely the desired combination of price, quantity, and other contract terms. This, implicitly, is how economists have handled the problem. Additional sophistication occasionally creeps in by the recognition of costs of attaining, processing, and evaluating information; the consumer then would engage in such information processing to the point at which the expected marginal benefits of the additional information are equated to the marginal costs of its acquisition.

The point made here is simply that consumers enter into contracts to serve their own self-interest. The paradigm of contract remains, even in this case, an essentially competitive relation.

3. Critiques of the positions taken by Kessler and Lord Diplock are offered below by Rakoff and Trebilcock. Their objection is to the equation of monopoly power within the market place with the use of standard forms.

Rakoff, 'Contracts of Adhesion', 1219–24

What gives Kessler's line of analysis its rhetorical force is its apparent ability to account for the well-known features of the practice to be explained. Why are contracts of adhesion offered take-it-or-leave-it? More importantly, why are they accepted on that basis? Why are they not read? Why are their terms so often unfavourable to the adhering party? All of these questions seem to be answered by viewing contracts of adhesion as deals crammed down the throats of helpless consumers by self-serving wielders of vast economic power. At a deeper level, Kessler's analysis derives additional force from its apparent ability to explain why the substantial growth of standard form contracts is historically coincident with the rise of modern business enterprise—to explain it, that is, if one grants Kessler his premise that the growth of large firms is the result of "the innate trend of competitive capitalism towards monopoly."

But there exists a different view of modern business history, a view that emphasizes the growth not of enterprises' external power, but rather of their organizing ability and internal organization. Monopoly, indeed, is an abstract concept defined, for all its apparent flavor, only by reference to the institution of the market. In order to understand standard form contracting, one must consider not only the use of standard forms in the market, but also the more complex institutional realities that give rise to such forms in the first place.

A NEW ANALYSIS

The Practice of Using Contracts of Adhesion

The development and use of contracts of adhesion represents one facet of the domination of the modern economy by business organizations. Firms create standard form contracts in part to stabilize their external market relationships, and in part to serve the needs of a hierarchical and internally segmented structure. . . .

. . . A dominant feature in the growth of the modern business firm over the past century and a half has been the replacement of market transactions by managerial coordination. In the production of goods, for example, the path from raw material to consumer commonly has been reduced by vertical integration to require only one, or a very few, transactions. Similarly integrated systems exist in many other sectors of economic life. In part, this phenomenon reflects the fact that market transactions are not cost free. It takes money to develop the relevant information, negotiate the deal, and draft the contract. But there is more. Dealing with an outsider in the marketplace introduces uncertainties into the productive process: suppliers may not ship materials as needed; buyers may delay payments and thus threaten cash flow. Internal administration of the sequential steps involved in production and distribution, and internal processing of the inevitable disputes, allow for greater coordination and predictability, and hence lower costs. When complete integration is not possible, output and requirements contracts, franchise arrangements, and the like will often help to accomplish the same goals.

Integration has its limits, however. At the end of the economic chain is a market between the firm and the consumer that, absent rationing, will remain a market. Yet here, too, the firm will attempt to tame the market; it will try to reduce the costs of contract formation, minimize uncertainty and liability for uncertainty, and gain some command over the remaining disputes.

Standard form documents, if legally enforceable, provide a means by which business firms can administer transactions that occur on the firms' "final" markets in an effort to achieve these goals. Standardization is valuable; it reduces transaction costs. The possibilities transcend mere standardization, however, for firms can draft the terms so as to stabilize the incidents of doing business. . . . Limits on liability for consequential damages allow the firm to reduce the potential losses on any transaction and to calculate better the risks that remain. Short time limits for making claims . . . facilitate the closing of accounts and reduce the need for contingency funds. Finally, if legal liabilities are set lower than the obligations that the firm recognizes in its actual practice, the gap can provide room to manoeuvre in the face of inevitable adversity. The enterprise can build a reputation for allowing customers substantial recourse in matters of return, repair, or alteration without committing itself to maintain the policy in any particular case. . . .

Form documents promote efficiency within a complex organizational structure. First, the standardization of terms, and of the very forms on which they are recorded, facilitates co-ordination among departments. The costs of communicating special understandings rise rapidly when one department makes the sale, another delivers the goods, a third handles collections, and a fourth fields complaints. Standard terms make it possible to process transactions as a matter of routine; standard forms, with standard blank spaces, make it possible to locate rapidly whatever deal has been struck on the few customized items. Second, standardization makes possible the efficient use of expensive managerial and legal talent. Standard forms facilitate the diffusion to underlings of management's decisions regarding the risks the organization is prepared to bear, or make it unnecessary to explain these matters to subordinates at all. Third, the use of form contracts serves as an automatic check on the consequences of the acts of wayward sales personnel. The pressure to produce may tempt salesmen to make bargains into which the organization is unwilling to enter; the use of standard form contracts to state the terms of the deal obviates much of the need for, and expense of, internal control and discipline in this regard. . . .

The take-it-or-leave-it approach to form contracts is thus fundamentally grounded not only on the efficiencies of mass distribution, but also on substantial institutional rigidities. Firms do not want to negotiate individualized contracts, because doing so entails bearing not only the costs of the particular negotiations, but also the economic and institutional costs of modifying an organizational structure geared to the standardized terms.

Accordingly, no assumption of even partial market control is needed to explain why firms use contracts of adhesion. Even in a competitive market, firms will refuse to bargain their standard terms in situations in which two individuals would find it worthwhile to dicker over identical matters.

Rakoff is concerned that Kessler has paid no account to the internal organizational structures of firms and the role that these structures may play in the use of standard form contracts with ultimate consumers. Rakoff is clearly considering large organizations, whereas Kessler is perhaps thinking more of the proliferation of standard-form contracts across the contractual environment.

The following extract from Trebilcock focuses more on the issue of standard form contracts in relation to consumers and the role of monopoly power. Trebilcock's principal justification for the use of standard-form contracts *not* being an incidence of the use/misuse of monopoly power is that standard-form contracts help to reduce transaction costs, so benefiting both producer and consumer. Trebilcock makes the point that, if the market for particular goods is competitive, a firm offering harsh standard-form terms will be forced to redraft them in the light of consumers switching their purchasing preferences to other competitive firms.

M. Trebilcock, 'An Economic Approach to Unconscionability', 398–9

. . . the proposition that the use of consumer standard-form contracts is the result of the concentration of market power is entirely without factual foundation. The reason why such contracts are used is exactly the same as for their use in the commercial context, that is to "facilitate the conduct of trade," or in economic terms, to reduce transaction costs. If an agreement had to be negotiated and drafted from scratch every time a relatively standard transaction was entered into the costs of transacting for all parties involved would escalate dramatically. Moreover, it is a matter of common observation that standard forms are used (for this reason) in countless contexts where no significant degree of market concentration exists. Dry-cleaners have standard form dry-cleaning agreements, hotels standard registration forms, [etc.]. . . . The fact that in these cases a supplier's products are offered on a take-it-or-leave-it basis is evidence not of market power but of a recognition that neither producer nor consumer interests are served by incurring the costs involved in negotiating separately every transaction. Moreover, even the presence of dickering between parties, standing alone, is ambiguous as between the presence or absence of competition. Dickering may, for example, be merely a reflection of attempts by a monopolist to price discriminate among consumers by ascertaining and exploiting different demand elasticities. The use of standard forms is a totally spurious proxy for the existence of market power. The real measure of market power is not whether a supplier presents his terms of a take-it-or-leave-it basis but whether the consumer, if he decides to "leave it," has available to him a workably competitive range of alternative sources of supply. Whether this is or is not so simply cannot be derived intuitively from the fact that a particular supplier is offering non-negotiable standard-form terms. It is a matter for independent inquiry. If the market is workably competitive, any supplier offering uncompetitive standard-form terms will have to reformulate his total package of price and non-price terms to prevent consumers (at least consumers at the margin, which are the decisive consideration in such a market) from switching their business to other competitors.

Goldberg offers us a different perspective on consumer behaviour in the face of a competitive product market. His view is that consumers will not simply switch their allegiance in a competitive product market to a producer of goods who offers more favourable standard-form contracts, for two reasons. First, the information required by the consumer to behave in this way will not be easy to acquire and collate; second, a producer can react to this behaviour by departing from his particular standard-form contracts to suit that customer.

V. Goldberg, 'Institutional Change and the Quasi-Invisible Hand', 485–6

We might expect competition in the market to constrain the firm's power in this arena. After all, the firm makes its price in this arena too, and if the industry is reasonably competitive we would expect that this competition would shield the price taker from the firm's power. Why will not competition among producers protect the contract term taker as well? The answer is twofold. On the one hand the cost of acquiring and processing information on contract terms is much greater than for price; unless the firm intentionally makes the particular term an important selling point—as is sometimes the case with the length or inclusiveness of the warranty—few, if any, customers will perceive the existence of variations in terms. Any movement toward contractual equilibrium due to the aggressive bargain-seeking of a few customers will be slow indeed due to both (1) the fewness of customers who will find it worthwhile to pay the costs of acquiring information, and (2) the ease with which a producer can "contract term discriminate"—renegotiate the terms for the few aggressive customers while keeping the high information barrier for other customers virtually intact. The second answer is that the "aggressive bargain-seeking customer" is usually just a minor figure in the equilibrating process. More important, in general, is the role of new entry (or exit) of producers. If the firms in an industry are making profits because they have written standardized contract terms that are very favorable to them, they will attract new entrants into the industry. The entry will continue until excess profits are bid away. The benefits to the firms of the standardized terms will be capitalized into the firms' value. Thus, while competition between producers will in the long run yield zero profits, the firm will be able to attain a capital gain (or prevent a capital loss) by choosing the appropriate standard contract terms.

This does not necessarily mean, however, that the industry as a whole will be better off or that the industry's gains will come at the expense of the consumer. It might well be that the equilibrium terms arrived at are optimal for both producers and consumers, but there is no reason to presume this to be true.

4. Rakoff and Trebilcock also offer a perspective on consumer behaviour. Rakoff offers us the picture of consumers who realize that more obligations and risks within the transaction are being imposed upon them, but are unable to do anything about it. Trebilcock, however, suggests measures that consumers could take to force firms to change their standard form contracts.

Rakoff, 'Contracts of Adhesion', 1125–7

3. *The Form and the Adherent.*—Customers know well enough that they cannot alter any individual firm's standard document. They are largely members of the society that spawns business firms, and they understand the institutional arrangements behind the take-it-or-leave-it stance. If they do not, and if they attempt to bargain the form terms, the salesman will explain his lack of authority to vary the form. Haggling, the customer finds, requires penetrating the hierarchical structure of the firm in the hope of finding someone who will deal—a daunting and perhaps prohibitively costly endeavor. And there may in fact be no one at any level who is willing to bargain. "We cannot make an exception for one customer"—the language of standardization becomes a moral claim.

Ultimately, in transactions involving organizational hierarchies, bargaining ceases to be the expected, or even appropriate, consumer behavior.

Shopping is still possible. But for most consumer transactions, the close reading and comparison needed to make an intelligent choice among alternative forms seems grossly arduous. Moreover, many of the terms concern risks that in any individual transaction are unlikely to eventuate. It is notoriously difficult for most people, who lack legal advice and broad experience concerning the particular transaction type, to appraise these sorts of contingencies. And the standard forms—because they are drafted to cover many such contingencies—are likely to be long and complex, even if each term is plainly stated. Once form documents are seen in the context of shopping (rather than bargaining) behavior, it is clear that the near-universal failure of adherents to read and understand the documents they sign cannot be dismissed as mere laziness. In the circumstances, the rational course is to focus on the few terms that are generally well publicized and of immediate concern, and to ignore the rest. The ideal adherent who would read, understand, and compare several forms is unheard of in the legal literature and, I warrant, in life as well.

Customers do shop some terms, but within a limited compass. That compass is defined largely by immediacy of impact (cash or credit), by ease of comparability (size of downpayment), and, to a certain extent, by the customs and practices of the trade (warranty terms in some industries at some times). As the last example indicates, businesses can and occasionally do undertake to combat otherwise-rational consumer apathy in order to "sell" new form terms. This is an expensive proposition, however, because the firm must both underwrite the additional risks comprehended by the new term and bear the cost of stimulating shopping behavior. At times, special business needs will make the expense worthwhile. Ordinarily, it is preferable to compete in regard to terms that already engage the customers' attention—most notably price.

The predictable consequence is that over time more and more risks are shifted to the adhering party. Drafting parties introduce contracts of adhesion to minimize their exposure to external risks and to further internal organizational aims. Adherents respond not by reading, but instead by focusing on a few terms. The firms compete in regard to those items. The incentive for the firms is to save whatever they can with defensive form terms and employ the savings to compete with respect to the shopped terms.

Trebilcock, 'An Economic Approach to Unconscionability', 412–13

It does not follow that the supplier has unconstrained bargaining power to impose any terms that he wishes on a consumer. One of the most important determinants of whether contract terms in such circumstances might be considered fair, in the sense of having been effectively disciplined by market forces, is whether at the *margin* of the market, there are *enough* consumers who are sensitive to the content of these clauses to bring effective pressure to bear on suppliers to modify them in an acceptable way. Non-economists often overlook the importance of marginal analysis in this context. For example, if only 10 per-cent of the buyers of insurance policies or dry-cleaning services studied all terms scrupulously before contracting and were influenced in their choice of policy by their evaluation of the so-called fine print clauses, and if no supplier of insurance or dry-cleaning services was able to "term discriminate" between these con-sumers and other consumers in the market, there would be strong competitive pressures on each supplier to adjust the terms of his contracts so as to avoid los-ing this potential business. Perhaps more important than the impact of marginal consumers on the initial formulation of standard form contract terms is their impact on the subsequent enforcement of these terms. For example, no matter how draconian the exculpatory clauses in insurance policies or dry-cleaning con-tracts, few, if any, suppliers in either market will be able to survive the market reactions likely to be engendered by a supplier treating these clauses as defining the limits of his required performance. A dry cleaner who loses or ruins half the suits that are brought in for cleaning is likely to find little long-term solace in exculpatory clauses on his dry-cleaning tickets (even if enforceable).

A difficulty with Trebilcock's suggestion about the role of consumers at the margin is how they would identify each other in the market-place and co-ordinate action as a group. Trebilcock goes on to offer us some suggestions as to the role legislation could play in regulating contract terms which mis-lead consumers and terms which diverge from the reasonable expectations of the consumer. The problem of 'unfair surprise' is precisely one where the unconscionability provision of the Uniform Commercial Code has offered a useful control mechanism. There is also some legislation in the UK which purports to do this. For example, the Unfair Contract Terms Act 1977, s. 3(2)(b)(i), dictates that a party purporting by use of a contract term in a standard form contract to render a performance substantially different from that reasonably expected of him can only rely upon that contract term in so far as it satisfies a test of reasonableness. Schedule 2 to the same Act gives some guidelines for applying the reasonableness test; one of these guidelines is whether the consumer knew or ought reasonably to have known of the existence and extent of the contract terms. Although not strictly applicable to s. 3 of the Act, the Schedule 2 guidelines are proving influential in shaping the overall judicial approach to the legislation. For a fuller discussion of the Unfair Contract Terms Act 1977, see Chapter 11.

Trebilcock, 'An Economic Approach to Unconscionability', 417–18

A modest proposal would be for the doctrine of unconscionability to penalize contractual documents which in their wording or organization are apt to mis-

lead consumers. It is clear that a number of warranties or guaranties are deceptive forms of advertising. For example, warranties that in the bold print offer
"life-time" guarantees of, *e.g.*, mufflers or carpets, when "life-time" in the fine
print is defined as meaning as long as the product happens to last, are clearly
deceptive. Similarly, in the case of "guarantees" which take more rights away
from the consumer than he would have had at law without any guarantee at
all....

A more expansive formulation of a rule against unfair surprise might impose
conspicuousness, intelligibility, and specific assent requirements with respect to
clauses creating substantial divergences from the reasonable expectations of
the consumer as reflected in terms available to other consumers at the margin
of the market. Such a rule would of course avoid outright prohibitions of such
clauses but instead would attach conditional prohibitions which could be
avoided by compliance with the required standards of conspicuousness, etc.
Thus, such a rule would avoid imposing preferences on the parties while at the
same time improving, hopefully, the quality of information in the market, or at
least the thickness of the margin of sophisticated consumers whose actions
"make" the market.

5. One of the difficulties with the type of economic analysis propounded
by Trebilcock is that it does not offer a solution to the very special problems encountered by low-income consumers. To such consumers, the purchase of a defective consumer good may constitute a disaster. They may
also be forced, through lack of resources, to 'choose' low-cost, low-
standard goods, without the benefit of sellers' warranties. Finally, for a
number of reasons including lack of transport facilities, inaccessibility of
cheap credit, and non-participation in the banking system, the poor may
often pay more for consumer goods and basic necessities than the better-
off, thus locking them into a vicious circle of poverty (see generally
F. Williams, *Why the Poor Pay More* (London, Macmillan/National
Consumer Council, 1977). To such consumers, Trebilcock's notion of
negotiation at the margins by assertive consumers is almost completely
meaningless.

VI. INCOMPLETE CONTRACTS

It is common to view contract as a vehicle for *planned* exchange. In the last
three sections of this chapter, we shall be concentrating on understanding
some aspects of the 'planning' element in contract. The discussion of the
distinction between discrete and relational exchanges in Chapter 2 highlighted briefly how the role of planning may vary according to the nature of
the transaction. Macneil, for example, has argued that, in the context of

relational contracts, planning focuses more on structures and processes which facilitate the continuation and performance of the ongoing relation. There is limited specific planning of substance. Conversely, discrete exchanges may be almost exhaustively planned, leaving only very remote contingencies which are beyond the scope of reasonable planning (see I. Macneil, 'A Primer of Contract Planning', (1975) 48 *S. Cal. L. Rev.* 627). Of course, this 'ideal' of planned exchange is, for various reasons, not always achieved.

We can contrast the practice of planning, therefore, with the widespread reality of incompleteness. In doctrinal terms, an incomplete contract is one which is sufficiently certain to avoid the fate which befell the putative hire-purchase arrangement in *Scammell* v. *Ouston*, but which comes before the court for adjudication because it lacks some (sufficiently clear) provision on a particular contingency which has arisen and brought the parties into conflict. According to Schwartz, there are five causes of incompleteness:

A. Schwartz, 'Relational Contracts in the Courts: An Analysis of Incomplete Agreements and Judicial Strategies', (1992) 21 *J. Leg. St.* 271 at 278–81

First, contract language sometimes is ambiguous or vague. Second, parties may inadvertently overlook a contracting problem. Third, the costs of solving the problem may exceed the parties' private gain from a solution. Relational scholars sometimes claim that contracts are incomplete because the future is imperfectly knowable. This claim seems largely coextensive with the cost claim. Commercial parties commonly are aware of the various contingencies that can arise. Some of these contingencies may seem sufficiently remote or the costs of dealing with them sufficiently great as to make neglect the best response. The contract is incomplete with respect to the set of such contingencies that actually materializes. Fourth, a contract is incomplete because of asymmetric information. This cause is important in relational contexts but is insufficiently appreciated. To understand its effects, one must realize that parties often want to condition performance on later states of the world or actions. . . . As an example of conditioning on future actions, an employer may prefer to make the employee's pay a function of the effort he expends on the job. . . .

Fifth, and finally, contracts may be incomplete because parties prefer anonymity. For example, suppose that workers come in three types: poor (but just acceptable), average, and good. The poor worker wants to conceal his ability, and the average worker is indifferent (the average or "pooling" wage is appropriate for him). If the portions of the three types are roughly similar, the employer will begin by paying the average wage to all unless the good worker can credibly disclose her ability. When she cannot, the labor contract is incomplete: a complete contract would condition the wage on each worker's actual type.

In sum, contracts can be incomplete because of (1) the inevitable limitations of language, (2) party inadvertence, (3) the costs of creating contract terms, (4) asymmetric information, and (5) a preference on one side of the transaction for anonymity (that is, pooling). The courts' ability to complete contracts partly turns on the cause of incompleteness to which a contract is prey.

Notes

1. Given the prefatory comments about the varied significance and role of planning in discrete and relational contracts, it is to be expected that incompleteness too may well differ in form and significance, depending upon the nature of the transaction. Schwartz specifically mentions relational contracts in the context of cause 4. It is useful also to consider the impact of cost (cause 3). However, as Schwartz implies, not only will it be prohibitively expensive to plan exhaustively a relation which is expected to evolve over time, but in fact it may be inimical to the nature of the relation itself—that is, to its sensitivity to later circumstances. Thus the 'ideal' of completeness at the outset is not only unattainable but undesirable. Hadfield reinforces this point by contrasting the classical and relational approaches to completeness, pointing out that courts may have difficulty in reconciling the prima facie nature of a contractual relationship and the flexibility which the parties to a relational contract will certainly wish to retain.

G. Hadfield, 'Problematic Relations: Franchising and the Law of Incomplete Contracts', (1990) 42 *Stan. L. Rev.* 927 at 927–8

In reality, few contracts can be complete. Accordingly, classical contract law has always provided for the accidental failure of completeness resulting from linguistic ambiguity, or from the absence of provisions specifying the performances required under certain, perhaps unanticipated, conditions. More recently, however, contract scholars have recognized that the failure of completeness is not always a mere stumble on the classical path. Often, contracts are necessarily and intentionally incomplete because mutual desires for flexible, but bounded, responses to uncertain future conditions limit the scope and precision of verifiable terms. Moreover, incomplete contracts often exist deeply embedded in an ongoing relationship. The parties are not strangers; much of their interaction takes place "off the contract," mediated not by visible terms enforceable by a court, but by a particular balance of cooperation and coercion, communication and strategy.

The confluence of contract and relation makes commitment problematic.

Contracts modify an existing relational balance, incorporating the legal system into the relationship. Yet precisely because the relational balance is difficult to alter privately, incompletely specified contractual commitments are vulnerable to unintended modifications; the private relational balance is there to insinuate itself back into place through the gaps in the incomplete contract. To the extent that courts cannot distinguish between the derogation of a commitment in an incomplete contract and an exercise of the flexibility which is a part of that commitment, incomplete contracts cannot fully function in their role as anchor for many complex transactions.

2. A model for understanding judicial interventions into incomplete contracts is suggested by Kronman in the following extract. He offers two contrasting reasons for implying terms into contracts—economic efficiency and distributive justice—using as his example the implied (and unexcludable/disclaimable) warranty (or implied term) of habitability which applies in landlord/tenant relationships under US law. It is possible to assess Kronman's arguments concerning implied terms without considering in detail the equivalent provisions of English law concerning landlord and tenant relationships.

A. Kronman, 'Paternalism and the Law of Contract', (1983) 92 *Yale LJ* 763 at 766–72

In many transactions, various standard terms are implied as a matter of law. These legally-implied provisions establish a set of ready-made contract terms, and whenever the parties would have included similar provisions in their agreement, they are made better off by being spared the time and expense of having to do so. If in most transactions of a particular sort the parties prefer the standard terms the law provides, the reduction in their transaction costs is likely to exceed the increased costs incurred by the few who would prefer other implied terms and must contract out of the regime to which they will otherwise be legally subject. The legal implication of standard terms is therefore perfectly consistent with the goal of promoting efficiency by reducing transaction costs. What appears indefensible from an economic point of view is the decision to make a standard term (like the warranty of habitability) nondisclaimable, for this can make a difference only where the parties would agree to waive the warranty if they could, and in every case of this sort, the prohibition against waiver seems to reduce the parties' welfare. Such a prohibition might therefore be thought justifiable only on noneconomic grounds.

The inefficiency of nondisclaimable warranties, however, is not as obvious as this overly simple argument suggests. If we regard the warranty of habitability as a device for allocating the risk that an undetected condition will render the premises uninhabitable, it is indeed difficult to understand why, from a strictly economic point of view, the warranty should be made nondisclaimable. The warranty is a form of insurance and the tenant's decision to solicit or refuse its inclusion in the lease will depend, in theory at least, on which of the parties is able, at least expense, to insure against or take steps to prevent the feared event. This assumes, however, that when he signs the contract, the landlord does not know of any latent condition that will make the property uninhabitable. If he knows that such a condition exists, but denies that it does or fails to disclose it, the tenant's agreement to waive the warranty of habitability can hardly be characterized as an efficient allocation of risk based upon his preference for self-insurance. If the landlord has lied to the tenant, there is no economic justification for enforcing their bargain; doing so would only give others an incentive to spend more on fraud protection (a deadweight loss from society's point of view). It is no answer to say that the tenant "takes the risk" of his landlord's fraud when he agrees to waive the warranty, for this would be like saying that I take the risk of being forced to sign a contract at gunpoint when I go out unarmed and should therefore be held to any promises extorted in this way. No economist would say that it is efficient to enforce an agreement of the latter sort, and the reasons for refusing to do so are just as strong when the agreement has been procured through deliberate misrepresentation. Even if the landlord has done nothing more than fail to disclose his knowledge of the latent condition, there is no economic justification for enforcing the lease, unless his knowledge is the fruit of a deliberate and socially productive search. . . .

A second and quite different justification for refusing to permit the voluntary waiver of certain warranties, such as the warranty of habitability, follows from the idea that in some circumstances a prohibition of this sort may be an essential part of a program of distributive justice. Many, including myself, have defended the view that private law norms may legitimately be used to redistribute wealth when alternative methods of doing so are likely to be more costly or intrusive. The distributive justification for making certain contractual entitlements inalienable by prohibiting their waiver is simply an extension of this idea and is implicit in the familiar and widely accepted notion of an adhesive contract.

Where there is a striking imbalance in the bargaining power of the parties to a contract, so that one is able to dictate terms to the other—to insist that the exchange be on his terms or not at all—the contract is said to be one of adhesion. Consumer contracts are often characterized as adhesive, since the consumer has little or no control over the terms of the agreement. In recent years, courts and legislatures have intervened in the exchange process, with increasing frequency, to correct the imbalance of bargaining power that contracts of this sort appear to involve. Typically, the first step has been the judicial or statutory implication of warranty terms that increase the consumer's rights under the contract, giving him what he wants but has no power to demand. But so long as the party with the greater bargaining power can force

Contract, Power, and Justice

the other to waive whatever liability these implied terms create, he can easily restore the original imbalance the warranty is meant to correct. At this point, a court or legislature determined to achieve greater equality in bargaining power may be tempted to make the implied warranty nondisclaimable.

The attack on contracts of adhesion rests upon an unstated conception of distributive fairness; though often overlooked, it is this conception that gives the attack its appeal. Many contracts are contracts of adhesion in the general sense that one party is able to dictate terms to the other, but this alone does not make an agreement objectionable. Suppose, for example, that my neighbor owns a painting I happen to covet. I offer him $5000 for it. He responds, "$10,000 and no warranties regarding its authenticity. Take it or leave it." Clearly, the fact that I lack bargaining power and must adhere to the terms he proposes does not by itself justify a judicial or legislative effort to tip the balance in my favor. The imbalance in this case, which stems from the fact that he owns the painting and I do not, is unobjectionable because we do not care how control over the painting is distributed.

We feel differently about the distribution of control over society's available housing stock, and inequalities of bargaining power in this context therefore seem a more appropriate target for judicial or legislative attack. The distribution of housing matters more to us than the distribution of paintings: Only the first is likely to seem important from the standpoint of most theories of distributive justice. Those contracts of adhesion that disturb us do so, then, because they reflect an underlying distribution of power or resources that offends our conception of distributive fairness; when distributive concerns are weak or nonexistent, contracts of adhesion are less troubling and the concept of adhesion itself loses meaning.

It is therefore misleading to describe the nondisclaimable warranty of habitability as simply a device for correcting an imbalance in bargaining power. More accurately, it is an instrument of redistribution that seeks to shift control over housing from one group (landlords) to another (tenants) in a way that furthers the widely shared goal of insuring everyone shelter of at least a minimally decent sort. To achieve this goal, the warranty must be made nondisclaimable, for if it is not, tenants—poor tenants in particular—will routinely be required to waive their rights to habitable premises, thereby restoring whatever distributional inequities exist at the outset.

Liverpool City Council v. *Irwin*
[1977] AC 239

The tenants of a council maisonette, situated in a fifteen-storey, purpose-built, ten-year-old block of flats, withheld their rent from the council in protest at the conditions in the block. The complaints of the defendant tenants, and the others who were part of the 'rent strike', were that there were defects in the flats themselves, such as overflowing cisterns, and principally that the Council was under a duty to keep in repair and maintain the common parts of the building. These common parts were identified as lifts, staircases, and rubbish chutes, and the tenants claimed that the Council's duty extended to the provision of lighting in these areas. The Council began proceedings for possession of the defendants' flat due to non-payment of rent. The defendants filed a defence and counterclaimed for damages and an injunction alleging that the Council was in breach of an obligation implied by law to keep the common parts in repair, in breach of an implied covenant to allow quiet enjoyment of the property and in breach of the statutory covenant implied by the Housing Act 1961, s. 32.

In the County Court, the judge granted possession to the Council but also held that the Council was in breach of an implied covenant to keep the common parts of the property repaired, in breach of the covenant for quiet enjoyment and in breach of the repairing covenant implied under the Housing Act 1961, s. 32. He awarded the defendants nominal damages.

The Council appealed to the Court of Appeal. The defendants did not pursue their argument on the existence of an implied covenant for quiet enjoyment before the Court of Appeal or the House of Lords. The Court of Appeal found for the Council, but differed in their reasons for doing so. The majority (Roskill and Ormrod LJJ) found that there was no implied covenant to keep the common parts in repair. Lord Denning MR found that there was such an implied covenant, but that the Council were not in breach of it (Lord Denning's reasoning is examined more fully in the extracts from Lord Wilberforce's judgment). The Court of Appeal was unanimous in holding that there was no breach of the Housing Act 1961. The defendants appealed to the House of Lords, which upheld the decision of the Court of Appeal, but not the reasoning of the majority on the implied covenant point. Their Lordships found that there *was* an implied covenant but that the Council was not in breach of it. They held that with regard to defects within the flats the Council was in breach of its obligation under the Housing Act 1961, s. 32.

Lord Wilberforce I consider first the tenants' claim in so far as it is based on contract. The first step must be to ascertain what the contract is. . . . We look first at documentary material. As is common with council lettings there is no formal demise, or lease or tendency agreement. There is a document headed "Liverpool Corporation, Liverpool City Housing Dept." and described as "Conditions of Tenancy." This contains a list of obligations upon the tenant— he shall do this, he shall not do that, or he shall not do that without the corporation's consent. . . . At the end there is a form for signature by the tenant stating that he accepts the tenancy. On the landlord's side there is nothing, no signature, no demise, no covenant: the contract takes effect as soon as the tenants sign the form and are let into possession.

We have then a contract which is partly, but not wholly, stated in writing. In order to complete it, in particular to give it a bilateral character, it is necessary to take account of the actions of the parties and the circumstances. As actions of the parties, we must note the granting of possession by the landlords and reservation by them of the "common parts"—stairs, lifts, chutes, etc. As circumstances we must include the nature of the premises, viz., a maisonette for family use on the ninth floor of a high block, one which is occupied by a large number of other tenants, all using the common parts and dependent upon them, none of them having any expressed obligation to maintain or repair them.

To say that the construction of a complete contract out of these elements involves a process of "implication" may be correct; it would be so if implication means the supplying of what is not expressed. But there are varieties of implications which the courts think fit to make and they do not necessarily involve the same process. Where there is, on the face of it, a complete, bilateral contract, the courts are sometimes willing to add terms to it, as implied terms: this is very common in mercantile contracts where there is an established usage: in that case the courts are spelling out what both parties know and would, if asked, unhesitatingly agree to be part of the bargain. In other cases, where there is an apparently complete bargain, the courts are willing to add a term on the ground that without it the contract will not work—this is the case, if not of *The Moorcock* (1889) 14 P.D. 64 itself on its facts, at least of the doctrine of *The Moorcock* as usually applied. This is, as was pointed out by the majority in the Court of Appeal, a strict test—though the degree of strictness seems to vary with the current legal trend—and I think that they were right not to accept it as applicable here. There is a third variety of implication, that which I think Lord Denning MR favours, or at least did favour in this case, and that is the implication of reasonable terms. But though I agree with many of his instances, which in fact fall under one or other of the preceding heads, I cannot go so far as to endorse his principle; indeed, it seems to me, with respect, to extend a long, and undesirable, way beyond sound authority.

The present case, in my opinion, represents a fourth category, or I would rather say a fourth shade on a continuous spectrum. The court here is simply concerned to establish what the contract is, the parties not having themselves fully stated the terms. In this sense the court is searching for what must be implied.

What then should this contract be held to be? There must first be implied a letting, that is, a grant of the right of exclusive possession to the tenants. With this there must, I would suppose, be implied a covenant for quiet enjoyment, as a necessary incident of the letting. The difficulty begins when we consider the common parts. We start with the fact that the demise is useless unless access is obtained by the staircase; we can add that, having regard to the height of the block, and the family nature of the dwellings, the demise would be useless without a lift service; we can continue that, there being rubbish chutes built into the structures and no other means of disposing of light rubbish, there must be a right to use the chutes. The question to be answered—and it is the only question in this case—is what is to be the legal relationship between landlord and tenant as regards these matters.

There can be no doubt that there must be implied (i) an easement for the tenants and their licensees to use the stairs, (ii) a right in the nature of an easement to use the lifts, (iii) an easement to use the rubbish chutes.

But are these easements to be accompanied by any obligation upon the landlord, and what obligation? There seem to be two alternatives. The first, for which the council contends, is for an easement coupled with no legal obligation, except . . . as regards the safety of those using the facilities. . . . The alternative is for easements coupled with some obligation on the part of the landlords as regards the maintenance of the subject of them, so that they are available for use.

My Lords, in order to be able to choose between these, it is necessary to define what test is to be applied. . . . In my opinion such obligation should be read into the contract as the nature of the contract itself implicitly requires, no more, no less: a test, in other words, of necessity. The relationship accepted by the corporation is that of landlord and tenant: the tenant accepts obligations accordingly, in relation inter alia to the stairs, the lifts and the chutes. All these are not just facilities, or conveniences provided at discretion: they are essentials of the tendency without which life in the dwellings, as a tenant, is not possible. To leave the landlord free of contractual obligation as regards these matters, and subject only to administrative or political pressure, is, in my opinion, inconsistent totally with the nature of this relationship. The subject matter of the lease (high rise blocks) and the relationship created by the tenancy demand, of their nature, some contractual obligation on the landlord.

I do not think that this approach involves any innovation as regards the law of contract. . . .

It remains to define the standard. My Lords, if, as I think, the test of the existence of the term is necessity the standard must surely not exceed what is necessary having regard to the circumstances. To imply an absolute obligation to repair would go beyond what is a necessary legal incident and would indeed be unreasonable. An obligation to take reasonable care to keep in reasonable repair and usability is what fits the requirements of the case. Such a definition involves—and I think rightly—recognition that the tenants themselves have their responsibilities. What it is reasonable to expect of a landlord has a clear relation to what a reasonable set of tenants should do for themselves. . . .

I would hold therefore that the landlords' obligation is as I have described. And in agreement, I believe, with your Lordships I would hold that it has not been shown in this case that there was any breach of that obligation. On the main point therefore I would hold that the appeal fails. . . .

As regards the obligation under the Housing Act 1961, section 32, again I am in general agreement with Lord Denning MR. The only possible item which might fall within the covenant implied by this section is that of defective cisterns in the maisonette giving rise to flooding or, if this is prevented, to insufficient flushing. I do not disagree with those of your Lordships who would hold that a breach of the statutory covenant was committed in respect of this matter for which a small sum of damages may be awarded. I would allow the appeal as to this matter and dismiss it for the rest.

LORD CROSS This appeal turns chiefly upon whether the council was under any, and if so what, contractual obligation to their tenants. The printed conditions of tenancy dated July 11, 1966, imposed a great many express obligations upon the tenants but did not expressly impose any obligations of any kind upon the council.

It has been argued that the council should not be taken to have accepted any legal obligations of any kind. After all, this was a distinguished city council which expected its tenants happily to rely on it to treat them reasonably without having the temerity to expect the council to undertake any legal obligations to do so. I confess that I find this argument and similar arguments which I have often heard advanced on behalf of other organisations singularly unconvincing.

Clearly, there was a contractual relationship between the tenants and the council with legal obligations on both sides. Those of the tenants are meticulously spelt out in the council's printed form which mentions none of the council's obligations. But legal obligations can be implied as well as expressed. In order to discover what, if any, are the council's implied obligations, all the surrounding circumstances must be taken into account.

Amongst the most important surrounding circumstances are the following. This was a block 15 storeys high which was built to be let to parents with young children. The lifts and staircases were obviously provided by the council as being necessary amenities for their tenants which they impliedly gave the tenants and their families and visitors a licence to use. . . .

Could it in reality have been contemplated by the council or their tenants that the council undertook no responsibility to take, at any rate, reasonable care to keep the lifts in order and the staircases lit? No doubt the tenants also owed a duty to use the lifts and staircases reasonably; indeed, so much was clearly implied in the printed terms of the tenancy. Can a pregnant woman accompanied by a young child be expected to walk up 15, or for that matter nine, storeys in the pitch dark to reach her home? Unless the law, in circumstances such as these, imposes an obligation upon the council at least to use reasonable care to keep the lifts working properly and the staircase lit, the whole transaction becomes inefficacious, futile and absurd. I cannot go so far as Lord Denning MR and hold that the courts have any power to imply a term into a contract merely because it seems reasonable to do so. Indeed, I think that such a proposition is contrary to all authority. To say, as Lord Reid said in *Young & Marten Ltd.* v. *McManus Childs Ltd.* [1969] 1 A.C. 454, 465, that ". . . no warranty ought to be implied in a contract unless it is in all the circumstances reasonable" is, in my view, quite different from saying that any warranty or term which is, in all the circumstances, reasonable ought to be implied in a contract. I am confident that Lord Reid meant no more than that unless a warranty or term is in all the circumstances reasonable there can be no question of implying it into a contract, but before it is implied much else besides is necessary, for example that without it the contract would be inefficacious, futile and absurd. . . .

I find it difficult to think of any term which it could be more necessary to imply than one without which the whole transaction would become futile, inefficacious and absurd as it would do if in a 15 storey block of flats or maisonettes, such as the present, the landlords were under no legal duty to take reasonable care to keep the lifts in working order and the staircases lit.

Notes

1. Lord Wilberforce identifies three situations in which a court may decide to imply terms into a contract. The first of these concerns a term to which both parties would agree if asked. This is reminiscent of Kronman's exposition of the transaction cost approach to the implication of terms. The second situation is that the court can imply a term into a contract if without that term the contract would not work. This too can be equated with the transaction cost approach outlined by Kronman. The implication of a term in these circumstances is called a term implied in fact. The test the courts use is one of necessity and business efficacy. The third of Lord Wilberforce's situations concerned the type of term to be implied in the contract between the City Council and the tenants. It was a term that would create a legal duty on the part of the City Council and as such is called a term implied in law. The House of Lords makes it clear that a term implied in these circumstances can only be imposed on the basis of necessity. The suggestion made by the Master of the Rolls in the Court of Appeal that such terms can be implied because it would be reasonable to do so is expressly rejected. Reasonableness is seen as only the standard by which compliance with the term is judged and not as determining its existence. For further details on recent developments in this area see A. Phang, 'Implied Terms Revisited', [1990] *JBL* 394; and 'Implied Terms in English Law: Some Recent Developments', [1993] *JBL* 242.

2. The term implied in *Liverpool City Council* v. *Irwin* cannot be simply equated with Kronman's other approach based on distributive justice. There are several competing factors in the case which have to be identified. First, as the House of Lords points out, there is the question of whether a

tenancy in one of the flats was workable unless the staircases, etc., were maintained, and, secondly, there was the conduct of the tenants and the other local residents to take into account. Should the City Council be liable for maintenance, notwithstanding acts of vandalism? This last point raises all manner of questions about the allocation of resources in local government and what tenants can expect from public-housing authorities. It would be unworkable and a serious imposition on the City Council to expect the authority to have an absolute duty to maintain and repair. The House of Lords is not really adjudicating on a situation where distributive justice or inequality of bargaining power is the contract issue, but one where issues of individual responsibility (the tenants) and state responsibility (the Council) for the conduct of irresponsible tenants and acts of vandalism by unknown third parties come into potential conflict. On the other hand, duties and standards in the context of public housing are issues which go beyond mere transaction costs; otherwise an economist may be tempted to say that for the below-market rent paid for the flats the tenants could not expect the City Council to undertake responsibility for the common parts. In reality, then, Kronman's model provides us with a starting-point for looking at judicial strategies rather than a complete model.

3. The House of Lords appears to be saying that the courts will use the same test to determine whether a term should be implied at law or in fact, i.e. a test of necessity. It has been doubted whether necessity is really a convincing way of describing the term implied by the House of Lords in *Liverpool City Council* v. *Irwin*. Treitel is of the view that the term imposed on the City Council was not necessary for the existence of the contract, i.e. it did not pass the business efficacy test. He further supports this by referring to the Sale of Goods Act 1979. This Act, along with other legislation such as the Supply of Goods and Services Act 1982, implies certain terms into contracts for the sale and supply of goods and services. A selection of illustrative terms from these statutes is set out below after the brief quotation from Treitel.

"Necessity" cannot, for example, justify the complex implied term of fitness of goods for particular purpose, set out in section 14(3) of the Sale of Goods Act 1979: it is perfectly possible to imagine a workable contract of sale which did not contain such a term. (G. Treitel, *The Law of Contract*, 8th edn. (London, Sweet and Maxwell, 1991), 191)

The Sale of Goods Act 1979

13. Sale by description.

(1) Where there is a contract for the sale of goods by description, there is an implied condition that the goods will correspond with the description.

(2) If the sale is by sample as well as by description it is not sufficient that the bulk of the goods corresponds with the sample if the goods do not also correspond with the description.

(3) A sale of goods is not prevented from being a sale by description by reason only that, being exposed for sale or hire, they are selected by the buyer.

14. Implied terms about quality or fitness.

(1) Except as provided by this section and section 15 below and subject to any other enactment, there is no implied condition or warranty about the quality or fitness for any particular purpose of goods supplied under a contract of sale.

(2) Where the seller sells goods in the course of a business, there is an implied condition that the goods supplied under the contract are of merchantable quality, except that there is no such condition—

(a) as regards defects specifically drawn to the buyer's attention before the contract is made; or

(b) if the buyer examines the goods before the contract is made, as regards defects which that examination ought to reveal.

(3) Where the seller sells goods in the course of a business and the buyer, expressly or by implication, makes known—

(a) to the seller, or

(b) where the purchase price or part of it is payable by instalments and the goods were previously sold by a credit-broker to the seller, to that credit-broker, any particular purpose for which the goods are being bought, there is an implied condition that the goods supplied under the contract are reasonably fit for that purpose, whether or not that is a purpose for which such goods are commonly supplied, except where the circumstances show that the buyer does not rely, or that it is unreasonable for him to rely, on the skill or judgment of the seller or credit-broker.

(4) An implied condition or warranty about quality or fitness for a particular purpose may be annexed to a contract of sale by usage.

(6) Goods of any kind are of merchantable quality within the meaning of subsection (2) above if they are as fit for the purpose or purposes for which goods of that kind are commonly bought as it is reasonable to expect having regard to any description applied to them, the price (if relevant) and all the other relevant circumstances.

15. Sale by sample.

(1) A contract of sale is a contract for sale by sample where there is an express or implied term to that effect in the contract.

(2) In the case of a contract for sale by sample there is an implied condition—

(a) that the bulk will correspond with the sample in quality;

(b) that the buyer will have a reasonable opportunity of comparing the bulk with the sample;

(c) that the goods will be free from any defect, rendering them unmerchantable, which would not be apparent on reasonable examination of the sample.

(3) In subsection (2)(c) above "unmerchantable" is to be construed in accordance with section 14(6) above. . . .

55. Exclusion of implied terms.

(1) Where a right, duty or liability would arise under a contract of sale of goods by implication of law, it may (subject to the Unfair Contract Terms Act 1977) be negatived or varied by express agreement, or by the course of dealing between the parties, or by such usage as binds both parties to the contract.

(2) An express condition or warranty does not negative a condition or warranty implied by this Act unless inconsistent with it.

The Supply of Goods and Services Act 1982

4. Implied terms about quality or fitness.

(1) Except as provided by this section and section 5 below and subject to the provisions of any other enactment, there is no implied condition or warranty about the quality of fitness for any particular purpose of goods supplied under a contract for the transfer of goods.

(2) Where, under such a contract, the transferor transfers the property in goods in the course of a business, there is (subject to subsection (3) below) an implied condition that the goods supplied under the contract are of merchantable quality.

(3) There is no such condition as is mentioned in subsection (2) above—

(a) as regards defects specifically drawn to the transferee's attention before the contract is made; or

(b) if the transferee examines the goods before the contract is made, as regards defects which that examination ought to reveal.

(4) Subsection (5) below applies where, under a contract for the transfer of goods, the transferor transfers the property in goods in the course of a business and the transferee, expressly or by implication, makes known—

(a) to the transferor, or

5. Implied terms where transfer is by sample.

(1) This section applies where, under a contract for the transfer of goods, the transferor transfers or agrees to transfer the property in the goods by reference to a sample.

(2) In such a case there is an implied condition—

(a) that the bulk will correspond with the sample in quality; and

(b) that the transferee will have a reasonable opportunity of comparing the bulk with the sample' and

(c) that the goods will be free from any defect, rendering them unmerchantable, which would not be apparent on reasonable examination of the sample.

(3) In subsection (2)(c) above "unmerchantable" is to be construed in accordance with section 4(9) above.

(4) For the purposes of this section a transferor transfers or agrees to transfer the property in goods by reference to a sample where there is an express or implied term to that effect in the contract concerned. . . .

8. *Implied terms where hire is by description.*

(1) This section applies where, under a contract for the hire of goods, the bailor bails or agrees to bail the goods by description.

(2) In such a case there is an implied condition that the goods will correspond with the description.

(3) If under the contract the bailor bails or agrees to bail the goods by reference to a sample as well as a description it is not sufficient that the bulk of the goods corresponds with the sample if the goods do not also correspond with the description.

(4) A contract is not prevented from falling within subsection (1) above by reason only that, being exposed for supply, the goods are selected by the bailee.

9. *Implied terms about quality or fitness.*

(1) Except as provided by this section and section 10 below and subject to the provisions of any other enactment, there is no implied condition or warranty about the quality or fitness for any particular purpose of goods bailed under a contract for the hire of goods.

(2) Where, under such a contract, the bailor bails goods in the course of a business, there is (subject to subsection (3) below) an implied condition that the goods supplied under the contract are of merchantable quality.

(3) There is no such condition as is mentioned in subsection (2) above—

(a) as regards defects specifically drawn to the bailee's attention before the contract is made; or

(b) if the bailee examines the goods before the contract is made, as regards defects which that examination ought to reveal.

(4) Subsection (5) below applies where, under a contract for the hire of goods, the bailor bails goods in the course of a business and the bailee, expressly or by implication, makes known—

(a) to the bailor in the course of negotiations conducted by him in relation to the making of the contract, or

(b) to a credit-broker in the course of negotiations conducted by that broker in relation to goods sold by him to the bailor before forming the subject matter of the contract, any particular purpose for which the goods are being bailed.

(5) In that case there is (subject to subsection (6) below) an implied condition that the goods supplied under the contract are reasonably fit for that purpose, whether or not that is a purpose for which such goods are commonly supplied.

(6) Subsection (5) above does not apply where the circumstances show that the bailee does not rely, or that it is unreasonable for him to rely, on the skill or judgment of the bailor or credit-broker.

(7) An implied condition or warranty about quality or fitness for a particular purpose may be annexed by usage to a contract for the hire of goods.

(8) The preceding provisions of this section apply to a bailment by a person who in the course of a business is acting as agent for another as they apply to a bailment by a principal in the course of a business, except where that other is not bailing in the course of a business and either the bailee knows that fact or reasonable steps are taken to bring it to the bailee's notice before the contract concerned is made.

(9) Goods of any kind are of merchantable quality within the meaning of subsection (2) above if they are as fit for the purpose or purposes for which goods of that kind are commonly supplied as it is reasonable to expect having regard to any description applied to them, the consideration for the bailment (if relevant) and all the other relevant circumstances. . . .

11. Exclusion of implied terms, etc.

(1) Where a right, duty or liability would arise under a contract for the transfer of goods or a contract for the hire of goods by implication of law, it may (subject to subsection (2) below and the 1977 Act) be negatived or varied by express agreement, or by the course of dealing between the parties, or by such usage as binds both parties to the contract.

(2) An express condition or warranty does not negative a condition or warranty implied by the preceding provisions of this Act unless inconsistent with it.

(3) Nothing in the preceding provisions of this Act prejudices the operation of any other enactment or any rule of law whereby any condition or warranty (other than one relating to quality or fitness) is to be implied in a contract for the transfer of goods or a contract for the hire of goods.

4. The approach of the House of Lords in this case can be seen as using a test of necessity if we consider the facts of the particular contract; it is inconceivable that dwellings could be let in a fifteen-storey block of flats without some provision being made for the maintenance of stairways and

lifts. The alternative is that all the tenants would be individually responsible, and that is unworkable. Statutes such as the Sale of Goods Act 1979 deal with particular types of contract and use a standardized model as the basis for allocating risks. Once we move away from an individual situation to a collective one, it becomes much more difficult to define in advance what will be a necessary implication in every contract. In that sense, all we can say is that contracts of this type are likely to raise particular problems. Terms implied to deal with these problems can then be more fairly described as 'reasonable implications' rather than 'necessary implications'. As the comments of Collins in the next extract indicate, terms implied in this statutory context are more likely to go some way towards Kronman's model of distributive justice than those implied in an individual case such as *Liverpool City Council* v. *Irwin*.

H. Collins, 'Implied Duty to Give Information During Performance of Contracts', (1992) 55 *MLR* 556 at 558–9

Implied terms are usually treated by the English courts as default rules, that is, rules to govern the contractual relation in the absence of express agreement. The courts try to impute these default rules to the presumed intent of the parties. This fits into the economic analysis of default rules which suggests that, to minimise transaction costs, the rules should be those which the parties would have negotiated, were the costs of negotiation low or absent. . . .

. . . [I]t must be recognised that implied terms can also serve as a technique by which courts impose obligations on parties in particular standard types of contractual relations for the purpose of establishing a just and fair balance of obligations. These implied terms, often said to be implied by law, suggest a model for the contractual relation which will be presumed to govern the relation in the absence of express contrary provision. The implied terms are not those which were perhaps intended, but rather those which are reasonable or reasonably necessary. The origin of these terms may lie in an appreciation of how a fair allocation of risks between the parties may be achieved, or they may be based on the goal of promoting the successful performance of contracts. Many of these model contracts have been consolidated in statutes such as the Sale of Goods Act 1979.

5. If statutes such as the Sale of Goods Act 1979 and the Supply of Goods and Services Act 1982 can be explained on the basis that Collins suggests, it may seem strange that both statutes, in ss. 55 and 11 respectively, contain provisions which allow the parties to agree to contract out of these implied terms. On this basis there is nothing to stop one contracting party, subject to the rules on incorporation and onerous terms looked at earlier in this chapter as well as the rules on exclusion clauses considered in Chapter 11, from using a contract of adhesion which has the effect of causing the other

party to give up his statutory rights contained in these implied terms. The disclaimable nature of these can be explained by reference to their background. These state-supplied rules, and, indeed, terms implied on the basis of Lord Wilberforce's three situations, are supposed to reflect the actual or presumed intentions of the parties. In order to satisfy the demands of freedom of contract, therefore, such terms must in principle be disclaimable.

In the context of judicially implied terms, historically the courts have taken seriously the freedom of contract ideal and tended to favour implying terms when it could be said that both parties would derive something from the implication and would have agreed to it, or that without the implication of a term the contract would fail and freedom of contract would not be satisfied. The freedom of contract ideal equates with Kronman's transaction-cost model. The courts were less prepared to imply a term when all that could be said was that the contract would be more workable as a co-operative venture. As Chapters 2 and 8 have shown, the freedom of contract ideal has gradually been eroded by concerns about the role of contract within a welfare state, etc. *Liverpool City Council* v. *Irwin* is an illustration of this concern, as is the Unfair Contract Terms Act 1977, referred to above. This Act will be dealt with in detail in Chapter 11.

The move away from the implication of terms to satisfy the freedom of contract ideal will not necessarily result in an implication based on Kronman's other ideal of distributive justice. This was illustrated by our analysis of the result in *Liverpool City Council* v. *Irwin*. Instead, it may lead simply to a broader evaluation of the contract relationship which may or may not result in terms which reflect distributive justice.

6. The ability, within limits, to disclaim implied terms is simply one example of the wider principle that the express terms of a contract will prevail over the implied terms. However, although a term may only be implied in law if it is not contrary to the express terms of the contract, sometimes the judges have endeavoured to construe the terms of a contract in order to leave space for an implied term. A good example is *Johnstone* v. *Bloomsbury HA* ([1991] 2 WLR 1362), where the Court of Appeal held that the presence in a junior doctor's contract of employment of a term requiring him to work for 40 hours a week and to be available on call for up to an average of a further 48 hours a week did not preclude the implication of a term imposing a duty on the employer not to endanger the employee's health. The fact that the doctor was available for 48 hours did not mean that the Health Authority needed to find work to occupy him throughout the whole period (see E. MacDonald, 'Express and Implied Terms and Exemptions', (1991) 107 *LQR* 555; A. Phang, 'Implied Terms in English Law: Some Recent Developments', [1993] *JBL* 242 at 252). For further discussion of other aspects of this case, see Chapter 11.

VII. CLASSIFICATION OF THE TERMS OF THE CONTRACT

The classification of the terms of the contract is important in English law because it is a necessary step towards determining the remedial consequences of a breach of those terms.

R. Brownsword, 'Retrieving Reasons, Retrieving Rationality? A New Look at the Right to Withdraw for Breach of Contract', (1992) 5 *JCL* 83 at 83–4

In which circumstances should an innocent party to a commercial contract have the right to withdraw for breach? In other words, when should the innocent party have the option of discharging itself (and the contract-breaker) from any further primary obligations under the contract? Subject to a particular term being designated as a condition by virtue of legislation, precedent, or express agreement, and subject to the right to withdraw being expressly reserved, English law treats withdrawal as an exceptional form of relief, to be available only where damages would not be an adequate remedy. Accordingly, if we follow this approach, the critical question (in the absence of prior determination by law or by agreement) is to identify just when and why damages would not adequately compensate the innocent party for the breach. This sounds straightforward enough. Yet, as is well known, the question of the right to withdraw for breach has, for some time, been a vexed matter in the English law of contract.

To implement the principle that the right to withdraw for breach should be available only where damages would not be adequate, a familiar litany of tests and approaches has been suggested. Thus, if we follow the traditional classification approach, the test is whether the breach goes to the root of the contract, or whether it strikes at an essential or a fundamental term; if we apply the modern *Hong Kong* [*Hong Kong Fir Shipping Co. Ltd.* v. *Kawasaki Kisen Kaisha Ltd.* [1962] 2 QB 26] approach . . . the question is whether the actual consequences of the breach have deprived the innocent party of substantially the whole benefit of what has been bargained for; while, if we adopt the test proposed by Buckley LJ in the *Decro Wall* case, the question is whether 'the consequences of the breach [are] such that it would be unfair to the injured party to hold him to the contract and leave him to the remedy in damages as and when a breach or breaches may occur' (*Decro-Wall International SA* v. *Practitioners in Marketing Ltd.* [1971] 2 All ER 216). In other words, the law suggests a number of criteria for assessing the adequacy of damages, in particular, the importance of the term which has been breached (given the surrounding contractual circumstances and the presumed intentions of the parties), the seriousness of the actual consequences of the breach, and the fairness of denying to the innocent party the option of withdrawal.

Bunge Corporation v. Tradax SA
[1981] 2 All ER 513

The buyers agreed to purchase from the sellers 15 tons of soyabean meal, to be shipped from the United States. There was a chain of contracts between the sellers and the buyers involving various sub-buyers. The contract of shipment was just one of the links in the contract chain. The buyers were required to provide a ship at a nominated port and, by clause 7 of the contract, to give '15 consecutive days' notice' of the readiness of the ship to load. The buyers needed to give notice by 13 June but in fact did not give notice until 17 June. The sellers claimed that late notice was a breach of contract which entitled them to treat the contract as at an end. They also claimed damages from the buyer.

An award of damages was made at arbitration, but reversed by the Commercial Court on the grounds that the term requiring the giving of notice of readiness to load was an innominate term and that the buyers' lateness did not amount to a breach of contract. The Court of Appeal held that the term was a condition and also restored the award of damages. This finding was upheld by the House of Lords.

LORD SCARMAN In *Hong Kong Fir Shipping Co Ltd* v. *Kawasaki Kisen Kaisha Ltd* the Court of Appeal rediscovered and reaffirmed that English law recognises contractual terms which, on a true construction of the contract of which they are part, are neither conditions nor warranties but are, to quote Lord Wilberforce's words in *Bremer Handelsgesellschaft mbH* v. *Vanden Avenne-Izegem* [1978] 2 Lloyd's Rep 109 at 113, 'intermediate'. A condition is a term the failure to perform which entitles the other party to treat the contract as at an end. A warranty is a term breach of which sounds in damages but does not terminate, or entitle the other party to terminate, the contract. An innominate or intermediate term is one the effect of non-performance of which the parties expressly or (as is more usual) impliedly agree will depend on the nature and the consequences of breach. In the *Hong Kong Fir* case the term in question provided for the obligation of seaworthiness, breach of which it is well known may be trivial (e.g. one defective rivet) or very serious (e.g. a hole in the bottom of the ship). It is inconceivable that parties when including such a term in their contract could have contemplated or intended (unless they expressly say so) that one defective rivet would entitle the charterer to end the contract or that a hole in the bottom of the ship would not. I read the *Hong Kong Fir* case as being concerned as much with the construction of the contract as with the consequences and effect of breach. The first question is always, therefore, whether, on the true construction of a stipulation and the contract of which it is part, it is a condition, an innominate term, or only a warranty. If the stipulation is one which on the true construction of the contract the parties have not made a condition, and breach of which may be attended by trivial, minor or very grave consequences, it is innominate, and the court (or an arbitrator) will, in the event of dispute, have the task of deciding whether the breach that has arisen is such as the parties would have said, had they been asked at the time they made their contract, 'It goes without saying that, if that happens, the contract is at an end.'

Where, therefore, as commonly happens, the parties do not identify a stipulation as a condition, innominate term or warranty, the court will approach the problem of construction in the way outlined by Upjohn LJ ([1962] 2 QB 26 at 63–64):

'Where, however, on the true construction of the contract, the parties have not made a particular stipulation a condition, it would be unsound and misleading to conclude that, being a warranty, damages is a sufficient remedy.'

Unless the contract makes it clear, either by express provision or by necessary implication arising from its nature, purpose and circumstances ('the factual matrix' as spelt out, for example, by Lord Wilberforce in his speech in *Reardon Smith Line Ltd* v *Hansen-Tangen* [1976] 3 All ER 570 at 573–575), that a particular stipulation is a condition or only a warranty, it is an innominate term the remedy for a breach of which depends on the nature, consequences and effect of the breach. . . .

The difficulty in the present case is, as counsel's excellent argument for the appellants revealed, to determine what the true construction is to the completed cl 7 of GAFTA form 119, which the parties incorporated in their contract. After some hesitation, I have concluded that the clause was intended as a term the *buyer's* performance of which was the necessary condition to performance by the seller of his obligations. The contract, when made, was, to use the idiom of Diplock LJ (in *Hong Kong Fir* [1962] 2 QB 26 at 65 . . ., 'synallagmatic', i.e. a contract of mutual engagements to be performed in the future, or, in the more familiar English/Latin idiom, an executory contract. The seller needed sufficient notice to enable him to choose the loading port; the parties were agreed that the notice to be given him was 15 days; this was a mercantile contract in which the parties required to know where they stood not merely later with hindsight but at once as events occurred. Because it makes commercial sense to treat the clause in the context and circumstances of this contract as a condition to be performed before the seller takes his steps to comply with bargain, I would hold it to be not an innominate term but a condition.

LORD LOWRY The term in question in *Hong Kong Fir* was one relating to seaworthiness, and the entire court agreed that it was not a condition but a term the remedy for a breach of which might be rescission (with or without damages) or merely damages for the breach. Secondly Diplock LJ introduces the discussion by saying that there are many contractual undertakings of a more complex character which cannot be categorised as being conditions or warranties. . . . And the description which has since been applied to this kind of term provides a conclusive answer to the appellants' contention. It is 'intermediate' because it lies in the middle *between* a condition and a warranty (just as the remedy for its breach lies somewhere between the remedies for breach of a condition and breach of a warranty), and it is 'innominate' because it is not *called* a condition or a warranty but assumes the character of each in turn.

It is by construing a contract (which can be done as soon as the contract is made) that one decides whether a term is, either expressly or by necessary implication, a condition, and not by considering the gravity of the breach of that term (which cannot be done until the breach is imminent or has occurred). The latter process is not an aid to construing the contract, but indicates whether rescission or merely damages is the proper remedy for a breach for which the innocent party might be recompensed in one way or the other according to its gravity. . . .

The 'wait and see' method, or, as my noble and learned friend Lord Wilberforce has put it, the 'gravity of the breach' approach, is not the way to identify a condition in a contract. This is done by construing the contract in the light of the surrounding circumstances. By his illuminating analysis Diplock LJ shed a new light on old and accepted principles; he did not purport to establish new ones.

The second general point which I desire to mention concerns stipulations as to time in mercantile contracts, in regard to which it has been said that, broadly speaking, time will be considered to be of the essence. To treat time limits thus means treating them as conditions, and he who would do so must pay respect to the principle enunciated by Roskill LJ in *Cehave NV* v. *Bremer Handelsgesellschaft mbH* [1976] QB 44 at 71 that contracts are made to be performed and not to be avoided.

The treatment of time limits as conditions in mercantile contracts does not appear to me to be justifiable by any presumption of fact or rule of law, but rather to be a practical expedient founded on and dictated by the experience of businessmen. . . .

The law having been established, why should we regard the term here in question as a condition? I start by expressing my full agreement with the reasons given in your Lordships' speeches. Among the points which have weighed with me are the following. 1. There are enormous practical advantages in certainty, not least in regard to string contracts where today's buyer may be tomorrow's seller. 2. Most members of the string will have many ongoing contracts simultaneously and they must be able to do business with confidence in the legal results of their actions. 3. Decisions would be too difficult if the term were innominate, litigation would be rife and years might elapse before the results were known. 4. The difficulty of assessing damages is an indication in favour of condition . . . 5. One can at least say that recent litigation has provided indications that the term is a condition. Parties to similar contracts should (failing a strong contra-indication) be able to rely on this: . . . 6. To make 'total loss' the only test of a condition is contrary to authority and experience, when one recalls that terms as to the date of sailing, deviation from a voyage and the date of delivery are regarded as conditions, but that failure to comply with them does not always have serious consequences. 7. Nor need an implied condition pass the total loss test: see 6 above. 8. If the consequences of breach of condition turn out to be slight, the innocent party may treat the condition as an innominate term or a warranty. 9. While the sellers could have made time of the essence, if it were not so already, this would require reasonable notice, which might well not be practical either in a string contract or at all. . . .

The only arguments against treating the term as a condition appear to me to be based on generalities, whereas the considerations which are peculiar to this contract and similar contracts tell in favour of its being a condition.

For these reasons, and for the reasons given by my noble and learned friends, I would concur in dismissing both the appeal and the cross-appeal. . . .

LORD ROSKILL . . . My Lords, the relevant phrase 'give at least 15 consecutive days' notice' consists only of six words and two digits. But the able arguments of which your Lordships have had the benefit have extended over three full days. The appellants' arguments may be summarised thus. They submitted that this term was not a condition but was what has come to be described since *Hong Kong Fir Shipping Co Ltd* v. *Kasawaki Kisen Kaisha Ltd* as an 'innominate' obligation (neither a condition nor a warranty), and that when a term is an innominate obligation the question whether or not a breach gives the innocent party the right to rescind depends on whether the innocent party was thereby deprived 'of substantially the whole benefit which it was intended he should obtain from the contract'. This last quotation is from the judgment of Diplock LJ in the *Hong Kong Fir* case [1962] 2 QB 26 at 70. It was further argued that since the respondents accepted that they could not show that admitted breach by the appellants in giving a late notice had deprived them of substantially the whole benefit which it was intended they should obtain from the contract, the respondents had no right to rescind on account of that late notice. Much reliance was also placed by counsel for the appellants on the ensuing passage in Diplock LJ's judgment: 'and the legal consequences of a breach of such an undertaking, *unless provided for expressly in the contract*, depend on the nature of the event to which the breach gives rise . . .' (my emphasis). There was, counsel argued, no such 'express' provision in this contract. Counsel also placed reliance on the application of the principle enunciated in the *Hong Kong Fir* case, which was a case of a time charterparty relating to an unseaworthy ship, to contracts for the sale of goods, such as the present, by the Court of Appeal in *Cehave NV* v. *Bremer Handelsgesellschaft mbH,* a decision approved in your Lordships' House in *Reardon Smith Line Ltd* v. *Hansen-Tangen.* The principles enunciated in the first two cases mentioned were, he said, of general application and pointed the way to a new and now correct approach to the question how a term in a contract alleged on the one hand to be a condition and on the other hand to be an 'innominate term' should be approached.

My Lords, it is beyond question that there are many cases in the books where terms the breach of which do not deprive the innocent party of substantially the whole of the benefit which he was intended to receive from the contract were nonetheless held to be conditions any breach of which entitled the innocent party to rescind. . . .

My Lords, I find nothing in the judgment of Diplock LJ in the *Hong Kong Fir* case which suggests any departure from the basic and long-standing rules for determining whether a particular term in a contract is or is not a condition and there is much in the judgment of Sellers LJ, with which Upjohn LJ expressly agreed, to show that those rules are still good law and should be maintained. They are enshrined in the oft-quoted judgment of Bowen LJ in *Bentsen* v. *Taylor, Sons & Co (No 2)* [1893] 2 QB 274 at 281:

'There is no way of deciding that question except by looking at the contract in the light of the surrounding circumstances, and then making up one's mind whether the intention of the parties, as gathered from the instrument itself, will best be carried out by treating the promise as a warranty sounding only in damages, or as a condition precedent by the failure to perform which the other party is relieved of his liability.'

That well-known passage will be found quoted by Sellers LJ in the *Hong Kong Fir* case [1962] 2 QB 26 at 60. . . .

My Lords, the judgment of Diplock LJ in the *Hong Kong Fir* case is, if I may respectfully say so, a landmark in the development of one part of our law of contract in the latter part of this century. Diplock LJ showed by reference to detailed historical analysis, contrary to what had often been thought previously, that there was no complete dichotomy between conditions and warranties and that there was a third class of term, the innominate term. But I do not believe he ever intended his judgment to afford an easy escape route from the normal consequences of rescission to a contract breaker who had broken what was, on its true construction, clearly a condition of the contract by claiming that he had only broken an innominate term. Of course when considering whether a particular term is or is not a condition it is relevant to consider to what other class or category that term, if not a condition, might belong. But to say that is not to accept that the question whether or not a term is a condition has to be determined solely by reference to what has to be proved before rescission can be claimed for breach of a term which has already been shown not to be a condition but an innominate term. . . .

My Lords, your Lordships' House had to consider a similar problem in relation to a different clause (cl 21) in a different GAFTA contract in *Bremer Handelsgesellschaft mbH* v *Vanden Avenne-Izegem*. . . . Lord Wilberforce said ([1978] 2 Lloyd's Rep 109] at 113):

'Automatic and invariable treatment of a clause such as this runs counter to the approach, which modern authorities recognise, of treating such a provision as having the force of a condition (giving rise to rescission or invalidity), or of a contractual term (giving rise to damages only) according to the nature and gravity of the breach. The clause is then categorised as an innominate term. This doctrine emerged very clearly in *Hong Kong Fir Shipping Co. Ltd.* v. *Kawasaki Kisen Kaisha Ltd.* in relation to the obligation of seaworthiness, and was as applied to a contract for sale of goods made on GAFTA form 100 in *The Hansa Nord*, a decision itself approved by this House in *Reardon Smith Line* v. *Hansen-Tangen*. In my opinion, the clause may vary appropriately and should be regarded as such an intermediate term: to do so would recognise that while in many, possibly most, instances, breach of it can adequately be sanctioned by damages, cases may exist in which, in fairness to the buyer, it would be proper to treat the cancellation as not having effect. On the other hand, always so to treat it may be often be unfair to the seller, and unnecessarily rigid.' . . .

My Lords, I venture to doubt whether much help is necessarily to be derived in determining whether a particular term is to be construed as a condition or as an innominate term by attaching a particular label to the contract. Plainly there are terms in a mercantile contract, as your Lordships' House pointed out in *Bremer Handelsgesellschaft mbH* v. *Vanden Avenne-Izegem*, which are not to be considered as conditions. But the need for certainty in mercantile contracts is often of great importance and sometimes may well be a determining factor in deciding the true construction of a particular term in such a contract.

To my mind the most important single factor of counsel's submission for the respondents is that until the requirement of the 15 consecutive days' notice was fulfilled the respondents could not nominate the 'one Gulf port' as the loading port, which under the instant contract it was their sole right to do. I agree with counsel that in a mercantile contract when a term has to be performed by one party as a condition precedent to the ability of the other party to perform another term, especially an essential term such as the nomination of a single loading port, the term as to time for the performance of the former obligation will in general fall to be treated as a condition. Until the 15 consecutive days' notice had been given, the respondents could not know for certain which loading port they should nominate so as to ensure that the contract goods would be available for loading on the ship's arrival at that port before the end of the shipment period.

It follows that in my opinion the umpire, the board of appeal and the Court of Appeal all reached the correct conclusion, and for the reasons I have given I would dismiss the appellants' appeal.

Notes

1. The remedy for breach of particular contract terms depends on how they are designated. This designation, it appears, is either made expressly or impliedly by the parties at the outset of the contract or through the intervention of the court to hold that a particular term has a particular designation. The court will use both previous case law and statutory designa-

tions of particular terms (e.g. in the Sale of Goods Act 1979) to decide which consequences flow from breach. The approach of the House of Lords in this case was to look at the contract at the time it was made and decide at that point the designation of the term. As their Lordships decided that it was a condition, then the remedy was damages and a right to terminate the contract; if they had decided that it was a warranty, then damages would have been the only remedy. What is now accepted as a supplemental approach to the traditional conditions/warranties approach was evolved by Lord Diplock in *Hong Kong Fir*. He argued that there is a third class of term—innominate or intermediate terms. The designation of the term as an innominate one gives the court the right to assess the seriousness of the breach, and to decide whether the remedy is damages and a right to terminate the contract or just damages.

The debate about the desirability of innominate terms as a classification usually centres around the competing claims of certainty and justice. The use of the condition/warranty dichotomy allows the parties to designate in advance what the particular remedies for breach will be, and to this end achieves a measure of certainty. However, in circumstances where the breach of a term labelled condition is trivial in consequence, for example, the party in breach could assert that a right to damages and termination would be unfair and unjust. The innocent party had no valid reason to terminate. The innominate terms approach overcomes this problem by allowing an assessment of the seriousness of the breach to be made at the time of the breach. This, of course, does little to achieve certainty.

2. Lord Lowry's judgment gives us the clearest reasons why a clause as to 'readiness to load' should be afforded the status of a condition. His criteria would seem to point towards the need for certainty in commercial relationships. All the judgments in the House of Lords appear influenced by the fact that the contract at issue was one in a chain of other contracts whereas the contract in *Hong Kong Fir* was a single long-term contract between two parties. The House of Lords point to the seaworthiness clause in *Hong Kong Fir* as being capable of breach on different levels of seriousness, for example, from a hole in the hull to a missing rivet. The implication is that a time clause such as readiness to load can only be breached in one way, through being late. However, there are surely degrees of lateness just as there are degrees of breach of the seaworthiness clause. It is not hard to conceive of a situation where notice is given, for example, two hours after the 15-day deadline has expired. This would make little difference even in a chain of contracts situation. What distinguishes the reasoning of the House of Lords in *Bunge* is its formalist adherence to the nature of the contract as planned by the parties, so that, in effect, even a trivial breach becomes inexcusable. The contrasting approach was taken by the House of Lords in *Reardon Smith Line Ltd.* v. *Hansen Tangen*, where

the fact that there was an error in the description of where a ship had been built could not be used by the party not in breach as an excuse to escape from a transaction which had turned out to be unprofitable. This is an example of what Adams and Brownsword (*Understanding Contract Law* (London, Fontana, 1987), 139) call the 'bad faith principle': 'a party should not be permitted to use a trivial breach as an excuse for withdrawal from a contract when the real reason for withdrawal is not the breach itself.' This leaves the courts juggling with two competing approaches: respecting the parties' planning at the inception of the contract and manipulating the doctrines in order to minimize *post hoc* opportunism to take advantage of a change in the market for the contract good.

To police this opportunism, whilst at the same time taking into account the behaviour of the party in breach, Brownsword proposes an approach to the right to withdraw which focuses, in cases where the right to withdraw is not conferred by statute, by case law, or by express agreement between the parties, on whether the innocent has good reasons for withdrawal.

R. Brownsword, 'Retrieving Reasons, Retrieving Rationality? A New Look at the Right to Withdraw for Breach of Contract', (1992) 5 *JCL* 83 at 92–3

The fact that there has been a breach of contract raises the possibility that the innocent party might have the right to withdraw. The mere fact of breach, however, is not sufficient reason. Breach warrants compensatory damages, but not necessarily the option of withdrawal. What kind of reasons, then, might an innocent party advance to support an argument in favour of the right to with-draw? Without any claim to being exhaustive of possible good reasons, six arguable grounds for the right to withdraw may be suggested as follows:

(1) the contract-breaker evinces, through the breach, a lack of commitment to the contract as a source of obligation (for example, the breach is inten-tional/calculating, or fraud/dishonesty is involved);

(2) the breach raises concerns about the competence of the contract-breaker (for example, the breach involves negligence);

(3) the breach, although unintentional and non-negligent, renders performance under the contract radically different from that envisaged at formation;

(4) proving (or quantifying) losses flowing from the breach gives rise to difficul-ties which put the innocent party at risk;

(5) the breach gives rise to concern about the contract-breaker's ability to meet future claims; and,

(6) the breach gives rise to concern about the *innocent party's* own ability to perform either the contract in question or another associated contract.

Without arguing the point, let us suppose that an innocent party claiming a right to withdraw for good reason must make out a prima facie case under any one of these heads. Further, let us suppose that the right to withdraw only obtains where the innocent party (i) acts in good faith, and (ii) has reasonable grounds for believing that the particular supporting reason applies. Accordingly, once a prima facie case has been made out, the onus shifts to the contract-breaker to rebut the innocent party's claim. This could be done by showing either a lack of good faith or a lack of reasonable grounds. The former might involve dishonesty or the like, but, crucially, if the innocent party has relied on collateral economic reasons—and, thus, is not seeking withdrawal '*for* breach'—this would constitute a lack of good faith and would disqualify withdrawal.

3. There is an argument for saying that after *Bunge* v. *Tradax* there should only be two types of term and not three: conditions which give rise to a remedy in damages and a right to terminate the contract and a second type of terms, breach of which gives rise to at least damages and possibly a right to terminate depending on the seriousness of the breach (see F. Reynolds, 'Discharge of Contract by Breach', (1981) 97 *LQR* 541). However, this runs counter to the stated views of the House of Lords in *Bunge*, which clearly lays down that there are three types of term. It would also prevent the parties from deciding at the outset of their contractual relationship that breach of some terms, no matter how serious, will result only in an award of damages. There would not seem to be any reason why they should not agree to this.

4. Termination, in the sense of the right of the innocent party to withdraw from the contract and to treat it as at an end on the grounds of a breach by the other party (termed 'rescission' throughout *Bunge*), should be distinguished from the other 'self-help' remedy of rescission *ab initio*. In the Australian case of *McDonald* v. *Dennys Lascelles Ltd.* ((1933) 48 CLR 457 at 476–7), Justice Dixon explained the distinction in the following terms:

When a party to a simple contract, upon a breach by the other contracting party of a condition of the contract, elects to treat the contract as no longer binding upon him, the contract is not rescinded as from the beginning. Both parties are discharged from the further performance of the contract, but rights are not divested or discharged which have already been unconditionally acquired. Rights and obligations which arise from the partial execution of the contract and causes of action which have accrued from its breach alike continue unaffected. When a contract is rescinded because of matters which affect its formation, as in the case of fraud, the parties are to be rehabilitated and restored, so far as may be, to the position they occupied before the contract was made. But when a contract, which is not void or voidable at law, or liable to be set aside in equity, is dissolved at the election of one party because the other has not observed an essential condition or has committed a breach going to its root, the contract is determined so far as it is executory only and the party in default is liable for damages for its breach.

This distinction has also been drawn in England by the House of Lords in *Johnson* v. *Agnew* ([1980] AC 367). The distinction explains why, once a contract has been rescinded, for example, for misrepresentation, no action can lie in damages for breach of contract, but when a contract has been terminated for breach, an action for damages also exists in respect of that breach, since the contractual duties which have been broken have not been wiped out with retrospective effect.

5. The debate about the need for commercial certainty and its antithesis—flexibility—in cases such as *Bunge* contains assumptions about the way commercial parties plan their relationships. The underlying assumptions of the structures of classical contract law are that parties plan for certainty of remedies and legal sanctions consequent on certain events. Innominate terms can be seen as a departure from such a system of rational planning, which explains why the House of Lords was adamant that there must be a core of terms which the parties can assume will attract a particular remedy at the outset of their relationship whatever the nature of the breach. In Chapter 2 we referred to the work of Stewart Macaulay. In the extract below, Macaulay describes a very different type of contract planning to that envisaged by those who focus on the condition/warranty/innominate term debate as a means of exposing the expectations placed on the law of contract by commercial parties.

S. Macaulay, 'Non-Contractual Relations in Business: A Preliminary Study', (1963) 28 *Am. Soc. Rev.* 55 at 56–65

Tentative Findings

It is difficult to generalize about the use and nonuse of contract by manufacturing industry. However, a number of observations can be made with reasonable accuracy at this time. The use and nonuse of contract in creating exchange relations and in dispute settling will be taken up in turn.

The creation of exchange relationships. In creating exchange relationships, businessmen may plan to a greater or lesser degree in relation to several types of issues. Before reporting the findings as to practices in creating such relationships, it is necessary to describe what one can plan about in a bargain and the degrees of planning which are possible.

People negotiating a contract can make plans concerning several types of issues: (1) They can plan what each is to do or refrain from doing; e.g., S might agree to deliver ten 1963 Studebaker four-door sedan automobiles to B on a certain date in exchange for a specified amount of money. (2) They can plan what effect certain contingencies are to have on their duties; e.g., what is to happen to S and B's obligations if S cannot deliver the cars because of a strike at the Studebaker factory? (3) They can plan what is to happen if either of them fails to perform; e.g., what is to happen if S delivers nine of the cars two weeks late? (4) They can plan their agreement so that it is a legally enforceable contract—that is, so that a legal sanction would be available to provide compensation for injury suffered by B as a result of S's failure to deliver the cars on time.

As to each of these issues, there may be a different degree of planning by the parties. (1) They may carefully and explicitly plan; e.g., S may agree to deliver ten 1963 Studebaker four-door sedans which have six cylinder engines, automatic transmissions and other specified items of optional equipment and which will perform to a specified standard for a certain time. (2) They may have a mutual but tacit understanding about an issue; e.g., although the subject was never mentioned in their negotiations, both S and B may assume that B may cancel his order for the cars before they are delivered if B's taxi-cab business is so curtailed that B can no longer use ten additional cabs. (3) They may have two inconsistent unexpressed assumptions about an issue; e.g., S may assume that if any of the cabs fails to perform to the specified standard for a certain time, all S must do is repair or replace it. B may assume S must also compensate B for the profits B would have made if the cab had been in operation. (4) They may never have thought of the issue; e.g., neither S nor B planned their agreement so that it would be a legally enforceable contract. Of course, the first and fourth degrees of planning listed are the extreme cases and the second and third are intermediate points. Clearly other intermediate points are possible; e.g., S and B neglect to specify whether the cabs should have automatic or conventional transmissions. Their planning is not as careful and explicit as that in the example previously given.

The following diagram represents the dimensions of creating an exchange relationship just discussed with "X's" representing the example of S and B's contract for ten taxi-cabs.

	Definition of Performances	Effect of Contingencies	Effect of Defective Performances	Legal Sanctions
Explicit and careful	X			
Tacit agreement		X		
Unilateral assumptions			X	
Unawareness of the issue				X

In larger firms such "boiler plate" provisions are drafted by the house counsel or the firm's outside lawyer. In smaller firms such provisions may be drafted by the industry trade association, may be copied from a competitor, or may be found on forms purchased from a printer. In any event, salesmen and purchasing agents, the operating personnel, typically are unaware of what is said in the fine print of the back of the forms they use. . . .

This type of standardized planning is very common. Requests for copies of the business documents used in buying and selling were sent to approximately 6,000 manufacturing firms which do business in Wisconsin. Approximately 1,200 replies were received and 850 companies used some type of standardized planning. With only a few exceptions, the firms that did not reply and the 350 that indicated they did not use standardized planning were very small manufacturers such as local bakeries, soft drink bottlers and sausage makers.

While businessmen can and often do carefully and completely plan, it is clear that not all exchanges are neatly rationalized. Although most businessmen think that a clear description of both the seller's and buyer's performances is obvious common sense, they do not always live up to this ideal. . . .

It is likely that businessmen pay more attention to describing the performances in an exchange than to planning for contingencies or defective performances or to obtaining legal enforceability of their contracts. Even when a purchase order and acknowledgment have conflicting provisions printed on the back, almost always the buyer and seller will be in agreement on what is to be sold and how much is to be paid for it. The lawyers who said businessmen often commit their firms to significant exchanges too casually, stated that the performances would be defined in the brief letter or telephone call; the lawyers objected that nothing else would be covered. Moreover, it is likely that businessmen are least concerned about planning their transactions so that they are legally enforceable contracts. For example, in Wisconsin requirements contracts—contracts to supply a firm's requirements of an item rather than a definite quantity—probably are not legally enforceable. Seven people interviewed reported that their firms regularly used requirements contracts in dealings in Wisconsin. None thought that the lack of legal sanction made any difference. . . .

Law suits for breach of contract appear to be rare. Only five of the 12 purchasing agents had ever been involved in even a negotiation concerning a contract dispute where both sides were represented by lawyers; only two of ten sales managers had ever gone this far. None had been involved in a case that went through trial. . . .

Tentative Explanations

Two questions need to be answered: (A) How can business successfully operate exchange relationships with relatively so little attention to detailed planning or to legal sanctions, and (B) Why does business ever use contract in light of its success without it?

Why are relatively non-contractual practices so common? In most situations contract is not needed.[1] Often its functions are served by other devices. Most problems are avoided without resort to detailed planning or legal sanctions because usually there is little room for honest misunderstandings or good faith differences of opinion about the nature and quality of a seller's performance. Although the parties fail to cover all foreseeable contingencies, they will exercise care to see that both understand the primary obligation on each side. Either products are standardized with an accepted description or specifications are written calling for production to certain tolerances or results. Those who write and read specifications are experienced professionals who will know the customs of their industry and those of the industries with which they deal. Consequently, these customs can fill gaps in the express agreements of the parties. Finally, most products can be tested to see if they are what was ordered; typically in manufacturing industry we are not dealing with questions of taste or judgment where people can differ in good faith.

When defaults occur they are not likely to be disastrous because of techniques of risk avoidance or risk spreading. One can deal with firms of good reputation or he may be able to get some form of security to guarantee performance. One can insure against many breaches of contract where the risks justify the costs. Sellers set up reserves for bad debts on their books and can sell some of their accounts receivable. Buyers can place orders with two or more suppliers of the same item so that a default by one will not stop the buyer's assembly lines.

Moreover, contract and contract law are often thought unnecessary because there are many effective non-legal sanctions. Two norms are widely accepted. (1) Commitments are to be honored in almost all situations; one does not welsh on a deal. (2) One ought to produce a good product and stand behind it. . . .

The final type of non-legal sanction is the most obvious. Both business units involved in the exchange desire to continue successfully in business and will avoid conduct which might interfere with attaining this goal. One is concerned with both the reaction of the other party in the particular exchange and with his own general business reputation. Obviously, the buyer gains sanctions insofar as the seller wants the particular exchange to be completed. Buyers can withhold part or all of their payments until sellers have performed to their satisfaction. If a seller has a great deal of money tied up in his performance which he must recover quickly, he will go a long way to please the buyer in order to be paid. Moreover, buyers who are dissatisfied may cancel and cause sellers to lose the cost of what they have done up to cancellation. Furthermore, sellers hope for repeat for orders, and one gets few of these from unhappy customers. . . .

---

¹ The explanation that follows emphasizes a *considered* choice not to plan in detail for all contingencies. However, at times it is clear that businessmen fail to plan because of a lack of sophistication; they simply do not appreciate the risk they are running or they merely follow patterns established in their firm years ago without reexamining these practices in light of current conditions.

Not only do the particular business units in a given exchange want to deal with each other again, they also want to deal with other business units in the future. And the way one behaves in a particular transaction, or a series of transactions, will color his general business reputation. Blacklisting can be formal or informal. Buyers who fail to pay their bills on time risk a bad report in credit rating services such as Dun and Bradstreet. Sellers who do not satisfy their customers become the subject of discussion in the gossip exchanged by purchasing agents and salesmen, at meetings of purchasing agents' associations and trade associations, or even at country clubs or social gatherings where members of top management meet. . . .

Not only are contract and contract law not needed in many situations, their use may have, or may be thought to have, undesirable consequences. Detailed negotiated contracts can get in the way of creating good exchange relationships between business units. If one side insists on a detailed plan, there will be delay while letters are exchanged as the parties try to agree on what should happen if a remote and unlikely contingency occurs. In some cases they may not be able to agree at all on such matters and as a result a sale may be lost to the seller and the buyer may have to search elsewhere for an acceptable supplier. Many businessmen would react by thinking that had no one raised the series of remote and unlikely contingencies all this wasted effort could have been avoided.

Even where agreement can be reached at the negotiation stage, carefully planned arrangements may create undesirable exchange relationships between business units. Some businessmen object that in such a carefully worked out relationship one gets performance only to the letter of the contract. Such planning indicates a lack of trust and blunts the demands of friendship, turning a cooperative venture into an antagonistic horse trade. Yet the greater danger perceived by some businessmen is that one would have to perform his side of the bargain to its letter and thus lose what is called "flexibility." Businessmen may welcome a measure of vagueness in the obligations they assume so that they may negotiate matters in light of the actual circumstances.

Adjustment of exchange relationships and dispute settlement by litigation or the threat of it also has many costs. The gain anticipated from using this form of coercion often fails to outweigh these costs, which are both monetary and non-monetary. Threatening to turn matters over to an attorney may cost no more money than postage or a telephone call; yet few are so skilled in making such a threat that it will not cost some deterioration of the relationship between the firms.

Notes

1. Macaulay refers to a 'boiler plate' clause. This is a term sometimes given to standard provisions governing performance, risk, and breach.

2. Critics of empirical work in contract have sometimes pointed out that different industries and different types of contractual relationship may produce different models of behaviour. The contractual relationships examined by Macaulay occur within specific industries related to manufacturing where there was a history of past dealing and an expectation of future dealing between the parties. These expectations to a large extent determined the use or non-use of legal sanctions. In contrast, the majority of the litigated cases on conditions, warranties, and innominate terms have come from the maritime field. It is possible that there is not the same homogeneity of interest in producing a good product or expectation of future dealings in these contracts as there is in the manufacturing industries. There is also the international nature of maritime trade, which would tend to undermine the existence of a set of generally adhered to 'rules of the game' and therefore to reinforce the need to deal through formal contract. This may account for the apparent readiness to litigate in maritime contracts as opposed to the disadvantages identified by Macaulay in the context of manufacturing contracts.

Questions

1. Is the decision of the Court of Appeal in *Interfoto* in conflict with the principle of freedom of contract? If so, why do you think the Court of Appeal chose to resolve the case by interfering in the bargain the parties appeared to have made?

2. What justifications exist for the doctrine of 'implied terms'? What conception of contractual justice do you think is exemplified by the House of Lords approach to implied terms in *Liverpool City Council* v. *Irwin*?

3. Do the analyses of standard form contracts presented in this chapter provide a convincing justification for regulating them separately from two-party transactions negotiated on an individual basis? If so, in what respects would you expect the treatment of standard form contracts to differ? You may wish to return to this question when you have studied the EC Directive on Unfair Contract Terms in Chapter 11.

4. Do you think it significant that the majority of cases on the classification of the terms of the contract have occurred in the context of shipping contracts? What factors do you think explain this phenomenon?

5. In what key respects do 'neo-classical' and relational contract theories differ in their approach to the contents of the contract? Does the work of Macaulay provide empirical support to either theory?

11

Exclusion Clauses

I. INTRODUCTION

Many of the themes of power and justice introduced and discussed in the preceding three chapters in Part III are brought together in this chapter in an analysis of exclusion clauses. Exclusion clauses are found very frequently in standard form contracts as well as in individually negotiated contracts; they are terms whereby one party seeks to disclaim or reduce his or her responsibility under the contract, for example, by excluding liability for breach of contract or by restricting the range of remedies available for breach of contract. The nature of exclusion clauses and the arguments surrounding the case for and against control are dealt with in Section II. Some sense of the almost infinite variety of possible exclusion clauses will be gained from the cases discussed in Sections III and IV.

The debate surrounding exclusion clauses as a contractual phenomenon comprises two distinct stages of analysis. First, it must be decided whether it is appropriate and necessary to subject exclusion clauses to any form of legal restraint. At this stage, the approach to be taken will depend upon an analysis of the nature and purpose of exclusion clauses. Should arguments based on the principles of freedom of contract and *laissez-faire* prevail, and are exclusion clauses simply efficient mechanisms for allocating risk whether they appear in standard form contracts or individually negotiated agreements? Alternatively, do the requirements of contractual justice demand intervention by the state, at least to protect the consumer who has not in any real sense 'consented' to the imposed terms in a standard-form contract? If it is concluded that some form of interventionism, however limited, is called for, the second stage of analysis requires an assessment of the appropriate form of regulation.

Many legal systems have developed special statutory regimes to deal with the problems raised by exclusion clauses. For example, in the United Kingdom, the Unfair Contract Terms Act 1977 operates by giving the judges a role in controlling the exclusion of liability in certain types of contract, in particular consumer contracts. It also prohibits without exception terms which seek to exclude or restrict liability for negligence which causes death or personal injury. Other systems offer a more general framework of control covering all 'onerous', 'unfair', or 'unconscionable' clauses. One example is §2-203 of the US Uniform Commercial Code, already discussed in Chapter 9. The European Community Directive on Unfair Contract Terms, when enacted into UK law, will inevitably lead to an at least partial refocusing of the system of control presently in force, and the emphasis will be placed directly on the controlling of the objectionable aspects of standard form contracts through lists of presumptively unfair types of clauses (see Section V).

These types of approach essentially depend upon a combination of statutory and judicial action and are concerned with individual cases, not general contractual regimes. Exceptionally, 'class actions' by consumer organizations may be provided for (see the Unfair Contract Terms Directive). We considered in Chapter 8 some of the difficulties attendant upon the judicial control of contract power and we return to these issues in Section II, where we also touch briefly upon alternative remedies such as administrative control of standard form contracts and systems of prior approval. However, these are matters which properly belong within a work on consumer protection rather than on the law of contract, as does an analysis of approaches based on informational strategies which aim to ensure that consumers know and understand the contractual terms by which they are bound. The issue of 'plain-language terms' is touched upon in Section V.

II. THE NATURE OF EXCLUSION CLAUSES AND THE PROBLEM OF CONTROL

Exclusion, exception, exemption, or exculpatory clauses can be seen as diminishing the risks which are borne by one party under a contract. Von Mehren offers an analysis of exclusion clauses which is centred around the related concepts of risk and insurance.

A. von Mehren, 'General Limits on the Use of Contract', in 'A General View of Contract', *International Encyclopedia of Comparative Law*, **(Tübingen/The Hague, Mohr/Nijhoff, 1982), vol. vii, ch. 1, p. 41**

Contracts almost invariably involve an allocation of risks between the parties. A contract to sell or to supply thus may shift various risks, for example, those relating to injury to persons and to the loss, damage, or destruction of objects or those attendant on changes in the value of money or variations in supply and demand. Each of these occurrences has, of course, the effect of increasing or reducing a person's total wealth. Are there then limits—and, if so, what are they—to the extent to which parties can, by contract, allocate risks in a way that departs from the allocations made by the general law of, *e.g.* contract, property, or tort?

Exculpatory provisions can operate in one of two general contexts: either they are an integral part of an insurance operation, in which case they serve to *pool* risk, or they are not connected with an insurance operation, in which event they serve to *shift* risk. Where an employer agrees to pay a higher wage in return for a provision in the employment contract excluding his normal liability for work-connected accidents and providing that the union will insure its members against these risks, the exculpation clause serves to pool risk as it constitutes an integral part of an overall insurance scheme. On the other hand, where such a clause in a contract of employment is not connected with an agreement providing for insurance of the risk in question, the clause shifts the risk from one party to the other. Of course, the party to whom the risk is shifted remains free to insure against it.

Exculpation provisions that form an integral part of an insurance operation are to be evaluated as part of that operation. Where insurance is permitted, an exculpatory clause that forms part of the insurance operation thus does not present difficulties. However, in most cases these clauses are not directly connected with insurance. They then raise the question of the extent to which risk allocations contained in the general law of contract and tort are within the domain of private ordering. These allocations presumably serve commutative justice; can they be displaced by private agreement?

Except where risks are placed by the legal order to deter or to encourage conduct—in which event the purpose of the rule may preclude risk allocations—parties should, for the most part, be free to allocate all the risks inherent in a transaction. Two limitations to this general freedom are required. The first regards the comparable qualifications of the parties as self-insurers and reinsurers. A party subject to a risk is necessarily either a self-insurer or a reinsurer. Complex and variable considerations bear on the question of which party to a given transaction should play these roles; for the most part, the legal order is prepared to leave the matter to private ordering, supplemented by optional rules of law that operate where no provision is made by the parties for the allocation of a given risk. However, where parties to a given type of transaction are, as a class, distinctly poorer self-insurers or reinsurers than other parties as a class, risk-placing rules may rest on that consideration and be mandatory. For example, both psychologically and economically, employers as a class are presumably better self-insurers and reinsurers than are employees. Accordingly, clauses in employment contracts excluding employer liability for work-connected injuries suffered by employees may well be denied enforcement. A second limitation upon party freedom to allocate risks inherent in a transaction may exist where the allocation by law serves a special social purpose such as promoting innovation or investment in an area where society wishes to encourage these.

Notes

1. Von Mehren's principal justification for denying the freedom of contracting parties to depart from general allocations of risk—namely the asymmetrical ability to insure—invites legal systems to draw a primary line of distinction between consumer contracts and commercial contracts, on the grounds that in the former case the consumer is less likely than a commercial contractor to be able to obtain, for a reasonable price, alternative cover against the risks of faulty performance by a supplier of goods or services. Although 'risk' and 'insurance' are here used as general abstract terms, von Mehren's argument does find an echo in s. 11(4)(b) of the Unfair Contract Terms Act 1977, which cites insurability as one aspect of the reasonableness test against which the validity of certain contract terms are to be measured (see Section IV below).

2. A more 'classical' assessment of the prima facie undesirability of exclusion clauses is put forward by Coote, who points to the importance of promise-keeping and of prohibiting unlawful behaviour as strong arguments against exclusion clauses.

B. Coote, *Exception Clauses* (London, Sweet and Maxwell, 1964), 138

Given the premise that exception clauses enable the promisor to escape liability for breach of his contractual promises, there is no doubt much to be said for a restrictive judicial attitude. If that is their effect, not only do exception clauses lessen the control exercised by the courts over the legal relations of the parties; they also conflict with some of the traditional theories of the nature of contract, for example, that promises should be kept and that the obligations created by the will of the parties should be enforceable by the courts. Similarly, where the courts have through the law of tort, or by implied-by-law terms in contract, sought to regulate conduct, exception clauses must appear to take away the ordinary sanctions against unlawful behaviour. When exception clauses are looked at in this way, the remarkable thing is not that they are regarded with disfavour but rather that they are permitted at all.

3. The 'distributive justice' argument against allowing the exclusion of terms implied by law was put forward by Kronman in Chapter 10. That such arguments can generate a perceived need for judicial intervention was echoed by Lord Denning MR in the Court of Appeal in *George Mitchell*. There he was discussing the legal position in relation to exclusion clauses before the advent of the Unfair Contract Terms Act 1977.

Mitchell (George) (Chesterhall) Ltd. v. *Finney Lock Seeds Ltd.*
[1983] 1 All ER 108 at 113–14

None of you nowadays will remember the trouble we had, when I was called to the Bar, with exemption clauses. They were printed in small print on the back of tickets and order forms and invoices. They were contained in catalogues or timetables. They were held to be binding on any person who took them without objection. No one ever did object. He never read them or knew what was in them. No matter how unreasonable they were, he was bound. All this was done in the name of 'freedom of contract'. But the freedom was all on the side of the big concern which had the use of the printing press. No freedom for the little man who took the ticket or order form or invoice. The big concern said, 'Take it or leave it.' The little man had no option but to take it. The big concern could and did exempt itself from liability in its own interest without regard to the little man. It got away with it time after time. When the courts said to the big concern, 'You must put it in clear words,' the big concern had no hesitation in doing so. It knew well that the little man would never read the exemption clauses or understand them.

It was a bleak winter for our law of contract. It is illustrated by two cases, *Thompson* v. *London Midland and Scottish Rly Co* [1930] 1 KB 41, (in which there was exemption from liability, not on the ticket, but only in small print at the back of the timetable, and the company were held not liable) and *L'Estrange* v. *F Graucob Ltd* [1934] 2 KB 394, (in which there was complete exemption in small print at the bottom of the order form, and the company were held not liable).

The secret weapon

Faced with this abuse of power, by the strong against the weak, by the use of the small print of the conditions, the judges did what they could to put a curb on it. They still had before them the idol, 'freedom of contract'. They still knelt down and worshipped it, but they concealed under their cloaks a secret weapon. They used it to stab the idol in the back. This weapon was called 'the true construction of the contract'. They used it with great skill and ingenuity. They used it so as to depart from the natural meaning of the words of the exemption clause and to put on them a strained and unnatural construction. In case after case, they said that the words were not strong enough to give the big concern exemption from liability, or that in the circumstances the big concern was not entitled to rely on the exemption clause. If a ship deviated from the contractual voyage, the owner could not rely on the exemption clause. If a warehousman stored the goods in the wrong warehouse, he could not pray in aid the limitation clause. If the seller supplied goods different in kind from those contracted for, he could not rely on any exemption from liability. If a shipowner delivered goods to a person without production of the bill of lading, he could not escape responsibility by reference to an exemption clause. In short, whenever the wide words, in their natural meaning, would give rise to an unreasonable result, the judges either rejected them as repugnant to the main purpose of the contract or else cut them down to size in order to produce a reasonable result.

Notes

1. The use of techniques of construction in order to restrict the ambit of exclusion clauses will be discussed in Section III. We shall also discuss the other common law technique of control—the test of incorporation. It can be argued that some exclusion clauses cause 'unfair surprise' because they are outside the norm. Such clauses have been subject to the 'red-hand' rule (cf. *Interfoto Picture Library Ltd.* v. *Stiletto Visual Programmes Ltd.*, [1988] 1 All ER 348, extracted in Chapter 10).

2. One of the difficulties with the strict construction techniques applied by the courts prior to the adoption of the Unfair Contract Terms Act 1977 was that they did not distinguish between consumer contracts and commercial contracts, or between individually negotiated arrangements and exclusion clauses found in standard-form contracts. Although Lord Denning MR seeks to create a sense of injustice by juxtaposing the 'little man' and the 'big concern', the examples which he gives at the end of the extract are of commercial arrangements where the type of interventionism which he was advocating might well have resulted in the disturbance of long-established allocations of risk and responsibility and patterns of insurance cover.

Conventional wisdom has it that consumers should be protected against exclusion clauses, imposed upon them in standard-form contracts on a 'take-it-or-leave-it' basis. However, the following extract from Schwartz appears to challenge the assumption that consumers 'want' product warranties and that the state should intervene to prohibit disclaimers of such warranties. A product warranty is a term in a contract for the sale of goods or the supply of services under which, for example, the seller or supplier promises that the goods or services are free from defects and of merchantable quality. Examples from the Sale of Goods Act 1979 and the Supply of Goods and Services Act 1982 are extracted in Chapter 10.

A. Schwartz, 'A Re-examination of Nonsubstantive Unconscionability', (1977) 63 *Va. L. Rev.* 1053 at 1056–9

POVERTY

A contracting party's poverty is commonly thought to militate in four ways against enforcing an agreement. First, poverty may impede the buyer's efforts to purchase a "fair" contract. The cost of a contract reflects, among other things, the agreement's allocation of risk between buyer and seller. For example, a contract disclaiming product warranties usually is cheaper than a contract providing such warranties. Although an affluent buyer often can pay the premium necessary to induce a seller to assume significant risk under a contract, a poor buyer may experience great difficulty in trying to buy away disfavored terms.

Second, poverty is thought to correlate strongly with a buyer's lack of commercial sophistication. A poor consumer, therefore, is often said to be at a disadvantage relative to more affluent parties in understanding and negotiating contracts. Third, poverty may restrict the flow of commercial information to poor consumers. If sellers provide less information in ghetto markets than in other markets, even a poor consumer skilled in bargaining may be unable to evaluate the terms of a proposed agreement. Fourth, poverty may exacerbate the consequences of certain contract clauses. An acceleration clause, for example, may bear more harshly upon a poor consumer than upon an affluent consumer. . . .

Prohibiting Particular Contract Clauses

Prohibiting a contract clause because a poor buyer finds it difficult to purchase more favorable terms yields a nonoptimal result. Assume, for example, that a retailer is offering two contracts that are identical except for one clause: the first contract, which costs $100, includes a warranty against product defects, while the second contract, which costs $90, includes a disclaimer of the warranty. The hypothetical retailer has customers for both contracts, but the state, by statute or judicial opinion, later bans the warranty disclaimer. Under these circumstances, the prohibition against warranty disclaimers neither helps nor hurts those customers who would have purchased warranty coverage. The prohibition, however, harms the customers who would have purchased a contract disclaiming all warranties. These consumers apparently value the insurance against product defects provided by a warranty less than they value other uses for their $10. Therefore, the prohibition against disclaimers yields a nonoptimal result: some buyers regard themselves as worse off than before the ban, and no buyers regard themselves as better off.

This result is particularly undesirable because banning warranty disclaimers is likely to affect the poor more adversely than the affluent. A poor person spends a large percentage of his income on goods for which his demand is income-inelastic, *e.g.*, food, shelter, and clothing. As his income rises, he will begin to purchase goods for which his demand is more income-elastic. Analysis indicates that a poor person's demand for warranty protection is probably more income-elastic than that for "necessities." Many of the contract clauses that are now of concern, such as warranty disclaimers, shift purchase risks to buyers. Poor people generally are more risk averse than rich people because they cannot withstand large losses. The poor, however, may lose relatively less than the middle class when purchase risks materialize because, in the circumstances discussed here, the poor have less at stake. For example, middle class buyers who default may lose valuable property, while poor buyers have much less property to lose. Also, accidents may cause middle class buyers to lose wages, while poor buyers on welfare may lose no income at all. Because a poor person, thus, is probably more anxious than a rich person to forego the insurance a warranty affords, prohibiting warranty disclaimers or other contract clauses will beat more harshly upon the poor than upon the affluent. Therefore, a contracting party's poverty, other things being equal, should militate in favor of, rather than against, enforcing a contract clause.

Note

Schwartz's conclusions on the position of the poor appear to run counter to the findings of the 'poor pay more' literature discussed in Chapter 10. They do not take account of the distributional arguments advanced by Kronman. Schwartz also appears to be making certain dubious assumptions about the extent to which both poor and affluent buyers value their interest in personal safety, an interest which may be threatened if warranty disclaimers are permitted.

Schwartz's conclusions are seriously challenged by Farber, who uses a wider frame of economic analysis. He takes account of factors such as the difficulties which consumers experience in acquiring information and their restricted ability to calculate risks.

D. Farber, 'Contract Law and Modern Economic Theory', (1983) 78 *NwUL Rev.* 303 at 329–33

Warranty Disclaimers.—One of the best-established restrictions on freedom of contract is the rule restricting the enforceability and scope of warranty disclaimers. All goods carry an implied warranty of suitability for their ordinary uses. Defects in the goods resulting in injury or property damage when the goods are put to their ordinary use constitute a breach of this implied warranty. Under a long-standing common law rule, now embodied in the Uniform Commercial Code, attempts to disclaim liability for personal injury resulting from such product defects are ineffective. In a world of perfect information, such a restriction on freedom of contract would make very little sense. Having complete knowledge of the products and warranty terms offered on the market, consumers would choose the combination of product, warranty term, and price best suited to their needs. Competition would force sellers to offer those terms sought by consumers. If any justification for the legal restrictions on warranty disclaimers exists, therefore, it must be based on the absence of perfect information.

The absence of perfect information, however, would not necessarily result in overuse of disclaimers. If competition over warranty terms were effective, disclaimers could serve a variety of useful functions. Warranties provide a form of consumer insurance against accidents. Some consumers may not wish to purchase such insurance coverage. They may already have other insurance, they may be more willing than the average consumer to take risks, or they may be especially careful and thus less likely than the average consumer to become involved in an accident. On the other hand, sellers would have a strong incentive to offer full warranties as an option. By providing additional warranty coverage, a seller could provide a signal to consumers about product quality. If consumers find it difficult to assess the quality of a product before purchasing that product, the seller could use the warranty as an inexpensive means of overcoming consumer ignorance. Given effective competition, warranty coverage would be an available option, which some consumers might waive.

Unfortunately, several significant barriers exist to effective competition over warranty terms. First, consumers find it difficult to understand the legal language used in warranties. Second, apart from the difficulty of interpreting the language of the warranty, assessing its value may also be quite difficult. In order to determine the value of warranty coverage for a particular product, one would need to determine the accident rate associated with that product and the extent of loss associated with each possible accident. The accident rate will be affected by the design of the product, the manufacturer's quality control and sources of materials and parts, and the level of care of the particular consumer using the product. Gathering such information about a particular product is likely to be quite difficult and costly. Gathering information about a sufficient number of firms to allow comparison is obviously an even more costly and difficult undertaking. . . .

In addition to these information costs, consumers also may face special difficulties in processing the information they do have available. An area of study known as "cognitive psychology" recently has received increasing attention from economists. Psychologists have developed a large body of experimental data suggesting that the ability of most individuals to process information about risks is limited in three respects. First, individuals are extremely unsophisticated about statistical theory. They tend to assign far too much weight to small samples. In general, they tend to assume that the data they possess represents the real situation; thus, they overlook other evidence suggesting the unreliability of their data. In short, they fail to anticipate properly the likelihood of future surprises.

Second, substantial evidence exists that individuals tend to underestimate the likelihood that low probability events will occur. For example, when asked about the probability of their being involved in an automobile accident in the next year, the majority of individuals selected odds of one in one hundred or greater. The real figure is one in ten.

Finally, individual decision making appears to be quite sensitive to the way in which the question that they are deciding is framed. For example, one experiment showed that doctors assess the desirability of an operation differently when told that the survival rate is eighty-five percent than when they are told the death rate is fifteen percent. In another experiment, use of seat belts varied depending on whether individuals were told the probability of an accident per trip or the probability of experiencing an accident in their lifetime.

This failure of individuals to assess risk accurately could be expected to lead consumers to undervalue sharply the benefits of warranty coverage. Apart from individuals' cognitive limitations, emotional factors also may play a part. Considering the hazards associated with purchase of a product might be a substantial source of cognitive dissonance that consumers would prefer to avoid.

Despite the barriers to acquiring and processing information about product warranties, some consumers may manage to acquire and process such information effectively. Professor Priest recently has argued that these consumers provide a sufficient check on the market and that manufacturers will tailor warranty terms to meet these consumers' needs. Several economic theorists have pointed out, however, that these "marginal" consumers may or may not be representative of the average consumer. For example, consumers who take the trouble to shop for good warranty terms may be less careful when using goods or have less insurance than other individuals. Contract terms tailored to the needs of the marginal consumer thus may not be well suited to the needs of the vast number of consumers.

Notes

1. The classic work on the consumer product warranties referred to by Farber is G. Priest, 'A Theory of the Consumer Product Warranty', (1981) 90 *Yale LJ* 1297.

2. The role of consumers at the margin was discussed in the section on standard-form contracts in Chapter 10. As Farber notes, it is difficult to extrapolate any general trends from the existence of a small number of consumers who actively resist the imposition of unfavourable terms and who negotiate individually tailored deals with suppliers. These consumers may in fact tell us little about what the law should do to protect the ordinary passive consumer who accepts imposed terms, and the consumers at the margin may do little to improve market conditions in favour of the mass of consumers.

We can take this discussion of whether exclusion clauses are fair and should be permitted, or should be controlled, further with the following synthesis by Beale of the circumstances in which 'known and understood' exclusion clauses (i.e. those which do not cause 'unfair surprise') should be permitted.

H. Beale, 'Unfair Contracts in Britain and Europe', [1989] *CLP* 197 at 205–8

It seems to me that when we are talking about a known and understood clause which the customer cannot get changed, the real reasons for saying that it may be unfair rest on one of two other grounds. One is that we feel that there are, as a matter of social policy, certain obligations which suppliers should not be able to escape and, correspondingly, certain rights of which the customer should not be deprived. The German Standard Business Terms Act of 1976 makes this assumption explicit. Art. 9 provides that terms in standard terms of business shall be void if they put the other party at an unreasonable disadvantage, and then states that unreasonable disadvantage is presumed if the clause is incompatible with the fundamental idea behind the legal rule from which it deviates. . . .

I am quite happy to accept that some prohibitions on exclusion clauses can be justified on this reasoning—the ban on exclusions of liability for death or personal injury caused by negligence, for example. I am more concerned with clauses which, by general consensus, may be fair in at least some circumstances, for instance because the customer can insure more cheaply. I would repeat the question raised by Professor Hellner: why do we assume that the rule provided by the general law should be the benchmark? To take a single instance, should sellers who deliver late always be liable for the consequential losses suffered by the buyer? The empirical evidence, though of course it is very scanty, suggests that this may not be what business people expect; and I begin to doubt whether there is anything "naturally right" about the seller having to take this responsibility when we find that in Swedish law, compensation for consequential loss caused by delay is not normally granted.

The other explanation is the one which I find much more persuasive. This is to say that the clause is unfair if, although it is compensated by a lower price, it exposes the customer to an unacceptable degree of risk. But what is unacceptable? Brownsword has recently suggested that to judge the fairness of contracts we should use a test derived from Rawls: are the terms

"such that they could be accepted by rational agents who, without knowing on which side of the transaction they might stand, had to imagine themselves as parties to the transaction?"

Brownsword argues that contracts which fail this test should not be upheld unless the losing party was consciously engaged in risk-taking. If we assume that most people are normally risk-averse, this test may work where there is exploitation of the traditional value-for-money sense. But I do not think we can use the Rawl test for harsh terms which are off-set by a lower price. If we ask whether the other party would have been prepared to enter the transaction on the same terms, we shall not get any conclusive answer. It depends upon the individual's preferences, on how averse she is to taking risks, on how serious the loss would be compared to her overall wealth.

What I think we are really saying is that a known and understood risk is nonetheless unacceptable when, not only was this customer reluctant to take it, but so would most customers be. We have moved, perhaps almost without noticing it, from controlling unfairness to promoting better, more efficient contract terms, giving the customer the rights she would have preferred and would have been prepared to pay the direct cost of, but did not get because of the costs involved in getting the standard form changed.

We now have an obvious difficulty. If we cannot assume that the general law necessarily provides the "right" answer, and if we are dealing with questions of customer preference, how is customer preference to be determined? For the reasons already given, we cannot rely on the fact that this individual customer was dissatisfied but could not secure anything better. It is not even conclusive that there appears never to have been any negotiation over the clause, even if there is some body, a trade association for instance, with whom the suppliers might have been expected to negotiate. First, the absence of negotiation or any change in the clause over time may mean that there is no margin of aware customers to bring pressure for change; but equally it might indicate that, though there are enough aware customers, the clause is acceptable to them. Secondly, if the marginal customers were dissatisfied, the supplier may have made the change unilaterally, without negotiation—it would be in its own interests to do so. . . .

What I believe we can do is to look to see whether it is likely that there is a sufficient margin of customers who are aware of the impact of the clause to exert pressure on the supplier should the terms offered not be what the customers want. The more prominent the clause, the more readily comprehensible it is, the easier it is to understand the risks it entails, and the greater the perceived probability of the risk, the more likely that customers will know enough and will bother to complain if they do not find what they want. In consumer contracts, at least, one might take into account whether the contract is one that is likely to be entered by those articulate middle-class persons who seem so ready to complain. So again, conspicuousness and intelligibility come to the fore, but this time in a different role, as creating at least a mild presumption that the clause is acceptable. . . .

If on the facts this presumption cannot be made, we then have to fall back on the normal criteria for determining whether an allocation of risk is efficient. If the clause is one excluding or limiting liability for some event which the supplier could more easily prevent than the customer, would there still be adequate incentives for the supplier to take precautions if the clause were upheld? Which party is in the better position to effect insurance or to carry the risk? How serious is the loss and what is the relative wealth of the parties? But it follows from what I said earlier that these questions should not be asked in relation to the particular customer concerned, but in relation to the run of customers.

Notes

1. The works referred to by Beale are: J. Hellner, 'Consequential Loss and Exemption Clauses', (1981) 1 *OJLS* 13; R. Brownsword, 'Liberalism and

the Law of Contract', (1989) *Archiv für Rechts- und Sozialphilosophie, Beiheft* 36, 86.

2. Beale proposes a twofold categorization of offensive and unfair terms. This is a well-established division, and is summarized by Duggan.

R. Duggan, 'Good Faith and the Enforceability of Standardized Terms", (1980) 22 *Wm. & M.L. Rev.* 1 at 4–5

. . . the use of standardized forms threatens two distinct abuses, each associated with one of the definitive characteristics. The one abuse, "surprise," occurs when the content of the standardized term diverges from the expectations of the nondrafter. This abuse follows as an inevitable consequence of the abstract generality of standardized terms. Standardized terms cannot achieve a uniform regulation of an indefinitely large number of future transactions without disregarding the unique interests of the particular nondrafter in the individual transaction. The concerted efforts of the education system and advertising industry notwithstanding, many nondrafters, whether consumers or merchants, approach transactions with distinct expectations. The other abuse, denominated "imbalance," refers to standardized terms which, by reference to some yet undefined standard, are too harsh to warrant enforcement. Given the drafter's complete control over the content of the standardized form, his profit motive, unless constrained by competition (unlikely in our highly regulated economy) or by legislative restraints, invariably will generate excessively one-sided terms.

This twofold classification also illustrates how the control of exclusion clauses cuts across the conventional distinction between procedural and substantive unfairness. The traditional common law forms of control discussed in the next chapter attach principally to the moment of formation and the process leading to formation. To a large extent, as we shall see, the statutory system set up by the Unfair Contract Terms Act 1977 is also still dominated by the moment of formation, in that this provides the point of temporal reference at which reasonableness is to be judged. However, the statutory framework also gives judges a power not hitherto held to enquire into the precise nature of the bargain between the contracting parties.

3. A test of the fairness of 'known and understood' clauses along the lines advocated by Beale makes it possible to draw a broad distinction between the differing circumstances of consumer transactions and commercial transactions, but without making an absolute division between the two. This permits a flexibility of judicial response to individual transactions which is based, as Beale emphasizes, on an assessment of the normal run of contracts in the market in question. As we shall see, there is a consistent tension within the case law on the Unfair Contract Terms Act between

seeing the reasonableness test as an individualized assessment of the balance of contractual justice in any given contract and as a general test of the fairness of certain widely used standard forms containing allocations of risk and responsibility.

4. Beale's approach would place extensive demands upon the judge in terms of a sophisticated assessment of market conditions. We considered in Chapter 8 some of the advantages and disadvantages of giving judges a role in the control of contract power. You can make an assessment of the role of the courts in England in the control of exclusion clauses after reading Sections III and IV. First, we conclude this section with a brief review of some alternative approaches to harsh terms in standard form contracts offered by Swedish and Israeli Law.

R. Cranston, *Consumers and the Law*, 2nd edn. (London, Weidenfeld and Nicholson, 1984), 80–1

A third approach to standard form contracts is that a public agency is authorized to take legal action to have offending terms declared void and their use prohibited. It might also be envisaged that the agency will seek voluntary action by businesses by negotiation and by drafting model contracts. Swedish legislation along these lines has operated since 1971. Under the Act Prohibiting Improper Contract Terms, the Consumer Ombudsman examines standard form contracts and standardized terms except in matters such as banking and insurance, and intervenes when he thinks that a clause is improper, i.e. 'it gives entrepreneurs an advantage or deprives consumers of a right and thereby causes such one-sided relations in the parties' rights and obligations under the contract that a reasonable balance between the parties no longer exists'. The Act deliberately excludes any requirement that impropriety be manifest. Terms can be referred to the Market Court which can issue an injunction against their future use. Certain clauses are deemed to be improper. Other clauses against which action has been taken include those which enable a business more than three weeks to decide whether to go through with a transaction and those which give a business the categorical right to cancel a contract and forfeit a deposit for delay in payment. Also subject to review and criticized in the preparatory work for the Act are clauses which allow the contractual price to be raised (except for changes in taxation).

Prior approval of standard form contracts is a fourth technique of consumer protection. It has not been widely used, and at most a few agreements like credit agreements must contain clauses presented in a form which, it is assumed, will be understood by and visible to consumers. Consumer groups have drawn up a number of model standard form contracts, mainly for publicity purposes, and with the hope that consumers would use them when they wanted work done, but they have been given short shrift by businesses which regard them as unfairly loaded against them. Prior approval of standard form contracts could proceed on a broad front as in Israel, where there is an administrative board to which businesses can apply to have restrictive terms in standard form contracts approved. In carrying out its task the Board must consider if, in the light of the surrounding circumstances, the clause is prejudicial to consumers or gives an unfair advantage to suppliers likely to prejudice consumers. Failure to approve renders the term(s) unenforceable, while approval prevents subsequent invalidation for a period of five years. Although certainty about the validity of their terms would seem an advantage, businesses have failed to obtain ratification, perhaps through fear that many clauses would be struck down. If the procedure is to be used some sort of mandatory provision must be introduced. In those few cases where standard form contracts have been submitted, and the Supreme Court has become involved, it has adopted a conservative interpretation and has been reluctant to invalidate restrictive terms in purely commercial contexts. The Israeli system would break down in the event that even a relatively small proportion of the standard form contracts in existence were submitted to it.

III. COMMON LAW CONTROLS ON EXCLUSION CLAUSES

In 1964, Coote made the following observation:

B. Coote, *Exception Clauses* (London, Sweet and Maxwell, 1964), 137

To the observer coming to the subject from outside, the attitudes of the English courts to exception clauses must seem a strange mixture of contradictions. In principle, the common law has allowed freedom of exclusion to an extent greater than in most judicial systems. In practice, English judges have for the most part viewed the exception clauses themselves with disfavour, and by and large have accorded to them the narrowest effect possible.

Benevolence in practice towards the 'victims' of exclusion clauses was personified by Lord Denning MR, whose hostile views on such clauses can be glimpsed from the brief extract from *George Mitchell* above. Although the advent of the Unfair Contract Terms Act has clearly influenced the assiduousness with which judges have sought out and applied common-law techniques of control, there remain two hurdles which an exclusion clause must surmount, before the application of the Act can be an issue. These are 'incorporation' and 'interpretation' or 'construction'.

Like any other contract term, the exclusion clause must be effectively incorporated into the contract, either by signature, by inclusion in a contractual document of which the plaintiff has effective notice (the 'ticket cases'), or by a consistent course of dealing (*McCutcheon* v. *David MacBrayne Ltd.* [1946] 1 All ER 430). It is a moot point whether, in the light of the statutory controls under the Act, the courts would now be prepared to apply the 'red hand' rule to the incorporation of 'surprise' terms by the giving of notice with the same eagerness as it was applied in *Interfoto* (Ch. 10).

Perhaps the harshest rule, from the perspective of contractual justice, is that which ties the consumer to contractual clauses included in or referred to in documents which he or she has signed (*L'Estrange* v. *F. Graucob Ltd.*), even though the consumer may have no knowledge or understanding of the content or effect of the clauses in question. In her feminist critique of one of the standard American Contracts casebooks (Dawson, Harvey, and Henderson, *Cases and Comments on Contracts*, 12th edn. (Mineola, NY, Foundation Press, 1982)) Frug offers a rereading of the traditional assent doctrine which binds a person signing a document to such clauses unless there has been a misrepresentation of their content or meaning by the other party (see *Curtis* v. *Chemical Cleaning and Dyeing Co.* [1951] 1 KB 805). Frug's analysis focuses on the explanatory force of a feminist critique which identifies gender stereotypes in traditional contract doctrines, as applied by the courts. As analysed by Frug, the cases on assent and signature, although devoid of any obvious 'gender factor', start to echo the paternalistic story-telling of the Court of Appeal in *Barclays Bank* v. *O'Brien* discussed in Chapter 9.

Frug, *Postmodern Legal Feminism* (New York, Routledge, 1992), 95–102

Allied Van Lines, Inc. v. *Bratton* M.-J. [351 So. 2d 344 (Fla. 1977)] . . . involves companion cases brought against a national moving company by two householders—both women—after their household goods were destroyed in transit. Both women sought relief from provisions in standardized agreements that limited their carrier's liability for loss and damage. Mrs. Bratton and Mrs. McKnab argued that these provisions should not be enforced against them because, although they had signed the carrier's forms, they had not actually read or agreed to the terms. The court in *Allied* rejected Mrs. Bratton's argument; it disregarded her ignorance of the restrictive terms in the carrier's bill of lading and held that her signature was sufficient to bind her to the agreement. In contrast, the court held that Mrs. McKnab's signature did not bind her. The carrier's agent had advised Mrs. McKnab incorrectly that the agreement gave her no choice regarding the amount of insurance coverage available to her. This misstatement, the court held, relieved Mrs. McKnab of the presumption of assent that her signature on the agreement would otherwise have warranted. By granting relief to Mrs. McKnab, *Allied* indicates to readers that standardized agreements need not always be binding. In denying relief to Mrs. Bratton, however, the court in *Allied* demonstrates that standardized agreements are often enforceable.

[The position of the plaintiffs in *Allied Van Lines* v. *Bratton* equates with the position of the two women plaintiffs in *L'Estrange* v. *Graucob* (Mrs Bratton) and *Curtis* v. *Chemical Cleaning and Dyeing Co.* (Mrs McKnab). The two American women both enjoyed the same fate as their opposite numbers in the English decisions.]

In this section, I will discuss two different interpretations of *Allied* that demonstrate [my] claims about the significance of gender. The first interpretation, which I call a traditional reading of the case, is an elaboration of the rationale the court presents in support of its decision. Readers who interpret *Allied* in the traditional manner are unlikely to acknowledge that gender-related ideas are a factor in their reading of the case. Yet, as I will show, gender-related ideas are implicated in this interpretation. I label the second interpretation a feminist reading, because gender-related ideas are overtly recognized in this interpretation. In addition, this reading is characterized by its opposition to *Allied* and to the traditional interpretation of the decision.

The traditional interpretation of *Allied* leads to a conclusion that, by and large, standardized contracts are legitimate, fair, and benign. Several aspects of the decision invite this favorable view. Thus, for example, the court frames the question of standardized contract enforceability as an issue of whether the individual householders agreed to the standardized terms. By discussing the legitimacy of the agreements in the language of assent, the court implies that individual householders have the ability to avoid the severity of the terms of standardized contracts if they simply adequately assert themselves. Mrs. Bratton "realized that she was signing a contract," the decision reports. Moreover, the carrier's agent did not "prevent" her from reading the document. She "simply did not read . . . or even ask questions . . .". The court indicates that, because Mrs. Bratton deliberately chose both to sign the documents and not to read them, she voluntarily relinquished her right to judicial protection against the harshness of the standardized form. . . .

The particular form of standardized agreement at issue in the case contributes to the view that Mrs. Bratton should be held responsible for her own loss. Unlike many standardized contracts . . . the standardized documents Mrs. Bratton failed to read actually offered her the choice of more insurance if she wanted it. Mrs. Bratton was not stuck with a form document that offered her only one set of terms. Traditional readers are more likely, therefore, to feel critical of Mrs. Bratton's conduct than to feel critical of standardized agreements.

The contrast between the court's treatment of Mrs. McKnab and Mrs. Bratton also conveys the benign nature of standardized agreements to traditional readers. The rationale that locked Mrs. Bratton into her agreement protected Mrs. McKnab. Although the court seemed ready to hold Mrs. McKnab responsible for her signature—she too "knew" she was "signing a contract"— ultimately the court is persuaded that the conduct of the carrier's agent "prevent[ed] [her] from exercising her right to choose adequate coverage." The court referred to prior conversations between Mrs. McKnab and the agent in which she had alerted him to her desires for maximum insurance coverage. Readers can infer from this that the agent's misstatement to Mrs. McKnab was deliberately deceptive. . . . Because the court relieved Mrs. McKnab of liability for her signature on the grounds that the agent prevented her from assenting freely to the standardized form, the *Allied* decision assures readers that the law of standardized agreements can be flexible and particularized. It will protect someone like Mrs. McKnab who actively seeks to protect herself, but it will not protect someone who is negligently passive, like Mrs. Bratton. . . . An active/passive distinction between the conduct of both the two women and the two agents, therefore, provides readers an explanation for the different treatment the women receive. . . .

The form of legal analysis that the court utilized in *Allied* also legitimates, for traditional readers, the legal doctrine dealing with standardized agreements. Because the court judged the enforceability of Mrs. Bratton's agreement by her signature, rather than by an examination of her actual knowledge of the contents of the standard form, the *Allied* court seems scrupulously neutral and objective. . . . the court in *Allied* did not inquire into inequality of bargaining power to determine the enforceability of the standardized agreements. Nor did it consider the justice of permitting a national moving company to limit its liability for loss of an individual householder's belongings. By avoiding these approaches, the court in *Allied* also avoided the troublesome question of whether setting aside standardized agreements violates the principle of judicial neutrality regarding the substance of contracts. . . .

All of the justifications for the *Allied* decision advanced so far are reinforced by gender-related ideas. Readers can convince themselves that Mrs. Bratton could have avoided the limited liability of which she complained by attributing a restrictive notion of self to her that is customarily linked with men. The court in *Allied* protects Mrs. McKnab's "masculine" attempt to be autonomous, aggressive, and self-reliant, and the court denies Mrs. Bratton relief because she didn't try to conduct her affairs in a similarly "masculine" way. If traditional readers implicitly recognize Mrs. McKnab's conduct as masculine and Mrs. Bratton's conduct as feminine, accepting *Allied* will be as natural as the superiority of "male" traits sometimes seems. Indeed, the gendered view of self implied in the opinion tends to prevent readers from being troubled by the complicated issue the case poses about the power of standardized contracts. . . .

The gender-related insight regarding the "male" notion of self underlying the *Allied* rationale will provide feminist readers with a basis for developing a critique of the traditional analysis. Mrs. Bratton's idea of self apparently did not conform to the view, commonly linked with men, that individuals should allow the assertive, self-centred aspects of their personality to dominate their conduct. The self-reliant view of personhood underlying *Allied* permitted the court to believe that Mrs. Bratton was free to choose whether or not to agree to the carrier's form, that her agent did not "prevent" her from reading the bill of lading before she signed it. But footnotes to the opinion reveal that Mrs. Bratton testified at trial that she did not read the document because "the house was really cold; and the men were tired. They were in a hurry to get out." Although some people might feel free in such a situation to ignore the workers' discomfort in order to pause to study carefully the moving company's documents, it is not surprising that Mrs. Bratton could not. Women are socialized to consider and value others' feelings above their own, and Mrs. Bratton simply acted like a woman in this situation. Because feminist readers are sympathetic to characteristics commonly associated with women, the court's refusal to evaluate the substantive content of Mrs. Bratton's standardized contract will not seem like a neutral judgment to these readers but a preference for male rather than female personality traits. . . .

As the feminist reading of *Allied* implies, the court's analysis in *Allied* might have been different if the court had valued feminine as well as masculine personality traits. The court could have considered whether Mrs. Bratton's agent should have extended more sensitivity and compassion to her by understanding her sympathy for him and his men, by informing her about the insurance option, and by preventing her from signing without indicating the liability coverage she wanted. The court could have considered whether the agent should have been as solicitous of Mrs. Bratton as she was of him. . . .

Although both the traditional and the feminist readers will be disadvantaged in their later reading of the standardized contract material if they are not exposed to alternative readings of *Allied*, the feminist reading is less likely to receive attention. It is, therefore, particularly important to emphasize how this reading will benefit traditional readers. A feminist reading will help these readers see the legal issue in standardized contract situations not as a question of assent but as a question of power. The court in *Allied* utilized individual consent as the exclusive standard by which to evaluate contract enforceability. The court assumed, in justifying this standard, that individuals could make informed judgments about the wisdom of contracts, that they could obtain full access to all the knowledge they need to exercise their consent wisely. . . .

The feminist reader of *Allied*, who is sensitive to the subordinate status of women, would challenge this single-minded focus on a consumer's obligation to inform herself about her contracts as misleading. The focus on knowledge masks the power exercised in contractual dealings. Mrs. Bratton's agent exercised power over her through his physical control over her bill of lading and through his familiarity, derived from prior experience, with its contents. But because he was a man, the agent also had power over Mrs. Bratton that she, as a woman, was socialized to acknowledge. By requiring Mrs. Bratton to assume full responsibility for informing herself about her bill of lading, the *Allied* court not only required her to challenge the agent's control over what she needed to know about the bill of lading, but also to challenge the control he as a man had over her as a woman.

A feminist reading of *Allied* exposes these forms of power. Moreover, it reveals that traditional contract doctrine, by treating the parties as if they had an adversarial relationship, implicitly rejects the more cooperative way in which many women have traditionally experienced power and knowledge. The major form of power available to most women, given the kind of work they have done, has been the power to nurture and share. Women primarily occupied with family responsibilities have learned to live in the context of relationships that are trusting and interdependent. In this sphere, many women do not respect or adhere to the traditional male view of power as force, authority, and domination. Given the concern she stated she felt for the workers, Mrs. Bratton earned her own self-respect by recognizing the workers' discomfort and doing what she did to ease their situation. Had she been in the agent's position at that point, she would have spoken to the householder about the insurance option; she would have recognized the householder's need to know and would have helped her.

By analyzing Mrs. Bratton's claim as a question of whether she *agreed* to the challenged terms, the *Allied* court sought to have Mrs. Bratton act unauthentically—to reject her own sense of self and be "more like a man." The court's assent analysis does more than simply deny the extent of the agent's power over Mrs. Bratton; it also prevents her from being able to exercise power in her own way. Thus, the act of framing the *Allied* issue in terms of assent is itself a form of power over Mrs. Bratton and others like her. Mrs. Bratton cannot adequately defend herself as long as the standardized contract issue is discussed as it is in *Allied*. Feminist readers, because of their sympathy—indeed, their empathy—for Mrs. Bratton and because of their opposition to the outcome of her case, will recognize that the court's rhetoric of freedom of choice in *Allied* is simply another way of exercising power.

A feminist reading of the decision reveals the aspects of the *Allied* opinion that foster traditional ideas about gender—aspects that in turn constrain readers' lives. Moreover, it exposes and stands in opposition to the domination of traditional legal doctrine. If readers understand that utilizing assent doctrine is a form of power over Mrs. Bratton's situation, they will be empowered to question and challenge the use of that doctrine. Indeed, by suggesting a way to oppose an outcome that would otherwise seem unassailable, the oppositional stance of feminist analysis becomes a source of power for the willing reader.

Note

Frug identifies what she sees as the 'traditional' approach to standard form contracts and the inclusion of exclusion clauses in such contracts, regarding it as engendering a culture of individual responsibility in which the assertive consumer is rewarded with enhanced protection under the law. In contrast, stereotypically feminine behaviour is not protected, a result which contrasts with the protection accorded to Mrs O'Brien by the Court of Appeal in *Barclays Bank* v. *O'Brien* (Chapter 9), who was protected against the threat of undue influence because she was a woman, even though her individual conduct was not stereotypically feminine.

The second hurdle which any exclusion clause must surmount under the common law—the interpretation of the clause—will probably be a less fraught exercise in the post-Act era. The common law rules on interpretation require that the clause must cover the breach at issue. In other words, the clause must effectively protect the party seeking to rely upon it from the consequences of the breach which has in fact occurred. Although the *contra proferentem* rule, whereby the ambiguities in an exclusion clause are to be construed to the disadvantage of the party seeking to rely upon it, remains 'good law', the days of strained constructions of the type highlighted by Lord Denning in *George Mitchell* (*supra*) must surely be past. The final ghosts of 'fundamental breach', whereby courts sought to outlaw exclusions of liability in respect of terms which were fundamental to the contract or in respect of particularly serious breaches of the contract, were finally laid to rest by s. 9 of the Unfair Contract Terms Act and the House of Lords in *Photo Production Ltd.* v. *Securicor Transport Ltd.* ([1980] 1 All ER 556). The second important rule of construction is that stated by the Privy Council in *Canada SS Lines Ltd.* v. *The King* ([1952] AC 192), whereby general words contained in an exclusion clause will not normally operate successfully to exclude liability for negligence. To put it another way, if the party using the exclusion clause wishes to escape from or restrict liability for negligence, he or she must use very clear words to do so. An example of the continuing common law approach to exclusion clauses (or better, on the facts of that case, to limitation clauses) is given in the extracts below from the *George Mitchell* decision in the House of Lords.

The weakness of an approach to the control of exclusion clauses based purely on the techniques of incorporation and construction is that it rewards the ingenious and careful drafter of contract clauses, and offers courts no mechanisms whereby they can correct serious imbalances of contract power. It leaves the parties free to agree upon exclusions of liability or, less desirably, allows one party exercising superior bargaining power to impose disadvantageous contract terms upon another, provided these are comprehensively (but not necessarily clearly) drafted. It is for this reason that Parliament intervened; first in 1973 to restrict the ability of those supplying goods to exclude liability for breach of the key implied terms in contracts of sale, and then, in 1977, to introduce a more comprehensive set of restrictions on clauses and notices purporting to exclude liability for breach of contract and for negligence.

IV. THE UNFAIR CONTRACT TERMS ACT 1977

A. The Scope of the Act

1. The title of this piece of legislation is very misleading. It does not purport to control all unfair terms. It is not restricted to contracts, but applies also to certain non-contractual notices. It applies only to those *contract* terms which attempt to exempt or restrict liability for breach of contract or negligence, and in relation to these terms it does not apply a standard of fairness. It controls terms within its scope in two ways, depending upon their nature: it prohibits certain terms absolutely and subjects others to a test of reasonableness.

The Act requires a contract term to be examined on two levels. First, it is necessary to decide whether a particular term is subject to the control of the Act. In other words, is it a term which purports to exclude or restrict liability? If the term is within the Act, the second task is to determine the type of control applicable. Set out below are some sections from the Act which pertain to the first question and which give, in relation to the second question, some flavour of the type of control exercisable over the various types of term. It is not our intention to give a detailed account of the operation of every section of the Act; rather, we try to give an overview of the type of clause caught by the Act, indicating the way in which clauses are controlled in general terms. Such detail as we give on each section can be found in Table. 2 on p. 644.

The Unfair Contract Terms Act 1977

1. Scope of Part I.

(1) For the purposes of this Part of this Act, "negligence" means the breach—

(a) of any obligation, arising from the express or implied terms of a contract, to take reasonable care or exercise reasonable skill in the performance of the contract;

(b) of any common law duty to take reasonable care or exercise reasonable skill (but not any stricter duty);

(c) of the common duty of care imposed by the Occupiers' Liability Act 1957 or the Occupier's Liability Act (Northern Ireland) 1957.

(2) This Part of this Act is subject to Part III; and in relation to contracts, t he operation of sections 2 and 4 and 7 is subject to the exceptions made by Schedule I.

(3) In the case of both contract and tort, sections 2 to 7 apply (except where the contrary is stated in section 6(4)) only to business liability, that is liability for breach of obligations or duties arising—

(a) from things done or to be done by a person in the course of a business (whether his own business or another's); or

(b) from the occupation of premises used for business purposes of the occupier; and references to liability are to be read accordingly but liability of an occupier of premises for breach of an obligation or duty towards a person obtaining access to the premises for recreational or educational purpose, being liability for loss or damage suffered by reason of the dangerous state of the premises, is not a business liability of the occupier unless granting that person such access for the purposes concerned falls within the business purposes of the occupier.

(4) In relation to any breach of duty or obligation, it is immaterial for any purpose of this Part of this Act whether the breach was inadvertent or intentional, or whether liability for it arises directly or vicariously.

2. Negligence liability.

(1) A person cannot by reference to any contract term or to a notice given to persons generally or to particular persons exclude or restrict his liability for death or personal injury resulting from negligence.

(2) In the case of other loss or damage, a person cannot so exclude or restrict his liability for negligence except in so far as the term or notice satisfies the requirement of reasonableness.

(3) Where a contract term or notice purports to exclude or restrict liability for negligence a person's agreement to or awareness of it is not of itself to be taken as indicating his voluntary acceptance of any risk.

3. Liability arising in contract.

(1) This section applies as between contracting parties where one of them deals as consumer or on the other's written standard terms of business.

(2) As against that party, the other cannot by reference to any contract term—

(a) when himself in breach of contract, exclude or restrict any liability of his in respect of the breach; or

(b) claim to be entitled—

(i) to render a contractual performance substantially different from that which was reasonably expected of him, or

(ii) in respect of the whole or any part of his contractual obligation, to render no performance at all,

except in so far as (in any of the cases mentioned above in this subsection) the contract term satisfies the requirement of reasonableness.

4. Unreasonable indemnity clauses.

(1) A person dealing as consumer cannot by reference to any contract term be made to indemnify another person (whether a party to the contract or not) in respect of liability that may be incurred by the other for negligence or breach of contract, except in so far as the contract term satisfies the requirement of reasonableness.

(2) This section applies whether the liability in question—

(a) is directly that of the person to be indemnified or is incurred by him vicariously;

(b) is to the person dealing as consumer or to someone else.

5. "Guarantee" of consumer goods.

(1) In the case of goods of a type ordinarily supplied for private use or consumption, where loss or damage—

(a) arises from the goods proving defective while in consumer use; and

(b) results from the negligence of a person concerned in the manufacture or distribution of the goods,

liability for the loss or damage cannot be excluded or restricted by reference to any contract term or notice contained in or operating by reference to a guarantee of the goods.

(2) For these purposes—

(a) goods are to be regarded as "in consumer use" when a person is using them, or has them in his possession for use, otherwise than exclusively for the purposes of a business; and

(b) anything in writing is a guarantee if it contains or purports to contain some promise or assurance (however worded or presented) that defects will be made good by complete or partial replacement, or by repair, monetary compensation or otherwise.

(3) This section does not apply as between the parties to a contract under or in pursuance of which possession or ownership of the goods passed.

6. Sale and hire-purchase.

(1) Liability for breach of the obligations arising from—

(a) section 12 of the Sale of Goods Act 1979 (seller's implied undertakings as to title, etc.);

(b) section 8 of the Supply of Goods (Implied Terms) Act 1973 (the corresponding thing in relation to hire-purchase),

cannot be excluded or restricted by reference to any contract term.

(2) As against a person dealing as consumer, liability for breach of the obligations arising from—

(a) section 13, 14 or 15 of the 1979 Act (seller's implied undertakings as to conformity of goods with description or sample, or as to their quality or fitness for a particular purpose);

(b) section 9, 10 or 11 of the 1973 Act (the corresponding things in relation to hire-purchase),

cannot be excluded or restricted by reference to any contract term.

(3) As against a person dealing otherwise than as consumer, the liability specified in subsection (2) above can be excluded or restricted by reference to a

contract term, but only in so far as the term satisfies the requirement of reasonableness.

(4) The liabilities referred to in this section are not only the business liabilities defined by section 1(3), but include those arising under any contract of sale of goods or hire-purchase agreement.

7. *Miscellaneous contracts under which goods pass.*

(1) Where the possession or ownership of goods passes under or in pursuance of a contract not governed by the law of sale of goods or hire-purchase, subsections (2) to (4) below apply as regards the effect (if any) to be given to contract terms excluding or restricting liability for breach of obligation arising by implication of law from the nature of the contract.

(2) As against a person dealing as consumer, liability in respect of the goods' correspondence with description or sample, or their quality or fitness for any particular purpose, cannot be excluded or restricted by reference to any such term.

(3) As against a person dealing otherwise than as consumer, that liability can be excluded or restricted by reference to such a term, but only in so far as the term satisfies the requirement of reasonableness.

(3A) Liability for breach of the obligations arising under section 2 of the Supply of Goods and Services Act 1982 (implied terms about title etc. in certain contracts for the transfer of the property in goods) cannot be excluded or restricted by reference to any such term.

(4) Liability in respect of—

(a) the right to transfer ownership of the goods, or give possession; or

(b) the assurance of quiet possession to a person taking goods in pursuance of the contract,

cannot (in a case to which subsection (3A) above does not apply) be excluded or restricted by reference to any such term except in so far as the term satisfies the requirement of reasonableness. . . .

12. *"Dealing as consumer".*

(1) A party to a contract "deals as consumer" in relation to another party if—

(a) he neither makes the contract in the course of a business nor holds himself out as doing so; and

(b) the other party does make the contract in the course of a business; and

(c) in the case of a contract governed by the law of sale of goods or hire-purchase, or by section 7 of this Act, the goods passing under or in pursuance of the contract are of a type ordinarily supplied for private use or consumption.

(2) But on a sale by auction or by competitive tender the buyer is not in any circumstances to be regarded as dealing as consumer.

(3) Subject to this, it is for those claiming that a party does not deal as consumer to show that he does not.

13. Varieties of exemption clause.

(1) To the extent that this Part of this Act prevents the exclusion or restriction of any liability it also prevents—

  (a) making the liability or its enforcement subject to restrictive or onerous conditions;

  (b) excluding or restricting any right or remedy in respect of the liability, or subjecting a person to any prejudice in consequence of his pursuing any such right or remedy;

  (c) excluding or restricting rules of evidence or procedure;

and (to that extent) sections 2 and 5 to 7 also prevent excluding or restricting liability by reference to terms and notices which exclude or restrict the relevant obligation or duty.

(2) But an agreement in writing to submit present or future differences to arbitration is not to be treated under this Part of this Act as excluding or restricting any liability.

2. It can be seen from the above provisions, in particular ss. 2, 3, and 13, that the Act does not employ any particular conception of an excluding or limiting term; rather, it bases its policing function on monitoring a particular type of market behaviour. For example, it relies on ss. 3 and 13 to pull into the ambit of the Act clauses which are not caught in their specific subject-matter by other provisions such as s. 6. This approach has several points in its favour. First, to attempt to proscribe clauses excluding or restricting liability on a clause-by-clause basis would invite the contract draftsman to attempt to circumvent the legislation. Second, there has been a debate for some time about the status of excluding or limiting terms; the generally accepted view is that such clauses, depending upon their scope, provide a defence to allegations of breach of contract or negligence. A more marginal approach is to regard such clauses not as a defence but as providing a definition of the contract obligation. The main proponent of this view has been B. Coote (*Exception Clauses* (London, Sweet and Maxwell, 1964); 'Unfair Contract Terms Act 1977', (1978) 41 *MLR* 312). By avoiding an overarching conceptual definition of excluding or restricting terms, the Act avoids the situation of breaches of contract being drafted as non-breaches. For example, s. 3(2)(b) is drafted sufficiently widely to prevent a seller defining his or her performance in terms which render it not what the buyer reasonably expected. An illustration of the definitional approach to exclusion clauses is provided by Yates.

D. Yates, *Exclusion Clauses in Contracts*, 2nd edn. (London, Sweet and Maxwell, 1982), 124–5

. . . suppose a seller contracts to sell a blue G. T. Brooklands 2,000 Special motor car, but provides in the written sale agreement that he accepts no responsibility whatsoever if the vehicle should be of a different colour, model, make and engine capacity, and any statements made by the seller as to these matters are not intended to be, and should not be, relied upon by the buyer. There seems little logic in a court holding that the seller had promised to deliver a blue G. T. Brooklands 2,000 Special, but that if he delivered a green Boneshaker 1,500 he would not be liable because the exclusion provided a defence. The simple fact is that the seller has promised nothing at all in respect of colour, model, make and engine capacity. He has merely promised to deliver "a car."

If s. 3(2)(b) were applied, the seller's clauses would be permissible only in so far as they satisfied the requirement of reasonableness. The criterion for establishing the reasonableness of an excluding or limiting term is something which is looked at later in this chapter. S. 3 does appear to use a double test of reasonableness—the substitute performance and the clause authorizing the substitute performance both have to be reasonable—and it must be asked how a clause purporting to authorize a performance outside the bounds of reasonable expectation can itself be anything other than unreasonable. This will not always be the case: the substitute performance offered may be superior to that which was originally contracted for if, for example, replacement is offered rather than repair.

3. A difficulty with devising legislation to focus on outcomes and on types of market behaviour rather than on specific clauses is that it then becomes possible to ensnare within the Act clauses that were not intended to be regulated. A good example of this is provided by Cheshire and Fifoot.

Cheshire, Fifoot, and Furmston's *Law of Contract*, 12th edn. (London, Butterworths, 1991), 184

Suppose for instance a supplier of machine tools provided in his standard printed conditions that payment terms are 25 per cent with order and 75 per cent on delivery and that he should be under no obligation to start manufacture until the initial payment is made. Such a provision may now have to pass the test for reasonableness under section 3(2)(b)(ii).

A clause of this type would presumably have little difficulty in passing the reasonableness test once within the Act, but, as Cheshire and Fifoot comment, 'it is not a good argument for putting hurdles on a motorway that most cars will drive through them'.

4. S. 3 is not the only section we need to consider in this context; s. 13 also is widely drafted, in line with the regulation of market behaviour ethos, to catch any terms which, while not drafted necessarily as exclusions or restrictions of liability, have the effect of restricting remedies or rendering them different to obtain (e.g. imposing time limits) or generally place restrictions on the other contracting party in relation to the liability or its

enforcement. The example given by MacDonald raises the issue of how far the courts should go in drawing clauses into the ambit of the Act through s. 13.

E. Macdonald, 'Exclusion Clauses: The Ambit of S. 13(1) of the Unfair Contract Terms Act 1977', (1992) *LS* 277 at 283

Consideration can be given to the situation where there is a direct contractual relationship between [a] house purchaser and [a] surveyor and the purchaser has contracted for a low level of inspection, short of that undertaken in a full structural survey. The purchaser could have contracted for some other level of inspection, at greater cost; up to that of a full structural survey. The surveyor may have chosen to state the level of inspection by stating that he will 'look at X but that does not include Y'. If that is the case then, when faced with a claim of negligent breach, s 13 . . . would seem inevitably to bring the 'but that does not include Y' clause within s 2(2) of the Unfair Contract Terms Act 1977. If the relevant clause is there to distinguish one level of service from another, then surely the clause should not necessarily be brought within the Act?

5. Judicial guidance on the scope of the Act has been limited. The accepted position seems to be that taken by the Court of Appeal in *Phillips Products Ltd.* v. *Hyland.* The plaintiffs hired a JCB excavator and its driver (the first defendant) from Hamstead (the second defendants) on contract terms offered by the latter. These were not terms drafted by Hamstead themselves, but by the Construction Plant-Hire Association (CPA) to which they belonged. The plaintiffs had hired plant from the defendants on two previous occasions, and it was accepted at the trial that the conditions in question were incorporated into the contract. At the centre of the dispute was Condition 8 of the Contract which read:

Handling of Plant
When a Driver or Operator is supplied by the owner to work the Plant, he shall be under the direction and control of the Hirer. Such Drivers or Operators shall for all purposes in connection with their employment in the working of the Plant be regarded as the servants or agents of the Hirer who alone shall be responsible for all claims arising in connection with the operation of the Plant by the said Drivers or Operators. The Hirer shall not allow any other person to operate such Plant without the Owner's previous consent to be confirmed in writing.

It was accepted that the disputed Condition had been seen and read by the plaintiffs. The excavator was hired on the occasion in question to 'back-fill' a drain. One of the plaintiffs' employees offered to help the defendants' driver, but it was made clear to him by the driver that he did not want any interference in the way he carried out his job. In the course of doing his job, the driver drove into the plaintiffs' premises and damaged them. The argument at trial concerned the defendants' liability in tort. As no one was injured in the accident, their liability fell to be assessed under s. 2(2) of the Act. As will be seen from later extracts from this case, the case could have been argued as a breach of contract case under s. 7, as it involved a contract of hire. As far as the scope of the Act was concerned, the Court of Appeal was faced with an argument from the defendants that this condition, which was part of a standard-form contract made on the terms laid down by the CPA, defined their liability and the liability of the plaintiffs and did not operate as an exclusion or a restriction, so that there was no application of s. 2(2) of the Act.

Slade LJ rejected this argument in the following terms:

Phillips Products Ltd. v. *Hyland*
[1987] 2 All ER 620 at 625–6

SLADE LJ Subsection (1) does not apply because there was, fortunately, no death or personal injury. Section 2(2), set out as incorporating the relevant wording of sub-s (1), provides that in case of other loss or damage a person cannot *by reference to any contract term* exclude or restrict his liability for negligence except in so far as the term satisfies the requirement of reasonableness. The argument for Hamstead is that they do not, by reference to condition 8, '*exclude or restrict*' their liability for negligence. Condition 8, it is stressed, is not an 'excluding' or 'restricting' clause. It may have an *effect* on the liability for negligence which would otherwise have existed if there were, as there was in the present case, negligence. . . . Nevertheless, the condition does not, it is said, amount to an attempt by either party to the contract to '*exclude or restrict*' liability: it is simply an attempt on their part to divide and allocate the obligations or responsibilities arising in relation to the contract by *transferring* liability for the acts of the operator from the plant owners to the hirers fail. A transfer, it is suggested, is not an exclusion; hence the hirers at the s 2(2) hurdle. . . .

However, the question for this court is . . . whether or not the provisions of condition 8 'exclude or restrict' Hamstead's liability for negligence within the meaning of s. 2(2) of the 1977 Act. . . . We are unable to accept that, in the ordinary sensible meaning of words in the context of s 2 and the 1977 Act as a whole, the provisions of condition 8 do not fall within the scope of s 2(2). A transfer of liability from A to B necessarily and inevitably involves the exclusion of liability so far as A is concerned. . . . In applying s 2(2), it is not relevant to consider whether the form of a condition is such that it can aptly be given the label of an 'exclusion' or 'restriction' clause. There is no mystique about 'exclusion' or 'restriction' clauses. To decide whether a person 'excludes' liability by reference to a contract term, you look at the effect of the term. You look at its substance. The effect here is beyond doubt. Hamstead does most certainly purport to exclude its liability for negligence by *reference to* condition 8. Furthermore, condition 8 purports to 'exclude or restrict the relevant obligation or duty' within the provisions of s 13(1) of the 1977 Act.

The exhortation to look at the substance of the clause and not at its form was perhaps to be expected. The Act is built on this type of approach, and such sentiments were expressed by the Law Commission in their 1975 Report, from which the Act itself emerged.

Law Commission, *Second Report on Exemption Clauses* (1976), para. 146

We do not propose to define exemption clauses in general terms; we regard this expression not as a legal term of art but as a convenient label for a number of provisions which may be mischievous in broadly the same way. Their mischief is that they deprive or may deprive the person against whom they may be invoked either of certain specific rights which social policy requires that he should have (for example the right of a buyer in a consumer sale to be supplied with goods of merchantable quality, or the right of a person to whom a service has been supplied to a reasonable standard of care and skill on the part of the supplier) or of rights which the promisee reasonably believed that the promisor had conferred upon him. It is with the last class of restriction or exclusion that we are concerned here. We propose that a term should be subject to control if it has the effect of enabling the promisor to offer in purported fulfilment of the contract a performance which is substantially different from that which the promisee reasonably expected when he entered into the contract, or if it has the effect of enabling the promisor to refuse to render any performance.

Notwithstanding these comments, we still lack any detailed yardstick against which to measure substance. A subsequent case saw Slade LJ's dictum applied to a contract of employment. In *Johnstone* v. *Bloomsbury Health Authority*, the Court of Appeal examined a provision in a junior hospital doctor's contract of employment that he should be available to work 48 hours overtime per week in addition to the requirement of a basic 40-hour week. Another aspect of the case was considered in Chapter 10, but the Court was also required to determine whether this clause was within the scope of the Act for the purposes of determining whether the claim should be struck out. The Act applies to contracts of employment only in so far as the protection of the employee is concerned. The junior doctor had established to the satisfaction of a majority of Court of Appeal that a term should be implied into his contract to the effect that the Health Authority owed him a duty of care in tort not to put at risk his health and safety in the way it exercised the overtime provision. The Act could potentially be applied in two ways to the overtime clause. On one level, the clause could be said to be contrary to s. 2(1) of the Act as a voluntary assumption of risk of death or personal injury, or it could be brought within The Act by s. 13 as a provision which restricted the duty of care owed by the authority. As s. 13 only extends the liability created by other sections and does not in itself create liability, the Court of Appeal then had to go on and establish under which section liability would be created. The court looked at s. 2.

Johnstone v. *Bloomsbury Health Authority*
[1991] 2 All ER 293 at 301

[STUART SMITH LJ] When considering the operation of s 2 of the 1977 Act the court is concerned with the substance and not the form of the contractual provision. In *Phillips Products Ltd* v. *Hyland* [1987] 2 All ER 620 at 626 Slade LJ said:

'In applying s 2(2), it is not relevant to consider whether the form of a condition is such that it can aptly be given the label of an "exclusion" or "restriction" clause. There is no mystique about "exclusion" or "restriction" clauses. To decide whether a person "excludes" liability by reference to a contract term, you look at the effect of the term. You look at its substance.'

In *Smith* v. *Eric S Bush (a firm)*, *Harris* v. *Wyre Forest DC* [1989] 2 All ER 514 at 530, this approach was approved: see per Lord Griffiths.

If . . . the defendants are entitled to succeed on the submissions they advanced . . . it is arguable that they can only do so because the effect of [the term requiring doctors to work overtime] must be construed as an express assumption of risk by the plaintiff (a plea of volenti not fit injuria) or because it operates to restrict or limit the ambit and scope of the duty of care owed by the authority. If that is the correct analysis, then the substance and effect, though not the form, of the term is such that it can properly be argued to fall within s 2(1) of the 1977 Act. For this reason, in my judgment, para 4(i) of the reply should not be struck out.

Note

For further suggestions of how the Act may be invoked in contracts of employment see L. Dolding and C. Fawlk, 'Judicial Understanding of the Contract of Employment', (1992) 55 *MLR* 562.

6. The test constructed by Slade LJ in *Phillips Products Ltd.* v. *Hyland* and applied in *Johnstone* is criticized for its potential breadth by Macdonald, who suggests that a more appropriate test would be one based on the expectations of the parties.

E. Macdonald, 'Exclusion Clauses: The Ambit of S. 13(1) of the Unfair Contract Terms Act 1977', (1992) 12 *LS* 277 at 293

An example will help to further illustrate how the 'expectations test' would function. . . . One example considered above [see p.] looked at the situation where there is a direct contractual relationship between the house purchaser and the surveyor and the surveyor stated the level of service by stating that he would look at X 'but that does not include Y'. It was suggested that, in an action based on the surveyor's negligent breach, the 'but that does not include Y' clause should not automatically be brought within s 2 of the Unfair Contract Terms Act 1977 as it would seem to be by s 13. . . . The 'expectations test' does not necessarily lead to that conclusion. It would be a matter of how clearly the existence of the different levels of service was explained to the purchaser and how the clause was embodied in the contract document, e.g. how close it was to the statement of the apparent obligation to look at everything encompassed within X, and whether it was in the same size type. The difference in price charged for the different levels of service would provide one indication that the lower level had been taken into account in the parties' reasonable expectations of performance.

The application of the reasonableness test, which is examined below, may result in similar questions being asked at that stage about the availability of different types of service, etc. There is a risk that a clause will only be assessed for reasonableness under the Act once it has been declared unreasonable for the purposes of bringing it within the scope of the Act.

The absence of a conceptual underpinning to the Act is the root cause of many of the problems discussed above. However, it is an unavoidable consequence of enacting legislation to deal with particular market behaviour and the results of that behaviour. The approach of the legislation has its attractions, and they have to be weighed against the disadvantages.

7. The Act does not apply to all contracts—a tribute perhaps to effective lobbying on the part of certain commercial groupings. In particular, Schedule 1 excludes from the application of ss. 2–4 and 7 *inter alia* contracts of insurance, contracts in relation to interests in land, and contracts concerned with intellectual property and securities.

B. The Nature of the Control

Table 2. *Summary of the provisions of UCTA*

Liability	UCTA section no.	Type of control	Class of person protected	Class of person controlled
Negligence by reference to contract term or notice	1(1)	Total ban or a test of reasonableness	Any person	Person in business—see ss. 1(3) and 14
Causing death or personal injury	2(1)	Total ban	As above	As above
Other damage	2(2)	Reasonableness in ss. 11(1) and 11(4)	As above	As above

Liability	UCTA section no.	Type of control	Class of person protected	Class of person controlled
Indemnity for any loss or damage through negligence	4	As above	Person dealing as a consumer, s. 12	Person in business—see ss. 1(3) and 14; look also at s. 12(1)(b)
Negligence in manufacture or distribution of goods ordinarily supplied for private use	5	Total ban	Person whose goods prove defective whilst in consumer use	As above
Contract liability When in breach	3(2)(a)	Reasonableness in ss. 11(1)and 11(4)	Person dealing as a consumer or on another's written standard terms of business	Person in business—see ss. 1(3) and 14; look also at s. 12(1)(b)
Rendering a contractual performance substantially different from that which was reasonably expected	3(2)(b)(i)	As above	As above	As above
Rendering no contractual performance in respect of whole or part of contractual obligation	3(2)(b)(ii)	As above	As above	As above
Indemnity for breach of contract	4	As above	Person dealing as a consumer —s. 12	As above
Implied undertakings in contracts for the sale and supply of goods				
Title in sale of goods and HP contracts	6(1)	Total ban	Any person	Any person
Description or sample in sale of goods and HP contracts	6(2)	As above	Person dealing as a consumer— see s. 12 incl. s. 12(1)(c) on type of goods	Person in business—see ss. 1(3) and 14; look also at s. 12(1)(b)

Table 2. *Cont.*

Liability	UCTA section no.	Type of control	Class of person protected	Class of person controlled
As above	6(3)	Reasonableness test under s. 11(2) and sch. 2	Person *who is not a consumer*	Any person
Quality or fitness for purpose in contract for the sale of goods or HP of goods	6(2)	Total ban	Person dealing as a consumer —see s. 12 incl. 12(1)(c) on type of goods	Person in business—see ss. 1(3) and 14, look also at sec. 12(1)(b)
As above	6(3)	Reasonableness test under s. 11(2) and sch. 2	Person *who is not a consumer*	Person in business—see ss. 1(3) and 14

Other contracts of supply not governed by the SGA 1979:

Title to goods	7(4)	Reasonableness test under s. 11(2) and sch. 2	Any person	Person in business—see ss. 1(3) and 14
Description, fitness, sample or quality	7(2)	Total ban	Person dealing as a consumer —see s. 12 incl. 12(1)(c) on type of goods	Person in business—see ss. 1(3) and 14
As above	7(3)	Reasonableness test under s. 11(2) and sch. 2	Person *who is not a consumer*	Person in business—see ss. 1(3) and 14

Misrepresentation

Amends Misrepresentation Act 1967, s. 3, and therefore applies to all contracts, not just those covered by UCTA	8	Reasonableness in ss. 11(1) and 11(4)	Any person	Any person

1. As will be seen from Table 2, the Act controls clauses falling within its ambit in two ways: either by means of a total ban or by the application of a test of reasonableness. The test applied depends upon (a) the effect and context of the term or notice and (b) the parties concerned. For example, some sections apply to 'any person' (e.g. 2(1), which places a total ban

upon clauses attempting to exclude liability for death or personal injury caused by negligence), whereas some apply only where a person is dealing as a consumer (e.g. s. 4, under which attempts to gain indemnification for breach of contract are subject to a test of reasonableness if the other party is dealing as a consumer). Within this broad spectrum there exist several subdivisions. For example, in some instances, different levels of protection are provided in relation to the same type of term depending upon the status of the other contracting party (cf. e.g. ss. 6(1), 6(2), and 6(3)), including a class defined as 'persons *not* dealing as consumers'. Two further subdivisions of contracting party are persons using goods for a 'consumer use' (s. 5) and persons who, while not consumers, are dealing on another's written standard terms of business (s. 3).

The intention of the legislature appears to be to provide tiered levels of protection turning on the status of the person seeking to escape from the clause, the status of the person relying upon the clause (see s. 1(3) on business liability), and the type of liability for which exclusion or limitation is sought. The result is a complex network of rules which result in all cases in the two alternative forms of protection: total ban or application of the reasonableness test. In the case of the latter test, the legislation provides certain general guidelines for some cases (e.g. terms caught by ss. 6 and 7), but not for others. There is no judicial power to amend or to adjust the contract in any way (compare the position with the extract from Cranston in Section II above).

While the spirit of the legislation in this respect is to be commended, it is difficult to see whether it produces more satisfactory results than the broad general approach under the US UCC. The reasonableness test is dealt with below, and it will be seen from that discussion that the approach of the courts in this area has done little to alter contracting behaviour, except where the clauses which have been litigated belong to an industry standard-form contract such as that of the Plant Hire Contractors, where any necessary redrafting of the documents will have an impact on all who use it. Outside such fields, the enquiries undertaken by the courts are too individualistic to allow any coherent principles to be drawn out.

2. The sections dealing with the reasonableness test are s. 11 and Schedule 2.

11. The "reasonableness" test.

(1) In relation to a contract term, the requirement of reasonableness for the purposes of this Part of this Act, section 3 of the Misrepresentation Act 1967 and section 3 of the Misrepresentation Act (Northern Ireland) 1967 is that the term shall have been a fair and reasonable one to be included having regard to the circumstances which were, or ought reasonably to have been, known to or in the contemplation of the parties when the contract was made.

(2) In determining for the purposes of section 6 or 7 above whether a contract term satisfies the requirement of reasonableness, regard shall be had in particular to the matters specified in Schedule 2 to this Act; but this subsection does not prevent the court or arbitrator from holding, in accordance with any rule of law, that a term which purports to exclude or restrict any relevant liability is not a term of the contract.

(3) In relation to a notice (not being a notice having contractual effect), the requirement of reasonableness under this Act is that it should be fair and reasonable to allow reliance on it, having regard to all the circumstances obtaining when the liability arose or (but for the notice) would have arisen.

(4) Where by reference to a contract term or notice a person seeks to restrict liability to a specified sum of money, and the question arises (under this or any other Act) whether the term or notice satisfies the requirement of reasonableness, regard shall be had in particular (but without prejudice to subsection (2) above in the case of contract terms) to—

(a) the resources which he could expect to be available to him for the purpose of meeting the liability should it arise; and

(b) how far it was open to him to cover himself by insurance.

(5) It is for those claiming that a contract term or notice satisfies the requirement of reasonableness to show that it does.

Schedule 2
"guidelines" for application of reasonableness test

The matters to which regard is to be had in particular for the purposes of sections 6(3), 7(3) and (4), 20 and 21 are any of the following which appear to be relevant—

(a) the strength of the bargaining positions of the parties relative to each other, taking into account (among other things) alternative means by which the customer's requirements could have been met;

(b) Whether the customer received an inducement to agree to the term, or in accepting it had an opportunity of entering into a similar contract with other persons, but without having to accept a similar term;

(c) whether the customer knew or ought reasonably to have known of the existence and extent of the term (having regard, among other things, to any custom of the trade and any previous course of dealing between the parties);

(d) where the term excludes or restricts any relevant liability if some condition is not complied with, whether it was reasonable at the time of the contract to expect that compliance with that condition would be practicable;

(e) whether the goods were manufactured, processed or adapted to the special order of the customer.

The Sch. 2 guidelines apply only to clauses caught by ss. 6 and 7. This seems to have the effect of creating three reasonableness tests within the

Act. What is more likely, however, is that the courts will graft onto the reasonableness tests applied under ss. 11(1) and 11(3) the type of question asked by Sch. 2 in the context of the operation of s. 11(2).

3. The first case in which the House of Lords was asked to consider the reasonableness test was *George Mitchell*. The case was actually brought as an action under the Supply of Goods (Implied Terms) Act 1973, s. 55 of which was amended by the Unfair Contract Terms Act 1977 and contained a reasonableness test identical to that found in Sch. 2 of the latter Act.

Mitchell (George) (Chesterhall) Ltd. v. *Finney Lock Seeds Ltd.*
[1983] 2 All ER 737

The appellants were seed merchants. They had supplied the respondent farmers with seed for a number of years, and on this occasion the contract was for 20 lb. of Dutch winter cabbage seed. The contract was made in December 1973, and contained the exclusion and limitation clauses set out in the judgment of Lord Bridge extracted below. The seed was in fact supplied by a company related to the appellants. Owing to its negligence, the respondents were supplied with autumn cabbage seed, which was itself of very poor quality. In any event, autumn cabbage could not be grown in the part of Scotland where the respondents' farm was situated. The crop had to be ploughed in, and the respondents claimed £61,513, which was described as all their loss arising from the appellants' breach of contract. The trial judge held that the clauses upon which the appellants sought to rely did not cover the situation in hand. This view was supported by a majority of the Court of Appeal, which also found unanimously against the appellants on the issue of whether the clause in question satisfied the statutory reasonableness test. The House of Lords unanimously decided that the clause did cover the breach but that it did not pass the reasonableness test.

Lord Bridge The issues in the appeal arise from three sentences in the conditions of sale indorsed on the appellants' invoice and admittedly embodied in the terms on which the appellants contracted. For ease of reference it will be convenient to number the sentences. Omitting immaterial words they read as follows:

'[1] In the event of any seeds or plants sold or agreed to be sold by us not complying with the express terms of the contract of sale . . . or any seeds or plants proving defective in varietal purity we will, at our option, replace the defective seeds or plants, free of charge to the buyer or will refund all payments made to us by the buyer in respect of the defective seeds or plants and this shall be the limit of our obligation. [2] We hereby exclude all liability for any loss or damage arising from the use of any seeds or plants supplied by us and for any consequential loss or damage arising out of such use or any failure in the performance of or any defect in any seeds or plants supplied by us or for any other loss or damage whatsoever save for, at our option, liability for any such replacement or refund as aforesaid. [3] In accordance with the established custom of the seed trade any express or implied condition, statement or warranty, statutory or otherwise, not stated in these Conditions is hereby excluded.'

I will refer to the whole as 'the relevant condition' and to the parts as 'clauses 1, 2 and 3' of the relevant condition.

The first issue is whether the relevant condition, on its true construction in the context of the contract as a whole, is effective to limit the appellants' liability to a refund of £201.60, the price of the seeds (the common law issue). The second issue is whether, if the common law issue is decided in the appellants' favour, they should nevertheless be precluded from reliance on this limitation of liability pursuant to the provisions of the modified s. 55 of the Sale of Goods Act 1979 which is set out in para. 11 of Sch. 1 to the Act and which applies to contracts made between 18 May 1973 and 1 February 1978 (the statutory issue). . . .

In the Court of Appeal, the common law issue was decided in favour of the appellants by Lord Denning MR, who said ([1983] 1 All ER 108 at 113):

'On the natural interpretation, I think the condition is sufficient to limit the seed merchants to a refund of the price paid or replacement of the seeds.'

Oliver LJ decided the common law issue against the appellants primarily on a ground akin to that of Parker J, albeit somewhat differently expressed. Fastening on the words 'agreed to be sold' in cl. 1 of the relevant condition, he held that the clause could not be construed to mean 'in the event of the seeds sold or agreed to be sold by us not being the seeds agreed to be sold by us'. Clause 2 of the relevant condition he held to be 'merely a supplement' to cl. 1. He thus arrived at the conclusion that the appellants had only succeeded in limiting their liability arising from the supply of seeds which were correctly described as Finneys Late Dutch Special but were defective in quality. As the seeds supplied were not Finneys Late Dutch Special, the relevant condition gave them no protection. Kerr LJ, in whose reasoning Oliver LJ also concurred, decided the common law issue against the appellants on the ground that the relevant condition was ineffective to limit appellants' liability for a breach of contract which could not have occurred without negligence on the appellants' part, and that the supply of the wrong variety of seeds was such a breach.

The Court of Appeal, however, was unanimous in deciding the statutory issue against the appellants. . . .

. . . The *Ailsa Craig* case drew an important distinction between exclusion and limitation clauses. This is clearly stated by Lord Fraser ([1983] 1 All ER 101 at 105):

'There are . . . authorities which lay down very strict principles to be applied when considering the effect of clauses of exclusion or of indemnity. . . . In my opinion these principles are not applicable in their full rigour when considering the effect of conditions merely limiting liability. Such conditions will of course be read contra proferentem and must be clearly expressed, but there is no reason why they should be judged by the specially exacting standards which are applied to exclusion and indemnity clauses.' . . .

. . . The relevant condition applies to 'seeds'. Clause 1 refers to 'seeds sold' and 'seeds agreed to be sold.' Clause 2 refers to 'seeds supplied'. As I have pointed out, Oliver LJ concentrated his attention on the phrase 'seeds agreed to be sold'. I can see no justification, with respect, for allowing this phrase alone to dictate the interpretation of the relevant condition, still less for treating cl. 2 as 'merely a supplement' to cl. 1. Clause 2 is perfectly clear and unambiguous. The reference to 'seeds agreed to be sold' as well as to 'seeds sold' in cl. 1 reflects the same dichotomy as the definition of 'sale' in the Sale of Goods Act 1979 as including a bargain and sale as well as a sale and delivery. The defective seeds in this case were seeds sold and delivered, just as clearly as they were seeds supplied, by the appellants to the respondents. The relevant condition, read as a whole, unambiguously limits the appellants' liability to replacement of the seeds or refund of the price. . . .

. . . In agreement with Lord Denning MR, I would decide the common law issue in the appellants' favour.

The statutory issue turns, as already indicated, on the application of the provisions of the modified s. 55 of the Sale of Goods Act 1979, as set out in para. 11 of Sch. 1 to the Act. The 1979 Act is a pure consolidation. The purpose of the modified s. 55 is to preserve the law as it stood from 18 May 1973 to 1 February 1978 in relation to contracts made between those two dates. The significance of the dates is that the first was the date when the Supply of Goods (Implied Terms) Act 1973 came into force containing the provision now re-enacted by the modified s. 55, the second was the date when the Unfair Contract Terms Act 1977 came into force and superseded the relevant provisions of the 1973 Act by more radical and far-reaching provisions in relation to contracts made thereafter. . . .

The contract between the appellants and the respondents was not a 'consumer sale', as defined for the purpose of these provisions. The effect of cl. 3 of the relevant condition is to exclude, inter alia, the terms implied by ss. 13 and 14 of the Act that the seeds sold by description should correspond to the description and be of merchantable quality and to substitute therefore the express but limited obligations undertaken by the appellants under cll. 1 and 2. The statutory issue, therefore, turns on the words in s. 55(4) 'to the extent that it is shown that it would not be fair or reasonable to allow reliance on' this restriction of the appellants' liabilities, having regard to the matters referred to in subs. (5).

This is the first time your Lordships' House has had to consider a modern statutory provision giving the court power to override contractual terms excluding or restricting liability, which depends on the court's view of what is 'fair and reasonable'. . . . But the several provisions of the Unfair Contract Terms Act 1977 which depend on 'the requirement of reasonableness', defined in s. 11 by reference to what is 'fair and reasonable', albeit in a different context, are likely to come before the courts with increasing frequency. It may, therefore, be appropriate to consider how an original decision what is 'fair and reasonable' made in the application of any of these provisions should be approached by an appellate court. It would not be accurate to describe such a decision as an exercise of discretion. But a decision under any of the provisions referred to will have this in common with the exercise of a discretion, that, in having regard to the various matters to which the modified s. 55(5) of the 1979 Act, or s. 11 of the 1977 Act direct attention, the court must entertain a whole range of considerations, put them in the scales on one side or the other and decide at the end of the day on which side the balance comes down. There will sometimes be room for a legitimate difference of judicial opinion as to what the answer should be, where it will be impossible to say that one view is demonstrably wrong and the other demonstrably right. It must follow, in my view, that, when asked to review such a decision on appeal, the appellate court should treat the original decision with the utmost respect and refrain from interference with it unless satisfied that it proceeded on some erroneous principle or was plainly and obviously wrong. . . .

The . . . other question of construction debated in the course of the argument was the meaning to be attached to the words 'to the extent that' in subs-s. (4) and, in particular, whether they permit the court to hold that it would be fair and reasonable to allow partial reliance on a limitation clause and, for example, to decide in the instant case that the respondents should recover, say, half their consequential damage. I incline to the view that, in their context, the words are equivalent to 'in so far as' or 'in circumstances in which' and do not permit the kind of judgment of Solomon illustrated by the example.

But for the purpose of deciding this appeal I find it unnecessary to express a concluded view on this question.

My Lords, at long last I turn to the application of the statutory language to the circumstances of the case. Of the particular matters to which attention is directed by paras (a) to (e) of s. 55(5), only those in paras (a) to (c) are relevant. As to para (c), the respondents admittedly knew of the relevant condition (they had dealt with the appellants for many years) and, if they had read it, particularly cl. 2, they would, I think, as laymen rather than lawyers, have had no difficulty in understanding what it said. This and the magnitude of the damages claimed in proportion of the price of the seeds sold are factors which weigh in the scales in the appellants' favour.

The question of relative bargaining strength under para. (a) and of the opportunity to buy seeds without a limitation of the seedsman's liability under para. (b) were interrelated. The evidence was that a similar limitation of liability was universally embodied in the terms of trade between seedsmen and farmers and had been so for very many years. The limitation had never been negotiated between representative bodies but, on the other hand, had not been the subject of any protest by the National Farmers' Union. These factors, if considered in isolation, might have been equivocal. The decisive factor, however, appears from the evidence of four witnesses called for the appellants, two independent seedsmen, the chairman of the appellant company, and a director of a sister company (both being wholly-owned subsidiaries of the same parent). They said that it had always been their practice, unsuccessfully attempted in the instant case, to negotiate settlements of farmers' claims for damages in excess of the price of the seeds, if they thought that the claims were 'genuine' and 'justified'. This evidence indicated a clear recognition by seedsmen in general, and the appellants in particular, that reliance on the limitation of liability imposed by the relevant condition would not be fair or reasonable.

Two further factors, if more were needed, weigh the scales in favour of the respondents. The supply of autumn, instead of winter, cabbage seed was due to the negligence of the appellants' sister company. Irrespective of its quality, the autumn variety supplied could not, according to the appellants' own evidence, be grown commercially in East Lothian. Finally, as the trial judge found, seedsmen could insure against the risk of crop failure caused by supply of the wrong variety of seeds without materially increasing the price of seeds.

My Lords, even if I felt doubts about the statutory issue, I should not, for the reasons explained earlier, think it right to interfere with the unanimous original decision of that issue by the Court of Appeal. As it is, I feel no such doubts. If I were making the original decision, I should conclude without hesitation that it would not be fair or reasonable to allow the appellants to rely on the contractual limitation of their liability

I would dismiss the appeal.

Notes

1. The clause at issue in this case was a limitation clause. Limitation clauses, it appears, are given special treatment by both the common law and legislation. S. 11(4) of the Act gives two additional guidelines for application to limitation clauses which are not included in relation to exclusion clauses: these are the resources which the party seeking to rely upon the clauses has available to meet any liability and the possibility of insuring against that liability. Lord Bridge also cited with approval the statement of Lord Fraser in *Ailsa Craig Fishing* v. *Malvern Fishing Co. Ltd.* ([1983] 1 All ER 101 at 105) to the effect that limitation clauses should be treated less severely than exclusion clauses. There would appear to be certain assumptions behind this differential treatment. The position taken by the House of Lords in *Ailsa Craig* is that limitation clauses are in less need of control as

they reflect the contract price paid, a calculation of risk, and the possibility of insurance for either of the parties. It is difficult to see why these are not considerations that apply equally to exclusion clauses. There would seem to be no reason why a clause limiting liability in *George Mitchell* to the replacement of the seeds or the refund of the purchase price (£201.60 as against a loss of £61,513.78 = 0.33%) should be any more of an agreed and considered resolution of these questions than a total exclusion would be. The view that limitation clauses are less in need of control through an interventionist approach than exclusion clauses because they represent an attempt by the parties to apportion risk between themselves is simply unsupportable.

2. The reasonableness test, according to s. 11(1) of the Unfair Contract Terms Act 1977, has to be applied to the clause taking into account the circumstances at the time the contract was made. This avoids any consideration of the reasonableness of purporting to exclude liability for the damage *actually* suffered, and focuses instead on the clause and the potentiality of its width.

3. According to s. 11(5), the burden of proving reasonableness falls on the party purporting to rely upon the clause. Lord Bridge asserts that findings on the issue of reasonableness are issues for the first instance judge, whose discretion on the issue of reasonableness should not be interfered with by an appellate court unless it was exercised on plainly incorrect principles or was obviously wrong. This limits the precedent value of decided cases on the reasonableness test. As Lord Bridge points out, there is room for considerable difference of judicial opinion on such questions. There is no certainty that what one judge considers to be unreasonable in a particular context will be followed by another in a later case.

4. The fact that there is no weighting placed on the guidelines given in the Act, or even an insistence that they be applied, further undermines the likelihood of any certainty in the application of the reasonableness test. We commented on judicial examinations of market power in relation to *Interfoto* in Chapter 10. The analysis in *George Mitchell* centred on the appellants' practice, when farmers had previously brought claims, of negotiating with a view to reaching a settlement rather than of seeking to rely strictly upon their limitation clause. This was taken by the court to be a recognition by the sellers that their clause was not reasonable. However, the sellers' practice of negotiating claims could just as easily be supported by a desire to maintain good customer relations. It is hard to see how, if the reasonableness of the clause is to be assessed at the time the contract was made, the conduct of the sellers on this point could be considered to be admissible evidence. One point of value for future cases that can be gleaned from *George Mitchell* is that sellers will be unlikely again to raise as

evidence their settlements of previous claims in order to show how reasonably they behaved.

Phillips Products Ltd. v. *Hyland*
[1987] 2 All ER 620

See above for the facts of this case. The issue as to whether or not condition 8 of the contract between the parties fell within the ambit of the Act has already been dealt with, leaving only the application of the reasonableness test to be discussed. Having decided that point in favour of the plaintiffs, the Court of Appeal was then asked to reassess the approach taken by the judge at first instance to the issue of reasonableness. This the Court refused to do, using as the basis for its decision the dictum of Lord Bridge in *George Mitchell* on the role of appellate courts. The Court of Appeal upheld the decision at first instance that the clause was unreasonable. In doing so, the Court was anxious to limit the effect of the decision by confining it to its own facts.

SLADE LJ Does the condition, on the evidence and in the context of the contract as a whole, satisfy the 'requirement of reasonableness, as defined by s. 11(1) and elsewhere in the 1977 Act? . . .

As the judge pointed out, all the relevant circumstances were known to both parties at that time. The task which he therefore set himself was to examine all the relevant circumstances and then ask himself whether, on the balance of probabilities, he was satisfied that condition 8, in so far as it purported to exclude Hamstead's liability for Mr Hyland's negligence, was a fair and reasonable term. As to these matters, his conclusions as set out in his judgment were as follows:

'What then were the relevant circumstances? Firstly, the second defendants carried on the business of hiring out plant and operators. In contrast the first defendants were steel stockholders, and as such had no occasion to hire plant except on the odd occasions when they had building work to be done at their premises. There had been apparently only three such occasions: one in 1979, one in July 1980 when the drainage trench was dug and the final occasion when the damage was done in August 1980. Secondly, the hire was to be for a very short period. It was arranged at very short notice. There was no occasion for the plaintiffs to address their mind to all the details of the hiring agreement, nor did they do so. The inclusion of condition 8 arose because it appeared in the second defendants' printed conditions. It was not the product of any discussion or agreement between the parties. Thirdly, there was little if any opportunity for the plaintiffs to arrange insurance cover for risks arising from the first defendant's negligence. In so far as the first defendant was to be regarded as the plaintiffs' servant it might have been an easy matter to ensure that the plaintiffs' insurance policies were extended, if necessary, to cover his activities in relation to third party claims. Any businessman customarily insures against such claims. He does not usually insure against damage caused to his own property by his own employees' negligence. Thus to arrange insurance cover for the first defendant would have required time and a special and unusual arrangement with the plaintiffs' insurers. Fourthly, the plaintiffs played no part in the selection of the first defendant as the operator of the JCB. They had to accept whoever the second defendant sent to drive the machine. Further, although they undoubtedly would have had to, and would have had the right to, tell the JCB operator what job he was required to do, from their previous experience they knew they would be unable in any way to control the way in which the first defendant did the job that he was given. They would not have had the knowledge to exercise such control. All the expertise lay with the first defendant. I do not think condition 8 could possibly be construed as giving control of the manner of operation of the JCB to the plaintiffs. Indeed in the event the first defendant made it perfectly plain to Mr Pritchard, the plaintiffs' builder, that he would brook no interference in the way he operated his machine. Those being the surrounding circumstances, was it fair and reasonable that the hire contract should include a condition which relieved the second defendants of all responsibility for damage caused, not to the property of a third party but to the plaintiff's own property, by the negligence of the second defendants' own operators? This was for the plaintiffs in a very real sense a "take it or leave it" situation. They needed a JCB for a simple job at short notice. In dealing with the second defendants they had the choice of taking a JCB operator under a contract containing some 43 written conditions or not taking the JCB at all. The question for me is not a general question whether any contract of hire of the JCB could fairly and reasonably exclude such liability, but a much more limited question as to whether this contract of hire entered into in these circumstances fairly and reasonably included such an exemption. I have come to the conclusion that the second defendants have failed to satisfy me that condition 8 was in this respect a fair and reasonable term.' . . .

We were told that the guidelines in Sch. 2 to the Act were not applicable in this case. It would seem, on a study of the provisions of the Act to which we were not referred in argument, that this may have been wrong. The contract here was a contract of hire. Normally in such a contract, and, it would seem consistently with the provisions of the general conditions in this case, the hirer takes possession of the article hired. Therefore, it appears to us that s. 7(3) (which we do not think it necessary to quote) would apply and thus render Sch. 2 applicable. On this basis the guidelines *would* fall to be considered. Fortunately, however, in view of the way in which the case has been argued on both sides, no difficulty arises on this account. The guideline in paras (*d*) is, on any footing, irrelevant. The guidelines in paras (*a*), (*b*) and (*c*) were argued as factors properly to be taken into account, even though not because of the guidelines themselves. The guideline in para. (*e*) would no doubt have been mentioned in argument if counsel on either side had thought that it affected the decision as to 'fair and reasonable' in this case.

In approaching the judge's reasons and conclusions on the issue, four points have, in our judgment, to be borne in mind.

Firstly, as the judge himself clearly appreciated, the question for the court is not a general question whether or not condition 8 is valid or invalid in the case of any and every contract of hire entered into between a hirer and a plant owner who uses the relevant CPA conditions. The question was and is whether the exclusion of Hamstead's liability for negligence satisfied the requirement of reasonableness imposed by the 1977 Act in relation to *this particular contract.*

Secondly, we have to bear in mind that the relevant circumstances, which were or should have been known to or contemplated by the parties, are those which existed when the contract was made. Section 11(1) is specific on that point. Hence, evidence as to what happened during the performance of the contract must, at best, be treated with great caution. As we have indicated, such evidence was adduced at the trial, apparently without objection. At best, it could probably be used to show, by evidence of conduct and absence of objection to that conduct, what the attitude of the parties would have been in that respect, what they would have contemplated, at the time when they made the contract.

Thirdly, the burden of proof falling on the owner under s. 11(5) of the 1977 Act is, in our judgment, of great significance in this case in the light, or rather in the obscurity, of the evidence and the absence of evidence on issues which were, or might have been, relevant on the issue of reasonableness. One particular example is the matter of insurance. The insurance position of all the parties was canvassed to some extent in oral evidence at the trial, but such evidence seems to us to have been singularly imprecise and inconclusive.

Finally, by way of approach to the issue of reasonableness, it is necessary to bear in mind, and strive to comply with, the clear and stern injunction issued to appellate courts by Lord Bridge . . . in *George Mitchell* (*Chesterhall*) *Ltd* v *Finney Lock Seeds Ltd* [on interfering with lower court decisions].

. . . [C]riticism has been made by Hamstead's counsel of some parts of the judge's reasoning. . . . It may be that the judge placed more stress than we would think right on the lack of opportunity of Mr Phillips to study and understand the conditions, and in particular condition 8. But this is the very sort of point to which Lord Bridge referred in saying that there is room for a legitimate difference of judicial opinion.

Against this, there is to be set the fact, as it appeared at the trial, that the general conditions with their 43 clauses were adopted by and used by all the members of the trade association to which Hamstead belonged. (Counsel has told us that there is other material which might alter the picture, but we cannot go beyond the evidence which was in fact before the judge.) Thus, we think he was justified in saying that in dealing with Hamstead this was for Phillips in a very real sense a 'take it or leave it situation'. As he said, they needed a JCB for a simple job at short notice and, in dealing with Hamstead, had the choice of taking a JCB operator under the general conditions or not taking the JCB at all. Even if Mr Phillips had understood and had been worried by the effect of condition 8 before he arranged for the conclusion of the earlier contracts or before he authorised Mr Pritchard to conclude the contract in August 1980 now in question, it is reasonable to assume, on the evidence as it stood, that he would not have thought that there was much that he could do about it, except to take the conditions offered. It is fair to say that we were told that various changes had been made, including the alterations to some of the general conditions since the coming into force of the Act and that the position today might be very different. But counsel for Hamstead necessarily and realistically accepts that we have to deal, as the judge had to deal, with the contractual terms as they were and with the facts as to relevant considerations as they were given in evidence at the trial: not as the terms are now or as the relevant facts might have appeared to be if further evidence had been given.

As appears from the passage which we have cited, other matters which influenced the judge in his decision on unreasonableness, and which we think were clearly relevant factors to be weighted in the balance, were that the hirers could play no part in the selection of the operator who was to do the work. Nor did the general conditions contain any warranty by Hamstead as to his fitness or competence for the job. Furthermore, despite the words in condition 8 'he shall be under the direction and control of the Hirer', we think it reasonable to infer that the parties, when they made the contract, would have assumed that the operator would be the expert in the management of this machine and that he would not, and could not be expected to, take any instructions from anyone representing the hirers as to the manner in which he would operate the machine to do the job, once the extent and nature of the job had been defined to him by the hirers; in short they would tell him what to do but not how to do it. If such evidence is admissible, which we do not find it necessary to decide, this inference would be strongly supported by the evidence of what actually happened on the site before the accident occurred.

It may be that in several respects this is a very special case on its facts, its evidence and its paucity of evidence. But on these facts and on the available evidence, we are wholly unpersuaded that the judge proceeded on some erroneous principle or was plainly and obviously wrong in his conclusion that Hamstead had not discharged the burden on them of showing that condition 8 satisfied the requirement of reasonableness in the context of this particular contract of hire. It is important therefore that our conclusion on the particular facts of this case should not be treated as a binding precedent in other cases where similar clauses fall to be considered but the evidence of the surrounding circumstances may be very different.

Notes

1. The comments by Slade LJ on whether the court should use the Sch. 2 guidelines for the reasonableness test which would apply if the contract were one caught by s. 7 of the Act, or whether the s. 11(1) reasonableness test should be used, with the clause being treated as one caught by s. 2(2) of the Act, are an indication that these two tests are unlikely to remain sep-

arate. In cases where the s. 11(1) test is applicable, the guidelines will probably be applied in practice as factors to be taken into account.

2. The obvious inference to be drawn from the fact that the contract was made on the CPA terms is that, if the plaintiffs had consulted other hire companies, they would probably have been unable to hire the plant without the offending condition 8. The Law Commission in its Second Report on Exemption Clauses in Contracts (1975) (No. 69, para. 152) took the view that this type of industry-wide standard-form contract was no less of a take-it-or-leave-it imposed 'contract of adhesion' than one drafted by an individual firm. There was, in their view, unlikely to be much thought given to the content of the terms in each individual transaction in either case; nor was the contract likely to have been drafted with a particular transaction in mind. As we saw in Chapter 10, the use of standard-form contracts is a device which can result in lower transaction costs and a lower contract price precisely because the agreement is not tailor-made for a particular contract. Industry standard terms are often drafted after consultation with all interested parties in that industry, including both consumers of the good or service concerned and the relevant suppliers. The contract terms arrived at are, in many cases, designed to form the basis of a relational contract where the outline of the relationship is planned but aspects of it will develop and change as the contract progresses. Consequently, there is inbuilt flexibility. These industry-standard terms are more likely to contain an even-handed approach to issues of insurance or bargaining power than terms produced by an individual company for its own use. It is interesting that the evidence on the issue of insurance, and in particular on who could insure, was so peremptorily dismissed by the Court of Appeal as imprecise and inconclusive. Those who draft industry-standard terms must do so with issues such as the availability of insurance in the forefront of their minds.

3. In relational contracts, the injunction in the Act to assess the reasonableness of the clause at the time the contract was made is likely to prove difficult to accomplish, as the contract terms may well have been varied and developed since the contract was made.

4. In this case, the contractual relationship was of short duration and there was likely to be little need for contract adaptation during the relationship. As the Court of Appeal was keen to point out, the consideration of the reasonableness of any clause can only take account of the particular situation in hand, and is not an assessment of the reasonableness of a clause *per se*. This accounts for the Court of Appeal's attempt to limit the precedent value of its conclusions. The difficulty with this approach is that the philosophy behind the drafting of industry-standard terms and individual

company terms is different. Any determination of the reasonableness of a clause contained in an industry-standard document is likely to have serious repercussions, whatever the wishes of the Court of Appeal.

Smith v. *Eric S. Bush*
[1989] 2 All ER 514

The facts are set out in the judgment of Lord Griffiths.

LORD GRIFFITHS . . . [The] facts of [*Smith* v. *Eric S. Bush*] are similar to hundreds of thousands of house purchases that take place every year. It concerns the purchase of a house at the lower end of the market with the assistance of finance provided by a building society. The purchaser applies for finance to the building society. The building society is required by statute to obtain a valuation of the property before it advances any money (see s. 13 of the Building Societies Act 1986). This requirement is to protect the depositors who entrust their savings to the building society. The building society therefore requires the purchaser to pay a valuation fee to cover or, at least, to defray the cost of obtaining a valuation. This is a modest sum and certainly much less than the cost of a full structural survey; in the present case it was £36.89. If the purchaser pays the valuation fee, the building society instructs a valuer, who inspects the property and prepares a report for the building society giving his valuation of the property. The inspection carried out is a visual one designed to reveal any obvious defects in the property which must be taken into account when comparing the value of the property with other similar properties in the neighbourhood. If the valuation shows that the property provides adequate security for the loan, the building society will lend the money necessary for the purchaser to go ahead . . . .

The building society may either instruct an independent firm of surveyors to make the valuation or use one of its own employees. In the present case, the building society instructed the appellants, an independent firm of surveyors. . . . The building society may or may not send a copy of the valuer's report to the purchaser. In this case the building society was the Abbey National and they did send a copy of the report to the purchaser, Mrs Smith. I understand that this is now common practice among building societies. The report, however, contained in red lettering and in the clearest terms a disclaimer of liability for the accuracy of the report covering both the building society and the valuer. Again, I understand that it is common practice for other building societies to incorporate such a disclaimer of liability.

Mrs Smith did not obtain a structural survey of the property. She relied on the valuer's report to reveal any obvious serious defects in the house she was purchasing. It is common ground that she was behaving in the same way as the vast majority of purchasers of modest houses. They do not go to the expense of obtaining their own structural survey; they rely on the valuation to reveal any obvious serious defects and take a chance that there are no hidden defects that might be revealed by a more detailed structural survey.

The valuer's report said 'the property has been modernised to a fair standard . . . no essential repairs are required' and it valued the property at £16,500. If reasonable skill and care had been employed when the inspection took place, it would have revealed that as a result of removing the chimney breasts in the rooms the chimneys had been left dangerously unsupported. Unaware of this defect and relying on the valuer's report, Mrs Smith bought the house for £18,000 with the assistance of a loan of £3,500 from the building society.

After she had been living in the house for about 18 months, one of the chimney flues collapsed and crashed through the bedroom ceiling and floor causing damage for which Mrs Smith was awarded £4,379.97 against the surveyors who had carried out the valuation.

[The House of Lords decided that the disclaimer of liability was caught by s. 2(2) of the Act as a notice, without contractual force, purporting to exclude liability for negligence. There was no contractual relationship between Mrs Smith and the valuer because the valuer was instructed by and acting for the building society. To reach the decision that the Act applied to the notice, the House of Lords first concluded that a valuer in this context owed a duty of care in tort to the purchaser who relied on the valuation. It then held that liability would exist but for the disclaimer, thus bringing the disclaimer within the scope of the Act by a combination of ss. 1(1)(b) and 13(1).

Their Lordships then went on to apply the reasonableness test to the disclaimer.]

Finally, the question is whether the exclusion of liability contained in the disclaimer satisfies the requirement of reasonableness provided by s. 2(2) of the 1977 Act. The meaning of reasonableness and the burden of proof are both dealt with in s. 11(3), which provides:

'In relation to a notice (not being a notice having contractual effect), the requirement of reasonableness under this Act is that it should be fair and reasonable to allow reliance on it, having regard to all the circumstances obtaining when the liability arose or (but for the notice) would have arisen.'

It is clear, then, that the burden is on the surveyor to establish that in all the circumstances it is fair and reasonable that he should be allowed to rely on his disclaimer of liability.

I believe that it is impossible to draw up an exhaustive list of the factors that must be taken into account when a judge is faced with this very difficult decision. Nevertheless, the following matters should, in my view, always be considered.

(1) Were the parties of equal bargaining power? If the court is dealing with a

one-off situation between parties of equal bargaining power the requirement of reasonableness would be more easily discharged than in a case such as the present where the disclaimer is imposed on the purchaser who has no effective power to object.

(2) In the case of advice, would it have been reasonably practicable to obtain the advice from an alternative source taking into account considerations of costs and time? In the present case it is urged on behalf of the surveyor that it would have been easy for the purchaser to have obtained his own report on the condition of the house, to which the purchaser replies that he would then be required to pay twice for the same advice and that people buying at the bottom end of the market, many of whom will be young first time buyers, are likely to be under considerable financial pressure without the money to go paying twice for the same service.

(3) How difficult is the task being undertaken for which liability is being excluded? When a very difficult or dangerous undertaking is involved there may be a high risk of failure which would certainly be a pointer towards the reasonableness of excluding liability as a condition of doing the work. A valuation, on the other hand, should present no difficulty if the work is undertaken with reasonable skill and care. It is only defects which are observable by a careful visual examination that have to be taken into account and I cannot see that it places any unreasonable burden on the valuer to require him to accept responsibility for the fairly elementary degree of skill and care involved in observing, following up and reporting on such defects. Surely it is work at the lower end of the surveyor's field of professional expertise.

(4) What are the practical consequences of the decision on the question of reasonableness? This must involve the sums of money potentially at stake and the ability of the parties to bear the loss involved, which, in its turn, raises the question of insurance. There was once a time when it was considered improper even to mention the possible existence of insurance cover in a lawsuit. But those days are long past. Everyone knows that all prudent, professional men carry insurance, and the availability and cost of insurance must be a relevant factor when considering which of two parties should be required to bear the risk of a loss. We are dealing in this case with a loss which will be limited to the value of a modest house and against which it can be expected that the surveyor will be insured. Bearing the loss will be unlikely to cause significant hardship if it has to be borne by the surveyor but it is, on the other hand, quite possible that it will be a financial catastrophe for the purchaser who may be left with a valueless house and no money to buy another. If the law in these circumstances denies the surveyor the right to exclude his liability, it may result in a few more claims but I do not think so poorly of the surveyors' profession as to believe that the floodgates will be opened. There may be some increase in surveyors' insurance premiums which will be passed on to the public, but I cannot think that it will be anything approaching the figures involved in the differ-

ence between the Abbey National's offer of a valuation without liability and a valuation with liability discussed in the speech of my noble and learned friend Lord Templeman. The result of denying a surveyor, in the circumstances of this case, the right to exclude liability will result in distributing the risk of his negligence among all house purchasers through an increase in his fees to cover insurance, rather than allowing the whole of the risk to fall on the one unfortunate purchaser.

I would not, however, wish it to be thought that I would consider it unreasonable for professional men in all circumstances to seek to exclude or limit their liability for negligence. Sometimes breathtaking sums of money may turn on professional advice against which it would be impossible for the adviser to obtain adequate insurance cover and which would ruin him if he were to be held personally liable. In these circumstances it may indeed be reasonable to give the advice on a basis of no liability or possibly of liability limited to the extent of the adviser's insurance cover.

In addition to the foregoing four factors, which will always have to be considered, there is in this case the additional feature that the surveyor is only employed in the first place because the purchaser wishes to buy the house and the purchaser in fact provides or contributes to the surveyor's fees. No one has argued that if the purchaser had employed and paid the surveyor himself, it would have been reasonable for the surveyor to exclude liability for negligence, and the present situation is not far removed from that of a direct contract between the surveyor and the purchaser. The evaluation of the foregoing matters leads me to the clear conclusion that it would not be fair and reasonable for the surveyor to be permitted to exclude liability in the circumstances of this case. I would therefore dismiss this appeal.

It must, however, be remembered that this is a decision in respect of a dwelling house of modest value in which it is widely recognised by surveyors that purchasers are in fact relying on their care and skill. It will obviously be of general application in broadly similar circumstances. But I expressly reserve my position in respect of valuations of quite different types of property for mortgage purposes, such as industrial property, large blocks of flats or very expensive houses. In such cases it may well be that the general expectation of the behaviour of the purchaser is quite different. With very large sums of money at stake prudence would seem to demand that the purchaser obtain his own structural survey to guide him in his purchase and, in such circumstances with very much larger sums of money at stake, it may be reasonable for the surveyors valuing on behalf of those who are providing the finance either to exclude or limit their liability to the purchaser.

Notes

1. The reasonableness test was applied on the basis of s. 11(3). The Sch. 2 guidelines were not applicable there. However, the factors which Lord

Griffiths identified as being in need of consideration are similar to the guidelines.

2. The reasonableness test in this context does not have to be applied to the clause at the time the contract was made, but at the point when liability arises. This is the only instance under the Act where this approach is used. This allows the House of Lords to take into account the damage done because of the negligence and the costs involved in repair, all factors used by Lord Griffiths.

3. Once again, the precedent value of the decision is restricted by the assertion that this is a decision made in the context of house ownership for those not in a high-income bracket. Indeed, references of this sort are also made in the context of the discussion elsewhere in the decision as to whether an alternative source of independent advice should have been sought. Lord Griffiths believes that the clause could pass the reasonableness test if the purchase concerned commercial property or larger domestic property. This non-interventionist stance with regard to commercial buyers and higher-income consumers is at odds with the approach of the court in *Phillips* v. *Hyland*, where little indication was given that commercial parties would be left to look after themselves.

4. For an interim assessment of the effect of the Unfair Contract Terms Act 1977, see J. Adams and R. Brownsword, 'The Unfair Contract Terms Act: A Decade of Discretion' ((1988) 104 *LQR* 94). A recent review of the problems of applying the reasonableness test is I. Brown and A. Chandler, 'Unreasonableness and the Unfair Contract Terms Act' ((1993) 109 *LQR* 41).

V. THE EC DIRECTIVE ON UNFAIR CONTRACT TERMS

On 5 April 1993, the Council of Ministers of the European Community adopted Directive 93/13/EEC on unfair terms in consumer contracts (OJ 1993 L95/29). This Directive represents the first significant incursion of the EC's harmonization of laws programme into the field of general contract law, and it contains a uniform framework for the regulation of a class of terms in consumer contracts defined as 'unfair' which must be enacted into the domestic laws of the Member States before 31 December 1994.

The Directive was adopted using the legal basis of Article 100A EC. This empowers the Council of Ministers to enact measures aimed at the completion of the internal market—an area in which goods, services, and factors of production (labour, capital, and enterprise) can flow freely. Consequently, the origins of the Directive lie as much in the economic sphere, with the aim to promoting competition on a 'level playing-field', as they do in the sphere of consumer protection.

A proposal for a Council Directive was first put forward by the Commission in September 1990 (OJ 1990 C243/2) and it encountered widespread criticism (e.g. H. Brandner and P. Ulmer, 'The Community Directive on Unfair Terms in Consumer Contracts: Some Critical Remarks on the Proposal Submitted by the EC Commission', (1991) 28 *CML Rev.* 647). A revised proposal was submitted in March 1992 (OJ 1992 C73/7) which took into account many of the criticisms. What was originally a 'blacklist' of prohibited terms annexed to the Directive was transformed into the 'indicative list' of the types of term which might be likely to fall foul of the unfairness test, and it is stressed throughout that the Directive is intended to provide a minimum framework from which the Member States may depart in order to give enhanced protection to consumers. With a number of further amendments, this proposal was adopted in April 1993.

The Directive cuts across the existing emphasis on exclusion clauses by setting up a structure of control for all contract terms deemed unfair, regardless of their particular function in the contract. The breadth of the control offered is illustrated by the indicative list in the Annex.

Council Directive 93/13/EEC
Unfair Terms in Consumer Contracts

[Recitals omitted]

Article 1

1. The purpose of this Directive is to approximate the laws, regulations and administrative provisions of the Member States relating to unfair terms in contracts concluded between a seller or supplier and a consumer.

2. The contractual terms which reflect mandatory statutory or regulatory provisions and the provisions or principles of international conventions to which the Member States or the Community are party, particularly in the transport area, shall not be subject to the provisions of the Directive.

Article 2

For the purposes of this Directive:
  (a) 'unfair terms' means the contractual terms defined in Article 3;
  (b) 'consumer' means any natural person who, in contracts covered by this Directive, is acting for purposes which are outside his trade, business or profession;
  (c) 'seller or supplier' means any natural or legal person who, in contracts covered by this Directive, is acting for purposes relating to his trade, business or profession, whether publicly owned or privately owned.

Article 3

1. A contractual term which has not been individually negotiated shall be regarded as unfair if, contrary to the requirement of good faith, it causes a significant imbalance in the parties' rights and obligations arising under the contract, to the detriment of the consumer.

2. A term shall always be regarded as not individually negotiated where it has been drafted in advance and the consumer has therefore not been able to influence the substance of the term, particularly in the context of a pre-formulated standard contract.

The fact that certain aspects of a term or one specific term have been individually negotiated shall not exclude the application of this Article to the rest of a contract if an overall assessment of the contract indicates that it is nevertheless a pre-formulated standard contract.

Where any seller or supplier claims that a standard term has been individually negotiated, the burden of proof in this respect shall be incumbent on him.

3. The Annex shall contain an indicative and non-exhaustive list of the terms which may be regarded as unfair.

Article 4

1. Without prejudice to Article 7, the unfairness of a contractual term shall be assessed, taking into account the nature of the goods or services for which the contract was concluded and by referring, at the time of conclusion of the contract, to all the circumstances attending the conclusion of the contract and to all the other terms of the contract or of another contract on which it is dependent.

2. Assessment of the unfair nature of the terms shall relate neither to the definition of the main subject matter of the contract nor to the adequacy of the price and remuneration, on the one hand, as against the services or goods supplied in exchange, on the other, in so far as these terms are in plain intelligible language.

Article 5

In the case of contracts where all or certain terms offered to the consumer are in writing, these terms must always be drafted in plain, intelligible language. Where there is doubt about the meaning of a term, the interpretation most favourable to the consumer shall prevail. This rule on interpretation shall not apply in the context of the procedures laid down in Article 7(2).

Article 6

1. Member States shall lay down that unfair terms used in a contract concluded with a consumer by a seller or supplier shall, as provided for under their national law, not be binding on the consumer and that the contract shall con-

tinue to bind the parties upon those terms if it is capable of continuing in existence without the unfair terms.

2. Member States shall take the necessary measures to ensure that the consumer does not lose the protection granted by this Directive by virtue of the choice of the law of a non-Member country as the law applicable to the contract if the latter has a close connection with the territory of the Member States.

Article 7

1. Member States shall ensure that, in the interests of consumers and of competitors, adequate and effective means exist to prevent the continued use of unfair terms in contracts concluded with consumers by sellers or suppliers.

2. The means referred to in paragraph 1 shall include provisions whereby persons or organizations, having a legitimate interest under national law in protecting consumers, may take action according to the national law concerned before the courts or before competent administrative bodies for a decision as to whether contractual terms drawn up for general use are unfair, so that they can apply appropriate and effective means to prevent the continued use of such terms.

3. With due regard for national laws, the legal remedies referred to in paragraph 2 may be directed separately or jointly against a number of sellers or suppliers from the same economic sector or their associations which use or recommend the use of the same general contractual terms or similar terms.

Article 8

Member States may adopt or retain the most stringent provisions compatible with the Treaty in the area covered by this Directive, to ensure a maximum degree of protection for the consumer.

Article 9

The Commission shall present a report to the European Parliament and to the Council concerning the application of this Directive five years at the latest after the date in Article 10(1).

Article 10

1. Member States shall bring into force the laws, regulations and administrative provisions necessary to comply with this Directive no later than 31 December 1994. They shall forthwith inform the Commission thereof.

These provisions shall be applicable to all contracts concluded after 31 December 1994.

2. When Member States adopt these measures, they shall contain a reference to this Directive or shall be accompanied by such reference on the occasion of their official publication. The methods of making such a reference shall be laid down by the Member States.

3. Member States shall communicate the main provisions of national law which they adopt in the field covered by this Directive to the Commission.

Article 11

This Directive is addressed to the Member States.

Annex
Terms Referred to in Article 3(3)

1. Terms which have the object or effect of:

(a) excluding or limiting the legal liability of a seller or supplier in the event of the death of a consumer or personal injury to the latter resulting from an act or omission of that seller or supplier;

(b) inappropriately excluding or limiting the legal rights of the consumer *vis-à-vis* the seller or supplier or another party in the event of total or partial non-performance or inadequate performance by the seller or supplier of any of the contractual obligations, including the option of offsetting a debt owed to the seller or supplier against any claim which the consumer may have against him;

(c) making an agreement binding on the consumer whereas provision of services by the seller or supplier is subject to a condition whose realization depends on his own will alone;

(d) permitting the seller or supplier to retain sums paid by the consumer where the latter decides not to conclude or perform the contract, without providing for the consumer to receive compensation of an equivalent amount from the seller or supplier where the latter is the party cancelling the contract;

(e) requiring any consumer who fails to fulfil his obligation to pay a disproportionately high sum in compensation;

(f) authorizing the seller or supplier to dissolve the contract on a discretionary basis where the same facility is not granted to the consumer, or permitting the seller or supplier to retain the sums paid for services not yet supplied by him where it is the seller or supplier himself who dissolves the contract;

(g) enabling the seller or supplier to terminate a contract of indeterminate duration without reasonable notice except where there are serious grounds for doing so;

(h) automatically extending a contract of fixed duration where the consumer does not indicate otherwise, when the deadline fixed for the consumer to express this desire not to extend the contract is unreasonably early;

(i) irrevocably binding the consumer to terms with which he had no real opportunity of becoming acquainted before the conclusion of the contract;

(j) enabling the seller or supplier to alter the terms of the contract unilaterally without a valid reason which is specified in the contract;

(k) enabling the seller or supplier to alter unilaterally without a valid reason any characteristics of the product or service to be provided;

(l) providing for the price of goods to be determined at the time of delivery or allowing a seller of goods or supplier of services to increase their price without in both cases giving the consumer the corresponding right to cancel the contract if the final price is too high in relation to the price agreed when the contract was concluded;

(m) giving the seller or supplier the right to determine whether the goods or services supplied are in conformity with the contract, or giving him the exclusive right to interpret any term of the contract;

(n) limiting the seller's or supplier's obligation to respect commitments undertaken by his agents or making his commitments subject to compliance with a particular formality;

(o) obliging the consumer to fulfil all his obligations where the seller or supplier does not perform his;

(p) giving the seller or supplier the possibility of transferring his rights and obligations under the contract, where this may serve to reduce the guarantees for the consumer, without the latter's agreement;

(q) excluding or hindering the consumer's right to take legal action or exercise any other legal remedy, particularly by requiring the consumer to take disputes exclusively to arbitration not covered by legal provisions, unduly restricting the evidence available to him or imposing on him a burden of proof which, according to the applicable law, should lie with another party to the contract.

2. *Scope of subparagraphs (g), (j) and (l)*

(a) Subparagraph (g) is without hindrance to terms by which a supplier of financial services reserves the right to terminate unilaterally a contract of indeterminate duration without notice where there is a valid reason, provided that the supplier is required to inform the other contracting party or parties thereof immediately.

(b) Subparagraph (j) is without hindrance to terms under which a supplier of financial services reserves the right to alter the rate of interest payable by the consumer or due to the latter, or the amount of other charges for financial services without notice where there is a valid reason, provided that the supplier is required to inform the other contracting party or parties thereof at the earliest opportunity and that the latter are free to dissolve the contract immediately.

Subparagraph (j) is also without hindrance to terms under which a seller or supplier reserves the right to alter unilaterally the conditions of a contract of indeterminate duration, provided that he is required to inform the consumer with reasonable notice and that the consumer is free to dissolve the contract.

(c) Subparagraphs (g), (j) and (l) do not apply to:
  – transactions in transferable securities, financial instruments and other products or services where the price is linked to fluctuations in a stock exchange quotation or index or a financial market rate that the seller or supplier does not control;
  – contracts for the purchase or sale of foreign currency, traveller's cheques or international money orders denominated in foreign currency;
(d) Subparagraph (l) is without hindrance to price-indexation clauses, where lawful, provided that the method by which prices vary is explicitly described.

Notes

1. We have not included the Preamble to the Directive, but it should be noted that it will be a key aid to the construction of the Directive itself by both the European Court of Justice and national courts. If, for example, a Member State were to choose not to employ the term 'good faith' which is used as an aspect of the 'unfairness' standard in Article 3(1), deeming such a term to be meaningless within the framework of its domestic law of obligations, the Directive and its Preamble will still be available for use by domestic courts as aids to the construction of the national implementing legislation (Case C-106/89 *Marleasing SA* v. *La Comercial Internacional de Alimentacion* [1990] ECR I-4135). Of particular assistance in this respect would be the section of the Preamble which appears to give some criteria for the application of the good faith test which are not explicitly included in Article 4(1) of the Directive itself, which simply refers to unfairness taking into account all the circumstances of the case. The Preamble states:

'. . . in making an assessment of good faith, particular regard shall be had to the strength of the bargaining positions of the parties, whether the consumers had an inducement to agree to the term and whether the goods or services were sold or supplied to the special order of the consumer; . . . the requirement of good faith may be satisfied by the seller or supplier where he deals fairly and equitably with the other party whose legitimate interests he has to take into account.'

2. The scope of the Directive differs sharply from that of the Unfair Contract Terms Act. It applies to all 'unfair' terms within 'consumer' contracts. This raises a number of points: (1) no sectors have successfully lob-

bied for exclusion as 'special cases', in contrast to the position under the Act; (2) the scope of the Directive is determined by the term 'consumer' defined—somewhat narrowly—in Article 2(b); (3) as is indicated by the Annex, the potential scope of application of the Directive is much broader than the Act, which is principally focused on 'exclusion clauses'; this point is consider further below in note 5; (4) those areas of *non-contractual* liability covered by the Act are not covered by the Directive; (5) the nature of the control, which focuses on 'unfairness', 'good faith' and a 'significant imbalance' clearly differs from the approach employed by the Act. In one respect the two systems of control are the same: unfairness, like reasonableness in most of the cases applying under the Act, is to be judged at the time of the conclusion of the contract.

3. The terms subject to control are all those which are not individually negotiated. This differs from the earlier version of the Directive, where the control was not limited to the undickered aspects of standard-form contracts. The burden of proof falls on the seller/supplier to demonstrate that a particular term is individually negotiated (Article 3(2)).

4. The approach of the Directive, including the breadth of the control and the use of the good faith principle as an element of the standard of unfairness indicates the strong influence of the German AGB-Gesetz (Standard Form Contracts Act) of 1976. The test employed is rather vague, and the failure to include the criteria mentioned in the Preamble in the Directive itself (see note 1 above) is somewhat puzzling. Article 4(2) also appears largely to exclude issues of price from consideration although the scope of that provision is not entirely clear. In applying the standard of unfairness, English judges may be influenced by the experience of both civil law and other common law jurisdictions (e.g. the UCC in the United States) in applying a statutorily recognised principle of good faith. It should not necessarily be assumed that a good faith or unfairness standard will be any more favourable to the consumer than a reasonableness standard.

In two significant respects, the Directive offers a clearly less favourable regime to the consumer than the Unfair Contract Terms Act. First, it makes no mention of the burden of proof as regards the standard of unfairness, except obliquely in the passage from the Preamble quoted in note 1, which refers to the requirement of good faith being satisfied by the seller/supplier. However, in the absence of clear words it must be assumed that the burden of proof rests upon the plaintiff consumer. The Act, in contrast, places the burden upon the party who seeks to argue that his or her terms are reasonable. Second, as the list of terms included in the Annex is merely indicative, there are no terms under the Directive which are absolutely prohibited. In contrast, the Act outlaws completely, for example, terms whereby a party seeks to exclude his or her liability for negligence (s.2(1)).

Whatever form implementing legislation in the United Kingdom ultimately takes (see note 9), it need not preclude more stringent protection for the consumer (see Article 8), as the Preamble expressly recognises that only 'minimum harmonization' of national laws is possible at this time, providing only a basic irreducible minimum of consumer protection throughout the European Community. It would not, for example, be a breach of Community law by the UK for this form of control to be retained.

5. The wider ambit of direct judicial control of the terms of the contract is apparent from the types of terms included in the Annex. One type of term which is now likely to be subject to the unfairness standard are liquidated damages clauses, discussed in Chapter 14, Section IV—at least in so far as they are included in consumer contracts. Provisions in contracts whereby the party in breach is required to pay a prefixed sum of money, rather than the innocent party waiting for an award of damages to be fixed by the court are unenforceable as 'penalties' if they do not constitute a genuine preestimate of the damage likely to be suffered by the innocent party. This type of clause would now appear to fall within category (e) listed in the Annex. Liquidated damages clauses in certain consumer contracts are already subject to specific forms of control in the Consumer Credit Act 1974, but the use of a general standard of unfairness will be an innovation for English law. This type of control can be compared to the proposal considered by Ham (see Chapter 14) to extend the doctrine of unconscionability (see Chapter 9) to cover excessive liquidated damages clauses.

6. The requirement of 'plain and intelligible language' in consumer contracts, although reminiscent of the judicial approach to construction in the days before the Unfair Contract Terms Act, is none the less an innovation for English law, in the sense that it will become a basic statutory standard for the drafting of consumer contracts. What is not clear is how the failure to draft terms in plain and intelligible language is to be penalized under the framework of the Directive, except through the admonition that cases of ambiguity will be adjudicated in favour of the consumer.

7. The remedy to be made available is the severance of offending clauses in the case of actions brought on individual contracts (Article 6(1)). The Directive also envisages the extension of representative actions to consumer groups enabling them to bring collective actions before the courts or competent national administrative bodies, resulting in a declaratory remedy. This collective approach to law enforcement in the consumer protection field could allay some of the doubts expressed elsewhere in this chapter and in the earlier discussions of contractual justice (Ch. 8) and standard form contracts (Ch. 10) about the effectiveness of consumer pressure and individual litigation as means of changing market conditions. This provision, if properly implemented, could lead to an explosion of test-

case litigation, but, as note 10 below shows, there is some doubt as to whether it will be implemented in the UK. Broadly the same test of unfairness is to be applied in the context of both abstract collective and specific individual litigation, although the rule of interpretation concerning plain language is excluded in the former case.

8. The Directive does not opt for the more radical approach to contract remedies used in the Nordic countries, under which courts have a generalized power to adjust terms in contracts which operate unfairly, and are allowed to take into account the changed circumstances of the parties post formation in choosing which approach to take (see T. Wilhelmsson, 'Control of Unfair Contract Terms and Social Values: EC and Nordic Approaches', (1993) 16 *JCP* 435.

9. At the time of writing the form of the UK implementing legislation was not entirely clear, although in October 1993 the Department of Trade and Industry issued a Consultation Paper indicating that a minimalist approach might be taken. This would involve re-enacting the Directive in very similar terms in the form of a statutory instrument, under the authority of s. 2(2) of the European Communities Act 1972. This would leave the Unfair Contract Terms Act untouched, and create parallel systems of control for those terms falling within the scope of both measures. This approach would create confusion and uncertainty, and has been criticized. For example, Reynolds argues ('Unfair Contract Terms', (1994) 110 *LQR* 3) that this would create a situation of 'nightmarish complexity' which is inimical to the philosophy of consumer law which requires 'simple and "user-friendly" rules'. Reynolds also suggests that the approach might infringe the UK's obligations under Community law, in particular under Article 5 EC, which requires the UK to refrain from any measures which might inhibit the achievement of the EC's objectives. This was interpreted, as Reynolds comments, in the case of *Commission* v *France (French Merchant Seamen)* (Case 167/73 [1974] ECR 359 at 372) to mean that a Member State should not maintain in force an inconsistent legal regime as this might create a 'state of uncertainty as to the possibility available [to Community citizens] of relying on Community law'.

It is strongly arguable that a more effective response to the needs of consumers would be for the whole field of 'unfair terms' to be regulated in a uniform manner, perhaps using different standards of unfairness for consumer and commercial contracts. Such an approach requires more parliamentary time, unlikely to be available before the expiry of the deadline for implementation of the Directive at the end of 1994.

10. The minimalism of the proposed Regulations can be seen perhaps most strongly in the approach taken to Article 7(2) on representative or collective actions. The DTI paper suggests that this provision should not be

implemented at all in the legislation, as UK law contains no general provision for representative actions. Consequently, it is argued that Article 7(2) has no effect in the UK. It is questionable whether such an approach would survive the scrutiny of the European Court if it were asked to evaluate the compatibility of a measure drafted in these terms with the obligation on the UK loyally to implement the Directive, pursuant to Article 5 and 189(3) EC. This will require an assessment of whether the result to be achieved by the Directive, namely enhanced consumer protection, requires the UK to develop a novel remedial structure in the private law context.

11. For further commentary on the Directive see M. Dean, 'Unfair Contract Terms: The European Approach', (1993) 56 *MLR* 581.

Questions

1. Do you find the arguments for controlling exclusion clauses within contracts convincing? Justify your answer by reference to the materials in both Chapters 8 and 11.

2. Would you agree with the statement that the Unfair Contract Terms Act, as interpreted in subsequent cases, does not provide a framework for dealing with most types of objectionable market behaviour which result in the insertion of terms into the contract which unfairly prejudice one party?

3. Why do you think the House of Lords in *George Mitchell* was anxious to place limits upon the role of appellate courts in relation to the Unfair Contract Terms Act? Is this abstentionist approach consistent with the arguments put forward by Reiter in Chapter 8 about the role of the judges?

4. What do you think will be the principal problems which will be encountered in delimiting the respective scope of the Unfair Contract Terms Act and any Regulations adopted for the purpose of implementing the EC Directive? Do you consider there to be a fundamental conflict in basic philosophy between the two measures?

5. Does the regulation of exclusion clauses provide an example of the transformation of contract law discussed by Collins in Chapter 8, or is it an example of merely tinkering with the existing system?

PART IV

The Ending of Contracts

12

Risk and the Discharge of Contracts

I. INTRODUCTION

As the introductory extracts in this chapter indicate, contractual behaviour is intimately concerned with risk-taking, with the law of contract providing a framework within which risks can be allocated between the parties or allowed to run their course. The type of risks which are the subject of this chapter are those which, when they occur (e.g. the destruction of the subject-matter of contract), are apt to render the performance of the contract something quite different from what the parties agreed or, indeed, literally impossible. We shall discuss the circumstances in which contracting on the basis of a mistaken assumption, or the occurrence of a particular event for which the parties have not planned, can lead to the contract being treated as *void* ab initio *for common mistake* (in the first case) or as *discharged for frustration* (in the second case). We shall also discuss a number of different policy approaches which can help explain the behaviour of courts in deciding whether the parties should be held to their promises or should be excused from them, where performance of a contract becomes either impossible or much more difficult as a consequence of changed circumstances or of the revelation of the underlying mistaken assumption of the parties. In particular, we shall look at judicial strategies used in some jurisdictions to allocate the losses stemming from the occurrence of risks which render contracts commercially impracticable or exceptionally burdensome for one party. Finally, this leads into a discussion of contract planning for risks, focusing in particular on *force majeure* clauses. A *force majeure* clause is one by which a promisor seeks to avoid taking the burden of risks over which he has no control, hence the use of the French legal term, which is the broad functional equivalent of the doctrine of frustration. Such a clause may typically provide that 'the promisor shall not be responsible for any losses occasioned by any Act of God, war, riot, strike, breakdown of machinery, fire or any cause contemplated by the term *force majeure*'.

We begin with a number of introductory comments on the nature of risk.

I. Macneil, 'A Primer of Contract Planning', (1975) 48 *S. Cal. L. Rev.* 627 at 667

The man-made concept of risk is a recognition that human beings are in a constant state of partial ignorance about the future, including future losses. We know with certainty from past experience that losses of various kinds will occur, but we do not know where, when, how, to whom, or how bad they will be. This state of partial ignorance we call risk. It disappears from our minds as soon as we know for sure either that the loss will occur or that it will not occur, simply because certainty is the opposite of risk. Risk is thus reduced whenever man acquires more certain knowledge about the occurrence or non-occurrence of future losses.

Except to the extent that he may be controlled by negative instincts such as the so-called death-wish, man seeks to avoid both losses and risks of loss. He does many things to try to avoid losses, from brushing his teeth in the morning to fighting massive, if commonly futile, wars. He tries to eliminate risks not only by seeking to eliminate causes of losses, but also by using various techniques to acquire more certain information concerning future losses. Organized efforts along these lines in the world of commerce and family matters have come to be called risk management. Risk planning in connection with contracts is simply one facet of risk management in the economic world.

Like legal framework planning, planning for contractual risks (whether or not they are legal framework risks) calls for special awareness on the part of a lawyer participating in contract planing. Except in specialized contracts such as insurance, contractual risk planning is very likely not to be central to the purpose of the parties in entering the contractual relationship. When risk planning is not a central purpose of the contract, it may be seen by the parties in the same light as any other "trouble" planning, namely something distasteful and disruptive to the relationship, perhaps to be put up with, but never to be liked; in short, it is a lawyer's job. It is not surprising, therefore, that lawyers commonly are involved heavily with contractual risk planning.

J. Swan, 'The Allocation of Risk in the Analysis of Mistake and Frustration', in B. Reiter and J. Swan (eds.), *Studies in Contract Law* (Toronto, Butterworths, 1980), 182–4

The making of any bargain necessarily involves the creation of a risk that subsequent events will cause the bargain to turn out to be less advantageous to one party than might have been hoped at the time it was made. This is as true of those bargains made in grocery shopping as it is of the bargain for the long term supply of coal, oil or uranium involving millions of dollars. It is obvious that the extent of the risks created by any contract is a function of both the size of the contract in terms of the assets or other financial resources of the parties and the period of time between the making of the contract and final performance. The risk that a loaf of bread bought in a supermarket one day may be on sale for half price the next is trivial and, in any case, since the contract of sale is fully executed when the loaf has been paid for, there is no possibility of breach by either party. The risks that are created by a long-term contract for the supply of uranium at a fixed price are large. The price may change over the period. Governmental interference may affect the demand or supply of uranium. These changes may make it advantageous for one party to escape his obligations and such an escape may be breach of the contract.

Most parties realize that the making of any contract creates risks and they may provide in the contract that the risks that they have foreseen will be allocated between them. The law of contracts provides a wide range of devices which the parties can use to achieve an allocation. These include conditions, warranties, escalator clauses, options to cancel, and so on. Even when the parties have not allocated a particular risk, the law may, so to speak, fill in the blanks and impose a particular risk on one party or the other. This can be seen in many areas: the implied conditions of quality under The Sale of Goods Act, the device of the 'implied conditions,' . . . the doctrine of frustration and rules regarding mistake. It is important to remember that this elaboration of the contract obligations has two features. The first is that whether the legislative or judicial interference is said to be based on the implication of a term or the imposition of a just solution on the parties, there has been an assignment of a risk to one side or the other. The second is that the parties are, in general, free to allocate the risk if they happen to think about it and so provide in their agreement.

Notes

1. Sociologists have suggested that the essence of risk is that it is calculable. In that sense, it can be contrasted with hazard or chance (see further on this U. Beck, 'From Industrial Society to the Risk Society: Questions of Survival, Social Structure and Ecological Enlightenment', (1992) 9(1) *Theory, Culture and Society* 97; and Ewald, 'Insurance and Risk', in Burchell *et al.* (eds.), *The Foucault Effect* (Brighton, Harvester/Wheatsheaf, 1991), 197). It is this quality of 'risk' which links it closely to insurance and which permits the shifting of the burden of a risk onto someone who has planned for it or who is paid to assume it. In the allocation of risks under contracts, insurance (which includes not only the conclusion of formal insurance contracts with third parties but also the ability to raise prices to cover losses (self-insurance)) and insurability will frequently play an important role in determining the conduct of the parties. It can also influence the court in the adjudication of the allocation of losses, as we saw in the discussion of the reasonableness test under the Unfair Contract Terms Act 1977 in Chapter 11. In this chapter, the role of insurance will come

through most clearly in the discussion of the economic analysis of frustration undertaken by Posner and Rosenfield which focuses on the role of the superior risk-bearer.

2. Common mistake and frustration operate in a sense as the emergency tool-kit of risk allocation within the law of contract. Judges will naturally prefer to adjudicate the rights and duties of the parties to a contract on the basis of the allocations of risk which they have made. Sometimes, as Swan noted (above), they can also do this by using the doctrine of implied terms. More recently, the recognition of the concept of factual benefit in *Williams* v. *Roffey* ([1990] 1 All ER 512) has opened the door to a more generous approach to the enforceability of contractual modifications—in particular the type of modifications which occur when external events such as price fluctuations make it much more difficult for one party to perform a contract. As we shall see, the sphere of application of both common mistake and frustration in English law is relatively narrow, although the present position is that the test for common mistake, at least in equity, is more generous than that for frustration. However, as is now well recognized, mistake and frustration in fact operate on the same terrain. As H. Havighurst comments (*The Nature of Private Contract* (Littleton, Colo., Rothman, 1961), 62), frustration 'is concerned with a mutual mistake as to the future and is not basically different from mutual mistake with respect to an existing fact'.

It should be noted that this quotation adopts the US practice of using the term 'mutual' mistake for what in English law would conventionally be termed 'common' mistake. This difference in terminology recurs at several junctures in this chapter. For further clarification of terminology see also Chapter 5.

The point made by Havighurst is illustrated in more detail by the next section.

II. FRUSTRATION AND MISTAKE: TWO PARALLEL DOCTRINES

Amalgamated Investment v. *John Walker* [1976] 2 All ER 509

The defendants owned a commercial property which they wished to sell. The property was advertised by estate agents instructed by the defendants 'as suitable for occupation or redevelopment'. An offer was made by a consortium of two companies, of which the plaintiff company was one. When the offer was made, the offerors made it clear that they possessed an office development permit which might be used in connection with a redevelopment of the property. The defendants must then have known that the offer was made with a view to redevelopment. The defendants accepted an offer of £1,710,000. The plaintiffs made the usual search enquiries before contracts were exchanged. This included asking a specific question about whether the property was designated as a listed building. The defendants answered this question in the negative. The contract for the sale was signed on 25 September 1973. On 26 September 1973 the Department of Environment informed the defendants that the property had been designated a listed building. The case proceeded on the basis of two issues, common mistake and frustration. Plowman V-C at first instance rejected both pleas from the plaintiffs. The Court of Appeal dismissed the plaintiff's appeal.

BUCKLEY LJ The judge found as a fact that the value of the property with no redevelopment potential was probably £1,500,000 less than the contract price. So the effect of the building being put into the list was this: that so long as it remained listed and 'listed building consent' could not be obtained, the value of the property was depreciated from the £1,700,000 odd, which was the sale price, to something of the order of £200,000. The judge also found as a fact that the defendants knew at all material times that the purchasers were buying the property for redevelopment. . . .

Plowman V-C held that there was no common mistake. He said:

'In my judgment, however, the issue of mistake does not arise. The relevant event, in my opinion, was the actual listing of the warehouse and not some preliminary step in the process of listing taken within the four walls of the Department, which might or might nor result in executive action, although no doubt it probably would.'

He therefore treated the building as having been listed on the day when the list was signed by the head of the relevant branch in the Ministry; that is to say, after the date of the contract. So, on that finding, the contract was not entered into in reliance on any, or under any, common mistake of the parties, for at the time when the contract was entered into the building was not a listed building.

He dealt with the alternative ground for frustration of the contract, which was taken before him, in this way:

'One therefore starts with this (and I quote Lord Radcliffe) ". . . frustration is not to be lightly invoked as the dissolvent of a contract". Let me then try to apply some of the tests proposed by the House of Lords [he is there referring to *Davis Contractors Ltd* v. *Fareham Urban District Council* [1956] AC 666]] to the facts of this case. Can it be said that the parties must have made their contract on the footing that the warehouse would not be listed in the future? I can see nothing in the contract to suggest that that must be the case. In my judgment the plaintiffs took the risk under the contract, and it seems to me impossible to maintain that the contract ceased to apply when the property was listed. They could have provided against the risk by an appropriate provision in the contract, but they did not do so. Again, is the contract which the parties made, on its true construction, wide enough to apply to the situation which arose when the property was listed? The answer to that must, in my judgment, be yes, and I can see nothing in the contract to support the contrary view. Would the thing undertaken, if performed, be a different thing from that contracted for? Or, again, can the plaintiffs say, "This was not the bargain we made"? (Non haec in foedera veni.) Not in my judgment. The plaintiffs undertook to purchase 33, Commercial Road, and if the purchase is completed, they will have done the very thing which they undertook to do, no more and no less. They took the risk under the contract of the property being listed, and it has turned out badly for them, but as Lord Simonds said, ". . . it by no means follows that disappointed expectations lead to frustrated contracts".'

So Plowman V-C held that the contract stood and that the purchasers were liable for the full purchase price, and that the contract should be carried out.

It has been contended before us that there was here a common mistake of fact on a matter of fundamental importance, in consequence of which the contract ought to be set aside. . . .

Counsel for the plaintiffs says that they bought the property as property which was ripe for development and that the defendants sold on the same basis, and that by reason of the decision to list the property the property was not in fact ripe for development. Therefore he says there was a common mistake as to the nature of the property, and the purchaser is entitled to rescission. . . .

. . . The crucial date, in my judgment, is the date when the list was signed. It was then that the building became a listed building, and it was only then that the expectations of the parties (who no doubt both expected that this property would be capable of being developed, subject always of course to obtaining planning permission, without it being necessary to obtain listed building permission) were disappointed. For myself, I entirely agree with the conclusion which the learned judge reached on this part of the case. In my judgment, there was no mutual mistake as to the circumstances surrounding the contract at the time when the contract was entered into. The only mistake that there was was one which related to the expectation of the parties. They expected that the building would be subject only to ordinary town planning consent procedures, and that expectation has been disappointed. But at the date when the contract was entered into I cannot see that there is any ground for saying that the parties were then subject to some mutual mistake of fact relating to the circumstances surrounding the contract. Accordingly, for my part, I think that the learned judge's decision on that part of the case is one which should be upheld.
. . .

I now turn to the alternative argument which has been presented to us in support of this appeal, which is on frustration. Counsel for the plaintiffs has relied on what was said in the speeches in the House of Lords in *Davis Contractors Ltd* v. *Fareham Urban District Council*, and it may perhaps be useful if I refer to what was said by Lord Radcliffe:

'So, perhaps, it would be simpler to say at the outset that frustration occurs whenever the law recognises that, without default of either party, a contractual obligation has become incapable of being performed because the circumstances in which performance is called for would render it a thing radically different from that which was undertaken by the contract.'

That is a passage which was referred to by Plowman V-C in the course of his judgment. Then, a little later on, after referring to *Denny, Mott and Dickson Ltd* v. *James B Fraser & Co Ltd* [[1944] AC 265], Lord Radcliffe said:

'It is for that reason that special importance is necessarily attached to the occurrence of any unexpected event that, as it were, changes the face of things. But, even so, it is not hardship or inconvenience or material loss itself which calls the principle of frustration into play. There must be as well such a change in the significance of the obligation that the thing undertaken would, if performed, be a different thing from that contracted for.'

Now, the obligation undertaken to be performed in this case by the defendants was to sell this property for the contract price and, of course, to show a good title and so forth. The defendants did not warrant in any way that planning permission could be obtained for the development of the property. No doubt both parties considered that the property was property which could advantageously be developed and was property for which planning permission would probably be satisfactorily obtained. But there was no stipulation in the contract relating to anything of that kind; nor, as I say, was there any warranty on the part of the defendants. . . . . I have reached the conclusion that there are not here the necessary factual bases for holding that this contract has been frustrated. It seems to me that the risk of property being listed as property of architectural or historical interest is a risk which inheres in all ownership of buildings. In many cases it may be an extremely remote risk. In many cases it may be a marginal risk. In some cases it may be a substantial risk. But it is a risk, I think, which attaches to all buildings and it is a risk that every owner and every purchaser of property must recognise that he is subject to. The purchasers in the present case bought knowing that they would have to obtain planning permission in order to develop the property. The effect of listing under the sections of the 1971 Act to which I have referred makes the obtaining of planning permission, it may be, more difficult, and it may also make it a longer and more complicated process. But still, in essence, the position is that the would-be developer has to obtain the appropriate planning permissions, one form of permission being the 'listed building permission'. The plaintiffs, when they entered into the contract, must obviously be taken to have known that they would need to get planning permission. They must also, in my judgment, be taken to have known that there was the risk, although they may not have regarded it as a substantial risk, that the building might at some time be listed, and that their chances of obtaining planning permission might possibly be adversely affected to some extent by that, or at any rate their chances of obtaining speedy planning permission. But, in my judgment, this is a risk of a kind which every purchaser should be regarded as knowing that he is subject to when he enters into his contract of purchase. It is a risk which I think the purchaser must carry, and any loss that may result from the maturing of that risk is a loss which must lie where it falls. Moreover, the plaintiffs have not yet established that they will be unable to obtain all the necessary planning permissions, including 'listed building permission'. So it has not yet, I think, been established that the listing of this building has had the drastic effect which the figures I have mentioned suggest that it may have had. It may well turn out to be the case that 'listed building permission' will be obtainable here and the purchasers will be able to carry into effect the development which they desire.

For these reasons I reach the conclusion, as I say, that the necessary facts have not been established in this case to found a claim that the contract has been frustrated.

For these reasons, I would dismiss this appeal.

Notes

1. It seems from Buckley LJ's judgment that English contract law applies the frustration doctrine to risks which arise during the running of the contract. For risks which occur prior to the contract, the common mistake doctrine is used. The plaintiffs in the above case were precluded from arguing common mistake, as the risk—or the mistake that was made regarding the sale and purchase of a listed building which was thought not to be listed—occurred after the contract was made. This meant that the issue was one of frustration. Later cases in this chapter will explain in more detail what tests each doctrine uses.

2. The basic root of the two doctrines is pointed out by Kull.

A. Kull, 'Mistake, Frustration and the Windfall Principle of Contract Remedies', (1991) 43 *Hastings LJ* 1 at 2

Mistake and frustration are . . . two names for the same problem. We may hypothesize perfect knowledge about the present moment but not about the future. Every contract is influenced by a "mutual mistake" as to the proposed exchange of values, if only because present values inescapably reflect projected but unknowable future values. Every agreement is to some extent "frustrated" in that the precise cost and value of either side's performance can never be known in advance. We form contracts in the knowledge that our information is imperfect, and we do not expect to anticipate with exactness the precise cost or value, at the time of performance, of what we are either to give or to receive. At a profounder level . . . *every* party to a contract "is aware, at the time the contract is made, that he has only limited knowledge with respect to the facts to which the [transaction] relates"; being human, he necessarily "treats his limited knowledge as sufficient".

III. MISTAKE

Bell v. *Lever Brothers*
[1932] AC 161

Bell and Snelling (the 'appellants') were appointed, respectively, Chairman and Vice-Chairman of the Board of Directors of a subsidiary company of Lever Brothers for a period of five years. In return they were paid salaries of £8,000 and £6,000 p.a. respectively, under five-year contracts of service with Lever. During their period of service, both Bell and Snelling engaged in business on their own account, in breach of a term of their service agreement prohibiting them from making any private profit on their own account. On reorganization of the subsidiary company, Lever made agreements with Bell and Snelling to terminate their contracts of service, paying them £30,000 and £20,000 respectively as compensation for their resigning voluntarily from their appointments. When Lever discovered the earlier breaches of contract by the defendants, they brought proceedings to have the compensation agreements set aside and to recover the money paid. Their case was based partly on fraud, which was rejected on the facts by the jury, and on mistake. Crucial findings of fact by the jury in relation to the significance of the earlier breaches are set out in the speech of Lord Warrington. Most crucial is the finding that when Bell and Snelling negotiated their compensation agreements they had forgotten about their earlier breaches of duty.

The claim based on unilateral mistake (i.e. a mistake by Lever as to the terms of the contract) failed largely because it was held that Bell and Snelling were under no obligation to disclose their breaches of duty. The claim for common mistake is dealt with in the extracts from the speeches of the Law Lords below. Note that some of the speeches refer to common mistake here as mutual mistake. What also makes the case extremely confusing is that the decision of the House of Lords is partly based on the question of whether Lever had effectively amended their pleadings and their case in order to incorporate the claim of common mistake. That they had not done so is at the root of Lord Blanesburgh's judgment. The important aspects of the case, therefore, are slightly submerged and need to be clearly identified as:

the 'test' of common mistake;
the application of this test to the facts of *Bell* v. *Lever Brothers*.

LORD BLANESBURGH . . . the appellants have not had the opportunity of showing by evidence the extent to which Levers received consideration for the settlement agreements over and above their release from liability the further payments for which, on the hypothesis, it was by all parties assumed that they remained liable. The mistake must go to the whole consideration. I have already indicated the general nature of the further advantages derived by Levers from the settlement agreements, as these appear on the record, but this aspect of the case has not been developed in evidence, because in the action as fought it was not either relevant or necessary so to do. It may be, indeed I am far from saying that, even on the existing record, the appellants have not sufficient evidence on this point to displace the new plea altogether. But here again it would, I think, be unfair to leave them exposed to the hazard of the amendment with that answer to it quite undeveloped. . . .

My Lords, I confess that I arrive without reluctance at this conclusion of the whole matter. It appears to me to accord with a sound view both of justice and of fairness. I should have deemed it unfortunate if the appellants had been left in enjoyment of the profit accruing from the offending transactions and if they had not been required to pay the nominal damage which the jury considered these transactions occasioned to Niger. But that result has not followed. For both the profit and the damage they remain accountable, as is wholesome.

Further acceptance, however, by your Lordships' House of the orders appealed from would have meant that, after the complete failure of the grave charges of fraud preferred against officials whose ability and services had brought to Niger advantages of untold value, these officials, the appellants, would have been left exposed to the same consequences as if the charges had all been true. Speaking only for myself I feel relieved to be able to take a view of equity and procedure which shields the appellants from such a consequence.

[Lord Blanesburgh accepted the appeal.]

LORD WARRINGTON The questions material to the issue of mistake as put to the jury and their answers thereto were as follows:—

3 (*b*). Did the defendants or either of them commit breaches of contract or duty towards the plaintiffs in entering into the contracts referred to as C.T.C., R. T. D., and G. S. 2 or any of them as private transactions on their own account and for their own benefit?

Answer: Yes.

4 (*a*). Were the plaintiffs (Levers) entitled to determine the contracts of service with the defendants or either of them?

Answer: Yes.

(1.) In January, 1928.

Answer: Yes.

And (2.) in March, 1929. If so, would the plaintiffs (Levers) have elected to exercise such right at either of such dates?

Answer: Yes.

(*b*) Similar questions and answers as to the position of the Niger Company in reference to the offices therein held by the defendants respectively.

5. When Levers entered into the agreements of March 19, 1929, did they

know of the actings of either of the defendants in regard to the dealings C. T. C., R. T. D., G. S. 2?

Answer: No.

If Levers had so known would they have made these agreements or either of them?

Answer: No.

At the date of the respective interviews prior to these agreements had the defendant Bell or the defendant Snelling in mind their actings in respect of these transactions?

Answer: No.

The final question was put to the jury at the suggestion of the learned judge, and obviously is only relevant to the issue whether there was a mutual mistake. No objection to it was taken on the part of the appellants. Moreover, it is quite obvious that an argument founded on unilateral mistake had not the slightest chance of success, and it must have been clear to both parties that the learned judge was going to deal with the case as one of mutual as distinguished from unilateral mistake. I will assume for the present that either on the pleadings as rightly understood, or on the manner in which the case was conducted, or on the assumption that all the evidence reasonably likely to be forthcoming on the point was before the Court, the learned judge was entitled to deal with the matter on the footing of mutual mistake, and will consider the case of that footing. . . .

. . . It is in my opinion clear that each party believed that the remunerative offices, compensation for the loss of which was the subject of the negotiations, were offices which could not be determined except by the consent of the holder thereof, and further believed that the other party was under the same belief and was treating on that footing.

The real question, therefore, is whether the erroneous assumption on the part of both parties to the agreements that the service contracts were undeterminable except by agreement was of such a fundamental character as to constitute an underlying assumption without which the parties would not have made the contract they in fact made, or whether it was only a common error as to a material element, but one not going to the root of the matter and not affecting the subject of the consideration.

With the knowledge that I am differing from the majority of your Lordships, I am unable to arrive at any conclusion except that in this case the erroneous assumption was essential to the contract which without it would not have been made.

It is true that the error was not one as to the terms of the service agreements, but it was one which having regard to the matter on which the parties were negotiating—namely, the terms on which the service agreements were to be prematurely determined and the compensation to be paid therefor, was in my opinion as fundamental to the bargain as any error one can imagine.

The compensation agreed to be paid was in each case the amount of the full salary for the two years and a half unexpired with the addition in Mr. Bell's case of 10,000*l.* and in Mr. Snelling's of 5000*l.* It is difficult to believe that the jury were otherwise than correct in their answer to the second branch of the group of questions numbered 5—namely, that had Levers known of the actings of the appellants in regard to the dealings in question they would not have made the agreements now impeached or either of them. It is true that such a finding is not in the strict sense one of fact, but it is an inference which the jury were entitled to draw from the evidence and from all the circumstances of the case, it is one which the learned judge and the Court of Appeal have also drawn, and, if I may say so with respect, it is one I should draw myself. I also agree with the learned judge that looking at the matter from the side of the appellants the existence of an agreement giving them rights which could only be compromised by compensation was in the same way the root and basis of the cancellation agreements.

In my opinion, therefore, assuming that the point was open, the appeal on the main question ought to be dismissed. . . .

This case seems to me to raise a question as to the application of certain doctrines of common law, and I have therefore not thought it necessary to discuss or explain the special doctrines and practice of Courts of equity in reference to the rescission on the ground of mistake of contracts, conveyances and assignments of property and so forth, or to the refusal on the same ground to decree specific performance, though I think, in accordance with such doctrines and practice, the same result would follow.

[Lord Warrington rejected the appeal.]

LORD ATKIN Having made this discovery it naturally occurred to Levers that instead of spending 50,000*l.* to cancel the two service agreements they might, if they had known the facts, have got rid of them for nothing. They therefore claimed the return of the money from the appellants, as well as the amount of the profits made; and on August 7, 1929, issued the writ in the present action, claiming damages for fraudulent misrepresentation and concealment, an account of the defendants' dealings in cocoa, and repayment of money paid under a mistake of fact. . . .

My Lords, the rules of law dealing with the effect of mistake on contract appear to be established with reasonable clearness. If mistake operates at all it operates so as to negative or in some cases to nullify consent. The parties may be mistaken in the identity of the contracting parties, or in the existence of the subject-matter of the contract at the date of the contract, or in the quality of the subject-matter of the contract. These mistakes may be by one party, or by both, and the legal effect may depend upon the class of mistake above mentioned. Thus a mistaken belief by A, that he is contracting with B, whereas in fact he is contracting with C, will negative consent where it is clear that the intention of

A. was to contract only with B. So the agreement of A. and B. to purchase a specific article is void if in fact the article had perished before the date of sale.

Mistake as to quality of the thing contracted for raises more difficult questions. In such a case a mistake will not affect assent unless it is the mistake of both parties, and is as to the existence of some quality which makes the thing without the quality essentially different from the thing as it was believed to be. Of course it may appear that the parties contracted that the article should possess the quality which one or other or both mistakenly believed it to possess. But in such a case there is a contract and the inquiry is a different one, being whether the contract as to quality amounts to a condition or a warranty, a different branch of the law. The principles to be applied are to be found in two cases which, as far as my knowledge goes, have always been treated as authoritative expositions of the law. The first is *Kennedy* v. *Panama Royal Mail Co.* (1867) LR 2 QB 580.

In that case the plaintiff had applied for shares in the defendant company on the faith of a prospectus which stated falsely but innocently that the company had a binding contract with the Government of New Zealand for the carriage of mails. On discovering the true facts the plaintiff brought an action for the recovery of the sums he had paid on calls. The defendants brought a cross action for further calls. Blackburn J., in delivering the judgment of the Court (Cockburn C.J., Blackburn, Mellor and Shee JJ.), said: "The only remaining question is one of much greater difficulty. It was contended by Mr. Mellish, on behalf of Lord Gilbert Kennedy, that the effect of the prospectus was to warrant to the intended shareholders that there really was such a contract as is there represented, and not merely to represent that the company *bonâ fide* believed it; and that the difference in substance between shares in a company with such a contract and shares in a company whose supposed contract was not binding, was a difference in substance in the nature of the thing; and that the shareholder was entitled to return the shares as soon as he discovered this, quite independently of fraud, on the ground that he had applied for one thing and got another. And, if the invalidity of the contract really made the shares he obtained different things in substance from those which he applied for, this would, we think, be good law. . . .

There is, however, a very important difference between cases where a contract may be rescinded on account of fraud, and those in which it may be rescinded on the ground that there is a difference in substance between the thing bargained for and that obtained. It is enough to show that there was a fraudulent representation as to any part of that which induced the party to enter into the contract which he seeks to rescind; but where there has been an innocent misrepresentation or misapprehension, it does not authorize a rescission unless it is such as to show that there is a complete difference in substance between what was supposed to be and what was taken, so as to constitute a failure of consideration. For example, where a horse is bought under a belief that it is sound, if the purchaser was induced to buy by a fraudulent representation as to the horse's soundness, the contract may be rescinded. If it was induced by an honest misrepresentation as to its soundness, though it may be clear that both vendor and purchaser thought that they were dealing about a sound horse and were in error, yet the purchaser must pay the whole price unless there was a warranty; and if there was a warranty, he cannot return the horse and claim back the whole price, unless there was a condition to that effect in the contract:

The Court came to the conclusion in that case that, though there was a misapprehension as to that which was a material part of the motive inducing the applicant to ask for the shares, it did not prevent the shares from being in substance those he applied for.

[Lord Atkin considered *Smith* v. *Hughes* and concluded:]

In these cases I am inclined to think that the true analysis is that there is a contract, but that the one party is not able to supply the very thing whether goods or services that the other party contracted to take; and therefore the contract is unenforceable by the one if executory, while if executed the other can recover back money paid on the ground of failure of the consideration. . . .

. . . It is essential . . . to keep in mind the finding of the jury acquitting the defendants of fraudulent misrepresentation or concealment in procuring the agreements in question. Grave injustice may be done to the defendants and confusion introduced into the legal conclusion, unless it is quite clear that in considering mistake in this case no suggestion of fraud is admissible and cannot strictly be regarded by the judge who has to determine the legal issues raised. . . .

. . . I have come to the conclusion that it would be wrong to decide that an agreement to terminate a definite specified contract is void if it turns out that the agreement had already been broken and could have been terminated otherwise. The contract released is the identical contract in both cases, and the party paying for release gets exactly what he bargains for. It seems immaterial that he could have got the same result in another way, or that if he had known the true facts he would not have entered into the bargain. A buys B's horse; he thinks the horse is sound and he pays the price of a sound horse; he would certainly not have bought the horse if he had known as the fact is that the horse is unsound. If B has made no representation as to soundness and has not contracted that the horse is sound, A is bound and cannot recover back the price. A buys a picture from B; both A and B believe it to be the work of an old master, and a high price is paid. It turns out to be a modern copy. A has no remedy in the absence of representation or warranty. A agrees to take on lease or to buy from B an unfurnished dwelling-house. The house is in fact uninhabitable. A would never have entered into the bargain if he had known the fact. A has no remedy, and the position is the same whether B knew the facts or not, so long as he made no representation or gave no warranty. . . .

This brings the discussion to the alternative mode of expressing the result of a mutual mistake. It is said that in such a case as the present there is to be implied a stipulation in the contract that a condition of its efficacy is that the facts should be as understood by both parties—namely, that the contract could not be terminated till the end of the current term. The question of the existence of conditions, express or implied, is obviously one that affects not the formation of contract, but the investigation of the terms of the contract when made. A condition derives its efficacy from the consent of the parties, express or implied. They have agreed, but on what terms. One term may be that unless the facts are or are not of a particular nature, or unless an event has or has not happened, the contract is not to take effect. . . .

Sir John Simon formulated for the assistance of your Lordships a proposition which should be recorded: "Whenever it is to be inferred from the terms of a contract or its surrounding circumstances that the consensus has been reached upon the basis of a particular contractual assumption, and that assumption is not true, the contract is avoided: i.e., it is void ab initio if the assumption is of present fact and it ceases to bind if the assumption is of future fact."

I think few would demur to this statement, but its value depends upon the meaning of "a contractual assumption," and also upon the true meaning to be attached to "basis," a metaphor which may mislead. When used expressly in contracts, for instance, in policies of insurance, which state that the truth of the statements in the proposal is to be the basis of the contract of insurance, the meaning is clear. The truth of the statements is made a condition of the contract, which failing, the contract is void unless the condition is waived. The proposition does not amount to more than this that, if the contract expressly or impliedly contains a term that a particular assumption is a condition of the contract, the contract is avoided if the assumption is not true. But we have not advanced far on the inquiry how to ascertain whether the contract does contain such a condition. Various words are to be found to define the state of things which make a condition. "In the contemplation of both parties fundamental to the continued validity of the contract," "a foundation essential to its existence," "a fundamental reason for making it," are phrases found in the important judgment of Scrutton L.J. in the present case. The first two phrases appear to me to be unexceptionable. They cover the case of a contract to serve in a particular place, the existence of which is fundamental to the service, or to procure the services of a professional vocalist, whose continued health is essential to performance. But "a fundamental reason for making a contract" may, with respect, be misleading. The reason of one party only is presumedly not intended, but in the cases I have suggested above, of the sale of a horse or of a picture, it might be said that the fundamental reason for making the contract was the belief of both parties that the horse was sound or the picture an old master, yet in neither case would the condition as I think exist. Nothing is more dangerous than to allow oneself liberty to construct for the parties contracts which they have not in terms made by importing implications which would appear to make the contract more businesslike or more just. The implications to be made are to be no more than are "necessary" for giving business efficacy to the transaction, and it appears to me that, both as to existing facts and future facts, a condition would not be implied unless the new state of facts makes the contract something different in kind from the contract in the original state of facts. Thus, in *Krell* v. *Henry* [1900–3] All ER Rep. 20, Vaughan Williams L.J. finds that the subject of the contract was "rooms to view the procession": the postponement, therefore, made the rooms not rooms to view the procession. . . .

We therefore get a common standard for mutual mistake, and implied conditions whether as to existing or as to future facts. Does the state of the new facts destroy the identity of the subject-matter as it was in the original state of facts? To apply the principle to the infinite combinations of facts that arise in actual experience will continue to be difficult, but if this case results in establishing order into what has been a somewhat confused and difficult branch of the law it will have served a useful purpose.

I have already stated my reasons for deciding that in the present case the identity of the subject-matter was not destroyed by the mutual mistake, if any, and need not repeat them.

[Lord Atkin accepted the appeal.]

LORD THANKERTON In the absence of fraud, which the jury has negatived, I am of opinion that neither a servant nor a director of a company is legally bound forthwith to disclose any breach of the obligations arising out of the relationship, so as to give the master or the company the opportunity of dismissal; on subsequent discovery, the master or company will not be entitled to hold the dismissal as operating from the date of the breach, but will be liable for wages or salary earned by the servant during the intervening period. . . .

Turning next to the question of mutual error or mistake, I think that the respondents' contention may be fairly stated as follows—namely, that in concluding the agreements of March, 1929, all parties proceeded on the mistaken assumption that the appellants' service agreements were not liable to immediate termination by Lever Brothers by reason of the appellants' misconduct, and that such common mistake involved the actual subject-matter of the agreements, and did not merely relate to a quality of the subject-matter.

The cases on this branch of the law are numerous, and in seeking the principle on which they rest I will at first confine my attention to those which relate to innocent mutual mistake on formation of the contract, as it appears to me that the cases relating to facts arising subsequently to the formation of the contract may be found to rest on a somewhat different principle. . . .

The service agreements of both appellants were then existing as binding legal contracts, although it was in the power of Lever Brothers, had they then known of the appellants' breach of contract, to have terminated the contracts; but, until the exercise of such power, the contracts remained binding. It is also clear that an essential purpose of the agreements of March, 1929, was to secure the termination of these service agreements. The mistake was not as to the existence of agreements which required termination—for such did exist—but as to the possibility of terminating them by other means.

A clear exposition of the principles to be applied in such a case as the present is to be found in the judgment of the Court of Queen's Bench (Cockburn C.J., Blackburn, Mellor and Shee JJ.), in *Kennedy* v. *Panama, &c., Co.*, delivered by Blackburn J. . . . .

The respondents' contention in the present appeal is that the service agreements surrendered to them are not the service agreements paid for, in respect that they were immediately defeasible by them. Blackburn J. proceeds [in *Kennedy*]:

"There is, however, a very important difference between cases where a contract may be rescinded on account of fraud, and those in which it may be rescinded on the ground that there is a difference in substance between the thing bargained for and that obtained. It is enough to show that there was a fraudulent representation as to *any part* of that which induced the party to enter into the contract which he seeks to rescind; but where there has been an innocent misrepresentation or misapprehension, it does not authorize a rescission unless it is such as to show that there is a complete difference in substance between what was supposed to be and what was taken, so as to constitute a failure of consideration". . . .

. . . In the present case, there being no obligation to disclose, the appellants, if they had had their misconduct in mind, would have been entitled to say nothing about it, and the respondents, in the absence of fraud, would have been bound by the contracts, even though, if they had known, they would not have entered into the contracts, but would have terminated the service agreements. I have difficulty in seeing how the fact that the appellants did not remember at the time is to put the respondents in a better position.

The phrase "underlying assumption by the parties," as applied to the subject-matter of a contract, may be too widely interpreted so as so include something which one of the parties had not necessarily in his mind at the time of the contract; in my opinion it can only properly relate to something which both must necessarily have accepted in their minds as an essential and integral element of the subject-matter. In the present case, however probable it may be, we are not necessarily forced to that assumption. . . .

In *Scott* v. *Coulson* it was common ground that at the date of the contract for sale of the life policy both parties supposed the assured to be alive, the result being that the plaintiffs were willing to accept as the best price they could get for the policy a sum slightly in advance of its surrender value and very much below the sum due on the death of the assured. As a matter of fact the assured was dead. It was therefore clear that the subject-matter of the contract was a policy still current with a surrender value and that accordingly the subject-matter did not exist at the date of the contract. *Couturier* v. *Hastie* ((1856) 5 HL as 673), where the cargo sold was held not to have existed at the date of sale, and *Strickland* v. *Turner* ((1852) 7 Ex. 208), where the annuitant was in fact dead at the date of sale of the annuity, were cases where the subject-matter was not in existence at the date of the contract. There are many other cases to the same effect, but I think that it is true to say that in all of them it either appeared on the face of the contract that the matter as to which the mistake existed was an essential and integral element of the subject-matter of the contract, or it was an inevitable inference from the nature of the contract that all the parties so regarded it.

In the present case the terms of the contracts throw no light on the question, and, as already indicated, I do not find sufficient material to compel the inference that the appellants, at the time of the contract, regarded the indefeasibility of the service agreements as an essential and integral element in the subject-matter of the bargain.

[Lord Thankerton accepted the appeal. Viscount Hailsham delivered a speech rejecting the appeal.]

Notes

1. A difficulty with *Bell* v. *Lever Brothers* is that it turns in part on scarcely believable findings of fact by the jury. Lord Blanesburgh's judgment contains an extract from the jury's findings. It appears that the jury believed Bell and Snelling when they said that they had forgotten their earlier breaches of duty. This made an action for anything other than common mistake virtually unsustainable. The jury also found as a fact that Lever Brothers would not have entered into the agreement with Bell and Snelling had they known the true facts. This finding is used by Adams and Brownsword in their discussion of common mistake (which appears after *Grist* v. *Bailey* below) to explain the findings of the two dissenting Law Lords. However, if the findings of fact had been otherwise, we might have been strongly tempted to say that Lever Brothers were not deprived of substantially the whole benefit of their agreement with Bell and Snelling when they found out that they could have disposed with their services without compensating them. Had Lever Brothers known of or found out about their breaches of duty and tried to dismiss Bell and Snelling, the two executives might well have refused to leave quickly or quietly without some financial incentive. Had Lever Brothers had to resort to the formal mechanism open to them to dismiss the two executives, this would have taken longer and might have occasioned adverse publicity.

2. We have divided our analysis of mistake into two parts. In Chapter 5 we looked at offer and acceptance problems of mistake: issues of mistake as to terms, as to the identity of one of the parties to the contract, mistakes made by one party with the knowledge of the other party, and mistakes made when the parties are at cross-purposes with each other. Here we are looking at a mistake shared by both parties. We can pull our thoughts on mistake together by looking at a number of different scenarios:

(a) A and B make a contract for the sale of a horse. B believed he is buying a horse with a proven record as a race-winner. A knows of B's belief and knows that it is wrong. This is clearly a mistake as to terms which renders the contract void *ab initio*.

(b) A and B make a contract for the sale of a horse which A warrants to be a proven race-winner. It turns out not to be. A is in breach of contract and B can get the appropriate remedy.

(c) A and B make a contract for the sale of a horse. B tells A he is a famous racehorse owner and A accepts a cheque from him. B sells the horse to C and his cheque bounces. B disappears. A can recover his horse from C only if he can show that B's identity was crucial to him when he chose the buyer of his horse, and was not just an issue of security of payment. Only if this is the case will the contracts between A and B and hence B and C be void, so rendering C liable to A in conversion.

(d) A and B make a contract for the sale of a horse. Unbeknown to them, the horse died earlier that day. A and B have made the same mistake— that the horse exists. Cases of this type, where the subject-matter has ceased to exist before the contract is made, are called *res extincta* cases. The contract in this case would be void. The only exception to this would be if A had warranted to B that the horse existed (see *McRae* v. *Commonwealth Disposals*, (1951) 84 *CLR* 377); in that situation, B would be entitled to view A as in breach of contract.

(e) A and B make a contract for the sale of a black horse. A has two black horses. At the time of making the contract with B, A has in mind only his black shire horse and has forgotten that he also owns a black race-horse. B, however, has in mind only A's black racehorse. It would appear that this creates a situation similar to *Raffles* v. *Wichelhaus (The Ships Peerless)* ((1864) 2 H. & C. 906) and *Scriven Brothers* v. *Hindley* ([1913] 3 KB 564) (see Ch. 5).

(f) A and B make a contract for the sale of a horse. Both are under the impression that the horse is qualified to run in the 1995 Grand National. The price of the horse reflects this impression. The horse turns out not to be so qualified. This is a mistake shared by both parties and is a mistake as to the quality of the horse. The test that B has to satisfy to have the contract set aside is that given in *Bell* v. *Lever Brothers* by Lord Atkin: 'Does the state of the new facts destroy the identity of the subject matter as it was in the original state of facts?' The mistake that B has made is one of overvaluing in the same way that Lever Brothers overvalued the services of Bell and Snelling. The test that Lord Atkin offers is couched in the language of the extinction of the subject matter. If Lever Brothers could not satisfy this test, then, bearing in mind also the examples he gives of the sale of a sound/unsound horse and an old master/modern copy, it is hard to see what factual situation would satisfy the test.

The harshness of this position has been the subject of judicial attention in the form of the invocation of the equitable jurisdiction of the courts. *Grist* v. *Bailey* offers a rather more generous test for common mistake in equity. If the test for equitable mistake is satisfied, the contract is voidable and can be set aside by the court; this differs from a contract which is void *ab initio*, and allows the court considerable flexibility in designing an appropriate remedy.

Grist v. *Bailey*
[1967] 1 Ch. 532

The defendant had contracted to sell to the plaintiff a freehold property. The property was described as 'subject to the existing tenancy'. The price agreed between the plaintiff and the defendant was £850. In fact the property was not subject to a tenancy, as the tenants, Mr and Mrs Brewer, had died and their son had no tenancy rights, and consequently its value was £2,250. The plaintiff brought an action for specific performance against the defendant. The defendant claimed by way of a defence that the contract was void for mistake at common law or *voidable in equity*.

GOFF J [T]he defence maintained that the agreement had been entered into under a common mistake of fact, and there was a counterclaim on the same grounds to have the agreement rescinded or set aside. . . .

In these circumstances, the first question which arises is one of law, namely, what is the effect of common mistake? The leading case on this subject is *Bell* v. *Lever Bros. Ltd.* This, of course, is binding upon me and if exhaustive is really fatal to the defendant, since it lays down very narrow limits within which mistake operates to avoid a contract. It was there held that mistake as to the quality of the subject-matter of the contract must be such as to make the actual subject-matter something essentially different from what it was supposed to be: see *per* Lord Atkin.

In that case the plaintiffs sought to recover large sums which they had paid by way of compensation for the determination of certain contracts of service which, though they did not know it, they were entitled to rescind. The case as pleaded was not one of mutual mistake, and Lord Blanesburgh held it was too late to amend, and Lord Atkin doubted whether amendment was permissible, but on the assumption that the pleadings were amended to raise this issue they and Lord Thankerton all agreed that the case must fail.

I should have thought that this was more fundamental than any mistake made in the present case, and moreover the examples of the horse, picture and garage given by Lord Atkin in his speech would in my judgment apply to prevent any mistake, as to the nature of the tenancy affecting the property, being sufficient to avoid the present agreement.

Mr. Godfrey has argued, however, that there is a wider principle in equity, in support of which he quotes Cheshire & Fifoot on Contract, 5th ed. (1960), p. 184, *Solle* v. *Butcher* [[1950] 1 KB 671], particularly the judgment of Denning L.J. and *Huddersfield Banking Co. Ltd.* v. *Henry Lister & Son Ltd.* [[1895] 2 Ch. 373]. . . .

In *Solle* v. *Butcher*, as it seems to me, Denning L.J. clearly drew a distinction between the effect of mistake at law which, where effective at all, makes the contract void, and in equity, where it is a ground for rescission or for refusing specific performance; and, as it further seems to me, he clearly thought that this was wider than the jurisdiction at law. His Lordship said:

"The principle so established by *Cooper* v. *Phibbs* [(1877) LR 2 HL 149] has been repeatedly acted on; . . . It is in no way impaired by *Bell* v. *Lever Bros. Ltd.*, which was treated in the House of Lords as a case at law depending on whether the contract was a nullity or not. If it had been considered on equitable grounds, the result might have been different."

Denning L.J. laid down the equitable rule in these terms:

"A contract is also liable in equity to be set aside if the parties were under a common misapprehension either as to facts or as to their relative and respective rights, provided that the misapprehension was fundamental and that the party seeking to set it aside was not himself at fault."

Bucknill L.J. did not specifically refer to *Bell* v. *Lever Bros. Ltd.*, but he laid down the principle in similar terms, saying:

"there was a common mistake of fact on a matter of fundamental importance, namely, as to the identity of the flat with the dwelling-house previously let at a standard rent of £140 a year, and that the principle laid down in *Cooper* v. *Phibbs* applies."

Mr. Baden Fuller has submitted that there is no difference between law and equity and no case which suggests that *Bell* v. *Lever Bros. Ltd.* does not cover the whole field, save what he describes as one casual remark of Denning L.J. in *Solle* v. *Butcher*, . . .

. . . I cannot dismiss what Denning L.J. said in *Solle* v. *Butcher* as a mere dictum. It was in my judgment the basis of the decision and is binding on me; and . . . I think Bucknill L.J. took the same view. . . .

Then I have to decide first, was there a common mistake in this case; secondly, was it fundamental; and perhaps thirdly, was the defendant at fault? . . .

It is clearly established . . . that the defendant did not know that either Mr. or Mrs. Brewer had died. Even if Mr. Bailey knew that Mrs. Brewer was dead, as to which I have no evidence, I am bound to infer that he did not know that Mr. Brewer was also dead. Mr. Ginn did not know that either was dead, and Mr. Rider said that he first learned that Mr. Brewer was dead after the date of the agreement, and that he then learned that Mr. Terry Brewer was in occupation. Mr. Rider further gave evidence that so far as investment was concerned his mind went no further than that the sort of prices they were discussing were prices relevant to a tenant remaining there, and that he assumed all along there was a protected tenant and that when the purchase was completed they would have a protected tenant, and again that he would never have expected to get this property for anything like £850 with vacant possession. He said he made his offer on the basis that there was a protected tenant and that he would stay there.

Such being the state of the evidence, in my judgment there was a common mistake, namely, that there was still subsisting a protected tenancy in favour of Mr. or Mrs. Brewer; and it is to be remembered that the language of clause 7 of the agreement is "subject to the existing tenancy thereof." In my view, this was nonetheless a common mistake, though the parties may have differed in their belief as to who the tenant was, whether Mr. or Mrs. Brewer, although that may have a bearing on materiality.

Then, was it fundamental? In view of Mr. Rider's own evidence to which I have referred, and the evidence of Mr. Cooper Hurst, a surveyor called on behalf of the defendant, that in his opinion the vacant possession value as at August, 1964, was £2,250, in my judgment it must have been, if Mr. Terry Brewer had no rights under the Rent and Mortgage Interest Restrictions Acts, 1920 to 1957.

This was the case pleaded in paragraph 3 of the defence and counterclaim, but it depends upon showing that Mrs. Brewer was the contractual tenant, since then her husband became statutory tenant, and the effect of the Increase of Rent and Mortgage Interest (Restrictions) Act, 1920, s. ;12 (1) (*g*) was spent, leaving no protection for Mr. Terry Brewer: (. . .)

The onus of proving the premise upon which that way of presenting her case depends is upon the defendant, and in my opinion she has failed to discharge it. . . .

There remains one other point, and that is the condition laid down by Denning L.J. that the party seeking to take advantage of the mistake must not be at fault. Denning L.J. did not develop that at all and it is not, I think, with respect, absolutely clear what it comprehends. Clearly, there must be some degree of blameworthiness beyond the mere fault of having made a mistake, but the question is, how much, or in what way? I think each case must depend on its own facts, and I do not consider that the defendant or her agents were at fault so as to disentitle them to relief.

It was argued that the vendor should know who her tenants are, but this was a case of a long-standing and informal tenancy, the rent under which was paid simply by attendance in the outer office, where it was received by some junior boy or girl, and Mr. Brewer had but recently died.

The result, in my judgment, is that the defendant is entitled to relief in equity, . . .

. . . I order rescission. It is clear that this, being equitable relief, may be granted unconditionally or on terms, and Mr. Godfrey, on behalf of the defendant, has offered to submit to a term that the relief I have ordered should be on condition that the defendant is to enter into a fresh contract at a proper vacant possession price, and, if required by the plaintiff, I will impose that term.

Notes

1. The parties here had made a mistake of fact as to whether there was a protected tenancy in existence or not. If their mistake had been one concerning the meaning of the relevant landlord and tenant legislation, then their mistake would have been one of law and not of fact and consequently would have been outside the remit of contract law. The dividing line between a mistake of fact and a mistake of law is not always a clear one. In *Solle* v. *Butcher*, a case discussed in *Grist* v. *Bailey*, the mistake made was one as to whether or not the current statutory provisions on rent control applied to the letting of a flat. Denning and Bucknill LJJ held that the mistake made was one of fact, but Jenkins LJ held that it was a mistake of law. Perhaps if the parties here had been mistaken as to what was sufficient to create a protected tenancy under the legislation, then Goff J might have declared it to be a mistake of law.

2. The test of mistake in equity appears to be that there must be a fundamental mistake and the party seeking to set aside the contract must not be at fault. Goff J was of the view that the mistake in *Grist* v. *Bailey* would not satisfy the *Bell* v. *Lever Brothers* test of new facts destroying old facts. This would seem to be an accurate appraisal of the situation. The defendant had undervalued her house if sold with vacant possession. Her mistake was no more serious than that of Lever Brothers or, in the examples given by Lord Atkin, of the buyer of a painting and a horse. However her mistake was serious enough for it to be assessed by Goff J as fundamental for the purposes of equitable intervention. We are not given a definition of 'fundamental', but it seems that it is less serious than the loss of the 'identity of the subject-matter'. This would appear to give a rather different meaning to 'fundamental' than that offered by normal usage. One academic writer (A. Phang, 'Common Mistake in English Law: The Proposed Merger of Common Law and Equity', (1989) 9 *LS* 291) has advocated merging the two doctrines of common mistake into one, on the grounds that they are so

similar. The merged doctrine would render contracts voidable and then the remedy would be created by legislative intervention if necessary.

This rides roughshod over two key points. First, the two doctrines are conceived of as being separate by the judges, as we can see from *Grist* and from the judgment of Steyn J in *Associated Japanese Bank* v. *CDN* (below). Second, while we may not find it easy to identify specifically the ambit of equitable mistake, that in itself is not a sufficient ground for merging the two doctrines. Traditionally their starting-points are different. The common law doctrine is an assessment of the effect of the new facts on the old situation. The starting-point for equitable mistake is that it is inequitable not to give relief, a point emphasized by the second limb of the test in equity, namely that the person seeking to have the contract set aside must not herself be at fault.

3. The requirement that the party seeking to set the contract aside should not be at fault is not without its difficulties. It could mean either that the party seeking to set the contract aside should not be in any way responsible for creating the mistake or that the party seeking to set the contract aside should not have passed up any opportunities to verify the correctness of the situation as it appeared to be.

4. Goff J in *Grist* v. *Bailey* applies the doctrine of equitable mistake expounded by the Court of Appeal led by Denning LJ in *Solle* v. *Butcher*. For an argument that *Solle* v. *Butcher* itself rests on misconceived reasoning, see J. Cartwright, '*Solle* v. *Butcher* and the Doctrine of Mistake in Contract' ((1987) 103 *LQR* 584).

5. In the extract below, Adams and Brownsword apply their analytic framework of market individualism and consumer welfarism to judicial pronouncements on mistake.

J. Adams and R. Brownsword, *Understanding Contract Law* (London, Fontana, 1987), 109–13

[T]he fact that common mistake and frustration deal with a similar problem is of more than passing interest. The occurrence of some unsuspected or unexpected risk, like the cancellation of the procession, often turns a satisfactory arrangement into an extremely bad bargain. Consequently, the doctrines of common mistake and frustration are potential avenues of escape from contracts and, as we shall see, this makes them important arenas for the conflict between market-individualism and consumer-welfarism. . . .

Common mistake: the 'hawks' and the 'doves'

In a famous American case, *Sherwood* v. *Walker* [6 Mich 568] (1887), the plaintiff purchased a cow, known as 'Rose 2d of Aberlone', from the defendants. If the cow had been a breeder, she would have been worth at least $750; whereas if the cow had been barren, her value would have been only $80 as beef. The parties agreed upon a value for beef price, and the plaintiff duly tendered $80. However, by this time the defendants had discovered that Rose was not barren, but was with calf, and they argued that the contract should be set aside on the grounds of common mistake. The majority of the Supreme Court of Michigan found in favour of the defendants holding that the difference between a beef cow (worth $80) and a breeding cow (worth at least $750) went beyond a question of mere quality and affected the substance of the whole consideration.

It is not altogether easy to contrast the dissent in *Sherwood* with the majority view, for the dissent was predicated on the assumption that the buyer purchased the cow on the basis of a speculative hunch that the cow might not be barren, and both views are couched in a terminology deriving from Roman law (Dig. 18.1.9). Nevertheless, both sides of the court started with the market-individualist premise that contracts are not lightly to be discharged, and with the concomitant principle that common mistakes as to quality are no ground for relief.

In England, there are two contrasting approaches to common mistake. First, there is the so-called 'common law' approach, which tackles the problem along the market-individualist lines of *Sherwood*. Accordingly, relief for common mistake is regarded as exceptional. This is the mews of the 'hawks'. Secondly, there is the so-called 'equitable' approach, which applies the very different ideas associated with consumer-welfarism. Relief for common mistake is judged here in the light of principles of fairness: this is the 'dovecote'.

In the leading case on the common law approach, *Bell* v. *Lever Brothers Ltd* (1932) . . . Lord Atkin approached both the common mistake and non-disclosure questions in a textbook market-individualist manner, though presented in a *form* which derives from Roman law (see Dig. 18.1.9). . . .

If we assume that the thinking of all judges concerned in *Sherwood* and *Bell* was market-individualist, then there is evidently some scope for disagreement within the market-individualist camp. Given that relief for common mistake must not jeopardize the security of market transactions, the question is how the minority in *Bell* (in the House of Lords) and the majority in *Sherwood* could defend their softer approach. An attractive argument is that while market-individualists should not allow common mistake to be used to re-negotiate the terms of a transaction, it is safe to release a party from a contract which, had the true facts been known, he would not have been prepared to make *on any terms* (an alternative way of putting it is to say that the mistake went beyond the risks exchanged by formation). Applying this argument, the majority in *Sherwood* seem to have stretched common mistake to the limit, for this looks like a re-negotiation case. With regard to *Bell*, however, the dissenting Law Lords seem to have good grounds for saying that, had the facts been known, Levers would not have entered into the golden hand-shake agreements *at all*.

Hence, the uncompromising view of the majority was inappropriate. This prompts the mischievous thought that the market-individualists (judged by their own standards) got it wrong in both *Sherwood* and *Bell.*

Alongside the common law approach to common mistake runs the equitable approach, which is usually traced to the majority decision of the Court of Appeal in *Solle* v. *Butcher* (1950). . . .

The *Solle* approach does not start with market-individualist thinking. Rather, it turns on consumer-welfarist ideas of reasonableness and fair play between the parties. In *Solle* itself, Lord Denning was struck by the unreasonableness of the plaintiff first advising the defendant that the rent could lawfully be set at £250 and then turning round 'quite unashamedly' (per Denning LJ at p. 695) and trying to take advantage of the parties' common misapprehension. No court of conscience could stand by and let this happen.

In the next case Steyn J attempts to pull together the two strands of authority dealing with common mistakes.

Associated Japanese Bank v. *Crédit du Nord SA*
[1988] 3 All ER 902

B concluded a sale and leaseback arrangement with the Associated Japanese Bank (AJB) for four machines, as a means of raising capital. AJB required B to find a guarantor of his obligations. A guarantee was provided by Crédit du Nord SA (CDN). The sale by B to AJB was for more than £1,000,000. After paying the first quarter's rent under the lease, B was arrested. It was discovered that the machines did not exist. AJB claimed, as they were entitled to under the lease, the whole of the outstanding amount from B. B was declared bankrupt. AJB sued CDN under the guarantee. Two principal arguments were advanced by the defendants to deny liability:

(1) The guarantor was not liable due to the non-fulfilment of an express or implied condition precedent of the guarantee that the machines existed.

(2) The guarantee was void *ab initio* for common mistake because the machines had never existed or, alternatively, the guarantee was voidable in equity for the same reason and was not enforceable.

Steyn J concluded that, as a matter of construction, the guarantee assumed that the machines existed on the basis of an express or implied condition precedent. Having reached this conclusion, he found for CDN. However, he then went on to consider the position in mistake, because counsel had advanced arguments under that head. He decided that the common law test of common mistake was satisfied and that, if it was not, the contract would have been voidable in equity for mistake.

STEYN J Throughout the law of contract two themes regularly recur: respect for the sanctity of contract and the need to give effect to the reasonable expectations of honest men. Usually, these themes work in the same direction. Occasionally, they point to opposite solutions. The law regarding common mistake going to the root of a contract is a case where tension arises between the two themes. That is illustrated by the circumstances of this extraordinary case. . . .

THE COMMERCIAL BACKGROUND

Before I turn to the sequence of events which led to the present dispute, a brief sketch of the commercial background should be given. The principal transaction was a sale and leaseback of equipment. That is a transaction whereby a person who owns equipment raises money by selling the equipment to another for cash and leases it back for a fixed term. It is to be distinguished from a direct lease where the lessor buys the equipment from a third party and leases it to the user, the lessee, for a fixed term. . . .

THE CONSTRUCTION POINT

The first question to be considered is whether the guarantee was expressly made subject to a condition precedent that the four machines existed. The factual matrix, which is relevant to this question of construction, is that both parties, the creditor and the guarantor, were induced to commit themselves by information supplied by the lease brokers employed by Mr Bennett. That information included the statement, which was made expressly or by necessary implication, that the four machines existed. And it matters not that AJB thought that Mr Bennett owned the machines, while CDN thought that AJB owned the machines. The fact is that both parties were informed, and believed, that the machines existed. Against that contextual scene, CDN provided a guarantee to AJB—

'in consideration of your leasing 4 Textile Compression Packaging machines to British Consolidated Engineering Company . . . pursuant to a Leasing Contract dated 29th February 1984 . . .'

The only other provision of the guarantee which is relevant to this question of construction is cl 6 of the guarantee. It reads as follows:

'*This Guarantee and your rights under it shall not be affected or prejudiced* by your holding or taking any other or further securities or by your varying releasing or omitting or neglecting to enforce any such securities or by your giving time for payment or granting any other indulgence to or making any other arrangements with or accepting any composition from the Lessee or *subject to our prior consent to any such variation by your varying the terms of the Leasing Contract made between yourselves and the Lessee or by the substitution of any other goods comprised in such contract.*' (My emphasis.)

On behalf of AJB it was submitted that the words 'subject to our prior consent' govern only variations of the lease other than variations entailing a substitution of goods. In other words, it was submitted that consent of the guarantor was required for any variation except one of the most important of all variations, viz substitution of goods. That interpretation is not justified by the language of cl 6, and it is a wholly unreasonable interpretation. I reject it. Clause 6 of the guarantee therefore contemplated the existence of the machines, and made provision for a right of substitution only if the guarantor granted consent. Against that background the question is whether it was *expressly* agreed that the guarantee would only become effective if there was a lease of four existing machines. The point is not capable of elaborate analysis. It is a matter of first impression. On balance, my conclusion is that, sensibly construed against its objective setting, the guarantee was subject to an express condition precedent that there was a lease in respect of four existing machines. If this conclusion is right, AJB's claim against CDN as guarantor or as sole or principal debtor under cl 11 fails.

If my conclusion about the construction of the guarantee is wrong, it remains to be considered whether there was an *implied* condition precedent that the lease related to four existing machines. In the present contract such a condition may only be held to be implied if one of two applicable tests is satisfied. The first is that such an implication is necessary to give business efficacy to the relevant contract, ie the guarantee. In other words, the criterion is whether the implication is necessary to render the contract (the guarantee) workable. That is usually described as the *Moorcock* test (see *The Moorcock* (1889) 145 PD 64). It may well be that this stringent test is not satisfied because the guarantee is workable in the sense that all that is required is that the guarantor who assumed accessory obligations must pay what is due under the lease. But there is another type of implication which seems more appropriate in the present context. It is possible to imply a term if the court is satisfied that reasonable men, faced with the suggested term which was ex hypothesi not expressed in the contract, would without hesitation say, 'Yes, of course, that is so obvious that it goes without saying': see *Shirlaw v Southern Foundries (1926) Ltd* [1939] 2 KB 206 at 227 per MacKinnon LJ. Although broader in scope than the *Moorcock* test, it is nevertheless a stringent test, and it will only be permissible to hold that an implication has been established on this basis in comparatively rare cases, notably when one is dealing with a commercial instrument such as a guarantee for reward. Nevertheless, against the contextual background of the fact that both parties were informed that the machines existed, and the express terms of the guarantee, I have come to the firm conclusion that the guarantee contained an implied condition precedent that the lease related to existing machines. Again, if this conclusion is right, AJB's claim against CDN as guarantor or as sole or principal debtor under cl 11 fails. . . .

Notwithstanding these conclusions, which are determinative of the case, I will now consider the arguments as to common or mutual mistake which played such a large part at the hearing of this case.

MISTAKE

The common law regarding mutual or common mistake

There was a lively debate about the common law rules governing a mutual or common mistake of the parties as to some essential quality of the subject matter of the contract. Counsel for CDN submitted that *Bell v Lever Bros Ltd* authoritatively established that a mistake by both parties as to the existence of some quality of the subject matter of the contract, which makes the subject matter of the contract without the quality essentially different from the subject matter as it was believed to be, renders the contract void ab initio. Counsel for AJB contested this proposition. He submitted that at common law a mistake even as to an essential quality of the subject matter of the contract will not affect the contract unless it resulted in a total failure of consideration. It was not clear to me that this formulation left any meaningful and independent scope for the application of common law rules in this area of the law. In any event, it is necessary to examine the legal position in some detail.

The landmark decision is undoubtedly *Bell v Lever Bros Ltd*. Normally a judge of first instance would simply content himself with applying the law stated by the House of Lords. There has, however, been substantial controversy about the rule established in that case. It seems right therefore to examine the effect of that decision against a somewhat wider framework. In the early history of contract law, the common law's preoccupation with consideration made the development of a doctrine of mistake impossible. Following the emergence in the nineteenth century of the theory of consensus ad idem it became possible to treat misrepresentation, undue influence and mistake as factors vitiating consent. Given that the will theory in English contract law was cast in objective form, judging matters by the external standard of the reasonable man, both as to contract formation and contractual interpretation, it nevertheless became possible to examine in what circumstances mistake might nullify or negative consent. But even in late Victorian times there was another powerful policy consideration militating against upsetting bargains on the ground of unexpected circumstances which occurred before or after the contract. That was the policy of caveat emptor which held sway outside the field of contract law subsequently codified by the Sale of Goods Act in 1893. Nevertheless, principles affecting the circumstances in which consent may be vitiated gradually emerged. The most troublesome areas proved to be two related areas, viz common mistake as to an essential quality of the subject matter of the contract and post-contractual frustration. . . .

. . . *Bell v Lever Bros Ltd* was a vitally important case: . . . Lord Atkin held ([1932] AC 161 at 218:

'. . . a mistake will not affect assent unless it is the mistake of both parties, and is as to the existence of some quality which makes the thing without the quality essentially different from the thing as it was believed to be.' . . .

Lord Blanesburgh's speech proceeded on different lines. It must not be forgotten that the issue of common mistake was only put forward at the eleventh hour. Lord Blanesburgh would have refused the necessary amendment, but he expressed his 'entire accord' with the substantive views of Lord Atkin and Lord Thankerton (see [1932] AC 161 at 198–199). The majority were therefore in agreement about the governing principle.

It seems to me that the better view is that the majority in *Bell v. Lever Bros Ltd* had in mind only mistake at common law. That appears to be indicated by the shape of the argument, the proposed amendment placed before the House of Lords (see [1932] AC 161 at 191) and the speeches of Lord Atkin and Lord Thankerton. But, if I am wrong on this point, it is nevertheless clear that mistake at common law was in the forefront of the analysis in the speeches of the majority.

The law has not stood still in relation to mistake in equity. Today, it is clear that mistake in equity is not circumscribed by common law definitions. A contract affected by mistake in equity is not void but may be set aside on terms. . . . It does not follow, however, that *Bell v. Lever Bros Ltd* is no longer an authoritative statement of mistake at common law. On the contrary, in my view the principles enunciated in that case clearly still govern mistake at common law. It is true that in *Solle v. Butcher* Denning LJ interpreted *Bell v. Lever Bros Ltd* differently. He said that a common mistake, even on a most fundamental matter, does not make the contract void at law. That was an individual opinion. Neither Bucknill LJ (who agreed in the result) nor Jenkins LJ (who dissented) even mentioned *Bell v. Lever Bros Ltd*. In *Magee v. Pennine Insurance Co Ltd* [1969] 2 QB 507 at 514 Lord Denning MR returned to the point. About *Bell v. Lever Bros Ltd* he simply said: 'I do not propose . . . to go through the speeches in that case. They have given enough trouble to commentators already.' He then repeated his conclusion in *Solle v. Butcher*. Winn LJ dissented. Fenton Atkinson LJ agreed in the result but it is clear from his judgment that he did not agree with Lord Denning MR's interpretation of *Bell v. Lever Bros Ltd* (see [1969] 2 QB 507 at 517–518). Again, Lord Denning MR's observation represented only his own view. With the profoundest respect to the former Master of the Rolls, I am constrained to say that in my view his interpretation of *Bell v. Lever Bros Ltd* does not do justice to the speeches of the majority.

When Lord Denning MR referred in *Magee v Pennine Insurance Co Ltd* to the views of commentators he may have had in mind comments in Cheshire and Fifoot *Law of Contract* (6th edn, 1964) p. 196. In substance the argument was that the actual decision in *Bell v. Lever Bros Ltd* contradicts the language of the speeches. If the test was not satisfied there, so the argument runs, it is difficult to see how it could ever be satisfied: see the latest edition of this valuable textbook for the same argument (Cheshire, Fifoot and Furmston *Law of Contract* (11th edn, 1986) pp. 225–226). This is a point worth examining because at first glance it may seem persuasive. *Bell v. Lever Bros Ltd* was a quite exceptional case; all their Lordships were agreed that common mistake had not been pleaded and would have required an amendment in the House of Lords if it were to succeed. The speeches do not suggest that the employees were entitled to keep both the gains secretly made and the golden handshakes were very substantial. But there are indications in the speeches that the so-called 'merits' were not all in favour of Lever Bros. The company was most anxious, because of a corporate merger, to terminate the two service agreements. There was apparently a doubt whether the voidability of the service agreements if revealed to the company *at the time of the severance contract* would have affected the company's decision. . . . Lord Atkin clearly regarded it as a hard case on the facts, but concluded 'on the whole' that the plea of common mistake must fail (see [1932] AC 161 at 223). It is noteworthy that Lord Atkin commented on the scarcity of evidence as to the subsidiaries from the boards of which the two employees resigned (see [1932] AC 161 at 212). . . . Lord Blanesburgh emphasised that Lever Bros secured the *future* co-operation of the two employees for the carrying through of the amalgamation (see [1932] AC 161 at 181). And the burden, of course, rested squarely on Lever Bros. With due deference to the distinguished authors who have argued that the actual decision in *Bell v. Lever Bros Ltd* contradicts the principle enunciated in the speeches it seems to me that their analysis is altogether too simplistic, and that the actual decision was rooted in the particular facts of the case. In my judgment there is no reason to doubt the substantive reasons emerging from the speeches of the majority.

No one could fairly suggest that in this difficult area of the law there is only one correct approach or solution. But a narrow doctrine of common law mistake (as enunciated in *Bell v. Lever Bros Ltd*), supplemented by the more flexible doctrine of mistake in equity (as developed in *Solle v. Butcher* and later cases), seems to me to be an entirely sensible and satisfactory state of the law: . . .

It might be useful if I now summarised what appears to me to be a satisfactory way of approaching this subject. Logically, before one can turn to the rules as to mistake, whether at common law or in equity, one must first determine whether the contract itself, by express or implied condition precedent or otherwise, provides who bears the risk of the relevant mistake. It is at this hurdle that many pleas of mistake will either fail or prove to have been unnecessary. Only if the contract is silent on the point is there scope for invoking mistake. That brings me to the relationship between common law mistake and mistake in equity. Where common law mistake has been pleaded, the court must first consider this plea. If the contract is held to be void, no question of mistake in equity arises. But, if the contract is held to be valid, a plea of mistake in equity may still have to be considered: see *Grist v. Bailey* . . . . Turning now to the approach to common law mistake, it seems to me that the following propositions are valid although not necessarily all entitled to be dignified as propositions of law.

The first imperative must be that the law ought to uphold rather than destroy apparent contracts. Second, the common law rules as to a mistake regarding the quality of the subject matter, like the common law rules regarding commercial frustration, are designed to cope with the impact of unexpected and wholly exceptional circumstances on apparent contracts. Third, such a mistake in order to attract legal consequences must substantially be shared by both parties, and must relate to facts as they existed at the time the contract was made. Fourth, and this is the point established by *Bell v. Lever Bros Ltd*, the mistake must render the subject matter of the contract essentially and radically different from the subject matter which the parties believed to exist. . . . The principles enunciated by Lord Atkin and Lord Thankerton represent the ratio decidendi of *Bell v. Lever Bros Ltd*. Fifth, there is a requirement which was not specifically discussed in *Bell v. Lever Bros Ltd*. What happens if the party who is seeking to rely on the mistake had no reasonable grounds for his belief? An extreme example is that of the man who makes a contract with minimal knowledge of the facts to which the mistake relates but is content that it is a good speculative risk. In my judgment a party cannot be allowed to rely on a common mistake where the mistake consists of a belief which is entertained by him without any reasonable grounds for such belief: cf *McRae v. Commonwealth Disposals Commission*. That is not because policy and good sense dictate that the positive rules regarding common mistake should be so qualified. . . . More importantly, a recognition of this qualification is consistent with the approach in equity where fault on the part of the party adversely affected by the mistake will generally preclude the granting of equitable relief.

Applying the law to the facts

It is clear, of course, that in this case both parties, the creditor and the guarantor, acted on the assumption that the lease related to existing machines. If they had been informed that the machines might not exist, neither AJB nor CDN would for one moment have contemplated entering into the transaction. That, by itself, I accept, is not enough to sustain the plea of common law mistake. I am also satisfied that CDN had reasonable grounds for believing that the machines existed. That belief was based on CDN's discussions with Mr Bennett, information supplied by National Leasing, a respectable firm of lease brokers, and the confidence created by the fact that AJB were the lessors.

The real question is whether the subject matter *of the guarantee* (as opposed to the sale and lease) was essentially different from what it was reasonably believed to be. The real security of the guarantor was the machines. The existence of the machines, being profit-earning chattels, made it more likely that the debtor would be able to service the debt. More importantly, if the debtor defaulted and the creditor repossessed the machines, the creditor had to give credit for 97½% of the value of the machines. If the creditor sued the guarantor first, and the guarantor paid, the guarantor was entitled to be subrogated to the creditor's rights in respect of recovery against the debtor: see Goff and Jones *Law of Restitution* (3rd edn, 1986) pp. 533–536). No doubt the guarantor relied to some extent on the creditworthiness of Mr Bennett. But I find that the prime security to which the guarantor looked was the existence of the four machines as described to both parties. For both parties the guarantee of obligations under a lease with non-existent machines was essentially different from a guarantee of a lease with four machines which both parties at the time of the contract believed to exist. The guarantee is an accessory contract. The non-existence of the subject matter of the principal contract is therefore of fundamental importance. Indeed the analogy of the classic res extincta cases, so much discussed in the authorities, is fairly close. In my judgment, the stringent test of common law mistake is satisfied; the guarantee is void ab initio. . . .

Equitable mistake

Having concluded that the guarantee is void ab initio at common law, it is strictly unnecessary to examine the question of equitable mistake. Equity will give relief against common mistake in cases where the common law will not, and it provides more flexible remedies, including the power to set aside the contract on terms. It is not necessary to repeat my findings of fact save to record again the fundamental nature of the common mistake, and that CDN was not at fault in any way. If I had not decided in favour of CDN on construction and common law mistake, I would have held that the guarantee must be set aside on equitable principles. Unfortunately, and counsel are not to blame for that, the question of the terms (if any) to be imposed (having regard particularly to sums deposited by Mr Bennett with CDN) were not adequately explored in argument. If it becomes necessary to rule on this aspect, I will require further argument.

Notes

1. Steyn J decided in favour of the defendants on the grounds that the guarantee of the lease assumed that the machines existed. An assumption of this sort is called a 'condition precedent'. In other words, he looked at the contract between the parties and decided that the risk of the machines not existing was not a risk which was accepted by CDN. They had intended only to enter into a guarantee of a lease for machines which existed, as evidenced by clause 6 of the guarantee. According to Steyn J, this clause demonstrated that they had sought to guarantee a lease of existing machines. Once Steyn J had made these findings on the construction of the contract, they were determinative of the issue. His findings on common mistake are, strictly speaking, *obiter dicta*.

2. Steyn J alludes briefly in his judgment to the *res extincta* cases. His position appears to be that the non-existence of the machines—the

subject-matter of the original lease contract—was sufficiently fundamental to him to hold that a secondary contract to guarantee the financial obligations of the lessee was void on the basis of the test in *Bell* v. *Lever Brothers*. He was not holding that the non-existence of the machines made this a *res extincta* case, because, of course, the guarantee contract in question was to guarantee obligations under the lease contract which *still* existed. The non-existence of the machines does not render the lease contract void in itself; it simply means that the defendants, CDN, would not be able to sell the machines if the lessee defaulted, and would be left only with their obligation to pay AJB under the guarantee.

3. In the extract below, Treitel compares *Bell* v. *Lever Brothers* and *Associated Japanese Bank* v. *CDN*, and examines Steyn J's grounds for distinguishing the two cases. It is apparent from the extract that the decision in *Bell* v. *Lever Brothers* can be justified on the basis that Lever Brothers did derive some benefit from their contract with Bell and Snelling, and that it would be unfair to deprive Bell and Snelling of the entire amount of their termination agreement on account of their breaches of duty. The only difficulty with justifying the decision on such arguments is that they appear to be considerations most suitable to an assessment in equity rather than at law. For himself, Treitel takes the line that *Bell* v. *Lever Brothers* upholds the sanctity of contract—shades of the market-individualist approach identified by Adams and Brownsword.

G. Treitel, 'Mistake in Contract', (1988) 104 *LQR* 501 at 504–7

There remains the question just how the *Associated Japanese Bank* case is to be distinguished from *Bell* v. *Lever Bros. Ltd.* . . . . Steyn J. . . . distinguishes *Bell* v. *Lever Bros. Ltd.* on the ground that it was "a quite exceptional case" and that the actual decision was "rooted in the facts of the particular case." Those facts were that Lever Bros. Ltd. derived benefits from the contract in dispute: they were "most anxious, because of a corporate merger, to terminate the two service agreements"; that it was not clear that they would not have entered into the disputed contract if they had known of the voidability of the service agreements (see [1932] A.C. 161 at p. 236 *per* Lord Thankerton); and that they were interested in securing the future co-operation of Bell and Snelling in carrying through the proposed merger. One can also, so far as the merits of the case are concerned, make the point that the rule of law entitling Lever Bros. Ltd. to dismiss Bell and Snelling without notice and without compensation would, if it had been applied in that case, have operated with Draconian effect. Bell and Snelling had, through their work for the subsidiary company of which they were officers, substantially increased the profitability and capital value of that company. In comparison with these matters, the benefits which they had derived from their breaches of duty were trivial. There was no question that they were liable to hand these benefits over to Lever Bros. Ltd.; indeed, they offered to do so when the true facts came to light. . . . All this is not to condone their undoubted lapses from strict principles of commercial morality; but a penalty of £50,000 for such lapses would have been unduly severe. . . . It is perhaps not fanciful to suggest that in *Bell* v. *Lever Bros. Ltd.* a narrow doctrine of mistake corrected an injustice that would have flowed from the rule of law under which a relatively trivial breach, which caused the innocent party no loss, nevertheless gave that party a ground for rescinding the contract.

In the *Associated Japanese Bank* case, there were no similar factors which could be said, on the "merits," to tip the balance in favour of upholding the contract. There was, moreover, an explicit finding that both parties believed that the machines existed, and that *neither* of them would, if aware of the true facts, have "for one moment contemplated entering into the transaction." . . . But Steyn J. in the *Associated Japanese Bank* case concedes that his finding on this point was "not enough to sustain the plea of common mistake." He further finds that the defendants had reasonable grounds for holding their mistaken belief; but while this may be a necessary condition to support a plea of mistake, it is clearly not a sufficient one. "The real question," he continues, "is whether the subject-matter *of the guarantee* (as opposed to the sale and lease) was essentially different from what it was reasonably believed to be." He concludes that there was such an essential difference, principally because "the real security of the guarantor was the machines." . . . A more serious problem is that, while the "security" [of the machines] might make the guarantee "essentially different" from the defendants' point of view, it is hard to see how they could have had this effect from the point of view of the plaintiffs, who were no doubt concerned for their own security but may be supposed to have been indifferent as to the security of the defendants. No doubt the plaintiffs also thought that their security lay in part in the existence of the machines, but that security was believed by them to arise under other contracts than that in suit: under the sale and lease back, not under the guarantee. It was presumably because the plaintiffs did not regard that security as adequate that they sought the further security of a bank guarantee. The conclusion that the plaintiffs, no less than the defendants, regarded the subject-matter as it was as essentially different from the subject-matter as it was believed to be can perhaps be most easily explained by looking at the transaction as a whole and not at the guarantee in isolation. There is a hint of this approach in Steyn J.'s description of the guarantee as an "accessory contract" so that the "non-existence of the subject-matter of the principal contract is . . . of fundamental importance. Indeed, the analogy of the classic *res extincta* cases . . . is very close." . . .

The *Associated Japanese Bank* case can no doubt he distinguished from *Bell* v. *Lever Bros. Ltd.* by describing the latter case as "quite exceptional"; but greater difficulty arises from the well-known examples given by Lord Atkin in the latter case of mistakes which would not make a contract void at law, such as the sale of a horse mistakenly believed to be sound, or of a dwelling house mistakenly believed to be inhabitable or of a picture mistakenly believed to be an old master, but in fact a modern copy (see [1932] A.C. 161 at p. 224). These examples seem to show that Lord Atkin, at least, did not confine himself to the special facts before him, but intended to formulate principles of more general application. While there is no direct conflict between the cases, the difference in result illustrates the conflict of policies, described at the beginning of the *Associated Japanese Bank* case: "respect for the sanctity of contract" prevailed in *Bell* v. *Lever Bros. Ltd.*, but yielded in the *Associated Japanese Bank* case to "the need to give effect to the reasonable expectations of honest men." The fact that each policy has its own validity accounts for the interest of this branch of the law and for the impossibility of explaining the authorities by reference to any single set of sharp distinctions.

4. Steyn J decides that if he had not found in favour of the defendants on the basis of the construction point or in common mistake he would have found for the defendants on the basis of equitable mistake. As this is merely an addendum to his judgment, it still leaves unanswered the questions as to how the requirement that the mistake be 'fundamental' is satisfied under the equitable jurisdiction, and what type of settlement the judge would have imposed had he used the equitable jurisdiction to set the contract aside on terms.

5. Steyn J describes the test for a common mistake of quality laid down by the House of Lords in *Bell* v. *Lever Brothers* as one which requires the subject-matter of the contract to be 'essentially and radically different from the subject matter which the parties believed to exist'. As the next section on frustration will show, this is a virtually identical test to that used by the courts when deciding whether a contract has been frustrated, i.e. whether subsequent events have made the contract incapable of performance through the fault of neither party. After we have examined the frustration doctrine, we will consider whether the tests for initial and subsequent impossibility should be the same.

IV. FRUSTRATION: THE BASIC DOCTRINAL STRUCTURE

A. The Basis of Frustration

The modern doctrine of frustration evolved during the nineteenth century as a departure from the principle that the conclusion of a contract engendered a strict duty to perform regardless of the circumstances. The leading case is *Taylor* v. *Caldwell* ((1863) B. & S. 826, 122 ER 826), which involved a contract for the hire of a music hall by an impresario for four days for the purpose of holding concerts. The hall was destroyed by fire before the first of the concerts was held; neither party was at fault. Both parties were excused from further performance and the contract was discharged. The justification in legal doctrine for this departure from the strict enforceability of contracts has remained uncertain.

In *National Carriers Ltd.* v. *Panalpina (Northern) Ltd.*, the House of Lords reviewed the juristic basis of frustration in a case in which they were asked to settle the uncertain question of whether the doctrine of frustration could apply to a lease.

National Carriers Ltd. v. *Panalpina (Northern) Ltd.*
[1981] AC 675

LORD ROSKILL My Lords, what is now called the doctrine of frustration was first evolved during the 19th century when notwithstanding the express language in which the parties had concluded their bargain the courts declined in the event which occurred to hold them to the strict letter of that bargain. *Taylor* v. *Caldwell*, is perhaps the most famous mid-19th century case, in which the relevant principle was laid down by Blackburn J. (as he then was) giving the judgment of the Court of Queen's Bench. The dispute in that case arose under a document which was expressed in the language of the lease but which was held to be a licence. There was no demise of the premises. But the licensee was relieved of his obligation to pay "rent" because of the fire which destroyed the premises and so made performance impossible. One can find what might be called anticipatory traces of the doctrine enunciated in *Taylor* v. *Caldwell* in some of the earlier 19th century cases, principally in relation to contracts of personal service made impossible of performance by death or illness, but no useful purpose would be presently served by reviewing them. What is important is not what happened before *Taylor* v. *Caldwell* but what happened thereafter.

The doctrine evolved slowly especially in the field of commercial law. It was invoked in the Coronation cases. As late as *Matthey* v. *Curling* [1922] 2 A.C. 180, Younger L.J. (as he then was) said in the Court of Appeal, at p. 210, that the doctrine of frustration was not one to be extended, a view much falsified in the event. . . .

[Having reviewed the law on time charterparties, Lord Roskill continued:]

My Lords, I mention these matters for three purposes: first to show how gradually but also how extensively the doctrine has developed; secondly to show how, whenever attempts have been made to exclude the application of the doctrine to particular classes of contract, such attempts, though sometimes initially successful, have in the end uniformly failed and thirdly, albeit I hope without unnecessary reference to a mass of decided cases—many in your

Lordships' House—the doctrine has at any rate in the last half century and indeed during and since the first World War been flexible, to be applied whenever the inherent justice of a particular case requires its application. The extension in recent years of government interference in ordinary business affairs, inflation, sudden outbreaks of war in different parts of the world, are all recent examples of circumstances in which the doctrine has been invoked, sometimes with success, sometimes without. Indeed the doctrine has been described as a "device" for doing justice between the parties when they themselves have failed either wholly or sufficiently to provide for the particular event or events which have happened. The doctrine is principally concerned with the incidence of risk—who must take the risk of the happening of a particular event especially when the parties have not made any or any sufficient provision for the happening of that event? When the doctrine is successfully invoked it is because in the event which has happened the law imposes a solution, casting the incidence of that risk on one party or the other as the circumstances of the particular case may require, having regard to the express provisions of the contract into which the parties have entered. The doctrine is no arbitrary dispensing power to be exercised at the subjective whim of the judge by whom the issue has to be determined. Frustration if it occurs operates automatically. Its operation does not depend on the action or inaction of the parties. It is to be invoked or not to be invoked by reference only to the particular contract before the court and the facts of the particular case said to justify the invocation of the doctrine. . . .

LORD HAILSHAM At least five theories of the basis of the doctrine of frustration have been put forward at various times . . . . The first is the "implied term" or "implied condition" theory on which Blackburn J. plainly relied in *Taylor* v. *Caldwell*, as applying to the facts of the case before him. To these it is admirably suited. The weakness, it seems to me, of the implied term theory is that it raises once more the spectral figure of the officious bystander intruding on the parties at the moment of agreement. . . . In *Embiricos* v. *Sydney Reid & Co.* [1914] 3 K.B. 45, 54 Scrutton J. appears to make the estimate of what constitutes a frustrating event something to be ascertained only at the time when the parties to a contract are called on to make up their minds, and this I would think to be right, both as to the inconclusiveness of hindsight which Scrutton J. had primarily in mind and as to the inappropriateness of the intrusion of an officious bystander immediately prior to the conclusion of the agreement.

Counsel for the respondent sought to argue that *Taylor* v. *Caldwell*, could as easily have been decided on the basis of a total failure of consideration. This is the second of the five theories. But *Taylor* v. *Caldwell* was clearly not so decided, and in any event many, if not most, cases of frustration which have followed *Taylor* v. *Caldwell* have occurred during the currency of a contract partly executed on both sides, when no question of total failure of consideration can possibly arise.

In *Hirji Mulji* v. *Cheong Yue Steamship Co. Ltd.* [1926] A.C. 497, 510 Lord Sumner seems to have formulated the doctrine as a ". . . device [sic], by which the rules as to absolute contracts are reconciled with a special exception which justice demands" and Lord Wright in *Denny, Mott & Dickson Ltd.* v. *James B. Fraser & Co. Ltd.* [1944] A.C. 265, 275 seems to prefer this formulation to the implied condition view. The weakness of the formulation, however, if the implied condition theory, with which Lord Sumner coupled it, be rejected, is that, though it admirably expresses the purpose of the doctrine, it does not provide it with any theoretical basis at all.

Hirji Mulji v. *Cheong Yue Steamship Co. Ltd.* is, it seems to me, really an example of the more sophisticated theory of "frustration of the adventure" or "foundation of the contract" formulation, said to have originated with *Jackson* v. *Union Marine Insurance Co. Ltd.* (1874) L.R. 10 C.P. 125 . . . . This, of course, leaves open the question of what is, in any given case, the foundation of the contract or what is "fundamental" to it, or what is the "adventure." Another theory, of which the parent may have been Earl Loreburn in *F. A. Tamplin Steamship Co. Ltd.* v. *Anglo-Mexican Petroleum Products Co. Ltd.* [1916] 2 A.C. 397, is that the doctrine is based on the answer to the question: "What in fact is the true meaning of the contract?": see p. 404. This is the "construction theory." In *Davis Contractors Ltd.* v. *Fareham Urban District Council* [1956] A.C. 696, 729 Lord Radcliffe put the matter thus, and it is the formulation I personally prefer:

". . . frustration occurs whenever the law recognises that without default of either party a contractual obligation has become incapable of being performed because the circumstances in which performance is called for would render it a thing radically different from that which was undertaken by the contract. Non haec in foedera veni. It was not this that I promised to do."

. . . my approach to the question involves me in the view that whether a supervening event is a frustrating event or not is, in a wide variety of cases, a question of degree, and therefore to some extent at least of fact, whereas in your Lordships' House in *Tsakiroglou & Co. Ltd.* v. *Noblee Thorl G.m.b.H.* [1962] A.C. 93 the question is treated as one at least involving a question of law, or, at best, a question of mixed law and fact. . . .

LORD WILBERFORCE

1. The doctrine of frustration of contracts made its appearance in English law in answer to the proposition, which since *Paradine* v. *Jane*, Aleyn 26, had held the field, that an obligation expressed in absolute and unqualified terms, such as an obligation to pay rent, had to be performed and could not be excused by supervening circumstances. Since *Taylor* v. *Caldwell*, it has been applied generally over the whole field of contract.

2. Various theories have been expressed as to its justification in law: as a device by which the rules as to absolute contracts are reconciled with a special exception which justice demands, as an implied term, as a matter of

construction of the contract, as related to removal of the foundation of the contract, as a total failure of consideration. It is not necessary to attempt selection
of any one of these as the true basis: my own view would be that they shade
into one another and that a choice between them is a choice of what is most
appropriate to the particular contract under consideration. One could see, in
relation to the present contract, that it could provisionally be said to be appropriate to refer to an implied term, in view of the grant of the right of way, or to
removal of the foundation of the contract—viz. use as a warehouse. In any
event, the doctrine can now be stated generally as part of the law of contract;
as all judicially evolved doctrines it is, and ought to be, flexible and capable of
new applications. . . .

LORD SIMON Frustration of a contract takes place when there supervenes an
event (without default of either party and for which the contract makes no sufficient provision) which so significantly changes the nature (not merely the
expense or onerousness) of the outstanding contractual rights and/or obligations from what the parties could reasonably have contemplated at the time of
its execution that it would be unjust to hold them to the literal sense of its stipulations in the new circumstances; in such case the law declares both parties to
be discharged from further performance.

Notes

1. Frustration applies to contracts generally. There is no class of contracts
which cannot, at least in theory, be held to be frustrated. It had been
argued that a lease, because it conveys an estate in land, could not be frustrated. This estate would survive even if the lessee were prevented from
actually *using* the land during the entire duration of the lease; this was the
position supported by the Court of Appeal in *Cricklewood Property and
Investment Trust Ltd.* v. *Leighton's Investment Trust Ltd.* ([1943] KB 493).
However, recognizing that the reality of a lease is an agreement to occupy
and use premises in return for rent, the House of Lords reversed the position in *National Carriers*, holding that a lease could be frustrated in exceptional circumstances, stressing that this would 'hardly ever' be the case.

On the facts of *National Carriers*, a lease for ten years was held not to be
frustrated when access to the property was blocked for twenty months,
four-and-a-half years before the end of the term. For further detailed discussion see J. Price, 'The Doctrine of Frustration and Leases' ((1988) 10 *J.
Leg. Hist* 90).

2. The 'implied term' approach to frustration requires the court to imply a
term into the contract providing that performance will be excused and the
contract discharged if the frustrating event occurs. While nominally faithful to the classical premiss that judges complete and interpret contracts
and do not make or destroy them, in practice this approach is fatally

flawed. Lord Hailsham hints at certain difficulties inherent in using the officious bystander test. Atiyah expands upon these points:

P. S. Atiyah, *An Introduction to the Law of Contract,* 4th edn. (Oxford, Clarendon Press, 1989), 254–6

The traditional theory is to explain frustration as based on the presumed intention of the parties, or in other words as based on an implied term in the original contract. In contrast to the implied term in cases of common mistake, which is a condition precedent, the implied term in cases of frustration would be a condition subsequent. Support for this theory is to be found in numerous judgments from the mid-nineteenth century right down to the present day. But there were always serious weaknesses in the implied-term theory, weaknesses which in fact exist in any attempt to base the consequences of a contract on the intention of the parties. In particular, it was always well established that the actual intentions of the particular parties did not matter—it was the intention which could be attributed to them as *reasonable men* which was determinative. Again, a problem arose from the fact that frustration was generally held only to be a possible legal conclusion if it was caused by some *unanticipated* or perhaps *unforeseen* event. But then how was it possible to attribute an implied intention to the parties with regard to something which they just had not foreseen?

For these and similar reasons, the implied-term theory became unpopular with some judges, particularly those who favoured greater candour as to the nature of the judicial function. Some judges began to say that it was not the intention of the parties which decided whether a contract was frustrated, but the court which exercises the necessary power of declaring the contract at an end. What happens is that the court decides what is reasonable in the circumstances of the case, and says that the parties ought to be discharged or not, according to these circumstances.

This theory was originally put forward by a distinguished Lord of Appeal, Lord Wright, in three cases in the 1940s, and it later attracted the support of Lord Denning. After various vicissitudes, it was substantially adopted in the speech of Lord Radcliffe in *Davis Contractors* v. *Fareham UDC.* . . . Lord Radcliffe's view, like that of Lord Wright, was that frustration depends on the operation of a rule of law, rather than the intention of the parties, but Lord Radcliffe went on to define a little more precisely when and how this rule of law would operate. According to this view, which has now been repeatedly endorsed by the House of Lords in later cases, a contract is frustrated when events have occurred which have changed the substance of the obligations assumed by the parties, so that to compel them to perform would be to make them do something radically different from what they contracted to do. Of course, even this approach does not discard the intention of the parties as an irrelevancy altogether. Because the whole point of the doctrine, as thus formulated, is to enable the parties to insist that they should only be legally obliged to perform what they had intended to perform, not something radically different. What the new formulation does effectively do is to depart from the literalness which might once have insisted that parties had to do something they never intended to do, merely because the contract might literally appear to oblige them to do so.

The rejection of the implied-term theory eventually took place when the principle of freedom of contract was at a low ebb, but earlier attempts to discard it by judges like Lord Wright and Lord Denning were frigidly received by traditional-minded judges like Lord Simon and Lord Simonds. It remains to be seen whether the modern resurgence of freedom-of-contract principles will lead to attempts to resuscitate the implied-term theory here, on the ground (for instance) that it is not the function of the law to 'impose' solutions on contracting parties. But it is desirable to point out that earlier support for the implied-term theory was often based on a serious misconception. It seems to have been thought (by judges like Lord Simon and Lord Simonds) that if the power to declare a contract frustrated was (as Lord Denning suggested) a power to qualify the literal terms of the contract, then this would replace certainty in the law with arbitrary, discretionary justice. The judge would be imposing *his* views on the parties, instead of enforcing their *own* intentions. But this was a serious mistake. Like all rules of law, the rules relating to frustration are a mixture of firm principle and of judicial discretion. Judges do not have a wide-ranging discretion to do whatever they think just; but they do, and must have, the power to decide borderline cases, and most lawyers think that when they do so, they are exercising a discretion. But these borderline cases are relatively unusual cases, taking the law as a whole, though they may be common in the appeal courts. And clearly, as the doctrine of frustration is refined and applied, precedents will multiply, and the law will become clearer, even though there will always be difficulties of application in some cases. In this respect there is no difference between the doctrine of frustration and any other set of rules of contract law.

See further on the problems of the exercise of judicial discretion in the implication of terms, L. Trakman, 'Frustrated Contracts and Legal Fictions' ((1983) 46 *MLR* 39).

3. It would appear from *National Carriers* that the House of Lords has now finally moved away from the implied term doctrine towards a construction or rule-of-law approach to frustration. Since *National Carriers*, the House of Lords has become somewhat impatient with constantly being asked to reconsider the precise theoretical basis of frustration, and it prefers to adopt the pragmatic nuts-and-bolts approach of Lord Radcliffe in *Davis* v. *Fareham UDC*.

Lord Roskill in *Pioneer Shipping Ltd.* v. *BTP Tioxide Ltd.*
[1981] 2 All ER 1030 at 1046

I venture to offer certain preliminary observations. First, I hope I shall not be thought discourteous or unappreciative of the industry involved in the preparation of counsel's arguments if I say that today massive citation of authority in cases where the relevant legal principles have been clearly and authoritatively determined is of little or no assistance and should be firmly discouraged. Some citation merely lengthens hearings and adds to costs without in any way leading to the avoidance of judicial error. In National Carriers Ltd v Panalpina (Northern) Ltd your Lordships' House recently reviewed the doctrine of frustration and, by a majority, held that it was susceptible of application to leases. It is clear, reading the speeches of your Lordships, that the House approved the now classic statement of the doctrine by Lord Radcliffe in Davis Contractors Ltd v Fareham Urban District Council [1956] AC 696 at 729, whatever may have been said in other cases at earlier stages of the evolution of the doctrine of frustration:

'. . . frustration occurs whenever the law recognises that, without default of either party, a contractual obligation has become incapable of being performed because the circumstances in which performance is called for would render it a thing radically different from that which was undertaken by the contract. Non haec in foedera veni. It was not this that I promised to do.'

It should therefore be unnecessary in future cases, where issues of frustration of contracts arise, to search back among the many earlier decisions in this branch of the law when the doctrine was in its comparative infancy. The question in these cases is not whether one case resembles another, but whether, applying Lord Radcliffe's enunciation of the doctrine, the facts of the particular case under consideration do or do not justify the invocation of the doctrine, always remembering that the doctrine is not lightly to be invoked to relieve contracting parties of the normal consequences of imprudent commercial bargains.

4. The difficulty with the 'radically different' test is its application in practice. In *National Carriers*, Lord Simon points to two key elements: that the contractual obligations of the parties after the alleged frustrating event should be different in nature, not simply more onerous; and that the doctrine, while applied strictly, should be used to do justice between the parties. The English law doctrine of frustration has not drifted into a broader notion of commercial impracticability as an excuse for non-performance, as has occurred in the United States. Furthermore, the legal consequences of frustration remain as drastic as ever: the contract is discharged, with the parties relieved from performing any accrued or future contractual duties. No practice of judicial adjustment of contracts has developed.

5. Only unanticipated risks can lead to the frustration of a contract. By definition, if the parties have expressly anticipated a risk they will have allocated it (e.g. through a *force majeure* clause). One of the difficulties for a court, however, is that even if the parties have not expressly dealt with a

particular risk they may have allocated it by default, e.g. by *not* including a *force majeure* clause. There is no general requirement that a frustrating event must be unforeseeable, since even the most improbable catastrophes such as wars are foreseeable as general risks, even if not in specific terms. However, the presence of a *force majeure* clause covering the relevant risk will preclude recourse to the doctrine of frustration.

B. The Operation of the Frustration Doctrine

Through the process of gradual development noted by the House of Lords in *National Carriers*, there has evolved a doctrine of frustration potentially applicable to any type of contract and in any circumstances which satisfy the strict test of radical change of circumstances. Frustration rarely succeeds as a defence, but it has been discussed relatively frequently by the appellate courts in recent years. Thus, in addition to contracts for the sale of land and leases, already used as illustrations in this chapter, recent cases have involved contracts of employment, contracts for services, building contracts, and charter parties amongst other types of contract. In addition, the range of allegedly 'frustrating events' which have been cited have included the following:

(1) major public events such as the world wars, other regional conflicts, the closing of the Suez canal, and the cancellation of the coronation of King Edward VII;

(2) general economic trends such as inflation and currency fluctuations;

(3) supervening illegality such as a prohibition on trading with the enemy during wartime;

(4) administrative action such as the issue of a compulsory purchase order;

(5) physical impossibility attendant upon the destruction of the thing contracted for; and

(6) changes in the personal circumstances of one of the contracting parties such as death or illness.

In this section we shall discuss a recent Court of Appeal decision which gives us an opportunity to draw together many of the key elements in the operation of the frustration doctrine.

J. Lauritzen AS v. Wijsmuller BN (The Super Servant Two)
[1990] 1 Lloyd's Rep. 1

In July 1980, the parties concluded a contract under which the defendants undertook to transport a drilling rig (the *Dan King*) purchased by the plaintiffs from Japan to a location off Rotterdam. The defendants had two specialized, semi-submersible barges which they could use to effect the transportation. Delivery of the rig was to be between 20 June and 20 August 1981. On 29 January 1981 one of the barges belonging to the defendant—the *Super Servant Two*—sank while it was being used for another of the defendant's other contracts, and on 16 February 1981 the defendants decided that they could not reschedule the work of the other barge—the *Super Servant One*—to allow it to complete the contract with the plaintiffs which it claimed to be frustrated. The parties entered into 'without prejudice' negotiations under which they arranged for the defendants to transport the plaintiffs' drilling rig by another means at greater expense to both parties. The plaintiffs sought recovery of the additional costs, claiming that the defendants were in breach of their original transportation contract; the defendants countered by arguing that the loss of the *Super Servant Two* meant that the original contract was discharged for frustration, thus protecting them from any liability and giving them a claim for additional expenditure resulting from the revised arrangements. They argued in the alternative that the loss of the ship was covered by a *force majeure* clause allowing them to cancel the contract in certain eventualities. A trial of certain preliminary issues was concerned with whether the events as pleaded by the parties amounted to frustration of the contract, and whether the *force majeure* clause applied. Mr Justice Hobhouse at first instance ([1989] 1 Lloyd's Rep. 148) essentially held in favour of the plaintiffs on these points, and the defendants appealed. Only the frustration point is discussed in these extracts; we shall return to the problem of *force majeure* clauses in Section VI below.

A key obstacle to success by the defendants on the frustration point was the Privy Council decision in *Maritime National Fish Ltd.* v. *Ocean Trawlers Ltd.* ([1935] AC 524). The defendants in that case operated a fleet of five trawlers, three of which they owned and two of which they chartered from other owners, including one from the plaintiffs. When the defendants were granted only three licences to use otter trawls by the government, instead of the five they had requested, they chose not to allocate one of the licences to the trawler chartered from the plaintiffs. They argued that the charter was frustrated, but the Privy Council held that it was not, since it was the choice of the defendants to allocate the licences to the other boats.

BINGHAM LJ The argument in this case raises important issues on the English law of frustration. Before turning to the specific questions I think it helpful to summarize the established law so far as relevant to this case.

The classical statement of the modern law is that of Lord Radcliffe in *Davis Contractors Ltd. v. Fareham Urban District Council.* . . . As Lord Reid observed in the same case (at p. 721):

. . . there is no need to consider what the parties thought or how they or reasonable men in their shoes would have dealt with the new situation if they had foreseen it. The question is whether the contract which they did make is, on its true construction, wide enough to apply to the new situation: if it is not, then it is at an end.

Certain propositions, established by the highest authority, are not open to question:

1. The doctrine of frustration was evolved to mitigate the rigour of the common law's insistence on literal performance of absolute promises . . . . The object of the doctrine was to give effect to the demands of justice, to achieve a just and reasonable result, to do what is reasonable and fair, as an expedient to escape from injustice where such would result from enforcement of a contract in its literal terms after a significant change in circumstances . . . .

2. Since the effect of frustration is to kill the contract and discharge the parties from further liability under it, the doctrine is not to be lightly invoked, must be kept within very narrow limits and ought not to be extended. . . .

3. Frustration brings the contract to an end forthwith, without more and automatically . . . .

4. The essence of frustration is that it should not be due to the act or election of the party seeking to rely on it . . . . a frustrating event must be one outside event or extraneous change of situation . . . .

5. A frustrating event must take place without blame or fault on the side of the party seeking to rely on it . . . .

The doctrine of frustration depends on a comparison between circumstances as they are or are assumed to be when a contract is made and circumstances as they are when a contract is, or would be, due to be performed. It is trite law that disappointed expectations do not of themselves give rise to frustrated contracts. To frustrate, an event must significantly change—

. . . the nature (not merely the expense or onerousness) of the outstanding contractual rights and/or obligations from what the parties could reasonably have contemplated at the time of [the contract's] execution . . . [*National Carriers Ltd.* sup., at p. 700, per Lord Simon of Glaisdale].

Had the *Dan King* contract provided for carriage by *Super Servant Two* with no alternative, and that vessel had been lost before the time for performance, then assuming no negligence by Wijsmuller (as for purposes of this question we must), I feel sure the contract would have been frustrated. The doctrine must avail a party who contracts to perform a contract of carriage with a vessel which, through no fault of his, no longer exists. But that is not this case. The *Dan King* contract did provide an alternative. . . . Wijsmuller have not alleged that when the *Dan King* contract was made either vessel was earmarked for its performance. That, no doubt, is why an option was contracted for. Had it been foreseen when the *Dan King* contract was made that *Super Servant Two* would be unavailable for performance, whether because she had been deliberately sold or accidentally sunk, Lauritzen at least would have thought it no matter since the carriage could be performed with the other. . . . the present case does not fall within the very limited class of cases in which the law will relieve one party from an absolute promise he has chosen to make.

. . . Wijsmuller's argument is subject to other fatal flaws. If . . . the contract was frustrated when Wijsmuller made or communicated their decision on Feb. 16, it deprives language of all meaning to describe the contract as coming to an end automatically. It was, indeed, because the contract did not come to an end automatically on Jan. 29, that Wijsmuller needed a fortnight to review their schedules and their commercial options. I cannot, furthermore, reconcile Wijsmuller's argument with the reasoning or the decision in *Maritime National Fish Ltd.*. In that case the Privy Council declined to speculate why the charterers selected three of the five vessels to be licensed but, as I understand the case, regarded the interposition of human choice after the allegedly frustrating event as fatal to the plea of frustration. If Wijsmuller are entitled to succeed here, I cannot see why the charterers lost there. . . .

I reach the same conclusion as the Judge for the reasons which he lucidly and persuasively gave.

The [other] issue between the parties was short and fundamental`: what is meant by saying that a frustrating event, to be relied on, must occur without the fault or default, or without blame attaching to, the party relying on it?

[Counsel for the defendants'] answer was that a party was precluded from relying on an event only when he had acted deliberately or in breach of an actionable duty in causing it. Those conditions were not met here since it was not alleged Wijsmuller sank *Super Servant Two* deliberately and at the material time Wijsmuller owed Lauritzen no duty of care. . . .

[Counsel for the plaintiffs] argued for a less restrictive approach. He relied on what Lord Justice Griffiths, as he then was, said in *The Hannah Blumenthal*, [1983] 1 A.C. 854 at p. 882.

[*Denmark Productions Ltd. v. Boscobel Productions Ltd.* [1969] 1 Q.B. 699] best illustrates what is meant by default in the context of frustration. The essence of frustration is that it is caused by some unforeseen supervening event over which the parties to the contract have no control and for which they are therefore not responsible. To say that the supervening event occurs without the default or blame or responsibility of the parties is, in the context of the doctrine of frustration, but another way of saying it is a supervening event over which they had no control. The doctrine has no application and cannot be invoked by a contracting party when the frustrating event was at all times within his control; still less can it apply in a situation in which the parties owed a contractual duty to one another to prevent the frustrating event occurring.

I do not pause to ask whether Lord Justice Griffith's opinion is formally binding upon us since in my judgment it clearly indicates the path which the law should follow. When, in *Bank Line Ltd.* [[1949] AC 435 at 452] Lord Sumner made his famous observation that "Reliance cannot be placed on a self-induced frustration", he was contrasting a self-induced frustration with one arising "without blame or fault on either side". As the Judge observed (at p. 156)—

... in some respects the doctrine of frustration and the concept of "self-inducement" are simply opposite sides of the same coin.

Wijsmuller's test would, in my judgment, confine the law in a legalistic strait-jacket and distract attention from the real question, which is whether the frustrating event relied upon is truly an outside event or extraneous change of situation or whether it is an event which the party seeking to rely on it had the means and opportunity to prevent but nevertheless caused or permitted to come about. A fine test of legal duty is inappropriate; what is needed is a pragmatic judgment whether a party seeking to rely on an event as discharging him from a contractual promise was himself responsible for the occurrence of that event.

Lauritzen have pleaded in some detail the grounds on which they say that *Super Servant Two* was lost as a result of the carelessness of Wijsmuller, their servants or agents. If those allegations are made good to any significant extent Wijsmuller would (even if my answer to [the first question] is wrong) be precluded from relying on their plea of frustration.

I would answer this question also as the Judge did and would therefore dismiss the appeal.

Notes

1. It might seem at first glance that this is the archetypal case of frustration—the loss or destruction of the means by which the contract is to be performed. In fact, as Bingham LJ points out, if the parties had nominated the *Super Servant Two* as the means of carrying the drilling rig in their original contract, the loss of the barge could have resulted in the contract being automatically discharged for frustration. In the event, there are two separate reasons why the defendants would have been unable to claim frustration on the facts as alleged, even if these had been proven. The second issue dealt with by Bingham LJ is the simpler of the two to understand, and that is the requirement that the frustration must not be induced by some act or default on the part of the party seeking to claim frustration. Even if the loss of the barge did not amount to a breach of contract or of a duty of care owed to the plaintiffs, if it could be proved that the defendants were

responsible for the loss of the ship, this would be sufficient to preclude the defence of frustration. Bingham LJ proposes a broad and pragmatic test for assessing the issue of responsibility in that context. Hobhouse J. at first instance suggested that an event is not 'supervening' if it occurs within one party's control and is not one of the hazards of everyday life. He contrasted the case of an opera singer who carelessly catches a cold (one of life's hazards) and is thus unable to perform her contract with an impresario, and an opera singer who is unable to sing because she strained her voice singing for another impresario (a matter within the sphere of control of the singer).

2. The more controversial issue concerns the conclusion reached by both Hobhouse J and the Court of Appeal that the loss of the *Super Servant Two* did not automatically discharge the contract. What brought the performance of the contract into doubt was the decision of the defendants not to reschedule the work of the *Super Servant One* in order to perform the contract with the plaintiffs. To their minds, this placed the case on all fours with the *Maritime National* case, a decision which had been criticized by Treitel (*The Law of Contract*, 7th edn. (London, Sweet and Maxwell, 1987), 700 ff.), who had argued that the crucial factor in that case was that the licence-holders could have satisfied all the contracts they held with other trawler-owners if they had chosen to allocate the available licences to those trawlers. In a case like this, the supplier in the position of the defendants must inevitably disappoint someone—he or she cannot absorb the loss internally. Certainly the decision of the Court of Appeal does seem quite harsh. For to view the choice of the defendants as to which of the contracts it would fulfil and which ones it would not as an element of fact which disentitles them from relying upon the doctrine of frustration 'leaves a seller or supplier of goods in an impossible position where his source of supply partially fails because of an unforeseen event. Indeed, in many ways it would be preferable if the source of supply failed completely because then the seller could invoke frustration as an excuse for non-performance' (McKendrick, 'Frustration and Force Majeure: Their Relationship and a Comparative Assessment', in E. McKendrick (ed.), *Force Majeure and Frustration of Contract* (London, Lloyd's of London Press, 1991), 42).

The decision seems all the more unfair to the defendants when it is contrasted with the approach of the courts in cases in which the partial failure of supplies had been foreseen in the sense that it was covered by a *force majeure* clause in each of the contracts concluded by the supplier. In such cases, the courts have held that the supplier has a discretion to choose which contracts to fulfil and which ones to cancel using the *force majeure* clause. This was a line of cases discussed by the courts in *The Super Servant Two* but declared to be inapplicable. Hobhouse J was, in contrast, unsympathetic to the situation of the defendants, stating that 'It is within the promisor's control how many contracts he enters into and the risk should be his . . . . If the promisor wishes [to be discharged from his obligations] he must bargain for the inclusion of a suitable *force majeure* clause in the contract' ([1989] 1 Lloyd's Rep. 148 at 158).

A conclusion of this nature pushes the parties very strongly towards the detailed planning of contracts, including the use of *force majeure* clauses. This is, of course, of little assistance to those who have not already based their contractual behaviour on the assumption that market choices of this nature will disqualify the chooser from relying upon the doctrine of frustration. However, as we have mentioned before in our commentary upon *Williams* v. *Roffey* ([1990] 1 All ER 512) in Chapter 6, there is in this context a link between frustration and the modification of contractual obligations. The recognition of a more generous test of factual benefit in order to allow the enforceability of contractual modifications made when a contract proves to be uneconomical for one party (e.g. because of changed economic circumstances which do not amount to frustration) is wholly consistent with a strict test of frustration. Thus, in addition to planning, contracting parties are pushed, by the interaction of consideration and frustration doctrine, towards the renegotiation of contracts—a strategy which works perfectly so long as the party to whom the contract has become more burdensome can persuade the other party to come to the bargaining table, and can successfully effect a alteration of the problematic terms.

3. Not surprisingly, Treitel returns to the offensive in the latest edition of his textbook, attacking the decision on its reasoning if not its conclusion.

G. Treitel, *The Law of Contract*, 8th edn. (London, Sweet and Maxwell, 1991), 805–6

Three grounds for the decision appear from the judgments but it is submitted with great respect that none of them is wholly convincing. First, it was said that the *Maritime National Fish* case had established that a party could not rely on frustration where his failure or inability was due to his "election"; and that the Court in *The Super Servant Two* should follow that decision. It is, however, submitted that the two cases are readily distinguishable: in the *Maritime National Fish* case it was possible for the charterer to perform *all* the contracts which he had made with the owners of the other trawlers, even though only three licences had been allocated to him; while in *The Super Servant Two* it was no longer possible, after the loss of the ship, for the carrier to perform all the contracts which he had made to carry drilling rigs during the period in question. Secondly, it was said that, if the carrier were given the choice which of the contracts he would perform, frustration of the other or others could only come about as a result of the exercise of that choice, and such a position would be inconsistent with the rule that frustration occurs automatically, *without* any election by either party. Again, it is submitted that this line of reasoning is not conclusive since the rule that frustration operates automatically is subject to qualification precisely in cases of allegedly self-induced frustration: . . . for example, . . . the imprisonment of an employee is a circumstance on which the employer, but not the employee, can rely as a ground of discharge, so that discharge cannot in such cases be described as automatic. . . . Moreover, the element of "election" could be eliminated if the question which of the contracts was to be discharged were left to be determined, not by the free choice of the promisor, but by a rule of law: *e.g.* by a rule to the effect that the various contracts should for this purpose rank in the order in which they were made. It may, from this point of view, be relevant that, in *The Super Servant Two*, some of the contracts which the carrier chose to perform (by the use of his other ship during the relevant period) had not been made "at any rate finally" until *after* the contract with the plaintiffs, and that, even after the loss of the *Super Servant Two*, the carrier had continued to negotiate for extra fees to be paid under one of those contracts, "before finally allocating the *Super Servant One* to the performance of these contracts." [Third ground omitted.]

The key question to be answered in respect of a decision such as this is whether it satisfies even those requirements for the operation of the doctrine of frustration imposed by the House of Lords in cases like *National Carriers*, namely that, while not being a doctrine which should be lightly invoked, it should none the less be sufficiently flexible to allow justice to be done as between the parties and it should be responsive to changing circumstances.

4. One issue raised by *The Super Servant Two* which deserves further analysis is whether in fact the solution adopted by the Court of Appeal is the most efficient one. For it discourages a party in the position of the defendants from making full use of the time available for transportation activities by its barges. By retaining flexibility in their scheduling of the barges to perform the various contracts which they had concluded, the defendants made themselves more vulnerable to damaging consequences in the event of the loss of one of their craft, amounting to a partial failure of supply. With a result such as that reached in *The Super Servant Two*, suppliers of transportation will be encouraged not to use the full capacity of their barges. Alternatively, even if they were unable to persuade customers to accept a *force majeure* clause in their contracts, suppliers might, through a rule such as the one applied here, be encouraged to insure against the risk of loss, either through self-insurance (e.g. raising prices) or the conclusion of an insurance policy. This analysis would be consistent with the views of Posner and Rosenfield on the risk falling upon the least cost avoider—i.e. the party best able to take out insurance, a point discussed in Section V.

5. For further comment on *The Super Servant Two* see E. McKendrick, 'The Construction of *Force Majeure* Clauses and Self-Induced Frustration', ([1990] *LMCLQ* 153); A. Chandler, 'Self-Induced Frustration, Foreseeability and Risk' ((1990) 41 *NILQ* 362); and S. Hedley, 'Carriage by Sea: Frustration and *Force Majeure*' ([1990] *CLJ* 209).

6. As amply revealed by *The Super Servant Two*, the test for frustration is strict. It is worth recalling the facts of *Bell* v. *Lever Brothers* and *Associated Japanese Bank* v. *CDN* to consider whether the test for initial impossibility/common mistake is as strict and, if it is, whether it should be. It seems that the wording of the two tests has gradually moved closer together, and it now appears from Steyn J's judgment in *Associated Japanese Bank* v. *CDN* that the test of 'radically different' will suffice for common mistake. As far as the judicial approach to frustration is concerned, we can say that a strict test pushes the parties towards using initial planning and *force majeure* clauses to cover the risk of the occurrence of the event, or towards renegotiating the contract. In the case of common mistake, there is an argument that the test should be more generous. First, if the parties contract on the basis that X is a fact, then neither of them is likely to have thought planning was necessary to cover the eventuality that X was an incorrect fact. It may also be that they cannot then renegotiate the contract, as they may not, without the existence of X, wish to be linked in the market. However, this view assumes that X is a crucial fact. The more generous the test that is applied, the more likely it is that facts which are not crucial will operate to allow the contract to be set aside. Moreover, the more generous the test, the less care a party is likely to take in checking that the jointly assumed facts are correct.

An alternative argument is that the ability to check the existence of facts should impose a stricter test than subsequent impossibility where, by definition, the event that has occurred is one that neither party foresaw or planned against. As to whether the application of the two tests is different or not, we cannot offer a definitive answer: common mistake is rarely pleaded, and we have little information about the difference of the requirements of common law and equity.

C. The Remedial Structure

Parties who plan for the occurrence of a particular event by deciding either that one party will take the risk that it may occur or that it will be covered by a *force majeure* clause create their own remedial structure within the contract to deal with questions such as how prepaid deposits and part-completed work are dealt with. Parties can also include a clause to deal with the consequences of frustration, in the event that the contract is discharged for frustration.

1. If a contract is found to be frustrated, then, in the absence of any of the above, the parties are forced to use the remedial structure offered by the Law Reform (Frustrated Contracts) Act 1943. In order to understand the approach of legislation it is necessary to look briefly at the common-law background. The common law is also relevant for contracts where the Act does not apply, (e.g. s. 2(5): the Act does not apply to contracts of insurance). The common law treats frustration as discharging a contract from the time of the frustrating event onwards, and not as if it rendered the contract void *ab initio*. Consequently, any elements of performance due but not carried out prior to the frustrating event remain due regardless of the fact that future performance is obviated. This may have the result of burdening one party but not the other.

2. The example most often used to illustrate this is *Chandler* v. *Webster* ([1904] 1 KB 493). The contract was for the hire of a room to watch the coronation procession of King Edward VII. Under the contract, the hire charge for the room was £141 15s., payable before the procession took place. The plaintiff paid the defendant £100, but before he had paid the balance, the coronation was cancelled due to the illness of the King—an event which gave rise to a considerable volume of litigation on frustration, as will be seen from the next section. The King's illness and the cancellation of the coronation were held to frustrate the contract. The plaintiff sought to recover his £100 and the defendant counterclaimed for the outstanding balance. The Court of Appeal rejected the plaintiff's claim for the return of the price paid, and held him liable to the defendant for the outstanding part of the price. The plaintiff's arguments that money paid under total failure of consideration was recoverable were rejected on the grounds that there could be a total failure of consideration only if a contract was void *ab initio*. The defendant was excused from all further performance because the contract was discharged. The plaintiff would not have had to pay the balance had it fallen due after the frustrating event.

3. Some aspects of the decision in *Chandler* v. *Webster* were overruled by the House of Lords in *Fibrosa Spolka Akcyjna* v. *Fairbairn, Lawson, Combe, Barbour Ltd.* ([1943] AC 32). It decided that a total failure of consideration could occur not only where a contract was void *ab initio* but also where performance or part-performance had been rendered on a basis which failed. The facts of *Fibrosa* were that part payment had been rendered by the appellants to the respondents for machines to be manufactured by the respondents and delivered to Poland. Before manufacture was completed, the contract was frustrated by the German occupation of Poland. The appellants were allowed to recover their £1,000 on the grounds that the basis for the contract had failed.

While mitigating some of the harshness of the common law approach,

Fibrosa did not solve all the problems. The respondents may have felt aggrieved, for example, that there was no provision made for the retention of any of the £1,000 as an allowance for their expenditure. The position of a party faced with partial but not total failure of consideration was not improved.

4. The Law Reform [Frustrated Contracts] Act 1943 makes some attempt to solve these problems. There is no statement of what the Act intends to achieve. Alternative bases that have been supported are 'a flexible machinery for the adjustment of loss' (A. Haycroft and D. Waksman, 'Restitution and Frustration', [1984] *JBL* 207 at 225) and the 'prevention of the unjust enrichment of either party', per Goff J in *BP* v. *Hunt* ([1982] 1 All ER 925 at 937). As will be seen from our discussion of the Act, one of the things that it is least likely to be praised for is its flexibility. A more appropriate comment about its purpose may be simply to say that it is intended to prevent the situation whereby loss lies where it falls.

Law Reform (Frustrated Contracts) Act 1943, s. 1(2)

All sums paid or payable to any party in pursuance of the contract before the time when the parties were so discharged (in this Act referred to as "the time of discharge") shall, in the case of sums so paid, be recoverable from him as money received by him for the use of the party by whom the sums were paid, and, in the case of sums so payable, cease to be so payable:

Provided that, if the party to whom the sums were so paid or payable incurred expenses before the time of discharge in, or for the purpose of, the performance of the contract, the court may, if it considers it just to do so having regard to all the circumstances of the case, allow him to retain or, as the case may be, recover the whole or any part of the sums so paid or payable, not being an amount in excess of the expenses so incurred.

This section deals with money paid or payable under a frustrated contract. Money that has been paid prior to the frustrating event is recoverable, but the court can order that some of the money is retained to cover any expenses incurred prior to frustration 'if it considers it just to do so'. Money which should have been paid prior to the frustrating event, but which has not been, is no longer payable. However, if the party to whom the money is owed has incurred expenses, the court may order that a sum is payable 'if it considers it just'. In each case the sum awarded by the court cannot exceed the amount actually paid or the amount payable in advance. The factors that the court will take into account in assessing the sum are not given. The chapter on remedies will show that when seeking a remedy the party concerned is expected to mitigate his loss; the same is presumably true in this context. The court will consider whether the expenses can be defrayed through other contracts, etc. A much more extensive discussion of the scope of this section is offered by E. McKendrick, 'The Consequences of Frustration: The Law Reform (Frustrated Contracts) Act 1943', in McKendrick (ed.), *Force Majeure and Frustration of Contract* (London, Lloyd's of London Press, 1991), 51.

5. The position with regard to benefits other than money acquired by one party from the other before discharge is dealt with by the Law Reform (Frustrated Contracts) Act 1943, s. 1(3).

Where any party to the contract has, by reason of anything done by any other party thereto in, or for the purpose of, the performance of the contract, obtained a valuable benefit (other than a payment of money to which the last foregoing subsection applies) before the time of discharge, there shall be recoverable from him by the said other party such sum (if any), not exceeding the value of the said benefit to the party obtaining it, as the court considers just, having regard to all the circumstances of the case and, in particular,—

> (a) the amount of any expenses incurred before the time of discharge by the benefited party in, or for the purpose of, the performance of the contract, including any sums paid or payable by him to any other party in pursuance of the contract and retained or recoverable by that party under the last foregoing subsection, and
>
> (b) the effect, in relation to the said benefit, of the circumstances giving rise to the frustration of the contract.

This subsection depends on a finding by the court of a valuable benefit (a term which is not defined) and the placing of a value on it which the court considers to be a just sum. The time at which the benefit is to be valued is not given. The subsection does refer to the conferring of a valuable benefit 'before the time of discharge', but it also refers to the effect of the circumstances of frustration on the valuable benefit. The case which most clearly considers the application of s. 1(3) is *BP* v. *Hunt*. The case reached the House of Lords, but the fullest examination of the section occurred in the first instance judgment of Goff J ([1982] 1 All ER 925). His judgment was reversed on appeal on other grounds. The facts of *BP* v. Hunt are complicated and Goff J's judgment is very long. We have simplified the facts as far as possible and extracted the judgment to show only Goff J's decision on s. 1(3).

BP Exploration Co (Libya) v. *Hunt (No. 2)*
[1982] 1 All ER 925

In December 1957 the Libyan Government granted the defendant a concession to explore and drill for oil in a specified area of Libya. The defendant did not have the resources in terms of knowledge or equipment to exploit the concession himself, and so in 1960 he entered into a contract with the plaintiffs. The contract involved a transfer of half of the concession to the plaintiffs, who would then exploit and drill for oil in the whole concession and make down-payments in oil and money to the defendant. Once oil was found, the plaintiffs, under the agreement, could claim some of their expenditure out of the defendant's share of the oil. Under the arrangement, if oil was not found, then the plaintiffs bore the costs and consequently the risk. Oil was found in large quantities in 1967. However, in 1971, there was a revolution in Libya and the new Libyan government expropriated the plaintiffs' half share and in 1973 did the same to the defendant's half-share. The plaintiffs brought an action for frustration and claimed an award of a just sum under s. 1(3) for a valuable benefit conferred on the defendant prior to frustration of the contract. Goff J held that the contract was frustrated and that the plaintiffs were entitled to an award under s. 1(3).

GOFF J The Act is *not* designed to do certain things. (i) It is not designed to apportion the loss between the parties. There is no general power under either s 1(2) or s 1(3) to make any allowance for expenses incurred by the plaintiff (except, under the proviso to s 1(2), to enable him to enforce pro tanto payment of a sum payable but unpaid before frustration); and expenses incurred by the defendant are only relevant in so far as they go to reduce the net benefit obtained by him and thereby limit any award to the plaintiff. (ii) It is not concerned to put the parties in the position in which they would have been if the contract had been performed. (iii) It is not concerned to restore the parties to the position they were in before the contract was made. A remedy designed to prevent unjust enrichment may not achieve that result; for expenditure may be incurred by either party under the contract which confers no benefit on the other, and in respect of which no remedy is available under the Act.

An award under the Act may have the effect of rescuing the plaintiff from an unprofitable bargain. This may certainly be true under s 1(2), if the plaintiff has paid the price in advance for an expected return which, if furnished, would have proved unprofitable; if the contract is frustrated before any part of that expected return is received, and before any expenditure is incurred by the defendant, the plaintiff is entitled to the return of the price he has paid, irrespective of the consideration he would have recovered had the contract been performed. Consistently with s 1(2), there is nothing in s 1(3) which necessarily limits an award to the contract consideration. But the contract consideration may nevertheless be highly relevant to the assessment of the just sum to be awarded under s 1(3); this is a matter to which I will revert later in this judgment. . . .

Claims under s 1(3)

General. In contract, where an award is made under s 1(3), the process is more complicated. First, it has to be shown that the defendant has, by reason of something done by the plaintiff in, or for the purpose of, the performance of the contract, obtained a valuable benefit (other than a payment of money) before the time of discharge. That benefit has to be identified, and valued, and such value forms the upper limit of the award. Secondly, the court may award to the plaintiff such sum, not greater than the value of such benefit, as it considers just having regard to all the circumstances of the case, including in particular the matters specified in s 1(3)(*a*) and (*b*). In the case of an award under s 1(3) there are, therefore, two distinct stages: the identification and valuation of the benefit, and the award of the just sum. The amount to be awarded is the just sum, unless the defendant's benefit is less, in which event the award will be limited to the amount of that benefit. The distinction between the identification and valuation of the defendant's benefit, and the assessment of the just sum, is the most controversial part of the Act. It represents the solution adopted by the legislature of the problem of restitution in cases where the benefit does not consist of a payment of money; but the solution so adopted has been criticised by some commentators as productive of injustice, and it certainly gives rise to considerable problems, to which I shall refer in due course.

Identification of the defendant's benefit. In the course of the argument before me, there was much dispute whether, in the case of services, the benefit should be identified as the services themselves, or as the end product of the services. One example canvassed (because it bore some relationship to the facts of the present case) was the example of prospecting for minerals. If minerals are discovered, should the benefit be regarded (as counsel for Mr Hunt contended) simply as the services of prospecting, or (as counsel for BP contended) as the minerals themselves being the end product of the successful exercise? Now, I am satisfied that it was the intention of the legislature, to be derived from s 1(3) as a matter of construction, that the benefit should in an appropriate case be identified as the end product of the services. This appears, in my judgment, not only from the fact that s 1(3) distinguishes between the plaintiff's performance and the defendant's benefit, but also from s 1(3)(*b*) which clearly relates to the product of the plaintiff's performance. Let me take the example of a building contract. Suppose that a contract for work on a building is frustrated by a fire which destroys the building and which, therefore, also destroys a substantial amount of work already done by the plaintiff. Although it might be thought just to award the plaintiff a sum assessed on a quantum meruit basis, probably a rateable part of the contract price, in respect of the work he has done, the effect of s 1(3)(*b*) will be to reduce the award to nil, because of the effect, in relation to the defendant's benefit, of the circumstances giving rise to the frustration of the contract. It is quite plain that, in s 1(3)(*b*), the word 'benefit' is intended to refer, in the example I have given, to the actual improvement to the building, because that is what will be affected by the frustrating event; the subsection therefore contemplates that, in such a case, the benefit is the end product of the plaintiff's services, not the services themselves. This will not be so in every case, since in some cases the services will have no end product; for example, where the services consist of doing such work as surveying, or transporting goods. In each case it is necessary to ask the question: what benefit has the defendant obtained by reason of the plaintiff's contractual performance? But it must not be forgotten that in s 1(3) the relevance of the value of the benefit is to fix a ceiling to the award. If, for example, in a building contract, the building is only partially completed, the value of the partially completed building (ie the product of the services) will fix a ceiling for the award; but the stage of the work may be such that the uncompleted building may be worth less than the value of the work and materials that have gone into it, particularly as completion by another builder may cost more than completion by the original builder would have cost. In other cases, however, the actual benefit to the defendant may be considerably more than the appropriate or just sum to be awarded to the plaintiff, in which event the value of the benefit will not in fact determine the quantum of the award. I should add, however, that, in a case of prospecting, it would usually be wrong to identify the discovered mineral as the benefit. In such a case there is always (whether the prospecting is successful or not) the benefit of the prospecting itself, ie of knowing whether or not the land contains any deposit of the relevant minerals; if the prospecting is successful, the benefit may include also the enhanced value of the land by reason of the discovery; if the prospector's contractual task goes beyond discovery and includes development and production, the benefit will include the further enhancement of the land by reason of the installation of the facilities, and also the benefit of in part transforming a valuable mineral deposit into a marketable commodity.

I add by way of footnote that all these difficulties would have been avoided if the legislature had thought it right to treat the services themselves as the benefit. In the opinion of many commentators, it would be more just to do so; after all, the services in question have been requested by the defendant, who normally takes the risk that they may prove worthless, from whatever cause. In the example I have given of the building destroyed by fire, there is much to be said for the view that the builder should be paid for the work he has done, unless he has (for example by agreeing to insure the works) taken on himself the risk of destruction by fire. But my task is to construe the Act as it stands. On the true construction of the Act, it is in my judgment clear that the defendant's benefit must, in an appropriate case, be identified as the end product of the plaintiff's services, despite the difficulties which this construction creates, difficulties which are met again when one comes to value the benefit. . . .

Valuing the benefit.   Since the benefit may be identified with the product of the plaintiff's performance, great problems arise in the valuation of the benefit. First, how does one solve the problem which arises from the fact that a small service may confer an enormous benefit, and conversely, a very substantial service may confer only a very small benefit? The answer presumably is that at the stage of valuation of the benefit (as opposed to assessment of the just sum) the task of the court is simply to assess the value of the benefit to the defendant. For example, if a prospector after some very simple prospecting discovers a large and unexpected deposit of a valuable mineral, the benefit to the defendant (namely, the enhancement in the value of the land) may be enormous; it must be valued as such, always bearing in mind that the assessment of a just sum may very well lead to a much smaller amount being awarded to the plaintiff. But conversely, the plaintiff may have undertaken building work for a substantial sum which is, objectively speaking, of little or no value, for example, he may commence the redecoration, to the defendant's execrable taste, of rooms which are in good decorative order. If the contract is frustrated before the work is complete, and the work is unaffected by the frustrating event, it can be argued that the defendant has obtained no benefit, because the defendant's property has been reduced in value by the plaintiff's work; but the partial work must be treated as a benefit to the defendant, since he requested it, and valued as such. Secondly, at what point in time is the benefit to be valued? If there is a lapse of time between the date of the receipt of the benefit, and the date of frustration, there may in the meanwhile be a substantial variation in the value of the benefit. If the benefit had simply been identified as the services rendered, this problem would not arise; the court would simply award a reasonable remuneration for the services rendered at the time when they were rendered, the defendant taking the risk of any subsequent depreciation and the benefit of any subsequent appreciation in value. But that is not what the Act provides: s 1(3)(*b*) makes it plain that the plaintiff is to take the risk of depreciation or destruction by the frustrating event. If the effect of the frustrating event on the value of the benefit is to be measured, it must surely be measured on the benefit as at the date of frustration. For example, let it be supposed that a builder does work which doubles in value by the date of frustration, and is then so severely damaged by fire that the contract is frustrated; the valuation of the residue must surely be made on the basis of the value as at the date of frustration. However, does this mean that, for the purposes of s 1(3), the benefit is always to be valued as at the date of frustration? For example, if goods are transferred and retained by the defendant till frustration when they have appreciated or depreciated in value, are they to b valued as at the date of frustration? The answer must, I think, generally speaking, be in the affirmative, for the sake of consistency. . . .

. . . I should record that the court is required to have regard to the effect, in relation to the defendant's benefit, of the circumstances giving rise to the frustration of the contract. I have already given an example of how this may be relevant, in the case of building contracts; and I have recorded the fact that this provision has been the subject of criticism. There may, however, be circumstances where it would not be just to have regard to this fact or, for example, if, under a building contract, it was expressly agreed that the work in progress should be insured by the building-owner against risks which include the event which had the effect of frustrating the contract and damaging or destroying the work.

Assessment of the just sum.   The principle underlying the Act is prevention of the unjust enrichment of the defendant at the plaintiff's expense. Where, as in cases under s 1(2), the benefit conferred on the defendant consists of payment of a sum of money, the plaintiff's expense and the defendant's enrichment are generally equal; and, subject to other relevant factors, the award of restitution will consist simply of an order for repayment of a like sum of money. But where the benefit does not consist of money, then the defendant's enrichment will rarely be equal to the plaintiff's expense. In such cases, where (as in the case of a benefit conferred under a contract thereafter frustrated) the benefit has been requested by the defendant, the basic measure of recovery in restitution is the reasonable value of the plaintiff's performance: in a case of services, a quantum meruit or reasonable remuneration, and in a case of goods, a quantum valebat or reasonable price. Such cases are to be contrasted with cases where such a benefit has not been requested by the defendant. In the latter class of case, recovery is rare in restitution; but if the sole basis of recovery was that the defendant had been incontrovertibly benefited, it might be legitimate to limit recovery to the defendant's actual benefit, a limit which has (perhaps inappropriately) been imported by the legislature into s 1(3) of the Act. However, under s 1(3) as it stands, if the defendant's actual benefit is less than the just or reasonable sum which would otherwise be awarded to the plaintiff, the award must be reduced to a sum equal to the amount of the defendant's benefit.

A crucial question, on which the Act is surprisingly silent, is this: what bearing do the terms of the contract, under which the plaintiff has acted, have on the assessment of the just sum? First, the terms on which the work was done may serve to indicate the full scope of the work done, and so be relevant to the sum awarded in respect of such work. For example, if I do work under a contract under which I am to receive a substantial prize if successful, and nothing if I fail, and the contract is frustrated before the work is complete but not before a substantial benefit has been obtained by the defendant, the element of risk taken by the plaintiff may be held to have the effect of enhancing the amount of any sum to be awarded. Secondly, the contract consideration is always relevant as providing some evidence of what will be a reasonable sum to be awarded in respect of the plaintiff's work. Thus if a prospector, employed for a fee, discovers a goldmine before the contract under which he is employed is frustrated (for example, by illegality or by his illness or disablement) at a time when his work was incomplete, the court may think it just to make an award in the nature of a reasonable fee for what he has done (though of course the benefit obtained by the defendant will be far greater), and a rateable part of the contract fee may provide useful evidence of the level of sum to be awarded. If, however, the contract had provided that he was to receive a stake in the concession, then the just sum might be enhanced on the basis that, in all the circumstances, a reasonable sum should take account of such a factor. . . . Thirdly, however, the contract consideration, or a rateable part of it, may provide a limit to the sum to be awarded. To take a fairly extreme example, a poor householder or a small businessman may obtain a contract for building work to be done to his premises at considerably less than the market price, on the basis that he cannot afford to pay more. In such a case, the court may consider it just to limit the award to a rateable part of the contract price, on the ground that it was the understanding of the parties that in no circumstances (including the circumstances of the contract being frustrated) should the plaintiff recover more than the contract price or a rateable part of it. Such a limit may properly be said to arise by virtue of the operation of s 2(3) of the Act. But it must not be forgotten that, unlike money, services can never be restored, nor usually can goods, since they are likely to have been either consumed or disposed of, or to have depreciated in value; and since, ex hypothesi, the defendant will only have been prepared to contract for the goods or services on the basis that he paid no more than the contract consideration, it may be unjust to compel him, by an award under the Act, to pay more than that consideration, or a rateable part of it, in respect of the services or goods he has received. It is unnecessary for me to decide whether this will always be so; but it is likely that in most cases this will impose an important limit on the sum to be awarded: indeed it may well be the most relevant limit to an award under s 1(3) of the Act.

Notes

1. Goff J decides that the benefit conferred must be valued at the time of frustration. Earlier in his judgment he indicates that, in his view, the basis of the Act is an avoidance of unjust enrichment, and this must influence his decision on this point. If the benefit has been destroyed by the frustrating event (e.g. fire in construction works), then there is no unjust enrichment to be dealt with, as the benefit has been destroyed. This will operate so as to place the risk of the type of frustrating event on the person conferring the benefit. For example, if the frustrating event is fire, which destroys the benefit, rather than enemy occupation, which makes completion presently impossible, the person conferring the benefit will be worse off. In effect, Goff J is raising s. 1(3)(*b*), the provision which draws attention to the effect of frustrating event on the benefit, from a factor to be taken into account in assessing a just sum to a factor to be taken into account when valuing the benefit. If the legislature had intended the destruction of benefits to result in a nil award for the party who conferred the benefit, then it could have provided much more simply for this.

2. For a further critique of Goff J's reasoning see A. Haycroft and D. Waksman, 'Restitution and Frustration' ([1984] *JBL* 207).

3. For a comparative insight into the remedial structure, see A. Stewart and J. Carter, 'Frustration Contracts and Statutory Adjustment: The Case for a Reappraisal' ([1990] *CLJ* 66).

V. THE POLICY BASIS OF FRUSTRATION AND RELATED DOCTRINES

A. Introduction

From time to time, the difficulties faced by courts in determining whether performance of a contract should be excused on grounds of frustration become evident when courts decide cases involving the same 'frustrating event' differently. Such is the case with the so-called 'coronation cases'— *Krell* v. *Henry* and *Herne Bay Steam Boat Co.* v. *Hutton*—which arose out of the postponement of the coronation of King Edward VII (see also *Chandler* v. *Webster* discussed in the previous section). It is with a discussion of these two cases that we begin this section on the policy issues underlying frustration. We also examine some American literature which seeks to explain how the courts resolve the difficulties of applying so-called excuse doctrine which, in the United States, is slightly more generous to the promisor seeking to be discharged from performance. We shall also comment briefly upon the idea of extending the range of 'excuses' in the consumer context to encompass the illness or unemployment of the consumer debtor who then is unable to meet his or her payment obligations under hire purchase or loan contracts.

B. Resolving Hard Cases

Krell v. *Henry*
[1900–3] All ER Rep. 20

The plaintiff was a tenant of some rooms in Pall Mall, London, which overlooked the route which the coronation processions to be held on 26 and 27 June 1902 were to follow. He agreed to let the defendant have possession of the rooms for the purpose of viewing the processions, for the sum of £75, £25 of which was paid in advance by way of deposit. The coronation was postponed because of the illness of the King, and the processions did not take place. The plaintiff sued the defendant to recover the balance of the payment due for the hire of the rooms. The judge at first instance found for the defendant, holding also that he was entitled to the return of his £25 deposit. The plaintiff appealed.

VAUGHAN WILLIAMS LJ The real question in this case is the extent of the application in English law of the principle of the Roman law which has been adopted and acted on in many English decisions, and notably in *Taylor* v. *Caldwell*. That case at least makes it clear that

"where, from the nature of the contract, it appears that the parties must from the begin-ning have known that it could not be fulfilled unless, when the time for the fulfilment of the contract arrived, some particular specified thing continued to exist, so that when entering into the contract they must have contemplated such continuing existence as the foundation of what was to be done; there, in the absence of any express or implied warranty that the thing shall exist, the contract is not to be construed as a positive contract, but as subject to an implied condition that the parties shall be excused in case, before breach, performance becomes impossible from the perishing of the thing without default of the contractor."

Thus far it is clear that the principle of the Roman law has been introduced into the English law. The doubt in the present case arises as to how far this principle extends. . . .

I do not think that the principle of the civil law as introduced into the English law is limited to cases in which the event causing the impossibility of perfor-mance is the destruction or non-existence of some thing which is the subject-matter of the contract or of some condition or state of things expressly specified as a condition of it. I think that you first have to ascertain, not neces-sarily from the terms of the contract, but if necessary from necessary infer-ences, drawn from surrounding circumstances recognised by both contracting parties, what is the substance of the contract, and then to ask the question whether that substantial contract needs for its foundation the assumption of the existence of a particular state of things. If it does, this will limit the operation of the general words, and in such case if the contract becomes impossible of performance by reason of the non-existence of the state of things assumed by both contracting parties, as the foundation of the contract, there will be no breach of the contract thus limited. . . .

. . . the plaintiff exhibited on his premises, third floor, 56A, Pall Mall, an announcement to the effect that windows to view the royal coronation proces-sions were to be let, and that the defendant was induced by that announcement to apply to the housekeeper on the premises, who said that the owner was willing to let the suite of rooms for the purpose of seeing the royal procession for both days, but not nights, of June 26 and 27. In my judgment, the use of the rooms was let and taken for the purpose of seeing the royal processions. . . . It was a licence to use rooms for a particular purpose and none other. And in my judgment the taking place of those processions on the days proclaimed along the proclaimed route, which passed 56A, Pall Mall, was regarded by both contracting parties as the foundation of the contract. I think that it cannot reasonably be supposed to have been in the contemplation of the contracting parties, when the contract was made, that the coronation would not be held on the proclaimed days, or the processions not take place on those days along the proclaimed route; and I think that the words imposing on the defendant the obligation to accept and pay for the use of the rooms for the named days, although general and unconditional, were not used with reference to the possibility of the particular contingency which afterwards occurred.

It was suggested in the course of the argument that if the occurrence, on the proclaimed days, of the coronation and the processions in this case were the foundation of the contract, and if the general words are thereby limited or qualified, so that in the event of the non-occurrence of the coronation and processions along the proclaimed route they would discharge both parties from further performance of the contract, it would follow that if a cabman was engaged to take someone to Epsom on Derby-day at a suitable enhanced price for such a journey, both parties to the contract would be discharged in the contingency of the race at Epsom for some reason becoming impossible, but I do not think this follows, for I do not think that in the cab case the happening of the race would be the foundation of the contract. No doubt the purpose of the engager was to go to see the Derby, and that the price was proportionately high; but the cab had no special qualifications for the purpose which led to the selection of the cab for this particular occasion. Any other cab would have done as well. Moreover, I think that, under the cab contract, the hirer, even if the race went off, could have said: "Drive me to Epsom, I will pay you the agreed sum, you have nothing to do with the purpose for which I hired the cab"—and that if the cabman refused he would have been guilty of a breach of contract, there being nothing to qualify his promise to drive the hirer to Epsom on a particular day, whereas, in the case of the coronation, there is not merely the purpose of the hirer to see the coronation processions, but it is the coronation processions and the relative position of the rooms which is the basis of the contract as much for the lessor as the hirer; and I think that if the King, before the coronation day and after the contract, had died, the hirer could not have insisted on having the rooms on the days named. It could not in the cab case be reasonably said that seeing the Derby race was the foundation of the contract, as viewing the processions was of the licence in this case, whereas, in the present case, where the rooms were offered and taken, by reason of their peculiar suitability from the position of the rooms for a view of the coronation processions, surely the view of the coronation processions was the foundation of the contract, which is a very different thing from the purpose of the man who engaged the cab—viz., to see the race—being held to be the foundation of the contract.

Each case must be judged by its own circumstances. In each case one must ask oneself, first: What, having regard to all the circumstances, was the foundation of the contract?; secondly: Was the performance of the contract prevented?; and thirdly: Was the event which prevented the performance of the contract of such a character that it cannot reasonably be said to have been in the contemplation of the parties at the date of the contract? If all these questions are answered in the affirmative (as I think they should be in this case), I think both parties are discharged from further performance of the contract. . . . The test seems to be, whether the event which causes the impossibility was or might have been anticipated and guarded against. . . .

. . . we have to ask ourselves whether the object of the contract was frustrated by the non-happening of the coronation and its processions on the days proclaimed . . . .

When once this is established, I see no difficulty whatever in the case. . . . I think this appeal ought to be dismissed.

Herne Bay Steam Boat Co. v. *Hutton*
[1900–3] All ER Rep. 627

Even the notes in the Law Reports suggest that it is difficult to reconcile *Krell* v. *Henry* with this case. This time the contract was for hire of a pleasure-boat by the defendant from the plaintiff owners for the purposes of viewing a Naval Review of the Fleet at Spithead on 28 June involving the newly crowned King. Again the event was cancelled owing to the King's illness, and the plaintiffs claimed the balance of £200 for the hire of the boat. The defendant counterclaimed for return of the £50 he had paid by way of a deposit, and succeeded at first instance. The plaintiffs' appeal was allowed.

VAUGHAN WILLIAMS LJ I am of opinion that this appeal must be allowed. . . . This contract, I think, placed the ship at the disposal of the defendant for those particular days . . . .

The defendant when hiring this boat had the object in view of taking people to see the Naval Review, and on the next day of taking them round the fleet and also round the Isle of Wight. But it does not seem to me that, because those purposes of the defendant became impossible, it is a legitimate inference that the happening of the Naval Review was contemplated by both parties as the foundation of the contract, so as to bring the case within the doctrine of *Taylor* v. *Caldwell*. On the contrary, when the contract is properly considered, I think that the purposes of the defendant, whether of going to the review or going round the fleet or the Isle of Wight with a party of paying guests, do not make those purposes the foundation of the contract within the meaning of *Taylor* v. *Caldwell*.

Having expressed this view, I do not know that there is any advantage to be gained by in any way defining what are the circumstances which might or might not constitute the happening of a particular contingency the foundation of the contract. I will only say I see nothing to differentiate this contract from a contract by which some person engaged a cab to take him on each of three days to Epsom to see the races, and for some reason, such as the spread of an infectious disease or an anticipation of a riot, the races are prohibited. In such a case it could not be said that he would be relieved of his bargain. So in the present case it is sufficient to say that the happening of the Naval Review was not the foundation of this contract.

ROMER LJ I am of the same opinion. . . . The ship itself had nothing to do with the review or the fleet. It was only a carrier of passengers to see it, and many other ships would have done just as well. It is similar to the hiring of a cab or other vehicle, on which, though the object of the hirer was stated, that statement would not make the object any less a matter for the hirer alone, and would not affect the person who was letting the vehicle for hire. There was not here, by reason of the review not taking place, a total failure of the consideration, nor anything like a total destruction of the subject-matter of the contract. Nor can I on this contract imply any condition which would relieve the defendant from liability to carry out the contract. Conditions are only implied to carry out the presumed intentions of the parties, and I cannot find any such presumed intention here. It follows that in my opinion, so far as the plaintiffs are concerned, the objects of the passengers on this voyage with regard to sightseeing do not form the subject-matter or essence of the contract.

Notes

1. Brownsword offers a reconciliation of the two cases which focuses on the critical differences between the two defendants, namely that *Henry* was a consumer and *Hutton* was not. Henry therefore deserved protection and Hutton did not.

R. Brownsword, 'Towards a Rational Law of Contract', in T. Wilhelmsson (ed.), *Perspectives of Critical Contract Law* (Aldershot, Dartmouth, 1993, 241 at 246–7

For many years, the standard response has been that the cases are reconcilable. Orthodoxy has it that the contract in *Krell v. Henry* was frustrated because the defendant was deprived of substantially the whole benefit of his bargain. Granted, he could have made use of the room on the days in question; but he surely would not have contemplated hiring the rooms were it not for the planned coronation processions. In *Herne Bay*, by contrast, the defendant was not wholly deprived of what he had bargained for. Not only did he have the use of the boat, the fleet actually remained anchored at Spithead notwithstanding the postponement of the coronation. The received wisdom, therefore, is that the cases are distinguishable, the difference being a matter of degree—Henry got no part of his bargain, but Hutton got at least some part of his bargain.

Whilst this strikes me as a plausible explanation of *Krell v. Henry*, it surely ignores the most important point about the *Herne Bay* case. The fact of the matter was that Mr. Hutton was a businessman from Southampton who hired the boat, not for his own pleasure, but for his own profit. His intention was to cram as many paying passengers as possible into the boat, to take such paying passengers as frequently as possible around the bay. His venture, in other words, was a purely commercial speculation—his grievance simply that of an entrepreneur who finds his anticipated profit diminished. It follows that the distinction between the two cases is not one of degree, but one of kind. Whereas Hutton hired the boat while dealing in the course of a business, Henry did not. Accordingly, the fact that the fleet remained anchored at Spithead (a fact much emphasized in the orthodox account) was entirely irrelevant; the contract in the *Herne Bay* case could not have been frustrated *even if the fleet had sailed away.* For, following *Davis Contractors Ltd. v. Fareham UDC*, it is now settled that a plea of frustration cannot succeed on grounds of purely economic loss; and, with the benefit of hindsight, it is clear that his was the sole basis for Hutton's argument.

2. We shall return to the difficulties of reconciling these two cases when we discuss Posner and Rosenfield's economic approach to risk, for they admit that these are 'hard cases' not readily explicable using their theory of the 'superior risk-bearer'.

3. Instead of drawing an analogy between the destruction of the music hall (*Taylor* v. *Caldwell*) and the 'destruction' of the subject-matter of the hire contract, in *Krell* v. *Henry* Vaughan Williams LJ chose a much broader rationale for his judgment, stating that 'the object of the contract was frustrated by the non-happening of the Coronation', a rationale which could potentially justify a wide range of excuses for non-performance, depending upon how the concept of 'object' is understood. In fact, the loosening of the language of frustration evident from this has not proved particularly influential, because, as *Herne Bay* shows, as well as later cases such as *Amalgamated Investments* v. *John Walker*, the English judges have not inclined towards a broad notion of frustration of purpose even where the performance loses much of its value for one party. *Krell* v. *Henry* has achieved a much higher standing in the United States as a leading case on frustration of purpose and as one of the landmarks in the liberalizing process under which the modern doctrines of frustration and impracticability have taken shape (see e.g. A. Kull, 'Mistake, Frustration and the Windfall Principle of Contract Remedies', (1991) 43 *Hastings LJ* 1 at 22 ff.). The position in the USA is well stated by Judge Sloss in the leading case on commercial impracticability, *Mineral Park Land Co.* v. *Howard* ((1916) 172 Cal. 289 p. 458): 172 Cal. 289, 156, p. 458 (1916)): 'A thing is impossible in legal contemplation when it is not practicable; and a thing is impracticable when it can be done only at excessive and unreasonable cost.'

Impracticability is also enshrined as an excuse for delay in delivery or non-delivery with respect to contracts for the sale of goods in §2-615 of the Uniform Commercial Code. In fact, although it offers at first sight a flexible doctrine for a complex world, commercial impracticability has relatively rarely been applied in practice, due to difficulties in applying the rather uncertain test. American commentators frequently have recourse to citing Corbin: 'Where neither custom nor agreement determines the allocation of a risk, the court must exercise its equity powers and pray for the wisdom of Solomon' (*Corbin on Contracts*, §1333, at 371–2, (1962)).

C. Competing Theories of Excuse Doctrines

It is against this background of apparent indeterminacy of doctrine that we can assess some of the main theories used to explain and predict the behaviour of the courts when they are asked to excuse the performance of the contract because of radically changed circumstances. For these purposes, it is unnecessary to draw any distinction between common mistake and the cluster of doctrines associated with frustration, since, as we have seen, these are all essentially concerned with the same issue.

R. Posner and A. Rosenfield, 'Impossibility and Related Doctrines in Contract Law: An Economic Analysis', (1977) 6 *J. Leg. St.* 83 at 89–92, 95–8, 103–4, 110–11

The economics of impossibility. The typical case in which impossibility or some related doctrine is invoked is one where, by reason of an unforeseen or at least unprovided-for event, performance by one of the parties of his obligations under the contract has become so much more costly than he foresaw at the time the contract was made as to be uneconomical (that is, the costs of performance would be greater than the benefits). The performance promised may have been delivery of a particular cargo by a specified delivery date—but the ship is trapped in the Suez Canal because of a war between Israel and Egypt. Or it may have been a piano recital by Gina Bachauer—and she dies between the signing of the contract and the date of the recital. The law could in each case treat the failure to perform as a breach of contract, thereby in effect assigning to the promisor the risk that war, or death, would prevent performance (or render it uneconomical). Alternatively, invoking impossibility or some related notion, the law could treat the failure to perform as excusable and discharge the contract, thereby in effect assigning the risk to the promisee.

From the standpoint of economics . . . discharge should be allowed where the promisee is the superior risk bearer; if the promisor is the superior risk bearer, nonperformance should be treated as a breach of contract. "Superior risk bearer" is to be understood here as the party that is the more efficient bearer of the particular risk in question, in the particular circumstances of the transaction. Of course, if the parties have expressly assigned the risk to one of them, there is no occasion to inquire which is the superior risk bearer. . . .

A party can be a superior risk bearer for one of two reasons. First, he may be in a better position to prevent the risk from materializing. . . . Discharge would be inefficient in any case where the promisor could prevent the risk from materializing at a lower cost than the expected cost of the risky event. In such a case efficiency would require that the promisor bear the loss resulting from the occurrence of the event, and hence that occurrence should be treated as precipitating a breach of contract.

But the converse is not necessarily true. It does not necessarily follow from the fact that the promisor could not at any reasonable cost have prevented the risk from materializing that he should be discharged from his contractual obligations. Prevention is only one way of dealing with risk; the other is insurance. The promisor may be the superior insurer. If so, his inability to prevent the risk from materializing should not operate to discharge him from the contract, any more than an insurance company's inability to prevent a fire on the premises of the insured should excuse it from its liability to make good the damage caused by the fire.

To understand how it is that one party to a contract may be the superior (more efficient) risk bearer even though he cannot prevent the risk from materializing, it is necessary to understand the fundamental concept of risk aversion. Compare a 100 percent chance of having to pay $10 with a one percent chance of having to pay $1000. The expected cost is the same in both cases, yet not everyone would be indifferent as between the two alternatives. Many people would be willing to pay a substantial sum to avoid the uncertain alternative—for example, $15 to avoid having to take a one percent chance of having to pay $1000. Such people are risk averse. The prevalence of insurance is powerful evidence that risk aversion is extremely common, for insurance is simply trading an uncertain for a certain cost. Because of the administrative expenses of insurance, the certain cost (that is, the insurance premium) is always higher, often much higher, than the uncertain cost that it avoids—the expected cost of the fire, of the automobile accident, or whatever. Only a risk-averse individual would pay more to avoid bearing risk than the expected cost of the risk.

The fact that people are willing to pay to avoid risk shows that risk is a cost. Accordingly, insurance is a method (alternative to prevention) of reducing the costs associated with the risk that performance of a contract may be more costly than anticipated. It is a particularly important method of cost avoidance in the impossibility context because the risks with which that doctrine is concerned are generally not preventable by the party charged with nonperformance. As mentioned, if they were, that would normally afford a compelling reason for treating nonperformance as a breach of contract. . . .

The factors relevant to determining which party to the contract is the cheaper insurer are (1) risk-appraisal costs and (2) transaction costs. The former comprise the costs of determining (a) the probability that the risk will materialize and (b) the magnitude of the loss if it does materialize. The amount of risk is the product of the probability of loss and of the magnitude of the loss if it occurs. Both elements—probability and magnitude—must be known in order for the insurer to know how much to ask from the other party to the contract as compensation for bearing the risk in question.

The relevant transaction costs are the costs involved in eliminating or minimizing the risk through pooling it with other uncertain events, that is, diversifying away the risk. This can be done either through self-insurance or through the purchase of an insurance policy (market insurance). . . .

The foregoing discussion indicates the factors that courts and legislatures might consider in devising efficient rules for the discharge of contracts. An easy case for discharge would be one where (1) the promisor asking to be discharged could not reasonably have prevented the event rendering his performance uneconomical, and (2) the promisee could have insured against the occurrence of the event at lower cost than the promisor because the promisee (a) was in a better position to estimate both (i) the probability of the event's occurrence and (ii) the magnitude of the loss if it did occur, and (b) could have self-insured, whereas the promisor would have had to buy more costly market insurance. As we shall see, not all cases are this easy. . . .

The costs of particularized inquiry. . . . A broad standard makes it difficult to predict the outcome of particular cases. If the purpose of contract law (so far as relevant here) is to supply standard contract terms in order to economize on negotiation, it will be poorly served by a legal standard so vague and general that contracting parties will encounter great difficulty in trying to ascertain the judicially implied terms of their contract; if the allocation of risks in the contract is unclear, neither party will know which risks he should take steps to prevent or insure against because he will be held liable if they materialize. . . .

The proper use of the sort of general standard developed earlier in this section is to guide not the decision of particular cases but the formulation of rules to decide groups of similar cases. Our effort in the next part is to show that a set of such rules—rules consistent with the general standard developed earlier—is implicit in the judicial decisions applying impossibility and related doctrines. . . .

. . . the purpose of an economically based discharge doctrine is to supply those contract terms that the parties would have adopted if they had negotiated expressly over them. This proposition has two important corollaries: (1) the doctrine is properly limited to contingencies not specifically provided for in the contract; (2) terms expressly negotiated by the parties must be honored— they may if they wish contract to do the "impossible."

. . . [A] common issue in the impossibility area is the effect of wars or other unexpected events on transportation contracts. To illustrate the relative abilities of the parties to bear risk in cases of this sort, consider the effect on shipping contracts of the closing of the Suez Canal by the Egyptian government in 1956. The closing required ships passing between Atlantic ports and ports in the Middle East to sail around Africa, a longer and more expensive voyage, and gave rise to voluminous litigation. The general result was the enforcement of the shipping contracts. For example, in *Transatlantic Financing Corp. v. United States* [(1966) 363 F. 2d 312] a shipowner argued that its contract with the United States to transport wheat from the U.S. to Iran was discharged by the closing of the Suez Canal. The issue was framed by Judge Wright as follows:

First, a contingency—something unexpected—must have occurred. Second, the risk of the unexpected occurrence must not have been allocated either by agreement or by custom. Finally, occurrence of the contingency must have rendered performance commercially impracticable.

The court found that the closing of the canal was unexpected and that the risk of its occurrence had not been expressly allocated between the parties. It then addressed the ultimate question: was the closing grounds for discharge?

To answer the question, Judge Wright sought to determine which party—the owner of the ship or the government—was the superior risk bearer. His answer addressed itself to the precise elements of our economic framework:

Transatlantic was no less able than the United States to purchase insurance to cover the contingency's occurrence. If anything, it is more reasonable to expect owner-operators of vessels to insure against the hazards of war. They are in the best position to calculate the cost of performance by alternative routes (and therefore to estimate the amount of insurance required), and are undoubtedly sensitive to international troubles which uniquely affect the demand for and cost of their services.

This passage makes the decision on whether to discharge the contract turn on an examination of the key economic parameters that we have identified. The shipowner is the superior risk bearer because he is better able to estimate the magnitude of the loss (a function of delay, and of the value and nature of the cargo, which are also known to the shipowner) and the probability of the unexpected event. Furthermore, shipowners who own several ships and are engaged in shipping along several different routes can spread the risks of delay on any particular route without purchasing market insurance or forcing their shareholders to diversify their common-stock portfolios. And the shipping company could, if it desired, purchase in a single transaction market insurance covering multiple voyages. Of course, the shipper in the particular case—the United States Government—was well diversified too, but decision should (and here did) turn on the characteristics of shippers as a class, if an unduly particularistic analysis is to be avoided. . . .

Doubtful Cases

In many individual, and perhaps some classes of, cases economic analysis—at least of the casual sort employed by the judges and lawyers in contract cases—will fail to yield a definite answer, or even a guess, as to which party is the superior risk bearer. A good example is provided by the coronation cases. Neither party was in a superior position to foresee the event (the illness of

Edward VII) that prevented completion of the contract. To be sure, the building owner had a superior ability to compute the loss, which depended on his ability to rerent the rooms on short notice, and could in principle have bought a single insurance policy on Edward's health at lower cost than the renters could have insured. However, the renters may well have been superior self-insurers: enforcing the contracts would have spread the loss among a relatively large number of renters rather than concentrate it on a relatively few building owners. It is not surprising that the courts divided on whether discharge should be allowed.

The choice in doubtful cases between treating nonperformance as breach or as discharge is similar to the choice in tort law between strict liability and no liability for unavoidable accidents. Pending definitive empirical study, we are inclined to consider the strict-liability solution better in the contract context. . . .

The performing party to a contract is generally the superior risk bearer. Typically, though not invariably, he is better able both to prevent the occurrence of the event rendering performance uneconomical and, if it cannot be prevented at reasonable cost, to estimate the probability of its occurrence. Often, too, he is at least as able as the payor to estimate the magnitude of the loss if the event occurs. . . . Finally, the performer can often self-insure at low cost simply by diversifying the risk across the full range of his contractual obligations.

The performer is not always the superior risk bearer; otherwise there would be no place in contract law for impossibility and related doctrines. But as long as the performer is *generally* the superior risk bearer, assigning the risk to him in cases of doubt—that is, refusing discharge in those cases—can be expected to yield correct results more often than the contrary rule. Accordingly, one is not surprised to find that the courts indeed treat discharge as an excuse, so that nonperformance is a breach of contract unless the case fits one of the exceptions to liability carved out by the impossibility or some other excuse doctrine.

Notes

1. Posner and Rosenfield distinguish between individual cases and groups of cases, seeking to limit the explanatory force of their theory to typical groups of cases where plaintiffs and defendants typically display particular characteristics. The theory starts to break down either in cases like *Transatlantic Financing*, where the shipper does not conform to the norm, or in *sui generis* cases like the coronation cases, in which Posner and Rosenfield resort to bland assertions about promisors. On the other hand, an efficiency-based theory such as this is always useful, if only as a starting point, because it helps us to identify at least some of the important questions. For example, to return to *The Super Servant Two*, it is not difficult to see the defendant barge-owners as the superior risk-bearer, better able to

determine the probability that the barge might sink and the magnitude of the costs (of finding suitable alternative transportation) if the risk should materialise. Both self-insurance and market insurance would probably have been available to the defendants.

2. This analysis ignores, of course, the other social values which might be pursued through contract law. Other commentators have suggested that excuse doctrine, as a departure from freedom of contract under which parties are free to allocate risks amongst themselves, is part of the 'safety net' offered by contract law, just like the principle of unconscionability. A doctrine of frustration can operate as 'an insurance principle limiting individual catastrophic losses. The social policy of risk sharing . . . seems to play a role in contract law' (D. Farber, 'Contract Law and Modern Economic Theory', (1983) 78 *NwUL Rev.* 303 at 336)

In the context of a broader analysis of the principles governing the termination of contracts generally, Hillman puts forward four fairness norms which, he argues, explain judicial approaches to doctrines such as frustration.

R. Hillman, 'An Analysis of the Cessation of Contractual Relations', (1983) 68 *Cornell L. Rev.* 617 at 618–19. © Copyright 1983, Cornell University.

Determining the right of cessation . . . requires further investigation into the meaning of fairness in the cessation context. Four interrelated fairness norms figure prominently in such analysis. A first norm dictates that courts should favor the party with greater equities. Courts effectuate this comparative equities norm by balancing one party's reliance interest and potential gains from performance with the prospect of economic harm to the other party from performance.

A second fairness norm dictates that a party should not knowingly cause harm to another without justification. This harm-avoidance norm insulates a contracting party from severe economic loss resulting either from the other party's attempted cessation or enforcement of the contract in the absence of countervailing harm to that other party.

A third fairness norm is that a party must act reasonably to avoid harming itself. The reasonableness inquiry requires a comparison of a party's conduct to that of similarly situated parties or general community standards. If a party's conduct was unreasonable, the harm the party suffered by reason of cessation or performance is not caused by the other party and therefore the courts will discount it in the balancing process.

A final fairness norm is that each party should benefit from an agreement roughly according to the contract allocation. Courts demonstrate the significance of this reciprocity norm when they consider expected benefits, as well as prospective harm, in balancing interests even when the parties' rights are uncertain because of an unclear cessation approach or because of a gap in the agreement.

Notes

1. In a feminist analysis of impossibility doctrine, Frug contrasts the two articles extracted above. Of the Posner and Rosenfield superior risk-bearer standard she says:

M. J. Frug, *Postmodern Legal Feminism* (New York, Routledge, 1992), 116

Like a phallus, this conceptual proposal is singular, daunting, rigid, and cock-sure. The purpose of the "superior risk bearer" standard, as they see it, is to permit courts to decide impossibility cases as if the singular legitimate deci-sional objective is to facilitate efficient contract planning. . . . Because the pro-posal is focused on a single goal, because it is confidently predicated on an abstract model of contractual relations, and because of its clearly decisive, on or off remedial implications, the characteristics of the Posner/Rosenfield impossibility standard correspond to stereotypical male virtues.

In contrast Hillman's approach is more typically feminine.

Frug, *Postmodern Legal Feminism*, 116–17

Hillman's article presents a sharply contrasting approach to impossibility doctrine. . . . Hillman proposes that courts apply impossibility doctrine to serve a number of goals besides the facilitation of future contract planning. . . . Because Hillman's impossibility proposal is characterized by a concern for mul-tiple objectives, by an appreciation of contextualized relationships, and by a desire to achieve flexibility and sharing in the administration of contract reme-dies, his proposal neatly fits the popular interpretation of Carol Gilligan's depic-tion of the virtuous feminine attitudes toward justice. . . . Simply by concretizing and disaggregating an abstract model of contractual relations and by pointing out the merit of expanding conventional remedial options, Hillman's articles offer a critique of the male model which is both powerful and also reminiscent of typical feminine criticisms of masculinity. That is, Hillman's equitable approach suggests the element of *arbitrariness* in imposing the "superior risk bearer" standard in situations where it might have little to do with what the par-ties actually intended.

2. Frug also criticizes Posner and Rosenfield for taking the discrete exchange as the model of contractual relations. In contrast, Hillman draws explicitly in his work on the relational contract theories of Macneil and

others. Applying relational contract analysis to situations where a continuing contractual relationship has become exceptionally onerous for one party as a result of changes for which the contract contains no planning mechanism lends two key insights. First, it may no longer be meaningful to talk of the allocation of risk between two parties whose relationship is based on principles of co-operation as well as market competition. Second, relational contract analysis calls into question the stark nature of the remedy of discharge, lending support to the argument that the appropriate judicial response in some cases of impracticability is to reformulate or adjust the contract.

Campbell and Harris make the first point very clearly, thereby indicating the unhelpful role which law can play in the context of long-term contracts.

D. Campbell and D. Harris, 'Flexibility in Long-Term Contractual Relationships: The Role of Cooperation', (1993), 20 *JL&S* 166 at 171–2

. . . Here we are dealing . . . with a co-operative response to failures in . . . planning. The classical law is clear about the response that should follow any such failure. This is liability and, indeed, efficient liability, because a firm that cannot make correct long-term decisions should be driven out of business. However, . . . failures under these circumstances lead rather to extra-legal strategies to keep the long-term relationship alive in all but the most acute circumstances.

There is a rather good example of this, widely known and discussed, based on Westinghouse's difficulties over uranium supply contracts in the 1970s. Westinghouse undertook very large long-term uranium supply contracts whilst leaving themselves without full cover of their own supplies. Shifts in the costs of all energy sources—in which the successful cartelization of oil prices by the Organization of Petroleum Exporting Countries (OPEC) played some part, made these contracts potentially ruinous, even for a corporation of the size of Westinghouse. So desperate was the industry as a whole that litigation was instituted by Westinghouse's buyers which Westinghouse tried to defend by a plea of commercial impracticability under UCC 2–615. Joskow has shown that Westinghouse made a number of what one might politely term 'non-optimal decisions' over these supply contracts, and, relying on an analysis of impossibility in contract derived from Posner, he became rather warm in saying that Westinghouse should not be excused performance but should bear the costs of its non-optimal decisions. When, it would seem, the court's adjudication denied Westinghouse relief under 2–615, this was welcomed thus by Maughmer, who shared Joskow's reasoning and amplified his tone:

The extension of relief to Westinghouse via section 2–615 would have created serious inroads in contract law from both a legal and an economic viewpoint. By applying strict tests and cautious interpretations to the elements of section 2–615, courts are able, as a matter of policy, to protect the legal and economic functions of contracts.

Thus the law on 2–615 is now authoritatively stated to be that commercial impracticability is basically a dead letter, for if Westinghouse going bust in order to perform a contract is not a case of commercial impracticability, then nothing ever can be, and Joskow's analysis is taken to be evidence of the value of the Posnerian defence of the classical law of presentiated risk allocation.

All this is very fine, except that a consultation of the list of corporations wound up for insolvency in the United States of America in the 1970s will not yield Westinghouse's name and, indeed, none of the heralded protection of the function of contracts took place. When the court seemed to declare the UCC irrelevant to the solution of this crisis in the energy economy of the United States of America, Westinghouse reached a set of completely renegotiated contracts of supply with its buyers on terms as favourable as the generally adverse business conditions allowed and things continued much as before (though in a changed international energy economy). What one imagines happened is that the buyers realized that they could gain no possible advantage from the liquidation of Westinghouse for, as even Joskow recognized, Westinghouse's pricing and supply policies were designed in good faith to encourage its buyers and thus expand the nuclear energy industry. No alternative more favourable supplier could conceivably become available, especially not after Westinghouse's trauma. Once freed from the panic of the oil crisis and the competitive suspicion and hostility into which the mutually destructive idea of holding Westinghouse to its contracts or of Westinghouse abandoning its buyers led, a sensible co-operative adjustment to the changed circumstances took place.

Note

The works referred to in this extract are: P. Joskow, 'Commercial Impossibility: The Uranium Market and the Westinghouse Case' ((1977) 6 *J. Leg. St.* 119); J. Maughmer, 'Commercial Impracticability as a Contractual Defence', ((1979) 47 *U. Miss.–Kan. City L. Rev.* 655).

3. The second insight of relational contracting is explored further by Halpern.

S. Halpern, 'Application of the Doctrine of Commercial Impracticability: Searching for "The Wisdom of Solomon"', (1987) 135 *U. Penn. L. Rev.* 1123 at 1172–3

When the focus becomes the "contractual entity," specifically, the "mutual reliance and consensual reciprocity inherent in contract," traditional sanctions and excuse doctrines become irrelevant and inappropriate. This is so because they "aim not at continuing the contractual relations but at picking up the pieces of broken contracts and allocating them between the parties on some basis deemed equitable." A contract, particularly a long-term contract, is an inherently incomplete, evolving mechanism rather than an embodiment of fully formulated intent—"[c]omplete consent is a mirage."

The relational model enshrines cooperation, placing specific unilateral economic needs in a subordinate position and consigning to damnation "opportunistic" advantage taking. The analogue is marriage or an on-going partnership and primacy is accorded the goal of continuing the relationship. From these assumptions, both a greater receptivity to arguments of impracticability and frustration, divorced from an intent-based analysis, and some form of equitable adjustment by the court when the parties cannot agree, follow axiomatically. Only a small logical synapse need then be bridged to impose a duty upon an advantaged party to accede to a reasonable proposed modification offered by the disadvantaged party. The fact that the result of such adjustment is the creation of a compromise that neither party may have wanted becomes secondary to the goal of fairly maintaining the relationship. The new operative fiction then is that the law is doing merely what the parties would have done *in the interest of the relationship* had they been required to deal with the matter at its inception.

Just as with the "efficiency" solution, however, the relational adjustment approach to risk allocation raises serious capability problems. The specter of ad hoc jurisprudence and unpredictability and a radical tilting of the precarious balance to be maintained among the conflicting norms haunt its application. Yet, the capability problem, and the balance among competing interests, could in time be ameliorated as experience accumulates. The unique power of our incremental case system, notwithstanding its toll on scholarly patience, is that coherent doctrine frequently can emerge as boundaries are adumbrated through judicial experience. Of greater significance is the conceptual problem inherent in applying a relational-based solution to situations in which the relational norms have been subordinated by the parties.

Notes

1. There is little evidence as yet in the common-law jurisdictions of courts 'taking' the power to adjust contractual relationships. The case of *Aluminium Company of America* v. *Essex Group* ('ALCOA') ((1980) 499 F. Supp. 53), in which a Pennsylvania judge adjusted the price mechanism for a long-term supply of aluminium, has been widely criticized by academic commentators in the USA and rarely followed by the judges. In England, there is the decision in *Staffordshire Area Health Authority* v. *South Staffordshire Waterworks Co.* ([1978] 3 All ER 769) in which the Court of Appeal, led by Lord Denning MR, effectively discharged a 1929 agreement for the supply of water at a fixed price made apparently in perpetuity, so that the parties could negotiate a more realistic deal. However, again that decision appears to stand alone. To

find a more consistent practice of judicial adjustment of contracts, it is necessary to look to the Nordic countries such as Sweden and Finland, where there is a wide range of consumer legislation under which the consumer debtor is protected against unforeseen changes in circumstances. There have also been proposals in these countries to develop a more explicit principle of social *force majeure* as a general excuse doctrine in consumer contracts. We shall look at this in the next section.

2. The difficulty with the relational contract analysis, as Halpern notes, is that it must fall away where the parties conclusively demonstrate that what they want is not a marriage model but a conventional contract model. The parties may well choose to elevate other goals such as competition above the value of co-operation.

D. Consumers, Hardship, and Social *Force Majeure*

In Chapter 8 we looked at Wilhelmsson's discussion of the importance of need-oriented general principles in the modern private law. In this section we shall review some of the arguments surrounding a specific proposal to recognize such a general principle—social *force majeure*. The objective of such a principle is that a consumer debtor who is unable to meet his or her payment obligations under hire purchase contracts, credit card agreements, loans, etc. could be (partially) relieved from payment in the event of unanticipated illness, unemployment, change in family circumstances such as divorce, or some other factor causing poverty and economic hardship. Such a general principle is not universally accepted in the Nordic countries, although it underlies consumer legislation already in place which protects consumer debtors in such circumstances on a partial basis; it could also be said to underlie UK legislation such as the Consumer Credit Act 1974, s. 129(2)(a), which allows courts to alter payment schedules for consumer credit agreements. There is also a precedent for general judicial intervention in the sphere of private law, since the Swedish and Finnish contracts legislation allow the judge to intervene to alter unfair terms in consumer standard form contracts.

The idea of social *force majeure* is closely linked to the objectives of the advanced welfare systems existing in the Nordic countries.

T. Wilhelmsson, *Critical Studies in Private Law* (Deventer, Kluwer, 1992), 181

In the ideology of the welfare state, one of the chief goals given for social development is the attempt to increase citizens' security by creating safeguards against the consequences of illness, unemployment and old age. A principle of social force majeure appears to be a means, albeit relatively unimportant, of furthering this goal. The discussion of the principle thus also implies specification of the extent to which this element of welfare-state ideology should be allowed to influence the law of contract.

Wilhelmsson, a leading proponent of social *force majeure*, has identified the basic framework for the application of general principle.

T. Wilhelmsson, ' "Social Force Majeure": A New Concept in Nordic Consumer Law', (1990) 13 *JCP* 1 at 7–8

The principle of social force majeure could be applied when the following four conditions are fulfilled:

1. The consumer is affected by some *special occurrence* such as an unfavourable change in his health (physical or mental illness, personal injury), work (unemployment, reduced work, strike and lockout), housing (termination of lease) or family (divorce, death or injury of family member). The list is not exhaustive; other occurrences may be relevant, too.
2. There is a *causal connection* between this occurrence and the consumer's difficulties in paying. If the occurrence has not led to economic difficulties for the person concerned—if he is wealthy and has other resources—he may not invoke the principle of social force majeure.
3. If the consumer *foresaw* the special occurrence when he concluded the contract, he cannot rely on it.
4. If the occurrence was caused by the *fault* of the consumer, he is also prevented from invoking the principle of social force majeure.

There are various legal consequences which may be attached to social force majeure. . . .

— Many of the acts, such as the legislation on interest, prescribe that social force majeure should lead to a *mitigation of the sanctions* imposed on a consumer who has not been able to pay on time. It therefore seems quite natural that social force majeure should form a relevant defence against, e.g., the liability to pay damages in case of delay.
— In some cases, when avoidance of a contract would cause economic losses to the consumer, social force majeure should *prevent the other party from avoiding* the contract, at least for some time. Such a consequence would be especially important in the case of permanent contracts concerning necessary utilities like electricity, telephone, and heating. . . .
— In some cases . . . one might recognize the right of the consumer to *withdraw* from a binding contract or to *terminate* a long term contract when he is hit by social force majeure.

He then goes on to address some of the chief arguments made by critics of the principle.

Wilhelmsson, ' "Social Force Majeure" ', *JCP* 10–12

One strategy of opposing a general principle of social force majeure, as well as specific statutes referring to instances of social force majeure, lies within the tradition of defending the "purity" of private law. . . . The problem of social force majeure should not be dealt with in the legislation on consumer sales; it is a problem for *social legislation*.

As such the argument is unanalytical and not very convincing. . . . The argument, however, may be given a material interpretation, referring to the different ways in which the protection offered by private law and social law are financed. Social law distributes resources from public funds but in private law the recognition of one party's needs as legally relevant is always effected at the other party's expense. One may therefore as an argument against a principle of social force majeure make the claim that it is not the responsibility of private parties to finance the supporting of other parties even if those parties are in a socially and economically difficult situation.

In some cases this argument seems very convincing. In relationships between individuals, or even between individuals and small firms, there is obviously often little room for a solution which takes into account the special needs of one party at the expense of the other. The situation is different, however, when one is dealing with a typical relationship in consumer law, that between an individual and a large enterprise. As a matter of fact several of the well-known arguments concerning enterprise liability in the doctrine of private law could easily be used for imposing a "duty to take into account the other party's needs" on such large enterprises. Such a duty may be based on, e.g., the bureaucratic image and economic power of large enterprises and the idea that there should be some tie between power and responsibilities. One may also refer to the well-known possibility of dispersal of risk; an enterprise may often in its price policy be able to arrange for the loss to be borne by a large number of consumers. Finally one could argue, at least in some cases, that liability follows from causing the problem in the first place. If the developing "credit card society" causes problems for persons not able to function properly in that society, then the finance companies, which have made this development possible, should have some responsibility for taking care of the problems. . . .

Social elements in private law are often claimed to be *counterproductive*. For instance, regulations protecting unemployed debtors may in effect make it harder for unemployed persons to obtain credit. Such a critique against protective private law rules does not, however, necessarily affect the principle of social force majeure. As the principle attaches relevance only to difficulties arising after the conclusion of the contract (one may use the term "subsequent needs"), difficulties which were not foreseen by the consumer, the discriminatory effect of the principle in the contract-making phase is probably bearable. It may lead to creditors being more cautious when granting credits; such an effect is, however, not to be regretted.

The claim has been made that the principle of social force majeure is a rather *ineffective* means of protection with limited practical importance. This is obviously true. Even if the doctrine achieves an undisputed position in Nordic law, this would, of course, solve but a very small portion of the problems connected with the overindebtedness of consumers. . . . However, the practical importance of the doctrine may grow if the Consumer Ombudsmen took more frequent steps towards getting social force majeure clauses written into important standard form contracts.

In spite of this possible development, other types of measures, such as informal and easily accessible bankruptcy proceedings resulting in definitive reduction of the debts of the consumer, would, however, still be needed and would certainly also be much more important means of reducing problems connected with the overindebtedness of consumers. . . . The principle should not be seen as the only means of dealing with overindebtedness in connection with illness and unemployment but as one measure complementing other types of measures with the same purpose.

Furthermore, one should not appraise the principle of social force majeure only on the basis of its direct practical effect. The ideological value of the principle should not be overlooked. The principle embodies notions which make it possible to take unemployment and other similar occurrences into account in the legal discourse; it makes these occurrences visible within the realm of private law. The concepts of law are brought closer to the concepts of reality. The argumentation is forced out into the open; it can no longer hide behind the abstract conceptualism of private law. The arguments in a particular case would obviously be affected if the problem were to be described not just in the conventional terms of creditor and debtor, but as a problem concerning the relationship between, e.g., an unemployed debtor and a commercial bank.

Note

Brief details of the role of the Consumer Ombudsman in the Nordic countries can be found in Chapter 11.

VI.   *FORCE MAJEURE* CLAUSES

J. McInnis, 'Frustration and Force Majeure in Building Contracts', in E. McKendrick (ed.), *Force Majeure and Frustration of Contract* **(London, Lloyd's of London Press, 1991), 157–9**

Force majeure is the concept whereby the law recognises that a contracting party may, without fault on its part, provide an excuse for non-performance when circumstances beyond its control render performance impossible. Thus, the clause itself seeks to define, in advance of certain stipulated events, the mutual rights and duties of the parties if those events, which, by definition, are beyond their control, occur. While these clauses frequently occur in practice, their scope and drafting vary considerably in terms of objects and effects.

The purpose of including a *force majeure* clause in one's contract is to seek to limit one's exposure to damages for non-performance. Hence the purpose is to provide a legal standard against which future risks may be allocated. The motivation for parties may be the fear that the court will neither imply a term into a contract excusing performance nor employ the doctrine of frustration.

Most *force majeure* clauses are drafted in two parts. The first part will provide for a list of specified events whose occurrence will excuse performance; examples may include strikes, accidents to machinery, war, licence restrictions or acts of God. The second part of the clause will usually purport to address all other causes howsoever arising. The specificity of the drafting will vary depending upon the circumstances. Current usage may also see the operation of the clause in two stages. Thus, the contract may provide for a set time frame, which, in the case of a stipulated *force majeure* event occurring, is automatically extended by a further set period of time. . . .

The courts construe *force majeure* clauses strictly. In *Lebeaupin* v. *Richard Crispin & Co.* [[1920] 2 KB 714] Mr Justice McCardie stated: "I take it that a *force majeure* clause should be construed in each case with a close attention to the words which precede or follow it, and with a due regard to the nature and general terms of the contract." Thus, by applying a strict rule of interpretation, here the *ejusdem generis* rule, the court denied that the event which was alleged to fall within the compass of the *force majeure* clause did fall within its compass. The criticism of a strict approach to the construction of *force majeure* clauses is that it may not reflect the true intent of the parties or the risks either intended to assume. The reason for this is that many factors are involved in the negotiation of a contract which may preclude either party from being able to draft an all-inclusive clause which provides for every possible event.

Apart from utilising strict rules of interpretation to limit *force majeure*, the law imposes other requirements which reduce the scope of *force majeure* clauses. For example, the obligor must not be at fault and the occurrence of the event must be beyond his control. Obligors must also show that there was no reasonable action that could have been taken to prevent or mitigate the outcome. Thus, where a party to a joint-venture agreement failed to establish that it had taken all reasonable steps to avoid a strike, that party was held to be precluded from relying upon a *force majeure* clause in the agreement.

One last factor that circumscribes the scope of *force majeure* may be referred to, which is that the specific event alleged must be the actual cause of the non-performance. Contractors will be familiar with the difficulty of trying, for example, to attribute delay to discrete events! The cumulative effect of these limitations by the courts is to define very narrowly the ambit of operation of *force majeure*.

One result of these limitations is that contractors are forced to devote additional time to negotiations over their contractual provisions and their eventual length, in effect, creating a "battle of the forms". To win in this battle requires contractors to see that "any foreseeable calamity, however remote, [is] . . . anticipated by careful 'tiger-day' clauses in the drafting of the contract".

Notes

1. In *The Super Servant Two*, the defendants sought to invoke the doctrine of frustration because it was doubtful whether they were protected against being in breach of contract for failure to provide a barge for transportation of the rig by the terms of their contract. These included a clause permitting cancellation in certain conditions:

17. Cancellation

17.1. Wijsmuller has the right to cancel its performance under this Contract whether the loading has been completed or not, in the event of force majeure (sic), Acts of God, perils or danger and accidents of the sea, acts of war, war-like-operations, acts of public enemies, restraint of princes, rulers or people or seizure under legal process, quarantine restrictions, civil commotions, blockade, strikes, lockout, closure of the Suez or Panama Canal, congestion of harbours or any other circumstances whatsoever, causing extra-ordinary periods of delay and similar events and/or circumstances, abnormal increases in prices and wages, scarcity of fuel and similar events, which reasonably may impede, prevent or delay the performance of this contract.

17.2. In the event that Wijsmuller has the right to terminate its performance under this Contract under this clause or clause 4, and the voyage has begun, Wijsmuller shall tender redelivery of the Cargo at a convenient port or place to be determined after consultation with the Principal and when uncontactable to be determined after consultation with the authorised representative of the Principal on board the Transportation Unit, and such delivery shall constitute good delivery under the terms of this Contract.

If Wijsmuller exercises its right under this clause, all payments due to Wijsmuller under the terms of this Contract will be deemed earned by Wijsmuller and the last instalment of the Contract sum as more specifically described in the Conditions of Particular Application of this contract will be reduced or increased pro rata to the distance actually sailed or to be sailed to such convenient port or place and the distance in the normal course of the voyage i.e. between the port or place of delivery and the stated port or place of redelivery of the Cargo.

Bingham LJ held, agreeing with Mr Justice Hobhouse, that the defendants could not invoke the clause if they had not exercised reasonable care when the barge was in their control. However, in principle, such a clause would cover the loss of the barge even *before* the performance of the contract was due. It did not apply only to events occurring during the performance of the contract.

2. It is not always easy to distinguish between a *force majeure* clause and an exclusion clause, subject to the special rules of judicial construction and statutory control which we discussed in Chapter 11. A *force majeure* clause does not exempt the party seeking to rely upon it from a liability which has already arisen; it is not a defence. It restricts the range of the contractual duties owed by that party, typically by providing for a right of cancellation or compulsory adjustment of the contract in the event of a particular occurrence. However, if one follows the Coote theory of exclusion clauses as definitions of, rather than defences, against liability, it appears that the line between the two is quite fine. Indeed, since the courts now approach the construction of the Unfair Contract Terms Act 1977 in such a way as to include within its scope all clauses which have the *effect* of excluding liability, there seems no reason in principle why s. 3(2)(b)(iii), which subjects to the reasonableness test terms in written standard terms of business which appear to give one party the right to render no performance at all to the reasonableness test, should not apply to *force majeure* clauses.

One difference between *force majeure* clauses and ordinary exclusion clauses which one would expect to find is that the former apply only to external events, without the agency of the party seeking protection. However in *The Super Servant Two*, Bingham LJ held that (a) *force majeure* clauses could be drafted to cover events involving a lack of care on the part of the party seeking protection (this was in fact the case with clause 17) but that (b) the rules of construction in *Canada SS Lines Ltd.* v. *The King* ([1952] AC 192) would apply to such a clause, thus requiring very clear words to 'excuse' the party claiming protection from his or her negligence. Commentators have retorted that, if Bingham LJ is right, it follows that clause 17 is not a true *force majeure* clause but rather an exclusion clause (see W. Swadling, 'Judicial Construction of Force Majeure Clauses', in E. McKendrick (ed.), *Force Majeure and Frustration of Contract* (London, Lloyd's of London Press, 1991), 18).

3. Goldberg believes that there is not, or at least should not be, any difference between the application of impossibility doctrine and the interpretation and enforcement of *force majeure* clauses.

V. Goldberg, 'Impossibility and Related Excuses', (1988) 144 *J. Inst. Th. Econ.* 100 at 100–1

The importance of the impossibility defense is circumscribed by the ability of the parties to contract around the law. If the law were too liberal in excusing performance, the parties could narrow the range of acceptable excuses by explicit contractual language. Conversely, if the law were too niggardly, the parties could enumerate additional circumstances that would justify discharge of the contractual obligations. If the law were badly out of line in either direction, the problems could be vitiated by proper drafting of *force majeure* clauses. Such clauses, which are very common, will suspend or discharge a promisor's obligations for "acts of God".

Indeed, it should not really matter whether we frame the problem of excuse in terms of implementing the parties' decision ("Does the fire constitute an act of God that excuses performance as per the initial agreement?") or of identifying the conditions that would justify excusing performance ("Does the fire make performance impossible?"). Even if a contract had no *force majeure* clause, a court might infer that the parties would have included one had they thought of it. That is, instead of recognizing an impossibility defense, the courts could achieve the same result by interpretation of a *force majeure* clause, express or implied.

Regardless of how the doctrine is labelled, courts, when considering a plea to excuse performance, should be constrained by the fundamental question: what would the parties have chosen? I will argue that, as a general rule, parties would not agree to excuse performance because of changed market conditions (neither supply nor demand shocks). The fact that market prices have doubled or tripled would be irrelevant. Parties are more likely to excuse performance if the supervening events adversely effect the costs of performing this particular contract for reasons that are essentially unrelated to overall market conditions.

Looked at from this perspective, the questions posed by way of preliminary issues in *The Super Servant Two* appear misconceived. If the loss of one barge out of two is sufficient to trigger the application of the *force majeure* clause, then it should also be sufficient to excuse the defendants from performance under the general law of frustration.

4. In *The Super Servant Two*, the barges provided by the defendants were specialized means of transportation offering the best method for getting the rig from its place of manufacture to its final location. In those circumstances, it is to be anticipated that the defendants would seek to protect themselves through a *force majeure* clause. Yates explains the incidence of such clauses in commercial contracts in the following terms:

D. Yates, 'Drafting Force Majeure and Related Clauses', (1991) 3 *JCL* 186 at 187

Force majeure clauses are particularly common in long-term construction contracts, such as shipbuilding agreements, turnkey projects, public works, infrastructure projects, joint ventures, management and marketing agreements, long-term transport contracts, and other contracts requiring a regular performance of services or delivery of goods from a particular source of supply. They are encountered infrequently in short term contracts involving a single transaction, where the parties may be willing as a matter of commercial practice either to take the risk of a major disaster affecting performance, or to hedge against it by, for example, taking out market insurance or pricing the goods so as to underwrite any potential losses over time on a turnover and profit related basis.

The *Super Servant Two* contract would appear to fall into the first category.

Questions

1. Is there a consistency of approach between both the tests and the policies used by English judges when they apply the doctrines of common mistake and frustration? Would you suggest any changes to achieve greater consistency?

2. Why do you think that the English courts apply stricter rules on the discharge of contracts for mistake and frustration than those which have developed in the United States?

3. Relational contract theory suggests that the parties will seek to avoid situations where one party finds it excessively difficult to perform a contract by compromising their differences. Is there a close and consistent relationship between the rules on discharge and those which apply to determine the enforceability of variations of contract (see Ch. 6)?

4. To what extent does the concept of social *force majeure* come into conflict with the paradigm notion of bargain?

5. Comparing the judicial approaches to the discharge of contracts and the interpretation and application of *force majeure* clauses, to what extent do you think the law encourages parties to plan their relationships in advance?

13

Performance, Breach, and Termination

I. INTRODUCTION

The performance of contracts is the norm. The existence of rules governing breach of contract and regulating the remedies of the innocent party presupposes the existence of a duty to perform contracts. The extent of that duty is determined by the contents of the contract, which, as we have seen, is composed in part of the matters agreed by the parties (or imposed by one party in some cases), plus any terms implied in law and in fact. Some legal systems imply a general duty of good faith in performance (see §205 of the US Restatement (Second) of Contracts and §242 of the German Civil Code) which conditions the manner in which contracts must be performed.

Breach of a contract generally occurs where one party either fails to perform, performs late, or performs defectively. *Complete non-performance* normally gives rise to a right on the part of the innocent party to terminate the contract, on the grounds of substantial failure of performance (for the meaning of termination, see Ch. 10) or on the grounds of repudiation. *Late* or *defective performance* entitles the innocent party to damages to make good any loss, and may give rise to a right to terminate the contract, according to the principles discussed in Chapter 10. As we saw in Chapter 12, if, for example, the non-performance of the contract is the consequence of a frustrating event, or performance is rendered impossible because the parties made a mistake, this does not give rise to a breach, as the contract is *discharged*.

It should not be inferred from these comments that a party who has not rendered performance will only be responsible and thence guilty of breach of contract if he or she is at fault. The general premiss of the common law of contract (although not a premiss shared with a civil-law system such as that in Germany) is that responsibility for breach of contract will arise without regard to fault on the part of the promisor. If a manufacturer delivers a defective good directly to a purchaser on the basis of a contract of sale, it does not matter how the goods come to be defective. The manufacturer will be responsible. This is not, however, a universal truth: under a contract for medical services, for example, a doctor promises only to take reasonable care, using her professional skills, to bring about the desired result. She does not *guarantee* a particular result (e.g. the success of a vasectomy operation: *Thake* v. *Maurice* [1986] QB 644). Von Mehren suggests some factors which might influence the choice between strict and fault liability, where this is possible, but concludes overall that the arguments for and against each position are not decisive.

A. von Mehren, 'A General View of Contract', in *International Encyclopedia of Comparative Law* (Tübingen/The Hague, Mohr/Nijhoff, 1982), vol. vii, ch. 1, p. 84

If a party believes there is a significant risk that future circumstances beyond his control could render his performance significantly more difficult, he would, unless he is a risk preferrer, bargain for the fault principle (where the legal order does not supply it as an optional rule) so far as his own performance was concerned. Conversely, a risk averse or risk neutral party who believes that future circumstances beyond the other party's control could render that party's performance significantly more difficult would prefer the strict liability rule which provides insurance against nonperformance and also avoids informational difficulties that may attach to the fault rule's operation. Each of these parties would presumably have to make price concessions to obtain the rule preferred by him. It seems, therefore, that neither principle has a clear claim to represent the solution that the parties would normally reach if they were to regulate the issue explicitly in their contract. The strict liability principle perhaps has a certain appeal from the perspective of the administration of justice as litigation of the issue of fault, which can be costly, is avoided. On the other hand, there may well be social objections to requiring obligors to insure their promised performances unless they are well enough advised or sufficiently experienced to provide otherwise in the contract.

Within limits, the parties are free to depart from the background rules of breach and liability laid down by the general law and to design their own contracts. For example, they may include exclusion clauses or *force majeure* clauses which affect the allocation of risks and obligations. They may also plan a remedial structure enhancing or reducing the right of the innocent party to terminate the contract in the event of breach by the other party, or setting in advance the sums payable in the form of compensation in the event of certain types of breach. The general objective of such structures, whether planned or arising under the general law, is to provide incentives to the parties to perform the contract effectively and punctually. In discussing certain aspects of breach, this chapter focuses on the role of the self-help remedy of termination, and in particular on termination as a right of the innocent party faced with an anticipatory breach or repudiation of a contract. Harris offers us a general evaluation of termination as a remedy.

D. Harris, 'Incentives to Perform, or Break Contracts', [1992] *CLP* 29 at 35–6

The most powerful incentive to perform provided by the general law . . . comes from the rules on termination for breach. . . . Termination is a unilateral act which does not require prior approval from the court. If the defendant disputes whether the plaintiff was entitled to terminate, he must bring proceedings and allow the plaintiff the favoured defence position in the litigation. Termination is a potent form of self-help by which the plaintiff can avoid having to begin litigation with its costs and uncertainties. He can also act quickly, and may be able to avoid the risk of the defendant's insolvency. If the plaintiff is entitled to terminate, there is no judicial power to control his choice, whether under the court's discretion or by a test of reasonableness: the sole issue is whether the plaintiff was legally entitled to terminate. The plaintiff is under no obligation to give the defendant any reasons for his decision to terminate. The court will uphold his decision if he can later show that at the time there were legal grounds for his action.

Fear of termination provides the defendant with a powerful incentive not to commit a serious breach because the loss which termination may impose on the defendant can greatly exceed any damages recoverable by the plaintiff. So the defendant's fear of his own potential loss may give him a most powerful incentive not to break the contract. By terminating the contract, the plaintiff cuts off further performance on both sides. He notifies the defendant that he will not accept any further performance from him, and at the same time he releases himself (the plaintiff) from any remaining obligations to perform his side of the contract. (After termination, the only liability of the plaintiff is for any breach of contract which he had committed before the time of termination.) So the defendant may lose all the benefit or profit which he expected from performance of the plaintiff's remaining obligations. If the defendant had incurred expenditure in performing (or preparing to perform) his side, he may lose all the benefit of that expenditure if it is not saleable to a third party. So by terminating, the plaintiff is empowered in some circumstances to impose a heavy loss on the defendant: it is the fear of this which provides the defendant with the strongest incentive to perform. For instance, if the buyer justifiably rejects goods which are of no interest to any one else because they were designed to suit the buyer's unique requirements, the seller will be left in the position of bearing the whole cost of manufacture. His fear of wasting his effort may be more powerful in encouraging performance than his fear of liability in damages. Fear of his own loss may exceed his fear of paying for the plaintiff's loss. But the remedy of termination brings *both* losses to bear on the defendant: he cannot recover his own loss to date, but the plaintiff can still sue him for damages for the plaintiff's loss in not getting the benefit of the defendant's complete performance.

Looking at the other side of the equation, Rosett points to the dilemma faced by the innocent party whose contract has been repudiated by the other side.

A. Rosett, 'Partial, Qualified and Equivocal Repudiation of a Contract', (1981) 81 *Colum. L. Rev.* 93 at 93–4

Few prospects are more threatening for a party to an important contract than that raised by the other party's statement that he will not perform. And yet, the power to repudiate a contractual obligation, thereby limiting risks and reducing overall transaction costs, actually encourages the making of contracts. From an economic perspective, less-than-optimal choices can be improved if parties can call off bad deals. Thus, recognition of a party's power to terminate an onerous agreement contributes to the economic efficiency of contract.

In addition, the social institution of contract remains workable in part because the potential promisemaker knows that he has options; he will always have a way out. To remain civilized, contract must be tolerable; its tendency for insatiable demands must be controlled. There must be some way to liquidate obligations, pay off mistakes, and try again. Repudiation serves this function. Repudiation enhances the moral dimension of contract as well, for there would be little moral significance in fulfilling a contractual obligation that one is powerless to abrogate. The more interesting human moral dilemmas are not about the captains who go down with their ships, but about those who wrestle with the tough questions: whether now is the time to abandon ship, and how to salvage as much as possible from the disaster.

For over a century, authorities in the law of contracts have struggled with the legal consequences of repudiation, particularly when it precedes the time of performance. Gradually, a clear set of principles, . . . has developed. Yet these principles are not easily applied to many of the crises lawyers regularly encounter when counseling clients. However clear the principles may appear, in practice a lawyer may have difficulty advising a client how to behave in a specific situation.

Uncertainties may arise in even the simplest cases: a buyer is told by a seller that the promised goods will not be coming; an owner watches a contractor pull his construction crew and equipment off the job; an employee under contract is informed that "your services will not be required." Whenever a transaction goes sour, the party who believes the contract has been repudiated must decide whether he is justified in cancelling the deal, stopping his own performance, and mitigating the consequences of breach by promptly finding a substitute in the market. Is a repudiation always a present breach of contract that gives rise to a claim for damages measured by the injured party's expectations? Is it a failure of a condition that suspends the other party's obligation to perform? Or does it have both effects?

Notes

1. Rosett's comments are made in the context of American law, where problems of repudiation are dealt with in the Restatement (Second) of Contracts, but they are equally applicable to English law.

2. Two points emerge from Rosett's analysis. First, although it might at first sight seem destructive to allow one party to pull out of a contract, leaving the other party to terminate and to claim damages instead, Rosett argues that it might bring about a net increase in welfare overall for a bad bargain to be brought to an end prematurely. For example, the respective capacities of the parties may be better used elsewhere in the market-place, and not in a contract linking them together. Second, despite long experience with problems of repudiation in the courts, uncertainties remain for the innocent party in knowing how to respond to the statements and acts of the other party.

3. The next case deals with the dilemmas faced by an innocent party where the contract-breaker has repudiated the contract even before the time for performance is due (anticipatory breach).

II. ANTICIPATORY BREACH

Fercometal SARL v. Mediterranean Shipping Co. SA (The Simona)
[1988] 2 All ER 742

LORD ACKNER

The facts

These can be shortly stated. On 11 June 1982 the charterers entered into a charterparty with the owners for the carriage of a part cargo of 6,000 tonnes of hot rolled steel coils from Durban to Bilbao in the vessel Simona. Box 19 in the charterparty, which was headed 'Cancelling date (Cl. 10)', contained the words 'LAYCAN 3/9 JULY, 1982'.

So far as material, cl 10 provided:

'Should the vessel not be ready to load (whether in berth or not) on or before the date indicated in Box 19, Charterers have the option of cancelling this contract, such option to be declared, if demanded, at least 48 hours before vessel's expected arrival at port of loading . . .' . . .

On 2 July the charterers received a telex message from the owners requesting an extension of the cancelling date, so as to cover the cargo loading dates from 13 to 16 July. Within a couple of hours there was a conversation between Mr Schweitzer, the managing director of the charterers, and Mr Storm, the managing director of the owners in South Africa. In that conversation Mr Schweitzer pressed on Mr Storm the gravity of the situation regarding the delivery of the steel to Spain before August, because of the holiday period in Spain which commenced in the early part of that month. Mr Storm suggested that the cargo be overcarried to North Europe and then brought back south, by which time the holidays would be over in Spain. This, however, was not acceptable and shortly after this conversation and on the same day a telex was sent from the charterers to the owners stating that the proposed new loading dates were not acceptable and, accordingly, that the charterers were cancelling the contract. Again, on that day, 2 July, the charterers lined up the fixture of the Leo Tornado, subject to the cancelling of the Simona. This vessel was 'spot' at Durban and would be taking only the charterers' steel. In the words of the arbitrators, she was a 'better bet for making Spain before the holidays'.

It is common ground that the action of the charterers in giving the notice purporting to cancel the contract was premature. It constituted an anticipatory breach and repudiation of the charterparty, because the right of cancellation could not be validly exercised until the arrival of the cancellation date, some seven days hence. It is equally common ground that this repudiation was not accepted by the owners. On 5 July the owners had a change of heart and telexed that the Simona would start loading on 8 July. Although it was possible at the time this telex was received to withdraw the notice of cancellation of the charterparty, since the notice had not been accepted, and to refrain from fixing the Leo Tornado, the charterers did not by this stage trust the owners. They preferred to confirm the fixture of the Leo Tornado, which in any case assured them of a speedier arrival time at Bilbao. They accordingly on that day confirmed the fixture. . . .

On 8 July the Simona arrived in the morning and tendered notice of readiness. The charterers rejected this notice, indorsing it 'vessel off charter 2/7', and on that day they began loading steel into the Leo Tornado. The owners' notice of readiness was in fact a false notice of readiness, because they were not able immediately to load the charterers' cargo. They were then loading other cargo, namely the copper and/or the granite.

[The charterers rejected the owners' notice on 8 July and began to load the cargo onto the substitute ship. The owners brought a claim for dead freight. The claim went to arbitration, where it was upheld on the grounds that the charterers had wrongfully repudiated the contract which relieved the owners from complying with their own obligations. Consequently it did not matter that the owners had failed to present the ship ready to load and would not affect their claim for damages. The charterers appealed to the High Court and were successful. The shipowners challenged this decision unsuccessfully in the Court of Appeal and then appealed again to the House of Lords. Their appeal was allowed by the House of Lords.]

The effect of a repudiation

The earlier authorities, when faced with a wrongful neglect or refusal, were concerned to absolve the 'innocent party' from the need to render useless performance, which the repudiating buyer had indicated he no longer wanted. In *Jones v Barkley* (1781) 99 ER 434 one finds the seeds of the later doctrine of accepted anticipatory breach. Lord Mansfield CJ said (99 ER 434 at 439–440):

'One need only state what the agreement, tender, and discharge, were, as set forth in the declaration. It charges, that the plaintiffs offered to assign, and to execute and deliver a general release, and tendered a draft of an assignment and release, and offered to execute and deliver such assignment, but the defendant absolutely discharged them from executing the same, *or any assignment and release whatsoever.* The defendant pleads, that the plaintiff did not actually execute an assignment and release; and the question is, whether there was a sufficient performance. Take it on the reason of the thing. The party must shew he was ready; but, if the other stops him on the ground of an intention not to perform his part, it is not necessary for the first to go farther, and do a nugatory act.' (Lord Mansfield CJ's emphasis.)

In *Cort and Gee v Ambergate Nottingham and Boston and Eastern Junction Rly Co* (1851) 17 QB 127 the plaintiffs agreed to manufacture a quantity of iron chairs for the defendant's railway. The defendant, having accepted some of the chairs, informed the plaintiffs that it had as many chairs as it required and that no further chairs would be accepted. The plaintiffs thereupon treated themselves as discharged from all further obligations and commenced proceedings against the defendant for wrongfully refusing to accept the chairs. They pleaded that from the time of making of the contract until the defendant's refusal they were ready and willing to perform their obligations, but that they had been discharged from further performance of the contract by the defendant's repudiation. The defendant denied that an oral renunciation prior to the time for performance excused the plaintiffs from the need to show that they were ready and willing to perform at the time set for performance. Thus, the question was: what sort of readiness and willingness (if any) does a plaintiff have to show in order to maintain an action for wrongful repudiation? It was held that the plaintiff's averment was sufficient and Lord Campbell CJ said (17 QB 127 at 144):

'In common sense the meaning of such an averment of *readiness and willingness* must be that noncompletion of the contract was not the fault of the plaintiffs, and that they were disposed and able to complete it if it had not been renounced by the defendants.' (Lord Campbell CJ's emphasis.)

The above case and some of the earlier ones were considered in *Hochster v De la Tour* (1853) 2 E & B 678, where a courier sued his employer who had written in before the time for performance had arrived that his services were no longer required. This was a clear anticipatory breach since, before the time had arrived at which the defendant was bound to perform his contractual obligation, he had evinced an intention no longer to be bound by his contractual obligations. At the conclusion of his judgment Lord Campbell CJ said (2 E & B 678 at 693–694):

'If it should be held that, upon a contract to do an act on a future day, a renunciation of the contract by one party dispenses with a condition to be performed in the meantime by the other, there seems no reason for requiring that other to wait till the day arrives before seeking his remedy by action: and the only ground on which the condition can be dispensed with seems to be, that the renunciation may be treated as a breach of the contract.'

Frost v Knight (1872) LR 7 Exch 111 was a case of a breach of promise to marry the plaintiff as soon as his (the defendant's) father should die. During the father's lifetime the defendant refused absolutely to marry the plaintiff and the plaintiff sued him, his father still being alive. When the case was argued before the Court of Exchequer Kelly CB concluded that there could be no actual breach of a contract by reason of non-performance so long as the time for the performance had not yet arrived (see LR 5 Exch 322). On appeal to the Exchequer Chamber Cockburn CJ said (LR 7 Exch 111 at 114):

'The promisee has an inchoate right to the performance of the bargain, which becomes complete when the time for performance has arrived. In the mean time he has the right to have the contract kept open as a subsisting and effective contract. Its unimpaired and unimpeached efficacy may be essential to his interests. His rights acquired under it may be dealt with by him in various ways for his benefit and advantage. Of all such advantage the repudiation of the contract by the other party, and the announcement that it never will be fulfilled, must of course deprive him. It is therefore quite right to hold that such an announcement amounts to a violation of the contract *in omnibus*, and that upon it the promisee, if so minded, may at once treat it as a breach of the entire contract, and bring his action accordingly.'

The innocent party's option

When one party wrongly refuses to perform obligations, this will not automatically bring the contract to an end. The innocent party has an option. He may either accept the wrongful repudiation as determining the contract and sue for damages or he may ignore or reject the attempt to determine the contract and affirm its continued existence. Cockburn CJ in *Frost v Knight* (1872) LR 7 Exch 111 at 112–113 put the matter thus:

'The law with reference to a contract to be performed at a future time, where the party bound to performance announces prior to the time his intention not to perform it . . . may be thus stated. The promisee, if he pleases, may treat the notice of intention as inoperative, and await the time when the contract is to be executed, and then hold the other party responsible for all the consequences of non-performance: but in that case he keeps the contract alive for the benefit of the other party as well as his own; he remains subject to all his own obligations and liabilities under it, and enables the other party not only to complete the contract, if so advised, notwithstanding his previous repudiation of it, but also to take advantage of any supervening circumstance which would justify him in declining to complete it. On the other hand, the promisee may, if he thinks proper, treat the repudiation of the other party as a wrongful putting an end to the contract, and may at once bring his action as on a breach of it; and in such action he will be entitled to such damages as would have arisen from the non-performance of the contract at the appointed time, subject, however, to abatement in respect of any circumstances which may have afforded him the means of mitigating his loss.' . . .

The way in which a 'supervening circumstance' may turn out to be to the advantage of the party in default, thus relieving him from liability, is illustrated by *Avery v Bowden*, where the outbreak of the Crimean war between England and Russia made performance of the charterparty no longer legally possible. The defendant, who prior to the outbreak of the war had in breach of contract refused to load, was provided with a good defence to an action for breach of contract, since his repudiation had been ignored. As pointed out by Parker LJ in his judgment ([1987] 2 Lloyd's Rep 236 at 240 [in the Court of Appeal in this case]), the law as stated in *Frost v Knight* has been reasserted in many cases since, and in particular in *Heyman v Darwins Ltd* [1942] AC 356 at 361, where Viscount Simon LC said:

'The first head of claim in the writ appears to be advanced on the view that an agreement is automatically terminated if one party "repudiates" it. That is not so. As SCRUTTON, L.J., said in *Golding* v. *London & Edinburgh Insurance Co., Ltd.* ((1932) 43 Ll LR 487 at 488): "I have never been able to understand what effect the repudiation by one party has unless the other accepts it." If one party so acts or so expresses himself, as to show that he does not mean to accept and discharge the obligations of a contract any further, the other party has an option as to the attitude he may take up. He may, notwithstanding the so-called repudiation, insist on holding his co-contractor to the bargain and continue to tender due performance on his part. In that event, the co-contractor *has the opportunity of withdrawing from his false position, and even if he does not, may escape ultimate liability because of some supervening event not due to this own fault which excuses or puts an end to further performance.*' (Parker LJ's emphasis.)

If an unaccepted repudiation has no legal effect ('a thing writ in water and of no value to anybody': per Asquith LJ in *Howard v Pickford Toll Co Ltd* [1951] 1 KB 417 at 421), how can the unaccepted acts of repudiation by the charterers in this case provide the owners with any cause of action? It was accepted in the Court of Appeal by counsel then appearing for the owners that it was an inevitable inference from the findings made by the arbitrators that the Simona was not ready to load the charterers' steel at any time prior to the charterers notice of cancellation on 12 July. Counsel who has appeared before your Lordships for the owners has not been able to depart from this concession. Applying the well-established principles set out above, the anticipatory breaches by the charterers not having been accepted by the owners as terminating the contract, the charterparty survived intact with the right of cancellation unaffected. The vessel was not ready to load by close of business on the cancelling date, viz 9 July, and the charterers were therefore entitled to and did give what on the face of it was an effective notice of cancellation. . . .

. . . When A wrongfully repudiates his contractual obligations in anticipation of the time for their performance, he presents the innocent party, B, with two choices. He may either affirm the contract by treating it as still in force or he may treat it as finally and conclusively discharged. There is no third choice, as a sort of via media, to affirm the contract and yet be absolved from tendering further performance unless and until A gives reasonable notice that he is once again able and willing to perform. Such a choice would negate the contract being kept alive for the benefit of *both* parties and would deny the party who unsuccessfully sought to rescind the right to take advantage of any supervening circumstance which would justify him in declining to complete.

Towards the conclusion of his able address, counsel for the owners sought to raise what was essentially a new point, argued before neither the arbitrators, Leggatt J nor the Court of Appeal. He submitted that the charterers' conduct had induced or caused the owners to abstain from having the ship ready prior to the cancellation date. Of course, it is always open to A, who has refused to accept B's repudiation of the contract, and thereby kept the contract alive, to contend that, in relation to a particular right or obligation under the contract, B is estopped from contending that he, B, is entitled to exercise that right or that he, A, has remained bound by that obligation. If B represents to A that he no longer intends to exercise that right or requires that obligation to be fulfilled by A and A acts on that representation, then clearly B cannot be heard thereafter to say that he is entitled to exercise that right or that A is in breach of contract by not fulfilling that obligation. If, in relation to this option to cancel, the owners had been able to establish that the charterers had represented that they no longer required the vessel to arrive on time because they had already fixed the Leo Tornado and, in reliance on that representation, the owners had given notice of readiness only after the cancellation date, then the charterers would have been estopped from contending they were entitled to cancel the charter-party. There is, however, no finding of any such representation, let alone that the owners were induced thereby not to make the vessel ready to load by 9 July. . . .

. . . The non-readiness of the vessel by the cancelling date was in no way induced by the charterers' conduct. It was the result of the owners' decision to load other cargo first.

In short, in affirming the continued existence of the contract, the owners could only avoid the operation of the cancellation clause by tendering the vessel ready to load on time (which they failed to do), or by establishing (which they could not) that their failure was the result of the charterers' conduct in representing that they had given up their option, which representation the owners had acted on by not presenting the vessel on time. I would therefore dismiss the appeal with costs.

Notes

1. The facts of this case require some amplification. The charterers' actions in purporting to cancel the contract amounted to wrongful repudiation; their right to cancel under the contract had not yet arisen, and the shipowners' conduct in saying that they might not have the ship ready by 9 July did not amount to conduct giving the charterers themselves the right to terminate the contract and to seek a remedy for anticipatory breach. The shipowners had the right to elect whether to accept the charterers' repudiation or to carry on and perform the contract. They elected to carry on and perform the contract. However, it was an agreed fact that they were never ready to do so; this in turn gave the charterers the right to cancel under the contract. Lord Ackner quotes Asquith LJ as saying that an unaccepted repudiation is a 'thing writ in water and of no value to anybody'—here the conduct of the charterers in purporting to cancel the contract was rendered a thing 'writ in water' by the shipowners' refusal to accept it, and consequently the contract between the charterers and the ship owners proceeded as if nothing had happened.

It is clear that both parties here wanted the best of both worlds. The charterers made a better bargain in relation to the substitute ship and its time of arrival at the ultimate destination, and wished to escape from their contract with the first shipowners. The first shipowners wanted to load other cargo first but also still wanted to deal with the charterers. Had the shipowners asserted that the ship would not be able to take the cargo of the charterers at all, that would have been conduct giving rise to anticipatory breach and termination. Their argument that the charterers would not have provided the cargo even if the ship had been ready on the appointed day is unsuccessful because the ship was not ready and the charterers were able to exercise their contractual right to cancel. The contract was unaffected by the charterers' by then obvious desire to ship their cargo on another vessel. On the principle of the balance of equities, suggested by Hillman in Chapter 12, we can say that the shipowners received their just deserts: the charterers would not have looked for another vessel if they had not lost their faith in the shipowners when the latter began to shift their position over the availability of loading. A rather different view of the shipowners' conduct is taken by Atiyah in the extract below.

2. In the extract below, Atiyah offers a comparison of termination and formation of contract. He also highlights the difficulties that can be experienced by both parties. It may be difficult for the innocent party to assess whether there is conduct amounting to repudiation or whether treating the conduct as a repudiation might result in an action by the other party for wrongful repudiation. It is also hard to tell whether an attempt at

repudiation has been rejected by the other party who is still expecting and offering performance.

P. S. Atiyah, *An Introduction to the Law of Contract*, 4th edn. (Oxford, Clarendon Press, 1989), 420–2

Rescission, termination, and formation of contract

Although the courts do not appear to have explicitly recognized it, the principles governing the cases of rescission and termination for breach are closely parallel to the principles governing the formation of a contract, and therefore also to the principles governing the termination of a contract by agreement. In the first place, it is not what a party intends that matters, but the reasonable interpretation that may be (and is) placed upon his words and behaviour by the other party. In the second place, a repudiation (or sometimes a different kind of breach or ground for rescission) is treated very much like a contractual offer in that it has no legal effect until it is *accepted*. The other party is entitled either to accept or to affirm the contract, and thus, in effect, to reject the proposed repudiation or grounds for rescission. Thirdly, an acceptance may itself be express, or may be inferred from conduct. And fourthly, a party may be held to have accepted or rejected a repudiation (or other breach or grounds for rescission) even where he does not mean to do so, because he has led the other to believe that he means to do so, and thereby induced him to act to his prejudice. This last possibility may be treated as an illustration of estoppel. . . .

These attempts to treat rescission and termination for breach as closely as possible to the principles governing the formation of contracts and termination by agreement possibly reflect the classical tradition. They seem prompted by a desire to see legal rights as deriving from the exercise of choices, and intentional behaviour, rather than from conduct. They probably work well enough in most cases; but they do give rise to a number of difficulties. First, it must be appreciated that in this field—unlike the case of formation or termination of contract by express agreement—an 'acceptance' or a 'rejection' by inference from conduct is perhaps more often the rule than the exception. Thus it is often difficult to say whether a contract has been 'affirmed' so that the innocent party has lost his right to rescind or terminate. . . .

A . . . source of difficulty is that the innocent party is often placed in a dilemma, following a repudiation or breach, which does not always seem adequately allowed for by the courts. In a case like the *Fercometal* case, for instance, where the charterer wrongfully repudiates by saying that he cannot load the ship when loading is due, the innocent party is often placed in difficulties. On the one hand, he wants to claim damages for this breach, as he thinks it to be; but on the other hand, in the immediate hurly-burly of commercial activity it is not always clear what is a breach and what is a justified demand. So in such a case the shipowner may be desperately trying to do two things at once.

He is trying to keep the contract alive, and so must be ready to perform if at the last minute the charterer says he will perform after all; and at the same time he is trying to ensure that if the charterer fails to load, there may still be time to load the ship with another cargo. The innocent party can easily slip up in this situation, and may then be penalized either by reduced damages or even by being told that he cannot sue at all—as in the *Fercometal* case itself.

Further thoughts on the 'offer' theory of termination are provided by A. Shea, 'Discharge from Performance of Contracts by Failure of Condition' ((1979) 42 *MLR* 623 at 631–2); and P. Nienaber, 'The Effect of Anticipatory Repudiation: Principle and Policy' ([1962] *CLJ* 213 at 220–3).

3. Lord Ackner summarizes the doctrine of anticipatory breach as giving the innocent party the right of election between accepting the repudiation and suing for damages before the time for performance is due or affirming the contract and waiting until performance is due. The doctrine of anticipatory breach is not without its critics. For example, Williston never supported it throughout his career.

E. Tabachnik, 'Anticipatory Breach of Contract', [1972] *CLP* 149 at 149–50

The doctrine has had to weather severe attacks from eminent contract lawyers. Professor Williston denounced it as "illogical and unjust" and added "that the matter was so plain that theoretical discussion was hardly possible."[1] Opposition to the doctrine proceeds on the premise that a promise cannot be broken until the time for its performance arrives. The problem may be stated in the terms of a leading case. In April the defendant contracts to employ the plaintiff as his courier and it is provided that the plaintiff's service is to begin on June 1 and to continue for three months thereafter. The defendant then repudiates the contract on May 11 and the plaintiff brings an action for damages on May 22, *i.e.* before the time of performance has arrived. It is asserted in the name of logic that one cannot in May breach a contract which is only to be performed in June.

There are other arguments for rejecting the doctrine—it can seem harsh to the party in breach that he finds himself liable in damages before he finds himself liable to perform. There is also the question of price fluctuation in contracts for the supply of goods and services in the future—is the court to assess damages on the basis of the delivery price or the current price?

4. Despite these objections, the doctrine of anticipatory breach has become firmly entrenched in both the United Kingdom and the USA (see

---

[1] Williston, *Contracts* (rev. ed.), para. 1307. See also Williston on "Repudiation of Contracts," 14 Harv. L.R. (1901), 317 and 421; reprinted in *Selected Readings on the Law of Contract*, p. 1044.

UCC §2–610). Several justifications can be put forward for the doctrine. The nineteenth-century approach, as evidenced in *Hochster* v. *De la Tour* ((1853) ER 922 at 926) is that the parties 'impliedly promise that in the meantime [*i.e. in the period before performance is due*] neither will do anything to the prejudice of the other inconsistent with that relation'. The idea of justifying the 'anticipatory breach' doctrine on the basis of an implied term echoes the nineteenth-century approach to the frustration doctrine mentioned in Chapter 12 (*Taylor* v. *Caldwell* (1863) 3 B. & S. 826).

Fried justifies the doctrine by focusing on the moral worth of the promise; having promised to be bound, the parties should view themselves as exactly that and not seek an early exit from their obligations.

C. Fried, *Contract as Promise* (Cambridge, Mass., Harvard University Press, 1981), 128–30

On January 2 Brenda contracts with Arthur that he work for her beginning July 1. On March 1 she wrongfully tells him that she has hired somebody else and that the job will not be available. On June 15 Arthur takes another, lower-paying job in some distant place to which he removes. On July 1 Brenda writes Arthur stating that since he has not presented himself for work under their agreement she considers herself released from all obligation. Arthur would nonetheless like to sue for the difference between the wages he is receiving and the higher wages promised in the contract with Brenda.

Brenda's claim will be that Arthur's working for her was the condition of any obligation that she might have, and that since he has disabled himself from fulfilling this condition, she is released and cannot be sued. The suggestion is obviously outrageous. What blocks it? Common sense suggests that Brenda cannot insist on the performance of a condition when she herself is in default and Arthur has not waived his rights arising from her breach. Once again we see the importance of not being in the wrong—and Brenda is clearly in the wrong. But what if Brenda says she is *not* in the wrong? What if she says she was perfectly prepared to take on Arthur on July 1, which is all the contract required her to do? Brenda says she is not in breach because her obligations only arose on July 1, at which date she was fully ready to perform. If her answer were allowed to stand, an obvious injustice would result. What is it and how is it to be avoided?

One device is to say that in fact Brenda's obligations do not begin on July 1 but arise with the making of the contract. These earlier obligations are said to be obligations of cooperation, noninterference, and the like. Her statement of March 1 is a breach of these obligations to act with loyalty to her undertaking from the moment of its formation. . . . A less forced way to get at the felt injustice of Brenda's claim is to say that Brenda, having announced her intention to breach on March 1, cannot complain if Arthur takes her at her word. That certainly is how we feel about the matter, but the response does seem a little too perfunctory to stand as an explanation.

The purpose of contractual obligation is to provide assurances into the future. Brenda has done that on January 2. Her declaration of March 1 contradicts this assurance. Can Arthur be blamed if he does not ignore Brenda's repudiation? It is after all more useful for him to set about finding alternative employment immediately. Waiting until July 1 might mean missing splendid opportunities, and although Brenda will eventually have to respond in damages, what is gained if he does forgo an earlier alternative? So utility is on the side of allowing Arthur to take Brenda at her word. But is it fair? Brenda, after all, might say that she might have changed her mind at any time—as in fact she eventually did. The simplest answer is the best. Arthur is entitled to rely on Brenda's word given in the contract of January 2. On March 1 she says something meaning Arthur no longer to expect that she will fulfill her promise. It would be unfair to Arthur to penalize him for seeking to protect his interests in the face of her threat. If you create an expectation intending another person to act upon it, it is a kind of entrapment then to claim that the other person's acting as you meant him to act constitutes a violation of *your* rights. You are not estopped if you do something you have a perfect right to do—for example, leaving your window open in the summer, even if you have reason to believe that somebody might take advantage of this to burglarize your house. (At least you are not estopped against the burglar.) But Brenda has not done something within her rights or something neutral, such as leaving a window open; she has threatened to act in violation of her obligations to Arthur. She has done so meaning him no longer to expect that she will fulfill her obligations. The entrapment lies in her than blaming Arthur for protecting himself against this wrongful threat. Arthur's failure to show up at Brenda's on July 1, his failure to comply with what may have been a condition in the January 1 contract, therefore will not under these circumstances foreclose him from claiming any of the rights he may have.

In holding Brenda to her repudiation we . . . allow the extinction of a contractual right by a voluntary act that is inconsistent with the assertion of that right and that undermines the actor's moral title to insist on the promise. We say that Brenda's bad faith maneuvers estop her from enforcing the contract, and estoppel is a nonpromissory act that weakens or extinguishes promissory rights.

Note

This extract displays the classic elements of Fried's contract philosophy explained in Chapter 2.

5. Perhaps a simpler view is to see the anticipatory breach doctrine as an obvious consequence of the executory contract. If an exchange of promises

suffices as consideration for a contract, then it would seem logical to say that liability to perform arises from that moment. Atiyah describes the decision in *Hochster* v. *De la Tour* in exactly these terms.

P. S. Atiyah, *The Rise and Fall of Freedom of Contract* (Oxford, Oxford University Press, 1979), 426–7

. . . in *Hochster* v. *De la Tour* . . . it was held for the first time that a plaintiff can sue for damages at once in the event of a repudiation of the contract by the defendant, even though the repudiation and the action both occur prior to the time fixed for performance. There are arguments of a policy nature both for and against any such rule, but for present purposes the interesting thing about the decision is the light it throws on the judicial perception of a contract in 1853. This decision, in a sense, represents the apotheosis of the executory contract. Not only does the contract create a right prior to any performance, but it is even possible to sue and recover damages prior to the date set for performance. What has happened here is that the Court has conceptualized the contract as a thing that is 'made'—'there is a relation constituted between the parties' says Campbell C.J.—and if the thing can be 'made' prior to performance, there is no reason why it should not also be 'broken' prior to performance. The executory contract has been reified, as thought it were a box which is first made and then broken.

There are, as Atiyah alludes, several policy justifications for the anticipatory breach doctrine. First, a party who has prepaid for future performance may need to recover his payment in order to enable him to enter into a replacement contract with a third party. Second, if a party who receives notice of repudiation has no remedy until the time for performance is due, that party is likely to do nothing in terms of arranging substitute performance and will wait until performance is due in the hope that it is offered. By allowing an action for damages at the time of repudiation, this extra loss is avoided. Both these policy justifications operate in favour of the innocent party as we would expect. The party in breach is offering not merely defective performance but no performance at all. The balance of the equities (see Hillman, Ch. 12) rests with the innocent party.

III. REPUDIATION AND PERFORMANCE

Lord Ackner refers to the innocent party as having two options when faced with a repudiation—either treat the contract as at an end and sue for damages or affirm the contract and wait until performance is due before seeking a remedy. There is a third option—the innocent party can carry on and perform the contract. The next case we look at is concerned with purported repudiation during performance of the contract, where the innocent party takes this third option. This involves the court working through a number of earlier authorities in order to establish the limits on the exercise of this third option.

Clea Shipping Corporation v. Bulk Oil International Ltd. (The Alaskan Trader)
[1984] 1 All ER 129

The *Alaskan Trader* was chartered by its owners to the hirers for a period of roughly two years and two weeks. Ten months into the charter, the ship broke down. It was clear that the necessary repairs would take many months. The charterers indicated that they had no further use for the ship. Their decision may have been influenced by the fact that the rate for commercial freight carriage had dropped considerably. The owners repaired the ship and nearly six months later it was ready for use. The ship was offered to the charterers but they declined to use it, treating the charterparty as if it were at an end. The owners could have treated the charterers' conduct as a repudiation but they declined to do so. The ship was left with the crew on board, waiting to be used by the charterers until the charterparty expired. The charterers paid the hire charges during this period, but when the charterparty had expired they sought, through arbitration, to recover this cost. The findings of the arbitrator are set out in the judgment of Lloyd J.

LLOYD J The owners argued that they were entitled to retain the hire, since they had kept the vessel at the disposal of the charterers throughout the period. They relied on the decision of the House of Lords in *White & Carter (Councils) Ltd v McGregor* [1962] AC 413, and the decision of Kerr J in *Gator Shipping Corp v Trans-Asiatic Oil Co Ltd SA and Occidental Shipping Establishment, The Odenfeld* [1978] 2 Lloyd's Rep 357. The charterers on the other hand argued that the owners ought, in all reason, to have accepted the charterers' conduct as a repudiation of the charter, and claimed damages. Even if no alternative employment could be found for the vessel, it would have been a great deal cheaper to lay the vessel up, rather than maintain her with a full crew on board. They relied on the decision of the Court of Appeal in *Attica Sea Carriers Corp v Ferrostaal Poseidon Bulk Reederei GmbH, The Puerto Buitrago* [1976] 1 Lloyd's Rep 250.

The arbitrator, having heard all the arguments which I have heard, and been referred to all the cases, upheld the charterers' contention . . . . Having concluded that the owners were not obliged to accept the charterers' repudiation in October 1980, before the repairs had been carried out, he continued:

'30. The position was very different when the vessel was tendered ready for service after completion of repairs. The Charterers refused to accept the vessel and made it clear they never would. At that stage there was nothing contingent or anticipatory about the Charterers' action. It was clear that the Charter was dead. The Owners however did not accept that the moribund condition of the Charter was equivalent to termination in the legal sense. They contended that all was required of the vessel under the Charter was that she should be at the Charterers' disposal; the hire thereby fell due and it would be unjust to permit the Charterers to avoid a debt by requiring the Owners to accept repudiation and claim damages. There is a superficial logic in this argument but it is apt to lead to absurd situations. In this case the Owners contend that they kept the vessel with a full crew and engine ready for over 7 months, waiting for orders which they well knew would never come. I am satisfied that this commercial absurdity is not justified by a proper interpretation of the decided cases. I consider that the analogy of a contract between master and servant applies more closely to a time charter than the analogy of a simple debt. The Owner supplies the vessel and crew; the Charterer supplies fuel oil, pays disbursements and gives orders. The Charterers were also able to satisfy me that at that stage the Owners had no legitimate interest in pursuing their claim for hire rather than a claim for damages. In these respects the present case differs materially from the case of *White & Carter* v. *McGregor*, and is more closely analogous to the case of *The Puerto Buitrago*, where the judgments of Lord Denning MR and Orr LJ are particularly in point. I considered that the decision in *The Odenfeld* turned on the highly unusual circumstances of that case.

31. I am satisfied on this basis that the Charter was terminated around the time the vessel was finally ready for service. . . .'

Counsel for the owners now seeks to persuade me that the arbitrator was wrong in law. He submits that in a case of repudiation the innocent party has an unfettered right to elect whether to accept the repudiation or not. Here the owners chose not to accept the repudiation. Provided they continued to keep the vessel at the disposal of the charterers, as they did, they were entitled to their hire. The arbitrator was wrong in law in holding that the owners *ought* to have accepted the charterers' repudiation by midnight on 8 April 1981.

Although the argument ranged far and wide, the appeal can, in my view, be decided quite simply. But, before stating my decision, I should first refer to the relevant decisions which are binding on me, or of strong persuasive force.

In *White & Carter v McGregor* the plaintiffs agreed to display advertisements for the defendant's garage on litter bins in the neighbourhood for a period of three years. The very same day the defendant said he did not wish to go on with the contract. The plaintiffs declined to accept the repudiation. They went ahead with the contract, and sued for the agreed price in debt. It was held by the House of Lords that they were justified. The minority, while conceding that an unaccepted repudiation does not put an end to the contract, nevertheless held that the plaintiffs' only remedy lay in damages, since it was obviously not a suitable case for specific performance. Lord Hodson, with whom Lord Tucker agreed, drew no distinction between anticipatory breach and breach at the date of performance. In either case the innocent party has an unfettered right of election. He said ([1962] AC 413 at 445):

'When the assistance of the court is not required the innocent party can choose whether he will accept repudiation and sue for damages for anticipatory breach or await the date of performance by the guilty party. Then, if there is failure in performance, his rights are preserved. It may be unfortunate that the appellants have saddled themselves with an unwanted contract causing an apparent waste of time and money. No doubt this aspect impressed the Court of Session but there is no equity which can assist the respondent. It is trite that equity will not rewrite an improvident contract where there is no disability on either side. There is no duty laid on a party to a subsisting contract to vary it at the behest of the other party so as to deprive himself of the benefit given to him by the contract. To hold otherwise would be to introduce a novel equitable doctrine that a party was not to be held to his contract unless the court in a given instance thought it reasonable so to do. In this case it would make an action for debt a claim for a discretionary remedy. This would introduce an uncertainty into the field of contract which appears to be unsupported by authority either in English or Scottish law save for the one case viz *Langford & Co Ltd v Dutch* (1952 SC 15) on which the Court of Session ([1961] SLT 144) founded its opinion and which must, in my judgment, be taken to have been wrongly decided.'

Lord Reid agreed with Lord Hodson and Lord Tucker that on the facts the plaintiffs' claim in debt must succeed. But his speech contains two important observations on the law. First, he pointed out that it is only in rare cases that the innocent party will be able to complete performance of his side of the contract, without the assent or co-operation of the party in breach. Obviously, if the innocent party cannot complete performance, he is restricted to his claim for damages. A buyer who refuses to accept delivery of the goods, and thereby prevents property passing, cannot, in the ordinary case, be made liable for the price. The peculiarity of *White & Carter v McGregor* as Lord Reid pointed out, was that the plaintiffs could completely fulfil their part of the contract without any co-operation from the defendant.

The second observation which Lord Reid made as to the law was that a party might well be unable to enforce his contractual remedy if 'he had no legitimate interest, financial or otherwise, in performing the contract rather than claiming damages'. Lord Reid did not go far in explaining what he meant by legitimate interest except to say that the de minimis principle would apply. Obviously it would not be sufficient to establish that the innocent party was acting unreasonably. . . . As Lord Reid said ([1962] AC 413 at 430):

'It might be, but it never has been, the law that a person is only entitled to enforce his contractual rights in a reasonable way and that a court will not support an attempt to enforce them in an unreasonable way. One reason why that is not the law is no doubt because it was thought that it would create too much uncertainty to require the court to decide whether it is reasonable or equitable to allow a party to enforce his full rights under a contract. . . .'

Nor does Lord Reid go far in explaining the juristic basis on which the court can confine the plaintiff's remedy to a claim for damages. All he says is that, in the absence of legitimate interest, 'that might be regarded as a proper case for the exercise of the general equitable jurisdiction of the court' (see [1962] AC 413 at 431). . . .

It is clear that, on the facts, no attempt had been made by the defendant to establish absence of legitimate interest. Accordingly, counsel for the owners was right when he submitted that the two observations which I have mentioned were both, strictly speaking, obiter. I further accept that the language used by Lord Reid is tentative. . . .

The next case is *Hounslow London BC v Twickenham, Garden Developments Ltd* [1971] 1 Ch 233, a case relied on strongly by counsel for the charterers. That case concerned a building contract between a firm of contractors and the local borough council. The council sought to terminate the contract, but the contractors refused to accept the repudiation. They relied on *White & Carter v McGregor*. Megarry J analysed the speeches in that case, and drew attention to the two observations, or limitations, in the speech of Lord Reid. He described both limitations as important. As to the first, he held that the building contract in the case before him contemplated the passive, if not active, cooperation of both parties in its performance. Accordingly, the case fell within the first of Lord Reid's limitations, and it was unnecessary for him to consider the second limitation as to legitimate interest. . . .

The next case, on which counsel for the charterers relied, is *The Puerto Buitrago*. In that case a vessel suffered an engine breakdown in the course of her service under a demise charter. There was a provision in the charter that the vessel should be dry-docked before redelivery, and any repairs found to be necessary were to be carried out at charterers' expense. The repairs were estimated to cost $2m. The value of the vessel when repaired would only have been $1m. The charterers declined to carry out the repairs. They purported to redeliver the vessel in her unrepaired state. The owners refused to accept redelivery. They argued that the charterers were bound to repair the vessel, and that hire continued to be payable until they had. The Court of Appeal decided in favour of the charterers. They held, on a preliminary question of law, that the obligation to repair was not a condition precedent to the right to redeliver. But they went on to consider three other questions of law which had been agreed between the parties, but which only arose if they were wrong on the first question of law. For the purpose of the fourth question, they assumed that the charterers were in breach by insisting on redelivering the vessel without first repairing her. On that assumption the fourth question was whether the owners were obliged to accept the charterers' conduct as a repudiation. The owners argued that they were not. They relied on *White & Carter v McGregor*. The Court of Appeal rejected the owners' argument. Lord Denning MR said that *White & Carter v McGregor* has—

'no application whatever in a case where the plaintiff ought, in all reason, to accept the repudiation and sue for damages—provided that damages would provide an adequate remedy for any loss suffered by him. The reason is because, by suing for the money, the

edy lies in damages. The fact that the owners' remuneration in this case, called hire, is payable in advance makes no difference. Counsel for the owners, on the other hand, argued that the owners earned their hire simply by holding the vessel and the services of their master and crew at the charterers' disposal. He concedes that in the case of master and servant, where the master has wrongly dismissed the servant, the servant cannot earn remuneration by holding himself at the disposal of his master. He is confined to his remedy in damages. But counsel for the owners submits that a time charter is different. In view of my decision on the legitimate interest point, it is unnecessary for me to decide between these rival arguments, or to explore the nature of a time charter contract any further. All I will say is that, at first blush, there seemed much to be said for the argument of counsel for the charterers. I say no more, because in *The Odenfeld* Kerr J found a similar argument unimpressive.

For the reasons I have given I would dismiss the owners' appeal and uphold the award.

Notes

1. The charterers here had purported to repudiate the contract for breach of the 'seaworthiness' clause. It may seem that the ship was unavailable for use for a large part of the charter period, but as we saw in Chapter 10, repudiation, once performance has begun, can only occur if a condition has been breached or if the consequences of the breach of an innominate term are held sufficiently serious to justify termination. The facts of this case did not fit into either these categories, and consequently the charterers were themselves in breach by rejecting future performance of the contract.

2. A central feature of the judgment in *The Alaskan Trader* is the discussion of *White and Carter (Councils) Ltd.* v. *McGregor*, the facts of which are given by Lloyd J, was a majority decision of the House of Lords. It is interesting that subsequent discussion of this case appears to have been confined, in both the case above and the earlier authorities discussed by Lloyd J, to Lord Reid's judgment. Lord Reid was joined in the majority by Lord Hodson, with whom Lord Tucker agreed. It is clear from the brief extract of Lord Hodson's judgment given by Lloyd J that he took a much more straightforward view than Lord Reid. The view of Lords Hodson and Tucker of the innocent party's right of election is that it is completely unfettered. It does not matter that performance, unwanted by the party in breach, may result in an inefficient use of resources. It is simply the innocent party's right based on the contract. It is only Lord Reid who imposes the requirement that the innocent party must have a legitimate interest in performing and must be able to perform without the co-operation of the injured party.

Counsel for the owners sought to challenge the applicability of this part of Lord Reid's judgment on the grounds that it was *obiter*. It is true that the defendants in *White and Carter (Councils)* did not attempt to challenge the legitimate interest of the plaintiffs in performing the contract. However, this hardly makes Lord Reid's comment *obiter*; if he had thought the plaintiffs did not satisfy either of the criteria he laid down, he would not have decided the way he did. What is far more likely to render his comments *obiter* is if the ratio is drawn instead from all the judgments of all three judges in the majority.

3. It is clear that Lord Reid's proposition in *White and Carter (Councils)* that a legitimate interest in performance is required by the innocent party is taken as a definite requirement by subsequent cases. Lloyd J makes the point that legitimate interest is not defined by Lord Reid. Nor is it defined in subsequent cases. The point is not expanded upon by Lloyd J, as he accepts the arbitrator's finding that the owners had no legitimate interest. The nearest we get to a definition is that an innocent party can have a legitimate interest even if his behaviour in performing the contract is unreasonable *but* not if his behaviour is 'wholly' unreasonable. The difference, for the innocent party, between being able to carry on and perform the contract and suing instead at the time of breach or at the time of performance is the difference between the contract price and an action for damages. It must follow that there is some connection between legitimate interest and the adequacy of damages. This point is picked up by Lloyd J in his discussion of *The Odenfeld*; he refers to one of the grounds influencing Kerr J in his finding of a legitimate interest as being 'the difficulty in calculating damages'. It is hard to see how a legitimate interest couched in this way is present in *White and Carter (Councils)*. Surely, damages would have been adequate. Some thoughts on how the facts of *White and Carter (Councils)* might support the counterposition are offered by Diamond.

A. Diamond, 'Commerce, Customers and Contracts', (1978) 11 *Melb. UL Rev.* 563 at 575–6

I do not believe that the appellants inflated their loss at all. I believe that if they had sued for damages they would have been able to prove their loss at the full amount and so would have obtained judgment for the same sum.

Why do I think this? Because the contract was a renewal contract: for the previous three years the garage proprietor's advertisements had been exhibited. They were still out on the bins when the renewal contract was signed and cancelled. So I do not think that the agents had to make any fresh plates and send men out to fix them. The most they had to do was their routine inspection and maintenance of all the litter bins, and they probably would not have saved much money if this contract had come to end without any renewal contract being signed. Moreover, I doubt if they could have relet the sites (though here I must admit I am less sure of my ground); my guess is that there were probably more lampposts than litter bins anyway. Accordingly, in my view it is more than likely that the three years' renewal rental was nearly all pure profit.

Why, then, did the advertising agents deliberately claim the price rather than sue for damages? I think we can see the answer if we look at the question from their point of view. They carry on business throughout Britain. They enter into a large number of contracts, and no doubt have a fair number of defaults. They evidently have a fair number of cancellations too, judging by the warning that the contract is non-cancellable specifically printed on their forms. Each time they sue, are they to call evidence in every case of their loss, of the availability of sites in the particular municipal area, of details of current lettings? How expensive and time-consuming this would be. What they want to be able to do is to issue summonses in the local courts for fixed sums of money and, in most cases, to get default judgments. I must say I don't blame them.

If these were sufficient reasons to allow the innocent party to perform the contract instead of accepting repudiation and suing for damages, this would be tantamount to saying that performance is everything. However, English contract law reflects a choice between performing a contract and paying damages for non-performance, in that damages are the primary remedy for breach. If performance were so very important, then we would expect specific performance to be the primary remedy. The focus on performance as a right of the innocent party reflects the view of two of the majority— Lords Hodson and Tucker in *White and Carter (Councils)*. In the next chapter we look in more detail at specific performance as a remedy. If the rights of the innocent party in this context are not to be alien to the rest of English contract law, it is hard to see a context in which there will be a legitimate interest in performing after repudiation and in asserting that damages are not an adequate remedy. For a sharply critical account of the judgments in *White and Carter (Councils)* see A. Goodhart, 'Measure of Damages when a Contract Is Repudiated' ((1962) 78 *LQR* 263).

4. As we shall discuss in the next chapter, contract law recognizes, along with the right to sue for damages, the principle of mitigation of loss as incumbent upon the innocent party. To satisfy this requirement, the innocent party has to do all that is reasonable to minimize the loss to himself. Failure to comply with this duty results in no remedy being given for the avoidable loss. However, the duty to mitigate in English law only arises once breach has been accepted; the duty to mitigate does not apply to anticipatory breach or repudiation until the innocent party accepts the breach and treats the contract as at an end. Lloyd J points out that this often criticized aspect of the mitigation rule does not apply in the United States. The common law position has been largely abandoned in favour of a rule that there is a general duty to mitigate whether or not breach is accepted (UCC §2-610(a)). For a discussion of the relative merits of the

common law and UCC positions, see C. Goetz and R. Scott, 'The Mitigation Principle toward a General Theory of Contractual Obligation' ((1983) 69 *Va. L. Rev.* 967 at 993–5) and T. Jackson, ' "Anticipatory Repudiation" and the Temporal Element of Contract Law: An Economic Inquiry into Contract Damages in Cases of Prospective Non-Performance' ((1978) 31 *Stan. L. Rev.* 69).

The adoption of a mitigation principle in relation to all breaches of contract, whether accepted or not, would leave an innocent party virtually no room to claim that he had a legitimate interest in performing the contract. If we elaborate upon the facts of *White and Carter (Councils)* as set out in *The Alaskan Trader*, we can construct a situation whereby the plaintiffs argue that they cannot allow the bins to carry no advertisements because that will damage their market impact as an advertising receptacle with future advertisers. But the defendants could raise the argument that the bins previously carried advertisements for products they considered environmentally harmful, and that they do not wish to be thought to be associated in any way with them. Even in this scenario, it is hard to see that the plaintiffs could not have found some alternative advertising or, if they could not, to return to the previous point, that their position could not have been protected by an award of damages. Any other finding would remove from the defendants the ability to get out of the contract and pay damages rather than to accept unwanted performance. The absence of a mitigation principle provides the innocent party with little incentive to abandon a repudiated contract and look for a contract performance from a third party. The ability to be able to look elsewhere and so avoid an inefficient waste of resources was identified by Atiyah in the earlier extract as one of the advantages of the doctrine of election. An innocent party is unlikely to do this unless there is an obviously better bargain available.

5. The second of Lord Reid's criteria is that the innocent party has to be able to complete the contract without the assistance of the other party. Lloyd J refers to the *Hounslow* case as deciding that assistance should be defined as active or passive co-operation. Once this qualification is imposed, it becomes hard to see how performance after attempted repudiation can be justified. In the *Hounslow* case, the passive co-operation was the conduct of the council in allowing the contractors to enter the land. We could also couch passive co-operation in that case in terms of the council not suing the contractor for trespass. If we apply the passive element of co-operation to the facts of *White and Carter (Councils)* we can see that there must have been a potential action for breach of copyright, for the use of the defendants' advertisements on the bins once their consent had been withdrawn, which the defendants did not take. In *The Alaskan Trader* the co-operation point was left undecided by Lloyd J, but from the last paragraph of his judgment it seems that he favours the view that co-operation was

needed by the charterers. The analogy offered is that of a master and servant contract. This, he seems to feel, is probably insufficient to support performance, because merely getting the ship ready and holding it for the owners' instructions would not, on the analogy of a master and servant contract, be rewarded by anything more than an award of damages. A further level of co-operation is required to satisfy a contract for services; this is the actual use of those services.

6. See further on *The Alaskan Trader*, J. Carter and G. Marston, 'Repudiation of Contract: Whether Election Fettered' ([1985] *CLJ* 18).

Questions

1. Is the approach taken by English law to the choices faced by the innocent party in a situation of anticipatory breach 'efficient' in the economic sense?

2. Should the court take the same approach to repudiation where it occurs once the performance of the contract has begun?

14

Remedies for Breach of Contract

I. INTRODUCTION

When a contractual relationship breaks down, the innocent party looks for a remedy. Remedies go to the very essence of contract: according to D. Campbell and D. Harris ('Flexibility in Long-Term Contractual Relationships', (1993) 20 *JL&S* 166 at 168), using the legal form of contract as the basis of an exchange of goods provides a 'state-underwritten guarantee of a remedy in the event of breach'. The first choice to be made is between punishing the guilty party for the breach and giving relief to the innocent party.

E. Farnsworth, 'Legal Remedies for Breach of Contract', (1970) 70 *Colum. L. Rev.* 1145 at 1145–7

If a society were seriously concerned with compelling men to keep their promises, it might be expected to treat a breach of contract as a crime and to punish defaulting promisors. Ours has not done so, and in this we are representative of mankind as a whole. . . .

If a society were seriously concerned with the compulsion of promisors, it might at least be expected to impose civil penalties for breach of contract if it chose not to impose criminal ones. The state, rather than exact the penalty itself, might simply allow the promisee to claim a sum of money designed to punish the defaulting promisor. . . . [C]ourts in this country, as in most of the rest of the world, expressly reject the notion that remedies for breach of contract have punishment as a goal, and with rare exceptions, refuse to grant "punitive damages" for breach of contract. In so refusing they confidently claim to be blind to fault, and they purport not to distinguish between aggravated and innocent breach. So Holmes said, "If a contract is broken the measure of damages generally is the same, whatever the cause of the breach." The skeptical reader may well ask whether even men of judicial temperament are immune from the temptation to depart from a rule so oblivious of blame and, indeed, [there are] some exceptions to the rule . . . In its essential design, however, our system of remedies for breach of contract is one of strict liability and not of liability based on fault, and this would be a strange design indeed if it were a system directed at the compulsion of promisors.

Our system, then, is not directed at *compulsion* of *promisors* to *prevent* breach; rather, it is aimed at *relief* to *promisees* to *redress* breach. It is not much concerned with the question suggested by Frost's lines: How can men be made to keep their promises? It is instead preoccupied with a different question: How can men be encouraged to deal with those who make promises? Perhaps it is more seemly for a system of free enterprise to promote the use of contract by encouraging promisees to rely on the promises of others, rather than by compelling promisors to perform their promises out of fear that the law will punish their breaches. In any event, this at least adds to the celebrated freedom to make contracts, a considerable freedom to break them as well.

Note

Farnsworth's work refers to the United States but is equally applicable to English law.

In earlier chapters, we have seen examples of the types of remedy for which the parties can look to the court, as well as some of the available self-help remedies, which the innocent party may use provided he or she has legitimate grounds. Remedies provided by the courts can be broken down into two groups:

specific relief: the court orders the performance of the promise (e.g. specific performance; injunction; action for the price);

substitutionary relief: the court orders the transfer from the party in breach to the innocent party of a substitute for the performance, normally damages

We have reviewed numerous examples of actions for breach of contract in which the innocent party has sought relief in the form of compensatory damages, and a smaller number of cases in which the innocent party has sought specific performance of a promise (e.g. *Beswick* v. *Beswick* [1968] AC 58, Ch. 7) or brought an action for the price (e.g. *White and Carter (Councils) Ltd.* v. *McGregor* [1962] AC 413, Ch. 13). In Chapters 10 and 13 we have also looked at examples of the self-help remedies to which the innocent party may resort. While the innocent party may not physically force the other party to perform her promise, he may withhold performance or bring the contract to an end in certain circumstances where a breach has occurred. The threat of such actions may be sufficient to persuade the other party to comply.

This, therefore, is the basic remedial structure provided by the law of contract. A number of additional points need, however, to be made before we move on to consider these remedies in detail. *First,* the parties may (and often do) deviate from the structure provided by the general law by setting up a specific remedial system in their own contract. Examples

include giving the innocent party a more extensive right to terminate or
cancel the contract for breach by the other party than is available under
the general law; providing for liquidated damages—i.e. an 'agreed' amount
to be payable in the event of a certain contingency occurring such as delay
(e.g. £*x* per day); or contracting out of the jurisdiction of the courts by providing for disputes under the contract to be resolved by an arbitrator. The
latter point of procedure is excluded from this book, as are issues of court
process and enforcement. We shall, however, provide some analysis of the
effectiveness and appropriateness of the remedial structure offered by the
common law, and of the judicial and legislative rules which limit the ability
of the parties to plan their own remedies.

Second, even though judicial and self-help legal remedies are available
under the general law or within the contract as agreed between the parties,
if a dispute arises under the contract they may well seek to resolve it without recourse to the law. It is unlikely that a contractor will ever take steps to
commence legal proceedings the moment a problem arises under his or
her contract, and consequently non-legal sanctions, even where they are
not the only sanctions used, are the logical precursors of legal sanctions.
Parties will almost always try to negotiate with a contract-breaker or seek
to persuade her to perform her promise, perhaps using threats not to deal
with her again or threats to her trade reputation. We shall consider the role
of non-legal sanctions and their relationship to legal remedies in the next
section.

Third, in addition to the types of remedy which we focus upon in this
chapter, the role of other fields of law should be mentioned. While breaking a contract does not itself constitute the commission of a crime
(although it may simultaneously constitute the commission of a tort), the
criminal law does play a supplementary role in the field of contract remedies. The criminal law, for example, protects tenants against harassment
by their landlords (Protection of Eviction Act 1977, as amended by s. 29 of
the Housing Act 1988), and in the context of consumer law there are criminal sanctions in the Trade Descriptions Act 1968 and the Consumer
Protection Act 1987, Parts II–IV, to maintain standards of safety and fair
dealing (see generally B. Harvey and D. Parry, *The Law of Consumer
Protection and Fair Trading*, 4th edn. (London, Butterworths, 1992), 231 ff.
and 339 ff.). Alternatively, administrative remedies may be available.
Complaints to administrative authorities such as the various Ombudsmen,
or local authority trading standards bodies, may offer an opportunity of
recourse to those consumers who consider themselves victims of a breach
of contract but unable to have effective recourse to self-help or judicial
action (e.g. because of the prohibitive cost of litigation).

According to von Mehren, it is possible to identify a variety of objectives
served by the contract remedial structure.

A. von Mehren, 'Relief', in 'A General View of Contract', *International Encyclopedia of Comparative Law* (Tübingen/The Hague, Mohr/Nijhoff, 1982), vol. vii, ch. 1, p. 86

Remedies can be designed and administered to serve one or more of six principal ends: (1) ensuring that the institution of contract will serve, even if difficulties respecting performance arise, to move resources to their economically most efficient use; (2) punishing the defaulting party; (3) providing "incentives for parties who have made a contract . . . to act in a way that is close to . . . what they would have agreed upon" had they foreseen the contingency at the time of contracting; (4) releasing the aggrieved (or nondefaulting) party from a relationship that has wholly or partially broken down; (5) compensating the aggrieved party for the diminishment of his existing wealth resulting from reliance on the broken contract (reliance interest); (6) allocating gains or losses expectable under the contract (expectation interest).

We can consider in the course of this chapter the extent to which these ends are successfully met by the structure of legal remedies, or by the non-legal sanctions to which parties have recourse; whether it is appropriate for contract remedies to incorporate an element of punishment for the contract breaker; and whether it is important for remedies to serve social and economic goals other than that of 'efficiency'.

II. NON-LEGAL SANCTIONS

H. Havighurst, *The Nature of Private Contract* (Littleton, Colo., Rothman, 1961), 68–76

Without legal sanctions for breach of a promise the contract institution would be under a disability, but we should not be confronted with the spectacle of a wolf eating himself up. . . .

The first and foremost reason that contract is less dependent upon law is that whereas the opportunity to take a man's pocketbook, his wife or his life, apart from law—to borrow a phrase once used by Holmes in another connection—is open to "the whole world of the unscrupulous," the opportunity to injure a man by breaking a contract is open only to those with whom he has chosen to deal. Although in the whole population there are many more persons with no inhibitions in the matter of breaking contracts than there are thieves, relation disrupters and cutthroats, yet when one is in a position to refuse to deal, it is easier to prevent an evil person from doing him injury through breach of contract than it is to stop a depredation upon these other interests. A man by selection can limit the circle of those in a position to hurt him by failing to keep a promise. . . .

The second reason why contract can exist without law is because the furtive breach of a promise is seldom possible, and consequently social sanctions are more effective.

This is not true of depredations upon property or the person. The burglar operates in the dark; the robber often wears a mask. For lesser offenses concealment is still easier. When there is a substantial hope of avoiding discovery, quite a number of persons will take the risk.

But the means of escaping detection are not as a rule open to one who commits a breach of contract. In the case of some kinds of agreements, to be sure, such as an implied promise by an employee to be honest and loyal to his employer, an undetected breach is not impossible; but these are rare. The breaker of the typical indisputable promise must be brazen. And I submit that the quality of cold-blooded brazenness in the human being is more uncommon than dishonesty. Thus quite apart from law, many persons who will furtively steal will not openly refuse to keep a promise as to which it is impossible to manufacture a plausible ground of dispute. . . . I should not be surprised if a burglar sometimes plies his trade in order to obtain funds to meet his contract obligations.

Furthermore, although the social sanctions applicable to breach of contract are not so severe as those attaching to detected dishonesty, they are substantial, tangible and certain. The man who does not keep his promises is not exactly a pariah, but he loses much that the great majority of people find essential to an agreeable existence. Anyone who has a history of failing to keep his word is stamped as unworthy of trust, and his chance of future benefit through contract is diminished. If he fails to pay a debt, he loses credit standing; if as the operator of a business he fails to carry out an undertaking to a customer, he loses goodwill. For inducing the performance of a contract, the fear of the credit man and the fear of a customer who can take his business elsewhere are for many persons spurs more poignant than the fear of the sheriff. . . .

. . . If non-legal sanctions are working there is no need for legal enforcement, and if they completely break down the threat of civil action alone will never bring about performance. But it is when non-legal sanctions become impaired and yet do not break down completely that the legal sanction becomes important. If non-legal sanctions accomplish a substantial part of the work of inducing performance, even the mild pressure created by the threat of civil process may do the rest.

It is relevant to our study to consider where the non-legal pressures break down in whole or in part. I see five circumstances contributing to such a result. In any given case of a breakdown, several of these circumstances usually intermingle and all are matters of degree:

(1) The debtor dies. You may protest that death is not a matter of degree, but the susceptibility of the decedent's successors to non-legal sanctions for paying his creditors will vary. In every case, I think, their force is less than conscience

and the social pressures upon the maker of the promise. But the procedures prescribed by law upon death are to a large extent designed for the creditor's protection. Legal sanctions applicable to the court-appointed personal representative are highly effective. An executor, while acting as an executor, does tend to live by law.

(2) Evil men, without conscience and not responsive to any relevant social pressures, succeed in entering the circle of the trusted. This is usually attributable to the creditor's ignorance or poor judgment.

(3) The debtor is subject to little competitive pressure. This circumstance is usually recognized as affecting the ability to set the terms of a contract and is referred to as bargaining power. But it is likewise significant in its bearing upon the non-legal consequences of breach. To the extent that others are clamoring to deal with him, the debtor can afford a disruption of his relation with the creditor and can risk a diminution of his reputation for fair dealing.

(4) The debtor, because of insolvency or for some other reason, finds it impossible or difficult to perform.

(5) Controversy develops. This may relate to the subject matter of the contract or to something entirely different. If the controversy relates to the contract, it could arise, on account of a misunderstanding as to the meaning of language but this is seldom the cause. Disputes concerning the meaning of language usually come into the picture when the lawyers come into it. Differences come about mainly because one party does not measure up to the other party's expectation based upon past practices or upon evaluations of character, or because of a miscalculation with respect to events either before or after the making of the contract. Whenever a dispute arises, subjects for argument can nearly always be found. . . .

Non-legal pressures upon an alleged debtor do not entirely cease when controversy develops; but to the extent that it is genuine, conscience no longer troubles, and to the extent that others can be made to believe in the justice of his defense, social pressures are reduced.

Notes

1. Havighurst suggests that legal sanctions may be used where disputes arise about the meaning of a contract, in particular if lawyers have become involved. The extracts from Macaulay below and from Beale and Dugdale (Section IV(C) below) indicate that, at least in those areas of business which have been studied empirically, recourse to law is very much a last resort.

2. A further factor underlying the importance of non-legal sanctions is that not all exchange relationships take the form of binding contracts. This may be, of course, because it is the policy of the law that certain types of agreement should not be binding (e.g. social and domestic agreements or

collective agreements), because the parties have specifically excluded legal enforceability (e.g. *Rose and Frank & Co.* v. *J. R. Crompton & Bros. Ltd.* [1925] AC 445), or because the parties are indifferent to enforceability and so never succeed in concluding a formally binding contract. Charny's typology of non-legal sanctions is sensitive not only to the interaction of the two types of sanction (non-legal and legal) but also to the interaction of legally enforceable and unenforceable commitments.

D. Charny, 'Non-legal Sanctions in Commercial Relationships', (1990) 104 *Harv. L. Rev.* 373 at 392–4

A Typology of Nonlegal Sanctions

The nonlegal sanction for breach of a commitment is the sacrifice of something valuable to the breaching party—a value often called the "bond" posted by that party. Three types of bonds are common in commercial transactions. The simplest type of nonlegal sanction is the sacrifice of *a relationship-specific prospective advantage.* The committing party places a particular asset under the control of another party; that party will confiscate or destroy the asset if the promisor breaches. The posting of collateral for a loan provides a familiar, albeit imperfect, example. Other examples include a franchisor's rendering the franchisee's investment worthless by revoking the right to use a trademark and a bank's destroying a small business by cutting off a line of credit or calling a note payable on demand. A particularly important and common form of relationship-specific prospective advantage is the opportunity to deal again with the same transactor—the "repeat deal." The asset posted is the value of future dealings; if one party breaches, the other party will terminate the relationship and refuse to deal with the breacher again, destroying the asset.

A second type of nonlegal sanction is loss of *reputation* among market participants. The promisor develops a reputation for reliability among market participants who are potential transactors. If the promisor improperly breaches his commitments, he damages his reputation and thereby loses valuable opportunities for future trade. Familiar examples of reputational bonds include trademarks in consumer markets and credit ratings for individual and corporate borrowers.

A third type of nonlegal sanction is the sacrifice of *psychic and social goods.* The breaching promisor may suffer loss of opportunities for important or pleasurable associations with others, loss of self-esteem, feelings of guilt, or an unfulfilled desire to think of himself as trustworthy and competent. An unsavory businessperson may be snubbed at the local club or suffer pangs of guilt during the Sunday sermon. Encouraging trust among workers or long-term customers is one function of the "corporate culture" of firms and of the feeling of responsibility to clientele that may develop at schools, banks, or other "quasi-public" institutions.

These three types of nonlegal sanctions operate side-by-side with legal sanctions. Most commercial relationships involve some commitments that are legally enforceable; some commitments that are legally enforceable but are also, or primarily, enforced by nonlegal sanctions; and some commitments that are enforced exclusively by nonlegal sanctions. For example, commitments regarding consumer product quality are legally enforceable under warranty provisions. However, nonlegal sanctions—particularly the manufacturer's reputation in consumer markets—are the major determinant of the manufacturer's adherence to commitments to maintain product quality above minimal standards. The warranty provisions cover only basic features of the goods, and for many products it is too costly for consumers to sue to enforce even these basic commitments.

Indeed, contracts that formally provide for legal sanctions depend upon nonlegal sanctions for their effectiveness whenever the legal sanctions are ineffective in inducing the promisor to perform. Though the contract is legally enforceable as a formal matter, the promisor may be judgment-proof or the promisee may not find it worthwhile to sue if breach occurs. For example, Macaulay's often-cited data that merchants rarely sued when sales contracts were breached suggest that those contracts were primarily enforced through nonlegal sanctions. On this interpretation of the data, the legally enforceable contract formally stated the parties' obligations, but nonlegal pressures—particularly concern with business reputation—actually induced compliance.

It is worth quoting in Macaulay in full on the settlement of disputes.

S. Macaulay, 'Non-contractual Relations in Business: A Preliminary Study', (1963) 28 *Am. Soc. Rev.* 55 at 61

Business exchanges in non-speculative areas are usually adjusted without dispute. Under the law of contracts, if B orders 1,000 widgets from S at $1.00 each, B must take all 1,000 widgets or be in breach of contract and liable to pay S his expenses up to the time of the breach plus his lost anticipated profit. Yet all ten of the purchasing agents asked about cancellation of orders once placed indicated that they expected to be able to cancel orders freely subject to only an obligation to pay for the seller's major expenses such as scrapped steel. All 17 sales personnel asked reported that they often had to accept cancellation. One said, "You can't ask a man to eat paper [the firm's product] when he has no use for it." A lawyer with many large industrial clients said,

Often businessmen do not feel they have "a contract"—rather they have "an order." They speak of "cancelling the order" rather than "breaching our contract." When I began practice I referred to order cancellations as breaches of contract, but my clients objected since they do not think of cancellation as wrong. Most clients, in heavy industry at least, believe that there is a right to cancel as part of the buyer-seller relationship.

There is a widespread attitude that one can back out of any deal within some very vague limits. Lawyers are often surprised by this attitude.

Disputes are frequently settled without reference to the contract or potential or actual legal sanctions. There is a hesitancy to speak of legal rights or to threaten to sue in these negotiations. Even where the parties have a detailed and carefully planned agreement which indicates what is to happen if, say, the seller fails to deliver on time, often they will never refer to the agreement but will negotiate a solution when the problem arises apparently as if there had never been any original contract. One purchasing agent expressed a common business attitude when he said,

if something comes up, you get the other man on the telephone and deal with the problem. You don't read legalistic contract clauses at each other if you ever want to do business again. One doesn't run to lawyers if he wants to stay in business because one must behave decently.

Or as one businessman put it, "you can settle any dispute if you keep the lawyers and accountants out of it. They just do not understand the give-and-take needed in business." All of the house counsel interviewed indicated that they are called into the dispute settlement process only after the businessmen have failed to settle matters in their own way. Two indicated that after being called in house counsel at first will only advise the purchasing agent, sales manager or other official involved; not even the house counsel's letterhead is used on communications with the other side until all hope for a peaceful resolution is gone.

Law suits for breach of contract appear to be rare. Only five of the 12 purchasing agents had ever been involved in even a negotiation concerning a contract dispute where both sides were represented by lawyers; only two of ten sales managers had ever gone this far. None had been involved in a case that went through trial.

Note

D. Harris and C. Veljanovski, ('Remedies under Contract Law', (1983) 5 *L. & Pol. Q.* 97 at 98) comment: 'The law of contract is analogous to the law of divorce; parties resort to it as the parting shot in the final breakdown of their relationship.' In many, if not all, business contexts, the parties will not resort to law unless they are certain that their commercial relationship with the other is irretrievable.

III. SELF-HELP LEGAL REMEDIES

Self-help remedies are available under the general law of contract. The parties may also, through the terms of their contract, agree to enhance or limit the scope of the remedies under the general law. Such remedies can include the right to terminate or cancel the contract, in the event of breach or in other circumstances, agreed rights to deductions from the price, the right of the innocent party to withhold performance, the taking of deposits, and other analogous incentive measures agreed between the parties. According to Harris, self-help remedies provide powerful incentives in all cases to the would-be contract breaker not to renege on his promise. As we saw in Chapter 13, the self-help remedy of termination is a particularly potent tool in that it can lead to the contract breaker bearing not only the loss suffered by the innocent party in respect of the contract but also any accrued expenditure on the preparation of the contract, which is not recoverable now that it has been terminated. If the contract-breaker has prepared a particular good for sale to the innocent party which cannot be sold to a third party, all that expenditure will be wasted. Self-help remedies agreed between the parties may have an even more swingeing effect.

D. Harris, 'Incentives to Perform, or Break Contracts', [1992] *CLP* 29 at 41–4

A special clause in the contract may give the plaintiff a much wider power to terminate for breach. The parties may provide, either expressly or by implication, that *any* breach by the defendant of a particular obligation, irrespective of the actual consequences of the breach in question, should entitle the plaintiff to terminate. Under this clause the plaintiff need not prove that he has suffered (or will suffer) any loss as a result of the breach, and he may choose to terminate without being subject to any test of reasonableness, such as under the rules of mitigation. Where the plaintiff has in fact suffered no loss or only trivial loss, the court may endeavour to interpret the clause so as to avoid giving the plaintiff this drastic remedy, but if the clause is clearly expressed it will be enforced despite the harsh outcome for the defendant. . . . Unless the clause expressly provides, the plaintiff need give the defendant no opportunity to cure the breach, even though it could be easily corrected without inconveniencing the plaintiff. The consequences of termination under a special clause in the contract are the same as under the general law applicable to a serious breach. By terminating, the plaintiff may in certain circumstances be able to impose a heavy loss on the defendant even though he (the plaintiff) suffers only trivial loss from the breach. There need be no proportionality between the loss to the plaintiff and the loss imposed on the defendant by the remedy. A minor breach by the defendant may entitle the plaintiff to terminate despite the fact that he has received nearly all the benefit of the defendant's performance: he can avoid paying for it, and yet may retain the benefit without payment where it is not capable of being returned to the defendant—as in the case of services rendered to the plaintiff, or building work on the plaintiff's land. . . .

Analogous to the fear of termination is the fear of giving the plaintiff a ground on which he can temporarily withhold performance of an obligation on his side. If the plaintiff's obligation is to depend on the defendant completing one of his obligations, the plaintiff has a temporary remedy for the defendant's failure to perform. The plaintiff is entitled to suspend his performance until he gets the benefit of the specified performance from the defendant. It does not matter that the plaintiff could not prove any loss from the defendant's breach. This form of 'self-help' remedy depends on the plaintiff negotiating a clause in the contract which give him this built-in security against the defendant's failure to perform. . . .

Some of the most powerful incentives to perform arise under the so-called 'forfeiture' clauses. . . . The word 'forfeiture' is used confusingly to cover several different types of clause: their common feature is that the plaintiff, by a 'self-help' remedy, is unilaterally entitled to *extinguish* a possessory or proprietorial right of the defendant or some contractual right previously enjoyed by him. The simplest type of forfeiture is where the plaintiff holds a sum of money which he has received from the defendant, or which he holds on the defendant's account: the clause provides that, upon a breach by the defendant, the plaintiff may 'forfeit' the money: this means that, without any need for a judicial order, the plaintiff may release himself from the defendant's claim to the money so that the plaintiff thereupon becomes entitled to retain and use it as its absolute and beneficial owner.

The use of the term 'deposit' is traditionally understood to entitle the recipient to act in this way if the payer defaults in a specified obligation. The recipient can forfeit the deposit without having to prove that he has suffered any loss through the breach in question. The language in the cases accepts that a deposit is obviously designed as an incentive to perform. No controls over deposits are found at common law, but a Privy Council decision hints that the amount of a deposit might have to satisfy a test of reasonableness. . . For many years, the courts were willing to grant relief against . . . 'forfeiture' clauses in only two situations: first, in landlord and tenant cases, there has been a long history of equitable relief against forfeiture of leasehold interests, viz. where a clause in the lease entitled the landlord to repossess the premises if the tenant failed to pay an instalment of the rent. In the second situation, the contract-breaker is purchasing land by paying the price by instalments: it is clearly established that if under such a contract the purchaser defaults in payment of an instalment of the price, the court has jurisdiction to relieve him against a clause providing for forfeiture of the instalments already paid: the relief is given by granting him an extension of time within which he could pay the instalment now due.

In the last few decades, there have been attempts to widen the range of situations in which the courts will grant some relief to the defendant against a forfeiture clause. But the House of Lords has recently restricted relief to situations where the right liable to be forfeited is a proprietary or possessory interest. This is not restricted to interests in land or chattels, but extends to interests in other personal property, for example patent rights. But if the right to be forfeited is a 'mere contractual' right, the common law can give no relief to the defendant when the plaintiff exercises his right to forfeit strictly in accordance with the terms of the clause. It does not matter that the loss of the defendant's right is out of all proportion to any loss suffered by the plaintiff from the breach. . . . The forfeiture requires no prior judicial action. This enables the astute drafts-man to draft a clause which provides the defendant with the strongest possible incentive to perform his obligation.

It should be noted that the relief granted when the courts do intervene against forfeiture is very limited. The courts seldom do more than give the con-tract-breaker more time in which to remedy his default: normally time in which to pay the sum he had failed to pay on time.

Notes

1. Harris comments upon the lack of judicial control upon the use of for-feitures and deposits in contracts. In the next section we shall examine a case (*Jobson* v. *Johnson*) which perhaps evidences a move towards a wider equitable control by the courts over creditors' remedies in the form of for-feitures, etc. The relative unwillingness of the courts to intervene in this context contrasts with the continued vibrancy of the long-established dis-tinction between liquidated damages clauses and penalty clauses consid-ered in Section IV. Special protection is, however, given to consumers who conclude hire-purchase agreements and related contracts under the Consumer Credit Act 1974.

2. Macneil suggests that the use of securities and deposits is to be distin-guished in origin from the principle of the enforcement of promises. This may perhaps explain in part the reluctance of courts to intervene.

I. Macneil, 'A Primer of Contract Planning', (1975) 48 *S. Cal. L. Rev.* 627 at 678–9

Planning to keep ahead of the game: security and forfeitures. In planning self-help remedies the lawyer may often advantageously utilize the forfeiture or security root or basis of legal reinforcement of contracts. This root, to be distinguished from the enforcement-of-promise root, traces historically to the giving of hostages or property as assurance that an expected, although not necessarily promised, performance would occur. The purest modern example is probably the pawning of goods. Although there is no promise by the borrower to repay the loan, if he does not do so the goods pawned are forfeited. The working principle of the security-forfeiture root may be said to be keeping ahead of the game. When it is working at its best from the viewpoint of the protected party, that party is always ahead, or at least not behind, no matter what the other party does about performance. For example, an owner who has contracted to have a building erected on his property under a contract with no progress payments typically is increasingly ahead of the game as the contract is performed. Should the contractor stop performance, the chances are often excellent that the value of the partially completed building will equal or exceed any loss the owner may suffer because of nonperformance. The consequences of such an arrangement are manifold. Because the forfeiting of the security is within the control of the beneficiary, the arrangement constitutes a form of self-help remedy available in the event of nonperformance. Thus the beneficiary of the forfeiture-security arrangement need rely less on the promise root of assurance. And the arrangement may result in the beneficiary being left after nonperformance by the other party with more than is needed to protect any of his restitutionary, reliance, and expectation interests.

3. The difference which drafting can make to the effectiveness of self-help remedies is well illustrated by *Lombard North Central plc* v. *Butterworth*.

Lombard North Central plc v. *Butterworth*
[1987] Q.B. 527

The defendant, who was an accountant, purchased a computer on hire-purchase terms, concluding a lease arrangement with the plaintiff finance company. Payment was to involve an initial sum of £584.04 and nineteen subsequent quarterly repayments. Of these only five were made, and of these three were late, before the plaintiffs lost patience with the defendant when the sixth payment was six weeks overdue. They repossessed and resold the computer (for just £172.88) and brought an action claiming the unpaid fourteen instalments less the sum recovered on resale. They succeeded at first instance and in the Court of Appeal. The key provisions of the contract are set out at the beginning of Mustill LJ's judgment and require some explanation. The effect of clause 2 (punctual payment is 'of the essence' of the lease) is crucial to the success of the plaintiffs' case. If the wording of clause 2 makes that term a condition of the contract, any breach of which gives the innocent party a right to terminate the contract and claim damages *under the common law*. This then means that it is unnecessary for the plaintiffs to rely upon their *contractual* rights to cancel and claim damages under clauses 5 and 6. The difficulty for the plaintiffs lay in the similarity between the latter clauses and those considered by the Court of Appeal in *Financings Ltd* v. *Baldock*, discussed by Nicholls LJ. It will become apparent from the judgments that the members of the Court of Appeal reluctantly allowed the plaintiffs to take advantage of the careful drafting of their contract, which allows them to make full use of the right to terminate the contract for breach of condition, and to claim damages for their loss of bargain in circumstances where, if clause 2 had been disregarded, the conduct of the hirer would not have been sufficient to give rise at common law to a right to terminate. In so doing, the plaintiffs also avoided falling foul of the law on penalties (see Section IV) which had restricted the ability of the finance company in *Financings Ltd.* v. *Baldock* to claim full damages for loss of bargain.

MUSTILL LJ The hiring agreement contained the following material provisions:

'THE LESSEE . . . AGREES . . .

2 (a) to pay to the lessor: (i) punctually and without previous demand the rentals set out in Part 3 of the Schedule together with Value Added Tax thereon punctual payment of each which shall be of the essence of this Lease . . .

5. IN THE EVENT THAT (*a*) the Lessee shall (i) make default in the due and punctual payment of any of the rentals or of any sum of money payable to the Lessor hereunder or any part thereof . . . then upon the happening of such event . . . the Lessor's consent to the Lessee's possession of the Goods shall determine forthwith without any notice being given by the Lessor, and the Lessor may terminate this Lease either by notice in writing, or by taking possession of the goods . . .

6. IN THE EVENT that the Lessor's consent to the Lessee's possession of the goods shall be determined under clause 5 hereof (*a*) the Lessee shall pay forthwith to the Lessor: (1) all arrears of rentals; and (ii) all further rentals which would but for the determination of the Lessor's consent to the Lessee's possession of the Goods have fallen due to the end of the fixed period of this Lease less a discount thereon for accelerated payment at the rate of 5 per cent per annum; and (iii) damages for any beach of this Lease and all expenses and costs incurred by the Lessor in retaking possession of the Goods and/or enforcing the Lessor's rights under this Lease together with such Value Added Tax as shall be legally payable thereon; (*b*) the Lessor shall be entitled to exercise any one or more of the rights and remedies provided for in clause 5 and sub clause (*a*) of this clause and the determination of the Lessor's consent to the Lessee's possession of the Goods shall not affect or prejudice such rights and remedies and the Lessee shall be and remain liable to perform all outstanding liabilities under this Lease notwithstanding that the Lessor may have taken possession of the Goods and/or exercised one or more of the rights and remedies of the Lessor. (*c*) any right or remedy to which the Lessor is or may become entitled under this Lease or in consequence of the Lessee's conduct may be enforced from time to time separately or concurrently with any other right or remedy given by this Lease or now or hereafter provided for or arising by operation of law so that such rights and remedies are not exclusive of the other or others of them but are cumulative.' . . .

On 18 May 1984 the plaintiffs commenced the present action by specially indorsed writ. The material parts read:

4. Pursuant to Clause 5 of the said Lease Agreement the Plaintiff terminated its consent to the Defendant's possession of the said Computer and Printer by a notice in writing dated the 20th day of December 1982 and by virtue of the Defendant's default under the said Lease Agreement the same has been determined.

5. Pursuant to Clause 6 of the said Lease Agreement and by virtue of the determination of consent to possession pursuant to Clause 5 thereof the Plaintiff is entitled to claim (a) all of his rentals (b) all further rentals which would have been payable had the Lease Agreement continued for the full period and (c) damages for breach of the Lease Agreement.

6. The Plaintiff has recovered possession of the said Computer and Printer in accordance with its entitlement to do so under Clause 5 of the said Lease Agreement and the net proceeds of sale amounted to £172.85. Calculating the amounts due to the Plaintiff the Defendant will be given credit for this sum and an allowance will be made for accelerated receipt of the payment due under the said Lease Agreement as provided in Clause 6 thereof.

7. The Defendant has failed to pay the sums referred to in paragraph 5 hereof and the Plaintiff is entitled under the Lease or alternatively as damages for breach of the Lease, the sum of £6,869.97.'

The sum of £6,869.97 was arrived at by adding the amount of the unpaid instalment and value added tax, and the 13 rentals due after termination, and then giving credit for the net proceeds of sale and an allowance of £1,221.49 for accelerated receipt. The pleading concluded with claims for £6,869.97 under para 7, interest and 'damages for breach of contract'. . . .

Three issues were canvassed before us. (1) Is cl 6 of the agreement to be disregarded, on the ground that it creates a penalty? . . . (2) Apart from cl 2(*a*) of the agreement, was the [judge at first instance] correct in holding that the conduct of the defendant amounted to a wrongful repudiation of the contract, and that the sum claimed was recoverable in damages? (3) Does the provision in cl 2(*a*) of the agreement that time for payment of the instalments was of the essence have the effect of making the defendant's late payment of the outstanding instalment a repudiatory breach?

As to the first two issues, I need say only that I have had the advantage of reading in draft the judgment to be delivered by Nicholls LJ, and that I am in such entire agreement with his conclusions and reasons that it is unnecessary to add any observations of my own.

I would, however, wish to deal with the third point. . . .

The reason why I am impelled to hold that the plaintiffs' contentions are well-founded can most conveniently be set out in a series of propositions. (1) Where a breach goes to the root of the contract, the injured party may elect to put an end to the contract. Thereupon both sides are relieved from those obligations which remain unperformed. (2) If he does so elect, the injured party is entitled to compensation for (a) any breaches which occurred before the contract was terminated and (b) the loss of his opportunity to receive performance of the promisor's outstanding obligations. (3) Certain categories of obligation, often called conditions, have the property that any breach of them is treated as going to the root of the contract. On the occurrence of any breach of condition, the injured party can elect to terminate and claim damages, whatever the gravity of the breach. (4) It is possible by express provision in the contract to make a term a condition, even if it would not be so in the absence of such a provision. (5) A stipulation that time is of the essence, in relation to a particular contractual term, denotes that timely performance is a condition of the contract. The consequence is that delay in performance is treated as going to the root of the contract, without regard to the magnitude of the breach. (6) It follows that where a promisor fails to give timely performance of an obligation in respect of which time is expressly stated to be of the essence, the injured party may elect to terminate and recover damages in respect of the promisor's outstanding obligations, without regard to the magnitude of the breach. (7) A term of the contract prescribing what damages are to be recoverable when a contract is terminated for a breach of condition is open to being struck down as a penalty, if it is not a genuine covenanted pre-estimate of the damage, in the same way as a clause which prescribes the measure for any other type of breach. No doubt the position is the same where the clause is ranked as a condition by virtue of an express provision in the contract. (8) A clause expressly assigning a particular obligation to the category of condition is not a clause which purports to fix the damages for breaches of the obligation, and is not subject to the law governing penalty clauses. (9) Thus, although in the present case cl 6 is to be struck down as a penalty, cl 2(*a*)(i) remains enforceable. The plaintiffs were entitled to terminate the contract independently of cl 5, and to recover damages for loss of the future instalments. This loss was correctly computed by the master.

These bare propositions call for comment. The first three are uncontroversial. The fourth was not, I believe, challenged before us, but I would in any event regard it as indisputable. That there exists a category of term, in respect of which any breach whether large or small entitles the promisee to treat himself as discharged, has never been doubted in modern times, and the fact that a term may be assigned to this category by express agreement has been taken for granted for at least a century. . . .

The fifth proposition is a matter of terminology, and has been more taken for granted than discussed. That making time of the essence is the same as making timely performance a condition was, however, expressly stated by Megaw and Browne LJJ in *Bunge Corp v Tradax SA* [1981] 2 All ER 513 at 532, 536, 539, and the same proposition is implicit in the leading speeches of Lord Wilberforce and Lord Roskill in the House of Lords.

The sixth proposition is a combination of the first five. There appears to be no direct authority for it, and it is right to say that most of the cases on the significance of time being of the essence have been concerned with the right of the injured party to be discharged, rather than the principles on which his damages are to be computed. Nevertheless, it is axiomatic that a person who establishes a breach of condition can terminate and claim damages for loss of the bargain, and I know of no authority which suggests that the position is any different where late performance is made into a breach of condition by a stipulation that time is of the essence. . . .

. . . The seventh is uncontroversial, and I would add only the rider that when deciding on the penal nature of a clause which prescribes a measure of recovery for damages resulting from a termination founded on a breach of condition, the comparison should be with the common law measure, namely with the loss to the promisee resulting from the loss of his bargain. If the contract permits him to treat the contract as repudiated, the fact that the breach is comparatively minor should in my view play no part in the equation.

I believe that the real controversy in the present case centres on the eighth proposition . . . I acknowledge, of course, that by promoting a term into the category where all breaches are ranked as breaches of condition, the parties indirectly bring about a situation where, for breaches which are relatively small, the injured party is enabled to recover damages as on the loss of the bargain, whereas without the stipulation his measure of recovery would be different. But I am unable to accept that this permits the court to strike down as a penalty the clause which brings about this promotion. To do so would be to reverse the current of more than 100 years' doctrine, which permits the parties to treat as a condition something which would not otherwise be so. I am not prepared to take this step. . . .

. . . I conclude that the plaintiffs are entitled to retain the damages which the master has awarded. This is not a result which I view with much satisfaction, partly because the plaintiffs have achieved by one means a result which the law of penalties might have prevented them from achieving by another. . . . Nevertheless, it is the answer to which, in my view, the authorities clearly point. Accordingly, I would dismiss the appeal.

NICHOLLS LJ. Shortly stated, the two issues raised on this appeal are whether the sums payable under cl 6 of the lease agreement constituted a penalty and, if so, whether the conduct of the hirer (the defendant) amounted to a repudiation of the agreement that was accepted by the owner (the plaintiffs). . . .

. . . The ratio of the decision of this court in *Financings Ltd v Baldock* [1963] 2 QB 104 was that when an owner determines a hire-purchase agreement in exercise of a right so to do given him by the agreement, in the absence of repudiation he can recover damages for any breaches up to the date of termination but not thereafter, and a 'minimum payment' clause which purports to oblige the hirer to pay larger sums than this is unenforceable as a penalty. Lord Denning MR said ([1963] 2 QB 104 at 110):

'Undoubtedly the cases in the past give rise to some conflict, and, therefore, I will try to state the matter on principle. It seems to me that, when an agreement of hiring is terminated by virtue of a power contained in it and the owner retakes the vehicle, he can recover damages for any breach up to the date of termination, but not for any breach thereafter, for the simple reason that there are no breaches thereafter.'

In my view, applying the principle enunciated in *Financings Ltd v Baldock* to this case leads inescapably to the conclusion that in the absence of a repudiatory breach cl 6(a) is a penalty in so far as it purports to oblige the defendant, regardless of the seriousness or triviality of the breach which led to the plaintiffs terminating the agreement by retaking possession of the computer, to make a payment, albeit a discounted payment, in respect of rental instalments which had not accrued due prior to 20 December 1982. . . .

The claim for damages

I turn to the second issue, which is whether the loss really sustained by the plaintiffs in this case by reason of the defendant's defaults in payment of the instalments amounted to loss of the whole hiring transaction. It would have so amounted if, but only if, the defendant's conduct amounted to a repudiation of the lease agreement and that repudiation was accepted by the plaintiffs.

I preface this issue with a reminder of the commercial realities of this lease transaction. In so doing I do not seek to ascribe to the transaction any legal characteristics other than those set forth in the lease agreement entered into by the parties. But in considering whether a hirer's conduct amounts to repudiation the commercial setting and object of the agreement must be of prime importance. The plaintiffs are a well-known finance company. Their business is to provide finance for, amongst other matters, the acquisition by customers of goods, whether by hire purchase or lease or otherwise. They do not themselves supply the goods. They adopt the normal practice of finance companies: they purchase the goods chosen by the customer from the supplier and pay for them, and then let them to the customer on hire purchase or hire or as the case may be.

In these circumstances, it was a matter of importance to the plaintiffs that the agreed instalments should be paid, and should be paid promptly. I can see no reason to doubt that the interest charges were calculated by reference to the agreed hire instalment dates, on the footing that the instalments would be paid regularly and with reasonable promptness. To the plaintiffs a hirer who is repeatedly and significantly late with his payments, and who has to be chased with reminders and warnings, time after time, is an unattractive hirer whose transaction may eventually become an unprofitable one, in which event the plaintiffs will lose substantially the whole benefit intended to be acquired by it under the agreement. . . .

. . . I have come to the conclusion that the court is not entitled to draw the inference that [by the time the plaintiffs gave notice of termination] the defendant had evinced an intention not to adhere to, not to be bound by, his obligation under the lease agreement to pay the instalments and to do so promptly and regularly. In reaching this conclusion I have in mind the commercial objective of this agreement as far as the plaintiffs were concerned, as described above. But, given the bare facts I have mentioned, the plaintiffs' action was too hasty. The three 1981 instalments had been paid promptly, the first three of the 1982 instalments had been paid belatedly or very belatedly but they had been accepted, and when notice of termination was given on 20 December 1982 only one instalment, the one due on 19 November, was outstanding. Without more I do not think those facts justify a finding of repudiation by 20 December 1982.

Thus far I have reached my conclusion regarding repudiation without giving any weight or effect to the provision in cl 2(*a*) of the lease, that punctual payment of each rental instalment was of the essence of the lease.

I must now consider a further submission advanced by the plaintiffs that, time of payment having been made of the essence by this provision, it was open to the plaintiffs, once default in payment of any one instalment on the due date had occurred, to treat the agreement as having been repudiated by the defendant, and claim damages for loss of the whole transaction, even though in the absence of this provision such a default would not have had that consequence. On this, the question which arises is one of construction: on the true construction of the clause, did the 'time of the essence' provision have the effect submitted by the plaintiffs? In my view, the answer to that question is Yes. The provision in cl 2(*a*) has to be read and construed in conjunction with the other provisions in the agreement, including cll 5 and 6. So read, it is to be noted that failure to pay any instalment triggers a right for the plaintiffs to terminate the agreement by retaking possession of the goods (cl 5), with the expressed consequence that the defendant becomes liable to make payments which assume that the defendant is liable to make good to the plaintiffs the loss by them of the whole transaction (cl 6). Given that context, the 'time of the essence' provision seems to me to be intended to bring about the result that default in punctual payment is to be regarded (to use a once fashionable term) as a breach going to the root of the contract, and, hence, as giving rise to the consequences in damages attendant on such a breach. I am unable to see what other purpose the 'time of the essence' provision in cl 2(*a*) can serve or was intended to serve or what other construction can fairly be ascribed to it. . . .

Mustill LJ's illuminating analysis leaves no escape from the conclusion that parties are free to agree that a particular provision in their contract shall be a condition such that a breach of it is to be regarded as going to the root of the contract and entitling the innocent party (1) to accept that breach as a repudiation and (2) to be paid damages calculated on that footing.

I have to say that I view the impact of that principle in this case with considerable dissatisfaction, for this reason. As already mentioned, the principle applied in *Financings Ltd v Baldock* was that when an owner determines a hire-purchase agreement in exercise of a power so to do given him by the agreement on non-payment of instalments, he can recover damages for any breaches up to the date of termination but (in the absence of repudiation) not thereafter. There is no practical difference between (1) an agreement containing such a power and (2) an agreement containing a provision to the effect that time for payment of each instalment is of the essence, so that any breach will go to the root of the contract. The difference between these two agreements is one of drafting form, and wholly without substance. Yet under an agreement drafted in the first form, the owner's damages claim arising on his exercise of the power of termination is confined to damages for breaches up to the date of termination, whereas under an agreement drafted in the second form the owner's damages claim, arising on his acceptance of an identical breach as a repudiation of the agreement, will extend to damages for loss of the whole transaction.

Nevertheless . . . I can see no escape from the conclusion that such is the present state of the law. This conclusion emasculates the decision in *Financings Ltd v Baldock*, for it means that a skilled draftsman can easily side-step the effect of that decision. Indeed, that is what has occurred here.

Notes

1. To Nicholls and Mustill LJJ, the conclusion that clause 2 allows the plaintiffs to terminate the agreement for reasons which at common law do not amount to a repudiation *and* to claim damages for loss of bargain, notwithstanding the decision in *Financings Ltd* v. *Baldock*, was one which gave them, as judges, no satisfaction. It has also been seen by some commentators as an unwelcome coda to the reassertion of the centrality of commercial certainty by the House of Lords in *Bunge* v. *Deutsche Tradax* ([1981] 2 All ER 513; see Ch. 10). See e.g. G. Treitel, 'Damages on Rescission for Breach of Contract' ([1987] *LMCLQ* 143); W. Bojczuk, 'When Is a Condition Not a Condition?' ([1987] *JBL* 353 at 358–62). The main argument of principle that is behind the decision in *Lombard* is one of freedom of contract: the parties are free to order their contracts as they wish, provided they do not offend against the law on penalties (see Section IV). The damages for breach claimed by the plaintiffs are not based on the agreed measure contained in clause 6, but on the general common law expectation measure (see further Section V). Consequently, the plaintiffs sidestep the law on penalties completely by (as it were) 'contracting into' the treatment of conditions elaborated in *Bunge* v. *Tradax*, claiming loss of bargain damages for a breach which did not, without clause 2, entitle termination of the contract since it was not repudiatory.

2. Treitel points out ([1987] *LMCLQ* 143 at 144–5) that the reason for preventing the finance company in *Financings Ltd.* v. *Baldock* from claiming full loss of bargain damages was that the right to terminate came only from the contract, and that consequently the only right to bargain damages likewise flowed from the contract. But since the relevant clause was stuck

down as a penalty, this left the finance company unable to sue for bargain damages, as it was the exercise of the contractual right to terminate which caused the loss of the bargain. Common law damages would not be available other than for lost expenditure resulting from the delay, as there was no common law right to terminate for what was not a repudiatory breach. Equally, argues Treitel, the right to terminate in *Lombard* comes from the contract, and consequently should be treated in the same way. The difficulty is that the contract-drafters have fed the right to terminate in *Lombard* back into the common law bargain measure of damages by creating a term of the contract which goes to its root, making the breach into a repudiatory one.

3. Beale, in contrast, has more sympathy with the general aim of the drafters of the *Lombard* contract. He contrasts this with the similar aim but different approach of the drafters of ICE contracts.

H. Beale, 'Penalties in Termination Provisions', (1988), 104 *LQR* 355 at 355–9

The Institution of Civil Engineers' Conditions of Contract (5th ed, revised 1979) provide in clause 63 that in certain circumstances the employer may:

"enter upon the site and expel the contractor therefrom without thereby avoiding the contract or releasing the contractor from any of his obligations or liabilities . . ."

thus, in effect, bringing the contract to an end. Clause 63(4) then provides that the contractor will be liable to the employer for any amount by which the cost of having the work completed by another contractor and "damages for delay in completion (if any) and all other expenses" exceed the sum which would have been due to the contractor upon completion by him, and this amount "shall be deemed a debt due by the contractor to the employer . . ." The circumstances in which this power is exercisable include some events which would be fundamental breaches at common law, such as "abandonment of the contract" and others which might not, such as failing to remove defective work within 14 days of a written notice condemning it or subletting part of the work in defiance of the engineer's consent. The clause is an attempt to give the employer better protection than is available at common law, but a little known decision of the Court of Appeal, *Capital Finance Co. Ltd*. v. *Donati* (1977) 121 S.J. 270, and dicta by Nicholls L.J. in *Lombard North Central Plc* v. *Butterworth* [1987] Q.B. 527 at pp. 540–543, show that such a clause may be a trap. If the employer determines the contract because of some default by the contractor which is held not to be sufficiently serious to justify termination at common law, the employer may find itself unable to claim the additional costs of completion by another contractor or compensation for delay despite the provisions of clause 63(4), because the latter will be void as a penalty. . . .

. . . [D]rafters of contracts such as the I.C.E. Conditions have relied on the alternative device of stating expressly that damages for loss of bargain shall be recoverable. Even in *Financings* itself there are hints that such an approach would work if the clause attempted to impose liability for no more than the actual loss. . . .

There is logic in saying that a clause entitling a party to recover for losses which it could not recover in the absence of the clause must be a penalty, but it is not compelling. There is no doubt that the finance house does suffer a loss if the goods repossessed have so far depreciated that they are worth less than the present value of the outstanding payments, and it has been recognised that this is a loss against which the owner "is entitled to protect himself". . . . The same must be true in the construction contract cases. Why do the courts not allow recovery? . . . The most probable explanation is that a clause simply giving a right to terminate for a minor breach does not make it clear enough to the other party that if he commits such a breach he may not only lose the goods or have his employment determined but may also be liable for loss of bargain damages. . . .

If this is correct, there is no reason not to uphold a clause which specifically states that further damages will be payable—the other party is put on notice, and in a much clearer way than if compliance with every term is made "of the essence" as in *Lombard*. . . .

Termination clauses have an important function in planning contracts so as to give one party protection and the other party an incentive to perform, while making the parties' rights more certain. Hedging the use of such clauses about with so many restrictions that they are difficult to employ except where the common law recognises that there has been a fundamental breach leaves too much to the court's assessment of what breaches are serious and which are not, and too little to the parties' choice. A clause which clearly states that in the event of certain breaches the contract may be terminated and various further sums, not exceeding the actual loss to the terminating party, must then be paid should be enforced unless there is good reason not to do so.

In the consumer context there may be good reasons for not enforcing such clauses, at least where, as in all the cases, the clause is contained in a standard form contract. First, a consumer may not notice or may not understand even an explicit clause and may be taken unfairly by surprise. Secondly, it has been shown that the combination of competition among suppliers and consumer ignorance about the terms which are on offer may lead to standard form contracts containing inefficiently harsh terms—terms which consumers would have paid more to have had changed in their favour, had they appreciated the effect of the clauses. . . . This might justify refusal to enforce even clear clauses in standard form contracts, if the court were convinced that a different clause would have been agreed had the clause been negotiated specifically. These problems are less likely in a non-consumer context. Accountants buying computers for business might be expected to understand the terms offered, and even if not all of them do so, it is likely that enough business customers will be aware of any terms they find objectionable, and complain, to put pressure on suppliers to offer better terms. There is therefore less of a case for refusing to enforce the clause as written. There would be no case for refusing when the clause is, like clause 63 of the I.C.E. conditions, in a contract which is thoroughly familiar to contractors and is sponsored by associations representing both sides of the industry.

IV. REMEDIES AGREED BETWEEN THE PARTIES BUT REQUIRING JUDICIAL ACTION

The commonest type of remedy agreed between the parties, but requiring judicial action if the contract breaker resists enforcement, is the liquidated damages clause. Such a clause commonly provides that, in the event of breach, the contact breaker will pay a certain sum or sums (no more, no less), either fixed or calculable in advance. The seriousness of the breach or the degree of delay in performance, to take two common examples, may affect the amount payable. They represent an attempt by the parties to cut down the costs of recovering damages in the event of breach. Ease of enforcement is ensured in many contracts, since the innocent party may be empowered to deduct the liquidated damages from price payable, making the liquidated damages clause akin to a self-help remedy and putting the onus on the contract breaker to bring proceedings. Problems of proof are avoided, the parties can fix the measure of damages (as in the ICE Conditions of Contract extracted by Beale above), and it is arguably also possible for the parties to agree the inclusion of loss which would be irrecoverable at common law because it is 'too remote' (see Section VI). The only test which a liquidated damages clause must pass is that it must be a genuine pre-estimate of loss. If not, the clause will be classed as a penalty and struck down under the court's equitable jurisdiction. The injured party is then left to claim unliquidated compensatory damages in the normal way (Section V).

A. Liquidated Damages Clauses

Liquidated damages clauses are very widely used, especially in long-term commercial contracts (engineering, construction, shipping, retail distribution, franchising, etc.), but they also occur in sales transactions such as hire-purchase and instalment sales—in which context they may also affect consumers. Parliament has intervened through the Consumer Credit Act 1974 to control the use of, for example, minimum payment clauses in hire purchase transactions.

The reasons for the use of liquidated damages provisions are summarized by Sweet.

J. Sweet, 'Liquidated Damages in California', (1972) 60 *Cal. L. Rev.* 84 at 86–7

First, consider the use of liquidation clauses in the model of a negotiated contract. Both contracting parties often wish to control their risk exposure, and permitting them to do so encourages risk-taking. The performing party may also wish to avoid the feared irrationality of the judicial process in determining actual damages. He may also be fearful that the court will give insufficient consideration to legitimate excuses for nonperformance, that the court may be unduly sympathetic to plaintiff's claim that any loss he incurred should be paid for by the party whose nonperformance caused the loss, or that the court may consider contract breach an immoral act.

There are also reasons why the nonperforming party as well may wish to use a liquidated damages clause. Sometimes a breach will cause damage, but the amount of damages cannot be proven under damage rules. For example, in wartime procurement contracts it may be impossible to establish the damages caused by delayed or defective performance by the contractor. Without an enforceable clause purporting to liquidate damages, the nonperforming party may fear that the performing party will have insufficient incentive to perform if the latter realizes that damages he has caused are not sufficiently provable to be collected. Such a clause is a penalty in that its principal function is to coerce performance. Yet if it is reasonable—not disproportionate to actual, although unprovable, damages or to the contract price—it will be enforced. Without a liquidated damages clause there is also a danger the contractor may recover the full contract price despite a breach that caused some unprovable losses. Thus while the nonperforming party may be motivated principally by the penalty aspects of the clause, he may to a lesser degree be motivated by the desire to prevent what appears to him to be unjust enrichment.

Liquidated damages clauses may also be inserted to improve upon what the parties believe to be a deficiency in the litigation process: the cost and difficulty of judicially proving damages. Through a liquidation clause the parties attempt to use contract to settle the amount of damages involved and thus improve the normal rules of damages. Also, when the clause is phrased in such a way as to indicate that the breaching party will pay a specified amount if a particular breach occurs, troublesome problems involved in proving causation and foreseeability may be avoided. This was extremely helpful, for example, in wartime procurement contracts, where not only was it almost impossible to establish the amount of damages, but it was equally impossible to establish that delayed or defective performance by the contractor caused any particular loss and that the loss was reasonably foreseeable at the time the contract was made. Finally, it is unlikely that either would later dispute the amount of damages recoverable as the result of his breach.

In the adhesion contract situation there are some similarities in objectives; the desire to control the irrationality and expense of the litigation process and the need to know the extent of risk exposure are still involved. There are, however, obvious additional objectives of the stronger party. He can dictate the terms of the contract; if he is the performing party, he is likely to use the contract clause to limit his exposure almost to the vanishing point, and if he is the nonperforming party, he may try to use a penalty clause to coerce performance, or he may try to use a genuine liquidation clause to make vindication of his legal rights as convenient and inexpensive as possible. In the adhesion context, then, the stronger party may try to limit his own liability and to set an agreed amount that is sufficiently high to coerce performance. In the event performance is not rendered, the clause may obtain a settlement or win the case.

The Privy Council has recently reviewed the law governing the distinction between penalties and liquidated damages clauses.

Philips Hong Kong Ltd. v. *The Attorney General of Hong Kong* (1993) 61 BLR 41

In 1986 Philips entered into a contract with the Hong Kong Government to design, supply, install, and commission a computerized supervisory system for certain roads and tunnels which were part of a complex road-construction project involving in all seven separate contracts. The network of construction contracts was linked together by a set of Key Dates, which designated the points at which each contact interfaced with the work programmes under the other contracts. Clause 27 of the Philips contract imposed an express obligation on Philips to meet its Key Dates, and clause 29 provided:

(a) that liquidated damages (varying between HK$60,655 and HK $77,818) would be payable *per diem* if the Key Dates were not met; and

(b) that additional liquidated damages of HK$74,104 would be payable *per diem* if the whole programme of work were not completed on time.

Philips brought an action seeking a declaration that the liquidation damages clauses were penal and therefore unenforceable. It succeeded at first instance, but failed when the Government appealed to the Court of Appeal of Hong Kong. Philips's appeal to the Privy Council failed.

LORD WOOLF [Clause 29] provides

"29. Liquidated damages for delay

29.1 If the Contractor shall fail to complete the Works or any Section thereof or shall fail to achieve a Specified Degree of Completion within the time prescribed by Clause 27 or extended time, or shall fail to complete or shall unduly delay the Tests on Completion then the Contractor shall pay to the Employer the sum or sums stated in the Appendix to the Form of Tender as liquidated damages for such default and not as a penalty for every day or part of a day which shall elapse between the time prescribed by Clause 27 or extended time, as the case may be, and the date of completion of the Works or the relevant Section thereof or the relevant Specified Degree of Completion.

29.2 The Employer may, without prejudice to any other method of recovery, deduct the amount of such damages from any monies due or which may become due to the Contractor whether under this or any other Contract with the Employer.

29.3 The payment or deduction of such damages shall not relieve the Contractor from his obligation to complete the Works or from any other of his obligations and liabilities under the Contract.

29.4 If before completion of the Works, any Section of the Works is required by the Employer and capable of occupation or use by the Employer and has been confirmed by the Engineer as completed pursuant to Clause 31 (Taking Over), the liquidated damages (if any) prescribed for delay to the whole of the Works shall for any period of delay after such certification be reduced in the proportion which the value of the Section so certified bears to the whole of the Works:

Provided that—. . .

Notwithstanding any provisions of this Clause or of the Contract providing for the reduction in liquidated damages for the early completion of any Section of the Works the resulting amount of liquidated damages shall not be less than the minimum amount of liquidated damages as stated is [sic] the Form of Tender." . . .

The consequences of Philips' approach to determining whether a provision in a contract as to liquidated damages is unenforceable

In these proceedings Philips are seeking to obtain no more than a ruling of the courts as to the legal position under the contract. They reserve the right to investigate the question as to whether the amount claimed is in fact excessive at the arbitration when the evidence can be fully investigated. Their Lordships have reservations as to the propriety and the practicality of Philips doing this. . . .

At this stage Mr Nicholas Dennys QC does not suggest on behalf of Philips that the sum claimed by the Government by way of liquidated damages is in fact exorbitant in view of the very substantial delay which in fact occurred in the execution of this contract by Philips. Instead he bases his argument on what could have happened in a number of different hypothetical situations. He suggests that if one or more of those situations had happened, the sum which would then be payable by way of liquidated damages would be wholly out of proportion to any loss which the Government was likely to suffer in that situation and that this is sufficient to establish that the provisions are penal in effect. If Philips' approach is correct this would be unsatisfactory. It would mean that it would be extremely difficult to devise any provision for the payment of liquidated damages in the case of a contract of this sort which would not be open to attack as being penal. As is the case with most commercial contracts, there is always going to be a variety of different situations in which damage can occur and even though long and detailed provisions are contained in a contract it will often be virtually impossible to anticipate accurately and provide for all the possible scenarios. Whatever the degree of care exercised by the draftsman it will still be almost inevitable that an ingenious argument can be developed for saying that in a particular hypothetical situation a substantially higher sum will be recovered than would be recoverable if the plaintiff was required to prove his actual loss in that situation. Such a result would undermine the whole purpose of parties to a contract being able to agree beforehand what damages are to be recoverable in the event of a breach of contract. This would not be in the interest of either of the parties to the contract since it is to their advantage that they should be able to know with a reasonable degree of certainty the extent of their liability and the risks which they run as a result of entering into the contract. This is particularly true in the case of building and engineering contracts. In the case of those contracts provision for liquidated damages should enable the employer to know the extent to which he is protected in the event of the contractor failing to perform his obligations.

As for the contractor, by agreeing to a provision for liquidated damages, he is seeking to remove the uncertainty as to the extent of his liability under the contract if he is unable to comply with his contractual obligations. That he may be unable to comply with those obligations is always a risk which a contractor has to face and there are substantial advantages from his point of view in being able to quantify accurately the amount of his liability if matters do not proceed according to plan. As Mr Richard Fernyhough QC [counsel for the Government] submitted, the liquidated damages clause enables the contractor when quoting for a contract to take account of the possible liability which he may be under in determining a price which he quotes for undertaking the contract, particularly where the amount of loss actually suffered by the employer will be difficult to quantify. It therefore makes commercial sense for both sides of the contract to remove the uncertainty by including a liquidated damages clause in the contract. However this will only be the result if the inclusion of a clause providing for liquidated damages will reduce and not increase the risk of a dispute and possible litigation in the event of the contractor failing to fulfil his contractual obligations.

What then is the position? Is it sufficient for a contractor to identify hypothetical situations where the effect of the application of the clause may be to produce a sum payable to the employer substantially in excess of the damage which the employer is likely to suffer in order to defeat the intended effect of a clause freely entered into by the parties providing for the payment of liquidated damages?

The court's approach to liquidated damages provisions in contracts
Although there is a good deal of disagreement as to how the penalty jurisdiction grew up (see the Law Commission Working Paper No 61, *Penalty Clauses*

and Forfeiture of Monies Paid) it is recorded in the judgment of Kay LJ in *Law* v *Local Board of Redditch* [1892] 1 QB 127 at 133 that originally it was by the Courts of Equity that relief was granted. They did so where a sum of money was agreed to be paid as a penalty for non-performance of a collateral contract where the actual damage which would be sustained could be estimated. In such circumstances the Courts would limit the sum recoverable to the actual loss suffered. The principle would be applied in particular where the penalty was agreed to be paid for the non-payment of a sum of money under a bond. This limited application of the principle was subsequently extended to other situations by the courts of common law, but the principle was always recognised as being subject to fairly narrow constraints and the courts have always avoided claiming that they have any general jurisdiction to rewrite the contracts that the parties have made.

Guidance as to what are the constraints is authoritatively set out in the speech of Lord Dunedin in *Dunlop Pneumatic Tyre Co Ltd* v *New Garage & Motor Co* [1915] AC 79 at 86, when he said:

". . . I shall content myself with stating succinctly the various propositions which I think are deducible from the decisions which rank as authoritative:

1. Though the parties to a contract who use the words 'penalty' or 'liquidated damages' may prima facie be supposed to mean what they say, yet the expression used is not conclusive. The Court must find out whether the payment stipulated is in truth a penalty or liquidated damages. This doctrine may be said to be found passim in nearly every case.

2. The essence of a penalty is a payment of money stipulated as in terrorem of the offending party; the essence of liquidated damages is a genuine covenanted pre-estimate of damage (*Clydebank Engineering and Shipbuilding Co* v *Don José Ramos Yzquierdo y Castaneda* [1905] AC 6.)

3. The question whether a sum stipulated is penalty or liquidated damages is a question of construction to be decided upon the terms and inherent circumstances of each particular contract, judged of as at the time of the making of the contract, not as at the time of the breach (*Public Works Commissioner* v *Hills* [1906] AC 368 and *Webster* v *Bosanquet* [1912] AC 394).

4. To assist this task of construction various tests have been suggested, which if applicable to the case under consideration may prove helpful, or even conclusive. Such are:

   (a) It will be held to be penalty if the sum stipulated for is extravagant and unconscionable in amount in comparison with the greatest loss that could conceivably be proved to have followed from the breach. (Illustration given by Lord Halsbury in *Clydebank* case [1905] AC 6).

   (b) It will be held to be a penalty if the breach consists only in not paying a sum of money, and the sum stipulated is a sum greater than the sum which ought to have been paid (*Kemble* v *Farren* (1829) 6 Bing 141) . . .

   (c) There is a presumption (but no more) that it is penalty when 'a single lump sum is made payable by way of compensation, on the occurrence of one or more or all

of several events, some of which may occasion serious and others but trifling
damage' (Lord Watson in *Lord Elphinstone* v *Monkland Iron and Coal Co* (1886) 11
App Cas 332).

On the other hand:

(d) It is no obstacle to the sum stipulated being a genuine pre-estimate of damage,
that the consequences of the breach are such as to make precise pre-estimation
almost an impossibility. On the contrary, that is just the situation when it is probable that pre-estimated damage was the true bargain between the parties
(*Clydebank* case [1905] AC 6 *per* Lord Halsbury at 11; *Webster* v *Bosanquet*, *per*
Lord Mersey at 398)."

Lord Denning did criticise this restricted view of the application of the principle
in *Bridge* v *Campbell Discount Co* [1962] AC 600 at 629, but his views were not
shared by the other members of the House. . . .

[His Lordship referred to the decision of] the High Court of Australia in
AMEV UDC Finance Ltd v *Austin* (1986) 162 CLR 170, a case to which reference is made, . . . for the general approach which was adopted as to what
should be the approach of the court to alleged penalties. It was a case in which
a finance company tried unsuccessfully to rely on general equitable principles
relating to relief against penalties as against guarantors of a hirer when the
finance company had determined a hiring agreement. Mason and Wilson JJ in
a point judgment, having admirably surveyed the decisions as to penalties
decided both in this country and in other Commonwealth countries, referred to
the advantages of allowing the parties to contracts greater latitude to determine for themselves the consequences of breaches or the termination of their
contracts, and then went on to say (p 193):

"But equity and the common law have long maintained a supervisory jurisdiction, not to
rewrite contracts imprudently made, but to relieve against provisions which are so
unconscionable or oppressive that their nature is penal rather than compensatory. The
test to be applied in drawing that distinction is one of degree and will depend on a number of circumstances, including (1) the degree of disproportion between the stipulated
sum and the loss likely to be suffered by the plaintiff, a factor relevant to the oppressive-
ness of the term to the defendant, and (2) the nature of the relationship between the
contracting parties, a factor relevant to the unconscionability of the plaintiff's conduct in
seeking to enforce the term. The courts should not, however, be too ready to find the
requisite degree of disproportion lest they impinge on the parties' freedom to settle for
themselves the rights and liabilities following a breach of contract. The doctrine of
penalties answers, in situations of the present kind, an important aspect of the criticism
often levelled against unqualified freedom of contract, namely the possible inequality
of bargaining power. In this way the courts strike a balance between the competing
interests of freedom of contract and protection of weak contracting parties: see
generally Atiyah, *The Rise and Fall of Freedom of Contract* (1979), especially Chapter
22."

It should not be assumed that, in this passage of their judgment, Mason and
Wilson JJ were setting out some broader discretionary approach than that indi-

cated as being appropriate by Lord Dunedin. On the contrary, earlier in their judgment they had noted that the "*Dunlop* approach" had been eroded by recent decisions and they stated that there was much to be said for the view that the courts should return to that approach. . . . [His Lordship also cited with approval] the view of Dickson J in the Supreme Court of Canada in *Elsey* v *J G Collins Insurance Agencies Ltd* (1978) 83 DLR at 15 where he said:

"It is now evident that the power to strike down a penalty clause is a blatant interference with freedom of contract and is designed for the sole purpose of providing relief against oppression for the party having to pay the stipulated sum. It has no place where there is no oppression."

Such views are in accord with those expressed by Lord Justice Diplock in *Robophone Facilities Ltd* v *Blank* [1966] 1 WLR 1428. He said (at 1447) that the "court should not be astute to descry a 'penalty clause'". These statements assist by making it clear that the court should not adopt an approach to provisions as to liquidated damages which could, as indicated earlier, defeat their purpose.

Except possibly in the case of situations where one of the parties to the contract is able to dominate the other as to the choice of the terms of a contract, it will normally be insufficient to establish that a provision is objectionably penal to identify situations where the application of the provision could result in a larger sum being recovered by the injured party than his actual loss. Even in such situations so long as the sum payable in the event of non-compliance with the contract is not extravagant, having regard to the range of losses that it could reasonably be anticipated it would have to cover at the time the contract was made, it can still be a genuine pre-estimate of the loss that would be suffered and so a perfectly valid liquidated damage provision. The use in argument of unlikely illustrations should therefore not assist a party to defeat a provision as to liquidated damages. As the Law Commission stated in Working Paper No 61 (page 30):

"The fact that in certain circumstances a party to a contract might derive a benefit in excess of his loss does not . . . outweigh the very definite practical advantages of the present rule upholding a genuine estimate, formed at the time the contract was made of the probable loss."

A difficulty can arise where the range of possible loss is broad. Where it should be obvious that, in relation to part of the range, the liquidated damages are totally out of proportion to certain of the losses which may be incurred, the failure to make special provision for those losses may result in the "liquidated damages" not being recoverable. . . . However, the court has to be careful not to set too stringent a standard and bear in mind that what the parties have agreed should normally be upheld. Any other approach will lead to undesirable uncertainty especially in commercial contracts.

The case for the appellant

In seeking to establish that the sum described in the Philips contract as liquidated damages was in fact a penalty, Philips has to surmount the strong inference to the contrary resulting from its agreement to make the payments as
liquidated damages and the fact that it is not suggesting in these proceedings
that the sum claimed is excessive in relation to the actual loss suffered by the
Government. The fact that the issue has to be determined objectively, judged
at the date the contract was made, does not mean what actually happens subsequently is irrelevant. On the contrary it can provide valuable evidence as to
what could reasonably be expected to be the loss at the time the contract was
made. Likewise, the fact that two parties who should be well capable of protecting their respective commercial interests agreed the allegedly penal provision suggests that the formula for calculating liquidated damages is unlikely to
be oppressive. The position is similar in relation to the evidence relied on by
the Government in this case as to their reasons for seeking to quantify their loss
in the manner set out in the contract. As the test is objective such evidence is
far from conclusive but it can at least provide the explanation as to why
the particular formula was adopted so that the court can evaluate that explanation. . . .

Here the Government in its evidence provides an explanation as to how the
liquidated damages were calculated. So far as the missing of Key Dates was
concerned, the amount of damages was calculated by applying a formula to
what was anticipated would be the value of the interfacing contracts. (The
actual value of the contracts was higher.) In the case of delay in completion of
the whole of the Philips contract the calculation was partly based on a formula
applied to the total value of the Philips contract in accordance with a manual of
instructions for contracts of this nature which the Government had prepared.
This was a perfectly sensible approach in a situation such as this where it
would be obvious that substantial loss would be suffered in the event of delay
but what that loss would be would be virtually impossible to calculate precisely
in advance. In the case of a governmental body the nature of the loss it will suffer as the result of the delay in implementing its new road programme is especially difficult to evaluate. The Government reasonably adopted a formula
which reflected the loss of return on the capital involved at a daily rate, to
which were added figures for supervisory staff costs, the daily actual cost of
making any alternative provision and a sum for fluctuations. Except for the
"alternative provision", the appropriate figures were calculated by reference to
the estimated final contract sum.

Philips argues this approach falls down because wholly unfairly it can and
most probably will result in the Government receiving at least double compensation. It is suggested that this can happen because the Government will
receive liquidated damages both for the delay which causes a Key Date to be

missed and again when the same delay results in the date for completion not being met. It is suggested it can also happen as a result of the same delay causing two or more Key Dates to be missed. (Liquidated damages will continue to be paid in respect of the earlier Key Date after the later date is missed.) As to the first example, the Government's response is that the two categories of liquidated damages are to cover different heads of loss so it is perfectly proper for payments to be made under each head. Where a Key Date is missed, the loss to which the liquidated damages primarily relate is the added expense to which the Government will be put in compensating the interfacing contractor whose contract is delayed. It is for this reason that the figure for liquidated damages is calculated on the value of the interfacing contract or contracts and accordingly increases with the number of those contracts which would be affected by the date being missed. . . .

Philips also rely on two other points to establish the provisions were penal. The first was that the provisions should be assumed to be penal because, in the words of Lord Watson in *Dunlop* (supra) at p 94, "a single lump sum is payable . . . on the occurrence of one or more or all of several events . . ." However, a different situation exists here to which the presumption does not apply. In this case the only event giving rise to the liability to pay liquidated damages is delay. Although that delay may be caused by any number of different circumstances, this is not a case of different causes of loss being compensated by the same figure of liquidated damages. . . .

The second point arises due to the presence of the minimum payment provision. . . . There can conceivably be circumstances where it is so obvious, before completion of the works as a whole, that the actual loss which will be sustained will be less than a specified minimum figure that to include that minimum figure in a provision for the payment of liquidated damages on a reducing sliding scale will have the effect of transforming an otherwise perfectly proper liquidated damages provision into a penalty, in so far as it prevents the liquidated damages from being reduced below that figure. However this is certainly not such a case. . . .

To conclude otherwise involves making the error of assuming that, because in some hypothetical situation the loss suffered will be less than the sum quantified in accordance with the liquidated damage provision, that provision must be a penalty, at least in the situation in which the minimum payment restriction operates. It illustrates the danger which is inherent in arguments based on hypothetical situations where it is said that the loss might be less than the sum specified as payable as liquidated damages. Arguments of this nature should not be allowed to divert attention from the correct test as to what is a penalty provision— namely is it a genuine pre-estimate of what the loss is likely to be?—to the different question, namely are there possible circumstances where a lesser loss would be suffered? Here the minimum payment provision amounted to about 28% of the daily rate of liquidated damages payable for non-completion of the whole works by Philips. The Government point out that if there is delay in completion it will continue inevitably to incur expenses of a standing nature irrespective of the scale of the work outstanding and that those expenses will continue until the work is completed. This being a reasonable assumption and there being no ground for suggesting that the minimum payment limitation was set at the wrong percentage, its presence does not create a penalty.

Notes

1. *Philips* can be taken as a typical example of the use of liquidated damages in large-scale construction contracts. The only special factual feature of this case is that the Hong Kong Government chose not to appoint a main contractor with overall responsibility for the road construction, but to conclude contracts directly with the companies responsible for the various works. This was, according to the Privy Council, because the Government wished to exercise greater control over the whole project, which was worth over HK$649 million. The litigation is also somewhat unusual in that it involves an attempt to have certain clauses declared unenforceable in advance of their use—that is, to ask the court to consider their validity in abstract. This approach has a certain attraction, in that it would enable the parties to clarify their rights and duties in advance; it ought to be possible for a court to assess a liquidated damages clause before it is used, as Lord Woolf cites with approval the proposition (point 3 of Lord Dunedin's classic guidelines) that the question whether a clause is a liquidated damages clause or a penalty is to be judged *as at the time of the making of the contract, not as at the time of the breach.* This could be taken as strong encouragement towards this sort of test-case litigation, yet in *Philips* Lord Woolf seriously questions the propriety of the plaintiff's approach. This attitude must be attributable to the marked reluctance of common law courts to make hypothetical judgments rather than to resolve actual disputes.

2. The burden of proving that a given clause is a penalty falls on the party seeking to avoid its effects. Philips fails to prove its case, since identifying certain circumstances in which the sums payable under the liquidated-damages clause would be substantially in excess of the actual loss of the defendant was insufficient.

3. According to Lord Dunedin in *Dunlop*, a penalty clause is one stipulated 'as in terrorem of the offending party'. The utility of this distinction has been doubted by the Law Commission (*Penalty Clauses and Forfeiture of Monies Paid*, Working Paper No. 61 (1975), 4) and by Lord Radcliffe in *Bridge* v. *Campbell Discount Co. Ltd.*

The Law Commission points to the necessary coercive force of the law of contract as a spur to performance rather than breach. In *Bridge* Lord Radcliffe commented:

I do not myself think that it helps to identify a penalty, to describe it as in the nature of a threat 'to be enforced in terrorem' . . . it obscures the fact that penalties may quite readily be undertaken by the parties who are not in the least terrorised by the prospect of having to pay them and yet are, as I understand it, entitled to claim the protection of the court when they are called upon to make good their promises. ([1962] AC 600 at 622)

A liquidated damages clause can be an incentive to perform without being coercive in the sense of threatening. However, as we shall see, economists argue that the law on penalties as it stands at present does not make the most of the incentives which the law could offer to ensure performance.

4. The alternative policy justification for striking down penalties offered by Lord Dunedin—and one that appears to attract the approval of both Lord Woolf and the Australian and Canadian judges he cites—is that of unconscionability. Given the limited role ascribed to unconscionability in English law, it is not surprising that the application of the penalties doctrine, at least to commercial contracts, encounters some opposition from commentators as an anomaly.

D. Harris, *Remedies in Contract and Tort* (London, Weidenfeld and Nicolson, 1988), 115

What is the purpose today of the law on penalties? It seems that its only justification is to protect a weaker party against the unconscionable use of a superior bargaining strength. If this is its purpose, it is hard to justify limiting judicial scrutiny to this one type of clause. Any type of clause can be drafted unfairly, but the law has never attempted overall control. For instance, no attempt is made by common law or equity to control the price (a debt) or the power to cancel the contract (terminate for breach) or many other types of remedy specified in the contract. The existing law on penalties can easily be evaded by the clever draftsman producing clauses which fall outside its scope. If abuse of a stronger bargaining position is the real evil, it should be attacked directly by a principle which aims at any manifestation of the abuse instead of one which aims selectively at penalty clauses and ignores all other types of clause. Nowadays the need for protection is mainly confined to consumer contracts, and here the courts unfortunately tend to take the view that it should be left to Parliament to provide the necessary protection to consumers. There is almost no prospect of a general doctrine of unconscionability being developed by English judges.

A similar point is made by Mueller in the US context.

R. Mueller, 'Contract Remedies: Business Fact and Legal Fantasy', [1967]
Wis. L. Rev. **833 at 838**

Let us re-examine our broad denial of freedom to contract in the sanctions area, not in terms of such meaningless words as "liquidated damages" or "penalties," but in terms of modern commercial realities. Why should parties not be permitted to agree to their own definitions of loss if they do so in arm's length bargaining? If the law will not question the adequacy of consideration, why should it question damages or damage formulae agreed upon in good faith? Obviously the question of unequal bargaining power is always involved here, but where is it not in the law of contract? Widening the opportunity for the parties to set damages in advance and encouraging them to do so might save society huge sums now spent each day on the too often futile pursuit of "actual" loss.

The better view is surely to view liquidated damages clauses as limited to terms which are genuine pre-estimates of damage. In that sense, they are permissible departures from the common law principle that the innocent party will be compensated for what he has lost, departures which do not drift too far towards the unacceptable goal of punishing the contract-breaker for breaching his promise.

5. An important practical point can be linked to this objection to interference with the freedom of contract of the parties. In most commercial contracts, the quid pro quo for the inclusion of a liquidated damages clause is an increase in price: the party under the obligation self-insures across a range of contracts which he or she concludes against the risk that he may default on one. Striking down a liquidated damages clause on the grounds that it is a penalty should, therefore, logically be accompanied by a restoration to the innocent party of the cost of including the clause which has proved futile (see Harris, *Remedies in Contract and Tort*, 115–16).

6. To avoid the law on penalties, the parties will often seek to 'entrench' their clauses as liquidated damages clauses. An example is clause 47 of the Institution of Civil Engineers' *Conditions of Contract* (6th edn., 1991).

Liquidated damages for delay

47 (1) (a) Where the whole of the Works is not divided into Sections the Appendix to the Form of Tender shall include a sum which represents the Employer's genuine pre-estimate (expressed per week or per day as the case maybe) of the damages likely to be suffered by him if the whole of the Works is not substantially completed within the time prescribed by Clause 43 or by any extension thereof granted under Clause 44 or by any revision thereof agreed under Clause 46(3) as the case may be.

(b) If the Contractor fails to complete the whole of the Works within the time so prescribed he shall pay to the Employer the said sum for every week or day (as the case may be) which shall elapse between the date on which the prescribed time expired and the date the whole of the Works is substantially completed.

Provided that if any part of the Works is certified as complete pursuant to Clause 48 before the completion of the whole of the Works the said sum shall be reduced by the proportion which the value of the part so completed bears to the value of the whole of the Works.

(2) (a) Where the Works is divided into Sections (together comprising the whole of the Works) which are required to be completed within particular times as stated in the Appendix to the Form of Tender sub-clause (1) of this Clause shall not apply and the said Appendix shall include a sum in respect of each Section which represents the Employer's genuine pre-estimate (expressed per week or per day as the case may be) of the damages likely to be suffered by him if that Section is not substantially completed within the time prescribed by Clause 43 or by any extension thereof granted under Clause 44 or by any revision thereof agreed under Clause 46(3) as the case may be.

(b) If the Contractor fails to complete any Section within the time so prescribed he shall pay to the Employer the appropriate stated sum for every week or day (as the case may be) which shall elapse between the date on which the prescribed time expired and the date of substantial completion of that Section.

Provided that if any part of that Section is certified as complete pursuant to Clause 48 before the completion of the whole thereof the appropriate stated sum shall be reduced by the proportion which the value of the part so completed bears to the value of the whole of that Section.

(c) Liquidated damages in respect of two or more Sections may where circumstances so dictate run concurrently.

(3) All sums payable by the Contractor to the Employer pursuant to this Clause shall be paid as liquidated damages for delay and not as a penalty.

(4) (a) The total amount of liquidated damages in respect of the whole of the Works or any Section thereof shall be limited to the appropriate sum stated in the Appendix to the Form of Tender. If no such limit is stated therein then liquidated damages without limit shall apply.

(b) Should there be omitted from the Appendix to the Form of Tender any sum required to be inserted therein either by sub-clause (1)(a) or by sub-clause (2)(a) of this Clause as the case may be or if any such sum is stated to be "nil" then to that extent damages shall not be payable.

As point 1 of Lord Dunedin's guidance indicates, such attempts are probably futile.

7. A further objection to the law on penalties is its somewhat anomalous scope. It is not difficult to avoid the law on penalties by skilful drafting, as there are a whole range of terms commonly included in contracts, such as reductions for prompt or early payment of a debt or payments due in the event of occurrences other than a breach of contract, which are not generally subject to the law on penalties. *Bridge* v. *Campbell Discount Co. Ltd.* illustrates the potential for unfairness. Bridge bought a car on hire-purchase terms but, finding himself unable to meet the payments, returned the car. Under the terms of the hire-purchase agreement, he was obliged to make a 'minimum payment'—that is, to make up the payments already made to two-thirds of the hire-purchase price, supposedly in compensation for depreciation. This clause would only be subject to the law on penalties if the minimum payment were due on breach. If the hirer had simply lawfully terminated the agreement, as was his right under the contract, rather than defaulting on payments and waiting for the finance company to repossess the car, the clause would appear to escape scrutiny. Yet such a clause is clearly not an attempt to pre-estimate loss through depreciation since, on the contrary, the extra payment becomes smaller as the agreement progresses and the depreciation increases. On this point the members of the House of Lords were agreed. They divided on the other issues of whether the hirer had exercised his right to terminate (the majority said he had not, thus avoiding the difficult question) and if he had, whether he would have been entitled to relief (only Lords Denning and Devlin said that he definitely was).

B. Towards a Wider Penalties Doctrine?

In a recent case, the Court of Appeal appears to have extended slightly the scope of the penalties doctrine, at the same time dovetailing it more closely with the principle of relief against forfeiture.

Jobson v. *Johnson*
[1989] 1 All ER 621

The defendant bought shares in Southend United Football Club from the vendors (the Rubin brothers), arranging payment in instalments. After making an initial payment of £40,000 and paying a further £100,000 in instalments, the defendant defaulted on the payments. The agreement provided that, in the event of default, the defendant must retransfer the shares to the vendors for £40,000 (clause 6(b) of the side agreement). Accordingly the plaintiff, as assignee of the Rubins, brought an action for specific performance of the agreement. In normal circumstances, this would have been a case for relief against forfeiture, giving the defendant more time to pay. However, because of a procedural failure on his part, this line of argument was barred. The defendant continued to defend the claim, arguing that the retransfer clause was a penalty and therefore unenforceable, and appealed to the Court of Appeal against an order for specific performance on these grounds.

DILLON LJ In this court the plaintiff does not challenge the judge's ruling that cl 6(b) is a penalty clause. That ruling was, in my judgment, plainly right for a combination of two reasons: (1) the repurchase of the shares under cl 6(b) was to be at the fixed price of £40,000 if there was default in payment of any instalment, without regard to how much the defendant had already paid; it would make no difference if the default was in the payment of the second, the last, or an intermediate instalment, and (2) there was also cl 6(a) of the side-letter providing for repurchase at an even lower price than £40,000 in the event of default in the payment of the first instalment under the side-letter, ie default when the defendant had only paid the £40,000 under the sale agreement. The plain reading of cl 6 is therefore that the defendant was to be punished for any default by being bound to retransfer substantially all the shares to the Rubins at a fixed price which was bound to be less, and could be very much less, than the defendant had paid. The retransfer price under either part of cl 6 could not have been based on a genuine pre-estimate either of the Rubins's loss or of the value of the shares.

The penal effect of cl 6(b) would of course be all the greater if, having enforced a retransfer of the shares for £40,000 under that paragraph, the plaintiff as assignee of the Rubins would remain entitled to sue the defendant to recover additionally all the unpaid instalments under the side-letter as varied by the variation agreement. For my part, however, I would hold as a matter of construction of the side-letter that retransfer of the shares under cl 6(b) was to be in lieu of all other remedies and would preclude the plaintiff recovering any unpaid instalments, whether those unpaid at the date when the retransfer was called for or those which would only have become payable subsequently.

We have therefore to consider what the basis is of the court's approach to penalty clauses, and we have had the benefit of very interesting historical argument on each side. . . .

. . . any court, English or Scottish, when faced with a claim for a sum of money payable on default which it identifies as a penalty, must refuse to enforce the penal part of the sum and must give judgment for the claimant merely for the actual damages suffered by the claimant, with, as appropriate, interest and costs. Where the penalty is a sum of money, the relief, once the penalty has been identified, does not involve a consideration of the circumstances of the defendant, or of the factors which might be appropriate to a grant of relief against forfeiture. . . . Giving judgement for the actual damage without further inquiry into the circumstances was . . . in my judgment . . . the correct course. . . .

Does it make any difference, then, that the penalty in the present case is not a sum of money? In principle, a transaction must be just as objectionable and unconscionable in the eyes of equity if it requires a transfer of property by way of penalty on a default in paying money as if it requires a payment of an extra, or excessive, sum of money. There is no distinction in principle between a clause which provides that if a person makes default in paying a sum of £100 on a certain day he shall pay a penalty of £1,000, and a clause which provides that if a person makes default in paying a sum of £100 on a certain day he shall by way of penalty transfer to the obligee 1000 shares in a certain company for no consideration. Again, there should be no distinction in principle between a clause which requires the defaulter, on making default in paying money, to transfer shares for no consideration, and a clause which in like circumstances requires the defaulter to sell shares to the creditor at an undervalue. In each case the clause ought to be unenforceable in equity in so far as it is a penalty clause. . . .

[Dillon LJ considered one of the few available authorities on this point—*Re Dagenham (Thames) Dock Co., ex parte Hulse* ((1873) 8 Ch. App. 1022)—in which the purchase of certain land was subject to a repossession clause in favour of the vendor if the purchaser defaulted on the second instalment of the purchase price. In that case, the purchaser (and subsequently the insolvent purchaser's liquidator) defaulted on the payment, and the court offered the vendor the sale of the land by the court with the unpaid instalment to be satisfied out of the proceeds.]

In the context of the present case, relief by way of an extension of time for the defendant to pay the unpaid purchase money and interest is just the relief which would have been considered on the defendant's counterclaim if the counterclaim had not been struck out. Moreover, it is the sort of relief to which the documents which, in breach of his undertaking, the defendant failed to disclose might have been marginally relevant, in that they might have indicated what period he would realistically have required to raise the necessary amount of money. Therefore in my judgment it is not open to this court to grant that form of relief on this appeal. It does not necessarily follow, however, in my judgment, that this court is therefore bound to enforce the penal clause, cl 6(b) of the side-letter, in all its rigour and without regard to its penal consequences. . . .

. . . [A] clause identified by the courts as a penalty clause cannot be enforced so as to enable a party to recover or retain more than his actual loss.

What then should the court do in the present case? It is not, in my judgment, open to the court to decree specific performance of the sale of the shares to the plaintiff, but at a higher price than the £40,000, so as to recoup to the defendant what he has actually paid for the shares, since that would involve the court making a new contract between the parties.

One possibility that might have been considered is that the court, while refusing specific performance, should, as in the money penalty cases such as . . . *Bridge* v. *Campbell Discount Co Ltd* [1962] AC 600, enter immediate judgment for the plaintiff against the defendant for the amount of the plaintiff's loss, viz all the unpaid instalments under the variation agreement with interest from default in respect of each instalment until judgment. That however is disclaimed by counsel for the plaintiff and has not been sought at any earlier stage. Moreover, if cl 6(b) of the side-letter is wholly unenforceable, the plaintiff could sue the defendant for the unpaid instalments and interest in a fresh action and would be entitled to summary judgment under RSC Ord 14.

There remain two other alternatives. Counsel for the plaintiff concedes that in the circumstances of this case the plaintiff is not entitled to any unpaid vendor's lien under the general law on the shares which have been transferred to the defendant under the sale agreement. If I am right, however, that the remedy of repurchase of the shares under cl 6(b) of the side-letter is an alternative, and not in addition to, the recovery of the unpaid instalments, the repurchase is in substance a security for the payment of the unpaid instalments and interest.

Accordingly, the court could, I apprehend, follow the course taken by Lord Romilly MR in *Re Dagenham (Thames) Dock Co* and offer the plaintiff an order for sale of the 62,566 shares by the court, and payment of the unpaid instalments and interest out of the proceeds as in the ordinary case of a vendor's lien.

Alternatively, by analogy to the power which the court has had for a very long time to direct an inquiry as to damages in a penalty case so as to ensure that there is no enforcement beyond the plaintiff's actual loss, the court could, in my judgment, direct inquiries to ascertain

[if the the total net sum due on the shares exceeded their present value. If that were the case, but not otherwise, the court would enforce the retransfer clause].

These two alternatives should, in my judgment, be offered to the plaintiff, but they cannot be forced on him. If neither is acceptable to him the appeal must, in my judgment, be allowed and the order for specific performance must be discharged since otherwise the court would be lending its machinery to the enforcement of the penal effects of a clause which has been clearly identified as a penalty clause. But in that event, as mentioned above the plaintiff will be free to bring a fresh action for payment.

[NICHOLLS LJ]

Equitable relief

In considering this appeal it is right to have in mind that the legal principles applicable today regarding penalty clauses in contracts and those applicable regarding relief from forfeiture stem from a common origin. A penalty clause in a contract, as that expression is normally used today, is a provision which, on breach of the contract, requires the party in default to make a payment to the innocent party of a sum of money which, however it may be labelled, is not a genuine pre-estimate of the damage likely to be sustained by the innocent party, but is a payment stipulated in terrorem of the party in default. For centuries equity has given relief against such provisions by not permitting the innocent party to recover under the penal provision more than his actual loss. . . .

Likewise with forfeiture. Take the simple case of a provision for forfeiture of a lease on non-payment of rent. That provision was regarded by equity as a security for the rent. So that, where conscience so required, equity relieved against the forfeiture on payment of the rent with interest. . . . In *Thompson v Hudson* (1869) LR 4 HL 1 at 15 Lord Hatherley LC summarised the underlying principle as follows:

'I take the law to be perfectly clear . . . namely, that where there is a debt actually due, and in respect of that debt a security is given, be it by way of mortgage or be it by way of stipulation that in case of its not being paid at the time appointed a larger sum shall become payable, and be paid in either of those cases Equity regards the security that has been given as a mere pledge for the debt, and it will not allow either a forfeiture of the property pledged, or any augmentation of the debt as a penal provision, on the ground that Equity regards the contemplated forfeiture which might take place at Law with reference to the estate as in the nature of a penal provision, against which Equity will relieve when the object in view, namely, the securing of the debt, is attained, and regarding also the stipulation for the payment of a larger sum of money, if the sum be not paid at the time it is due, as a penalty and a forfeiture against which Equity will relieve.'

. . . [A] penalty clause in a contract is, in practice, a dead letter. An obligation to make a money payment stipulated in terrorem will not be enforced beyond the sum which represents the actual loss of the party seeking payment, namely, principal, interest and, if appropriate, costs, in those cases where (to use modern terminology) the primary obligation is to pay money, or where the primary obligation is to perform some other obligation, beyond the sum recoverable as damages for breach of that obligation. (For convenience I shall hereafter refer to that sum as 'the actual loss of the innocent party'.) Hence normally there is no advantage in suing on the penalty clause. . . .

Although in a practice a penalty clause in a contract as described above is effectively a dead letter, it is important in the present case to note that, contrary to the submissions of counsel for the defendant, the strict legal position is not that such a clause is simply struck out of the contract, as though with a blue pencil, so that the contract takes effect as if it had never been included therein. Strictly, the legal position is that the clause remains in the contract and can be sued on, but it will not be enforced by the court beyond the sum which represents, in the events which have happened, the actual loss of the party seeking payment. There are many cases which make this clear. . . .

. . . [A]s the law has developed, a distinction has arisen between the enforcement of penalty clauses in contracts and the enforcement of forfeiture clauses. A penalty clause will not be enforced beyond the sum which equals the actual loss of the innocent party. A forfeiture clause, of which a right of re-entry under a lease on non-payment of rent is the classic example, may also be penal in its effect. Such a clause frequently subjects the defaulting party, in the event of non-payment of rent or breach of some other obligation, to a sanction which damnifies the defaulting party, and benefits the other party, to an extent far greater than the actual loss of the innocent party. For instance, the lease may be exceedingly valuable and the amount of unpaid rent may be small. But in such a case the court will lend its aid in the enforcement of the forfeiture, by making an order for possession, subject to any relief which in its discretion the court may grant to the party in default. Normally the granting of such relief is made conditional on the payment of the rent with interest and costs. If that condition is not complied with, and subject to any further application by the tenant or other person in default for yet more time, the forfeiture provision will be enforced. Thus the innocent party is in a better position when seeking to enforce a forfeiture clause than when seeking to enforce a penalty clause in a contract.

This is not the occasion to attempt to rationalise the distinction. One possible explanation is that the distinction is rooted in the different forms which the relief takes. In the case of a penalty clause in a contract equity relieves by cutting down the extent to which the contractual obligation is enforceable: the 'scaling-down' exercise, as I have described it. In the case of forfeiture clauses equitable relief takes the form of relieving wholly against the contractual forfeiture provision, subject to compliance with conditions imposed by the court. Be that as it may, I see no reason why the court's ability to grant discretionary relief against forfeiture should deprive a defendant of the relief automatically granted in respect of a penalty clause if, exceptionally, a contractual provision has characteristics which enable a defendant to pray in aid both heads of relief.

Property and not money

I return to penalty clauses. The scaling-down exercise which is carried out automatically by equity is straightforward when the penalty clause provides for payment of a sum of money. More difficult, and more unusual, is the case where the penal obligation triggered by the breach is an obligation to transfer property to the party not in default, as under cl 6(b). Even in such a case there is no difficulty where the value of the property at the time when the court is making its order does not exceed the actual loss of the innocent party. In that event there can be no more objection to the court specifically enforcing the obligation to transfer the property than there would be to the court making an order for the payment of a sum of money stipulated in a (pecuniary) penalty clause where, in the event, that sum does not exceed the actual loss of the innocent party. The difficulty arises where the value of the property agreed to be transferred exceeds the actual loss of the innocent party. A precisely comparable scaling-down exercise would not provide an acceptable solution, at any rate where the property consists of a single piece of land, or a block of shares in a company such as Southend United Football Club Ltd, whose shares are not traded in one of the securities markets. It could not be right to order specific performance of cl 6(b) in part only, namely in respect of the reduced number of shares whose value does not exceed the actual loss of the plaintiff. That, indeed, would be to make a new bargain for the parties.

In the present case we do not know what is the current value of the shares comprised in cl 6(b), even in approximate terms. I shall return later to the question of what, in that circumstance, can and should be done. For the moment it is sufficient to note that, apart from the difference between shares and money, cl 6(b) possesses all the essential characteristics of a penalty clause. In principle, and subject to the complication arising from the difficulty of 'scaling-down' an obligation to transfer shares, there can be no difference between an obligation to pay a stipulated sum of money arising on a default and an obligation to transfer specified property arising on a default. The essential vice is the same in each case. In principle, so far as this can be achieved, the parties' respective positions should be no better, or worse, than they would be if cl 6(b) had stipulated for payment of money rather than a transfer of shares.

A forfeiture clause

Clause 6(b), however, is something of a hybrid. It possesses the essential characteristics of a penalty clause in a contract. It also possesses features which resemble those of a forfeiture provision. Clause 6(b) provided that if the purchaser failed to pay all the agreed instalments, he would retransfer to the vendors a slice (44.9%) of the issued share capital of the company equal to the slice the vendors had sold to him. In substance cl 6(b) is equivalent to a right to re-take the property being sold in default of payment of the full price. . . .

. . . In the present case cl 6(b) is a term intended to provide the unpaid vendors with some 'security' against non-payment by giving them an alternative remedy (repossession of their former slice in the company) in the event of default in payment of all the instalments. That is a situation in which, par excellence, equity in its discretion, and having regard to all the circumstances, may grant relief. Such relief would normally be on terms that the primary obligation for which this alternative remedy is 'security' is performed within a reasonable time, albeit later than stipulated in the agreement. . . .

I think, therefore, that cl 6(b) is a clause in respect of which Harman J had jurisdiction to grant relief. The most obvious form which the relief might have taken was to relieve the defendant from complying with cl 6(b) if he paid the balance of the price with interest and costs, as occurred in *Re Dagenham*

(*Thames*) *Dock Co, ex p Hulse*. The contrary conclusion, that the court had no jurisdiction to give relief, would mean that if the defendant's claim for relief had not been struck out at the trial, and if the defendant had been able and willing to pay the outstanding instalments with interest and costs at once in full, the court could still not have given him any relief in respect of cl 6(b), however deserving his case. That is not an acceptable conclusion.

Procedurally it is established practice for a claim by a defendant for relief from forfeiture to be the subject of a counterclaim. Whether that is an issue which can be raised only in a counterclaim as distinct from in a defence is not a matter which calls for consideration in this case, because in the present case the claim for relief from forfeiture was made, in the normal way, in a counter-claim and it was this counterclaim that was struck out by the judge. Thus the defendant's claim for relief from forfeiture was the issue which the judge barred the defendant from pursuing. Against that order of the judge there has been no appeal.

The consequence of no claim for relief

However, I am unable to accept that in the absence of a claim for discretionary relief from forfeiture it follows that the court must or should now specifically enforce cl 6(b) in its entirety, whatever the value of the shares. As I have said, I see no reason why there should not be an order for specific performance of cl 6(b) if the shares do not exceed in value the actual loss of the plaintiff . . . . If, on the other hand, the shares are now worth more than the amount of the plaintiff's loss, the court has available to it a means of ensuring that the purpose for which cl 6(b) was included in the main agreement is duly fulfilled without either party otherwise being prejudiced. Clause 6(b) was intended to provide the vendors with a form of 'security' if the purchase defaulted in paying the full price. If the shares are now worth more than the actual loss of the plaintiff, ex hypothesi a sale of the shares will realise a sum which is sufficient to put the plaintiff in the financial position he would have occupied if the defendant had not defaulted. If the shares are now sold and the plaintiff is duly paid the amount of his actual loss, with the surplus proceeds being paid to the defendant, the plaintiff will have obtained from cl 6(b) everything for which it was provided as 'security'.

In my view that is the course which the court can and should take. It is the equivalent in the different circumstances of this case to the automatic scaling-down of a (pecuniary) penalty clause. Clause 6(b) is being enforced, in favour of the plaintiff and against the defendant, but in a form modified to preclude it from operating penally. As I have said, it would not be right to order the transfer to the defendant of a reduced number of shares. Nor would it be right to order the transfer of all the shares, to the prejudice of the defendant, or to refuse to grant any specific relief with regard to the shares, to the prejudice of the plaintiff, when by ordering (if the plaintiff so requests) that the shares be sold, the court can enforce cl 6(b) to an extent, or in a manner, that would give the plaintiff everything for which cl 6(b) was intended to be 'security' and yet still prevent the clause operating punitively against the defendant. If the court orders a sale it will be granting a limited form of specific relief in respect of the defendant's obligations under cl 6(b). . . .

Conclusion

For these reasons I would make an order in the terms outlined by Dillon LJ. I agree also with what he says on the irrecoverability of the unpaid instalments if the plaintiff chooses to take an order for the enforcement of cl 6(b) in the manner discussed above. . . .

I regret to find myself differing from Kerr LJ in that I am unable to agree with the alternative course proposed by him. That course would restore the parties, so far as is now possible, to their pre-contract positions. That approach does not accord with the established equitable principle relating to penalty clauses, whereunder equity confines the sum recoverable under a penalty clause to the loss actually suffered by the innocent party by reason of the breach of contract.

KERR LJ I respectfully differ on one aspect of this puzzling case from the conclusions reached in the judgments of Dillon and Nicholls LJJ, which I have had the great advantage of reading. This concerns the choice of remedies to which the plaintiff should now be entitled.

It is common ground that cl 6(b) is penal in its nature. . . .

However, it does not follow that a penalty clause is illegal in the same way as, for instance, provisions imposing unlawful restraints of trade. These are simply struck down, or 'blue-pencilled', because they are prohibited on the ground of public policy, unless it is possible to sever the good from the bad. Penalty clauses falling within the principles considered in the *Dunlop Tyre* case are not in the same category. In my view, the combined effect of law and equity on penalty clauses is simply that they will not be enforced in favour of a plaintiff without first giving to the defendant a proper opportunity to obtain relief against their penal consequences.

This is of particular importance in relation to the relevant provision in the present case. I respectfully agree with the analysis of Nicholls LJ in the section of his judgment headed 'A forfeiture clause' that this is the true nature of cl 6(b). . . . it is in my view much closer to what is commonly referred to as a 'forfeiture' than a 'penalty' clause. It follows a fortiori that cl 6(b) is not *necessarily* unenforceable, but merely that the defendant must be given a proper opportunity of seeking appropriate relief before there can be any question of enforcing the provisions.

This analysis is also supported by the course which this action would have taken but for the fact that the defendant's counterclaim for relief came to be struck out due to his own fault, and I did not understand anyone to suggest the contrary. The normal course of events would have been that the defendant would have been granted relief from the obligation to retransfer the shares, but on terms that he must pay the then outstanding instalments in full, together with interest and the plaintiff's costs. . . . However, if it should then have turned out that the defendant was unwilling or unable to abide by these terms, after he had been given every reasonable opportunity to do so, then an order for the retransfer of the shares on the terms of cl 6(b) would have been made. This is an everyday situation in the context of provisions for forfeiture in leases, and it is also the basis on which the law of mortgages and the equity of redemption have developed. It seems to work well in practice and to cause little injustice. Thus, if in the present case the value of the shares in January 1987 had been greatly in excess of the outstanding instalments when Harman J was dealing with the matter, then Mr Johnson, the defendant, would no doubt have been willing and able to raise the amount of the outstanding instalments together with interest and costs, if necessary by borrowing on the security of the shares, in order to obtain relief in the normal way.

However, the defendant chose not to pursue this course. He evidently preferred to let his counterclaim be struck out. Perhaps he was unwilling to comply with an order which would have forced him to reveal his financial circumstances; or it may be that the then value of the shares made a claim for relief unattractive; or perhaps he had both considerations in mind. In the result, the stage of considering and formulating the terms on which relief should be granted was never reached.

In these unusual circumstances, but only with considerable doubt, I respectfully agree with the judgments of Dillon and Nicholls LJJ that it was at any rate premature to grant immediate specific performance of a forfeiture clause which, for the reasons already stated, was also penal in its nature.

But more than a year has passed since then. Although both parties were somewhat cagey about explaining the present position, it is clear that circumstances have changed. On behalf of the defendant, counsel intimated to us, as I understood him, that the shares were now worth far more than the total outstanding purchase price and that the defendant would have no difficulty in raising the necessary sum to be granted relief on usual terms to obtain their release from escrow. On behalf of the plaintiff, counsel did not contradict these veiled references to the present value of the shares, but he reminded us repeatedly that we had no evidence of their value and must not speculate about it. He also pointed out that counsel for the defendant was careful not to suggest that there was any way whereby the defendant's struck-out counterclaim for relief could now somehow be revived.

If one accepts that the order for specific performance made by Harman J cannot stand, as I do albeit with doubt, what is the appropriate course which this court should now take? Two things appear clear. First, the rights of the plaintiff cannot be prejudiced by the defendant's failure to pursue the offer of relief which the court was bound to, and did, grant to him. If this process had run its normal course, then the plaintiff would have obtained an order for payment by the defendant of all the outstanding instalments, together with interest and costs, within a reasonable time, or alternatively for the retransfer of the shares pursuant to cl 6(b) in default of compliance.

Secondly, it is plain that whereas in January 1987 the issue may have been largely about money, at any rate so far as the defendant was concerned, it is now solely about the right to the shares. Both sides are clearly most anxious to obtain them and interested in little else. That is why counsel for the defendant took pains to let us know, although perhaps he should not have done so, that the defendant was now willing, able and extremely keen to comply with any order as to payment if he is permitted to retain the shares. It is equally the reason why counsel on behalf of the plaintiff not only formally declined the court's offer of a monetary judgment, but also made no response to counsel for the defendant's offer of more or less readily available cash in full.

Quite apart from the fact that the counterclaim for relief has been struck out, I agree that it is now far too late for the defendant to seek relief in the normal way. I say that, because in my view the plea in the defence that cl 6(b) is a penal provision obliges the court to offer relief to the defendant, without the need for any formal counterclaim. It follows inevitably, once it is clear that the plaintiff is seeking to enforce a penalty clause. I also agree that, given that the order of Harman J cannot stand, it is necessary for this court to reach an appropriate conclusion in equity. To this end the judgments of Dillon and Nicholls LJJ have offered the choice of two remedies to the plaintiff. The first is an order for the sale of the shares by the court and payment of the unpaid instalments and interest out of the proceeds, no doubt together with costs in the ordinary way, and obviously leaving it open to the plaintiff to sue thereafter for any balance of the price which may still be outstanding. The second is an inquiry as to the value of the shares, and an order to the effect of cl 6(b) in the event that their present value is less than the total net sum presently due from the defendant; but not otherwise.

In my view neither of these alternatives offers sufficient justice to the plaintiff in the exceptional circumstances of this case. The first alternative differs little from simply granting relief to the defendant in the usual way, save that this would be accompanied by what would in effect be an auction of the shares, in which both parties as well as outsiders could compete. The second alternative is almost certainly unrealistic and not a worthwhile offer in practice, since it is to be suspected that the present value of the shares greatly exceeds all monetary sums to which the plaintiff is now entitled.

In these circumstances it seems to me that, in equity, the plaintiff is entitled to a further alternative. This would be an order giving effect to cl 6(b), but on terms that the plaintiff repays to the defendant, perhaps with interest, the £160,000 which he has received under the agreement. In my view a further option to this effect would do justice to the plaintiff without contravening any principle of equity. It would give effect to the unenforceability of cl 6(b) because of its penal nature, but without simply 'blue-pencilling' it, which would be wrong. Secondly, it would provide some compensation to the plaintiff for having lost the opportunity of obtaining an order in terms of cl 6(b) because the normal process of an application for relief from forfeiture was frustrated by the defendant's decision to allow his counterclaim to be struck out. Above all, it would result in equitable restitution to both parties, without enforcing or 'blue-pencilling' cl 6(b). There is nothing penal about a provision that, in the event of a failure by the defendant to pay any instalment of the price, the plaintiff is to be entitled to rescind the contract and to recover the goods against a refund of all sums received by him. . . . Clause 6(b) is penal, because its operation takes no account of the sums already received, and to that extent it is unenforceable. But it is enforceable to the extent that it is not a penalty, by requiring full resti-tution by the plaintiff as a condition of its enforcement. That would not be a case of 'mending men's bargains', but the enforcement of a penal forfeiture clause by the removal of its penal element, and in a situation where relief from forfeiture can no longer be claimed by the defendant.

Subject to offering this further alternative to the plaintiff I therefore agree that the order of Harman J should be set aside and that the defendant's appeal should be allowed to this extent.

Notes

1. There are a number of points on which all three judges are agreed. These include the penal nature of the clause—a point which will be consid-ered further below—and the ability of and necessity for the court to give relief in circumstances such as these, even though the defendant had missed his 'first stop' remedy—relief against forfeiture—by failing to dis-close certain documents. In other words, because of the hybrid nature of the clause—part penalty clause, part forfeiture clause—the defendant was essentially given two bites at the cherry in terms of obtaining relief, although all three judges were at pains to stress that the relief awarded was only a 'scaling-down' exercise. The essence of the disagreement between Dillon and Nicholls LJJ on the one hand and Kerr LJ on the other was the extent to which the plaintiff's contractual right to specific performance of the retransfer clause should be scaled down.

2. It is perhaps surprising that the Court of Appeal should have been will-ing to extend the law on penalties to retransfer clauses such as clause 6(b), and even more surprising that so little reasoning is offered to justify the conclusion that there is no real difference in nature between an obliga-tion to pay money and an obligation to transfer property. The case for extending the scope of the court's jurisdiction in respect of remedial

clauses agreed between the parties negotiating at arm's length, as here, seems insubstantial, in particular when there is no suggestion of procedural impropriety. See further D. Harris, 'Penalties and Forfeiture: Contractual Remedies Specified by the Parties' ([1990] *LMCLQ* 158).

3. The members of the Court of Appeal, although they were not unanimous as regards the orders they wished to make, none the less appeared to see nothing strange in having to delve deep into their judicial imaginations in order to devise an 'appropriate' form of relief for the defendant. Where Kerr LJ differed both in attitude and approach to reasoning from the others was in his more cynical evaluation of the defendant's conduct. He gives the reader strong hints that there was more to the relationship between defendant and plaintiff than met the eye, particularly in view of their evident reluctance to bring the real value of the shares at the date of trial into the public domain.

4. The case gives additional judicial guidance on the effects of a finding that a clause is a penalty. It is consistent with the view that the judicial role in this context is the scaling down of remedies contractually agreed for the members of the Court of Appeal to reject the 'blue pencil' test of striking out the clause in its entirety. A penalty is therefore to be distinguished from a clause which offends the rules on illegality or restraint of trade. According to the court, it is simply a clause which is rendered partially unenforceable, so far as is necessary.

C. The Economic Analysis of Penalties

Posner has described the common law approach to the non-enforcement of penalty clauses, albeit freely negotiated between the parties, as 'a major unexplained puzzle in the economic theory of the common law' (R. Posner, 'Some Uses and Abuses of Economics in Law', (1979) 46 *U. Chi. L. Rev.* 281 at 290). *Jobson* v. *Johnson* illustrates the court taking a very one-dimensional view based on the type of clause used; according to the Court of Appeal, the plaintiffs could not have made a genuine pre-estimate of their loss as they did not incorporate a sliding scale into the retransfer clause so that later default would increase the price at which the plaintiffs would be entitled to repurchase the shares. The following extract from Ham advocates a much more wide-ranging enquiry. Ham's final position echoes the link drawn by Harris above between the control of penalty clauses and the doctrine of unconscionability. Ham treats penalty clauses specifically as an issue of procedural fairness based on the conduct of the respective parties.

A. Ham, 'The Rule Against Penalties in Contract: An Economic Perspective', (1990) 17 *Melb. UL Rev.* 649 at 650, 653–61, 668–90

The basic philosophy of the economic analysis of legal rules is that individuals are rational agents aiming to maximize their well-being and make the best agreement possible, subject to the constraints imposed upon them by the law and the other party. My argument is that only the parties themselves have sufficient information at the time of forming the contract to be able to formulate the optimal damages clause taking all relevant subjective and objective factors into account. Therefore, in commercial transactions which are fully negotiated between parties of comparable bargaining strength, the optimal rule is to enforce all stipulated damage agreements. The courts still have an important role, however, in ensuring that the contract is fully and fairly negotiated and that one party is not taking unconscionable advantage of the other. . . .

. . . [T]he court's quantification of loss is important for three reasons: First, it is this assessment that is the alternative to that stipulated by the parties, hence its perceived shortcomings may motivate the parties to negotiate their own pre-estimate of loss. Secondly, should the pre-estimate be struck down as a penalty it is the court's assessment that is substituted as the recoverable amount. Thirdly, in deciding whether an agreed sum is 'extravagant and unconscionable' in comparison with the greatest probable loss, the courts must assess what that loss might be by their own criteria. . . .

Freedom of contract is one of the principles that underlies contract law, yet its rationale is seldom examined. It is based on the standard assumptions of economic analysis. To simplify matters we assume that all benefits and costs can be measured in dollar values, including 'non-economic' considerations. It is individuals themselves who determine the dollar values to be placed on the benefits and costs of an agreement. Furthermore, individuals will maximize the difference between their benefits and their costs; utility maximization. It follows that left to themselves, parties on equal terms will reach the agreement that maximizes the benefits to both sides. Such an outcome is desirable because it is efficient; that is, from a given pool of resources, the net benefit to the overall community is maximized. . . .

[The Doctrine of Efficient Breach]

. . . [B]usiness certainty requires that promises should be kept. However, breach should be encouraged when, relative to performance, it yields a net gain to the parties (*i.e.* a Pareto-improvement). Circumstances frequently change between the time of formation and the time of performance. If the situation becomes such that the opportunity cost of performance to one party is greater than the other party's gain from the contract, then there is clearly a net sum gain if the contract is not performed. Encouraging the breach of such inefficient contracts will not, in principle, deter the formation of future contracts because the victim of breach is always fully compensated and hence is indifferent between damages and performance. The breaching party is able to fully compensate the innocent promisee for losses sustained due to the former's breach, and still gain him or herself. Thus breach will benefit both parties and is 'efficient'. . . .

Breach may be involuntary, to avoid greater loss, or it may be voluntary, motivated by greater profits (from a higher offer, for example) than those expected from performance. Thus, in a contract for the product of goods, costs may be uncertain until after the contract is made. In this case breach will be efficient if the seller's production costs exceed the value of the goods to the buyer. . . .

The Effect of Penalties

Proposition 5: 'Excessive' liquidated damages may prevent breach even when such breach would be optimal.

The penalty doctrine aims to prevent unfair recovery in excess of justifiable and quantifiable loss and to prevent inefficient performance through fear of a penalty when breach is preferable.

Economists have developed models to show the ideal response to a change in circumstances assuming partial performance is possible. A penalty clause acts as a means of forcing inefficient performance as this is preferable (less costly) to paying a still larger penalty. So a penalty clause is analogous to an award of specific performance as both, whether by direct court order or by the deterrent effect of an '*in terrorem*' clause, result in performance of the contract that one party sought to breach causing the other party to initiate litigation. Specific performance is only awarded by the courts when ordinary money damages are inadequate, and cannot substitute for performance. As a penalty has the same effect, it can be argued that similar criteria should be applied to their enforcement. That is, even when a stipulated sum has been found to be a penalty, the courts should enforce it if there is evidence that damages as assessed by the court would be inadequate. . . .

THE COURT'S ASSESSMENT OF DAMAGES

The Costs of the Penalty Doctrine

Proposition 6: Shortcomings in the court's assessment of loss may cause an optimal, efficient liquidated damages claim to appear excessive.

For a number of reasons the court's assessment of loss to the plaintiff may differ from that actually suffered. This may mean that a stipulated damages clause that would fully compensate is not enforced, and an inadequate court award is substituted. Thus the court's inference of unfairness in their attitude to agreed damages clauses for what they consider to be excessive amounts may not be warranted, and refusing to enforce such clauses may impose more costs than it removes.

Traditional damage measures provide quite adequate compensation in purely commercial transactions, as losses can be objectively evaluated either on the basis of lost profits from anticipated breach, or to reflect the difference between contract and market prices. The principles of compensation are harder to apply in two other possible cases. First, when the promised performance has a market value but the promisee attaches an additional idiosyncratic value to performance which he or she has contracted for by paying a premium on the market price. Evaluated after breach, such subjective loss is regarded as too speculative and uncertain to be recovered in the courts. Of course, such a limitation is justified where the costs of establishing idiosyncratic value exceed the costs of an inaccurate measure of damage. Secondly, limitations are imposed on the recovery of consequential loss and even reasonably foreseeable loss that is too uncertain to quantify. This avoids the difficult process of quantifying uncertain loss, but at the plaintiff's expense. Even when the parties have attempted to resolve the uncertainty with a stipulated sum, as efficiency dictates, the penalty doctrine increases transaction costs again by relating this sum to the maximum uncertain loss possible before enforcing the agreement.

Parties who know they may be disadvantaged by such rules can unambiguously gain if liquidated damages clauses that compensate fully are always enforced. 'In the absence of evidence of unfairness or other bargaining abnormalities, efficiency would be maximized by the enforcement of the agreed allocation of risks embodied in a liquidated damages clause'. Efficiency is enhanced through minimization of transaction costs if agreements negotiated *ex-ante* are enforced.

Apart from the limitations of compensation by the courts, such damages awards are not the best way of insuring against loss from breach because litigation is an inherently expensive and uncertain process. The seller already knows the probability of breach and could set the premium accordingly if he or she were to directly insure the buyer. A third party insurance company would have to devote significant resources to finding this probability out. Further, a seller may be able to influence the probability of breach for the best result. The penalty doctrine prevents parties from self-insuring idiosyncratic value like this.

More general enforcement of stipulated damage agreements would considerably reduce the time and expense of litigation. Proof of damage sustained, frequently a complex and expensive process, would no longer be necessary. In addition, if liability is not a major issue, then out of court settlements may be promoted due to the greater predictability of the outcome as the problem of valuation uncertainty has been removed.

The penalty doctrine undoubtedly increases transaction costs at the time of forming the contract. The threat of subsequent judicial review and non-enforcement of a clause means the parties must spend extra time and effort to frame their liquidated damages clause so that it fits the requirements imposed by the penalty doctrine and the courts will enforce it. . . .

The Presumption of Unfairness

Penalty clauses are assumed by the courts to be unfair or unconscionable because such an agreement could only have been reached by an abuse of the bargaining process. They assume that compensation in excess of actual loss is unjust and oppressive. This begs the question of whether the courts do in fact award full compensation and of whether such full recovery is always the best result. These issues have already been discussed but even if we accept the court's assumptions, there are problems.

First, the reasoning in decisions assessing a stipulated damages clause often comes close to conflicting with the fundamental principle that the law will neither inquire into the adequacy of consideration nor, as a rule, offer relief from what has turned out simply to be a bad bargain.

Secondly, the unfairness rationale is a *post hoc* judgment of the bargain which ignores the risk allocation made at the time of contracting. The entire bargaining process should be taken into account. The risk of breach should be recognized as a factor in determining the contract price. A premium may be paid by the buyer in order to get the seller to accept some of his or her risk in the form of an agreed damages clause for a sum greater than that the courts would award. To call an agreed remedy 'unfair' either neglects its role in shifting risk or implies inadequate consideration for the shift. Neither assertion is justified.

Stipulated damages clauses are often used where the real loss, including the subjective elements, is difficult to assess in advance but a pre-estimate can be made which averages out the risk of over- and under-compensation. The question of whether a sum is coercive becomes irrelevant when the innocent party is indifferent between the money and performance. By inflating the measure of agreed damages the innocent party signals the other party that he or she values performance highly. By making a rational choice to minimize his or her own costs the breaching party will only breach when the cost of performance of contract risks and deprives one party of a benefit he or she contracted for. . . .

SUMMARY AND CONCLUSIONS

. . . We have seen that a number of factors might induce the parties to negotiate a liquidated damages clause: (1) if expected damages are readily calculable but the parties believe that negotiation of a liquidated damages clause will save potential litigation or settlement costs should breach occur, (2) the expected damages are uncertain or difficult to establish and the parties may wish to eliminate the uncertainty of the amount that can be recovered and the expense of litigation to find it by setting liability in advance, (3) parties have different degrees of risk aversion and wish to negotiate liquidated damages so that the less risk-averse party at least partially insures the more risk-averse against loss from breach, (4) one party may attach unusual and subjective value to performance which would be rejected by a court as too fanciful to recover, (5) parties may desire a different allocation of the risks of and gains from breach than that which flows from the court's approach.

If the parties are risk-neutral they will only provide for a given contingency (for example, by stipulating a liquidated damages clause in the case of that contingency) if the adverse consequences of failing to provide for the occurrence of that event are sufficient to justify the sure costs of including such provisions and the expected cost of verifying the occurrence. Factors which must be taken into account are the difficulty of reaching agreement over an issue, the probability and magnitude of a particular loss occurring, the cost of verifying the occurrence of an event, and the importance of the transaction to the parties. The introduction of risk means that the allocation of the risk of loss due to this contingency must also be considered. In essence the issue is whether the costs of litigation and the risk of undercompensation exceed the costs of negotiating in advance.

The costs of negotiating a liquidated damages clause are greatly increased by the current uncertainty over what is required for a clause to be enforceable. Negotiation is more difficult as there are no clear guidelines and after breach there is almost always sufficient doubt for the breaching party to challenge the agreed sum on which the injured party seeks to rely. . . .

The penalty doctrine is a longstanding principle of the general law originally developed to combat unfair bargaining and extortionate 'penalty' clauses. However, with the development of the doctrine of unconscionability and the enactment of trade practices and consumer protection legislation, better ways have evolved to deal with such problems without the cost of striking out some fair and legitimate clauses. As with any attempt to correct a failure of the market, the most efficient approach is to address the problem (*i.e.* unfair clauses) as directly as possible. In this case, this means examining the bargaining process and the relationship of the parties (via the doctrines of duress and unconscionability) rather than looking merely at the end product, the agreed sum.

The adverse effects of the penalty doctrine have been discussed at length. It runs against the principle of freedom of contract not to enforce the fairly bargained agreements and risk allocations reached by the parties. The penalty doctrine may remove the need to prove unfairness, but it also makes it necessary to show what damage could have been suffered, which may be more difficult. Perhaps more importantly, the measure of damage used by the courts may not be fully compensatory. Expectation damages do not allow for the parties' attitudes to risk as they are calculated after breach. . . . In short, the parties themselves are in the best position to know what value they want to protect and how to allocate risk. Further reasons to enforce liquidated damages are the conflicting roles it plays and the frequently neglected factor that such clauses are 'paid for' in the contract price.

The conflict between the roles of incentive maintenance and the allocation of risk arises because differences in attitude to risk mean that one party can insure the other so that he or she is indifferent between breach or performance. Thus the costs of the breach are not borne by the party responsible for imposing them. Again, the parties can resolve this best among themselves by partial insurance, through liquidated damages clauses, to compromise between the two roles according to their priorities. This is impossible for the court to achieve, after breach, because it lacks the necessary information and because after breach uncertainty is resolved and the parties have an incentive to lie to maximize their gains.

In addition, as we have seen, parties wishing to be protected by an agreed damages clause in excess of what a court might award generally have paid a 'premium' on the contract price in return for this extra insurance. Hence they do have an interest in this secondary agreement to see that, if there is breach of the base agreement, they get what they bargained for and the clause is enforced. Currently, of course, such premiums are heavily discounted by the probability that they will not be enforced.

The conclusion to be drawn from all the foregoing considerations is that stipulated damage agreements should be enforced when the parties have comparable information unless there is evidence of duress or unconscionable conduct.

Note

See also S. Rea, 'Efficiency Implications of Penalties and Liquidated Damages' ((1984) 13 *J. Leg. St.* 147); D. Farber, 'Contract Law and Modern Economic Theory' ((1983) 73 *NwUL Rev.* 303); C. Goetz and R. Scott, 'Liquidated Damages, Penalties and the Just Compensation Principle: Some Notes on an Enforcement Model and a Theory of Efficient Breach' ((1977) 77 *Colum. L. Rev.* 554); K. Clarkson, R. Miller, and T. Muris, 'Liquidated Damages and Penalties: Sense or Nonsense' ([1978] *Wis. L. Rev.* 351).

As Ham points out at the beginning of the extract, his analysis of penalty/liquidated damages clauses and their desirability rests on certain assumptions regarding the market-place and the bargaining strength of contracting parties. It must be the case that in some industries a shortage of potential contractors or purchasers restricts the inclusion or subsequent enforcement of liquidated damage clauses. A rather different picture is offered by the following extract. Beale and Dugdale used a sample (19) drawn from engineering firms in Bristol and found widespread non-use of liquidated damages and instead an emphasis on the co-operative use of non-legal sanctions. We can obviously express several caveats concerning the accuracy of these findings. The study was on one sector of industry in one area and the sample was small. Moreover, liquidated damages are only reported on in relation to one facet of contracting, late delivery. However, the respondents to the Beale and Dugdale survey appear to have been engaged in relational contracts, and appear to have created performance norms outside the legal framework. These findings are in a sense rendered more valuable by being drawn from one industry: they give a more realistic picture of market behaviour.

H. Beale and A. M. Dugdale, 'Contracts between Businessmen: Planning and the Use of Contractual Remedies', (1975) 2 *BJLS* 45 at 53–5

Delivery dates were planned by express agreement in almost all contracts. Deliveries were nevertheless often delayed beyond the planned date, and yet such situations gave rise to few serious disputes and only one in which legal action was likely. The explanation did not however appear to lie in the use of contract law in planning and regulating the effect of such delays. In the standard form contracts and informal exchanges there was no planning of devices to encourage performance, such as liquidated damages clauses, other than that the price was usually payable after delivery, nor of simple remedies other than cancellation. The main methods of dealing with delay were completely extra-legal. Sellers would try when giving delivery dates to give themselves ample "lee time"; buyers would employ "progress chasing", the constant application of pressure especially through higher management and sometimes through the ultimate customer. . . .

General contract law provides that the buyer shall have the right to cancel for late delivery of goods unless this right is excluded by the contract. Cancellation is a simple remedy which the aggrieved party can normally operate without the court's assistance, and it was not surprising to find it used fairly frequently. In the case of standard items which could be resold the sellers would accept this without protest. With non-standard items most sellers said that they would expect compensation for the work done, especially if the delay was not their fault, but in practice a buyer was unlikely to cancel an order for a non-standard item because even if the design costs already incurred did not prevent it it was unlikely that the goods could be obtained more quickly from another supplier.

In contrast the buyer is similarly entitled to damages for consequential loss caused by late delivery, but it appeared that such consequential losses were seldom claimed and almost never paid: the most that would happen is that the seller might if he thought the delay was his fault waive the operation of a price escalation clause or absorb the higher cost of quicker transport whether by air freight or the roof of the managing director's car. The reason for this general position does not appear to be the difficulty of claiming such losses: the buyer has the simple remedy of "set off", or deduction of his losses from the price, but only one buyer claimed that he did this occasionally and no one else appeared to have heard of the practice. It seemed that the situation was caused by an interplay of related commercial facts and practices. On the one hand buyers were expected to guard against delay by planning schedules so that deliveries could be late without causing loss; on the other sellers were bound by an "unwritten law" that the buyer must be notified in advance of any likely delay, to enable the buyer to reschedule (only one contract required this). If this could not solve the problem the buyer might well have alternative sources of supply or be able to use other materials. Even if the buyer did suffer a loss it was generally recognized that the seller should not be liable for delays which were not his fault, and it seemed to be the general view that it was far safer to refuse any claim for consequential loss for fear of creating a precedent. Finally in some cases it would not be possible to claim serious consequential losses from a small supplier without the risk of bankrupting him. Thus although there was potential scope for making a claim in a few cases, it was almost unknown for such a claim to be paid. We were told of one dispute in which a claim had been made and the seller had gone as far as retaining counsel, but this case also involved allegations that the goods were defective.

It was only in the specifically negotiated contracts that liquidated damages clauses (clauses agreeing in advance the compensation payable for late delivery) were found. These clauses appear to be convenient ways both of encouraging timely performance and of avoiding disputes about compensation, and are commonly thought by lawyers to be attractive to the business community, but the criticisms made to us may explain why they are not more commonly used, particularly in standard conditions. Sellers clearly wished to avoid any liability for delay, but in most cases of negotiated sales they could not get away with excluding their liability altogether as they attempt to do in their "back of order" conditions. They might therefore prefer a liquidated damages clause instead of full liability at common law. But this would not be the case if they thought that the customer was unlikely to press any claim for consequential loss, for instance because of a close relationship between the two firms, or was unlikely to be able to prove any loss, for instance because the project for which the goods were required was almost certain to be running late, or because the goods were required for a non-profit making purpose such as "defence".

Buyers might have been expected to favour liquidated damages just to avoid having to prove their losses. But again there were criticisms. Firstly, sellers would not usually accept liquidated damages clauses unless delays caused by *force majeure* were excepted, and *force majeure* clauses were so wide that the buyer would receive no compensation for much of the delay. Several buyers said that they preferred to preserve their common law rights even though they would not usually exercise them. Secondly, the administrative costs of enforcing liquidated damages clauses are relatively high because keeping track of delays and investigating the causes requires a lot of manpower.

Nor when a liquidated damages clause had been agreed did buyers seem very keen to make use of the remedy. We were told that often a negotiated settlement would be reached under which only part of the sum due would be paid. This seems to destroy one advantage of the device, and apparently another advantage was also sometimes thrown away: the buyer can normally "set off" liquidated damages due against the price and pay only the balance, yet we were told of a buyer claiming liquidated damages long after paying the price in full. Our impression is that in the area of delay at least the main reason for liquidated damages was not to obtain compensation but to discipline the other party. One experienced officer told us that he favoured liquidated damages not because he wanted damages but because he wanted a realistic delivery date in the first place and to be told of any likely delay well in advance; in negotiated contracts he would ensure that the operation of the *force majeure* clause excusing the seller was conditioned on prompt notification of the excusable delay.

Thus in both negotiated and non-negotiated contract situations, late delivery seems to be regarded as primarily a commercial problem to be solved commercially rather than a legal problem susceptible to solution by the use of planning. Not surprisingly most buyers and sellers seemed to regard delivery dates as targets rather than firm promises.

V. JUDICIAL REMEDIES FOR BREACH OF CONTRACT

We have concentrated in the initial sections of this chapter on the self-help, extrajudicial and extralegal aspects of contract remedies, on the assumption that these aspects are very important in practice. In this section we move on to consider the framework of remedies awarded by the courts to an action brought by the innocent party. As we noted in the introduction to this chapter, the court can choose between giving specific or substitutional relief. In English law, the jurisdiction to compel performance derives from equity, and takes the form of the remedy of specific performance or, alternatively, some form of injunction. An action for the price (i.e. an action in debt) is also a form of specific relief. Compensatory damages can be awarded at common law or, exceptionally, under the court's equitable jurisdiction. These are the principal remedies available to the courts.

We shall consider first the link between the nature of the remedies awarded and the nature of the contractual obligation. What interests is the enforcement of contractual promises intended to protect, and what type of remedies best protect these interests? Second, we look at specific performance, and its relationship to damages. Third, we consider the precise nature of the normal measure of damages (expectation), and exceptional situations where alternative measures of compensation (reliance-based or restitutionary damages) might be more appropriate. Finally, we consider the various general limitations which are placed on the recovery of compensatory damages—remoteness of damage, mitigation of loss, contributory negligence, and irrecoverable loss.

A. The Protection of Interests and Contract Remedies

The usual remedy awarded for breach of contract by the courts in common law jurisdictions is compensatory 'expectation' damages, i.e. damages placing the party sustaining loss by reason of a breach of contract 'so far as money can do it . . . in the same situation . . . as if the contract had been performed' (per Parke B in *Robinson* v. *Harman* (1848) 1 Exch. 850 at 855). In other words, the disappointed party is to be awarded the money equivalent of his loss of bargain, including loss of profit. In the exceptional situations where specific performance can be and is awarded, it is likewise the loss of bargain which is protected through the compulsion of the performance of the contract. According to Atiyah, the ascendancy of the expectation damages measure (loss of bargain) is closely linked to the rise of the executory contract in the late eighteenth and early nineteenth century. He links it also to the growth of the mitigation rule, which promoted efficient allocations of resources by encouraging the disappointed promisee to seek performance from a third party and to look to the promisor to make up any deficiency (Atiyah, *The Rise and Fall of Freedom of Contract*, rev. edn. (Oxford, Oxford University Press, 1985), 424 ff). Atiyah's historical work shows a connection between the underlying aims of contract remedies and the various competing conceptions of the nature of the contractual obligation which have been featured throughout this book (see in particular Ch. 6). In other words, it may be consistent to protect the disappointed party's loss of bargain if bargain is seen as the central pillar of contract. But if, as some now argue, it is patterns of reasonable reliance which determine the extent to which promises are enforceable, it is not so clear why the innocent party should be awarded more than she has *lost* in reliance upon the unperformed promise rather than what she *would have gained* in the event of proper performance.

The link between the interests protected by the contractual obligation and the interests protected by contract remedies was first clearly identified in 1936 by Fuller and Perdue in their seminal work, 'The Reliance Interest in Contract Damages'. They commence their analysis by arguing against expectation damages as the appropriate remedy for breach of contract.

L. Fuller and W. Perdue, 'The Reliance Interest in Contract Damages', (1936–7) 46 *Yale LJ* 52 at 52–7

The proposition that legal rules can be understood only with reference to the purposes they serve would today scarcely be regarded as an exciting truth. The notion that law exists as a means to an end has been commonplace for at least half a century. There is, however, no justification for assuming, because this attitude has now achieved respectability, and even triteness, that it enjoys a pervasive application in practice. . . . We are still all too willing to embrace the conceit that it is possible to manipulate legal concepts without the orientation which comes from the simple inquiry: toward what end is this activity directed? Nietzsche's observation, that the most common stupidity consists in forgetting what one is trying to do, retains a discomforting relevance to legal science.

In no field is this more true than in that of damages. In the assessment of damages the law tends to be conceived, not as a purposive ordering of human affairs, but as a kind of juristic mensuration. The language of the decisions sounds in terms not of command but of discovery. We *measure* the *extent* of the injury; we *determine* whether it was *caused* by the defendant's act; we *ascertain* whether the plaintiff has included the *same item* of damage twice in his complaint. . . .

It is, as a matter of fact, clear that the things which the law of damages purports to "measure" and "determine"—the "injuries", "items of damage", "causal connections", etc.—are in considerable part its own creations, and that the process of "measuring" and "determining" them is really a part of the process of creating them. . . . For example, one frequently finds the "normal" rule of contract damages (which awards to the promisee the value of the expectancy, "the lost profit") treated as a mere corollary of a more fundamental principle, that the purpose of granting damages is to make "compensation" for injury. Yet in this case we "compensate" the plaintiff by giving him something he never had. This seems on the face of things a queer kind of "compensation". We can, to be sure, make the term "compensation" seem appropriate by saying that the defendant's breach "deprived" the plaintiff of the expectancy. But this is in essence only a metaphorical statement of the effect of the legal rule. In actuality the loss which the plaintiff suffers (deprivation of the expectancy) is not a datum of nature but the reflection of a normative order. It appears as a "loss" only by reference to an unstated *ought*. Consequently, when the law gauges damages by the value of the promised performance it is not merely measuring a quantum, but is seeking an end, however vaguely conceived this end may be.

It is for this reason that it is impossible to separate the law of contract damages from the larger body of motives and policies which constitutes the general law of contracts. It is, unfortunately for the simplicity of our subject, impossible to assume that the purposive and policy-directed element of contract law has been exhausted in the rules which define contract and breach. If this were possible the law of contract damages would indeed be simple, and we would have but one measure of recovery for all contracts. Of course this is not the case. What considerations influence the setting up of different measures of recovery for different kinds of contracts? What factors explain the rather numerous exceptions to the normal rule which measures damages by the value of the expectancy? It is clear that these questions cannot be answered without an inquiry into the reasons which underlie (or may underlie) the enforcement of promises generally. . . .

THE PURPOSES PURSUED IN AWARDING CONTRACT DAMAGES

It is convenient to distinguish three principal purposes which may be pursued in awarding contract damages. These purposes, and the situations in which they become appropriate, may be stated briefly as follows:

First, the plaintiff has in reliance on the promise of the defendant conferred some value on the defendant. The defendant fails to perform his promise. The court may force the defendant to disgorge the value he received from the plaintiff. The object here may be termed the prevention of gain by the defaulting promisor at the expense of the promisee; more briefly, the prevention of unjust enrichment. The interest protected may be called the *restitution interest*. For our present purposes it is quite immaterial how the suit in such a case be classified, whether as contractual or quasi-contractual, whether as a suit to enforce the contract or as a suit based upon a rescission of the contract. These questions relate to the superstructure of the law, not to the basic policies with which we are concerned.

Secondly, the plaintiff has in reliance on the promise of the defendant changed his position. For example, the buyer under a contract for the sale of land has incurred expense in the investigation of the seller's title, or has neglected the opportunity to enter other contracts. We may award damages to the plaintiff for the purpose of undoing the harm which his reliance on the defendant's promise has caused him. Our object is to put him in as good a position as he was in before the promise was made. The interest protected in this case may be called the *reliance interest*.

Thirdly, without insisting on reliance by the promisee or enrichment of the promisor, we may seek to give the promisee the value of the expectancy which the promise created. We may in a suit for specific performance actually compel the defendant to render the promised performance to the plaintiff, or, in a suit for damages, we may make the defendant pay the money value of this performance. Here our object is to put the plaintiff in as good a position as he would have occupied had the defendant performed his promise. The interest protected in this case we may call the *expectation interest*. . . .

It should not be supposed that the distinction here taken between the reliance and expectation interests coincides with that sometimes taken between "losses caused" (damnum emergens) and "gains prevented" (lucrum cessans). In the first place, though reliance ordinarily results in "losses" of an affirmative nature (expenditures of labor and money) it is also true that opportunities for gain may be foregone in reliance on a promise. Hence the reliance interest must be interpreted as at least potentially covering "gains prevented" as well as "losses caused". (Whether "gains prevented" through reliance on a promise are properly compensatable in damages is a question not here determined. Obviously, certain scruples concerning "causality" and "foreseeability" are suggested. It is enough for our present purpose to note that there is nothing in the definition of the reliance interest itself which would exclude items of this sort from consideration.) On the other hand, it is not possible to make the expectation interest entirely synonymous with "gains prevented". The disappointment of an expectancy often entails losses of a positive character.

It is obvious that the three "interests" we have distinguished do not present equal claims to judicial intervention. It may be assumed that ordinary standards of justice would regard the need for judicial intervention as decreasing in the order in which we have listed the three interests. The "restitution interest," involving a combination of unjust impoverishment with unjust gain, presents the strongest case for relief. If, following Aristotle, we regard the purpose of justice as the maintenance of an equilibrium of goods among members of society, the restitution interest presents twice as strong a claim to judicial intervention as the reliance interest, since if A not only causes B to lose one unit but appropriates that unit to himself, the resulting discrepancy between A and B is not one unit but two.

On the other hand, the promisee who has actually relied on the promise, even though he may not thereby have enriched the promisor, certainly presents a more pressing case for relief than the promisee who merely demands satisfaction for his disappointment in not getting what was promised him. In passing from compensation for change of position to compensation for loss of expectancy we pass, to use Aristotle's terms again, from the realm of corrective justice to that of distributive justice. The law no longer seeks merely to heal a disturbed status quo, but to bring into being a new situation. It ceases to act defensively or restoratively, and assumes a more active role. With the transition, the justification for legal relief loses its self-evident quality. It is as a matter of fact no easy thing to explain why the normal rule of contract recovery should be that which measures damages by the value of the promised performance.

Fuller and Perdue's definition of the reliance interest which is to be protected extends beyond negative wasted expenditure to include opportunities forgone in reliance upon promises. It is the protection of the lost opportunity element which underlies one of the reasons for the pragmatic adoption of the expectation *measure* of damages by Fuller and Perdue as the best way, in practice, of protecting the reliance *interest* within the contractual obligation.

Fuller and Perdue, 'The Reliance Interest in Contract Damages', 60–2

What reasons can be advanced? In the first place, even if our interest were confined to protecting promisees against an out-of-pocket loss, it would still be possible to justify the rule granting the value of the expectancy, both as a cure for, and as a prophylaxis against, losses of this sort.

It is a cure for these losses in the sense that it offers the measure of recovery most likely to reimburse the plaintiff for the (often very numerous and very difficult to prove) individual acts and forbearances which make up his total reliance on the contract. If we take into account "gains prevented" by reliance, that is, losses involved in foregoing the opportunity to enter other contracts, the notion that the rule protecting the expectancy is adopted as the most effective means of compensating for detrimental reliance seems not at all far-fetched. Physicians with an extensive practice often charge their patients the full office call fee for broken appointments. Such a charge looks on the face of things like a claim to the promised fee; it seems to be based on the "expectation interest". Yet the physician making the charge will quite justifiably regard it as compensation for the loss of the opportunity to gain a similar fee from a different patient. This foregoing of other opportunities is involved to some extent in entering most contracts, and the impossibility of subjecting this type of reliance to any kind of measurement may justify a categorical rule granting the value of the expectancy as the most effective way of compensating for such losses. . . .

. . . Whatever tends to discourage breach of contract tends to prevent the losses occasioned through reliance. Since the expectation interest furnishes a more easily administered measure of recovery than the reliance interest, it will in practice offer a more effective sanction against contract breach. It is therefore possible to view the rule measuring damages by the expectancy in a quasi-criminal aspect, its purpose being not so much to compensate the promisee as to penalize breach of promise by the promisor. The rule enforcing the unrelied-on promise finds the same justification, on this theory, as an ordinance which fines a man for driving through a stop-light when no other vehicle is in sight.

In seeking justification for the rule granting the value of the expectancy there is no need, however, to restrict ourselves by the assumption, hitherto made, that the rule can only be intended to cure or prevent the losses caused by reliance. A justification can be developed from a less negative point of view. It may be said that there is not only a policy in favor of preventing and undoing the harms resulting from reliance, but also a policy in favor of promoting and facilitating reliance on business agreements. As in the case of the stop-light ordinance we are interested not only in preventing collisions but in speeding traffic. Agreements can accomplish little, either for their makers or for society, unless they are made the basis for action. When business agreements are not only made but are also acted on, the division of labor is facilitated, goods find their way to the places where they are most needed, and economic activity is generally stimulated. These advantages would be threatened by any rule which limited legal protection to the reliance interest. Such a rule would in practice tend to discourage reliance. The difficulties in proving reliance and subjecting it to pecuniary measurement are such that the business man knowing, or sensing, that these obstacles stood in the way of judicial relief would hesitate to rely on a promise in any case where the legal sanction was of significance to him. To encourage reliance we must therefore dispense with its proof. For this reason it has been found wise to make recovery on a promise independent of reliance, both in the sense that in some cases the promise is enforced though not relied on (as in the bilateral business agreement) and in the sense that recovery is not limited to the detriment incurred in reliance.

The juristic explanation in its final form is then twofold. It rests the protection accorded the expectancy on (1) the need for curing and preventing the harms occasioned by reliance, and (2) on the need for facilitating reliance on business agreements.

Notes

1. Fuller and Perdue have been criticized for the 'lightness' with which they assert their bold normative propositions about the hierarchy of interests within contract, and for their blind assumption of the key role of the reliance interest. As T. Rakoff puts it:

Fuller never considers the possibility that there might be social policies of the sort he discusses that would support the expectation measure on its own, rather than mediately through protection of the reliance interest. (He never considers, for example, that courts might want, as a matter of policy to encourage the profit motive *per se*). ('Fuller and Perdue's *The Reliance Interest* as a Work of Legal Scholarship', [1991] *Wis. L. Rev.* 203 at 214)

While their support for the primacy of the reliance interest has been followed by contract scholars such as Atiyah, there have equally been many attempts since the publication of 'The Reliance Interest' to argue on theoretical grounds for the award of expectation damages, on the grounds that this follows from the nature of the contractual obligation either as an act of promising (e.g. Fried) or as a efficient exchange (e.g. Posner). These arguments will be examined further below.

2. Burrows's main criticism of Fuller and Perdue is that their first reason for pragmatically advocating the expectation measure as a surrogate for proof of the reliance interest is rather weak. He much prefers their second

argument, based on encouraging reliance and exchange (A. Burrows, *Remedies for Torts and Breach of Contract* (London, Butterworths, 2nd Edition, 1994), 19. However, the second point should not be overstated: Fuller and Perdue are not drifting into advocating the centrality of the expectation interest as a means of encouraging 'people to perform their side of a bargain, thereby upholding the working of the market economy under which goods and services find their way to where they are most wanted' (Burrows, *Remedies for Torts . . .* , 19); rather, their argument is closely related to one of the pragmatic reasons for supporting the enforce-ability of purely executory contracts identified by Atiyah, ('Contracts, Promises and the Law of Obligations', in *Essays on Contract*, rev. edn. (Oxford, Clarendon Press, 1988), 35–6). In another context, Atiyah, like Fuller and Perdue, is arguing that *reliance* is best encouraged through the protection of *expectation*, in this case though the application of a criterion of enforceability (consideration) under which a bare exchange of promises is recognized as a binding contract. In other words, the measure of dam-ages, like the criterion of enforceability, can be applied instrumentally to achieve other ends, such as the protection of reliance.

3. The thrust of Atiyah's support for the protection of the reliance interest has a number of dimensions. First, as we commented above, he has observed a historical link between the 'rise and fall' of the freedom of con-tract principle and the fate of expectation damages in judicial practice. Second, in a related observation, he notes that the theoretical ascendancy of the expectation loss is not matched by practice, both because of the unwillingness of the courts to award expectation damages in certain cir-cumstances (e.g. against consumers—see *Rise and Fall*, 754–9) and because of the application of the mitigation principle in cases such as *Lazenby Garages Ltd.* v. *Wright* ([1976] 2 All ER 770). In that case, a garage-owner who resold a second-hand car without loss of profit to a third party after the defendant had refused to take delivery of the car he had purchased was denied any damages for breach for contract. Finally, Atiyah has cited the empirical evidence of business contracting gathered by authors such as Macaulay, Beale, and Dugdale to observe that businessmen tolerate and indeed expect a high degree of promise-breaking, and consequently do not expect to receive their loss of bargain for every contract broken. These fac-tors, coupled with his position on the importance of protecting reliance in exchange relationships, leads Atiyah to conclude that the question of dam-ages available in a case such as *Lazenby* v. *Wright* should be decided on the basis of wasted expenditure (e.g. in making the second sale) rather than on the basis of loss of bargain discounted by the duty to mitigate.

4. Ultimately, as Pettit asserts, whatever the pragmatic arguments in favour of protecting the *reliance interest* through the expectation measure,

the decision to advocate the protection of one particular interest rather than another is one which must be driven by a value judgment. He states his position as follows, making no attempt to conceal that it is a subjective judgment.

M. Pettit, 'Private Advantage and Public Power: Reexamining the Expectation and Reliance Interests in Contract Damages', (1987) 38 *Hastings LJ* 417 at 426–8

Logic does not resolve the choice between reliance and expectation. Complete protection of the promisee's reliance interest (including lost opportunities) would mean compensation for all losses suffered by the promisee by reason of the promisor's conduct from promise through breach. If the starting point from which to measure loss is the promisee's status at the time the promise was made, then reliance damages provide full compensation, and expectation damages are supercompensatory. But advocates of the expectation measure can also claim the compensation principle. If the starting point for measuring loss is the value of the promise, then the expectation measure provides no more than exact compensation for actual loss.

What should be the base level from which losses are measured? Expectation supporters can point out that it is the breach alone and not the initial promise that is the wrong to be compensated for. If no wrong had been committed (the promise had been kept), the promisee would have been in, say, position X. Because of the wrong the promisee is in position Y. Compensatory damages, therefore, should be X minus Y. Reliance supporters can reply that expectation is a strange kind of compensation because in fact the promisee never actually occupied position X. Expectation damages make the promisee better off than the promisee had ever been before. By using the time of promise as the starting point we can take account of the effect of all the actions of the promisor—you cannot break a promise without making it first. Reliance supporters can argue that their measure makes contract remedies consistent with tort remedies, so that we have one compensation rule for breaches of civil obligations. Expectation advocates can counter that the presence of a promise makes contract different from tort, and uniformity would mean treating unequal things equally.

Although the choice between the expectation and reliance principles cannot be resolved by purely analytic means, the analysis of the difference between the two measures helps to clarify what is and what is not at stake in making the choice. That difference is what I have called the "extra advantage" that the nondefaulting party would have received from the defaulter beyond what he would have obtained elsewhere; the contract may have provided for this extra advantage for many different reasons. My own view is that implementation of this private advantage is not a proper use of the power of the state.

Critics might respond that as long as no one has exploited an improper advantage (for example, by exertion of vastly superior bargaining power, deception, duress, or the like) there is no reason why the extra advantage should not be enforced. My view is that, even when the bargaining process displays no identifiable flaw, this kind of private advantage should not become an object of state enforcement. There is no doubt that my view reflects certain fundamental philosophical and political biases. My conclusion reflects an underlying belief that, more often than not, it is the stronger actors in our society who seek to employ state power to enforce this privately negotiated "extra" advantage. This belief is certainly subject to intuitive challenge and empirical contradiction.

Fried's theory of promising constitutes one of the notable attempts since Fuller and Perdue to give a theoretically grounded justification for the expectation measure of damages.

C. Fried, *Contract as Promise* (Cambridge, Mass., Harvard University Press, 1981), 17–21

What a promise is worth

If I make a promise to you, I should do as I promise; and if I fail to keep my promise, it is fair that I should be made to hand over the equivalent of the promised performance. In contract doctrine this proposition appears as the expectation measure of damages for breach. The expectation gives the victim of a breach no more or less than he would have had had there been no breach—in other words, he gets the benefit of his bargain. Two alternative measures of damage, reliance and restitution, express the different notions that if a person has relied on a promise and been hurt, that hurt must be made good; and that if a contract-breaker has obtained goods or services, he must be made to pay a fair (just?) price for them. . . .

The insistence on reliance or benefit is related to disputes about the nature of promising. As I have argued, reliance on a promise cannot alone explain its force: There is reliance because a promise is binding, and not the other way around. But if a person is bound by his promise and not by the harm the promisee may have suffered in reliance on it, then what he is bound to is just its performance. Put simply, I am bound to do what I promised you I would do— or I am bound to put you in as good a position as if I had done so. To bind me to do no more than to reimburse your reliance is to excuse me to that extent from the obligation I undertook. If your reliance is less than your expectation . . . then to that extent a reliance standard excuses me from the very obligation I undertook and so weakens the force of an obligation I chose to assume. Since by hypothesis I chose to assume the obligation in its stronger form (that is, to render the performance promised), the reliance rule indeed precludes me from incurring the very obligation I chose to undertake at the time of promising. The most compelling of the arguments for resisting this conclusion and for urging that we settle for reliance is the sense that it is sometimes harsh and ungenerous to insist on the full measure of expectancy. . . . The harshness comes about because in the event the promisor finds the obligation he assumed too burdensome.

This distress may be analyzed into three forms [(1) and (2) omitted].

Finally there is the most troublesome ground of regret: (3) The promisor made no mistake about the facts or probabilities at all, but now that it has come time to perform he no longer values the promise as highly as when he made it. He regrets the promise because he regrets the value judgment that led him to make it. . . . Compassion may lead a promisee to release an obligation in such a case, but he releases as an act of generosity, not as a duty, and certainly not because the promisor's repentance destroys the force of the original obligation. The intuitive reason for holding fast is that such repentance should be the promisor's own responsibility, not one he can shift onto others. It seems too easy a way of getting out of one's obligations. Yet our intuition does not depend on suspicions of insincerity alone. Rather we feel that holding people to their obligations is a way of taking them seriously and thus of giving the concept of sincerity itself serious content. Taking this intuition to a more abstract level, I would say that respect for others as free and rational requires taking seriously their capacity to determine their own values. . . . If we decline to take seriously the assumption of an obligation because we do not take seriously the promisor's prior conception of the good that led him to assume it, to that extent we do not take him seriously as a person. We infantilize him, as we do quite properly when we release the very young from the consequences of their choices.

Notes

1. A number of Fried's critics (e.g. Atiyah, 'The Liberal Theory of Contract', in *Essays on Contract*, rev. edn. (Oxford, Clarendon, 1988), 124; Pettit, 'Private Advantage and Public Power', 429) have pointed out that the thrust of his argument on promise-keeping seems to support the use of specific performance as the primary remedy for breach of contract rather than to address the debate between the various measures of damages. The relationship between the two remedies is taken up below.

2. Pettit also repudiates Fried's argument on political grounds, continuing his theme that the ability of private individuals to enlist state power to enforce private advantages should be strictly limited.

Pettit, 'Private Advantage and Public Power', 431

The rhetoric of promise-keeping and personal autonomy comes easily to those who seek to enforce the promises of others. Those with the power to negotiate favorable contracts naturally support rules that enforce those contracts to the fullest extent. But the importance of promise-keeping is not the only moral value involved in choosing a contract damages measure. One could argue in moral terms that a person should not insist on obtaining the full advantage resulting from another person's miscalculation of current market conditions, for example. Promisees seeking to enlist state power to effectuate promised advantages cannot persuasively rest their claims on any natural or necessary affinity between the expectation measure of contract damages and shared notions of morality.

Economists have also addressed the problems raised by the determination of the appropriate measure of damages for breach of contract. Some, such as Goetz and Scott, have reached conclusions which echo the findings of Fuller and Perdue (C. Goetz and R. Scott, 'Enforcing Promises: An Examination of the Basis of Contract', (1980) 89 *Yale LJ* 1261 at 1284 ff). They argue that perhaps the principal social rationale of promising is to produce beneficial reliance, which they define as the reliance placed by promisees on promises with the prospect of increasing their wealth in the future. They also define an interest called 'detrimental reliance', which is the situation which occurs when a promise relied upon by the promisee is broken, leaving the promisee worse off than before the promise was made. To protect both elements of reliance so defined, Goetz and Scott opt for a damages formula under which expectation damages can be awarded as 'a good proxy for the prospective net reliance damage formulation' which they have developed (p. 1284).

Other economists have focused on the problem of contractual behaviour, treating the measure of contractual damages as one element in the decision of every promisor whether to breach or to perform her contracts. Given that the award of expectation damages is, at least in conventional legal doctrine, the primary measure of damages for breach of contract, the task of the economist is then to determine whether or not it is efficient. It is only efficient on the model propounded by economists such as Posner if parties are encouraged to perform when breach would be inefficient and encouraged to default if breach would be efficient. Linzer explains how the theory of efficient breach works.

In the context of contracts, efficiency theory suggests that promisors who breach increase society's welfare if their benefit exceeds the losses of their promisees. Such failure to perform, the so-called efficient breach of contract, is illustrated by the following. Assume that Athos owns a woodworking factory capable of taking on one more major project. He contracts to supply Porthos with 100,000 chairs at $10 per chair, which will bring Athos a net profit of $2 per chair, or $200,000 on the contract. Before any work takes place, Aramis, who sells tables, approaches Athos. Although there are several chair factories in the area, only Athos's factory can make tables. If Athos will supply Aramis with 50,000 tables, Aramis will pay him $40 per table. Athos can produce the tables for $25, so he can make a net profit of $750,000 if he uses his factory for Aramis's tables. But to do so, he must breach his contract with Porthos. There are other chair factories, and Porthos will be able to get the chairs from one of them—for example, from D'Artagnan's. Let us assume that because of his distress situation Porthos will have to pay D'Artagnan 20% more than Athos's price for comparable chairs, and that Porthos will sustain $100,000 in incidental administrative costs and consequential costs such as damages for delay to his customers. Even with these costs, Porthos will lose only $300,000 because of Athos's breach, and Athos can reimburse him in full and still make $450,000 profit, over twice the profit from his contract with Porthos.

As one might expect, efficiency theorists applaud the Athoses of the world for breaching their contracts. Thus, Richard Posner sets up a similar illustration and notes that "if damages are limited to loss of expected profit, there will be an incentive to commit a breach. There should be . . . . The expectation rule thus assures that the product ends up where it is most valuable. . . ."

Although these positions conflict with the notion of *pacta sunt servanda* and with the moral view . . . they do make some sense. People generally enter into commercial contracts and routine labor contracts for purely economic reasons and can therefore be fully compensated with damages for injuries caused by breach. If we prevent Athos from building tables for Aramis, we force him to waste his resources, with no economic benefit to Porthos. Therefore, while it would be possible to restrain Athos by making his breach of contract a crime, by imposing punitive damages or penalties on him, or by ordering specific performance, the law does not do this. . . . Thus, despite our concern for holding parties to their word, at least in the conventional market situation that we have illustrated, law, economics, and arguably common sense all condone the deliberate and willful breach.

Notes

1. Other dimensions of the economic analysis of the measure of damages have been explored. For example, D. Farber ('Contract Law and Modern Economic Theory', (1983) 78 *NwUL Rev.* 303 at 321) argues for the expectation measure as the means of preserving a high level of future contracting activity. Anything less than the full performance value will operate as a disincentive to future contractual exchanges. A. Polinsky (*An Introduction to Law and Economics*, 2nd edn. (Boston, Little, Brown, 1989), 60–5)

identifies the importance of contract remedies matching the risk allocation between the parties, and concludes in favour of a general acceptance of the expectation measure over the reliance measure.

2. Linzer points to the interesting fact that both promise theory (the 'moral view') and efficiency theory conclude in favour of the centrality of the expectation interest in the contractual obligation and in contract remedies, albeit for very different reasons. The moral view supports the expectation interest on the grounds that promises should not be *broken*, while efficiency theory takes the same position on the grounds that contracts are and should be *breakable*.

3. Efficiency theory in the analysis of contract remedies has received general criticism from Ian Macneil. We extract here his conclusions on these issues. We interpolate into these conclusions some of the examples which he gives in the body of the text.

I. Macneil, 'Contract Remedies: A Need for Better Efficiency Analysis', (1988) 144 *J. Inst. Th. Econ.* 6 at 28–9

The efficiency model is too often applied to the analysis of contract remedies without proper attention to its own requirements. Procedurally, there is great and virtually universal failure to make clear what assumptions are being made. This is an extremely serious problem since a very wide range of assumptions, many of them quite complex, are required in the analysis of contract law.

This procedural failing runs over into, and also causes, substantive failings in analysis. These include the following: (1) omission of aspects of contract behavior likely, or even sure, to have systematic effect on efficiency [e.g. co-operative behaviour in the context of relational contracts]. (2) Failure to recognize the pervasive effect of contract remedies on behavior other than that studied. (3) Failure to recognize that the extremely limited hypothetical situations used in proofs limit the kinds of contracts to which conclusions may properly be addressed, and hence remedies which can be recommended on efficiency grounds [e.g. many hypothetical cases used by academics cite examples of discrete transactions only]. (4) Failure to recognize the limited impact legal rules have on the behavior of participants in contracts. (5) Failure to consider all significant transaction costs likely to have systematic effects on contract behavior and legal remedies. (6) Lack of realism in assessing transaction costs. (7) Failure adequately to recognize that the introduction of real, rather than assumed, transaction costs, into the model deprives the model of its deductive positivist nature and renders it only as good as the empirical demonstrations of the real costs. . . .

Cure of these errors in efficiency analysis of contract remedies can lead only to the following: much greater complexity or conclusions of extremely limited nature or both, and extreme modesty in advocating particular contract remedies on efficiency grounds. This outcome severely limits the utility of efficiency analysis of contract remedies. If such cures are effected, a relational approach to contracts and their remedies in which efficiency analysis is reached only by working to it through the relations, rather than assuming them away *ab initio*, may seem more attractive than it now does as a tool of economic analysis. Such an approach lacks the false clarity and false positivism of the efficiency model as it is currently used in analyzing contract remedies. I believe, however, that it will lead to more realistic and effective analysis of the material and necessarily social aspects of contracts and contract remedies. This I believe also to be the true role of economics, not simply the refined analysis of scarcity.

Notes

1. We shall return to the theory of efficient breach and Macneil's critique below.

2. Macneil's criticisms apply to the application of efficiency theory to contract remedies generally—not only to the determination of the measure of damages.

B. Specific Performance

The award of an expectation-based remedy leaves the courts a choice between substitutionary relief (an award of damages) and specific relief (specific performance). Included within specific relief is an award of the contract price. We looked at examples of this remedy in *White and Carter (Councils) Ltd.* v. *McGregor* in Chapter 13. In both English and US law the primary form of relief is an award of damages. The entrenchment of this position can be seen from the writings of Oliver Wendell Holmes, amongst others: 'The duty to keep a contract of common law means a prediction that you must pay damages if you do not keep it—and nothing else' ('The Path of the Law', (1897) 10 *Harv. L. Rev.* 457 at 462). The difficulties confronting those who advocate specific performance as the principal remedy for the expectation interest are set out by Schwartz.

A. Schwartz, 'The Case for Specific Performance', (1979) 89 *Yale LJ* 271 at 274

Specific performance is the most accurate method of achieving the compensation goal of contract remedies because it gives the promisee the precise performance that he purchased. The natural question, then, is why specific performance is not routinely available. Three explanations of the law's restrictions on specific performance are possible. First, the law's commitment to the compensation goal may be less than complete; restricting specific performance may reflect an inarticulate reluctance to pursue the compensation goal fully. Second, damages may generally be fully compensatory. In that event, expanding the availability of specific performance would create opportunities for promisees to exploit promisors by threatening to compel, or actually compelling, performance, without furthering the compensation goal. The third explanation is that concerns of efficiency or liberty may justify restricting specific performance, despite its greater accuracy; specific performance might generate higher transaction costs than the damage remedy, or interfere more with the liberty interests of promisors.

Traditionally, specific relief has not been available for certain types of contract and is not awarded where damages would be adequate. These caveats are currently shifting ground, and we shall consider whether these limitations should now be couched more broadly in terms of whether the courts consider specific relief desirable or not. We also consider the grounds which are used to justify the primacy of damages.

The first of Schwartz's explanations is not explored any further by him, and nor will it be by us. The previous section showed the extent of the commitment of the law of contract to the award of expectation-based remedies. As we have seen, doubts about *why* courts should award the expectation interest and the argument advanced by commentators such as Atiyah that in reality the full expectation is rarely awarded both question the reality of that commitment. Moreover, the existence of the duty to mitigate is an important limitation upon the ability to recover full compensation, as is the exclusion of certain types of loss from damages awards as irrecoverable loss. This is not the case with specific performance because, as Schwartz points out, specific performance is the most accurate remedy, giving the promisee the precise performance he purchased.

The theory of efficient breach was explained in the previous section. It also helps to explain why, from an economist's viewpoint, damages should be the primary remedy rather than specific performance. The link between the theory of efficient breach and the award of damages rather than specific performance is explained by Macneil, building on the example used by Linzer (above) of the Four Musketeers.

I. Macneil, 'Efficient Breach of Contract: Circles in the Sky', (1982) 68 *Va. L. Rev.* 947 at 950–3

The simple-efficient-breach analysis is fallacious. The assumption that it is economically efficient for Athos to build tables rather than chairs by no means leads to the conclusion that breach is the economically efficient result. Rather, that result is obtained through the *nonperformance* of the contract to build chairs, and the substitution of the contract to build tables. Since breach is far from the only way to avoid performance of the chair contract, no conclusion can be deduced that breach is any more (or less) efficient than other ways of securing the efficient result of nonperformance.

Underlying the simple-efficient-breach analysis is the assumption that the expectation damages rule will lead to the making of tables rather than chairs and that the specific performance rule will lead to the making of chairs rather than tables. Neither assumption is valid. This may be shown by assuming a world in which all relations between the parties can be conducted without transaction costs. They have the usual property and other legal entitlements to start with and can trade them costlessly. Using Linzer's illustration of the Four Musketeers, Aramis's offer of the table contract has created an opportunity for someone to make at least an additional $250,000. Under the expectation damages rule, that someone is Athos. If Athos is subject only to damages in the amount of the $300,000 that Porthos loses from the breach, Athos will breach and pay Porthos $300,000. Under that rule he will make tables, not chairs, and efficiency will be served.

If there are no transaction costs the cause of economic efficiency is served equally well by the specific performance rule. Athos will promptly tell Porthos about the new contract and will agree to pay Porthos something between $0 and $250,000 (over and above his costs of $300,000) for a release from the chair contract. Since this is a world without transaction costs, they will, of course, make a deal. Once again, while wealth distribution will be different, efficiency will be served.

Free of transaction costs, *neither* of these rules leads to more efficient use of resources than the other in the kinds of situations concerning efficiency theorists. It is, therefore, illogical to conclude that either a right to specific performance or a right to expectation damages will lead to such a result in the real world. Whatever "direction" towards or away from efficiency either of these rules has depends entirely upon the relative transaction costs each will generate.

It is clear then that the simple-efficient-breach conclusion about the inefficiency of the specific performance rule is logically indefensible on the basis of what it purports to be—a deduction from the efficiency model. The conclusion of inefficiency can be defended only on the basis that the transaction costs of securing nonperformance of the first agreement under the specific performance rule are always higher than under the expectation damages rule.

Macneil seeks to show that specific performance can satisfy the criteria of the efficient breach theory, but he does this by assuming that the contractual relationship between the parties has zero transaction costs. Macneil's whole credo of contract centres on the concept of relational contract (see Ch. 2). Once he adds the facets of relational contract to his example the arguments of the economists he opposes come into play. Macneil points out that the question of the efficiency of a damages remedy as opposed to specific performance centres on transaction costs. The economists who seek to show that damages are aptly the primary remedy seek to do so by alluding to the transaction costs of each remedy. Macneil can only answer this by asserting that the appropriate transaction costs can only be quantified by empirical inquiry and not by micro-economic models (at p. 957).

Traditionally, transaction costs in this context are divided into pre- and post-breach costs.

(i) *Pre-breach transaction costs.* One of the primary exponents of the case for limiting the availability of specific performance on the grounds of pre-breach transaction costs is Kronman. He takes a position described by Schwartz (above) as intention justification theory; in other words, the limits on the availability of specific performance placed by the courts mean that the remedy is available in situations where the parties would want it and not in others where, if specific performance were available, one or other of the parties would bargain to secure its exclusion as a remedy from the contract.

A. Kronman, 'Specific Performance', (1978) 45 *U. Chi. L. Rev.* 351 at 365–9

When would the parties to a contract freely agree to a judicially enforceable provision giving the promisee an option to specifically enforce the other party's promise? Other things equal, a promisee will always prefer to have such a provision included in the contract for it gives him an additional right which he would not otherwise possess. Other things equal, a promisor will always prefer a contract without such a provision—a contract, in other words, which he may unilaterally breach on the condition that he make a subsequent compensatory payment to the promisee. Consequently, a promisee intent upon writing a specific performance provision—a property rule—into the contract will have to pay to secure the promisor's consent. Similarly, a promisor must make a payment of some sort in order to exclude a provision for specific enforcement from the contract. If and only if the benefit which the promisee realizes from a specific performance provision exceeds the cost of the provision to the promisor will the provision be included in the final contract.

When the subject matter of a contract is unique, the risk is greater that the promisee's money damage remedy will be undercompensatory. Since a right to compel specific performance reduces this risk, promisees—as a class—should be willing to pay more for a provision giving them a right of this sort when there is no developed market generating information about the value of the subject matter of their contract.

However, if a specific performance provision is likely to be more beneficial to a promisee when the subject matter of his contract is unique, it is also likely to be more costly to his promisor under the same circumstances. In the first place, a right in the promisee to compel specific performance increases the probability of costly negotiations for transfer of the promisee's contract rights. This of course always reinforces the promisor's preference for a money damages rule. However, a promisor is likely to regard this reason as especially compelling where the subject matter of his contract is unique, since the lack of information about substitutes will almost certainly make the parties' negotiations longer and more complicated and thus more costly.

Second, if the promisee is entitled to specifically enforce the promisor's obligation, the promisor who wishes to breach will have to make a release payment to the promisee and buy his way out of the contract. The amount of the release payment demanded by the promisee will be greater than what the promisor would have to pay the promisee under a money damages rule. . . .

The cost of a specific performance provision to the promisor will be determined, in part, by his own estimate of the likelihood that he will want to breach the contract. If he fully intends to perform, and thinks breach unlikely, a promisor will be less hostile to a contract with a specific performance provision than he would otherwise be. One important factor influencing the promisor's thinking in this regard is the probability that he will receive a better offer for his goods or services in the interim between formation of the contract and performance. The higher the probability, the greater the likelihood he will want to breach. The probability of receiving an attractive alternative offer may be especially low where the subject matter of the contract is unique. In this case there is by definition no developed market, transactions are spotty at best, and therefore a promisor will often justifiably think it highly unlikely that he will receive any alternative offer (let alone a better one) for the promised goods or services. Indeed, where the subject matter of his contract is genuinely unique, a promisor may estimate the likelihood of a preferable alternative offer as close to zero, and thus be nearly indifferent as to what remedies the promisee will enjoy in the highly unlikely event of breach. . . .

In the case of a contract for non-unique goods or services, by contrast, the existence of a developed market increases the likelihood that the promisor will receive alternative offers before he has performed the contract. The promisor will therefore be anxious to retain the freedom and flexibility enjoyed under a money damages rule.

Moreover, the promisor will be especially anxious in this case to avoid the additional transaction costs that would be incurred if he had to negotiate a voluntary transfer of the promisee's contract rights. Although these costs will tend to be smaller where the subject matter of the contract is not unique, they can never be less than some fixed minimum (the cost of contacting the promisee, notifying him of an intention to breach, obtaining a release statement of some sort, and so on). Where there is an established market in the goods or services involved, prices will ordinarily be grouped rather closely around a single point.

The probability is therefore greater that any alternative offer the promisor does receive will not be sufficiently high to cover the cost of negotiating a release plus the amount he must pay the promisee for the release. Thus the likelihood increases that a promisor who has agreed to a specific performance provision will find himself in the undesirable position of having to decline an alternative offer that he would accept under a money damages rule. In some cases the alternative offer will cover the release payment but will be refused solely because the transaction costs of negotiating a transfer of the promisee's contract rights are prohibitively high. The promisor should therefore be willing to make a small payment to the promisee, perhaps in the form of a slightly reduced contract price, in order to exclude a specific performance provision and thus avoid these potential transaction costs.

Schwartz criticizes Kronman's position on unique goods on the grounds that he does not assess the market for unique goods accurately. According to Schwartz, the market for unique goods is likely to be more developed than Kronman thinks: the scarcity of unique goods causes sellers to increase price rather than output. The latter would be the response in a market for non-unique goods if demand increases. The desire to be able to increase the price in this way encourages sellers to retain their freedom to breach contracts.

Schwartz uses the demise of the unique-goods argument for specific performance as the most appropriate remedy for contracts where no adequate substitute performance is available to argue that specific performance should be one of a range of remedies readily available to contracting parties. His point is that remedies are 'context-dependent' ('The Case for Specific Performance', 366), and that it is impossible on the basis of intention justification theories to determine in advance which remedies parties want in particular situations. Parties should, then, have the choice of a range of remedies. The difficulty with this approach is that it does not demonstrate why, in cases where there is substitutionary relief available, specific performance is as efficient a remedy. Rather, it shows us that in some, but not all, cases of unique goods, specific performance will be the desired remedy.

(ii) *Post-breach transaction costs.* An example of the post-breach transaction costs argument is set out in the next extract by Schwartz, who then offers his own critique of it. In Schwartz's critique the term 'cover costs' refers to the need for one of the parties to find and obtain an alternative to what was promised under the contract.

Schwartz, 'The Case for Specific Performance', 285–91

For example, suppose that a buyer (B1) contracts with a seller (S) to buy a widget for $100. Prior to delivery, demand unexpectedly increases. The widget market is temporarily in disequilibrium as buyers make offers at different prices. While the market is in disequilibrium, a second buyer (B2) makes a contract with S to purchase the same widget for $130. Subsequently, the new equilibrium price for widgets is $115. If specific performance is available in this case, B1 is likely to demand it, in order to compel S to pay him some of the profit that S will make from breaching. B1 could, for example, insist on specific performance unless S pays him $20 ($15 in substitution damages plus a $5 premium). If S agreed, B1 can cover at $115, and be better off by $5 than he would have been under the damage remedy, which would have given him only the difference between the cover price and the contract price ($15). Whenever S's better offer is higher than the new market price, the seller has an incentive to breach, and the first buyer has an incentive to threaten specific performance in order to capture some of the seller's gains from breach.

The post-breach negotiations between S and B1 represent a "dead-weight" efficiency loss; the negotiations serve only to redistribute wealth between S and B1, without generating additional social wealth. If society is indifferent as to whether sellers or buyers as a group profit from an increase in demand, the law should seek to eliminate this efficiency loss. Limiting buyers to the damage remedy apparently does so by foreclosing post-breach negotiations.

This analysis is incomplete, however. Negotiation costs are also generated when B1 attempts to collect damages. If the negotiations by which first buyers (B1 here) capture a portion of their sellers' profits from breach are less costly than the negotiations (or lawsuits) by which first buyers recover the market contract differential, then specific performance would generate lower post-breach negotiation costs than damages. This seems unlikely, however. The difference between the contract and market prices is often easily determined, and breaching sellers have an incentive to pay it promptly so as not to have their extra profit consumed by lawyers' fees. By contrast, if buyers can threaten specific performance and thereby seek to capture some of the sellers' profits from breach, sellers will bargain hard to keep as much of the profits as they can. Therefore, the damage remedy would probably result in quick payments by breaching sellers while the specific performance remedy would probably give rise to difficult negotiations. Thus the post-breach negotiation costs associated with the specific performance remedy would seem to be greater than those associated with the damage remedy.

This analysis makes the crucial assumption, however, that the first buyer, B1, has access to the market at a significantly lower cost than the seller; though both pay the same market price for the substitute, B1 is assumed to have much lower cover costs. If this assumption is false, specific performance would not give rise to post-breach negotiations. Consider the illustration again. Suppose that B1 can obtain specific performance, but that S can cover as conveniently as B1. If B1 insists on a conveyance, S would buy another widget in the market for $115 and deliver on his contracts with both B1 and B2. A total of three transactions would result: S-B1; S-B2; S2-S (S's purchase of a second widget). None of these transactions involves post-breach negotiations. Thus if sellers can cover conveniently, the specific performance remedy does not generate post-breach negotiation costs.

The issue, then, is whether sellers and buyers generally have similar cover costs. Analysis suggests that they do. Sellers as well as buyers have incentives to learn market conditions. Because sellers have to "check the competition," they will have a good knowledge of market prices and quality ranges. Also, when a buyer needs goods or services tailored to his own needs, he will be able to find such goods or services more cheaply than sellers in general could, for they would first have to ascertain the buyer's needs before going into the market. However, in situations in which the seller and the first buyer have already negotiated a contract, the seller is likely to have as much information about the buyer's needs as the buyer has. Moreover, in some markets, such as those for complex machines and services, sellers are likely to have a comparative advantage over buyers in evaluating the probable quality of performance and thus would have lower cover costs. Therefore, no basis exists for assuming that buyers generally have significantly lower cover costs than sellers. It follows that expanding the availability of specific performance would not generate higher post-breach negotiation costs than the damage remedy. . . .

. . . [S]erious objections may be made to this conclusion:

the first objection assumes that sellers breach partly because their cover costs are higher than those of their buyers; it then argues that when cover costs do diverge, allowing specific performance seemingly is less efficient than having damages be the sole remedy. Returning to the widget hypothetical, let Cb = the first buyer's (B1's) cover costs; Cs = the seller's cover costs. Assume that S has higher cover costs than B1, *i.e.*, Cs > Cb. If specific performance were available, B1 could threaten to obtain it, so as to force S to pay him part of the cover cost differential. Cs – Cb. If B1 made a credible threat, S would be better off negotiating than covering. Because only the availability of specific performance enables B1 to force this negotiation, one could argue that it is less efficient than having damages as the sole remedy.

This objection is incorrect, even if differential cover costs influence seller decisions to breach. A credible threat by B1 to seek specific performance would usually require preparing or initiating a lawsuit. This would entail costs of lost business time, lost goodwill and lawyer's fees, and these costs usually exceed any cover cost differential (Cs – Cb) that may exist. This is because the magnitude of cover costs—and hence of the differential—are low in relation to legal costs. Locating and arranging for substitute transactions are routine, relatively inexpensive business activities. Since the legal and related costs necessary for a credible threat commonly exceed the cover cost differential, it would rarely pay buyers to threaten specific performance to capture part of this differential. Thus no post-breach negotiations would be engendered by any differences in the parties' cover costs.

The second objection to the conclusion that post-breach negotiation costs are no higher under specific performance than under damages follows from the fact that in some cases sellers cannot cover at all. In these cases, buyers can always compel post-breach negotiations by threatening specific performance. There are two situations in which a seller cannot cover: if he is a monopolist or if the goods are unique. In either event the first buyer would also be unable to cover. If neither the seller nor the first buyer can cover, no reason exists to believe that there would be higher post-breach negotiation costs with specific performance than with damages. If specific performance were available, B1 and S would negotiate over B1's share of the profit that S's deal with B2 would generate, or B1 would insist on a conveyance from S and then sell to B2. If only the damages remedy is available, B1 would negotiate with S respecting his expected net gain from performance rather than over the contract market difference, because he could not purchase a substitute. This expected gain is often difficult to calculate, and easy for the buyer to exaggerate. There is no reason to believe that negotiations or litigation over this gain would be less costly than the negotiations over division of the profit that B2's offer creates, or the costs of a second conveyance between B1 and B2. Thus even when the seller cannot cover, specific performance has not been shown to generate higher post-breach negotiation costs than damages. Moreover, when neither party can cover—the case under discussion—buyers have a right to specific performance under current law.

To summarize, if the initial buyer has access to the market at a significantly lower cost than the seller, a damages rule generates lower post-breach negotiation costs than a rule that makes specific performance routinely available. It seems likely, however, that both parties will be able to cover at similar, relatively low cost, or that neither will be able to cover at all. In either event, post-breach negotiation costs are similar under the two rules. . . .

The final objection to the conclusion that post-breach negotiation costs are no higher under specific performance than under damages applies in the context of unexpectedly rapid inflation. Suppose that a promisee would realize $3,000 profit from a construction project that he contracted to buy for $10,000. Suppose also that, at the time he made the contract, the promisor anticipated that the project would cost him $8,000, and that unanticipated inflation raised the promisor's costs to $15,000. In the event that the promisee's anticipated profits from completion of the project do not similarly increase, the promisee's best strategy would be to threaten specific performance so as to force the promisor to share part of the $7,000 cost savings that the promisor would realize from breaching. Although the promisee loses $3,000 from breach, the promisor saves $7,000. The negotiations over division of the net $4,000 savings that breach makes possible are a deadweight efficiency loss. If only the damage remedy were available to the promisee, however, the promisee could still force such negotiations because he would retain the power to impose a $7,000 loss on the promisor.

The standard damage measure for breach of a construction contract is the difference between the contract price and the new market price. In the hypothetical, the new market price would be $17,000 ($15,000 cost plus the contractor's $2,000 profit), and the contract price is $10,000. Thus specific performance and the damages remedy create identical incentives for the parties to engage in costly post-breach negotiations in the event of unexpected inflation.

Notes

1. The remedy of damages incorporates the doctrine of mitigation, which operates as a limitation on the extent of the remedy; the effect of the doctrine is to pass the cost of cover to the promisee. In the absence of this doctrine, incentives to cover pass to the promisor. It might seem that only the empirical investigation advocated by Macneil can provide an answer to such issues as who has lower cover costs, the promisee or the promisor. On this basis the economists' case for the primacy of damages may seem unproven. However, a point which both Schwartz and Macneil have overlooked is whether limitations on the recovery of compensatory damages such as the rules on remoteness and mitigation of damage have in themselves an incentive value for efficient behaviour. We consider these rules below.

2. An alternative argument in favour of specific performance is that certain types of loss may not be calculable in monetary terms. To a certain extent, specific performance is already awarded in cases which concern unique goods, but it is arguable that more use could be made of it in cases concerning fungible goods. Harris, Ogus, and Phillips identify an area of loss they describe as the 'consumer surplus', which they define as 'the subjective value obtained from a "good" over and above the utility associated with its market price' (see D. Harris, A. Ogus, and J. Phillips, 'Contract Remedies and the Consumer Surplus', (1979) 95 *LQR* 581 at 582). Below they explain how this subjective value is calculated.

D. Harris, A. Ogus, and J. Phillips, 'Contract Remedies and the Consumer Surplus', (1979), 95 *LQR* 581 at 583

It is, of course, difficult to measure utility, but generally economists avoid the conceptual problem by measuring utility in terms of the maximum amount a consumer would pay for a particular purchase. For instance, if a purchaser can buy a plot of land for £1,000, when he would be prepared to pay up to £1,500 for it, the extra £500 represents his "consumer surplus." Without using this term, an intending bidder at an auction thinks in this way when he decided beforehand what is the maximum bid he is prepared to make: the difference between any lower price he pays and the higher price he is prepared to pay measures the consumer surplus expected at that time. Therefore willingness to pay, rather than market price, is the appropriate measure for estimating the value of a purchase, and the consumer surplus is the difference between this value and the market price.

Specific performance may overcome the problem of valuing the consumer surplus, although it will be of no assistance in cases where performance is no longer possible. It is also difficult to use arguments based on the consumer surplus to deal with commercial contracts, where the value of a good over its market price is likely to be future profit which is not difficult to calculate.

(iii) *Judicial approaches to specific performance.* We referred earlier to the existence of evidence that the judiciary are becoming more willing to grant specific rather than substituting relief. The following case is interesting in that it concerns the sale of oil, which is not a unique good. None the less, the plaintiffs are able to obtain an injunction to ensure the continuance of its supply. The award of an injunction in this context is, as Goulding J points out, the equivalent in effect to making an award of specific performance.

Sky Petroleum Ltd. v. *VIP Petroleum Ltd.*
[1974] 1 All ER 954

The plaintiffs had made a contract with the defendants under which, for a period of ten years from 1970, the plaintiffs were to buy all their petrol and diesel from the defendants. The contract could be terminated at three months' notice by either party and incorporated a fixed price. The defendants sought to terminate the contract, alleging a breach by the plaintiffs of the credit provisions of the contract. The plaintiffs sought an interlocutory injunction (best described as a temporary remedy providing interim resolution of the contract dispute) to protect their petrol and diesel supply.

GOULDING J This is a motion for an injunction brought by the plaintiff company, Sky Petroleum Ltd, as buyer, under a contract dated 11th March 1970 made between the defendant company, VIP Petroleum Ltd, as seller, of the one part and the plaintiff company of the other part. . . .

After the making of the agreement, it is common knowledge that the terms of trade in the market for petroleum and its different products changed very considerably, and I have little doubt that the contract is now disadvantageous to the defendant company. After a long correspondence, the defendant company, by telegrams dated 15th and 16th November 1973, has purported to terminate the contract under a clause therein providing for termination by the defendant company if the plaintiff company fails to conform with any of the terms of the bargain. What is alleged is that the plaintiff company has exceeded the credit provisions of the contract and has persistently been, and now is, indebted to the defendant company in larger amounts than were provided for . . . . [T]hat dispute . . . involves not only a question of construction of the contract, but also certain disputes on subsequent arrangements between the parties and on figures in the accounts. I cannot decide it on motion and the less I say about it the better.

What I have to decide is whether any injunction should be granted to protect the plaintiff company in the meantime. There is trade evidence that the plaintiff company has no great prospect of finding any alternative source of supply for the filling stations which constitute its business. The defendant company has indicated its willingness to continue to supply the plaintiff company, but only at prices which, according to the plaintiff company's evidence, would not be serious prices from a commercial point of view. There is, in my judgment, so far as I can make out on the evidence before me, a serious danger that unless the court interferes at this stage the plaintiff company will be forced out of business. In those circumstances, unless there is some specific reason which debars me from doing so, I should be disposed to grant an injunction to restore the former position under the contract until the rights and wrongs of the parties can be fully tried out. . . .

Now I come to the most serious hurdle in the way of the plaintiff company which is the well-known doctrine that the court refuses specific performance of a contract to sell and purchase chattels not specific or ascertained. That is a well-established and salutary rule and I am entirely unconvinced by counsel for the plaintiff company when he tells me that an injunction in the form sought by him would not be specific enforcement at all. The matter is one of substance and not of form and it is, in my judgment, quite plain that I am for the time being specifically enforcing the contract if I grant a injunction. However the ratio behind the rule is, as I believe, that under the ordinary contract for the sale of non-specific goods, damages are a sufficient remedy. That, to my mind, is lacking in the circumstances of the present case. The evidence suggests, and indeed it is common knowledge, that the petroleum market is in an unusual state in which a would-be buyer cannot go out into the market and contract with another seller, possibly at some sacrifice as to price. Here, the defendant company appears for practical purposes to be the plaintiff company's sole means of keeping its business going, and I am prepared so far to depart from the general rule as to try to preserve the position under the contract until a later date. I therefore propose to grant an injunction.

Notes

1. Goulding J refers to 'specific goods'. Specific goods are defined in the Sale of Goods Act 1979, s. 61, as goods 'identified and agreed upon at the time the contract is made'. The goods supplied by the defendants were clearly not specific; the fuel supplied over the ten-year period of the contract would have been produced or refined, etc. by the defendants as required by the plaintiffs. The 1979 Act attaches the remedy of specific performance to an action for breach of contract to deliver specific goods (s. 52). It had been assumed that, by exclusion, the court did not have the power to order specific performance in the case of unascertained goods. However, Goulding J ignores this remedial framework, and appears to hold that that state of the oil market in effect designated the goods 'commercially unique'.

This approach has its attractions; the oil market was so volatile that it would have been difficult to ascertain the precise effect of the defendants' conduct on the plaintiffs. It was not clear that a substitute source of supply was available or at what price. If a category of 'commercially unique' goods is recognized, however, courts will have to undertake a complex analysis of the market in that commodity to reach the conclusion that its structure is such that an award of damages would be inadequate. This was only a first instance decision, and on an interlocutory point. It is by no means clear that other judges will accept the principle of commercial uniqueness. For a review of decisions on commercial uniqueness since *Sky Petroleum*, see A. Burrows, 'Specific Performance at the Cross Roads' ((1984) 4 *LS* 102 at 104.

2. It is clear from *Sky Petroleum* that a principle guiding the availability of specific performance as a remedy is the inadequacy of damages. We need to know what makes an award of damages inadequate. Is it sufficient that damages are difficult or impossible to calculate, or is there some other underlying principle? In Chapter 7 we mentioned *Beswick* v. *Beswick* ([1968] AC 58). The facts were briefly that a widow was awarded a remedy of specific performance to enforce an annuity contracted for by her late husband in her favour. She recovered not in her own right as a third party but on behalf of her husband's estate as the administratrix.

Here we are concerned with the type of recovery she is awarded rather than with the privity of contract problems surrounding the fact of recovery. The estate on behalf of which the widow recovered had suffered only nominal damage, and an award in these terms might have been expected. However, the House of Lords rejected an award of damages as inadequate. The scope of their decision has long been a matter of debate. All five Lords rejected an award of damages on the ground that a 'just result' required something more.

We can interpret 'just result' in several ways. First, we can look at the case in its narrow context as a way of circumventing the privity of contract rule. The House of Lords may have felt that injustice was caused because in this context damages can only ever be nominal, as the promisee's own loss will always be nominal and will not match the loss of the third party. Second, we can focus on the multiplicity of actions point. Once a decision to award more than nominal damages is made, damages cannot be quantified as no one knows how long the widow will live. She might then have to sue for each annuity payment individually. Third, we can say that the House of Lords is making a value judgement about the conduct of the party in breach. Not to award specific performance would have allowed him to obtain a very good bargain indeed, namely his uncle's coal business at very low cost. To put it another way, it could be argued that, in any case where specific performance would produce a 'more just' solution, it should be awarded.

This third possibility was alluded to most clearly by Lord Pearce. It would have the effect of reversing the remedies structure; instead of beginning with damages and deciding whether they would be adequate to remedy the breach, the court would begin by assessing what was required for a just result and awarding specific performance if it was appropriate. *Beswick* v. *Beswick* has remained a 'hard case'; the third view has not been judicially adopted. It is interesting that Goulding J rested his decision in *Sky Petroleum* on the 'commercial uniqueness' of petroleum fuel and *Beswick* v. *Beswick* was not discussed.

3. A traditional objection to awards of specific performance is that in certain contexts, e.g. employment contracts, this remedy is an unwanted intrusion on personal liberty and freedom. As Ogus points out, this is increasingly not a position adopted by the courts and legislature.

A. Ogus, 'Remedies: English Report', in D. Harris, and D. Tallon (eds.), *Contract Law Today* (Oxford, Oxford University Press, 1991), 243 at 256

There are several specific legislative provisions which involve the reinstatement of dismissed employees and the courts seem to have been influenced by them when, without statutory compulsion, they have effectively ordered an employer to re-engage an individual or an association to admit a person as member. At the same time, they obviously consider that the difficulties involved in supervising the performance of some contracts have been exaggerated. It is the plaintiff, rather than the court, who must, in the first instance, monitor performance, and an officer of the court can be appointed to investigate allegations of non-compliance. The greater willingness to order specific performance in such cases accords with the view expressed by some that the courts have a positive, regulatory role in a mixed economy and that the enforcement of standards is not the exclusive province of the executive.

The infringement of liberty argument against specific performance is reinforced by observations that judicial involvement in enforcing this remedy will be too costly. However, this seems a very weak argument; the availability of specific performance as a remedy in this context may lead to less litigation and less judicial involvement than at present.

C. Expectation-Based Damages: Measure of Damages

From the perspective of doctrine, the dominant remedy for breach of contract is expectation-based damages. The plaintiff may recover his loss of bargain, less any costs avoided because of the breach. A useful starting-point for considering the scope of recoverable expectation loss is provided by the exercise on *Naughton* v. *O'Callaghan* ([1990] 3 All ER 191) in Chapter 5. Review this exercise before continuing with this section. In this section we consider some of the issues raised by putting into practice the deceptively simple statement of principle that contract damages are expectation-based and compensatory in nature.

First we consider the basic reference point for the loss of bargain: cost of cure versus difference in value. We then examine briefly the limited recoverability of certain types of non-pecuniary or intangible loss such as mental distress and physical discomfort.

The first question to be answered is: 'What measure of damages will mend a bargain?' Is it the cost of bringing the defective performance up to scratch (the 'cost of cure') or is it the difference in value between the defective performance rendered and the value of the performance on the open market if it had been property rendered? Some statutory guidance is available on the correct basis for assessing damages, such as s. 18 of the Landlord and Tenant Act 1927, which provides that damages for breach by a tenant of her covenant under a lease to repair the premises are to be fixed on a difference-in-value basis. Likewise, part IV of the Sales of Goods Act 1979 on actions for breach of contract provides, in the case of damages for non-acceptance of goods by the buyer (s. 50(3)), non-delivery by the seller (s. 51(3)), and breach of warranty by the seller (s. 53(5)), that the recoverable loss is to be assessed on a difference-of-value basis. Moreover, the existence of the doctrine of mitigation, which requires a buyer or seller who receives no performance to go out into the market-place to secure substitute goods or to make a substitute sale if at all possible, speaks in favour of this approach. However, the rules in the Sale of Goods Act are merely prima facie rules and in appropriate cases courts may award cost of use damages.

The next case, however, demonstrates that the court may refuse to award cost of cure damages, even if it is apparent that the guilty party has quite cynically breached the contract hoping to derive a windfall profit.

Tito v. *Waddell (No. 2)*
[1977] Ch. 106

The defendants had been granted exclusive licences to mine phosphate on Ocean Island, a small Pacific island. They covenanted with the defendants, the owners of the island who had moved to another island, that they would replant the land, after mining, with indigenous trees and shrubs, in order to restore it as nearly as possible to its pre-mining operations state. In breach of contract, the defendants failed to replant the island. In the course of an exceedingly lengthy judgment, Megarry VC rejected the plaintiffs' claim for specific performance of the defendants' replanting obligations. He then went on to consider the measure of damages in respect of the breach of the replanting obligation. The plaintiffs sought damages to cover the cost of replanting, at an estimated A\$73,140 per acre. The defendants rejected this contention, claiming that, as the Ocean Islanders had no intention of returning to the island, the damages should be purely nominal.

MEGARRY VC In the absence of any clear authority on the matter before me, I think I must consider it as a matter of principle. I do this in relation to the breach of a contract to do work on the land of another, whether to build, repair, replant or anything else: and I put it very broadly. First, it is fundamental to all questions of damages that they are to compensate the plaintiff for his loss or injury by putting him as nearly as possible in the same position as he would have been in had he not suffered the wrong. The question is not one of making the defendant disgorge what he has saved by committing the wrong, but one of compensating the plaintiff. In the words of O'Connor L.J. in *Murphy* v. *Wexford County Council* [1921] 2 I.R. 230, 240:

"You are not to enrich the party aggrieved; you are not to impoverish him; you are, so far as money can, to leave him in the same position as before."

Second, if the plaintiff has suffered monetary loss, as by a reduction in the value of his property by reason of the wrong, that is plainly a loss that he is entitled to be recouped. On the other hand, if the defendant has saved himself money, as by not doing what he has contracted to do, that does not of itself entitle the plaintiff to recover the saving as damages; for it by no means necessarily follows that what the defendant has saved the plaintiff has lost.

Third, if the plaintiff can establish that his loss consists of or includes the cost of doing work which in breach of contract the defendant has failed to do, then he can recover as damages a sum equivalent to that cost. It is for the plaintiff to establish this: the essential question is what his loss is.

Fourth, the plaintiff may establish that the cost of doing the work constitutes part or all of his loss in a variety of ways. The work may already have been done before he sues. Thus he may have had it done himself, as in *Jones* v. *Herxheimer* [1950] 2 K.B. 106. Alternatively, he may be able to establish that the work will be done. This, I think, must depend on all the circumstances, and not merely on whether he sues for specific performance. An action for specific performance is doubtless one way of manifesting a sufficient intention that the work shall be done: but there are others. Thus the plaintiff may be contractually bound to a third party to do the work himself, as in *Conquest* v. *Ebbetts* [1896] A.C. 490. . . .

. . . I have already mentioned the case of the plaintiff who does the work himself before he sues: I cannot see that it matters that he did it without being under any obligation to do it. After all, he contracted for valuable consideration that it should be done. Suppose, then, that he has not done it but states that he intends to do it. Of course, he may not be believed: but if he is, why should not his loss be measured by what it will cost him to do the thing that the defendant ought to have done but did not do? In some cases, the circumstances may demonstrate a sufficient fixity of intention in the plaintiff's resolve, as where the property is his home and will be highly inconvenient or nearly uninhabitable until the work is done. In such a case I cannot think that it matters that the house could be made convenient or inhabitable by doing cheaper or less idiosyncratic work: what matters is the work to which the plaintiff is entitled under the contract. . . .

. . . Whatever the circumstances, if the plaintiff establishes that the contractual work has been or will be done, then in all normal circumstances it seems to me that he has shown that the cost of doing it is, or is part of his loss, and is recoverable as damages. . . . In the words of Denning J. in *Westminster* (*Duke*) v. *Swinton* [1948] 1 K.B. 524, 534, "The real question in each case is: What damage has the plaintiff really suffered from the breach?" In the end, the question seems to me to come down to a very short point. The cost is a loss if it is shown to be a loss. . . . .

Does the Chancery Amendment Act 1858 (Lord Cairns' Act) make any difference? [Counsel for the plaintiffs] Mr. Macdonald submitted that where a contract was one in which the court can order specific performance but refuses to do so, the damages that would be awarded in substitution for specific performance under the Act must be a real substitute; therefore, he said, in this case they should equal the cost of doing the work. . . . I readily accept this proposition as far as the word "therefore"; but I cannot see that the conclusion follows. When the court refuses to order the doing of some expensive but largely futile work, the difference in the value of the property to the plaintiff with the work done and without it may be great or it may be small. He may or may not be able to establish that although on the market the difference is negligible, there are reasons, whether idiosyncratic or not, why it is a matter of great moment to him. In damages one always comes back to the fundamental question, that of the loss or injury that the plaintiff has suffered, and the sum of money that will compensate him for it. Whatever may be the position in other cases, I cannot see that on the facts of this case it makes any difference whether the damages are awarded at common law or under the Act.

I turn to Mr. Macdonald's secondary contention, founded on a suitable proportion of the cost of replanting as representing what the British Phosphate Commissioners would have paid to be released from their obligation to replant. This contention did not emerge until very late in the proceedings. It was on Day 96 that Mr. Macdonald first cited *Wrotham Park Estate Co. Ltd.* v. *Parkside Homes Ltd.* [1974] 1 W.L.R. 798 . . . . In [that] case, houses had been built on land without the prior approval of the plaintiffs which a restrictive covenant made requisite. On the facts of the case a mandatory injunction to demolish the houses was refused, and damages in substitution therefor were held to be recoverable under the Act of 1858. Brightman J. resolved the difficult question of the appropriate quantum of damages by holding that the plaintiffs should recover 5 per cent. of the defendants' expected profit from their venture. . . .

I find great difficulty in seeing how these cases help Mr. Macdonald. If the plaintiff has the right to prevent some act being done without his consent, and the defendant does the act without seeking that consent, the plaintiff has suffered a loss in that the defendant has taken without paying for it something for which the plaintiff could have required payment, namely, the right to do the act. The court therefore makes the defendant pay what he ought to have paid the plaintiff, for that is what the plaintiff has lost. The basis of computation is not, it will be observed, in any way directly related to wasted expenditure or other loss that the defendant is escaping by reason of an injunction being refused: it is the loss that the plaintiff has suffered by the defendant not having observed the obligation to obtain the plaintiff's consent. Where the obligation is contractual, that loss is the loss caused to the plaintiff by the breach of contract.

In the present case, the loss caused to the plaintiffs by the British Phosphate Commissioners' failure to replant is the diminution in the value of their land resulting from that failure, or, if it is established that the land would be replanted, the cost of replanting. In the latter case, no doubt, the British Phosphate Commissioners might well have been willing to pay something to be released from their obligation to replant, though that something would probably be rather less than the total estimated cost of replanting. But the point is that not unless the British Phosphate Commissioners would be liable to replant or pay damages equal to the cost of replanting would there be any liability from which the British Phosphate Commissioners would seek release on the basis of paying a sum equal to the discounted cost of replanting. If Mr. Macdonald establishes that liability, he does not need his less favourable secondary contention: if Mr. Macdonald fails to establish that liability, there is no foundation on which to base his secondary contention. Of course, until it has been determined whether or not some burden exists, the person who would be subject to that burden may always be willing to pay something to be relieved of the risk: but I do not think that this can affect the measure of damages in the case which determines that the burden does exist. In any case, the two authorities in question seem to me to be a long way away from a case where the issue is not one of invading the property rights of another without consent, but of breach of a contract to replant his land.

(b) QUANTUM. I return, then, to Mr. Macdonald's primary contention. Have the plaintiffs shown that the cost of replanting represents the loss to them caused by the failure to perform the replanting obligation? Only one answer to that question seems possible, and that is No. The plaintiffs own small scattered plots of land; there is nothing to establish that the owners of neighbouring plots of land, who are not parties to these proceedings, would procure the replanting of their plots rather than keep any damages for themselves or other purposes; the Banabans are now well established in Rabi, over 1,500 miles away; and there they have an island over 10 times the size and unaffected by mining, as contrasted with the much smaller Ocean Island with some five-sixths of it mined.

Let me suppose that these circumstances had been explicitly put to each of the plaintiffs, coupled with the possibility that replanting would be held not to involve demolishing pinnacles and putting down soil, and the certainty that only a relatively small part of the island was subject to any replanting obligation. If the witness had nevertheless strongly asserted a firm intention to spend any damages on replanting his land, I should even then have been slow to accept his answer unless he gave convincing reasons for taking such a course. A mere general assertion of a desire to have the land replanted could carry very little weight in such circumstances. As it is, there was no evidence on behalf of any of the plaintiffs that came near to satisfying me that the cost of replanting represented a loss to him or her which could form the basis of an award of damages. . . .

[Six months later, after the parties had failed to agree the quantum of damages, Megarry VC gave judgment on the damages recoverable by the plaintiffs in respect of the breach of the replanting obligation.]

What was agreed was that without further evidence and without further argument, and on the basis of rusticum judicium [a rough-and-ready form of calculation derived from maritime law] I should decide the measure of damages for the plaintiffs who have succeeded in Ocean Island No. 1. I was asked to express my decision in the terms of a sum of money in Australian dollars for every acre of land, on the assumption that the amount of damages appropriate to each acre of land was the same, whatever its actual location and condition, and on the footing that all the land has ceased to be used by the British Phosphate Commissioners, so that the obligation to replant has arisen. . . .

I do not propose to discuss the basis of damages any further than appears in my judgment. Put broadly, what I have to consider is the loss caused to the owner of an acre of land by reason of the British Phosphate Commissioners' failure to replant it in accordance with the obligations in the . . . deeds, construed as I have construed them. . . . Rusticum judicium abjures any exact method of calculating the amount of damages, and I do not propose to attempt to set out any part of the process of arriving at a sum for damages which, in accordance with the judgment that I have already delivered, should be neither nominal or minimal, but nevertheless not very large. In broad terms, what I have to consider is the loss to the owner of a plot of land of the advantage of having his land in its present state planted with an appropriate mixture of coconuts, almonds and pandanus, with the consequent improvement in its appearance and such possibility as there is of edible fruit being produced in due time. On the whole, having regard to all the circumstances of the case, including the nature of the terrain, I think that an appropriate sum by way of damages is $A75 per acre. Let me emphasise that this sum in no way represents damages on the basis claimed by the plaintiffs, with its levelling of the pinnacles and importation of vast quantities of soil, for I have already rejected that basis of claim. Nor does it represent the cost of replanting the land on a more modest basis, for I have already held that the loss to the plaintiffs is not the cost of replanting the land but instead is the diminution in its value caused by the failure to replant it on that more modest basis. I say this merely in an attempt to avoid or curtail misunderstandings.

Notes

1. A key fact which helps to explain Megarry VC's decision both to refuse specific performance and to award only a very low level of damages was the complete impracticability of the task of replanting. It would have taken nearly twenty years before any replanted trees or shrubs would have begun to bear fruit. In other words, the cost of completion was disproportionate in comparison to the benefits thereby to be gained. In reality, moreover, the Ocean Islanders would not have undertaken the work. Consequently, while accepting that cost of cure could be an appropriate measure of damages in certain circumstances, Megarry VC held that the plaintiffs had failed to prove that this was the measure of the loss they suffered as a result of the breach of the replanting obligation. The judgment in *Tito* v. *Waddell* was approved by Oliver J in *Radford* v. *De Froberville* ([1978] 1 All ER 33), where it was held that the plaintiffs did intend to do what the defendants had failed to do, namely build a wall which the latter had promised to build. Consequently the cost of cure—the cost of building the wall—was awarded as damages rather than the much lower sum which represented the diminution in the value of the property.

2. *Tito* v. *Waddell* has, however, encountered criticism, despite this judicial approval. The first criticism concerns the requirement of proof of intent by the plaintiff to do the work. G. Jones ('The Recovery of Benefits Gained from a Breach of Contract', (1983) 99 *LQR* 443 at 450) comments: 'to say that a defendant is liable for the cost of replanting only if the plain-

tiff intends to replant must seem strange to the businessman who knows what he has promised to do . . . such an argument makes a nonsense of the reasonable expectations of promisees.' What Jones appears to be suggesting is that expectation damages measures in this way are not in fact protecting the promisee's expectation interest, a criticism essentially shared by P. Birks ('Restitutionary Damages for Breach of Contract: Snepp and the Fusion of Law and Equity', [1987] *LMCLQ* 421) and E. McKendrick, who argues that the plaintiffs in *Tito* v. *Waddell* were under-compensated because of the approach taken by Megarry VC ('Promises to Perform: How Valuable?', (1992) 5 *JCL* 6 at 11). See also E. MacDonald, 'Breach of a Conceptual Obligation: Cost of Work or Market Value?' ([1988] *Conv.* 421).

3. Megarry VC takes a very narrow view of the plaintiffs' contention that at the very least an award of damages based on diminution of value would deprive them of the valuable benefit to be derived if the defendants had sought to buy off their obligation to replant. According to Jones, Megarry VC draws an unsustainable distinction between breaking a promise which incidentally creates an equitable obligation as well (i.e. a property right) and breaking a promise which is merely expressed as a contractual right. An alternative mechanism for measuring the value of the replanting to the Islanders, which would have fallen between the cost of replanting and the purely notional sum of A$75 per acre fixed upon by Megarry VC, is suggested by D. Harris, A. Ogus, and J. Phillips ('Contract Remedies and the Consumer Surplus', (1979) 95 *LQR* 581 at 590–4). It is based on the recognition of the subjective value of their homeland to the Islanders. One way of calculating the value of the consumer surplus is to assess how much the promisee could have demanded from the promisor as the cost of releasing him from his obligation, precisely the approach taken in *Wrotham Park Estate* and rejected in *Tito* v. *Waddell*.

4. The second major criticism of *Tito* v. *Waddell* concerns Megarry VC's strict adherence to what he sees as the 'compensatory aim' of contract damages. It is arguable that his formalist adherence to identifying the 'real loss' to the plaintiffs led him to forget the true purpose of contract remedies, to protect the interests which make up the various elements of the contractual obligation. Consequently, it is arguable that a more satisfactory balance, between avoiding giving the plaintiffs a windfall in terms of substantial damages which they had no intention of spending on replanting and protecting their reasonable expectation that the defendants would take the obligation to replant seriously while preventing the defendants from deriving a windfall profit from the award of merely nominal damages, would have been to make an award of restitutionary damages. It would thereby have been possible to deprive the defendants of the benefit of the breach of obligation, as suggested by Fuller and Perdue, by accepting that

in certain circumstances it is unnecessary for the benefit gained by the defendants to be matched directly by a loss suffered by the plaintiffs. L. Friedman ('Restitution of Benefits Obtained through Appropriation of Property or the Commission of a Wrong', (1980) 80 *Colum. L. Rev.* 504) contends that a restitutionary remedy in such circumstances has an important and extensive deterrent effect upon wrongdoers. Jones, while arguing in favour of such a remedy, acknowledges that it is difficult to state what its precise limits should be. In particular, he is concerned to see the development of a claim which dovetails with the insights offered by market economists such as Posner, who argue that the rules on remedies should not deter efficient breaches which allow resources to be reallocated to where they can be used more profitably.

G. Jones, 'The Recovery of Benefits Gained from a Breach of Contract', (1983) 99 *LQR* 443 at 456–7

. . . a restitutionary claim should only lie if the defendant has saved himself expense by failing to perform a collateral term of a contract which he has substantially performed; conversely there should be no restitutionary claims if he fails to perform at all. So if this limit is accepted, a plaintiff could recover the expense which a defendant saves from failing to leave the demised property in good repair or land levelled to a uniform grade but not the profits gained by an owner who, in breach of the terms of the charter, withdraws a ship and hires her to another at a higher freight rate. This distinction is pragmatically attractive to those who share Judge Posner's economic philosophy since it does not deter a defendant from non-performance when it would be profitable to do so.

The novelty of a restitutionary claim for profits might otherwise tempt judges to restrict its breadth, in particular to say that it should lie only if the defendant's breach was wilful. The English common law has consistently denied the relevance of the inquiry, why did the defendant fail to carry out his promise? . . . On balance, it is preferable to reject a bald distinction between wilful and non-wilful breach but to affirm that the remedy of an account of profits from a breach of contract is a remedy which it is in the discretion of the court to grant or refuse. The nature of the promisor's conduct may be a factor for the court in determining whether to grant an accounting but it should not be a decisive one.

The burden will be on the promisee to prove that the promisor could not have gained the profits in question except by breaking his contract with the promisee.

5. Cost of cure can only be used as the basis of measuring damages if it constitutes the monetary equivalent of what the promisor promised. Promises to carry out certain works on land owned by the promisee, as in *Tito* v. *Waddell* and *Radford* v. *De Froberville*, are obvious cases where

putting the plaintiff in the position he would have been in had the contract
been performed arguably involves giving him the money to carry out the
work in lieu of the defendant. A rather different situation obtains in the
context of contracts for professional services, where the promisor merely
promises to take reasonable care in the provision of his or her services and
does not warrant that any statements made are true. A good example is the
provision of a negligent survey report, which induces a person to purchase
a house believing it to be free of defects which require more than routine
maintenance. The surveyor does not promise that his report is true—he
merely promises to take reasonable care in its preparation. In that case, the
measure of damages is diminution in value: either the purchaser would not
have bought the house, had the report been prepared carefully, in which
case he is entitled to the cost of extricating himself from the transaction by
selling the house off at a lower price than the purchase price, or he would
have bought the house at a reduced price, in which case his loss is the extra
he has paid. He is not entitled to the cost of making the house good, since
the survey did not promise that the house was free from substantial defects
(*Philips* v. *Ward* [1956] 1 All ER 874; *Watts* v. *Morrow* [1991] 4 All ER 937).
Diminution in value is, in these cases, the true measure of the 'cost of completion' of the contract.

6. It can be assumed that one factor which induced the Ocean Islanders to
litigate the breach of the replanting obligation was the strong sense of
grievance at the loss of their homeland and the distress caused by the cavalier behaviour of the British Phosphate Commissioners. It is only within
very narrow limits that English law recognizes intangible harms such as
these, or such as physical discomfort, inconvenience, or mental distress
caused by a breach of contract, as recoverable losses. It has been thought
that cases such as *Jarvis* v. *Swan Tours Ltd.* ([1973] 1 All ER 71) heralded a
new era of generosity amongst the English judges as regards non-pecuniary loss, but the recent Court of Appeal decision in *Watts* v. *Morrow* has
set firm limits upon further expansion of this type of loss. Only in cases
where 'the subject matter of the contract . . . is to provide peace of mind or
freedom of distress' (per Purchas LJ in *Hayes* v. *James and Charles Dodd*
[1990] 2 All ER 815 at 826) are damages for 'pure' mental distress recoverable.

Contracts for the provision of package holidays offer perhaps the best
example of a settled practice of awarding damages for mental distress (e.g.
Jackson v. *Horizon Holidays Ltd.* [1975] 3 All ER 92). In the cases involving
the provision of negligent survey reports, where the purchasers may end
up living in houses which are quasi-building sites for many months while
necessary repairs are carried out, the basis for the award of non-pecuniary
damages is the physical discomfort suffered by the plaintiffs and, where

appropriate, mental distress consequent upon that discomfort. As Bingham LJ accepted in *Watts* v. *Morrow*, the foundation for the restriction of recoverable loss for breach of contract is one of policy, and awards for physical discomfort should be 'restrained', for reasons which Bingham LJ did not expand upon.

The closing down of avenues of recovery for mental distress means that the courts have now declined the opportunity to develop one area of doctrine which would have allowed them to recognize and compensate in respect of the so-called consumer surplus.

D. Reliance-Based Damages

Although the general principle of the law of contract damages is that of putting the innocent party in the position he would have been in had the contract been properly performed, there are circumstances in which the victim of a breach will fare better if he frames his claim in terms of what he has lost rather than what he has not gained. As a general proposition, English law also recognizes that, in the event of a breach of contract, the innocent party can always recover his wasted expenditure under the contract (or, indeed, wasted expenditure incurred in direct contemplation of the contract: *Anglia Television* v. *Reed* [1972] 1 QB 60). Normally such wasted expenditure will be recovered as an aspect of the gross profit resulting under the contract, but clearly a difficulty will arise for the plaintiff if he or she is unable to prove that any profit would have resulted from the contract—either because the contract was not a particularly good bargain for the plaintiff or because the defendant's breach of contract has now made it impossible to estimate what profits would have resulted.

However, one caveat should be attached to this analysis. English law allows the recovery of reliance loss without essentially departing from an expectation-based framework for contract remedies. Consequently, reliance damages are recoverable only to the extent, in principle, that the loss would have been recouped had the contract been performed. In other words, reliance damages are bargain-led in the sense that the innocent party cannot improve her position under a bad bargain by claiming for the protection of her reliance interest, rather than the expectation loss. Consequently, although in *C. & P. Haulage* v. *Middleton* ([1983] 3 All ER 94 at 98) Ackner LJ defined the measure of the reliance loss in the classic 'Fuller' terms as the innocent party 'asking to be put in the position he would have been in if the contract had never been made at all', this approach is limited by a countervailing principle that the innocent party will not, through an award of compensation, be put in a better position than if the contract had been performed. In a sense, this is the precise mirror image of the position propounded by Fuller and Perdue. They proposed the conventional award of expectation damages as the best means of protecting, in practice, the innocent party's reliance interest in the contractual obligation. The English position on reliance damages, as limited in these terms, seems to be protecting the innocent party's expectation interest (which may be very small or, indeed, negative if he has made a bad bargain) by awarding compensation based on a reliance measure.

As with any award of damages, one of the key questions is that of proof. If reliance loss is to be limited by the frame of expectation, the question arises as to who must prove the width of the frame. Is it for the innocent party to prove that she would have definitely recouped at least the expenditure or for the contract-breaker to prove that she would not have done so?

CCC Films (London) Ltd. v. *Impact Quadrant Films Ltd.*
[1984] 3 All ER 298

The defendants, who made films, granted the plaintiffs—the English subsidiary of a German company—a licence to exploit, distribute, and exhibit three films, in return for a payment of $12,000. When the money was paid, the defendants delivered the three films to the plaintiff's agent in London, who returned them to the defendants (on the 'bailment contract'), requesting them to arrange the sending of the films to the plaintiffs in Munich. In breach of the bailment contract, the films were sent by ordinary post and uninsured, and were lost in the post. The defendants also broke a number of subsequent agreements made with the plaintiffs to send replacement copies (the 'subsidiary agreements'), and consequently the plaintiffs were never able to exploit the licence. The plaintiffs conceded that they were unable to prove loss of profits on the licence, and consequently conventional expectation damages were unavailable. A claim for restitution of the price was also unavailable, as by delivering the films to the plaintiffs' agent in London the defendants had performed substantially the whole of their side of the bargain under the licence. The plaintiffs were therefore left with claiming wasted expenditure under the licence (the $12,000 fee) as reliance loss resulting from the breach of the bailment agreement and the subsidiary agreements. The judgment of Hutchinson J reviews many of the authorities on reliance loss.

In *Anglia Television* v. *Reed* an actor, a few days after entering into a contract to play the leading part in a television play which the plaintiffs were producing, repudiated the contract with the result that the production had to be abandoned. The plaintiffs claimed £2,750 wasted expenditure as damages for breach of contract. Of that sum £1,896 had been laid out by them before they entered into the contract and the issue was whether that sum as well as the post-contractual expenditure could be recovered. The Court of Appeal held that it could. It is important to note that no argument was advanced by the defendants to the effect that the expenditure, whether pre- or post-contract, was irrecoverable because the film would not have generated sufficient returns to cover the plaintiffs' outlay; nor, in the absence of any such contention, was there any argument as to where the burden of showing that the expenditure would not have been recouped lay. Lord Denning MR said ([1972] 1 QB 60 at 63–64):

'Anglia Television then sued Mr Reed for damages. He did not dispute his liability, but a question arose as to the damages. Anglia Television do not claim their profit. They cannot say what their profit would have been on this contract if Mr Reed had come here and performed it. So, instead of a claim for loss of profits, they claim for the wasted expenditure. They had incurred the director's fees, the designer's fees, the stage manager's and assistant manager's fees, and so on. It comes in all to £2,750. Anglia Television say that all that money was wasted because Mr Reed did not perform his contract . . . It seems to me that a plaintiff in such a case as this had an election: he can either claim for his loss of profits; or for his wasted expenditure. But he must elect between them. He cannot claim both. If he has not suffered any loss of profits—or if he cannot prove what his profits would have been—he can claim in the alternative the expenditure which has been thrown away, that is, wasted, by reason of the breach. That is shown by *Cullinane v British 'Rema' Manufacturing Co Ltd* [1954] 1 QB 292 at 303, 308. If the plaintiff claims the wasted expenditure, he is not limited to the expenditure incurred *after* the contract was concluded. He can claim also the expenditure incurred *before* the contract, provided that it was such as would reasonably be in the contemplation of the parties as likely to be wasted if the contract was broken. Applying that principle here, it is plain that, when Mr Reed entered into his contract, he must have known perfectly well that much expenditure had already been incurred on director's fees and the like. He must have contemplated—or, at any rate, it is reasonably to be imputed to him—that if he broke his contract, all that expenditure would be wasted, whether or not it was incurred before or after the contract. He must pay damages for all the expenditure so wasted and thrown away.' (Lord Denning MR's emphasis.) . . .

In *Cullinane* v. *British 'Rema' Manufacturing Co Ltd* the issue was whether the plaintiff could claim both diminution in value occasioned by breach of warranty and loss of profits or was required to elect between them. The majority of the Court of Appeal held that he must elect. Evershed MR said ([1954] 1 QB 292 at 303):

'As a matter of principle again, it seems to me that a person who has obtained a machine such as the plaintiff here obtained, which was mechanically in exact accordance with the order given, but was unable to perform a particular function which it was warranted to perform, may adopt one of two courses. He may, when he discovers its incapacity and that it is not what he wanted and is useless to him, claim to recover the capital cost he has incurred less anything he can obtain by disposing of the material that he got. A claim of that kind puts the plaintiff in the same position as though he had never made the contract at all. He is, in other words, back where he started, and, if it were shown that the profit-earning capacity was, in fact, very small, the plaintiff would probably elect so to base his claim. Alternatively, he may, where the warranty in question relates to performance, make his claim on the basis of the profit he has lost, because the machine as delivered fell short in its performance of that which it was warranted to do. If he chooses to base his claim on that footing, depreciation has nothing whatever to do with it.'

I interpret the passage I have just read and that cited from Lord Denning MR's judgment in *Anglia Television Ltd* v. *Reed* as indicating that in these cases the plaintiff has an unfettered choice: it is not only where he establishes by evidence that he cannot prove loss of profit or that such loss of profit as he can prove is small that he is permitted to frame his claim as one for wasted expenditure. I consider that when Lord Denning MR says, 'If he has not suffered any loss of profits—or if he cannot prove what his profits would have been—he can claim in the alternative the expenditure which has been thrown away', and when Evershed MR says, 'if it were shown that the profit-earning capacity was, in fact, very small, the plaintiff would probably elect so to base his claim', each is describing factors which would be likely to motivate the plaintiff to elect to claim on the lost expenditure basis rather than laying down what must be proved before such a claim can be entertained. In other words, I consider that those cases are authority for the proposition that a plaintiff may always frame his claim in the alternative way if he chooses. I reach this conclusion all the more readily when I reflect that to hold that there had to be evidence of the impossibility of making profits might in many cases saddle the plaintiff with just the sort of difficulties of proof that this alternative measure is designed to avoid.

It is, I think, important in this context to distinguish between the term 'loss of profit' and the term 'recovery of expenditure'. When Lord Denning MR speaks in *Anglia Television Ltd v Reed* of the plaintiffs not having suffered loss of profits or of it being impossible for them to prove what their profits would have been, he is referring, I believe, to profits after recoupment of expenditure, ie net profits. The plaintiffs in *Anglia Television Ltd* v. *Reed* were by the defendant's breach deprived of putting to the test whether and to what extent they would have (a) recouped their expenditure and (b) gone on to make a net profit and of how much. It may well be that they could have led some evidence as to the probabilities in relation at least to the first of these matters. They had a script and no doubt they had budget and profit forecasts which could have been reinforced by evidence as to their experience with other similar projects. It seems that they did not adduce any such evidence any more than did the plaintiffs in the present case, though Mr Brauner [who controlled the plaintiff company], with his vast experience in the film industry and the advantage of having viewed these films, could no doubt have given some general evidence as to his expectations. Nevertheless, the difficulties of proof would clearly be enormous and it is hard to envisage how the plaintiffs in the present case could in practice have proved a claim based on loss of profits.

It is, however, common ground that a claim for wasted expenditure cannot succeed in a case where, even had the contract not been broken by the defendant, the returns earned by the plaintiff's exploitation of the chattel or the rights which were the subject matter of the contract would not have been sufficient to recoup that expenditure. There is direct authority for that proposition, which, as I say, is accepted by both counsel, in the decision of the Court of Appeal in *C & P Haulage (a firm) v Middleton*. That was a case in which the plaintiffs sought to maintain a claim for the cost of work to premises from which he was later unlawfully evicted. The evidence established that the plaintiff was actually better off as a result of being evicted than he would have been had he been permitted to remain until the time when he could lawfully have been required to leave. Ackner LJ, having cited *Anglia Television Ltd v Reed*, went on as follows ([1983] 3 All ER 94 at 98–99):

'. . . The case which I have found of assistance, and I am grateful to counsel for their research, is *Bowlay Logging Ltd v Domtar Ltd* [1978] 4 WWR 105. It is a case in the British Columbia Supreme Court. Berger J, in a very careful and detailed judgment, goes through various English and American authorities and refers to the leading textbook writers, and I will only quote a small part of his judgment. He refers (at 116) to the work of Professor L L Fuller and William R Perdue Jr in "The Reliance Interest in Contract Damages" (1936) 46 Yale LJ 52 at 79: "We will not in a suit for reimbursement for losses incurred in reliance on a contract knowingly put the plaintiff in a better position than he would have occupied had the contract been fully performed." Berger J then refers to a case in 1949, *L Albert & Son v Armstrong Rubber Co* 178 F 2d 182, in which Learned Hand CJ, speaking for the Circuit Court of Appeal, Second Circuit, "held that on a claim for compensation for expenses in part performance the defendant was entitled to deduct whatever he could prove the plaintiff would have lost if the contract had been fully performed". What Berger J had to consider was this (at 105): "The parties entered into a contract whereby the plaintiff would cut timber under the defendant's timber sale, and the defendant would be responsible for hauling the timber away from the site of the timber sale. The plaintiff claimed the defendant was in breach of the contract as the defendant had not supplied sufficient trucks to make the plaintiff's operation, which was losing money, viable, and claimed not for loss of profits but for compensation for expenditures. The defendant argued that the plaintiff's operation lost money not because of a lack of trucks but because of the plaintiff's inefficiency, and, further, that even if the defendant had breached the contract the plaintiff should not be awarded damages because its operation would have lost money in any case." This submission was clearly accepted because the plaintiff was awarded only nominal damages, and Berger J said (at 117): "The law of contract compensates a plaintiff for damages resulting from the defendant's breach; it does not compensate a plaintiff for damages resulting from his making a bad bargain. Where it can be seen that the plaintiff would have incurred a loss on the contract as a whole, the expenses he has incurred are losses flowing from entering into the contract, not losses flowing from the defendant's breach. In these circumstances, the true consequence of the defendant's breach is that the plaintiff is released from his obligation to complete the contract—or in other words, he is saved from incurring further losses. If the law of contract were to move from compensating for the consequences of breach to compensating for the consequences of entering into contracts, the law would run contrary to the normal expectations of the world of commerce. The burden of risk would be shifted from the plaintiff to the defendant. The defendant would become the insurer of the plaintiff's enterprise. Moreover, the amount of the damages would increase not in relation to the gravity or consequences of the breach but in relation to the inefficiency with which the plaintiff carried out the contract. The greater his expenses owing to inefficiency, the greater the damages. The fundamental principle upon which damages are measured under the law of contract is restitutio in integrum. The principle contended for here by the plaintiff would entail the award of damages not to compensate the plaintiff but to punish the defendant." . . . if as a result of being kept out of these premises the appellant had found no other premises to go to for a period of time, his claim would clearly have been a claim for such loss of profit as he could establish his business suffered. In my judgment, the approach of Berger J is the correct one. It is not the function of the courts where there is a breach of contract knowingly, as this would be the case, to put the plaintiff in a better financial position than if the contract had been properly performed. In this case the appellant, if he was right in his claim, would indeed be in a better position because, as I already indicated, had the contract been lawfully determined, as it could have been in the middle of December, there would have been no question of his recovering these expenses.'

It is important, for reasons that I shall come to in a moment, to note that in that case, unlike *Bowlay Logging Ltd v Domtar Ltd* relied on by Ackner LJ, no question arose as to where the burden of proof lay on the issue whether the plaintiff would or would not have been better off had the contract been performed. . . .

The argument of counsel for the defendant proceeds on the basis that the cases of recovery of 'reliance expenditure' constitute strictly defined exceptions to the general principles. . . .

. . . He submits that *Cullinane v British 'Rema' Manufacturing Co Ltd* . . . is authority for the proposition that there must be before the court evidence that the plaintiff's expenditure would have been recouped by earnings resulting from the contract before the amount of the expenditure can be recovered as damages for breach of contract. This latter submission, which, if correct, would make that case an authority on the onus of proof, is not in my view correct. . . .

On this crucial question of where the onus of proof lies in relation to whether or not the exploitation of the subject matter of the contract would or would not have recouped the expenditure, there are, however, a number of cases which are more directly relevant. Counsel for the plaintiffs submits that *C & P Haulage v Middleton* is binding English authority for the view that the onus is on the defendant. I have already pointed out that in that case no question arose as to where the onus lay. I can find nothing in either judgment which justifies counsel's contention. He relies on the terms in which Ackner LJ cites the judgment of Berger J in *Bowlay Logging Ltd* v. *Domtar Ltd* and that of Learned Hand CJ in *L Albert & Son* v. *Armstrong Rubber Co.* But Ackner LJ was citing those passages as authority for the proposition that expenditure cannot be recovered in cases where, if the contract had been performed, the plaintiff would not have recouped his expenditure. He was in no way concerned with the question of burden of proof. The most that can be said is that, given that both cases contain clear statements to the effect that the onus was on the defendant and that the passage cited by Ackner LJ from *L Albert & Son* v. *Armstrong Rubber Co* contained an express assertion to that effect, the proposition is obviously one which did not strike Ackner LJ as being plainly erroneous, for he would otherwise presumably have said as much. To that extent, *C & P Haulage* v. *Middleton* assists counsel for the plaintiff, but it is not in my judgment English authority for the proposition that in these circumstances the onus lies on the defendant.

I turn, therefore, to the Canadian and American cases. In *Bowlay Logging Ltd* v. *Domtar Ltd* Berger J held that the onus of showing that the exploitation of the contract would have lost money lay on the defendant. In doing so, he based himself on the American cases of *L Albert & Son* v. *Armstrong Rubber Co* and *Dade County* v. *Palmer & Baker Engineers Inc* (1965) 339 F 2d 208, so it is those cases that I must consider.

In the former case, where a claim for damages for breach of contract in relation to the sale of some machines designed to recondition old rubber was advanced on the wasted expenditure rather than the loss of profit basis, Learned Hand CJ held that the onus was on the defendants, saying (at 189):

'In cases where the venture would have proved profitable to the promisee there is no reason why he should not recover his expenses. On the other hand, on those occasions in which the performance would not have covered the promisee's outlay, such a result imposes the risk of the promisee's contract upon the promisor. We cannot agree that the promisor's default in performance should under this guise make him an insurer of the promisee's venture; yet it does not follow that the breach should not throw upon him the duty of showing that the value of the performance would in fact have been less than the promisee's outlay. It is often very hard to learn what the value of the performance would have been; and it is a common expedient, and a just one, in such situations to put the peril of the answer upon the party who by his wrong has made the issue relevant to the rights of the other. On principle, therefore, the proper solution would seem to be that the promisee may recover this outlay in preparation for the performance, subject to the privilege of the promisor to reduce it by as much as he can show that the promisee would have lost, if the contract had been performed.'

The judgment in the *Dade County* case, while again being direct authority on the point, again favourable to counsel for the plaintiffs, is very brief and contains the bare statement: 'The burden is on the defendant to prove that full performance would have resulted in a net loss.'

I am, of course, not bound by any of these cases, but plainly they are of great persuasive authority. I am impressed by, and respectfully adopt, the reasoning of Learned Hand CJ in *L Albert & Son* v. *Armstrong Rubber Co* and I do so the more readily because, as I have already mentioned, that case and *Bowlay Logging Ltd* v. *Domtar Ltd* were relied on by Ackner LJ in *C & P Haulage* v. *Middleton* in a different context without eliciting from the Lord Justice any adverse comment on this point. Even without the assistance of such authorities, I should have held on principle that the onus was on the defendant. It seems to me that, at least in those cases where the plaintiff's decision to base his claim on abortive expenditure was dictated by the practical impossibility of proving loss of profit rather than by unfettered choice, any other rule would largely, if not entirely, defeat the object of allowing this alternative method of formulating the claim. This is because, notwithstanding the distinction to which I have drawn attention between proving a loss of net profit and proving in general terms the probability of sufficient returns to cover expenditure, in the majority of contested cases impossibility of proof of the first would probably involve like impossibility in the case of the second. It appears to me to be eminently fair that in such cases, where the plaintiff has by the defendant's breach been prevented from exploiting the chattel or the right contracted for and, therefore, putting to the test the question of whether he would have recouped his expenditure, the general rule as to the onus of proof of damage should be modified in this manner.

It follows that, the onus being on the defendants to prove that the expenditure incurred by the plaintiffs is irrecoverable because they would not have recouped their expenditure (and that onus admittedly not having been discharged), the plaintiffs are entitled to recover such expenditure as was wasted as a result of such breach or breaches of contract as they have proved.

This last hurdle, proof that expenditure on the main contract was wasted as a result of the breach of one or more of the subsidiary contracts, had seemed to me to be by no means the least formidable that the plaintiffs had to surmount. However, when, in the course of argument, I voiced my misgivings about it, counsel for the defendants (on reflection, I think, inevitably and rightly) made what he called at the time a 'provisional concession' to the following effect: that it was foreseeable that a total failure to deliver the tapes pursuant to one or more of the subsidiary contracts would render it difficult at least for the plaintiffs to exploit the films. He never sought to withdraw or modify this concession and, as I say, it appears to me to have been correctly made because there was evidence from Mr Brauner that the tapes were an essential prerequisite to any attempt at successful exploitation, and the defendants knew as much.

I therefore find (1) that the foreseeable result of the breach of their obligations imposed by one or more of the subsidiary contracts to deliver any of the tapes was that the expenditure incurred by the plaintiffs in acquiring the licence to exploit the tapes would be wasted, (2) that in the event that expenditure was wasted because, given that the receipt of the tapes was a necessary prerequisite to any exploitation, the plaintiffs were, by the breaches of the subsidiary contracts, prevented from undertaking any sort of exploitation of the rights for which they had paid $12,000, (3) that the onus of proving that, had the tapes been received, the plaintiffs would not have succeeded in recouping their expenditure, ie the $12,000 and any other exploitation expenditure, lay on the defendants and has not been discharged, and (4) that accordingly the plaintiffs are entitled to judgment for $12,000.

In case it is not clear, I should add that, had I been persuaded that the burden of proving that the expenditure would have been recouped lay on the plaintiffs, I should have found that that burden had not been discharged and that accordingly the plaintiffs were entitled to nominal damages only.

As it is, there will be judgment for the plaintiffs for $12,000.

Notes

1. It is somewhat misleading, in the light of the prefatory comments which we made about the expectation frame of reliance damages, for the courts to talk of a 'free election' between the expectation measure and the reliance measure. Perhaps it is better to view the assessment of damages as simply a calculation of the total loss which the plaintiff has suffered, including separate heads for wasted expenditure and loss of profit, with the task of the court being to ensure that the plaintiff does not recover twice for the same loss. Thus he can recover *either gross* profit *or* wasted expenditure plus *net* profit (see H. Beale, *Remedies for Breach of Contract* (London, Sweet and Maxwell, 1980), 156). However, it is now clear since *CCC Films* that the claim for wasted expenditure does have certain distinctive features, notably the placing of the onus of proof on the contract-breaker to demonstrate that the wasted expenditure would not have been recouped had the contract been performed. The explanation given by Hutchinson J for this conclusion is twofold; first, it can be derived from certain persuasive authorities which he cites (in particular the two US cases of *L. Albert and Son* and *Dade County*), which indicate that the defendant should bear the risk of loss resulting from his depriving the plaintiff of the opportunity of making a profit, at least to the extent that he is subject to a rebuttable presumption that the contract would have been sufficiently profitable for the wasted expenditure to be recouped. The second reason given is that the result chosen by Hutchinson J is 'eminently fair'.

2. The judgment of Hutchinson J and the authorities he cites give ample support to the thesis that the reliance measure of damages as applied in these cases is simply an instrumental technique for protecting the plaintiff's expectation interest. The cases cited support the view that breach of contract is not in itself a 'wrong' in the same way as a tort, since the award of compensation does not have the same restorative objective. The innocent party must throughout take most of the risk that he or she has made a bad bargain, subject only to the rules on onus of proof elaborated in *CCC Films*. Burrows comes close to arguing that the cases on reliance damages in fact protect 'the plaintiff's expectation interest, albeit in a different way than the expectation interest is normally protected' (*Remedies for Torts*

and Breach of Contract (London, Butterworths, 1987), 221), but steps back from this position on the grounds *inter alia* that

A. Burrows, *Remedies for Torts and Breach of Contract* (London, Butterworths, 2nd Edition, 1994), 254

. . . the reliance interest approach accords with there being a particularly strong case for legal intervention, resting on underlying 'tort' notions of corrective justice, when the plaintiff has been left not only less well off than if the contract had been performed, but also worse off than if no contract had been made. In contrast, taking the expectation interest approach, there is no obvious explanation for why the law should allow the plaintiff the benefit of a rebuttable presumption that he would have recouped his expenses.

3. The approach taken by Hutchinson J to the issue of burden of proof is two-pronged. He acknowledges that this is an issue on which there is no direct authority in English law, and consequently that this is a case of first impression. He bases his decision largely on the citation of persuasive authority, deriving additional support from the fact that the US cases which are directly on the point in question are implicitly approved by an English case which is binding upon him as to its own *ratio* (*C. & P. Haulage* v. *Middleton*). This reasoning seems formalist in the extreme. However, in addition, Hutchinson J does display a realist side to his judicial character, in that he boldly states the belief that it is 'eminently fair' that the defendants should bear the burden of it being unknown whether the lost expenditure would have been recouped by the contract.

4. Hutchinson J does not directly address the issue of the allocation of the burden of proof in circumstances where it is *not* evident from the facts that it is the defendant's breach which has made it difficult or impossible to assess loss of profit. Consequently the issue remains to be conclusively decided in a case where the plaintiff opts for the reliance measure rather than expectation damages because he fears that litigation focused on loss of profits will reveal how bad his bargain was.

5. At the end of his judgment, Hutchinson J refers to the 'foreseeable result of the breach'. Like other awards of damages, damages for wasted expenditure are subject to the general rules on limitation of compensatory damages including mitigation of loss and remoteness (see Section VI).

VI. LIMITATIONS ON COMPENSATORY DAMAGES

A. Introduction

We have noted in the previous sections that the award of 'compensatory' damages for breach of contract occurs within a framework of protecting the expectation interest. However, the contract-breaker's duty to make good loss arising from the breach is not unlimited. First, the innocent party must normally prove his loss, and prove that it was caused by the contract-breaker. Second, the innocent party is restricted by what J. Swan and B. Reiter (*Contracts, Cases, Notes and Materials*, 3rd edn. (Canada, Montgomery, 1985), 101) term 'the principle of avoidable harms': 'the plaintiff can recover compensation for those losses that in all the circumstances it is proper to charge to the defendant and which could not have been avoided had the plaintiff acted reasonably'.

In this section we shall look in some detail at the main restriction upon the recovery of consequential loss caused by a breach of contract, namely the requirement that the damage should not be too remote. Before doing so, we shall look briefly at two other aspects of the principle of avoidable harms, the requirement that the victim of a breach of contract must mitigate his loss and the limited application to contracts of the principle of contributory negligence.

B. The Doctrine of Mitigation

The doctrine of mitigation places a duty on the victim of a breach of contract to seek to secure an alternative performance of the obligations owed to him under the contract: to seek another buyer for goods refused by the original buyer or to seek another seller who can supply the goods which the original seller now refuses to supply. The prima facie measure of expectation damages is, as we have seen, the difference between the contract price and the market price, which can lead to the assessment of the plaintiff's damages at nil. In *The Soholt* ([1983] 1 Lloyd's Rep. 605) the defendants breached a contract to build and deliver a ship by delivering late. The plaintiffs refused late delivery at the contract price, but recovered no damages because it was reasonable for them to mitigate their loss by accepting late delivery as offered by the defendants at the contract price. This type of rule restricts the range of opportunistic behaviour which a party who is a victim of a breach of contract can engage in. Equally, economists assess the rule as one which provides an incentive to breach contracts, and to that extent it can be linked to the theory of efficient breach discussed in Sections III and IV. The doctrine of mitigation effectively protects the position of the contract-breaker who anticipates making a net profit from the breach by forcing the innocent party to secure the next best alternative available in the market-place. Seen from this angle, the mitigation doctrine is not so much an exception to the principle of the protection of expectation loss as a corner-stone of it. For the notion of expectation presupposes the operation of a market, and a rational value-maximizing contractor who will, logically, go out into the market-place to secure an alternative in the event of default by the other party.

In the light of this analysis, it is perhaps surprising that the doctrine of mitigation is not of universal application and that it does not apply, as we have seen, until a breach of contract has been accepted by the innocent party (see *White and Carter (Councils) Ltd.* v. *McGregor* [1962] AC 413). There is, as many have suggested, a strong case for the general application of the mitigation doctrine, as is the case in the United States.

C. Contributory Negligence

The concept of negligence is not one which operates easily within the framework of contractual obligations. There are many contracts where one party owes a strict obligation to the other to achieve a particular result, e.g. to supply certain goods on time or to supply goods without defects. On the other hand, there are cases in which either the nature of the contractual duty owed is one of reasonable care (e.g. a professional person's duty to take reasonable care in the provision of professional services) or a contractual duty is coterminous with a duty of care in tort and consequently both forms of liability can arise out of a breach of contract. It has now been established that a plaintiff cannot, in the latter case, avoid a defence of contributory negligence under the Law Reform (Contributory Negligence) Act 1945 by framing an action in contract rather than in tort (*Forsikringsaktieselskapet Vesta* v. *Butcher* [1988] 2 All ER 43). This seems eminently sensible, but it would seem that there is a less strong case for widening the scope of the 1945 Act to cover all cases of breach of contract, although this was suggested by the Law Commission (*Contributory Negligence as a Defence in Contract*, Working Paper No. 114, 1990). As *Lambert* v. *Lewis* ([1982] AC 225) shows, situations involving strict contractual duties can be dealt with using causation principles. In that case, a dealer supplied a defective trailer coupling, which broke and caused an accident. However, the customer had carried on using the coupling after it had become obvious that it was defective. The customer's claim against the dealer failed on the grounds that it was the failure to stop using the coupling which caused the accidents.

D. Remoteness of Damage

Coufos v. Czarnikow (The Heron II)
[1969] 1 AC 350

The respondents chartered the appellants' ship to convey a cargo of sugar to Basrah. The voyage should have taken twenty days, but the appellants, in breach of contract, made several stops on the way to Basrah, and arrived ten days late. The appellants knew that there was a market for sugar at Basrah but they did not know that the respondents intended to sell the cargo when it arrived. The cargo was sold on its arrival. However, the price per ton was lower than that which would have been realized ten days earlier if the cargo had arrived on time, as in the interim period another cargo of sugar had arrived and been sold. This forced the price down. The respondents sought to recover the difference in price as damages for breach of contract. The appellants admitted their liability for nine days' lost interest on the value of the sugar, but denied liability in relation to the fall in the market value of the sugar. The House of Lords found in favour of the respondents.

LORD REID . . . It may be well first to set out the knowledge and intention of the parties at the time of making the contract so far as relevant or argued to be relevant. The charterers intended to sell the sugar in the market at Basrah on arrival of the vessel. They could have changed their mind and exercised their option to have the sugar delivered at Jeddah but they did not do so. There is no finding that they had in mind any particular date as the likely date of arrival at Basrah or that they had any knowledge or expectation that in late November or December there would be a rising or a falling market. The shipowner was given no information about these matters by the charterers. He did not know what the charterers intended to do with the sugar. But he knew there was a market in sugar at Basrah, and it appears to me that, if he had thought about the matter, he must have realised that at least it was not unlikely that the sugar would be sold in the market at market price on arrival. And he must be held to have known that in any ordinary market prices are apt to fluctuate from day to day: but he had no reason to suppose it more probable that during the relevant period such fluctuation would be downwards rather than upwards—it was an even chance that the fluctuation would be downwards.

So the question for decision is whether a plaintiff can recover as damages for breach of contract a loss of a kind which the defendant, when he made the contract, ought to have realised was not unlikely to result from a breach of contract causing delay in delivery. I use the words "not unlikely" as denoting a degree of probability considerably less than an even chance but nevertheless not very unusual and easily foreseeable.

For over a century everyone has agreed that remoteness of damage in contract must be determined by applying the rule (or rules) laid down by a court including Lord Wensleydale (then Parke B.), Martin B. and Alderson B. in *Hadley* v. *Baxendale*. But many different interpretations of that rule have been adopted by judges at different times. So I think that one ought first to see just what was decided in that case, because it would seem wrong to attribute to that rule a meaning which, if it had been adopted in that case, would have resulted in a contrary decision of that case.

In *Hadley* v. *Baxendale* [(1854) 9 Exch. 528] the owners of a flour mill at Gloucester which was driven by a steam engine delivered to common carriers, Pickford & Co., a broken crankshaft to be sent to engineers in Greenwich. A delay of five days in delivery there was held to be in breach of contract and the question at issue was the proper measure of damages. In fact the shaft was sent as a pattern for a new shaft and until it arrived the mill could not operate. So the owners claimed £300 as loss of profit for the five days by which resumption of work was delayed by this breach of contract. But the carriers did not know that delay would cause loss of this kind.

Alderson B., delivering the judgment of the court, said:

"We find that the only circumstances here communicated by the plaintiffs to the defendants at the time the contract was made, were, that the article to be carried was the broken shaft of a mill, and that the plaintiffs were the millers of that mill. But how do these circumstances show reasonably that the profits of the mill must be stopped by an unreasonable delay in the delivery of the broken shaft by the carrier to the third person? Suppose the plaintiffs had another shaft in their possession put up or putting up at the time, and that they only wished to send back the broken shaft to the engineer who made it; it is clear that this would be quite consistent with the above circumstances, and yet the unreasonable delay in the delivery would have no effect upon the intermediate profits of the mill. Or, again, suppose that at the time of the delivery to the carrier, the machinery of the mill had been in other respects defective, then, also, the same results would follow."

Then, having said that in fact the loss of profit was caused by the delay, he continued:

"But it is obvious that, in the great multitude of cases of millers sending off broken shafts to third persons by a carrier under ordinary circumstances, such consequences would not, in all probability, have occurred."

Alderson B. clearly did not and could not mean that it was not reasonably foreseeable that delay might stop the resumption of work in the mill. He merely said that in the great multitude—which I take to mean the great majority—of cases this would not happen. He was not distinguishing between results which were foreseeable or unforeseeable, but between results which were likely because they would happen in the great majority of cases, and results which were unlikely because they would only happen in a small minority of cases. He continued:

"It follows, therefore, that the loss of profits here cannot reasonably be considered such a consequence of the breach of contract as could have been fairly and reasonably contemplated by both the parties when they made this contract."

He clearly meant that a result which will happen in the great majority of cases should fairly and reasonably be regarded as having been in the contemplation of the parties, but that a result which, though foreseeable as a substantial possibility, would only happen in a small minority of cases should not be regarded as having been in their contemplation. He was referring to such a result when he continued:

"For such loss would neither have flowed naturally from the breach of this contract in the great multitude of such cases occurring under ordinary circumstances, nor were the special circumstances, which perhaps, would have made it a reasonable and natural consequence of such breach of contract, communicated to or known by the defendants."

I have dealt with the latter part of the judgment before coming to the well known rule because the court were there applying the rule and the language which was used in the latter part appears to me to throw considerable light on the meaning which they must have attached to the rather vague expressions used in the rule itself. The rule is that the damages "should be such as may fairly and reasonably be considered either arising naturally, i.e., according to the usual course of things, from such breach of contract itself, or such as may reasonably be supposed to have been in the contemplation of both parties, at the time they made the contract, as the probable result of the breach of it."

I do not think that it was intended that there were to be two rules or that two different standards or tests were to be applied. The last two passages which I quoted from the end of the judgment applied to the facts before the court which did not include any special circumstances communicated to the defendants; and the line of reasoning there is that because in the great majority of cases loss of profit would not in all probability have occurred, it followed that this could not reasonably be considered as having been fairly and reasonably contemplated by both the parties, for it would not have flowed naturally from the breach in the great majority of cases.

I am satisfied that the court did not intend that every type of damage which was reasonably foreseeable by the parties when the contract was made should either be considered as arising naturally, i.e., in the usual course of things, or be supposed to have been in the contemplation of the parties. Indeed the decision makes it clear that a type of damage which was plainly foreseeable as a real possibility but which would only occur in a small minority of cases cannot be regarded as arising in the usual course of things or be supposed to have been in the contemplation of the parties: the parties are not supposed to contemplate as grounds for the recovery of damage any type of loss or damage which on the knowledge available to the defendant would appear to him as only likely to occur in a small minority of cases.

In cases like *Hadley* v. *Baxendale* or the present case it is not enough that in fact the plaintiff's loss was directly caused by the defendant's breach of contract. It clearly was so caused in both. The crucial question is whether, on the information available to the defendant when the contract was made, he should, or the reasonable man in his position would, have realised that such loss was sufficiently likely to result from the breach of contract to make it proper to hold that the loss flowed naturally from the breach or that loss of that kind should have been within his contemplation.

The modern rule of tort is quite different and it imposes a much wider liability. The defendant will be liable for any type of damage which is reasonably foreseeable as liable to happen even in the most unusual case, unless the risk is so small that a reasonable man would in the whole circumstances feel justified in neglecting it. And there is good reason for the difference. In contract, if one party wishes to protect himself against a risk which to the other party would appear unusual, he can direct the other party's attention to it before the contract is made, and I need not stop to consider in what circumstances the other party will then be held to have accepted responsibility in that event. But in tort there is no opportunity for the injured party to protect himself in that way, and the tortfeasor cannot reasonably complain if he has to pay for some very unusual but nevertheless foreseeable damage which results from his wrongdoing. I have no doubt that today a tortfeasor would be held liable for a type of damage as unlikely as was the stoppage of Hadley's Mill for lack of a crankshaft: to anyone with the knowledge the carrier had that may have seemed unlikely but the chance of it happening would have been seen to be far from negligible. But it does not at all follow that *Hadley* v. *Baxendale* would today be differently decided. . . .

. . . I would agree . . . that it is generally sufficient that that event would have appeared to the defendant as not unlikely to occur. It is hardly ever possible in this matter to assess probabilities with any degree of mathematical accuracy. But I do not find in that case or in cases which preceded it any warrant for regarding as within the contemplation of the parties any event which would not have appeared to the defendant, had he thought about it, to have a very substantial degree of probability.

But then it has been said that the liability of defendants has been further extended by *Victoria Laundry (Windsor) Ltd.* v. *Newman Industries Ltd.* ([1949] 2 KB 528). I do not think so. The plaintiffs bought a large boiler from the defendants and the defendants were aware of the general nature of the plaintiffs' business and of the plaintiffs' intention to put the boiler into use as soon as possible. Delivery of the boiler was delayed in breach of contract and the plaintiffs claimed as damages loss of profit caused by the delay. A large part of the profits claimed would have resulted from some specially lucrative contracts which the plaintiffs could have completed if they had had the boiler: that was rightly disallowed because the defendants had no knowledge of these contracts. But Asquith L.J. then said:

"It does not, however, follow that the plaintiffs are precluded from recovering some general (and perhaps conjectural) sum for loss of business in respect of dyeing contracts to be reasonably expected, any more than in respect of laundering contracts to be reasonably expected."

It appears to me that this was well justified on the earlier authorities. It was certainly not unlikely on the information which the defendants had when making the contract that delay in delivering the boiler would result in loss of business: indeed it would seem that that was more than an even chance. . . .

[In this part of his judgment, Lord Reid goes on to discuss the specific parts of Asquith LJ's judgment in *Victoria Laundry*; hence the references to numbered paragraphs. Phrases in inverted commas refer to phrases used by Asquith LJ]

But what is said to create a "landmark" is the statement of principles by Asquith L.J. This does to some extent go beyond the older authorities and in so far as it does so, I do not agree with it. In paragraph (2) it is said that the plaintiff is entitled to recover "such part of the loss actually resulting as was at the time of the contract reasonably foreseeable as liable to result from the breach." To bring in reasonable foreseeability appears to me to be confusing measure of damages in contract with measure of damages in tort. A great many extremely unlikely results are reasonably foreseeable: it is true that Lord Asquith may have meant foreseeable as a likely result, and if that is all he meant I would not object further than to say that I think that the phrase is liable to be misunderstood. For the same reason I would take exception to the phrase "liable to result" in paragraph (5). Liable is a very vague word but I think that one would usually say that when a person foresees a very improbable result he foresees that it is liable to happen.

I agree with the first half of paragraph (6). For the best part of a century it has not been required that the defendant could have foreseen that a breach of contract must necessarily result in the loss which has occurred. But I cannot agree with the second half of that paragraph. It has never been held to be sufficient in contract that the loss was foreseeable as "a serious possibility" or "a real danger" or as being "on the cards." It is on the cards that one can win £100,000 or more for a stake of a few pence—several people have done that. And anyone who backs a hundred to one chance regards a win as a serious possibility—many people have won on such a chance. . . . It appears to me that in the ordinary use of language there is wide gulf between saying that some event is not unlikely or quite likely to happen and saying merely that it is a serious possibility, a real danger, or on the cards. Suppose one takes a well-shuffled pack of cards, it is quite likely or not unlikely that the top card will prove to be a diamond: the odds are only 3 to 1 against. But most people would not say that it is quite likely to be the nine of diamonds for the odds are then 51 to 1 against. On the other hand I think that most people would say that there is a serious possibility or a real danger of its being turned up first and of course it is on the cards. If the tests of "real danger" or "serious possibility" are in future to be authoritative then the *Victoria Laundry* case would indeed be a landmark because it would mean that *Hadley* v. *Baxendale* would be differently decided today. I certainly could not understand any court deciding that, on the information available to the carrier in that case, the stoppage of the mill was neither a serious possibility nor a real danger. If those tests are to prevail in future then let us cease to pay lip service to the rule in *Hadley* v. *Baxendale*. But in my judgment to adopt these tests would extend liability for breach of contract beyond what is reasonable or desirable. From the limited knowledge which I have of commercial affairs I would not expect such an extension to be welcomed by the business community and from the legal point of view I can find little or nothing to recommend it. . . .

It appears to me that, without relying in any way on the *Victoria Laundry* case, and taking the principle that had already been established, the loss of profit claimed in this case was not too remote to be recoverable as damages. . . .

For the reasons which I have given I would dismiss this appeal.

LORD PEARCE . . . it was suggested in argument that there was or should be one principle of damages for both contract and tort and that guidance for one could be obtained from the other. I do not find such a comparison helpful. In the case of contract two parties, usually with some knowledge of one another, deliberately undertake mutual duties. They have the opportunity to define clearly in respect of what they shall and shall not be liable. The law has to say what shall be the boundaries of their liability where this is not expressed, defining that boundary in relation to what has been expressed and implied. In tort two persons, usually unknown to one another, find that the acts or utterances of one have collided with the rights of the other, and the court has to define what is the liability for the ensuing damage, whether it shall be shared, and how far it extends. If one tries to find a concept of damages which will fit both these different problems there is a danger of distorting the rules to accommodate one or other other and of producing a rule that is satisfactory for neither. . . .

The underlying rule of the common law is that "where a party sustains a loss by reason of a breach of contract, he is, so far as money can do it, to be placed in the same situation with respect to damages, as if the contract had been performed" (Parke B. in *Robinson* v. *Harman*). But since so wide a principle might be too harsh on a contract-breaker in making him liable for a chain of unforeseen and fortuitous circumstances, the law limited the liability in ways which crystallised in the rule in *Hadley* v. *Baxendale*. This was designed as a direction to juries but it has become an integral part of the law.

Since an Olympian cloud shrouded any doubts, difficulties and border-line troubles that might arise in the jury room and the jury could use a common sense liberality in applying the rule to the facts, the rule worked admirably as a general guidance for deciding facts. But when the lucubrations of judges who have to give reasons superseded the reticence of juries, there were certain matters which needed clarification. That service was well performed by the judgment of the Court of Appeal in the case of *Victoria Laundry (Windsor) Ltd.* v. *Newman Industries Ltd.* I do not think that there was anything startling or novel about it. In my opinion it represented (in felicitous language) the approximate view of *Hadley* v. *Baxendale* taken by many judges in trying ordinary cases of breach of contract.

It is argued that it was an erroneous departure from *Hadley* v. *Baxendale* in that it allowed damages where the loss was "a serious possibility" or "a real danger" instead of maintaining that the loss must be "probable," in the sense that it was more likely to result than not. . . .

. . . in my opinion the expressions used in the *Victoria Laundry* case were right. I do not however accept the colloquialism "on the cards" as being a useful test because I am not sure just what nuance it has either in my own personal vocabulary or in that of others. I suspect that it owes its attraction, like many other colloquialisms, to the fact that one may utter it without having the trouble of really thinking out with precision what one means oneself or what others will understand by it, a spurious attraction which in general makes colloquialism unsuitable for definition, though it is often useful as shorthand for a collection of definable ideas. It was in this latter convenient sense that the judgment uses the ambiguous words "liable to result." They were not intended as a further or different test from "serious possibility" or "real danger."

The whole rule in *Hadley* v. *Baxendale* limits damages to that which may be regarded as being within the contemplation of the parties. The first part deals with those things that "may fairly and reasonably be considered as arising naturally, i.e. according to the usual course of things." Those are presumed to be within the contemplation of the parties. As Lord Wright said in the case of the *Monarch Steamship* ([1949] AC 196 at 224):

"As reasonable businessmen each must be taken to understand the ordinary practices and exigencies of the other's trade or business. That need not generally be the subject of special discussion or communication.". . .

"Both parties were tacitly taken to be acquainted sufficiently with the general business position. The same is true in many cases of complicated consequences flowing from an unanticipated breach of contract, but the damages are not treated either as special or remote if they flow from the normal business position of the parties which the court assumes must be reasonably known to them. It would not be helpful to cite the familiar authorities which are numerous but depend primarily upon the facts of each case."

Even the first part of the rule however contains the necessity for the knowledge of certain basic facts, e.g. in *Hadley* v. *Baxendale* the fact that it was a mill shaft to be carried. On this limited basis of knowledge the horizon of contemplation is confined to things "arising naturally, i.e. according to the usual course of things."

Additional or "special" knowledge, however, may extend the horizon to include losses that are outside the natural course of events. And of course the extension of the horizon need not always *increase* the damages; it might introduce a knowledge of particular circumstances, e.g., a subcontract, which show that the plaintiff would in fact suffer *less* damage than a more limited view of the circumstances might lead one to expect. According to whether one categorises a fact as basic knowledge or special knowledge the case may come under the first part of the rule or the second. For that reason there is sometimes difference of opinion as to which is the part which governs a particular case and it may be that both parts govern it. . . .

The facts of the present case lead to the view that the loss of market arose naturally, i.e., according to the usual course of things, from the shipowner's deviation. The sugar was being exported to Basrah, where, as the respondents knew, there was a sugar market. It was sold on arrival and fetched a lower price than it would have done had it arrived on time. The fall in market price was not due to any unusual or unpredictable factor. . . .

I would dismiss the appeal.

Notes

1. The House of Lords unanimously decided that the shipowner was liable for the charterers' loss; it was not too remote. However, that seems to be where their unanimity ends. The two judgments that we have extracted evidence two distinctly different approaches to assessing the position of the shipowners.

Both Lord Reid and Lord Pearce find a common starting-point in the test offered by Alderson B in *Hadley* v. *Baxendale*; loss for which damages are recoverable must arise either naturally ('usual course of things') or must have been in the reasonable contemplation of the parties at the time the contract was made as not unlikely/liable to be/serious possibility (all formulations offered in *The Heron II*). Lord Reid appears at the start of his judgment to say that he does not support a two-limb test, but nevertheless his assessment of the shipowners' liability is based on such a test. According to Lord Pearce (Lord Hodson took a very similar position) the shipowners' liability arises on the first limb of the test: 'the facts of the present case lead to the view that the loss of market arose naturally'. For Lord Reid, whose position was echoed by Lord Morris and Lord Upjohn, liability arose on the basis of the second limb.

2. The House of Lords also differ in their formulation of the degree of likelihood with which the loss must be foreseeable in order to satisfy the second limb of the test. For Lord Reid the appropriate formulation is 'not unlikely'. This was shared by Lord Morris, who also added 'the result was liable to be', with which Lord Hodson concurred. Lords Pearce and Upjohn posit the test of 'serious possibility' or 'real danger' and assert that they do

not mean anything different from 'liable to result'. It is interesting that these two Lords are considerably less antagonistic towards the judgment of Asquith LJ in *Victoria Laundry* v. *Newman*. The House of Lords eschews any move towards a statistical calculation of the degree of likelihood, and it is possible that Lords Reid, Morris, and Hodson do not see their formulations as being the same as 'serious possibility' or 'real danger'. Lord Pearce condemns the phrase 'on the cards' as a meaningless colloquialism, but the formulations offered by the House of Lords in its place create little more, if any, meaning.

There would appear, then, to be considerable uncertainty surrounding the degree of likelihood required to be contemplated by the parties for the second limb of the test. The effect that this uncertainty has on the parties' calculation of risk, and consequently on the contract terms they agree upon at the outset of their relationship, is not clear. The economic models offered by Posner and Bishop, set out below, assume that the parties plan in advance around the remoteness rules. M. Eisenberg, 'The Principle of *Hadley* v. *Baxendale*' ((1992) 80 *Cal. L. Rev.* 563 at 566) describes the remoteness rules as akin to devices 'to limit sellers' liability. If the principle were dropped from the law, sellers could still limit liability by contractual provisions that preclude consequential damage'. On this basis the uncertainty will seriously interfere with the parties' ability to apportion risk. Lord Morris asserts that 'when parties enter into a contract they do not ordinarily at such time seek to work out or to calculate the exact consequences of a breach of their contract' ([1969] 1 AC 350 at 396). These sentiments seem to pervade the judgments of the House of Lords, and perhaps explain the general and vague terms in which the degree of likelihood is discussed.

3. It may seem strange that in *Hadley* v. *Baxendale* (for the facts see Lord Reid's judgment above) the court held that the loss of the mill-owners was too remote, despite a five-day delay in getting the shaft back to them, whereas in *The Heron II* a nine-day delay which caused the charterers to sell at a lower market price was not too remote, despite the fact that the shipowner did not know of the charterers' intention. As explained in note 1, Lord Pearce even went so far as to assert that the charterers' loss was a natural consequence of the delay. The shipowner in *The Heron II* had assumed that the charterers had already sold the cargo. It is not clear from the facts whether the intermediate arrival of the second ship, carrying a sugar cargo which forced down the price of sugar in the vital nine-day period, could have been within the reasonable contemplation of either party at the time they made the contract.

The apparent harshness of the decision in *The Heron II* exemplified by the readiness of the House of Lords to hold, with very little discussion of the facts, either that the drop in the market was foreseeable as not unlikely, etc. or that it was the natural consequence of the shipowners' delay, can be explained partly by judicial attitudes to time stipulations in commercial contracts. We saw in Chapters 10 and 13, as well as earlier in this chapter (*Lombard North Central* v. *Butterworth*) that the courts take time clauses very seriously; they are generally treated as conditions giving the innocent party the right to terminate the contract and to claim damages for breach irrespective of the effect of breach.

4. The judgments of the House of Lords refer to the differences between the remoteness tests in contract and tort. It is clear that the remoteness test in tort is much more developed than is the test in contract. In contract, the arena of liability is set by concepts such as privity of contract, consideration, and intention to create legal relations. As Lord Pearce points out, the parties to a contract are known to each other and can plan the risks that each is prepared to accept, subject only to the continuing uncertainty of the remoteness rules explained in note 2 above. In tort, the remoteness rule plays a role as a primary test of liability, and it also reflects general public policy concerns rather than merely the intentions of the parties involved. For an incisive discussion of the policies behind the tort and contract remoteness rules, see Burrows, *Remedies for Torts and Breach of Contract*, 2nd Edition, 1994, pp. 47–50.

5. Lord Pearce places the formulation of the remoteness rule in *Hadley* v. *Baxendale* in the context of jury assessment of damages. A more detailed analysis of the historical background of the decision in *Hadley* v. *Baxendale* is offered by Danzig.

R. Danzig, '*Hadley* v. *Baxendale*: A Study of the Industrialisation of the Law', (1975) 4 *J. Leg. St.* 249 at 277–83

I have suggested that the rule's utility for nineteenth-century judges and entrepreneurs was as a control mechanism. It tended to make damages both predictable and limited by constraining them to the bounds of the normal, in the absence of special notice leading to advance contemplation of an abnormal state of affairs. In another context Professor Posner suggests that the rule is of societal advantage because it increases the chances of optimization of precaution-taking. He describes the "general principle" of the case as "that where a risk of loss is known to only one party to the contract, the other party is not liable for the loss if it occurs," and then suggests that this principle "induces the party with knowledge of the risk either to take any appropriate precautions himself or, if he believes that the other party might be the more efficient loss avoider, to disclose the risk to that party."

He illustrates this advantage by the following hypothetical:

A commercial photographer purchases a roll of film to take pictures of the Himalayas for a magazine. The cost of development of the film by the manufacturer is included in the purchase price. The photographer incurs heavy expenses (including the hire of an airplane) to complete the assignment. He mails the film to the manufacturer but it is mislaid in the developing room and never found.

Compare the incentive effects of allowing the photographer to recover his full losses and of limiting him to recovery of the price of the film. The first alternative creates little incentive to avoid similar losses in the future. The photographer will take no precautions. He is indifferent as between successful completion of his assignment and the receipt of adequate compensation for its failure. The manufacturer of the film will probably not take additional precautions either; the aggregate costs of such freak losses are probably too small to justify substantial efforts to prevent them. The second alternative, in contrast, should induce the photographer to take precautions that turn out to be at once inexpensive and effective: using two rolls of film or requesting special handling when he sends the roll in for development. [*Economic Analysis of Law*, 3rd edn. (Boston, Little, Brown, 1986), 114–15]

It should be obvious that the rule's achievement of the advantages Professor Posner describes or the benefits I have noted earlier has been and continues to be premised on the viability of its underlying concepts of normalcy and notification. Yet the manner in which these concepts were pressed into service by the Exchequer panel is characteristic of the half-way industrialized period in which the case arose.

On the one hand, the panel helped to bring the law in phase with the industrializing economy. By its presumption of normalcy the rule invented in the case eroded the prior legal deference to idiosyncrasy and opened the prospect of a standardization of damages as a concomitant of the standardization of transactions effected by mass production. Moreover, in its emphasis on contemplation as the only alternative to natural damages, the rule signalled an evolution away from the pre-industrial emphasis on status and towards the more modern volitional concepts of contract. On the other hand, as developed in *Hadley v Baxendale*, these concepts were tainted by anachronism, and as they were applied over the following years their antique aspects became more salient.

Consider, first, the notification or "contemplation" branch of the rule. . . .

Whether viewed as a simple "notice" or a more exacting "contemplation" requirement, however, this portion of the rule in *Hadley v. Baxendale* runs counter to the tide of an industrializing economy. It was already somewhat out of date when expressed in the Exchequer opinion. For in *Hadley v. Baxendale* the court spoke as though entrepreneurs were universally flexible enough and enterprises small enough for individuals to be able to serve "notice" over the counter of specialized needs calling for unusual arrangements. But in mass-transaction situations a seller cannot plausibly engage in an individualized "contemplation" of the consequences of breach and a subsequent tailoring of a transaction. In the course of his conversion of a family business into a modern industrial enterprise, Baxendale made Pickfords itself into an operation where the contemplation branch of the rule in *Hadley v. Baxendale* was no longer viable. Even in the 1820's the Pickfords' operations were "highly complex."

The bulk of Pickfords' traffic was of an intermediate kind, which came on to the main north-south route from east and west. This was directed to certain staging points, sorted, and thence dispatched to its destination. Cross-traffic of this kind was tricky to organize, and required very clear methods of procedure. According to Joseph Baxendale, then a senior partner in Pickfords, a cargo of 15 tons might involve up to 150 consignees and thus the same number of invoices.

By 1865 the business had grown to the point where it left that contemporary chronicler of industry, Henry Mayhew, without words to "convey . . . to the reader's mind a fair impression of the gigantic scale upon which the operations of the firm are conducted." This was "an enormous mercantile establishment with a huge staff of busy clerks, messengers and porters. . . . It is divided into innumerable departments, the employees in each of which find it as much as they can comfortably do to master its details without troubling themselves about any other."

A century later most enterprises fragment and standardize operations in just this way. This development—and the law's recognition of it—makes it self-evidently impossible to serve legally cognizable notice on, for example, an air-line that a scheduled flight is of special importance or on the telephone company that uninterrupted service is particularly vital at a particular point in a firm's business cycle. . . .

The inadequacies of the rule are masked by still more fundamental phenomena which render the case of very limited relevance to the present economy. At least in mass-transaction situations, the modern enterprise manager is not concerned with his corporation's liability as it arises from a particular transaction, but rather with liability when averaged over the full run of transactions of a given type. In the mass-production situation the run of these transactions will average his consequential-damages pay-out in a way far more predictable than a jury's guesses about the pay-out. In other words, for this type of entrepreneur—a type already emerging at the time of *Hadley v. Baxendale*, and far more prevalent today—there is no need for the law to provide protection from the aberrational customer; his own market and self-insurance capacities are great enough to do the job. . . .

It is only for small-volume sellers, those who deal in custom-made transactions or with a small number of customers—*i.e.*, for those transactions most like early nineteenth century commerce—that the rule invented in *Hadley v. Baxendale* is arguably of commercial significance. These sellers also, of course, may limit their liability by contract or cushion their liability by insurance, but since their sales transactions are less routinized (and also often less professionalized) they are more likely to miscarry and their miscarriage is less likely to have been provided for through economic precautions such as insurance, or legal precautions effected as a result of consulting farsighted counsel. . . .

Even within this realm, however, it can be doubted that the rule much effects economic life. It is doubtful that it affects information flow at the time of the making of the contract, because by hypothesis the parties are not very accurate or self-conscious planners. A more sophisticated rationale for the rule in this context might focus on its effect on a seller not at the time of his entering a contract, but rather at the time of his deciding whether to voluntarily breach or to risk breaching. Only at that time and only where an option exists as to whether to breach or to increase the risk of breach, does it seem likely that a seller who has not opted for a limitation of liability clause will consult a lawyer, and consequently be affected by the legal rules. It can be argued that the societal gain from the rule in *Hadley v. Baxendale* stems from its improvement of the seller's calculus about whether to breach in this situation. . . .

But if this is its modern rationale, it is apparent that considerable thought ought to be given to restructuring the rule. Resting the seller's liability on whether the type of damages incurred was "normal" . . . seems undesirable because it lets an all-or-nothing decision ride on an indicator about which many sellers cannot, at the time of breach, speculate with confidence. Further, if the recoverability of a type of damages is established, a seller may often have no reasonable basis for determining the magnitude of the damages involved. On this dimension—obviously critical to any calculus of the care warranted to avoid breach—the rule has nothing to say. Lastly, if the rule were truly finely geared to optimizing the allocation of resources, it would place its emphasis on the damage known to the seller at the time of breach, rather than at the time of contract, at least where the breach was voluntary. When the rule was framed stress had to be placed on communication at the time of the making of a contract because that was the only occasion on which information exchange could be coerced without fear of imposing enormous transaction costs. Now the telephone and vastly improved telegraphic facilities make it possible to mandate discussion at the time of breach. Would it be desirable to move the focus of the rule to this point? On this question, some empirical evidence would be desirable. Do the average transaction costs associated with information exchange at the time of the contract multiplied by the number of instances in which such information is exchanged exceed the average transaction costs of information exchange at the time of voluntary breach multiplied by the number of occasions when breach is seriously considered? If so, there is much to be said for a revision in the rule.

Danzig's closing position is that the remoteness rules as formulated in *Hadley* v. *Baxendale* were supportable in their historical context but that their continued application is not; the requirements of an industrialized society with easy availability of information indicate a different formulation which focuses on the relevant time of knowledge as the moment of breach rather than the making of the contract.

6. Danzig provides a useful summary of Posner's position on the contract remoteness rules. Posner points to the inducements the rules offer for pre-

caution-taking and the efficient allocation of risk that results. Posner's position is not without its critics; see for example Eisenberg ('The Principle of *Hadley* v. *Baxendale*', 582–3). In Eisenberg's view, Posner overstates the risk of breach occurring and does not allow for the principle of self-interest; by asserting that allowing full recovery does not create incentives to avoid similar loss in the future, Posner is equating, in value terms, a liability claim and performance. Eisenberg feels that an innocent party will always value performance more highly than a liability claim and consequently, in situations where breach is likely, an innocent party will take precautions out of self-interest, regardless of whether liability rules are framed to induce precaution-taking.

7. In the extract below, Bishop offers us an analysis of contract remoteness rules based on the costs of passing information, where information about the plaintiffs' situation could have been passed by him to the defendant 'cheaply'. It is not clear whether 'cheaply' means that the cost of giving the information to the plaintiff is less than its value to the defendant or whether the cost of passing information is assessed against the transaction costs of the contractual relationship.

W. Bishop, 'The Contract—Tort Boundary and the Economics of Insurance', (1983) 12 *J. Leg. St.* 241 at 254–7

The line of cases *Hadley v. Baxendale*, . . . *Victoria Laundry*, and *Heron II* concerns a matter that is usually irrelevant in tort (at least as between strangers): the efficient transfer of information. The law of contract denies recovery to a plaintiff when four conditions are met:

1. The plaintiff possessed information unknown to the defendant.

2. The defendant, had he possessed that information, might have altered his behavior so as to make his breach less likely to occur.

3. The plaintiff could have conveyed the information to the defendant cheaply. (This condition is not mentioned in the cases, though it is clear that it is assumed by the courts to be fulfilled. Of course it is normally *not* fulfilled in tort.)

4. The plaintiff did not do so.

A good example of these rules in operation is the *Victoria Laundry* case. The defendant manufacturer of boilers contracted to supply them to the plaintiff laundry. In breach of contract the manufacturer delivered late. The laundry sought to recover damages for profit lost on an unusually lucrative dyeing contract. The court limited the plaintiff to such damages as would be normal in a case of this kind.

Less clear is *Heron II*. . . . Lord Reid thought that the circumstances (that the charterer might well wish to sell on arrival) ought to have been so clear to the shipowner that the latter ought to have realized the risk without explicit warning. This case is near the line, with everything depending on the circumstances the parties were in. If the circumstances were clear, then to require an explicit warning of the obvious would be wasteful of resources (here labor and time).

I take no position on the doctrinal controversy about whether affirmative assumption of risk or merely notice of risk is needed to found liability. I doubt that it really matters very much. Sometimes merely receiving notice, particularly notice of strikingly unusual risks, will be tantamount to affirmative assumption and sometimes not. It is unlikely that a uniform general rule for such cases would be appropriate. It seems that courts treat this, sensibly I think, as depending on the facts of each case.

The central point here is that where the four conditions above are met, the value of the information to the defendant is greater than the cost to the plaintiff of conveying that information to him. To encourage such efficient transfers of information is the purpose of the contract remoteness rule of *Hadley v. Baxendale*.

Note that the first limb of the rule in *Hadley* fits easily into this scheme. The normal case is one in which no information needs to be conveyed, since the defendant, knowing normal business conditions, already knows as much as the plaintiff. To require the plaintiff to inform the defendant of normal conditions would be inefficient, because the cost of transactions here, though low, is not zero. Any expenditure on information transfer is only wasted. . . .

It should be clear that the function of remoteness in the *Hadley v. Baxendale* line of contract cases is very different from the function of remoteness in tort. The tort measure of foreseeability seeks to define as too remote an event that no one would anticipate at all—one to which the ordinary observer would assign near zero probability. The contract measure of foreseeability will include as too remote many consequences which are merely unusual—ones that have quite substantial probabilities of occurring. The defining characteristics of an event that is too remote for the purposes of contract are those set out in conditions 1–4 above. These conditions have nothing to do with unforeseeability in the sense of very low probability. . . .

The promisors or defendants in *Hadley*, *Victoria Laundry*, and *Heron II* were insurers. Like all insurers they charged a price for that service. Like all insurers they wished to guard against "adverse selection," against high risk promisees obtaining low priced insurance. This is not just a distributional matter between promisor and promisee. If such adverse selection occurs, promisors will make fewer promises and ask higher prices for them. In consequence, planning becomes harder and more costly. So long as planning for the future is of value, this form of adverse selection will be disadvantageous for society.

In sum then, analytically the rule in *Hadley v. Baxendale* is a rule designed to minimize adverse selection. . . . cheap information is the best antidote to adverse selection problems. So in contract the promisor is entitled to assume "usual risks" unless he is notified to the contrary, whereupon he can demand and obtain a high price. . . .

Whether, as these economic models assert, the remoteness rules are an integral part of contract planning or not is, as usual, a question for empirical testing.

Questions

1. North American books and courses on contract law frequently begin, rather than end, with remedies. Why do you think this approach is taken and to what extent, if at all, would you argue that it provides a better representation of the essence of contract?

2. What policies underlie the approach of the English courts to the use of self-help remedies for breach of contract? Do you think that they have achieved a satisfactory balance between encouraging self-reliance through planning and ensuring the protection of the law against abuses of bargaining power in the construction of remedial systems?

3. Is the refusal of the Privy Council in *Philips* to consider the abstract fairness of a liquidated damages clause likely to have any impact on the usage of such clauses? What impact on liquidated damages is the EC Directive on Unfair Terms in Contracts (Ch. 11) likely to have?

4. Should plaintiffs be given a free choice between specific performance and damages?

5. Why do you think that the arguments of Fuller and Perdue, while greatly influential in the field of academic work, have not been incorporated into English judicial thinking on contract damages?

6. Is the *Hadley* v. *Baxendale* approach to contract remoteness sustainable under modern economic conditions?

Index